DEDICATION

To my wife, Janette, who
is my greatest blessing.

YOUR STUDY OF
THE

DOCTRINE AND COVENANTS MADE EASIER

PART 2
SECTION 43 THROUGH SECTION 93

SECOND EDITION

YOUR STUDY OF
THE

DOCTRINE AND COVENANTS MADE EASIER

PART 2
SECTION 43 THROUGH SECTION 93

SECOND EDITION

DAVID J. RIDGES

CFI, AN IMPRINT OF

CEDAR FORT
Publishing & Media

SPRINGVILLE, UTAH

ISBN 13: 978-1-4621-3896-8

Published by CFI, an imprint of Cedar Fort, Inc.
2373 W. 700 S., Springville, UT, 84663
Distributed by Cedar Fort, Inc., www.cedarfort.com

Library of Congress Control Number: 2020945612

Cover design by Shawnda T. Craig
Cover design © 2020 Cedar Fort, Inc.

Printed in the United States of America

10 9 8 7 6 5 4 3 2 1

Printed on acid-free paper

CONTENTS

SECTIONS

PREFACE

The Doctrine and Covenants is the Savior's book to us in our day. In it, He personally teaches us the "doctrines" and "covenants" necessary to live a righteous, rewarding life, and to successfully walk along the covenant path toward eventual exaltation in the highest degree of glory in the celestial kingdom. In the October 1986 general conference of the Church, in reference to the importance of understanding the doctrines of the gospel, Elder Boyd K. Packer said:

> True doctrine, understood, changes attitudes and behavior. The study of the doctrines of the gospel will improve behavior quicker than a study of behavior will improve behavior. ("Little Children," *Ensign*, Nov. 1986)

Briefly put, "doctrines" are the teachings of the plan of salvation, the answers to questions about the meaning and purpose of life, instructions, rules, facts, hows, whys, and commandments that, if followed, will lead to exaltation. In D&C 10:62, the Lord tells us that He is going to "bring to light the true points" of His doctrine. The Doctrine and Covenants does this.

This study guide is a brief, to-the-point help to a better understanding of the doctrines of the gospel and the ordinances of salvation required for celestial exaltation. The style is somewhat conversational to help you feel as if you were being guided through the Doctrine and Covenants in one of my classes. It is designed, in many cases, to give you instant understanding of basic doctrines and principles, as well as to provide you with the background to apply them in your life, which, in turn, will help you develop a deeper understanding and testimony of the gospel. Remember that the Holy Ghost is THE teacher. He will enlighten your mind and warm your heart as you pray and study this, the Savior's book to us.

INTRODUCTION

I have had a number of friends who have told me that they "don't get much out of reading the Doctrine and Covenants." This study guide is intended to remedy that. Through background and setting notes for each section, plus brief in-the-verse notes, along with the help of the Holy Ghost, I hope you will be enabled to feel and relive the excitement and effects of these revelations on the Prophet Joseph Smith and the early participants in the Restoration and see how they apply to you. Indeed, a key to understanding and enjoying studying the Doctrine and Covenants is seeing the application of its doctrines and teachings in your own life and in the lives of your family and friends. There are boundless applications and blessings available to us directly from the Savior through the study of this book of scripture. This study guide points many of them out.

As was the case with the first edition, this second edition comes in three volumes. This is part two. This new three-volume set contains many updates and much additional historical information based on research made available through the Joseph Smith Papers Project. I have used the 2013 edition of the Doctrine and Covenants, as published by The Church of Jesus Christ of Latter-day Saints, as the basic text. References to the Bible come from the King James Version, as published by The Church of Jesus Christ of Latter-day Saints. JST references refer to the Joseph Smith Translation of the Bible.

Every verse of the Doctrine and Covenants from section 43 through section 93 is included in this second volume. All the remaining verses of the Doctrine and Covenants are contained in parts one and three of this three-volume study guide set. All three volumes have background and setting notes for each section, as well as brief notes of explanation between and within the verses to clarify and help you learn and grow in your appreciation and understanding of this sacred volume of scripture. The notes within the verses are printed in italics and enclosed in brackets in order to make it easy for you to distinguish between the actual scripture text and my teaching comments. Notes between the verses are indented and printed in a different font than the scripture text. **Bold** is often used to highlight things for teaching purposes.

You may be aware, as mentioned above, that, as a result of recent research for the Joseph Smith Papers Project, there are a number of changes to the section headings in the 2013 printing of the Doctrine and Covenants compared to previous editions. Such adjustments, most of them minor, have been made to 78 sections. One example of this is found in sections 39 and 40, where the name "James Covel" is now used rather than "James Covill." Another example of these Joseph Smith Papers Project research-based changes is this: If you are using an edition of the Doctrine and Covenants prior to the 2013 edition, you will see a number of corrected or added dates for the sections in this study guide. For example, prior to the 2013 edition of the Doctrine and Covenants, the date given for section 80 is March 1832. Based on recent research, the date is now given as March 7, 1832. Furthermore, at the time I wrote the first edition of this study guide, the then-current research for when living the Word of Wisdom became a temple recommend requirement was documented as being in the 1930s under President Heber J. Grant. However, current research has established it as being in 1919, shortly after President Grant became the Prophet. That fact is included in the background notes for section 89 in this second edition of this study guide. The Second Edition of *Doctrine and Covenants Made Easier* incorporates these changes as well as adding hundreds of additional helps and clarifications to assist you in your study.

This study guide is designed to be a user-friendly, "teacher in your hand" introductory study of this portion of the Doctrine and Covenants, as well as a refresher course for more advanced students of the scriptures. It is also designed to be a quick-reference resource that will enable readers to look up a particular passage or block of scripture for use in lessons, talks, or personal study as desired. It is my hope that you will incorporate some of the notes given in this study guide into your own scriptures, whether paper copy or on digital devices, to assist you in reading and studying this portion of the Doctrine and Covenants in the future. Thus, your own scriptures will become one of your best tools in your continued study of the gospel.

—David J. Ridges

NOTE

In section 10, verse 62, the Savior specifically told us that He was going to restore "the true points of my doctrine." "Doctrines" are eternal truths, facts, or things in the plan of salvation that do not change, such as:

- Faith, repentance, baptism, and the gift of the Holy Ghost.

- The Godhead consists of the Father, the Son, and the Holy Ghost.

- The members of the Godhead are three separate beings.

- There are three kingdoms of glory; namely, the telestial, terrestrial, and celestial.

- In the celestial kingdom, there are three degrees.

- The highest degree of glory in the celestial is called "exaltation."

- Those who attain exaltation will live in their own eternal family unit and ultimately become gods.

- Heavenly Father is completely fair, thus everyone will ultimately get a perfect opportunity before the final judgment to hear, understand, and then accept or reject the gospel.

- The sins we have repented of will not even be mentioned on Judgment Day.

- Little children who die before the years of accountability will receive exaltation.

- Ordinance work for the dead is part of the Father's plan of happiness for His children.

- We are spirit children of Heavenly Parents.

- The Atonement of Christ works for our shortcomings and imperfections as well as our sins.

- Baptism is required for entrance into the celestial kingdom, except in the case of little children who die before the age of accountability and the intellectually handicapped who do not have sufficient understanding to be accountable.

- God will not allow His living prophets to lead us astray.

- And many, many more wonderful doctrines that help us understand the "whats," "whys" and "hows" of the Father's plan of salvation for us, His children.

In the Doctrine and Covenants, the Lord has indeed restored many true doctrines, which, among other things, enable us to better live the gospel because we better understand it. Throughout these three volumes of study guides for the Doctrine and Covenants, I will often add extra notes to point out and summarize the many doctrines given by the Savior for us as He said He would. You will see an example of this immediately after verse 2, next.

SECTION 43

Background

This revelation was given through the Prophet Joseph Smith at Kirtland, Ohio, in February 1831. The Church, as an official organization, was less than one year old (having been organized on April 6, 1830). At this point in time, members were moving from New York and other locations to the Kirtland, Ohio, area as commanded by the Lord in D&C 37:3; see also D&C 38:31–32.

One of the extremely important messages to us in this section is that the Lord will not allow His prophet to lead us astray. This is a "law," as stated by the Lord in verses four and five. In other words, we are 100 percent safe in following the living prophet.

As with many other revelations in the Doctrine and Covenants, specific current problems or circumstances led up to the giving of this revelation. Many of these early members were converted from Christian churches of the day. In some of these churches, it was accepted as common practice that any member of a congregation could receive revelation for any other member or members. They could also proclaim doctrine for their entire church. As you can

well imagine, such actions resulted in confusion and lack of doctrinal focus and clarity, and it was causing considerable trouble at the time of this revelation through Joseph Smith.

One notable example of this problem was that of a Mrs. Hubble, who claimed to be a prophetess of the Lord. She believed she was receiving revelations for the Church, including that she should become a teacher to the Church. The Prophet Joseph Smith spoke of her as follows:

"Soon after the foregoing revelation [D&C 42] was received, a woman [Mrs. Hubble] came making great pretensions of revealing commandments, laws and other curious matters; and as almost every person has advocates for both theory and practice, in the various notions and projects of the age, it became necessary to inquire of the Lord, when I received the following [D&C 43]" (*History of the Church*, 1:154).

In a footnote to the above quote, we learn that John Whitmer (the first official historian of the Church; see D&C 47:1) wrote of Mrs. Hubble. The footnote reads as follows:

"This woman's name, according to the history of the church kept by John Whitmer, was Hubble. 'She professed to be a prophetess of the Lord, and professed to have many revelations, and knew the

Book of Mormon was true, and that she should become a teacher in the church of Christ. She appeared to be very sanctimonious and deceived some who were not able to detect her in her hypocrisy; others, however, had the spirit of discernment and her follies and abominations were manifest.' John Whitmer's *History of the Church*, Ch. 3." (See Joseph Smith, *History of the Church*, 1:154, footnote 12. See also *The Joseph Smith Papers, Histories, Volume 2: Assigned Histories, 1831–1847*, ed. Karen Lynn Davidson and others [2012], 29; spelling, capitalization, and punctuation standardized; see also *The Joseph Smith Papers, Documents, Volume 1: July 1828–June 1831*, 257, note 95).

Thus, it was quite common at this point in the early history of the Church for members to claim revelation for the Church and to attempt to correct the prophet. The Lord gives clear correction to this in verses 1–6.

Among other teachings and doctrines given in this section, you will find the role of councils in the Church (verse 8), the importance of covenants as we "bind" ourselves to safe behaviors (verse 9), and the necessity for us to support and sustain the living prophet if we want heaven's guidance through him (verses 12–14). Verses 15–35 contain a warning that the elders of the Church are to give to the inhabitants of the earth in the last days.

In these last twenty verses, we will learn brief details about the Second Coming, the rule of the righteous with the Savior during the Millennium, the binding of Satan and his subsequent loosing for a "little season," the end of the earth, the resurrection of the righteous, and the final fate of the wicked.

We will now proceed to study section 43, using **bold** for teaching emphasis, [*brackets with italics*] for teaching notes within the verses, and indentation in a different font for teaching notes and comments between verses. Remember, as we begin, that the first issue addressed by the Lord is the issue of having one person only, namely the living prophet, authorized to receive commandments and doctrine for the whole Church.

1 O HEARKEN, ye elders of my church, and give ear to the words which I shall speak unto you.

2 For behold, verily, verily, I say unto you, that ye have received a commandment for a law [*section 42*] unto my church, through him [*Joseph Smith*] **whom I have appointed unto you to receive commandments and revelations from my hand**.

Doctrine

Verses 3–5. The Lord will not let the prophet lead the Church astray.

3 And **this ye shall know** assuredly—that **there is none other appointed unto you to receive commandments and revelations** until he be taken, if he abide in me.

Did you notice the last phrase of verse 3, above? It is an important part of understanding that the Lord will not allow the living prophet to lead us astray. It says, in effect, that the prophet will remain the Lord's mouthpiece to the Saints as long as he remains faithful and worthy. Verse 4, next, explains what would happen if the living prophet were to begin to stray. You will see that if this were to happen, the living prophet would have no more power except to appoint his successor—in other words, the prophet who would take his place. This is a very exact procedure and would leave no room for doubt or speculation on our part as to who our authorized prophet is. (This is one reason that it is so important for us to read and understand the Doctrine and Covenants. There is great security for us in so doing.)

4 But verily, verily, I say unto you, that **none else shall be appointed unto this gift** [to serve as the living prophet] **except it be through him**; for **if it** [the office of prophet] **be taken from him he shall not have power except to appoint another in his stead**.

In verse 5, next, the Lord leaves absolutely no doubt in our minds that the above fail-safe guarantee is solidly in place so that we can completely trust the official words and teachings of our living prophet. Simply put, it is a law of God.

5 And **this shall be a law unto you**, that ye **receive not the teachings of any that shall come before you** [except the living prophet] **as revelations or commandments** [in other words, as new doctrines or commandments to the whole Church];

Next, the Lord reminds us that this "law" is given to protect us from deception and confusion as to who gives us the final word of the Lord.

6 And **this I give unto you that you may not be deceived**, that you may know they [people other than the prophet who claim to receive revelation for the whole Church] are not of me.

One thing before we go on. We have never had our living prophet lead us astray. The reason is simple. He can't. The Lord will not allow it. If he were to attempt to do so, the Lord would remove him from office, as explained here in section 43, after requiring one last thing of him, namely, to appoint his replacement under the Lord's specific direction. Apostates, people who have left the Church, often claim that the current prophet is leading us astray. They obviously don't understand the "law" of the Lord given in verse 5, above. Thus, we know that we have no valid reason to believe their false claims and teachings.

Next, in verse 7, the Savior explains that He will have teachers and leaders in the Church, who are properly authorized and called of God, to teach and explain the revelations and commandments that have come through the living prophet.

7 For verily I say unto you, that **he that is ordained of me shall come in at the gate** [*come through proper channels; be properly called, authorized and sustained, and so forth*] **and be ordained** as I have told you before [*in D&C 42:11*], **to teach those revelations which you have received and shall receive through him** [*Joseph Smith; the living prophet*] whom I have appointed.

In verse 8, next, we are given a general format for councils in the Church. These can include ward councils, councils of presidencies, family councils, and so on. Perhaps you have noticed, especially in recent years, that the Brethren (General Authorities) have encouraged more use of councils in local church units in order to address local needs and concerns more effectively. One of the things they have especially emphasized is the need for each member of such councils to participate actively in the discussion and decision making for which such councils are designed by the Lord.

8 And now, behold, I give unto you a commandment, that when ye are assembled together **ye shall instruct and edify** [*build and strengthen*] **each other, that ye may know how to act and direct my church**, how to act upon the points of my law [*especially section 42; see D&C 42:2*] and commandments, which I have given.

The first two phrases of verse 9, next, explain the desired outcome of councils in the Church.

9 And **thus ye shall become instructed in the law of my church, and** be **sanctified** [*made pure, holy, fit to be in the presence of God; cleansed from sin*] by that which ye have received, and **ye shall bind yourselves** [*make covenants; compare with D&C 82:15*] **to act in all holiness before me**—

One of the important lessons we can gain from the last phrase in verse 9, above, is the symbolism involved in making covenants. When we make covenants with God, we are, in effect, "binding" ourselves to safe behaviors. In other words, we "bind" or tie ourselves to God when we are thinking rationally and wisely, so that later, when we are tempted to sin, we have extra incentive and strength to do what is right. Honest people are greatly strengthened by making covenants.

10 That inasmuch as ye do this, glory shall be added to the kingdom which ye have received [*one possible interpretation of this is "the Church will grow and prosper in your lives"*]. Inasmuch as ye do it not, it shall be taken, even that which ye have received [*perhaps meaning you will lose the blessings you have received, and possibly your membership in the Church*].

11 **Purge** [*cleanse*] **ye out the iniquity** [*the sin and evil*] **which is among you**; sanctify yourselves [*become more pure and holy*] before me;

In verses 12–14, next, these early members of the Church are taught the necessity on their part of supporting and sustaining the living prophet—in this case the Prophet Joseph Smith. Part of this support involves praying for him. Another aspect of support consists of donating for his temporal needs. For us in our day, in addition to our prayers, this includes the payment of tithes and offerings, which sustain our prophet's travels and ministry throughout the Church and the world.

12 And **if ye desire the glories of the kingdom** [*if you want the full blessings of the gospel*], appoint [*sustain; see D&C 43:12, footnote 12a*] ye my servant Joseph Smith, Jun., and **uphold him before me by the prayer of faith**.

13 And again, I say unto you, that **if ye desire the mysteries of the kingdom** [*the basic, simple, revealed truths and doctrines of the gospel, not strange, obscure mysteries; see Bible Dictionary under "Mystery"*], **provide for him food and raiment** [*clothing*], **and whatsoever thing he needeth to accomplish the work wherewith I have commanded him;**

14 And **if ye do it not he shall remain unto them that have received him** [*you will be left out, and those who do support him will become the Lord's people*], that I may reserve unto myself a pure people before me.

As mentioned in the introduction to this section, verses 15–35 explain the necessity of taking the gospel message to all the world. They provide brief glimpses into several doctrines of the Father's plan of salvation for His children, along with counsel to each of us as we do our part to spread the gospel. We will continue to use **bold** to point things out as we study these verses.

At first, the **bolded** portion of verse 15, next, may seem a bit arrogant. But when you stop to think about it, if our missionaries were to take time to learn the philosophies and teachings of the people they are teaching, they would have no time to actually study and teach the simple gospel message they are to present.

15 Again I say, hearken ye elders of my church, whom I have appointed: **Ye are not sent forth to be taught, but to teach** the children of men the things which I have put into your hands by the power of my Spirit;

16 And **ye are to be taught from on high.** Sanctify yourselves [*repent as needed and work on becoming more clean and pure*] and **ye shall be endowed with power** [*you will be given power from God to preach and spread the Church*], that ye may give even as I have spoken.

17 Hearken ye, for, behold, **the great day of the Lord is nigh at hand** [*the Second Coming is getting close*].

18 For **the day cometh that the Lord shall utter his voice out of heaven** [*perhaps including the "voice" of thunderings, lightnings, tempests, and waves in the last days; see verse 21; see also D&C 88:90*]; the heavens shall shake and the earth shall tremble, and the trump of God shall sound both long and loud [*signaling the Second Coming and the resurrection of the righteous; see D&C 88:92, 96–97*], and shall say to the sleeping nations [*perhaps meaning spiritually asleep*]: Ye saints arise and live [*the resurrection of the righteous dead, at the beginning of the Millennium*]; ye sinners stay and sleep until I shall call again [*the wicked must wait until the end of the thousand-year Millennium to be resurrected; see D&C 88:100–102*].

In verse 19, next, you will see a rather common phrase in the scriptures: "gird up your loins." It can mean "get dressed," "be ready for action," "be prepared," and so forth, depending on the context. In this verse, as you can see, it means to be prepared spiritually to meet the Savior.

19 Wherefore **gird up your loins** [*prepare yourselves*] lest ye be found among the wicked.

Next, in verse 20, the Savior tells the elders to preach the gospel every chance they get, and to warn all people to prepare to meet Christ at His coming. This applies to all of us as we have opportunities to share the gospel. We must be careful and appropriate as we do this, by following the Lord's counsel in D&C 38:41 to teach with "mildness and in meekness."

20 **Lift up your voices** [*speak up*] and spare not [*don't hesitate*]. Call upon the nations to repent, both old and young, both bond [*slaves, people in bondage*] and free, **saying: Prepare yourselves for the great day of the Lord**;

Verse 21 has a significant doctrinal statement by the Savior. We know that Jesus was resurrected and is a celestial being with a glorified, resurrected body of flesh and bones (see D&C 130:22). Most of the Christian churches teach that He is now a mysterious entity encompassed within the unfathomable Godhead, and that He is basically undefinable and incomprehensible to mortals. But, in the first line of verse 21, He clearly and simply states that He is a man. This is beautiful, clear, and understandable doctrine!

21 For if **I**, who **am a man** [*Jesus Christ; see verse 34*], do lift up my voice and call upon you to repent, **and ye hate** [*avoid, shrink away from; see* Webster's New World Dictionary, Second College Edition] **me**, what will ye say [*what excuses will you have for your wickedness*] when the day cometh when the

thunders shall utter their voices from the ends of the earth [*when natural disasters, earthquakes, plagues, pestilences, and such increase in the last days; see D&C 88:89–91*], **speaking to the ears of all that live, saying—Repent, and prepare for the great day of the Lord** [*the Second Coming and beginning of the Millennium*]?

In verses 21–27, the Lord explains why He is going to cause a great increase in frequency and intensity of natural disasters in the last days, leading up to His Second Coming, which will usher in the Millennium. These are often referred to as "signs of the times," meaning obvious signs and indicators that show us that the coming of the Lord is getting close. He explains in these verses that these signs are a wake-up call, a call to repentance, to the wicked and those who have strayed from God.

22 Yea, and again, when the **lightnings** shall streak forth from the east unto the west, and **shall utter forth their voices** unto all that live, and make the ears of all tingle that hear, **saying** these words—**Repent ye**, for the great day of the Lord is come?

23 And again, **the Lord shall utter his voice** out of heaven, saying: Hearken, O ye nations of the earth, and **hear the words of**

that God who made you.

In verses 24–25, next, the Lord explains that He has tried the gentle approach to gather His children to Him, but they have ignored those warm, gentle, pleasant invitations. Therefore, in effect, He has to raise His voice in order to get their attention. This is a demonstration of His mercy as He attempts to get more people to use their agency to choose to return to God, rather than being condemned on Judgment Day.

24 O, ye nations of the earth, **how often would I have gathered you** together as a hen gathereth her chickens under her wings [*symbolic of the warmth and security available to us in the arms of the Savior and His gospel*], but ye would not!

25 **How oft have I called upon you by** the mouth of **my servants**, and by the ministering of **angels**, and by **mine own voice**, and by the voice of **thunderings**, and by the voice of **lightnings**, and by the voice of **tempests**, and by the voice of **earthquakes**, and great **hailstorms**, and by the voice of **famines** and **pestilences** [*plagues, epidemics*] of every kind, and by the great sound of a **trump** [*including the pure, clear gospel truths*], and by the voice of **judgment**, and by **the voice of mercy** all the day long, and by the

voice of **glory and honor and the riches of eternal life** [*exaltation*], and **would have saved you with an everlasting salvation, but ye would not!**

26 Behold, **the day has come, when the cup of the wrath of mine indignation** [*righteous anger*] **is full** [*the last days have arrived during which the Lord will express His righteous anger upon the wicked inhabitants of the earth via natural disasters and such, as explained in verse 25, above*].

Having taught these elders (see verse 1) of the early Church what their basic message to the world is to be, Jesus now reaffirms that these are His words to them, and He invites them to move ahead with this vital work.

27 Behold, verily I say unto you, that **these are the words of the Lord your God**.

28 Wherefore [*therefore*], **labor ye, labor ye in my vineyard for the last time**—for the last time call upon the inhabitants of the earth.

Do you remember hearing that this is the "last dispensation" and that the Church will never go into apostasy (fall away) again? It is true, and verse 28, above, is one of the places in scripture where we learn that this is the case. These early missionaries are told that this is the "last time" that the gospel will be taught before the Savior comes (verse 29, next).

And, while we're on the subject of the Second Coming, it is important to note the caution, in verse 29, next, that Jesus gives concerning the timing of His coming. He will come in all His glory "in mine own due time"—in other words, when the timing is right. This makes it impossible to pin it down to a specific day, week, month, or even year. This is in complete harmony with Matthew 24:36 and Mark 13:32, where we are definitely told that no man can know the exact timing of the Second Coming.

29 For **in mine own due time** will I come upon the earth in judgment, and **my people** [*the faithful members of the Church*] **shall be redeemed and shall reign with me on earth** [*the righteous members of the Church will assist the Savior in governing the earth during the Millennium; see Revelation 20:4*].

Next, in verses 30–33, the Savior bears personal testimony to us that the Millennium will come, and He gives brief details of what will happen from that point to the end of the earth.

30 For **the great Millennium** [*the thousand years of peace*], of which I have spoken by the mouth of my servants, **shall come.**

Doctrine

Vs. 31. Satan will be bound during the Millennium and not allowed to tempt mortals then.

31 For **Satan shall be bound** [*will not be allowed to tempt people on earth during the Millennium (D&C 101:28)*], and when he is **loosed again** [*after the thousand years have ended; see D&C 88:110–11*] he shall only reign for **a little season** [*during which the final battle (the Battle of Gog and Magog) will take place; see D&C 88:111–15*], and then cometh the **end of the earth** [*meaning that the mortal earth will become a celestial planet, will be moved from this solar system back into the presence of the Father (see* Teachings of the Prophet Joseph Smith, *181) and will become the home of those who lived on it and who are judged worthy of celestial glory; see D&C 130:9–11*].

Doctrine

Vs. 32. When righteous mortals during the Millennium finish their earth life, they will die and be resurrected instantly.

Next, in verse 32, the Savior gives a detail about life for the righteous during the Millennium, which you have perhaps heard. It is that the righteous, after they have finished living out their mortal lives during the Millennium, will die and be resurrected instantly. We know from other scriptures that they will live to be one hundred years of age (Isaiah 65:20) and that they will actually die, but that they will not need to be buried in the ground because they will be resurrected immediately after they die (D&C 101:31).

32 And he that liveth in righteousness shall be changed in the twinkling of an eye, and the earth shall pass away so as by fire.

The last phrase of verse 32, above, could have dual meaning, referring both to the cleansing of the earth by fire at the time of the Savior's coming (see D&C 101:24–25; Matthew 3:12), as well as the celestialization of the earth after the Millennium and "little season" are over (see D&C 29:22–24).

Verse 33, next, could also have dual meaning, referring to the literal burning of the wicked at the Second Coming (they are burned, destroyed by His glory; see D&C 5:19, 2 Nephi 12:10, 19, 21), and their subsequently being turned over to Satan to suffer for their sins (see D&C 19:15–17). It certainly refers to the final state of sons of perdition (compare with D&C 76:44–48).

33 And the wicked shall go away into unquenchable fire, and their end [*their final situation*] no man knoweth on earth, nor ever shall know, until they come before me in judgment.

Finally, having given these early elders (and all of us) much counsel and instruction about the importance of sharing the gospel, and having explained several details about the plan of salvation that are vital for our understanding of the big picture and the purposes of life, Jesus now concludes, instructing them (and us) to take His words seriously.

We would do well to understand, from the Savior's approach in the above verses, that it is not enough simply to tell people to repent. Without a basic understanding of doctrines of the plan of salvation, people have no context in which to make repentance meaningful.

34 Hearken ye to these words. Behold, **I am Jesus Christ,** the Savior of the world. **Treasure these things up in your hearts,** and let the solemnities [*serious matters*] of eternity rest upon your minds [*take these things seriously, and keep the reality of living eternally firmly in mind*].

35 Be sober [*be serious-minded about serious things*]. **Keep all my commandments.** Even so. Amen.

SECTION 44

Background

The Joseph Smith Papers Project research gives helpful background information for section 44. We will quote from the 2018 *Doctrine and Covenants Student* Manual:

"Soon after arriving in Kirtland, Ohio, the Prophet Joseph Smith received the revelations recorded in Doctrine and Covenants 42, which outlined laws guiding the Church. Included was the commandment that the elders should 'go forth in the power of my Spirit, preaching my gospel, two by two. . . . And from this place ye shall go forth' (D&C 42:6, 8). The revelation recorded in Doctrine and Covenants 44 called for the elders of the Church to meet together before going forth to preach the gospel.

"The Prophet Joseph Smith acted on that instruction and sent a letter on February 22, 1831, to Martin Harris, who was still living in New York. The Prophet made reference to the revelation when he explained to Martin that 'the work is here breaking forth on the east, west, north, and south; you will also inform the Elders which are there that all of them who can be spared will come here without delay if possible, this by Commandment of the Lord as he has a great work for them all' (in *The Joseph Smith Papers, Documents, Volume 1: July 1828–June 1831*, 263;

punctuation and spelling standardized).

"In subsequent weeks during the spring of 1831, many of the Saints from New York gathered to Kirtland, Ohio. The fourth conference of the Church was held in June 1831, and many elders participated in the meetings of this conference, which prepared them to leave afterward to preach the gospel."

Thus, the fourth general conference of the Church was held June 3–6, 1831, in a schoolhouse on the outskirts of Kirtland and was the first such conference held in Ohio. The three previous general conferences were held in Fayette, New York, beginning on June 9, 1830, September 26, 1830, and January 2, 1831, respectively. At this point in time, membership in the Church is approaching two thousand.

Among other things in this section, we will be taught many of the purposes of conferences held by the Church. If we understand these purposes, we will have an even greater desire to attend. We will point out a number of these purposes and benefits, using **(1)**, **(2)**, and so on, and using **bold.** As you will see, many of these benefits are spiritual and eternal, as much or more so than physical.

First, in verse 1, next, the Lord instructs the Prophet and Sidney Rigdon to call the missionaries in from their various fields of labor to attend this conference.

1 BEHOLD, thus saith the Lord unto you my servants, **it is expedient** [*necessary*] in me **that the elders of my church should be called together**, from the east and from the west, and from the north and from the south, by letter or some other way.

2 And it shall come to pass, that inasmuch as they are faithful, and exercise faith in me, **(1) I will pour out my Spirit upon them** in the day that they assemble themselves together [*as they meet together in this conference*].

3 And it shall come to pass that **they shall go forth into the regions round about, and preach repentance** unto the people.

4 **And many shall be converted** [**(2)** *They will obtain greater power to spread the gospel*]**,** insomuch that **(3) ye shall obtain power to organize yourselves according to the laws of man** [*you will have greater power to organize Church units in various communities according to the laws of the land*];

5 That **(4) your enemies may not have power over you**; that **(5) you may be preserved in all things**; that **(6) you may be**

enabled to keep my laws; (7) that every bond may be broken wherewith the enemy seeketh to destroy my people.

Verse 6, next, reminds these Saints to take care of the poor and the needy among them. The "law" spoken of would likely be section 42, in which instructions were given for the implementation of the law of consecration, which contains provisions for the care of the needy (see D&C 42:30–31).

6 Behold, I say unto you, that ye must **visit the poor and the needy and administer to their relief**, that they may be kept until all things may be done according to **my law** which ye have received. Amen.

SECTION 45

Background

This revelation was given to the Church through Joseph Smith at Kirtland, Ohio, on March 7, 1831. At this point in time, the Church is just eleven months old and there are about two thousand members, most of whom have gathered or who are on their way to gather in the Kirtland, Ohio, area. During this time, Sidney Rigdon's mother and oldest brother will join the Church (see *Doctrine and Covenants Student Manual*, 1981, 91). Joseph Smith and Sidney Rigdon continue to work on what will become the Joseph Smith Translation of the Bible (JST), as instructed by the Lord in D&C 41:7. The Prophet's wife, Emma, is expecting twins. They will be born on April 30, 1831, but will only live about three hours before they pass away.

At this time, the Saints are facing many false rumors and much bad publicity. Wild stories about them are circulating freely, adding to the difficulty of gathering and worshipping the Lord in Ohio. Local civic leaders, ministers and their congregations, newspaper editors, and others have united in a joint effort to stop their friends and neighbors from being converted to this new religion. The Prophet Joseph Smith wrote of this as follows:

"At this age of the Church [*early in the spring of 1831*] many false reports, lies, and foolish stories, were published in the newspapers, and circulated in every direction, to prevent people from investigating the work, or embracing the faith. A great earthquake in China, which destroyed from one to two thousand inhabitants, was burlesqued [*twisted*] in some papers, as '"Mormonism" in China.' But to the joy of the Saints who had to struggle against every thing that prejudice and wickedness could invent, I received the following [*Doctrine and Covenants, section 45*]." (*History of the Church,* 1:158.)

One of the major messages we learn from this revelation is the importance of perspective during times of trials, disappointments, and hardships. It is as if the Lord were lifting the minds and hearts of these struggling Saints up to a "high mountain" from which they are permitted to see things as the Lord sees them, including the great blessings that await the righteous in the future. Afterward, they are, in effect, "returned" down to earth to daily life and struggles but are much better able to cope and progress. Perhaps you have had similar experiences in which the Lord has enabled you to "see" for a brief moment as He sees, thus empowering you to submit more cheerfully to trials and to have more joy and satisfaction in daily living. This is one of the great blessings of having the gospel in our lives with the accompanying gift of the Holy Ghost.

One of the great treasures in this section is found in verses 16–59, where the Savior quotes the Olivet Discourse (Matthew 24), in which He answered questions and pointed out many signs of the times to His disciples during the last week of His mortal life as they met on the Mount of Olives (see Matthew 24:3). Matthew 24 is one of the best-known chapters in the Bible dealing with the signs of the times (prophecies that will be fulfilled shortly before the Second Coming). The great value of these verses in section 45 in the Doctrine and Covenants is that we find more than three hundred words added to this discourse that are not found in Matthew 24.

As we proceed, we will be taught gospel vocabulary and many doctrines of the gospel, including numerous details of the plan of salvation. If you understand the gospel vocabulary and doctrinal concepts given in section 45, you will find that your understanding of many other passages in the scriptures is greatly enhanced. We will add an unusually large number of notes and considerable commentary as we study this section. You may wish to make several notes in your own Doctrine and Covenants, section 45, based on what we cover now.

First of all, in verse 1, the Savior identifies Himself and introduces Himself to us as the one giving this revelation.

Doctrine

Vs. 1. Jesus Christ is the Creator of the earth and the heavens and everything in them (except people because we are "offspring" [see Acts 17:29] **of Heavenly Parents, not "creations" like rocks, trees, horses, and the like.)**

1 **HEARKEN** [listen carefully], **O ye people of my church, to whom the kingdom** [the true Church with the true gospel of Jesus Christ here on earth] **has been given; hearken ye and give ear to him** [Jesus Christ] **who laid the foundation of the earth** [who created the earth], **who made the heavens and all the hosts thereof,** and **by whom all things were made which live, and move, and have a being** [Jesus is the creator of heaven and earth and everything in them].

Next, in the first part of verse 2, Christ warns us to be prepared to meet Him since we don't know when we might die. Alma 34:33 has essentially the same message for us.

In the last part of verse 2, we are likewise counseled to be prepared to meet the Savior. In the context of this section, this part of the verse seems to imply that the Second Coming will come a bit sooner than we expect, based on the signs of the times. We need to be ready or our souls will not be saved.

2 And again I say, **hearken unto my voice, lest death shall overtake you;** in an hour **when ye think not the summer shall be past** [you don't know when you are going to die and your mortal opportunities to prepare to meet God will be over; also, the Second Coming will arrive when you don't expect it], and **the harvest ended** [the

gathering of the righteous and the destruction of the wicked will be over], and **your souls not saved** [*unless you are prepared*].

Doctrine

Verses 3–5. If we are earnestly and honestly striving to live the gospel faithfully, we can plan on a pleasant Judgment Day.

Verses 3–5, next, go together. They are a most comforting reminder of the role of the Savior and His Atonement in making it possible for us to be saved, despite our inadequacies and imperfections.

To set the stage for understanding these three verses, we will take a bit of poetic license and imagine the following scenario: Suppose that you have just died and are waiting your turn to be judged. You find yourself fretting about things you did not complete while on earth despite your good intentions and honest desires to be good.

As you wait, you review your life. Despite the fact that you attended church faithfully, paid a full tithing (except for the tithing check still in your drawer, which you forgot to turn in last month), kept the Word of Wisdom, tried to be nice, didn't swear much (you're actually progressing on this), attended the temple pretty regularly and so on, you find yourself focusing on sins

and imperfections you haven't yet overcome. Just as you decide that you can't possibly make the celestial kingdom but hope to make the terrestrial, the door opens and it is your turn to be judged.

Embarrassed by your shortcomings and humbled by what you didn't get done on earth, you walk in to face the Savior to be judged, whispering with head bowed that He can save time by sending you to terrestrial glory without any further discussion. At this point, the Savior comes around the judgment bar of God, walks up to you, puts His arm around you, hugs you, and says:

3 **Listen to him** [*Jesus Christ*] **who is the advocate** [*our Mediator, "attorney," the one who wants us to win on Judgment Day*] **with the Father, who is pleading your cause before him** [*who wants you to be saved*]—

Next, still hugging you, He turns you to face the Father with Him,

4 Saying: **Father, behold the sufferings and death of him** [*Christ*] **who did no sin** [*in other words, consider My Atonement in behalf of this person (you)*], **in whom thou wast well pleased; behold the blood of thy Son which was shed,** the blood of him whom thou gavest that thyself might be glorified [*the purpose of the Atonement is to bring*

such people as you back to the Father permanently*];

5 Wherefore [*therefore, because of My Atonement*], **Father, spare** [*apply the law of mercy, rather than the law of justice to*] **these my brethren** [*in our scenario, "apply my Atonement to this, my sister, or to this, my brother"*] **that believe on my name, that they may come unto me and have everlasting life** [*the term "everlasting life" always means exaltation in the highest degree of glory in the celestial kingdom*].

Can you imagine your relief and gratitude when you realize that the Savior's Atonement applies fully to people like you! You have been honestly and sincerely striving to keep the commandments and to do good, and, as is the case with all who are accountable, you have been a bit slow on some things. Yet, at this glorious moment, you find complete fulfillment of Revelation 21:4, which says: "And God shall wipe away all tears from their eyes; and there shall be no more death, neither sorrow, nor crying, neither shall there be any more pain: for the former things [*mortal trials, sins, and so on*] are passed away." You have truly been cleansed from all your sins by the Savior's Atonement and stand pure and clean (sanctified) in His presence as He now judges you!

As we continue with section 45,

the Savior uses several gospel doctrinal vocabulary words and phrases as He reviews His role and sets in perspective the stage for the teachings given in verses 16–59.

6 Hearken, O ye people of my church, and ye elders **listen together** [*listen in unity of heart and purpose*], and **hear** [*obey*] my voice **while it is called today** [*while you still have time*], and harden not your hearts [*don't become prideful and insensitive to the gospel*];

7 For verily I say unto you that I am **Alpha and Omega** [*the "A" and the "Z" of the Greek alphabet, another way of saying the beginning and the end*], **the beginning and the end** [*Jesus has been involved in saving us since the beginning (including the council in heaven, the War in Heaven, and the creation of the earth), and will be there in the end, including as our final judge (John 5:22)*], **the light and the life of the world**—a light that shineth in darkness [*spiritual darkness*] and **the darkness comprehendeth it not.**

The word "comprehendeth," in verse 7, above, can have at least two meanings in this context. One is that those who are not spiritually sensitive do not understand the light of the gospel or even realize that it is there for them. They do not understand or appreciate spiritual things.

Another meaning of "comprehend" is to surround and overcome. It is comforting to know that spiritual darkness cannot ultimately win over Christ and the righteous. Perhaps you've noticed that, upon opening an outside door at night, darkness does not stream into the house and obliterate the light. Light always penetrates darkness rather than the other way around. Simple, powerful symbolism is in this natural state of things. The darkness of Satan and his evil hosts cannot overcome or "comprehend" Christ, the Light and Life of the world, nor the righteous, who are honestly striving to keep their covenants and live righteous lives.

8 I [*Jesus*] **came unto mine own, and mine own received me not** [*not just the Jews, but all who reject Him; see* Teachings of the Prophet Joseph Smith, *pages 14–15*]; **but unto as many as received me gave I power to do many miracles, and to become the sons of God** [*a scriptural vocabulary phrase meaning those who attain exaltation; see D&C 76:24, Mosiah 5:7*]; and even **unto them that believed on my name gave I power to obtain eternal life** [*this phrase always means "exaltation," the highest degree of glory in the celestial kingdom—in other words, becoming*

gods and living in the family unit forever].

Next, in verse 9, Jesus tells us why He restored His gospel in these last days.

9 And even so **I have sent mine everlasting covenant** [*the full gospel; see D&C 133:57*] **into the world, to be a light to the world,** and to be **a standard for my people** [*members of the Church*], **and for the Gentiles** [*in this context, all people who are not members of the Church*] **to seek to it, and to be a messenger before my face to prepare the way before me** [*including to prepare the way for the Second Coming*].

In verses 10–15, next, the Savior issues a wonderful invitation to all who join His Church. He says, in effect, that He will chat and reason with us, just as He did with prophets and Saints in ancient times. What an invitation! He will teach us so that the gospel makes sense and so that we can see the big picture and the reasons for keeping the commandments. We will continue to use **bold** to point things out.

10 Wherefore, come ye unto it [*the gospel of Jesus Christ*], and **with him that cometh I will reason as with men in days of old**, and I will show unto you my strong reasoning [*we will be able to see things as Christ sees them*].

11 Wherefore, **hearken ye together and let me show unto you even my wisdom**—the wisdom of him whom ye say is **the God of Enoch, and his brethren** [*the City of Enoch was taken up into heaven, as recorded in Moses 7:21; see also D&C 38:4*],

12 **Who were separated from the earth** [*who were taken up off the earth*]**, and were received unto myself**—a city reserved **until a day of righteousness shall come** [*the City of Enoch will come back down to earth at the beginning of the Millennium; see Moses 7:62–63*]—**a day that was sought for by all holy men** [*many of the righteous throughout history have wished that the Millennium would come during their lifetime*]**, and they found it** [*peace and righteousness on earth*] **not because of wickedness and abominations;**

By the way, when the City of Enoch was taken up, it included the buildings, ground, gardens, and domestic animals (see *Discourses of Brigham Young*, 105). The inhabitants of the City of Enoch were translated when taken up, and they were resurrected at the time of Christ's resurrection (see D&C 133:54–55.)

Verse 13, next, expresses the sentiments occasionally felt by many of the righteous. There

are times when it seems that no one else wants to live the gospel as thoroughly as they do, which leaves them feeling lonely and like strangers away from home for a season.

13 **And confessed** [*came to the conclusion*] **they were strangers and pilgrims on the earth** [*because of the wickedness on earth*];

14 **But obtained a promise that they should find it and see it in their flesh** [*as resurrected beings who will rule and reign with the Savior during the Millennium; see Revelation 20:4*].

15 Wherefore, hearken and **I will reason with you, and I will speak unto you and prophesy, as unto men in days of old** [*Jesus desires that we have the same perspective and opportunity to understand as He gave to Saints in ancient times*].

As mentioned previously, the Savior will now teach us what He taught His disciples, as recorded in Matthew, chapter 24. It was the last week of His mortal life, probably Tuesday (He will be crucified on Friday). The Savior's triumphal entry into Jerusalem two days earlier (Matthew 21) had set the entire city of Jerusalem into an uproar. City officials and priests, along with many others, were determined to destroy Jesus and His followers. (Much the same sentiments existed against the members of the Church in the hearts and efforts of residents of the Kirtland, Ohio, area at the time section 65 was given). The Master's disciples were very concerned about His safety, as well as their own future. They came to Him with two specific questions as He sat upon the Mount of Olives (Joseph Smith–Matthew 1:4):

1. When would the destruction of the temple in Jerusalem and the Jews take place?

2. What are the signs of His Second Coming and the destruction of the wicked?

We will now study His answers in verses 16–59.

16 And **I will show it plainly as I showed it unto my disciples** as I stood before them in the flesh [*on the Mount of Olives before His crucifixion and resurrection*], and spake unto them, saying: As **ye have asked of me concerning the signs of my coming**, in the day **when I shall come in my glory** in the clouds of heaven [*the Second Coming*], to fulfil the promises that I have made unto your fathers [*ancestors*],

17 For as ye have looked upon the long absence of your spirits from your bodies to be a bondage [*we will miss our physical bodies after we die and go to the spirit world*], **I**

will show unto you how the day of redemption shall come [*Jesus will teach us about how we will be redeemed, including how our spirits will get our physical bodies back in the resurrection*], **and also the restoration of the scattered Israel** [*Jesus will also teach us about the gathering of Israel In the last days in these verses*].

Next, in verses 18–24, Jesus answers the question as to what will happen to the Jews and to the temple in Jerusalem after He is crucified. Most of this took place within forty years of His death and resurrection.

18 And now **ye behold** [*right now you can see*] **this temple** which is in Jerusalem, **which ye call the house of God** [*the wording "which ye call" is significant; in effect, Jesus is saying that the temple, which is still referred to by the Jews as the house of the Lord, is not the house of the Lord; it has been defiled by wickedness, money changers, and so on and has been rejected by Christ*], and **your enemies** [*the Jews, the enemies of His righteous disciples who are listening to Him as he teaches them*] **say that this house shall never fall.**

19 But, verily [*truly*] I say unto you, that **desolation** [*terrible destruction*] **shall come upon this**

generation [*the Jews then living*] as a thief in the night [*it will catch them by surprise*], and **this people** [*the Jewish nation at the time of Christ*] **shall be destroyed and scattered among all nations** [*a part of the scattering of Israel*].

20 And **this temple** [*the temple in Jerusalem*] which ye now see **shall be thrown down** that there shall not be left one stone upon another.

> In about A.D. 70, the Romans literally burned the flammable components of the temple and then tore the above-ground portion of the building apart, stone by stone. It is helpful to note that when the Romans began destroying the Jewish nation, faithful Christians of the day heeded the word of the Lord (Matthew 24:16) and fled to Pella (about eighty miles north of Jerusalem, east of the Jordan River), and were thus spared the atrocities that were heaped upon the unbelieving Jews. We will include a longer note on this after verse 21, next.

21 And it shall come to pass, that **this generation of Jews shall not pass away until every desolation which I have told you concerning them shall come to pass.**

> A brief summary of the fulfillment of the Savior's prophecy about the "desolations" (verse 21, above) that would befall the Jews of that

day is found in the institute of religion *Doctrine and Covenants Student Manual*, 1981, page 93, quoting Smith and Sjodahl as follows (**bold** added for emphasis):

"In the year A.D. 66, Cestus Gallus marched into Judea and threatened Jerusalem. He might have taken the City, but he retreated and met with defeat near Beth-Horon. **The Christians in the City, remembering the words of our Lord, fled to the little city of Pella**, but the Jews were fired, by their temporary success, to renewed resistance. Vespasian was then sent from Rome to crush the rebellion. He took some of the strongholds of the Country and approached Jerusalem. Internal strife prevailed there, and such horrors were perpetrated that Vespasian decided to give his army a rest, while the Jews destroyed each other. Vespasian was elevated to the throne, and his son, Titus, was left to continue the conquest. **The siege began in the year A.D. 70.** Soon famine prevailed. Citizens who ventured outside the walls to search for roots to eat, if seized, were crucified by the Roman soldiers. Sometimes hundreds in that awful position could be seen from the walls. A trench was dug around the City, in order to make its isolation complete. Prisoners of war were cut open, while alive, to enable soldiers to search their bodies for gold which they might have swallowed. Six hundred thousand persons died within the walls, and the dead bodies, too numerous to be buried, were left in the houses. The Zealots, a fanatical sect whose members maintained that God would save them at the last moment, went about murdering and urging the people to resistance. Even Titus was sick at heart at the daily horrors he witnessed or heard of. At length **the temple became a fort**. Titus attacked it as such. **A Roman soldier**, contrary to order, **set fire to it**. After a while the scene was one of carnage and plunder. **Six thousand Jews perished in the flames**. In this awful war **more than a million and a half of the Jews perished, and many were sold into slavery, and thus 'scattered among all nations**.' (*Commentary*, 260–61.)"

As the Savior continued teaching his disciples, He confirmed their testimonies of the gospel by bearing His own to them, as recorded in verses 22–23, next.

22 **Ye say that ye know** that the end of the world cometh [*"end of the world" means "end of wickedness"; this phrase can refer to the destruction of the wicked in conjunction with the Second Coming and can also mean after the end of the Millennium and the "little season" that follows (D&C 88:110–15)*]; **ye say also that ye know** that the heavens and the earth shall pass away [*this earth will die and be resurrected (D&C 88:26) and, when it is*

celestialized (D&C 130:9–11), it will be moved from its current "heavens" (solar system and such) back into the presence of the Father where it was originally created. See statement by Brigham Young, Journal of Discourses, Vol. 17, pages 143–44, as follows: "When man fell, the earth fell into space, and took up its abode in this planetary system, and the sun became our light . . . When it (the earth) is glorified, it will return again into the presence of the Father"; see also* Teachings of the Prophet Joseph Smith, *page 181*)];

23 And **in this ye say truly, for so it is**; but these things which I have told you shall not pass away until all shall be fulfilled.

Next, in verses 24–25, we are briefly taught about the scattering and latter-day gathering of the Jews.

24 And **this I have told you concerning Jerusalem**; and when that day shall come [*the devastations upon the Jews in the years immediately following the crucifixion of Christ*], shall **a remnant** [*of the Jews*] be **scattered among all nations**;

Doctrine

Verses 25–53. The signs of the times are prophecies to be fulfilled in the last days

showing that the Second Coming of Christ is getting close.

25 But **they** [*the Jews*] **shall be gathered again** [*in the last days*]; **but** they **shall remain** [*will not be gathered to Christ*] **until the times of the Gentiles be fulfilled** [*until the Gentiles are gathered*]

> The phrase "times of the Gentiles" in verse 25, above, is a reference to the last days in which we live, at which time the gospel will be preached to the Gentiles. In this context, "Gentiles" means everyone except the Jews. According to the Savior's teaching in verse 25, in the last days, the gospel will be preached first to the Gentiles, meaning everyone except the Jews. Then, when the "times of the Gentiles" have been fulfilled—in other words, when the Gentiles have had a chance to hear the true gospel of Jesus Christ, then the Jews will get another opportunity. We are now living during the "times of the Gentiles." This is one of the "signs of the times" that is currently being fulfilled.
>
> Jesus continues now, teaching His disciples (and us) of additional signs of the times that will indicate that His Second Coming is getting close.

26 And in that day [*in the last days, before His coming*] shall be heard of **wars and rumors of wars** [*this sign is being fulfilled now, in our day*], and **the whole earth shall be in commotion** [*including political disasters as well as natural disasters, such as plagues and other calamities, which are now being fulfilled*], and **men's hearts shall fail them** [*people will give up hope, be depressed, and much despair will be everywhere, which is now also being fulfilled*], and **they shall say that Christ delayeth his coming until the end of the earth** [*things will get so bad that people will worry that there won't be anyone left on earth by the time the Savior comes*].

27 And **the love of men shall wax** [*grow*] **cold** [*people will not care about anyone but themselves—now being fulfilled*], and **iniquity** [*gross wickedness*] **shall abound** [*will be everywhere—now being fulfilled*].

28 And **when the times of the Gentiles is come in** [*when the time comes to preach the gospel to the Gentiles*], **a light** [*the restoration of the gospel through Joseph Smith*] **shall break forth among them that sit in darkness** [*spiritual darkness*], and it shall be **the fulness of my gospel**;

> The restoration of the gospel, spoken of in verse 28, above, is another sign of the times. It is basically fulfilled and continues to be fulfilled. The other part of verse 28, speaking of the gospel being

taken to "them that sit in darkness," is a sign of the times that is currently being fulfilled through the preaching of the gospel as we take it to all the world.

Next, in verse 29, we are told that many people will reject the gospel when it is preached to them in the last days. And, as you will see, the Savior explains why this will be the case.

29 **But they receive it not**; for they perceive not the light, and they turn their hearts from me **because of the precepts** [*the prevailing teachings, rules, laws, morals, and principles*] **of men**.

30 And **in that generation** [*the last days; the dispensation of the fullness of times*] **shall the times of the Gentiles be fulfilled**.

31 And there shall be men standing in that generation, that shall not pass [*will not die*] until they shall see an overflowing scourge; for **a desolating sickness shall cover the land**.

Many have suggested different possibilities as to what the "desolating sickness" spoken of in verse 31, above, might be. Some think it is AIDS. Some think it is antibiotic-resistant strains of germs. Yet others speculate that it could be an especially deadly form of flu, such as COVID-19, causing a worldwide plague. The

most "desolating" and destructive "sickness" of all is personal wickedness, which causes moral and spiritual darkness and the destruction of individuals and nations. We are seeing this now throughout the world. While we have not been told specifically what this "desolating sickness" is, we are left to wonder if it might be more spiritual than physical.

Next, in verse 32, the Lord tells us how to avoid the "overflowing scourge" and "desolating sickness" spoken of in verse 31.

32 But **my disciples** [*true followers*] **shall stand in holy places** [*including righteous homes, temples, church meetings, family history centers, seminaries and institutes, scripture reading, Church magazines, general conferences, and so on*], **and shall not be moved** [*will not be overcome*]; but among the wicked, men shall lift up their voices and curse God and die.

Next, the Savior lists additional signs of the times and explains what the reaction of the majority of earth's inhabitants will be.

33 And there shall be **earthquakes** also in divers [*various*] places, and **many desolations** [*devastating disasters*]; **yet men will harden their hearts against me**, and they **will take up the sword, one against another**,

and **they will kill one another.**

In verse 34, next, along with the first phrase of verse 35, the Savior stops quoting the Olivet Discourse (Matthew 24) for a moment and tells us how His disciples reacted to what He had just told them.

34 And now, when I the Lord had spoken these words unto my disciples, **they were troubled.**

There is a major message for us in what the Master tells His disciples next as to how they should react to the signs of the times. As you can see, He counsels them to "be not troubled" (the first part of verse 35). Instead, they should use the fulfillment of these prophecies to strengthen their testimonies.

Perhaps you have attended classes or been involved in discussions concerning the signs of the times in which the prevailing sentiment and feeling was that of fear and even an element of panic. If we follow the Savior's counsel (seen also in Joseph Smith—Matthew 1:23), we will avoid approaching these prophecies with fear and trepidation and instead look at them as faith and testimony builders as instructed by Jesus in the last part of verse 35, next.

35 And I said unto them: **Be not troubled,** for, **when all these things shall come to pass, ye may know that the promises which have been made unto you**

shall be fulfilled. [*In other words, you can know that the gospel is true because of the obvious fulfillment of so many prophecies.*]

36 And when the light [*including the restoration of the gospel, the fulfillment of these prophecies, and so forth*] shall begin to break forth, it shall be with them [*the people who live in the last days*] like unto a parable which I will show you—

Next, the Savior likens the signs of the times to the leaves sprouting on a tree, showing that summer is not far off. When we see the signs of the times being fulfilled, we know that the Second Coming is not far off.

37 **Ye look and behold** [*see*] **the fig-trees,** and **ye see them with your eyes** [*in other words, the evidence is obvious; there is no question as to what is happening*], and **ye say** when they begin to shoot forth [*when leaves begin to grow in spring*], and their leaves are yet tender, that **summer is now nigh at hand** [*summer is nearly here*];

38 **Even so it shall be in that day** [*in the last days*] **when they shall see all these things** [*the signs of the times being fulfilled; obvious evidence*], **then shall they know that the hour** [*for the Second Coming*] **is nigh** [*near*].

The word "fear," as used in verse 39, next, means living righteously, striving to stay on the covenant path, having respect and reverence for the Lord and for sacred things, including the scriptures. The message is that those who respect and study the scriptures and live the gospel will be familiar with the signs of the times. As they see them being obviously fulfilled, they will be looking forward to His coming.

39 And it shall come to pass that **he that feareth me shall be looking forth for the great day of the Lord to come,** even **for the signs of the coming of the Son of Man.**

Perhaps you've wondered why Jesus is often referred to in scripture as "the Son of Man" (verse 39, above) since you know that He is the Son of God and not the son of a mortal man. Did you notice that the word "Man" is capitalized? "Man" is short for "Man of Holiness," meaning Heavenly Father. Thus, Jesus is the "Son of Man of Holiness," or the Son of Heavenly Father. You can read this explanation in Moses 6:57. Sometimes, as in Matthew 20:28 and John 3:13, the phrase is "Son of man" (with "man" not capitalized), but it still means the same thing.

Next, in verses 40–43, the Savior tells us of yet more signs of the times, explaining that the righteous (spoken of in verse 39) will recognize them for what they are.

40 And **they** [*the righteous*] **shall see signs and wonders,** for they shall be shown forth **in the heavens above, and in the earth beneath** [*the signs of the times will be all around us*].

41 **And they shall behold** [*see*] **blood,** and **fire,** and **vapors of smoke.**

42 And **before the day of the Lord** [*Second Coming*] **shall come, the sun shall be darkened,** and the **moon** be **turned into blood,** and the **stars fall from heaven.**

In reference to verse 42, above, it is interesting to note that Joel 2:31 also speaks of the darkening of the sun and the moon being turned to blood as a prominent sign of the times. In the October 2001 general conference, in the Saturday morning session, President Gordon B. Hinckley taught that this has been fulfilled. He said (**bold** added for emphasis):

"The era in which we live is the fulness of times spoken of in the scriptures, when God has brought together all of the elements of previous dispensations. From the day that He and His Beloved Son manifested themselves to the boy Joseph, there has been a tremendous cascade of enlightenment poured out upon the world. The hearts of men have turned to their fathers in fulfillment of the words of Malachi. **The vision of Joel has been fulfilled wherein he declared**:

Joel 2:28–32

28 And it shall come to pass afterward, that I will pour out my spirit upon all flesh; and your sons and your daughters shall prophesy, your old men shall dream dreams, your young men shall see visions:

29 And also upon the servants and upon the handmaids in those days will I pour out my spirit.

30 And I will shew wonders in the heavens and in the earth, blood, and fire, and pillars of smoke.

31 The sun shall be turned into darkness, and the moon into blood, before the great and the terrible day of the LORD come.

32 And it shall come to pass, that **whosoever shall call on the name of the LORD shall be delivered**: for in mount Zion and in Jerusalem shall be deliverance, as the LORD hath said, and in the remnant whom the LORD shall call."

As soon as our living prophet said that these words of Joel had been

fulfilled, I accepted it on faith. We are now left to wait for additional inspired details as to how this prophecy has been fulfilled.

Next, beginning with verse 43, we are given specific details about the events leading up to and surrounding the actual Second Coming.

43 And **the remnant** [*of the Jews*] **shall be gathered unto this place** [*Jerusalem*];

44 And then **they shall look for me, and, behold, I will come**; and **they shall see me in the clouds of heaven, clothed with power and great glory** [*when the resurrected Christ comes this time, it will be with full power and glory, as opposed to the humble circumstances of His first coming and mortal ministry*]; **with all the holy angels** [*the hosts of heaven will accompany Him; this will be a very large group*]; and **he that watches not for me shall be cut off** [*another way of saying that the wicked will be destroyed at His coming*].

It is important as we study these verses to be aware that they are not all in exact chronological sequence. Jesus is reviewing and giving additional details. For instance, as we get to verses 48–53, we will be taught about the Savior appearing to the Jews on the Mount of Olives. This is not the Second Coming; rather, it is an appearance of the Lord prior to it, similar to the appearance of the Savior at Adam-ondi-Ahman (Daniel 7:9–14; D&C 116) and to the city of New Jerusalem, spoken of in verses 66–67 in this section.

As He continues to teach us and give us marvelous doctrinal details, Jesus speaks of the resurrection of the righteous, often called "the morning of the first resurrection," and likewise frequently referred to as "the resurrection of the just." From this we learn that the righteous dead will be resurrected before the wicked are destroyed at the time of His coming (see also D&C 86:7).

45 But **before the arm of the Lord shall fall** [*before the wicked are destroyed*], an angel shall sound his trump, and **the saints that have slept** [*the righteous, celestial quality who are already dead; see D&C 88:97–98*] **shall come forth to meet me** in the cloud [*the "cloud" spoken of in (D&C 34:7)*].

46 Wherefore, **if ye have slept in peace** [*if you died righteous or have become righteous and worthy through the postmortal spirit world work for the dead and are now faithful and worthy of celestial glory*] **blessed** [*happy*] **are you**; for as you now behold me and know that I am, **even so shall ye come unto me and your souls shall live**

[*your body and spirit will be reunited; (D&C 88:15)*], and **your redemption shall be perfected**; and the saints shall come forth from the four quarters of the earth [*the righteous dead will be resurrected from all over the earth*].

47 **Then shall the arm of the Lord fall upon the nations** [*then the wicked will be destroyed*].

It is encouraging to note that the righteous Saints who are still alive at the time of the Second Coming will also be caught up to meet the coming Lord (see D&C 88:96).

As mentioned previously, now the Savior goes back just a bit chronologically (in verse 48, next) and gives details about His appearance to the Jews on the Mount of Olives just outside of Jerusalem. This appearance to the Jews will occur before the actual Second Coming. President Ezra Taft Benson spoke of this as follows (**bold** added for emphasis):

"His **first appearance** will be to the righteous Saints who have gathered to the New Jerusalem. In this place of refuge they will be safe from the wrath of the Lord, which will be poured out without measure on all nations. . . .

"The **second appearance** of the Lord **will be to the Jews**. To these beleaguered sons of Judah, surrounded by hostile Gentile armies who again threaten to overrun

Jerusalem, the Savior—their Messiah—will appear and set His feet on the Mount of Olives, 'and it shall cleave in twain, and the earth shall tremble, and reel to and fro, and the heavens also shall shake' (D&C 45:48).

"The Lord Himself will then rout the Gentile armies, decimating their forces (see Ezek. 38, 39). Judah will be spared, no longer to be persecuted and scattered. . . .

"The **third appearance** of Christ will be **to the rest of the world.**

"All nations will see Him 'in the clouds of heaven, clothed with power and great glory; with all the holy angels . . .

"'And the Lord shall utter his voice, and all the ends of the earth shall hear it; and the nations of the earth shall mourn, and they that have laughed shall see their folly.

"'And calamity shall cover the mocker, and the scorner shall be consumed; and they that have watched for iniquity shall be hewn down and cast into the fire.' (D&C 45:44, 49–50.)

"Yes, come He will!" (Ezra Taft Benson, "Five Marks of the Divinity of Jesus Christ," *Ensign, December 2001*).

48 And **then shall the Lord set his foot upon this mount** [*the Mount of Olives*], and **it shall cleave in twain** [*it will split in two*

(see Zechariah 14:4–7)], and **the earth shall tremble, and reel to and fro** [*everyone on earth will feel this earthquake; the righteous will recognize it as a sign of the times*], and **the heavens also shall shake.**

In verses 49–50, next, He describes the awful awareness that will come upon the wicked as they realize that they have been caught up with.

49 And **the Lord shall utter his voice,** and **all** the ends of the earth **shall hear it**; and the nations of the earth **shall mourn,** and they that have laughed [*at the righteous and at morality and righteousness in general*] **shall see their folly** [*foolishness; lack of wisdom and foresight*].

50 And **calamity shall cover the mocker** [*who mocked sacred things*], and **the scorner** [*of righteousness*] **shall be consumed** [*will be burned*]; and **they that have watched for iniquity** [*in the righteous, in the leaders of the Church, in men and women of integrity; this can also mean those who constantly watch for new opportunities to commit sin*] **shall be hewn down and cast into the fire.**

In verses 51–53, next, the Savior returns to describing His appearance to the Jews on the Mount of Olives (before His actual Second

Coming to the entire world) and to their reaction upon seeing Him.

51 And **then shall the Jews look upon me and say: What are these wounds in thine hands and in thy feet?**

52 **Then shall they know that I am the Lord**; for **I will say unto them: These wounds are the wounds with which I was wounded in the house of my friends** [*in other words, these are the wounds that He received when those who should have been His friends crucified Him*]. **I am he who was lifted up** [*crucified*]. **I am Jesus** that was crucified. **I am the Son of God.**

53 And **then shall they weep** because of their iniquities [*they will be truly sorry for their wickedness*]; **then shall they lament** [*mourn*] **because they persecuted their king.**

Perhaps you can imagine and feel the tenderness of the scene described above as the Jews acknowledge and accept Jesus as the Christ, their Savior, and mourn for their sins. Elder Parley P. Pratt described this appearance of the Savior as follows (**bold** added for emphasis):

"Zechariah, chapter 14, has told us much concerning the great battle and overthrow of the nations who fight against Jerusalem, and he has said, in plain words, that the Lord shall come at the very time of the overthrow of that army; yes, in fact, even while they are in the act of taking Jerusalem, and have already succeeded in taking one-half the city, spoiling their houses, and ravishing their women. Then, behold, **their long-expected Messiah, suddenly appearing, shall stand upon the Mount of Olives**, a little east of Jerusalem, to fight against those nations and deliver the Jews. Zechariah says **the Mount of Olives shall cleave in twain**, from east to west, and one-half of the mountain shall remove to the north while the other half falls off to the south, suddenly forming **a very great valley into which the Jews shall flee for protection from their enemies** as they fled from the earthquake in the days of Uzziah, king of Judah; while the Lord cometh and all the Saints with Him. **Then will the Jews behold that long, long-expected Messiah, coming in power to their deliverance, as they always looked for him**. He will destroy their enemies and deliver them from trouble at the very time they are in the utmost consternation, and about to be swallowed up by their enemies. But what will be their astonishment when they are about to fall at the feet of their Deliverer and acknowledge him their Messiah! **They discover the wounds which were once made in his hands, feet, and side**; and on inquiry, at once recognize

Jesus of Nazareth, the King of the Jews, the man so long rejected. Well did the prophet say that **they shall mourn and weep**, every family apart, and their wives apart. But, thank heaven, **there will be an end to their mourning; for he will forgive their iniquities and cleanse them from uncleanness**" (Parley P. Pratt, *Voice of Warning*, 32–33; quoted in the *Doctrine and Covenants Student Manual*, 1981, 96–97).

Next, in verse 54, we are taught that those who have died and are worthy of terrestrial glory will have part in the first resurrection. The major resurrection at the beginning of the Millennium will take place in two parts—first, the celestial, and next, the terrestrial. The righteous dead, who are worthy of celestial glory, will be resurrected first (D&C 88:97–98). This is sometimes referred to as "the morning of the first resurrection." Then a major terrestrial resurrection will take place (D&C 88:99). This is sometimes referred to as the "afternoon of the first resurrection." Remember, this all takes place at or near the beginning of the Millennium.

54 And then shall the **heathen nations** [*a general term for those who will be in terrestrial glory; see notes included with D&C 76:71– 73 in this study guide for more information*] be redeemed, **and they that knew no law shall have**

part in the first resurrection; and it shall be tolerable for them [*perhaps implying that they will have a better experience on Judgment Day than the wicked; compare with D&C 75:22*].

Next, in verse 55, the Savior teaches us that Satan will be bound during the Millennium.

Doctrine

Vs. 55. Satan will be bound during the Millennium.

55 And **Satan shall be bound**, that he shall have no place in the hearts of the children of men.

Some Church members wonder whether Satan will be bound so that he cannot even try to tempt us or if the statement in verse 55, above, means that he will try but nobody will listen. Joseph Fielding Smith provided an answer as follows (**bold** added for emphasis):

"There are many among us who teach that the binding of Satan will be merely the binding which those dwelling on the earth will place upon him by their refusal to hear his enticings. This is not so. **He will not have the privilege during that period of time to tempt any man.** (D. & C. 101:28.)" (*Church History and Modern Revelation*, 1:192).

Next, the Lord refers back to the parable of the ten virgins, which

He gave as recorded in Matthew 25:1–13. This is one of those places in modern scripture that bless us with greater understanding of the Bible. For instance, in verse 57, below, the Savior explains what He meant by the "wise virgins."

56 And **at that day, when I shall come in my glory** [*the Second Coming*], **shall the parable be fulfilled which I spake concerning the ten virgins**.

57 For **they that are wise** and **have received the truth**, and **have taken the Holy Spirit for their guide**, and **have not been deceived**—verily I say unto you, they shall not be hewn down and cast into the fire, but shall abide the day [*they will not be destroyed at the Second Coming*].

Next, in verses 58–59, we are taught a few more details about how life will be during the Millennium.

Doctrine

Vs. 58. Children will grow up without sin during the Millennium.

58 And **the earth shall be given unto them** [*the "wise," as defined in verse 57, above*] **for an inheritance**; and **they shall multiply and wax strong** [*the population of*

righteous people will increase rapidly during the Millennium], and **their children shall grow up without sin unto salvation**.

The phrase "without sin," in verse 58, above, could have at least two meanings. It could mean that children will grow up without "sinning" during the thousand years of peace. It could also mean that children born during the Millennium will grow up in an environment that is essentially without sin—without the wickedness and the sins of telestial lifestyles surrounding them, such as those with which we are plagued in these last days. The point at the end of verse 58, above, is wonderful, namely that, in that millennial environment, children will grow up "unto salvation."

Doctrine

Vs. 59. Christ will be the King over the entire world during the Millennium.

59 For **the Lord** [*Christ*] **shall be in their midst**, and **his glory shall be upon them**, and **he will be their king** and **their lawgiver**.

The type of government described in the last phrase of verse 59, above, is a "theocracy," which means "government by God."

This is the end of the Savior's quoting what He taught his disciples on the Mount of Olives concerning

His Second Coming as recorded in Matthew 24. As mentioned previously, the quote consists of section 45, verses 16–33 and 35–59, and contains more than three hundred additional words not found in Matthew 24 in the Bible.

Next, in verse 60, Jesus tells Joseph Smith in particular, and the Church in general, that he will receive no further explanation of Matthew 24 until additional work is done on the Joseph Smith Translation of the Bible (JST).

60 And now, behold, I say unto you, **it shall not be given unto you to know any further concerning this chapter** [*Matthew 24*], **until the New Testament** [*part of the Joseph Smith Translation of the Bible*] **be translated,** and in it all these things shall be made known [*in other words, as you continue to work on the translation of the New Testament, you will learn much more about this*];

61 Wherefore I give unto you that ye may now translate it [*go ahead now and work on correcting the New Testament as it now stands in the King James Bible*], that ye may be prepared for the things to come.

It is interesting to note that the very next day after this revelation was given, Joseph Smith resumed work on what is sometimes referred to as the inspired translation of the Bible, with Sidney Rigdon serving as his scribe. Up to this time, the Prophet had been working on the Old Testament and had done work up to and including Genesis 19:35. As a result of this revelation (D&C 45:60–62), Joseph and Sidney immediately began to work on the New Testament (while finishing a bit more of the Old Testament). In fact, they began working on it on March 8, 1831, beginning with Matthew, and by April 7, 1831, they had finished to Matthew 9:2. (See the table on page 96 in Robert J. Matthews's *A Plainer Translation: Joseph Smith's Translation of the Bible.*)

We will pause for a moment and provide a bit of background for the Joseph Smith Translation of the Bible, or the "JST" as it is commonly referred to today. We will quote from the institute of religion student manual, *Church History in the Fullness of Times*, 2003, 117–18.

"Joseph Smith's inspired translation of the Bible was one of the pivotal developments of his work as a prophet, and it has had a profound influence on the Church. Joseph's knowledge about the principles of the gospel and God's work with his ancient prophets and people increased immensely through this project. He considered it an important 'branch' of his calling and labored diligently at it. When he and

Sidney Rigdon were at home in Ohio, this was their major preoccupation. The frequency with which the "translation" is referred to in the revelations and historical documents of the period underscores the importance of this project. The Prophet first began this work in New York in 1830. When he arrived in Ohio in February 1831, he continued his work in the Old Testament with the help of his scribe, Elder Rigdon. But early in March, Joseph was commanded to work on the translation of the New Testament (see D&C 45:60–61). During the next two years Joseph and Sidney continued their work on both the New and the Old Testaments. They optimistically pronounced their work finished on 2 July 1833. See *History of the Church,* 1:368."

"In addition to the great legacy left to the Church in the Joseph Smith Translation (JST) itself, numerous revelations now recorded in the Doctrine and Covenants came to the Prophet while he worked on the inspired translation. The study of the Bible stimulated him to inquire of the Lord about significant doctrinal and organizational matters. Doctrine and Covenants sections 76, 77, and 91 have direct links with the translation effort, 'and probably much of the information in sections 74, 84, 86, 88, 93, 102, 104, 107, 113, and 132.' It is probable that many others are indirectly connected. (Robert J. Matthews, *A Plainer Translation:*

Joseph Smith's Translation of the Bible—A History and Commentary (Provo: Brigham Young University Press, 1985), page 256; see also pages 264–65.)"

62 For verily I say unto you, that **great things await you** [*apparently referring to the additional revelations, spoken of above, triggered by questions arising from the work on the JST*];

As the Savior continues, He warns these early Saints about troubles in their own land, explaining that this is the reason He commanded them to move from their "eastern lands" to Ohio. (See D&C 37:3.) He also warns of future wars in the United States, no doubt including the Civil War as well as future troubles.

63 **Ye hear of wars in foreign lands; but**, behold, I say unto you, **they are nigh, even at your doors**, and **not many years hence ye shall hear of wars in your own lands.**

64 **Wherefore** [*this is why*] **I, the Lord, have said, gather ye out from the eastern lands**, assemble ye yourselves together ye elders of my church; go ye forth into the western countries [*the areas west of Kirtland, Ohio*], call upon the inhabitants to repent, and inasmuch as they do repent, build up churches [*units*

and congregations of the Church]
unto me.

Next, the importance of unity and harmony (verse 65) is emphasized for those who desire to be the people of the Lord. These qualities are essential for those who ultimately wish to become celestial—in other words, worthy to live in a Zion society, of which the New Jerusalem (verse 66) is an example.

65 And **with one heart** and with **one mind**, gather up your riches that ye may purchase an inheritance which shall hereafter be appointed unto you.

Doctrine

Verses 66–71. The city of New Jerusalem will be built before the Second Coming of Christ.

66 And **it shall be called the New Jerusalem**, a land of **peace**, a city of **refuge**, a place of **safety** for the saints of the Most High God;

We will take just a moment to learn a bit more about New Jerusalem, which is also referred to as "Zion" in this context.

A city named New Jerusalem will be built in Independence, Jackson County, Missouri (D&C 57:2–3). It is spoken of in a number of places in the scriptures, including verse 66, next, and in Moses 7:61–62 in the Pearl of Great Price. At this point (section 45), the Saints have not yet been told where this city of Zion, or New Jerusalem, is to be built. They will be told in a little more than four months, on July 20, 1831, as the Prophet Joseph Smith receives the revelation now known as D&C 57.

In the meantime, they are commanded to pool their resources in preparation for buying property for this city (verse 65, above). Perhaps one of the more important lessons we learn from this is that the Lord expects us to be obedient and to do our part to prepare for desired blessings that can come our way in the future.

Here is just a bit more about New Jerusalem. It will become one of two headquarters or capitals during the Millennium (Old Jerusalem will become the other one). Joseph Fielding Smith explained this as follows (**bold** added for emphasis):

"When Joseph Smith translated the Book of Mormon, he learned that America is the land of Zion which was given to Joseph and his children and that on this land the City Zion, or **New Jerusalem**, is to be built. He also learned that **Jerusalem in Palestine** is to be rebuilt and become a holy city. **These two cities**, one in the land of Zion and one in Palestine, are to **become capitals for the kingdom of God during the millennium**" (*Doctrines of Salvation*, 3:71).

We will learn more about New Jerusalem in verses 67–71.

67 And **the glory of the Lord shall be there**, and **the terror of the Lord also shall be there, insomuch tha**t [*such that*] **the wicked will not come unto it**, and **it shall be called Zion.**

68 And it shall come to pass among the wicked, that **every man that will not take his sword against his neighbor must needs flee unto Zion** [*including the stakes of Zion (see D&C 115:6)*] **for safety**.

69 And **there shall be gathered unto it out of every nation** under heaven; and it shall be **the only people that shall not be at war one with another.**

70 And **it shall be said among the wicked: Let us not go up to battle against Zion**, for the inhabitants of Zion are terrible; wherefore we cannot stand.

71 And it shall come to pass that **the righteous shall be gathered out from among all nations, and shall come to Zion, singing with songs of everlasting joy**.

It is important for us to realize that although New Jerusalem will be a literal city and that verses 65–71 apply to it, there is a much broader context for these verses. For instance, in D&C 115:6, we learn

that in our day the stakes of Zion are to serve as "a defense and for a refuge" from the troubles and devastations that will be poured out upon the earth before the Second Coming. Thus, the advantages and protections provided by "Zion" and described in these verses can easily apply to Saints all over the world as they gather to the stakes of Zion in their own lands in the last days. The Prophet Joseph Smith spoke of this. He spoke of more than one gathering place for the Saints as follows (**bold** added for emphasis):

"Without Zion, and a place of deliverance, we must fall; because the time is near when the sun will be darkened, and the moon turn to blood, and the stars fall from heaven, and the earth reel to and fro. Then, if this is the case, and if we are not sanctified and **gathered to the places God has appointed**, with all our former professions and our great love for the Bible, we must fall; we cannot stand; we cannot be saved; for **God will gather out his Saints from the Gentiles**, and **then comes desolation and destruction**, and **none can escape except the pure in heart who are gathered**." (*Teachings of the Prophet Joseph Smith*, 71.)

Next, in verse 72, the Lord counsels the Saints not to talk to nonmembers about New Jerusalem, about Jackson County, Missouri, as a gathering place until

He tells them to. As you can well imagine, such talk could alarm and alienate people, including the locals in Missouri, and cause many misunderstandings and problems.

72 And now I say unto you, **keep these things from going abroad unto the world** until it is expedient in me [*until it is wise in the Lord's sight*], that ye may accomplish this work in the eyes of the people, and in the eyes of your enemies, **that they may not know your works until ye have accomplished the thing which I have commanded you;**

73 **That when they shall know it** [*when the enemies of the Church (verse 72, above) become aware of it*], that **they may consider these things** [*perhaps meaning the power and protection of the Lord, which will be upon the Saints in the last days as they gather together and strive to live the laws and commandments of a Zion people*].

74 For **when the Lord shall appear he shall be terrible unto them, that fear may seize upon them, and they shall stand afar off and tremble.**

75 And **all nations** [*meaning the wicked in all nations*] **shall be afraid** because of the terror of the

Lord, and the power of his might. Even so. Amen.

SECTION 46

Background

This revelation was given through the Prophet Joseph Smith in Kirtland, Ohio, on March 8, 1831, just one day after the revelation recorded in section 45 was given. It deals with some important issues that require correction and additional instruction as the Church continues to grow. Remember, the Church is not quite one year old, and the converts come from several different religious backgrounds and persuasions that strongly affect their thinking as new members of the true Church. We see the Lord's patience and kindness as He gently teaches them.

Among other things at this period in the early history of the Church, particularly in the Kirtland, Ohio, region, some of the recent converts were exhibiting rather strange, even bizarre behaviors that they attributed to the manifestation of the Holy Ghost upon them. John Whitmer, David Whitmer's older brother, wrote "Some would fancy to themselves that they had the sword of Laban [see 1 Nephi 4:8–9], and would wield it as expert as a [soldier], . . . some would slide or scoot . . . [on] the floor, with the rapidity of a serpent, which the[y] termed sailing in the boat to the Lamanites, preaching the gospel. And many other vain and foolish manoeuvers (spelling in context) that are unseeming, and unprofitable to mention. Thus the devil blinded the eyes of some good and honest disciples" (in *The Joseph Smith Papers, Histories, Volume 2: Assigned Histories, 1831–1847*, 38).

In addition to these strange and false so-called spiritual manifestations among some members, the Saints in Kirtland had developed a practice of not allowing nonmembers of the Church to attend their worship services. Verses 3–6 will address this issue by instructing members not to exclude nonmembers from their public meetings.

Section 46 is probably best known for its listing of several gifts of the Spirit. As we study these spiritual gifts, you may wish to pay particular attention to which ones you may already have and which ones you feel you would like to strive to obtain according to the invitation of the Lord in verse 8.

President Dallin H. Oaks, while serving in the Quorum of the Twelve Apostles, taught us who can receive these gifts of the Spirit (**bold** added):

"**The Spirit of Christ is given to all men and women** that they may know good from evil, and manifestations of the Holy Ghost are given to lead earnest seekers to repentance and baptism. These are preparatory gifts. What we term spiritual gifts come next.

"**Spiritual gifts come to those who have received the gift of the Holy Ghost**. As the Prophet Joseph Smith taught, the gifts of the Spirit 'are obtained through that medium' [the Holy Ghost] and 'cannot be enjoyed without the gift of the Holy Ghost.' . . . (*Teachings of the Prophet Joseph Smith*, 243, 245)" ("Spiritual Gifts," *Ensign*, Sept. 1986, 68).

As we begin our verse-by-verse study, let's look first at verse 2. It is very important to anyone who has the stewardship to conduct meetings in the Church. While we know that there are guidelines and policies that are provided by the Church for the conducting of meetings, it is vital that those in charge listen to and follow the promptings of the Spirit as they preside and conduct.

1 HEARKEN, O ye people of my church; for verily I say unto you that these things were spoken unto you for your profit and learning.

2 But **notwithstanding those things which are written** [*in the handbooks, policy manuals, and such*], it always has been given to the elders of my church from the beginning, and ever shall be, to **conduct all meetings as** they are **directed and guided by the Holy Spirit.**

As you can no doubt see, the instructions given in verse 2, above, when followed, allow for meetings to better meet the needs of individuals in the congregation, class, quorum, or group. When the promptings of the Spirit are followed, it makes all the difference.

As mentioned in the background for this section, a practice of not admitting the public (unless they were serious investigators) to church meetings had become commonplace. The Lord addresses this issue directly in verses 3–6, next. We will point it out with **bold**.

3 Nevertheless **ye are commanded never to cast any one out from** [*prevent them from attending*] **your public meetings** [*there are obviously private meetings, such as temple, ward council, class presidency, and so forth, to which the public would not be invited*], **which are held before the world.**

4 **Ye are also commanded not to cast any one who belongeth to the church out of your sacrament meetings**; nevertheless, if any have trespassed, let him not partake [*of the sacrament*] until he makes reconciliation [*until he or she repents*].

5 And again I say unto you, **ye shall not cast any out of your sacrament meetings who are**

earnestly seeking the kingdom—I speak this concerning those who are not of the church [*in other words, nonmembers*].

6 And again I say unto you, **concerning your confirmation meetings** [*meetings held to confirm recently baptized individuals; we usually do this in sacrament meetings now; see D&C 46:6, footnote a*], that **if there be any that are not of the church, that are earnestly seeking after the kingdom, ye shall not cast them out.**

President Russell M. Nelson also emphasized that nonmembers are invited to our public meetings and added counsel as to whether or not they should be allowed to take the sacrament. He said (**bold** added):

"Because we invite all to come unto Christ, friends and neighbors are always welcome **but not expected to take the sacrament. However, it is not forbidden. They choose for themselves**. We hope that newcomers among us will always be made to feel wanted and comfortable. Little children, as sinless beneficiaries of the Lord's Atonement, may partake of the sacrament as they prepare for covenants that they will make later in life" ("Worshiping at Sacrament Meeting," *Ensign*, Aug. 2004, 28).

Verse 7, next, is a transition between verses 3–6, above, which deal with the conducting of meetings according to the promptings of the Spirit, and the topic of spiritual gifts, which begins with verse 8. Among other things, this whole section points out the significant role of the Holy Ghost in the true Church of Jesus Christ. The beginning of verse 7 points out that not only does the Holy Ghost prompt for the proper conducting of meetings in the Church, but also that it should be listened to "in all things." The whole verse is a formula for avoiding deception.

7 But ye are commanded **in all things to ask of God**, who giveth liberally [*generously*]; and **that which the Spirit testifies unto you** even so I would **that ye should do** in all holiness of heart [*with pure motives*], walking uprightly before me [*living righteously*], considering the end [*goal*] of your salvation, doing all things with prayer and thanksgiving [*gratitude*], **that ye may not be seduced** [*overcome, fooled, deceived*] **by evil spirits**, or **doctrines of devils**, or the **commandments of men**; for some are of men, and others of devils.

Did you notice, near the end of verse 7, above, that not all dangers come directly from the devil? In addition to the dangers of being "seduced by evil spirits" and "doctrines of devils," there are dangers of being "seduced" by the

philosophies, dangerous thinking, lack of wisdom, and foolish notions of other people.

As we move on to verse 8, next, we are taught that the gifts of the Spirit (given by the Holy Ghost; see verse 13) are key to avoiding any kind of deception.

8 Wherefore, **beware lest ye are deceived**; and **that ye may not be deceived seek ye earnestly the best gifts**, always remembering for what they are given [*including the purposes pointed out in verse 7, above*];

Did you notice in verse 8, above, that the Lord invites us to seek these spiritual gifts? While each member of the Church has been given at least one gift (verse 11), we are invited to seek additional gifts, choosing those that would be "best" for us. This can be a very important part of our personal spiritual growth and progression. We should obviously avoid seeking for those that could be damaging to us—for instance, seeking for the gift of tongues so that we can show off in testimony meeting or whatever. The last portion of verse 9 warns us against seeking these gifts for selfish or unwise purposes.

Also, verse 9, next, points out who will benefit from such gifts of the Spirit.

9 For verily I say unto you, **they**

are given for the benefit of those who love me and keep all my commandments, and him that seeketh so to do [*a comfort to those who are honestly striving to keep all the commandments but still fall short*]; that all may be benefited that seek or that ask of me, that ask and not for a sign that they may consume it upon their lusts [*to try to use these gifts to intentionally build one's self up in the eyes of others; to use to accomplish wicked or selfish goals*].

10 And again, verily I say unto you, I would that ye should **always remember**, and **always retain in your** minds what those gifts are, that are given unto the church.

Did you notice that the Lord gives many cautions in the above verses with respect to motives and the use of spiritual gifts? Perhaps you are aware that these gifts are often counterfeited by the devil. It is one of his ways of deceiving people. His list of counterfeits includes healings, prophecy, tongues, interpretation of tongues, false spirits, visions, dreams, gathering, and so forth. The Prophet Joseph Smith gave the following counsel on this matter (**bold** added):

"A man must have the discerning of spirits before he can drag into daylight this hellish influence and unfold it unto the world in all its soul-destroying, diabolical, and horrid colors; for **nothing is a greater injury to the children of men than to be under the influence of a false spirit when they think they have the Spirit of God**. Thousands have felt the influence of its terrible power and baneful effects. Long pilgrimages have been undertaken, penances endured, and pain, misery and ruin have followed in their train; nations have been convulsed, kingdoms overthrown, provinces laid waste, and blood, carnage and desolation are habiliaments [*usually spelled "habiliments," meaning attire, dress*] in which it has been clothed" (*History of the Church*, 4:573).

Next, in verses 11 and 12, we see an element of teamwork built into the Lord's giving of some gifts to one member, other gifts to another, and different gifts to yet another, and so forth. In other words, one person has one gift, another a different one, and others additional ones, and when they work together in harmony, all are benefited.

11 For **all have not every gift** given unto them; for **there are many gifts**, and to **every man is given a gift** by the Spirit of God.

12 **To some is given one**, and **to some is given another, that all may be profited thereby.**

Before we move ahead with our

study of the specific gifts of the Spirit referred to in section 46, beginning with verse 13, we will pause to note that there are other places in the scriptures where most of these same gifts are mentioned. In fact, if you are one who makes brief notes in the front or back of your scriptures for quick reference, or you have a "notes" section on your digital device, you may wish to turn there now and write the following note:

Gifts of the Spirit

D&C 46:8–29

1 Corinthians 12:3–11

Moroni 10:9–18

Romans 12:6–13 (including less commonly mentioned gifts)

Just one more observation, and then we will move on to verse 13. D&C 46, 1 Corinthians 12, and Moroni 10 basically review the same gifts of the Spirit. However, Moroni 10:14 mentions one not mentioned by the other two sources. It is the gift of seeing angels and ministering spirits.

Now, on to the gifts that are given by the Holy Ghost, mentioned in verses 13–25.

The gift of knowing that Jesus is the Christ

13 To some it is given by the Holy Ghost to know that Jesus Christ is the Son of God, and that he was crucified for the sins of the world.

The gift of believing the testimony of those who do know

14 To others it is given **to believe on their words,** that they also might have eternal life [*exaltation*] if they continue faithful. [*In other words, while they do not have their own sure testimony, if they keep the commandments because they believe others who do know for themselves, they will also gain exaltation in the highest degree in celestial glory.*]

The gift of leadership, including understanding and skillfully using the various organizations within the Church to save souls

15 And again, to some it is given by the Holy Ghost to know the differences of administration, as it will be pleasing unto the same Lord, according as the Lord will, suiting his mercies according to the conditions of the children of men. [*This gift is especially noticeable in the Prophet, General Authorities, General Auxiliary leaders, stake presidents, bishops, and local quorum and auxiliary leaders.*]

The gift of being able to distinguish between true philosophies and false philosophies, good ideas and bad ideas, wise counsel and foolish counsel, whether something is from God or from some other source

16 And again, it is given by the Holy Ghost to some **to know the diversities of operations**, whether they be of God, that the manifestations of the Spirit may be given to every man to profit withal. [*Sometimes a person with this gift will sense something wrong with a philosophy or idea being taught in a class at school or wherever, even if a complete understanding of what is wrong is not yet in place. This gift, along with other gifts of the Spirit, can be most valuable in distinguishing between the things of God and counterfeits.*]

Elder Marion G. Romney (who later served in the First Presidency) explained "the diversities of operations" as follows (**bold** added for emphasis):

"By the statement in the revelation on spiritual gifts, '. . . it is given by the Holy Ghost to some to **know the diversities of operations**, whether they be of God, . . . and to others the discerning of spirits,' it appears that there are some apparently supernatural manifestations which are not worked by the power of the Holy Ghost. The truth is there are many which are not. **The world today is full of counterfeits**. It has always been so. Away back in the days of Moses, when Aaron's rod became a serpent, then Pharaoh's wise men, sorcerers and magicians '. . . cast down every man his rod, and they became serpents. . . .' (Ex. 7:11–12.) Isaiah warned against seeking '. . . unto them that have familiar spirits, and unto wizards that peep, and that mutter: . . .' (Isa. 8:19.)

"The Saints were cautioned by the Lord to walk uprightly before him, doing all things with prayer and thanksgiving, that they might '. . . not be seduced by evil spirits, or doctrines of devils, or the commandments of men; . . .' (D&C 47:7.)

"These citations not only sustain the proposition that there are counterfeits to the gifts of the Spirit, but they also suggest the origin of the counterfeits. However, we are not required to rely alone upon their implications, plain as they are, for the Lord states specifically that **some of the counterfeits '. . . are of men, and others of devils.'** [D&C 46:7.]

"**Some of these counterfeits are crude and easily detected, but others closely simulate true manifestations of the spirit**. Consequently, people are confused and deceived by them.

Without a key [*such as the gift of knowing "the diversities of operations"*], **one cannot distinguish between the genuine and the counterfeit**" (In Conference Report, April 1956, 70–71).

The gift of wisdom

17 And again, verily I say unto you, to some is given, by the Spirit of God, the word of wisdom.

It is important to note that the "word of wisdom" spoken of in verse 17, above, is not the "Word of Wisdom" known as section 89 of the Doctrine and Covenants in which the Lord counsels the Saints to avoid tobacco, alcohol, and hot drinks (tea and coffee) and to make wise use of fruits and grains and the like. Rather, it is the gift of having wisdom, seeing through the facade, and getting to the root cause. It includes the gift of seeing ahead to the ultimate consequences of a particular course of action.

The gift of knowledge and the gift of teaching

18 To another is given the word of knowledge, that all may be taught to be wise and to have knowledge.

As indicated above, verse 18 can be viewed as having two gifts of the Spirit in it. Perhaps you have had the experience of having

an instructor who had the gift of knowledge (able to learn and retain knowledge) but who did not have the gift of teaching. Still, one who has the gift of knowledge can be a valuable resource in classes, scientific research, and business.

The gift of having faith to be healed

19 And again, to some it is given to have faith to be healed;

This is a marvelous gift for those who possess it. There are many healings because of this gift of the Spirit. Yet, many do not have it. Under such circumstances, it might be easy for one not possessing it to feel less important than one who has it. The Lord addressed this situation in section 42 of the Doctrine and Covenants as follows (**bold** added for teaching purposes):

D&C 42:43–44, 48–52

43 And whosoever among you are sick, and have not faith to be healed, but believe, shall be nourished with all tenderness, with herbs and mild food [*perhaps this could include wise use of medicines and medical care today*], and that not by the hand of an enemy.

44 And the elders of the church, two or more, **shall** be called, and shall pray for and

lay their hands upon them in my name [*administering to the sick*]; **and if they die they shall die unto me, and if they live they shall live unto me.**

48 **And again, it shall come to pass that he that hath faith in me to be healed, and is not appointed unto death, shall be healed.**

49 **He who hath faith to see shall see.**

50 **He who hath faith to hear shall hear.**

51 **The lame who hath faith to leap shall leap.**

52 **And they who have not faith to do these things, but believe in me, have power to become my sons** [*in other words, those who do not have the gift of having faith to be healed can still attain exaltation*]; **and inasmuch as they break not my laws thou shalt bear their infirmities.**

The gift of healing

20 **And to others it is given to have faith to heal.**

This gift applies both to healing physically as well as healing spiritually. Being healed spiritually, gaining a testimony, being converted to the Church, being healed of bitterness and anger, and so forth, are no doubt even more important than being healed physically in the eternal perspective.

A bit of a caution should perhaps go along with discussion of this gift. Those who have this gift are sometimes called upon to the point that they become the unofficial "designated blessers and healers" in a given ward or locality. As a result, those who would normally be called upon to administer to the sick, such as fathers, brothers, ministering brothers and sisters, and so forth, are excluded from consideration. There is, of course, no absolute rule that a "designated healer" should not be called, but wisdom should prevail.

By the way, the gift of healing is not limited to priesthood holders. Faithful women, including mothers, are often blessed with this gift and use it through their prayers of faith in behalf of the sick. The Prophet Joseph Smith spoke of faithful sisters healing the sick. He said "if the sisters should have faith to heal the sick, let all hold their tongues, and let everything roll on" (*Teachings of the Prophet Joseph Smith*, 224).

The gift of working miracles

21 **And again, to some is given the working of miracles;**

Here, as with the gift of healing, we may tend to think more in terms of the spectacular such as stopping rain or calming water, rather than the less conspicuous daily healings and miracles associated with these gifts. While there certainly are marvelous and obvious miracles—a definite blessing accompanying the gospel of Jesus Christ—if we don't pay attention, we may miss the "working of miracles" that abounds on a less-obvious level. For example, the gift of working miracles could be seen in the lessening of contention, the impression to call someone who has an urgent need to talk, the sudden inspiration to solve a problem on an assembly line, the avoidance of a traffic accident, the calming of a child in discomfort, and so on.

The gift of prophecy

22 And to others it is given to prophesy;

In John 16:13 we are taught that the Holy Ghost "shall shew you things to come." Therefore, we understand that, among other things, this gift (which all members can have and which must be kept within proper stewardship and realm of influence) can include the gift of knowing the future. Certainly, the First Presidency and the members of the Quorum of the Twelve have this gift for their stewardship over the entire world. We sustain them as "prophets, seers, and revelators." Other leaders within the Church can

have this gift for those within their stewardships. Parents can have it for their families.

As a personal example, I was working late on a Saturday evening, studying and making notes for a talk I was to give on the following day. However, my mind kept focusing on the fact that one of our daughters was not yet home and it was getting late. Suddenly, I was given to know that she would be driving in within the next few minutes, and I was able to concentrate on preparing the talk. Sure enough, within ten minutes, I heard the unmistakable sound of our big Ford pickup driving into the driveway. She was home.

A faithful member could have the gift of prophecy by way of a good feeling or an uncomfortable feeling dealing with whether to marry the person he or she is currently dating. The gift of prophecy could be helpful in choosing a career path in college, choosing between employment options, deciding whether to relocate, and so forth.

The gift of discerning of spirits

23 And to others the discerning of spirits.

Elder Stephen L Richards explained that in addition to sensing hidden evil or good, this gift also enables one who possesses it to see the good in others. This is perhaps one of the most important manifestations of this gift. Elder Richards said that this gift consists largely "of an acute sensitivity to impressions—spiritual impressions, if you will—to read under the surface as it were, to detect hidden evil, and more importantly to find the good that may be concealed. **The highest type of discernment is that which perceives in others and uncovers for them their better natures, the good inherent within them** [bold added for emphasis]. It's the gift every missionary needs when he takes the gospel to the people of the world. He must make an appraisal of every personality whom he meets. He must be able to discern the hidden spark that may be lighted for truth. The gift of discernment will save him from mistakes and embarrassment, and it will never fail to inspire confidence in the one who is rightly appraised" (In Conference Report, April 1950, 162).

The gift of tongues

24 And again, it is given to some to speak with tongues;

This gift was manifest on the day of Pentecost, when Peter and the Apostles spoke to the multitudes in their own language, and those in the crowds (from many different countries) heard the preaching in their own languages. (See Acts 2:4–13.)

One of the most common manifestation of this gift is found in how fast and effectively our missionaries learn to speak foreign languages as part of their missionary work. This happens much to the amazement of people outside the Church. Representatives of large corporations and government entities have more than once approached the Church to ask if we could train them in our techniques for teaching foreign languages so effectively. Obviously, it is a bit difficult to explain to them that they and their people would have to join the Church so that they could get the gift of the Holy Ghost in order to receive this gift. And even then, it would have to be in harmony with the will of the Lord for them to receive and use the gift.

On occasions this gift is manifest in the sudden ability of people to understand or speak and understand a foreign language that they do not know. I experienced this as a young missionary in Austria. A member of the First Presidency was touring our mission and spoke to a large gathering of Saints in Vienna. Having been on my mission sufficiently long to understand German quite well, my companion missionaries and I, were amazed and deeply touched when we realized that many of the members in the congregation who did not understand English were understanding the sermon without needing interpretation into German. The gift of tongues had come upon them, and testimonies were greatly strengthened.

On the other hand, speaking in tongues is perhaps one of the most misunderstood gifts of the Holy Ghost and is often used by Satan and his evil spirits to deceive, divert, and detour people from the true gospel of Jesus Christ.

Because the gift of tongues is often used by the devil to counterfeit spirituality and to deceive, the Prophet Joseph Smith taught, "Be not so curious about tongues, do not speak in tongues except there be an interpreter present; the ultimate design of tongues is to speak to foreigners, and if persons are very anxious to display their intelligence, let them speak to such in their own tongues. The gifts of God are all useful in their place, but when they are applied to that which God does not intend, they prove an injury, a snare and a curse instead of a blessing" (*History of the Church*, 5:31–32).

The gift of the interpretation of tongues

25 And to another is given the interpretation of tongues.

This gift usually appears in conjunction with the gift of tongues. Elder Bruce R. McConkie taught, "Tongues and their interpretation are classed among the signs and miracles which always attend the faithful and which stand as evidences of the divinity of the Lord's work. (Mormon 9:24; Mark 16:17; Acts 10:46; 19:6.) In their more

dramatic manifestations they consist in speaking or interpreting, by the power of the Spirit, a tongue which is completely unknown to the speaker or interpreter. Sometimes it is the pure Adamic language which is involved" (*Doctrinal New Testament Commentary*, 2:383).

This gift, as is the case with the gift of tongues, is most often found in the work of spreading the gospel throughout the earth. Certainly, those who work with translating the scriptures and Church curriculum materials into foreign languages for use as the Church spreads forth into all nations would experience this gift.

Next, in verse 26, we are reminded that all of these gifts of the Spirit are given for the benefit of God's children.

26 And all these gifts come from God, for the benefit of the children of God.

As you know, one of the responsibilities of the bishop of a ward is to keep the doctrine pure and to see that all things in the ward are done in accordance with established practices and policies of the Church. In order to do this, he doesn't necessarily have to have all the gifts of the Spirit himself, but he is given the ability to discern or distinguish between correct and proper use of gifts of the Spirit and counterfeit ones. This allows him to help his members avoid deception in any of many forms. This we are taught in verse 27, next.

27 And **unto the bishop** of the church, and unto such as God shall appoint and ordain to watch over the church and to be elders unto the church [*this would include General Authorities, stake presidents, and branch presidents*], are to have it **given** unto them **to discern all those gifts** lest there shall be any among you professing and yet be not of God. [*In other words, in case there are deceivers among them.*]

Next, in verse 28, we are reminded that these spiritual gifts are to be received and used under the direction of the Holy Ghost. As you can see, this is a vital control over this aspect of God's work with His children.

28 And it shall come to pass **that he that asketh in Spirit shall receive in Spirit**;

We understand from verse 29, next, that some have all these gifts. We suppose that this could refer to the prophet and other leaders, but we do not have a clear explanation from an authorized source. Therefore, we will apply Alma 37:11, which says, "Now these mysteries are not yet fully made known unto me; therefore I shall forbear." In other words, "I don't know; therefore, I won't say."

29 That **unto some it may be given to have all those gifts**, that there may be a head, in order that every member may be profited thereby.

Earlier we mentioned that there are a number of less-commonly mentioned gifts of the Spirit. We will pause here and consider some of these gifts. In D&C 46:11, above, the Lord tells us "there are many gifts." We will quote Romans 12:6–13 here and use **bold** to point out some of these gifts that are not often referred to in discussions of gifts of the Spirit.

Romans 12:6–13

6 **Having** then **gifts differing** according to the grace that is given to us, whether **prophecy**, *let us prophesy* according to the proportion of faith;

7 Or **ministry** [*the gift of ministering to the needs of others*], let us wait on our ministering: or he that teacheth, on **teaching** [*the gift of being an effective teacher*];

8 Or he that exhorteth, on **exhortation** [*the gift of effectively explaining the urgency of living the gospel*]: he that **giveth** [*the gift of generosity*], let him do it with simplicity; he that **ruleth** [*the gift of leadership*], with diligence; he that sheweth **mercy**

[*the gift of being merciful*], with cheerfulness.

9 Let **love** [*the gift of showing sincere love*] be without dissimulation. **Abhor that which is evil** [*the gift of having a natural aversion to evil*]; **cleave to that which is good** [*the gift of wanting to be around goodness*].

10 **Be kindly affectioned** [*the gift of being sincerely kind*] one to another with brotherly love; in honour **preferring one another** [*the gift of putting the needs of others ahead of one's own needs*];

11 **Not slothful in business** [*the gift of being skilled in business dealings*]; **fervent in spirit** [*the gift of being truly spiritual*]; **serving the Lord** [*the gift of loving to serve the Lord*];

12 Rejoicing in **hope** [*the gift of hope, which in turn brings happiness and optimism*]; **patient** [*the gift of patience*] in tribulation; continuing **instant in prayer** [*the gift of praying always, continuously in tune with heaven*];

13 **Distributing to the necessity of saints** [*the gift of skillfully caring for the needy*]; given to **hospitality** [*the gift of hospitality, of being a gracious host*].

Elder Marvin J. Ashton spoke of these "less conspicuous gifts" as follows:

"Let us review some of these less-conspicuous gifts: the gift of **asking**; the gift of **listening**; the gift of **hearing** and **using a still, small voice**; the gift of **being able to weep**; the gift of **avoiding contention**; the gift of **being agreeable**; the gift of **avoiding vain repetition**; the gift of **seeking that which is righteous**; the gift of **not passing judgment**; the gift of **looking to God for guidance**; the gift of **being a disciple**; the gift of **caring for others**; the gift of **being able to ponder**; the gift of **offering prayer**; the gift of **bearing a mighty testimony**; and the gift of **receiving the Holy Ghost**" ("'There Are Many Gifts,'" *Ensign*, November 1987, 20).

Next, in verse 30, we are given a clue about how to get our specific prayers answered. It is rather simple and quite important. In effect, it says that when we are inspired by the Holy Ghost as to what to ask for, it is the will of God; therefore, it will happen. You may wish to write a cross-reference next to verse 30 in your own scriptures to D&C 50:29–30.

30 He that asketh in the Spirit asketh according to the will of God; wherefore it is done even as he asketh.

Next, in verse 31, the Savior reminds us that all our prayers as well as official ordinances and so forth in the Church must be done in the name of Jesus Christ.

31 And again, I say unto you, **all things must be done in the name of Christ**, whatsoever you do in the Spirit;

The importance of expressing gratitude while still under the influence of the Spirit is emphasized next in verse 32. In D&C 59:21, we will again come across this emphasis on expressing gratitude to God for blessings received.

32 And **ye must give thanks unto God in the Spirit for whatsoever blessing ye are blessed with**.

The Savior closes this revelation by stressing the fact that we must be consistent in living the gospel in our daily lives. We must not be on again, off again followers of Christ.

33 And **ye must practise virtue and holiness before me continually**. Even so. Amen.

SECTION 47

Background

This revelation was given to John Whitmer, who was David Whitmer's older brother and one of the Eight Witnesses of the Book of Mormon. It was given through the Prophet Joseph Smith in Kirtland, Ohio, on March 8, 1831.

The heading to this section is an example of the minor changes that have been made to seventy-eight Doctrine and Covenants section headings in the 2013 edition compared to the headings in prior editions. We will show you both headings:

2013 Edition

Revelation given through Joseph Smith the Prophet, at Kirtland, Ohio, March 8, 1831. John Whitmer, who had already served as a clerk to the Prophet, initially hesitated when he was asked to serve as the Church historian and recorder, replacing Oliver Cowdery. He wrote, "I would rather not do it but observed that the will of the Lord be done, and if he desires it, I desire that he would manifest it through Joseph the Seer." After Joseph Smith received this revelation, John Whitmer accepted and served in his appointed office.

1989 Printing

Revelation given through Joseph Smith the Prophet, at Kirtland, Ohio, March 8, 1831. HC 1:166. Prior to this time Oliver Cowdery had acted as Church historian and recorder. John Whitmer had not sought an appointment as historian, but, being asked to serve in this capacity, he had said that he would obey the will of the Lord in the matter. He had already served as a secretary to the Prophet in recording many of the revelations received in the Fayette, New York, area.

Thus, in this revelation, John Whitmer was called to serve officially as Church historian and recorder. With Oliver Cowdery now on a mission to the Lamanites on the western frontier (see sections 30 and 32), Brother Whitmer's calling, as mentioned above, was to take over from Oliver as Church historian and recorder. His history, according to the latest research from the Joseph Smith Papers Project, consisted of ninety-six pages and spanned from 1831 to 1838. He gave much good and faithful service to the Church during most of these years, but toward the end of 1838, he became angry with Joseph Smith and refused to give the Church the history he had kept. For this and other reasons, he was excommunicated on March 10, 1838. He never returned to the Church but never denied his testimony of the Book of Mormon. In 1893 the Church finally obtained a copy of his history of the Church.

This revelation is a reminder to us that we are to be a record-keeping people and that the history of the Church is a vital part of the work of the Lord in these last days. Such has been the case in every dispensation of the gospel, beginning with Adam and Eve (see Moses 6:5).

We will now proceed with section 47, using **bold as usual** to point things out. You may wish to mark some of the bolded items in your own scriptures.

1 BEHOLD, it is expedient in me [*the Lord considers it necessary*] that my servant **John** [*Whitmer*] **should write and keep a regular history, and assist you, my servant Joseph, in transcribing all things which shall be given you**, until he is called to further duties.

2 Again, verily I say unto you that **he can also lift up his voice** [*speak*] **in meetings, whenever it shall be expedient** [*necessary, needed*].

3 And again, I say unto you that **it shall be appointed unto him to keep the church record and history continually**; for Oliver Cowdery I have appointed to another office [*including a mission to the Lamanites with Parley P. Pratt, Peter Whitmer Jr., and Ziba Peterson*].

4 Wherefore, **it shall be given him, inasmuch as he is faithful, by the Comforter, to write these things** [*in other words, this history is to be written under the direction of the Holy Ghost*]. Even so. Amen.

SECTION 48

Background

Early in 1831, the Saints began moving from the eastern United States, primarily New York, to settle in the Kirtland, Ohio, area as previously commanded by the Lord (see D&C 37:1–3). As they began arriving in Ohio, they had many questions, including whether or not Ohio was to be the place where New Jerusalem would be built. They had read about New Jerusalem in the Book of Mormon (for example, in Ether 13:6) and had recently been told more about it in D&C 42:9 and 62.

They were also wondering whether to buy land in the Kirtland area for the Saints to settle and build on as they arrived from the east. Should they plan on settling permanently in Ohio, or was it to be a temporary situation? In answer to these and other questions, the Lord gave the revelation contained in section 48 to Joseph Smith in Kirtland sometime in March 1831.

One of the lessons we can learn from this revelation is the importance of having faith and following the Lord's instructions, even if He only answers part of our question about a particular concern. For instance, as stated above, these Saints wanted to know if they were to settle permanently in Ohio. In verses 1 and 3, below, the Lord tells them three times that they will be there "for the

present time." He could no doubt have told them that they would be in Kirtland for five years, as he did about six months later (see D&C 64:21), but He chose not to. Thus, we are reminded that one of the most important lessons we are to learn during mortality is to walk by faith and not demand complete answers before we start walking.

1 IT is necessary that ye should remain **for the present time** in your places of abode, as it shall be suitable to your circumstances.

2 And inasmuch as ye have lands, ye shall impart to the eastern brethren [*perhaps meaning that if they already have land in Ohio, they should share their land with incoming Saints so they too have land to settle on*];

3 And inasmuch as ye have not lands, let them buy **for the present time** in those regions round about, as seemeth them good, for it must needs be necessary that they have places to live **for the present time**.

Next, in verses 4–6, the Lord refers to "the city," meaning the city of New Jerusalem. Again, these Saints are expected to walk by faith and be obedient to the instructions of the Lord, without having all of their questions answered, including their wanting to know the location where New Jerusalem is to be built. By the way, they will be given a hint in about three months that Missouri will be "the land, which I will consecrate unto my people" (D&C 52:2–3), and then, in D&C 57:1–3, which was given in July 1831, they will finally be told that Independence, Missouri, is "the place for the city of Zion," meaning the New Jerusalem.

Thus, in this revelation, these early members of the Church are counseled to acquire land needed "for the present time" in Ohio, but also to save up as much money as they can appropriately come up with in order to be in a position eventually to buy land for the New Jerusalem. This is obviously a "curriculum" designed by our loving Savior for their growth and development, much the same as He does for each of us for our best good and development.

4 It must needs be necessary that ye **save all the money that ye can**, and that ye obtain all that ye can in righteousness, that in time ye may be enabled to purchase land for an inheritance, even the city [*New Jerusalem*].

5 **The place** [*the location for New Jerusalem*] **is not yet to be revealed**; **but** after your brethren come from the east **there are to be certain men appointed, and to them it shall be given to know the place**, or to them it shall be revealed.

In verse 5, above, and 6, next, notice how the Lord in His mercy and kindness gives these faithful Saints a bit more information about the eventual gathering to Zion, which, in this context, is another name for the New Jerusalem. This provides hope and encouragement as they walk in faith to fulfill what the Lord has instructed.

6 And **they shall be appointed to purchase the lands**, and to make a commencement to **lay the foundation of the city** [*the city of Zion—in other words, New Jerusalem*]; and **then shall ye begin to be gathered** with your families, every man according to his family, according to his circumstances, and **as is appointed to him by the presidency and the bishop** of the church, **according to the laws and commandments which ye have received, and which ye shall hereafter receive** [*more instructions are coming*]. Even so. Amen.

SECTION 49

Background

This is a fascinating revelation in which the Lord refuted a number of ideas and doctrines taught by a congregation of the Shaking Quakers, who lived not far from Cleveland, Ohio, about fifteen miles southwest of Kirtland. This revelation was given in Kirtland, Ohio, through the Prophet Joseph Smith on May 7, 1831, and was addressed to Sidney Rigdon, Parley P. Pratt, and Leman Copley. Brother Copley had been a member of the Shaking Quaker congregation before his conversion to the Church. Although Brother Copley had been baptized into the restored Church, he still felt that many of the teachings of the Shakers were true.

The Shaking Quakers (United Society of Believers in Christ's Second Appearing) were respectable and industrious citizens. Among other things, they had excellent schools, built fine furniture, invented the clothespin and flat broom as we know them today, washed hands often (unusual in that day), thus avoiding many of the epidemics of the times, and lived together in a type of united order. Many people not of their beliefs sent their own children to the Shaker schools because of the excellent education provided.

The Shaking Quakers originated in England, probably in the late 1700s, and immigrated to America in 1774 because of persecution. They were led by a woman named Ann Lee, who had been converted in England at age twenty-two to the "Shakers" (so called by many because they worshipped through dancing, shaking, clapping, whirling, chanting, and twisting, which they believed caused their sins to drop from their souls, thus leaving them clean before God).

Ann Lee married at age twenty-six and quickly had four children, three of whom died in infancy, and one of whom, Elizabeth, died at the age of six. Grief-stricken, she came to the conclusion that total denial of physical passion and desire was the only path to peace for her devastated soul. She decided that sexual relations and the institution of marriage were the basic cause of all evil. She claimed to have had a vision in which she saw Adam and Eve defy God's commands and engage in sexual relations, which purportedly led to their expulsion from the Garden of Eden. She thus concluded that sex was evil and the primal cause of the separation of mankind from God. Her husband eventually ended their marriage after thirteen years.

She proclaimed herself to be Christ, who had come the second time, this time coming in the form of a woman. Ann Lee served as the leader of the Shaking Quakers from about 1754 up to the time of her death near Albany, New York, on September 8, 1784, at the age of forty-eight. Shortly before her death, she told her followers that the Shakers would move to Ohio. Subsequently, a substantial number of them moved to Ohio and established a community of Shakers near Cleveland.

The teachings of the Shakers, as

established in America by Ann Lee, included the doctrine that Christ's Second Coming had already taken place and that He had come this time in the form of a woman (Ann Lee), the forbidding of the touching of members of the opposite sex (including the shaking of hands), the teaching that men and women are equals, that baptism was not necessary, that pork should not be eaten (many Shakers refused to eat any meat at all), and that celibacy (intentional avoidance of marriage as a matter of religion) was the highest form of worshipping God.

As we go through section forty-nine now, we will use **bold** to point things out, including the Lord's direct responses to the teachings of the Shaking Quakers.

1 **HEARKEN unto my word**, my servants **Sidney** [*Rigdon*], and **Parley** [*Pratt*], and **Leman** [*Copley*]; for behold, verily I say unto you, that I give unto you a commandment that you shall **go and preach my gospel which ye have received, even as ye have received it** [*in other words, don't water it down or change it*], **unto the Shakers.**

The three brethren mentioned in verse 1, above, did go as instructed, attending a Shaker service and receiving permission to read this revelation to the Shakers

at the end of that meeting. Their message was rejected.

2 Behold, I say unto you, that **they desire to know the truth in part, but not all,** for they are not right before me and must needs repent.

It is interesting to note, in verses 3 and 4, next, that as the Lord instructs these three, He cautions Leman Copley not to cave in to the teaching and persuasion of his former associates in the Shaker community. Sadly, he wavered over the next few years, leaving and then coming back to the Church at least twice. He eventually joined with apostates who had left the Church. He died estranged from the Church in Ohio at about age eighty-one.

3 Wherefore, I send you, my servants Sidney and Parley, to preach the gospel unto them.

4 And **my servant Leman shall be ordained unto this work, that he may reason with them, not according to that which he has received of them** [*not reverting back to his old Shaker beliefs*], **but according to that which shall be taught him by you my servants;** and by so doing I will bless him, otherwise he shall not prosper.

Next, the Savior quotes His Father and identifies Himself as He begins addressing specific incorrect beliefs of the Shakers.

He first assures them that He has not yet come to earth for the Second Coming.

5 Thus saith the Lord; **for I am God, and have sent** [*note that this is past tense, in other words, it has already been done*] **mine Only Begotten Son** into the world for the redemption of the world, and have decreed that **he that receiveth him shall be saved**, and **he that receiveth him not shall be damned** [*stopped in progression*]—

6 And they have done unto **the Son of Man** [*Christ*] even as they listed [*just as they desired*]; and he **has taken his power on the right hand of his** [*the Father's*] **glory**, and **now reigneth in the heavens**, and **will reign till he descends on the earth** to put all enemies under his feet, **which time is nigh at hand** [*the Second Coming is getting close*]—

7 I, the Lord God, have spoken it; **but the hour and the day no man knoweth, neither the angels in heaven, nor shall they know until he comes.**

Remember that one of the beliefs of the Shakers was that they did not need baptism. In other words, their faithful members did not have sins.

8 Wherefore, I will that all men shall repent, for **all are under sin**, except those which I have reserved unto myself, holy men that ye know not of.

Joseph Fielding Smith explained the phrase "holy men that ye know not of" in verse 8, above. He said that they "are translated persons such as John the Revelator and the Three Nephites, who do not belong to this generation and yet are in the flesh in the earth performing a special ministry until the coming of Jesus Christ" (*Church History and Modern Revelation*, 1:209).

9 Wherefore, I say unto you that **I have sent unto you mine everlasting covenant** [*the restored gospel of Jesus Christ*], even that which was from the beginning.

10 And that which I have promised I have so fulfilled, and the nations of the earth shall bow to it; and, if not of themselves, they shall come down, for that which is now exalted of itself shall be laid low of power.

11 Wherefore, **I give unto you** [*Sidney, Parley, and Leman*] **a commandment that ye go among this people** [*the Shakers*], **and say unto them**, like unto mine Apostle of old, whose name was Peter:

12 **Believe on the name of the Lord Jesus, who** was on the

earth, and **is to come**, the beginning and the end;

13 **Repent and be baptized in the name of Jesus Christ**, according to the holy commandment, **for the remission of sins**;

14 And whoso doeth this shall **receive the gift of the Holy Ghost, by the laying on of the hands of the elders of the church**.

15 And again, verily I say unto you, that **whoso forbiddeth to marry is not ordained** [*authorized*] **of God**, for **marriage is ordained of God unto man** [*in other words, celibacy is a false doctrine*].

16 Wherefore, **it is lawful that he should have one wife, and they twain shall be one flesh** [*they should have children*], and **all this that the earth might answer the end** [*purpose*] **of its creation** [*in other words, if people don't have children, the spirit children of our Heavenly Parents cannot come to earth to obtain bodies and continue to progress*];

17 And **that it might be filled with the measure of man** [*that the earth might be populated*], according to his creation before the world was made [*as intended for the spirits who were created in premortality*].

Next, the Lord addresses the issue of whether or not to eat meat. This is an important verse for members of the Church who may wonder if we should avoid meat except in times of cold or famine (especially with respect to the proper interpretation of D&C 89:12–13).

18 And **whoso forbiddeth to abstain from meats, that man should not eat the same, is not ordained** [*authorized, approved*] **of God**;

As mentioned above, verse 18 provides a vital clarification regarding the eating of meat. It is okay to eat meat if we want to. And in case readers do not understand the wording in verse 18, above, our modern prophets have provided D&C 49, footnote 18a, making sure members of the Church realize that the Lord does not endorse abstinence from meat as a teaching of the true Church. We will reread verse 18, here, substituting the wording in footnote 18a for the wording as it stands. When we do so, it reads,

"And whoso **biddeth** [*requires*] to abstain from meats, that man should not eat the same, is not ordained of God."

Verse 19, next, confirms the interpretation of verse 18 given by the Brethren. You may also wish to make a cross-reference here to D&C 59:16–20 in your own scriptures since in them the Lord again teaches this principle.

19 For, behold, the **beasts** of the field and the **fowls** of the air, **and that which cometh of the earth, is ordained** [*authorized by the Lord*] **for the use of man for food** and for **raiment** [*clothing*], and that he might have in abundance.

20 **But it is not given that one man should possess that which is above another**, wherefore the world lieth in sin [*selfishness is an underlying reason for much of the sin and wickedness in the world*].

21 And **wo be unto man that sheddeth blood or that wasteth flesh and hath no need**.

Next, the Master addresses the false teaching of Ann Lee that Jesus will come in the form of a woman and also explains that the Second Coming will not be low key by way of a traveling man who announces himself as the Savior. In other words, the Second Coming will be just as spectacular and all-encompassing as foretold in prophecy.

22 And again, verily I say unto you, that **the Son of Man** [*Christ*] **cometh not in the form of a woman, neither of a man traveling on the earth.**

23 Wherefore, **be not deceived**, but continue in steadfastness, looking forth for the **heavens to be shaken**, and the **earth to tremble** and to **reel to and fro** as a drunken man, and for the **valleys to be exalted**, and for the **mountains to be made low**, and for the **rough places to become smooth**—and all this when the angel shall sound his trumpet [*in other words, all this will happen when the Savior comes; thus, it will be spectacular, and none will miss it or have any doubt about it*].

Having addressed specific false doctrines, the Savior now gives these three representatives of the Church (and the Shaking Quakers and all of us) some prophecies that will be fulfilled preceding His coming, and He tenderly invites them to repent and ask Him for help in understanding the true gospel. He assures them that He will "open the door" for them and support them in their mission.

24 But before the great day of the Lord shall come [*before the Second Coming of Christ*], **Jacob** [*Israel*] **shall flourish** in the wilderness [*the apostate world*], and **the Lamanites shall blossom as the rose** [*a wonderful prophecy that is being fulfilled dramatically in our day*].

25 **Zion shall flourish** upon the hills and rejoice upon the mountains, and shall be assembled together unto the place which I have appointed. [*Among other things,*

this verse can mean that the Church will grow dramatically and spread throughout the world before the Second Coming.]

26 Behold, I say unto you, **go forth as I have commanded you**; repent of all your sins; ask and ye shall receive; knock and it shall be opened unto you.

27 Behold, **I will go before you and be your rearward** [*your protection*]; and **I will be in your midst, and you shall not be confounded** [*stopped, confused*].

28 Behold, **I am Jesus Christ**, and I come quickly. Even so. Amen.

The word quickly, as used in verse 28, above, does not necessarily mean "right away." It might better be understood as meaning that when the Savior comes, it will happen suddenly or "quickly," and there will be no time left for repenting.

SECTION 50

Background

This revelation was given through the Prophet Joseph Smith in Kirtland, Ohio, on May 9, 1831. During this period of time in the early days of the Church, there were many so-called "spiritual manifestations" among the Saints. The problem was that many of these "manifestations" were strange and even bizarre. And so, the Saints were not sure whether they came from God or the devil. One of Satan's well-used tools is the counterfeiting of revelation and spiritual manifestations.

For instance, after Parley P. Pratt had returned from the mission to the American Indians west of Missouri (see D&C 32) in late March 1831, he visited several branches of the Church around Kirtland and was dismayed to see what he considered to be disgusting spiritual manifestations among the members. He wrote, "As I went forth among the different branches, some very strange spiritual operations were manifested, which were disgusting, rather than edifying. Some persons would seem to swoon away, and make unseemly gestures, and be drawn or disfigured in their countenances. Others would fall into ecstacies, and be drawn into contortions, cramp, fits, etc. Others would seem to have visions and revelations, which were not edifying, and which were not congenial to the doctrine and spirit of the gospel. In short, a false and lying spirit seemed to be creeping into the Church.

"All these things were new and strange to me, and had originated in the Church during our absence, and previous to the arrival of President Joseph Smith from New York.

"Feeling our weakness and inexperience, and lest we should err in judgment concerning these spiritual phenomena, myself, John Murdock, and several other Elders, went to Joseph Smith, and asked him to inquire of the Lord concerning these spirits or manifestations.

"After we had joined in prayer in his translating room, he dictated in our presence the following revelation [section 50]:—(Each sentence was uttered slowly and very distinctly, and with a pause between each, sufficiently long for it to be recorded, by an ordinary writer, in long hand.

"This was the manner in which all his written revelations were dictated and written. There was never any hesitation, reviewing, or reading back, in order to keep the run of the subject; neither did any of these communications undergo revisions, interlinings, or corrections. As he dictated them so they stood, so far as I have witnessed; and I was present to witness the dictation of several communications of several pages each. . . .)" (*Autobiography of Parley P. Pratt*, 61–62).

The Prophet Joseph Smith spoke of these strange manifestations in Kirtland. He said, "Soon after the Gospel was established in Kirtland, and during the absence of the authorities of the Church, many false spirits were introduced, many strange visions were seen, and wild, enthusiastic notions were entertained; men ran out of doors under the influence of this spirit, and some of them got upon the stumps of trees and shouted, and all kinds of extravagances were entered into by them; one man pursued a ball that he said he saw flying in the air, until he came to a precipice, when he jumped into the top of a tree, which saved his life; and many ridiculous things were entered into, calculated to bring disgrace upon the Church of God, to cause the Spirit of God to be withdrawn, and to uproot and destroy those glorious principles which had been developed for the salvation of the human family." (*History of the Church*, 4:580. See also *Manuscript History of the Church*, vol. C-1, page 1311, josephsmithpapers.org.)

What we learn from section 50 will be valuable in helping us avoid deception ourselves. First, in verses 1 and 2, we will be taught that there are indeed many evil and false spirits who attempt to deceive. In other words, such things are not merely the product of wild imaginations.

1 HEARKEN [*listen carefully*], O ye elders of my church, and **give ear to the voice of the living God**; and attend to the words of wisdom which shall be given unto you, according as ye have asked and are agreed **as touching the church, and the spirits which**

have gone abroad in the earth.

2 Behold, verily I say unto you, that **there are many spirits which are false spirits, which have gone forth in the earth, deceiving the world.**

Revelation 16:14 reminds us that evil spirits have power to work miracles.

Revelation 16

14 For **they are the spirits of devils, working miracles,** which go forth unto the kings of the earth and of the whole world, to gather them to the battle of that great day of God Almighty.

President Boyd K. Packer of the Quorum of the Twelve warned us on several occasions that Satan and his evil spirits strive constantly to deceive us by counterfeiting true revelation. He said, "Be ever on guard lest you be deceived by inspiration from an unworthy source. You can be given false spiritual messages. There are counterfeit spirits just as there are counterfeit angels. (See Moro. 7:17.) . . .

"The spiritual part of us and the emotional part of us are so closely linked that [it] is possible to mistake an emotional impulse for something spiritual. We occasionally find people who receive what they assume to be spiritual

promptings from God, when those promptings are either centered in the emotions or are from the adversary" ("The Candle of the Lord," *Ensign,* Jan. 1983, 55–56).

In another talk, President Packer spoke of the importance of distinguishing between a temptation from the devil and a true revelation from the Lord:

"There can be counterfeit revelations, promptings from the devil, temptations! As long as you live, in one way or another the adversary will try to lead you astray. . . .

"The Prophet Joseph Smith said that 'nothing is a greater injury to the children of men than to be under the influence of a false spirit when they think they have the Spirit of God' [*Teachings of the Prophet Joseph Smith,* 205]. . . .

"If ever you receive a prompting to do something that makes you feel uneasy, something you know in your mind to be wrong and contrary to the principles of righteousness, do not respond to it!" ("Personal Revelation: The Gift, the Test, and the Promise," *Ensign,* Nov. 1994, 61).

Continuing now with section 50, the Savior tells us what Satan is trying to do to us.

3 And also **Satan hath sought to deceive you,** that he might overthrow you.

Next, Jesus reminds these Saints

that He is aware of them and the evil things taking place among them. He assures the faithful of exaltation and warns the guilty of coming judgments.

4 Behold, **I, the Lord**, have looked upon you, and **have seen abominations in the church** [*among the members*] that profess my name [*who claim to be faithful members*].

5 But **blessed are they who are faithful** and endure, whether in life or in death, for **they shall inherit eternal life** [*exaltation*].

6 But **wo unto them that are deceivers and hypocrites** [*people who want to look good but don't want to be good*], for, thus saith the Lord, I will bring them to judgment.

Next, in verse 7, we will find an important and reassuring lesson. Perhaps you have worried about a friend or loved one who was raised in a home or under circumstances where they did not get a fair chance to understand the gospel or see it in action. Perhaps there was much hypocrisy, including devastating abuse. Perhaps an acquaintance has been severely offended by hypocrisy on the part of an active member of the Church. Verse 7 reminds us that God is completely fair, and that victims of bad example and hypocrisy will "be reclaimed." In

other words, they will be given a completely fair opportunity to understand and accept or reject the gospel, either in this life or the next. And, according to the Lord, they will be "reclaimed." This is most comforting!

Doctrine

Verses 7. God is completely fair. Those who do not get a completely fair set of opportunities to hear, understand, and accept or reject the gospel either later in this life or in the next life, will get them before the final judgment day.

7 Behold, verily I say unto you, there are **hypocrites among you**, who **have deceived some**, which has given the adversary power; but behold **such shall be reclaimed**;

As you know from experience, all the wicked do not get punished during their mortal lives. In fact, some seem to prosper despite sinning and breaking God's commandments. Verse 8, next, reminds us that all such will eventually have their day of reckoning.

8 But **the hypocrites shall be detected and shall be cut off** [*from the full blessings of the gospel*], **either in life or in death**, even as I will; and wo unto them who are

cut off from my church, for the same are overcome of the world [*in other words, they have given in to sin and the ways of the world*].

9 Wherefore, **let every man beware lest he do that which is not in truth and righteousness before me**.

Beginning with verse 10, next, the Savior deals directly with the question that led to the giving of this revelation; namely, how to tell if spiritual manifestations come from God or from the devil. Jesus tells these men that He will reason with them the same way they would reason with each other, and that He will use simple logic to help them understand Him.

10 And now **come**, saith the Lord, by the Spirit, unto the elders of his church, and **let us reason together**, that ye may understand;

11 **Let us reason even as a man reasoneth one with another face to face**.

12 Now, **when a man reasoneth he is understood of man**, because he reasoneth as a man; **even so will I, the Lord, reason with you that you may understand**.

Next, the Lord uses a question-answer format to teach these early members and leaders how to tell whether or not the manifestations they are witnessing are from the Holy Ghost or the devil and his evil spirits.

Question

13 Wherefore, I the Lord ask you this question—unto what were ye ordained [*what were you called to do*]?

Answer

14 To **preach my gospel by the Spirit**, even the Comforter [*the Holy Ghost, which brings peace and harmony—unlike the strange manifestations they've seen*] which was sent forth to teach the truth [*in clear, easily recognizable terms*].

Question

15 **And then received ye spirits which ye could not understand, and received them to be of God** [*and you accepted strange and weird manifestations to be from God*]; and **in this are ye justified?**

Answer

16 Behold **ye shall answer this question yourselves** [*in other words, the answer is obvious—no, you were not justified in believing that such strange things had come from God*]; nevertheless, **I will be merciful unto you**; he that is weak among you hereafter shall be made strong [*if they keep learning these lessons—a kind reminder that these*

*elders are still learning and that the
Lord is merciful and patient*].

Question

**17 Verily I say unto you, he that
is ordained of me and sent forth
to preach the word of truth by
the Comforter, in the Spirit of
truth, doth he preach it by the
Spirit of truth or some other
way?**

Perhaps you've noticed that when
the Holy Ghost is present, testifying of the truthfulness of the gospel, helping you understand gospel principles, and so forth, there
is a sweet feeling of peace, calm,
and assurance that attends it. This
is opposite the unsettling, jangling,
and boisterous spirit that attends
the types of "spiritual" manifestations these brethren were concerned about.

Answer

**18 And if it be by some other way
it is not of God.** [*In other words,
when you stop and think about it, it is
easy to tell the difference.*]

Question

19 And again, he that receiveth the
word of truth, **doth he receive it
by the Spirit of truth** [*the peace
and calm that attend the testifying
of the Holy Ghost*] **or some other
way?**

Answer

**20 If it be some other way it is
not of God.**

Remember, the Lord told them He
would reason with them "as a man
reasoneth one with another face
to face" (verse 11). We are seeing
this and will see it again in verse
21, next.

Question

**21 Therefore, why is it that ye
cannot understand and know,
that he that receiveth the word
by the Spirit of truth receiveth
it as it is preached by the Spirit
of truth?** [*In other words, the Holy
Ghost does not do wild and weird
things like jumping on stumps and
shouting, twisting grotesquely, rolling and uttering strange sounds, and
so forth, that are opposite the peace
that accompanies the Spirit.*]

Next, in verses 22–25, the Savior
summarizes this lesson on distinguishing between the truth from
God and attempted deceptions
from the devil and his evil spirits.
We will summarize each point at
the beginning of the relevant verse.

Point 1

**When the Holy Ghost is
involved, gospel understanding
is the result** (as opposed to not
understanding the meaning and
messages of strange and weird
manifestations).

Point 2

When the Holy Ghost is involved, both the preacher and the hearer are edified (built up, strengthened in personal righteousness and understanding of the gospel).

Point 3

When the Holy Ghost is involved, there is rejoicing and harmony.

22 **Wherefore, he that preacheth and he that receiveth, understand one another, and both are edified and rejoice together**.

Point 4

Darkness is felt when the Holy Ghost is not involved.

23 And **that which doth not edify is not of God, and is darkness.**

Point 5

Things from God produce spiritual light and understanding. There is a progression from one level of understanding and light to the next. This progress continues for the faithful until they have all light and perfect understanding (see D&C 88:49, which tells the faithful that the day will come when they will actually comprehend God).

24 **That which is of God is light** [*that which comes from God produces light and understanding in our minds and hearts*]; and **he that receiveth light, and continueth in God, receiveth more light**; and **that light groweth brighter and brighter until the perfect day** [*until the person knows all things and becomes a god*].

Point 6

Spiritual light and truth from God enable us to chase deception and spiritual darkness out of our lives.

25 And again, verily I say unto you, and I say it that you may **know the truth**, **that you may chase darkness from among you;**

Next, in verse 26, the Savior explains that in order to be greatest in His kingdom, one must be the humble servant of everyone. This seems to be the exact opposite of the arrogance and self-serving attitude seen commonly among worldly, powerful leaders.

26 **He that is ordained of God and sent forth, the same is appointed to be the greatest**, notwithstanding [*even though*] he **is the least and the servant of all.**

One of the reasons such people (verse 26, above) are the

"greatest" is that the humble work of spreading the gospel enables sincere converts to eventually become gods, the greatest reward in the universe! We see this in verse 27, next.

27 Wherefore, **he is possessor of all things**; for **all things are subject unto him, both in heaven and on the earth** [*terms used to describe gods; see D&C 132:20*], **the life and the light, the Spirit and the power, sent forth by the will of the Father through Jesus Christ, his Son** [*all blessings and rewards of the gospel come through Jesus Christ's mission and Atonement*].

Next, we are reminded of the necessity of personal purity in order to progress in the gospel. Such purity is available through the Atonement of Jesus Christ.

28 **But no man is possessor of all things except he be purified and cleansed from all sin.**

Personal purity leads to power in prayer, as explained in verses 29–30, next.

29 And **if ye are purified** and cleansed from all sin, **ye shall ask whatsoever you will in the name of Jesus and it shall be done.**

30 **But know this, it shall be given you what you shall ask**

[*in other words, if you are close to the Spirit, the Holy Ghost will inspire you as to what you may properly ask for*]; and as ye are appointed to the head, the spirits shall be subject unto you.

You may wish to cross-reference verse 30, above, with D&C 46:30, which carries a similar message regarding knowing if something is proper to pray for.

Next, the Savior teaches more about distinguishing between that which comes from God and that which comes from evil sources and gives instruction as to how to handle the situation when you become aware that something may be false or evil. Such falsehood or evil could come from other people as well as from evil spirits or the devil.

31 Wherefore, it shall come to pass, that **if you behold** [*see, sense*] **a spirit manifested that you cannot understand**, and you receive not that spirit, **ye shall ask of the Father in the name of Jesus; and if he give not unto you that spirit** [*if the situation or person does not bring light, understanding, rejoicing, edification, and so forth as explained in verses 22–25*], **then you may know that it is not of God.**

32 And **it shall be given unto you, power over that spirit**

[*including teachings, philosophies, persons, evil spirits*]; **and you shall proclaim against that spirit with a loud** [*firm, definite*] **voice that it is not of God**—

Note the caution given here, next, to basically avoid arrogance and ego building, which are not in harmony with the ways of God.

33 **Not with railing accusation,** that ye be not overcome, **neither with boasting nor rejoicing,** lest you be seized [*overpowered*] therewith.

Next, we are reminded of the importance of giving credit to God and avoiding the mistake of thinking we have power by ourselves to accomplish such things.

34 He that receiveth of God, **let him account it of God**; and let him rejoice [*humbly*] that he is accounted of God worthy to receive [*such help in discriminating between good and evil and dealing effectively with it*].

In the final verses of this section, the Savior gives tender and somewhat personal counsel to several of the elders who asked Joseph Smith to inquire of the Lord concerning these matters. He also bears witness to them that Joseph Smith is His prophet, and He forgives them of their sins, thus giving them a fresh start and encouragement to continue learning and growing.

35 And **by giving heed and doing these things which ye have received, and which ye shall hereafter receive** [*more help and instructions come to those who obey initial counsel*]—**and the kingdom is given you of the Father, and power to overcome all things which are not ordained of him** [*which do not come from God*]—

36 And behold, verily I say unto you, **blessed are you who are now hearing these words of mine from the mouth of my servant** [*Joseph Smith*], for **your sins are forgiven you**.

37 Let my servant Joseph Wakefield, in whom I am well pleased, and my servant Parley P. Pratt go forth among the churches and strengthen them by the word of exhortation [*counseling and teaching, urging obedience to God's commandments*];

38 And also my servant John Corrill, or as many of my servants as are ordained unto this office, and let them labor in the vineyard [*the mission field, the earth, the Church*]; and let no man hinder them doing that which I have appointed unto them—

In verse 39, next, the Lord expresses dissatisfaction with Edward Partridge, who was ordained as the first bishop of the Church (see D&C 41:9). He also gently reminds Bishop Partridge that he can be forgiven.

While we do not know for sure what the problem was, we do know that it was the bishop's responsibility to help the Saints moving into the area to get settled. It may be that he was not following counsel in fulfilling his responsibilities in this regard. In D&C 51:1–2, Edward Partridge is told that he must do things the way the Lord instructs, implying that perhaps he was ignoring some counsel and trying to do things his own way. We will see when we get to D&C 85:8 that Bishop Partridge was severely chastised for refusing to follow instructions. He did repent and was faithful to the end.

39 Wherefore, in this thing my servant **Edward Partridge is not justified** [*his behavior is not pleasing to God*]; nevertheless **let him repent and he shall be forgiven**.

One important message for us in verse 40, next, is that we must first learn to walk in faith and obedience before gaining more knowledge. Otherwise, we would be overwhelmed.

40 Behold, **ye are little children and ye cannot bear all things now; ye must grow in grace and in the knowledge of the truth.**

Next, the Master tenderly encourages all of us who feel our

weaknesses and inadequacies by reminding us that we can achieve exaltation because of His Atonement.

41 **Fear not, little children, for you are mine**, and **I have overcome the world** [*Christ's Atonement has overcome all things for the righteous*], and **you are of them that my Father hath given me**;

42 **And none of them that my Father hath given me shall be lost.** [*This includes the fact that no power in earth or hell can tear the righteous away from the Savior, who will bring them safely to the Father.*]

Next, Jesus explains that He and His Father are united in purpose and work, and that those of us who accept and follow Him are, in effect, united with Him in purpose and work. In other words, if we unite with Christ, we are uniting with the Father.

43 And **the Father and I are one.** I am in the Father and the Father in me; and **inasmuch as** [*if*] **ye have received me, ye are in me and I in you.**

It is comforting and significant to know, as taught in verse 44, next, that the Savior is often in our midst. He is not an absentee God nor an uninterested deity who has finished His work and gives no more revelation and scripture as is taught by many religions.

44 Wherefore, **I am in your midst**, and **I am the good shepherd** [*the One we can safely follow back into the fold*], and **the stone of Israel** [*the promised Messiah, the sure foundation*]. **He that buildeth upon this rock shall never fall.**

According to verses 45–46, we can plan on seeing the Savior, whether in this life or the next. It will happen. In the context of this section, this is beautiful assurance and encouragement to continue walking in faith until that day comes.

45 And **the day cometh that you shall hear my voice and see me, and know that I am**.

46 **Watch, therefore, that ye may be ready.** Even so. Amen.

SECTION 51

Background

This is another example of an exact date, May 20, 1831, now being available because of research on the Joseph Smith Papers Project, whereas, editions of the Doctrine and Covenants prior to the 2013 edition simply said "May 1831" in the heading.

In this section, we will learn more about the law of consecration. This revelation was given through the Prophet Joseph Smith at Thompson, Ohio, not far from Kirtland. It was given at the request of Bishop Edward Partridge, who had the main responsibility for dividing up community property and funds among the Saints as they continued to move into the Kirtland, Ohio, area from the eastern states, especially those Saints from Colesville, New York. In section 42, given about three months before, the basics of the law of consecration had been given by the Lord. Now, more details were needed about how to actually live the law of consecration.

Perhaps you have attended a class or heard a discussion in which the "united order" or "law of consecration" was said to be basically similar to communism. Nothing could be farther from the truth. As we study this revelation, we will see foundational principles upon which the law of consecration is based. Among other things, we will see that the individual is top priority (opposite of communism), allowances are made to accommodate and foster individual talents and personalities (opposite of communism), and that private ownership of property is an integral part of living the law of consecration (opposite of communism).

First, the Lord addresses thirty-seven-year-old Bishop Edward Partridge, the first bishop of the Church, and provides basic principles and guidelines throughout the revelation for implementing the law of consecration. This action in

Ohio is, in effect, a preparatory education that will be valuable for the Saints as they later relocate to Missouri and begin building a Zion society. We will note these principles as we come to them.

1 HEARKEN unto me, saith the Lord your God, and **I will speak unto my servant Edward Partridge, and give unto him directions**; for it must needs be that he receive directions how to organize this people.

2 **For it must needs be** [*it is necessary*] **that they be organized according to my laws** [*the law of consecration, basically, the laws of the celestial kingdom*]; if otherwise, they will be cut off.

Principle
There is not flat equality in the living of the law of consecration. Individual differences and wishes are respected and encouraged. (Obviously, all are expected to live the same basics of the gospel of Jesus Christ.)

3 **Wherefore, let my servant Edward Partridge, and those whom he has chosen, in whom I am well pleased, appoint unto this people their portions** [*assign the lands, means, and resources*], every man equal **according to** his

family, according to his **circumstances** and his **wants** and **needs**.

Principle
Private ownership of property is a vital part of the law of consecration.

4 And let my servant Edward Partridge, when he shall appoint a man his portion, **give unto him a writing** [*a deed to his property*] **that shall secure unto him his portion, that he shall hold it**, even this right and this inheritance in the church, until he transgresses and is not accounted worthy by the voice of the church, according to the laws and covenants of the church, to belong to the church.

5 And **if he shall transgress and is not accounted worthy to belong to the church, he shall not have power to claim that portion which he has consecrated unto the bishop for the poor and needy of my church**; therefore, he shall not retain the gift, **but shall only have claim on that portion that is deeded unto him.**

6 And thus **all things shall be made sure, according to the laws of the land** [*the deeds are to be handled in accordance with the laws of the land*].

President J. Reuben Clark Jr. explained the principle of private ownership of property as applied in the United Order. He said, "One of the places in which some of the brethren are going astray is this: There is continuous reference in the revelations to equality among the brethren, but I think you will find only one place where that equality is really described, though it is referred to in other revelations. That revelation (D&C 51:3) affirms that every man is to be 'equal according to his family, according to his circumstances and his wants and needs.' (See also D&C 82:17; 78:5–6.) Obviously, this is not a case of 'dead level' equality. It is 'equality' that will vary as much as the man's circumstances, his family, his wants and needs, may vary" (In Conference Report, October 1942, 55).

President Clark went on to say, "The fundamental principle of this system was the private ownership of property. Each man owned his portion, or inheritance, or stewardship, with an absolute title, which he could alienate, or hypothecate, or otherwise treat as his own. The Church did not own all of the property, and the life under the United Order was not a communal life, as the Prophet Joseph himself said (*History of the Church*, 3:28). The United Order is an individualistic system, not a communal system" (In Conference Report, October 1942, 57).

7 And **let that which belongs to this people be appointed unto this people** [*probably an instruction to Bishop Partridge to stop holding back on giving deeds and to go ahead and do it. When we get to section 85, we will see that he had deep concerns and was holding back as to whether or not it was wise to have private ownership of property with legal deeds*].

8 And the money which is left unto this people—let there be an agent appointed unto this people, to take the money to provide food and raiment [*clothing*], **according to the wants** of this people.

In verse 8, above, we are again reminded that "wants" are important too in implementing the law of consecration. Many people have the mistaken notion that living the United Order would be a very basic lifestyle, almost a survival-only type of living. This would not be the case in a successful United Order.

Principle

Living the law of consecration requires honest people who are unselfish and united in harmony with each other— in other words, it requires celestial-quality individuals.

9 And let every man deal honestly, and be alike among this

people, and **receive alike, that ye may be one** [*united*], even as I have commanded you.

An explanation of the terms "be alike" and "receive alike," in verse 9, above, is given in the *Doctrine and Covenants Student Manual*, 1981, page 111, as follows (**bold** added for emphasis): "Under the united order everyone was alike in that they were independent and had full opportunity to use their gifts and talents in building the kingdom of God. They were also alike in that all had equal opportunity to benefit from whatever talents and abilities existed in the community. The idea that everyone was alike in goods possessed or income received is an erroneous one. The order was united in love, purpose, and commitment, but **unity does not mean sameness**. A man with seven children has needs different from those of couples just beginning married life."

10 **And let that which belongeth to this people** [*the Colesville Branch*] **not be taken and given unto that of another church** [*branch of the Church*].

An explanation of the word "church" as used in verse 10, above, is given in the *Doctrine and Covenants Student Manual*, 1981, page 111, as follows: "The word 'church' in this paragraph stands for 'Branch,' as in Sec. 20:81,

45:64, and elsewhere. The meaning conveyed is that the property owned by the Colesville Branch could not be claimed by any other Branch. (Smith and Sjodahl, *Commentary*, 299.)"

As you can see, the Lord is giving Bishop Partridge rules and instructions that will very carefully control the living of the law of consecration among these Saints. Otherwise, there would be much misunderstanding, contention, and disharmony as a result.

11 Wherefore, **if another church** [*branch*] **would receive money of this church** [*as a loan*], **let them pay unto this church again** [*pay it back*] according as they shall agree;

12 And **this shall be done through the bishop or the agent**, which shall be appointed **by the voice of the church** [*the principle of common consent; see section 26*].

Principle

There is to be a bishop's storehouse where supplies are to be housed for distribution to the poor and needy.

13 And again, **let the bishop appoint a storehouse unto this church** [*similar to our bishop's storehouses today*]; **and let all things both in money and in**

meat [*food*], **which are more than is needful** for the wants of this people, **be kept in the hands of the bishop**.

Principle

Those whose callings require full-time service in the Church can have their needs and the needs of their families taken care of out of the funds and resources of the Church. (This can include some missionaries and some General Authorities today.)

14 And let him also reserve unto himself for his own wants, and for the wants of his family, as he shall be employed in doing this business.

15 And thus I grant unto this people a privilege of organizing themselves according to my laws [*according to the basic principles of the law of consecration*].

16 And I consecrate unto them this land for a little season [*the Saints will be in the Kirtland area for about five years; see D&C 64:21*], until I, the Lord, shall provide for them otherwise, and command them to go hence [*they will eventually be commanded to move to Missouri*];

There is great wisdom in what the Lord tells these members in verse

17, next. It can apply to many other situations also. The Lord tells them to settle down and live as if they were going to be in Ohio for many years, even though they know from revelation that they will only be there for "a little season" (verse 16, above, and in section 48).

17 And the hour and the day is not given unto them [*they don't yet know when they will be commanded to move again*], wherefore [*therefore*] **let them act upon this land** [*Ohio*] **as for years**, and **this shall turn unto them for their good**.

Next, in verse 18, the Lord says that the same principles given to Bishop Partridge will likewise apply in other settings. Then He explains that those who can successfully live the law of consecration will be qualified and worthy of exaltation.

18 Behold, **this shall be an example** unto my servant Edward Partridge, **in other places, in all churches** [*branches of the Church*].

19 And **whoso is found a faithful, a just, and a wise steward** shall enter into the joy of his Lord, and **shall inherit eternal life** [*exaltation, which is the highest degree of glory in the celestial kingdom*].

20 Verily, I say unto you, I am Jesus Christ, who **cometh quickly,**

in an hour you think not. Even so. Amen.

Just a thought in closing: it is interesting that, even though we have the signs of the times and other scriptures that alert us to the closeness of the Second Coming of Christ, He will still come at a time when we don't quite expect Him (see verse 20, above). One message we learn from this is that we need to be doing our best to live the gospel continuously and not risk periods of being intentionally less valiant in the gospel.

SECTION 52

Background

This revelation was given on June 6, 1831 (see heading in 2013 edition of the Doctrine and Covenants), in Kirtland, Ohio, through the Prophet Joseph Smith. The Church had just finished holding a four-day conference in Kirtland, which began on June 3 and finished on June 6. This revelation was given on the last day of this conference. During the conference, several of the brethren were ordained to the office of high priest, the first time this specific office was conferred upon men in this dispensation.

It was also during this conference that Joseph Smith revealed that John the Revelator (the Apostle who had served with Peter and James in the First Presidency and who was translated and is still on earth) was, at that time (1831) working with the lost ten tribes, preparing them for their return. John Whitmer, who served for a time as church historian, wrote, "The Spirit of the Lord fell upon Joseph in an unusual manner. And [Joseph] prophesied that John the Revelator was then among the ten tribes of Israel . . . to prepare them for their return from their long dispersion" (in *The Joseph Smith Papers, Histories, Volume 2: Assigned Histories, 1831–1847*, ed. Karen Lynn Davidson and others [2012], 39. See also *History of the Church*, 1:176.)

In this revelation, the Saints were told by the Lord that the next conference of the Church was to be held in Missouri. This was a brief but exciting hint that Missouri was to be significant in the future of the Church. Also, twenty-eight missionaries were specifically named and called to go forth and preach the gospel.

An important part of this section for us is verses 14–19, in which the Lord provides a pattern for avoiding deception. We will note eight specific points in this pattern when we get to them.

First, in verse 2, the Lord tells these elders what they should be doing between now and the next conference, which is to be held in Missouri. As usual, we will use **bold** for emphasis as well as a suggestion for things you might wish to mark in your own scriptures.

1 BEHOLD, thus saith the Lord unto the elders whom he hath called and chosen in these last days, by the voice of his Spirit—

2 Saying: **I, the Lord, will make known unto you what I will that ye shall do from this time until the next conference, which shall be held in Missouri**, upon the land which I will consecrate unto my people, which are a **remnant of Jacob** [*Israel*], and those who are heirs according to the covenant.

You may wish to make a brief note in your own scriptures to the side of verse 2 explaining that "Jacob" is another name for "Israel." He was Abraham's grandson and the father of the twelve tribes of Israel. Israel is the covenant people through whom the gospel and priesthood covenants are to be taken to all the world. (See Abraham 2:9–11.) These faithful Saints in Kirtland are among the first of "scattered Israel" who are being gathered in the last days according to the covenant and promise of the Lord to do so. Thus, they are at the very forefront of the promised latter-day gathering of Israel.

Next, Joseph and Sidney are told to leave for Missouri as soon as possible.

3 Wherefore, verily I say unto you, **let my servants Joseph Smith, Jun., and Sidney Rigdon** take their journey as soon as preparations can be made to leave their homes, and **journey to the land of Missouri.**

4 And inasmuch as they are faithful unto me, it shall be made known unto them what they shall do;

5 **And it shall also**, inasmuch as they are faithful, **be made known unto them the land of your inheritance** [*Missouri; see verse 42—in other words, if Joseph and Sidney are faithful, they will be guided by the Lord and will be told where the Saints will eventually settle in Missouri*].

It may sound a bit strange to hear the Lord say, in effect, "if the Prophet and Church leaders are faithful . . ." (verses 4 and 5, above), but it is an important reminder that they too have agency. As noted in D&C 43:3–5, the Lord will never allow them to lead us astray. Verse 6, next, reemphasizes this fact.

6 And **inasmuch as they are not faithful, they shall be cut off**, even as I will, as seemeth me good.

Next, several brethren are also instructed to leave on missions to

Missouri. In verse 9, they will be cautioned to preach and teach only that which is in the scriptures and what the Prophet Joseph Smith has taught as prompted by the Holy Ghost. In other words, they should avoid preaching personal opinions as doctrine—good advice for us today!

7 And again, verily I say unto you, let my servant **Lyman Wight** and my servant **John Corrill** take their journey speedily;

8 And also my servant **John Murdock**, and my servant **Hyrum Smith**, take their journey unto the same place [*Missouri*] by the way of Detroit.

9 And let them journey from thence [*from there*] preaching the word by the way, **saying none other things than that which the prophets and Apostles have written** [*in other words, the scriptures*], and that which is taught them by the Comforter [*the Holy Ghost*] through the prayer of faith.

10 **Let them go two by two** [*a precedent for modern missionary work*], and thus **let them preach** by the way in every congregation, **baptizing by water, and the laying on of the hands** [*confirming*] by the water's side.

In verse 11, next, we learn that the Lord will cut His work short with His righteous power—in other words, the Second Coming will come a little sooner than we think. Otherwise, according to Matthew 24:22, no one would still be alive at the Second Coming. Matthew wrote, "And except those days should be shortened, there should no flesh be saved; but for the elect's sake, those days shall be shortened." In D&C 84:97, the Lord again states that His work "shall be cut short in righteousness."

11 For thus saith the Lord, **I will cut my work short in righteousness,** for the days come that I will send forth judgment unto victory [*the day is coming when plagues and pestilences will be sent forth upon the earth, which, along with the Second Coming, will ultimately lead to the destruction of the wicked and the triumph of righteousness at the beginning of the Millennium*].

Next, in verses 12 and 13, Lyman Wight is given a warning and reminded that if he remains faithful, he will have major leadership responsibilities here on earth and be a "ruler over many things," which can imply that he can be a god in the next life.

12 **And let my servant Lyman Wight beware, for Satan desireth to sift him as chaff.**

Chaff (verse 12) is the husk that is

rubbed away from kernels of grain in the threshing process. Grain can be separated from the chaff through rubbing the grain between the hands and then tossing it into the wind. The wind blows the chaff away, and the grain kernels fall to the floor. The imagery in verse 12 is that Satan wants to blow Lyman every which way, like chaff in the wind, and separate him or "sift" him away from the Church.

13 And behold, **he that is faithful shall be made ruler over many things**.

It is sad to note that, although Lyman Wight did much good in the Church for a few more years (including being ordained an Apostle in 1841), his strong will and fiery temper began to cause trouble. He eventually left the Church and led about 150 members astray who followed him from Wisconsin to Texas. He died in Texas in 1858, having tried unsuccessfully to get the Church to join him there.

Satan desires to "sift" all of us "as chaff" (verse 12). In other words, he desires to deceive us and lead us away from the Church and God. Next, in verses 14–19, The Lord gives us a pattern for avoiding deception. First, we will call your attention to eight points in this pattern. Then we will do a bit more with it.

14 And again, **I will give unto you a pattern in all things,**
that ye may not be deceived; for Satan is abroad in the land, and he goeth forth deceiving the nations—

15 Wherefore he that **[1] prayeth**, whose spirit **[2] is contrite** [*desires correction as needed from God through the scriptures, the Holy Ghost, or others, including Church leaders*], the same is accepted of me if he **[3] obey mine ordinances**.

16 He that speaketh, whose spirit is contrite, whose **[4] language is meek** and **[5] edifieth** [*builds others up and strengthens them*], the same is of God if he **[6] obey mine ordinances**.

17 And again, he that **[7] trembleth under my power** [*is humble and shows respect for God*] shall be made strong, and shall bring forth fruits of praise and wisdom, **[8] according to the revelations and truths which I have given you** [*lives in strict harmony with God's revealed word*].

18 And again, **he that** is overcome and **bringeth not forth fruits, even according to this pattern, is not of me**.

19 Wherefore, **by this pattern ye shall know the spirits in all cases under the whole heavens**

[*this pattern applies to all forms of deception, including people, philosophies, politics, groups, media, and so forth*].

Now, we will list these eight points again, along with brief commentary on each. In effect, if a person who is trying to persuade you toward a certain conclusion, course of action, belief, or whatever conforms to all eight points in this pattern, then you can rest assured that you will not be deceived by him or her.

(1) The person prays to God faithfully.

(2) The person humbly desires correction as needed.

(3) The person is living in harmony with the covenants he or she has made with God, including faithful church attendance, tithe paying, temple attendance, and so forth.

(4) The person's language is gentle and pleasant, not caustic and bitter.

(5) What you are hearing edifies you—in other words, brings you peace, light, and understanding (see D&C 50:22–24).

(6) The person keeps covenants made with God via ordinances such as baptism, sacrament, and in the temple.

(7) The person is humble and respects and carefully follows the leaders of the Church through whom the Lord extends His power and authority to all the world.

(8) The person's teachings and life are in strict harmony with the scriptures and the words of the modern prophets and Apostles.

20 **And the days have come** [*perhaps meaning that there will be extra persuasive deception in the last days preceding the Second Coming*]; **according to men's faith it shall be done unto them**.

In reference to the last phrase of verse 20, above, it is helpful to remember that "faith" usually implies action on our part. Thus, if we exercise "faith"—in other words, the "action" of studying and applying the principles of avoiding deception given by the Lord in this revelation—we will receive the extra help needed from the Holy Ghost to avoid being deceived.

Next, the Lord calls several more elders to serve missions to Missouri. You will probably recognize several of the names in this list of missionaries.

21 Behold, this commandment is given unto all the elders whom I have chosen.

22 And again, verily I say unto you, let my servant **Thomas B. Marsh** and my servant **Ezra Thayre** take their journey also,

preaching the word by the way unto this same land.

23 And again, let my servant **Isaac Morley** and my servant **Ezra Booth** take their journey, also preaching the word by the way unto this same land.

24 And again, let my servants **Edward Partridge** and **Martin Harris** take their journey with my servants **Sidney Rigdon** and **Joseph Smith, Jun**.

25 Let my servants **David Whitmer** and **Harvey Whitlock** also take their journey, and preach by the way unto this same land.

26 And let my servants **Parley P. Pratt** and **Orson Pratt** [*these are brothers*] take their journey, and preach by the way, even unto this same land.

27 And let my servants **Solomon Hancock** and **Simeon Carter** also take their journey unto this same land, and preach by the way.

28 Let my servants **Edson Fuller** and **Jacob Scott** also take their journey.

29 Let my servants **Levi W. Hancock** and **Zebedee Coltrin** also take their journey.

30 Let my servants **Reynolds Cahoon** and **Samuel H. Smith** also take their journey.

Just a quick note about Reynolds Cahoon (verse 30, above). In 1834, he and his wife had their seventh child, a boy. They asked the Prophet Joseph Smith to give him a name and blessing. As the Prophet prepared to do their bidding, he asked them what name they wanted him to give the infant. They declined to give one, instead asking Joseph to choose one. During the blessing, the Prophet named the baby "Mahonri Moriancumer Cahoon." You can perhaps imagine the surprise of the parents at now having a son named Mahonri Moriancumer Cahoon! At the end of the blessing, Joseph explained to them that the Lord had just revealed to him during the blessing that the name of the brother of Jared in the Book of Mormon was Mahonri Moriancumer. This event was recorded in an early Church publication, *The Juvenile Instructor*, as follows:

"While residing in Kirtland Elder Reynolds Cahoon had a son born to him. One day when President Joseph Smith was passing his door he called the Prophet in and asked him to bless and name the baby. Joseph did so and gave the boy the name of Mahonri Moriancumer. When he had finished the blessing he laid the child on the bed, and turning to Elder Cahoon he said, the name I have given your son is the name of the brother of Jared; the Lord has just shown [or revealed] it to me. Elder William F. Cahoon, who was standing near heard the Prophet make this statement to his father; and this was the first time the name of the brother of Jared was known in the Church in this dispensation" ("The Jaredites," *Juvenile Instructor,* 1 May 1892, 282; see also *Book of Mormon Student Manual,* 1979, 478).

31 Let my servants **Wheeler Baldwin** and **William Carter** also take their journey.

32 And let my servants **Newel Knight** and **Selah J. Griffin** both be ordained, and also take their journey.

In verse 33, next, the Lord gives interesting counsel; namely, that these missionaries should take different routes as they preach the gospel en route to Missouri. When you stop to think about it, if they all followed the same path to Missouri, the first would do most of the preaching, and as others came along, there would be little opportunity left for effective preaching.

33 Yea, verily I say, let all these take their journey unto one place [*Missouri*], in their **several courses**, and **one man shall not build upon another's foundation, neither journey in another's track** [*in other words, go separate ways, but all end up in Missouri*].

34 **He that is faithful, the same shall be kept and blessed with much fruit** [*much success*].

35 And again, I say unto you, let my servants **Joseph Wakefield** and **Solomon Humphrey** take their journey into the **eastern lands**;

It is interesting to note, in verse 35, above, that Elder Wakefield and Elder Humphrey were not sent to Missouri with the others but rather to the "eastern lands." This meant New York. In verse 36, next, they are told to stick to the scriptures as they preach about the restoration. The "families" mentioned apparently refer to relatives in Stockholm, New York.

They went and had considerable success, including baptizing John Smith, a future patriarch to the Church, and George A. Smith, who would become an Apostle. Both of these converts were relatives of Solomon Humphrey.

36 Let them labor with their families [*relatives*], **declaring none other things than the prophets and Apostles**, that which they have seen and heard and most assuredly believe, that the prophecies may be fulfilled.

37 **In consequence of transgression**, let that which was bestowed upon **Heman Basset** be taken from him, and placed upon the head of **Simonds Ryder**.

Heman Basset (verse 37, above) left the Church shortly after this revelation was given. He was seventeen years old at this time and had already shown signs of being easily deceived. He had been living a type of "united order" with about one hundred others on Isaac Morley's farm in Kirtland before his baptism into the Church. He claimed to have had a revelation handed to him by an angel. Levi Hancock, who heard Heman tell the story of his vision, said, "Basset would behave like a baboon. He said he had a revelation he had received in Kirtland from the hand of an angel, he would read it and show pictures of a course of angels declared to be Gods, then would testify of the truth of the work and I believed it all, like a fool" (Levi Ward Hancock, autobiography, 18). During the conference of the Church immediately preceding this revelation (section 52), the Prophet Joseph Smith had sternly warned Heman. He said, "Heamon Basset you sit still the Devil wants to sift you" (Levi Ward Hancock, autobiography, quoted above).

Just a brief note about Simonds Ryder (verse 37, above). He was a member for just three months. Among his stated reasons for leaving the Church was that the Prophet misspelled his name on his call to go to Missouri to preach. His name was spelled "Rider" rather than "Ryder."

38 And again, verily I say unto you, let Jared Carter be ordained a priest, and also George James be ordained a priest.

Next, the Lord instructs the men who had not been called on missions to Missouri to take good care of the members in Ohio, to preach the gospel in the surrounding area, and to work for their own living rather than depending on contributions from the Church for their support.

39 Let the residue of the elders [the remaining men] **watch over the churches** [the branches of the Church], **and declare the word** [preach the gospel] in the regions round about them; and **let them labor with their own hands that there be no idolatry nor wickedness practiced** [this word was spelled "practised" in editions of the Doctrine and Covenants prior to the 2013 edition. Just another example of the many relatively insignificant changes and corrections made in the 2013 edition by the Church. For more information on these changes, go online to Gospel Library/Scriptures/About the Scriptures/Adjustments to the Scriptures].

An explanation of the word "idolatry" (verse 39, above,) is found in the Doctrine and Covenants Student Manual, 1981, page 113, as follows:

"This instruction was given to those elders not assigned to go as missionaries to Missouri. These men were assigned to stay home and be the priesthood leaders for the Saints in Kirtland. By laboring with their own hands for their support rather than being paid for their priesthood service, these brethren would help prevent idolatry and priestcraft from springing up in the Church (see 2 Nephi 26:29). Modern readers may wonder at the use of the word idolatry, since idolatry is often thought of as a practice that went out of existence centuries ago. But in the preface to the Doctrine and Covenants, the Lord warned that one of the characteristics of the last days would be that 'every man walketh in his own way, and after the image of his God . . . whose substance is that of an idol' (D&C 1:16), and Paul defined covetousness as idolatry (see Ephesians 5:5; Colossians 3:5). In other words, when a man sets his heart on natural things, or prestige, or power to the point that God is no longer supreme, then that becomes as god to him. He worships, or gives his allegiance to, those things. This verse suggests that if the elders who remained in Ohio did not labor with their own hands, they might be guilty of this kind of covetousness, or idolatry."

40 And **remember in all things the poor and the needy, the sick and the afflicted,** for **he that doeth not these things, the same is not my disciple** [*is not a true follower of Christ*].

41 And again, let my servants Joseph Smith, Jun., and Sidney Rigdon and Edward Partridge **take with them a recommend from the church** [*similar to a temple recommend today, certifying that you are a member of the Church in good standing; see D&C 52:41, footnote a*]. And let there be one obtained for my servant Oliver Cowdery also.

42 And thus, even as I have said, if ye are faithful ye shall **assemble yourselves together to rejoice upon the land of Missouri,** which is **the land of your inheritance** [*a hint that they will be gathering there sometime in the future*], which is now the land of your enemies.

43 But, behold, **I, the Lord, will hasten the city** [*the city of New Jerusalem or Zion; see D&C 42:35*] **in its time** [*when the time is right*] and will crown the faithful with joy and with rejoicing.

44 Behold, **I am Jesus Christ, the Son of God,** and **I will lift them up** [*reward them with exaltation*] at **the last day** [*on the final judgment day*]. Even so. Amen.

SECTION 53

Background

This revelation was given through the Prophet Joseph Smith to a merchant named Algernon Sidney Gilbert in Kirtland, Ohio, on June 8, 1831. Brother Gilbert was baptized in 1830 and was about forty-one years old at the time of this revelation. He had a desire to know what the Lord wanted him to do in the Church and asked the Prophet to inquire for him. Joseph did and this revelation was the result.

A. Sidney Gilbert will live another three years and then die of cholera in Missouri after having hosted in his home several members of Zion's Camp (the little army of Saints that marched from Kirtland to Missouri in 1834 to assist members there who had been driven out by mobs) who were afflicted with the disease. He was known as a generous and good man as well as a skilled businessman. In fact, he was a business partner to Newel K. Whitney and co-owner of the Newel K. Whitney Store in Kirtland.

As you will see in this revelation, the Lord will request that Brother Gilbert move to Missouri and use his business skills to serve as an agent to the Church there. He will assist Bishop Edward Partridge (the first bishop in the Church) in handling the temporal affairs and needs of the Church.

Even though this revelation is given to a specific individual, you will see a number of lessons that can apply to all of us. For example, in verse 1, we are again reminded that God does hear our individual prayers and that He does know our thoughts and the desires of our hearts. In both verses 1 and 2, the Savior personally introduces Himself to Brother Gilbert, a sweet reminder that the Savior is humble and personable as described by Moroni in Ether 12:39.

1 BEHOLD, I say unto you, my servant Sidney Gilbert, that **I have heard your prayers**; and **you have called upon me that it should be made known unto you, of the Lord your God, concerning your calling and election** [*what the Savior wants Sidney to do now*] **in the church**, which I, the Lord, have raised up in these last days [*Jesus bears personal testimony to Brother Gilbert that this is His church*].

2 Behold**, I, the Lord**, who was crucified for the sins of the world, **give unto you a commandment that you shall forsake the world** [*avoid low worldly standards and behaviors and, instead, keep the commandments of God and the covenants you have made with Him*].

Next, in verse 3, the Master instructs Sidney Gilbert to be ordained an elder and to preach the first principles of the gospel, namely, faith, repentance, baptism, and the gift of the Holy Ghost.

3 **Take upon you mine ordination, even that of an elder**, to **preach faith** and **repentance** and **remission of sins**, according to my word, and **the reception of the Holy Spirit by the laying on of hands**;

> The instruction in verse 3, above, for Sidney to teach that the gift of the Holy Ghost is given by the "laying on of hands" is particularly important, because so many people in his day (and ours) believed that the receiving of the Spirit was a matter of "happening" rather than a gospel ordinance.
>
> Next, Brother Gilbert is called to be an agent to assist the bishop in handling the business and material needs of the members. In response to this, over the next three years until he dies, he will set up stores from which the Saints can purchase goods and supplies.

4 And also to **be an agent unto this church** in the place which shall be appointed by the bishop, according to commandments which shall be given hereafter.

> In verse 5, below, Sidney Gilbert is instructed to travel with the Prophet and Sidney Rigdon to Missouri. He will build a store in Independence, Missouri, which will eventually be broken into by mobs, and

they will toss the merchandise out into the streets. He will build another store in Liberty, Missouri, and will again care for the needs of the Saints.

5 And again, verily I say unto you, you shall **take your journey with my servants Joseph Smith, Jun., and Sidney Rigdon**.

> Brother Gilbert's generosity as a merchant is described by Parley P. Pratt as he prepared to depart from Liberty, Missouri, on another mission. He said:
>
> "I next called on Sidney A. Gilbert, a merchant, then sojourning in the village of Liberty—his store in Jackson County having been broken up, and his goods plundered and destroyed by the mob. 'Well,' says he, 'brother Parley, you certainly look too shabby to start a journey; you must have a new suit; I have got some remnants left that will make you a coat,' etc. A neighboring tailoress and two or three other sisters happened to be present on a visit, and hearing the conversation, exclaimed, 'Yes, brother Gilbert, you find the stuff and we'll make it up for him.' This arranged, I now lacked only a cloak; this was also furnished by brother Gilbert" (*Autobiography of Parley P. Pratt,* 108).
>
> As we continue, verse 6, next, reminds us once again of the role of faith in moving ahead in obedience to the Lord's commands,

even when we do not know for sure what is going to happen next.

6 Behold, **these are the first ordinances which you shall receive;** and **the residue shall be made known in a time to come** [*the Lord will tell him more and give additional help and instructions when the time is right*], according to your labor in my vineyard.

Finally, as this revelation closes, we are reminded that remaining true and faithful to the end is a vital part of the gospel.

7 And again, I would that ye should learn that **he only is saved who endureth unto the end.** Even so. Amen.

SECTION 54

Background

Given through the Prophet Joseph Smith to Newel Knight, this revelation was received in Kirtland, Ohio, on June 10, 1831. Brother Knight was five years older than the Prophet and was the son of Joseph and Polly Knight, who had been generous to Joseph and Emma Smith on many occasions. Joseph had become acquainted with the Joseph Knight family while boarding with Isaac Hale's family in Harmony, Pennsylvania, prior to bringing the gold plates home. The Knights had been converted to the Church, along with several others in Colesville, New York.

In December 1830, the Lord had commanded the Saints to move to Ohio (see D&C 37:2). By this time, in June 1831, Newel Knight and a number of other members from New York had moved to Ohio and were living in Thompson not far from Kirtland. Newel was serving as president of the Thompson Branch of the Church, a group of about 60.

Problems had arisen in Thompson, which led Brother Knight to ask Joseph Smith to request counsel from the Lord. This resulted in the receiving of what is now known as section 54. Briefly put, the problem was that the rest of the Colesville Branch had now arrived in Thompson, and Leman Copley (perhaps you remember him from the background given along with section 49) had agreed to live the law of consecration by donating his large farm for the Colesville Saints to settle and build on. He had done this by covenant, as is required by the law of consecration. However, shortly after they arrived, he backed out of the agreement with encouragement from Ezra Thayre. This, of course, left the Colesville Saints in a difficult predicament, so they asked Newel Knight to go to the Prophet and find out what they should do. As you will see, after giving instructions on the seriousness of covenant breaking, the Lord instructs these faithful members to go on to Missouri. In verse 1, next, the Savior identifies Himself and introduces Himself.

1 BEHOLD, **thus saith the Lord**, even Alpha and Omega [*the "A" and the "Z" of the Greek alphabet, another scriptural term for the Savior*], **the beginning and the end**, even **he who was crucified for the sins of the world**—

Next, in verse 2, Brother Knight is instructed to continue in his calling as branch president of the Colesville Saints. According to the *Doctrine and Covenants Student Manual*, 1981, page 115, Brother Knight is one of those leaders spoken of in D&C 38:34–36 who were to be sustained to take care of "the poor and the needy."

2 Behold, verily, verily, **I say unto you**, my servant **Newel Knight, you shall stand fast** [*continue to serve diligently*] **in the office** whereunto I have appointed you.

3 And if your brethren [*the members of the Thompson Branch*] desire to escape their enemies, let them **repent** of all their sins, and **become truly humble** before me and **contrite** [*be open and receptive to correction as needed*].

Next, the Lord explains to Brother Knight that the covenant his people made with Him and Leman Copley for land on which to settle

as a part of the law of consecration has been broken (by Leman Copley), and thus is no longer in effect. In other words, they are no longer bound by it.

4 And **as the covenant which they made unto me has been broken, even so it has become void and of none effect**.

Verses 5 and 6, next, serve as a brief but important lesson concerning the two parties involved in a covenant that is broken. The guilty party is in serious trouble with the Lord, whereas the party that did its best to keep the covenant will obtain mercy (in other words, will ultimately receive great blessings from the Lord one way or another. Their exaltation is not in jeopardy because the other person or people involved in the covenant chose to break it).

5 And **wo to him by whom this offense cometh**, for **it had been better for him that he had been drowned in the depth of the sea**.

6 But **blessed are they who have kept the covenant and observed the commandment** [*kept their part of the agreement*], **for they shall obtain mercy**.

In verses 7–10, next, the Savior tells Brother Knight to take his branch to Missouri, to handle leadership and expenses according to their best judgment, and, for the time being, to stop trying to live the law of consecration (United Order). In its place, they are to live "like unto men" (verse 9) until the time comes (in Missouri) to live the law of consecration again.

7 Wherefore, **go to now and flee the land**, lest your enemies come upon you; and **take your journey**, and appoint whom you will to be your leader, and to pay moneys for you.

8 And thus you shall **take your journey into the regions westward, unto the land of Missouri**, unto the borders of the Lamanites.

> The "borders of the Lamanites" (verse 8, above) was a common term in that day for the western frontier. Many Indian tribes lived west of the Missouri River. Thus, Jackson County, Missouri, was on the extreme western edge of civilization at that time.

9 And **after you have done journeying** [*upon arriving in Missouri*], behold, I say unto you, **seek ye a living like unto men** [*don't keep striving to live the law of consecration, for now*], until I prepare a place for you.

10 And again, **be patient in tribulation** until I come; and, behold, I come quickly, and **my reward is with me** [*among other things, this phrase can mean that living the*

gospel of Jesus Christ carries with it its own rewards, independent of other benefits and blessings], and **they who have sought me early shall find rest to their souls**. Even so. Amen.

> This group of more than sixty faithful Colesville Saints followed instructions and traveled the almost nine hundred miles to Missouri, arriving in Independence, Missouri, near the end of July 1831.

SECTION 55

Background

> This revelation was given to W. W. Phelps, age thirty-nine, through the Prophet Joseph Smith, on June 14, 1831, at Kirtland, Ohio. William Wines Phelps had not been baptized at the time of this revelation to him. A newspaper editor and printer by trade, he had read an announcement in a newspaper on March 26, 1830, that the Book of Mormon was about to come off the press and would be for sale. He later met Parley P. Pratt, from whom he purchased a copy on April 9, 1830. After reading the book, he desired to meet Joseph Smith and consequently left for Kirtland, Ohio, to do so.
>
> Having just recently arrived in Kirtland with his family, he met the Prophet and, through him, asked what the Lord desired him to do now. Section 55 contains the Lord's answer. After the

Savior introduces Himself to him, he is instructed to be baptized, confirmed, and ordained an elder. Shortly after this revelation, he will be baptized and ordained an elder.

1 BEHOLD, **thus saith the Lord** unto you, my servant William, yea, **even the Lord of the whole earth**, thou art called and chosen; and **after thou hast been baptized** by water, which if you do with an eye single to my glory [*meaning with pure motives*], **you shall have a remission of your sins and a reception of the Holy Spirit by the laying on of hands**;

2 And **then thou shalt be ordained by the hand of my servant Joseph Smith, Jun., to be an elder** unto this church, to preach repentance and remission of sins by way of baptism in the name of Jesus Christ, the Son of the living God.

Next, William is told that after he has been properly baptized and confirmed and has received the Melchizedek Priesthood through ordination to the office of elder in the Church, he will have the power to confer the gift of the Holy Ghost by the laying on of hands.

3 And on whomsoever you shall lay your hands, if they are contrite before me, **you shall have power to give the Holy Spirit**.

As you can see in verse 4, next, the Lord will put Brother Phelps right to work, using his talents and skills for printing and writing to bless the lives of children in the Church, as well as adults.

4 And again, you shall be ordained to **assist my servant Oliver Cowdery to do the work of printing**, and of **selecting and writing books for schools in this church, that little children also may receive instruction** before me as is pleasing unto me.

Brother Phelps commented on his role in making the gospel available to children. He said:

"As a people we are fast approaching a desired end, which may literally be called a beginning. Thus far, we cannot be reproached with being backward in instruction. By revelation, in 1831, I was appointed to 'do the work of printing, and of selecting and writing books for schools in this church, that little children might receive instruction;' and since then I have received a further sanction. We are preparing to go out from among the people, where we can serve God in righteousness; and the first thing is, to teach our children; for they are as the Israel of old. It is our children who will take the kingdom and bear it off to all the world. The first commandment with promise to Israel was, 'Honor thy father and thy mother, that thy days may be long in the land, which the Lord thy God giveth thee.' We will instruct our children in the paths of righteousness; and we want that instruction compiled in a book" (*Times and Seasons*, November 1, 1845, 1015).

In Missouri, Brother Phelps printed the Book of Commandments (the precursor to the Doctrine and Covenants) and the first Church newspaper, *The Evening and the Morning Star.* Later, back in Kirtland, he helped prepare and print the 1835 edition of the Doctrine and Covenants. He helped Emma Smith prepare the first hymn book for the Church. He wrote several of our Church hymns, including

- "The Spirit of God"

- "Now Let Us Rejoice"

- "Redeemer of Israel"

- "Now We'll Sing with One Accord"

- "Praise to the Man"

- "Adam-ondi-Ahman"

- "Gently Raise the Sacred Strain"

- "O God, the Eternal Father"

- "If You Could Hie to Kolob"

Continuing with section 55, next, in verse 5, William W. Phelps will be instructed to go to Missouri with Joseph Smith and Sidney Rigdon.

5 And again, verily I say unto you, for this cause [*to serve as a printer for*

the Church, as well as to carry out his other assignments*] you shall **take your journey with my servants Joseph Smith, Jun., and Sidney Rigdon**, that you may be planted [*a word which symbolizes being "planted in the Lord's vineyard to do His work*] in the land of your inheritance [*Missouri*] to do this work.

6 And again, let my servant **Joseph Coe** also **take his journey with them**. The residue shall be made known hereafter [*the Lord will tell them more when they get there*], even as I will. Amen.

Forty-eight-year-old Joseph Coe, born on November 12, 1784, was an early convert from New York. He joined the Saints in the Kirtland area in early 1831 and traveled to Missouri with the Prophet, Sidney Rigdon and others as instructed in verse 6, above. He was one of the eight elders present when Sidney Rigdon dedicated Missouri for the gathering of the Saints. Over time, he had disagreements with Joseph Smith that eventually led him to join with others in an attempt to overthrow Joseph as the Prophet. He was finally excommunicated in December 1838.

SECTION 56

Background

This revelation was given to the Prophet Joseph Smith at Kirtland,

Ohio, on June 15, 1831. Perhaps you've noticed that there were several revelations given in June 1831. In fact, sections 52 through 56 were all given during that time.

We mentioned in the background to section 52 that many pairs of missionaries were called to go on missions to Missouri and preach along the way as they traveled. One of these sets of missionaries was Thomas B. Marsh and Ezra Thayre (D&C 52:22). In the background to section 54, we mentioned that Ezra Thayre was part of the problem that had arisen in Thompson, Ohio, near Kirtland over the consecration of a large farm for the settling of the Saints arriving from Colesville, New York.

The problem leading up to this revelation is that rebellious Ezra Thayre is embroiled in controversy in Thompson and doesn't particularly want to go to Missouri on a mission, even though the Lord has called him to go. As a result, he is dragging his feet on preparations to leave on the mission, which in turn has caused Thomas Marsh great concern because he does want to go. Consequently, Brother Marsh has gone to the Prophet Joseph, who has gone to the Lord for counsel on the matter. In verses 1–4, you will see the seriousness of making and then breaking covenants.

1 **HEARKEN, O ye people who profess my name** [*who claim to be members of the Lord's Church*], **saith the Lord your God**; for behold, **mine anger is kindled against the rebellious**, and **they shall know mine arm** [*symbolic of power in scriptural symbolism*] **and mine indignation** [*anger*], in the day of visitation [*punishment*] and of wrath upon the nations.

Some people wonder how God, who is perfect and righteous, can have "indignation" (verse 1, above). This type of anger is sometimes called "righteous indignation" and is often seen in the Lord's "parenting" situations when His children have not responded to a gentle approach. Therefore, He speaks and counsels in ways that are more likely to get their attention and appropriate response leading to repentance. When they still refuse to change their ways, the law of justice is eventually put into action, and wayward children often see that as anger. It is important to keep in mind that His "anger" or "indignation" is not out-of-control anger as is often the case with mortal parents. Rather, it is perfectly controlled and is mercifully designed to provide additional chances for the rebellious and wicked to come to their senses and repent.

Next, in verse 2, Jesus teaches a simple, basic doctrine.

2 And **he that will not take up his cross and follow me, and**

keep my commandments, the same shall not be saved [*will not be given exaltation, which is the highest of all blessings available on Judgment Day*].

The phrase "take up his cross," as used in verse 2, above, means to do whatever is necessary in order to follow Christ and keep His commandments and our covenants with Him. "Cross," of course, symbolizes trials and hardships encountered.

Next, in verse 3, we see the phrase "in mine own due time," which reminds us that the Lord is patient and that His punishments of His "children" come according to His timetable, not ours. Perhaps this is one of the reasons that some members who are striving to keep the commandments find themselves wondering why the wicked are not punished. They will be if they don't eventually repent. But in the meantime, as you have no doubt noticed, some of them do wake up spiritually and repent, bringing much joy in heaven as well as on earth. (Compare with D&C 18:13, 15.)

3 Behold, I, the Lord, command; and he that will not obey shall be cut off **in mine own due time**, after I have commanded and the commandment is broken.

Next, we find a brief lesson on the fact that some commandments and instructions can be revoked if

people refuse to obey. This sometimes comes as a surprise to people who have the notion that once God says something, it cannot be revoked. We must carefully differentiate between "eternal laws," which cannot be revoked (such as the necessity of repenting, the necessity for an atonement, the law of justice, the law of mercy, and so forth) and commandments that can be revoked if people use their agency to disobey (such as the case here with Ezra Thayre, who is rebelling against going on a mission, thus leaving Thomas Marsh without a companion). Ezra Thayre would seem to have increased accountability since he was ordained a high priest at the fourth general conference of the Church held in June in Kirtland.

You may wish to make a cross-reference in your own scriptures next to verse 4, below, that sends you to D&C 58:30–33, which likewise deals with God's "revoking" instructions and blessings when people chose not to obey.

4 Wherefore **I, the Lord, command and revoke, as it seemeth me good**; and all this to be answered upon the heads of the rebellious [*the law of accountability*], saith the Lord.

5 **Wherefore** [*this is why*], **I revoke the commandment** which was given unto my servants Thomas B. Marsh and

Ezra Thayre [*D&C 52:22*], **and give a new commandment** unto my servant Thomas, that he shall take up his journey speedily [*don't keep waiting for Ezra Thayre*] to the land of Missouri, and **my servant Selah J. Griffin shall also go with him**.

The *Doctrine and Covenants Student Manual*, 1981, page 117, helps us understand what is happening in verses 6–8, next.

"In these verses the Lord changed the assignments given in Doctrine and Covenants, section 52, verses 22 and 32. Selah J. Griffin, formerly assigned to Newel Knight, was assigned to Thomas B. Marsh. Newel Knight was called to go with the Colesville Saints to Missouri, and Ezra Thayre was released from his missionary calling."

6 For behold, **I revoke the commandment which was given unto my servants Selah J. Griffin and Newel Knight** [*D&C 52:32*], in consequence of the stiffneckedness of my people which are in Thompson, and their rebellions.

7 Wherefore, **let my servant Newel Knight remain with them** [*as their leader, rather than going on a preaching mission to Missouri with Selah Griffin*]; and as many [*of the Thompson Branch*] as will go [*to Missouri*] may go, that are contrite before me, and be led by him to the land which I have appointed.

8 And again, verily I say unto you, that my servant **Ezra Thayre must repent** of his **pride**, and of his **selfishness**, and **obey the former commandment** which I have given him concerning the place upon which he lives [*the farm in Thompson, Ohio*].

9 And **if he will do this**, as there shall be no divisions made upon the land, **he shall be appointed still to go to the land of Missouri;**

10 **Otherwise he shall receive the money which he has paid, and shall leave the place**, and shall be cut off out of my church [*excommunicated*], saith the Lord God of hosts;

One possible explanation of verse 10, above, is that Ezra Thayre, in addition to supporting Leman Copley (who went back on his covenant to consecrate his large farm in Thompson for the settling of the Colesville Branch) appears to have given a sum of money to the Church. If he decides to leave the Church and the Thompson area, the money would be paid back.

Next, in verse 11, the Lord assures that His words given above will be fulfilled.

11 And **though the heaven and the earth pass away, these words shall not pass away, but shall be fulfilled**.

12 And if my servant Joseph Smith, Jun., must needs pay the money [*pay back Ezra Thayre; see verse 10, above*], behold, I, the Lord, will pay it unto him again in the land of Missouri, that those of whom he shall receive may be rewarded again according to that which they do;

It appears that Brother Thayre repented and remained faithful for a time, because he was again called to serve a mission with Thomas B. Marsh, this time on January 25, 1832 (D&C 75:31). He served this mission faithfully. He continued faithful in the Church until the Martyrdom of the Prophet Joseph Smith in 1844, at which time he refused to follow the leadership of the Quorum of the Twelve under Brigham Young. The last we hear of Ezra Thayre is that he was serving as a high priest in the Reorganized Church of Jesus Christ of Latter Day Saints in Michigan in 1860.

13 For according to that which they do they shall receive, even in lands [*in Missouri*] for their inheritance.

Next, we are reminded of the danger of making our own rules and enjoying wickedness rather than following the Lord's counsel.

14 Behold, thus saith the Lord unto my people—**you have many things to do and to repent of**; for behold, your sins have come up unto me, and are not pardoned, **because you seek to counsel in your own ways** [*you are making your own rules*].

15 And **your hearts are not satisfied**. And **ye obey not the truth, but have pleasure in unrighteousness**.

Sometimes it seems that the rich are the most likely to become prideful and selfish and to leave God. However, in verses 16 and 17, next, we are taught that the poor can also succumb to the temptation of being arrogant and prideful and of justifying their own unrighteousness.

16 **Wo unto you rich men**, that will not give your substance to the poor, for your riches will canker your souls [*will make spiritual "sores" upon your souls*]; and this shall be your lamentation [*this is what you will say, with great regret*] in the day of visitation [*when you are punished for your sins*], and of judgment [*on Judgment Day*], and of indignation [*when you feel the righteous anger of God*]: The harvest is past, the summer is ended [*my opportunities to repent are over*], and my soul is not saved!

17 **Wo unto you poor men**, whose hearts are not broken [*who are not humble*], whose spirits are not contrite [*who do not desire correction as needed from the Lord*], and whose bellies are not satisfied, and whose hands are not stayed [*stopped*] from laying hold upon [*stealing*] other men's goods, whose eyes are full of greediness, and who will not labor with your own hands!

18 But **blessed are the poor who are pure in heart**, whose hearts are broken, and whose spirits are contrite, **for they shall see the kingdom of God coming in power and great glory unto their deliverance**; for the fatness [*wealth; the best*] of the earth shall be theirs.

19 **For behold, the Lord shall come**, and **his recompense** [*reward*] **shall be with him**, and he shall reward every man, and the poor [*the righteous poor*] shall rejoice;

20 **And their generations** [*posterity*] **shall inherit the earth** [*compare with Matthew 5:5 and D&C 45:56–58*] from generation to generation, forever and ever. And now I make an end of speaking unto you. Even so. Amen.

SECTION 57

Background

Finally, the long-awaited day has arrived! The Prophet is in Missouri with other Church leaders and missionaries who have likewise traveled the approximately nine hundred miles from Kirtland. In this revelation, given to the Prophet Joseph Smith in "Zion" (Jackson County, Missouri) on July 20, 1831, the Lord reveals the location where Zion, the New Jerusalem, is to be built. The "center place" for the city of Zion is Independence, Missouri (see verse 3). Imagine the excitement and feelings of humility in the hearts of these brethren as they find themselves standing on this holy ground!

Leading up to this marvelous day, the Lord had given several revelations in which He gave hints and clues about this city of Zion, the city of New Jerusalem. For example, in the Book of Mormon, members of the Church had read about a New Jerusalem that would be located in America (see 3 Nephi 20:22; 21:23–24; Ether 13:2–10). In September 1830, the Lord had told the Saints that no one at that time knew where the city of Zion would be built (Hiram Page had claimed to know), but that it would be built "on the borders by the Lamanites" (D&C 28:9). And in D&C 42:62, the Lord told faithful members that He would tell them, when the time was right, "where the New Jerusalem shall be built."

Having departed from Kirtland on June 19, 1831, and arrived in Independence, Missouri, on July 14, 1831, with his traveling companions, the Prophet Joseph now spent time contemplating and wondering "When will the wilderness blossom as the rose; when will Zion be built up in her glory, and where will thy Temple stand unto which all nations shall come in the last days?" (in *Manuscript History of the Church*, vol. A-1, page 127, josephsmithpapers.org).

Now, with great rejoicing in their hearts, these elders receive the message through their Prophet that they are standing on the land of Zion, the place for the gathering of the Saints, and that the temple is to be built on a spot not far from the courthouse.

1 **HEARKEN, O ye elders of my church, saith the Lord your God, who have assembled yourselves together, according to my commandments, in this land,** which is **the land of Missouri,** which **is the land which I have appointed and consecrated for the gathering of the saints.**

2 Wherefore, **this is the land of promise,** and **the place for the city of Zion.**

3 And thus saith the Lord your

God, if you will receive wisdom here is wisdom. Behold, the place which is now called **Independence is the center place; and a spot for the temple is lying westward, upon a lot which is not far from the courthouse.**

Apostle Bruce R. McConkie informed us that this temple will be built before the Second Coming of Christ. He Said, "As to the temple unto which all nations shall come in the last days, **it shall be built in the New Jerusalem before the Second Coming**, all as a part of the preparatory processes that will make ready a people for their Lord's return" (*A New Witness for the Articles of Faith*, 595).

We will include a quote from the 2018 *Doctrine and Covenants Student Manual*, chapter 21, which informs us that the temple in New Jerusalem will consist of a complex of 24 temples. "About two years after he received the revelation recorded in Doctrine and Covenants 57, the Prophet Joseph Smith received additional revelation concerning the spot where the temple would be constructed. In 1833, the Prophet had a plat map drawn for the city of Zion that depicted **a temple complex of 24 buildings** to be constructed next to each other in Independence (see *History of the Church*, 1:357–59). The gathering to and the building up of the city of Zion, or New Jerusalem, as declared by the Lord, will begin at 'the place of the temple' (D&C 84:4)."

Continuing our study of section 57, we move on to verse 4. In D&C 48:4, the Lord had told the members in Kirtland to begin saving money to purchase land for the New Jerusalem, or Zion. Now, in verses 4–6, the Church is instructed to begin actually buying land in this part of Missouri.

4 **Wherefore**, it is wisdom that **the land should be purchased by the saints**, and also **every tract lying westward**, even unto the line [*the border*] running directly between Jew [*the Indians, or Lamanites*] and Gentile [*the Missourians*];

The use of the word "Jew" in verse 4, above, can be a bit confusing unless we stop to recall the origins of the Lamanites. As you know, Lehi and his group came from Jerusalem in 600 B.C. Regardless of specific genealogy, they were "Jews," politically and geographically. Since the Lamanites are descendants of Lehi and Sariah, they too can be referred to as "Jews."

5 And also **every tract bordering by the prairies, inasmuch as my disciples are enabled to buy lands**. Behold, this is wisdom, that they may obtain it for an everlasting inheritance.

It is interesting to note that land was available for purchase in this part of Missouri for $1.25 per acre. We will include a quote from the institute of religion *Church History Student Manual,* which describes this.

"The price of land and its ready availability also attracted the Saints. In 1831 whole sections of this undeveloped country could be purchased for $1.25 per acre. The Lord directed the brethren to purchase as much land as they were able (see D&C 57:3–5; 58:37, 49–52; 63:27), and Sidney Rigdon was appointed to 'write a description of the land of Zion' (D&C 58:50) to be circulated among eastern Saints in a quest for funds. Sidney Gilbert was appointed 'an agent unto the Church' to receive money from contributors and buy lands (D&C 57:6). Edward Partridge, already serving as a bishop, was commanded to divide the purchased land among the gathering Saints as 'their inheritance' (D&C 57:7). The Lord also cautioned regarding Zion, 'Let all these things be done in order. . . . And let the work of the gathering be not in haste, nor by flight' (D&C 58:55–56)." (*Church History in the Fulness of Times,* 1989, 107.)

6 And **let my servant Sidney Gilbert** [*the merchant spoken of in section 53; see background to section 53 in this study guide for more information about him*] **stand in the**

office to which I have appointed him [*D&C 53:4*], **to receive moneys, to be an agent unto the church, to buy land in all the regions round about**, inasmuch as can be done in righteousness, and as wisdom shall direct.

7 **And let my servant Edward Partridge** stand in the office to which I have appointed him [*the first bishop in the Church; see D&C 41:9*], and **divide unto the saints their inheritance** [*portion out the land purchased in Missouri to the arriving Saints*], even as I have commanded; and also those whom he has appointed to assist him.

As previously mentioned, Sidney Gilbert was a skilled businessman and merchant. In verse 8, next, the Lord gives him specific instructions concerning his responsibilities in Missouri.

8 And again, verily I say unto you, **let** my servant **Sidney Gilbert** plant himself in this place, and **establish a store, that he may sell goods without fraud** [*the Saints were subject to being cheated by local merchants who saw a chance to raise prices exorbitantly as members of the Church arrived in Missouri*], that he may **obtain money to buy lands** for the good of the saints, and that he may **obtain whatsoever things the disciples**

[*members of the Church*] **may need** to plant them [*establish themselves*] in their inheritance [*in Missouri*].

Next, we see an important reminder that we are to conduct the business of the Church in accordance with the laws of the land in which it is being established. We suspect that the "license" was a business license required by local or state law at the time.

9 And also **let my servant Sidney Gilbert obtain a license**—behold here is wisdom, and whoso readeth let him understand—that he may send goods also unto the people, even by whom he will as clerks employed in his service;

10 And **thus provide for my saints**, that my gospel may be preached unto those who sit in darkness [*spiritual darkness; without the gospel*] and in the region and shadow of death.

You may recall from the background given for section 55, in this study guide as well as in the notes for that section, that William W. Phelps was, among other things, a printer by trade. In response to the instructions given by the Lord next, in verses 11–13, he established the first printing press for the Church in Missouri and published the first newspaper, the *Evening and the Morning Star*. He will also help select and prepare the revelations for the Book of Commandments (in effect, the first edition of the Doctrine and Covenants).

11 And again, verily I say unto you, **let my servant William W. Phelps** be planted in this place [*make this his home*], and **be established as a printer unto the church**.

12 And lo, if the world receive his writings—behold here is wisdom—**let him obtain whatsoever he can obtain in righteousness, for the good of the saints**.

13 And **let my servant Oliver Cowdery assist him**, even as I have commanded, in whatsoever place I shall appoint unto him, **to copy**, and to **correct**, and **select**, that all things may be right before me, as it shall be proved by the Spirit through him.

14 And thus **let those of whom I have spoken be planted** [*make their homes here*] **in the land of Zion, as speedily as can be, with their families**, to do those things even as I have spoken.

15 And **now concerning the gathering**—Let the bishop [*Edward Partridge (verse 7)*] and the agent [*Sidney Gilbert (verse 6)*] make preparations for those families which have been commanded to come to this land [*particularly the members of the Colesville Branch, who, at this time, are en route to Missouri, being led by Newel Knight; see D&C 56:7*], as soon as possible, and plant them in their inheritance.

16 **And unto the residue** [*those not specifically addressed in this revelation*] of both elders and members **further directions shall be given hereafter**. Even so. Amen.

Just a quick note about Kirtland before we move on: Perhaps you recall that the Lord had already told the Church that Kirtland, Ohio, was to be the gathering place "for the present time" (D&C 48:1, 3), thus indicating that it was a temporary gathering place. They were to position themselves financially to "purchase land for an inheritance, even the city," meaning the city of New Jerusalem (D&C 48:4), whose location was yet to be revealed (D&C 48:5). Now that the location of the city of Zion has been revealed (D&C 57:1–3), the money being collected will make its way to Bishop Partridge and will be used as instructed.

We know from D&C 64:21 that Kirtland was to serve as a "stronghold" for five years. Thus, over the next approximately five years, we will have, in effect, two headquarters for the Church—Kirtland and Jackson County, Missouri. If you keep this in mind, it will help avoid confusion regarding background and setting of several of the next revelations in the Doctrine and Covenants.

One other note. The Prophet Joseph Smith also revealed that Jackson County, Missouri, was the location of the Garden of Eden. According to Wilford Woodruff, President Brigham Young once said, "Joseph, the Prophet, told me that the Garden of Eden was in Jackson County, Missouri. When Adam was driven out he went to the place we now call Adam-ondi-Ahman, Daviess County, Missouri. There he built an altar and offered sacrifices" (Cowley, *Wilford Woodruff: History of His Life and Labors,* 481; see also 545–46).

SECTION 58

Background

This revelation was given through the Prophet Joseph Smith in Zion, Jackson County Missouri, on Monday, August 1, 1831, about eleven days after the revelation (section 57) designating Independence, Missouri, as the "center place" of Zion. Likewise, in section 57, many of these elders, including Edward Partridge, the first bishop of the Church, were commanded to "plant" themselves in Missouri now. This commandment to stay in Missouri now came as a shock to many of these men who had planned on returning shortly to

their families, whom they had left back in Ohio just a month previously.

A quote from *Revelations in Context* helps us understand how difficult these commandments to remain in Missouri actually were for these early Saints. Bishop Partridge wrote to his wife, Lydia, and "broke the news that he wouldn't be returning to Ohio that summer and instead asked that she and their five daughters join him on the Missouri frontier. Additionally, instead of being able to return to Ohio to help them move that fall, he wrote, 'Brother Gilbert or I must be here to attend the sales in Dec. [and] not knowing that he can get back by that time I have thought it advisable to stay here for the present contrary to [my] expectations.' He also warned that once she joined him in Missouri, 'We have to suffer [and] shall for some time many privations here which you [and] I have not been much used to for year[s]' [Letter, Aug. 5, 1831, in Edward Partridge letters, 1831–1835, Church History Library].

"Lydia willingly obeyed the revelation to move, packing her home and gathering her five daughters to travel west to a place she had never seen before" (Sherilyn Farnes, "A Bishop unto the Church," in *Revelations in Context*, 79–80. See history.lds.org).

Most of these members had already recently moved from New York to Kirtland in the dead of winter, only to be told shortly after their arrival in Ohio that they were now to move to Missouri. We will be taught many lessons as we study section 58, beginning with the topic of tribulation and blessings and continuing with the topic of perspective in verses 1–4. You may wish to mark these verses in your own scriptures and place a brief note something to the effect of "tribulation and blessings" out to the side. Remember, the Savior is our teacher.

1 HEARKEN, O ye elders of my church, and give ear to my word, and **learn of me** [*Jesus*] what I will concerning you, and also concerning this land unto which I have sent you.

2 For verily I say unto you, **blessed is he that keepeth my commandments, whether in life or in death**; and **he that is faithful in tribulation, the reward of the same is greater in the kingdom of heaven.**

3 **Ye cannot behold with your natural eyes, for the present time, the design** [*plan*] **of your God concerning those things which shall come hereafter** [*right now you can't see what I see for the future of this land of Zion*], **and the glory which shall follow after much tribulation.**

4 For **after much tribulation come the blessings.** Wherefore **the day cometh that ye** [*the faithful*] **shall be crowned with much glory**; the hour is not yet, but is nigh at hand.

It is clear from the above verses that tribulation, properly endured, can lead to substantial personal growth and the highest blessings from God. A common but mistaken notion among some belief systems is that trials and tribulation are a result of personal transgression. In a very real way, the Lord is telling these faithful though imperfect Saints that the tribulations they have endured and will yet endure for the gospel's sake are a "curriculum" for their learning and growth. While we can't always see noble purposes in tribulation, the Lord can. And, in verse 3, He reminds us that we are not yet capable of seeing as He does during many of our trials and tribulations. So, we have to simply go forward with faith.

In verses 5–6, next, He tells us that one of the purposes of tribulation is that of teaching us obedience in the face of opposition.

5 **Remember this, which I tell you before, that you may lay it to heart** [*in scriptural symbolism, "heart" is the center of feelings and tends to be the basis for most behavior*], **and receive that which is to follow.**

In verses 6–9, the Savior gives several specific reasons for sending these Saints to Missouri at this time. We will number these reasons as we point them out. We can apply these to ourselves as we accept callings and responsibilities that severely tax our energies and resources.

6 Behold, verily I say unto you, **for this cause I have sent you** [*on this difficult journey to Jackson County, Missouri, among other things*]— **[1] that you might be obedient,** and **[2] that your hearts might be prepared to bear testimony of the things which are to come**;

7 And also **[3] that you might be honored in laying the foundation** [*for the growth of the Church*], and in **[4] bearing record of the land upon which the Zion of God shall stand** [*in other words, bearing record that the long-promised Zion will be established*];

8 And also **[5] that a feast of fat things** [*meaning the "very best"—in other words, the restored gospel of Jesus Christ*] **might be prepared for the poor**; yea, a feast of fat things, of wine on the lees well refined [*the very best*], **[6] that the earth may know that the mouths of the prophets shall not fail** [*so that the inhabitants of the earth may know that the words of prophets will be fulfilled*];

9 Yea, **a supper of the house of the Lord** [*a feast of the true gospel, prepared by God through His servants*], well prepared, **[7] unto which all nations shall be invited** [*the gospel will be preached to all people*].

Next, in verses 10–11, we are told that the gospel will go forth in two distinctive waves (after the early Saints have laid the foundation; see verse 7). In other words, the Lord says that there is an order as far as to whom the gospel will be preached in the last days. The first group is the "rich and the learned, the wise and the noble" (verse 10). After that, it will go to the economically severely disadvantaged and to those who are severely spiritually "blind and deaf" (verse 11).

While these are relative terms, it appears that there have been many converts since the beginning of the restoration who are among the "noble and great" spoken of by Abraham (Abraham 3:22). As such people have joined the Church and provided strength and resources, the Church has been positioned to take the gospel to all people. This is a rather interesting and exciting prophecy to see being fulfilled in our day.

10 **First, the rich and the learned, the wise and the noble;**

11 And **after that** cometh the day of my power; **then shall the poor**, the **lame**, and the **blind**, and

the **deaf**, come in unto the marriage of the Lamb [*the full gospel and its benefits, a reference to the parable given in Matthew 22:1–14*], and **partake of the supper of the Lord**, prepared for the great day to come.

12 Behold, I, the Lord, have spoken it.

In verse 13 and the first phrase of verse 14, the Lord reiterates that the reason He sent them to Missouri is so that the testimony of the restored gospel can go from Zion into all the world.

13 And **that the testimony might go forth from Zion**, yea, from the mouth of the city of the heritage of God—

14 Yea, **for this cause I have sent you hither** [*here to Missouri*], and have selected my servant Edward Partridge, and have appointed unto him his mission in this land.

Verses 14–16 contain strong words for Edward Partridge, whose responsibilities as bishop include dividing out tracts of land upon which the incoming Saints can settle and build. He is called to repentance and warned that he won't get another chance if he chooses not to be obedient to instructions. While we don't know for sure what the problem was, verse 17 leads us to suspect that the chastisement had to do with

the allocating of Church-owned property to incoming members and that perhaps he was refusing to give written deeds to them (as instructed in D&C 51:4). We will deal more with this issue when we get to section 85, verse 8. Perhaps it was an entirely different problem, such as not properly using his counselors or listening to them (verse 18). Someday, we will know.

15 But **if he repent not of his sins**, which are **unbelief** and **blindness of heart**, let him take heed lest he fall.

16 Behold **his mission is given unto him, and it shall not be given again**.

17 And **whoso standeth in this mission** [*the calling of bishop*] **is appointed to be a judge in Israel**, like as it was in ancient days, **to divide the lands of the heritage of God unto his children**;

18 And to judge his people by the testimony of the just, and **by the assistance of his counselors**, according to the **laws of the kingdom** [*including private ownership of property in the United Order*] which are given by the prophets of God.

19 For verily I say unto you, **my law shall be kept on this land** [*the land of Zion*].

In the next several verses, we will be taught a number of mini lessons. We will point several of these out as we go. Many of these will probably be familiar to you. If not, once you hear them, you will notice them often in the sermons of Church leaders and in class discussions, as well as in sacrament meetings and so forth.

Lesson

Those in leadership positions must be humble enough to let God guide and direct them.

20 Let no man think he is ruler; but let God rule him that judgeth, according to the counsel of his own will, or—in other words, him that counseleth or sitteth upon the judgment seat.

Lesson

Being a loyal member of the Church is not an excuse for breaking the laws of the land.

21 Let no man break the laws of the land, for **he that keepeth the laws of God hath no need to break the laws of the land.**

Lesson

Respect and uphold the government in the land in which you live. (Some government, no matter how imperfect, is almost always better than no government.)

22 Wherefore, be subject to the powers that be [*man-made governments*], **until he** [*Christ*] **reigns whose right it is to reign, and subdues all enemies under his feet** [*this includes the millennial reign of Christ*].

Lesson

Keep a wise perspective between the laws of God and the laws of governments.

23 Behold, **the laws which ye have received from my hand are the laws of the church**, and in this light [*being subject to governments and so forth*] ye shall hold them forth. Behold, here is wisdom [*there is wisdom in doing this*].

24 And now, as I spake concerning my servant **Edward Partridge, this land** [*Zion, in Missouri*] **is the land of his residence**, and those whom he has appointed for his counselors; and also the land of the residence of him whom I have appointed to keep my storehouse [*the bishop's storehouse; see D&C 51:13*];

Lesson

There are many matters that are best left up to individuals and the Lord.

25 Wherefore, let them bring their families to this land, as they shall counsel between themselves and me.

Lesson

It is not necessary for us to be commanded in everything we do. We have a mind, and the Lord expects us to use it.

26 For behold, **it is not meet** [*necessary, wise*] **that I should command in all things**; for **he that is compelled in all things**, the same **is a slothful and not a wise servant**; wherefore he receiveth no reward.

27 Verily I say, **men should** be anxiously [*energetically, with sincere dedication*] engaged in a good cause, and **do many things of their own free will**, and bring to pass much righteousness;

28 **For the power is in them** [*they are capable of this*], wherein **they are agents unto themselves** [*they have moral agency*]. And inasmuch as men do good they shall in nowise lose their reward.

29 But **he that doeth not anything until he is commanded, and receiveth a commandment with doubtful heart, and keepeth it with slothfulness, the same is damned** [*does not progress*].

Lesson

Personal accountability is a basic principle of the gospel of Christ.

30 **Who am I** that made man, saith the Lord, **that will hold him guiltless that obeys not my commandments?** [*In other words, what kind of a god would our God be if He did not hold people accountable for how they use their agency?*]

Lesson

Do not blame the Lord when you, yourself, are responsible for not receiving promised blessings. He can command and revoke, depending on our response to His commandments.

31 **Who am I, saith the Lord, that have promised and have not fulfilled?**

32 **I command and men obey not; I revoke and they receive not the blessing.**

33 **Then they say in their hearts: This is not the work of the Lord, for his promises are not fulfilled** [*in other words, they blame God*]. But **wo unto such**, for their reward lurketh beneath, and not from above.

As we continue, the Lord gives instructions for consecrating material means to the Church as the

Saints gather in Missouri. Martin Harris is given instructions to do so as an example to others.

34 And now I give unto you **further directions concerning this land** [*Zion, Jackson County, Missouri*].

35 It is wisdom in me that my servant **Martin Harris should be an example unto the church, in laying his moneys before the bishop of the church** [*the law of consecration in action*].

36 And also, **this is a law unto every man that cometh unto this land** [*Zion, Jackson County, Missouri*] **to receive an inheritance; and he shall do with his moneys according as the law** [the law of consecration] **directs.**

37 And it is wisdom also that **there should be lands purchased in Independence**, for the place of the storehouse [*the bishop's storehouse*], and also for the house of the printing.

Lesson

The Lord expects us to listen to the Holy Ghost and to exercise our agency in many things concerning our personal lives. Many decisions are left up to us.

38 And **other directions concerning my servant Martin Harris shall be given him of the Spirit, that he may receive his inheritance as seemeth him good** [*whatever he decides is fine*];

Next, in verse 39, Martin Harris is given a warning to the effect that he is still afflicted with pride. In D&C 5:24 and 32, he was warned that he needed to be humble. It appears that he is still struggling with this problem at this time.

39 And let him repent of his sins, for **he seeketh the praise of the world.**

40 And also **let my servant William W. Phelps stand in the office to which I have appointed him** [*"as a printer unto the church" (D&C 57:11)*], and receive his inheritance in the land;

41 And **also he hath need to repent**, for I, the Lord, am not well pleased with him, for he **seeketh to excel** [*perhaps meaning that he wants to get ahead at the expense of others, an attitude that does not fit in with the law of consecration*], **and he is not sufficiently meek before me.**

Having counseled the above brethren to repent, the Savior now gently reminds them (and all of us) that once we have truly repented, our sins will not be brought up again. This includes on Judgment Day.

You may be interested to know that even in the case of members who are excommunicated, when they return to membership through baptism and confirmation, their original baptism and confirmation dates are put on their new membership records, thus preserving their privacy regarding their past problems and adhering to the Lord's promise in verse 42, next, wherein He says, "I, the Lord, remember them no more."

For those who have thus repented and been cleansed by the Atonement of Christ, the day of final judgment will be a pleasant experience, as taught in the last half of 2 Nephi 9:14 (**bold** added for emphasis).

2 Nephi 9:14

Wherefore, we shall have a perfect knowledge of all our guilt, and our uncleanness, and our nakedness; **and the righteous shall have a perfect knowledge of their enjoyment, and their righteousness, being clothed with purity, yea, even with the robe of righteousness.**

Verses 42 and 43 go together. You may wish to mark them in some way that indicates that they go together.

Lesson

When we truly repent, we are forgiven, and our sins will not be brought up again, not even on final Judgment Day.

42 Behold, he who has repented of his sins, the same **is forgiven,** and **I, the Lord, remember them no more.**

43 **By this ye may know if a man repenteth of his sins**—behold, **he will confess them** and **forsake them** [*stop doing them*].

Occasionally, over the years in classes, a student has asked me if verse 42 really means that God forgets our sins or simply that He will never bring them up to us again if we have truly repented. While the important thing is that He "remembers them no more," the technical answer may reside in D&C 82:7, in which we are told that if we commit the same sins we once repented of, "the former sins return."

Another question quite often brought up in classes has to do with what sins require that a member confess them to the bishop. Obviously, confession to the Lord and forsaking are required (see verse 43, above), and a member can confess anything of concern to his or her bishop or stake president. But a general guideline is that any sin that violates the commitments and issues involved in a temple recommend interview would need to be confessed to a person's bishop. Breaking the law of chastity, violating the Word of Wisdom, failure to pay tithing, criminal activity, preaching false doctrine, failure to sustain general or local officers in the Church, child abuse, and spouse abuse are among the sins that should be confessed to the bishop or stake president. Once such sins have been properly confessed to one's bishop or stake president, they do not need to be confessed again in additional temple recommend interviews over the years.

Yet another issue that has come up in class discussions over my years of teaching is whether it is permissible to confess to another bishop if a member is not comfortable confessing to his or her own bishop. The answer is simple. Our own bishop is the only one who has the keys of stewardship over us. While another bishop may be kind and a member may feel more comfortable going to him, he has no authority for that person, and thus, the requirement for confession is not met by visiting with him. One alternative is to go to one's stake president, who also has keys and authority to hear confessions from the members of his stake. In the case of a student, for instance, who may be away to college, he or she could confess to the home ward bishop or the college ward bishop.

In the remainder of this section, the Lord deals with a number of issues, including the matter of collecting money with which to purchase land in Missouri. First, He points out that the main gathering to Missouri will not take place for many years and that He will carefully control it when the time comes.

44 And now, verily, **I say concerning the residue of the elders** [*the ones not called to settle at this time in Missouri*] **of my church, the time has not yet come, for many years, for them to receive their inheritance in this land** [*Missouri*], except they desire it through the prayer of faith, only as it shall be appointed unto them of the Lord.

45 For, behold, **they shall push the people together from the ends of the earth.** [*In other words, there is much missionary work to be done before Zion is established in Missouri.*]

The **bolded** phrase in verse 45, above, is a quote from Deuteronomy 33:17, which speaks of Joseph's (who was sold into Egypt) posterity, pointing out the missionary duties of Ephraim and Manasseh. We will quote this Bible verse here. You will see that one word is different. The Doctrine and Covenants uses "from" rather than "to." In this verse in

Deuteronomy, Joseph is told in his father's blessing that his posterity will play a major role in the gathering of Israel in the last days.

Deuteronomy 33:17

His [*Joseph who was sold into Egypt*] glory is like the firstling of his bullock, and his horns are like the horns of unicorns [*"wild ox" in the Hebrew Old Testament*]: with them he shall push the people together **to** the ends of the earth: and they are the ten thousands of Ephraim, and they are the thousands of Manasseh.

Next, in verses 46–48, the Lord instructs the missionaries who are not called to settle in Missouri that they are to do much missionary work in the area, as well as along the way when they finally return to their homes in the Kirtland area.

46 Wherefore, assemble yourselves together; and **they who are not appointed to stay in this land** [*Missouri*], **let them preach the gospel in the regions round about**; and **after that let them return to their homes.**

47 **Let them preach by the way** [*as they travel home*], and bear testimony of the truth in all places, and call upon the rich, the high and the low, and the poor to repent.

48 And **let them build up churches** [*branches of the Church*], inasmuch as the inhabitants of the earth will repent.

It is clear that the Church could not afford to purchase much land in Missouri at this time and that many more converts would be needed to finance the building up of Zion there. It is also a basic principle of the gospel that the sacrifices of the members, including financial sacrifices, bring strength and personal testimony into the lives and hearts of the members. This principle applies in the lives of members today as they pay tithes and offerings and reap the blessings of heaven.

Next, the members in Ohio are instructed to continue sacrificing and donating money for the purchase of land in Missouri.

49 And **let there be an agent appointed** by the voice of the church [*sustained by the members*], unto the church **in Ohio, to receive moneys to purchase lands in Zion** [*Jackson County, Missouri*].

Next, Sidney Rigdon is instructed to make a written description of the land on which Zion will be built and to write an official letter to all the branches of the Church at the time, requesting help in collecting money for purchasing land in Missouri.

50 And I give unto my servant **Sidney Rigdon** a commandment,

that he **shall write a description of the land of Zion, and a statement of the will of God**, as it shall be made known by the Spirit unto him;

Brother Rigdon did write a description of the land, but his first attempt was not accepted by the Lord, as indicated a few weeks later in D&C 63:56. His second attempt was accepted. In volume one of *History of the Church,* we have a description of the land of Zion that was given by Joseph Smith in early August 1831. Whether this is a copy of Sidney Rigdon's description, we don't know, but we will include it here for your information.

Description of the Land of Zion.

"As we had received a commandment for Elder Rigdon to write a description of the land of Zion, we sought for all the information necessary to accomplish so desirable an object. The country is unlike the timbered states of the East. As far as the eye can reach the beautiful rolling prairies lie spread out like a sea of meadows; and are decorated with a growth of flowers so gorgeous and grand as to exceed description; and nothing is more fruitful, or a richer stockholder in the blooming prairie than the honey bee. Only on the water courses is timber to be found. There in strips from one to three miles in width, and following faithfully the meanderings of the streams, it grows in luxuriant forests. The forests are a mixture of oak, hickory, black walnut, elm, ash, cherry, honey locust, mulberry, coffee bean, hackberry, boxelder, and bass wood; with the addition of cottonwood, butterwood, pecan, and soft and hard maple upon the bottoms. The shrubbery is beautiful, and consists in part of plums, grapes, crab apple, and persimmons.

Agricultural Products; Animals, Domestic and Wild.

"The soil is rich and fertile; from three to ten feet deep, and generally composed of a rich black mold, intermingled with clay and sand. It yields in abundance, wheat, corn, sweet potatoes, cotton and many other common agricultural products. Horses, cattle and hogs, though of an inferior breed, are tolerably plentiful and seem nearly to raise themselves by grazing in the vast prairie range in summer, and feeding upon the bottoms in winter. The wild game is less plentiful of course where man has commenced the cultivation of the soil, than in the wild prairies. Buffalo, elk, deer, bear, wolves, beaver and many smaller animals here roam at pleasure. Turkeys, geese, swans, ducks, yea a variety of the feathered tribe, are among the rich abundance that grace the delightful regions of this goodly land—the heritage of the children of God.

The Climate.

"The season is mild and delightful nearly three quarters of the year, and as the land of Zion, situated at about equal distances from the Atlantic and Pacific oceans, as well as from the Alleghany and Rocky mountains, in the thirty-ninth degree of north latitude, and between the sixteenth and seventeenth degrees of west longitude [from Washington], it bids fair—when the curse is taken from the land—to become one of the most blessed places on the globe. The winters are milder than the Atlantic states of the same parallel of latitude, and the weather is more agreeable; so that were the virtues of the inhabitants only equal to the blessings of the Lord which He permits to crown the industry of those inhabitants, there would be a measure of the good things of life for the benefit of the Saints, full, pressed down, and running over, even an hundred-fold. The disadvantages here, as in all new countries, are self-evident—lack of mills and schools; together with the natural privations and inconveniences which the hand of industry, the refinement of society, and the polish of science, overcome" (*History of the Church*, 1:197–98).

Next, in verse 51 (as mentioned above), Sidney Rigdon is instructed to write a letter from the Church to all branches, which includes a request for money from the members to assist in buying land in Missouri.

51 **And an epistle** [*an official letter*] **and subscription** [*request for funds*], **to be presented unto all the churches to obtain moneys,** to be put into the hands of the bishop, of himself or the agent, as seemeth him good or as he shall direct, **to purchase lands for an inheritance for the children of God** [*the righteous members of the Church*].

52 For, behold, verily I say unto you, **the Lord willeth that the disciples** [*members of the Church*] **and the children of men** [*non-members*] **should open their hearts,** even **to purchase this whole region of country,** as soon as time will permit.

In verse 53, next, we see a warning that if the members of the Church fail to purchase the land needed in Missouri, it will only be obtained through the shedding of blood. Over time, there was considerable reluctance on the part of a number of members in other areas to donate money to buy land in Missouri. As you know, there was much violence against the Saints in Missouri. In our day, there is considerable acquiring of land in Missouri, including in Adam-ondi-Ahman, due to the generous donations and tithing of the members of the Church, as well as through income to the Church from business ventures that bring in money from sources outside the Church.

53 Behold, here is wisdom. **Let them do this lest they receive none inheritance, save it be by the shedding of blood.**

54 And again, **inasmuch as there is land obtained, let there be workmen sent forth** of all kinds [*with all kinds of skills*] unto this land, to labor for the saints of God.

In verses 55–56, next, the Master reminds these early members of the Church that the instructions given above must be carried out with wisdom and order. Part of doing these things "in order" would include purchasing land such that the Church would have clear legal title to it. Also, it was vital that the Saints themselves be as well prepared as possible to settle and build when they arrived in Missouri rather than "fleeing" helter-skelter to Zion.

55 **Let all these things be done in order;** and let the privileges of the lands [*probably meaning the advantages and blessings of settling on such fertile and sacred land*] be made known from time to time, by the bishop or the agent of the church.

56 And **let the work of the gathering be not in haste, nor by flight;** but let it be done as it shall be counseled by the elders of the church at the conferences, according to the knowledge which they receive from time to time.

Next, in verse 57, Brother Rigdon is instructed to dedicate the land of Zion, which includes the "spot for the temple." Joseph Smith himself will dedicate the temple site.

57 And **let my servant Sidney Rigdon consecrate and dedicate this land, and the spot for the temple, unto the Lord.**

The Prophet Joseph Smith recorded the dedication of the land by Sidney and the dedication of the temple site by him. He wrote,

"On the second day of August, I assisted the Colesville branch of the Church to lay the first log, for a house, as a foundation of Zion in Kaw township, twelve miles west of Independence. The log was carried and placed by twelve men, in honor of the twelve tribes of Israel. At the same time, through prayer, the land of Zion was consecrated and dedicated by Elder Sidney Rigdon for the gathering of the Saints. It was a season of joy to those present, and afforded a glimpse of the future, which time will yet unfold to the satisfaction of the faithful" (*History of the Church*, 1:196).

"On the third day of August, I proceeded to dedicate the spot for the Temple, a little west of Independence, and there were also present Sidney Rigdon, Edward Partridge, W. W. Phelps, Oliver Cowdery, Martin Harris and Joseph Coe." (*History of the Church*, 1:199. See also *Manuscript History of the Church*, vol. A-1, page 139, josephsmithpapers.org.)

As the Lord finishes this revelation, He instructs Joseph Smith and others to finish up and then journey back to Kirtland. Remember, as mentioned in the notes at the end of section 57 in this book, that there will, in effect, be two headquarters or gathering places for the Saints over the next five years—Kirtland, Ohio, and Missouri.

58 And let a conference meeting be called; and **after that let my servants Sidney Rigdon and Joseph Smith, Jun., return** [*to Ohio*], **and also Oliver Cowdery with them**, to accomplish the residue [*the rest*] of the work which I have appointed unto them in their own land [*Ohio*], and **the residue** [*in Missouri, see verse 61*] as **shall be ruled by the conferences**.

59 And **let no man return** [*to Ohio*] **from this land** [*Missouri*] **except he bear record by the way**, of that which he knows and most assuredly believes [*all who*

return to Ohio should do missionary work as they travel back].

60 **Let that which has been bestowed upon Ziba Peterson** [*possibly his license to preach the gospel*] **be taken from him**; and let him stand as a member in the church, and labor with his own hands, with the brethren, **until he is sufficiently chastened for all his sins; for he confesseth them not, and he thinketh to hide them.**

Just a quick note about Ziba Peterson (verse 60, above). In October 1830 he was called to go on a mission to the Lamanites along with Parley P. Pratt, Oliver Cowdery, and Peter Whitmer Jr. (See D&C 32:1–3.) He left from Fayette, New York, on October 17, 1830, and he and his companions traveled some 1,500 miles, preaching along the way and arriving in Independence, Missouri, in December 1830. They preached the gospel there and to the Indians across the Missouri River as late as April 1831.

Sadly, even though he responded to the chastisement in verse 60, above, and three days later confessed his sins, he withdrew from the Church in May 1833 and was excommunicated on June 25, 1833 (see *History of the Church*, 1:367). He never came back. He eventually moved his family to California, where he died in 1849 in Placerville.

61 **Let the residue** [*remainder*] **of the elders** of this church, **who are coming to this land** [*Missouri*], some of whom are exceedingly blessed even above measure, also hold a conference upon this land [*see verse 58, above*].

62 And **let my servant Edward Partridge** [*the bishop*] **direct the conference** which shall be held by them.

63 And **let them also return, preaching the gospel by the way**, bearing record of the things which are revealed unto them.

64 For, verily, **the sound** [*of gospel preaching*] **must go forth from this place into all the world**, and unto **the uttermost parts of the earth**—the **gospel must be preached unto every creature**, with signs [*blessings and miracles*] following them that believe.

President Spencer W. Kimball explained the preaching of the gospel to "the uttermost parts of the earth." He said:

"It seems to me that the Lord chose his words when he said 'every nation,' 'every land,' 'uttermost bounds of the earth,' 'every tongue,' 'every people,' 'every soul,' 'all the world,' 'many lands.'

"Surely there is significance in these words!

"Certainly his sheep were not limited to the thousands about him and with whom he rubbed shoulders each day. A universal family! A universal command! . . .

"I feel that when we have done all in our power that the Lord will find a way to open doors. That is my faith. . . .

"With the Lord providing these miracles of communication [radio, television, cassette tape players, satellites and receiving stations, and so on], and with the increased efforts and devotion of our missionaries and all of us, and all others who are 'sent,' surely the divine injunction will come to pass . . . (D&C 58:64.) And we must find a way. . . .

"Using all the latest inventions and equipment and paraphernalia already developed and that which will follow, can you see that perhaps the day may come when the world will be converted and covered?

"If we do all we can . . . I am sure the Lord will bring more discoveries to our use. He will bring a change of heart into kings and magistrates and emperors, or he will divert rivers or open seas or find ways to touch hearts. He will open the gates and make possible the proselyting" ("When the World Will Be Converted," *Ensign*, October 1974, 5, 10–11, 13).

65 And **behold the Son of Man**

[the "Son of Man of Holiness"—in other words, the Son of God; see Moses 6:57] **cometh**. Amen.

SECTION 59

Background

This revelation was given in Zion, Jackson County, Missouri, on Sunday, August 7, 1831, which was the day Polly Knight was buried.

This was a particularly tender occasion. Polly Knight was the wife of Joseph Knight Sr. and the mother of Newel Knight. Newel had just led the Thompson Branch (which included his parents) from the Kirtland area to Missouri (as instructed by the Lord in D&C 54:7–8). The Thompson Branch consisted primarily of members who had been converted in Colesville, New York, had gathered to Kirtland, and had then been instructed by the Lord to move on to Missouri.

The Prophet Joseph Smith knew the Knights well. In 1826, he had become well acquainted with them. They lived in Colesville, New York, at the time, and Joseph met them while boarding with the Isaac Hale family in Harmony, Pennsylvania (about fifteen miles from Colesville). During this time, Joseph occasionally lodged with the Knights, who listened attentively as he recounted his visions to them. It was Joseph Knight Sr.

who loaned Joseph Smith a horse and buggy with which to bring the gold plates home from the Hill Cumorah in September 1827. The Knights believed his testimony and joined the Church shortly after it was organized on April 6, 1830. They were humble stalwarts in the faith.

Polly Knight's health had not been good for some time prior to beginning the nearly nine hundred-mile journey from Ohio to Missouri, but she insisted on going because she wanted to plant her feet on the sacred soil of Zion before she passed away. We will quote the Institute of Religion's *Church History in the Fulness of Times* manual for more detail on this:

"The journey to Missouri was not an easy one. This was particularly true for the Colesville Saints who left Thompson, Ohio, carrying their belongings and provisions in twenty-four wagons. At Wellsville, Ohio, they left the wagons and traveled by steamboat down the Ohio River to the junction of the Mississippi River. They then traveled up the Mississippi River to St. Louis. At St. Louis, Newel Knight and his company and some of the Prophet's companions elected to journey by steamboat on the Missouri River. This necessitated a wait of several days before passage could be secured.

"The case of Polly Knight illustrates the strong feelings of many members of the Church. Sister

Knight, mother of Newel and a member of the Colesville branch, risked her life making the trip to Zion. Polly's health was failing, but her anxiety to see the promised land was so great that she refused to be left behind in Ohio. Nor would she remain with friends along the route for rest and recuperation. Her son wrote, 'Her only, or her greatest desire, was to set her feet upon the land of Zion, and to have her body interred in that land.' Fearing that she might die at any time on the journey, Newel left the boat on one occasion and went ashore to purchase lumber for a coffin. He later reported that 'the Lord gave her the desire of her heart, and she lived to stand upon that land.' Polly died within two weeks of her arrival in the land of Zion and was the first Latter-day Saint to be buried in Missouri. The Lord gave these consoling words: 'Those that live shall inherit the earth, and those that die shall rest from all their labors, and their works shall follow them; and they shall receive a crown in the mansions of my Father, which I have prepared for them' (D&C 59:2)." (*Church History in the Fulness of Times*, 2003, 104–5.

Section 59 is perhaps best known for its verses dealing with the Sabbath and the blessings of Sabbath Day observance (verses 9–17). We will move ahead now with our verse-by-verse study. As mentioned above, Polly Knight had died, having walked upon the soil

of the land of Zion. It is Sunday, August 7, 1831, the day they buried her, and verses 1–2 have direct reference to her and her faithfulness in coming to Zion.

1 BEHOLD, **blessed**, saith the Lord, **are they who have come up unto this land** [*Missouri*] **with an eye single to my glory** [*with proper motives*], according to my commandments.

2 For those that live shall inherit the earth, and **those that die shall rest from all their labors, and their works shall follow them; and they shall receive a crown in the mansions of my Father, which I have prepared for them**.

Verses 3–8 give counsel and encouragement. They also emphasize that the Ten Commandments are still in force.

3 Yea, **blessed are they whose feet stand upon the land of Zion, who have obeyed my gospel**; for they shall receive for their reward the good things of the earth, and it shall bring forth in its strength.

Perhaps you've heard someone complain that there are too many commandments and that there doesn't seem to be much freedom in living the gospel. People who think this do not understand freedom. They fail to realize that it is the breaking of God's commandments that limits freedom and reduces options. Verse 4, next, is a clear lesson on the fact that commandments are great blessings. In effect, they are the "instruction manual" for true human freedom and happiness. They bring us from spiritual darkness and confusion into the light of the gospel and eternal perspective and understanding. They enable us to exercise our moral agency in ways that lead to the highest blessings and most satisfying lifestyle in the universe, namely, godhood. The truly wise seek the commandments of God. The foolish reject them until they are bound by consequences.

4 And **they shall** also **be crowned with blessings** from above, yea, and **with commandments not a few**, and with revelations in their time—they that are faithful and diligent before me.

Next, in verse 5 and the first part of verse 6, we see similar wording to that in Matthew 22:37–39.

5 Wherefore, I give unto them a commandment, saying thus: **Thou shalt love the Lord thy God with all thy heart, with all thy might, mind, and strength**; and in the name of Jesus Christ thou shalt serve him.

6 **Thou shalt love thy neighbor as thyself.** Thou shalt not steal; neither commit adultery, nor kill, nor do anything like unto it.

Did you notice an important doctrine that the Savior added here in the Doctrine and Covenants? We will quote Matthew 22:37–39 here so you can pick it out.

Matthew 22:37–39

37 Jesus said unto him, Thou shalt love the Lord thy God with all thy heart, and with all thy soul, and with all thy mind.

38 This is the first and great commandment.

39 And the second is like unto it, Thou shalt love thy neighbour as thyself.

The answer to our question is that He added, "and in the name of Jesus Christ thou shalt serve him."

Continuing with our study, you have probably observed that many people today claim that the Ten Commandments are outdated, that they do not apply in modern society. In the last part of verse 6, the Savior clearly indicates that they are still in force. We will repeat verse 6 here and use **bold** to emphasize this point.

Doctrine

The Ten Commandments are still in force today.

6 Thou shalt love thy neighbor as thyself. **Thou shalt not steal;**

neither **commit adultery, nor kill,** nor do anything like unto it.

A most important principle is taught in the last phrase of verse 6, above. It is that we must avoid "anything like unto it." This is the answer when someone says, in effect, that the scriptures do not mention a specific sin, and therefore it is not forbidden. For example, a student once said to me in class that there is no specific mention in the scriptures of certain types of sexual physical intimacy other than adultery or fornication; therefore, any sexual activity, other than actual adultery or fornication must be permissible. The simple answer to him and the entire class was to quote D&C 59:6: "nor do anything like unto it." He was somewhat startled and disappointed and exclaimed, "Oh, so there is something in there about it!"

Next, in verse 7, we find that we are commanded to have gratitude. This may sound a bit strong, that is, to refer to it as a commandment. But the wording is "Thou shalt," the same as in the Ten Commandments. Remember, "commandments" are given for our good (verse 4, above), and gratitude is one of the most healing and beneficial of all human attributes. No wonder we are commanded to express it. We will see more about gratitude in verse 21.

7 Thou shalt thank the Lord thy God in all things.

One of the most important and beneficial of all personal sacrifices we can give is mentioned next, in verse 8.

8 Thou shalt offer a sacrifice unto the Lord thy God in righteousness, even that **of a broken heart and a contrite spirit.**

The words "broken heart" and "contrite spirit" in verse 8, above, obviously mean humility. However, if we take a closer look, we can find additional fine-tuned meanings in these expressions.

One of my students, while pondering the phrase "broken heart," asked if it meant that truly righteous people should be crying most of the time—an interesting observation with a definite "no" for an answer. As we chatted, we used the comparison of a "well-broken" or "well-trained" horse, strong and powerful with much spirit and energy but very quickly yielding to the slightest touch of the reins or directions of the "master." Thus, one way of looking at "broken heart" is that of having our hearts willingly and easily controlled by the "Master" through His gospel and our eagerness to keep His commandments.

The word "contrite" can be defined as being "humble" or "meek," but it has the additional fine-tuned scriptural meaning of seeking correction as needed. Thus, having a "contrite spirit" includes the desire to receive correction from the Lord as needed in order to grow and progress.

Next, in verses 9–17, the Savior teaches these Saints and all of us about the purposes of the Sabbath. As expressed in verse 9, a major benefit of keeping the Sabbath holy is that of keeping ourselves more nearly "unspotted" or untarnished by the world.

Doctrine

Where possible, we should go to church on the Sabbath day.

9 And **that thou mayest more fully keep thyself unspotted from the world, thou shalt** [a commandment] **go to the house of prayer** [the church] and offer up thy sacraments **upon my holy day;**

Perhaps you are acquainted with someone who claims that he or she can get closer to God by going to the mountains, or wherever, on Sunday than by going to church. While it may be true that we can have spiritual thoughts and experiences among God's creations in nature and feel close to Him, there is a major flaw in such thinking. The problem is that such a person is making his or her own rules and is completely ignoring the "thou shalt" of verse 9. It is not an optional matter for those who desire salvation.

10 For verily this is a day appointed unto you to **rest from your labors,** and to **pay thy devotions unto the Most High;**

11 **Nevertheless thy vows shall be offered up in righteousness on all days and at all times** [we must live the gospel all week, not just on Sunday];

12 But remember that **on this, the Lord's day, thou shalt offer thine oblations and thy sacraments** unto the Most High, **confessing thy sins unto thy brethren** [in this context, this likely includes making peace with people you have offended], **and before the Lord.**

The word "oblations," as used in verse 12, above, means "offerings, whether of time, talents, or means, in service of God and fellowman," as stated in D&C 59:12, footnote b.

From verses 13–15, next, we see that it is up to us to make the Sabbath a special day of dedication to the Lord and personal growth toward Him. The focus should be on what to do on the Sabbath in order to accomplish this goal rather than focusing on what we can't or shouldn't do. It is to be a pleasant day of "rejoicing . . . with cheerful hearts and countenances." In fact, if we fill the Sabbath with appropriate things, there will probably not be time to do things that violate the purpose of the Sabbath.

As an Apostle, President Russell M. Nelson taught us how to more readily keep the Sabbath Day holy. He said:

"How do we hallow the Sabbath day? In my much younger years, I studied the work of others who had compiled lists of things to do and things not to do on the Sabbath. It wasn't until later that I learned from the scriptures that my conduct and my attitude on the Sabbath constituted a sign between me and my Heavenly Father. With that understanding, I no longer needed lists of dos and don'ts. When I had to make a decision whether or not an activity was appropriate for the Sabbath, I simply asked myself, 'What sign do I want to give to God?' That question made my choices about the Sabbath day crystal clear. . . .

"How can you ensure that your behavior on the Sabbath will lead to joy and rejoicing? In addition to your going to church, partaking of the sacrament, and being diligent in your specific call to serve, what other activities would help to make the Sabbath a delight for you? What sign will you give to the Lord to show your love for Him?" ("The Sabbath Is a Delight," *Ensign* or *Liahona*, May 2015, 130).

13 And **on this day thou shalt do none other thing**, only let thy food be prepared with singleness of heart that thy fasting may be perfect, or, in other words, **that thy joy may be full**.

14 Verily, **this is fasting and prayer, or in other words, rejoicing and prayer**.

15 And inasmuch as ye **do these things with thanksgiving, with cheerful hearts and countenances**, not with much laughter, for this is sin, but with a glad heart and a cheerful countenance—

There are some words and phrases in verses 13–15, above, that can help us keep the Sabbath day holy. We will take time to take a closer look at some of them here.

Singleness of heart (verse 13)

This phrase is considered by some to mean "simplicity." Yet others define it as meaning "with specific purpose." Thus, in a family or as an individual where it means "simplicity," meal preparation might be simple and easy, with minimal effort to prepare and clean up.

On the other hand, for those to whom it means "specific purpose," the focus might intentionally include a more elaborate meal, with the desired result of attracting the family to join together and spend more time in food and conversation, during which family ties are strengthened and the family counsels together one with another.

In either case or in any of several other scenarios, if the focus in the heart is on keeping the Sabbath, the meal preparation will most likely be appropriate. This is one of those matters where we are taught correct principles and expected to govern ourselves. John Taylor explained that the Prophet Joseph Smith said, "I teach the people correct principles, and they govern themselves" (In *Journal of Discourses*, 10:57–58).

Fasting (verse 13)

President Joseph F. Smith taught the following about fasting:

"Now, while the law requires the Saints in all the world to fast from 'even to even' and to abstain both from food and drink, it can easily be seen from the Scriptures, and especially from the words of Jesus, that it is more important to obtain the true spirit of love for God and man, 'purity of heart and simplicity of intention,' than it is to carry out the cold letter of the law. The Lord has instituted the fast on a reasonable and intelligent basis, and none of his works are vain or unwise. His law is perfect in this as in other things. Hence, those who can are required to comply thereto; it is a duty from which they cannot escape; but let it be remembered that the observance of the fast day by abstaining twenty-four hours from food and drink is not an absolute rule, it is no iron-clad law to us, but it is left with the people as a matter of conscience, to exercise wisdom and discretion. Many are subject to weakness, others are delicate in health, and others have nursing babies; of such it should not be required to fast. Neither should parents compel their little children to fast. I have known children to cry for something to eat on fast day. In such cases, going without food will do them no good. Instead, they dread the day to come, and in place of hailing it, dislike it; while the compulsion engenders a spirit of rebellion in them, rather than a love for the Lord and their fellows. Better teach them the principle, and let them observe it when they are old enough to choose intelligently, than to so compel them.

"But those should fast who can, and all classes among us should be taught to save the meals which they would eat, or their equivalent, for the poor. None are exempt from this; it is required of the Saints, old and young, in every part of the Church. It is no excuse that in some places there are no poor. In such cases the fast donation should be forwarded to the proper authorities for transmission to such stakes of Zion as may stand in need" (*Gospel Doctrine*, 243–44).

There is perhaps another aspect of "fasting" that may be seen in the context of verse 13. It is the added dimension that "fasting" can also mean "fasting" from the things of the world—the daily work and toil, entertainments and so forth—that use up much of our time and attention during the week.

Not with much laughter (verse 15)

There is a tendency on the part of some people to never take sacred things seriously. For them, "laughter" is a means of brushing serious matters aside. D&C 88:69 speaks of "excess of laughter," and D&C 88:121 associates "laughter" with "light-mindedness," which is another term for not taking sacred things seriously. Thus, we understand that "laughter," in the context of the Sabbath, can mean showing irreverence and disrespect for the sacred purposes of the Lord's "holy day."

As we continue with section 59, the Savior teaches us the benefits of keeping the Sabbath holy.

16 Verily I say, that **inasmuch as ye do this** [*keep the Sabbath day holy*]**, the fulness of** [*everything in*] **the earth is yours, the beasts of the field** and the **fowls of the air,** and **that which climbeth upon the trees and walketh upon the earth**;

17 Yea, and **the herb**, and **the good things which come of the earth**, whether **for food** or for **raiment** [*clothing*], or for **houses,** or for **barns**, or for **orchards**, or

for **gardens**, or for **vineyards**;

In verses 18–19, next, the Savior tells us one of the major purposes of His creations for us. We will use **bold** to point it out.

18 Yea, all things which come of the earth, in the season thereof, are made for the benefit and the use of man, both **to please the eye and to gladden the heart**;

19 Yea, for food and for raiment, for taste and for smell, to strengthen the body **and to enliven the soul.**

20 And **it pleaseth God** [*it makes God happy*] **that he hath given all these things unto man**; for unto this end [*purpose; "to please the eye and to gladden the heart . . . and to enliven the soul"*] were they made to be used, with judgment [*wisdom and common sense*], not to excess, neither by extortion [*to take by force, overcharge, greediness*].

In the note accompanying verse 7, we mentioned that we would return to the topic of gratitude when we got to verse 21. It is significant to note that the importance of gratitude is pointed out rather dramatically in verse 21. If you look carefully, you will see that the Lord groups all other commandments into one but places gratitude into a category of its own. Thus, gratitude is mentioned exclusively, in effect being compared in importance to all the other commandments combined. While we need to be careful not to go overboard in our analogy here, it is obvious that the Lord considers gratitude to be one of the most important and saving attributes. Failing to have and express gratitude is apparently one of the most serious and damaging of all human traits.

21 And **in nothing doth man offend God, or against none is his wrath kindled, save** [*except*] **those who confess not his hand in all things** [*who do not express gratitude*]**, and obey not his commandments.**

The phrase "the law and the prophets," as used in verse 22, next, means the Bible, specifically the Old Testament. The "law" consists of the first five books of the Old Testament (Genesis, Exodus, Leviticus, Numbers, and Deuteronomy). The "prophets" is a reference, basically, to the rest of the Old Testament and includes the words of the prophets such as Isaiah, Jeremiah, Ezekiel, and so forth.

22 Behold, **this is according to the law and the prophets** [*in other words, what the Lord has explained in the above verses is also taught in the Bible*]; wherefore, trouble me no more concerning this matter.

In closing, the Master reminds us of the rewards that come to the righteous. As you can see, we do not have to wait until the next life to receive one of the greatest rewards of all.

23 But learn that he who doeth the works of righteousness shall receive his reward, even **peace in this world and eternal life** [*exaltation*] **in the world to come.**

24 I, the Lord, have spoken it, and the Spirit beareth record. Amen.

Before we leave section 59, we will include one more quote regarding keeping the Sabbath day holy. President Spencer W. Kimball taught,

"The Sabbath is a holy day in which to do worthy and holy things. Abstinence from work and recreation is important, but insufficient. The Sabbath calls for constructive thoughts and acts, and if one merely lounges about doing nothing on the Sabbath, he is breaking it. To observe it, one will be on his knees in prayer, preparing lessons, studying the gospel, meditating, visiting the ill and distressed, writing letters to missionaries, taking a nap, reading wholesome material, and attending all the meetings of that day at which he is expected" ("The Sabbath—A Delight," *Ensign*, January 1978, 4).

SECTION 60

Background

This revelation was given through the Prophet Joseph Smith in Jackson County, Missouri, on August 8, 1831. A number of Saints, including the Prophet and other Church leaders, had come to Missouri, as commanded by the Lord. They had dedicated the land of Zion for the eventual gathering of the Lord's people (D&C 58:57), had dedicated a temple site, and had accomplished other things as instructed. Having completed these assigned tasks, many of them had been instructed by the Lord to return east (D&C 58:46, 58, 63) to their homes and responsibilities in the Kirtland, Ohio, area for a season.

As you no doubt have observed, one of the main focuses of the Restoration at this point in time is that of missionary work. It is vital for the continued establishment of the Church that there be a large influx of new converts. The Lord has sent many of His "noble and great" (Abraham 3:22) spirits to earth and placed them in strategic locations where they can be found by these early missionaries. When these faithful ones from our premortal life hear the gospel, they will recognize it as the truth and will join the Church. But first, these early missionaries must find them.

Thus, in this revelation, the Lord gives specific instructions to those brethren who are now to return from Jackson County, Missouri, to their homes in the East. They are told to go out of their way to make every reasonable effort to preach the gospel as they travel rather than simply focusing on getting home.

By the way, if you look at a map, you will see that much of the journey between Missouri and Ohio could be made by river (particularly the Missouri, Mississippi, and Ohio Rivers). This helps understand the use of the "craft" (boat) mentioned in verse 5. Waterways were indeed the preferred mode of travel for many in that day.

As we begin our specific study of the verses in this section, you will see that the Lord emphasizes the importance of preaching and spreading the gospel as they travel. This focus certainly applies to us also in our day.

1 BEHOLD, thus saith the Lord unto the elders of his church, who are to return speedily to the land from whence they came [*back east to the Kirtland area*]: Behold, **it pleaseth me, that you have come up hither** [*to Missouri*];

2 But **with some I am not well pleased,** for **they will not open their mouths** [*to preach the gospel*], but **they hide the talent** [*the gospel; the ability to teach the gospel*] which I have given unto them,

because of the fear of man. Wo unto such, for mine anger is kindled against them.

> As you can see from verse 2, above, it is a serious matter not to share the gospel when the opportunity is available. From verse 3, next, it appears that some of the twenty-eight elders called by the Lord to come to Missouri (see section 52) and preach the gospel en route did not do an adequate job of it in the eyes of the Lord. Now, as they return to Ohio, they are being given a chance to do better.

3 And it shall come to pass, **if they are not more faithful** unto me, **it shall be taken away, even that which they have** [*perhaps meaning their calling to serve missions or the small "talent" they have, which can be developed more if they will be obedient*].

4 For **I, the Lord, rule in the heavens above, and among the armies of the earth** [*in other words, the Lord has the power to help them succeed with their missions*]; and in the day when I shall make up my jewels [*a scriptural phrase meaning exaltation; jewels are symbolic of the best; the imagery is that they will become jewels in the Lord's crown of glory on the final Judgment Day*], all men shall know what it is that bespeaketh [*foretells; indicates by obvious signs;*

represents] the power of God.

5 But, verily, **I will speak unto you concerning your journey unto the land** [*Ohio*] **from whence you came. Let there be a craft made, or bought, as seemeth you good, it mattereth not unto me**, and take your journey speedily for the place which is called St. Louis [*go straight to St. Louis before you stop to preach the gospel*].

> There is perhaps an important message for us couched in verse 5, above. The phrase "it mattereth not unto me" may be a bit of a surprise to some who believe that there is always a right and wrong for every situation we face. Similar verses are found in D&C 61:22, 62:5, 63:44, and 80:3. In this case, the Lord is saying that it makes no difference to Him whether these brethren buy a boat or build one themselves.
>
> In applying this principle to our lives, there may be situations and decisions we face in which we seek an answer from the Lord but can't seem to get one. For example, suppose you had two job offers, one for a position with a company in Rochester, New York, and one in San Diego, California. You pray and receive a peaceful feeling about the job in Rochester. Therefore, you assume that you should get a negative feeling when praying about the opportunity in San

Diego. You pray and get a peaceful feeling. Confused, you try again, with the same result. You must make a decision soon, and in an attempt to draw closer to the Spirit, you turn to the scriptures, opening your Doctrine and Covenants to a random page. It is section 60. As you read, "it mattereth not unto me" jumps out at you, and you now realize that either job would be fine with the Lord. He will use you in the Church no matter which location you settle in. With great relief, you offer a prayer of gratitude and proceed with making your choice.

Next, in verses 6 and 7, the Savior instructs the Prophet, Sidney, and Oliver to travel straight to Cincinnati before they begin preaching, whereas others are told to get off the river at St. Louis and begin preaching (verse 8).

Notice also that they are to preach "without wrath" (verse 7). As you have perhaps noticed, some preachers in some religions seem to believe that preaching should be fiery, with much loud condemnation of the wicked. This is not to be the mode of preaching for these true servants of God.

6 And from thence let my servants, Sidney Rigdon, Joseph Smith, Jun., and Oliver Cowdery, take their journey for Cincinnati;

7 And in this place let them lift up their voice and declare my word with loud voices [speaking up so people can hear], **without wrath** or doubting, lifting up holy hands upon them. For **I am able to make you holy** [clean, pure, without sin, worthy of blessings], **and your sins are forgiven you.**

We find another beautiful and simple "gem" couched in verse 7, above. It is a marvelous understatement by our humble Savior as He says, "I am able to make you holy."

8 And let the residue [the others] **take their journey** from St. Louis, **two by two**, and preach the word, **not in haste** [don't hurry along home], among the congregations of the wicked, until they return to the churches [the branches of the Church] from whence they came.

We have to be a bit careful with the phrase "congregations of the wicked" as used in verse 8, above. It is clear that many wicked, riotous, and rebellious people had come west and settled on the fringes of society where they could live their chosen lifestyle in relative freedom. However, there were many good people also, with Christian standards and virtues, who had settled in these western lands. The term "wicked" is sometimes used to mean those who do not have the gospel. We find this use of the word in the Doctrine and Covenants. We will take time to point this out.

D&C 88:52–53

52 And whoso receiveth not my voice is not acquainted with my voice, and is not of me.

53 And by this you may know the righteous from **the wicked**, and that the whole world groaneth under sin and darkness even now.

A quote from the 2018 *Doctrine and Covenants Student Manual*, chapter 22, further helps us in understanding the use of "wicked" here:

"The phrase 'congregations of the wicked' as used in Doctrine and Covenants 60:8 and other revelations (see also D&C 61:33; 62:5) does not necessarily mean that all people in these places were guilty of gross wickedness. Rather, the phrase likely refers to people who did not have a knowledge or understanding of the restored gospel of Jesus Christ."

As we continue, it is helpful to recall that these missionaries baptized a number of people and established branches of the Church along the way as they traveled from Ohio to Missouri. Now, as they return to Ohio, it is likely that they will visit many of these converts again and thus strengthen the little branches as they go, as indicated in verse 9, next.

9 And **all this for the good of the churches** [*branches of the Church*]; for this intent have I sent them.

We see a principle of the law of consecration in action in verses 10–11, next. Bishop Edward Partridge is handling the consecrated funds of the "united order" in Missouri and is instructed by the Lord to supply money to these missionaries to help with their needs as they return to Ohio. Those who are able to pay the money back after they get home are requested to do so. Those who can't are not required to. No one will tell them who can and who can't. It is up to them to decide. This illustrates the fact that a very high level of personal honesty and integrity is required to successfully live the law of consecration. It is a celestial law, and we must be able to live it in order to qualify for the celestial kingdom.

Similarly, no one tells us exactly how much fast offering to pay. It is up to us. We decide.

10 **And let my servant Edward Partridge impart of the money** which I have given him, **a portion unto mine elders who are commanded to return;**

11 And **he that is able, let him return it** by the way of the agent [*men assigned to assist the bishop in handling the funds of the Church*]; and **he that is not, of him it is not required.**

12 And **now I speak of the residue** [*others*] who are to come unto this land [*Missouri; see verse 14*].

As you can see, verses 13–14, next, contain good counsel for today's missionaries as well as for these early elders in 1831.

13 Behold, **they have been sent to preach my gospel among the congregations of the wicked**; wherefore, **I give unto them a commandment**, thus: **Thou shalt not idle away thy time, neither shalt thou bury thy talent that it may not be known**.

14 And after thou hast come up unto the land of Zion, and hast proclaimed my word, thou shalt speedily return, **proclaiming my word** among the congregations of the wicked, **not in haste, neither in wrath nor with strife**.

The Lord explains that shaking "off the dust of thy feet," in verse 15, next, is a "testimony against" those who reject the missionaries. In this context, it appears to be a witness that they had a valid chance to hear and accept the gospel but rejected it. In a way it can be considered a curse in the sense that people who reject the gospel are "cursed" by their own choice to continue living in spiritual darkness and ignorance of the plan of salvation.

15 And **shake off the dust of thy feet against those who receive thee not**, not in their presence, lest thou provoke them, but in secret; and **wash thy feet, as a testimony against them** in the day of judgment.

As a follow-up to verse 15, above, we will include two quotes from the 1981 *Doctrine and Covenants Student Manual* here.

"The ordinance of washing the dust from one's feet was practiced in New Testament times and was re-instituted in this dispensation (see D&C 88:139–40; John 11:2; 12:3; 13:5–14). The action of shaking or cleansing the dust from one's feet is a testimony against those who refuse to accept the gospel (see D&C 24:15; 84:92; 99:4). Because of the serious nature of this act, Church leaders have directed that it be done only at the command of the Spirit. President Joseph Fielding Smith explained the significance of the action as follows: 'The cleansing of their feet, either by washing or wiping off the dust, would be recorded in heaven as a testimony against the wicked. This act, however, was not to be performed in the presence of the offenders, "lest thou provoke them, but in secret, and wash thy feet, as a testimony against them in the day of judgment." The missionaries of the Church who faithfully perform their duty are under the obligation of leaving their testimony with all with whom they come in contact in their work. This testimony will stand as a witness against those who reject the message, at the judgment.' (*Church History and Modern Revelation*, 1:223.)" *Doctrine and Covenants Student Manual*, 1981, 130–31).

"Cursings as well as blessings may be administered by the power and authority of the priesthood (see D&C 124:93) and include the sealing up of the unbelieving and rebellious to punishment (see D&C 1:8–9). The act of cleansing the feet as a testimony against those who reject the servants of the Lord is an ordinance of cursing and is not just a demonstration that a witness of the truth has been given and has been rejected. Through this cleansing ordinance, those who rejected the truth are on their own, and those who preached the gospel to them are no longer responsible for them before the Lord (see D&C 88:81–82). It is apparent in this and other scriptures given later in the Doctrine and Covenants that this ordinance is to be performed only when the Lord expressly commands it (see also D&C 75:20–22)" (*Doctrine and Covenants Student Manual*, 1981, 50).

16 Behold, this is sufficient for you, and the will of him [*Christ*] **who hath sent you.**

17 And by the mouth of my servant Joseph Smith, Jun., it shall be made known concerning Sidney Rigdon and Oliver Cowdery

[*Sidney and Oliver will be told more about their specific responsibilities by the Prophet*]. The residue [*the others*] hereafter. Even so. Amen.

SECTION 61

Background

This revelation was given through the Prophet Joseph Smith at McIlwaine's Bend, on the bank of the Missouri River, Friday, August 12, 1831.

Section 61 stirs much interest in the minds of members today on the subject of "curses on the waters." It also is subject to misinterpretation and misapplication because it is not kept in its proper context.

We will first give some historical background and then strive to differentiate between verses that apply to Joseph Smith's day and to those that have application in our day. Since many verses apply specifically to the 1830s, it becomes a problem when they are applied to our day.

In early August 1831, several leaders and elders were instructed to return to Ohio (D&C 58:46, 58, 63). In D&C 60:5, they were told to buy or build watercraft, whichever they preferred, in which to travel by river as they pursued their journey home. Their first destination was St. Louis. On August 9, Joseph Smith, along with ten others began their journey in canoes down the Missouri River. We will quote again from the 2018 institute manual for Doctrine and Covenants:

On August 9, 1831, the Prophet Joseph Smith and 10 elders departed Independence, Missouri, in canoes heading down the Missouri River for St. Louis. The river was difficult to navigate due to the many fallen trees submerged in the river. During the first few days of traveling, there was some conflict that arose in the group, and feelings of discord were present for a time. On the third day of the journey, a submerged tree nearly capsized the canoe that Joseph Smith and Sidney Rigdon were in. At the Prophet's urging, the group camped on the banks of the Missouri River at a place called McIlwaine's Bend. After leaving the river to make camp, William W. Phelps saw in broad daylight 'the Destroyer, in his most horrible power, ride upon the face of the waters' (*Manuscript History of the Church*, vol. A-1, page 142, josephsmithpapers. org). That evening the group discussed their difficulties, resolved their contentious feelings, and forgave one another. The next morning the Prophet received the revelation recorded in Doctrine and Covenants 61."

With these things in mind, we will now proceed with our study of this revelation. First, the Savior re-

minds these brethren of His power and stewardship, which gives Him power to forgive sins (which He does in verse 2).

1 BEHOLD, and **hearken unto the voice of him** [*Jesus Christ*] **who has all power, who is from everlasting to everlasting, even Alpha and Omega, the beginning and the end** [*involved in all things relating to our salvation, from premortality to the final judgment*].

2 Behold, verily [*listen carefully*] **thus saith the Lord** unto you, O ye elders of my church, who are assembled upon this spot [*on the bank of the Missouri River, by McIlwaine's Bend; see heading to section 61 in your Doctrine and Covenants*], **whose sins are now forgiven you,** for **I, the Lord, forgive sins, and am merciful unto those who confess their sins with humble hearts;**

Verse 2, above, must have been very comforting and humbling to those in the group who had been short-tempered and disagreeable with each other. Apparently, they had made peace with each other by now (see verse 20).

Next, in verse 3, they are instructed to be more missionary-minded.

3 But verily I say unto you, that **it is not needful for this whole company of mine elders to be**

moving swiftly upon the waters, whilst the inhabitants on either side are perishing in unbelief.

4 Nevertheless, **I suffered** [*allowed*] it [*probably a reference to W. W. Phelps's vision of Satan riding upon the waters—see heading to this section*] **that ye might bear record**; behold, **there are many dangers upon the waters, and more especially hereafter** [*this can include things such as pollution, acid rain, warfare, tidal waves, oil spills, and so forth in the last days*];

5 For I, the Lord, have decreed in mine anger **many destructions upon the waters**; yea, and **especially upon these waters** [*the Missouri and Mississippi Rivers; the destruction can include cholera and disastrous flooding*].

> Verse 6, next, applies to the elders to whom the Lord was speaking in this revelation and can easily apply to missionaries today in the islands and elsewhere who are required to travel by water as they do their work.

6 Nevertheless, **all flesh is in mine hand** [*the Lord has all power to help and bless us*], and **he that is faithful among you shall not perish by the waters.**

7 Wherefore, it is expedient [*necessary*] that my servant Sidney Gilbert and my servant William W. Phelps be in haste upon their errand and mission [*to purchase a printing press and bring it back to Missouri*].

> According to what the Lord says next, we understand that the perils and problems that these men had experienced during the previous day were allowed in order to humble them and help them learn to work together in harmony. In context, the last phrase of verse 8 indicates that disharmony and bickering can be a serious form of wickedness.

8 Nevertheless, **I would not suffer** [*allow*] **that ye should part** [*go your separate ways to fulfill your assignments*] **until you were chastened** [*scolded*] for all your sins, **that you might be one** [*be united in harmony with each other*], **that you might not perish in wickedness**;

9 But now, verily I say, it behooveth me [*it is the Lord's will*] that ye should part. Wherefore let my servants Sidney Gilbert and William W. Phelps take their former company, and let them take their journey in haste that they may fill their mission [*to buy a printing press and take it back to Missouri*], and **through faith they shall overcome**;

The word "faith" in the last phrase of verse 9, above, is a reminder that faith is a major tool for us to use in obtaining the Lord's help.

10 And **inasmuch as they are faithful they shall be preserved, and I, the Lord, will be with them**.

11 And let the residue [*the others*] take that which is needful for clothing.

12 Let my servant Sidney Gilbert take that which is not needful [*the leftover clothing and equipment*] with him, as you shall agree [*you decide*].

Having addressed immediate needs and given instructions, the Lord now invites these men, in effect, to come to "class" and let Him teach them about the land and the water and the cursings and blessings pronounced upon them. He will reason with them and teach them as He did His people in ancient times—see for example Isaiah 1:18, where He reasons together with them. First, in verse 13, He reminds them that commandments are given for their benefit.

13 And now, behold, **for your good I gave unto you a commandment concerning these things**; and **I, the Lord, will reason with you as with men in days of old.**

14 Behold**, I, the Lord, in the beginning blessed the waters** [*Genesis 1:20–22*]; **but in the last days,** by the mouth of my servant John [*the Apostle, who recorded the Book of Revelation*], **I cursed the waters** [*Revelation 8:8–11; 16:3–4*].

15 Wherefore, **the days will come that no flesh shall be safe upon the waters** [*this can apply to Joseph Smith's day, indicating that there will be times during flooding that no travelers will be safe on these rivers; it could also refer to the last days, when, because of warfare, tidal waves, severe pollution, terrorists, and so on, no one will be safe traveling to a particular destination on the water; see also Moses 7:66*].

Joseph Fielding Smith taught about these verses as follows:

"In the beginning the Lord blessed the waters and cursed the land, but in these last days this was reversed, the land was to be blessed and the waters to be cursed. A little reflection will bear witness to the truth of this declaration. In the early millenniums of this earth's history, men did not understand the composition of the soils, and how they needed building up when crops were taken from them. The facilities at the command of the people were primitive and limited, acreage under cultivation was limited, famines were prevalent and the luxuries which we have today were not obtainable. Someone may rise up and say that the soil in those days was just as productive as now, and this may be the case. It is not a matter of dispute, but the manner of cultivation did not lend itself to the abundant production which we are receiving today. It matters not what the causes were, in those early days of world history there could not be the production, nor the varieties of fruits coming from the earth, and the Lord can very properly speak of this as a curse, or the lack of blessing, upon the land. In those early periods we have every reason to believe that the torrents, floods, and the dangers upon the waters were not as great as they are today, and by no means as great as what the Lord has promised us. The early mariners among the ancients traversed the seas as they knew them in that day in comparative safety. . . . Today this manner of travel in such boats would be of the most dangerous and risky nature. Moreover, we have seen the dangers upon the waters increase until the hearts of men failed them and only the brave, and those who were compelled to travel the seas, ventured out upon them. In regard to the Missouri-Mississippi waters, we have seen year by year great destruction upon them, and coming from them. Millions upon millions of dollars, almost annually are lost by this great stream overflowing its banks. Many have lost their lives in these floods as they sweep over the land, and

even upon this apparently tranquil or sluggish stream there can arise storms that bring destruction. Verily the word of the Lord has been, and is being, fulfilled in relation to those waters. While the Lord has spoken of the sea heaving itself beyond its bounds, and the waves roaring, yet we must include the great destruction upon the waters by means of war, and especially by submarine warfare as we have learned of it in recent years" (*Church History and Modern Revelation*, 1:224; see also Genesis 3:17–19; Ether 7:23–25; 9:16, 28; Revelation 16:1–6; Alma 45:16; D&C 59:3; 16–19).

Verse 16, next, seems to apply to Joseph Smith's day.

16 And it shall be said in days to come that **none is able to go up to the land of Zion** [*Missouri*] **upon the waters, but he that is upright in heart** [*righteous*].

Next, in verse 17, the Lord continues explaining the "blessings and curses" referred to above.

17 And, as **I, the Lord, in the beginning cursed the land** [*Genesis 3:17*], even so **in the last days have I blessed it**, in its time, for the use of my saints, that they may partake the fatness thereof.

The Lord states that He "has blessed" the land "in the last days." Verse 17, above, is a clear reference to this fact. Perhaps you've noticed that agricultural science has now made it possible to grow abundant crops in much smaller gardens and upon much smaller farms. Surely, this is a clear sign that the Lord has blessed the land in the last days.

Verses 18–29, next, seem to primarily refer to the travels of the Saints in Joseph Smith's day upon the Missouri, Mississippi, and Ohio Rivers.

18 And **now I give unto you a commandment** that what I say unto one I say unto all, that **you shall forewarn your brethren concerning these waters** [*the rivers upon which the Saints often traveled*], that they come not in journeying upon them, lest their faith fail and they are caught in snares;

19 I, the Lord, have decreed, and **the destroyer** [*Satan*] **rideth upon the face thereof**, and I revoke not the decree.

20 **I, the Lord, was angry with you yesterday** [*because of their disharmony and ill feelings toward each other; see notes in Background*], **but today mine anger is turned away.**

21 Wherefore, let those concerning whom I have spoken, that should take their journey in haste—again I say unto you, let them take their journey in haste.

Verse 22, next, is important in understanding this section. As previously stated, it is prophesied that there will be special dangers upon the waters in the last days, and there are. But verse 22 clearly shows that all water is not dangerous, and from it we understand that most water use and travel is just fine, as long as common sense is used.

22 And **it mattereth not unto me**, after a little, if it so be that they fill their mission, **whether they go by water or by land**; **let this be** as it is made known unto them **according to their judgments** [*common sense and wisdom*] hereafter.

23 And now, **concerning my servants, Sidney Rigdon, Joseph Smith, Jun., and Oliver Cowdery, let them come not again upon the waters, save it be upon the canal**, while journeying unto their homes [*they journeyed as instructed, arriving in Kirtland in late August*]; or in other words they shall not come upon the waters to journey, save upon the canal.

24 Behold, **I, the Lord, have appointed a way for the journeying of my saints**; and behold, this is the way—that **after they leave the canal they shall journey by land**, inasmuch as they are commanded to journey and

go up unto the land of Zion [*Missouri*];

25 And they shall do like unto the children of Israel, pitching their tents by the way.

26 And, behold, this commandment you shall give unto all your brethren.

> Verses 27–28, next, are a reminder that, when prompted by the Holy Ghost, a faithful priesthood holder could be allowed to command and the water will obey. (See D&C 61:27, footnote a.) It is also possible that these verses could apply specifically to the Prophet Joseph Smith.

27 Nevertheless, **unto whom is given power to command the waters**, unto him **it is given by the Spirit** to know all his ways;

28 Wherefore, **let him do as the Spirit of the living God commandeth him**, whether upon the land or upon the waters, as it remaineth with me to do hereafter.

29 And unto you is given the course for the saints, or the way for the saints of the camp of the Lord, to journey [*as stated in verse 24*].

> In verses 30–31, Joseph Smith and his two traveling companions are told to go straight to Cincinnati before they start to preach. Cincinnati was just a village at this time, with many dwelling there who had fled civilization to the east after having broken the law.

30 And again, verily I say unto you, my servants, **Sidney Rigdon, Joseph Smith, Jun., and Oliver Cowdery, shall not open their mouths** [*preach the gospel*] in the congregations of the wicked **until they arrive at Cincinnati;**

31 **And in that place they shall lift up their voices unto God against that people**, yea, unto him whose anger is kindled against their wickedness, **a people who are well–nigh ripened for destruction** [*just about ready to be destroyed*].

32 **And from thence** [*from Cincinnati*] let them [*Joseph, Sidney, and Oliver*] **journey for the congregations of their brethren** [*they may travel on home to Kirtland*], **for their labors even now are wanted more abundantly among them than among the congregations of the wicked** [*they are wanted urgently back home*].

33 And now, **concerning the residue** [*the other elders in this group of eleven to whom this revelation was given*], **let them journey and declare the word** among the congregations of the wicked,

inasmuch as it is given [*they should take time to preach along the way from here, as inspired by the Spirit*];

34 And **inasmuch as** [*if*] **they do this they shall rid their garments** [*be relieved of the responsibility for the sins of these people*], and **they shall be spotless before me** [*they will be forgiven of their own sins*].

The phrase "they shall rid their garments" in verse 34, above, is seen in other forms elsewhere in scripture. For example, in 2 Nephi 9:44, Jacob says, "I take off my garments, and I shake them before you," symbolizing that he is "shaking their sins off his clothing" that they have now heard the gospel, and that their souls are in their own hands. He has fulfilled his duty by preaching it to them. Therefore, their sins are no longer his responsibility. In Jacob 2:2, he teaches his people in order "that I might rid my garments of your sins." Likewise, King Benjamin assembled his people in order to teach them, in order "that I might rid my garments of your blood."

Next, in verse 35, the remaining elders are told that they can stay together as a group en route home to Ohio, or they can split up and go two by two. However, Reynolds Cahoon and Samuel H. Smith (the Prophet's younger brother) are to stay together regardless of what the other four decide to do.

35 And **let them journey together, or two by two**, as seemeth them good, only let my servant **Reynolds Cahoon, and my servant Samuel H. Smith**, with whom I am well pleased, **be not separated until they return to their homes,** and this for a wise purpose in me [*the Lord doesn't tell them why; they are to take it on faith*].

36 And now, verily I say unto you, and what I say unto one I say unto all, **be of good cheer, little children; for I am in your midst, and I have not forsaken you;**

Verse 36, above, is a pleasant reminder that the Savior is often among us, as He said to these men. ("I am in your midst.")

37 And **inasmuch as you have humbled yourselves before me, the blessings of the kingdom** [*ultimately exaltation*] **are yours.**

38 Gird up your loins [*prepare for the journey*] and be watchful and be sober [*be serious about their responsibilities*], looking forth for the coming of **the Son of Man** [*Jesus, the Son of Man of Holiness (Son of the Father); see Moses 6:57*], for he **cometh in an hour you think not.**

The end of verse 38, above, is another reminder that no one knows the exact timing of the Savior's

Second Coming. It can be cross-referenced to Matthew 24:36 and Mark 13:32.

The Prophet Joseph Smith likewise taught that no one knows the timing. He said, "Jesus Christ never did reveal to any man the precise time that He would come. Go and read the Scriptures, and you cannot find anything that specifies the exact hour He would come; and all that say so are false teachers" (*History of the Church*, 6:254).

39 **Pray always that you enter not into temptation**, that you may abide [*be able to survive*] the day of his coming, **whether in life or in death**. Even so. Amen.

SECTION 62

Background

Given August 13, 1831, at Chariton, Missouri, on the bank of the Missouri River, this revelation through the Prophet Joseph Smith was given to his group, who were returning to the Kirtland area from Missouri, and a group of elders who were on their way to Missouri. The Prophet gave background for this revelation as follows:

"On the 13th [August] I met several of the Elders on their way to the land of Zion, and after the joyful salutations with which brethren meet each other, who are actually 'contending for the faith once delivered to the Saints,' I received

the following: [section 62]" (*History of the Church* 1:205).

The *Doctrine and Covenants Student Manual*, 1981, page 132, has a quote in which these elders coming from Kirtland to Missouri are identified. It reads,

"Reynolds Cahoon named them as follows: Hyrum Smith, John Murdock, Harvey Whitlock, and David Whitmer (see *Journal History*, 13 August 1831)."

This is a short section that contains sweet insights into the Savior's personal attention and care for His humble followers here on earth.

1 BEHOLD, and hearken, O ye elders of my church, saith the Lord your God, even **Jesus Christ, your advocate, who knoweth the weakness of man and how to succor them who are tempted**.

We will mention two things from verse 1, above. First, the term "advocate" in this context means "one who wants us to succeed and does everything in his power to help us."

Second, the word "succor" means "to hurry to help someone in distress or need."

2 And verily **mine eyes are upon those who have not as yet gone up unto the land of Zion**; wherefore **your mission is not yet full**

[*these elders have not yet completed their mission*].

Next, the Master tells them (John Murdock, David Whitmer, Harvey Whitlock, and Hyrum Smith—the Prophet's older brother) that their testimonies are recorded in heaven.

3 Nevertheless, ye are blessed, for **the testimony which ye have borne is recorded in heaven for the angels to look upon**; and they rejoice over you, and your sins are forgiven you.

We find ourselves hoping that verse 3, above, applies likewise to us. If it does, we may be able to hope that our loved ones who have already died might be able to read our testimonies when we bear them, provided that they too are recorded in heaven.

Next, the Savior instructs these men to continue on to Missouri and to hold a sacrament meeting when they get there.

4 And now **continue your journey. Assemble** yourselves **upon the land of Zion**; and **hold a meeting** and **rejoice together**, and **offer a sacrament unto the Most High.**

Did you notice in verse 4, above, that one of the major purposes of church meetings is so that we have an opportunity to get together and enjoy one another's company?

5 And then you may return [*to Kirtland*] to bear record, yea, even altogether, or two by two, as seemeth you good, **it mattereth not unto me** [*see note for D&C 60:5 for more on this*]; only **be faithful, and declare glad tidings unto the inhabitants of the earth, or among the congregations of the wicked.**

Remember, as pointed out previously, that the term "wicked," as used in this context (verse 5, above), doesn't always mean evil, truly wicked people. Rather, it can simply mean people who don't have the gospel. This is a much different meaning than we use today.

6 Behold, I, the Lord, have brought you together that the promise might be fulfilled, that the faithful among you should be preserved and rejoice together in the land of Missouri. **I, the Lord, promise the faithful and cannot lie.**

It helps, as we continue to verse 7, to understand that John Murdock was so sick and weak at this time that he was unable to continue the journey to Jackson County. After the Lord's counsel to them in verse 7, these four men pooled their money and bought a horse for Brother Murdock to ride the rest of the way to Zion.

7 I, the Lord, am willing, **if any among you desire to ride upon horses, or upon mules, or in chariots, he shall receive this blessing**, if he receive it from the hand of the Lord, **with a thankful heart in all things** [*another reminder of the importance of gratitude*].

8 These things remain with you to do according to judgment and the directions of the Spirit.

> The phrase "the kingdom is yours," in verse 9, next, is most reassuring. It is another way of saying that if we keep sincerely progressing, we can make it to celestial exaltation despite present weaknesses and imperfections.

9 Behold, **the kingdom is yours**. And behold, and lo, I am with the faithful always. Even so. Amen.

SECTION 63

Background

In editions previous to the 2013 edition of the Doctrine and Covenants, the date of this revelation was given as "late in August 1831." However, based on research for the Joseph Smith Papers Project, the date is now known to be August 30, 1831. It was given through Joseph Smith in Kirtland, Ohio. The Prophet had now arrived back in Kirtland, having traveled the nine hundred miles from Jackson County, Missouri, in nineteen days.

Although many members of the Church in the Kirtland area were faithful and deeply committed to the Lord and His newly restored Church, some were not. They claimed to be members and wanted the blessings of the gospel but were not keeping the commandments. In fact, while the Prophet was gone to Missouri, many in Kirtland had grumbled, and some had apostatized. Some apparently wanted more obvious evidence from God that this was His church. Lustful thinking and sexual immorality also seem to have become a problem among some of the members in Kirtland. These conditions among the members in Ohio seem to make up the background and setting for verses 1–21. The wicked and rebellious in the Kirtland area receive a severe chastisement from the Savior Himself in these verses.

Continuing on, beginning with verse 22, the Lord gives these members specific instructions concerning Kirtland as well as Zion (in Jackson County, Missouri), giving much prophecy and pointing their minds forward to the time of His Second Coming and the Millennium. He gives encouragement to the righteous (example: verses 47–49) and warns all of the members not to be among the "foolish virgins" (verse 54).

The revelation concludes with specific instructions to Sidney Rigdon about his written description of Zion (verses 55–56) and a clear reminder of the importance of missionary work, the seriousness of covenants, the necessity of respect for the name of God, and the need for patience with themselves as the Saints strive to overcome sins and shortcomings.

It's a good idea at times as you are studying the scriptures to "step back," so to speak, and look for major messages and patterns. By so doing, you give the Spirit additional opportunities to teach you. Section 63 lends itself nicely to this approach in studying. If you "step back" and look at this section from an overall perspective, you will see an interesting pattern in how the Savior is dealing with the problems among the Saints in Kirtland. It is similar to how He sometimes deals with us as we have need to repent. In a very real sense, this is a pattern for parenting.

Pattern for Parenting

First—He explains the problems (verses 1–21).

Second—He gives them specific things to do and gives counsel that will help them repent and overcome the problems (verses 22–46, 55–66).

Third—He gives them something to look forward to by pointing their minds ahead to the blessings and rewards of obedience and living the gospel (verses 47–54).

With this in mind, we will use **bold** to point out the problems He addresses in the text of verses 1–21. We will go through these verses first without commentary, other than using **bold** for emphasis, so that you can see at a glance what the Lord's concerns are. Then we will repeat the verses and add commentary. You may wish to read just the **bolded** words and phrases the first time through.

1 **HEARKEN**, O ye people, and open your hearts and give ear from afar; and listen, **you that call yourselves the people of the Lord,** and hear the word of the Lord and his will concerning you.

2 Yea, verily, I say, **hear the word of him whose anger is kindled against the wicked and rebellious;**

3 Who willeth to take even them whom he will take, and preserveth in life them whom he will preserve;

4 Who buildeth up at his own will and pleasure; and destroyeth when he pleases, **and is able to cast the soul down to hell.**

5 Behold, **I, the Lord, utter my voice, and it shall be obeyed.**

6 Wherefore, verily I say, **let the wicked take heed,** and **let the rebellious fear and tremble**; and **let the unbelieving hold their lips**, **for the day of wrath shall come** upon them as a whirlwind, and all flesh shall know that I am God.

7 And **he that seeketh signs shall see signs, but not unto salvation**.

8 Verily, I say unto you, **there are those among you who seek signs**, and there have been such even from the beginning;

9 But, behold, **faith cometh not by signs, but signs follow those that believe**.

10 Yea, **signs come by faith, not by the will of men, nor as they please, but by the will of God**.

11 Yea, signs come by faith, unto mighty works, for **without faith no man pleaseth God**; and **with whom God is angry he is not well pleased**; wherefore, **unto such he showeth no signs, only in wrath unto their condemnation**.

12 Wherefore, **I, the Lord, am not pleased with those among you who have sought after signs and wonders for faith, and not for the good of men unto my glory**.

13 Nevertheless, I give commandments, and **many have turned away from my commandments and have not kept them**.

14 **There were among you adulterers and adulteresses; some of whom have turned away from you, and others remain with you** that hereafter shall be revealed.

15 **Let such beware and repent speedily, lest judgment shall come upon them as a snare, and their folly shall be made manifest, and their works shall follow them in the eyes of the people**.

16 And verily I say unto you, as I have said before, **he that looketh on a woman to lust after her, or if any shall commit adultery in their hearts, they shall not have the Spirit, but shall deny the faith and shall fear**.

17 Wherefore, I, the Lord, have said that **the fearful, and the unbelieving, and all liars, and whosoever loveth and maketh a lie, and the whoremonger, and the sorcerer, shall have their part in that lake which burneth with fire and brimstone, which is the second death**.

18 Verily I say, that **they shall not have part in the first resurrection**.

19 And now behold, I, the Lord,

say unto you that **ye are not justified, because these things are among you**.

20 **Nevertheless, he that endureth in faith and doeth my will, the same shall overcome, and shall receive an inheritance upon the earth when the day of transfiguration shall come**;

21 **When the earth shall be transfigured**, even according to the pattern which was shown unto mine Apostles upon the mount; of which account the fulness ye have not yet received.

As you can see, there are many problems among the Saints in Ohio at this point in Church history, not unlike those among members today. As mentioned previously, we will now repeat verses 1–21, adding commentary. First, the Lord addresses the members who call themselves faithful members but who are actually not.

1 **HEARKEN**, O ye people, and open your hearts and give ear from afar; and listen, **you that call yourselves the people of the Lord** [*implying that they "call" themselves Saints but are not*], and hear the word of the Lord and his will concerning you.

Next, in verses 2–6, the Lord gives a concise, to-the-point warning and lesson about the reality of His

role in disciplining the rebellious. Such strong wording from a loving God is often needed to get the attention of people who think they are doing rather well but in reality are blinded to the dangers of the direction their life is taking. In D&C 95:1, the Savior reminds us that "whom I love I also chasten that their sins may be forgiven, for with the chastisement I prepare a way for their deliverance in all things out of temptation."

2 Yea, verily, I say, **hear the word of him** [*Christ*] **whose anger is kindled against the wicked and rebellious**;

3 **Who willeth to take even them whom he will take** [*remove from the earth*], **and preserveth in life them whom he will preserve**;

4 **Who buildeth up** at his own will and pleasure; **and destroyeth** when he pleases, **and is able to cast the soul down to hell** [*Jesus is our final judge; see John 5:22*].

5 Behold, **I, the Lord, utter my voice, and it shall be obeyed**.

6 **Wherefore** [*therefore*], verily I say, **let the wicked take heed, and let the rebellious fear and tremble**; and **let the unbelieving hold their lips** [*including that they should stop murmuring and complaining*], for the day of wrath [*punishments*] shall come upon

them as a whirlwind, and **all flesh shall know that I am God**.

Next, in verses 7–12, the topic of seeking signs is addressed. This is a context-sensitive issue. Faith-obedience brings "signs" or blessings, which are appropriate and strengthen testimony and build character. Signs that are demanded as proof of God's existence or as obvious evidence of His involvement are inappropriate and a sign of rebellion and arrogance on the part of those who demand them.

Thus, the "signs" spoken of here, which are out of order, are those that people demand from God before they will be obedient. In effect, they are saying, "Show me the blessings, and then I will obey the commandments. Bless me first and then I will pay tithing. Bless me first and then I will donate money to buy land in Zion." Demanding evidence from God first, before obedience, hardens and damages the soul. On the other hand, faith softens the soul and makes it moldable and pliable in the hands of the Master. When people move ahead with faith, before the blessings or results are known, they grow in character and strength toward God.

7 And **he that seeketh signs shall see signs, but not unto salvation** [*in other words, those who arrogantly demand proof of potential blessings before they will obey God will*

ultimately see plenty of evidence that God exists when He punishes them; see last part of verse 11].

8 Verily, I say unto you, **there are those among you who seek signs**, and there have been such even from the beginning;

Next, we are reminded that faith in the hearts and actions of the righteous does produce signs, and that God carefully controls these miracles and blessings so that they are truly a benefit to His Saints.

9 But, behold, **faith cometh not by signs, but signs follow those that believe**.

10 Yea, **signs come by faith, not by the will of men, nor as they please, but by the will of God**.

11 Yea, signs come by faith, unto mighty works, for **without faith no man pleaseth God** [*no accountable person can be saved without faith*]; and **with whom God is angry he is not well pleased**; wherefore, **unto such he showeth no signs, only in wrath unto their condemnation** [*in the form of punishments and being stopped in personal progression*].

As this lesson on sign-seeking continues, we are reminded that it is usually the case that signs demanded by the wicked and rebellious are generally not the kind of signs that would be for the good of others. This could include such signs as would not foster spiritual growth and goodness, rather, the building up of one's self in the eyes of others, selfish pleasure, pride, and so forth.

12 Wherefore, **I, the Lord, am not pleased with those among you who have sought after signs and wonders for faith**, and **not for the good of men** unto my glory.

13 Nevertheless, I give commandments, and **many have turned away from my commandments and have not kept them**.

Next, in verses 14–16, the Lord addresses the spiritually damaging effects of lustful thinking and sexual immorality, which had apparently become a serious problem among some of the Ohio Saints. He mercifully also reminds these members that such sins can be repented of and thus forgiven.

14 **There were among you adulterers and adulteresses; some** of whom **have turned away from you, and others remain with you** that hereafter shall be revealed.

15 **Let such beware and repent speedily**, lest judgment shall come upon them as a snare, and **their folly shall be made manifest, and their works shall follow them in the eyes of the people**.

One of my students once asked why sexual intimacy outside of marriage is such a serious sin since science and modern medicine make it so easy and convenient to prevent conception. This question, of course, got the immediate full attention of everyone in class. I was most grateful for verse 16, next, in which the Lord gives an answer to this question.

16 And verily I say unto you, as I have said before [*in D&C 42:23*], **he that looketh on a woman to lust after her, or if any shall commit adultery in their hearts, they shall not have the Spirit, but shall deny the faith and shall fear**.

As you can see, from the bolded portion of verse 16, above, one reason that immoral behavior is so serious is that it drives the Spirit away, leaving people insensitive to spiritual things and vulnerable to becoming inactive in the Church, as well as living in fear of the punishments of God.

Next, in verse 17, we see a list of several sins that when not repented of will lead the sinner to being turned over to Satan to pay for his or her own sins and ultimately end up in the telestial kingdom on the day of final judgment (see also D&C 76:103 and Revelation 22:15).

17 Wherefore [*this is why*], I, the Lord, have said that **the fearful** [*afraid to do right*], and the **unbelieving**, and **all liars, and whosoever loveth and maketh a lie, and the whoremonger** [*people whose lives are centered on sexual immorality*], **and the sorcerer** [*including witchcraft, devil worship, and the occult*], **shall have their part in that lake which burneth with fire and brimstone** [*will be punished for their own sins; see D&C 19:15–17; 76:84–85*], **which is the second death** [*being cut off from living in the direct presence of God*].

18 Verily I say, that **they shall not have part in the first resurrection** [*telestials are not resurrected with the righteous but must wait until the end of the Millennium for resurrection; see D&C 88:100–101*].

Verse 19, next, uses the word "justified." In a general sense, as most often used in the scriptures (for example, see Moses 6:60), "justified" means those who are ratified at the final judgment as worthy to live forever in the presence of God and Christ in celestial glory.

The word "justified" as used in verse 19, next, means to "be right before God." In other words, to be worthy for the full blessings of the Lord.

19 And now behold, I, the Lord, say unto you that **ye are not justified** [*worthy to enter celestial glory*]**, because these things** [*the sins and concerns mentioned in the above verses*] **are among you**.

As you read verse 20, next, notice the encouragement given by the Savior to these members who are being chastised for their sins. It is not too late for them to "overcome" and be found worthy to "inherit the earth" (the earth will become the celestial kingdom for those of us who live worthy of obtaining celestial glory; see D&C 130:9–11).

20 Nevertheless, **he that endureth in faith and doeth my will, the same shall overcome** [*overcome sin and evil with the help of Christ and His Atonement*]**, and shall receive an inheritance upon the earth when the day of transfiguration shall come;**

21 **When the earth shall be transfigured,** even according to the pattern which was shown unto mine Apostles upon the mount [*the Mount of Transfiguration; see Matthew 17:1–3, 9*]; of which account the fulness ye have not yet received [*we have not yet been given a full account of what took place when Jesus was transfigured on the mountain about six months before His crucifixion and resurrection*].

Looking back at verses 20–21, the earth will actually go through two "transfigurations." One is when it is transfigured from a "telestial" globe to a "terrestrial" globe as it receives its "paradisiacal glory" at the beginning of the Millennium (Articles of Faith 1:10). The second is when it is changed into a celestial planet (D&C 130:9), moved back into the presence of the Father where it was first created (*Teachings of the Prophet Joseph Smith*, 181), and becomes the celestial kingdom for those from this earth who are worthy of celestial glory.

As we continue with verse 22, we see an insightful phrase reminding us of the Lord's kindness and patience with us. Notice that He says, "not by the way of commandment." Then, in verse 23, He says that there are special blessings for those who keep the commandments.

22 And now, verily I say unto you, that as I said that I would make known my will unto you, behold I will make it known unto you, **not by the way of commandment**, for **there are many who observe not to keep my commandments**.

23 **But unto him that keepeth my commandments I will give the mysteries of my kingdom** [*the doctrines, principles, and ordinances of the plan of salvation; not "mysterious and strange things"; see the Bible Dictionary under*

"Mystery"], **and the same** [*the gospel*] **shall be in him a well of living water, springing up unto everlasting life** [*bringing him to exaltation*].

Do you see the messages in verses 22–23, above? Certainly, one major message is that we can't be forced to heaven. Another is that those who have a good attitude toward studying the gospel and abiding by its teachings will want to live by every word from God, whether it comes by way of commandment or counsel. Attitude is critically important in becoming celestial.

Next, the Lord gives additional instructions concerning Zion in Jackson County, Missouri. Again, the Saints are reminded that the gathering to Missouri is to be done in order and with wisdom.

24 And now, behold, **this is the will of the Lord your God concerning his saints**, that **they should assemble** themselves together **unto the land of Zion, not in haste,** lest there should be confusion, which bringeth pestilence [*all kinds of trouble*].

A quote from the 2018 Doctrine and Covenants Student Manual helps us understand "not in haste" in verse 24, above.

"To manage the number of Saints gathering to Zion, Church leaders required those in Ohio desiring to go to Missouri to obtain a Church-issued certificate before they could migrate and participate in the law of consecration in Missouri. However, many enthusiastic members disregarded the instruction and went to Missouri in large numbers. A Church historian appointed by the Prophet Joseph Smith later wrote, 'The church immediately began to gather in Jackson County, and on this subject they became quite enthusiastic. They had been commanded not to go up in haste, nor by flight, but to have all things prepared before them. Money was to be sent up to the bishop, and as fast as lands were purchased, and preparations made, the bishop was to let it be known, that the church might be gathered in. But this regulation was not attended to, for the church got crazy to go up to Zion, as it was then called. The rich were afraid to send up their money to purchase lands, and the poor crowded up in numbers, without having any places provided, contrary to the advice of the bishop and others, until the old citizens began to be highly displeased' (John Corrill, *A Brief History of the Church of Christ of Latter Day Saints* [1839], 18–19, josephsmithpapers .org; see also *The Joseph Smith Papers, Histories, Volume 2: Assigned Histories, 1831–1847*, ed. Karen Lynn Davidson and others [2012], 146)."

25 Behold, the land of Zion—I, **the Lord, hold it in mine own hands** [*the Lord owns the whole earth, including Zion, and has power over it*];

26 Nevertheless, **I, the Lord, render unto Caesar the things which are Caesar's.** [*A reference to Luke 20:25. In effect, the Lord could clear the land of Zion and simply turn it over to the Saints; however, it is proper that the members purchase land in Zion from the legal owners. In other words, "Pay Caesar for the things Caesar owns." Respect man-made governments. Among other things, they prevent chaos and anarchy.*]

27 Wherefore, **I the Lord will that you should purchase the lands**, that you may have advantage of the world, that you may have claim on the world [*so that the civil government's legal system will be obligated to support their ownership of the land*], that they may not be stirred up unto anger.

28 For Satan putteth it into their hearts to anger against you, and to the shedding of blood.

Next, we see that there are basically just two options for obtaining the land on which to build Zion in Missouri.

29 Wherefore, the land of Zion shall not be obtained but [*except*]

by purchase or by blood [*bloodshed*], otherwise there is none inheritance for you.

30 And **if by purchase,** behold **you are blessed**;

31 And **if by blood**, as you are forbidden to shed blood, lo, your enemies are upon you, and **ye shall be scourged from city to city, and from synagogue to synagogue**, and but few shall stand to receive an inheritance.

> Next, in verse 32, we see that as people reject truth and righteousness, going against their consciences and the commandments of God, His Spirit withdraws, with the resulting wars and devastations described in verse 33. The world is experiencing this now.

32 I, the Lord, am angry with the wicked; **I am holding my Spirit from the inhabitants of the earth**.

33 **I have** sworn in my wrath, and **decreed wars** upon the face of the earth, **and the wicked shall slay the wicked**, and **fear shall come upon every man**;

> Left alone, verses 32–33, above, could be quite discouraging for the righteous. Verse 34, next, must be included with them for a complete picture. With it included, we see that the Saints will have difficulties because of the wickedness of the

world but that the Lord will be with them.

34 **And the saints also shall hardly escape; nevertheless, I, the Lord, am with them**, and will come down in heaven from the presence of my Father and consume the wicked with unquenchable fire [*a reference to the Second Coming*].

> It is important to understand the phrase, in verse 34, above, that says, "the Saints also shall hardly escape." The Prophet Joseph Smith addressed this subject. He said:
>
> "It is a false idea that the Saints will escape all the judgments, whilst the wicked suffer; for all flesh is subject to suffer, and 'the righteous shall hardly escape;' still many of the Saints will escape, for the just shall live by faith; yet many of the righteous shall fall a prey to disease, to pestilence, etc., by reason of the weakness of the flesh, and yet be saved in the Kingdom of God. So that it is an unhallowed principle to say that such and such have transgressed because they have been preyed upon by disease or death, for all flesh is subject to death; and the Savior has said, 'Judge not, lest ye be judged'" (*History of the Church*, 4:11).
>
> The messages and counsel of our current prophet and other Church leaders must also be included with

verses 32–34, above, if we are to avoid gloom, despair, and pessimism in our own lives. One of the strongest messages from them is for us to avoid getting caught up in gloom and doom. Rather, we are reminded that this is a wonderful time to be alive. President Gordon B. Hinckley said during general conference in October 2001 (**bold** added for emphasis):

"I do not know what we did in the preexistence to merit the wonderful blessings we enjoy. We have come to earth in this great season in the long history of mankind. **It is a marvelous age, the best of all**" ("Living in the Fulness of Times," *Ensign,* November 2001, 4).

Verse 35, next, tells us that, even though the Second Coming is close, it is not yet here. This may sound obvious, but remember that there were some in Joseph Smith's day, such as the Shaking Quakers (see heading to section 49 in your Doctrine and Covenants) who taught that the Savior had already come. Likewise, there are some today who teach that He is already here, that His Second Coming has occurred but that the Millennium has not yet begun.

35 And behold, **this** [*the Second Coming*] **is not yet, but by and by**.

As you know, there are usually many different messages and lessons we can get from a given verse or set of verses. What the Holy Ghost teaches us is determined by our situation and needs at the time or for future use. Therefore, as we read our scriptures, we get one message one time and another the next time, and so forth. There are many different messages we could get from verses 36–37, next. We will choose to read them for helps in surviving the last days and will use **bold** to point them out.

36 Wherefore, seeing that I, the Lord, have decreed all these things [*the last day's calamities and destructions leading up to the Second Coming*] upon the face of the earth, **I will that my saints should be assembled** upon the land of Zion [*in terms of our surviving the last days, this verse can mean for us to gather with the faithful Saints, in our branches, wards, and stakes, no matter where we live*];

37 And that every man should **take righteousness** in his hands [*use personal righteousness as a weapon to defend yourself against wickedness*] **and faithfulness** upon his loins [*clothe yourself with faithfulness to God*], **and lift a warning voice** unto the inhabitants of the earth [*explain and teach the gospel to those around you*]; and **declare both by word and by flight that desolation shall come upon the wicked** [*teach the gospel with words and by example as you*

avoid and flee (when necessary) the wickedness that is enveloping the world].

38 Wherefore, **let my disciples** [*members of the Church*] **in Kirtland arrange their temporal concerns**, who dwell upon this farm [*the farm in Kirtland upon which Titus Billings and others were living*].

Next, the Lord tells Titus Billings to sell the farm, mentioned in verse 38, above, and move to Jackson County, Missouri, in the spring, along with several other Saints currently living on that farm. (Some Saints were to remain in Kirtland until later). Brother Billings did so, leading a small company of Latter-day Saints to Zion in the spring and consecrating the proceeds from the sale of the farm to the Church in Zion. He died faithful to the Church, in Provo, Utah, on February 6, 1866, at age seventy-two. Obedience pays big dividends.

39 **Let my servant Titus Billings**, who has the care thereof, **dispose of** [*sell*] **the land**, that he may be prepared in the coming spring to take his journey up unto the land of Zion, with those that dwell upon the face thereof [*with others who live on the farm*], excepting those whom I shall reserve unto myself, that shall not go until I shall command them.

40 And let all the moneys which can be spared [*you decide how much you need for traveling and how much can be given for building Zion*], **it mattereth not unto me whether it be little or much**, be sent up unto the land of Zion, unto them whom I have appointed to receive.

Did you notice the important message in verse 40, above? The Lord said that it does not matter to Him how much or how little money is given in such donations. This can apply to us in the sense that it is up to us to decide how much we pay for fast offering, humanitarian aid, missionary fund, and so forth (except tithing in which it does matter; it is 10 percent). Perhaps you've noticed that the Brethren steadfastly avoid giving you a dollar amount to pay with respect to these other voluntary contributions to the Church. They likewise counsel local leaders of the Church to avoid setting quotas for temple attendance. It is up to each member to decide since it is a part of the law of consecration. And the law of consecration operates on celestial standards—in other words, on the basic goodness, generosity, unselfishness, honesty, and integrity of participants. The same principles apply to the visiting of the sick, the number of children to have and when to have them, seniors serving missions, and so forth.

Next, in verse 41, the Savior tells these Saints that He will instruct the Prophet as to who is to go to Missouri and who is to stay in Ohio for a season.

41 Behold, **I, the Lord, will give unto my servant Joseph Smith, Jun., power** that he shall be enabled **to discern** by the Spirit those **who shall go up unto the land of Zion, and** those of my disciples **who shall tarry** [*stay put*].

42 **Let my servant Newel K. Whitney retain his store** [*the Newel K. Whitney Store in Kirtland*], or in other words, the store, **yet for a little season.**

43 Nevertheless, **let him impart** [*donate*] **all the money which he can impart, to be sent up unto the land of Zion**.

44 Behold, **these things are in his own hands, let him do according to wisdom** [*he is free to decide for himself; another illustration of the principles of agency and integrity inseparably associated with the law of consecration.*]

45 Verily I say, **let him be ordained** [*set apart*] **as an agent unto the disciples that shall tarry** [*the Church members who remain in Ohio*], and let him be ordained unto this power;

Next, in verse 46, Newel K. Whitney and Oliver Cowdery are instructed to spread the word quickly among the branches of the Church in Ohio, explaining the need for donations to buy land in Zion, and to collect donations as they go. The present value as well as the eternal value of obedience to God's instructions is emphasized in verses 47–48.

46 And now **speedily visit the churches**, expounding [*explaining and teaching*] these things unto them, **with my servant Oliver Cowdery**. Behold, this is my will, **obtaining moneys** even as I have directed.

47 **He that is faithful and endureth shall overcome the world** [*will overcome the sins and temptations of the world*].

48 He that sendeth up treasures unto the land of Zion shall receive an inheritance in this world, **and his works shall follow him, and also a reward in the world to come.**

In verses 49–54, the Lord points the minds and hearts of these Saints to the future, to the Second Coming and the Millennium, giving them perspective as to the blessings that will someday come to the righteous. Such perspective gives strength that helps with present burdens and difficulties encountered because of obedience to God's commandments and counsel.

49 Yea, and **blessed are the dead that die in the Lord** [*who die righteous*], from henceforth, **when the Lord shall come** [*the Second Coming*], and old things shall pass away, and all things become new [*D&C 29:24*], **they shall rise from the dead** and shall not die after, **and shall receive an inheritance before the Lord, in the holy city.**

Among other possibilities, the "holy city" mentioned at the end of verse 49, above, could be a reference to Zion, or the New Jerusalem in Missouri, which will be one of two cities that will serve as headquarters for the Savior and His Church during the Millennium (see Ether 13:1–11).

Also, in Revelation 21:2, a "holy city" is spoken of that symbolizes the celestialized earth (see heading to Revelation 21 in your Bible); or, in other words, the celestial kingdom for those from this earth.

Either way, to "receive an inheritance before the Lord, in the holy city," verse 49, above, can be interpreted to mean that the faithful Saints can look forward to being with the Savior in the future, no matter what happens to them in this mortal life.

Next, we are taught that faithful Saints who are still alive when

the Savior comes will live during the Millennium to a specified age and then die. This answers the question sometimes asked as to whether mortals who live during the Millennium will actually die or simply be resurrected without dying. They will die but will be resurrected immediately, "in the twinkling of an eye" (see verse 51, and D&C 101:31).

50 And **he that liveth when the Lord shall come, and hath kept the faith** [*was faithful on earth*], blessed is he; nevertheless, **it is appointed to him to die at the age of man.**

How old is the "age of man" (verse 50, above)? Isaiah said that people will live to be one hundred years old during the Millennium (Isaiah 65:20). Joseph Fielding Smith also spoke of this. He said (**bold** added for emphasis):

"When Christ comes the saints who are on the earth will be quickened and caught up to meet him. This does not mean that those who are living in mortality at that time will be changed and pass through the resurrection, for mortals must remain on the earth until after the thousand years are ended. A change, nevertheless, will come over all who remain on the earth; they will be quickened so that they will not be subject unto death until they are old. Men shall die when they are **one hundred years of age**, and the change shall be made suddenly to the immortal state. Graves will not be made during this thousand years. . . . Death shall come as a peaceful transition from the mortal to the immortal state" (*Way to Perfection*, 298–99, 311).

51 Wherefore, **children shall grow up until they become old; old men shall die; but they shall not sleep in the dust** [*they will not be buried*], **but they shall be changed in the twinkling of an eye** [*resurrected immediately*].

52 Wherefore, **for this cause preached the Apostles unto the world the resurrection of the dead** [*perhaps meaning that the Savior's Apostles of old likewise preached about these things to strengthen faithful Saints back then in living the gospel despite difficulties and persecutions*].

53 **These things are the things that ye must look for** [*it helps us live the gospel when we understand and look forward to these things*]; and, **speaking after the manner of the Lord** [*speaking in terms of the Lord's time*], **they are now nigh at hand**, and in a time to come, even in **the day of the coming of the Son of Man.**

Next, the Lord uses imagery and symbolism from the parable of the ten virgins (Matthew 25:1–13) as

He explains that some members of the Church will be wise and some foolish when it comes to being prepared to meet the Savior. The righteous will not be completely separated from the wicked until the Second Coming.

54 And **until that hour** [*up until the Second Coming*] **there will be foolish virgins among the wise**; and **at that hour cometh an entire separation of the righteous and the wicked**; and in that day will I send mine angels to pluck out the wicked and cast them into unquenchable fire [*the wicked will be destroyed at the Second Coming*].

The topic now changes to the description of Zion in Jackson County, Missouri, which the Lord asked Sidney Rigdon to write (see D&C 58:50–51). As you will see in verses 55–56, his first attempt was not acceptable to the Lord. He will make another attempt and it will be accepted.

55 And now behold, verily I say unto you, **I, the Lord, am not pleased with my servant Sidney Rigdon**; he exalted himself in his heart, and received not counsel, but grieved the Spirit;

56 Wherefore **his writing** [*written description of Zion*] **is not acceptable unto the Lord**, and **he shall make another**; and if the Lord receive it not, behold he standeth

no longer in the office to which I have appointed him.

In a sense, the prospective missionaries spoken of in verse 57, next, could be like potential senior missionaries today. If they desire to serve, they are to make it known and they will be called on missions.

57 And again, verily I say unto you, **those who desire in their hearts**, in meekness, **to warn sinners to repentance, let them be ordained unto this power**.

58 For **this is a day of warning, and not a day of many words** [*missionaries need to preach the gospel simply and directly*]. For I, the Lord, am not to be mocked in the last days.

Next, in verses 59–60, the Lord reminds us of His power and influence over all things. One message we gain from this is that the wicked cannot successfully escape from Him and the consequences of sin. A more pleasant message is that it is completely safe for us to follow Him.

59 Behold, **I am from above**, and **my power lieth beneath. I am over all**, and **in all**, and **through all**, and **search all things** [*He knows all that is going on*], and the day cometh [*likely a direct reference to the Second Coming and the Millennium*] that

all things shall be subject unto me.

60 Behold, **I am Alpha and Omega, even Jesus Christ**.

While verses 61–64 can easily be used to preach against swearing and profanity and using the name of God in vain, there is another aspect of these verses in the context of this section that also fits.

As stated earlier, those addressed directly in this section are members of the Church. They have taken upon them the name of Christ, having made covenants with the Father in the Savior's name. They have, in effect, spoken His name with their lips as they have made covenants and taken His name upon them through baptism, and some of them have taken it "in vain" because they are now breaking their covenants and rebelling. They have offended the Spirit (verse 64) as they have mocked and ridiculed the sacred things that have come "from above," either by their complaining or their sinful acts.

Thus, taking "the name of the Lord . . . in vain" can mean making covenants and then breaking them, treating lightly "that which cometh from above" (the gospel of Jesus Christ, revelation, inspiration, the words of the prophets, and so forth).

61 Wherefore, **let all men beware how they take my name in their lips—**

62 For behold, verily I say, that **many there be who are under this condemnation** [*have committed this sin*], **who use the name of the Lord, and use it in vain**, having not authority [*among other things, perhaps meaning that they are not the leaders of the Church and do not have the authority to correct the Prophet and criticize the leaders*].

63 Wherefore, **let the church repent of their sins, and I, the Lord, will own them** [*Jesus will accept them now and on Judgment Day*]; otherwise they shall be cut off.

Elder James E. Talmage explained various aspects of taking the name of the Lord in vain. He said:

"1. We may take the name of God in vain by profane speech.

"2. We take it in vain when we swear falsely, not being true to our oaths and promises.

"3. We take it in vain in a blasphemous sense when we presume to speak in that name without authority.

"4. And we take his name in vain whenever we willfully do aught [anything] that is in defiance of his commandments, since we have taken his name upon ourselves" (In Conference

Report, October 1931, 53).

Yet another important message, in verse 64, next, is that we must speak about sacred things with reverence and respect, avoiding inappropriate humor involving deity and Church leaders, not reducing sacred and holy things to the common and crude.

64 Remember that **that which cometh from above is sacred, and must be spoken with care, and by constraint of the Spirit**; and in this there is no condemnation, and **ye receive the Spirit through prayer**; wherefore, without this there remaineth condemnation.

Joseph and Sidney followed the instructions given in verse 65, next, and accepted the invitation of John Johnson to live with him and his family on their farm in Hiram, Ohio, about thirty miles southeast of Kirtland. Joseph and Emma moved in with the Johnsons on September 12, 1831. The great revelation known as section 76, giving details about the three degrees of glory and perdition, will be given in the Johnson home in February 1832.

The John Johnson home has now been restored by the Church and is one of the prime Church history attractions in the Kirtland area.

65 **Let my servants, Joseph Smith, Jun., and Sidney Rigdon,**

seek them a home [*in the Kirtland area*], as they are taught through prayer by the Spirit.

In verse 66, the Savior gives a final word of counsel and comfort.

66 These things remain to overcome through patience [*the concerns and instructions addressed in this section must still be overcome, and patience will be needed*], **that such may receive a more exceeding and eternal weight of glory** [*it is worth overcoming sins and shortcomings*], **otherwise, a greater condemnation. Amen.**

Before we leave this section, it is worth taking another look at the word "patience" in verse 66, above. We will mention three aspects of patience here:

1. Patience with others, in order to work together with them in harmony.

2. Patience with yourself, so that you don't cripple personal progress with self-criticism and condemnation.

3. Patience with the leaders of the Church so that you don't find yourself criticizing them.

You may wish to read Alma 32 again and look at the important role of "patience," especially as emphasized in verses 41, 42, and 43.

SECTION 64

Background

This revelation through the Prophet Joseph Smith was given in Kirtland, Ohio, on September 11, 1831, just one day before Joseph moved his family to the John Johnson home in Hiram, Ohio, about thirty miles southeast of Kirtland. Sidney Rigdon likewise moved to the Johnson farm. One of the main reasons for the move was to have the uninterrupted time necessary to resume the translation of the Bible, which work had been temporarily set aside during the Prophet's recent travels to Missouri.

Sidney Rigdon was serving as scribe for Joseph during the inspired revision of the Bible. This work today is known as the Joseph Smith Translation of the Bible, or JST. As you have perhaps noticed, there are many footnotes in our Church's edition of the Bible that give corrections and additions to the Bible text. There is also a short section at the back of our Bible titled the "Joseph Smith Translation," which contains longer corrections and additions.

Joseph Fielding Smith gave some background to this section. He said:

"Because of interference and because he needed a quiet place in which to work, the Prophet on

September 12, 1831, moved to the home of John Johnson in the township of Hiram. This was in Portage County, Ohio, about thirty miles southeast of Kirtland. From the time he moved until early in October, the Prophet spent most of his spare time preparing for the continuation of the translation of the Bible. By translation is meant a revision of the Bible by inspiration or revelation as the Lord had commanded him, and which was commenced as early as June 1830. (D.H.C. 1:215.) Sidney Rigdon continued to write for the Prophet in the work of revision. The day before the Prophet moved from Kirtland he received an important revelation, section 64, as it now appears in the Doctrine and Covenants. This revelation contained a wealth of information, counsel and warning, for the guidance of the members of the Church. In it the Lord said: 'Behold, thus saith the Lord your God unto you, O ye elders of my church, hearken ye and hear, and receive my will concerning you. For verily I say unto you, I will that ye should overcome the world; wherefore I will have compassion upon you.' Then it is made known that the keys of the mysteries of the kingdom were to remain with Joseph Smith while he lived inasmuch as he should obey the Lord's ordinances. We learned in an earlier revelation that this same promise was made to him, with the warning that if he should fail he would still have power to appoint or ordain his successor, and

the Church was instructed that no other was appointed or would be, to give revelations for the Church and this was to be a law unto the Church. This might have saved some ambitious individuals from the pitfalls laid by the adversary, and some who were foolish enough to follow them, if they had been properly impressed with this plain and logical doctrine. (Sec. 43:3–6.) The Lord declared that there were some who had sought occasion against the Prophet, but without cause. This has been true in the case of each of his successors in the Presidency of the Church. The Lord pointed out the fact that the Prophet had sinned, nothing very grievous, but he had shown repentance, and there are 'sins unto death.' (See 64:7; 1 John 5:16.) A sin unto death merits no forgiveness" (Joseph Fielding Smith, *Church History and Modern Revelation,* 2:7–8).

Additional background that is helpful in understanding this section has to do with Ezra Booth (verse 15). He was a Methodist minister and close friend of John Johnson. He was converted to the Church in about May 1831 when he saw the Prophet Joseph Smith command Brother Johnson's wife, Elsa, to be healed. Ezra witnessed the immediate healing of her lame arm (see *History of the Church,* 1:215–16). Ezra was ordained a high priest on June 3, 1831, and served a mission to Missouri as instructed by the Lord in D&C 52:23 (given

June 7, 1831). He became upset about having to walk the entire distance to Missouri, preaching as they went. It was apparently not the comfort and attention to which he had become accustomed as a popular minister prior to joining the Church. He began to find fault with Joseph Smith and other leaders of the Church.

One of the things that seemed to bother Booth about Joseph Smith was that the Prophet's naturally pleasant and jovial personality was not serious enough for a true prophet of God. He felt that Joseph had a "spirit of lightness and levity, a temper of mind easily irritated, and an habitual proneness to jesting and joking" (in *The Joseph Smith Papers, Documents, Volume 2: July 1831–January 1833*, ed. Matthew C. Godfrey and others [2013], 60, note 332).

By September 1831, Ezra Booth was back in Kirtland and was in a condition of apostasy, criticizing the Prophet and rejecting the Church. He was excommunicated on September 6, 1831 (see *Church History in the Fulness of Times*, 2003, 114), and he formally denounced the Church at a Methodist camp meeting on September 12, 1831. He went on to become the first apostate to write and publish anti-Mormon literature, publishing nine articles against the Church in the *Ohio Star* newspaper from October to December 1831. Ezra Booth participated in the tarring and feathering of the Prophet Joseph Smith on the night of March 24, 1832, at the John Johnson farm in Hiram, Ohio.

Section 64 is perhaps best-known because of its counsel on forgiving others. You may wish to glance ahead and see if you recognize verses 9–11. As you will see, it has many other important messages also.

As we begin our verse-by-verse study, we feel the tenderness and compassion of the Savior in verses 1–4 as He forgives sins and encourages efforts to improve and do better.

1 BEHOLD, **thus saith the Lord your God unto you**, O ye elders of my church, hearken ye and hear, and **receive my will concerning you.**

2 For verily I say unto you, **I will that ye should overcome the world** [*the Savior wants us to succeed*]; wherefore [*this is one of the reasons*] **I will have compassion upon you.**

3 **There are those among you who have sinned; but verily I say, for this once, for mine own glory** [*because the Savior also has joy, happiness, and success as we repent; see first phrase of Mosiah 14:11*], **and for the salvation of**

souls, I have forgiven you your sins.

4 **I will be merciful unto you**, for I have given unto you the kingdom.

Next, in verse 5, we have another witness from the Savior Himself, that the living prophet, although not perfect, leads us under His direction. This verse, when coupled with D&C 43:3–4, serves as a reminder that the living prophet will never be allowed to lead us astray.

5 And **the keys of the mysteries of the kingdom shall not be taken from my servant Joseph Smith, Jun.**, through the means I have appointed [*in D&C 43:3–4*], **while he liveth, inasmuch as he obeyeth mine ordinances**.

The last phrase of verse 5 is important because it says, in effect, that the living prophet still has agency, and if he were to choose to disobey God and refuse to lead the Church according to the Lord's will, he would be removed from office.

Next, beginning with verse 6, the focus turns to forgiving others in order to receive forgiveness from the Lord.

6 **There are those who have sought occasion against him** [*Joseph Smith*] **without cause** [*they do not have a valid case against the Prophet*];

7 **Nevertheless, he has sinned** [*Joseph is not perfect*]; **but** verily I say unto you, **I, the Lord, forgive sins unto those who confess their sins before me and ask forgiveness**, who have not sinned unto death [*become sons of perdition; see D&C 76:31–35*]. [*In other words, Joseph confesses his sins and asks for forgiveness, and the Lord forgives him, just as is the case with you and me and all others who sincerely repent.*]

8 **My disciples, in days of old** [*followers of Christ in ancient times*], sought occasion [*had complaints*] against one another and **forgave not one another in their hearts**; and for this evil they were afflicted and sorely [*severely*] chastened [*disciplined*].

As stated in the background notes for this section, verses 9–11, next, are probably some of the most often-quoted in the Doctrine and Covenants. The doctrine is clear. We must forgive others and turn their judgment over to the Savior in order to be forgiven ourselves.

9 Wherefore, I say unto you, that **ye ought to forgive one another**; for **he that forgiveth not** his brother his trespasses **standeth condemned** [*stopped in personal progress; in trouble on Judgment Day*] before the Lord; for **there**

remaineth in him the greater sin.

10 I, the Lord, will forgive whom I will forgive, but of you it is required to forgive all men [*including yourself*].

The last phrase of verse 9, above, bears further comment. At first glance, it sounds unfair, especially in the case of serious and damaging actions against us by others. For instance, in cases of robbery, rape, child abuse, spouse abuse, and other traumatizing "trespasses" against someone, how can the victim be guilty of a "greater sin" by not forgiving the perpetrator? There are several possible answers to this question. We will consider two.

First, another term for sin, trespass is "spiritual damage." Thus, anger, hatred, desires for revenge, and so forth, if allowed to remain "in" us, can do "greater" damage over time than the original "trespass" against us. They can cripple spiritual and emotional growth as well as preventing healing.

Second, if those who have trespassed against us do get to the point where they are repenting and asking our forgiveness, and we refuse their pleas for forgiveness, we can do even "greater" damage to them than they did to us.

There is another question we must address with these verses. Does

forgiving mean allowing additional "trespasses"? Does the Lord require that we continue to be "walked on"? We find an answer by reading what Nephi was commanded by the Lord to do after repeated trespasses against him by Laman and Lemuel. He was commanded to "flee" his brethren (2 Nephi 5:5) and to go with those who would follow him to a place and situation in which they could have peace.

Yet another question must be considered. What if a person who has been severely traumatized by another's actions tries to forgive, prays for help, seeks counsel from others, reads the scriptures, and so forth, but still finds that he or she is emotionally incapable of forgiving? What then?

Mercifully, the answer is found in verse 11, next.

11 And ye ought to say in your hearts—let God judge between me and thee, and reward thee according to thy deeds.

In other words, they are invited to turn the burden of "judging" and punishing over to God and thus get on with their lives.

Over many years serving as a bishop and stake president, I found verse 11, above, to be most helpful in such situations. The major step for people who had not yet been able to muster the strength emotionally to forgive their "trespasser" was to turn things over to the Savior. I asked them if they felt that they could support the Savior's decision and actions with respect to their abuser. Usually, the immediate answer was "yes," which brought visible relief. In some cases, they had to pray for strength first over a period of time to simply turn the person or persons over to the Lord. Having taken this step, it was not long before they began seeing their "enemy" with pity and with a hope that he or she could someday change and avoid the misery that awaited them if they refused to repent.

Next, in verses 12–14, the Master explains the necessity of Church disciplinary action on occasions and that such action by Church leaders does not constitute lack of forgiving on their part (as commanded in verses 9–10, above); rather, it is sometimes necessary to meet the requirements of the Lord in preserving the strength and purity of the Church. We will learn more about this in section 102.

12 **And him that repenteth not of his sins, and confesseth them not, ye shall bring before the church**, and do with him as the scripture saith unto you, either by commandment or by revelation [*either according to the commandments and instructions already given, such as in D&C 42:24, 26, 75,*

80–91, or as directed by the Spirit at the time].

13 And this ye shall do that God may be glorified—**not because ye forgive not, having not compassion, but that ye may be justified in the eyes of the law, that ye may not offend him who is your lawgiver**—

14 Verily I say, **for this cause** [*in order not to disobey God*] **ye shall do these things**.

As mentioned in the background given in this study guide for this section, Ezra Booth apostatized after a few weeks in the Church. Both Ezra Booth and Isaac Morley are mentioned in verses 15–16, next. They served as companions (D&C 52:23) as they traveled on their missions to Missouri. They had both complained against Church leaders. Note that Isaac Morley is forgiven, but Ezra Booth is not. Ezra left the Church and fought against it, never coming back. In contrast, Isaac repented and remained faithful, serving as a patriarch, stake president, and high counselor through mobbings and persecutions in Missouri and Illinois and the trials and difficulties of moving west with the pioneers. He died true to the Church, in Fairview, Utah, on June 24, 1865, at age seventy-nine.

15 Behold, **I, the Lord, was angry with** him who was my

servant **Ezra Booth**, and **also** my servant **Isaac Morley**, for they kept not the law, neither the commandment;

16 **They sought evil in their hearts, and I, the Lord, withheld my Spirit**. They condemned for evil that thing in which there was no evil [*possibly a reference to the instruction from the Lord for Isaac Morley to sell his farm in Kirtland and consecrate the money from the sale to the Church as part of the law of consecration*]; nevertheless **I have forgiven my servant Isaac Morley** [*who repented and did sell his farm after all; see verse 20*].

17 And **also my servant Edward Partridge**, behold, he **hath sinned**, and **Satan seeketh to destroy his soul; but when these things are made known unto them, and they repent of the evil, they shall be forgiven**.

As is the case with so many verses in the Doctrine and Covenants, verse 17, above, has a simple but important message and reminder for all of us. It is that when we find out that we have been wrong, and if we humble ourselves and repent, we will be forgiven.

Next, the Lord requests that Sidney Gilbert (business partner to Newel K. Whitney and co-owner of the Newel K. Whitney store in

Kirtland) return to Zion in Jackson County, Missouri, to continue setting up a store there (see note accompanying D&C 53:4 in this study guide) and to handle other business affairs of the Church as needed.

18 And now, verily I say that **it is expedient in me that** my servant **Sidney Gilbert**, after a few weeks, **shall return upon his business, and to his agency in the land of Zion**;

19 And that which he hath seen and heard may be made known unto my disciples [*members of the Church, faithful followers of Christ*], that they perish not. And for this cause have I spoken these things.

Along with the background already given in the note following verse 14, above, verse 20, next, gives us an important insight as to why the Lord asked Isaac Morley to sell his farm in Kirtland and consecrate the money gained from the sale to the Church. The insight is that this apparently was a critical moment in Isaac's life. He seems to have been sorely tempted to keep the farm and the personal wealth it provided for him and his family. At first, he refused to sell but quickly rethought the issue and determined to be obedient and sell, thus strengthening his testimony by obedience during a moment of temptation. With the spiritual momentum gained by this act of obedience, he gained strength to endure faithfully for the rest of his life.

Watch now, in verse 20, as the Lord explains why He had Isaac Morley sell his farm.

20 And again, I say unto you, that my servant Isaac Morley may not be tempted above that which he is able to bear, and counsel wrongfully to your hurt, I gave commandment that his farm should be sold.

Frederick G. Williams also owned a farm in the area, but the Lord instructs him not to sell. It consisted of about 144 acres.

21 I will not that my servant Frederick G. Williams should sell his farm, for I, the Lord, will to retain a strong hold in the land of Kirtland, for the space of five years, in the which I will not overthrow the wicked, that thereby I may save some.

If we use our imagination, we might hear some members gossiping and complaining because Isaac Morley was told by the Prophet to sell his farm (verse 20), whereas Frederick G. Williams (an extra close friend of the Prophet and physician to Joseph and Emma and their family) was told to keep his farm (verse 21). Such chatter is folly! From what you know, you can readily see that

such criticism is foolish and shows lack of faith in the Lord's prophet. But how many situations do we run into where we do not have the understanding and insights that we have here? For example, one bishop may handle a seemingly similar situation completely differently than another bishop. This is just a reminder to have faith in the inspiration of the Lord to His leaders, and to avoid gossip and criticism.

Looking again at verse 21, above, we see two more messages. First, Kirtland is to remain a stronghold of the Church for another five years. During this time, a temple will be built. And when it is dedicated, on March 27, 1836 (D&C 109), marvelous manifestations will attend it. And just a week later, on April 3, 1836, the Savior, Moses, Elias, and Elijah will appear and bestow priesthood keys upon the Prophet and Oliver Cowdery (D&C 110). Obviously, these Saints didn't know all this when instructions were given to keep Kirtland as a headquarters of the Church for five years.

Thus, having some members remain in Kirtland while excitement for relocating to Missouri was running high was both a test of faith for those who were asked to remain, as well as a significant opportunity for the faithful to learn a lesson through blessings that came through obedience.

A second message is found at the

end of verse 21, above. It is that the Lord holds off on "smiting" the wicked and disobedient, because by being patient, He still might save some of them. It is well to keep this in mind when, at times, we are tempted to wish that the Lord would "smite" those who make life difficult and miserable for us.

In verse 22, next, the Lord tells these members that after five more years in Kirtland, all who wish to move to Missouri are welcome to do so, as long as they do it with humble and receptive hearts.

22 And **after that day** [*after five years; verse 21, above*]**, I, the Lord, will not hold any guilty that shall go with an open heart up to the land of Zion**; for **I, the Lord, require the hearts of the children of men**.

We ought not to miss the important message at the end of verse 22, above. The Lord requires our "hearts," our center of feelings and emotions. The mind is the center of rational thought and intellectual understanding, but we tend to act and behave based on our feelings. Thus, when we give our hearts to the Lord, we are giving our deepest loyalty to Him. We find ourselves wanting to obey Him rather than needing to obey Him in order to get blessings we want. When we give our hearts to Him, we find ourselves being truly good rather than playing it safe.

Next, we see another verse that is quite well-known. It deals with paying tithing so we don't get burned at the Second Coming.

23 Behold, **now it is called to-day until the coming of the Son of Man** [*this is your opportunity to prepare to meet God; compare with D&C 45:6 and Alma 34:32–33*], and verily **it is a day of sacrifice, and a day for the tithing of my people**; for **he that is tithed shall not be burned at his coming**.

Obviously, a person who lives in sin and wickedness but pays tithing to avoid being burned with the wicked when the Savior comes would not avoid burning. Such people, if there be any, would be forgetting that the Lord requires the "heart," as explained in verse 22.

24 For **after today** [*the time between now and the Second Coming*] **cometh the burning**—this is speaking after the manner of the Lord [*according to the symbolic language used by God*]—for verily I say, **tomorrow** [*when the Second Coming arrives*] **all the proud and they that do wickedly shall be as stubble**; and **I will burn them up**, for I am the Lord of Hosts; and I will not spare any that remain in Babylon [*symbolic of personal as well as mass wickedness*].

People often wonder how the

wicked will actually be burned. The scriptures have a simple answer. They will be burned by the glory of the coming Christ. We find this in D&C 5:19, as well as in 2 Nephi. We will quote 2 Nephi here (**bold** added for emphasis):

2 Nephi 12:10, 19, 21

10 O ye wicked ones, enter into the rock, and hide thee in the dust, for the fear of the Lord and the glory of his majesty shall smite thee.

19 And they shall go into the holes of the rocks, and into the caves of the earth, for the fear of the Lord shall come upon them and **the glory of his majesty shall smite them**, when he ariseth [*at the time of the Second Coming*] to shake terribly the earth.

21 To go into the clefts of the rocks, and into the tops of the ragged rocks, for the fear of the Lord shall come upon them and **the majesty of his glory shall smite them**, when he ariseth to shake terribly the earth.

25 Wherefore, **if ye believe me, ye will labor while it is called today** [*you will prepare to meet God now*].

Next, in verse 26, the Lord instructs Newel K. Whitney and Sidney Gilbert not to sell the Newel K. Whitney store in Kirtland (which they own together) until the five years (verse 21) are up. The Saints who remain in Kirtland will need its goods and services.

26 And **it is not meet** [*necessary*] **that** my servants, **Newel K. Whitney and Sidney Gilbert, should sell their store** and their possessions here; for this is not wisdom until the residue [*remaining members*] of the church, which remaineth in this place [*Kirtland*], shall go up unto the land of Zion [*Jackson County, Missouri*].

It appears that, in verses 27–33, next, the Lord is reminding Brothers Whitney and Gilbert that they will need to do business with non-members along with their business with and for the Church in Kirtland, and that the Lord will inspire them as they work to carry out their stewardships. The importance of their role in supplying goods and services for the Saints through their business skills and talents is emphasized in verse 30. That they will become tired and weary in carrying out their responsibilities is implied by verse 33.

27 Behold, it is said in my laws, or forbidden, to get in debt to thine enemies;

28 But behold, it is not said at any time that the Lord should not

take when he please, and pay as seemeth him good.

29 Wherefore, **as ye are agents, ye are on the Lord's errand; and whatever ye do according to the will of the Lord is the Lord's business**.

30 And **he hath set you to provide for his saints** in these last days, that they may obtain an inheritance in the land of Zion.

31 And behold, I, the Lord, declare unto you, and my words are sure and shall not fail, that they shall obtain it.

32 But all things must come to pass in their time.

33 Wherefore, **be not weary in well-doing**, for ye are laying the foundation of a great work. And **out of small things proceedeth that which is great**.

34 Behold, **the Lord requireth the heart and a willing mind**; and the willing and obedient shall eat the good of the land of Zion [*symbolic of obtaining the blessings of the Lord temporally and physically*] in these last days.

35 And **the rebellious shall be cut off out of the land of Zion, and shall be sent away, and shall not inherit the land** [*symbolic of the fact that the wicked will not "inherit" a place in the kingdom of God*].

36 For, verily I say that **the rebellious are not of the blood of Ephraim** [*symbolic of all those who come into the Church and make and keep covenants, regardless of which tribe of Israel they come from*], wherefore they shall be plucked out.

In verses 37–40, next, the Lord symbolically and literally presents the Church, the righteous Saints, and the pure gospel of Jesus Christ, as the standard against which all things are to be judged.

37 Behold, **I, the Lord, have made my church in these last days like unto a judge** sitting on a hill, or in a high place, to judge the nations.

38 For it shall come to pass that **the inhabitants of Zion shall judge all things pertaining to Zion**.

39 And **liars and hypocrites shall be proved by them, and they who are not Apostles and prophets shall be known**.

40 And **even the bishop, who is a judge, and his counselors, if they are not faithful in their stewardships shall be condemned,**

and others shall be planted in their stead [*all leaders of the Church are subject to obeying the principles and commandments of the gospel; there is no "privilege because of position" in the Church, as is the case in almost all man-made governments and organizations*].

Finally, in verses 41–43, the Savior prophesies about the successful gathering of Israel in the last days. We are watching this even now as it happens before our very eyes!

41 For, behold, I say unto you that **Zion shall flourish**, and **the glory of the Lord shall be upon her**;

42 And **she shall be an ensign** [*a flag, a signal to gather; a rallying point*] unto the people, and **there shall come unto her out of every nation under heaven**.

43 And **the day shall come when the nations of the earth shall tremble because of her, and shall fear because of her terrible** [*mighty and strong*] **ones**. The Lord hath spoken it. Amen.

SECTION 65

Background

This revelation was given in Hiram, Ohio, thirty miles southeast of Kirtland on October 30,1831. The Prophet Joseph Smith said

that he received it as a prayer "in the fore part of October" (*History of the Church*, 1:218).

A number of revelations were received by the Prophet while he and his family, along with Sidney Rigdon, were living on the John Johnson farm. Many of these revelations were given as a result of questions that came up in the minds of Joseph and Sidney as they continued the work of translating the Bible (known today as the JST, or the Joseph Smith Translation) in the Johnson home. Perhaps the most notable of these revelations is section 76 (the three degrees of glory and perdition), which was occasioned by working on John 5:29 as they were translating the New Testament.

One of the main messages in this section is that the kingdom of God is going forth as a result of the restoration of the gospel so that the kingdom of heaven can come.

We will see the term "kingdom of God" in verses 2, 5, and 6. The Prophet Joseph Smith explained his role in setting up the kingdom of God in the last days as follows:

"The ancient prophets declared that in the last days the God of heaven should set up a kingdom which should never be destroyed, nor left to other people [Daniel 2:44]; and the very time that was calculated on, this people were struggling to bring it out. . . .

"I calculate to be one of the instruments of setting up the kingdom of Daniel by the word of the Lord, and I intend to lay a foundation that will revolutionize the whole world. . . . It will not be by sword or gun that this kingdom will roll on: the power of truth is such that all nations will be under the necessity of obeying the Gospel" (*History of the Church*, 6:364–65).

Basically, the "kingdom of God" (verse 2) means the Church here on earth. The "kingdom of heaven" (verse 6) means Christ's millennial kingdom, which will be set up on earth when He comes again and which will be the ruling government for all nations and people during the thousand years.

Remember, the Prophet Joseph Smith said that this revelation came in the form of a prayer when it was given to him.

1 HEARKEN, and lo, a voice as of one sent down from on high, who is mighty and powerful, whose going forth is unto the ends of the earth, yea, whose voice is unto men—**Prepare ye the way of the Lord**, make his paths straight.

2 **The keys of the kingdom of God are committed unto man on the earth** [*by way of the restoration of the gospel, through Joseph Smith*], and from thence [*"thence," likely meaning the small beginnings*

in New York] shall the gospel roll forth unto the ends of the earth, as the stone which is cut out of the mountain without hands [*Daniel 2:34–35*] shall roll forth, until it has filled the whole earth.

3 **Yea, a voice crying—Prepare ye the way of the Lord, prepare ye the supper of the Lamb** [*the restored gospel is the "supper of the Lamb" to be offered to all people; see the parable in Matthew 22:1–14*], **make ready for the Bridegroom** [*prepare for the coming of Christ who is the "Bridegroom"*].

Verse 4, next, in this prayer, contains a request for all of us to preach the gospel.

4 **Pray unto the Lord, call upon his holy name, make known his wonderful works among the people.**

In verse 5, next, we see, through this prayer, that the gospel is to be restored and offered to all people upon the earth in preparation for the coming of the Lord, at which time the Savior will come in full glory.

5 **Call upon the Lord, that his kingdom may go forth upon the earth, that the inhabitants thereof may receive it, and be prepared for the days to come, in the which the Son of Man**

[*Christ, "Son of Man of Holiness" (Heavenly Father); see Moses 6:57*] **shall come** down in heaven, **clothed in the brightness of his glory, to meet the kingdom of God** [*the Church*] **which is set up on the earth**.

6 Wherefore [*the prayer continues*], **may the kingdom of God** [*the Church*] **go forth, that the kingdom of heaven may come**, that thou, O God, mayest be glorified in heaven so on earth, that thine enemies may be subdued; for thine is the honor, power and glory, forever and ever. Amen.

In conclusion, we will include a quote from Elder James E. Talmage of the Quorum of the Twelve in which he explained the terms "kingdom of God" and "kingdom of heaven." He said:

"The expression 'Kingdom of God' is used synonymously with the term 'Church of Christ'; but the Lord had made plain that He sometimes used the term 'Kingdom of Heaven' in a distinctive sense. In 1832 He called attention to that in these words, addressing Himself to the elders of the Church [D&C 65:1–6]:

"As Christ gave power to bear off the kingdom in his day, so has he given the same power in this day.

"Such was the prayer, such is the prayer, prescribed for this people to pray, not to utter in words only, not to say only, but to pray—that the Kingdom of God may roll forth in the earth to prepare the earth for the coming of the Kingdom of Heaven. That provision in the Lord's prayer, 'Thy kingdom come, thy will be done on earth as it is in heaven' has not been abrogated [*annulled, done away with*]. We are praying for the Kingdom of Heaven to come, and are endeavoring to prepare the earth for its coming. The Kingdom of God, already set up upon the earth, does not aspire to temporal domination among the nations. It seeks not to overthrow any existing forms of government; it does not profess to exercise control in matters that pertain to the governments of the earth, except by teaching correct principles and trying to get men to live according to the principles of true government, before the Kingdom of Heaven shall come and be established upon the earth with a King at the head. But when He comes, He shall rule and reign, for it is His right" (In Conference Report, April 1916, 128–29).

SECTION 66

Background

The 2013 edition of the Doctrine and Covenants heading for this section is another example of the great value of the research being done for the Joseph Smith Papers Project. If you have a prior edition, the heading for this section is:

"Revelation given through Joseph Smith the Prophet, at Orange, Ohio, October 25, 1831. HC 1:219–221. This was the first day of an important conference. In prefacing this revelation, the Prophet wrote: 'At the request of William E. McLellin, I inquired of the Lord, and received the following.'"

The heading in the 2013 edition reflects additional research.

Revelation given through Joseph Smith the Prophet, at Hiram, Ohio, October 29, 1831. William E. McLellin had petitioned the Lord in secret to make known through the Prophet the answer to five questions, which were unknown to Joseph Smith. At McLellin's request, the Prophet inquired of the Lord and received this revelation.

Brother McLellin was slightly less than a month younger than Joseph Smith (having been born on January 18, 1806). He was a widower and had been a school teacher in Paris, Tennessee. He had heard the gospel preached by Harvey Whitlock and David Whitmer, had traveled to Independence, Missouri, to see Joseph Smith but missed him, and had subsequently joined the Church, being baptized in Jackson County, Missouri, by Hyrum Smith on August 20, 1831. He was ordained an elder on August 24, 1831, and then left the next day for Tennessee, traveling with Hyrum Smith on a missionary journey. William preached his first sermon as an elder in the Church on August 28. After spending some time in Tennessee, he left for Kirtland, Ohio, with Hyrum Smith and finally met the Prophet Joseph Smith in October 1831.

After becoming acquainted with the Prophet, William E. McLellin asked him to inquire of the Lord for him (which resulted in section 66). William had approached the Lord previously in secret prayer and specifically asked Him to answer five questions for him through Joseph Smith. He shared this information with no one, but after the revelation of the Lord through Joseph, Brother McLellin wrote, "I now testify in the fear of God, that every question which I had thus lodged in the ears of the Lord of Sabbath, were answered to my full and entire satisfaction" (William E. McLellin, in Susan Easton Black's *Who's Who in the Doctrine & Covenants*, 191).

As we proceed with our study of this brief section, we will see that William E. McLellin has many good attributes and much potential but also that he has some weaknesses about which the Lord warns him.

He will be called as a member of the Quorum of the Twelve Apostles in 1835, but, sadly, he will go into apostasy and will be excommunicated in 1838.

The Joseph Smith Papers Project gives us some additional information about William. We will quote from the 2018 *Doctrine and Covenants Student Manual*:

"William served the Lord faithfully for a time, and in 1835 he was called to serve as a member of the Quorum of the Twelve Apostles. Sadly, William did not heed the Lord's counsel to continue faithful to the end and later apostatized and turned against the Prophet Joseph Smith. When he was excommunicated from the Church in May 1838, he admitted that he had 'quit praying, and keeping the commandments, and indulged himself in his lustful desires' (Joseph Smith, in *Manuscript History of the Church*, vol. B-1, page 796, josephsmithpapers.org."

1 BEHOLD, thus saith the Lord unto my servant William E. McLellin—**Blessed are you, inasmuch as you have** [*because you have*] **turned away from your iniquities** [*sins*], **and have received my truths**, saith the Lord your Redeemer, the Savior of the world, even of as many as believe on my name.

In verse 2, next, the Savior bears His personal testimony to Brother McLellin as to the truthfulness of the restored gospel.

2 Verily I say unto you, **blessed are you for receiving mine everlasting covenant** [*for being baptized and confirmed*], even **the fulness of my gospel, sent forth unto the children of men** [*inhabitants of the earth*], that they might have life [*eternal life, exaltation*] and be made partakers of the glories which are to be revealed in the last days, as it was written [*prophesied*] by the prophets and Apostles in days of old.

Next, the Master reminds William McLellin that he needs to improve. It is a much-needed blessing to have our faults pointed out, but, as you probably know, it takes a humble person to accept such correction. Brother McLellin will have difficulty accepting it.

3 Verily I say unto you, my servant William, that **you are clean, but not all; repent, therefore, of those things which are not pleasing in my sight**, saith the Lord, for **the Lord will show them unto you** [*so he can repent—a great kindness from God*].

4 And **now, verily, I, the Lord, will show unto you what I will concerning you**, or what is my will concerning you.

The Lord now asks William to do missionary work and gives specific instructions.

5 Behold, verily I say unto you, that **it is my will that you should proclaim my gospel from land to land, and from city to city**, yea, in those regions round about where it has not been proclaimed [*in areas where no one has yet formally preached the gospel*].

6 **Tarry not many days** [*don't stay long*] **in this place** [*the Kirtland area*]; **go not up unto the land of Zion** [*Missouri*] **as yet; but inasmuch as you can send** [*money*], **send; otherwise, think not of thy property**.

7 **Go unto the eastern lands**, bear testimony in every place, unto every people and in their synagogues, reasoning with the people.

8 **Let my servant Samuel H. Smith** [*Joseph Smith's younger brother*] **go with you**, and forsake him not, and give him thine instructions; and he that is faithful shall be made strong in every place; and **I, the Lord, will go with you**.

William did go to "the eastern lands" (verse 7) and preached in Pennsylvania, but his mission was cut short because of disobedience and sickness.

In verse 9, next, William is told by the Lord that he will be privileged to have the gift of healing (one of the gifts of the Spirit mentioned in D&C 46:20), and in verses 9–10, he is counseled in things that he particularly needs, including patience. He is specifically told to avoid adultery.

9 **Lay your hands upon the sick, and they shall recover**. Return not till I, the Lord, shall send you. **Be patient** in affliction. **Ask**, and ye shall receive; knock, and it shall be opened unto you.

10 **Seek not to be cumbered** [*possibly meaning to avoid distractions that would take him away from his missionary work*], **forsake all unrighteousness. Commit not adultery—a temptation with which thou hast been troubled**.

11 **Keep these sayings**, for they are true and faithful [*play close attention to what the Lord has said, and be obedient, because it deals with exact and specific issues for William*]; **and thou shalt magnify thine office, and push many people to Zion** [*a reference to Deuteronomy 33:13–17, in which Joseph's (Joseph, who was sold into Egypt) posterity is blessed to lead the gathering of Israel in the last days*] with songs of everlasting joy upon their heads.

12 **Continue in these things even unto the end, and you shall have**

a crown of eternal life [*symbolism meaning exaltation*] at the right hand [*the covenant hand, symbolic of receiving promised blessings from God through personal worthiness*] of my Father, who is full of grace and truth [*is full of help and truth*].

13 Verily, thus saith the Lord your God, your Redeemer, even Jesus Christ. Amen.

SECTION 67

Background

This revelation was given at Hiram, Ohio, in November 1831 through the Prophet Joseph Smith. The Prophet had called a special conference, held at the John Johnson home, during which the top priority business was preparing sixty-five revelations for publication in what was to be known as the "Book of Commandments." The plan was to print ten thousand copies (later reduced to 3,000) of this book of scripture in Missouri, on a printing press set up by William W. Phelps and Oliver Cowdery, as commanded by the Lord in D&C 57:11–14. The Book of Commandments was the predecessor to what we now know as the Doctrine and Covenants.

During the first day of this conference, on November 1, 1831, the Lord gave His own "preface" (see D&C 1:6) to the Book of Commandments. It is now section 1 of the Doctrine and Covenants.

During the conference, there was some criticism by William E. McLellin (and apparently others; see verse 5) of the wording in the revelations. As you will see, in section 67, verses 5–8, the Lord invited anyone who cared to challenge the wording of the revelations given through Joseph Smith to choose the least significant revelation from the Book of Commandments and try to come up with a better one. William E. McLellin volunteered to take up the challenge. Of him, Joseph Smith wrote (**bold** added for emphasis):

"After the foregoing was received [section 67], **William E. M'Lellin**, as the wisest man, in his own estimation, **having more learning than sense**, endeavored to write a commandment like unto one of the least of the Lord's, but failed; it was an awful responsibility to write in the name of the Lord. The Elders and all present that witnessed this vain attempt of a man to imitate the language of Jesus Christ, renewed their faith in the fulness of the Gospel, and in the truth of the commandments and revelations which the Lord had given to the Church through my instrumentality" (*History of the Church*, 1:226; see also in *Manuscript History of the Church*, vol. A-1, page 162, josephsmithpapers.org).

We will proceed now with section 67. First, in verses 1–2, the Savior assures these elders that their prayers have been heard, that He knows them personally, and that He has power to bless them.

1 BEHOLD and hearken, O ye elders of my church, who have assembled yourselves together [*for the conference that began on November 1, 1831*], **whose prayers I have heard**, and whose **hearts I know**, and whose **desires have come up before me**.

2 Behold and lo, **mine eyes are upon you**, and the heavens and the earth are in mine hands, and **the riches of eternity** [*including exaltation*] **are mine to give**.

We do not know what the blessing was that is referred to in verse 3, next. But there is a lesson for us in it; namely, that fear can stand in the way of receiving desired blessings.

3 Ye endeavored to believe that ye should receive the blessing which was offered unto you; but behold, verily I say unto you **there were fears in your hearts**, and verily **this is the reason that ye did not receive**.

Next, beginning with verse 4, the Lord offers a tangible testimony that the revelations given through Joseph Smith are from Him. The

testimony is a simple one. No man can duplicate the revelations that come from God. Man-made attempts are hollow and empty. They may have words, but they do not have the Spirit.

4 And now **I, the Lord, give unto you a testimony of the truth of these commandments** [*the sixty-five revelations given through the Prophet Joseph Smith, which were to make up the Book of Commandments*] which are lying before you [*which the Prophet and others were preparing for publication*].

5 **Your eyes have been upon my servant Joseph Smith, Jun.**, and **his language you have known**, and **his imperfections you have known**; and you have sought in your hearts knowledge that you might express beyond his language [*you think you can do a better job of writing than he has done*]; this you also know.

Next, in verses 6–8, comes the challenge from the Lord to the Prophet's critics among this group of elders.

6 Now, **seek ye out of the Book of Commandments** [*the sixty-five revelations about to be published*], even **the least that is among them**, and **appoint him that is the most wise among you**;

7 Or, **if there be any among you that shall make one like unto it, then ye are justified in saying that ye do not know that they are true;**

8 **But if ye cannot make one like unto it, ye are under condemnation if ye do not bear record that they are true.**

9 For **ye know that there is no unrighteousness in them**, and that which is righteous cometh down from above, from the Father of lights [*the Father; the source of light; the same expression is used in the Bible in James 1:17*].

10 And again, verily I say unto you that it is your privilege, and a promise I give unto you that have been ordained unto this ministry, that **inasmuch as you strip yourselves from jealousies and fears, and humble yourselves before me, for ye are not sufficiently humble**, the veil shall be rent and **you shall see me and know that I am**—not **with the carnal neither natural mind, but with the spiritual.**

There is more than one scriptural meaning for the phrase to "see [God]." This is explained in the last part of verse 10, above, combined with verses 11–14, next.

Of course, it is possible to literally see God, as was the case with

Joseph Smith. Some have seen the Father and many have seen the Savior literally. In order to have this experience, a person must be "quickened" (verse 11) by the Holy Ghost. Otherwise, their mortal bodies would not survive the occasion (verse 12; compare with Moses 1:11).

All can "see" the Savior in the sense spoken of in verse 10, above. Through the power of the Holy Ghost, we can know that Jesus is the Christ and "see" the reality of His existence. We can "see" His tenderness, mercy, kindness, and charity for us. We can feel His love and understand His gospel. All this and more is "seeing" the Savior with our "spiritual" mind (end of verse 10).

We will **bold** what we have said in the above notes as taught in the next verses.

11 For **no man has seen God at any time in the flesh** [*literally*], **except quickened by the Spirit of God.**

12 **Neither can any natural man** [*unprepared mortal*] **abide** [*survive*] **the presence of God**, neither after the carnal mind [*the spiritually unprepared mind*].

Next, the Savior tells the men to whom this revelation specifically applies that they are not yet prepared to literally see angels, let alone the Savior.

13 **Ye** [*some of the men in the room with Joseph Smith*] **are not able to abide the presence of God now, neither the ministering of angels**; wherefore, **continue in patience** until ye are perfected.

14 **Let not your minds turn back** [*don't give up hope*]; and **when ye are worthy, in mine own due time** [*when the timing is right according to the wisdom of the Lord*], **ye shall see and know** that which was conferred upon you by the hands of my servant Joseph Smith, Jun. Amen.

Two more notes before we leave section 67.

First, Elder Orson F. Whitney spoke of the Lord's challenge, given in section 67, to write a revelation. He said:

"Well, one of them, who thought himself the wisest, and who possessed some learning, took up the challenge and actually attempted to frame a revelation; but it was a flat failure. He could utter, of course, certain words, and roll out a mass of rhetoric; but the divine spirit was lacking, and he had to acknowledge himself beaten.

"It is not so easy to put the spirit of life into things. Man can make the body, but God alone can create the spirit" (In Conference Report, April 1917, 42).

Second, William E. McLellin (by the way, we find several different spellings of his name in historical documents) served a mission with Parley P. Pratt in the winter of 1832. He became a member of the high council in Clay County, Missouri, in 1834. On February 15, 1835, he was called to be a member of the Quorum of the Twelve Apostles.

In 1835 he wrote a letter criticizing the First Presidency, and he left the Church in August 1836. In 1838 he was excommunicated, after which he joined in mobbing and robbing the Saints in Missouri and in driving them from the state. Entries and notes found in the *History of the Church*, 3:215, tell of McLellin's activities while the Prophet and others were held in jails in Missouri. We will quote two of these here. One is an entry by the Prophet. The second is a footnote.

"During our trial William E. McLellin, accompanied by Burr Riggs and others, at times were busy in plundering and robbing the houses of Sidney Rigdon, George Morey, the widow Phebe Ann Patten, and others, under pretense or color of law, on an order from General Clark, as testified to by the members of the different families robbed" (*History of the Church*, 3:215).

"While the brethren were imprisoned at Richmond it is said that 'McLellin, who was a large and active man, went to the sheriff and asked for the privilege of flogging the Prophet. Permission was granted on condition that Joseph would fight. The sheriff made known to Joseph McLellin's earnest request, to which Joseph consented, if his irons were taken off. McLellin then refused to fight unless he could have a club, to which Joseph was perfectly willing; but the sheriff would not allow them to fight on such unequal terms. McLellin was a man of superficial education, though he had a good flow of language. He adopted the profession of medicine.'—Mill. Star, 36:808, 809" (*History of the Church*, 3:215, footnote).

William E. McLellin eventually moved to Illinois and then on to Kirtland, Ohio, where, in early 1847, he Joined with Martin Harris, who was organizing a new church called the Church of Christ. William soon visited David Whitmer in Richmond, Missouri, encouraging him to be the prophet of this new church. The church apparently died out by the end of 1849.

On June 5, 1869, McLellin joined the Hedrickites, an apostate church set up by Granville Hedrick after the martyrdom of the Prophet Joseph Smith. He left that church by November 1869. His wife joined the Reorganized Church of Jesus Christ of Latter Day Saints (note that it is "Latter Day Saints" rather than "Latter-day Saints," as is the spelling for our church)

and they moved to Independence, Missouri, in 1870. William E. McLellin died on April 24, 1883, at age seventy-seven. Despite his opposition to the First Presidency and his bitterness toward the Church, he bore witness to his dying day of the truthfulness of the Book of Mormon.

SECTION 68

Background

This revelation was given through the Prophet Joseph Smith in Hiram, Ohio, on November 1, 1831. It was given at the request of Orson Hyde, Luke S. Johnson, Lyman E. Johnson, and William E. McLellin. Perhaps you've noticed that several revelations were given in Hiram. If you turn to the front of your Doctrine and Covenants to the "Chronological Order of Contents" and count the revelations given in Hiram (at the John and Elsa Johnson home), you will count sixteen!

Among many doctrines in section 68, perhaps the most widely known and often-quoted are the instructions to teach children to understand repentance, faith, baptism, the gift of the Holy Ghost (verse 25), and the doctrine that children may be baptized at age eight (verse 25).

The Prophet Joseph Smith gave a brief background to this section. He said:

"As the following Elders—Orson Hyde, Luke Johnson, Lyman E. Johnson, and William E. M'Lellin—were desirous to know the mind of the Lord concerning themselves, I inquired, and received the following [section 68]: (*History of the* Church, 1:227).

First, in verse 1, next, Orson Hyde is told that he is to teach the gospel "from people to people, and from land to land." This was literally fulfilled, including his dedicating the Holy Land for the gathering of the Jews.

1 MY servant, **Orson Hyde, was called by his ordination to proclaim the everlasting gospel, by the Spirit of the living God, from people to people, and from land to land**, in the congregations of the wicked [*a phrase often used to mean people who don't have the gospel*], in their synagogues, reasoning with and expounding [*explaining*] all scriptures unto them.

A quote from the *Doctrine and Covenants Student Manual*, 1981, pages 143–44, gives additional detail about the travels of Orson Hyde, as prophesied in verse 1, above.

"The prophecy in this verse was literally fulfilled. Orson Hyde proclaimed the gospel 'from people to people, from land to land.' In 1832, he and Samuel H. Smith traveled in the States of New York, Massachusetts, Maine, and Rhode Island—two thousand miles—on foot. In 1835 he was ordained an Apostle, and in 1837 he went on a mission to England. In 1840 he was sent on a mission to Jerusalem. He crossed the Ocean, traveled through England and Germany, visited Constantinople, Cairo, and Alexandria, and, finally, reached the Holy City. On October 24th, 1841, he went up on the Mount of Olives and offered a prayer, dedicating Palestine for the gathering of the Jews. (Smith and Sjodahl, *Commentary*, 409.)"

Next, the Savior gives instructions to missionaries as they go forth.

2 And, behold, and lo, **this is an ensample** [*example*] **unto all those** who were ordained unto this priesthood, **whose mission is appointed unto them to go forth—**

3 And this is the ensample unto them, that **they shall speak as they are moved upon by the Holy Ghost** [*teach according to the promptings of the Spirit*].

Next, in verses 4–5, the Lord explains the significance of teaching by the Spirit.

4 And **whatsoever they shall speak when moved upon by the Holy Ghost shall be scripture**, shall be **the will of the Lord**, shall be **the mind of the Lord**, shall be

the word of the Lord, shall be **the voice of the Lord**, and **the power of God unto salvation** [*will lead those who listen and obey to salvation in celestial glory*].

Verse 4, above, is a good example of a verse of scripture that must be interpreted in context. The word "scripture" is defined concisely as that which is being taught by the missionary and which, when followed, will lead to salvation.

Often in our gospel conversations, the term "scripture" is used to mean the word of the Lord to the whole Church, in fact, to the entire world. If this definition is applied to the word "scripture" in verse 4, then the phrase "whatsoever they shall speak" must be limited to the living prophets, seers, and revelators, and more specifically, to **the** prophet (the President of the Church). Elder Harold B. Lee addressed this issue. He said:

"It is not to be thought that every word spoken by the General Authorities is inspired, or that they are moved upon by the Holy Ghost in everything they read and write. Now you keep that in mind. I don't care what his position is, if he writes something or speaks something that goes beyond anything that you can find in the standard church works [the scriptures], unless that one be the prophet, seer, and revelator—please note that one exception—you may immediately say, 'Well, that is his own

idea.' And if he says something that contradicts what is found in the standard church works (I think that is why we call them 'standard'—it is the standard measure of all that men teach), you may know by that same token that it is false, regardless of the position of the man who says it" ("The Place of the Living Prophet, Seer, and Revelator" address delivered to seminary and institute of religion faculty, July 8 1964, 14; quoted in *Doctrine and Covenants Student Manual*, 1981, 144).

Joseph Fielding Smith also spoke on this matter. He said:

"When one of the brethren stands before a congregation of the people today, and the inspiration of the Lord is upon him, he speaks that which the Lord would have him speak. It is just as much scripture as anything you will find written in any of these records, and yet we call these the standard works of the Church. We depend, of course, upon the guidance of the brethren who are entitled to inspiration.

"There is only one man in the Church at a time who has the right to give revelation for the Church, and that is the President of the Church. But that does not bar any other member in this Church from speaking the word of the Lord, as indicated here in this revelation, section 68, but a revelation that is to be given as these revelations are given in this book, to the

Church, will come through the presiding officer of the Church; yet, the word of the Lord, as spoken by other servants at the general conferences and stake conferences, or wherever they may be when they speak that which the Lord has put into their mouths, is just as much the word of the Lord as the writings and the words of other prophets in other dispensations" (*Doctrines of Salvation*, 1:186).

5 Behold, **this is the promise of the Lord** unto you, O ye my servants.

Verses 6–12 can generally be read as advice and counsel to missionaries today.

6 Wherefore, **be of good cheer**, and **do not fear**, for **I the Lord am with you, and will stand by you**; and **ye shall bear record of me, even Jesus Christ, that I am the Son of the living God, that I was, that I am, and that I am to come.**

7 **This is the word of the Lord** unto you, my servant Orson Hyde, and also unto my servant Luke Johnson, and unto my servant Lyman Johnson, and unto my servant William E. McLellin, and **unto all the faithful elders of my church—**

8 **Go ye into all the world, preach the gospel to every creature,** **acting in the authority which I have given you, baptizing in the name of the Father, and of the Son, and of the Holy Ghost.**

9 And **he that believeth and is baptized shall be saved, and he that believeth not shall be damned** [*stopped in progression*].

10 And **he that believeth shall be blest with signs following, even as it is written** [*the scriptures contain many promises and blessings to those who are baptized and faithfully keep their covenants*].

11 And **unto you it shall be given to know the signs of the times, and the signs of the coming of the Son of Man** [*the Holy Ghost will teach missionaries many things, including how to understand and recognize the "signs of the times," which are prophecies that will be fulfilled in the last days, indicating that the Second Coming is getting close*];

12 And of as many as the Father shall bear record, to you shall be given power to seal them up unto eternal life [*those who accept baptism can then work faithfully toward the sealing ordinances available in temples*]. Amen.

The topic now changes, and verses 13–21 deal with the office of bishop, more particularly, with the calling of Presiding Bishop of the Church. It is helpful to know that at this time in the history of the Church, there was only one bishop and that was Bishop Edward Partridge, who had been called as bishop in February 1831 (see D&C 41:9).

First, in verse 14, the Lord explains that there will be other bishops called in the future, and He explains that they are to be worthy high priests, appointed by the First Presidency (verse 15). Perhaps you are aware in our day that before a bishop is called, the stake president receives a letter from the First Presidency, authorizing him to issue a call to a particular man, who has been approved by them to be called to serve as a bishop.

13 And now, concerning the items in addition to the covenants and commandments, they are these—

14 **There remain hereafter, in the due time of the Lord, other bishops to be set apart** unto the church, to minister even according to the first [*like Bishop Partridge did*];

15 Wherefore **they shall be high priests who are worthy**, and they shall be **appointed by the First Presidency** of the Melchizedek Priesthood, **except they be literal descendants of Aaron** [*Moses's older brother; see Exodus 7:7*].

16 And **if they be literal descendants of Aaron they have a legal right to the bishopric, if they are the firstborn among the sons of Aaron;**

17 For the firstborn holds the right of the presidency over this priesthood, and the keys or authority of the same.

18 No man has a legal right to this office [*Presiding Bishop of the Church*], to hold the keys of this priesthood, except he be a literal descendant and the firstborn of Aaron.

Elder Joseph Fielding Smith explained the phrase "except they be literal descendants of Aaron" in verse 15, above. He pointed out that this applies only to the office of Presiding Bishop of the Church. Furthermore, such a literal descendant of Aaron would have to be worthy and be called by the First Presidency. He could not simply walk into Church headquarters and announce that he is here and ready to begin serving as Presiding Bishop. Elder Smith taught:

"It has no reference whatever to bishops of wards. Further, such a one must be designated by the First Presidency of the Church and receive his anointing and ordination under their hands. The revelation comes from the Presidency, not from the patriarch, to establish a claim to the right to preside in this office. In the absence of knowledge concerning such a descendant, any high priest, chosen by the Presidency, may hold the office of Presiding Bishop and serve with counselors" (*Doctrines of Salvation*, 3:92–93).

"The office of Presiding Bishop of the Church is the same as the office which was held by Aaron. . . . It was this office which came to John the Baptist, and it was by virtue of the fact that he held the keys of this power and ministry that he was sent to Joseph Smith and Oliver Cowdery to restore that Priesthood, May 15, 1829. The person who has the legal right to this presiding office has not been discovered; perhaps is not in the Church, but should it be shown by revelation that there is one who is the 'firstborn among the sons of Aaron,' and thus entitled by birthright to this presidency, he could 'claim' his 'anointing' and the right to that office in the Church" (*Church History and Modern Revelation*, 1:259).

19 But, **as a high priest of the Melchizedek Priesthood has authority to officiate in all the lesser offices he may officiate in the office of bishop when no literal descendant of Aaron can be found, provided he is called and set apart and ordained unto this power, under the hands of the First Presidency** of the Melchizedek Priesthood.

20 And a literal descendant of Aaron, also, **must be designated by this Presidency**, and **found worthy**, and anointed, and **ordained under the hands of this Presidency, otherwise they are not legally authorized to officiate in their priesthood**.

These instructions (verses 15–21) regarding a literal descendant of Aaron and the office of Presiding Bishop may well be a matter that will come into play sometime in the future, and if and when it does, we will probably exclaim, "Oh, that is what it meant!"

21 But, by virtue of the decree concerning their right of the priesthood descending from father to son, **they may claim their anointing if at any time they can prove their lineage, or do ascertain it by revelation from the Lord under the hands of the above named Presidency**.

Verses 22–24, next, explain that the Presiding Bishop of the Church, should occasion demand, could not be tried for his membership in the Church, except by the First Presidency.

22 And again, **no bishop** [*Presiding Bishop*] or high priest who shall be set apart for this ministry [*who is called to serve as Presiding Bishop*] **shall be tried or condemned for any crime**

[*meaning worthiness issues, not civil law issues; see D&C 42:79, 84, 85, 86, 87*], **save it be before the First Presidency of the church**;

23 And inasmuch as he is found guilty before this Presidency, by testimony that cannot be impeached [*by evidence that cannot be refuted*], he shall be condemned;

24 And **if he repent he shall be forgiven**, according to the covenants and commandments of the church.

In verses 25–28, the topic now turns to the responsibility that parents in the Church have to teach their children to understand the basic commandments, ordinances, and principles of the gospel by the time they are eight years old.

As a bishop, one of my most pleasant duties was that of interviewing children for baptism. Time and time again, I was impressed (and sometimes almost startled) by the knowledge and depth of understanding of these young candidates for baptism. They were living proof that young children can indeed be taught by age eight as instructed by the Lord in these next verses.

25 And again, **inasmuch as parents have children in Zion**, or in any of her stakes which are organized, **that teach them not to understand the doctrine of repentance, faith in Christ the Son of the living God, and of baptism and the gift of the Holy Ghost by the laying on of the hands, when eight years old, the sin be upon the heads of the parents.**

As you will see, additional instructions for parents to teach their children are included in verse 28.

Before moving on, we will pause for a moment and consider the phrase "the sin be upon the heads of the parents" at the end of verse 25, above. Note that in this context the word "sin" is singular and not plural. Therefore, we understand it to be saying, in effect, "the sin of not teaching the gospel to their children." Otherwise, an unfortunate false doctrine arises that states that parents are responsible for all sins committed by their children if they did not teach them the gospel. President Spencer W. Kimball said:

"I have sometimes seen children of good families rebel, resist, stray, sin, and even actually fight God. In this they bring sorrow to their parents, who have done their best to set in movement a current and to teach and live as examples. But I have repeatedly seen many of these same children, after years of wandering, mellow, realize what they have been missing, repent, and make great contribution to the spiritual life of their community. The reason I believe this can take place is that, despite all the adverse winds to which these people have been subjected, they have been influenced still more, and much more than they realized, by the current of life in the homes in which they were reared. When, in later years, they feel a longing to recreate in their own families the same atmosphere they enjoyed as children, they are likely to turn to the faith that gave meaning to their parents' lives.

"There is no guarantee, of course, that righteous parents will succeed always in holding their children, and certainly they may lose them if they do not do all in their power. The children have their free agency.

"But if we as parents fail to influence our families and set them on the 'strait and narrow way,' then certainly the waves, the winds of temptation and evil will carry the posterity away from the path.

"'Train up a child in the way he should go; and when he is old, he will not depart from it.' (Prov. 22:6.) What we do know is that righteous parents who strive to develop wholesome influences for their children will be held blameless at the last day, and that they will succeed in saving most of their children, if not all" ("Ocean Currents and Family Influences," *Ensign*, November 1974, 111–12).

Brigham Young taught:

"If Brother Brigham shall take a wrong track, and be shut out of the Kingdom of heaven, no person will be to blame but Brother Brigham. I am the only being in heaven, earth, or hell, that can be blamed.

"This will equally apply to every Latter-day Saint. Salvation is an individual operation. I am the only person that can possibly save myself. When salvation is sent to me, I can reject or receive it. In receiving it, I yield implicit obedience and submission to its great Author throughout my life, and to those whom he shall appoint to instruct me; in rejecting it, I follow the dictates of my own will in preference to the will of my Creator" (*Discourses of Brigham Young*, 390).

26 For **this shall be a law unto the inhabitants of Zion, or in any of her stakes** which are organized.

In verse 27, next, the Lord specifically repeats what He said in verse 25, above, regarding the age for baptism and confirmation for young children.

27 And **their children shall be baptized for the remission of their sins when eight years old**, and receive the laying on of the hands [*be confirmed*].

In verse 28, the Savior adds additional items for parents to teach children.

28 And **they shall also teach their children to pray, and to walk uprightly before the Lord**.

In verses 29–31, the emphasis seems to be, among other things, on the importance of parents teaching by example and avoiding being lazy.

29 And the inhabitants of Zion shall also **observe the Sabbath day to keep it holy**.

30 And the inhabitants of Zion also shall remember their labors, inasmuch as they are appointed to **labor, in all faithfulness; for the idler shall be had in remembrance** [will be brought to judgment] **before the Lord**.

31 Now, I, the Lord, am not well pleased with the inhabitants of Zion, for **there are idlers among them**; and **their children are also growing up in wickedness; they also seek not earnestly the riches of eternity, but their eyes are full of greediness**.

32 **These things ought not to be**, and must be done away from among them; wherefore, let my servant Oliver Cowdery carry these sayings [the manuscript for the Book of Commandments; see D&C 69 section heading as well as 69:1] unto the land of Zion [Jackson County, Missouri].

33 And a commandment I give unto them—that **he that observeth not his prayers** before the Lord in the season thereof, let him be had in remembrance before the judge of my people.

34 **These sayings are true and faithful; wherefore, transgress them not, neither take therefrom** [don't minimize their importance nor water them down].

35 Behold, I am Alpha and Omega, and I come quickly. Amen.

SECTION 69

Background

This revelation was given in Hiram, Ohio, on November 11, 1831, through the Prophet Joseph Smith.

As stated in the background to section 67 in this study guide, sixty-five revelations had been approved (at a special conference held November 1, 1831, at Hiram) to be published as the Book of Commandments (the predecessor to the Doctrine and Covenants). The manuscript containing copies of these revelations was to be carried to Zion, in Jackson County, Missouri, by Oliver Cowdery. In addition, money that had been collected in the Kirtland area was also to be carried by Oliver to Missouri for the building up of the Church in Zion.

Since much of the journey to Zion would take Oliver through dangerous frontier territory, the Lord called John Whitmer to accompany him. This we see in verses 1–2, next. The remainder of the section, verses 3–8, deals primarily with John Whitmer's duties as Church historian. You may wish to read the background notes in this study guide for section 47, where you will see more detail about John Whitmer as historian for the Church.

1 HEARKEN unto me, saith the Lord your God, for my servant Oliver Cowdery's sake. It is not wisdom in me that he should be entrusted with [*have full responsibility for the safety of*] the commandments [*the manuscript for the Book of Commandments*] and the moneys which he shall carry unto the land of Zion, except one go with him who will be true and faithful [*like Oliver*].

2 Wherefore, I, the Lord, will that my servant, **John Whitmer, should go with my servant Oliver Cowdery;**

John Whitmer did accompany Oliver Cowdery as instructed. They started for Missouri on November 20, 1831, and arrived in Independence on January 5, 1832, after a long and difficult journey in winter cold.

B. H. Roberts gave additional

background for verses 1–2, above. He said:

"The fact was that much of the journey between Kirtland and Independence, or Zion, was through a sparsely settled country, the western portion of it through a frontier country where there is always a gathering, more or less, of lawless people; and it was at considerable risk that a person traveled through such a country, especially when alone and carrying money with him. It was wisdom then, for the sake of Oliver Cowdery, and to insure the safety of the money and the sacred things he was to carry with him, that one should go with him that would be a true and faithful companion, hence the appointment of John Whitmer" (*Comprehensive History*, 1:268n).

As mentioned above, in the background to this section, verses 3–8 contain instructions to John Whitmer, who was called by the Lord on March 8, 1831, to replace Oliver Cowdery as the Church Historian (D&C 47:1, 3–4). John Whitmer was one of the Eight Witnesses to the Book of Mormon and was an older brother to David Whitmer (one of the Three Witnesses).

3 And also that **he** [*John Whitmer*] **shall continue in writing and making a history** [*of the Church*] of all the important things which he shall observe and know concerning my church;

4 And **also that he receive counsel and assistance from my servant Oliver Cowdery and others.**

As you can see, in verse 5, next, missionaries scattered abroad were to send accounts and histories to Zion, where John Whitmer could use them in preserving and recording the history of the growing restored Church.

5 And also, **my servants who are abroad in the earth should send forth the accounts of their stewardships to the land of Zion;**

6 For **the land of Zion shall be a seat** [*headquarters*] and a place **to receive and do all these things** [*for the keeping of this history*].

Next, the Lord instructs John to do much traveling from place to place in the Church in order to gather and record details to be used in writing the history of the Church.

7 Nevertheless, **let my servant John Whitmer travel many times from place to place, and from church to church** [*from branch to branch*], that he may the more easily obtain knowledge [*for the history*]—

8 **Preaching** and **expounding** [*explaining*], **writing, copying, selecting, and obtaining all things which shall be for the**

good of the church, and **for the rising generations** [*the major purpose of keeping a history*] that shall grow up on the land of Zion, to possess it from generation to generation, forever and ever. Amen.

SECTION 70

Background

This revelation was given through the Prophet Joseph Smith at Kirtland, Ohio, on November 12, 1831.

Section 70 would be particularly difficult to understand without a knowledge of the background and setting. You will see this as we study it verse by verse.

As you know from the background notes to sections 67 and 69, the Book of Commandments (the first publication of revelations through Joseph Smith) was to be printed in Missouri. The printing press was set up in Independence by W. W. Phelps. Oliver Cowdery and John Whitmer were to take the manuscript for the Book of Commandments, along with money collected to help build Zion, to Independence. The plan was to print ten thousand copies. The number was later reduced to three thousand. The Book of Commandments contained sixty-five revelations, plus the Lord's "preface" (now section 1) and an appendix (now section 133).

As we study, you will see many attributes and character qualities required of those who desire to obtain celestial glory. These are the same qualities as are required of those who live the law of consecration.

First, though, in verses 1–4, the Lord names those men who are serving on what we could call "the scripture publication committee." He reminds them of their responsibility and stewardship.

1 BEHOLD, and **hearken** [*defined in the 1828 Noah Webster Dictionary (American Dictionary of the English Language) as "to give heed to what is uttered; to observe or obey"*], O ye inhabitants of Zion, and **all ye people of my church who are afar off, and hear the word of the Lord** [*in this context, the Book of Commandments*] which I give unto my servant **Joseph Smith, Jun.**, and also unto my servant **Martin Harris**, and also unto my servant **Oliver Cowdery**, and also unto my servant **John Whitmer**, and also unto my servant **Sidney Rigdon**, and also unto my servant **William W. Phelps**, by the way of commandment unto them.

2 For **I give unto them a commandment**; wherefore hearken and hear, for thus saith the Lord unto them—

3 **I, the Lord, have appointed them, and ordained them to be stewards over the revelations and commandments** which I have given unto them, and which I shall hereafter give unto them [*continuing revelation*];

4 And **an account of this stewardship will I require of them in the day of judgment**.

The main topic of verses 5–7, next, is what to do with the money that will come from sales of copies of the Book of Commandments.

5 Wherefore, I have appointed unto them, and **this is their business** in the church of God, **to manage them** and the concerns thereof, yea, **the benefits** [*proceeds from sales*] thereof.

6 Wherefore, a commandment I give unto them, that **they shall not give these things** [*the proceeds from sales of the Book of Commandments*] **unto the church, neither unto the world**;

Verse 16 tells them that they are to use this money in caring for themselves and their families.

Beginning with verse 7, next, we are given insights to the high character and unselfishness required of those who live the law of consecration. If you have wondered if you could live celestial law, you may wish to pay close attention to what we **bold** in the next verses as well as to the notes we add.

You will see that it is up to them to decide what is surplus.

7 Nevertheless, **inasmuch as** [*if*] **they receive more than is needful for their necessities** and their **wants**, it shall be given into my storehouse [*the bishop's storehouse, to assist the poor and the needy*];

8 And **the benefits shall be consecrated unto the inhabitants of Zion**, and unto their generations, inasmuch as they become heirs according to the laws of the kingdom.

9 Behold, **this** [*deciding what to keep for your own use and what to consecrate to the Church to bless the lives of others*] **is what the Lord requires of every man in his stewardship** [*based on what he or she personally owns and earns*], even as I, the Lord, have appointed or shall hereafter appoint unto any man.

10 And behold, **none are exempt from this law** [*of having a celestial attitude*] **who belong to the church of the living God** [*the true, real God, as opposed to dead idols—inanimate objects that are commonly worshipped in many religions*];

11 Yea, **neither the bishop, neither the agent who keepeth the Lord's storehouse, neither he who is appointed in a stewardship over temporal things** [*"none are exempt" (verse 10) from these rules—in other words, everyone who desires to attain celestial glory must develop celestial attitudes, feelings, and behaviors, regardless of where or how he or she serves*].

Next, in verse 12, the Lord explains that as the Saints live the law of consecration, there will be some who are occupied full time in managing temporal and spiritual aspects of the Church, and thus they and their families will need to be supported out of the funds and supplies of the Church.

12 **He who is appointed to administer spiritual things**, the same **is worthy of his hire** [*is worthy of being supported by the funds of the Church*], even as those who are appointed to a stewardship to **administer in temporal things**;

13 Yea, even more abundantly, which abundance is multiplied unto them **through the manifestations of the Spirit** [*the funds of the Church are to be allocated as directed by the Holy Ghost*].

The importance of having a Christlike, celestial attitude is again emphasized in verse 14, next.

14 Nevertheless, **in your temporal things** [*physical needs*] **you shall be equal**, and this **not grudgingly**, otherwise the abundance of the manifestations of the Spirit shall be withheld.

Verses 15–18 seem to refer mainly to the men named in verse 1, who are involved full time in their responsibilities for the preparation and publication of the Book of Commandments, and, thus, cannot work to support and sustain their families. This revelation explains why they are to keep the proceeds from the sale of copies of the Book of Commandments.

15 Now, this commandment [*to keep the money from sales of the Book of Commandments*] I give unto my servants **for their benefit** while they remain [*while they are so heavily involved in this work*], **for a manifestation of my blessings** upon their heads, and **for a reward** of their diligence and **for their security**;

16 **For food** and for **raiment** [*clothing*]; for an **inheritance**; for **houses** and for **lands**, in whatsoever circumstances I, the Lord, shall place them [*in whatever full-time callings the Lord gives them*], and whithersoever I, the Lord, shall send them.

17 For **they have been faithful**

over many things, and have done well inasmuch as they have not sinned.

18 Behold, **I, the Lord, am merciful and will bless them**, and they shall enter into the joy of these things [*they will have great satisfaction for jobs well done*]. Even so. Amen.

Before we leave this section, we will take a moment, as we did in section 51, to remind you that living the law of consecration preserves individuality and personal identity. There is private ownership of property and respect for and encouragement of the development and use of individual talents and abilities. Unselfishness, generosity, concern for the welfare of others, and Christlike attitudes are essential. Otherwise, it won't work.

President J. Reuben Clark Jr., of the First Presidency, explained that the "equality" in the law of consecration is not flat equality without consideration of individual wants, desires, and needs. He said:

"There is continuous reference in the revelations to equality among the brethren, but I think you will find only one place where that equality is really described, though it is referred to in other revelations. That revelation (D. & C. 51:3) affirms that every man is to be 'equal according to his family, according to his circumstances and his wants and needs.' (See also D. & C. 82:17; 78:5–6.) Obviously, this is not a case of 'dead level' equality. It is 'equality' that will vary as much as the man's circumstances, his family, his wants and needs, may vary" (In Conference Report, October 1942, 55).

SECTION 71

Background

This revelation was given to Joseph Smith and Sidney Rigdon, on December 1, 1831, while they were working on the translation of the Bible (the JST) at the John Johnson home in Hiram, Ohio.

In the background to section 64, we mentioned that a member of the Church by the name of Ezra Booth had apostatized from the Church and had written nine bitter and inflammatory anti-Mormon articles that had caused much sentiment against the Church in the Kirtland area. At the time of this revelation, Symonds Ryder, also an apostate and former member, had joined Ezra Booth in publicly attacking the Church.

As you know, we are generally counseled to ignore the efforts and writings of such people. Missionaries especially are so instructed. If we were to take our time and energy to rebut such attacks, it would take away from the time and energy we spend in serving others and fulfilling our responsibilities with our families, Church, employment, missionary work, and so forth. If we debated with every individual who desires to debate and confront us about the Church, there would be much more tension and animosity, and few would be able to hear the peaceful call of the Church to follow Christ.

Therefore, the instruction of the Lord to Joseph and Sidney in this revelation is unusual (verse 7). In fact, a friend of mine who was serving as a mission president at the time told me that a set of elders excitedly called him one day at his office and told them that they had just found a scripture that would allow them to debate the local minister in public. The minister had been causing much trouble for them as they attempted to do their missionary work in that area.

Curious and concerned, the president asked them to tell him what verse they were using. They pointed him to D&C 71:7. Luckily, my friend knew the background to this verse and counseled the elders that this was a special context-sensitive case, and it did not constitute a license for all missionaries to debate in public. Disappointed but understanding, the elders settled back and continued to follow the counsel in D&C 19:30 ("reviling not against revilers"), which does apply to the preaching of the gospel.

Going back to the background and setting for this section, because of the damage being done to the Church and individual members in Ohio, the Lord instructs Joseph and Sidney to go ahead and engage in public as well as private debate with these enemies of the gospel. They did, with much success, and in D&C 73:3, they will be told to go back to the work of translating the Bible.

1 BEHOLD, **thus saith the Lord unto you my servants Joseph Smith, Jun., and Sidney Rigdon, that the time has verily come** that it is necessary and expedient [*necessary*] in me **that you should open your mouths** in proclaiming my gospel, the things of the kingdom, expounding [*explaining*] the mysteries thereof out of the scriptures, according to that portion of Spirit and power which shall be given unto you, even as I will.

2 Verily I say unto you, **proclaim unto the world** [*to nonmembers*] **in the regions round about** [*in this part of Ohio*], and in the church [*among the members*] also, **for the space of a season** [*for a while*], even **until it shall be made known unto you** [*until the Lord asks them to stop*].

3 Verily **this is a mission for a season**, which I give unto you.

4 Wherefore, labor ye in my vineyard. **Call upon the inhabitants of the earth**, and bear record, and prepare the way for the commandments and revelations which are to come. [*In effect, the Lord is asking them to soften the attitudes and concerns held by nonmembers as a direct result of Ezra Booth's writings.*]

Verses 5–6, next, explain the importance of obedience.

5 Now, behold **this is wisdom**; whoso readeth, let him understand and receive also;

6 **For unto him that receiveth it shall be given more abundantly, even power.**

In verses 7–9, next, the Savior tells Joseph and Sidney that they will be blessed with success if they faithfully follow this counsel.

7 Wherefore, **confound your enemies; call upon them to meet you both in public and in private; and inasmuch as ye are faithful their shame shall be made manifest.**

8 Wherefore, **let them bring forth their strong reasons against the Lord.**

9 Verily, thus saith the Lord unto you—there is **no weapon that is formed against you shall prosper;**

Joseph Fielding Smith tells us what happened as Joseph and Sidney carried out the Lord's instructions at this time. He said:

"Quite generally the Lord counsels his servants not to engage in debates and arguments, but to preach in power the fundamental principles of the Gospel. This was a condition that required some action of this kind, and the Spirit of the Lord directed these brethren to go forth and confound their enemies, which they proceeded immediately to do, as their enemies were unable to substantiate their falsehoods and were surprised by this sudden challenge so boldly given. Much of the prejudice was allayed and some friends made through this action" (*Church History and Modern Revelation*, 1:269).

Next, in verse 10, we see that anyone who fights against the Lord's work will eventually be stopped, but that it will happen according to the wisdom and timing of the Lord.

10 And if any man lift his voice against you **he shall be confounded** [*stopped*] **in mine own due time.**

11 Wherefore, **keep my commandments; they are true and faithful** [*the commandments are, in effect, loyal and faithful "traveling companions," right on target, for us during our mortal sojourn, and will bring us safely home to God*]. Even so. Amen.

SECTION 72

Background

The heading to section 72 in the 2013 printing of the Doctrine and Covenants states that this section "is a compilation of three revelations received on the same day." They were given through the Prophet Joseph Smith in Kirtland, Ohio, on December 4, 1831. Verses 1–8 are the first revelation. Immediately after they were received, Newel K. Whitney was ordained a bishop. Then verses 9–23 were received, outlining the duties of a bishop, and verses 24–26 were given providing instructions for the gathering to Zion.

You will see that several practices of the Church today have their precedents in this section, such as requiring that a priesthood holder have a temple recommend or have a written recommendation from his bishop in order to perform an ordinance outside his own ward.

As background to the receiving of this revelation, Joseph Smith recorded that "several of the Elders and members assembled together to learn their duty, and for edification, and after some time had been spent in conversing about our temporal and spiritual welfare, I received the following: [D&C 72]" (*History of the Church*, 1:239).

The First Revelation Given This Day, Verses 1–8

1 HEARKEN, and **listen to the voice of the Lord**, O ye who have assembled yourselves together, who are the high priests of my church, to whom the kingdom and power have been given.

2 For verily thus saith the Lord, **it is expedient in me** [*it has become necessary*] **for a bishop to be appointed unto you**, or of you, unto the church in this part of the Lord's vineyard [*in the Kirtland, Ohio, area*].

3 And verily in this thing ye have done wisely, for **it is required of the Lord, at the hand of every steward, to render an account of his stewardship, both in time and in eternity**.

4 For **he who is faithful and wise in time is accounted worthy to inherit the mansions prepared for him of my Father**.

5 Verily I say unto you, **the elders of the church in this part of my vineyard** [*the Kirtland area*] **shall render an account of their stewardship unto the bishop, who shall be appointed of me** in this part of my vineyard.

At this point, some members of the Church in the Kirtland area were living the law of consecration, but the only bishop in the Church, Edward Partridge, was living in Zion in Missouri at that time. Thus, a bishop was needed in Kirtland. This sets the stage for Newell K. Whitney to be called as a bishop (verse 8).

6 **These things shall be had on record, to be handed over unto the bishop in Zion** [*Bishop Edward Partridge, the first bishop to be called in this dispensation (D&C 41:9), in effect, the Presiding Bishop of the Church*].

7 And the duty of the bishop shall be made known by the commandments which have been given, and the voice of the conference.

8 And now, verily I say unto you, my servant **Newel K. Whitney is the man who shall be appointed and ordained unto this power** [*to be bishop in Kirtland*]. This is the will of the Lord your God, your Redeemer. Even so. Amen.

As noted above, verses 9–23 were given after Newel K. Whitney was ordained a bishop. They give additional details about the duties of a bishop as well as more about the law of consecration, the need for "certificates" (equivalent to recommends today) to be carried by priesthood holders in order to function in their priesthood, and so forth.

The Second Revelation Given This Day, Verses 9–23

9 The word of the Lord, in addition to the law [*perhaps referring to the revelation given earlier that day, in which instructions were given to ordain Newel K. Whitney a bishop*] which has been given, **making known the duty of the bishop who has been ordained unto the church in this part of the vineyard** [*Kirtland*], **which is verily this—**

Next, specific duties of a bishop are listed. They still apply today.

10 To **keep the Lord's storehouse** [*the bishop's storehouse*]; to **receive the funds of the church** [*such as tithing, fast offering, humanitarian aid, missionary fund, and so forth today*] in this part of the vineyard;

11 To **take an account of the elders** as before has been commanded; **and to administer to their wants** [*administer welfare funds to the needy*], who shall pay for that which they receive, inasmuch as they have wherewith to pay;

12 That **this also may be consecrated** to the good of the church, **to the poor and needy.**

One of the things that we see in action, next, in verse 13 (which likewise is done in the Church today), is this: when a local ward or branch does not have sufficient fast offering funds to meet the needs of the poor and the needy among them, funds can be given from the general Church funds to assist the local bishop in meeting local needs.

13 **And he who hath not wherewith to pay,** an account shall be taken and handed over to **the bishop of Zion** [*Edward Partridge, the Presiding Bishop*], who **shall pay the debt out of that which the Lord shall put into his hands** [*general Church funds, particularly fast offering funds today*].

14 And **the labors of the faithful** [*those who are called to full-time service in the Church, such as General Authorities and missionaries today*] **who labor in spiritual things,** in administering the gospel and the things of the kingdom unto the church, and unto the world, **shall answer the debt unto the bishop in Zion** [*in other words, those who serve full time in the Church are not required to reimburse the Church for their support and the support of their families*];

15 **Thus it** [*the needed funds*] **cometh out of the church,** for according to the law [*the law of consecration*] **every man that**

cometh up to Zion must lay all things before [*must consecrate all he has to*] the bishop in Zion.

16 And now, verily I say unto you, that as **every elder in this part of the vineyard** [*in Kirtland*] **must give an account of his steward-ship unto the bishop in this part of the vineyard** [*Bishop Newel K. Whitney*]—

In verses 17–18, next, we see also that a "recommend" from Bishop Whitney, in Kirtland, was required in order for members who moved from Ohio to Zion, in Jackson County, Missouri, to participate in the law of consecration there.

17 **A certificate** [*equivalent to a recommend today*] from the judge or bishop [*Bishop Whitney*] in this part of the vineyard [*in the Kirtland area*], unto the bishop in Zion [*Bishop Partridge*], **rendereth every man acceptable, and answereth all things, for an inheritance, and to be received as a wise steward and as a faithful laborer** [*in Missouri*];

18 **Otherwise he shall not be accepted of the bishop** [*Bishop Partridge*] **of Zion.**

Next, the Lord instructs that every elder in the Ohio area who desires a "recommend" from Bishop Newel K. Whitney (and who doesn't live under his immediate supervision),

should bring a recommend from his branch president, and then Bishop Whitney can give him a recommend to be used in Missouri.

19 And now, verily I say unto you, **let every elder** who shall give an account unto the bishop of the church in this part of the vineyard [*Bishop Whitney in Kirtland*] **be recommended by the church or churches** [*the branch or branches of the Church*], **in which he labors,** that he may render himself and his accounts approved in all things.

Verses 20–22 refer specifically to the brethren in D&C 70:1–3 who had the direct responsibility to see that the Book of Commandments was published. They referred to themselves as the "Literary Firm" (*History of the Church*, 2:482–83). Because their responsibilities required their full time, they were to receive assistance from the funds of the Church to support themselves and their families.

20 And again, **let my servants who are appointed as stewards over the literary concerns of my church have claim for assistance upon the bishop or bishops in all things**—

21 **That the revelations** [*the Book of Commandments*] **may be published**, and go forth unto the ends of the earth; that they also may

obtain funds which shall benefit the church in all things;

22 That they also may render themselves approved in all things [*in order for them to be able to carry out their responsibilities*], and be accounted as wise stewards.

> According to verse 23, the pattern described in the above verses for "recommends" and so forth is to be applied throughout the Church as it grows and spreads throughout the earth.

23 And now, behold, **this shall be an ensample** [*example*] **for all the extensive** [*numerous*] **branches of my church, in whatsoever land they shall be established**. And now I make an end of my sayings. Amen.

> As the Church grows and as converts are baptized in areas where an organized branch of the Church does not exist, such converts won't have a branch president to give them a recommend for Bishop Whitney or Bishop Partridge. In verses 24–26, next, the Master explains how to handle this situation.

The Third Revelation Given This Day, Verses 24–26

24 A few words in addition to the laws of the kingdom, respecting the members of the church—**they that are appointed by the Holy Spirit to go up unto Zion**, and they who are privileged to go up unto Zion—

25 **Let them carry up unto the bishop a certificate from three elders** of the church, **or a certificate from the bishop**;

26 **Otherwise** he who shall go up unto the land of Zion **shall not be accounted as a wise steward** [*will not be allowed to participate in the Church and the law of consecration in Jackson County, Missouri*]. This is also an ensample [*example*]. Amen.

SECTION 73

Background

> This revelation was given to Joseph Smith and Sidney Rigdon, in Hiram, Ohio, on January 10, 1832. You may wish to read the background notes for section 71 in this study guide. In section 71, Joseph and Sidney had been told to put aside work on the translation of the Bible (the JST) for a season in order to face the wild rumors and falsehoods being circulated in the area as a result of nine anti-Mormon articles published by apostate Ezra Booth in a local newspaper. The articles ran from October to December and had done much damage to the Church.

> The Prophet wrote of the success

of their efforts in confronting the libel of Ezra Booth and others. He said: "From this time until the 8th or 10th of January, 1832, myself and Elder Rigdon continued to preach in Shalersville, Ravenna, and other places, setting forth the truth, vindicating the cause of our Redeemer; showing that the day of vengeance was coming upon this generation like a thief in the night; that prejudice, blindness and darkness filled the minds of many, and caused them to persecute the true Church, and reject the true light; by which means we did much towards allaying the excited feelings which were growing out of the scandalous letters then being published in the Ohio Star, at Ravenna, by the before-mentioned apostate, Ezra Booth. On the 10th of January, I received the following revelation [D&C 73] making known the will of the Lord concerning the Elders of the Church until the convening of the next conference" (*History of the Church*, 1:241).

Having successfully followed the instructions given in section 71, the Prophet and Sidney are now told to return to the work of translating the Bible (verse 3). Some verses in this section are directed to various elders serving missions in the Ohio area (see D&C 73, footnote 1a in your Doctrine and Covenants), whereas some instructions are specifically to Joseph and Sidney.

1 FOR verily, thus saith the Lord, it is expedient in me that **they** [*various missionaries in the Ohio area*] **should continue preaching the gospel, and in exhortation to the churches in the regions round about, until conference** [*to be held in Amherst, Ohio, January 25, 1832; see heading to section 74 in your Doctrine and Covenants*];

2 And **then**, behold, **it shall be made known** unto them, by the voice of the conference, **their several missions**.

Verses 3 and 4 are directed specifically to the Prophet and Sidney Rigdon.

3 Now, verily I say unto you my servants, Joseph Smith, Jun., and Sidney Rigdon, saith the Lord, **it is expedient to translate again**; [*they are to resume work on the translation of the Bible, which we know today as the Joseph Smith Translation of the Bible, or JST*]

4 And, inasmuch as it is practicable, to preach in the regions round about until conference; and **after that it is expedient to continue the work of translation until it be finished.**

Again, verse 5 appears to apply to several elders.

5 And **let this be a pattern unto**

the elders until further knowledge, even as it is written.

6 Now **I give no more unto you at this time**. Gird up your loins [*continue preparations for further assignments*] and be sober [*be serious about the work*]. Even so. Amen.

SECTION 74

Background

This section is yet another example of the great value coming to us from research for the Joseph Smith Papers Project. Editions of the Doctrine and Covenants prior to the 2013 edition give the date of this revelation as January 1832. It was actually sometime in 1830. A quote from the 2018 *Doctrine and Covenants Student Manual* shows that this is incorrect:

"When Church historian and recorder John Whitmer copied the revelation recorded in Doctrine and Covenants 74 into the official record book, he recorded the date as 1830 (see *The Joseph Smith Papers, Documents, Volume 1: July 1828–June 1831*, ed. Michael Hubbard MacKay and others [2013], 228). Years later, those editing the Prophet Joseph Smith's history mistakenly wrote that the Prophet received this revelation in January 1832 while he was making inspired revisions to the New Testament.

However, John Whitmer identified Wayne County, New York, as the place where Joseph Smith dictated the revelation and 1830 as the date when it was received. The Prophet's later history described this revelation as 'an Explanation of the epistle to the first Corinthians, 7th Chapter, 14th verse' (in *Manuscript History of the Church*, vol. A-1, page 178, josephsmithpapers.org). The passage in 1 Corinthians 7:14 had often been cited in Joseph Smith's day to justify infant baptism."

1 Corinthians 7:14 is the subject of this revelation. It is helpful, by way of background and setting for this revelation, to understand that the Jews had a traditional belief that little children were born unclean or unholy (see verse 6).

Verse 1, next, quotes 1 Corinthians 7:14 as it stands in the King James Bible.

1 FOR the unbelieving husband [*nonmember husband*] is sanctified [*helped toward being cleansed*] by the wife [*faithful member*], and the unbelieving wife [*nonmember*] is sanctified by the husband [*faithful member*]; else [*otherwise*] were your children unclean, but now are they holy.

Beginning with verse 2, next, the Lord explains the background to this verse. The law of circumcision was part of the law of Moses and was still being practiced by the Jews who had rejected Christ. Thus, if a woman joined the Church, set up by the Savior during His mortal ministry, her nonmember husband still wanted their children to be subject to the law of Moses, including the law of circumcision for males.

2 Now, **in the days of the Apostles the law of circumcision was had among all the Jews who believed not the gospel of Jesus Christ.**

3 And it came to pass that **there arose a great contention among the people** [*members of the Church*] **concerning the law of circumcision,** for **the unbelieving husband was desirous that his children should be circumcised and become subject to the law of Moses, which law was fulfilled** [*the law of Moses had now been fulfilled by Jesus Christ and the law of circumcision was no longer in force*].

4 And it came to pass that **the children, being brought up in subjection to the law of Moses, gave heed to the traditions of their fathers and believed not the gospel of Christ, wherein they became unholy.**

We see from verse 4, above, that the problem was that if children were brought up keeping the law of Moses, even though they may

have belonged to the true Church and attended its meetings, they still ended up believing the law of Moses and the false traditions of the Jews. Thus, they grew up to become "unholy" or unworthy of salvation.

Next, in verse 5, we are told that Paul had given his opinion that a woman or a man should not marry outside the Church unless they had an agreement that the children who were born to them would not be raised according to the law of Moses.

5 Wherefore, **for this cause the Apostle** [*Paul*] **wrote unto the church** [*wrote to the Corinthian members of the Church*], giving unto them a commandment, not of the Lord, but of himself [*expressing his opinion*], **that a believer should not be united** [*married*] **to an unbeliever; except the law of Moses should be done away among them,**

6 **That their children might remain without circumcision; and that the tradition might be done away,** which saith **that little children are unholy;** for **it was had among the Jews;**

Next, in verse 7, we are taught one of the most beautiful of all doctrines regarding little children. It will be repeated again in D&C 137:10.

7 But **little children are holy, being sanctified** [*saved; made holy and fit to be in the presence of God*] **through the atonement of Jesus Christ**; and this is what the scriptures mean [*such as Mosiah 3:16; Moroni 8; D&C 29:47, 50; and D&C 137:10*].

SECTION 75

Background

This revelation was given through the Prophet Joseph Smith at a conference held at Amherst, Ohio, about fifty miles east of Kirtland on January 25, 1832. It consists of two revelations given on the same day (similar to section 73, which consists of three revelations given on the same day). The first revelation is verses 1–22. The second, verses 23–36.

One of the significant things to watch as we study the Doctrine and Covenants is the gradual development of the structure of Church leadership as we know it today. Rather than organizing it all at once, the Lord did it step by step as the growth and development of the Church warranted it. In a way, it was similar to what happens in outlying areas of the Church today. First, there may be a few members, then a dependent branch with a minimum of leadership, then a branch with a branch president, then with a full branch presidency, and finally, a ward

with the full normal organization of officers and teachers.

For example, when the Church was organized on April 6, 1830, there were four priesthood offices to which men were ordained— deacon, teacher, priest, and elder (see D&C 20:38). And Joseph Smith was "called a seer, a translator, a prophet, an apostle of Jesus Christ, an elder of the church" (D&C 21:1).

In 1831, a new office was added, that of bishop. Edward Partridge was called to be the first bishop in February 1831 (D&C 41:9).

In 1832, at the time of this revelation (section 75), Joseph Smith was sustained and ordained as the President of the High Priesthood of the Church. Thus, he is now the "President of the Church." In early March 1832, he will get counselors for the first time, and on March 15, 1832, the Lord announced that the First Presidency held "the keys of the kingdom, which belong always unto the Presidency of the High Priesthood" (D&C 81:2).

In December 1833, the first patriarch was called (Joseph Smith's father, Joseph Smith Sr.).

In 1834, the first stake was organized at Kirtland on February 17.

In 1835, the Quorum of the Twelve Apostles was organized.

The above serves to remind us

that the Lord did things "line upon line" as He gradually established the organization of the Church as we know it today.

At the time of this revelation, some elders had approached the Prophet, concerned that they were having difficulty in getting people to understand the message of the Restoration as they preached and taught it. They asked Joseph to ask the Lord for counsel on this matter. As the Savior responds, He first identifies Himself to these elders in verse 1.

The First Revelation Given on This Day, Verses 1–22 (given to elders who had submitted their names to serve missions).

1 VERILY, verily, I say unto you, **I who speak** even **by the voice of my Spirit**, even **Alpha and Omega, your Lord and your God—**

"Alpha and Omega" (verse 1) are the first and last letters of the Greek alphabet—in other words, "A and Z." The symbolism is that all things are encompassed by the Savior. He knows all things and has all power to help us and bring us to exaltation if we are willing. He can help us in everything from A to Z in our lives.

Next, the Lord addresses these elders who have come to seek counsel from Him.

2 **Hearken, O ye who have given your names to go forth to proclaim my gospel,** and **to prune my vineyard** [*the imagery is that of cutting out the old dead wood of falsehood and apostasy, the false doctrines and philosophies of the world that stand in the way of new growth, as in pruning a fruit tree*].

3 Behold, I say unto you that **it is my will that you should go forth and not tarry** [*don't delay longer*], neither be idle but labor with your might—

4 **Lifting up your voices as with the sound of a trump** [*the imagery is that of a clear, easily discernible, simple, uncluttered message of the Restoration, like a trumpet or French horn in an orchestra is easy to pick out*], **proclaiming the truth according to the revelations and commandments which I have given you** [*as they preach, they should stick to the scriptures and revelations through the prophet*].

5 And thus, **if ye are faithful ye shall be laden with many sheaves** [*you will have a great harvest of souls*], and crowned with honor, and glory, and immortality, and eternal life [*exaltation in celestial glory*].

Verses 6–12 are directed to William E. McLellin and Luke Johnson.

In D&C 66:7 (given about three months previous to this revelation), the Lord had told Elder McLellin to go to the "eastern lands" to preach. He did go to Pennsylvania and preached some, but returned soon because of disobedience and illness. (You may wish to read more about William McLellin in the background notes for sections 66 and 67 in this study guide.) Now, the Lord revokes that mission for William and asks him to go south to preach.

One lesson that we learn from this change in missions for Brother McLellin is that the Lord keeps trying with us, even when we make mistakes, and even when our attitude is poor. He loves us and gives us every opportunity to succeed.

6 Therefore, verily I say **unto** my servant **William E. McLellin, I revoke the commission** [*mission call*] **which I gave unto him to go unto the eastern countries** [*the eastern United States*];

7 And **I give unto him a new commission** and a new commandment, in the which I, the Lord, **chasten him for the murmurings of his heart**;

8 And **he sinned; nevertheless, I forgive him** and say unto him again, **Go ye into the south countries** [*the Savior is giving him another chance to succeed*].

9 And let my servant Luke Johnson [*son of John and Elsa Johnson*] go with him, and proclaim the things which I have commanded them—

10 **Calling on the name of the Lord for the Comforter** [*the Holy Ghost*], **which shall teach them all things that are expedient** [*necessary*] **for them**—

11 **Praying always that they faint not** [*so they don't get too discouraged and give up*]; and **inasmuch as they do this, I will be with them even unto the end.**

12 Behold, this is the will of the Lord your God concerning you. Even so. Amen.

Verses 13–22 give instructions to several pairs of missionaries to serve in various parts of the United States.

13 And again, verily thus saith the Lord, let my servant **Orson Hyde** and my servant **Samuel H. Smith** take their journey into the eastern countries, and proclaim the things which I have commanded them; and inasmuch as they are faithful, lo, I will be with them even unto the end.

14 And again, verily I say unto my servant **Lyman Johnson**, and unto my servant **Orson Pratt**, they shall also take their journey

into the eastern countries; and behold, and lo, I am with them also, even unto the end.

15 And again, I say unto my servant **Asa Dodds**, and unto my servant **Calves Wilson**, that they also shall take their journey unto the western countries, and proclaim my gospel, even as I have commanded them.

16 And **he who is faithful shall overcome all things** [*with the help of the Atonement of Christ*]**, and shall be lifted up** [*given exaltation*] **at the last day** [*on the final Judgment Day*]**.

17 And again, I say unto my servant **Major N. Ashley**, and my servant **Burr Riggs**, let them take their journey also into the south country.

Verses 18–22 contain a context for shaking "off the dust of your feet as a testimony against them" (verse 20). The word "testimony" means "witness"—in other words, "evidence" that they rejected the missionaries.

In many conversations among members of the Church, the word "curse" enters into such discussions. In a sense, rejecting the gospel brings the "curse" of not having the gospel and its attendant blessings upon those who reject the missionaries. However, we

must be very careful in what we do with such words. Remember, God is completely fair, and all people will ultimately have had a fair chance to hear and understand the gospel before the day of final judgment. You may wish to read section 138, especially verses 30–34, to reaffirm this doctrine.

18 Yea, **let all those take their journey**, as I have commanded them, going **from house to house, and from village to village, and from city to city**.

19 **And in whatsoever house ye enter, and they receive you, leave your blessing upon that house**.

20 And **in whatsoever house ye enter, and they receive you not**, ye shall **depart speedily** from that house, and **shake off the dust of your feet as a testimony against them**.

21 And you shall be filled with joy and gladness; and **know this, that in the day of judgment you shall be judges of that house, and condemn them** [*unless they accept the gospel later; see D&C 138*];

22 And **it shall be more tolerable for the heathen** [*those who didn't get a chance to hear the gospel*] **in the day of judgment, than**

for that house; therefore, gird up your loins [*prepare to serve*] and be faithful, and ye shall overcome all things, and be lifted up [*receive exaltation*] at the last day. Even so. Amen.

Before we leave the subject of shaking dust off feet "as a testimony against them" (verse 20, above), we will include a quote from the *Doctrine and Covenants Student Manual*, 1981, pages 130–31 on this subject.

"The ordinance of washing the dust from one's feet was practiced in New Testament times and was reinstituted in this dispensation (see D&C 88:139–40; John 11:2; 12:3; 13:5–14). The action of shaking or cleansing the dust from one's feet is a testimony against those who refuse to accept the gospel (see D&C 24:15; 84:92; 99:4). Because of the serious nature of this act, Church leaders have directed that it be done only at the command of the Spirit. President Joseph Fielding Smith explained the significance of the action as follows: 'The cleansing of their feet, either by washing or wiping off the dust, would be recorded in heaven as a testimony against the wicked. This act, however, was not to be performed in the presence of the offenders, "lest thou provoke them, but in secret, and wash thy feet, as a testimony against them in the day of judgment." The missionaries of the Church who faithfully perform their duty are under the obligation

of leaving their testimony with all with whom they come in contact in their work. This testimony will stand as a witness against those who reject the message, at the judgment.' (*Church History and Modern Revelation*, 1:223.)"

In verses 23–28, the Lord gives instructions concerning how the families of missionaries should be cared for in their absence.

The Second Revelation Given on This Day, Verses 23–36

(given to a group of elders who wanted to know the Lord's will for them).

23 And again, thus saith the Lord unto you, **O ye elders** of my church, **who have given your names** [*in other words, the elders who requested this revelation*] **that you might know his will concerning you—**

24 Behold, I say unto you, that **it is the duty of the church to assist in supporting the families of those** [*who have already been called on missions*], **and also to support the families of those who are called** [*those who will yet be called*] and must needs be sent unto the world to proclaim the gospel unto the world.

25 **Wherefore, I, the Lord, give unto you this commandment**, that ye **obtain places for your**

families, inasmuch as [*if*] **your brethren are willing to open their hearts** [*in other words, if others who are not called to go on missions are willing to help support your families while you are gone*].

26 And **let all such as can obtain places for their families, and support of the church for them, not fail to go** [*on the missions to which they have been called*] into the world, whether to the east or to the west, or to the north, or to the south.

27 **Let them ask and they shall receive, knock and it shall be opened unto them, and be made known from on high, even by the Comforter** [*the Holy Ghost*], **whither they shall go.**

Next, because the Saints were generally poor in worldly means and goods at this time in Church history, it was difficult to find others who had the means themselves to support their own families plus others. Therefore, those who are unable to find support for their families, if they go on missions, are counseled to stay home and support them themselves. They will not lose blessings from the Lord by so doing.

28 And again, verily I say unto you, that **every man who is obliged to provide for his own family** [*who can't find others to support his family*], let him provide [*he should stay home and provide for them himself*], and **he shall in nowise lose his crown** [*he will not lose his salvation*]; **and let him labor in the church** [*he should serve faithfully in the Church at home*].

In a significant sense, the principle explained by the Savior in verse 28, above, could apply to any faithful members who desire to serve a mission but can't because of difficulties beyond their control. They are to stay home and serve faithfully in the Church there. They will not lose eternal blessings as a result.

Another general principle is taught in verse 29, next. Personal industry and diligence need to be developed by all who wish to become celestial.

29 **Let every man be diligent in all things.** And **the idler shall not have place in the church, except he repent and mend his ways.**

In the final verses of this section, several other missionary pairs are identified.

30 Wherefore, let my servant **Simeon Carter** and my servant **Emer Harris** be united in the ministry;

31 And also my servant **Ezra**

Thayre and my servant **Thomas B. Marsh**;

32 Also my servant **Hyrum Smith** and my servant **Reynolds Cahoon**;

33 And also my servant **Daniel Stanton** and my servant **Seymour Brunson**;

34 And also my servant **Sylvester Smith** and my servant **Gideon Carter**;

35 And also my servant **Ruggles Eames** and my servant **Stephen Burnett**;

36 And also my servant **Micah B. Welton** and also my servant **Eden Smith**. Even so. Amen.

SECTION 76

Background

This revelation includes a vision (consisting of six visions) given to the Prophet Joseph Smith and Sidney Rigdon while living at the home of John and Alice (Elsa) Johnson in Hiram, Ohio. The vision was given on February 16, 1832, and provides doctrinal details about the three degrees of glory and perdition (meaning complete loss, complete destruction). Section 76 is thus one of the major doctrinal sections of the Doctrine and Covenants.

One of the main reasons Joseph and Emma Smith, along with Sidney Rigdon, had moved into the John Johnson home was so that Joseph and Sidney would have time to continue work on the translation of the Bible (the *Joseph Smith Translation of the Bible*, or JST) as commanded by the Lord in D&C 45:60–61.

Joseph had started work on the JST in June 1830 and continued for about three years. During the work of translating, correcting, and revising, many questions came up in the Prophet's mind. As was his way, he turned to the Lord for answers.

The question that led to the vision recorded in section 76 had to do with the Christian concept of heaven and hell, and, in particular, John 5:29, which is usually interpreted as meaning that there is just one heaven and one hell. We will quote it here, including verse 28 for context:

John 5:28–29

28 Marvel not at this: for the hour is coming, in the which all that are in the graves shall hear his voice,

29 And shall come forth; they that have done good, unto the resurrection of life; and they that have done evil, unto the resurrection of damnation.

The question that came up in the Prophet's mind had to do with the problem of believing in just one heaven in view of the fact that there are so many different lifestyles and degrees of righteousness or wickedness among people.

Joseph Smith gave the background to this vision. He wrote:

"Upon my return from Amherst [Ohio] conference, I resumed the translation of the Scriptures. From sundry [various] revelations which had been received, it was apparent that many important points touching the salvation of man, had been taken from the Bible, or lost before it was compiled. It appeared self-evident from what truths were left, that if God rewarded every one according to the deeds done in the body the term 'Heaven,' as intended for the Saints' eternal home must include more kingdoms than one. Accordingly, on the 16th of February, 1832, while translating St. John's Gospel, myself and Elder Rigdon saw the following vision [D&C 76]" (*History of the Church*, 1:245).

About 12 other men were in the room at the Johnson home when the vision was given. Brother Philo Dibble was one of them, and he recorded the experience as follows:

"The vision which is recorded in the Book of Doctrine and Covenants was given at the house of 'Father Johnson,' in Hiram, Ohio, and during the time that Joseph and Sidney were in the spirit and saw the heavens open, there were other men in the room, perhaps twelve, among whom I was one during a part of the time—probably two-thirds of the time,—I saw the glory and felt the power, but did not see the vision.

"The events and conversation, while they were seeing what is written (and many things were seen and related that are not written,) I will relate as minutely as is necessary.

"Joseph would, at intervals, say: 'What do I see?' as one might say while looking out the window and beholding what all in the room could not see. Then he would relate what he had seen or what he was looking at. Then Sidney replied, 'I see the same.' Presently Sidney would say 'what do I see?' and would repeat what he had seen or was seeing, and Joseph would reply, 'I see the same.'

"This manner of conversation was reported at short intervals to the end of the vision, and during the whole time not a word was spoken by any other person. Not a sound nor motion made by anyone but Joseph and Sidney, and it seemed to me that they never moved a joint or limb during the time I was there, which I think was over an hour, and to the end of the vision.

"Joseph sat firmly and calmly all the time in the midst of a magnificent glory, but Sidney sat limp and pale, apparently as limber as a rag, observing which, Joseph remarked, smilingly, 'Sidney is not used to it as I am'" (*Juvenile Instructor*, May 1892, 303–4).

We mentioned earlier that this vision consisted of a series of six separate visions within the overall vision. The overall vision is recorded in verses 19–113. For purposes of study, the six visions within the vision can generally be grouped as given in the following list (you may wish to include this list as notes in your own scriptures):

Overall Vision
Verses 19–113

Six Visions within the Vision
1. **The Glory of the Son (verses 19–24)**

2. **The Fall of Lucifer (Satan) (verses 25–29)**

3. **The Sons of Perdition (verses 30–39, 43–49)**

4. **Celestial Glory (verses 50–70, 92–96)**

5. **Terrestrial Glory (verses 71–80, 87, 91, 97)**

6. **Telestial Glory (verses 81–89, 98–106, 109–12)**

We will now begin our verse-by-verse study of this section. In verses 1–10, we are taught about the glory and power of God. We are also given many insights as to the desire of God to bless us and show respect and honor toward us. This is almost unique in a world in which many Christian religions, along with numerous non-Christian religions, demean and debase mankind in order to elevate God.

1 **HEAR**, O ye heavens, and give ear, O earth, **and rejoice** ye inhabitants thereof, for **the Lord is God, and beside him there is no Savior**.

2 **Great is his wisdom, marvelous are his ways, and the extent of his doings none can find out**.

3 **His purposes fail not, neither are there any who can stay his hand** [*none can stop the Lord*].

4 **From eternity to eternity he is the same** [*He uses the same plan of salvation to save*], and his years never fail [*He will never cease to exist*].

5 For thus saith the Lord—**I, the Lord, am merciful and gracious unto those who fear** [*respect*] **me, and delight to honor those who serve me in righteousness and in truth unto the end**.

6 **Great shall be their reward and eternal shall be their glory**.

Before reading verse 7, next, it is helpful to check the Bible Dictionary (in our Latter-day Saint edition of the Bible) for the definition of "mystery." Otherwise, we might think that it means mysterious and obscure facts and details. It does not. We will use **bold** for emphasis.

Mystery

"Denotes in the N.T. [*New Testament*] **a spiritual truth that was once hidden but now is revealed, and that, without special revelation, would have remained unknown.** It is generally used along with words denoting revelation or publication (e.g., Rom. 16:25–26; Eph. 1:9; 3:3–10; Col. 1:26; 4:3; 1 Tim. 3:16). **The modern meaning of something incomprehensible forms no part of the significance of the word as it occurs in the N.T.** *See also* Alma 12:9–11; 40:3; D&C 19:10; 42:61–65; 76:5–10. On the other hand, there is no spiritual gain in idle speculation about things the Lord has not revealed. See Deut. 29:29; Alma 37:11."

7 And **to them will I reveal all mysteries**, yea, all the hidden mysteries of my kingdom from days of old, and for ages to come, will I make known unto them the good pleasure of my will concerning all things pertaining to my kingdom.

8 Yea, **even the wonders of eternity shall they know**, and things to come will I show them, even the things of many generations.

9 And **their wisdom shall be great, and their understanding reach to heaven**; and **before them the wisdom of the wise shall perish, and the understanding of the prudent shall come to naught** [*nothing*].

Verse nine, above, reminds us of the "wise," including many philosophers, highly educated individuals, the teachings of most other religions, Christian and non-Christian, and others who present their confusing and conflicting views about God and religion, completely missing the simple doctrines and truths of the true gospel of Jesus Christ. Thus, these "plain and simple things" (1 Nephi 13:29) are "mysteries" to them. And their teachings and mysterious wonderings and musings will come to nothing when exposed to the full light and wonderful intelligence of the pure gospel of Jesus Christ.

10 For **by my Spirit will I enlighten them** [*the righteous who "fear" God—verse 5*]**, and by my power will I make known unto them the secrets of my will— yea, even those things which eye has not seen, nor ear heard, nor yet entered into the heart of man.**

In verses 11–18, Joseph Smith and Sidney Rigdon tell us what led up to this vision.

11 **We, Joseph Smith, Jun., and Sidney Rigdon**, being in the Spirit [*working under the influence of the Holy Ghost*] on the sixteenth day of February, in the year of our Lord one thousand eight hundred and thirty–two—

12 **By the power of the Spirit our eyes were opened and our understandings were enlightened**, so as to see and understand the things of God—

13 Even those things which were from the beginning before the world was, which were **ordained of the Father** [*authorized and put into action*], **through his Only Begotten Son**, who was in the bosom of the Father [*who worked in complete harmony with the Father*], even from the beginning;

In verse 14, next, we are told that the Prophet and Sidney Rigdon saw the Savior and talked with Him during this vision.

14 **Of whom we bear record**; and the record which we bear is the fulness of the gospel of Jesus Christ, who is the Son, **whom we saw and with whom we conversed in the heavenly vision.**

15 For **while we were doing the work of translation** [*working on the translation of the Bible, which became the Joseph Smith Translation (the JST)*], which the Lord had appointed unto us, **we came to the twenty–ninth verse of the fifth chapter of John**, which was given unto us as follows—

16 **Speaking of the resurrection of the dead**, concerning those who shall hear the voice of the Son of Man [*speaking of those who will have had a fair chance to hear and understand the gospel by the day of final judgment*]:

17 **And shall come forth; they who have done good in the resurrection of the just; and they who have done evil, in the resurrection of the unjust.**

18 Now **this caused us to marvel, for it was given unto us of the Spirit.**

Did you notice the wonderful doctrine in verse 18? The Holy Ghost can cause us to wonder about things, to prepare us to be taught by the Spirit, and to receive answers from above to our prayers and wonderings.

Perhaps you have had the experience of wondering about something and then going to church and the sacrament meeting speaker or a teacher in one of your classes answered your question. It may have seemed to you that he or she was talking directly to you! And because you had been wondering about that very thing, the answer meant much more than it otherwise would have because you were prepared by the Spirit to hear it. In fact, you still remember it today. Such is the power of the Holy Ghost to prepare and teach us.

Next, the vision that Joseph Smith and Sidney Rigdon had of the Savior is described. Remember that the entire vision they had, consisting of six visions, goes from verse 19 to 113.

Vision #1
The Glory of the Son
(verses 19–24)

19 And while we meditated upon these things, the Lord touched the eyes of our understandings and they were opened, and the glory of the Lord shone round about.

20 And we beheld the glory of the Son, on the right hand of the Father, and received of his fulness;

From verse 21, next, we learn that they saw others, besides the Father and Son, in this vision.

21 And saw the holy angels, and them who are sanctified [*"sanctified" means those who have proven*

themselves worthy of living with God forever—compare with Moses 6:60] before his throne, worshiping God, and the Lamb, who worship him forever and ever.

The idea in the scriptures of worshipping God "forever and ever" is often misunderstood. It has caused some to wonder if they even want to go to heaven. It conjures up visions of standing on clouds, playing harps forever, and becoming terribly bored.

However, when we realize that "worshipping God" includes doing things that bring Him honor and glory, such as serving others, even creating our own worlds and using the same plan of salvation for our spirit children that He used for us, the term "worship" becomes exciting and fascinating, the complete opposite of boredom.

You may wish to mark verses 22–24 in your own scriptures. They are often quoted and are very powerful.

22 And now, after the many testimonies which have been given of him [*Christ*], **this is the testimony, last of all, which we give of him: That he lives!**

23 For we saw him, even on the right hand [*the covenant hand, symbolizing that the Savior kept the covenants He made with the Father to be the Redeemer*] **of God; and**

we heard the voice bearing record that he is the Only Begotten of the Father—

On occasions, students of the
gospel become confused at the
term "Only Begotten of the Father"
(verse 23, above). The confusion
comes when they consider the
fact that all of us are spirit sons
and daughters of God (as stated
in the proclamation on the family),
born to Him in the premortal life.
How can Christ be the "Only Begotten" when we too are begotten
spirit children of God?

The answer is simple and important. Jesus is the Only Begotten
of the Father in the flesh. In other
words, He is the only one whose father in mortality was God. President
Heber J. Grant explained this. He
said (**bold** added for emphasis):

"We believe absolutely that Jesus
Christ is the Son of God, begotten of God, the first-born in the
spirit and **the only begotten in
the flesh**; that He is the Son of
God just as much as you and I are
the sons of our fathers" (Heber J.
Grant, "Analysis of the Articles of
Faith," *Millennial Star,* January 5,
1922, 2).

24 **That by him** [*Christ*]**, and
through him, and of him, the
worlds are and were created**
[*all the worlds He has created or will
yet create*]**, and the inhabitants
thereof are begotten sons and
daughters unto God.**

Verse 24, above, answers an interesting question that often comes
up in gospel classes and discussions. The question is whether
Jesus is the savior of other worlds
in addition to ours. Can you pick
out the answer? It is found in the
last phrase, which states that the
inhabitants of all those worlds
("worlds without number" according to Moses 1:33) "are begotten
sons and daughters **unto** God."
The word "unto" is significant. It is
not "of." (We are all begotten spirit
sons and daughters "of" God.) It
is "unto," implying the action of
bringing them unto the Father
through the gospel and the Atonement. In other words, through our
Savior, the inhabitants of all of Father's worlds have the opportunity
to be brought back to the Father
and live with Him in celestial glory
forever. Thus, "begotten sons and
daughters unto God" is another
term for exaltation.

Just in case someone challenges
this interpretation of verse 24, it
is helpful to read verses 22–24
in poetic form, as written by the
Prophet Joseph Smith (who put
the whole vision in poetic form):

*And now after all of the proofs
    made of him,
By witnesses truly, by whom
    he was known,
This is mine, last of all, that he lives;
    yea, he lives!
And sits on the right hand of God
    on his throne.*

*And I heard a great voice bearing
record from heav'n,*

*He's the Saviour and Only
Begotten of God,*

*By him, of him, and through him,
the worlds were all made,*

*Even all that career [orbit] in
the heavens so broad.*

*Whose inhabitants, too, from the
first to the last,*

*Are sav'd by the very same
Saviour of ours;*

*And of course, are begotten Gods
daughters and sons*

*By the very same truths and the
very same powers.*

—Millennial Star, 4:49–55

Vision #2

The Fall of Lucifer
(verses 25–29)

**25 And this we saw also, and
bear record, that an angel of
God** [*Lucifer, Satan*] **who was in
authority** [*Lucifer held considerable
authority in premortality before he
rebelled*] **in the presence of God,
who rebelled against the Only
Begotten Son** [*Christ*] whom the
Father loved [*was able to bless with
His highest blessings*] and who was
in the bosom of the Father [*who
was in complete harmony and unity
with the Father*], **was thrust down**

**from the presence of God and
the Son,**

The word "loved" in the phrase
"whom the Father loved" in verse
25, above, must be understood
correctly. Otherwise, it sounds like
the Father loves some of His children more than others.

In an article titled "Divine Love,"
written for the February 2003
Ensign, then Elder Russell M.
Nelson described several different
types of "love" as it pertains to
God. Among other things, he
wrote (**bold** added for emphasis):

"While **divine love** can be called
perfect, infinite, enduring, and
universal, it **cannot correctly be
characterized as *unconditional*.**
The word does not appear in the
scriptures. On the other hand,
many verses affirm that **the higher levels of love the Father and
the Son feel for each of us—
and certain divine blessings
stemming from that love—are
conditional.**

"The resplendent bouquet of God's
love—including eternal life—includes **blessings for which we
must qualify**, not entitlements to
be expected unworthily."

With this instruction from Elder
Nelson in mind, we can define the
phrase "whom the Father loved"
as meaning "whom the Father
was enabled to bless because of
Christ's obedience."

We will now continue with the vision of the fall of Lucifer.

26 And was called Perdition [*which means complete loss, irreparably damaged*], for **the heavens wept over him**—he was **Lucifer, a son of the morning** [*all of us wept and were sorry to see him fall*].

By the way, the name "Lucifer" (verse 26) means "light bearer" or "light bringer" (common dictionary definitions). Continuing, we must be careful to read the last phrase of verse 26, above, exactly as it is. Some people inadvertently read it as "the son of the morning" rather than "a son of the morning." The difference is important. If it were "the son of the morning," it would imply that Lucifer was one of the highest in authority. Whereas "a son of the morning" implies that he was one of many who held authority and wielded influence in our premortal life. President George Q. Cannon of the First Presidency explained this. He said:

"Some have called him *the* son of the morning, but here it is *a* son of the morning—one among many, doubtless. This angel was a mighty personage, without doubt. The record that is given to us concerning him clearly shows that he occupied a very high position; that he was thought a great deal of, and that he was mighty in his sphere, so much so that when the matter was debated concerning the earth and the plan of salvation, he was of sufficient importance to have a plan, which he proposed as the plan by which this earth should be peopled and the inhabitants thereof redeemed. His plan, however, was not accepted; but it was so plausible and so attractive that out of the whole hosts of heaven one-third accepted his plan and were willing to cast their lot with him [Moses 4:1–4; D&C 29:36–37]. Now, the difference between Jesus and Lucifer was this: Jesus was willing to submit to the Father" (*Millennial Star,* September 5, 1895, 563–64; quoted in the *Doctrine and Covenants Student Manual,* 1981, 160).

27 And we [*Joseph Smith and Sidney Rigdon*] beheld, and lo, **he is fallen! is fallen, even a son of the morning!**

28 And while we were yet in the Spirit, the Lord commanded us that we should write the vision; for **we beheld Satan, that old serpent, even the devil, who rebelled against God, and sought to take the kingdom of our God and his Christ—**

29 Wherefore [*this is why*], **he maketh war with the saints of God,** and encompasseth them round about [*surrounds them with temptation to sin*].

The "war" referred to in verse 29, above, started with the War in Heaven (see Revelation 12:7–9), which started with the rebellion of Lucifer in premortality. It is still continuing here on earth. It will not be over until the final defeat of Satan and his evil followers in the battle of Gog and Magog, which will take place after the Millennium comes to an end. (See D&C 88:110–115.) The War in Heaven was a battle for our loyalty and, ultimately, for our souls. President Gordon B. Hinckley said (**bold** added for emphasis):

"The book of Revelation speaks briefly of what must have been **a terrible conflict for the minds and loyalties** of God's children" ("War and Peace," *Ensign*, May 2003, 78). He then went on to quote Revelation 12:7–9.

Next, we will study what the Prophet Joseph Smith and Sidney Rigdon saw regarding the sons of perdition.

Vision #3
The Sons of Perdition, sometimes referred to in gospel conversations as those who will end up in "outer darkness" (verses 30–39, 43–49)

This final place, reserved for the devil and those who follow him completely, is referred to variously as "hell," "perdition," and sometimes "outer darkness." You can find it referred to as "outer darkness" in "*Guide to the Scriptures*," under "Hell," where it says, "The scriptures sometimes refer to hell as outer darkness."

Before we move on, it is important to understand that Satan makes war (verse 30) against all of us who have lived beyond the age of accountability (see D&C 29:46–47). A key phrase in verse 30, next, is "made war <u>and</u> overcame." Satan cannot completely overpower and forever claim anyone without that person's consent. Thus, sons of perdition are those who have intentionally made unwise agency choices and have thus gradually turned themselves completely over to Lucifer.

For teaching purposes, we will number the qualifications for becoming sons of perdition as we go along.

30 And **we saw a vision of the sufferings of those with whom he [*Lucifer*] made war and overcame [*a gradual process*], for thus** came the voice of the Lord unto us:

31 Thus saith the Lord concerning all those who **[1] know my power,** and **[2] have been made partakers thereof,** and **[3] suffered themselves through the power of the devil to be overcome,** and to **[4] deny the truth** and **[5] defy my power**—

We will add some notes for each of the five items numbered in verse 31, above.

(1) "know my power"

In order to "know" God and His power, one must have the witness of the Holy Ghost. Joseph Smith taught this as follows: "All sins shall be forgiven, except the sin against the Holy Ghost; for Jesus will save all except the sons of perdition. What must a man do to commit the unpardonable sin? He must receive the Holy Ghost, have the heavens opened unto him, and know God, and then sin against Him. After a man has sinned against the Holy Ghost, there is no repentance for him. He has got to say that the sun does not shine while he sees it; he has got to deny Jesus Christ when the heavens have been opened unto him, and to deny the plan of salvation with his eyes open to the truth of it; and from that time he begins to be an enemy. This is the case with many apostates of the Church of Jesus Christ of Latter-day Saints" (*Teachings of the Prophet Joseph Smith*, 358).

(2) "have been made partakers thereof"

They are members of the Church, have received all ordinances, endowments, and such that we have available here in this life to prepare for exaltation. President Joseph F. Smith explained this (**bold** added for emphasis):

"And he that believes, is baptized, and receives the light and testimony of Jesus Christ . . . **receiving the fulness of the blessings of the gospel in this world**, and afterwards turns wholly unto sin, violating his covenants . . . will taste the second death" (*Gospel Doctrine*, 476–77).

(3) "suffered themselves through the power of the devil to be overcome"

They must exercise their moral agency to intentionally go against knowledge and truth. In other words, they must intentionally allow themselves to be overcome by Satan.

(4) "deny the truth"

They become complete liars, completely lacking integrity. In other words, they become totally dishonest, like Satan, denying the truth when they fully know it.

(5) "defy my power"

They don't simply go inactive. Rather, they fight against God and the Church, against all that is good, with the same evil energy with which Satan and his evil hosts fight truth and right.

Next, in verse 32, the Lord defines such people as being sons of perdition.

32 **They are** they who are **the sons of perdition,** of whom I say

that it had been better for them never to have been born;

From the last phrase of verse 32, above, we understand that sons of perdition do not come through the veil as such. Rather, they retrogress during this life and become sons of perdition.

33 For **they are vessels of wrath** [*have become full of anger, bitterness, and hatred of that which is good. In other words, they actually become like Satan. They think as he does, act as he does, and react against good as he does. This is the full opposite of becoming like Christ through following His commandments and striving to live His gospel*], **doomed to suffer the wrath of God, with the devil and his angels in eternity** [*they will ultimately be cast out completely with Satan and the evil spirits who followed him in the War in Heaven; see D&C 88:114*];

34 Concerning whom I have said **there is no forgiveness in this world nor in the world to come** [*in other words, this sin, often termed "the sin against the Holy Ghost," cannot be forgiven; the reason is simple: it is that, among other things, such individuals have become just like Satan and would not have any use for or interest in forgiveness if it were offered to them*]—

In verse 35, next, we see three more qualifications for becoming sons of perdition.

35 Having **[6] denied the Holy Spirit after having received it,** and having **[7] denied the Only Begotten Son of the Father,** having **[8] crucified him unto themselves and put him to an open shame.**

We will add notes for each of the three items listed in verse 35, above.

(6) "denied the Holy Spirit after having received it"

In order to become a son of perdition, one must have received the gift of the Holy Ghost. The following quote helps us understand this.

"To become a son of perdition one must sin against the Holy Ghost; but before that is possible, one must receive the gift of the Holy Ghost. Elder Melvin J. Ballard explained that 'unto the Holy Ghost has been given the right and the privilege of manifesting the truth unto men as no other power will. So that when he makes a man see and know a thing he knows it better than he shall ever know anything else; and to sin against that knowledge is to sin against the greatest light there is, and consequently commit the greatest sin there is.' (*Millennial Star*, 11 Aug. 1932, 499–500.)" (See also

Doctrine and Covenants Student Manual, 1981, 161.)

(7) "denied the Only Begotten Son of the Father"

After receiving a sure testimony that Jesus is the Christ, they reject Him completely, just as Satan has.

(8) "crucified him unto themselves and put him to an open shame"

They become so bitter that they themselves would gladly crucify Christ again if they had the opportunity. In other words, as stated above, they have become like Satan. They think as he does, hate as he does, and have the same desires and goals as he does. Brigham Young summarized the topic of becoming sons of perdition. He said:

"How much does it take to prepare a man, or woman . . . to become angels to the devil, to suffer with him through all eternity? Just as much as it does to prepare a man to go into the Celestial Kingdom, into the presence of the Father and the Son, and to be made an heir to his kingdom and all his glory, and be crowned with crowns of glory, immortality, and eternal lives" (*Journal of Discourses*, 3:93).

Additional information about the fate and ultimate condition of sons of perdition is given in verses 36–48.

36 These are **they** who **shall go away into the lake of fire and brimstone** [*there is no literal "lake of fire and brimstone"; brimstone is molten sulfur; thus, this phrase is symbolic of the worst, unimaginable suffering*], **with the devil and his angels** [*the evil spirits who followed him in the War in Heaven*]—

37 And **the only ones on whom the second death** [*being completely cut off from God's presence*] **shall have any power** [*the only ones who will not have at least some degree of glory and be free from Satan forever*];

38 Yea, verily, **the only ones who shall not be redeemed in the due time of the Lord** [*redeemed to at least telestial glory or better*], **after the sufferings of his wrath** [*after being punished for their own sins; see D&C 19:15–17*].

Before we read verse 39, next, we must be aware that everyone who has ever been born on earth will be resurrected. This includes those who become sons of perdition. (See 1 Corinthians 15:22, D&C 88:32.) Lucifer and the evil spirits who followed him (Revelation 12:4) will, of course, not get resurrected because they do not receive mortal bodies.

If we do not understand the above doctrine, we will be apt to interpret verse 39, next, as saying that everyone except sons of perdition will be resurrected. This would be false doctrine.

39 For all the rest [*all except those mortals who become sons of perdition*] shall be brought forth by the resurrection of the dead, **through the triumph and the glory of the Lamb** [*all who attain telestial, terrestrial, or celestial glory, will, at least to some degree, partake of the "triumph and glory" of Christ; they will all be completely free from Satan in the eternities, and will live in kingdoms of glory*], **who was slain,** who was in the bosom of the Father before the worlds were made [*whose Atonement was planned in the premortal councils*].

Verses 40–44 break from describing sons of perdition long enough to rejoice in the Atonement of Christ.

40 And **this is the gospel, the glad tidings,** which the voice out of the heavens bore record unto us—

41 **That he came into the world,** even Jesus, **to be crucified for the world,** and **to bear the sins of the world,** and **to sanctify** [*to make holy, to cleanse and make fit to be in the presence of God*] **the world,** and **to cleanse it from all unrighteousness;**

42 That **through him** [*Christ*] **all might be saved whom the Father had put into his power** [*through the means of the gospel and the Atonement*] **and made** [*made worthy of salvation*] **by him;**

43 **Who glorifies the Father** [*Christ brings honor and glory to the Father*], **and saves all** the works of his hands [*saves everyone, to one degree of glory or another*], **except those sons of perdition** who deny [*completely reject*] the Son after the Father has revealed him [*after they know full well that Jesus is the Christ*].

44 Wherefore [*therefore*], **he saves all except them—they shall go away into everlasting punishment,** which is **endless punishment,** which is **eternal punishment, to reign with the devil and his angels** [*including the wicked spirits who followed him in premortality*] **in eternity,** where their worm dieth not [*where they cannot cease to exist*], and the fire [*perhaps meaning spiritual agony*] is not quenched, which is their torment—

45 And **the end** thereof, **neither the place** thereof, **nor their**

torment, no man knows [*no mortal can comprehend how miserable they will be*];

46 Neither was it revealed, neither is, neither will be revealed unto man, **except to them who are made partakers thereof**;

47 Nevertheless, **I, the Lord, show it by vision unto many** [*including Joseph Smith and Sidney Rigdon; see verse 30, above*], but straightway shut it up again;

48 Wherefore, **the end**, the **width**, the **height**, the **depth**, and the **misery** thereof, **they understand not, neither any man except those who are ordained** [*not "foreordained" or "predestined" or "preselected" by God to this condemnation, but rather "ordained" or '"qualified for" by the law of justice*] **unto this condemnation** [*being stopped in spiritual progression*].

In a technical sense, there is another way to know what happens to them. Those who become gods will know all things. Therefore, they will know the final fate of sons of perdition. (This is by far the best way to find out!)

49 And **we heard the voice, saying: Write the vision**, for lo, **this is the end of the vision of the** sufferings of the ungodly.

Vision #4
Celestial Glory
(verses 50–70, 92–96)

These are faithful, baptized members of the Church, who have the gift of the Holy Ghost and strive to keep the commandments, thus qualifying them to be "washed and cleansed from all their sins" (verse 52). Little children who die before the age of accountability will be in the highest degree of glory in the celestial kingdom—in other words, in exaltation. We will discuss more about this when we get to D&C 137:10.

50 And again we bear record— for **we saw and heard**, and this is the testimony of the gospel of Christ **concerning them who shall come forth in the resurrection of the just** [*"resurrection of the just" is another term for those who gain celestial glory*]—

51 **They are they who [1] received the testimony of Jesus**, and **[2] believed on his name** and **[3] were baptized** after the manner of his burial, being buried in the water in his name, and this according to the commandment which he has given—

52 That by **[4] keeping the commandments** they might be **[5] washed and cleansed from all their sins**, and **[6] receive the Holy Spirit by the laying on of the hands** of him who is ordained and sealed unto this power;

53 And who **[7] overcome by faith**, and **[8] are sealed by the Holy Spirit of promise** [*the Holy Ghost*], which the Father sheds forth upon all those who are just and true.

We will add some notes to the numbered items in verses 51–53, above.

(1) "received the testimony of Jesus"

"Received" is an active verb, one that calls for action on our part. The action required here is that of receiving the gospel into one's life and sincerely striving to live in conformity to its commandments and covenants.

(2) "believed on his name"

"Belief" in this context is much more than mere acknowledging. It includes actively living the gospel and believing that it will lead to salvation because of the Atonement of Christ.

(3) "were baptized"

These people were baptized by immersion by those who had the priesthood authority to do so.

(4) "keeping the commandments"

Keeping the commandments leads to the cleansing expressed in number 5, next.

(5) "washed and cleansed from all their sins"

Although none of us will be perfect in all ways at the time we leave this mortal life, by striving sincerely and honestly to keep the commandments, we qualify to be cleansed from all sins by the Atonement of Jesus Christ. We are thus made pure, clean, and worthy to enter into the presence of God. Not only that, but we are also enabled to be comfortable in His presence (compare with 2 Nephi 9:14, last half of verse).

(6) "receive the Holy Spirit by the laying on of the hands"

The gift of the Holy Ghost is given at the time of confirmation. If we actively "receive" the Holy Ghost into our lives thereafter, He will guide us in all things throughout our lives. By following His promptings, we will be led to greater and greater understanding of the gospel and will be enabled to have the Atonement of Christ active in our lives. This leads to number 7, next.

(7) "overcome by faith"

The foregoing steps lead to overcoming the sins and temptations of the world through faith in the Lord Jesus Christ, thus qualifying us to receive number 8, next.

(8) "are sealed by the Holy Spirit of promise"

The Holy Ghost is the "Holy Spirit of promise." The name comes from the fact that He is the Holy Spirit that is promised by Jesus Christ to His worthy followers after baptism.

One of the roles of the Holy Ghost is to seal or ratify ordinances performed here on earth so that they are binding in heaven also. Thus, when a worthy member is "sealed by the Holy Spirit of promise," it means that he or she has proven worthy of exaltation and is "sealed up" for that blessing.

When ordinances are not performed by proper authority, or they are performed by proper authority but the person does not live worthily, the Holy Ghost does not seal them, thus, the ordinances are not binding in heaven. We are taught this clearly in the Doctrine and Covenants as follows:

D&C 132:7

7 And verily I say unto you, that the conditions of this law are these: All covenants, contracts, bonds, obligations, oaths, vows, performances, connections, associations, or expectations, that are not made and entered into and sealed by the Holy Spirit of promise, of him who is anointed, both as well for time and for all eternity, and that too most holy, by revelation and commandment through the medium of mine anointed, whom I have appointed on the earth to hold this power (and I have appointed unto my servant Joseph to hold this power in the last days, and there is never but one on the earth at a time on whom this power and the keys of this priesthood are conferred), **are of no efficacy, virtue, or force in and after the resurrection from the dead; for all contracts that are not made unto this end have an end when men are dead.**

Elder David A. Bednar taught, "The Holy Spirit of Promise is the ratifying power of the Holy Ghost. When sealed by the Holy Spirit of Promise, an ordinance, vow, or covenant is binding on earth and in heaven. (See D&C 132:7.) Receiving this 'stamp of approval' from the Holy Ghost is the result of faithfulness, integrity, and steadfastness in honoring gospel covenants 'in [the] process of time' (Moses 7:21). However, this sealing can be forfeited through unrighteousness and transgression" ("Ye Must Be Born Again," *Ensign or Liahona*, May 2007, 22).

Before we move on, you may wish to glance back over verses 51–53 and take note of the fact that it is not complicated to qualify for celestial glory. Some people get the notion that being a faithful, active member of the Church is too complex and difficult to understand and do. In reality, being faithful to God is the simplest of all lifestyles. Even children can do it (see D&C 68:25–28). Complexity enters in when people sin and try to hide it or rationalize sin away.

As we continue, we see a number of different terms for "exaltation" in verses 54–58 and in verses 66–67. "Exaltation" means attaining the highest degree of glory in the celestial kingdom and becoming gods. It is also referred to as "eternal life." We know that the terms in these next verses refer to exaltation, not just to entering one of the other levels in celestial glory (see D&C 131:1–4), because verse 58 says "they are gods." We will **bold** these words and phrases to point them out. A number of these terms may be familiar to you. (On a sad note, some apostates who

have broken off from our church have taken some of these terms as the names of the churches they have formed.)

54 They are they who are the church of the Firstborn.

55 They are they into whose hands the Father has given all things [*in other words, they have been given exaltation*]—

56 They are they who are priests and kings, who have received of his fulness, and of his glory;

Faithful women in the Church are also included in the context of verse 56, above. Elder Bruce R. McConkie said (**bold** added for emphasis):

"If righteous men have power through the gospel and its crowning ordinance of celestial marriage to become kings and priests to rule in exaltation forever, it follows that the women by their side (without whom they cannot attain exaltation) will be **queens and priestesses**. (Rev. 1:6; 5:10.) Exaltation grows out of the eternal union of a man and his wife. Of those whose marriage endures in eternity, the Lord says, "Then shall they be gods" (D. & C. 132:20); that is, **each of them, the man and the woman, will be a god. As such they will rule over their dominions forever** (*Mormon Doctrine*, 613).

57 And are **priests of the Most High, after the order of Melchizedek**, which was **after the order of Enoch**, which was **after the order of the Only Begotten Son** [*Jesus Christ*].

58 Wherefore, as it is written, **they are gods**, even the **sons of God** [*meaning that they have done all things necessary to become "heirs" of God—in other words, gods*]—

Rewards and blessings of exaltation in celestial glory are detailed in verses 59–70. Again, we will use **bold** to point these out.

59 Wherefore, **all things are theirs**, whether life or death, or things present, or things to come, all are theirs and **they are Christ's, and Christ is God's**.

60 And **they shall overcome all things**.

The word "shall," in verse 60, above, is important. In fact, it is very comforting. It lets us know that we will be allowed to continue progressing in the next life provided that we have qualified for that privilege during this life. None of us will be perfect when we die. There will be much progress and growth yet to be made after we pass away. However, once being judged worthy of exaltation on Judgment Day, those who receive

this blessing will go on to "overcome all things." The Prophet Joseph Smith taught this. He said (**bold** added for emphasis):

"When you climb up a ladder, you must begin at the bottom, and ascend step by step, until you arrive at the top; and so it is with the principles of the Gospel—you must begin with the first, and go on until you learn all the principles of exaltation. **But it will be a great while after you have passed through the veil before you will have learned them. It is not all to be comprehended in this world; it will be a great work to learn our salvation and exaltation even beyond the grave**" (*Teachings of the Prophet Joseph Smith*, 348).

61 Wherefore, **let no man glory in man** [*don't build your life upon the philosophies and false wisdom of man*], **but rather let him glory in God**, who shall subdue all enemies under his feet [*those who remain loyal to God are guaranteed to overcome all obstacles to exaltation*].

62 **These shall dwell in the presence of God and his Christ forever** and ever.

Next, in verse 63, we find that those who qualify for celestial glory will be privileged to accompany Christ as He comes to earth at the time of the Second Coming.

63 **These are they whom he shall bring with him, when he shall come in the clouds of heaven to reign on the earth** [*during the Millennium*] **over his people.**

64 **These are they who shall have part in the first resurrection.**

65 **These are they who shall come forth in the resurrection of the just.**

In the context of verses 64–65, above, the terms "first resurrection" and "resurrection of the just" both refer to those who will be in the celestial kingdom. Another term for this resurrection is "the morning of the first resurrection."

However, be aware that in a broader sense, the "first resurrection" includes all who will inherit the celestial and terrestrial kingdoms, since these resurrections will take place near the beginning of the Millennium (see D&C 88:96–99). First, the celestials will be resurrected, then the terrestrials, all near the front end of the Millennium. We will quote from the 2018 *Doctrine and Covenants Student Manual* for this:

"The Resurrection of the just is also known as the 'first resurrection' (D&C 76:64) and includes all those who will inherit the celestial and terrestrial kingdoms (see D&C 88:96–99). The First Resurrection began when the graves of the righteous were opened after the Resurrection of Jesus Christ (see Matthew 27:52–53; Mosiah 15:21–24; 3 Nephi 23:9–10). The Doctrine and Covenants refers to the First Resurrection as the time when the just will come forth from their graves at the Second Coming of Jesus Christ (see D&C 29:13; 45:54; 88:96–99). The Resurrection of the unjust, or the 'last resurrection' (D&C 76:85), will include those who will inherit the telestial kingdom and those who are sons of perdition, and it will occur at the end of the Millennium (see D&C 76:85; 88:32, 100–102)" (*Doctrine and Covenants Student Manual*, 2018, chapter 28, 76:50–119).

One more important technical point. Obviously, there will be many righteous people during the Millennium itself, including children who are born and who "shall grow up without sin unto salvation" (D&C 45:58). These will also inherit celestial glory, but their resurrection will occur at the end of their mortal millennial lives of 100 years (Isaiah 65:20), regardless of when, during the Millennium, they live. When referring to their resurrection, we say something to the effect that they are part of the "first resurrection," or, in other words, they will join the first resurrection when their turn comes.

66 **These are they who are come unto Mount Zion** [*symbolizing celestial glory, and including those*

who will dwell with Christ in New Jerusalem; see D&C 84:2], **and unto the city of the living God** [in this context, this means celestial kingdom; see Revelation 21, heading, and verse 2], **the heavenly place, the holiest of all** [celestial glory].

In addition to giving more names for exaltation, verse 67, next, contains an important doctrine. It is that "innumerable" people will attain exaltation.

67 These are they who have come to an **innumerable** company of angels, to **the general assembly** and **church of Enoch, and of the Firstborn**.

Revelation chapter seven also teaches that great numbers of people will enter exaltation. We will include it here and use **bold** to point this doctrine out.

Revelation 7:9

After this I beheld, and, lo, a great multitude, which no man could number, of all nations, and kindreds, and people, and tongues, stood before the throne, and before the Lamb, **clothed with white robes** [symbolic of celestial glory], **and palms in their hands** [palm fronds are symbolic of triumph and victory; thus, these have "overcome" all things and will receive exaltation];

Some may wonder how "innumerable" people can attain celestial glory when other scriptures say that only a few will make it. An example of this is found in Matthew 7:14, which says, "Strait is the gate, and narrow is the way, which leadeth unto life, and few there be that find it."

The answer is simple. Such scriptures as Matthew 7:14 are context sensitive. At various times in the history of the world, including our day, because of gross and widespread wickedness, "few" have been doing the things necessary to qualify for celestial glory.

However, "few there be that find it" would not have applied during the two hundred years of peace among the Nephites after the appearance and teaching of the resurrected Christ. Likewise, it will not apply during the Millennium when virtually all will join the Church and be faithful (see D&C 84:98).

Add to these numbers of righteous all the faithful from the Fall of Adam and Eve to the Second Coming, all the babies and children who have died before reaching the age of accountability (D&C 137:10), which is about 50–80 percent of the earth's total population, plus all those who accept the gospel in the spirit world (D&C 138:32, 58–59), and you have large numbers who will enter celestial glory and exaltation.

As we continue, we see more descriptive terms for those who attain exaltation.

68 These are they whose names are written in heaven [*in the "Book of Life"; see Revelation 3:5*], where God and Christ are the judge of all.

69 These are they who are just men made perfect [*a process*] through Jesus the mediator of the new covenant, who wrought out this perfect atonement through the shedding of his own blood.

President Russell M. Nelson, when he was an Apostle, taught about the process by which we become perfect. He said, "Brothers and sisters, let us do the best we can and try to improve each day. When our imperfections appear, we can keep trying to correct them. We can be more forgiving of flaws in ourselves and among those we love. We can be comforted and forbearing. The Lord taught, 'Ye are not able to abide the presence of God now . . . ; wherefore, continue in patience until ye are perfected' [D&C 67:13].

"We need not be dismayed if our earnest efforts toward perfection now seem so arduous and endless. Perfection is pending. It can come in full only after the Resurrection and only through the Lord. It awaits all who love him and keep his commandments. It includes

thrones, kingdoms, principalities, powers, and dominions [see D&C 132:19]. It is the end for which we are to endure. It is the eternal perfection that God has in store for each of us" ("Perfection Pending," *Ensign*, Nov. 1995, 88).

70 These are they whose bodies are celestial [*they will have celestial resurrected bodies*], whose glory is that of the sun, even the glory of God, the highest of all, whose glory the sun of the firmament is written of as being typical.

We will be taught that there are differences between the resurrected bodies of those who gain celestial glory and the bodies of those who go to other places when we study verse 78 and D&C 88:28–32.

We will also see additional blessings and details about those who attain celestial exaltation when we get to verses 92–96.

Next, we will study the vision of those who enter terrestrial glory.

<u>**Vision #5**</u>
Terrestrial Glory
(verses 71–80, 87, 91, 97)

71 And again, we saw the terrestrial world, and behold and lo, **these are they** who are of the terrestrial, **whose glory differs from that of the church of the Firstborn** [*celestial glory, specifically, exaltation; see verses 54 and*

67] who have received the fulness of the Father [*who have received exaltation*], **even as that of the moon differs from the sun** in the firmament. [*In other words, the terrestrial kingdom is as different in glory from the celestial kingdom as the moon is different from the sun*].

We will use numbers and **bold** to point out qualifications for terrestrial glory.

72 Behold, these are **[1] they who died without law**;

Verses 73 and 74 go together.

73 And also they who are **[2] the spirits of men kept in prison** [*in spirit prison*], **whom the Son visited** [*see 1 Peter 3:18–2; 4:6, D&C 138*], and preached the gospel unto them, that they might be judged according to men in the flesh [*so that they can be judged by the same standards as people on earth who have the gospel*];

74 **Who received not the testimony of Jesus in the flesh, but afterwards received it.**

75 **These are they who are [3] honorable men of the earth, who were blinded by the craftiness of men.**

76 **These are they who receive of his glory** [*they get some glory*],

but not of his fulness [*but not full glory like celestials*].

77 **These are they who receive of the presence of the Son** [*Jesus will visit them*], **but not of the fulness of the Father.**

78 Wherefore, **they are bodies terrestrial**, and not bodies celestial [*their resurrected bodies are terrestrial, not celestial*], and differ in glory as the moon differs from the sun.

In D&C 88:28–32, we are taught that there will be differences between celestial resurrected bodies and the resurrected bodies of those who are given terrestrial glory, telestial glory, and outer darkness (sons of perdition). Joseph Fielding Smith explained this. He said:

"In the resurrection there will be different kinds of bodies; they will not all be alike. The body a man receives will determine his place hereafter. There will be celestial bodies, terrestrial bodies, and telestial bodies, and these bodies will differ as distinctly as do bodies here. . . .

"Bodies will be quickened [*resurrected*] according to the kingdom which they are judged worthy to enter. . . .

"Some will gain celestial bodies with all the powers of exaltation and eternal increase. These bodies will shine like the sun as our Savior's does, as described by John. Those who enter the terrestrial kingdom will have terrestrial bodies, and they will not shine like the sun, but they will be more glorious than the bodies of those who receive the telestial glory.

"In both of these kingdoms there will be changes in the bodies and limitations. They will not have the power of increase, neither the power or nature to live as husbands and wives, for this will be denied them and they cannot increase.

"Those who receive the exaltation in the celestial kingdom will have the 'continuation of the seeds forever.' They will live in the family relationship. In the terrestrial and in the telestial kingdoms there will be no marriage. Those who enter there will remain 'separately and singly' forever.

"Some of the functions in the celestial body will not appear in the terrestrial body, neither in the telestial body, and the power of procreation will be removed" (*Doctrines of Salvation*, 2:286–88).

79 These are [4] they who are not valiant in the testimony of Jesus; wherefore, they obtain not the crown over the kingdom of our God [*"crown" is symbolic of exaltation, of ruling and reigning as gods*].

We will add some notes for the numbered items in verses 72 through 79.

(1) "they who died without law"

Elder Melvin J. Ballard explained this as follows:

"Now, I wish to say to you that those who died without law, meaning the pagan nations, for lack of faithfulness, for lack of devotion, in the former life, are obtaining all that they are entitled to. I don't mean to say that all of them will be barred from entrance into the highest glory. Any one of them who repents and complies with the conditions might also obtain celestial glory, but the great bulk of them will only obtain terrestrial glory" (Bryant S. Hinckley, *Sermons and Missionary Services of Melvin J. Ballard*, 251; quoted in the *Doctrine and Covenants Student Manual*, 1981, 164).

(2) "the spirits of men kept in prison, whom the Son visited . . . Who received not the testimony of Jesus in the flesh, but afterwards received it"

In short, this appears to mean those who had a valid opportunity to "receive" the gospel (to incorporate the gospel into their lives) during mortality, but who intentionally chose not to, and then "afterwards received it" (in the spirit world).

Since God is completely fair, we have to consider that such people would have had a completely fair opportunity to hear and understand the gospel before rejecting it. Also, since we understand that many in the spirit world mission field will accept the gospel and (when their temple work is completed by mortals) go on to celestial exaltation (D&C 138), we are compelled to believe that those spoken of in verses 73 and 74, who "afterwards received it," must yet lack something that would allow them to attain celestial glory and be comfortable there. Perhaps they are not as deeply committed as those who ultimately qualify for the celestial reward. We don't know. Thus, we will have to wait for additional knowledge from authorized sources before being able to answer all the questions that come up regarding these verses.

(3) "honorable men of the earth, who were blinded by the craftiness of men"

These are good and honorable people, who are honest, keep the law of chastity, keep their word, help others, and live respectable, clean lives. Yet, among other things, it appears that they do not want to be tied down by church obligations, time-consuming meetings, and so forth. Joseph Fielding Smith spoke of this category of people. He said:

"Into the terrestrial kingdom will go all those who are honorable and who have lived clean virtuous lives, but who would not receive the Gospel, but in the spirit world repented and accepted it as far as it can be given unto them. Many of these have been blinded by tradition and the love of the world, and have not been able to see the beauties of the Gospel" (*Church History and Modern Revelation*, 1:287–88).

He also said:

"All who enter this kingdom [*terrestrial glory*] must be of that class who have been morally clean." (*Answers to Gospel Questions*, 2:208–10.)

(4) "they who are not valiant in the testimony of Jesus"

Those who have a testimony but intentionally do not live according to it fall into this category. They still fulfill the other qualifications for terrestrial glory, such as being honorable and keeping the law of chastity, but they are not valiant and faithful in living the gospel, keeping their covenants, fulfilling their church obligations, and so forth.

Be careful not to imply from this that those who attain celestial glory must be perfect here on earth. That, of course, is not the case. But there is a big difference in attitude and loyalty between members who know the gospel is true and strive to live it and those who know the gospel is true but live it when it is convenient or fits their current needs.

Bruce R. McConkie summarized the qualifications for terrestrial glory as follows:

"To the terrestrial kingdom will go: 1. Accountable persons who die without law (and who, of course, do not accept the gospel in the spirit world under those particular circumstances which would make them heirs of the celestial kingdom); 2. Those who reject the gospel in this life and who reverse their course and accept it in the spirit world; 3. Honorable men of the earth who are blinded by the craftiness of men and who therefore do not accept and live the gospel law; and 4. Members of The Church of Jesus Christ of Latter-day Saints who have testimonies of Christ and the divinity of the great latter-day work and who are not valiant, but who are instead lukewarm in their devotion to the Church and to righteousness. (D. & C. 76:71–80.)" (*Mormon Doctrine*, 784).

By the way, it is interesting to note that those who enter celestial glory will live on this earth (D&C 130:9–11) after it has been celestialized and glorified, whereas those who go to terrestrial and telestial glory will live on other planets prepared for them. Joseph Fielding Smith taught this. He said (**bold** added for emphasis):

"This earth will become a celestial kingdom when it is sanctified. Those who enter **the terrestrial** kingdom will **have to go to some other sphere** which will be prepared for them. Those who enter **the telestial** kingdom, **likewise will have to go to some earth which is prepared for them**, and there will be **another place which is hell where the devil and those who are punished to go with him will dwell**. Of course, those who enter the telestial kingdom, and those who enter the terrestrial kingdom will have the eternal punishment which will come to them in knowing that they might, if they had kept the commandments of the Lord, have returned to his presence as his sons and his daughters. This will be a torment to them, and in that sense it will be hell" (*Answers to Gospel Questions*, 2:210).

80 And now **this is the end of the vision which we saw of the terrestrial**, that **the Lord commanded us to write** while we were yet in the Spirit.

Before we continue, we will mention one other question that occasionally comes up in gospel discussions. It asks why the Lord, as a matter of kindness and mercy, couldn't place all people into heaven, whether they are worthy or not. Brigham Young addressed this question. He said:

"Some might suppose that it

would be a great blessing to be taken and carried directly into heaven and there set down, but in reality that would be no blessing to such persons; they could not reap a full reward, could not enjoy the glory of the kingdom, and could not comprehend and abide the light thereof, but it would be to them a hell intolerable and I suppose would consume them much quicker than would hell fire. It would be no blessing to you to be carried into the celestial kingdom, and obliged to stay therein, unless you were prepared to dwell there (*Discourses of Brigham Young*, Deseret Book, 95).

We will now proceed to study the telestial glory.

Vision #6

Telestial Glory
(verses 81–89, 98–106, 109–112)

81 And again, we saw the glory of the telestial, which glory is that of the lesser, even **as the glory of the stars differs from that of the glory of the moon** in the firmament [*there is much difference between the telestial glory and the terrestrial glory*].

We will use numbers and **bold** to point out qualifications of those who receive telestial glory.

82 These are [1] they who received not the gospel of Christ, neither the testimony of Jesus.

83 These are [2] they who deny not the Holy Spirit [*they did not deny the Holy Ghost, therefore, they are not sons of perdition*].

We will add some notes for the numbered items in verses 82–83.

(1) "they who received not the gospel of Christ"

These are people who willfully rejected Christ and His full gospel after being given fair opportunities to accept it.

(2) "they who deny not the Holy Spirit"

In other words, they are wicked, but they did not deny the Holy Ghost, therefore, they do not qualify to be sons of perdition.

We will add additional numbers when we get to verses 99–101 and 103.

As we continue, we see details as to what happens to those who qualify for telestial glory.

84 These are they who are thrust down to hell.

These people will be turned over to Satan to suffer for their own sins because they were not willing to repent and allow Christ's Atonement to pay for their sins. See verse 106 and D&C 19:15–19. Elder Joseph Fielding Smith explained this. He said (**bold** added for emphasis):

"Into this kingdom will go all of those who have been unclean in their lives. See verses 98 to 112, in section 76. These people who enter there will be the unclean; the liars, sorcerers, adulterers, and those who have broken their covenants. Of these the Lord says: 'These are they who are cast down to hell and suffer the wrath of Almighty God, until the fulness of times, when Christ shall have subdued all enemies under his feet, and shall have perfected his work (D&C 76:106).' Yet **these, after they have been punished for their sins and having been turned over to the torments of Satan, shall eventually come forth, after the millennium**, to receive the telestial kingdom" (*Answers to Gospel Questions*, 12:208).

85 These are **they who shall not be redeemed from the devil until the last resurrection**, until the Lord, even Christ the Lamb, shall have finished his work.

In D&C 88:100–101, we are taught that those who receive telestial glory must wait until the end of the Millennium (the thousand years of peace) to be resurrected. Combining this reference with verse 85, above, we learn that telestials will be turned over to Satan to suffer for their sins during the time that the Millennium is going on upon the earth. They will not be redeemed from the devil until they are resurrected into telestial bodies.

86 These are **they who receive not of his fulness in the eternal world** [*they will not gain the blessings of celestial glory and exaltation*], **but of the Holy Spirit through the ministration of the terrestrial** [*the Holy Ghost can have influence in the telestial kingdom; also, those in the terrestrial kingdom can visit those in the telestial kingdom*];

Elder James E. Talmage summarized telestial glory as follows:

"There is another grade [*telestial*], differing from the higher orders as the stars differ from the brighter orbs of the firmament; this is for those who received not the testimony of Christ, but who, nevertheless, did not deny the Holy Spirit; who have led lives exempting them from the heaviest punishment [*perdition*], yet whose redemption will be delayed until the last resurrection. In the telestial world there are innumerable degrees comparable to the varying light of the stars. Yet all who receive of any one of these orders of glory are at last saved, and upon them Satan will finally have no claim" (James E. Talmage, *The Articles of Faith*, 92).

As you saw in verse 86, above, those who live in the terrestrial kingdom can visit the telestial kingdom. Next, in verse 87, we are taught that inhabitants of the celestial kingdom can visit people who live in the terrestrial glory. As you can see, there is no doctrine here to the effect that celestials can visit telestials.

87 And the terrestrial through the ministration of the celestial.

88 And also the telestial receive it [*the limited blessings for them as mentioned in verse 86, above*] **of** [*through*] **the administering of angels who are appointed to minister for them,** or who are appointed to be ministering spirits for them; for **they** [*those who go to telestial glory*] **shall be heirs of salvation** [*will receive a degree of salvation, not celestial, not terrestrial, but telestial, which is still so wonderful we cannot imagine it; see verse 89, next*].

With very few exceptions, the term "salvation," as used in the scriptures, means exaltation. One of the exceptions appears in verse 88, above. In this case, it means "salvation in telestial glory." Indeed, being free from Satan forever and being in a kingdom of glory that "surpasses all understanding" (verse 89, below) is "salvation." But this salvation is as a star compared to the sun, as far as celestial glory is concerned.

The Prophet Joseph Smith used the word "saved" in this sense. He taught (**bold** added for emphasis):

"But except a man be born again, he cannot see the kingdom of God. This eternal truth settles the question of all men's religion.

A man may be saved, after the judgment, **in the terrestrial kingdom, or in the telestial kingdom, but he can never see the celestial kingdom of God without being born of the water and the Spirit**. He may receive a glory like unto the moon [i. e. of which the light of the moon is typical], or a star [i. e. of which the light of the stars is typical], but he can never come unto Mount Zion, and unto the city of the living God, the heavenly Jerusalem, and to an innumerable company of angels; to the general assembly and Church of the First-born, which are written in heaven, and to God the judge of all, and to the spirits of just men made perfect, and to Jesus the Mediator of the new covenant, unless he becomes as a little child, and is taught by the Spirit of God" (*History of the Church,* 1:283–84).

89 And thus we saw, in the heavenly vision [*consisting of verses 19–113*], **the glory of the telestial, which surpasses all understanding** [*which is far more glorious and beautiful that any of us can imagine*];

The last phrase of verse 89, above, is a reminder that our Heavenly Father is merciful and kind. He is going to give even those who qualify only for telestial glory a reward that is far better than any of us can imagine! Elder John A. Widtsoe explained this. He said:

"The book [Doctrine and Covenants] explains clearly that the lowest glory to which man is assigned is so glorious as to be beyond the understanding of man. It is a doctrine fundamental in Mormonism that the meanest sinner, in the final judgment, will receive a glory which is beyond human understanding, which is so great that we are unable to describe it adequately. Those who do well will receive an even more glorious place. Those who dwell in the lower may look wistfully to the higher as we do here. The hell on the other side will be felt in some such way.

"The Gospel is a gospel of tremendous love. Love is at the bottom of it. The meanest child is loved so dearly that his reward will be beyond the understanding of mortal man" (*The Message of the Doctrine and Covenants*, 67).

Even though the main vision of the telestial glory ends with verse 89, there are additional qualifications for the telestial kingdom mentioned in verses 99–101 and 103. As mentioned previously, we will continue the use of **bold** and the numbering relating to telestial glory when we get to these verses. You may wish to look ahead to those verses now and then come back to verse 90 to continue your study of section 76.

90 And no man knows it except him to whom God has revealed it [*perhaps meaning that none can know these details about the three*

degrees of glory, exaltation, and perdition unless it is given them by revelation*].

91 And thus we saw **the glory of the terrestrial** which **excels in all things the glory of the telestial**, even in glory, and in power, and in might, and in dominion.

92 And thus we saw **the glory of the celestial**, which **excels in all things—where God, even the Father, reigns upon his throne forever and ever**;

93 Before whose throne all things bow in humble reverence, and give him glory forever and ever.

Verses 94–95, next, refer to exaltation, or, in other words, becoming gods and receiving "all that my father hath" (D&C 84:38).

94 **They who dwell in his presence are the church of the First-born** [*another term for exaltation*]; and **they see as they are seen** [*by the Father—verse 92*]**, and know as they are known** [*by the Father*]**, having received of his fulness and of his grace** [*having become gods*];

95 And **he makes them equal in power, and in might, and in dominion**.

96 And **the glory of the celestial is one** [*degree of glory*]**, even as

the glory of the sun is one.

97 And **the glory of the terrestrial is one** [*degree of glory*], even as the glory of the moon is one.

98 And **the glory of the telestial is one** [*degree of glory*], even as the glory of the stars is one; for as one star differs from another star in glory, even so differs one from another in glory in the telestial world [*the telestial kingdom has many different degrees of glory within it*];

99 For **[3] these are they who are of Paul, and of Apollos, and of Cephas**.

100 **These are they who say they are some of one and some of another**—some **of Christ** and some of **John**, and some of **Moses**, and some of **Elias**, and some of **Esaias** [*an ancient prophet who lived in the days of Abraham; see "Esaias" in the Bible Dictionary and D&C 84:11–13*], and some of **Isaiah**, and some of **Enoch**;

101 But **[4] received not the gospel, neither the testimony of Jesus** [*these two were already numbered in verse 82*]**, neither the prophets, neither the everlasting covenant**.

102 Last of all, these all are they who will not be gathered with the saints, to be caught up unto the church of the Firstborn, and received into the cloud.

103 **[5] These are they who are liars, and sorcerers, and adulterers, and whoremongers, and whosoever loves and makes a lie**.

We noted two qualifications for telestial glory as we studied verses 82–83. As you can see, we continued this numbering, beginning with verse 99, above. We will now add notes for items 3–5.

<u>(3) "these are they who are of Paul, and of Apollos, and of Cephas, of Christ, John, Moses, Elias, Esaias, Isaiah, and Enoch"</u>

Paul was, of course, a member of the Church. If you check Acts 18:24 and 19:1, 5, you will see that Apollos and Cephas likewise were faithful followers of Christ. So were the other prophets mentioned in verse 100. So, what is the message here?

Throughout the world's history, there have been various sects and religions who have claimed to believe the Bible, in which the words of Christ and the prophets are taught. Yet their creeds and teachings vary greatly. Also, there have been a number of members of the true Church who have broken away and set up their own false churches (based on the teachings of past prophets), and rejected the teachings of the living prophets.

Thus, many in the telestial kingdom will be those who claimed to believe but who did not live according to the full gospel. In fact, many of these groups have engaged in bloody battles against each other and in wars of hatred and vicious verbal opposition. They are not followers of Christ and have rejected the full gospel of the Savior. Elder James E. Talmage explained this. He said:

"We learn further that the inhabitants of this kingdom [telestial] are to be graded among themselves, comprising as they do the unenlightened among the varied opposing sects and divisions of men, and sinners of many types, whose offenses are not those of utter perdition: 'For as one star differs from another star in glory, even so differs one from another in glory in the telestial world; for these are they who are of Paul, and of Apollos, and of Cephas. These are they who say they are some of one and some of another—some of Christ, and some of John, and some of Moses, and some of Elias, and some of Esaias, and some of Isaiah, and some of Enoch; But received not the gospel, neither the testimony of Jesus, neither the prophets, neither the everlasting covenant'" (*Articles of Faith*, 369).

(4) received not the gospel, neither the testimony of Jesus, neither the prophets, neither the everlasting covenant

These are the wicked who rejected the Savior and His prophets and who refused to enter into the covenants of the gospel that are required of those who desire exaltation. They refused to repent when the principles of righteousness were explained to them and foolishly or blatantly continued in their wicked ways.

(5) These are they who are liars, and sorcerers, and adulterers, and whoremongers, and whosoever loves and makes a lie

As you can see, this verse (verse 103) has several qualifiers for telestial glory. It could be broken down into categories, including

• **Dishonesty** in any form.

• **The occult**, including witchcraft, fortune telling, and so on.

• **Sexual immorality**. The First Presidency said the following about illicit sex: "The doctrine of this Church is that sexual sin—the illicit sexual relations of men and women—stands, in its enormity, next to murder. The Lord has drawn no essential distinctions between fornication, adultery, and harlotry or prostitution. Each has fallen under His solemn and awful condemnation" (Heber J. Grant, J.

Reuben Clark Jr., David O. McKay, general conference, October 11, 1942).

• **Making illicit sex the central focus of life** (whoremongers).

• **Whoever "loves and makes a lie."** Possibilities for this category can include covenant breakers, who, in effect "lie" to God when they break their covenants. It can include those involved in illicit sex who love it and lie to try to cover it up. It can also include people who love gossip and love to pass on lies about others. All these are forms of dishonesty.

In Galatians, we find an expanded list of sins which, unrepented of, will lead to telestial glory. We will include it here for reference (**bold** added for emphasis):

Galatians 5:19–21

19 Now the works of the flesh are manifest, which are these [*now here are some of the worldly sins you must avoid*]*;* **Adultery, fornication, uncleanness, lasciviousness** [*lustful behavior, thinking and talking and all sexual immorality, including pornography*],

20 Idolatry [*idol worship*]**, witchcraft, hatred, variance** [*disharmony*]**, emulations** [*rivalry and other such behaviors based on jealousy and worldly*

ambitions]**, wrath** [*anger, loss of temper*]**, strife, seditions** [*stirring up unrighteous discontent with those in power, including government leaders and church leaders*]**, heresies** [*false doctrines*],

21 Envyings, murders, drunkenness, revellings [*riotous, drunken parties and lifestyles*]**,** and such like: of the which I tell you before [*I forewarn you*], as I have also told *you* in time past, that **they which do such things shall not inherit the kingdom of God** [*the celestial kingdom, or the terrestrial kingdom for that matter*].

Next, we are taught additional details about those who are consigned to the telestial kingdom.

104 These are they who suffer the wrath of God on earth.

105 These are they who suffer the vengeance of eternal fire [*they will be turned over to Satan to be punished for their own sins, since they refused to repent and thus accept the Savior's payment for them; see verse 106, next; also verses 84–86 and D&C 19:15–17*].

106 These are they who are cast down to hell and suffer the wrath of Almighty God, until the fulness of times [*until the end of the Millennium; see verse 85*], when

Christ shall have subdued all enemies under his feet, and shall have perfected his work;

> The question sometimes comes up as to whether the Savior will ever finish up His work assigned to Him by the Father and become a Heavenly Father to His own worlds. The answer is found in verses 107–8, next.

107 When **he** [*Christ*] **shall deliver up the kingdom, and present it unto the Father**, spotless, saying: I have overcome and have trodden the wine-press alone, even the wine-press of the fierceness of the wrath of Almighty God.

108 **Then shall he be crowned with the crown of his glory, to sit on the throne of his power** to reign forever and ever.

> A few more details about the telestial kingdom are given in verses 109–12, next.

109 But behold, and lo, **we saw the glory and the inhabitants of the telestial world**, that **they were as innumerable as the stars in the firmament of heaven, or as the sand upon the seashore**;

110 And heard the voice of the Lord saying: **These all shall bow the knee, and every tongue shall confess to him** who sits upon the throne forever and ever;

111 For **they shall be judged according to their works**, and every man shall receive according to his own works, his own dominion, in the mansions which are prepared;

112 And **they shall be servants of the Most High; but where God and Christ dwell they cannot come, worlds without end**.

> The question often comes up concerning verse 112, above, as to whether it is possible, after the final Judgment Day, to eventually progress from one degree of glory to another. At the time this study guide went to press, the instruction from the First Presidency and the Quorum of the Twelve Apostles to curriculum writers for the Church was that we do not have sufficient information from the Lord at this point to answer that question either yes or no.
>
> Verse 113, next, informs us that this is the end of the vision, which started in verse 19.

113 **This is the end of the vision which we saw**, which we were commanded to write while we were yet in the Spirit.

114 But **great and marvelous are the works of the Lord, and the mysteries of his kingdom which he showed unto us, which**

surpass all understanding in glory, and in might, and in dominion;

We find in verses 115–16, next, that there were many things that Joseph Smith and Sidney Rigdon saw that they were commanded not to write. Also, these brethren tell us that it would be impossible to put into words many of the things they saw.

115 Which he commanded us we should not write while we were yet in the Spirit, and are not lawful for man to utter;

116 Neither is man capable to make them known, for they are only to be seen and understood by the power of the Holy Spirit, which God bestows on those who love him, and purify themselves before him;

117 To whom he grants this privilege of seeing and knowing for themselves;

118 That through the power and manifestation of the Spirit, while in the flesh, they may be able to bear his presence in the world of glory.

119 And to God and the Lamb be glory, and honor, and dominion forever and ever. Amen.

We will learn more about the celestial kingdom and exaltation when we get to sections 131 and 132.

SECTION 77

Background

This revelation was given to the Prophet Joseph Smith in Hiram, Ohio, in March 1832 while he was working on the Book of Revelation for the inspired translation of the Bible (*the Joseph Smith Translation*, or JST).

He had begun his inspired translation and revision of the New Testament on March 8, 1831, and would complete his initial work on it in July 1832. He then continued reviewing and revising the translation until February 2, 1833.

Section 77 contains a series of questions and answers about the Apostle John's book of Revelation in the Bible. It provides many answers to questions that arise while striving to understand the vision given to the Apostle John while he was being held in a prison colony on the Isle of Patmos (Revelation 1:9) about A.D. 95 In fact, it serves as a key to unlocking many of the "hidden mysteries" of this marvelous book.

Joseph Smith explained that "John had the curtains of heaven withdrawn, and by vision looked through the dark vista of future ages, and contemplated events that should transpire throughout every subsequent period of time until the final winding up scene—[and] while he gazed upon the glories of the eternal world, saw an innumerable company of angels and heard the voice of God" (in *Manuscript History of the Church*, vol. C-1, Addenda, page 69, josephsmithpapers.org).

One of the main questions that arises among students of the book of Revelation has to do with determining what is symbolic and what is literal when it comes to the imagery used in John's writing. The revealed answers to questions, as given here through Joseph Smith, serve as invaluable keys in this matter.

As we proceed, we will include the verses from Revelation that are referenced in this section. For example, verses 1–3, next, refer to Revelation 4:6.

Revelation 4:6

6 And before the throne there was **a sea of glass** like unto crystal: and in the midst of the throne, and round about the throne, were **four beasts** full of eyes before and behind [*in front and back*].

1 Q. **What is the sea of glass** spoken of by John, 4th chapter, and 6th verse of the Revelation?

A. **It is the earth**, in its sanctified, immortal, and eternal state [*as a celestial planet*].

The Prophet taught more about this. He said:

"While at dinner, I remarked to my family and friends present, that when the earth was sanctified and became like a sea of glass, it would be one great urim and thummim, and the Saints could look in it and see as they are seen" (*History of the Church*, 5:279).

Also, in section 130, he taught:

D&C 130:9

9 This earth, in its sanctified and immortal state [*when it becomes a celestial kingdom*], **will be made like unto crystal and will be a Urim and Thummim to the inhabitants who dwell thereon**, whereby all things pertaining to an inferior kingdom, or all kingdoms of a lower order, will be manifest to those who dwell on it; and this earth will be Christ's.

Brigham Young spoke of this when he said:

"This Earth will become a celestial body—be like a sea of glass, or like a Urim and Thummim; and when you wish to know anything, you can look in this Earth and see all the eternities of God" (*Journal of Discourses*, 8:200).

2 Q. **What are** we to understand by **the four beasts**, spoken of in the same verse?

A. They are **figurative** [*symbolic*] **expressions**, used by the Revelator, John, in describing heaven, the paradise of God, the happiness of man, and of beasts, and of creeping things, and of the fowls of the air; that which is spiritual being in the likeness of that which is temporal; and that which is temporal in the likeness of that which is spiritual; the spirit of man in the likeness of his person, as also the spirit of the beast, and every other creature which God has created.

Did you notice other things also taught in verse 2, above, in addition to the fact that the beasts are symbolic? We will list two of them.

1. Beasts, creeping things, and fowls of the air have the capacity to be happy and will have that capacity eternally (see verse 3, next).

2. Spirit looks like the physical body it inhabits. Bruce R. McConkie spoke of this when he said:

"Man and all forms of life existed as spirit beings and entities before the foundations of this earth were laid. There were spirit men and spirit beasts, spirit fowls and spirit fishes, spirit plants and spirit trees. Every creeping thing, every herb and shrub, every amoeba and tadpole, every elephant and dinosaur—all things—existed as spirits, as spirit beings, before

they were placed naturally upon the earth" (*The Millennial Messiah*, 642–43; also quoted in the *Doctrines of the Gospel Student Manual*, 1981, 16).

3 Q. **Are the four beasts limited to individual beasts, or do they represent classes or orders?**

A. **They are limited to four individual beasts, which** were shown to John, to **represent** [*are symbolic of*] **the glory of the classes of beings** in their destined order or sphere of creation, **in the enjoyment of their eternal felicity** [*eternal happiness*].

The Prophet Joseph Smith taught that there are many beasts in heaven that would be entirely strange to us. He said that these animals come from other earths. We will quote the Prophet here:

"I suppose John saw beings there of a thousand forms, that had been saved from ten thousand times ten thousand earths like this,—strange beasts of which we have no conception: all might be seen in heaven. The grand secret was to show John what there was in heaven. John learned that God glorified Himself by saving all that His hands had made, whether beasts, fowls, fishes or men; and He will glorify Himself with them" (*Teachings of the Prophet Joseph Smith*, 291).

As we move on, imagine that

you were reading the book of Revelation with no outside help and were trying to figure out the "eyes and wings" spoken of in Revelation 4:8 ("eyes" are also spoken of in Revelation 4:6, as quoted above). We will give verse 8 here, using **bold** for emphasis:

Revelation 4:8

8 And **the four beasts had each of them six wings** about *him;* **and they were full of eyes** within: and they rest not day and night, saying, Holy, holy, holy [*in Hebrew, such things repeated three times symbolize the superlative, the very best*], Lord God Almighty, which was, and is, and is to come.

Without the revealed word of the Lord, as given in verse 4, next, we wouldn't be able to understand this verse. With it, we are greatly blessed.

4 Q. **What are we to understand by the eyes and wings**, which the beasts had?

A. **Their eyes are a representation** [*are symbolic*] **of light and knowledge**, that is, they are full of knowledge; and **their wings are a representation of power, to move, to act, etc**.

Have you ever wondered why many pictures of angels show them with wings? Verse 4,

above, helps us understand that symbolism. In ancient times, the fastest creatures were birds. With their wings, they were able to get from one place to another quickly. Since angels are able to instantly be wherever they are needed, it was logical for artists to picture them with wings, representing their ability to "move, to act" as needed in carrying out the work of God.

Next, verse 5 refers back to three verses in the fourth chapter of Revelation. We will quote them here:

Revelation 4:4, 10–11

4 And round about the throne *were* four and twenty seats: and upon the seats I saw **four and twenty elders sitting, clothed in white raiment** [*symbolic of celestial glory*]; and they had on their heads **crowns of gold** [*symbolic that they had qualified to receive exaltation*].

10 The four and twenty elders fall down before him that sat on the throne, and worship him that liveth for ever and ever, and cast their crowns before the throne, saying,

11 Thou art worthy, O Lord, to receive glory and honour and power: for thou hast created all things, and for thy pleasure

they are and were created.

5 Q. **What are** we to understand by **the four and twenty elders,** spoken of by John?

A. We are to understand that **these** elders whom John saw, **were elders who had been faithful in the work of the ministry and were dead; who belonged to the seven churches** [*wards or branches spoken of in Revelation 1:11*]**, and were then in the paradise of God.**

As you can see from the Prophet's answer in verse 5, above, in this case, the twenty-four elders were literal. In other words, they were real individuals who lived in the days during or after Christ's mortal mission and belonged to the seven wards or branches spoken of by John the Apostle in Revelation 1:11. It is highly likely that before his arrest and banishment to the prison colony on the Isle of Patmos (some fifty miles off the western coast of Turkey today), John visited these seven wards or branches of the Church located in what is now western Turkey.

Verse 6, next, has reference to Revelation 5:1.

Revelation 5:1

1 AND I saw in the right hand of him that sat on the throne **a book written within and on the backside, sealed with seven seals.**

6 Q. **What are we to understand by the book** which John saw, which was **sealed on the back with seven seals?**

A. We are to understand that **it contains the revealed will, mysteries, and the works of God;** the hidden things of his economy **concerning this earth during the seven thousand years of its** continuance, or its **temporal** [*subject to our current time system*] **existence.**

If you were to study Revelation 5, you would discover that "him" in verse 1 (quoted above) refers to the Father. Thus, the "book" could well be termed "the Father's plan"—in other words, the plan of salvation. "Right hand" symbolizes "covenant hand," thus teaching us that the Father's plan for us relies heavily on covenants. It is "sealed" because no one can carry out the Father's plan for us on the earth except Jesus Christ. Again, if you were to study verses 5–7 in Revelation 5, you would find that the "Lamb" (Jesus) is the one who takes the book from the Father's hand (verse 7). In other words, He accepts the mission from the Father to be our Savior and carry out the Atonement and all that goes with it in order to save us, if we accept it.

Did you also notice how long this earth will have, from the Fall of Adam and Eve to the final winding up scenes, concluding with the final judgment? It is seven thousand years. We have already used up about six thousand years, and still need a thousand for the Millennium. Thus, we know that the Second Coming is getting relatively close.

Next, verse 7 refers both to Revelation 5:1, above, and to chapter 6. As you will see, each seal represents one thousand years of the earth's temporal [*our time system*] history.

7 Q. **What are we to understand by the seven seals** with which it was sealed?

A. We are to understand that **the first seal contains the things of the first thousand years**, and **the second also of the second thousand years, and so on until the seventh**.

We will quote enough of Revelation 6 to give the basic idea for the answer given in verse 7, above, using **bold** as usual for emphasis. As you will see, the opening of each "seal" provides a brief sketch of events and conditions in that particular one-thousand-year period of the earth's history.

Revelation 6:1–12

1 AND **I saw when the Lamb opened one of the seals** [*the first seal, 4,000–3,000 B.C.*], and I heard, as it were, the noise of thunder, one of the four beasts saying, Come and see.

2 And I saw, and behold a white horse: and he that sat on him had a bow; and a crown was given unto him: and he went forth conquering, and to conquer.

3 And when he had opened **the second seal** [*3,000–2,000 B.C.*], I heard the second beast say, Come and see.

4 And there went out another horse *that was* red: and *power* was given to him that sat thereon to take peace from the earth, and that they should kill one another: and there was given unto him a great sword.

5 And when he had opened **the third seal** [*2,000–1,000 B.C.*], I heard the third beast say, Come and see. And I beheld, and lo a black horse; and he that sat on him had a pair of balances in his hand.

6 And I heard a voice in the midst of the four beasts say, A

measure of wheat for a penny, and three measures of barley for a penny; and *see* thou hurt not the oil and the wine.

7 And when he had opened **the fourth seal** [*1,000–0* B.C.], I heard the voice of the fourth beast say, Come and see.

8 And I looked, and behold a pale horse: and his name that sat on him was Death, and Hell followed with him. And power was given unto them over the fourth part of the earth, to kill with sword, and with hunger, and with death, and with the beasts of the earth.

9 And when he had opened **the fifth seal** [A.D. *0–1,000*], I saw under the altar the souls of them that were slain for the word of God, and for the testimony which they held:

10 And they cried with a loud voice, saying, How long, O Lord, holy and true, dost thou not judge and avenge our blood on them that dwell on the earth?

11 And white robes were given unto every one of them; and it was said unto them, that they should rest yet for a little season, until their fellowservants also and their brethren, that should be killed as they *were,* should be fulfilled.

12 And I beheld when he had opened **the sixth seal** [A.D. *1,000–2,000*], and, lo, there was a great earthquake; and the sun became black as sackcloth of hair, and the moon became as blood;

By the way, Revelation 8–9 and a few other chapters deal with things that will take place during the seventh seal before the Second Coming and the beginning of the Millennium. We will say more about this in a minute.

Next, in verse 8, the Lord gives information to us through His prophet Joseph Smith about the four powerful angels spoken of in Revelation 7:1.

Revelation 7:1

1 AND **after these things I saw four angels standing on the four corners of the earth** [*symbolic of all the inhabitants of the earth*], holding the four winds of the earth, that the wind [*symbolic of destruction*] should not blow on the earth, nor on the sea, nor on any tree.

8 Q. **What are** we to understand by **the four angels**, spoken of in the 7th chapter and 1st verse of Revelation?

A. We are to understand that **they are four angels sent forth from God, to whom is given power** over the four parts of the earth, **to save life and to destroy**; these are **they** who **have the everlasting gospel to commit to every nation, kindred, tongue, and people**; having power to shut up the heavens, to seal up unto life, or to cast down to the regions of darkness.

From the answer in verse 8, above, we understand, among other things, that there is much going on behind the scenes by way of angelic ministration and involvement in the work of spreading the gospel throughout the earth before the Second Coming.

We will prepare for verse 9, next, by including verse 3 also for context. You will see that the destruction of the wicked in the last days is not to be completed until the gathering of righteous Israel.

Revelation 7:2–3

2 And **I saw another angel ascending from the east,** having the seal of the living God: and he **cried with a loud voice to the four angels, to whom it was given to hurt the earth and the sea,**

3 **Saying, Hurt not the earth, neither the sea, nor the trees,** till we have sealed the servants of our God in their foreheads [*symbolic of loyalty*].

9 Q. What are we to understand by the angel ascending from the east, Revelation 7th chapter and 2nd verse?

A. We are to understand that **the angel ascending from the east is he to whom is given the seal** [*the power and authority*] **of the living God over the twelve tribes of Israel** [*includes all people throughout the earth in the last days who will accept the gospel and make and keep covenants*]; wherefore, he crieth unto the four angels [*he has power over the four angels spoken of in verse 8*] **having the everlasting gospel, saying: Hurt not the earth, neither the sea, nor the trees** [*perhaps meaning, among other things, not to let mankind destroy the earth's ecology before the righteous are successfully gathered*]**, till we have sealed the servants of our God in their foreheads** [*until righteous Israel has been gathered; in Bible symbolism, "forehead" means loyalty; therefore, this phrase can mean "until we have gathered those of Israel who will be completely loyal to God"*]. And, **if you will receive it, this is Elias which was to come to gather together the tribes of Israel and restore all things.**

One of the definitions of the word "Elias," in verse 9, above, is "any messenger from God sent to carry out a specific task." You may wish to turn to your Bible Dictionary in the back of your LDS Bible and read definition 3 under "Elias." Thus, the "Elias" in verse 9 could possibly be a "composite" of many different angels and messengers to be sent forth by God to assist with the restoration of the gospel and the gathering of Israel.

As the Prophet answers the question in verse 10, next, we find that the things spoken of in Revelation 7, including the gathering of Israel, are to happen during the sixth seal.

10 Q. What time are the things spoken of in this chapter [*chapter 7 of Revelation*] **to be accomplished?**

A. They are to be accomplished in the sixth thousand years, or the opening of the sixth seal [*which symbolizes the sixth thousand-year period of the earth's history*].

Just a word of caution. As we consider the seven one-thousand-year periods of the earth's temporal existence, spoken of in the book of Revelation, it is vital that we be careful not to try to exactly superimpose these time periods upon our calendar system. There are many questions as to the accuracy of our calendar system, especially as we go

back to the time of the Fall (read "Chronology" in your Bible Dictionary). Therefore, we don't know just where we are in the sixth seal, or, perhaps we are already in the beginning of the seventh seal. We don't know.

Next, we learn of the 144,000 spoken of in Revelation 7:4. The question as to just who these are often comes up. Perhaps you have heard the idea that there will only be 144,000 saved when the Savior comes. This is not true. We have an answer from the Lord through the Prophet Joseph Smith. As you will see, they are high priests from throughout the world, twelve thousand from each tribe of Israel, who will help with the gathering of Israel in the last days.

Revelation 7:4

4 And I heard the number of them which were sealed: *and there were* sealed an hundred *and* forty *and* four thousand of all the tribes of the children of Israel.

11 Q. What are we to understand by sealing the one hundred and forty-four thousand, out of all the tribes of Israel—**twelve thousand out of every tribe?**

A. We are to understand that those who are sealed are high priests, ordained unto the holy order of God, **to administer the**

everlasting gospel; for they are they who are ordained **out of every nation**, kindred, tongue, and people, by the angels to whom is **given power** over the nations of the earth, **to bring as many as will come to the church of the Firstborn** [*to the Church of Jesus Christ, and ultimately to exaltation in the celestial kingdom; see D&C 76:54, 67, 102*].

Perhaps you have heard at one time or another the attempts of someone to pin down the exact timing of the Second Coming. Often, such people are of the opinion that the Savior's Coming will be at the conclusion of the sixth seal, the end of the sixth thousand-year period.

A careful study of the answer to the question in verse 12, next, shows that this is not the case. Some things will be finished up in the beginning of the seventh seal, before the actual coming of Christ and the beginning of the Millennium. Thus, it would be impossible to calculate the exact timing of the Second Coming (see Matthew 24:36), even if we knew the exact time of the Fall of Adam.

You may wish to read Revelation 8:6–13 in your Bible as background for verse 12, next.

12 Q. **What are we to understand by the sounding of the trumpets, mentioned in the 8th chapter of Revelation**?

A. We are to understand that as God made the world in six days, and on the seventh day he finished his work, and sanctified it, and also formed man out of the dust of the earth, even so, **in the beginning of the seventh thousand years** will the Lord God sanctify the earth, and complete the salvation of man, and judge all things, and shall redeem all things, except that which he hath not put into his power, when he shall have sealed all things, unto the end of all things; and **the sounding of the trumpets of the seven angels are the preparing and finishing of his work, in the beginning of the seventh thousand years**— the preparing of the way **before the time of his coming**.

It appears that just in case we didn't get the message in verse 12, above, that the Savior will not come at the end of the sixth thousand years but rather sometime in the beginning of the seventh, it is repeated in verse 13, next.

You may wish to read Revelation chapter 9 in your Bible as background for verse 13, next. There are a great many signs of the times included in this chapter of Revelation.

13 Q. **When are the things** [*signs of the times*] **to be accomplished, which are written in the 9th chapter of Revelation?**

A. They are to be accomplished **after the opening of the seventh seal, before the coming of Christ.**

While we don't know the answer, it is sometimes interesting to read Revelation 8–9 and wonder whether we might already be in the beginning of the seventh seal.

Many people are puzzled by the "little book" mentioned in Revelation 10 that John is commanded to eat. It would seem a bit difficult to eat a book. We will include the relevant verses of Revelation, chapter 10, here.

Revelation 10:1–2, 8–11

1 AND **I saw another mighty angel come down from heaven,** clothed with a cloud: and a rainbow was upon his head, and his face was as it were the sun, and his feet as pillars of fire:

2 And **he had in his hand a little book** open: and he set his right foot upon the sea, and his left foot on the earth,

8 And **the voice which I heard from heaven spake unto me** [*John the Beloved Apostle*] again,

and said, Go and **take the little book** which is open in the hand of the angel which standeth upon the sea and upon the earth.

9 And **I went unto the angel, and said unto him, Give me the little book. And he said unto me, Take it, and eat it up**; and it shall make thy belly bitter, but it shall be in thy mouth sweet as honey.

10 And **I took the little book** out of the angel's hand, **and ate it up**; and it was in my mouth sweet as honey: and as soon as I had eaten it, my belly was bitter.

11 And **he said unto me, Thou must prophesy again before many peoples, and nations, and tongues, and kings**.

With the help of Joseph Smith, we find this imagery easier to understand.

14 Q. **What are we to understand by the little book which was eaten by John, as mentioned in the 10th chapter of Revelation?**

A. **We are to understand that it was a mission**, and an ordinance, **for him to gather the tribes of Israel**; behold, this is Elias, who, as it is written, must come and restore all things.

As with most missions (including ward and stake callings), there are many aspects of it that are "sweet" (Revelations 10:9) and some aspects that tend to make the "belly bitter" (give one indigestion).

Next, in verse 15, we are given key information that helps us understand Revelation 11, in which two "witnesses" (verse 3) "prophesy" for three and a half years among the Jews and then are killed (verse 7). By the way, the word "prophesy" in this context can mean to teach and instruct as well as to predict the future. We will include the relevant verses of Revelation chapter 11 here, with some explanatory notes as background for section 77, verse 15. These notes are taken from *Your Study of the New Testament Made Easier* by David J. Ridges.

Revelation 11:3–13

3 And **I will give power unto my two witnesses** [*two prophets to the Jews in the last days; D&C 77:15*]**, and they shall prophesy** [*serve, minister, prophesy, and so on*] **a thousand two hundred and threescore days** [*42 months or 3 1/2 years, about the same length as Christ's ministry*], clothed in sackcloth [*in humility*].

4 **These are the two olive trees** [*olive trees provide olive oil for lamps so people can be prepared to meet Christ; compare with the parable of the ten virgins in Matthew 25:1–13*]**, and the two candlesticks** [*hold light so people can see clearly*] standing before the God of the earth.

5 And **if any man will** [*wants to*] **hurt them** [*the two prophets*]**, fire** [*the power of God to destroy*] **proceedeth out of their mouth, and devoureth their enemies** [*the two prophets will be protected during their mission*]: and if any man will hurt them, he must in this manner be killed [*he will be killed by the power of God*].

6 **These** [*the two prophets*] **have power to shut heaven** [*have the power of God; compare with the Prophet Nephi in Helaman 10:5–10 and 11:1–6*], that it rain not in the days of their prophecy: **and have power over waters to turn them to blood, and to smite the earth with all plagues** [*to encourage people to repent; to deliver from evil, bondage, as with the plagues in Egypt*], as often as they will.

7 And **when they shall have finished their testimony** [*ministry*]**, the beast** [*Satan*] that ascendeth out of the bottomless

pit [*Rev. 9:1–2*] **shall make war against them** [*the two prophets*], **and shall overcome them, and kill them.**

8 And their dead bodies shall lie in the street of the great city [*Jerusalem*], which spiritually is called Sodom and Egypt [*is very wicked*], **where also our Lord was crucified.**

9 And they [*the wicked*] **of the people and kindreds and tongues and nations shall see their dead bodies three days and an half** [*perhaps symbolically tying in with their 3 1/2 year ministry as well as the Savior's three days in the tomb; the Savior was killed, too, by the wicked for trying to save them*], **and shall not suffer** [*allow*] **their dead bodies to be put in graves** [*many in eastern cultures believed that if the body is not buried, the spirit is bound to wander the earth in misery forever*].

10 And they that dwell upon the earth [*not just people in Jerusalem; implies that knowledge of the death of the two prophets will be known worldwide*] **shall rejoice over them, and make merry, and shall send gifts one to another** [*people all over the world will cheer and send gifts*

to one another to celebrate the deaths of these two prophets*]; **because these two prophets tormented them** [*the wicked*] that dwelt on the earth [*implies that these prophets' influence was felt and irritated the wicked far beyond Jerusalem*].

11 And after three days and an half the Spirit of life from God entered into them [*they are resurrected at this time; see McConkie, Doctrinal New Testament Commentary, 3:511*], **and they stood upon their feet; and great fear fell upon them which saw them.**

12 And they [*the wicked who were celebrating*] **heard a great voice from heaven saying unto them** [*the two slain prophets*], **Come up hither. And they ascended up to heaven in a cloud; and their enemies beheld** [*saw*] **them.**

13 And the same hour [*immediately*] **was there a great earthquake,** and the tenth part of the city fell, and in the earthquake were slain of men seven thousand: and the remnant were affrighted, and gave glory to the God of heaven [*perhaps implying that some of the wicked were converted as was the case with* *the Savior's resurrection and also when Lazarus was brought back from the dead; if so, the deaths of the two prophets bore immediate fruit in helping some begin returning to God]*

The question arises from reading the Bible as to whether these "witnesses" are prophets or missionaries, Jewish or LDS, or what? The answer to the question in verse 15, next, clears this up.

15 Q. **What is to be understood by the two witnesses,** in the eleventh chapter of Revelation?

A. **They are two prophets that are to be raised up to the Jewish nation in the last days, at the time of the restoration, and to prophesy to the Jews after they are gathered and have built the city of Jerusalem in the land of their fathers.**

Thus, we understand that these are to be members of the Church and, in fact, latter-day prophets. We have fifteen "prophets, seers, and revelators" in the Church today. They are the First Presidency and the Quorum of the Twelve Apostles. It appears that two of them, or their successors, will someday fulfill this prophecy.

Elder Bruce R. McConkie taught about these two prophets. He said that they would be "followers of that humble man Joseph Smith,

through whom the Lord of Heaven restored the fulness of his everlasting gospel in this final dispensation of grace. No doubt they will be members of the Council of the Twelve or of the First Presidency of the Church" (*Doctrinal New Testament Commentary*, 3:509).

SECTION 78

Background

This revelation was given through the Prophet Joseph Smith in Hiram, Ohio, on March 1, 1832. It deals primarily with the establishment of a "firm," later known as the "United Firm" in order "to manage the Church's storehouses and publishing efforts" (see *Doctrine and Covenants Student Manual*, 2018, chapter 29) and also with the personal righteousness and character traits required to live the law of consecration.

As background for section 78, the student manual quoted above additionally explains:

"In a revelation given in February 1831, the Lord commanded the Saints to establish a storehouse to gather surplus goods and money for the benefit of the poor (see D&C 42:34–35; see also D&C 51:13). Newel K. Whitney's mercantile store in Kirtland, Ohio, operated as one storehouse, and Sidney Gilbert established another in Independence, Missouri (see D&C 57:8–10; 72:8–10). These storehouses not only supplied the Saints with needed goods but also generated revenue to purchase land and finance the publication of the Lord's revelations to the Prophet Joseph Smith. Additionally, in November 1831, the Lord appointed Joseph Smith, Oliver Cowdery, John Whitmer, Sidney Rigdon, Martin Harris, and William W. Phelps as 'stewards over the revelations and commandments' (D&C 70:3). This group had the responsibility to oversee the publication of the revelations. For their labors, they were to receive compensation from the profits generated from the sale of the published revelations. The Lord instructed them to place any profits over and above their needs in His storehouse for the benefit of the Saints in Zion (see D&C 70:7–8).

"On March 1, 1832, the Prophet Joseph Smith met with a group of high priests in Kirtland, Ohio, possibly to discuss the Church's mercantile and publication efforts. During the meeting, the Prophet dictated the revelation recorded in Doctrine and Covenants 78. Subsequently, the United Firm was created to better manage the Church's property and financial endeavors, such as the storehouses. The part of the United Firm that managed the Church's publishing efforts was called the Literary Firm."

The Prophet received three other revelations about the same time. He explained: "Besides the work of translating [the translation of the Bible—the JST], previous to the 20th of March, I received the four following revelations: [D&C 78–81]" (*History of the Church*, 1:255).

You may be aware that in earlier editions of the Doctrine and Covenants, substitute names were used for several of the brethren in this section, as well as in section 82, verse 11, and in section 104, verses 26 and 43. Just in case this topic is brought up to you, we will quote Elder Orson Pratt's explanation of it:

"The names that were incorporated when it was printed, did not exist there when the manuscript revelations were given, for I saw them myself. Some of them I copied. And when the Lord was about to have the Book of Covenants given to the world it was thought wisdom, in consequence of the persecutions of our enemies in Kirtland and some of the regions around, that some of the names should be changed, and Joseph was called Baurak Ale, which was a Hebrew word; meaning God bless you. He was also called Gazelam, being a person to whom the Lord had given the Urim and Thummim. He was also called Enoch. Sidney Rigdon was called Baneemy. And the revelation where it read so many dollars into the treasury was changed to talents. And the City of New York was changed to Cainhannoch" (*Journal of Discourses*, 16:156).

Beginning with the 1981 edition of the Doctrine and Covenants, the use of these substitute names was done away with. Joseph Fielding Smith gave additional background for this section. He said (**bold** added for emphasis):

"During the early part of the year 1832, the Prophet and Sidney Rigdon continued the work of the revision of the scriptures [the JST]. At the time the Prophet was still residing in the house of Father John Johnson, at Hiram. It was during this time that this important revelation was given to the members of the Priesthood who were assembled imparting instructions in relation to the plan of **the 'united order'** or 'order of Enoch,' on which the promised Zion should be built. The Lord had revealed that it was only through obedience to his divine will, **the celestial law**, that Zion could be built. The members of the Church rejoiced when the Lord revealed to them the site on which the New Jerusalem, or City of Zion, should be built. Their enthusiasm, however, was not sufficient to carry them through to a conclusion in strict obedience to the divine will. In this revelation (section 78) the Lord reveals his will in words of wisdom to all those holding the High Priesthood" (*Church History and Modern Revelation*, 1:304–5).

As we study this revelation, you will see that unselfishness and charity are essential personal character traits for those who successfully live the "United Order" (see D&C 92:1) under the law of consecration. Such characteristics are part of celestial law (see verse 7). As noted above, this revelation was given to a number of priesthood brethren who had assembled with the Prophet in the John Johnson home. Beginning with verse 1, the Lord addresses these Melchizedek Priesthood holders and teaches them principles relating to the United Order and the law of consecration.

1 THE Lord spake unto Joseph Smith, Jun., saying: **Hearken unto me**, saith the Lord your God, **who are ordained unto the high priesthood of my church, who have assembled yourselves together**;

2 And **listen to the counsel of him who has ordained you from on high**, who shall speak in your ears the words of wisdom, that salvation may be unto you in that thing which you have presented before me, saith the Lord God.

Did you notice, in verse 2, above, that when hands are laid upon our heads by faithful priesthood holders here on earth, it is the same as the Savior Himself doing it?

3 For verily I say unto you, **the time has come, and is now at hand**; and behold, and lo, **it must needs be** [*it is necessary*] **that there be an organization** [*the United Firm; see D&C 92 heading (2013 edition)*] **of my people**, in **regulating and establishing the affairs of the storehouse for the poor of my people**, both in this place [*the Kirtland area*] and in the land of Zion [*in Jackson County, Missouri*]—

4 For a permanent and everlasting establishment and order unto my church, **to advance** the cause, which ye have espoused [*adopted as your own*], to **the salvation of man**, and to the glory of your Father who is in heaven [*compare with Moses 1:39*];

In verses 5–7, next, the Lord teaches us that in order to be prepared to live comfortably in celestial glory, we must learn to live the celestial laws embedded in the law of consecration and the United Order here on earth.

5 **That you may be equal in the bonds of heavenly things**, yea, **and earthly things** also, **for the obtaining of heavenly things**.

6 For **if ye are not equal in earthly things ye cannot be equal in obtaining heavenly things**;

7 For **if you will that I give unto you a place in the celestial world, you must prepare yourselves by doing the things which I have commanded you and required of you.**

We will take just a moment to review what it means to be "equal in earthly things" (verse 6, above). This must not be interpreted as taking away personality, individuality, individual talents, hobbies, interests, and so forth. President J. Reuben Clark Jr. explained this as follows (**bold** added for emphasis):

"One of the places in which some of the brethren are going astray is this: There is continuous reference in the revelations to equality among the brethren, but I think you will find only one place where that equality is really described, though it is referred to in other revelations. That revelation (D. & C. 51:3) affirms that every man is to be **'equal according to** his **family**, according to his **circumstances** and his **wants** and **needs.'** (See also D. & C. 82:17; 78:5–6.) **Obviously, this is not a case of 'dead level' equality. It is 'equality' that will vary as much as the man's circumstances, his family, his wants and needs, may vary**" (In Conference Report, October 1942, 55).

You may have noticed that through tithing, fast offering, humanitarian aid fund, perpetual education fund,

missionary fund, temple construction fund, and so on, and helping
one another through compassionate service, service projects, dedicating time and talents to temple
work, missionary service, and so
forth, we are much closer to living
the United Order today than some
members might realize. It is all
part of the law of consecration.

8 And now, verily thus saith the
Lord, **it is expedient** [*necessary*]
**that all things be done unto my
glory** [*which is bringing exaltation to people; see Moses 1:39*], **by
you who are joined together in
this order** [*the United Firm which
has just been organized at this point
in Church history for the poor and
needy members in the Kirtland area
and Jackson County, Missouri—see
verse 3*];

9 Or, in other words, **let my servant Newel K. Whitney** [*who was
called to serve as bishop in the Kirtland area; see D&C 72:2, 8*] and my
servant **Joseph Smith, Jun.**, and
my servant **Sidney Rigdon** sit in
**council with the saints which are
in Zion** [*help the Saints in Missouri
better understand the principles and
applications of the United Firm*];

10 **Otherwise Satan seeketh to
turn their hearts away from the
truth**, that they become blinded
and understand not the things
which are prepared for them.

11 Wherefore, a commandment I
give unto you, to **prepare and organize yourselves by a bond or
everlasting covenant that cannot be broken** [*by the Lord; see
D&C 82:10—nor by members without very serious consequences*].

As you can see, from verse 11,
above, covenants are an integral
part of living the United Firm under
the law of consecration. The seriousness of breaking covenants
made with God is pointed out in
verse 12, next.

12 And **he who breaketh it** [*the
covenant spoken of in verse 11,
above*] **shall lose his office and
standing in the church, and
shall be delivered over to the
buffetings of Satan until the day
of redemption.**

Elder Bruce R. McConkie defined
what it means to be turned over "to
the buffetings of Satan." He said:

"To be turned over to the buffetings of Satan is to be given into
his hands; it is to be turned over to
him with all the protective power of
the priesthood, of righteousness,
and of godliness removed, so that
Lucifer is free to torment, persecute, and afflict such a person
without let or hindrance" (*Mormon
Doctrine*, 108).

13 Behold, **this is the preparation wherewith I prepare
you**, and the foundation, and the

ensample [*example*] which I give unto you, **whereby you may accomplish the commandments which are given you**;

14 **That through my providence** [*help*], **notwithstanding the tribulation which shall descend upon you** [*a prophecy that the Saints in Ohio and Missouri will yet go through much trial and tribulation*], **that the church may stand independent above all other creatures beneath the celestial world** [*under heaven; a prophecy that the day will come when the Church will grow and be independent of all outside forces*];

Next, in verse 15, the Lord uses terms meaning exaltation to describe the reward of those who successfully and faithfully live in harmony with the law of consecration.

15 **That you may come up unto the crown** [*symbolic of being a ruler*] **prepared for you** [*exaltation*], and **be made rulers over many kingdoms** [*when they become gods; compare with D&C 132:19–20*], saith the Lord God, the Holy One of Zion [*in other words, Jesus Christ*], who hath established the foundations of Adam-ondi-Ahman [*the place (in Missouri) where Adam met with his posterity to bless them three years before he died; see D&C 107:53–56*];

16 **Who hath appointed Michael** [*Adam*] **your prince**, and established his feet, and set him upon high, **and given unto him the keys of salvation under the counsel and direction of the Holy One** [*Christ*], who is without beginning of days or end of life.

One of the doctrines taught in verse 16, above, is that Adam stands next to Christ in authority over this earth, having been given the "keys of salvation" under the direction of Christ. This correct view of Adam and his power and authority is a far cry from the commonly held view of him among many other faiths.

Next, the Lord speaks to these men, and to all of us, explaining that we have hardly even begun to see the blessings and advantages of living celestial laws. His kindness and charity are seen as He cheers us on and encourages us to take His hand and be led to celestial glory.

17 Verily, verily, I say unto you, **ye are little children, and ye have not as yet understood how great blessings the Father hath in his own hands and prepared for you**;

18 And **ye cannot bear all things now**; nevertheless, **be of good cheer, for I will lead you along. The kingdom is yours** and **the**

blessings thereof are yours, and **the riches of eternity are yours**.

Once again, we see the value and importance of gratitude as taught in verse 19, next. (Compare with D&C 59:21.)

19 And **he who receiveth all things with thankfulness shall be made glorious**; and the things of this earth shall be added unto him, even an hundred fold, yea, more.

20 Wherefore [*therefore*], **do the things which I have commanded you**, saith your Redeemer, even the Son Ahman [*Jesus Christ*], who prepareth all things before he taketh you [*perhaps meaning who has prepared everything in advance in order to successfully "lead us along" the covenant path (verse 18)*];

The name, "Son Ahman," found near the end of verse 20, above, is also used in D&C 95:17. It means "the Son of God." "Ahman" is the name of God in the pure language. Elder Orson Pratt explained this in some detail. He taught:

"There is one revelation that this people are not generally acquainted with. I think it has never been published, but probably it will be in the Church History. It is given in questions and answers. The first question is, 'What is the name of God in the pure language?' The answer says, 'Ahman.' 'What is

the name of the Son of God?' Answer, 'Son Ahman—the greatest of all the parts of God excepting Ahman'" (*Journal of Discourses*, 2:342).

21 For **ye are the church of the Firstborn**, and he will take you up in a cloud [*symbolic of being taken up to heaven; see Acts 1:9*], and appoint every man his portion.

The "church of the Firstborn," in verse 21, above, is another term for exaltation. We saw it in D&C 76:54, 67, and 102. Joseph Fielding Smith explained this term as follows:

"Those who gain exaltation in the celestial kingdom are those who are members of the Church of the Firstborn; in other words, those who keep all the commandments of the Lord (*Doctrines of Salvation*, 2:41).

22 And **he that is a faithful and wise steward shall inherit all things** [*will become a god*]. Amen.

SECTION 79

Background

This revelation was given through the Prophet Joseph Smith in Hiram, Ohio, on March 12, 1832. In the background to section 78 in this book, we mentioned that it was one of four revelations (sections 78–81) that the Prophet received prior to March 20, 1832, while residing at the home of John Johnson.

As is the case with all sections of the Doctrine and Covenants, there is at least one message that is of value for us by way of application in our own lives. Even though this section is brief, it has several.

As you can see, this revelation was given to Jared Carter. He was converted to the Church when he first read the Book of Mormon. He was baptized in Colesville, New York, by Hyrum Smith in February 1831 at age thirty. He moved with the Colesville Saints to Ohio. In the fall of 1831, Brother Carter left to serve a mission in the east and preached in Ohio, Pennsylvania, New York, and Vermont for five months. He then returned home to Ohio. Shortly after his return, he visited the Prophet Joseph Smith to ask about his next mission, and on March 12, 1832, he was given this revelation, section 79. In it, he is asked to serve a mission "again into the eastern countries" (verse 1).

1 VERILY I say unto you, that it is my will that my servant **Jared Carter should go again into the eastern countries**, from place to place, and from city to city, in the power of the ordination wherewith he has been ordained, **proclaiming glad tidings of great joy, even the everlasting gospel**.

In verse 2, next, we see two of the many functions of the Holy Ghost.

2 And **I will send upon him the Comforter** [*the Holy Ghost*], **which shall teach him the truth and the way whither he shall go**;

3 And **inasmuch as he is faithful, I will crown him again with sheaves** [*the Lord will give him another bountiful harvest of souls*].

4 Wherefore, **let your heart be glad**, my servant Jared Carter, and **fear not**, saith your Lord, even Jesus Christ. Amen.

Jared Carter left on this mission as instructed on April 25, 1832. This mission lasted six months and two days, and he brought seventy-nine souls into the Church. We will quote again from the 2018 *Doctrine and Covenants Student Manual*, chapter 29, for an inspiring account of John and Elizabeth Tanner, whom he helped bring into the true gospel. The source for this account is the Journal of Jared Carter, typescript, 20, Church History Library, Salt Lake City).

"Among those he helped convert to the restored gospel were John and Elizabeth Tanner. John Tanner was a wealthy businessman whose leg had been afflicted with sores. Jared Carter gave the following account of the healing of John Tanner: 'The Lord had mercy upon a lame man by the name of Tanner, who was so lame that he could not bear his weight . . . on one of his feet. He had been lame for months but we found he was a believer in the Book of Mormon. I asked him to endeavor to walk in the name of Christ [and] he agreed to undertake. I then took him by the hand and commanded him in the name of Christ to walk and by the power of Christ he was enabled to walk' (Journal of Jared Carter, 19). After his conversion, John Tanner moved to Ohio and donated thousands of dollars to pay the debt on the Kirtland Temple site and to finance its construction. This was an answer to the prayers of the Prophet Joseph Smith and other Church leaders."

SECTION 80

Background

This revelation was given to eighteen-year-old Stephen Burnett in Hiram, Ohio, on March 7, 1832. He had joined the Church at age sixteen in Warrensville, Ohio. A year later, he was ordained a high priest by Oliver Cowdery.

Both he and Eden Smith (verse 2) had been previously called to serve missions with different companions on January 25, 1832 (during a conference held at Amherst, Ohio; see D&C 75:35–36). We don't currently know whether or not he fulfilled that call.

1 VERILY, **thus saith the Lord unto** you my servant **Stephen Burnett** [*eighteen years old*]: **Go ye, go ye into the world and preach the gospel to every creature that cometh under the sound of your voice.**

We too are to help spread the gospel to all who come within our sphere of influence. Except when we are serving formally as missionaries, being a good example is often the best way to "preach." In so doing, we "cannot go amiss" (verse 3).

2 And inasmuch as you desire a companion, **I will give unto you my servant Eden Smith** [*about twenty-six years old*].

When we studied D&C 60:5, we mentioned that some decisions in our lives do not have a "right" answer. It "mattereth not" to the Lord. Therefore, we can do whatever we think is best and it will be fine with God. Verse 3, next, describes one such situation.

3 Wherefore, **go ye and preach my gospel, whether to the north or to the south, to the east or to the west, it mattereth not, for ye cannot go amiss** [*you can't go wrong*].

In verse 4, next, we are reminded of the importance of missionaries knowing the gospel and having their own testimony of the things they are teaching.

4 Therefore, **declare the things which ye have heard, and verily believe, and know to be true**.

5 Behold, this is the will of him who hath called you, your Redeemer, even Jesus Christ. Amen.

SECTION 81

Background

This revelation was given through the Prophet Joseph Smith on March 15, 1832, in Hiram, Ohio.

As you can see, the heading and introduction to this section in your Doctrine and Covenants is about as long as the seven verses of the revelation itself. This section is particularly significant because it represents a major step forward in organizing the First Presidency of the Church, which began with organizing the Presidency of the High Priesthood (verse 2). This step is the calling of counselors to serve with the Prophet, thus leading ultimately to the formal organizing of the First Presidency as the leading quorum of the Church (see D&C 107:22).

You can also see, from the information in the heading in your Doctrine and Covenants, that Jesse Gause (about twenty years older than the Prophet) was one of the two men originally called by the Lord to serve as counselors in the First Presidency. However, as noted in the heading, he apostatized and was excommunicated in December 1832. This is a sad reminder that Church leaders can misuse their agency even to the point of losing their membership.

Frederick G Williams was the one who replaced Jesse Gause in January 1833, a few weeks after Jesse Gause was excommunicated. Thus, his name was written into the transcription of this revelation for the first publication of the Doctrine and Covenants in 1835.

Brother Williams was born on October 28, 1787. He was eighteen years older than Joseph Smith (then twenty-six years old) and just over five years older than Sidney Rigdon, the other counselor (D&C 90:6).

By the way, the last half of verse 5 (**bolded** part) is one of the more often quoted verses in the Church. If you don't particularly recognize it now, you will no doubt recognize it in the future because of paying attention to it now.

As we proceed to study this section, we will be taught about the keys of the priesthood held by the First Presidency and will be given counsel that applies to any member of the Church called to serve as a counselor to a president.

1 **VERILY, verily, I say unto you** my servant **Frederick G. Williams**: Listen to the voice of him who speaketh, to the word of

the Lord your God, and **hearken to the calling wherewith you are called**, even **to be a high priest in my church, and a counselor unto my servant Joseph Smith, Jun.**;

2 Unto whom I have given **the keys of the kingdom**, which **belong always unto the Presidency of the High Priesthood** [*which gradually became the First Presidency*]:

One of the important lessons in verse 3, next, is that the Lord sustains His prophet. So also, should the counselors. So it is with any authorized presidency within the quorums and auxiliaries of the Church.

3 Therefore, verily **I acknowledge him** [*Joseph Smith*] **and will bless him, and also thee, inasmuch as** [*if*] **thou art faithful in counsel**, in the office which I have appointed unto you [*as a counselor*], **in prayer always, vocally and in thy heart, in public and in private**, also in thy ministry in proclaiming the gospel in the land of the living, and among thy brethren.

We often hear the counsel to "lift where you stand"—in other words, fulfill the calling you currently have to the best of your ability, even if it doesn't put you in the limelight. Verse 4, next, reflects this counsel.

4 And **in doing these things thou wilt do the greatest good unto thy fellow beings, and wilt promote the glory of him who is your Lord.**

As stated earlier, verse 5, next, contains sweet counsel for counselors, and for all of us as we sustain our leaders.

5 Wherefore, be faithful; stand in the office which I have appointed unto you; **succor the weak, lift up the hands which hang down, and strengthen the feeble knees.**

In conclusion, verse 6, next, can be seen as another reminder that it is not where we serve but how we serve that counts eternally.

6 And **if thou art faithful unto the end thou shalt have a crown** [*symbolic of exaltation*] **of immortality, and eternal life** [*exaltation*] in the mansions which I have prepared in the house of my Father.

7 Behold, and lo, **these are the words of Alpha and Omega** [*the one in charge of all things, under the direction of the Father*], even **Jesus Christ**. Amen.

SECTION 82

Background

This revelation was given through the Prophet Joseph Smith in Independence, Jackson County, Missouri, on April 26, 1832. We will quote the heading given for this section in the 2013 edition of the Doctrine and Covenants:

*"Revelation given to Joseph Smith the Prophet, in Independence, Jackson County, Missouri, April 26, 1832. The occasion was a council of high priests and elders of the Church. At the council, Joseph Smith was sustained as the President of the High Priesthood, to which office he had previously been ordained at a conference of high priests, elders, and members at Amherst, Ohio, January 25, 1832 (see the heading to section 75). This revelation reiterates instructions given in an earlier revelation (section 78) to establish a firm—known as the **United Firm** (under Joseph Smith's direction, the term "order" later replaced "firm")—to govern the Church's mercantile and publishing endeavors."*

We will quote from the 2018 *Doctrine and Covenants Student Manual*, chapter 30, for additional

background for this section. Note that the righteousness, dedication, integrity, and celestial character traits required to keep their covenants as members of the United Firm (see heading above) are the same as needed for successfully living the law of consecration and United Order.

"In 1832 the Church had two centers of growing membership: one in Kirtland, Ohio, and one in Jackson County, Missouri. To assist needy Saints and to generate revenue that could be used to purchase land in Zion (Jackson County) and publish the revelations, a storehouse was established in each location (see D&C 57:8–10; 72:8–10). In November 1831, the Lord appointed a group of Church leaders to be 'stewards over the revelations and commandments' (D&C 70:3) and see to their publication. Later, the Lord commanded that a 'firm' be organized to manage the literary and mercantile endeavors of the Church (see the section headings to D&C 78 and D&C 82).

"The Prophet Joseph Smith and other Church leaders had traveled to Independence, Missouri, in obedience to the Lord's commandment to 'sit in council with the saints which are in Zion' (D&C 78:9). They met to establish a 'firm' or 'order' that would oversee and regulate the mercantile and publishing endeavors of the Church. Church members who were invited to participate in the firm included Joseph Smith, Sidney Rigdon, Newel K. Whitney, and Martin Harris, all of whom resided in Kirtland, Ohio, and Edward Partridge, Sidney Gilbert, John Whitmer, Oliver Cowdery, and William W. Phelps, all of whom resided in Jackson County, Missouri (see D&C 78:9; 82:11). In 1833, two additional members—Frederick G. Williams and John Johnson—were added to the firm by revelation (see D&C 92:1–2; 96:6–9). The objective of the firm was to manage storehouses that would provide goods and money to help the poor as well as to generate revenue to purchase land for Zion and finance the publication of the Lord's revelations to the Prophet. One branch of the firm would operate in Independence and was to be called 'Gilbert, Whitney & Co.,' and one would operate in Kirtland and would be named 'Newel K. Whitney & Co.' (see 'Minutes, 26–27 April 1832,' page 25, josephsmithpapers.org).

"The members of the firm, or order, were to be united with one another in a covenant. Each received a stewardship over part of the business interests of the Church, and each could draw upon the resources of the firm to manage his stewardship. The successful operation of the business endeavors would generate a surplus that was to be kept in the Church's storehouses."

As you know, the law of consecration requires a "Zion" lifestyle and

celestial attributes, including a high degree of personal integrity, charity, and righteousness. It is a high goal for any of us to attain, but with the help of the Lord, we can. The members of the United Firm at this time were falling short of the requirements required to successfully carry it out. In section 82, the Master addresses many of these shortcomings and gives direction and encouragement. These personal qualities certainly apply to us if we desire to attain the celestial kingdom.

This section contains a number of familiar quotes often used in talks and gospel conversations—for example, verses 3, 7, and 10.

Verse 1, next, specifically refers to Sidney Rigdon and Bishop Edward Partridge. They'd had a disagreement with each other but had worked things out and made peace with each other by the time of this revelation. In this verse, we are reminded that in order to be forgiven by the Lord, we must forgive each other (Matthew 6:15, D&C 64:9–10).

1 VERILY, verily, I say unto you, my servants, that **inasmuch as you have forgiven one another your trespasses, even so I, the Lord, forgive you.**

Verse 2, next, contains a strict warning by a loving Savior to His people to repent and exercise more self-control and obedience to the commandments.

Remember that these members had just recently come to Missouri where the land was fertile and opportunities for future personal gain were abundant. For some, it was difficult to consecrate potential wealth to the Church. Also, the type of person required to succeed on the frontier of civilization was of necessity strong-willed. Because of this, they sometimes found it difficult to show obedience and loyalty to Church leaders.

2 Nevertheless, **there are those among you who have sinned exceedingly**; yea, even **all of you have sinned**; but verily I say unto you, **beware from henceforth, and refrain from sin** [*they are being given another chance*], **lest sore** [*severe*] **judgments** [*consequences, punishments*] **fall upon your heads.**

Verse 3, next, is much-quoted in the Church. It is, in effect, an equation and reminds us of our greater accountability to be obedient because of the knowledge, testimony, and rich blessings already given us by the Lord.

3 For of him **unto whom much is given much is required**; and **he who sins against the greater light shall receive the greater condemnation.**

Elder Neil L. Andersen of the Quorum of the Twelve Apostles explained verse 3, above, as follows: "As members of The Church of Jesus Christ of Latter-day Saints, having a witness of His reality not only from the Bible but also from the Book of Mormon; knowing His priesthood has been restored to the earth; having made sacred covenants to follow Him and received the gift of the Holy Ghost; having been endowed with power in His holy temple; and being part of preparing for His glorious return to the earth, we cannot compare what we are to be with those who have not yet received these truths. 'Unto whom much is given much is required' [D&C 82:3]" ("Never Leave Him," *Ensign*, Nov. 2010, 41).

In verse 4, next, the Master Teacher gives us the "why" of verse 3, above.

4 **Ye call upon my name for revelations, and I give them unto you** [*"much is given," including "greater light"*]; **and inasmuch as** [*if*] **ye keep not my sayings**, which I give unto you, **ye become transgressors**; and **justice and judgment are the penalty which is affixed unto my law** [*the law of justice is active for us unless we repent*].

Next, in the first part of verse 5, we are reminded that the counsel and instruction from the Lord in these revelations applies to us all.

5 Therefore, **what I say unto one I say unto all**: Watch, for the adversary [*the devil*] spreadeth his dominions, and darkness [*spiritual darkness*] reigneth;

6 And **the anger of God kindleth against the inhabitants of the earth**; and **none doeth good, for all have gone out of the way** [*everyone has the need and necessity to repent; compare to D&C 49:8, first half*].

Next, in verse 7, we find an important and serious doctrine. It is that if we have repented of certain sins but then commit them again, even years later, the "former sins return." In other words, we have to repent of that type of sin all over again. We have obviously not completely overcome it, or we would not have committed it again.

7 And now, verily I say unto you, I, the Lord, will not lay any sin to your charge; go your ways and sin no more; but **unto that soul who sinneth shall the former sins return**, saith the Lord your God.

Verses 8–15 go together and basically refer to the instruction of the Lord to the brethren mentioned to "bind" themselves by covenant to live in the United Firm in conformity to the law of consecration. See especially verses 11 and 15.

First, in verses 8–9, the Savior gives us a concise lesson in the

"why" of obedience to His commandments; namely, that He might bless us.

8 And again, I say unto you, **I give unto you a new commandment**, that you may understand my will concerning you;

9 Or, in other words, **I give unto you directions how you may act before me, that it may turn to you for your salvation**.

Verse 10, next, is perhaps the most well-known in this section and one of the best-known verses in the entire Doctrine and Covenants. It is an absolute guarantee that the Lord will keep His promises to us if we fulfill our part of the contract. You may wish to cross-reference verse 10 in your own Doctrine and Covenants with D&C 130:20–21.

10 **I, the Lord, am bound when ye do what I say; but when ye do not what I say, ye have no promise.**

Verses 11 and 12 go together.

11 Therefore, verily I say unto you, that **it is expedient** [*necessary*] **for** my servants **Edward Partridge** [*the bishop in Missouri*] and **Newel K. Whitney** [*the bishop in Kirtland*], **Sidney Gilbert** and **Sidney Rigdon**, and my servant **Joseph Smith**, and **John Whitmer** and **Oliver Cowdery**, and

W. W. Phelps and **Martin Harris to be bound together** [*in living the law of consecration in the United Firm in Missouri and Kirtland*] **by a bond and covenant that cannot be broken by transgression, except judgment shall immediately follow**, in your several stewardships—

12 **To manage the affairs of the poor**, and all things pertaining to the bishopric **both in the land of Zion and in the land of Kirtland**;

> Next, in verses 13–14, the Savior explains that while Kirtland will serve as a headquarters for the Church yet for a season (a total of about five years; see D&C 64:21), Zion, Jackson County, Missouri, will "increase" and "her borders" will be enlarged (verse 14).

13 For **I have consecrated the land of Kirtland in mine own due time** for the benefit of the saints of the Most High, and for a stake to Zion.

14 For **Zion must increase in beauty, and in holiness; her borders must be enlarged**; her stakes must be strengthened; yea, verily I say unto you, Zion must arise and put on her beautiful garments [*must "put on the priesthood"; compare with D&C 113:7–8*].

We understand verse 14, above, to be a prophecy that the Church will continue to grow from these small and humble beginnings in Kirtland and Missouri until it has filled the entire earth (Daniel 2:35). President Harold B. Lee spoke of this. He taught:

"Zion, as used here, undoubtedly had reference to the Church. At that time there was but a small body of Church members just beginning to emerge as an organization, after having experienced harsh treatment from enemies outside the Church. . . .

"To be worthy of such a sacred designation as Zion, the Church must think of itself as a bride adorned for her husband, as John the Revelator recorded when he saw in vision the Holy City where the righteous dwelled, adorned as a bride for the Lamb of God as her husband. Here is portrayed the relationship the Lord desires in his people in order to be acceptable to our Lord and Master even as a wife would adorn herself in beautiful garments for her husband.

"The rule by which the people of God must live in order to be worthy of acceptance in the sight of God is indicated by the text to which I have made reference. This people must increase in beauty before the world; have an inward loveliness which may be observed by mankind as a reflection in holiness and in those inherent qualities of sanctity. The borders of Zion, where the righteous and pure in heart may dwell, must now begin to be enlarged. The stakes of Zion must be strengthened. All this so that Zion may arise and shine by becoming increasingly diligent in carrying out the plan of salvation throughout the world" ("Strengthen the Stakes of Zion," *Ensign*, July 1973, 3).

15 **Therefore** [*because of what the Lord knows about the future growth of the Church*], I give unto you this commandment, that ye **bind yourselves by this covenant** [*in the "United Firm"*], and it shall be done according to the laws of the Lord [*it must be done according to the rules of the law of consecration*].

16 Behold, **here is wisdom** also in me **for your good**.

Next, in verses 17–19, the Savior defines what He means by "equal," as it relates to living the law of consecration, as it applies to the United Firm.

17 And you are to be **equal,** or **in other words, you are to have equal claims on the properties** [*held by the United Firm*], for the benefit of managing the concerns of your stewardships, **every man according to his wants and his needs**, inasmuch as his wants are just—

18 And all this for the benefit of the church of the living God, **that every man may improve upon his talent, that every man may gain other talents** [*surplus, above and beyond his wants and needs*], yea, even an hundred fold, **to be cast into the Lord's storehouse** [*the bishop's storehouse*], **to become the common property of the whole church**—

19 **Every man seeking the interest of his neighbor** [*a celestial character trait*], and **doing all things with an eye single to** [*focused on*] **the glory of God** [*whose "work and . . . glory" is to bless and benefit His children, leading them to exaltation; see Moses 1:39*].

20 **This order** [*the United Firm, run according to the law of consecration*] I have appointed to be **an everlasting order** [*the principles of the law of consecration are eternal*] unto you, and unto your successors, inasmuch as you sin not.

21 And **the soul that sins against this covenant, and hardeneth his heart against it, shall be dealt with according to the laws of my church** (see D&C 78:12), and shall be delivered over to the buffetings of Satan until the day of redemption [*see note for D&C 78:12 in this study guide*].

Some years ago, one of our daughters approached me, her scriptures in hand, with a puzzled look on her face. She said, in effect, "Dad, I thought that we were supposed to avoid associating with wicked people and making friends with them for fear of losing our own souls because of their influence on us." She was reading the Doctrine and Covenants and had just read verse 22, next.

22 And now, verily I say unto you, and this is wisdom, **make unto yourselves friends with the mammon of unrighteousness**, and they will not destroy you.

We sat down together, reread the verse, and then discussed the context created by the final phrase in the verse. Obviously, for these early Saints, this counsel was a life-and-death matter. Also, we are counseled not to deliberately provoke those who are enemies to the ways of righteousness. In fact, when we are friendly and kind toward such people, we have a better chance of preserving our own freedoms and way of life in addition to the better likelihood that some of them will desire to know more about the gospel.

You may have noticed on numerous occasions that the leaders of the Church strive to be friendly toward many whose lifestyles do not reflect gospel standards. The Savior spoke of this when He was accused of associating with sinners.

He replied, "They that be whole need not a physician, but they that are sick" (Matthew 9:12).

According to Wikipedia, the word "mammon" in Hebrew means "money" and has been adopted in modern Hebrew to mean "wealth."

Joseph Fielding Smith spoke of the Lord's counsel to "make . . . friends with the mammon of unrighteousness." He taught:

"The commandment of the Lord that the saints should make themselves 'friends with the mammon of unrighteousness' seems to be a hard saying when not properly understood. It is not intended that in making friends of the 'mammon of unrighteousness' that the brethren were to partake with them in their sins; to receive them to their bosoms, intermarry with them and otherwise come down to their level. They were to so live that peace with their enemies might be assured. They were to treat them kindly, be friendly with them as far as correct and virtuous principles would permit, but never to swear with them or drink and carouse with them. If they could allay prejudice and show a willingness to trade with and show a kindly spirit, it might help to turn them away from their bitterness. Judgment was to be left with the Lord" (*Church History and Modern Revelation*, 1:323).

In verse 23, next, the Lord reminds us that He is the final Judge and that He is the one who gives out punishments and rewards. He continues in verse 24 by reminding the Saints that the goal of eternal life can be attained by them.

23 Leave judgment alone with me, for it is mine and **I will repay**. Peace be with you; my blessings continue with you.

24 For even yet the kingdom is yours, and shall be forever, if you fall not from your steadfastness. Even so. Amen.

SECTION 83

Background

This revelation was given through the Prophet Joseph Smith in Independence, Missouri, on April 30, 1832. At this time, some members of the Church in Missouri were striving to live according to the principles of consecration. It appears that some questions had come up concerning property rights of women whose deceased husbands had consecrated their property to the Church. Whatever the case, this revelation was given to Joseph Smith as he sat in counsel with some of the brethren.

1 VERILY, thus saith the Lord, in addition to the laws of the church **concerning women and children, those who belong to the church, who have lost their husbands or fathers**:

2 Women have claim on their husbands for their maintenance, until their husbands are taken [*die*]; and if they are not found transgressors they shall have fellowship in the church.

3 And if they are not faithful they shall not have fellowship in the church [*they will lose their membership in the Church*]; **yet they may remain upon their inheritances according to the laws of the land** [*because the United Order includes private ownership of property; see D&C 51:4–5; thus their property belongs to them, not to the Church*].

4 All children have claim upon their parents for their maintenance [*for their daily physical needs*] **until they are of age.**

5 And **after that, they have claim upon the church**, or in other words upon the Lord's storehouse [*the bishop's storehouse*], **if their parents have not wherewith to give them inheritances** [*if the family can't help*].

6 And **the storehouse** [*bishop's storehouse*] **shall be kept** [*filled*] **by the consecrations of the church; and widows and orphans shall be provided for, as also the poor.** Amen.

SECTION 84

Background

This revelation was given through the Prophet Joseph Smith at Kirtland, Ohio, on September 22 and 23, 1832. The Prophet called this a revelation on priesthood.

This is one of the major doctrinal sections of the Doctrine and Covenants. Among other topics, it deals with:

• New Jerusalem

• The priesthood line of authority from Adam to Moses

• Melchizedek Priesthood

• Aaronic Priesthood

• The Oath and Covenant of the Priesthood

• The light of Christ

• The condemnation of the Church for not studying the Book of Mormon sufficiently

• Signs that follow believers

• Plagues of the last days

• **What it means to** "sing a new song"

• The Millennium

• The destruction of New York, Albany, and Boston, **if** they reject the gospel

Joseph Smith gave the background to section 84 as follows:

"As soon as I could arrange my affairs, I recommenced the translation of the Scriptures, and thus I spent most of the summer. In July, we received the first number of *The Evening and Morning Star,* which was a joyous treat to the Saints. Delightful, indeed, was it to contemplate that the little band of brethren had become so large, and grown so strong, in so short a time as to be able to issue a paper of their own, which contained not only some of the revelations, but other information also,—which would gratify and enlighten the humble inquirer after truth. . . .

"The Elders during the month of September began to return from their missions to the Eastern States, and present the histories of their several stewardships in the Lord's vineyard; and while together in these seasons of joy, I inquired of the Lord, and received on the 22nd and 23rd of September [1832], the following revelation on Priesthood: [D&C 84]" (*History of the Church*, 1:273, 286–87).

As mentioned at the beginning of the background for this section, this revelation was given over a period of two days. Apparently, as stated in verse 1, six elders were present on September 22 when the revelation began, but additional information from a note in an original handwritten copy of this revelation tells us that ten high priests were there during the latter part of the revelation. (See *The Joseph Smith Papers, Documents,*

Volume 2: July 1831–January 1833, ed. Matthew C. Godfrey and others [2013], 289–90.)

Since section 84 contains many revealed doctrines, we will point out a number of them by placing "**Doctrine**" at the beginning of the relevant verse or verses. These doctrines are examples of what the Savior told us in D&C 10:62–63, when He stated that He would bring back many of His "points of doctrine." They are likewise examples of the fulfillment of the prophecy found in 1 Nephi 13:40, in which the Lord said He would restore the "plain and precious things" that had been taken away from the Bible.

In verses 1–5, the Savior reviews the purposes of the Restoration and gives more detail about New Jerusalem and the temple that will someday be built in Independence, Missouri.

1 **A REVELATION of Jesus Christ** unto his servant Joseph Smith, Jun., and six elders, as they united their hearts and lifted their voices on high.

2 Yea, **the word of the Lord concerning his church, established** in the last days **for the restoration of his people,** as he has spoken by the mouth of his prophets, and **for the gathering of his saints** to stand upon Mount Zion, which shall be **the city of New Jerusalem.**

The temple lot, spoken of in verse 3, next, is currently owned by the Church of Christ Temple Lot, commonly called the Hedrickites—a church established by Granville Hedrick after the martyrdom of the Prophet Joseph Smith. The lot was laid out with corner stones under the direction of Joseph Smith and can easily be seen today. It is just across the parking lot from our visitors' center in Independence, Missouri.

3 **Which city shall be built, beginning at the temple lot,** which is appointed by the finger of the Lord, in the western boundaries of the State of Missouri [*see D&C 57:2–3*], and **dedicated by the hand of Joseph Smith, Jun., and others** [*see D&C 58:57*] with whom the Lord was well pleased.

Joseph Smith spoke of the dedication of the land of Zion by Sidney Rigdon and recorded that he, himself, dedicated the site for the temple. He said:

"On the second day of August [1831], I assisted the Colesville branch of the Church to lay the first log, for a house, as a foundation of Zion in Kaw township, twelve miles west of Independence. The log was carried and placed by twelve men, in honor of the twelve tribes of Israel. At the same time, through prayer, the land of Zion was consecrated and dedicated by Elder Sidney Rigdon for the gathering of the Saints. It was a season of joy to those present, and afforded a glimpse of the future, which time will yet unfold to the satisfaction of the faithful" (*History of the Church*, 1:196).

"On the third day of August, I proceeded to dedicate the spot for the Temple, a little west of Independence, and there were also present Sidney Rigdon, Edward Partridge, W. W. Phelps, Oliver Cowdery, Martin Harris and Joseph Coe" (*History of the Church*, 1:199).

Doctrine

A city called "New Jerusalem" will be built in Jackson County, Missouri, along with a temple.

4 Verily this is the word of the Lord, that the city New Jerusalem shall be built by the gathering of the saints, **beginning at this place,** even **the place of the temple, which temple shall be reared in this generation.**

5 For verily **this generation shall not all pass away until an house shall be built unto the Lord, and a cloud shall rest upon it, which cloud shall be even the glory of the Lord, which shall fill the house.**

Some critics of the Church have pointed at verses 4–5, above, and claimed that this is one prophecy that failed to come true. They have used it in their attempts to discredit the Prophet Joseph Smith. They claim that since a temple was not built in Independence, Missouri, during that "generation," Joseph Smith is a false prophet.

The interpretation of this aspect of these verses hinges on the definition of the word "generation." There are many different definitions of this word. Among others, it can mean the time from the marriage of a couple to the marriage of their children, or about twenty to thirty years. It is often used in scripture to mean one hundred years, as in the case of the Nephites after the visit of the resurrected Christ to them. They had peace for two generations, or two hundred years (see 4 Nephi 1:22) and were basically destroyed at the end of four generations, or four hundred years.

Another definition of "generation," and perhaps the one that best applies to verses 4–5, above, is the one used in Matthew 24:34, which refers to the signs of the times to be shown before the Second Coming. In this case, "generation" means an indefinite period of time in which prophesied events will take place. This definition of "generation" is also found in Joseph Smith—Matthew 1:34 and surrounding verses.

If we apply this last definition, there is no problem, because New

Jerusalem, including a temple, will indeed be built in Independence, Missouri, in this "generation," meaning in the time period from the restoration of the true Church, through Joseph Smith, up to the Second Coming. It is a true prophecy given through a true prophet of God, Joseph Smith. The faithful will rejoice when this takes place, and the critics of the Church will be disappointed.

We will include a quote from the 2018 *Doctrine and Covenants Student Manual* that summarizes the teachings in verses 2–5, above:

"During the Prophet Joseph Smith's first visit to Jackson County, Missouri, in July 1831, the Lord identified the area as 'the land which I have appointed and consecrated for the gathering of the saints' (D&C 57:1). He continued: 'Wherefore, this is the land of promise, and the place for the city of Zion. . . . The place which is now called Independence is the center place' (D&C 57:2–3). Joseph Smith and Sidney Rigdon soon dedicated the land of Zion and a site for a temple to be built. They were familiar with earlier revelations in which the Lord had indicated that the center place of Zion would be known as the city of the New Jerusalem, where God's people would gather and build a temple and where Jesus Christ would someday come to visit His people (see Ether 13:6, 8; D&C 42:9, 35–36; 45:66–67).

"In the months after Joseph and Sidney dedicated the land, hundreds of Church members arrived and settled in Jackson County. In September 1832, as recorded in Doctrine and Covenants 84, the Lord reaffirmed His will for the Saints to build 'the city of New Jerusalem' (D&C 84:2), beginning with the temple, which the Lord commanded should 'be reared in this generation' (D&C 84:4).

"However, by the end of 1833, the Latter-day Saints had been driven out of Jackson County by their enemies and eventually settled elsewhere. The Saints learned that their own transgressions had contributed to their expulsion from Zion (see D&C 101:1–6; 105:1–6). Neither the city of New Jerusalem nor the temple was built at that time, as commanded in Doctrine and Covenants 84:4–5. Several years later, after the Saints had established themselves in Nauvoo, Illinois, the Lord declared that they were excused from the commandment to build the city of New Jerusalem and the temple (see D&C 124:49–51). Nevertheless, the Lord's promises remain that Zion will one day be redeemed and the New Jerusalem will be built (see D&C 100:13; 105:9; 136:18)."

Next, in verses 6–16, we are given the direct line of authority from Moses back to Adam.

Doctrine, verses 6–16

The priesthood must be passed from one man to another by the laying on of hands. Moses had a direct line of priesthood authority going back to Adam.

We will use **bold** to point out this direct line of priesthood from Moses to Adam. But we need to call your attention to something before we continue. The first phrase of verse 6, next, **"And the sons of Moses,"** is the beginning of a sentence that skips all the way over to verse 31 where it continues with **"—for the sons of Moses and also the sons of Aaron shall offer an acceptable offering and sacrifice in the house of the Lord, which house shall be built unto the Lord in this generation, upon the consecrated spot as I have appointed—"**

Everything between the two quotes given above is parenthetical, like being in parentheses; in other words, it is basically a long explanation that could have a parenthesis at the beginning and one at the end. If you were to place these parentheses in your own scriptures as notes, you would have the following in parentheses, which is the priesthood line of authority for Moses back to Adam:

6 And the sons of Moses, **(according to the Holy Priesthood which he received under the hand of**

his father–in–law, Jethro;

. . . and continuing to verse 31 . . .

31 **Therefore, as I said concerning the sons of Moses)**—for the sons of Moses and also the sons of Aaron shall offer an acceptable offering and sacrifice in the house of the Lord, which house shall be built unto the Lord in this generation, upon the consecrated spot as I have appointed—

We will study the words of the Savior within these "parentheses," that is, verses 6 through the first part of verse 31, and then when we get to verse 31, we will study the concept that began with the first phrase of verse 6.

Priesthood Line of Authority of Moses Back to Adam

6 And the sons of **Moses**, according to the Holy Priesthood which he received under the hand [*by the laying on of hands*] of his father–in–law, **Jethro**;

7 And Jethro received it under the hand of **Caleb**;

8 And Caleb received it under the hand of **Elihu**;

9 And Elihu under the hand of **Jeremy**;

10 And Jeremy under the hand of **Gad**;

11 And Gad under the hand of **Esaias**;

12 And Esaias received it under the hand of God.

We don't know if verse 12, above, means that Esaias received the Melchizedek Priesthood from Abraham (verse 13, next), under the direction of God, or if it means he received it directly from God. We will continue with Abraham.

13 Esaias also lived in the days of **Abraham**, and was blessed of him—

14 Which Abraham received the priesthood from **Melchizedek**, who received it **through the lineage of his fathers** [*ancestors*], **even till Noah**;

Did you notice a change beginning with verse 14, above? Until that verse, each individual in the line of authority was given, but as of verse 14, we are apparently seeing a summary of many individuals from Melchizedek back to Noah. The same is true with verses 15–16, next.

15 And from **Noah till Enoch**, through the lineage of their fathers;

16 And from **Enoch to Abel**, who was slain by the conspiracy of his brother, who received the priesthood by the commandments of God, by the hand [*the laying on of hands*] of his father **Adam**, who **was the first man**—

Doctrine, verse 16

Adam was the first man.

As you can see, in the last part of verse 16, above, we have an important revealed truth as to the origin of man. The Savior simply says, "Adam . . . was the first man."

As you know, there are numerous theories as to how mankind came to be on this earth. Several years ago, the First Presidency at the time used the revealed word of God in an official statement on this matter. They said (**bold** added for emphasis):

"It is held by some that Adam was not the first man upon this earth, and that the original human being was a development from lower orders of the animal creation. These, however, are the theories of men. The word of the Lord declares that Adam was 'the first man of all men' (Moses 1:34), and we are therefore in duty bound to regard him as the primal [first] parent of our race. It was shown to the brother of Jared that all men were created in the beginning after the image of God; and whether we take this to mean the spirit or the body, or both, it commits us to the same conclusion: **Man began life as a human being**, in the likeness of our heavenly Father." (The First Presidency [Joseph F.

Smith, John R. Winder, and Anthon H. Lund], in James R. Clark, *Messages of the First Presidency,* 4:205–6.)

As we continue, we see two more doctrines—that the priesthood is essential to having the true church on earth and that the priesthood is eternal—along with much other instruction about the priesthood.

Doctrine, verse 17

The priesthood must be on earth in order for the Church of Jesus Christ to exist.

Doctrine, verse 17

The priesthood is eternal.

17 Which priesthood continueth in the church of God in all generations [*is always with the true Church when it exists on earth*]**, and is without beginning of days or end of years** [*is eternal*]**.**

18 And the Lord confirmed a priesthood also upon Aaron and his seed [*the Aaronic Priesthood*]**,** throughout all their generations, **which** priesthood also continueth and **abideth forever with the priesthood which is after the holiest order of God** [*the Melchizedek Priesthood*]**.**

Next, in verses 19–22, the Savior teaches us about the role and function of the Melchizedek

Priesthood. You may wish to bracket these verses in your own scriptures and place a note saying "Melchizedek Priesthood" along the bracket. The Savior will teach more about this in section 107.

Doctrine, verses 19–22

The Melchizedek Priesthood directs the Church and holds the keys of the "spiritual blessings of the church" (see also D&C 107:18).

19 And this greater priesthood [*Melchizedek*] **administereth the gospel** and **holdeth the key of the mysteries** [*the simple basics of the gospel, which are "mysteries" to most of the world because they do not have the full gospel of Christ; see Bible Dictionary under "Mystery"*] **of the kingdom,** even **the key of the knowledge of God.**

Joseph Fielding Smith taught the following about the Melchizedek Priesthood as explained in verse 19, above:

"It is the Holy Priesthood that unlocks the door to heaven and reveals to man the mysteries of the Kingdom of God. It is this Divine Authority which makes known the knowledge of God! Is there any wonder that the world today is groping in gross darkness concerning God and the things of his kingdom? We should also remember that these great truths are not made known even to members of the Church unless they place their lives in harmony with the law on which these blessings are predicated. (D. & C. 130:20–21.)" (*Church History and Modern Revelation*, 1:33).

Doctrine, verse 20

Through the ordinances of the Priesthood, "the power of godliness is manifest."

20 Therefore, **in the ordinances thereof, the power of godliness is manifest.**

Elder Todd D. Christofferson taught about "the power of godliness" as follows:

"Our covenant commitment to Him permits our Heavenly Father to let His divine influence, 'the power of godliness' (D&C 84:20), flow into our lives. He can do that because by our participation in priesthood ordinances we exercise our agency and elect to receive it. . . .

"In all the ordinances, especially those of the temple, we are endowed with power from on high. This 'power of godliness' comes in the person and by the influence of the Holy Ghost. . . .

". . . It is also the Holy Ghost, in His character as the Holy Spirit of Promise, that confirms the validity and efficacy of your covenants and seals God's promises upon

you" ("The Power of Covenants," *Ensign*, May 2009, 22).

Doctrine, verses 21–22

Without the authority and ordinances of the Melchizedek Priesthood, we cannot be taught the things necessary to bring "the power of godliness" into our lives.

21 And **without the ordinances thereof** [*without the ordinances of the Melchizedek Priesthood*]**, and the authority of the priesthood, the power of godliness is not manifest unto men in the flesh;**

22 For **without this** [*perhaps meaning the "power of godliness" (verse 21), which no doubt includes Melchizedek Priesthood ordinances and the personal righteousness arising out of living the gospel of Christ, plus the gift of the Holy Ghost, which comes to all faithful members via a Melchizedek Priesthood ordinance*] **no man can see the face of God, even the Father, and live.**

Next, we are told that Moses tried diligently to get his people to accept and live the gospel, inherent in the Melchizedek Priesthood-based Church of Jesus Christ.

23 Now **this** [*that without Melchizedek Priesthood ordinances and direction, the "power of godliness" is out*

of reach, as is the privilege of seeing God] **Moses plainly taught to the children of Israel** in the wilderness, **and sought diligently to sanctify his people** [*to make them holy and fit to be in the presence of God]* **that they might behold** [*see*] **the face of God** [*Exodus 19:10–11*];

24 **But they hardened their hearts and could not endure his presence** [*would have been killed by His glory if they had seen Him*]; therefore, the Lord in his wrath, for his anger was kindled against them, swore that they should not enter into **his rest** while in the wilderness, which rest **is the fulness of his glory**.

Doctrine, verse 24

(Last part of verse 24, above.) "Rest" means exaltation or being in the full presence of God (see also Alma 12:34).

Doctrine, verse 25

The Melchizedek Priesthood was taken from the children of Israel.

25 **Therefore, he took Moses out of their midst, and the Holy Priesthood** [*Melchizedek Priesthood*] **also;**

Doctrine, verses 26–28

A major purpose of the Aaronic Priesthood is that of preparing us for Melchizedek Priesthood ordinances and blessings.

26 And **the lesser priesthood** [*Aaronic Priesthood*] continued, which priesthood **holdeth the key of the ministering of angels and the preparatory gospel**;

27 Which gospel is **the gospel of repentance and of baptism, and the remission of sins**, and the law of carnal commandments [*part of the law of Moses involving rigid rites and laws, designed as a "schoolmaster" (Galatians 3:24) to raise them to the level where they could benefit from the Melchizedek Priesthood*], **which the Lord** in his wrath **caused to continue with the house of Aaron** [*the descendants of Aaron, brother of Moses*] among the children of Israel **until John** [*the Baptist*], **whom God raised up, being filled with the Holy Ghost from his mother's womb.**

28 For **he** [*John the Baptist*] **was baptized** while he was yet **in his childhood**, and was **ordained** [*not to the priesthood but perhaps blessed or set apart to carry out his earthly mission, possibly similar to*

the blessing of babies today] **by the angel of God at the time he was eight days old unto this power, to overthrow the kingdom of the Jews, and to make straight the way of the Lord before the face of his people, to prepare them for the coming of the Lord**, in whose hand is given all power.

As you can see, several important items were brought up in verses 26–28, above. In reference to "ministering of angels," in verse 26, we are taught that angels do much behind the scenes to prepare the way for people to join the Church. We also understand that there is much "ministering" by angels in assisting us in our family history work so that our dead ancestors can have the blessings of repentance and baptism (verse 27, next).

President Dallin H. Oaks, then an Apostle, spoke on the subject of the Aaronic Priesthood and the ministering of angels in the priesthood session of general conference in October 1998 as follows (**bold** added for emphasis):

"The scriptures recite numerous instances where an angel appeared personally. Angelic appearances to Zacharias and Mary (see Luke 1) and to King Benjamin and Nephi, the grandson of Helaman (see Mosiah 3:2; 3 Ne. 7:17–18) are only a few examples. **When I was young, I**

thought such personal appearances were the only meaning of the ministering of angels. As a young holder of the Aaronic Priesthood, I did not think I would see an angel, and **I wondered what such appearances had to do with the Aaronic Priesthood**.

"But **the ministering of angels can also be unseen**. Angelic messages can be **delivered by a voice** or merely by **thoughts** or **feelings communicated to the mind**. President John Taylor described 'the action of the angels, or messengers of God, upon our minds, so that the heart can conceive . . . revelations from the eternal world' (*Gospel Kingdom*, sel. G. Homer Durham [1987], 31.)

"Nephi described three manifestations of the ministering of angels when he reminded his rebellious brothers that (1) **they had 'seen an angel**,' (2) **they had 'heard his voice from time to time**,' and (3) also that **an angel had 'spoken unto [them] in a still small voice'** though they were 'past feeling' and 'could not feel his words' (1 Ne. 17:45). The scriptures contain many other statements that angels are sent to teach the gospel and bring men to Christ (see Hebrews 1:14; Alma 39:19; Moroni 7:25, 29, 31–32; D&C 20:35). **Most angelic communications are felt or heard rather than seen**.

"**How does the Aaronic Priesthood hold the key to the ministering of angels?** The answer is the same as for the Spirit of the Lord.

"**In general, the blessings of spiritual companionship and communication are only available to those who are clean**. As explained earlier, **through the Aaronic Priesthood ordinances of baptism and the sacrament, we are cleansed of our sins and promised that if we keep our covenants we will always have His Spirit to be with us. I believe that promise not only refers to the Holy Ghost but also to the ministering of angels**, for 'angels speak by the power of the Holy Ghost; wherefore, they speak the words of Christ' (2 Ne. 32:3.) So it is that **those who hold the Aaronic Priesthood open the door for all Church members who worthily partake of the sacrament to enjoy the companionship of the Spirit of the Lord and the ministering of angels**" ("The Aaronic Priesthood and the Sacrament," *Ensign,* November 1998, 39).

In the last part of verse 27 and in verse 28, next, we find revealed information about John the Baptist. It is not available other than through revelation from the Lord. Questions arise as to whether John had the gift of the Holy Ghost while still in the womb, and whether he was given the priesthood when he was eight days old. We will read a quote from Elder Bruce R. McConkie about these questions and then go on to verse 28. We will use **bold** for emphasis.

"We do know that 'he was **baptized** while he was yet in his childhood [meaning, **when he was eight years of age**], and was **ordained** by the angel of God at the time he was eight days old unto this power [note it well, **not to the Aaronic Priesthood**, but] to overthrow the kingdom of the Jews, and to make straight the way of the Lord before the face of his people, **to prepare them for the coming of the Lord**, in whose hand is given all power.' (D&C 84:24.) **We do not know when he received the Aaronic Priesthood**, but obviously it came to him after his baptism, at whatever age was proper, and before he was sent by one whom he does not name to preach and baptize with water" (*Mortal Messiah*, 384–85).

Next, we are taught some specifics about various Melchizedek and Aaronic Priesthood offices. Keep in mind that this was new information for the members in the beginning stages of the Restoration.

29 And again, the offices of **elder and bishop** [*must be ordained a high priest in order to serve as a bishop*] **are** necessary **appendages belonging unto** [*are categories within*] **the high priesthood** [*Melchizedek Priesthood*].

30 And again, **the offices of teacher and deacon are necessary appendages belonging to the lesser priesthood** [the Aaronic Priesthood], which priesthood was confirmed upon Aaron and his sons.

As previously mentioned, the Savior began a sentence at the beginning of verse 6 and then added much parenthetical information (verses 6–30). He now completes that sentence, explaining that "an acceptable offering and sacrifice" will once again be possible in the last days, because of the restoration of the gospel and the priesthood. Without proper priesthood authority, our "offerings" and "sacrifices," our ordinances and covenants, would not be valid. None of our ordinances of exaltation performed in temples would be in effect now or in eternity.

With true priesthood, because of the Restoration, authorized ordinances can once again be performed on earth by both Aaronic and Melchizedek Priesthood holders during this wonderful dispensation of the fullness of times.

Doctrine, verse 31

With the restoration of the priesthood, valid ordinances of salvation and exaltation can once again be performed on earth.

31 **Therefore, as I** [the Savior] said [at the beginning of verse 6] concerning the sons of Moses— for **the sons of Moses** [symbolic of Melchizedek Priesthood holders] and **also the sons of Aaron** [Aaronic Priesthood holders] **shall offer an acceptable offering and sacrifice in the house of the Lord**, which house shall be built unto the Lord in this generation, upon the consecrated spot as I have appointed—

A most significant phrase, defining who the latter-day "sons of Moses and of Aaron" are, is found in verse 32, next. As you will see, it defines them as our faithful priesthood holders today. There is important symbolism here.

32 And **the sons of Moses and of Aaron** shall be filled with the glory of the Lord, upon Mount Zion in the Lord's house, **whose sons are ye** [perhaps meaning Joseph Smith and the elders mentioned by the Lord in verse 1 of this section]; **and also many** [faithful priesthood holders in the last days] **whom I have called and sent forth to build up my church.**

A quote from the 2018 Doctrine and Covenants Student Manual, (which is an official publication of the Church and thus has doctrinal reliability) confirms who the sons of Moses and the sons of Aaron in verses 31 and 32, above, are (**bold** added for emphasis):

"In Doctrine and Covenants 84:31, the Lord continued the discussion that began in Doctrine and Covenants 84:5–6 regarding the role of 'the sons of Moses and also the sons of Aaron . . . in the house of the Lord,' including the latter-day temple that will be built in the city of New Jerusalem. **The sons of Moses are those who hold the Melchizedek Priesthood. The sons of Aaron are those who hold the Aaronic Priesthood.** These priesthood bearers will 'offer an acceptable offering and sacrifice in the house of the Lord' (D&C 84:31)." (For further details about these latter-day offerings, see Isaiah 66:20–21; Omni 1:26; D&C 13:1; 128:24.)

You may wish to cross-reference verse 32, here, with verse 34, below.

In verses 33–42, next, we have what is known as "the Oath and Covenant of the Priesthood." Here, again, you may wish to bracket or otherwise identify these verses and place a note out to the side that says, "Oath and Covenant of the Priesthood."

The Oath and Covenant of the Priesthood

Doctrine

Faithful Melchizedek Priesthood holders make

a covenant with God upon accepting and being ordained to the priesthood. The Father makes an "oath" with them that if they serve faithfully, they will receive all that He has (verse 38). This is known as "The Oath and Covenant of the Priesthood."

33 For whoso is faithful unto the obtaining these two priesthoods [*Aaronic and Melchizedek*] of which I have spoken, **and** the **magnifying their calling, are sanctified** by the Spirit [*are directed and prompted by the Holy Ghost, leading them to sanctification—being made holy and fit to be in the presence of God through the blessings of the Atonement; compare with Moses 6:60*] **unto the renewing of their bodies.**

The "renewing of their bodies," in verse 33, above, can have at least two meanings. One is that they will receive celestial bodies at the time they are resurrected (see D&C 88:28–29). Another possible meaning is that, on occasions when they are weary and tired, they will be carried by the power of the Lord to complete their work. They will know that they have been blessed far beyond their physical and mental capacities.

34 They become the sons of Moses and of Aaron and the seed of

Abraham [*symbolic of exaltation; in effect, the "heirs" of Abraham, who has already become a god; see D&C 132:29, 37*], and **the church and kingdom, and the elect of God.** [*All of these are terms meaning exaltation.*]

We will include two quotes here from the 1981 *Doctrine and Covenants Student Manual* that explain what it means to "become the sons of Moses and of Aaron."

"Who are the sons of Aaron and Levi today? They are, by virtue of the blessings of the Almighty, those who are ordained by those who hold the authority to officiate in the offices of the priesthood. It is written that those so ordained become the sons of Moses and Aaron" (Joseph Fielding Smith, *Doctrines of Salvation,* Bookcraft, 1956, 3:93; see also *Doctrine and Covenants Student Manual,* 1981, 184).

"'Sons of Moses,' and 'sons of Aaron' do not refer to their literal descendants only, for all who are faithful and obtain these Priesthoods, and magnify their calling, are sanctified by the Spirit and become the 'sons' of Moses and of Aaron, and the seed of Abraham, as well as the Church and Kingdom, and the elect of God (verse 34). Paul expresses this thought as follows, 'Know ye therefore that they which are of faith, the same are the children of Abraham' (Gal. 3:7). (Smith and Sjodahl,

Commentary, 504.)" (*Doctrine and Covenants Student Manual,* 1981, 184).

While verse 35, next, is generally understood to pertain to men as they accept the call to hold the Melchizedek Priesthood, it can, in a very important sense, pertain to all righteous members, male and female, who enter into or "receive" priesthood ordinances and covenants. D&C 132:19 makes it clear that when faithful men and women enter into covenants performed by "him who is anointed, unto whom I have appointed this power and the keys of this priesthood," if they continue to live worthy, they will enter exaltation and become gods (D&C 132:20).

In verses 35–38, the Master shows us a beautiful "progression" of steps leading to exaltation.

35 And also **all they who receive this priesthood receive me**, saith the Lord;

36 For **he that receiveth my servants receiveth me**;

37 And **he that receiveth me receiveth my Father**;

Doctrine, verse 38

It is possible to become gods.

38 And **he that receiveth my Father receiveth my Father's kingdom**; therefore [*for this*

reason] **all that my Father hath shall be given unto him**.

Next, in verse 39, we find the wording that leads to the term "Oath and Covenant of the Priesthood."

39 And this is according to **the oath and covenant which belongeth to the priesthood**.

40 Therefore, **all those who receive the priesthood, receive this oath and covenant of my Father, which he cannot break**, neither can it be moved [*compare with D&C 82:10*].

From verse 40, above, we learn that the "oath" is what the Father promises. His "oath and covenant" is to give those who "receive the priesthood" all that He has.

It doesn't take much analyzing to see that when we give our "all" and qualify to receive the Father's "all," we get the better bargain.

President Henry B. Eyring taught what it means to receive this oath and covenant. He said:

"Rising to the possibilities of the oath and covenant brings the greatest of all the gifts of God: eternal life [*exaltation*]. That is a purpose of the Melchizedek Priesthood. Through keeping the covenants as we receive the priesthood and renewing them in the temple ceremonies, we are

promised by an oath made by our Heavenly Father, Elohim, that we will gain the fulness of His glory and live as He lives. We will have the blessing of being sealed in a family forever with the promise of eternal increase . . .

". . . The very fact that you have been offered the oath and covenant is evidence that God has chosen you, knowing your power and capacity. He has known you since you were with Him in the spirit world. With His foreknowledge of your strength, He has allowed you to find the true Church of Jesus Christ and to be offered the priesthood. You can feel confidence because you have evidence of His confidence in you" ("Faith and the Oath and Covenant of the Priesthood," *Ensign*, May 2008, 61–62).

Verse 41, next, explains the seriousness of violating the covenants we make when accepting the Melchizedek Priesthood. President Marion G. Romney explained this verse as follows:

"Now, I do not think this means that all who fail to magnify their callings in the priesthood will have committed the unpardonable sin, but I do think that priesthood bearers who have entered into the covenants that we enter into—in the waters of baptism, in connection with the law of tithing, the Word of Wisdom, and the many other covenants we make—and then refuse to live up to these covenants will stand in jeopardy of losing the promise of eternal life" ("The Covenant of the Priesthood," *Ensign,* July 1972, 99).

41 But whoso breaketh this covenant after he hath received it, and altogether turneth therefrom, shall not have forgiveness of sins in this world nor in the world to come.

Because of the seriousness of this covenant, as stated in verse 41, above, it may be that some will decide not to enter into it. It appears that verse 42, next, addresses such persons, likely meaning both men and women who intentionally avoid the highest priesthood ordinances available in the temple because of the seriousness and accountability that accompany ordinances of exaltation.

42 And wo unto all those who come not unto this priesthood which ye have received, which I now confirm [*perhaps meaning "reconfirm," reassure that it is in force in your behalf*] upon you who are present this day [*Joseph Smith and the elders mentioned in verse 1*], by mine own voice out of the heavens; and even I have given the heavenly hosts and mine angels charge concerning you [*another reminder that there is much done for us, behind the scenes, by angels*].

In verses 43–44, next, we are counseled not to let our guard

down and to carefully live by the revealed word of God.

43 And I now give unto you a commandment to **beware concerning yourselves, to give diligent heed to the words of eternal life** [*exaltation*].

44 For you shall live by every word that proceedeth forth from the mouth of God.

Some major functions of the Light of Christ are explained in verses 45–47, next.

Doctrine, verses 45–47

Everyone born into the world is given the Spirit of Christ, sometimes called the Light of Christ. A major function of the Light of Christ (also sometimes called "conscience") is to lead all who will follow it to the gospel of Jesus Christ. If they listen and follow until they become members of the Church, they will receive the greater light and help of the gift of the Holy Ghost. It will, in turn, lead them home to the Father if they live according to its promptings.

45 For the word of the Lord is truth, and whatsoever is **truth is light** [*among other things, truth* brings *"light" and understanding into our souls*], and whatsoever is **light is Spirit** [*includes the fact that truth and light come to us from the Spirit of Christ*], even **the Spirit of Jesus Christ** [*often referred to as the Light of Christ*].

46 And **the Spirit giveth light to every man that cometh into the world; and the Spirit enlighteneth every man through the world, that hearkeneth to the voice of the Spirit** [*those who listen to the Spirit of Christ will receive enlightenment*].

47 And **every one that hearkeneth to the voice of the Spirit cometh unto God, even the Father** [*those who heed the promptings of the Spirit of Christ will be led home to the Father by eventually joining the Church of Jesus Christ and living the gospel*].

Elder Richard G. Scott taught about the Light of Christ as follows:

"The Light of Christ is that divine power or influence that emanates from God through Jesus Christ. It gives light and life to all things. It prompts all rational individuals throughout the earth to distinguish truth from error, right from wrong. It activates your conscience. Its influence can be weakened through transgression and addiction and restored through proper

repentance. The Light of Christ is not a person. It is a power and influence that comes from God and when followed can lead a person to qualify for the guidance and inspiration of the Holy Ghost" ("Peace of Conscience and Peace of Mind," *Ensign,* November 2004, 15.)

Verse 48, next, teaches us the result of following the Light of Christ. This result is available to all people. If they follow the Spirit of Christ, it will lead them to the true Church. If they join, they will be taught about the "covenant," which, in this context, includes the full gospel of Jesus Christ, with its attending covenants and ordinances.

48 And **the Father teacheth him** [*those who follow the Spirit of Christ and are led to the true Church*] **of the covenant which he has renewed and confirmed upon you** [*through the restoration of the gospel*], which is confirmed upon you for your sakes, and **not for your sakes only, but for the sake of the whole world** [*the restored gospel will ultimately be made available to all*].

Next, the Savior reviews the need for all to heed the influence of the Spirit of Christ upon them and come to the restored gospel.

49 And **the whole world lieth in sin, and groaneth under darkness** [*spiritual darkness*] **and**

under the bondage [*captivity*] of sin.

50 And **by this you may know they are under the bondage of sin, because they come not unto me.**

Did you notice the "equation" given in verse 50, above? Those who are not with Christ are being held captive by sin, whether they know it or not. It is just that simple.

51 For **whoso cometh not unto me is under the bondage of sin.**

Sometimes people are disturbed by the use of the term "wicked" (verse 53) in reference to the people in spirit prison. This is because they know that there are some wonderful and good people there (in the spirit prison, which I prefer to call the "spirit world mission field") who have not yet been taught the gospel, and they don't like to hear them referred to as wicked. Verses 52–53, next, show us that there is another scriptural meaning for the word "wicked" in addition to its use as a term for those involved in sin and gross evil. As you will see, "wicked" is sometimes used in scripture to refer to those who have not yet been taught the gospel.

52 And **whoso** receiveth not my voice **is not acquainted with my voice, and is not of me.**

53 And **by this you may know the righteous from the wicked,** and that the whole world groaneth under sin and darkness even now.

Next, in verses 54–59, an extremely serious matter is explained by the Savior. It is that the Saints have not treated seriously enough the things He has already given them. As you will see, this includes the Book of Mormon. We would do well to pay close attention ourselves to His words of reprimand and counsel.

54 And **your minds in times past have been darkened** because of unbelief, and **because you have treated lightly the things you have received—**

55 **Which vanity and unbelief have brought the whole church under condemnation.**

56 And **this condemnation resteth upon the children of Zion** [*the members in Missouri at this time*]**, even all.**

57 And **they shall remain under this condemnation until they repent and remember the new covenant, even the Book of Mormon and the former commandments which I have given them, not only to say, but to do** according to that which I have written—

President Ezra Taft Benson spoke of the importance of the Book of Mormon in each of our lives. He said:

"Every Latter-day Saint should make the study of this book a lifetime pursuit. Otherwise he is placing his soul in jeopardy and neglecting that which could give spiritual and intellectual unity to his whole life" ("The Book of Mormon Is the Word of God," *Ensign*, May 1975, 65).

58 That they may bring forth fruit meet for [*worthy of*] **their Father's kingdom; otherwise there remaineth a scourge and judgment to be poured out upon the children of Zion.**

The Saints who were settling in Missouri at the time of this revelation fully expected that the Church would be established there, never to be removed, and that it would continue to grow and flourish in Jackson County until the Second Coming.

As you can see, in verses 58 and 59, there is a stern warning from the Lord that if they do not "bring forth fruit meet for their Father's kingdom" (verse 58)—in other words, if they do not live in harmony with the celestial laws incorporated in the gospel, including the oath and covenant of the priesthood, they will be "scourged" (driven and plundered).

59 For shall the children of the kingdom pollute my holy land [*by their disobedience and lack of diligence in living the gospel*]**?** Verily, **I say unto you, Nay.**

Next, in verses 60–61, the Savior assures these brethren that if they heed the counsel and warning He has just given, and follow the counsel He gives next, they will be forgiven. In a way, this is a formula for spiritual success and applies to all of us.

60 Verily, verily [*a scriptural term meaning that what comes next is of key importance*]**, I say unto you who now hear my words,** which are my voice, **blessed are ye inasmuch as you** [*if you will*] **receive these things;**

61 For I will forgive you of your sins with this commandment— that you remain steadfast in your minds in solemnity and the spirit of prayer, in bearing testimony to all the world of those things which are communicated unto you.

We do not know who the men are that are with the Prophet as this revelation is given. It appears from the context that they were some of the leading brethren at the time. We learn from verse 62, next, that they are to continue preaching the gospel themselves and enlist the aid of others to continue taking the gospel to all the world. The General Authorities of the Church are continuing this same pattern of missionary work today.

62 Therefore, **go ye into all the world**; and **unto whatsoever place ye cannot go ye shall send** [*send others on missions to those places*], **that the testimony may go from you into all the world unto every creature.**

63 And **as I said unto mine Apostles, even so I say unto you, for you are mine Apostles, even God's high priests**; ye are they whom my Father hath given me; **ye are my friends;**

We don't want to miss what just happened at the end of verse 63, above. The Savior called them His "friends." From this point on in the Doctrine and Covenants, the Master will refer to these and other humble followers as "friends." This is a term of endearment and closeness that signifies a change in relationship as they become more righteous and faithful.

64 Therefore, **as I said unto mine Apostles I say unto you** again, that **every soul who believeth on your words, and is baptized by water for the remission of sins, shall receive the Holy Ghost.**

Next, in verses 65–73, the Savior

tells us of many of the miracles that will be evident in His church. While we understand these to be literal, there is value in also seeing spiritual symbolism in each of them. If you learn to see such symbolism, then you will often see the spiritual counterpart for literal healings. As you know, spiritual healing has eternal benefits that reach far beyond the literal healing of the physical body and mind. We will designate these spiritual counterparts to literal healings through notes in brackets.

Doctrine, verses 65–73

This is a day of miracles. Miracles, signs, and wonders are a quiet and sweet part of the gospel of Christ.

65 And **these signs shall follow them that believe—**

66 **In my name they shall do many wonderful works;**

67 In my name **they shall cast out devils** [*literal; symbolically could include that the pure gospel of Christ "casts out" evil thoughts, damaging philosophies, fears, confusion as to the purpose of life, and so forth*];

68 **In my name they shall heal the sick** [*literal; symbolically could include the healing of spiritual darkness and confusion, remorse and guilt, anger and hatred*];

69 **In my name they shall open the eyes of the blind** [*literal; often means healing the spiritually "blind"*], and **unstop the ears of the deaf** [*including the spiritually deaf*];

70 And **the tongue of the dumb** [*those who can't speak*] **shall speak** [*can also refer to the power of the Holy Ghost to help us express ourselves more effectively as we discuss the gospel with others, as well as when we speak and teach in church*];

71 And if any man shall administer **poison** unto them it **shall not hurt them** [*symbolically, "poison" could include false philosophies, false doctrines, confusing false political theories, and so forth*];

72 And the **poison of a serpent** [*can also be symbolic of the false doctrines put forth by Satan (the "serpent"), including Internet content that is leading some away from the Church today*] **shall not have power to harm them.**

Sacred experiences, including miracles, are often for our own private blessing and benefit and are usually best kept to ourselves or within a small number of family or close friends. They are not to be used for building ourselves up in the eyes of others. This is a real danger against which the Lord warns in verse 73, next.

73 But a commandment I give unto them, that **they shall not boast themselves of these things, neither speak them before the world**; for **these things are given unto you for your profit and for salvation.**

In verses 74–76, next, we are once again reminded of the importance of our sharing the gospel with others, and of their responsibility to accept it when they know it is true.

74 Verily, verily, I say unto you, **they who believe not on your words, and are not baptized in water in my name, for the remission of their sins, that they may receive the Holy Ghost, shall be damned** [*stopped in spiritual progress*]**, and shall not come into my Father's kingdom** [*celestial glory*] **where my Father and I am.**

75 And **this revelation** unto you, **and commandment, is in force** from this very hour **upon all the world,** and **the gospel is unto all who have not received it** [*the gospel is to be taken to all the world*].

76 But, verily I say **unto all those to whom the kingdom has been given** [*all the members of the Church*]**—from you it must be preached unto them** [*Church

leaders are to continue preaching the gospel to the members], **that they shall repent of their former evil works**; for they are to be upbraided [scolded, chastised] for their evil hearts of unbelief, and your brethren in Zion [in Missouri] for their rebellion against you at the time I sent you.

We will do one more thing with verse 76, above. The word "upbraided" may be familiar to you. "Upbraideth not" is used in James 1:5, which young Joseph Smith read in the Bible before going into the grove to pray. It comes from the ancient practice of jerking a child's braid upward as a means of scolding or disciplining. Thus, the word came to mean to "scold or chastise."

Again, in verse 77, next, the Savior refers to these men as His friends. He then goes on to tell them that they are getting the same advice as His disciples of old.

77 And again I say unto you, **my friends** (see also verse 63), for **from henceforth** [from now on] **I shall call you friends**, it is expedient [necessary] that I give unto you this commandment [to continue teaching the gospel to the members of the Church, as well as to the world], that ye become even as my friends [disciples] in days when I was with them [during the Savior's mortal ministry], traveling

to preach the gospel in my power;

78 **For I suffered** [allowed] **them not to have purse** [a money bag] **or scrip** [a bag for carrying food; see Bible Dictionary under "Scrip"], **neither two coats.**

79 Behold, **I send you out to prove the world** [to test the world by teaching them the gospel so that they can use their moral agency and be accountable for their actions], and **the laborer is worthy of his hire** [those who preach the gospel earn their blessings through hard work].

In verses 80–91, next, the Savior informs these early brethren that He will take care of those who go forth to preach the gospel. They will be fed, clothed, and assisted financially by people as they pursue their missionary journeys (verses 89–90). This required great faith on the part of these missionaries, and there was much success in bringing converts into the Church. Because of the success of these missionary efforts, the Church was greatly strengthened by the large influx of converts and positioned for significant continued missionary efforts into all the world.

For the most part, these verses must be understood in the context of these early missionary efforts. Otherwise, we would have missionaries going out today without proper preparation for taking care of their physical needs.

80 And **any man that shall go and preach** this gospel of the kingdom, **and fail not to continue faithful in all things, shall not be weary in mind, neither darkened** [*spiritually*], **neither in body, limb, nor joint**; and **a hair of his head shall not fall to the ground unnoticed** [*the Lord is watching over them*]. And **they shall not go hungry, neither athirst** [*this aspect of missionary work is taken care of today by the funds of the Church as well as by the financial support of family and friends of missionaries*].

Verses 81–84, next, are similar to Matthew 6:25–36, which, according to JST Matthew 6:25–27 and 3 Nephi 13:25–34, were addressed to the Savior's Apostles.

81 **Therefore, take ye no thought for the morrow**, for what ye shall eat, or what ye shall drink, or wherewithal ye shall be clothed.

82 **For, consider the lilies of the field,** how they grow, they toil not, neither do they spin; and the kingdoms of the world, in all their glory, are not arrayed like one of these.

83 **For your Father, who is in heaven, knoweth that you have need of all these things.**

84 Therefore, **let the morrow take thought for the things of itself**.

85 **Neither take ye thought beforehand what ye shall say; but treasure up in your minds continually the words of life** [*keep studying the gospel*], **and it shall be given you in the very hour that portion that shall be meted unto every man** [*with proper preparation, you will qualify to have the help of the Holy Ghost in determining what to teach to each person you meet*].

86 Therefore, **let no man among you**, for this commandment is unto all the faithful who are called of God in the church unto the ministry, **from this hour take purse or scrip**, that goeth forth to proclaim this gospel of the kingdom.

As previously mentioned, some could understand, based on verse 86, above, that none of our missionaries or general Church leaders today should take money and supplies with them as they go forth to preach the gospel. However, as you know, we believe in continuous revelation. Thus, this advice no longer applies. The Lord does not require that His servants today go without "purse or scrip," depending on the kindness and generosity of people throughout the world to travelers and missionaries. Rather, funds are made available to take care of their needs.

As the Savior continues teaching these brethren, we see that the message of the gospel as taught by the missionaries is to make people accountable and to provide them the option of using their agency wisely.

87 Behold, **I send you out to reprove the world of all their unrighteous deeds** [*to call the people of the earth to repentance*]**, and to teach them of a judgment which is to come** [*to teach them that they will someday face God on Judgment Day*].

Verse 88, next, is a favorite of missionaries, including senior missionaries, as they go forth into the unknown to serve. You may wish to mark it in your own scriptures.

88 And whoso receiveth you, there I will be also, for **I will go before your face. I will be on your right hand and on your left, and my Spirit shall be in your hearts, and mine angels round about you, to bear you up.**

89 **Whoso receiveth you receiveth me; and the same will feed you, and clothe you, and give you money.**

90 And **he who feeds you, or clothes you, or gives you money,**

shall in nowise lose his reward.

Verse 91, next, seems to refer more to members of the Church than to nonmembers. The message is clear. If we pay our tithes and offerings, which serve to help spread the gospel to all the world, we are true disciples (followers) of Christ. If we don't, we are not!

91 And **he that doeth not these things is not my disciple; by this you may know my disciples.**

Verses 92–95 are sensitive and must be kept in context. The context here appears to be that of a testimony that they tried to preach the gospel to the person or to the people but were rejected. Based on what we understand in the overall context of the scriptures, the Lord continues to reach out to people throughout their lives. See, for example, Jacob 6:4–5. You probably know several people who have come into activity later in life after having been less active or who had rejected earlier efforts to teach them the gospel. They are now faithful, committed Saints.

92 **He that receiveth you not, go away from him alone by yourselves** [*so you don't cause unnecessary trouble*]**, and cleanse your feet** even with water, pure water, whether in heat or in cold, and **bear testimony of it unto your Father** which is in heaven, and

return not again unto that man.

See section 60, verse 15, in this study guide for more concerning the washing of feet as mentioned in verse 92, above.

93 And in whatsoever village or city ye enter, do likewise.

Verse 94, next, seems to imply that some missionaries could be tempted to simply wash their feet a lot, thus getting off somewhat easy, rather than going to every effort to find and teach the honest in heart.

94 **Nevertheless, search diligently** [*for people who will listen to you*] and spare not [*don't spare any effort*]; and **wo unto that house, or that village or city that rejecteth you, or your words, or your testimony concerning me**.

95 **Wo** [*trouble*], I say again, **unto that house, or that village or city that rejecteth you, or your words, or your testimony of me**;

One of the signs of the times is given in verses 96–97, next. It is that, in the last days, as people reject the quiet, humble, gentle approach of the missionaries who are sent throughout the world to preach the gospel (see D&C 88:88–90), the Lord will "turn up the volume" via plagues, natural disasters, and so forth in order to get people's attention. Such things are the natural consequence,

decreed by God, for mass wickedness among the inhabitants of the earth.

<u>Doctrine, verses 96–97</u>

Things will continue to get worse until the Second Coming.

96 For **I, the Almighty, have laid my hands upon the nations, to scourge them for their wickedness.**

97 And **plagues shall go forth, and they shall not be taken from the earth until I have completed my work**, which shall be cut short in righteousness [*perhaps meaning that Christ will come a little sooner than expected (Joseph Smith—Matthew 1:47–48; could also mean that if the last days were not cut short by the Second Coming, none of the righteous would survive—compare with Matthew 24:22*]—

A major transition takes place between verse 97 and verse 98. The Savior now takes us from the plagues, pestilences, and devastations of the last days into the Millennium. Verse 98 teaches us that the time will come during the Millennium when virtually all people will have joined the Church and will live the gospel.

"Virtually all," for all practical

purposes, means "everyone." The reason we don't say "all people" is that, because of agency, a few will turn to wickedness even during the Millennium as stated by Isaiah in Isaiah 65:20.

Doctrine, verse 98

During the Millennium, the time will come when virtually all people on earth will accept and live the gospel.

98 Until all shall know me, who remain [*who were not destroyed by the Second Coming; see 2 Nephi 12:10, 19, 21, and who live during the Millennium*], even from the least unto the greatest, **and shall be filled with the knowledge of the Lord, and shall see eye to eye** [*will live in peace and harmony one with another*], **and shall** lift up their voice, and with the voice together **sing this new song**, saying:

Verses 99–103 describe conditions that will exist during the Millennium. But before we continue, we will take a moment to consider the phrase "sing this new song" at the end of verse 98, above.

Singing a "new song" can mean rejoicing about something that could not be celebrated before because it had not yet taken place. Symbolically, new converts could "sing a new song," rejoicing that they now belong to the true Church. First-time parents could

"sing a new song" that they are now parents. Missionaries could "sing a new song," rejoicing that they are now finally on their mission.

In this case, those who are present at the beginning of the Millennium can "sing a new song" of rejoicing that the Savior is finally here on earth and that millennial conditions of peace and harmony prevail.

On a personal note, some years ago as I entered the freeway on my way to teach my evening Book of Mormon class at the institute, a "new song" came into my mind—beautiful music I had never heard before (or since). It continued playing in my mind for about fifteen minutes. I enjoyed it but had no idea what it meant. That evening, during class, I noticed a new student sitting toward the back of the room in a rather large class. The Spirit was strong, and I taught a number of things I had not specifically prepared.

After class, the young lady came up, introduced herself to me, and said that I had been talking directly to her during the class and had specifically addressed her concerns about joining the Church. She was not a member but was investigating the Church. With her questions answered, she was determined to be baptized and asked me to confirm her, which I did two weeks later at her baptism conducted by the full-time missionaries.

As I traveled home after class, it occurred to me that the reason I'd had the "new song" playing in my mind before class was that the young investigator was soon going to be able to "sing a new song" in her life; namely, a song of rejoicing that she had found the true gospel of Jesus Christ and had become a member.

We will continue now with verses 99–102, which constitute "singing a new song" in celebration of the arrival of the Millennium, and describe some millennial conditions.

We will provide some possible explanatory notes. You could no doubt see additional possibilities and interpretations.

Doctrine, verses 99–102

The Millennium will come as prophesied.

99 The Lord hath brought again Zion [the Lord's kingdom has finally come again];

The Lord hath redeemed his people, Israel [righteous Israel have been set free from Satan and sin, and the thousand years of peace have been ushered in],

According to the election of grace [as prophesied because of the divine help of Christ and His Atonement],

Which was brought to pass by the faith

And covenant of their fathers [their ancestors].

100 The Lord hath redeemed his people;

And **Satan is bound** [not allowed to tempt at all; see D&C 101:28] **and time is no longer** [we don't have to wait any longer for the Millennium because it is here].

The Lord hath gathered all things in one [all things have been restored].

The Lord hath brought down Zion [the kingdom of heaven has come down upon the earth; see D&C 65:6] **from above.**

The Lord hath brought up Zion [the kingdom of God on earth; see D&C 65:6] **from beneath** [from the earth; in other words, the Church in heaven is now combined with the Church on earth].

101 The earth hath travailed and brought forth her strength [symbolically, the earth has gone into labor (as in childbirth) and has finally succeeded in bringing forth a righteous people; compare with 1 Nephi 21:18–21, where Isaiah prophesies that righteous people will cover the earth];

And **truth is established in her bowels** [*the entire earth is filled with the truths of the gospel*];

And **the heavens have smiled upon her** [*mother earth finally has the satisfaction of resting from the wickedness that has been upon her for so long; compare with Moses 7:48*];

And **she is clothed with the glory of her God** [*mother earth is wrapped with the warmth and glory of the Savior*];

For **he stands in the midst of his people** [*Jesus Christ rules and reigns among His people for a thousand years*].

The final "verse" of this "new song" (verse 102) is a song of gratitude to God.

102 **Glory, and honor, and power, and might,**

Be ascribed [*given*] **to our God; for he is full of mercy,**

Justice, grace and truth, and peace,

Forever and ever, Amen.

Verses 103–8, next, give practical instructions on how to share resources, including money given to them as they travel and preach.

103 And again, verily, verily, I say unto you, **it is expedient** [*wise, necessary*] that **every man who goes forth to proclaim mine everlasting gospel, that inasmuch as** [*if*] **they have families, and receive money by gift, that they should send it unto them** [*their families back home*] **or make use of it for their benefit** [*or use it themselves*], **as the Lord shall direct them,** for thus it seemeth me good.

104 And **let all those** [*missionaries*] **who have not families, who receive money** [*who receive donations from people in their mission fields*], **send it up unto the bishop in Zion** [*send it to Bishop Edward Partridge, in Jackson County, Missouri*], **or unto the bishop** [*Bishop Newel K. Whitney*] **in Ohio,** that it may be consecrated **for the bringing forth of the revelations** [*the Book of Commandments—the predecessor to the first Doctrine and Covenants*] **and the printing thereof, and for establishing Zion** [*and for building up the Church in Missouri*].

Verse 105, next, describes the purpose of our current Deseret Industries and of the Humanitarian Fund.

105 And **if any man shall give unto any of you a coat, or a suit,**

take the old [*your old coat or suit*] and cast [*give*] it unto the poor, and go on your way rejoicing.

The principle given in verse 106, next, is often seen in missionary companionships as well as in the assigning of ministering companionships.

106 And if any man among you be strong in the Spirit, let him take with him that is weak, that he may be edified [*strengthened and taught*] in all meekness, that he may become strong also.

The use of Aaronic Priesthood holders to assist and learn under the direction of Melchizedek Priesthood holders is exemplified in verse 107, next.

107 Therefore, take with you those who are ordained unto the lesser priesthood [*Aaronic Priesthood*], and send them before you to make appointments, and to prepare the way, and to fill appointments that you yourselves are not able to fill.

108 Behold, this is the way that mine Apostles, in ancient days, built up my church unto me.

Verses 109–10, next, teach the importance of each member of the Church fulfilling his or her calling, and of all working in peace and harmony with each other. Every member is needed in the Church.

You have likely heard this as a theme of a number of gospel sermons over the years.

109 Therefore, let every man stand in his own office, and labor in his own calling; and let not the head say unto the feet it hath no need of the feet; for without the feet how shall the body be able to stand?

110 Also the body [*the Church, the kingdom of God*] hath need of every member, that all may be edified [*strengthened and built up*] together, that the system may be kept perfect.

The last phrase of verse 110, above, is interesting. Perhaps you've noticed that the Lord does a "perfect" work (saving souls) using imperfect people, backed up by the "perfect" gospel in the "perfect system"—in other words, the Church.

Next, we see specific instructions relating to the duties of various priesthood offices.

111 And behold, the high priests should travel, and also the elders, and also the lesser priests [*priests in the Aaronic Priesthood*]; but the deacons and teachers should be appointed to watch over the church, to be standing ministers unto the church [*deacons and teachers should stay at*

home and function in the local wards and branches].

When I was a new bishop, I was told that it was my responsibility not only to wisely assist the poor and needy who approached me for help but also that I was to <u>seek out the poor and assist them</u> if appropriate. That caught me a bit by surprise. Verse 112, next, is the scriptural basis for that advice to me. I followed the counsel.

112 And **the bishop**, Newel K. Whitney, also **should travel round about and among all the churches, searching after the poor to administer to their wants** by humbling the rich and the proud [*the rich are often vulnerable to becoming prideful, and giving to the poor can help keep them humble*].

Verse 113, next, provides a basis for having some full- and part-time employees to help operate bishops' storehouses, Welfare Square, Deseret Industries, and so forth.

113 **He should also employ an agent** to take charge and to do his secular business as he shall direct.

While I was serving as a stake president, a member of my stake came to me one day, concerned about whether she should warn her relatives in New York to move elsewhere. She had just read verses 114–15, next, and was sincerely concerned for their safety. I pointed out to her that the word "if" was contained in both verses, and I asked if she had noticed that. She hadn't and was greatly relieved, realizing that there are many in these cities who have accepted the gospel. In fact, we now have temples in these areas!

114 Nevertheless, **let the bishop go unto the city of New York**, also to the city of **Albany**, and also to the city of **Boston, and warn the people of those cities** with the sound of the gospel, with a loud voice, **of the desolation and utter abolishment which await them if they do reject these things**.

115 For **if they do reject these things** the hour of their judgment is nigh, and their house shall be left unto them desolate.

The "if . . . then" nature of the above prophecy about New York, Albany, and Boston bears looking at a bit closer. As you read the scriptures, you will come across a number of such prophecies. One of them was the preaching of Jonah to the wicked city of Nineveh (Jonah 3). He told the wicked citizens of Nineveh that they would be destroyed in forty days (Jonah 3:4). If you read this chapter of Jonah in your Latter-day Saint Bible and pay close attention to the JST changes in the footnotes, you will see that the people repented after being warned by Jonah.

This was quite a disappointment to him (see Jonah 4). Apparently, he didn't understand the "if . . . then" principle of prophecy. The Lord explained it to him in Jonah 4:4–11.

Next, the Lord reassures Bishop Newel K. Whitney that He will watch over him as he goes on his mission to the east.

116 Let him trust in me and he shall not be confounded [*he won't be stopped from carrying out this assignment*]; **and a hair of his head shall not fall to the ground unnoticed.**

The Lord brings this revelation to a close by encouraging the missionaries to go forth and preach as He has instructed, pointing out that they are to warn the inhabitants of the earth of the destructions and devastations that will come in the last days. In verse 119, we see that as these signs of the times are fulfilled, they can strengthen our testimonies.

117 And verily I say unto you, the rest of my servants, go ye forth as your circumstances shall permit, in your several callings, unto the great and notable cities and villages, **reproving**

the world in righteousness [*standing as righteous witnesses against the wicked world*] of all their unrighteous and ungodly deeds, **setting forth clearly and understandingly the desolation of abomination in the last days.**

The phrase "desolation of abomination," found at the end of verse 117, above, is similar to the phrase "abomination of desolation" found in Joseph Smith—Matthew 1:12, 32. The Bible Dictionary defines this term as it applies to verse 117. We will quote it here:

Bible Dictionary: Abomination of Desolation

"Daniel spoke prophetically of a day when there would be 'the abomination that maketh desolate' (Dan. 11:31; 12:11), and the phrase was recoined in New Testament times to say 'the abomination of desolation, spoken of by Daniel the prophet' (Matt. 24:15).

"Conditions of desolation, born of abomination and wickedness, were to occur twice in fulfillment of Daniel's words. The first was to be when the Roman legions under Titus, in A.D. 70, laid siege to Jerusalem (Matt. 24:15; JS—M 1:12).

"Speaking of the last days, of the days following the Restoration of the gospel and its declaration 'for a witness unto all nations,' our Lord said: 'And again shall the abomination of desolation, spoken of by Daniel the prophet, be fulfilled' (JS—M 1:31–32). That is, Jerusalem again will be under siege.

"In a general sense, abomination of desolation also describes the latter-day judgments to be poured out upon the wicked wherever they may be. And so that the honest in heart may escape these things, the Lord sends His servants forth to raise the warning voice, to declare the glad tidings of the Restoration, lest 'desolation and utter abolishment' come upon them. The elders are commanded to reprove 'the world in righteousness of all their unrighteous and ungodly deeds, setting forth clearly and understandingly the desolation of abomination in the last days' (D&C 84:114, 117; 88:84–85)."

Continuing, we see that everyone in the world will have a chance to recognize and acknowledge the Lord because of the signs of the times that will be shown by nature in the last days.

118 For, with you saith the Lord Almighty, **I will rend their kingdoms; I will not only shake the earth, but the starry heavens shall tremble.**

119 For **I, the Lord, have put forth my hand to exert the powers of heaven**; ye cannot see it now, **yet a little while and ye shall see it, and know that I am, and that I will come and reign with my people.**

120 **I am Alpha and Omega**, the beginning and the end. Amen.

SECTION 85

Background

This is a revelation given through the Prophet Joseph Smith on November 27, 1832, at Kirtland, Ohio.

The heading to section 85 in the 2013 edition of the Doctrine and Covenants, given here, gives helpful additional background compared to the heading in the 1981 edition:

*Revelation given through Joseph Smith the Prophet, at Kirtland, Ohio, November 27, 1832. This section is an extract from a letter of the Prophet to William W. Phelps, who was living in Independence, Missouri. It answers questions about those Saints who had moved to Zion **but who had not followed the commandment to consecrate their properties** and had thus not received their inheritances according to the established order in the Church.*

A quote from the 2018 *Doctrine and Covenants Student Manual* gives valuable background information for this section:

"By November 1832, more than 800 Latter-day Saints had gathered to the land of Zion in Jackson County, Missouri (see *The Joseph Smith Papers, Documents, Volume 2: July 1831–January 1833*, ed. Matthew C. Godfrey and others [2013], 315). It was expected that Church members who settled in Zion would live according to the system of consecration commanded by the Lord (see D&C 42:30–36; 57:4–7; 58:19, 34–36; 72:15). This meant that a member would consecrate or dedicate property and resources to the Lord through a legal deed that was signed by both the member and the bishop. In return, the member was given, through another legal deed, property and resources called an 'inheritance' or 'stewardship' according to the needs and wants of the member's family. Saints who settled in Jackson County, Missouri, and were obedient to the law of consecration received an inheritance of land that had been purchased by Church agents" (*Doctrine and Covenants Student Manual*, 2018, chapter 32).

Some of the brethren living in Missouri wrote to the Prophet to ask him for counsel regarding the fact that some members who had moved to Jackson County were not living according to the law of consecration. Joseph Smith wrote a letter addressed to William W. Phelps, then living in Independence, Missouri, in which he answered this and other questions.

Section 85 is an extract from this letter. The Prophet introduced this letter as follows (**bold** used to point out the problem of not receiving deeds):

"In answer to letters received from the brethren in Missouri, I wrote as follows:

"*Kirtland, Nov. 27th, 1832.*

"Brother William W. Phelps:

". . . While I dictate this letter, I fancy to myself that you are saying or thinking something similar to these words:—'My God, great and mighty art Thou, therefore **show unto Thy servant what shall become of those who** are essaying [*attempting*] to **come up unto Zion**, in order to keep the commandments of God, **and yet receive not their inheritance by consecrations, by order of deed from the Bishop**, the man that God has appointed in a legal way, agreeably to the law given to organize and regulate the Church, and all the affairs of the same'" (*History of the Church*, 1:297).

First of all, in verse 1, next, the Prophet confirms that accurate records must be kept of the activities of the Church in Zion, including records of the consecration of property, and the redistribution of property to those living the law of consecration in Missouri. Clerks were appointed to keep such records. As you know, we have ward and stake clerks today, with similar responsibilities to keep accurate records.

1 **IT is the duty of the Lord's clerk**, whom he has appointed, **to keep a history, and a general church record of all things that transpire in Zion, and of all those who consecrate properties, and receive inheritances legally** [*according to the laws of the land, including written deeds that gave private ownership of property*] **from the bishop** [*from Bishop Partridge*];

2 **And also their manner of life, their faith, and works; and also of the apostates** [*people who leave the Church*] **who apostatize after receiving their inheritances** [*after having property deeded to them—compare with D&C 51:5*].

If you go back and read D&C 51:5, you will see that apostates would still own the land that had been deeded to them under the law of consecration.

Next, in verses 3–5, the Lord instructs that members moving to Missouri who were not willing to participate in the law of consecration were not to have their names entered in the records of the faithful in Zion. It appears also that no genealogies were to be kept of these people and their families, through which someone might try to make a legal claim on property owned by the Church.

3 **It is contrary to the will and commandment of God that those who receive not their inheritance by consecration** [*those who refuse to participate in the law of consecration*], **agreeable to his law**, which he has given, that he may tithe his people, to prepare them against the day of vengeance and burning, **should have their names enrolled with the people of God.**

4 **Neither is their genealogy to be kept, or to be had where it may be found on any of the records or history of the church.**

5 **Their names shall not be found, neither the names of the fathers, nor the names of the children written in the book of the law of God** [*the official tithing record of the Church; see October 1899 general conference explanation by Joseph F. Smith*], saith the Lord of Hosts.

In verse 6, next, Joseph Smith explains that he is receiving this revelation from the Holy Ghost. It reminds us that we sometimes feel the help and witness of the Holy Ghost in "every fiber of our being."

6 Yea, thus saith **the still small voice, which whispereth through and pierceth all things, and often times it maketh my bones to quake while it maketh manifest**, saying:

It helps to have a bit of history in advance before reading verses 7 and 8, next. In verse 8, Bishop Edward Partridge is told that he will be replaced if he doesn't repent and start following the program set up by the Lord, rather than trying to tell the leaders of the Church how to run things. If he doesn't repent, then one "mighty and strong" (verse 7) will be sent to replace him. Bishop Partridge repented, and so no one was needed to replace him.

7 And it shall come to pass that **I, the Lord God, will send one mighty and strong**, holding the scepter of power in his hand, clothed with light for a covering, whose mouth shall utter words, eternal words; while his bowels shall be a fountain of truth, **to set in order the house of God** [*in Missouri*]**, and to arrange by lot the inheritances of the saints** [*to distribute consecrated property fairly, by written deed*] **whose names are found, and the names of their fathers, and of their children, enrolled in the book of the law of God** [*whose names are properly recorded by the clerk (verse 1) in the records of the Church in Missouri, as those who are participating in the law of consecration*];

8 While **that man** [*Bishop Edward Partridge*], who was called of God and appointed [*to be the Presiding Bishop of the Church and to handle the law of consecration in Missouri*]**, that putteth forth his hand to steady the ark of God** [*who is trying to tell the Prophet and other Church leaders how to run the Church—in other words, is telling the Lord how to run things*]**, shall fall by the shaft of death, like as a tree that is smitten by the vivid shaft of lightning**.

We will include a rather lengthy official statement from the First Presidency of the Church (Joseph F. Smith, John R. Winder, and Anthon H. Lund) in 1905 explaining verses 7–8, above. We will add **bold** for emphasis. They wrote:

"It is to be observed first of all that the subject of **this whole letter** [the letter from Joseph Smith to W. W. Phelps, from which section 85 is taken], as also the part of it subsequently accepted as a revelation, **relates to the affairs of the Church in Missouri**, the gathering of the Saints to that land **and obtaining their inheritances under the law of consecration and stewardship**; and **the Prophet deals especially with the matter of what is to become of those who fail to receive their inheritances by order or deed from the bishop**. . . .

"It was while these conditions of rebellion, jealousy, pride, unbelief and hardness of heart prevailed among the brethren in Zion—

Jackson county, Missouri—in all of which Bishop Partridge participated, that the words of the revelation taken from the letter to William W. Phelps, of the 27th of November, 1832, were written. The 'man who was called and appointed of God' to 'divide unto the Saints their inheritance'—**Edward Partridge—was at that time out of order, neglecting his own duty, and putting 'forth his hand to steady the ark'**; hence, he was warned of the judgment of God impending, and the prediction was made that **another, 'one mighty and strong,' would be sent of God to take his place**, to have his bishopric—one having the spirit and power of that high office resting upon him, by which he would have power to 'set in order the house of God, and arrange by lot the inheritance of the Saints'; in other words, one who would do the work that Bishop Edward Partridge had been appointed to do, but had failed to accomplish. . . .

"And inasmuch as **through his repentance and sacrifices and suffering, Bishop Edward Partridge undoubtedly obtained a mitigation of the threatened judgment against him** of falling 'by the shaft of death, like as a tree that is smitten by the vivid shaft of lightning,' so the occasion for sending another to fill his station—'one mighty and strong to set in order the house of God, and to arrange by lot the inheritances of the Saints'—may

also be considered as having passed away and the whole incident of the prophecy closed" (Clark, *Messages of the First Presidency,* 4:112, 115, 117).

"This much, then, we have learned, viz., that Edward Partridge, the Bishop of the Church, was the one 'called and appointed, to divide by lot unto the Saints their inheritances.' But was Edward Partridge the one in 1832 who was 'putting forth his hand to steady the ark,' and threatened with falling 'by the shaft of death like as a tree that is smitten by the vivid shaft of lightning'? Undoubtedly. The brethren in those days were limited in their experience. The Church had been organized but as yesterday. The order of the Priesthood was not understood then, as it is understood today. The brethren composing it had been but recently brought together. Some of them were often in rebellion against the Prophet and the order of the Church because of these conditions; and it required instruction and time and experience to enable men to understand their duties and preserve their right relationship to each other as officers of the Church.

"Bishop Partridge was one of the brethren, who—though a most worthy man, one whom the Lord loved, and whom the Prophet described as 'a pattern of piety,' and 'one of the Lord's great men'—at times arrayed himself in opposition to the Prophet in those early days, and sought to correct him in his administrations of the affairs of the Church; in other words, 'put forth his hand to steady the ark'" (Clark, *Messages of the First Presidency,* 4:113).

We will explain the phrase "to steady the ark." We read about this in 2 Samuel 6:6–7. First, though, a bit more background. In Old Testament days, the Ark of the Covenant normally resided in the Tabernacle's Holy of Holies in Israel. It symbolized the earthly dwelling place of God. When it was in the Tabernacle, only the high priest could approach it. No other priests were allowed to.

It was taken from Israel by the Philistines (1 Samuel 4:10–11), but they sent it back to Israel because of troubles encountered while they possessed it (1 Samuel 5–6). King David arranged to have it picked up after the Philistines returned it and to have it carried by authorized priests back to its proper place. It was expressly forbidden for the Ark of the Covenant to be touched by an unauthorized person.

As it was being transported to another location, the cart upon which it was being transported passed over rough ground and the Ark started to tip. Uzzah tried to "steady the ark" and was struck dead (2 Samuel 6:6–7). Obviously, there is much more to the story. But for our purposes here, the point is that this phrase came to mean "one who tries to take things into his own hands" or "one who feels that the proper authorities of the Church are not doing their job correctly, therefore he takes it upon himself to straighten them out or take over their responsibilities."

On a sad note, several apostates from the Church, who have attempted to set up their own churches, have claimed that they were the "one mighty and strong" mentioned in verse 7 of this section sent by the Lord to get the church back on track.

We will now proceed with verse 9, next. You will see the phrase "book of remembrance." In the Topical Guide in our Latter-day Saint Bible, "book of remembrance" is cross-referenced with "book of life," which is mentioned in Revelation 3:5 as the record kept in heaven in which the names of those who receive exaltation are recorded.

9 And **all they who are not found written in the book of remembrance shall find none inheritance in that day** [*perhaps referring to Judgment Day*], **but they shall be cut asunder** [*destroyed*], **and their portion** [*reward*] **shall be appointed them among unbelievers, where are wailing and gnashing** [*grinding in agony*] **of teeth** [*see D&C 19:5; a description of*

those who receive the punishments of God reserved for the wicked].

Next, the Prophet Joseph Smith assures W. W. Phelps (to whom this revelation is being written) that he is not just giving his opinion but rather is giving the word of the Lord concerning the situation in Zion.

10 These things I say not of myself; therefore, as the Lord speaketh, he will also fulfil.

Verse 11, next, reminds us that there is no "privilege" in the Church of Jesus Christ because of position or rank in authority. None who fail to qualify will receive land in Missouri, symbolic of receiving "an inheritance" in celestial glory.

11 And **they** who are of the High Priesthood, **whose names are not found written in the book of the law** [*see verse 5, above*], or that are found to have **apostatized**, or to have been **cut off from the church**, as well as the lesser priesthood, or the members, in that day **shall not find an inheritance among the saints of the Most High;**

12 Therefore, it shall be done unto them as unto the children of the priest, as will be found recorded in the second chapter and sixty-first and second verses of Ezra.

We will include the above-mentioned verses of Ezra here. As you will see, they emphasize the importance of worthily having your name on the official records of the Church. We will add **bold** for emphasis:

Ezra 2:61–62

61 **And of the children of the priests**: the children of Habaiah, the children of Koz, the children of Barzillai; which took a wife of the daughters of Barzillai the Gileadite, and was called after their name:

62 **These sought their register** *among* those that were reckoned by genealogy, **but they were not found: therefore** were they, as polluted, **put from the priesthood**. [*In other words, their names were not on the records of the Church, therefore they could not hold the priesthood or have the blessings thereof.*]

SECTION 86

Background

This revelation was given through the Prophet Joseph Smith on December 6, 1832, in Kirtland, Ohio. It is a direct result of his work on the translation of the Bible (the JST). Verses 1–7 deal with the parable of the wheat and the tares. Verses 8–11 deal with the blessings of the priesthood, particularly the blessings promised in Abraham 2:9–11.

In Matthew 13:24–30, 36–43, Jesus gave the parable of the wheat and the tares. It helps to understand that tares are a weed that in its early and intermediate stages of growth looks like wheat. We read the following about tares in the Bible Dictionary:

Tares

"Matt. 13:25. The word denotes darnel grass, a poisonous weed, which, until it comes into ear, is similar in appearance to wheat."

Before studying this section, you may wish to read the parable of the wheat and the tares in your Bible. As mentioned above, it is found in Matthew 13:24–30, 36–43.

We will now study verses 1–7 verse by verse.

1 VERILY, **thus saith the Lord** unto you my servants, **concerning the parable of the wheat and of the tares**:

2 Behold, verily I say, **the field was the world,** and **the Apostles were the sowers** of the seed [*the Savior's Apostles planted the seeds of the gospel abroad*];

Verse 2, above, is different than Matthew 13:37, which says that the sower is the "Son of man," meaning Jesus. There is no

problem here because Jesus is in charge and His Apostles "sow" under His direction. "Whether by mine own voice or by the voice of my servants, it is the same" (D&C 1:38).

3 And **after they have fallen asleep** [*after the Apostles had died*] **the great persecutor of the church** [*Satan*], **the apostate, the whore** [*Satan; Satan's kingdom (1 Nephi 14:10–11); one who perverts that which is pure and righteous for evil purposes*], even **Babylon** [*the kingdom of the devil; the wicked of the earth*], **that maketh all nations to drink of her cup** [*who spreads evil throughout the world*], **in whose hearts the enemy, even Satan, sitteth to reign**—behold **he soweth the tares** [*plants evil and wickedness throughout the world; often disguises evil ("tares") to make it look good (makes it look like "wheat")*]; wherefore, **the tares choke the wheat** and **drive the church into the wilderness** [*symbolic of the apostasy that took place after the crucifixion and resurrection of Christ and the death of His Apostles*].

From verse 3, above, to verse 4, next, we see the transition from the apostasy and dark ages after Christ's mortal ministry to the restoration of the gospel through Joseph Smith. Then, in verse 5, we are told that angels are now anxious to begin the final destruction of the wicked. But in verses 6–7, the Lord requires them to wait until the time is right.

4 But behold, **in the last days, even now** [*in Joseph Smith's day*] while the Lord is beginning to bring forth the word [*in the early beginnings of the Restoration*], and the blade is springing up and is yet tender [*the gospel has been restored and the converts are like tender plants, with much to learn*]—

5 Behold, verily I say unto you, **the angels are crying unto the Lord day and night**, who are ready and waiting **to be sent forth to reap down the fields** [*the angels want to destroy the wicked now*];

There is much symbolism in verse 6, next, including that all of us have both "wheat" and "tares" growing within us. The Lord is kind not to root out all of our sins, weaknesses, imperfections, and so forth all at once, which would completely overwhelm us (compare with Jacob 5:65–66 in the Book of Mormon). Rather, with patience and kindness, He allows us to grow "line upon line, precept upon precept" (see 2 Nephi 28:30).

6 But the Lord saith unto them, **pluck not up the tares while the blade is yet tender** (for verily your faith is weak [*in other words, the members of the Church have*

much growing yet to do]), **lest you destroy the wheat also.**

Another important insight we gain from verse 6, above, is that the Lord, in His mercy, doesn't show us all of our weaknesses at the same time. Rather, He has the Holy Ghost point out some weakness now, and then when we have improved sufficiently on those matters, He points out additional things for us to work on. This approach is briefly mentioned at the end of Revelation 2:24, at the conclusion of encouragement and warnings given to the early Saints in Thyatira.

Revelation 2:24

24 But unto you I say, and unto the rest in Thyatira, as many as have not this doctrine, and which have not known the depths of Satan, as they speak; **I will put upon you none other burden.**

Among the many things we learn from verse 7, next, is that at the time of the Second Coming, the righteous will be taken up first and then the wicked will be burned. This is a different order than given in Matthew 13:30, where the tares are burned and then the wheat is gathered.

In other words, the correct order is that the righteous will be taken up at the time of the Second Coming, and then the wicked will be burned and the earth cleansed in preparation for the Millennium.

7 Therefore, **let the wheat and the tares grow together until the harvest is fully ripe**; then ye shall **first gather out the wheat** from among the tares, and after the gathering of the wheat, behold and lo, **the tares are bound in bundles, and the field remaineth to be burned**.

> Perhaps you have noticed that there are "wheat" and "tares" in almost every branch and ward in the Church. This will continue to be the case until the Second Coming, when there will be a complete separation of the righteous from the wicked. In the meantime, through kindness and patience on the part of the members, and with the help of the Holy Ghost, some "tares" will become converted and become "wheat."

> The last four verses of this revelation deal with encouragement for these brethren and others, including us, no doubt, to press forward with faith in continuing the restoration of the gospel and the carrying of it to all the world.

> President Russell M. Nelson, then of the Quorum of the Twelve Apostles, helps us understand verses 8–10, next, with the following quote (**bold** added for emphasis):

> "You are one of God's noble and great spirits, held in reserve to come to earth at this time. (See D&C 86:8–11.) In your premortal life you were appointed to help prepare the world for the great gathering of souls that will precede the Lord's second coming. **You are one of a covenant people. You are an heir to the promise that all the earth will be blessed by the seed of Abraham and that God's covenant with Abraham will be fulfilled through his lineage in these latter days**. (See 1 Ne. 15:18; 3 Ne. 20:25.)" ("Choices," *Ensign*, Nov. 1990, 73).

8 Therefore, **thus saith the Lord unto you, with whom the priesthood hath continued through the lineage of your fathers** [*meaning that the direct line of priesthood authority, which came from your "fathers," meaning Abraham, Isaac, Jacob, and so forth, was interrupted by the apostasy after Christ's death and now continues with you*]—

9 **For ye are lawful heirs** [*you have the right to the priesthood of Abraham, Isaac, and Jacob, as members of the house of Israel; see Abraham 2:9–11*], **according to the flesh** [*here in mortality as descendants of Abraham*], and have been hid from the world with Christ in God—

10 **Therefore your life and the priesthood have remained, and**

must needs remain through you and your lineage until the restoration of all things spoken by the mouths of all the holy prophets since the world began.

11 Therefore, **blessed are ye if ye continue in my goodness** [*they will receive many blessings and much happiness if they continue faithful*], **a light unto the Gentiles** [*they will be a light to all nonmembers in the world*], and **through this priesthood, a savior unto my people Israel** [*through performing valid priesthood ordinances, modern priesthood holders (along with the sisters who do work for the dead) become "saviors," and all people on earth can join the Church and become part of covenant Israel*]. The Lord hath said it. Amen.

SECTION 87

Background

This revelation was given at or near Kirtland, Ohio, on Christmas day, December 25, 1832, through the Prophet Joseph Smith.

If you have ever wanted "proof" to show others that Joseph Smith was indeed a true prophet of God, this section is an excellent choice.

Verse one is a prophecy that the Civil War would start with the rebellion of South Carolina. If you look again at the date it was given,

December 25, 1832, and then do a little research, you'll find that the Civil War was begun by South Carolina as Union troops housed in Fort Sumter, South Carolina, were fired upon on April 12, 1861. This specific prophecy was given about twenty-eight years before it was fulfilled! Joseph Smith was a prophet of God!

As we proceed to study this section, you will see that it covers much in addition to the Civil War. It is a prophecy on wars, and it covers the time from the beginning of the Civil War right up to the Second Coming. It foretells the rebellion and rising up of oppressed people everywhere, and the wars and bloodshed that will eventually be poured out upon the entire earth prior to the Millennium.

Please note in verse 1 that as the Lord reveals these things through Joseph Smith, He speaks of "wars" (plural), beginning with the Civil War (1861–1865).

1 VERILY, thus saith the Lord **concerning the wars that will shortly come to pass, beginning at the rebellion of South Carolina**, which will eventually terminate in the death and misery of many souls;

2 And the time will come that **war will be poured out upon all nations, beginning at this place** [*South Carolina*].

Note the incredible specifics given in verse 3, next. We will give one possible interpretation for the last half of the verse.

3 For behold, **the Southern States shall be divided against the Northern States**, and **the Southern States will call on other nations, even the nation of Great Britain**, as it is called [*plus France, Holland, and Belgium; at this point, it appears to begin a transition into World Wars I and II*], **and they** [*probably meaning Great Britain, France, Holland, Belgium, and so on*] **shall also call upon other nations** [*including the United States*], **in order to defend themselves against other nations** [*including Germany*]; and **then war shall be poured out upon all nations** [*likely meaning that after World War II, war will continue to be poured out upon the whole world until the Savior comes*].

Next, this prophecy indicates that "slaves" will rebel against their "masters." To think that this applies only to the slaves during the period of slavery in the Southern states would be far too narrow. There are "slaves" or oppressed people, cultures, and nations throughout the world who are rebelling against the shackles of tyranny and unrighteous dominion.

4 And it shall come to pass, after many days, **slaves shall rise up against their masters**, who shall be marshaled and disciplined for war [*there will be many rebellions and uprisings leading to fighting, civil wars, and so on as people struggle to gain basic civil rights*].

The word "remnants" is used in verse 5, next. "Remnant," as used in the scriptures, always refers to segments or portions of the house of Israel. You can verify this by looking through the references given in the Topical Guide, under "Remnant."

The reason we mention this is that some interpret verse 5 as being a prophecy about the Lamanites on the Western Hemisphere. No doubt it refers to many "remnants" of Israel including the Lamanites, but it is not limited to them. Thus, it appears that verse 5, among other possibilities, can be a prophecy that remnants of Israel throughout the world will become restless and will yearn for basic freedoms, thus "vexing" those in oppressive authority over them as part of their preparation to be gathered to the gospel.

5 And it shall come to pass also that **the remnants** [*of Israel*] **who are left** of the land **will marshal themselves** [*will organize themselves*], and **shall become exceedingly angry, and shall vex the Gentiles** [*their oppressors*] **with a sore vexation** [*will cause much*

trouble for the Gentiles who attempt to suppress them].

Verse 6, next, is a prophetic summary of the wars and turbulence among mankind as well as in nature, which will continue to increase in intensity until the Second Coming. These things will bear witness of the displeasure of God at the wickedness that continues to increase upon the earth. The wise will note this and seek God.

6 And **thus, with the sword** and by **bloodshed** the inhabitants of the earth shall mourn; and with **famine**, and **plague**, and **earthquake**, and the **thunder** of heaven, and the fierce and vivid **lightning** also, **shall the inhabitants of the earth be made to feel the wrath, and indignation, and chastening** [*scolding, punishing*] **hand of an Almighty God, until the consumption decreed** [*until the prophesied devastations*] **hath made a full end of all nations** [*until all man-made governments cease to exist and the Savior's millennial government takes over in conjunction with the Second Coming*];

Many people wonder why the "justice of God" doesn't fall upon the wicked sooner than it generally does. One of the reasons the Lord puts off the destruction of the wicked as long as possible is that

He may be able to save more of them. See D&C 64:21, last of the verse. That the wicked who have killed the Saints and stood in the way of the work of the Lord will eventually be caught up with if they don't repent is evidenced by verse 7, next. It gives the basic reason for the fulfilling of the signs of the times given in verse 6, above.

7 **That the cry of the saints, and of the blood of the saints, shall cease to come up into the ears of the Lord** of Sabaoth [*the Savior; "the creator of the first day"; see D&C 95:7*], **from the earth, to be avenged of their enemies** [*to have the law of justice put in force to punish the wicked*].

The word "Sabaoth" (verse 7, above) is defined in the Bible Dictionary in your Latter-day Saint Bible. We will include that definition here:

Sabaoth

"*Hosts.* The Lord of Sabaoth was a title of Jehovah; the hosts were the armies of Israel (1 Sam. 17:45), but also included the angelic armies of heaven (cf. Judg. 5:20; 2 Kgs. 6:17; Rom. 9:29; James 5:4; see also D&C 87:7; 88:2; 95:7; 98:2)."

Next, in verse 8, the Savior tells us what to do to be spiritually safe as the plagues and devastations of the last days sweep the earth.

8 Wherefore, **stand ye in holy**

places, and be not moved, until the day of the Lord come; for behold, it cometh quickly, saith the Lord. Amen.

"Holy places," no doubt include righteous homes, temples, sacrament meetings, other church meetings and classes, seminary and institute classes, the settings in which you study your scriptures and say your private prayers, and so forth.

SECTION 88

Background

Verses 1–126 of this revelation were given through the Prophet Joseph Smith at Kirtland, Ohio, over the course of a two-day conference held on December 27–28, 1832. Verses 127–37 were given on January 3, 1833. Verses 138–141 were added during the publication of the first Doctrine and Covenants in 1835.

We will include a quote from the 2018 *Doctrine and Covenants Student Manual* for background to section 88:

"On December 27, 1832, the Prophet Joseph Smith met with several Church leaders and other members in the 'translating room,' located upstairs in Newel K. Whitney's store in Kirtland, Ohio. He desired further divine instruction about the elders' duties and about how to build up Zion. As this

meeting, or conference, began, the Prophet explained that in order for revelation to be received, each person in the assembled group should exercise faith in God and be of one heart and mind. He proceeded to invite each person to take a turn praying aloud to know the Lord's will. The ensuing revelation was then dictated by Joseph Smith until 9:00 p.m. that evening, at which time they stopped for the night. The next morning the group reassembled and prayed, and the remainder of the revelation was received. Later, on January 3, 1833, the Prophet received additional revelation that was later added to the revelation he had received in December (see D&C 88:127–37). Beginning with the 1835 edition of the Doctrine and Covenants, the revelation that was given on January 3, 1833, was added to the one received on December 27–28, 1832, along with four more verses that were added at the end (see D&C 88:138–41).

"For many months before January 1833, Church leaders in Missouri had directed accusations and expressed unkind feelings toward Church leaders in Ohio. On January 11, 1833, Joseph Smith sent a letter to William W. Phelps in Independence, Missouri, and included a copy of the revelation recorded in Doctrine and Covenants 88:1–126 (and perhaps the portion in verses 127–37) and explained: 'I send you the olive leaf which we have plucked from the tree of

Paradise, the Lord's message of peace to us; for though our Brethren in Zion indulge in feelings towards us, which are not according to the requirements of the new covenant, yet we have the satisfaction of knowing that the Lord approves of us and has accepted us, and established His name in Kirtland for the salvation of the nations. . . . Let me say to you, seek to purify yourselves, and also all the inhabitants of Zion, lest the Lord's anger be kindled to fierceness. . . . The Brethren in Kirtland pray for you unceasingly, for knowing the terrors of the Lord, they greatly fear for you' (in *The Joseph Smith Papers, Documents, Volume 2: July 1831–January 1833*, ed. Matthew C. Godfrey and others (2013), 365, 367; capitalization, spelling, and punctuation standardized)."

This revelation is a "high mountain" experience for faithful members of the Church who desire to do right and strive to retain spirituality despite opposing forces all around them. It holds many keys for achieving spiritual peace.

Just a bit more about "high mountain" experiences. Many prophets throughout history have been taken up into a "high mountain" (example: 1 Nephi 11:1) where they have been shown many things from the Lord's perspective. The Holy Ghost and the scriptures can do similar things for us. When we see things as the Lord sees them,

it makes it much easier for us to successfully pass the tests and learn the lessons set out for us in our mortal "curriculum."

Joseph Smith had several "high mountain" experiences, including the First Vision, the visits and instructions of Moroni, the vision of the three degrees of glory and perdition (section 76), the appearance of Christ, Moses, Elias, and Elijah in the Kirtland Temple (section 110), and so forth. Yet, between these marvelous manifestations, he had to deal with the details, trials, and decisions of daily living as a husband, father, and friend, in addition to the responsibilities of being the Lord's prophet.

The Saints at this time in history were facing difficult times and were yet to have more intense opposition as enemies within and outside of the Church mounted persecution against them. The doctrines and perspectives given in section 88 served as a "high mountain" experience for them, enabling them to face their trials with intelligence and knowledge of the "big picture" as the Savior sees things, and thus they were empowered to succeed in their mortal missions. Section 88 can do the same thing for us.

As this section takes you up on this "high mountain," you will see that the Savior teaches a great many specific doctrines in the course of this revelation. We will point out a number of them as we go along.

First, in verses 1–2, Jesus tells these men, including the Prophet, that it pleases Him when His followers sincerely desire to know His will concerning them. This certainly applies to us also.

1 VERILY, **thus saith the Lord unto you who have assembled yourselves together to receive his will concerning you**:

2 Behold, **this is pleasing unto your Lord**, and **the angels rejoice over you**; the alms of **your prayers** [*prayers are "offerings" or "alms" to the Lord*] have come up into the ears of the Lord of Sabaoth [*the Savior; see notes for D&C 87:7 in this study guide*], and **are recorded in the book of the names of the sanctified** [*the Book of Life in which the names of the righteous are recorded in heaven; Revelation 3:5*], **even them of the celestial world**.

Next, in verses 3–4, the Savior explains that a major function of the Holy Ghost is to lead us to exaltation in the celestial kingdom.

3 Wherefore, **I now send** upon you **another Comforter**, even upon you my friends, that it may abide in your hearts, even **the Holy Spirit of promise** [*the Holy Ghost; the "Holy Spirit that was promised" by the Savior to his disciples; see Acts 1:5*]; which **other Comforter** is the same that I promised unto my disciples, as is recorded in the testimony of John.

Quoting from the 2018 *Doctrine and Covenants Student Manual* regarding "The Holy Spirit of Promise," referred to in verse 3, above:

"President Joseph Fielding Smith (1876–1972) explained: 'The Holy Spirit of Promise is not the Second Comforter. The Holy Spirit of Promise is the Holy Ghost who places the stamp of approval upon every ordinance that is done righteously; and when covenants are broken he removes the seal' (*Doctrines of Salvation* 1:55).

"While each of those who were present had previously received the gift of the Holy Ghost, they were then being promised that they could receive an assurance of eternal life through a manifestation of the Holy Ghost (see Ephesians 1:13–14; D&C 76:51–54; 132:7). The Holy Spirit of Promise is an assurance from the Holy Ghost that the ordinances and covenants necessary for salvation have been properly entered into and have been kept. In essence, it is a witness from the Spirit that a person has the promise of eternal life."

Doctrine, verse 4

A major function of the gift of the Holy Ghost is that of leading us to celestial exaltation.

4 **This Comforter** [*the Holy Ghost*] **is the promise which I give unto you of eternal life** [*the help they were promised that, when followed, leads to eternal life, which is another term for exaltation*], **even the glory** of **the celestial kingdom;**

Next, in verse 5, we are taught that the celestial kingdom is the highest glory, that exaltation is within that kingdom, and that God the Father lives in celestial glory.

Doctrine, verse 5

God the Father lives in celestial glory.

5 **Which glory** [*the celestial kingdom—verse 4, above*] **is that of the church of the Firstborn** [*means exaltation; see D&C 76:54, 67*], **even of God, the holiest of all** [*the Father*]**, through Jesus Christ his Son** [*the Holy Ghost (verse 4) leads us to celestial glory through Jesus Christ and the Atonement*]—

Having been taught the role of the Holy Ghost in leading us to celestial glory through Christ, we will now

be taught more about the Savior Himself. You have often seen Christ introduced as "Alpha and Omega" (example: D&C 84:120) and have had it explained that Alpha and Omega are the first and last letters of the Greek alphabet. The symbolism is that all things fall under Christ's direction and power.

Verse 6, next, exemplifies this as it describes Christ's overcoming of all things in order to serve as our Redeemer.

6 **He** that **ascended up on high,** as also **he descended below all things** [*D&C 122:8*]**,** in that **he comprehended all things** [*He encompassed and overcame all things necessary in order to save us*]**, that he might be in all and through all things** [*that He might provide an infinite Atonement*]**, the light of truth** [*Jesus is the "light of truth"*];

Perhaps you have wondered what holds all the planets and stars in their orbits such that they don't crash into each other and create total chaos in the universe. Verses 6–13, next, inform us that Jesus is the power that holds all things, both in the macrocosm as well as in the microcosm, in their proper orbits and relationships with each other. He not only created them, but His power also controls them and keeps them orderly.

Doctrine, verses 6–13

The Light of Christ is the power that holds all planets, stars, electrons, atomic particles, and so forth in their proper orbits and relationships with each other, thus preventing chaos in the universe. It controls all matter and energy in the universe.

7 Which truth shineth. This is the light of Christ. As also **he is in the sun** [*His power is evidenced by the performance of the sun*], and **the light of the sun**, and **the power thereof by which it was made**.

8 As also **he is in the moon**, and **is the light of the moon**, and **the power thereof by which it was made;**

9 As also **the light of the stars**, and **the power thereof by which they were made;**

10 And **the earth** also, and **the power thereof**, even the earth upon which you stand.

11 And **the light which shineth, which giveth you light, is through him who enlighteneth your eyes**, which is **the same light that quickeneth** [*increases, sharpens*] **your understandings;**

12 **Which light proceedeth forth from the presence of God to fill the immensity of space** [*the Light of Christ influences all things in space*]—

13 **The light which is in all things**, which **giveth life to all things**, which is **the law by which all things are governed**, even **the power of God** who sitteth upon his throne, who is in the bosom of eternity, who is in the midst of all things.

Joseph Fielding Smith taught about the Light of Christ. He said that the "Light of Christ is not a personage. It has no body. I do not know what it is as far as substance is concerned; but it fills the immensity of space and emanates from God. It is the light by which the worlds are controlled, by which they are made. It is the light of the sun and all other bodies. It is the light which gives life to vegetation. It quickens the understanding of men, and has these various functions as set forth in these verses.

"It is: 'The light which is in all things, which giveth life to all things, which is the law by which all things are governed, even the power of God who sitteth upon his throne, who is in the bosom of eternity, who is in the midst of all things.'

"This is our explanation in regard to the Spirit of Christ, or Light of Truth, which every man receives and is guided by. Unless a man had the blessings that come from this Spirit, his mind would not be quickened; there would be no vegetation grown; the worlds would not stay in their orbits; because it is through this Spirit of Truth, this Light of Truth, according to this revelation, that all these things are done.

"The Lord has given to 'every man that cometh into the world,' the guidance of the Light of Truth, or Spirit of Jesus Christ, and if a man will hearken to this Spirit he will be led to the truth and will recognize it and will accept it when he hears it" (*Doctrines of Salvation*, 1:52–53).

Having been shown the all-encompassing role of the Light of Christ, which, as you can see, is much more than our "conscience" (although that is a vital role of the Light of Christ), our attention is next turned to the Savior's role as Redeemer.

First, in verses 14–17, we see the Savior's role in providing resurrection for us.

14 Now, verily I say unto you, that **through the redemption which is made for you is brought to pass the resurrection from the dead.**

Doctrine, verse 15

The strict gospel definition of "soul" is the spirit and the body together.

15 And **the spirit and the body are the soul of man**.

Remember also that the spirit itself is composed of two things; namely, intelligence (D&C 93:29), and the spirit body, which is composed of spirit matter (D&C 131:7–8).

16 And **the resurrection from the dead is the redemption of the soul** [*the "soul," composed of the spirit and the physical body, is put back together, so to speak, at the time of resurrection*].

17 And **the redemption of the soul** [*the resurrection*] **is through him** [*Christ*] **that quickeneth all things** [*who gives life to all things as taught in verses 6–13, above*], in whose bosom [*in whose tender heart*] it is decreed that **the poor and the meek of the earth shall inherit it** [*the earth*].

Did you notice the doctrine taught at the end of verse 17, above? We will list it next.

Doctrine, verse 17

Those from this earth who earn celestial glory will live on it when it is glorified and becomes our celestial planet. See also D&C 130:9–11.

Next, beginning with verse 18, we will be taught what must happen to the earth in order for it to become a celestial planet, the celestial kingdom for those of us who attain celestial glory.

18 Therefore, **it must needs be sanctified from all unrighteousness** [*it has to be cleansed from all wickedness*], **that it may be prepared for the celestial glory** [*that it may become the celestial kingdom for us*];

19 For **after it hath filled the measure of its creation** [*after it has finished its work of hosting mankind, through the end of the Millennium and to the end of the "little season" after the Millennium; see D&C 88:111*], **it shall be crowned with glory** [*it will become a celestial planet*], **even with the presence of God the Father;**

> Joseph Smith taught that this earth "will be rolled back into the presence of God, and crowned with celestial glory" (*Teachings of the Prophet Joseph Smith*, 181).

20 **That bodies** [*in order that people who receive celestial bodies at the time of resurrection; see D&C 88:28–29*] **who are of the celestial kingdom may possess it forever and ever** [*so that resurrected mortals who are worthy of celestial glory can live on it forever*]; **for, for this intent was it made and created** [*this is the reason the earth was created in the first place*], and **for this intent are**

they sanctified [*made clean, pure, holy, and fit to be in the presence of God through the Atonement*].

Doctrine, verse 21

Those who do not qualify for celestial glory will have to live on other planets, terrestrial and telestial, which will be prepared for them.

21 And **they who are not sanctified through the law** [*those who refuse to be made pure and holy, fit to live in the presence of God through the laws and covenants of the gospel and Atonement of Christ*] which I have given unto you, **even the law of Christ, must inherit another kingdom** [*another planet*], even that of **a terrestrial** kingdom, **or that of a telestial** kingdom.

> Joseph Fielding Smith taught that "other earths, no doubt, are being prepared as habitations for terrestrial and telestial beings, for there must be places prepared for those who fail to obtain celestial glory, who receive immortality but not eternal life" (*Doctrines of Salvation*, 1:72).

Doctrine, verse 22

Those who have not qualified for celestial glory would be miserable if placed in the celestial kingdom.

22 For **he who is not able to abide** [*not able to live*] **the law of a celestial kingdom cannot abide** [*can't stand; would not be comfortable in*] **a celestial glory.**

Doctrine, verse 23

Those who have lived beneath the standards of terrestrial glory would be miserable if placed in the terrestrial kingdom.

23 And **he who cannot abide** [*live*] **the law of a terrestrial kingdom cannot abide a terrestrial glory.**

Doctrine, verse 24

Sons of perdition could not stand to live in a kingdom of glory.

24 **And he who cannot abide the law of a telestial kingdom cannot abide a telestial glory; therefore he is not meet** [*suited*] **for a kingdom of glory. Therefore** [*for this reason*] **he must abide a kingdom which is not a kingdom of glory** [*in other words, must live in outer darkness with Satan and the other sons of perdition*].

Next, we are taught that the earth is living the laws that will lead her to celestial glory. You may wish to read Moses 7:48–49, 58, and 61

to get the feel for the earth's desire to be a celestial planet. This brings up many interesting questions that will yet have to be answered, perhaps at the beginning of the Millennium, when "all things" shall be revealed (D&C 101:32–34).

25 And again, verily I say unto you, **the earth abideth** [*obeys*] **the law of a celestial kingdom,** for **it filleth the measure of its creation** [*it is fulfilling the purposes for which it was created*], and **transgresseth not the law—**

Doctrine, verse 26

The earth will die and will be resurrected to celestial glory.

26 **Wherefore** [*this is why*], **it shall be sanctified** [*it will be cleansed from the wickedness upon it, and be made pure and holy, a fit dwelling place for Christ and those from this earth who qualify for celestial glory; see D&C 130:9*]; yea, notwithstanding **it** [*the earth*] **shall die,** it **shall be quickened again** [*it will be resurrected*], and shall abide the power by which it is quickened [*it will be celestialized*], and **the righteous shall inherit it.**

The topic now turns to the righteous who will inherit the earth (end of verse 26, above).

27 For **notwithstanding** [*even though*] **they** [*all mortals*] **die,**

they also [*just like the earth does*] **shall rise again, a spiritual body** [*a resurrected body, consisting of intelligence, spirit, and physical body, permanently combined for eternity*].

Next, we are taught that there will be differences in resurrected bodies depending on whether they are celestial, terrestrial, telestial, or sons of perdition.

Doctrine, verses 28–32

There will be significant differences between the resurrected bodies of celestials, terrestrials, telestials, and sons of perdition.

28 They who are of a celestial spirit [*those who have lived worthy of celestial glory*] **shall receive the same body** [*the same type of body that they had on earth, with all the capabilities, including the powers of procreation*] which was **a natural body**; even ye shall receive **your bodies**, and **your glory shall be that glory by which your bodies are quickened** [*the type of resurrected body you receive will depend on which degree of glory you receive, or outer darkness*].

Some people have expressed a bit of concern that they really don't want to get their body ("your bodies"—verse 28, above) back in the resurrection because they had hoped for a better one.

Alma 40:23 assures us that our bodies will be perfect in the resurrection, that everything will be "perfect and proper." It is thus obvious that we will be delighted with what we get if we attain celestial resurrection.

Verse 29, next, continues the description of celestial, resurrected bodies.

29 Ye who are quickened [*resurrected*] **by a portion of the celestial glory** [*according to the laws of celestial glory*] **shall then receive of the same** [*will receive a celestial body*], **even a fulness** [*the kind of celestial, resurrected bodies that our Heavenly Parents have*].

Next, in verses 30–32, we are taught that terrestrials, telestials, and sons of perdition will receive resurrected bodies that will match their final destination on Judgment Day.

30 And they who are quickened [*resurrected*] **by a portion of** [*according to the laws of*] **the terrestrial glory shall then receive of the same, even a fulness** [*their resurrected bodies will have a "fullness" of terrestrial glory*].

31 And also they who are quickened [*resurrected*] **by a portion of** [*according to the laws of*] **the telestial glory** shall then **receive of the same, even a fulness** [*their resurrected bodies will reflect the completeness of telestial glory].

32 And **they who remain** [*mortals who become sons of perdition*] **shall also be quickened** [*will also be resurrected*]; nevertheless, **they shall return again to their own place** [*will be cast out with Satan and his evil spirits; see D&C 88:114*], to enjoy that which they are willing to receive, **because they were not willing to enjoy that which they might have received.**

Joseph Fielding Smith taught about the differences between resurrected bodies depending on which kingdom of glory people attain. He said:

"In the resurrection there will be different kinds of bodies; they will not all be alike. The body a man receives will determine his place hereafter. There will be celestial bodies, terrestrial bodies, and telestial bodies, and these bodies will differ as distinctly as do bodies here . . .

"Elder Orson Pratt many years ago in writing of the resurrection and the kind of bodies which would be raised in these kingdoms said: 'In every species of animals and plants, there are many resemblances in the general outlines and many specific differences characterizing the individuals of each species. So in the resurrection. There will be several classes of resurrected bodies; some celestial, some terrestrial, some telestial, and some sons of perdition. Each of these classes will differ from the others by prominent and marked distinctions . . .

"Some will gain celestial bodies with all the powers of exaltation and eternal increase. These bodies will shine like the sun as our Savior's does, as described by John. Those who enter the terrestrial kingdom will have terrestrial bodies, and they will not shine like the sun, but they will be more glorious than the bodies of those who receive the telestial glory.

"In both of these kingdoms there will be changes in the bodies and limitations. They will not have the power of increase, neither the power or nature to live as husbands and wives, for this will be denied them and they cannot increase.

"Some of the functions in the celestial body will not appear in the terrestrial body, neither in the telestial body, and the power of procreation will be removed" (*Doctrines of Salvation,* 2:286–88).

Verse 33, next, continues with the thought at the end of verse 32, above, in which we were taught that sons of perdition "were not willing to enjoy that which they might have received."

33 For **what doth it profit a man if a gift is bestowed upon him, and he receive not the gift?**

Behold, **he rejoices not in that which is given unto him, neither rejoices in him who is the giver of the gift**.

Verses 34–35, next, explain why those who refuse to live according to the laws of celestial glory cannot be cleansed by the Atonement of Christ. They serve as a brief course in the importance of having and understanding eternal law.

34 And again, verily I say unto you, **that which is governed by law is also preserved by law and perfected and sanctified** [*cleansed and made fit to dwell in the presence of God*] **by the same.**

35 **That which breaketh a law, and abideth not by** [*does not live according to*] **law, but seeketh to become a law unto itself** [*determines to make his or her own rules contrary to the laws of God*]**, and willeth** [*desires*] **to abide in sin, and altogether abideth in sin, cannot be sanctified by law, neither by mercy, justice, nor judgment. Therefore, they must remain filthy still.**

Perhaps you have wished at times that the Lord would explain more about how He creates things and organizes the universe. In verses 36 through 45, next, He does. He will, in effect, invite us into His "classroom" as He teaches us some laws and principles of creation.

Unless you are different from most, you probably will not quite understand it all. Therefore, He will pause at the end of verse 45, and in verse 46, He will ask us what He could compare these things to, which might make it easier for us to understand.

He begins with the basics.

36 **All kingdoms have a law given;**

37 **And there are many kingdoms; for there is no space in the which there is no kingdom** [*scientists are discovering more about this, that there is no such thing as "empty space"; rather, there are cosmic particles and forms of energy in what was once thought of as empty space*]; **and there is no kingdom in which there is no space, either a greater or a lesser kingdom.**

38 And **unto every kingdom** [*perhaps meaning that in every "domain," whether macroscopic or microscopic, whether referring to a planet, moon, solar system, galaxy atom, cell, or whatever*] **is given a law** [*all things are governed by the laws of God*]; **and unto every law there are certain bounds also and conditions** [*there are rules*

that govern the application of all laws].

39 All beings who abide not in those conditions [*who don't keep the laws and commandments of God*] **are not justified** [*ratified and approved to return to God's presence and live there forever in celestial glory*].

One thing that can help us understand the word "justified" as found in verse 39, above, is the use of the term as it relates to computers and word processing. "Justify," in document terminology, means to have the word processing software line up one or both margins of a document in a perfectly straight, vertical line.

In gospel terminology, "justify" can mean to be "lined up in perfect harmony with God." The Holy Ghost assists us in this endeavor, prompting us to do the things necessary to access the Atonement's cleansing and healing power so that we are ultimately "justified" or living in harmony with the laws of God and can thus enter His presence for eternity.

Next, in verse 40, we are taught more about celestial qualities and attributes. We are shown why celestials like to associate with celestials. In a sense also, it shows us why wicked people could not be happy in celestial glory.

We are shown that if we are honest, we love honesty. If we are virtuous, we love virtue. If we are merciful, we love to associate with those who are merciful. If we use clean language, we prefer to associate with those who use clean language themselves. If we love the light of the gospel, we choose friends who likewise respect and love the gospel.

The qualities listed are qualities that thrive in celestial glory and typify the attributes of God. Remember that those whose lifestyles and thinking reflect the opposites of these celestial traits could not be happy eternally with God. This is basic eternal law.

40 For intelligence cleaveth unto intelligence; wisdom receiveth wisdom; truth embraceth truth; virtue loveth virtue; light cleaveth unto light; mercy hath compassion on mercy and claimeth her own; justice continueth its course and claimeth its own [*the law of justice will rule over those who fail to qualify for the law of mercy; see Alma 42*]; **judgment goeth before the face of him** [*God*] **who sitteth upon the throne and governeth and executeth all things.**

41 He [*God*] **comprehendeth** [*encompasses*] **all things** [*the theme of verses 6–13, 36–45*], **and all**

things are before him, and all things are round about him; and he is above all things, and in all things, and is through all things, and is round about all things; and all things are by him, and of him, even God, forever and ever.

42 And again, verily I say unto you, **he hath given a law unto all things, by which they move in their times and their seasons;**

43 And **their courses** [*orbits*] **are fixed,** even **the courses of the heavens and the earth,** which comprehend the earth **and all the planets.**

44 And **they give light to each other in their times and in their seasons, in their minutes, in their hours, in their days, in their weeks, in their months, in their years—all these are one year with God, but not with man** [*God has a different time system than man does*].

Verse 45, next, summarizes the fact that the creations of God influence every aspect of our lives and bear witness of the existence of God to all who will pay attention (see verse 47; also see Moses 6:63).

45 **The earth rolls upon her wings,** and **the sun giveth his light by day,** and **the moon**

giveth her light by night, and the stars also give their light, as they roll upon their wings in their glory, in the midst of the power of God.

As mentioned previously, the Savior now pauses to ask these brethren what He could compare these things to in order for them to better understand.

46 **Unto what shall I liken these kingdoms, that ye may understand?**

The answer to the question posed by the Master, in verse 46, above, is given by Him in verse 47, next, and also in the parable given in verses 51–61.

47 Behold, all these are kingdoms [*all God's creations are "kingdoms" with their "bounds . . . and conditions" (verse 38), as set by God*], and **any man who hath seen any or the least of these** [*of God's creations*] **hath seen God moving in his majesty and power.** [*In other words, if we have seen His creations, we have, in effect, seen Him, implying that until we become more like Him, this will give us at least a start as far as comprehending how He does things is concerned.*]

48 **I say unto you, he hath seen him;** nevertheless, he [*Christ*] who came unto his own [*came to earth*] was not comprehended.

In verses 49–50, next, He encourages us by informing us that (if we are faithful) the day will come that we will be able to actually comprehend Him!

Doctrine, verses 49–50

Through personal faithfulness and worthiness, we can look forward to the day when we will actually comprehend God.

49 The light shineth in darkness [*in spiritual darkness on earth*], and the darkness comprehendeth it not; nevertheless, **the day shall come when you shall comprehend even God**, being quickened in him and by him.

50 **Then shall ye know that ye have seen me, that I am, and that I am the true light that is in you, and that you are in me; otherwise ye could not abound.**

The Master now gives a parable, in answer to the question He asked in verse 46, above, comprising verses 51–61. In this parable, He teaches that He will visit each of the many worlds He has created, and the worthy inhabitants of each will have the privilege of seeing Him. This does not mean that He will be born, live, be crucified, and then be resurrected on each of these other worlds. Rather, it means that He will visit them from

time to time. This parable ties in nicely with D&C 76:24, which informs us that the inhabitants of all of the Father's worlds are saved by the Atonement performed by the Savior on our world.

This parable has twelve worlds (verse 55), but they are symbolic of all the worlds Christ has and will create (see verse 61). It is interesting to note that in biblical symbolism, the number twelve represents God's perfect work.

51 **Behold, I will liken these kingdoms** [*the worlds He has created for the Father*] **unto a man** [*God*] **having a field** [*a world*], and **he sent forth his servants** [*His prophets and faithful members*] **into the field to dig in the field** [*to cultivate the gospel in that world*].

52 And **he** [*Christ*] **said unto the first** [*the servants on the first world*]: Go ye and labor in the field, and **in the first hour I will come unto you, and ye shall behold the joy of my countenance** [*in other words, Christ will visit them*].

53 **And he said unto the second** [*the prophets and faithful members on the second world*]: Go ye also into the field, and **in the second hour I will visit you with the joy of my countenance.**

54 And **also unto the third, saying: I will visit you;**

55 And **unto the fourth, and so on unto the twelfth** [*not a set number, twelve, but, among other things, symbolic of the perfect gospel of Jesus Christ upon all the Father's worlds*].

56 And **the lord of the field** [*Christ*] **went unto the first** [*man (verse 52), world, prophets, faithful members there*] **in the first hour, and tarried with him all that hour** [*perhaps implying that the Savior will visit them for their Millennium*], and he was made glad with the light of the countenance of his lord.

57 And **then he withdrew from the first that he might visit the second also, and the third, and the fourth, and so on unto the twelfth.**

58 **And thus they all received the light of the countenance of their lord, every man in his hour, and in his time, and in his season—**

59 **Beginning at the first, and so on unto the last**, and from the last unto the first, and from the first unto the last [*none will be left out*];

60 **Every man in his own order, until his hour was finished**, even according as his lord had commanded him, **that his lord might be glorified in him, and he in his lord, that they all might be glorified.**

61 Therefore, **unto this parable I will liken** [*compare*] **all these kingdoms** [*all the Father's worlds*], **and the inhabitants thereof** [*and all the inhabitants of these worlds; compare with D&C 76:24*]—**every kingdom in its hour, and in its time, and in its season** [*every one will get its turn as determined by God*], even according to the decree which God hath made.

At this point, the Savior does what He did with the Nephites in 3 Nephi 17:2–3, wherein He told the Nephites to go home and ponder overnight the things He had just told them. Here, likewise, He is, in effect, saying that it was obviously difficult for these brethren to comprehend what He had been teaching them, therefore, He invites them to think these things over and ponder them in their hearts. Perhaps you find yourself in the same situation, needing to think more about these wonderful insights that you can't comprehend completely. Don't miss the commandment that He gives at the end of verse 62, next, and the counsel in verses 63–64, to continue to pray and learn and grow toward the ability to comprehend these things.

62 And again, verily I say unto you, **my friends, I leave these sayings with you to ponder in your hearts, with this commandment which I give unto**

you, that ye shall call upon me while I am near—

63 **Draw near unto me and I will draw near unto you; seek me diligently and ye shall find me; ask, and ye shall receive; knock, and it shall be opened unto you.**

64 **Whatsoever ye ask the Father in my name it shall be given unto you, that is expedient for you** [*that will be necessary and good for you at this point in your growth and progression*];

65 And **if ye ask anything that is not expedient** [*good, wise, necessary*] **for you, it shall turn unto your condemnation** [*it will stop your progress*].

Just another comment about verse 65, above, before we move on. Perhaps you have met someone who has become caught up in the "mysteries" of the gospel and has forgotten to nourish the basics of faith and simplicity in living it. It is not uncommon for such people to eventually end up in apostasy. Perhaps this is a basic meaning of the wording in verse 65 in which the Savior warns not to "ask anything that is not expedient."

Next, in verses 66–68, after warning us not to get caught up in asking for things we ought not to, verse 65, above (the Holy Ghost will help you know what to pray for; see D&C 46:30; 50:30), the Lord instructs us how to prepare spiritually to understand and comprehend these things of God to a greater and greater extent.

We are taught that, while we are generally not allowed to see the Savior directly, at this point, we are nevertheless allowed to hear His "voice" through the Spirit and can thus learn and understand His teachings and thrive in our gospel growth.

66 Behold, **that which you hear is as the voice of one crying in the wilderness** [*perhaps meaning, among other things, a voice teaching truth in an apostate world*]—in the wilderness, because **you cannot see him**—my voice, because **my voice is Spirit; my Spirit is truth; truth abideth** [*lasts*] and hath no end [*there are absolute truths in the gospel that are not subject to the whims and fancies of men or to the limits of time*]; and if it [*perhaps meaning the Spirit*] be in you it [*truth*] shall abound [*flourish in you as you grow toward exaltation*].

The eye tends to focus the attention and resources of the mind and body. Therefore, the symbolism of the "eye" in verse 67, next, can mean that if you focus your spiritual "eye" on the things of God, you will continue to grow in spiritual knowledge and understanding until you become a god (compare with D&C 132:20).

67 And **if your eye be single to my glory** [*if you focus on the things of God*], **your whole bodies shall be filled with light** [*light and truth of the gospel*], and **there shall be no darkness in you**; and **that body which is filled with light comprehendeth all things** [*has become like God*].

68 **Therefore, sanctify** [*cleanse and purify*] **yourselves that your minds become single to God** [*so that the things of God are top priority in your lives*], **and the days will come that you shall see him; for he will unveil his face unto you**, and it shall be **in his own time, and in his own way, and according to his own will.**

The final three phrases of verse 68, above, deal with the privilege of literally seeing the Savior or the Father. That "he will unveil his face unto you." Did you notice that it does not necessarily happen when a person wants it but rather when it is wise and appropriate in the eyes of God? This appearance is sometimes referred to as the "other comforter."

Joseph Smith taught (**bold** added for emphasis):

"There are **two Comforters** spoken of. **One is the Holy Ghost**, the same as given on the day of Pentecost, and that all Saints receive after faith, repentance, and baptism. This first Comforter [is the] Holy Ghost. . . . **The other Comforter** spoken of is a subject of great interest and perhaps understood by few of this generation. After a person hath faith in Christ, repents of his sins, and is baptized for the remission of his sins, and receives the Holy Ghost, (by the laying on of hands), which is the first Comforter, then let him continue to humble himself before God, hungering and thirsting after righteousness, and living by every word of God, and the Lord will soon say unto him, Son, thou shalt be exalted. . . . When the Lord has thoroughly proved him, and finds that the man is determined to serve Him at all hazard, then the man will find his calling and election made sure, then it will be his privilege to receive the other Comforter. . . . Now what is this other Comforter? It **is no more or less than the Lord Jesus Christ Himself**; and this is the sum and substance of the whole matter, that **when any man obtains this last Comforter, he will have the personage of Jesus Christ to attend him or appear unto him from time to time, and even He will manifest the Father unto him**, and They will take up their abode with him, and the visions of the heavens will be opened unto him and the Lord will teach him face to face, and he may have a perfect knowledge of the mysteries of the kingdom of God" (in *Manuscript History of* the Church, vol. C-1, pages 8–9 [addenda], josephsmithpapers. org; spelling, punctuation, and capitalization standardized).

69 **Remember the great and last promise which I have made unto you** [*perhaps referring to the promise made in verse 68, above, that they would eventually be privileged to see God*]; **cast away your idle thoughts** [*perhaps referring to inappropriate thoughts that tend to slip into an idle mind*] **and your excess of laughter** far from you.

"Excess of laughter" generally means not taking important things seriously. This could easily be the meaning in verse 69, above. Certainly, we see pleasant examples of delightful humor and deep laughter on occasions in the talks and comments of our Prophet and other General Authorities today as well as in times past.

There seems to be a transition now from the Savior's "classroom" to practical instructions for these brethren in conducting the business of the Church in the Kirtland area. Remember, as background for these next verses, that these men have been doing much traveling on the Lord's errand. Next, He asks them to stay in Kirtland for a season.

70 **Tarry ye** [*stay*], tarry ye **in this place** [*Kirtland*], and **call a solemn assembly** [*hold a conference*], even

of those who are **the first laborers** [*of the first workers who are laying the foundation of the Church; see D&C 58:7*] **in this last kingdom** [*the dispensation of the fullness of times; the gospel has been restored for the last time, and the Church will continue until the Second Coming when the Savior will take over as "King of Kings and Lord of Lords." See Revelation 19:16*].

71 And **let those whom they have warned in their traveling** [*while on their missions and other travels*] call on the Lord, and **ponder the warning in their hearts which they have received**, for a little season.

Looking at the last half of verse 71, above, we see something that often happens to people after the missionaries have talked with them. They "feel" something in their hearts. The Holy Ghost is testifying to them. There is something different about the missionaries or the member who chatted with them about the gospel. We see at the end of verse 71 that this feeling often lasts for "a little season," but if they do not act upon it, it often dissipates and disappears.

In verses 118–41 of this section, the Lord will give instructions for establishing the School of the Prophets (verse 127), as it was called. It will begin on January 23, 1833, at Kirtland, Ohio. A number of the brethren came to Kirtland to attend the school. They were taught many things that would be helpful in carrying out their duties with their congregations, missionary work, and such, including the gospel, languages, history, and politics.

It appears that verse 72, next, may address their concerns about leaving their families and branches of the Church to attend this schooling, as well as the solemn assembly spoken of in verse 70, above. The Lord will provide people to watch over their "flocks" while they are gone.

72 Behold, and lo, **I will take care of your flocks, and will raise up elders and send unto them**.

73 **Behold, I will hasten my work in its time** [*the Lord will speed the growth of the Church along as appropriate, and this solemn assembly and other schooling is part of that process*].

As you no doubt have noticed, as stated in verse 73, the Lord is indeed "hastening" His work "in its time." It is happening all around us and at every turn!

As you will see, verses 74–80, next, provide more instruction about gathering together and teaching one another.

74 And **I give unto you, who are the first laborers in this last**

kingdom [*the dispensation of the fulness of times*] **a commandment** that you **assemble yourselves together**, and **organize yourselves**, and **prepare yourselves**, and **sanctify yourselves**; yea, **purify your hearts**, and **cleanse your hands and your feet before me, that I may make you clean**;

75 **That I may testify unto your Father, and your God, and my God, that you are clean from the blood of this wicked generation**; that I may fulfil this promise, this great and last promise [*possibly referring to the promise in verse 68 that the day would come when they would be privileged to see God*], which I have made unto you, **when I will** [*when the time and circumstances are right, according to God's will*].

76 **Also, I give unto you a commandment that ye shall continue in prayer and fasting** from this time forth.

Verses 77–80, next, could be considered to be the "curriculum" guide for the schooling that these brethren are to organize.

77 And I give unto you a commandment that you shall **teach one another the doctrine of the kingdom**.

78 **Teach ye diligently and my**

grace shall attend you, that you may be instructed more perfectly in theory, in principle, in doctrine, in the law of the gospel, in all things that pertain unto the kingdom of God, that are expedient [*necessary*] for you to understand;

79 Of things both in heaven and in the earth, and under the earth; things which have been, things which are, things which must shortly come to pass; things which are at home, things which are abroad; the wars and the perplexities of the nations, and the judgments which are on the land; and a knowledge also of countries and of kingdoms—

The importance of this education and schooling is pointed out in verse 80, next.

80 That ye may be prepared in all things when I shall send you again to magnify the calling whereunto I have called you, and the mission with which I have commissioned you.

The last half of verse 81, next, is often quoted in gospel discussions and sermons. It is a basic missionary scripture applied to "every member a missionary." "Warned" in this case could also be interpreted to mean "taught."

81 Behold, I sent you out to testify and warn the people, and it becometh every man who hath been warned to warn his neighbor.

Verse 82, next, emphasizes the principle of accountability.

82 Therefore [*after they have been taught and warned*], they are left without excuse, and their sins are upon their own heads.

Verse 83, next, teaches that the Savior is anxious to save souls and is readily available to help and bless us. It also reminds us of the importance of not waiting until it is too late to become involved in the gospel.

83 He that seeketh me early shall find me, and shall not be forsaken [*left without help*].

84 Therefore, tarry ye [*stay in Kirtland and study and prepare, as instructed in verses 77–80*], and labor diligently, that you may be perfected in your ministry to go forth among the Gentiles for the last time [*another reminder that this is the last dispensation before the Second Coming of Christ*], as many as the mouth of the Lord shall name [*the Lord will name those who are to participate in the School of the Prophets*], to bind up the law and seal up the testimony [*to preach the gospel and bear*

witness of God; compare with Isaiah 8:16–17], **and to prepare the saints for the hour of judgment which is to come** [*the punishments of God which are soon to come upon the world*];

85 **That their souls may escape the wrath of God, the desolation of abomination** [*the destruction of gross evil and punishment of God*] **which awaits the wicked, both in this world and in the world to come.** Verily, I say unto you, let those who are not the first elders [*the leading elders in the Church*] continue in the vineyard [*not come in to attend the School of the Prophets*] until the mouth of the Lord shall call them, **for their time is not yet come; their garments are not clean from the blood of this generation** [*they have not yet finished warning and preaching to the people to whom they were sent.*]

For more regarding the "desolation of abomination" mentioned in verse 85, above, see the notes for section 84, verse 117 in this study guide.

Once a person has been cleansed from sin and "set free" from past follies and evil through the Atonement of Christ, it is extremely important that he or she does not revert back to a life of sin as pointed out in verse 86, next.

86 **Abide ye in the liberty wherewith ye are made free; entangle not yourselves in sin, but let your hands be clean, until the Lord comes.**

Beginning with verse 87 and continuing through verse 116, we will be given much prophecy and detail about the final events leading up to the Second Coming; the taking up of the righteous to meet the coming Lord; the first, second, third, and fourth resurrections; the Millennium; the final battle after the Millennium; and the end of the War in Heaven as Satan and his evil followers are cast out completely.

These are "high mountain doctrines" that allow us to see things from the Lord's perspective. As mentioned in the notes at the beginning of this section, such perspectives provide strength, encouragement, and purpose as we press forward in our daily lives, sometimes battling discouragement and opposition to personal righteousness.

We begin with a summary of some signs of the times that will be fulfilled shortly before the Savior comes. Verse 87 seems to be a summary, and then, beginning with verse 88, we see a sequence.

87 **For not many days hence** and [*it won't be long before*] **the earth shall tremble and reel to and fro as a drunken man; and the sun shall**

hide his face, and shall **refuse to give light**; and **the moon shall be bathed in blood**; and **the stars shall become exceedingly angry**, and **shall cast themselves down as a fig that falleth from off a fig-tree.**

One of the first stages of the wind-up scenes before the Second Coming is the preaching of the gospel by missionaries. They will be sent to all the world. This is the gentle approach.

Then, as people become more and more wicked and violent, re-jecting the gentle message and invitation of the missionaries, the Lord will "turn up the volume" so to speak and have nature "speak up" in order to get people's attention and save more souls.

88 And **after your testimony cometh wrath and indignation upon the people.**

89 **For after your testimony cometh the testimony of earth-quakes**, that shall cause **groanings** in the midst of her [*probably meaning the earth*], and **men shall fall upon the ground and shall not be able to stand.** [*This will, of course, be terrifying, and will cause some to turn to God or back to God.*]

90 And **also cometh the testimony of** the voice of **thunderings**, and the voice of **lightnings**, and the voice of **tempests**, and the voice of **the waves of the sea heaving themselves beyond their bounds.**

91 And **all things** [*including nature, politics, breakdown of the family, uprisings, war, and personal wickedness*] **shall be in commotion**; and surely, **men's hearts shall fail them** [*people will give up hope; there will be much depression and despair*]; **for fear shall come upon all people.**

As we read verse 92, next, we see that the inhabitants of the earth will be unmistakably alerted that the Second Coming and destruc-tion of the wicked are here when that time arrives.

92 And **angels shall fly through the midst of heaven, crying with a loud voice, sounding the trump of God, saying: Prepare ye, prepare ye, O inhabitants of the earth; for the judgment** [*the prophesied punishments*] **of our God is come.** Behold, and lo, **the Bridegroom** [*the Savior*] **cometh; go ye out to meet him** [*a reference to the Parable of the Ten Virgins, given in Matthew 25:1–13, especially verse 6*].

We will include a quote here from the 2018 *Doctrine and Covenants Student Manual* regarding the "angels . . . sounding the trump of God" mentioned in verse 92, above:

"Seven trumpets, each sounded by a different angel, will signal key events surrounding the Second Coming of Jesus Christ. Among these events are the fall of "the mother of abominations" (see D&C 88:94, 105), the orderly resurrection of the dead (see D&C 88:95–102), the announcement that "the hour of [God's] judgment is come" (see D&C 88:103–4), and the proclamation that God's work is finished (see D&C 88:106). The seven angels will sound their trumpets a second time, and each will announce a review of 1,000 years of the earth's history, from the Fall of Adam to the Millennium (see D&C 88:108–10).

We do not know what the "great sign in heaven" will be, as spoken of in verse 93, next. But we do know that everyone will see it at the same time.

93 And immediately there shall appear a great sign in heaven, and **all people shall see it together** [*everyone will see it at the same time*].

The Prophet Joseph Smith spoke of the "sign in heaven," referred to in verse 93, above. He said:

"Then will appear one grand sign of the Son of Man in heaven. But what will the world do? They will say it is a planet, a comet, etc. But the Son of man will come as

the sign of the coming of the Son of Man, which will be as the light of the morning cometh out of the east" (*Teachings of the Prophet Joseph Smith,* 286; *Teachings of Presidents of the Church: Joseph Smith,* 252–53).

Next, in verse 94, the complete destruction of the wicked is foretold. As you can see, there is much use of scriptural symbolism in this verse. There are many different terms and phrases that mean Satan, his kingdom, his temptations, and so on. The sounding of the "trump" is a reminder that all will hear and no one will miss this.

94 And another angel shall sound his trump, saying: **That great church** [*the church of the devil; see 1 Nephi 14:10; the kingdom of the devil; 1 Nephi 22:22*]**, the mother of abominations** [*Satan and his evil kingdom*]**, that made all nations drink of the wine of the wrath of her fornication** [*which provided temptation toward sin, wickedness, and sexual sin for all in the world to partake of*]**, that persecuteth the saints of God,** that **shed their blood—she** [*Satan's kingdom, the "whore of all the earth"; 1 Nephi 14:10*] **who sitteth upon many waters, and upon the islands of the sea** [*1 Nephi 14:11*]**—behold, she is the tares of the earth** [*the deceiving false doctrines, philosophies, counterfeits of*

God's work, and so on; see notes for section 86 in this study guide]; **she** [*Satan's kingdom; the wicked of the world*] **is bound in bundles** [*prepared for burning*]; **her bands are made strong** [*God has decreed it, there is no escape*], **no man can loose them; therefore, she is ready to be burned.** And **he** [*the angel at the beginning of this verse*] **shall sound his trump both long and loud, and all nations shall hear it** [*everyone on earth will know that this is taking place*].

We do not know what the "silence in heaven for the space of half an hour" is, spoken of in verse 95, next. We do know that silence is an excellent attention getter (compare with 3 Nephi 10:1–2).

Some have thought that the "half an hour" might be in the Lord's time system (one thousand years on earth equals one day in heaven; see 2 Peter 3:8), which would make the "half an hour" into about twenty-one years of our time. They further speculate that during this twenty-one-year period there would be no revelation because of the "silence in heaven."

Suggesting that there would be no revelation is contrary to the fact that the Church will not go into apostasy again (Daniel 2:44–45). It will continue to spread throughout the world, with prophets, seers and revelators at the helm, right up until the kingdom of God (the

Church on earth) meets the kingdom of heaven (the Savior and the hosts of heaven) at the Second Coming; see D&C 65:6).

Thus, we are probably best off to consider the "half an hour" to be in our current time system unless told otherwise by a prophet.

95 And **there shall be silence in heaven for the space of half an hour**; and **immediately after shall the curtain of heaven be unfolded** [*the veil will be removed*], as a scroll is unfolded after it is rolled up, **and the face of the Lord shall be unveiled** [*everyone will see the coming Christ*];

Revelation 1:7 informs us that everyone will see the Savior at this time, including those who crucified Him.

Revelation 1:7

7 **Behold, he cometh with clouds; and every eye shall see him, and they** *also* **which pierced him**: and all kindreds of the earth shall wail because of him. Even so, Amen.

Elder Orson Pratt explained that everyone, including the dead, will see the Savior when He comes. He taught (**bold** added for emphasis):

"The second advent of the Son of God is to be something altogether of a different nature from anything that has hitherto transpired on the face of the earth, accompanied with great power and glory, something that will not be done in a small portion of the earth like Palestine, and seen only by a few; but **it will be an event that will be seen by all**—all flesh shall see the glory of the Lord; when he reveals himself the second time, **every eye, not only those living at that time in the flesh**, in mortality on the earth, **but also the very dead themselves**, they also who pierced him, those who lived eighteen hundred years ago, who were engaged in the cruel act of piercing his hands and his feet and his side, will also see him at that time" (In *Journal of Discourses*, 18:170).

Next, we are told that the righteous, faithful Latter-day Saints who are alive upon the earth at the time will be taken up to meet the coming Lord. They will need to be "quickened" or "transfigured" (see Moses 1:11) by the power of the Holy Ghost in order for their mortal bodies to withstand the presence of the Son of God, who will come in all His glory. By the way, it will be His glory that will destroy the wicked; see D&C 5:19; 2 Nephi 12:10, 19, 21.

Doctrine, verse 96

Faithful Saints who are alive on earth at the time of the Savior's coming will be transfigured and taken up to meet Him.

96 And the saints that are upon the earth, who are alive [*who are still mortal*], **shall be quickened and** be **caught up to meet him**.

Next, in verses 97–98, we are taught that the dead who are worthy of celestial glory (verse 98) will be resurrected and also caught up to meet Him. This is sometimes referred to as the "morning of the first resurrection."

By the way, a large group of the dead, who were worthy of celestial resurrection, was resurrected with the Savior at the time of His resurrection. This would have included Adam and Eve and all the righteous Saints down to the time of Christ's resurrection, including John the Baptist. See D&C 133:54–55.

Doctrine, verse 97

The righteous who died after the resurrection of Christ, who lived worthy of celestial glory, will be resurrected and taken up to meet the coming Lord.

97 And they who have slept in their graves shall come forth [*will be resurrected*], for their graves shall be opened; and **they also shall be caught up to meet him** in the midst of the pillar of heaven—

Verse 98, next, speaks of another

beautiful privilege for the faithful Saints, living and dead. Not only will they be caught up to meet the coming Savior, but they also will have the privilege of descending to the earth with Him as He comes to usher in the Millennium and begin His thousand-year reign on earth. Next time you see a painting of the coming of the Lord, you might picture yourself as one of the beings in the background who are coming down with Him.

At this point, those Saints who are still mortal will continue living on earth until they reach a hundred years of age (Isaiah 65:20). The Saints who are resurrected at this time will begin ruling and reigning with the Savior, as taught in Revelation 20:4.

Doctrine, verses 96–98

The living Saints at the time of the Second Coming, as well as the righteous who are still in the grave and who are resurrected at this time, will have the privilege of meeting the Savior as He comes and then descending to the earth with Him.

98 They [*both the living "saints" in verse 96 and the righteous dead who "have slept in their graves" in verse 97*] **are Christ's**, the first fruits, they **who shall descend with him** first, and they who are on the earth and in their graves, **who are first caught up to meet him**; and all this by the voice of the sounding of the trump of the angel of God [*as announced to the world by the angel blowing his horn*].

Verse 99, next, informs us that those who are worthy of terrestrial glory, who have already died, will be resurrected near the first of the Millennium, but after the celestial dead have been resurrected. This terrestrial resurrection is sometimes referred to as the "afternoon of the first resurrection." No terrestrials have yet been resurrected.

Doctrine, verse 99

Those who lived from the time of Adam and Eve up to the time of the Second Coming, who have already died and who earned terrestrial glory, will be resurrected sometime near the beginning of the Millennium but not until the celestial resurrection spoken of in verse 97, above, has taken place. No terrestrials from this earth have been resurrected yet.

99 And after this [*the events spoken of in verses 96–98*] another angel shall sound, which is the second trump; and then **cometh the redemption of those who are Christ's at his coming; who**

have received their part in that prison [*the spirit prison, as spoken of in D&C 76:73 during the vision of those who receive terrestrial glory (D&C 76:71–80)*] which is prepared for them, that they might receive the gospel, and be judged according to men in the flesh.

Verses 100–101, next, teach us that those who have earned telestial glory will not be resurrected until the end of the Millennium. Therefore, no telestials have been resurrected yet.

Doctrine, verses 100–101

Those who qualify for telestial glory will not be resurrected until the end of the Millennium. No telestials from this earth have been resurrected yet.

100 And again, another trump shall sound, which is the third trump; and then come the spirits of men who are to be judged, and are found under condemnation [*will be assigned to the telestial kingdom*];

101 And these are the rest of the dead; and they live not again until [*they will not be resurrected until*] the thousand years are ended, neither again, until the end of the earth.

There is one more resurrection, the very last one. It is spoken of in verse 102 and is the resurrection of mortals who become sons of perdition.

Doctrine, verse 102

Mortals from this earth who become sons of perdition will be the last to be resurrected.

102 And another trump shall sound, which is the fourth trump, saying: There are found among those who are to remain until that great and last day, even the end, who shall remain filthy still.

Verses 103–5, next, summarize the triumph of God over Satan as the kingdom of the devil, often referred to as "Babylon," falls at the time of the Second Coming.

103 And another trump shall sound, which is the fifth trump, which is the fifth angel who committeth the everlasting gospel—flying through the midst of heaven, unto all nations, kindreds, tongues, and people;

104 And this shall be the sound of his trump [*this is his message*], saying to all people, both in heaven and in earth, and that are under the earth—for every ear shall hear it, and every knee shall bow, and every tongue

shall confess [*ultimately, everyone, including those who follow Satan into perdition, sometimes referred to as outer darkness, will acknowledge that Jesus is the Christ; this does not necessarily mean that they will accept His gospel, rather that they will ultimately have to admit that He is who He says He is*], **while they hear the sound of the trump, saying: Fear God, and give glory to him who sitteth upon the throne, forever and ever; for the hour of his judgment is come.**

105 And again, **another angel shall sound his trump,** which is **the sixth angel, saying: She** [*Babylon, Satan's kingdom, the church of the devil, "the whore of all the earth"; see 1 Nephi 14:10*] **is fallen** who made all nations drink of the wine of the wrath of her fornication [*who spread gross wickedness throughout the whole world*]; **she is fallen, is fallen!** [*In other words, the wicked are finally destroyed and the thousand years of peace can begin!*]

You may wish to cross-reference verses 106–7, next, with D&C 76:106–8 in your own scriptures. These verses teach that Christ will ultimately finish His work with this world after the Millennium, the little season, and the final judgment and will turn it back over to the Father.

106 And again, **another angel shall sound his trump,** which is **the seventh angel** [*this is Adam; see verse 112; the number seven in scriptural symbolism represents completeness, perfection*], **saying: It is finished;** it is finished! [*Everything with respect to this world is complete*]. **The Lamb of God** [*Christ*] **hath overcome** [*has triumphed*] and **trodden the wine-press alone** [*Christ was the only one who could carry out the Atonement; thus, He had to do it alone*], even **the wine-press** [*symbolic of the terrible burden and pressure of suffering for all our sins*] **of the fierceness of the wrath of Almighty God** [*to satisfy the demands of the law of justice*].

107 And **then** [*after the world is finished up*] **shall the angels be crowned with the glory of his might,** and **the saints shall be filled with his glory, and receive their inheritance and be made equal with him** [*will receive exaltation, be made gods*].

Having been shown the final finish-up scenes for this world in the above verses, we are now taken back in time and given additional details about the final scenes, including the binding of Satan at the beginning of the Millennium, the "little season" after the Millennium is over, during which the battle of

Gog and Magog takes place (see Bible Dictionary under "Gog"), and the final banishing of Satan and his followers.

First, in verses 108–9, we are shown a bit more about how judgment will take place. Note how well-organized all of this is.

108 And **then shall the first angel** again sound his trump in the ears of all living, and **reveal the secret acts of men, and the mighty works of God in the first thousand years.**

109 And **then shall the second angel** sound his trump, and **reveal the secret acts of men, and the thoughts and intents of their hearts, and the mighty works of God in the second thousand years—**

110 **And so on, until the seventh angel** [Michael—in other words, Adam; see verse 112] **shall sound his trump;** and **he shall stand forth upon the land and upon the sea** [symbolic of Adam's position and authority over the whole earth, under the Savior], **and swear** [promise, covenant] **in the name of him who sitteth upon the throne** [in other words, he promised in the name of Jesus Christ; see verse 115], **that there shall be time no longer** [that there will be no more delay, the Millennium will now

begin]; and **Satan shall be bound** [will not be allowed to tempt and interfere on earth during the Millennium—compare with D&C 101:28], that old serpent, who is called the devil, **and shall not be loosed for the space of a thousand years.**

Next, in verses 111–13, we are shown the preparations for the final battle, the Battle of Gog and Magog, during which the war for our loyalty, which began with the War in Heaven, will be brought to a close.

By the way, Gog was the wicked king of Magog in ancient times who attacked Israel. Over time, "Gog and Magog" came to symbolize the forces of evil that fight against God. We will quote from the Bible Dictionary for a bit more about this.

Gog

"(1) A Reubenite (1 Chr. 5:4).

"(2) King of Magog, whose invasion of Israel was prophesied by Ezekiel (Ezek. 38; 39). The prophecy points to a time when the heathen nations of the north would set themselves against the people of God and would be defeated and led to recognize Jehovah as King. **All this appears to be at the second coming** of the Lord. **Another battle, called the battle of Gog and Magog, will occur at the end of the 1,000 years.** This is described by John in Rev. 20:7–9; see also D&C 88:111–116."

111 And then he shall be loosed for a little season, that he may **gather together his armies**.

Joseph Fielding Smith taught that there will be many mortals who will become sons of perdition at this time because they will know the Savior personally, having lived on earth with Him during the final years of the Millennium, and then turning wicked and joining forces with Satan when he is let loose after the Millennium is over.

Elder Smith said:

"After the thousand years Satan will be loosed again and will go forth again to deceive the nations. Because men are still mortal, Satan will go out to deceive them. Men will again deny the Lord, but in doing so they will act with their eyes open and because they love darkness rather than light, and so they become sons of perdition. Satan will gather his hosts, both those on the earth and the wicked dead who will eventually also be brought forth in the resurrection. Michael [*Adam*], the prince, will gather his forces and the last great battle will be fought. Satan will be defeated with his hosts. Then will come the end. Satan and those who follow him will be banished into outer darkness" (*Doctrines of Salvation*, 1:87).

112 And **Michael, the seventh

angel, even the archangel, shall gather together his armies**, even the hosts of heaven.

113 And **the devil shall gather together his armies**; even the hosts of hell, **and shall come up to battle against Michael and his armies**.

We see the final outcome of this battle in verses 114–15, next.

114 And **then cometh the battle of the great God** [*the Battle of Gog and Magog*]; and **the devil and his armies shall be cast away into their own place** [*outer darkness; perdition*]**, that they shall not have power over the saints any more at all.**

115 For **Michael** shall fight their battles, and **shall overcome him** [*Lucifer, Satan*] who **seeketh the throne of him who sitteth upon the throne, even the Lamb.**

Did you notice Lucifer's basic motivation for all the evil he has caused as mentioned in the last half of verse 15, above? He wanted to be the Redeemer, as stated also in Moses 4:1–3.

116 **This is the glory of God** [*as stated also in Moses 1:39*], and **the sanctified** [*those who obtain celestial glory*]; and they **shall not any more see death** [*perhaps meaning spiritual death, resulting from the

influence of Satan and his angels;
compare with Alma 12:16].

Verse 117, next, provides a transition between the "high mountain" doctrines given in the previous verses and specific instructions for setting up and running the "school of the prophets" (verse 127), which constitute verses 118–41.

117 Therefore, verily I say unto you, my friends, **call your solemn assembly** [*see verses 70–75*]**, as I have commanded you**.

Some are of the opinion that the "solemn assembly" referred to in verse 117, above, as well as in previous verses, is the same thing as the School of the Prophets. In any case, we will use **bold** along with just a few notes, letting the scriptures speak for themselves as we read the Lord's instructions for this School of the Prophets.

By the way, the brethren began meeting in this school on January 23, 1833. They met in an upper room of the Newel K. Whitney Store in Kirtland, Ohio, and had many marvelous manifestations and spiritual discussions there. Also, because many of these men chewed or smoked tobacco and Emma Smith had to clean up after them, this will provide the setting for the receiving of the Word of Wisdom, which we will study next in section 89.

You will likely recognize some of the next verses as often-quoted

in lessons and sermons.

118 **And as all have not faith, seek ye diligently and teach one another words of wisdom**; yea, **seek ye out of the best books words of wisdom; seek learning, even by study and also by faith**.

An important caution is given at the end of verse 118, above. It is that there is danger in basing one's studies solely upon the precepts, philosophies, theories, and teachings of men without the gospel as an anchor to the soul. Many have gone into intellectual apostasy because they failed to include faith in their studies.

119 **Organize yourselves; prepare every needful thing;** and **establish** a house, even **a house of prayer**, a house of **fasting**, a house of **faith**, a house of **learning**, a house of **glory**, a house of **order**, **a house of God**;

120 That your incomings may be in the name of the Lord; that your outgoings may be in the name of the Lord; that all your salutations may be in the name of the Lord, with uplifted hands unto the Most High [*in other words, that everything you do might be done under the direction and influence of the Spirit of the Lord*].

121 Therefore, **cease from all your light speeches, from all laughter, from all your lustful desires,**

from all your pride and light-mindedness, and from all your wicked doings.

Verse 121, above, is context sensitive. It contains instructions for conducting sessions of the School of the Prophets. While the instruction to avoid "lustful desires," "pride," "light-mindedness" (not taking serious things seriously), and "all your wicked doings" applies to all situations and settings, the instruction regarding "light speeches" and "laughter" would apply to sacred and serious settings where funny speeches and inappropriate laughter would ruin the spirit of the occasion. For example, this would apply to our temple worship. Our living prophets are marvelous examples of proper use of humor.

President Joseph F. Smith taught the following:

"The Lord has called upon us to be a sober-minded people, not given to much laughter, frivolity and light-mindedness, but to consider thoughtfully and thoroughly the things of his kingdom that we may be prepared in all things to understand the glorious truths of the gospel, and be prepared for blessings to come. . . .

". . . I believe that it is necessary for the Saints to have amusement, but it must be of the proper kind. I do not believe the Lord intends and desires that we should pull a long face and look sanctimonious and hypocritical. I think he expects us to be happy and of a cheerful countenance, but he does not expect of us the indulgence in boisterous and unseemly conduct and the seeking after the vain and foolish things which amuse and entertain the world. He has commanded us to the contrary for our own good and eternal welfare" (In Conference Report, October 1916, 70).

122 **Appoint** among yourselves **a teacher, and let not all be spokesmen at once;** but **let one speak at a time** and **let all listen unto his sayings,** that when all have spoken that all may be edified of all [*so that you can learn from each member of the class*], and that every man may have an equal privilege.

123 See that ye **love one another; cease to be covetous; learn to impart one to another as the gospel requires.**

124 **Cease to be idle; cease to be unclean; cease to find fault one with another; cease to sleep longer than is needful; retire to thy bed early, that ye may not be weary; arise early, that your bodies and your minds may be invigorated.**

125 And above all things, **clothe yourselves with the bond of**

charity, as with a mantle, which is **the bond of perfectness and peace**.

126 **Pray always, that ye may not faint** [*become overly discouraged*], until I come. Behold, and lo, I will come quickly, and receive you unto myself. Amen.

127 And again, **the order of** the house prepared for the presidency **of the school of the prophets, established for their instruction in all things that are expedient** [*important and necessary*] **for them**, even for all the officers of the church, or in other words, those who are called to the ministry in the church, beginning at the high priests, even down to the deacons—

128 And **this shall be the order of the house of the presidency** of the school: **He that is appointed to be president, or teacher, shall be found standing in his place**, in the house which shall be prepared for him.

129 Therefore, **he shall be first** in the house of God, **in a place that the congregation in the house may hear his words carefully and distinctly**, not with loud speech.

130 And when he cometh into the house of God, for **he should be first** in the house—behold, this is beautiful, **that he may be an example**—

131 **Let him offer himself in prayer** upon his knees before God, in token or remembrance of the everlasting covenant.

132 And when any shall come in after him, let the teacher arise, and, with uplifted hands to heaven, yea, even directly, salute his brother or brethren with these words:

133 Art thou a brother or brethren? I salute you in the name of the Lord Jesus Christ, in token or remembrance of the everlasting covenant, in which covenant I receive you to fellowship, in a determination that is fixed, immovable, and unchangeable, to be your friend and brother through the grace of God in the bonds of love, to walk in all the commandments of God blameless, in thanksgiving, forever and ever. Amen.

134 And **he that is found unworthy of this salutation** [*the greeting given in verse 133, above*] **shall not have place among you; for ye shall not suffer that mine house shall be polluted by him.**

135 And he that cometh in and is faithful before me, and is a brother, or if they be brethren, they shall salute [greet] the president or teacher with uplifted hands to heaven, with this same prayer and covenant, or by saying Amen, in token of the same.

136 Behold, verily, I say unto you, this is an ensample [example] unto you for a salutation to one another in the house of God, in the school of the prophets.

137 And ye are called to do this by prayer and thanksgiving [with gratitude], as the Spirit shall give utterance in all your doings in the house of the Lord, in the school of the prophets, that it may become a sanctuary, a tabernacle of the Holy Spirit to your edification.

138 And ye shall not receive any among you into this school save he is clean from the blood of this generation;

139 And he shall be received by the ordinance of the washing of feet, for unto this end [purpose] was the ordinance of the washing of feet instituted.

140 And again, the ordinance of washing feet is to be administered by the president, or presiding elder of the church.

141 It is to be commenced with prayer; and after partaking of bread and wine [the sacrament], he is to gird [dress] himself according to the pattern given in the thirteenth chapter of John's testimony concerning me. Amen.

SECTION 89

Background

This revelation was given through the Prophet Joseph Smith at Kirtland, Ohio, on February 27, 1833. It is known as the Word of Wisdom.

President Brigham Young gave the background for this revelation as follows:

"I think I am as well acquainted with the circumstances which led to the giving of the Word of Wisdom as any man in the Church, although I was not present at the time to witness them. The first School of the Prophets was held in a small room situated over the Prophet Joseph's kitchen, in a house which belonged to Bishop Whitney. . . . The brethren came to that place for hundreds of miles to attend school in a little room probably no larger than eleven by fourteen. When they assembled together in this room after breakfast, the first they did was to light their pipes and, while smoking, talk about the great things of the kingdom and spit all over the room, and as soon as the pipe was out of their mouths a large chew of tobacco would then be taken. Often when the Prophet entered the room to give the school instructions he would find himself in a cloud of tobacco smoke. This, and the complaints of his wife at having to clean so filthy a floor, made the Prophet think upon the matter, and he inquired of the Lord relating to the conduct of the Elders in using tobacco, and the revelation known as the Word of Wisdom was the result of his inquiry. You know what it is and can read it at your leisure" (*Journal of Discourses*, 12:158).

There are many important aspects to this revelation. For instance, as you study it you would do well to note that there are more "dos" than "don'ts" contained in it. Also, pay careful attention to the fact that it is not a system of vegetarianism. In fact, if you look at the verse summaries after the heading to section 89 in your Doctrine and Covenants, you will see that meat is clearly permitted (**bold** added for emphasis):

*10–17, Herbs, fruits, **flesh**, and grain are ordained for the use of man and of animals*;

We will deal more with this when we get to verses 12–13.

As you will see, in verse 2, the Word of Wisdom was not a commandment when it was first given. However, in a general conference of the Church held on September 9, 1851, President Brigham Young presented it to the members as a commandment. Still, many did not comply, perhaps not considering it to be as serious and important as other commandments. Finally, in 1919, under the direction of President Heber J. Grant (see 2018 *Doctrine and Covenants Student Manual*, chapter 35), the Word of Wisdom became a temple recommend item and thus began to be "locked in" as a vital part of being a faithful Saint. It has now become a commandment in the full sense of the word, just in time to protect us from "evils and designs which do and will exist in the hearts of conspiring men" (verse 4), such as the rampant drug culture, alcohol addiction, and sexual immorality, which often go with smoking and drinking.

President Joseph F. Smith explained why the Word of Wisdom was not given as a commandment at first. He said: "At that time, . . . if [the Word of Wisdom] had been given as a commandment it would have brought every man, addicted to the use of these noxious things, under condemnation; so the Lord was merciful and gave them a chance to overcome, before He brought them under the law" (in Conference Report, Oct. 1913, 14).

We will now proceed with our verse-by-verse study.

1 **A WORD OF WISDOM, for the benefit of the council of high priests** [*the School of the Prophets*], **assembled in Kirtland, and the church,** and **also the saints in Zion** [*the members at that time in Jackson County, Missouri*]—

2 To be **sent greeting; not by commandment or constraint** [*see background notes above for this section for when it became a commandment*], **but by revelation and the word of wisdom, showing forth the order and will of God in the temporal** [*physical*] **salvation of all saints in the last days**—

3 Given for **a principle with promise** [*explained in verses 18–21*], **adapted to the capacity of the weak and the weakest of all saints** [*in other words, there is ultimately no excuse for not living the Word of Wisdom*], **who are or can be called saints.**

Even though the Word of Wisdom serves as a law of health, some wonder why we are required to abstain completely from the harmful substances included in the Word of Wisdom rather than being allowed to use them with moderation. The Lord gives the reason next in verse 4. Perhaps you have noticed that, in many cases, the forbidden substances in the Word of Wisdom serve as a gateway to more harmful substances.

4 Behold, verily, thus saith the Lord unto you: **In consequence of evils and designs which do and will exist in the hearts of conspiring men in the last days, I have warned you, and forewarn you,** by giving unto you this word of wisdom by revelation—

President Ezra Taft Benson explained the warning given in verse 4, above:

"There is another part of this revelation [D&C 89] that constitutes a pertinent warning to this modern generation. 'In consequence of evils and designs which do and will exist in the hearts of conspiring men in the last days, I have warned you, and forewarn you, by giving unto you this word of wisdom by revelation.' (D&C 89:4.)

"The Lord foresaw the situation of today when motives for money would cause men to conspire to entice others to take noxious substances into their bodies. Advertisements which promote beer, wine, liquors, coffee, tobacco, and other harmful substances are examples of what the Lord foresaw. But the most pernicious example of an evil conspiracy in our time is those who induce young people into the use of drugs.

"My young brothers and sisters, in all love, we give you warning that Satan and his emissaries will strive to entice you to use harmful substances, because they well know if you partake, your spiritual powers will be inhibited and you will be in their evil power. Stay away from those places or people which would influence you to break the commandments of God. Keep the commandments of God and you will have the wisdom to know and discern that which is evil" ("A Principle with a Promise," *Ensign*, May 1983, 54–55).

5 That **inasmuch as any man drinketh wine or strong drink among you, behold it is not good, neither meet** [*proper; wise*] **in the sight of your Father**, only [*except*] in assembling yourselves together to offer up your sacraments before him [*in other words, except for use with the sacrament; and, as you know, we no longer use wine but rather water; compare with D&C 27:2*].

6 And, behold, **this should be wine, yea, pure wine of the grape of the vine, of your own make**.

7 And, again, **strong drinks are not for the belly**, but for the washing of your bodies.

Regarding the wine to be used for the sacrament at the time of this revelation, if you carefully read the heading to D&C 27 and verses 3 and 4, you will see that the wine they were to use was not to be "strong drink"; it was to be "new"—in other words, fresh juice, not fermented (see 2018 *Doctrine and Covenants Student Manual*, chapter 35).

8 **And again, tobacco is not for the body, neither for the belly, and is not good for man**, but is an herb for bruises and all sick cattle, to be used with judgment and skill.

The question is often asked as to where the words "tea" and "coffee" are found in the Word of Wisdom. The answer is "hot drinks" in verse 9, next.

9 And again, **hot drinks** are not for the body or belly.

The Joseph Smith Papers Project helps us understand what is meant by "hot drinks" in verse nine, above. We will quote from the 2018 *Doctrine and Covenants Student Manual*:

"The Prophet Joseph Smith and Hyrum Smith were reported to have specifically identified coffee and tea as the "hot drinks" mentioned in the Word of Wisdom, and President Brigham Young later confirmed this explanation (see *The Joseph Smith Papers, Documents, Volume 3: February 1833–March 1834*, 14)."

You can also read on page 186 of *True to the Faith*, published by the Church in 2004, that "the term 'hot drinks' refers to tea and coffee." You can also read on the same page that "Anything harmful that people purposefully take into their bodies is not in harmony with the Word of Wisdom. This is especially true of illegal drugs, which can destroy those who become addicted to them. Stay entirely away from them."

Another thing regarding the term "hot drinks" is that some members tend to think that since the word "hot" is used, it may be permissible to drink these products cold or iced. This is not so. Also, some members tend to believe that any hot drink, including hot chocolate, is against the Word of Wisdom. This also is not the case. Of course, any drink that is too hot and burns when you drink it is against the law of common sense, but it is not a matter of temple worthiness.

We must be careful not to add things to the Word of Wisdom that neither the Lord nor His prophets have added. For example, some add cola drinks and other caffeine drinks to the Word of Wisdom. While these might fit into the statement of the Brethren about "anything harmful" taken into our bodies, quoted above, we must be careful not to go beyond what the Lord has said by making these a matter of temple worthiness and imposing our own interpretations upon others.

Beginning with verse 10 and continuing through verse 17, we see many "dos" that, when followed, will provide better health.

10 And again, verily I say unto you, **all wholesome herbs** [*a word meaning "vegetables and plants" in Joseph Smith's day*] God hath ordained for the constitution, nature, and use of man—

11 **Every herb in the season thereof**, and **every fruit in the season thereof**; all these to be used with prudence and thanksgiving.

12 Yea, **flesh also of beasts and of the fowls of the air**, I, the Lord, have ordained [*authorized*] for the use of man with thanksgiving; **nevertheless they are to be used sparingly** [*"sparingly" seems to be the key word, here*];

Verse 13, next, is sometimes used to claim that the Word of Wisdom is a system of vegetarianism. We will quote from Elder John A. Widtsoe. He said:

"The Word of Wisdom is not a system of vegetarianism. Clearly, meat is permitted [see D&C 42:18]" (Widtsoe, *Evidences and Reconciliations*, 3:156–57; quoted in the *Doctrine and Covenants Student Manual*, 1981, 210).

If you will read D&C 49:18–19 and footnote 18a that was placed there by our Church leaders, you will again see that meat is not prohibited by the Word of Wisdom. You may also wish to read D&C 59:16–19, which likewise confirms this.

What, then, do we do with verse 13, next, which seems to say that meat should only be used in times of famine or cold? Let's read it first and then do a bit more with it.

13 And it is pleasing unto me that they should not be used, only in times of winter, or of cold, or famine.

Since we already have the answers, above, revealed through the Brethren that the Word of Wisdom is not a system of vegetarianism, we can take another look at verse 13 and see if we are reading it correctly.

At the time this revelation was given, there were groups in the Kirtland, Ohio, area who advocated not eating meat. One of these was the Shaking Quakers, all of whom avoided eating pork as a matter of religion, and many of whom likewise made abstinence from all meat a matter of religious belief. See heading to section 49. With this in mind, we might read verse 13, above, as follows:

"And it is pleasing unto me that they [*the flesh of beasts and . . . fowls—verse 12*] should not be used only in times of winter, or cold, or

famine as Ann Lee and the Shaking Quakers teach. Rather, they are to be used sparingly."

Whatever the case, we are wise if we follow our Church leaders on this matter. Of course, those whose bodies function best on a meat-free diet are welcome to follow such eating habits. But they must be cautious not to impose their preferences upon other members as the will of the Lord and the doctrine of the Church.

14 All grain is ordained [*approved*] **for the use of man and of beasts, to be the staff of life**, not only **for man** but **for the beasts of the field** [*domestic animals*], and **the fowls of heaven**, and **all wild animals** that run or creep on the earth;

15 And these [*perhaps meaning the wild animals mentioned in verse 14, above—we don't know for sure*] **hath God made for the use of man only in times of famine and excess of hunger.**

16 All grain is good for the food of man; as **also the fruit of the vine**; that which yieldeth fruit, **whether in the ground** [*such as potatoes, radishes, carrots, and so forth*] **or above the ground—**

It is interesting that modern animal science studies have verified that the grains recommended for specific animals, in verse 17, next, are correct.

17 Nevertheless, wheat for man, and **corn for the ox,** and **oats for the horse,** and **rye for the fowls and for swine, and for all beasts of the field** [*domestic animals*], and **barley for all useful animals,** and for mild drinks, as also other grain.

In verse 3, above, we were told that the Word of Wisdom is "a principle with promise." The promised blessings are given in verses 18–21, next. This is an important part of the Word of Wisdom that unfortunately is often left out of discussions and conversations about it.

18 **And all saints who remember to keep and do these sayings, walking in obedience to the commandments** [*an additional stipulation for receiving these blessings*], **shall receive health in their navel and marrow to their bones** [*a biblical phrase meaning "the support and blessings of the Lord," as was the case with Daniel and his three companions; see Daniel 1:6–20; see also Proverbs 3:7–10*];

19 **And shall find wisdom and great treasures of knowledge, even hidden treasures** [*meaning, among other things, will have better knowledge and stronger testimonies of the gospel*];

It is not uncommon for people who have physical limitations and disabilities, who faithfully keep the Word of Wisdom, to be a bit disappointed when they read verse 20, next. While better health and strength are obviously a major benefit of keeping the Word of Wisdom, verse 20 has a symbolic meaning that applies to all the faithful and that is even more important eternally than mortal strength and stamina. We will add it as a note to the end of the verse.

20 **And shall run and not be weary, and shall walk and not faint.** [*They will be strengthened by the Lord and will not be stopped in pursuing the path to exaltation. Compare with Isaiah 40:28–31.*]

Verse 20, above, should be read in the context of verse 21, next.

21 **And I, the Lord, give unto them a promise, that the destroying angel shall pass by them, as the children of Israel, and not slay them.** Amen.

President J. Reuben Clark Jr. spoke of these promises as follows (**bold** added for emphasis):

"This does not say and this does not mean, that to keep the Word of Wisdom is to insure us against death, for death is, in the eternal plan, coequal with birth. This is the eternal decree. [1 Cor. 15:22; 2 Nephi 9:6.] But it does mean that the destroying angel, he who comes to punish the unrighteous for their sins, as he in olden time afflicted the corrupt Egyptians in their wickedness [Ex. 12:23, 29], shall pass by the Saints, 'who are walking in obedience to the commandments,' and who 'remember to keep and do these sayings.' **These promises do mean that all those who qualify themselves to enjoy them will be permitted so to live out their lives that they may gain the full experiences and get the full knowledge which they need in order to progress to the highest exaltation in eternity**, all these will live until their work is finished and God calls them back to their eternal home, as a reward" (In Conference Report, October 1940, 17–18).

SECTION 90

Background

This revelation was given to the Prophet Joseph Smith on March 8, 1833, in Kirtland, Ohio. In this revelation (see verse 6), the Lord instructed that Sidney Rigdon and Frederick G. Williams were to be "equal with thee (Joseph Smith) in holding the keys of this last kingdom." As a result, ten days later, on March 18, 1833, they were ordained as counselors in the Presidency of the High Priesthood (which later became known as the First Presidency). Joseph Smith described how this took place:

"I laid my hands on Brothers Sidney and Frederick, and ordained them to take part with me in holding the keys, of this last kingdom, and to assist in the presidency of the high priesthood, as my counselors; after which, I exhorted the brethren to faithfulness, and diligence in keeping the commandments of God, and gave much instruction for the benefit of the saints, with a promise, that the pure in heart should see a heavenly vision; and, after remaining a short time in secret prayer, the promise was verified; for many present had the eyes of their understanding opened by the Spirit of God so as to behold many things. . . .

"After [partaking of the sacrament] many of the brethren saw a heavenly vision of the Savior, and concourses of angels, and many other things, of which each one has a record of what he saw" (in *Manuscript History of the Church*, vol. A-1, page 281, josephsmithpapers.org; spelling standardized).

The "Presidency of the High Priesthood" became known as the "First Presidency" by 1835. (See *The Joseph Smith Papers, Documents, Volume 3: February 1833–March 1834*, 26).

In verse one, we see that the humble Prophet of the Restoration, Joseph Smith Jr., had been feeling his inadequacies and had pled with the Lord for forgiveness of his sins.

1 **THUS saith the Lord**, verily, **verily I say unto you my son** [*a term of closeness and endearment*], **thy sins are forgiven thee, according to thy petition**, for **thy prayers and the prayers of thy brethren have come up into my ears**.

In verses 2–3, next, we are told once more that this is the last time the gospel will be restored again before the Second Coming. This is significant because every other time throughout the history of the earth that the gospel was restored, the Church eventually went into apostasy and had to be restored again. It will not happen this time (see Daniel 2:45–46).

Joseph Smith and his successors hold the priesthood keys of authority to administer and direct the Church, and will continue to hold them until they turn them over to the Savior at the council at Adam-ondi-Ahman, shortly before the Second Coming; see Daniel 7:14.

2 Therefore, **thou art blessed from henceforth that bear the keys of the kingdom** given unto you; **which kingdom is coming forth for the last time**.

3 Verily I say unto you, **the keys of this kingdom shall never be taken from you, while thou art in the world, neither in the world to come**;

The word "oracles," as used in verses 4–5, next, means both "revelations" and "the prophets through whom revelations are received." Verse 5 emphasizes the accountability of all who receive the revelations of God through His living oracles.

4 Nevertheless, **through you shall the oracles be given** to another, yea, even **unto the church**.

5 And **all they who receive the oracles of God, let them beware how they hold them** [*respond to them*] **lest they are accounted as a light thing, and are brought under condemnation thereby**, and stumble and fall when the storms descend, and the winds blow, and the rains descend, and beat upon their house [*in other words, when the temptations of the devil try to steer them away from following the revelations of God through His prophets*].

Sidney Rigdon and Frederick G. Williams are addressed, beginning in verse 6, next.

6 And again, verily **I say unto** thy brethren, **Sidney Rigdon and Frederick G. Williams, their sins are forgiven them also**, and they are accounted as **equal with thee in holding the keys of this last kingdom**;

These brethren, along with the

Prophet, now form what we know as the "Quorum of the First Presidency." The two counselors function under the direction of the Prophet, but not independently. When the Prophet dies, the Quorum of the First Presidency is dissolved.

In order to understand the last phrase of verse 6, above, it is helpful to know that each new Apostle is given all the keys of the priesthood at the time he is ordained an Apostle and set apart to serve in the Quorum of the Twelve. Thus, each of the fifteen "prophets, seers, and revelators" who serve as the First Presidency and the Twelve today holds all of the priesthood keys. However, only the Prophet has the authority to exercise all of the keys. They are dormant in the others until if and when they become the President of the Church. Otherwise, there would be no one on earth to give the new Prophet the keys after the previous President of the Church has passed away.

Next, beginning with verse 7, these counselors to the Prophet are given more on-the-job training, including instructions about the purposes of the School of the Prophets.

7 As **also through your administration the keys of the school of the prophets** [see D&C 88:118–141], which I have commanded to be organized;

8 **That thereby they** [the brethren chosen to attend the School of the Prophets] **may be perfected in their ministry** for the salvation of Zion, and of the nations of Israel, and of the Gentiles, as many as will believe;

9 That **through your administration they may receive the word** [you are to teach them], and through their administration [they are to teach others] the word may go forth unto the ends of the earth, unto the Gentiles first, and then, behold, and lo, they shall turn unto the Jews.

Next, the Savior gives these men an overview of the impact that their work will have upon the world.

10 And **then cometh the day when the arm of the Lord shall be revealed in power in convincing the nations, the heathen nations, the house of Joseph, of the gospel of their salvation.**

11 For it shall come to pass **in that day**, that **every man shall hear the fulness of the gospel in his own tongue**, and **in his own language**, through those who are ordained unto this power, **by the administration of the Comforter** [all will be given a chance to be taught under the direction and power of the Holy Ghost], **shed forth**

upon them for the revelation of Jesus Christ [*to bear testimony to them that Jesus is the Christ*].

The message given in verse 11, above, is of tremendous importance. Among other things, it certifies that God is completely fair. It states basically that every individual who ever comes to earth, who lives beyond the years of accountability (D&C 68:25–28, 137:10), will have the opportunity to hear and understand the gospel under the direction and power of the Holy Ghost, who will bear witness to them that Jesus is the Christ. Whether this happens for them in this life or in the spirit world mission field, the outcome is the same.

Once they have received this completely fair opportunity to hear and understand the gospel of Jesus Christ, under the direction and influence of the Holy Ghost, they are then free to accept it or reject it.

Knowing this is comforting to those who worry about whether a loved one has had a fair chance to understand the gospel.

Verses 12–18, next, appear to be directed specifically to the First Presidency.

12 And now, verily I say unto you, I give unto you a commandment that you **continue in the ministry and presidency**.

13 And **when you have finished the translation of the prophets** [*the JST work on the Old Testament*], **you shall from thenceforth preside over the affairs of the church and the school** [*the School of the Prophets*];

14 And **from time to time**, as shall be manifested by the Comforter, **receive revelations to unfold the mysteries of the kingdom**;

15 And **set in order the churches** [*supervise the wards and branches of the Church*], and **study and learn, and become acquainted with all good books, and with languages, tongues, and people**.

16 And **this shall be your business and mission in all your lives, to preside in council, and set in order all the affairs of this church and kingdom**.

Next, these brethren are reminded that they are still subject to temptation and must humbly strive to live the gospel themselves. Position does not give privilege as far as yielding to sin and temptation are concerned.

17 **Be not ashamed** [*don't be embarrassed to do what is right*], **neither confounded** [*stopped from performing your duties*]; **but be admonished** [*accept correction*] **in all your high-mindedness and**

pride, for it bringeth a snare upon your souls.

18 Set in order your houses; keep slothfulness and uncleanness far from you.

Unfortunately, both Sidney Rigdon and Frederick G. Williams eventually apostatized and left the Church, both having been trapped in the "snare" of pride and high-mindedness (verse 17, above).

Next, in verses 19–23, the Prophet is given specific instructions that he is to carry out. First, a home is to be provided for President Williams and his family.

19 Now, verily I say unto you, let there be a place provided, as soon as it is possible, for the family of thy counselor and scribe, even Frederick G. Williams.

20 And let mine aged servant, Joseph Smith, Sen. [sixty-one years old at this time], continue with his family upon the place where he now lives; and let it not be sold until the mouth of the Lord shall name.

21 And let my counselor, even Sidney Rigdon, remain where he now resides until the mouth of the Lord shall name.

22 And let the bishop [Newel K. Whitney] search diligently to obtain an agent [to assist with managing the temporal affairs and needs of the Church in Ohio and the surrounding areas], and let him be a man who has got riches in store [he needs to be a man with considerable wealth available to him]— a man of God, and of strong faith—

23 That thereby he may be enabled to discharge [pay] every debt; that the storehouse of the Lord [the bishop's storehouse] may not be brought into disrepute before the eyes of the people.

24 Search diligently, pray always, and be believing, and all things shall work together for your good, if ye walk uprightly and remember the covenant [to live the law of consecration] wherewith ye have covenanted one with another.

In order to understand verse 25, next, we must know the context. Otherwise, we would think that the Lord is telling us to limit our families to very few children. First, the verse:

25 Let your families be small, especially mine aged servant Joseph Smith's, Sen., as pertaining to those who do not belong to your families;

The last phrase of verse 25, above, is a clue as to the meaning of "let your families be small." Because of the large numbers of Saints gathering in the Kirtland area at this time in history, it was common for a number of families to move in temporarily with other families, thus overloading the capability of the host families to care for all under their roof.

The generosity of the Prophet's father was apparently taking a heavy toll on him and his family, therefore, he was counseled to place tighter limits on the number of people he invited to live with him and his family.

Also, as we look at verse 26, next, we see a hint that some of the "guests" may have been taking advantage of the situation.

26 That those things that are provided for you, to bring to pass my work, be not taken from you and given to those that are not worthy—

27 And thereby you be hindered in accomplishing those things which I have commanded you.

Specific instructions are given to the Prophet in verses 28–31 regarding Sister Vienna Jaques. She had recently traveled alone from Boston to Kirtland at the age of forty-three after having glanced through the Book of Mormon and becoming convinced by a vision that it was worth reading.

After meeting the Prophet and being taught further by him, she was baptized. She returned to Boston, converted many family members, and returned to Kirtland with her valuables, which included $1,400 in savings that she consecrated to the Church on March 8, 1833, the day of this revelation to the Prophet.

By the way, she remained faithful despite going through all the Missouri persecutions of the Saints. At age sixty, she drove her own team and wagon across the plains, arriving in the Salt Lake Valley on October 2, 1847. She died at age ninety-six in her own home in Salt Lake City.

28 And again, verily I say unto you, it is my will that my handmaid Vienna Jaques should receive money to bear her expenses, and go up unto the land of Zion [*she is to be given sufficient money back from what she consecrated to the Church to enable her to go to Jackson County, Missouri, and settle with the Saints there*];

29 And the residue of the money [*the remainder of the $1,400 plus, which she consecrated to the Church in Kirtland*] **may be consecrated unto me, and she be rewarded in mine own due time.**

30 Verily I say unto you, that it is

meet in mine eyes [*it is the Lord's will*] **that she should go up unto the land of Zion, and receive an inheritance from the hand of the bishop** [*she is to be given land and supplies by Bishop Partridge when she arrives in Zion*];

31 **That she may settle down in peace inasmuch as she is faithful, and not be idle** [*a major principle in living the law of consecration*] **in her days from thenceforth**.

Verses 32–33 hint that some members in Missouri were complaining and grumbling because Joseph Smith was still living in Kirtland, and they felt that he was ignoring them by not coming to Missouri to live and help build up Zion.

32 And behold, verily I say unto you, that ye shall **write this commandment, and say unto your brethren in Zion, in love greeting** [*in kindness and gentleness*], **that I have called you also to preside over Zion in mine own due time** [*in other words, tell the brethren in Zion that I will have you come to Missouri when the time is right*].

33 Therefore, **let them cease wearying me concerning this matter**.

Verse 34, next, informs us that the attitude on the part of many in

Missouri is improving. Still, verse 35 tells us of specific concerns dealing with William E. McLellin (see sections 66 and 67), Sidney Gilbert (the bishop's agent and assistant in Zion), and Bishop Edward Partridge (who was told in D&C 85:8 that he must stop trying to "steady the ark" by refusing to issue written deeds to those living the law of consecration—D&C 51:4–5—among other things).

34 Behold, I say unto you [*Joseph Smith*] that **your brethren in Zion begin to repent, and the angels rejoice over them**.

35 **Nevertheless, I am not well pleased with many things**; and **I am not well pleased with my servant William E. McLellin**, neither with my servant **Sidney Gilbert**; and **the bishop** [*Edward Partridge*] **also**, and **others have many things to repent of**.

36 But verily I say unto you, that **I, the Lord, will contend** [*will continue to work*] **with Zion, and plead with her strong ones** [*the local leaders of the Church in Missouri at this time*], **and chasten her until she overcomes and is clean before me**.

37 For **she shall not be removed out of her place** [*the city of Zion, New Jerusalem, and the temple will yet be built, as prophesied, in*

Independence, Missouri; see D&C 84:3–5]. **I, the Lord, have spoken it. Amen.**

SECTION 91

Background

This revelation was given through the Prophet Joseph Smith on March 9, 1833, in Kirtland, Ohio.

As you can see in the heading to section 91 in your Doctrine and Covenants, the Prophet was working on the inspired translation of the Bible, more particularly on the revising and correcting of the Old Testament at this time. The question came up as to whether or not he should translate the Apocrypha.

The Old Testament Apocrypha consists of fifteen ancient texts that were not included in the Hebrew Bible but that were included in the Greek Old Testament referred to as the Septuagint. They were considered scripture by some but not by others.

They ultimately became part of the Christian Bible until Martin Luther came along and placed them in a different section in the Bible referred to as the "Apocrypha." They are of questionable value and validity and are contained in some editions of the Bible but not in others today. The King James version of the Bible used by Joseph Smith in his inspired translation of the

Bible contained the Apocrypha, located between the Old Testament and the New Testament. Thus, his question to the Lord as to whether or not he should translate it.

They are books in addition to the thirty-nine books of the Old Testament. These apocryphal books are

1. The First Book of Esdras
2. The Second Book of Esdras
3. Tobit
4. Judith
5. The Rest of the Chapters of the Book of Esther
6. The Wisdom of Solomon
7. Ecclesiasticus or the Wisdom of Jesus son of Sirach
8. Baruch
9. A Letter of Jeremiah
10. The Song of the Three
11. Daniel and Susanna
12. Daniel, Bel, and the Snake
13. The Prayer of Manasseh
14. The First Book of the Maccabees
15. The Second Book of the Maccabees

The Lord's answer is found next in section 91.

1 VERILY, thus saith the Lord unto you concerning the Apocrypha—**There are many things contained therein that are true, and it is mostly translated correctly**;

2 **There are many things contained therein that are not true**, which are interpolations by the hands of men.

3 Verily, I say unto you, that **it is not needful that the Apocrypha should be translated** [*in other words, you don't need to include the Apocrypha in your JST work on the Bible*].

4 Therefore, **whoso readeth it, let him understand, for the Spirit manifesteth truth**;

5 And **whoso is enlightened by the Spirit shall obtain benefit therefrom**;

6 And **whoso receiveth not by the Spirit, cannot be benefited. Therefore it is not needful that it should be translated**. Amen.

SECTION 92

Background

This revelation was given to the Prophet Joseph Smith on March 15, 1833, in Kirtland, Ohio. It was given to Frederick G. Williams regarding his duties in the United Firm in Kirtland (see heading to section 92 in the 2013 edition of the Doctrine and Covenants).

Frederick G. Williams had recently been called to be a counselor in the First Presidency, to serve with Joseph Smith and Sidney Rigdon (see D&C 81:1).

Although this revelation consists of just two verses, it contains at least two messages that apply to all of us. They are that each of us should "be a lively member" in the Church (verse 2), and that by keeping the commandments we have been given, we qualify for eternal blessings (verse 2).

1 VERILY, thus saith the Lord, **I give unto the united order** [*the formal organization of those in the Ohio area who were living the law of consecration*], organized agreeable to the commandment previously given, **a revelation and commandment concerning my servant Frederick G. Williams, that ye shall receive him into the order** [*the United Firm. See background notes for section 82 in this study guide*]. **What I say unto one I say unto all.**

Verse 2 is specifically addressed to President Williams, recently appointed as a counselor in the First Presidency.

2 And again, I say unto you my

servant Frederick G. Williams, **you shall be a lively member** in this order; and **inasmuch as you are faithful in keeping all former commandments you shall be blessed forever.** Amen.

SECTION 93

Background

This revelation was given through the Prophet Joseph Smith in Kirtland, Ohio, on May 6, 1833. It is a powerful revelation about our potential to become like our Heavenly Father. It is a "high mountain" revelation in the sense that it takes us up into a "high mountain," as it were (compare to Nephi's experience in 1 Nephi 11:1), and lets us see things as the Lord does, thus giving us knowledge and perspective that enable us to make better decisions and draw closer to the Lord in our daily living, especially when we are faced with opposition. (See notes about "high mountain experiences" in the background for section 88.)

At this time, opposition to the Church and the faithful members was mounting, both in Missouri and in Kirtland. This revelation provided additional strength and perspective for enduring the increasing opposition from within and from outside the Church.

In early April, a mob of about three hundred men had gathered in Missouri and attempted to organize to drive the Saints from their land. Also, some members of the Church had apostatized in both Ohio and Missouri and were a source of persecution against the Saints.

The Prophet provided information about the mob in Missouri as follows:

"In the month of April, the first regular mob rushed together, in Independence, to consult upon a plan, for the removal, or immediate destruction, of the Church in Jackson county. The number of the mob was about three hundred. A few of the first Elders met in secret, and prayed to Him who said to the wind, 'Be still,' to frustrate them in their wicked designs. The mob, therefore, after spending the day in a fruitless endeavor to unite upon a general scheme for 'moving the Mormons out of their diggings' (as they asserted), became a little the worse for liquor and broke up in a regular Missouri 'row,' showing a determined resolution that every man would 'carry his own head'" (*History of the Church*, 1:342).

In this revelation, we will be given many doctrines and insights that can help us maintain a steady course on the covenant path toward exaltation.

First, in verses 1–5, the Savior bears witness of His existence, and the fact that the faithful can know, without doubt, that He exists.

1 VERILY, thus saith the Lord: It shall come to pass that **every soul who forsaketh his sins** and **cometh unto me**, and **calleth on my name** [*both by praying and by making covenants in the name of Jesus Christ and keeping them*], and **obeyeth my voice,** and **keepeth my commandments, shall see my face and know that I am**;

Regarding the privilege of literally seeing the Savior, D&C 88:68 reminds us that it will be "in his own time, and in his own way, and according to his own will." Thus, it could be during this life or in the next.

The most powerful witness of all that the Savior exists comes not by literally seeing Him but rather through the witness of the Holy Ghost. Thus, all who fulfill the requirements spelled out in verse 1, above, can "see" the Savior and "know" now by the power of the Holy Ghost that He is.

Next, the Master reminds us that everyone born on earth is blessed with a conscience and has the Light of Christ to guide and direct them in every aspect of living. You may wish to refer back to D&C 88:6–13 to gain further insights as to the powerful influence of the Light of Christ. As you will see, it is much more than a conscience.

Doctrine, verse 2

Everyone has a conscience plus much more because of the Light of Christ.

2 And that **I am the true light that lighteth every man that cometh into the world**;

Next, the Savior teaches us that He and His Father work together in perfect harmony with each other.

3 And that **I am in the Father, and the Father in me, and the Father and I are one**—

We see much of symbolism, next, as Jesus explains how He is both the "Father" and the "Son." You may wish to read Mosiah 15:1–5 before going on. In effect, Jesus is the "Father" of our salvation. He is the "Father" of our being "born again." We are His "children" symbolically (see Mosiah 5:7) because He is the "Father of our salvation," because He carried out the Atonement in our behalf. He is the Father of our salvation in the same sense that George Washington is the "father" of our country.

He is the "Son" because He is literally the Son of God the Father.

4 **The Father** [*of our salvation*] **because he** [*Heavenly Father*] **gave me of his fulness** [*because the Father gave Him all power and authority to be our Redeemer*], and **the Son**

because I was in the world and made flesh my tabernacle, and dwelt among the sons of men.

Next, in verse 5, Jesus teaches, in effect, that He came on earth to live in order to teach about His Father, and that the Father's love and mercy are plainly shown by the plan of salvation.

5 **I was in the world** [*Jesus came to earth to perform His mortal mission*] **and received of my Father** [*received all that was needed from the Father in order to carry out His mission*]**, and the works of him** [*the Father*] **were plainly manifest**.

John the Baptist kept a record, but we do not have it in the Bible. Someday we will get it (see verses 6 and 18). In the meantime, verses 6–18, next, give us excerpts from his record. This is an example of the restoration of an ancient record through pure revelation and is similar to the Book of Moses in the Pearl of Great Price.

As we study these verses, you will get a better feeling for the greatness of John the Baptist. In fact, Jesus said, "Among them that are born of women there hath not risen a greater than John the Baptist" (Matthew 11:11). It is hoped that you will feel the greatness of his testimony by the power of the Holy Ghost.

6 And **John** [*the Baptist*] **saw and bore record of the fulness of my glory**, and the fulness of John's record [*the complete record kept by John the Baptist*] is hereafter to be revealed.

7 And **he bore record, saying: I saw his** [*Christ's*] **glory, that he was in the beginning, before the world was**;

8 Therefore, **in the beginning the Word** [*Jesus Christ*] **was**, for **he was the Word, even the messenger of salvation**—

9 **The light and the Redeemer of the world; the Spirit of truth**, who came into the world, because **the world was made by him, and in him was the life of men and the light of men**.

10 **The worlds** [*worlds without number—compare with Moses 1:33*] **were made by him; men were made by him; all things were made by him, and through him, and of him**.

11 And **I, John, bear record that I beheld his glory, as the glory of the Only Begotten of the Father, full of grace and truth, even the Spirit of truth, which came and dwelt in the flesh, and dwelt among us**.

Next, in verses 12–13, John the Baptist teaches us, in effect, that

Jesus began with the veil and learned and grew as part of His mortal experience.

12 And I, John, saw that he received not of the fulness at the first, but received grace for grace;

13 And he received not of the fulness at first, but continued from grace to grace, until he received a fulness;

Apostle James E. Talmage taught that Jesus had the veil over the memory of His premortal life when He began His mortal life on earth, just as we do. He said:

"Over His mind had fallen the veil of forgetfulness common to all who are born to earth, by which the remembrance of primeval existence is shut off. The Child grew, and with growth there came to Him expansion of mind, development of faculties, and progression in power and understanding. His advancement was from one grace to another, not from gracelessness to grace; from good to greater good, not from evil to good, from favor with God to greater favor, not from estrangement because of sin to reconciliation through repentance and propitiation" (*Jesus the Christ*, 111).

On this same subject, President Lorenzo Snow taught:

"When Jesus lay in the manger, a helpless infant, He knew not that He was the Son of God, and that formerly He created the earth. When the edict of Herod was issued, He knew nothing of it; He had not power to save Himself; and His father and mother had to take Him and fly into Egypt to preserve Him from the effects of that edict. Well, He grew up to manhood, and during His progress it was revealed unto Him who He was, and for what purpose He was in the world. The glory and power He possessed before He came into the world was made known unto Him" (In Conference Report, April 1901, 3.)

14 And thus he was called the Son of God, because he received not of the fulness at the first.

Next, in verse 15, John the Baptist tells us about the marvelous witness given to him at the time he baptized the Savior.

15 And I, John, bear record, and lo, the heavens were opened, and the Holy Ghost descended upon him in the form of a dove, and sat upon him, and there came a voice out of heaven saying: This is my beloved Son.

We learn from the teachings of Joseph Smith that the phrase "in the form of a dove," as given in verse 15, above, is symbolic rather than literal. The dove represented the fact that the Holy Ghost was present and came upon the Savior. The

Prophet Joseph Smith, speaking of John the Baptist, taught (**bold** added for emphasis):

"He was entrusted with the important mission, and it was required at his hands, to baptize the Son of Man. Whoever had the honor of doing that? Whoever had so great a privilege and glory? Whoever led the Son of God into the waters of baptism, and had the privilege of **beholding the Holy Ghost descend in the form of a dove, or rather in the *sign* of the dove**, in witness of that administration? The sign of the dove was instituted before the creation of the world, a witness for the Holy Ghost, and the devil cannot come in the sign of a dove. **The Holy Ghost is a personage, and is in the form of a personage. It does not confine itself to the *form* of the dove, but in *sign* of the dove. The Holy Ghost cannot be transformed into a dove**; but the sign of a dove was given to John to signify the truth of the deed, as the dove is an emblem or token of truth and innocence (*Teachings of the Prophet Joseph Smith*, 275–76).

16 And **I, John, bear record that he received a fulness of the glory of the Father;**

17 And **he received all power, both in heaven and on earth, and the glory of the Father was with him**, for he dwelt in him.

In verse 18, next, the Savior informs us that we will yet be given the full record kept by John the Baptist if we are faithful.

18 And **it shall come to pass, that if you are faithful you shall receive the fulness of the record of John.**

Perhaps you have noticed that the majority of those in the world who believe in God do not know what they worship. Consequently, they do not really know how to worship, nor do they realize that they can become like God.

Next, in verse 19, the Savior tells us why He revealed John the Baptist's teachings and testimony to us (given above), as well as why He gives us the teachings in verses 20–39, next.

19 **I give unto you these sayings that you may understand and know how to worship**, and **know what you worship, that you may come unto the Father in my name, and in due time receive of his fulness** [*become like the Father—in other words, receive exaltation in celestial glory*].

20 For **if you keep my commandments you shall receive of his fulness** [*will be exalted*], **and be glorified in me as I am in the Father**; therefore, I say unto you, **you shall receive grace for grace**

[this will come step by step, with the help (the grace) of God].

21 And now, verily I say unto you, **I was in the beginning with the Father, and am the Firstborn** *[Jesus is the firstborn of all the Father's spirit children; see Colossians 1:13–15]*;

22 And **all those who are begotten through me** *[who are "born again" through the Atonement of Christ]* **are partakers of the glory of the same** *[receive exaltation]*, **and are the church of the Firstborn** *[another term for exaltation; see D&C 76:58, 94]*.

23 **Ye were also in the beginning with the Father;** that which is Spirit, even the Spirit of truth *[we will do more with this when we get to verse 29]*;

> Next, the Savior defines pure truth.

24 And **truth is knowledge of things as they are, and as they were, and as they are to come;**

25 And **whatsoever is more or less than this is the spirit of that wicked one** *[the devil]* **who was a liar from the beginning.**

26 **The Spirit of truth is of God. I am the Spirit of truth** *[compare with D&C 88:6–13]*, and

John bore record of me, saying: He received a fulness of truth, yea, even of all truth;

27 And **no man receiveth a fulness** *[no one receives all the Father has to give—exaltation]* **unless he keepeth his commandments.**

> Next, in verses 28–29, the Savior teaches us that gaining exaltation is a step-by-step process that began in our premortal existence. As we obeyed the commandments of God back then, and as we obey them now, we gradually and definitely progress toward exaltation.
>
> In fact, in the context of this lesson from the Master Teacher, "intelligence" will be defined as the behavior of forsaking "that evil one" (verse 37)—in other words, avoiding evil and following the light brought by the gospel of Jesus Christ.

28 **He that keepeth his commandments receiveth truth and light, until he is glorified in truth and knoweth all things** *[has become a god]*.

29 **Man was also in the beginning with God. Intelligence, or the light of truth, was not created or made, neither indeed can be.**

> Verse 29, above, is an important doctrine of the plan of salvation. It teaches us that we have always

existed. The basic part of us, intelligence, "was not created or made." The Prophet Joseph Smith explained this. He said:

"Is it logical to say that the intelligence of spirits is immortal, and yet that it has a beginning? The intelligence of spirits had no beginning, neither will it have an end" (*History of the Church*, 6:311).

30 **All truth is independent in that sphere in which God has placed it, to act for itself, as all intelligence also** [*in other words, we had agency in premortality also; see D&C 29:36*]; otherwise there is no existence.

31 Behold, **here is the agency of man**, and **here is the condemnation of man** [*here is how man gets himself in trouble*]; because **that** [*the truths of the gospel*] **which was from the beginning is plainly manifest unto them, and they receive not the light** [*they reject the gospel*].

32 And **every man whose spirit receiveth not the light is under condemnation** [*is accountable and is thus being slowed or stopped in his progress*].

Doctrine, verses 33–34

We cannot have the highest satisfaction and joy until our spirit and body are permanently joined in exaltation.

33 For man is spirit. The elements are eternal, and **spirit and element, inseparably connected, receive a fulness of joy** [*the only way to receive the highest joy and happiness—in other words, the "fulness" (verse 27) of the Father—is to be resurrected into a celestial body (D&C 88:28–29) and to enter into exaltation*];

34 And **when separated** [*without resurrection*], **man cannot receive a fulness of joy.**

Next, we are reminded that we are a "temple" in which the Spirit of God can reside. We must keep our "temple" clean.

35 **The elements are the tabernacle of God** [*the Father has a resurrected body of "flesh and bones, as tangible as man's"; see D&C 130:22*]; yea, **man is the tabernacle of God, even temples**; and **whatsoever temple is defiled, God shall destroy that temple.**

Verses 36 and 37, next, go together. They teach that true "intelligence" is the behavior of forsaking evil. We are empowered to forsake evil by the "light and truth" that we accept from God. (In this context, "intelligence" has nothing to do with IQ.)

Doctrine, verses 36–37

True intelligence, in the eternal, spiritual sense, is the behavior of forsaking evil.

36 **The glory of God is intelligence**, or, **in other words, light and truth.**

37 **Light and truth forsake that evil one** [*Satan and his temptations*].

> As you will see, when we get to verse 39, the devil's major goal and focus is to take "light and truth" away from us.
>
> But first there are important and interesting doctrines taught in verse 38, next.

38 **Every spirit of man was innocent in the beginning** [*we all started out innocent as spirits in premortality*]; and God having redeemed man from the fall, **men became again, in their infant state, innocent before God** [*we all became innocent again when we were born into mortality*].

> As we study the implications of what is taught in verse 38, above, we conclude that since we were "innocent" when we were born as spirit children of Heavenly Parents (we know we have "parents" in heaven because it is so stated in "The Family: A Proclamation to the World"; see *Ensign* or *Liahona*,

Nov. 2010, 129), and since we became "again" innocent upon mortal birth, then we must not have remained "innocent" throughout our premortal education as spirits.

That this was the case is evident from the War in Heaven. This, then, brings up the question as to whether we could sin, repent, be forgiven and thus progress during our premortal probation. In other words, did the Atonement of Christ work for us there? The answer is "yes." We will provide two quotes in support of this answer.

The first quote is from the 1979 New Testament student manual, *The Life and Teachings of Jesus and His Apostles*, used by the institutes of religion of the Church. We read (**bold** added for emphasis):

"Some accounts that we have of the premortal life teach that we 'were on the same standing' (Alma 13:5), and that we were 'innocent' in the beginning (D&C 93:38). **We were given laws and agency, and commandments to have faith and repent from the wrongs that we could do there. '. . . Man could and did in many instances, sin before he was born.'** (Smith, *The Way to Perfection,* 44.)

"'God gave his children their agency even in the spirit world, by which the individual spirits had the privilege, just as men have here, of choosing the good and rejecting the evil, or partaking of the evil to suffer the consequences of their sins. . . . Some even there were more faithful than others in keeping the commandments of the Lord. . . .

"'The spirits of men . . . had an equal start, and we know they were all innocent in the beginning; but the right of free agency which was given to them enabled some to outstrip others, and thus, through the eons of immortal existence, to become more intelligent, more faithful, for they were free to act for themselves, to think for themselves, to receive the truth or rebel against it.' (Smith, *Doctrines of Salvation,* 1:58–59.)" (Quoted in *Life and Teachings of Jesus and His Apostles,* 336.)

The second quote is from Elder Jeffrey R. Holland. He said:

"We could remember that even in the Grand Council of Heaven [in the premortal realm] He loved us and was wonderfully strong, that we triumphed even there by the power of Christ and our faith in the blood of the Lamb" ("'This Do in Remembrance of Me,'" *Ensign,* November 1995, 68).

Revelation 12:11 teaches the same doctrine.

Revelation 12:11

11 And **they** [*premortal spirits*] **overcame him** [*the devil*] **by**

the blood of the Lamb [*the Atonement of Christ*], **and by the** word of their testimony; **and they** [*righteous mortals who applied the Atonement to their lives on earth*] **loved not their lives unto the death.**

Verse 39, next, summarizes the efforts of the adversary to take light and truth—in other words, "intelligence" (verses 36–37, above), away from us.

39 And **that wicked one** [*Satan*] cometh and **taketh away light and truth, through disobedience, from the children of men** [*people*]**, and because of the tradition of their fathers.**

There is a transition now, and in verses 40–53, the Savior gives instructions to the Prophet and others. He reproves some of the leaders for not taking proper care in teaching their children and setting their own houses in order. There is good counsel for all parents here.

40 But **I have commanded you to bring up your children in light and truth.**

41 **But verily I say unto you, my servant Frederick G. Williams** [*a counselor to the Prophet in the First Presidency*]**, you have continued under this condemnation;**

42 **You have not taught your children light and truth, according to the commandments;** and that wicked one hath power, as yet, over you, and this is the cause of your affliction.

43 And now a commandment I give unto you—**if you will be delivered you shall set in order your own house**, for there are many things that are not right in your house.

44 Verily, **I say unto my servant Sidney Rigdon, that in some things he hath not kept the commandments concerning his children**; therefore, **first set in order thy house**.

45 Verily, I say unto my servant Joseph Smith, Jun., or in other words, **I will call you friends, for you are my friends**, and **ye shall have an inheritance with me** [*this is very encouraging and gives hope during this time of being called to repentance*]—

46 I called you servants for the world's sake, and **ye are their servants for my sake**—

47 **And now, verily I say unto Joseph Smith, Jun.—You have not kept the commandments, and must needs stand rebuked before the Lord**;

48 **Your family must needs repent and forsake some things, and give more earnest heed unto your sayings**, or be removed out of their place.

As mentioned above, the advice given to specific brethren above can apply to all of us.

49 **What I say unto one I say unto all; pray always lest that wicked one have power in you, and remove you out of your place** [*in the kingdom of God*].

50 My servant **Newel K. Whitney** [*the bishop in Kirtland*] also, a bishop of my church, **hath need to be chastened, and set in order his family, and see that they are more diligent and concerned at home, and pray always**, or they shall be removed out of their place.

51 Now, I say unto you, **my friends, let my servant Sidney Rigdon go on his journey**, and make haste, and also proclaim the acceptable year of the Lord [*a phrase meaning to preach the gospel of Christ*], and the gospel of salvation, as I shall give him utterance; **and by your prayer of faith with one consent I will uphold him.**

Did you notice at the end of verse 51, above, that the Lord says that our prayers in behalf of others have an effect on the blessings they receive?

Sidney Rigdon had been the main scribe, assisting the Prophet with the translation of the Bible (the JST). With him gone on a preaching journey, Frederick G. Williams was to take over as scribe. You can see from verses 52–53, next, that the Lord is anxious for them to continue with the translation of the Bible and with the School of the Prophets (see D&C 88:118–41).

52 And **let my servants Joseph Smith, Jun., and Frederick G. Williams make haste also** [*in the work of translating the Bible*]**,** and it shall be given them even according to the prayer of faith; and inasmuch as you keep my sayings you shall not be confounded in this world, nor in the world to come.

53 And, verily I say unto you, that it is my will that you should **hasten to translate my scriptures** [*The JST*]**, and to obtain a knowledge of history, and of countries, and of kingdoms, of laws of God and man** [*in the school of the prophets*]**, and all this for the salvation of Zion.** Amen.

The Joseph Smith Papers, Documents, Volume 3: February 1833–March 1834, 166, tells us that they diligently finished the translation of the Bible (the JST) on July 2, 1833, a short two months after verses 52 and 53, above, were given them by the Lord.

Sources

Anderson, Richard Lloyd. *Investigating the Book of Mormon Witnesses.* Salt Lake City: Deseret Book, 1981.

Barrett, Ivan J. *Joseph Smith and the Restoration.* Provo, UT: Brigham Young University, 1982.

Black, Susan Easton. *Who's Who in the Doctrine and Covenants.* Salt Lake City: Bookcraft, 1997.

Book of Mormon Student Manual. Salt Lake City: The Church of Jesus Christ of Latter-day Saints (Institutes of Religion), 1982.

Cannon, George Q. *Life of Joseph Smith the Prophet.* Good Press, 1888.

————. *Life of Joseph Smith the Prophet.* Salt Lake City: Deseret News Press, 1907.

Church History in the Fulness of Times. Salt Lake City: The Church of Jesus Christ of Latter-day Saints (Institutes of Religion), 1989, 2003.

Clark, James R. (Compiler.) *Messages of the First Presidency of The Church of Jesus Christ of Latter-day Saints.* 6 vols. Salt Lake City: Bookcraft, 1965–75.

Conference Reports of The Church of Jesus Christ of Latter-day Saints. Salt Lake City: The Church of Jesus Christ of Latter-day Saints, 1898 to the present.

Cowley, Matthias F. *Wilford Woodruff: History of His Life and Labors.* 2d ed. Salt Lake City: Bookcraft, 1964.

Doctrine and Covenants Student Manual. Salt Lake City: The Church of Jesus Christ of Latter-day Saints (Institutes of Religion), 1981, 2018.

Doctrines of the Gospel Student Manual. Salt Lake City: The Church of Jesus Christ of Latter-day Saints (Institutes of Religion), 1981.

Doxey, Roy W. (Compiler.) *Latter-day Prophets and the Doctrine and Covenants.* Salt Lake City: Deseret Book, 1978.

"The Family: A Proclamation to the World." *Ensign or Liahona,* Nov. 2010, 129.

Hancock, Levi Ward. Autobiography. Typescript. L. Tom Perry Special Collections, Harold B. Lee Library, Brigham Young University, Provo, Utah.

Hinckley, Bryant S. *Sermons and Missionary Services of Melvin J. Ballard.* Salt Lake City: Deseret Book, 1949.

Joseph Smith Papers, The. Salt Lake City: Church Historian's Press. See also josephsmithpapers.org. (These books consist of several volumes now [2020] and will consist of more than 30 volumes when they are complete.)

Journal of Discourses. 26 vols. London: Latter-day Saints' Book Depot, 1854–86.

Kimball, Spencer W. *The Teachings of Spencer W. Kimball.* Edited by Edward L. Kimball. Salt Lake City: Bookcraft, 1982.

Lang, W. *History of Seneca County [Ohio], from the Close of the Revolutionary War to July, 1880.* Woburn, MA: Unigraphic, 1973.

Latter-day Saints' Millennial Star, The. Manchester, Liverpool, and London, England: The Church of Jesus Christ of Latter-day Saints, 1840–1970.

Life and Teachings of Jesus and His Apostles: New Testament Student Manual, The. Salt Lake City: The Church of Jesus Christ of Latter-day Saints, 1979.

Ludlow, Daniel H. *Encyclopedia of Mormonism.* Edited by Daniel H. Ludlow. 5 vols. New York: Macmillan, 1992.

Lundwall, N. B. *Temples of the Most High.* Salt Lake City: Bookcraft, 1971.

Matthews, Robert J. *A Plainer Translation: Joseph Smith's Translation of the Bible—A History and Commentary.* Provo, Utah: Brigham Young University Press, 1975.

McConkie, Bruce R. *Doctrinal New Testament Commentary.* 3 vols. Salt Lake City: Bookcraft, 1965–73.

————. *The Millennial Messiah: The Second Coming of the Son of Man.* Salt Lake City: Deseret Book, 1982.

————. *Mormon Doctrine.* 2d ed. Salt Lake City: Bookcraft, 1966.

————. *The Mortal Messiah: From Bethlehem to Calgary.* 4 vols. Salt Lake City: Deseret Book, 1979–81.

————. *The Promised Messiah: The First Coming of Christ.* Salt Lake City: Deseret Book, 1978.

McGavin, Cecil E. *Historical Background of the Doctrine and Covenants.* Salt Lake City: Literary Licensing, 2011.

Otten, L. G. *Historical Background and Setting for each section of the Doctrine and Covenants.* Privately published, 1970.

Pratt, Parley P. *Autobiography of Parley P. Pratt.* Salt Lake City: Deseret Book, 1938–1985.

Proctor, Scott and Maurine. *The Revised and Enhanced History of Joseph Smith by His Mother.* Salt Lake City: Bookcraft, 1996.

Revelations in Context. Edited by Matthew McBride and James Goldberg (2016). See history.lds.org.

Roberts, B. H. *A Comprehensive History of The Church of Jesus Christ of Latter-day Saints, Century One.* 6 vols. Salt Lake City: Deseret Press, 1930.

Smith, Hyrum M. and Janne M. Sjodahl. *Doctrine and Covenants Commentary.* Salt Lake City: Deseret Book, 1951.

Smith, Joseph. *History of The Church of Jesus Christ of Latter-day Saints.* Edited by B. H. Roberts. 2d ed. rev., 7 vols. Salt Lake City: The Church of Jesus Christ of Latter-day Saints, 1932–51.

————. *Teachings of the Prophet Joseph Smith.* Selected by Joseph Fielding Smith. Salt Lake City: Deseret Book, 1976.

Smith, Joseph F. *Gospel Doctrine.* Salt Lake City: Deseret Book, 1939.

Smith, Joseph Fielding. *Answers to Gospel Questions.* Compiled by Joseph Fielding Smith Jr. 5 vols. Salt Lake City: Deseret Book, 1957–66.

————. *Church History and Modern Revelation—A Course Study for Melchizedek Priesthood Quorums.* Salt Lake City: The Council of the Twelve Apostles of The Church of Jesus Christ of Latter-day Saints, 1946.

————. *Doctrines of Salvation.* Compiled by Bruce R. McConkie. 3 vols. Salt Lake City: Bookcraft, 1954–56.

————. *Way to Perfection.* Salt Lake City: Deseret Book, 1975.

Smith, Lucy Mack. *History of Joseph Smith by His Mother, Lucy Mack Smith.* Salt Lake City: Bookcraft, 1958.

Talmage, James E. *The Articles of Faith.* Salt Lake City: Deseret Book, 1984.

Talmage, James E. *Jesus the Christ.* Salt Lake City: Deseret Book, 1977.

Teachings of Presidents of the Church—Wilford Woodruff. Salt Lake City: The Church of Jesus Christ of Latter-day Saints, 2004.

————. *Jesus the Christ.* Salt Lake City: Deseret Book, 1977.

Times and Seasons. Commerce (later Nauvoo), Illinois, 1839–46.

Widtsoe, John A. *Evidences and Reconciliations.* Salt Lake City: Bookcraft, 1943.

————. *The Message of the Doctrine and Covenants.* Salt Lake City: Bookcraft, 1978.

————. *The Word of Wisdom: A Modern Interpretation.* Salt Lake City: Deseret Book, 1938.

Young, Brigham. *Discourses of Brigham Young.* Selected by John A. Widtsoe. Salt Lake City: Deseret Book, 1954.

Additional sources for the notes given in this work are as follows:

- The Standard Works of The Church of Jesus Christ of Latter-day Saints.
- Footnotes in the Latter-day Saint version of the King James Bible.
- The Joseph Smith Translation of the Bible.

- The Bible Dictionary in the back of the Latter-day Saint version of the King James Bible.

- Various dictionaries.

- Various student manuals provided for our institutes of religion.

- Other sources as noted in the text.

ABOUT THE AUTHOR

David J. Ridges was raised in southeastern Nevada until his family moved to North Salt Lake City, Utah, when he was in fifth grade. He is the second of eight children.

Brother Ridges graduated from Bountiful High, served a two-and-a-half-year German-speaking mission to Austria, attended the University of Utah and BYU, and then graduated from BYU with a major in German and a physics minor. He later received a master's degree in educational psychology with a Church History minor from BYU.

He taught seminary and institute of religion as his chosen career for thirty-five years. He taught BYU Campus Education Week, Especially for Youth, Adult Religion, and Know Your Religion classes for over twenty-five years.

Brother Ridges has served as a Sunday School and seminary curriculum writer. He has had many callings, including Gospel Doctrine teacher, bishop, stake president, and patriarch. He and Sister Ridges have served two full-time, eighteen-month CES missions. He has written over forty books, which include several study guides for the standard works, Isaiah, Revelation, and many doctrinal publications on gospel topics such as the signs of the times, plan of salvation, and temples.

Brother and Sister Ridges met at the University of Utah. They were married in the Salt Lake Temple, are the parents of six children, and have sixteen grandchildren and one great-granddaughter so far. They make their home in Springville, Utah.

Scan to visit

www.davidjridges.com

NOTES

NOTES

NOTES

NOTES

NOTES

NOTES

YOUR STUDY OF
THE

DOCTRINE AND COVENANTS MADE EASIER

PART 1
SECTION 1 THROUGH SECTION 42

SECOND EDITION

YOUR STUDY OF
THE

DOCTRINE AND
COVENANTS
MADE EASIER

PART 1
SECTION 1 THROUGH SECTION 42

SECOND EDITION

BONUS SECTION

A BRIEF CHRONOLOGY
OF MAJOR CHARACTERS
IN EARLY CHURCH HISTORY

DAVID J. RIDGES

CFI, AN IMPRINT OF

CEDAR FORT
Publishing & Media

SPRINGVILLE, UTAH

ISBN 13: 978-1-4621-3895-1

Published by CFI, an imprint of Cedar Fort, Inc.
2373 W. 700 S., Springville, UT, 84663
Distributed by Cedar Fort, Inc., www.cedarfort.com

Library of Congress Control Number: 2020945612

Cover design by Shawnda T. Craig
Cover design © 2020 Cedar Fort, Inc.

Printed in the United States of America

10 9 8 7 6 5 4 3 2 1

Printed on acid-free paper

DEDICATION

To my wife, Janette, who
is my greatest blessing.

CONTENTS

SECTIONS

BONUS SECTION

PREFACE

The Doctrine and Covenants is the Savior's book to us in our day. In it, He personally teaches us the "doctrines" and "covenants" necessary to live a righteous, rewarding life, and to successfully walk along the covenant path toward eventual exaltation in the highest degree of glory in the celestial kingdom. In the October 1986 general conference of the Church, in reference to the importance of understanding the doctrines of the gospel, Elder Boyd K. Packer said:

> True doctrine, understood, changes attitudes and behavior. The study of the doctrines of the gospel will improve behavior quicker than a study of behavior will improve behavior. ("Little Children," *Ensign*, Nov. 1986)

Briefly put, "doctrines" are the teachings of the plan of salvation, the answers to questions about the meaning and purpose of life, instructions, rules, facts, hows, whys, and commandments that, if followed, will lead to exaltation. In D&C 10:62, the Lord tells us that He is going to "bring to light the true points" of His doctrine. The Doctrine and Covenants does this. It also includes covenants required for celestial glory and exaltation.

This study guide is a brief, to-the-point help to a better understanding of the Doctrine and Covenants with its accompanying doctrines of the gospel and the ordinances of salvation required for celestial exaltation. The style is somewhat conversational to help you feel as if you were being guided through the Doctrine and Covenants in one of my classes. It is designed, in many cases, to give you instant understanding of basic doctrines and principles, as well as to provide you with the background to apply them in your life, which, in turn, will help you develop a deeper understanding and testimony of the gospel. Remember that the Holy Ghost is THE teacher. He will enlighten your mind and warm your heart as you pray and study this, the Savior's book directly to us.

INTRODUCTION

Welcome to the Second Edition of *Your Study of the Doctrine and Covenants Made Easier.* As was the case with the first edition, this second edition comes in three volumes. This is part 1. In compiling this second edition, I have incorporated many updates and much additional historical information and corrections based on recent research made available through the Joseph Smith Papers Project. I have added thousands of brief clarifications and helps to my notes and commentary for the first edition of this study guide. I have used the 2013 edition of the Doctrine and Covenants, as published by The Church of Jesus Christ of Latter-day Saints, as the basic text. References to the Bible come from the King James Version, as published by The Church of Jesus Christ of Latter-day Saints. JST references refer to the Joseph Smith Translation of the Bible.

Every verse of the Doctrine and Covenants, from section 1 through section 42, is included in this volume, Part 1. All the remaining verses of the Doctrine and Covenants are contained in Parts 2 and 3. All three volumes have background and setting notes for each section, as well as brief notes of explanation between and within the verses to clarify and help you learn and grow in your appreciation and understanding of this sacred volume of scripture. The notes within the verses are printed in italics and enclosed in brackets in order to make it easy for you to distinguish between the actual scripture text and my teaching comments. Notes between the verses are indented and are printed in a different font than the scripture text. **Bold** is often used to highlight things for teaching purposes.

You may be aware that, as a result of recent research, including for *The Joseph Smith Papers* publications, there are a number of changes to the section headings in the 2013 printing of the Doctrine and Covenants compared to previous editions. Such adjustments, most of them minor, have been made to 78 sections. One example of this is found in sections 39 and 40, where the name "James Covel" is now used rather than "James

Covill." The Second Edition of *Doctrine and Covenants Made Easier* incorporates these changes. You can read more about these changes by going online to Gospel Library/Study Helps/About the Scriptures/ Adjustments to the Scriptures, browsing down the page to "Doctrine and Covenants and Pearl of Great Price," and continuing to read from that point on.

This work is intended to be a user-friendly, "teacher in your hand" introductory study of this portion of the Doctrine and Covenants, as well as a refresher course for more advanced students of the scriptures. It is also designed to be a quick-reference resource which will enable readers to look up a particular passage of scripture for use in lessons, talks, or personal study as desired. It is my hope that you will write some of the notes given in this book in your own scriptures, whether paper copy or on digital devices, to assist you in reading and studying this portion of the Doctrine and Covenants in the future. Thus, your own scriptures will become one of your best tools in your continued study of the gospel.

—David J. Ridges

SECTION 1

Background

This section is not the first revelation, chronologically, in the Doctrine and Covenants. In fact, the Lord had already given over 60 recorded revelations to the Church and individuals by this time. The Lord gave this revelation as "my preface unto the book of my commandments" (D&C 1:6). Thus, section 1 was to be the Lord's preface to the revelations already given and still serves that purpose for us with our edition of the Doctrine and Covenants. This revelation was given on November 1, 1831, at a special conference of elders of the Church, held in Hiram, Ohio, at the home of John and Elsa Johnson. At this point, the Church was just over one and one-half years old (having been officially organized on April 6, 1830), and the Prophet Joseph Smith was 25 years of age. One of the matters considered at this conference was that of publishing the revelations received thus far in book form. This publication was to be known as the "Book of Commandments," and the decision was made to print 10,000 copies. Later, it was decided to print 3,000 copies. It would contain 65 sections (what we now know as D&C, sections 2 through 66).

The Joseph Smith Papers publications inform us that, during the conference, a committee consisting of Sidney Rigdon, Oliver Cowdery, and William E. McLellin was asked to write a preface for the Book of Commandments (see *The Joseph Smith Papers, Documents, Volume 2, July 1831– January 1833*, ed. Matthew C. Godfrey and others [2013], 104). When they presented their work to the conference, the group rejected it, and they asked Joseph Smith to go to the Lord for help. Here again, *The Joseph Smith Papers* publications help.

"After [Joseph Smith] and the elders bowed in prayer, [Joseph], who was 'sitting by a window,' dictated the preface 'by the Spirit,' while [Sidney] Rigdon served as scribe. 'Joseph would deliver a few sentences and Sidney would write them down [recalled William E. McLellin], then read them aloud, and if correct, then Joseph would proceed and deliver more'" (in *The Joseph Smith Papers, Documents, Volume 2, July 1831– January 1833*, 104).

Preparations to print the Book of Commandments were made, and by the summer of 1833, the printing was well under way in Missouri. However, in the course of events, the printing press and most of the copies of the Book of Commandments were destroyed by mobs and the printing was held up for a time.

By the summer of 1835, the Prophet Joseph had received a number of additional revelations from the Lord. In a conference of the Church, held on August 17, 1835, approval was given to print the 65 revelations in the Book of Commandments again, and to include 37 new revelations also in this publication. Rather than calling this printing the "Book of Commandments," it was named "The Doctrine and Covenants." It had a total of 102 sections and is known as the 1835 edition of the Doctrine and Covenants.

As mentioned above, section 1 was given by the Lord as His preface to the Doctrine and Covenants. Sixty-five sections precede this one chronologically, but this revelation is listed first, because it is the Savior's preface to His book of scripture to us, namely, the Doctrine and Covenants. It is also interesting to note that section 133 was given at the same special conference of elders in Hiram, Ohio. It was given two days after section 1, on November 3, 1831, and was first included in the Doctrine and Covenants as an appendix (see heading to section 133). Thus, in a sense, sections 1 and 133 serve as "bookends" to this sacred book of scripture.

We will move ahead now in our study of section 1. As you will see, in addition to being the Lord's preface, it can also be viewed as the Savior's personal testimony to all of us.

Many doctrines and principles are taught in this section. We will point out many of these through the use of **bold**, for emphasis in the scripture text itself, as well as through indented notes between verses and the use of explanatory notes in [*brackets*] within the verses.

Note: In section 10, verse 62, the Savior specifically told us that He was going to restore "the true points of my doctrine." "Doctrines" are eternal truths, facts, things in the plan of salvation that do not change, such as:

• Faith, repentance, baptism, gift of the Holy Ghost.

• The Godhead consists of the Father, the Son, and the Holy Ghost.

• The members of the Godhead are three separate beings.

• There are three kingdoms of glory, namely, the telestial, terrestrial, and celestial.

• In the celestial kingdom, there are three degrees.

• The highest degree of glory in the celestial is called "exaltation."

• Those who attain exaltation will live in their own eternal family unit and ultimately become gods.

• Heavenly Father is completely

fair, thus everyone will ultimately get a perfect opportunity before the final judgment to hear, understand, and then accept or reject the gospel.

- The sins we have repented of will not even be mentioned on Judgment Day.

- Little children who die before the years of accountability will receive exaltation.

- Ordinance work for the dead is part of the Father's plan of happiness for His children.

- We are spirit children of Heavenly Parents.

- The Atonement of Christ works for our shortcomings and imperfections as well as our sins.

- Baptism is required for entrance into the celestial kingdom, except in the case of little children who die before the age of accountability and the intellectually handicapped who do not have sufficient understanding to be accountable.

- God will not allow His living prophets to lead us astray.

- And many, many more wonderful doctrines that help us understand the whats, whys, and hows of the Father's plan of salvation for us, His children.

In the Doctrine and Covenants, the Lord has indeed restored many true doctrines, which, among other things, enable us to better live the gospel because we better understand it. Throughout these three study guides for the Doctrine and Covenants, I will often add extra notes to point out and summarize the many doctrines given by the Savior for us, as He said He would. You will see an example of this before verse one, next.

Just one more thing. As you can see, the very first word in this revelation, given by the Savior, is "hearken." This is a powerful word meaning to both "listen" and "obey." President Russell M. Nelson, of the Quorum of the Twelve Apostles at the time, explained that "the Hebrew language of the Old Testament in most instances uses **the same term for both hearkening** (to the Lord) **and obedience** (to His word)" ("Listen to Learn," *Ensign*, May 1991, 24).

Doctrine

Verse 1. God always knows what we are doing.

1 **HEARKEN** [*a strong word, often used in scriptures to mean "listen and obey," as in 1 Nephi 4:32, Genesis 3:17, 21:12, and Acts 27:21*], O ye people of my church, saith the voice of him [*Jesus Christ*] who dwells on high, and **whose eyes are upon all men**; yea, verily I say: Hearken ye people from afar; and ye that are upon the

islands of the sea, listen together.

One of the major messages given in verse 2, next, is that God is completely fair. Everyone will be given a perfect opportunity, before the final judgment, to both hear and understand the gospel. Then, each can use personal agency to accept or reject it. We will use **bold** to emphasize this fact.

Doctrine

Verse 2. Everyone will ultimately get a perfect opportunity before the final Judgment Day, to hear, understand, and then accept or reject the gospel.

2 For verily **the voice of the Lord is unto all** men, and there is **none** to **escape**; and there is **no eye** that **shall not see, neither ear that shall not hear, neither heart that shall not be penetrated.**

As you can see from verse 2, above, it is not enough to physically "hear" the gospel or "see" things related to it. Rather, each "heart" must be "penetrated." In other words, each of God's children must have the opportunity to truly understand it. For many, that opportunity comes in this mortal life. For many others, it will not come until they hear the gospel preached in the spirit world (see D&C 138, especially verses 32–34). After the gospel has "penetrated" the heart, each can accept it or rebel against it. Thus, each will be treated fairly at the final judgment while individual agency is preserved.

Doctrine

Verse 3. All sins that have not been repented of will eventually be exposed and brought to light.

3 And the **rebellious shall be pierced with much sorrow**; for **their iniquities** [*wickedness*] **shall be spoken upon the housetops** [*all wicked deeds will be exposed; perhaps this might include news media reports and gossip in our day, as well as unrepented-of evil being revealed on Judgment Day*], and **their secret acts shall be revealed.**

Doctrine

Verse 4. The gospel will go forth to all people.

4 And the **voice of warning shall be unto all people**, by the mouths of my disciples [*faithful leaders and members of the Church*], whom I have chosen in these last days.

As you can see in verse 5, next, the Savior is very emphatic that nothing will stop the spread of the gospel in the last days.

5 And **they shall go forth and none shall stay** [*stop*] **them**, for I the Lord have commanded them.

Next, the Savior tells us that the Doctrine and Covenants is His instruction to us and to all the world.

6 Behold, **this is mine authority** [*perhaps referring back to "the voice of the Lord," verse 2, and "the voice of warning," verse 4*]**, and the authority of my servants** [*perhaps meaning these revelations are authorized by the Lord; can also include the authority of the priesthood, under which the work goes forth; see footnote 6a*]**, and my preface unto the book of my commandments, which I have given them to publish unto you, O inhabitants of the earth**.

Joseph Fielding Smith commented on verse 6, above, as follows:

"The Doctrine and Covenants is distinctively peculiar and interesting to all who believe in it, [in] that **it is the only book in existence which bears the honor of a preface given by the Lord himself**. . . . It was not written by Joseph Smith, but was dictated by Jesus Christ, and contains his and his Father's word to the Church and to all the world that faith in God, repentance from sin, and membership in his Church might be given to all who will believe, and that once again

the New and Everlasting covenant might be established" (*Church History and Modern Revelation*, 1:252).

Next, Jesus bears His own personal witness to us that every prophesy in the Doctrine and Covenants will be fulfilled.

Doctrine
Verse 7. The words and promises of God will all be fulfilled, guaranteed.

7 **Wherefore, fear and tremble, O ye people, for what I the Lord have decreed in them** [*the revelations in the Doctrine and Covenants*] **shall be fulfilled**.

Verses 8–11, next, refer to the power "to seal both on earth and in heaven" (verse 8). In the context of this section, this refers particularly to the wicked who reject the gospel. In the larger context of the scriptures, this sealing power can refer to the specific sealing power and priesthood keys held by modern prophets and apostles. These verses as well as others in this section are a "voice of warning" (see verse 4) to all the world.

Doctrine
Verse 8. The official acts of God's authorized servants are valid in heaven as well as on earth.

8 And verily I say unto you, that **they who go forth**, bearing these tidings unto the inhabitants of the earth, **to them is power given to seal both on earth and in heaven**, the unbelieving and rebellious [*the wicked; see verse 9*];

Doctrine

Verse 9. The preaching of the gospel to the world makes the wicked accountable and unable to avoid the punishments of God (unless they repent).

9 Yea, verily, **to seal them up** [*to make them accountable*] **unto the day when the wrath of God** [*the punishments of God*] **shall be poured out upon the wicked without measure** [*without limit*]—

> Next, in verse 10, we are taught that we are, in effect, writing part of the script for our own judgment day, based on the way we treat others.

Doctrine

Verse 10. How we treat others will have a significant impact on how we are rewarded or punished by the Lord on the day of final judgment.

10 Unto the day when the Lord shall come to recompense [*pay;*

reward] unto every man according to his work, and **measure** [*give out; pay; reward*] **to every man according to the measure which he has measured to** [*according to what he has done to*] **his fellow man**.

11 Wherefore **the voice of the Lord is unto the ends of the earth** [*the gospel will be preached to all the world*], **that all that will hear** [*so that all who want to hear*] **may hear**:

Doctrine

Verse 12. The Second Coming of Christ is getting close.

12 Prepare ye, prepare ye for that which is to come, for **the Lord is nigh** [*the Second Coming is getting close; see D&C 1:12, footnote b*];

> Along with the doctrine given us by the Lord, Himself, that His coming is close, comes the caution not to set a time in our own minds for this great event. Matthew 24:36 tells us: "But of that day and hour knoweth no *man*, no, not the angels of heaven, but my Father only." Therefore, while we know that we live in the last days and that the Savior's coming is "nigh," we must continue with living and not postpone some things in anticipation of it.

Doctrine

Verses 13 and 14. The wicked will be destroyed at the time of the Second Coming.

In verse 13, next, we see the phrase, ". . . his sword is bathed in heaven." Isaiah 34:5–6 gives us a possible explanation of this phrase as used in the Doctrine and Covenants. If you read these verses from Isaiah, you will see that the imagery involved is that of the sword of destruction, wielded by the powers of heaven, in harmony with the law of justice. The sword is bathed in the blood of the wicked, who are destroyed by the coming of Christ. We will include these Isaiah verses here for you to read now, then go on to verse 13.

Isaiah 34:5–6

5 For my sword shall be bathed [*bathed in blood; see verse 6, next*] in heaven [*in other words, the wicked will be destroyed*]: behold, **it shall come down upon Idumea** [*Edom; the world—see D&C 1:36; means the wicked and rebellious in the world*], and upon the people of my curse [*who have cursed themselves through personal wickedness*], to judgment.

6 The sword of the LORD is filled with blood [*bathed in blood*], it is made fat with fatness [*covered with fat like a knife used in animal sacrifices*], and with the blood of lambs and goats, with the fat of the kidneys of rams: for the LORD hath a sacrifice in Bozrah [*the capital of Edom, a country southeast of Palestine; symbolic of the world and the wickedness of its inhabitants*], and a great slaughter in the land of Idumea [*the wicked world; in other words, the sword of the Lord is going to come down upon the wicked of the world*].

13 And the anger of the Lord is kindled, and **his sword is bathed in heaven, and it shall fall upon the inhabitants** [*the wicked inhabitants*] **of the earth.**

In D&C 133:46–51, we find similar imagery referring to the blood of the wicked. In this case, the blood of the wicked is "sprinkled upon my [*Christ's*] garments" (verse 51) as the wicked are destroyed at His coming. In other words, His clothing is "dyed red" (verses 46 and 48), symbolically, by the blood of the wicked, as they are destroyed at the Second Coming.

We understand the "wicked," referred to here, to be those who are living at or below a telestial lifestyle (briefly described in D&C 76:103), who are turned over to Satan to suffer for their own sins, and who will not be resurrected until the end of the Millennium (see D&C 76:84–85; 88:100–101).

Next, the "voice of warning" continues as the Savior explains that there will ultimately be a complete separation of the righteous from the wicked.

14 And **the arm** [*symbolic of power, as used in scriptural symbolism*] **of the Lord shall be revealed**; and the day cometh that **they who will not** [*who refuse to*] **hear the voice of the Lord, neither the voice of his servants, neither give heed to the words of the prophets and apostles, shall be cut off** from among the people;

President Henry B. Eyring taught the great value of heeding the words of the prophets. "Every time in my life when I have chosen to delay following inspired counsel or decided that I was an exception, I came to know that I had put myself in harm's way. Every time that I have listened to the counsel of prophets, felt it confirmed in prayer, and then followed it, I have found that I moved toward safety" ("Finding Safety in Counsel," *Ensign*, May 1997, 25).

Next, in verses 15 and 16, we are warned about what some people do that gets them cut off from the Lord's covenant people.

15 For they have **strayed from mine ordinances**, and have **broken mine everlasting covenant** [*among other things, this can mean that they have broken their eternal covenants which, if kept, lead to peace and happiness, on earth as well as in eternity*];

16 **They seek not the Lord to establish his righteousness** [*they do not want to do God's will or they ignore it; their motives are often evil*], but **every man walketh in his own way** [*everyone does his own thing, makes his own rules; spiritual anarchy*], and after the image of his own god [*sets his own priorities in life*], whose image is in the likeness of the world [*gets caught up in worldliness*], and whose substance is that of an idol [*worldliness is like idol worship*], which waxeth [*grows*] old and shall perish in Babylon [*the wicked will die in their sins*], even Babylon the great [*Satan's kingdom; spiritual wickedness; see D&C 133:14*], which shall fall.

Next, the Savior tells us what He has available for us, as well as all the inhabitants of the world, so that we do not get caught up in the ways of the world, as explained in the previous verses.

First, Jesus bears His own personal witness to us that Joseph Smith was called of God and taught to be the prophet of the Restoration.

Doctrine

Verse 17. Joseph Smith was a true prophet, called of God.

17 Wherefore, I the Lord, knowing the calamity [*disasters, destructions*] which should [*will*] come upon the inhabitants of the earth, **called upon my servant Joseph Smith, Jun., and spake unto him from heaven, and gave him commandments**;

Doctrine

Verse 18. Many Church leaders and members will successfully take the blessings of the gospel restored by Joseph Smith to all the world.

18 And also gave commandments to others [*including early leaders of the Church who assisted Joseph Smith in the Restoration, as well as missionaries and members in our day*], **that they should proclaim these things unto the world**; and all this that it might be fulfilled, which was written by the prophets [*for instance, in 1 Corinthians 1:27*]—

19 The weak things of the world [*including the missionaries and all Church members*] **shall come forth and break down the mighty and strong ones** [*ultimately, the gospel*

truths will triumph over all falsehood and error, no matter how "strong" and "mighty" they are made to look], that man should not counsel his fellow man [*so that we do not have to rely solely on the philosophies of men*], neither trust in the arm of flesh—

Next, in verses 20–23, we are taught four specific benefits of having the gospel of Jesus Christ in our lives and hearts.

20 But that every man might speak in the name of God the Lord, even the Savior of the world; [*including the privilege of having a testimony and speaking and teaching by the power of the Holy Ghost; see 2 Nephi 32:2–3*]

21 That faith also might increase in the earth;

22 That mine everlasting covenant [*the full gospel of Jesus Christ, with its truths, covenants, and ordinances*] **might be established**;

23 That the fulness of my gospel might be proclaimed by the weak and the simple unto the ends of the world, and before kings and rulers.

The phrase "the weak and the simple," in verse 23, above, is comforting. It is a reminder that one does not have to have advanced educational degrees or power and position in society to effectively preach and spread the gospel.

In the beginning of verse 24, next, the Savior reminds us again (as in verse 6) that this "preface" to the Doctrine and Covenants is given by His authority. Then, in verses 24–28, He goes on to give us five specific purposes of the Doctrine and Covenants. We will number these and point them out through the use of **underlined bold**.

24 Behold, **I am God and have spoken it; these commandments are of me**, and were given unto my servants in their weakness, after the manner of their language, **(1) that they might come to understanding** [*we must understand the gospel before we can live it and obtain its marvelous blessings*].

25 And **(2) inasmuch as they erred it might be made known** [*if we are in error, in actions or thoughts, we can't change unless we are taught correct doctrines and principles*];

26 And **(3) inasmuch as they sought wisdom they might be instructed** [*wisdom means, among other things, to make decisions in the present that will make a better future; those who desire to be wise need and desire instruction from wiser and higher sources*];

27 And **(4) inasmuch as they sinned they might be chastened** [*told what they are doing wrong*], **that they might repent** [*we can't repent and come unto Christ unless we are made aware of our sins*];

28 And **(5) inasmuch as they were humble they might be made strong, and blessed from on high, and receive knowledge from time to time** [*one of the great blessings of faithful membership in the Church is receiving on-going revelation, strength, and blessings from on high*].

Next, in verse 29, Jesus again bears record to us of Joseph Smith, His prophet, and bears witness that the Book of Mormon is true.

29 And after having received the record of the Nephites [*the gold plates*], yea, even **my servant Joseph Smith, Jun., might have power to translate** through the mercy of God, **by the power of God, the Book of Mormon.**

It would seem to this author that President Russell M. Nelson, with his world-wide contacts in the world of medicine, has played and continues to play a major role in fulfilling the prophecy given in verse 30, next; namely that the Church will be brought "forth out of obscurity." The word "obscure" means that few people know about it. Under President Nelson's direction, the Church has taken very significant strides in being widely known, not only for its missionary work, but also for its humanitarian aid and construction of temples.

Doctrine

Verse 30. The Church will continue going forth, becoming more and more prominent throughout the world.

30 And also those to whom these commandments were given, might have power to lay the foundation of this church, and to bring it forth out of obscurity and out of darkness, the only true and living [*having ongoing revelation and true priesthood authority, as well as the gift of the Holy Ghost*] **church upon the face of the whole earth**, with which I, the Lord, am well pleased, speaking unto the church collectively and not individually—

Verses 31–32, next, form a vital and beautiful "mini sermon." The Savior, in effect, tells us that while He "cannot look upon sin with the least degree of allowance," He can look upon sinners with a great degree of compassion because of His Atonement, if they repent.

Doctrine

Verses 31 and 32. Sin, itself, is, ultimately, completely unacceptable, as far as the eternal laws governing returning to God's presence are concerned. However, because of the Atonement of Christ, through proper repentance and living the gospel thereafter, sins can be forgiven completely and one can return to the presence of God completely sinless, pure, and clean.

31 For I the Lord cannot look upon sin with the least degree of allowance;

32 Nevertheless, he that repents and does the commandments of the Lord [*it is not enough to merely stop sinning, but we must start doing good, including keeping the commandments*] **shall be forgiven;**

Perhaps you've noticed, on occasion, that people who once had a testimony, but who turn to sin, lose much more than their testimony if they do not repent. They also lose the "light" in their countenance, as well as the light of gospel knowledge. They can hardly engage in a gospel conversation like they once could. It is as if something has been taken out of their soul. It has, according to verse 33, next.

Doctrine

Verse 33. It is possible to have one's testimony and gospel knowledge taken away.

33 And he that repents not, from him shall be taken even the light which he has received; for my Spirit shall not always strive with man, saith the Lord of Hosts.

Next, in verse 34 and in the first part of verse 35, Jesus tells us again, as He did in verse 2, that He will make sure that all people, no matter who or where they are, will receive the opportunity to be taught the gospel. This counteracts a common false philosophy among some groups and cultures that some people, no matter what, will be held in higher position by the Lord than all others. This belief, often referred to as "predestination," seemed to be very prominent among the Jews at the time of Christ's ministry on earth. See Matthew 3:9.

Doctrine

Verses 34 and 35. The Lord considers all people to have equal worth and value, and thus all will ultimately have an equal opportunity to hear and understand the gospel of Jesus Christ before final judgment.

34 And again, verily I say unto

you, O inhabitants of the earth: I the Lord am willing to make these things known unto all flesh [*all people*];

35 For **I am no respecter of persons** [*the Lord considers one person just as important as another; one soul is just as valuable as another*], and will that [*desire that*] all men shall know that **the day speedily cometh; the hour** is not yet [*in 1831, at the time of this revelation*], but **is nigh at hand, when peace shall be taken from the earth, and the devil shall have power over his own dominion**.

The last lines of verse 35, above, combined with the first lines of verse 36, next, prophesy, in effect, that in the last days, there will not be much "gray area." It appears that people will have to choose sides. The devil will have great and wide-open power over his followers, and the humble followers of Christ will have great power and blessings come upon them. No one will be successful in stopping the progress of the Church and the blessings of God from coming upon His Saints (see also verse 5, above). People will either be swept along in the flood of evil, or they will become stronger and stronger in living the gospel. There will be little middle ground left.

36 And also **the Lord shall have power over his saints, and shall**

reign in their midst, and shall come down in judgment upon Idumea, or the world.

Finally, the Savior invites us to be nourished and strengthened by the revelations contained in the Doctrine and Covenants and promises that the Holy Ghost will attend those who study them. He also teaches the vital lesson that the words of His prophets are to be considered His own. A passage of scripture with the same basic message can be found in D&C 124:45–46.

37 **Search these commandments**, for they are true and faithful [*perhaps meaning that they will not disappoint nor let you down*], and **the prophecies and promises which are in them shall all be fulfilled.**

Doctrine

Verse 38. There is no difference in authority between the words of the Lord and the words of His authorized servants.

38 **What I the Lord have spoken, I have spoken, and I excuse not myself;** and though the heavens and the earth pass away, **my word shall not pass away, but shall all be fulfilled, whether by mine own voice or by the voice of my servants, it is the same.**

39 For behold, and lo, the Lord is God, and **the Spirit beareth record,** and **the record is true** [*the Savior is bearing His testimony directly to you and me*], and **the truth abideth** [*lasts*] **forever and ever** [*whereas false philosophies ultimately are exposed by truth and come to an end*]. Amen.

SECTION 2

Background

Chronologically, this section is the earliest in the Doctrine and Covenants and was given September 21, 1823, by the angel Moroni. Imagine how satisfying it must have been for Moroni to appear to Joseph Smith in 1823 and begin the great work of bringing forth the Book of Mormon after having waited approximately 1400 years (since he finished engraving on the gold plates and buried them In the Hill Cumorah about A.D. 421)!

On the evening of September 21, 1823 (about three and one-half years after the First Vision), as Joseph Smith, then seventeen, prayed for forgiveness of his sins and to learn his standing with God, Moroni appeared to him, telling him of the gold plates and showing him a vision of where they were deposited in the Hill Cumorah (see Joseph Smith—History 1:29–42). During this appearance, Moroni taught him much and quoted many scriptures, including the three verses that comprise this section of the Doctrine and Covenants.

As Joseph Smith tells us in Joseph Smith—History 1:36–39, Moroni quoted from Malachi 4:5–6, "but with a little variation from the way it reads in our Bibles" (Joseph Smith—History 1:36). In order for you to see the different wording used by Moroni, we will include Malachi 4:5–6 here, from the Bible, along with section 2 of the Doctrine and Covenants. We will use **bold** to point out some of the differences in Moroni's wording compared to the wording in the Bible. Then we will go through section 2 again and add some commentary.

D&C 2:1

1 Behold, I will reveal unto you the Priesthood, by the hand of Elijah the prophet, before the coming of the great and dreadful day of the Lord.

Malachi 4:5

5 Behold, I will send you Elijah the prophet before the coming of the great and dreadful day of the LORD:

D&C 2:2–3

2 And he shall **plant in the hearts of the children the promises made to the fathers**, and **the hearts of the children**

shall turn to their fathers.

3 If it were not so, the whole earth would be utterly wasted at his coming.

Malachi 4:6

6 And he shall turn the heart of the fathers to the children, and the heart of the children to their fathers, lest I come and smite the earth with a curse.

Now, as stated above, we will go through section 2 again, adding some brief commentary.

The fulfillment of the promise given in D&C 2:1, next, took place on Easter Sunday, April 3, 1836, in the Kirtland Temple, as recorded in D&C 110. Elijah appeared to Joseph Smith and Oliver Cowdery and committed to them the priesthood keys of sealing families together for eternity.

Elder David A. Bednar, of the Quorum of the Twelve Apostles, explained who Elijah was and why he returned in our day:

"Elijah was an Old Testament prophet through whom mighty miracles were performed. He sealed the heavens, and no rain fell in ancient Israel for 3½ years. He multiplied a widow's meal and oil. He raised a young boy from the dead, and he called down fire from heaven in a challenge to the prophets of Baal. (See 1 Kings 17–18.) At the conclusion of Elijah's mortal ministry, he 'went up by a whirl-wind into heaven' (2 Kings 2:11) and was translated.

"'We learn from latter-day revelation that Elijah held the sealing power of the Melchizedek Priesthood and was the last prophet to do so before the time of Jesus Christ' (Bible Dictionary, 'Elijah'). . . .

"Elijah appeared with Moses on the Mount of Transfiguration (see Matthew 17:3) and conferred this authority upon Peter, James, and John. Elijah appeared again with Moses and others on April 3, 1836, in the Kirtland Temple and conferred the same keys upon Joseph Smith and Oliver Cowdery" ("The Hearts of the Children Shall Turn," *Ensign* or *Liahona*, Nov. 2011, 24).

In the Bible Dictionary, in the back of our LDS Bible, under "Elijah," we are told the following (**bold** added for emphasis):

"We learn from latter-day rev-elation that **Elijah held the seal-ing power of the Melchizedek Priesthood** and was the last prophet to do so before the time of Jesus Christ. He appeared on the Mount in company with Moses (also translated) and con-ferred the keys of the priesthood on Peter, James, and John (Matt. 17:3). **He appeared again, in company with Moses and others, on April 3, 1836, in the Kirtland (Ohio) Temple and conferred the**

same keys upon Joseph Smith and Oliver Cowdery. All of this was in preparation for the com-ing of the Lord, as spoken of in Malachi 4:5–6 (D&C 110:13–16). As demonstrated by his miracu-lous deeds, **the power of Elijah is the sealing power of the priest-hood** by which things bound or loosed on earth are bound or loosed in heaven. Thus **the keys of this power are once again operative on the earth and are used in performing all the ordi-nances of the gospel for the liv-ing and the dead**."

Doctrine

Verses 1–3. The sealing power of the priesthood is necessary in order for ordinances, including eternal marriage, to be valid in eternity.

1 BEHOLD, I will reveal unto you the Priesthood [*the sealing keys and power of the Melchizedek Priesthood*]**, by the hand of Elijah the prophet**, before the coming of the great and dreadful day of the Lord [*before the Second Coming of Christ with its accompanying tre-mendous and dreaded-by-the-wick-ed destruction*].

The change in wording given by Moroni for verse 2, next, indicates that in the last days people will have a great interest in studying and learning about their ancestors, which will be placed in the hearts of people by the Lord. Certainly, this is happening now, as people throughout the world respond to this desire to study their ancestry. Millions access the Church's family history website and come to family history centers to search for information about their family trees. This feeling in the heart is often referred to as "the Spirit of Elijah" and includes the desire among members of the Church to do the temple work for their ancestors.

In a Priesthood Genealogy Seminary, held in 1973, Harold B. Lee said that this uniting of families through the sealing keys restored by Elijah applies also to living families.

2 And he [Elijah] shall plant in the hearts of the children the promises made to the fathers, and the hearts of the children shall turn to their fathers.

Joseph Fielding Smith explained the phrase "the promises made to the fathers" in verse 2, above, as follows:

"This expression has reference to certain promises made to those who died without a knowledge of the Gospel, and without the opportunity of receiving the sealing ordinances of the Priesthood in matters pertaining to their exaltation. According to these promises, the children in the latter days are

to perform all such ordinances in behalf of the dead" (*Improvement Era*, July 1922, 829–31).

President Russell M. Nelson of the Quorum of the Twelve Apostles explained what the promises or covenants were that God made with Abraham and others:

"The covenant God made with Abraham and later reaffirmed with Isaac and Jacob is of transcendent significance. It contained several promises, including

"• Jesus the Christ would be born through Abraham's lineage.

"• Abraham's posterity would be numerous, entitled to an eternal increase, and also entitled to bear the priesthood.

"• Abraham would become a father of many nations.

"• Certain lands would be inherited by his posterity.

"• All nations of the earth would be blessed by his seed.

"• And that covenant would be everlasting—even through 'a thousand generations' [*Deuteronomy 7:9; 1 Chronicles 16:15; Psalm 105:8*].

"Some of these promises have been fulfilled; others are still pending. . . .

". . . We have received, as did they of old, the holy priesthood and the everlasting gospel. We have the right to receive the fulness of the gospel, enjoy the blessings of the priesthood, and qualify for God's greatest blessing—that of eternal life.

"Some of us are the literal seed of Abraham; others are gathered into his family by adoption. The Lord makes no distinction. Together we receive these promised blessings—if we seek the Lord and obey His commandments" ("Covenants," *Ensign* or *Liahona*, Nov. 2011, 87–88).

Finally, in the last verse of section 2, we are taught how absolutely vital the sealing power of the Melchizedek Priesthood is as restored by Elijah. Without this, the earth would be "wasted" and would fail to fulfill its ultimate purpose. Among possible ways to interpret verse 3, next, we will consider one, as follows:

In Moses 1:39, the Lord tells us that His whole purpose is to "bring to pass the **immortality** and **eternal life** of man."

"Immortality" means living forever as a resurrected being. All who have ever lived or who will live as mortals will be resurrected because of Christ's resurrection and Atonement (see 1 Corinthians 15:22).

"Eternal life" means exaltation in the highest degree of glory in the celestial kingdom, which means

living in the family unit forever (see D&C 131:1–4 and 132:19–20). Without the sealing power of the Melchizedek Priesthood, we could not be sealed together as families forever; therefore, we could not attain eternal life, which is exaltation. Thus, the "work and . . . glory" of God (Moses 1:39) would be frustrated, and the earth would fail to fulfill its purposes. In other words, as far as uniting families together eternally, the earth would be "wasted."

3 If it were not so [*if worthy families were not sealed together eternally through the sealing power of the priesthood*], **the whole earth would be utterly wasted at his coming**.

Joseph Smith taught the following concerning the message in verse 3, above:

"The greatest responsibility in this world that God has laid upon us is to seek after our dead. The Apostle says, 'They without us cannot be made perfect;' (Heb. 11:40) for it is necessary that the sealing power should be in our hands to seal our children and our dead for the fulness of the dispensation of times—a dispensation to meet the promises made by Jesus Christ before the foundation of the world for the salvation of man.

"Now, I will speak of them. I will meet Paul half way. I say to you,

Paul, you cannot be perfect without us. It is necessary that those who are going before and those who come after us should have salvation in common with us; and thus hath God made it obligatory upon man. Hence, God said, 'I will send you Elijah the prophet before the coming of the great and dreadful day of the Lord; and he shall turn the heart of the fathers to the children, and the heart of the children to their fathers, lest I come and smite the earth with a curse.' (*Mal. 4:5.*)" (*Teachings of the Prophet Joseph Smith,* 356).

SECTION 3

Background

This section was given in July 1828 at Harmony, Pennsylvania. In December 1827, Joseph Smith and his wife, Emma, had moved from the Palmyra, New York, area to Harmony, Pennsylvania, to the home of Emma's parents in order for Joseph to work on translating the gold plates in a peaceful environment. They soon purchased a small home nearby from Emma's brother, Jesse, which was located on 13 acres next to the Susquehanna River, where Joseph could continue the work. By this time, they were expecting their first of nine children.

In February 1828, Martin Harris, a prominent Palmyra businessman and friend of Joseph and his family, came and served as scribe for him as he translated. Martin's assistance was welcomed, and the work of translation went forward at a good pace. By June 14, 1828, they had 116 manuscript pages of translation written on what was called "foolscap" paper (roughly the dimensions of legal-sized paper today).

During the translation of the plates, Martin had asked Joseph if he could take the pages of translation to Palmyra, where he hoped to use them as evidence to stop the wagging tongues of his wife, Lucy, and others who had spread damaging rumors about him and his association with Joseph Smith. Being a highly respected citizen and a man of strict integrity, such reputation-damaging rumors and accusations, including that he had been deceived and had fallen under Joseph Smith's spell, were especially painful.

Joseph had asked the Lord about Martin's request through the Urim and Thummim. The Lord said not to give the pages to him. Martin persisted and asked a second time. Joseph asked the Lord again. The Lord turned down the request again. Now, with 116 pages of manuscript completed, Martin begged again, and Joseph asked the Lord for the third time, upon which he was told that Martin could take the 116 pages on the condition that he agree in writing to show them only to his "wife; his brother, Preserved Harris; his parents, Nathan and Rhoda Harris; and his wife's sister, Mary Harris Cobb (see *The Joseph Smith Papers, Documents, Volume 1: July 1828–June 1831*, ed. Michael Hubbard MacKay and others [2013], 6, footnote 25)." Martin joyfully agreed to these terms and left for Palmyra with the precious pages on June 14, 1828.

The next day, June 15, 1828, a baby boy was born to Joseph and Emma. The infant died that same day, and it was two weeks before Emma was out of danger of dying herself from the difficulties of the birth. During these trying days, Joseph stayed faithfully by her side, doing all he could to nurse her back to health. After two weeks, Emma asked if Martin had returned with the 116 pages. He hadn't. Emma was concerned, and after another week, she assured Joseph that she would be all right. She encouraged him to go to Palmyra in search of Martin and the manuscript.

Joseph left for Palmyra (actually, his parents lived in Manchester, a smaller community next to Palmyra), and upon arriving at his parents' home, sent for Martin, who lived in Palmyra. After several hours, Martin finally came, and in a traumatic scene, he explained to Joseph that the 116 pages were lost.

With a heavy heart, the young Prophet Joseph Smith returned to Harmony. There, he was met by Moroni, who took the plates and

the Urim and Thummim. Shortly, the angel appeared again and gave him the Urim and Thummim, through which he received what we know as section 3 of the Doctrine and Covenants, after which Moroni took the Urim and Thummim and left.

With this as a brief background, perhaps you can understand and feel the deep impact of the lesson Joseph Smith was taught by the Lord in this revelation. As difficult as it was, Joseph learned his lesson well and never again went against the instructions of God.

By the way, this section goes with section 10. At the time section 10 was given, the gold plates and the Urim and Thummim had been returned to Joseph Smith, and he was privileged to continue the work of translation. We will discuss that background further when we get there.

There are many possible lessons for us to learn from section 3, including

1. The aftermath of disobedience to God is ugly.

2. Don't question or go against the counsel of the Lord.

3. Don't yield to peer pressure, no matter how convincing the argument, if it goes counter to God's counsel (verses 6–7).

4. Through obedience and faithfulness, we can have the help

of God in all times of trouble (verse 8).

5. God is patient and merciful and still wants us to succeed, even when we have slipped up (verse 10).

6. The definition of "wicked" doesn't always mean deeply evil (verses 12–13).

We will now go through this section verse by verse. Remember as you read that the Prophet Joseph is receiving this through the Urim and Thummim and that he has been brought to the depths of despair and humility by the loss of the 116 manuscript pages.

1 **THE works, and the designs** [*plans*]**, and the purposes of God cannot be frustrated** [*stopped*], neither can they come to naught [*nothing*].

2 For **God doth not walk in crooked paths** [*implying, "like you have done, Joseph"*], neither doth he turn to the right hand nor to the left, neither doth he vary from that which he hath said [*He keeps His word*], therefore his paths are straight, and **his course is one eternal round**.

The phrase "one eternal round," as used in verse 2, above, basically means "the same," or, "God is always reliable; you can trust Him, depend on Him." An expanded definition could be that

God always uses the same laws, principles, covenants, and ordinances to do His work of making exaltation available to His mortal children. Another way to look at it might be that you can always depend on God, just as you can depend on the exactness of an unvaried course, if you are going around a perfect circle. Yet another way to look at it might be that God uses the same plan of salvation for each "round" of creation, or each world to which He sends a group of His spirit children.

3 Remember, remember that **it is not the work of God that is frustrated** [*stopped; interfered with*]**, but the work of men**;

One thing we can learn from verse 3, above, is that by following God, we will always succeed, but when we detour and follow the ways of man, we will be frustrated or, in other words, stopped in achieving our eternal goals.

Next, in verse 4, we see a number of paths that can take us away from God.

4 For although a man may have many revelations [*such as you, Joseph, have had, including the First Vision*], and have power to do many mighty works, yet **if he boasts in his own strength**, and **sets at naught** [*ignores*] **the counsels of God**, and **follows after the dictates of his own will** [*makes*

his own rules; does what he wants to] **and carnal desires** [*influenced by cares of the world*], he must fall and incur the vengeance of a just God upon him [*in other words, the punishment he brings upon himself is fair*].

5 Behold**, you have been entrusted with these things** [*the gold plates, the Urim and Thummim, the work of translating, and so on*], but **how strict were your commandments**; and remember also the promises which were made to you, if you did not transgress them.

In verse 5, above, the Lord refers to "strict" commandments that had been given to Joseph Smith. Among other things, we understand these to refer to Moroni's instructions to the Prophet as he told him about the gold plates and eventually turned them over to him. We will include three verses here that contain some of these commandments and warnings:

Joseph Smith—History 1:42, 46, and 59

42 Again, **he told me, that when I got those plates** of which he had spoken—for the time that they should be obtained was not yet fulfilled—**I should not show them to any person; neither the breastplate with the** Urim and Thummim; only to those to whom I should be commanded to show them; if I did I should be destroyed. While he was conversing with me about the plates, the vision was opened to my mind that I could see the place where the plates were deposited, and that so clearly and distinctly that I knew the place again when I visited it.

46 By this time, so deep were the impressions made on my mind, that sleep had fled from my eyes, and I lay overwhelmed in astonishment at what I had both seen and heard. But what was my surprise when again I beheld the same messenger at my bedside, and heard him rehearse or repeat over again to me the same things as before; and **added a caution to me**, telling me that **Satan would try to tempt me** (in consequence of the indigent circumstances [*poor financial status*] of my father's family), **to get the plates for the purpose of getting rich**. This he forbade me, saying that I must have no other object in view in getting the plates but to glorify God, and **must not be influenced by any other motive than that of building his kingdom**; otherwise I could not get them.

59 At **length the time arrived for obtaining the plates**, the Urim and Thummim, and the breastplate. On the twenty-second day of September, one thousand eight hundred and twenty-seven, having gone as usual at the end of another year to the place where they were deposited, **the same heavenly messenger delivered them up to me with this charge**: that I should be responsible for them; that **if I should let them go carelessly, or through any neglect of mine, I should be cut off**; but that if I would use all my endeavors to preserve them, until he, the messenger, should call for them, they should be protected.

We will now return to the text of section 3. These verses are certainly a lesson in parenting. The Lord is telling His young prophet the truth, with love and strictness, and with no room for misunderstanding. Yet these verses are leading up to the tenderness and encouragement of verse 10.

6 And behold, **how oft you have transgressed the commandments and the laws of God, and have gone on in the persuasions of men** [*the ways of the world*].

Verse 7, next, contains a strong warning against yielding to negative peer pressure.

7 For, behold, **you should not have feared man more than God**. Although men set at naught [*ignore*] the counsels of God, and despise his words—

8 Yet **you should have been faithful**; and **he would have extended his arm and supported you against all the fiery darts of the adversary**; and **he would have been with you in every time of trouble**.

Perhaps one important lesson we learn from verse 8, above, is that we won't be spared from trials and troubles in this life, but through faithfulness to God, we can receive His support as we go through them.

The people of Alma provide us with an example of this kind of support from God as follows:

Mosiah 24:14–15

14 And **I will also ease the burdens which are put upon your shoulders, that even you cannot feel them** upon your backs, even while you are in bondage; and this will I do that ye may stand as witnesses for me hereafter, and that ye may know of a surety that I, the Lord God, do visit my people in their afflictions.

15 And now it came to pass that **the burdens which were laid**

upon **Alma and his brethren were made light**; yea, the Lord did strengthen them that they could bear up their burdens with ease, and **they did submit cheerfully and with patience** to all the will of the Lord.

We return now to section 3. Notice the encouragement given in verses 9 and 10, as well as the warning in verse 11.

9 Behold, thou art Joseph, and thou wast chosen to do the work of the Lord, but because of transgression, **if thou art not aware thou wilt fall**.

Doctrine

Verse 10. God is merciful. (This may sound too simple, but some religions and people teach that God is only a God of justice, vengeance, and punishment.)

10 But **remember, God is merciful; therefore, repent** of that which thou hast done which is contrary to the commandment which I gave you, **and thou art still chosen, and art again called to the work;**

11 **Except thou do this, thou shalt be delivered up and become as other men, and have no more gift**.

Perhaps this is a good place to pause and consider another

lesson we can learn from the above verses, combined with some of the history behind both sections 3 and 10 of the Doctrine and Covenants, which deal with the loss of the 116 manuscript pages.

The lesson is that wise parents do not always immediately restore privileges lost by disobedient children. There is wisdom in letting them go without for a period of time, during which growth and internal change can take place. It appears that the Lord used this approach on Joseph Smith at this point in the restoring of the gospel.

Rather than immediately restoring the privilege and responsibility of translating the gold plates, the Lord gave him hope and encouragement in verses 9 and 10, above, but made him wait to actually begin the work again, without knowing when the gift of translating would be restored.

Remember that the section we are studying, section 3, was given in July 1828. As mentioned previously, it was at this time that the angel took the gold plates and the Urim and Thummim from Joseph in consequence of the loss of the 116 pages. The Prophet's mother, Lucy Mack Smith, informs us that the angel returned the plates and Urim and Thummim to him on September 22, 1828. We read this in *History of Joseph Smith, by His Mother, Lucy Mack Smith*, chapter 26. Section 10 of the Doctrine and Covenants was given to the Prophet in conjunction with returning to him the privilege of translating. As you can see in the heading to section 10 in the 2013 edition of the Doctrine and Covenants, section 10 was received "likely around April, 1829, though portions may have been received as early as the summer of 1828." In section 10, Joseph is instructed on how to proceed with the translation. We will turn to his mother's account for the details, beginning with her record of what happened after Joseph found out that Martin Harris had lost the 116 manuscript pages and had returned home to Harmony, Pennsylvania. We will continue to use **bold** for teaching purposes.

History of Joseph Smith by His Mother, Lucy Mack Smith, chapter 26.

"On leaving you," said Joseph, "I returned immediately home. Soon after my arrival, I commenced humbling myself in mighty prayer before the Lord, and, as I was pouring out my soul in supplication to God, that if possible I might obtain mercy at his hands and be forgiven of all that I had done contrary to his will, an angel stood before me, and answered me, saying, that I had sinned in delivering the manuscript into the hands of a wicked man, and, as I had ventured to become responsible for his faithfulness, I would of necessity have to suffer the consequences of his indiscretion, and I must now give up the Urim and Thummim into his (the angel's) hands.

"This I did as I was directed, and as I handed them to him, he remarked, '**If you are very humble and penitent, it may be you will receive them again; if so, it will be on the twenty-second of next September.**'"

The Prophet's mother gives additional commentary and then continues by saying that she will now continue with Joseph's account of what happened.

"After the angel left me," said he, "I continued my supplications to God, without cessation, and **on the twenty-second of September, I had the joy and satisfaction of again receiving the Urim and Thummim**, with which I have again commenced translating, and Emma writes for me, but the angel said that the Lord would send me a scribe, and I trust his promise will be verified. The angel seemed pleased with me when he gave me back the Urim and Thummim, and **he told me that the Lord loved me, for my faithfulness and humility."**

We will now continue with section 3. Next, the Lord will give us a definition of a "wicked man." There are certainly additional lessons for us here. We will use **bold** to point out this definition.

12 And when thou deliveredst up that which God had given thee sight and power to translate [*in other words, the 116 manuscript pages*], thou deliveredst up that which was sacred into the hands of **a wicked man** [*referring to Martin Harris*],

13 Who has **set at naught the counsels of God**, and has **broken the most sacred promises** which were made before God, and has **depended upon his own judgment** and **boasted in his own wisdom.**

14 And this is the reason that thou hast lost thy privileges **for a season—**

15 For thou hast suffered [*allowed*] the counsel of thy director to be trampled upon from the beginning.

16 **Nevertheless** [*in spite of what you have done*], **my work shall go forth**, for inasmuch as [*since*] the knowledge of a Savior has come unto the world, through the testimony of the Jews [*through the Bible*], even so shall the knowledge of a Savior come unto **my people—**

As you can see, there is a dash at the end of verse 16, and again at the end of verse 17. This alerts us to the fact that verse 17 contains the definition for "my people." The people spoken of in verse 17 are all Book of Mormon people and were descendants of Nephi and his younger brothers, Jacob and Joseph, plus Zoram, who was Laban's servant. Thus, in this context, "my people" means the descendants of the Book of Mormon people who live in these latter days.

17 And to the Nephites, and the Jacobites, and the Josephites, and the Zoramites, through the testimony of their fathers [*ancestors, such as Lehi, Sariah, Nephi, Jacob, Alma, and so on*]—

In verse 18, next, the Lord refers to the descendants of Laman, Lemuel, and Ishmael. We usually refer to these people as Lamanites. In this verse, the Lord gives a brief review of the Book of Mormon, in which the Nephites were destroyed by the Lamanites.

18 And this testimony [*the Book of Mormon*] shall come to the knowledge of the Lamanites, and the Lemuelites, and the Ishmaelites, who dwindled in unbelief because of the iniquity [*wickedness*] of their fathers, whom the Lord has suffered [*allowed*] to destroy their brethren the Nephites, because of their [*the Nephites'*] iniquities and their abominations [*extreme wickedness*].

19 And for this very purpose are these plates [*the gold plates*] preserved, which contain these records [*the account of the Lord's dealings with the peoples of the Western Hemisphere*]—that the promises of the Lord might be fulfilled, which he made to his people [*the Book of Mormon people*];

Next, the Lord gives specific things that reading and studying the Book of Mormon can do for the Lamanites. You will see many benefits for you also.

Doctrine

Verse 20. The Lamanites will come to know of God's dealings with their ancestors and of God's promises to them today.

20 And that the Lamanites might come to the knowledge of their fathers [*ancestors*], and

that they might **know the promises of the Lord,** and that they may **believe the gospel** and **rely upon the merits of Jesus Christ** [*rely upon the Atonement of Christ and His gospel*], and **be glorified** [*receive exaltation in celestial glory; see footnote 20e, which refers to Moroni 7:26, where "sons of God" means exaltation, as explained in the Topical Guide*] **through faith in his name,** and **that through their repentance they might be saved.** Amen.

SECTION 4

Background

According to *The Joseph Smith Papers* publications, Joseph Smith Sr. and his son Samuel traveled from their home near Palmyra, New York, to Harmony, Pennsylvania, in January, 1829, to visit Joseph Smith Jr. and his wife, Emma. During this visit, Joseph's Father asked for a revelation concerning his possible role in God's work. (See *The Joseph Smith Papers, Documents, Volume 1: July 1828–June 1831*, ed. Michael Hubbard MacKay and others [2013], 5.)

While Father Smith was there, the Lord did indeed give him a revelation through his son, Joseph. This is the first recorded revelation given by the Lord to another person, through Joseph Smith, the

Prophet. Later in the Doctrine and Covenants, we will study many such revelations given to individuals by the Lord through the Prophet Joseph Smith.

During the years since the First Vision in the spring of 1820, Joseph's father had supported him despite severe persecution. On the evening of September 21, 1823, Moroni appeared to the seventeen-year-old Joseph Smith Jr., telling him of the gold plates buried in Hill Cumorah and teaching him of the important work he was to do. The angel appeared two more times that night and again the next day, at which time Joseph was instructed to tell his father all that had transpired during Moroni's visit. He did so, and his father replied, saying to him "that it was of God, and told me to go and do as commanded by the messenger." (See Joseph Smith—History 1:49–50.)

It must have been a tender scene as the young Prophet Joseph gave this revelation from the Savior to his father, Joseph Smith Sr. In it we find counsel and instruction which readily applies to all of us.

Verse 1 of section 4 is very similar to verse 1 of sections 6, 11, 12, and 14. It is a major theme at this point of the Restoration. The "marvelous work" spoken of is "about to come forth." It hasn't come forth yet, but is right on the threshold. The translation of the gold plates has been slowed since the loss of the 116 pages by Martin Harris but will move along rapidly once Oliver Cowdery arrives on the scene in early April 1829. The translation will be completed in late June 1829. It will be published and available for sale by March 26, 1830.

The Church is not yet organized but will be on April 6, 1830. Thus, indeed, at this point in Church history, "a marvelous work is about to come forth." We will continue to use **bold** for teaching emphasis.

1 NOW behold, **a marvelous work is about to come forth** among the children of men [*among the people of the earth*].

Verse 2, while given to Joseph Smith Sr., certainly applies to all of us. There are many things we can learn from it, including that we need to be one hundred percent committed to the Lord. A partial commitment won't do. Another thing is the comforting fact that our best is good enough to enable us to be free of sin on the final day of judgment.

Doctrine

Verse 2. If we do our best in serving God, we will indeed be made free from sin and thus stand clean and pure before the Savior on the day of final judgment. In other words, because of our best

effort, coupled with the Savior's Atonement, we will be worthy to enter celestial glory. Our best will be good enough.

2 Therefore, O ye that embark [*go forth*] **in the service of God,** see that ye **serve him with all** your **heart, might, mind** and **strength, that ye may stand blameless before God at the last day** [*final Judgment Day*].

In conjunction with verse 2, above, perhaps you have noticed that some people are afflicted with what might be termed "the re-deciding syndrome." In other words, their commitment to the Lord and to the Church, their covenants, and so on, are not one hundred percent. As a result, they find themselves constantly "re-deciding" whether or not to go to church, whether or not to pay tithing, minister to their assigned families, read scriptures, avoid inappropriate media, movies, music, and so on. Such "re-deciding" promotes stagnation, stifles progress, and causes instability.

3 Therefore, **if ye have desires to serve God ye are called to the work;**

The question sometimes arises with respect to verse 3, above, as to whether or not it refers to formal callings in the Church, including full-time missionaries, or what?

As you have no doubt noticed, proper interpretation of verses of scripture depends on the context in which the verse is found.

In this case, there is no Church yet at this time In Church history. The priesthood has not been restored yet. There are no formal callings in the Church yet. The context is that of missionary work. The "field is white, already to harvest" (verse 4).

George Albert Smith, who later became the eighth president of the Church, explained that this verse applies to missionary work as follows:

"It is not necessary for you to be called to go into the mission field in order to proclaim the truth. Begin on the man who lives next door by inspiring confidence in him, by inspiring love in him for you because of your righteousness, and your missionary work has already begun" (In Conference Report, Oct. 1916, 50–51).

Verse 4, next, can be seen as the beginning of the fulfillment of the prophecy given in Daniel 2:35, 44–45, which foretells the spreading of the gospel to fill the whole earth. The "field is white," meaning ready to harvest. The grain (the "wheat," symbolic of faithful converts) is ready to be harvested and brought into the Lord's "barn." See Matthew 13:24–30, which is the parable of the wheat and the tares, and in which "barn" symbolizes the Church and kingdom of

God—ultimately, celestial glory.

Verse 4 also explains the reward of personal salvation that comes to those who faithfully help with the "harvest" of souls by bringing people to Christ, who brings them to the Father.

4 For behold **the field is white already to harvest**; and lo, **he that thrusteth in his sickle** [*a cutting tool, used anciently to harvest grain*] **with his might**, the same layeth up in store [*stores up personal blessings*] that he perisheth not [*spiritually*], but **bringeth salvation to his soul**;

There are many possible approaches to studying verses 5 and 6, next. First, we will **bold** the personal qualities we need to develop in order to successfully "thrust in [our] sickle" in the latter-day harvesting of souls.

5 And **faith, hope, charity** and **love**, with an **eye single to the glory of God** [*having pure motives, not doing it for personal profit or gain*], qualify him for the work.

6 Remember **faith, virtue, knowledge, temperance, patience, brotherly kindness, godliness, charity, humility, diligence**.

Next, we will go through verses 5 and 6 again, this time adding a bit more commentary.

5 And **faith** [*a principle of action, doing; actual movement on our part*], **hope** [*optimism, confidence that there is good in people, and that there will be some who will listen; also, humble confidence in ourselves, that we can do the work, with the help of the Lord*], **charity and love** [*inspired, Christlike love for people, which radiates from the member-missionary and touches hearts*], **with an eye single to the glory of God** [*while there are many personal benefits to those who share the gospel, the chief motivation for sharing it should be bringing joy to God*], **qualify him for the work**.

6 Remember **faith** [*keeps us trying when otherwise we might give up*], **virtue** [*personal purity; uplifting thoughts about others*], **knowledge** [*of the doctrines and principles of the gospel, plan of salvation, and so on*], **temperance** [*self-control; using wisdom*], **patience** [*it often requires much patience over long periods of time to bring people to Christ*], **brotherly kindness** [*kind acts are often the very best method of "preaching"*], **godliness** [*trying our best to reflect God in our behaviors and thoughts*], **charity** [*"the pure love of Christ"—see Moroni 7:47*], **humility** [*the opposite of arrogance and the "holier than thou" attitude which quickly alienates others*], **diligence** [*wise persistence;*

not giving up; missionary work often requires hard work].

Finally, we will go through verses 5 and 6 one more time, pointing out another possible lesson learned from them. One of the wonderful things about studying and restudying the scriptures is that there are many different messages imbedded in them. One time we see this message. Another time through, we see that message. The Holy Ghost inspires and directs our minds and hearts such that, over a lifetime of study, we can receive a multitude of personal instructions and messages from the same passage of scripture.

This time through verses 5 and 6, we will point out that verse 5 emphasizes personal qualities needed in order for us to do the work. Verse 6 emphasizes "people skills," or, in other words, how to work successfully with others in promoting and furthering the work of the Lord. Another way to put it might be to say that verse 6 shows us how to lead others in a Christ-like way. You can come up with many more definitions, as well as counsel for leaders, from the words in verse 6.

5 And faith, hope, charity and love, with an eye single to the glory of God, **qualify him** for the work.

6 Remember **faith** [*in others*], **virtue** [*so that others will respect you*], **knowledge** [*so that others can look*

up to you, trust you, and so that you can teach them correctly*], **temperance** [*not given to wild mood swings, etc., that destroy confidence in leaders*], **patience** [*allowing people to fail and try again until they succeed*], **brotherly kindness** [*is felt as much or more than observed; instills confidence in followers*], **godliness** [*when they watch you, they understand God better*], **charity** [*radiates to and encourages others; gives them strength to succeed*], **humility** [*helps people want to follow you; they know you know you are not perfect*], **diligence** [*they know you are going to keep helping them until they succeed; thus they are less likely to give up*].

In verse 7, next, the Lord exemplifies verses 5 and 6, above. He encourages Joseph Smith Sr., as well as all of us, to turn constantly to Him. In other words, He says, "Turn to Me and I will help you. Thus, your work will become My work."

They are strong words of assurance.

Doctrine

Verse 7. Action is often required on our part to access God's help.

7 **Ask**, and ye shall **receive**; **knock**, and it shall be **opened** unto you. Amen.

SECTION 5

Background

This revelation was given to the Prophet Joseph Smith at the request of Martin Harris. About 7–8 months before, Martin had lost the 116 manuscript pages. Now, in March 1829, several months after the angel had returned the plates and the Urim and Thummim to Joseph, Harris came to Harmony, Pennsylvania, to visit the Prophet and to request the privilege of seeing the gold plates (see verses 1 and 24).

Many years ago, when I was first studying the background and history of this section of the Doctrine and Covenants and realized that Martin Harris had actually come back to make such a request, I was appalled that he would be so bold as to return to where he had caused so much trouble and heartache, let alone make such a request.

However, as I thought about it, my heart changed, and I found myself grateful that Martin Harris had returned. I realized that all of us make mistakes and that each of us can humble ourselves, come back, and receive rich blessings precluded by previous behaviors. I became aware of a tremendous lesson to be found in section 5; namely that the Savior is infinitely forgiving. He will counsel, instruct, help, and offer the previously lost blessings again.

Much of the instruction in section 5 is to Joseph Smith, telling him just what to say to Martin (starting with verse 2). As you can understand, this was a kindness of the Lord to Joseph, who was in a rather awkward situation with this influential friend of the Smith family. Harris was a prominent Palmyra businessman, who was 23 years older than the young Prophet, and who had provided substantial financial help and support that had significantly helped Joseph to proceed with the work.

First, in verse 1, we see that a major purpose of Martin's visit was to actually verify that Joseph had the gold plates.

1 BEHOLD, I say unto you, that as my servant **Martin Harris has desired a witness** at my hand, **that you, my servant Joseph Smith, Jun., have got the plates** of which you have testified and borne record that you have received of me;

2 And now, behold, **this shall you say unto him—he who spake unto you, said unto you** [*in other words, in effect, tell him that I told you to tell him . . .*]: I, the Lord, am God, and have given these things unto you, **my servant** [*a kind reassurance to Joseph of his standing with the Lord*] **Joseph Smith, Jun.**, and have commanded you that you should stand as a witness of these things;

3 And I have caused you that you should enter into **a covenant** with me, **that you should not show them except to those persons to whom I commanded you**; and **you have no power over them except** [*unless*] **I grant it unto you**.

4 And **you have a gift to translate the plates**; and this is the first gift that I bestowed upon you; and I have commanded that you should **pretend to no other gift until my purpose is fulfilled in this**; for I will grant unto you **no other gift until it** [*the translation of the Book of Mormon plates*] **is finished**.

Remember that these are the things the Lord told Joseph to tell Martin (verse 2). The Lord is showing kindness here in helping Martin understand why Joseph is under such strict covenant and obligation not to show anyone the plates unless commanded to do so by the Lord Himself.

In addition, Joseph himself is being taught and reminded of the importance of the work of translating and how vital strict obedience is on his part.

Next, in verses 5–7, both Joseph and Martin are reminded of the tremendous importance of this work of translation for the whole world! It is preliminary to much more that will take place in the restoration of the gospel.

Doctrine

Verse 5. Trouble and woe are the natural aftermath of refusal to obey God's commandments.

5 **Verily, I say unto you, that woe shall come unto the inhabitants of the earth if they will not hearken unto** [*listen to and obey*] **my words**;

6 For **hereafter** [*after you finish the translation*] **you shall be ordained** [*including being ordained an apostle; see footnote 6a, which refers to D&C 20:2*] **and go forth and deliver my words unto the children of men** [*a scriptural term meaning "people"*].

7 Behold, **if they will not believe my words** [*contained in the Book of Mormon*]**, they would not believe you**, my servant Joseph, if it were possible that you should show them all these things [*including the gold plates and the Urim and Thummim*] which I have committed unto you.

8 Oh, this unbelieving and stiffnecked [*prideful; not humble; not teachable*] generation—mine anger is kindled against them.

9 Behold, verily I say unto you, I have reserved those things which I have entrusted unto you, my

servant Joseph, for a wise purpose in me, and it shall be made known unto future generations [*perhaps meaning, among other things, that great numbers in future generations will understand the importance of the Book of Mormon*];

> Sometimes, members of the Church wonder why the Lord does not seem to reveal spectacular new doctrines through our modern prophets. The answer seems to be given in verse 10; namely, that He has already revealed the doctrines through the Prophet Joseph Smith. The emphasis in the revelations to our modern "prophets, seers, and revelators" is more how to implement the plan of salvation and save souls rather than the revealing of new doctrine.

Doctrine

Verse 10. Joseph Smith was the prophet chosen by the Lord to restore the doctrines of the gospel in the last days.

10 But this generation shall have my word through you [*Joseph Smith*];

> Verse 11, next, must have quickly gained Martin's full attention. Three special witnesses were to be called by the Lord, who would be shown the things Martin desired to see.

11 And in addition to your [*Joseph Smith's*] testimony, **the testimony of three** of my servants, whom I shall call and ordain, **unto whom I will show these things** [*the things mentioned in D&C 17:1*], and they [*the words of testimony from these three witnesses*] shall go forth with my words [*especially the Book of Mormon*] that are given through you [*Joseph Smith*].

> Next, the Lord gives additional details as to the special witness that will be given to the three men chosen to be witnesses to the Book of Mormon. In verse 12 we learn that Jesus will personally bear witness of these things to them from heaven.

12 Yea, **they** [*the Three Witnesses*] **shall know of a surety that these things are true**, for **from heaven will I declare it unto them**.

> Next, Joseph and Martin are told that these three witnesses will literally see the things being spoken of. In D&C 17:1, we are informed that "these things" were the gold plates, breastplate, sword of Laban, Urim and Thummim, and the Liahona.

13 I will give them power that **they may behold** [*see*] and **view these things** as they are;

14 And **to none else will I grant this power, to receive this same testimony among this generation,**

in this the beginning of the rising up and the coming forth of my church out of the wilderness [*symbolic of the earth without the gospel*]— clear as the moon, and fair as the sun, and terrible as an army with banners [*symbolizing that none will stop the coming forth and spreading of the restored gospel*].

15 And **the testimony of three witnesses** will I send forth of [*as a witness for*] my word.

Next, the Lord teaches that He will also bear witness, through the Holy Ghost, to all who will believe in the Book of Mormon. This same promise obviously applies to all His words, in other scriptures as well as through His living prophets today.

Doctrine

Verse 16. Baptism and confirmation are prerequisites to being truly "born again."

16 And behold, **whosoever believeth on my words, them will I visit with the manifestation of my Spirit**; and they shall be born of me, even of water and of the Spirit [*in other words, they will be baptized and receive the gift of the Holy Ghost, through which they will then be spiritually reborn*]—

17 And **you must wait yet a little while** [*for baptism, etc.*], for ye are not yet ordained [*you don't yet have the priesthood authority necessary*]—

18 And **their** [*the three special witnesses*] **testimony shall also go forth** unto the condemnation of [*will stand as a witness against*] this generation if they harden their hearts against them;

The first half of verse 19, next, speaks of a devastating plague, which could easily include the withdrawal of the Spirit. The last half of the verse give us a clue as to how the wicked will be destroyed at the Second Coming of Christ.

Doctrine

Verse 19. At the Second Coming, the wicked will be destroyed by the glory of Christ as He comes. Their physical bodies cannot survive the full glory of the Savior at that time.

19 For **a desolating scourge** [*perhaps meaning spiritual sickness, which is the worst plague of all*] **shall go forth among the inhabitants of the earth**, and shall continue to be poured out from time to time, if they repent not, until the earth is empty, **and the inhabitants thereof are consumed away and utterly**

destroyed by the brightness of my coming.

As you just read at the end of verse 19, above, we are told that the wicked will be burned by the glory of the coming of Christ. They will not be able to withstand His presence as He comes in full glory, which will be the case at the Second Coming. Second Nephi tells us the same thing as follows:

2 Nephi 12:10, 19, 21

10 O ye wicked ones, enter into the rock, and hide thee in the dust, for the fear of the Lord and the glory of his majesty shall smite thee.

19 And they shall go into the holes of the rocks, and into the caves of the earth, for the fear of the Lord shall come upon them and **the glory of his majesty shall smite them**, when he ariseth to shake terribly the earth.

21 To go into the clefts of the rocks, and into the tops of the ragged rocks, for the fear of the Lord shall come upon them and the majesty of **his glory shall smite them**, when he ariseth to shake terribly the earth.

We will now return to Doctrine and Covenants, section 5. The Savior, in effect, is telling us that just as

the inhabitants of Jerusalem were warned of coming destruction, so also the inhabitants of the world are being warned, and everything prophesied will come to pass.

20 Behold, **I tell you these things, even as I also told the people of the destruction of Jerusalem**; and **my word shall be verified** at this time as it hath hitherto been verified.

Next, the Lord gives Joseph Smith a strong commandment to do better, still using tender terminology ("my servant Joseph") as He does so.

21 And now I command you, my servant Joseph, to repent and **walk more uprightly** before me, and to yield to the persuasions of men no more [*certainly a strong reference, perhaps among other things, to his previous giving in to Martin Harris concerning the 116 pages*];

22 And that you **be firm in keeping the commandments** wherewith I have commanded you; and **if** you do this, behold I grant unto you eternal life [*exaltation*], **even if you should be slain**.

We can learn more from verse 22, above. For one thing, some people have come to believe that if you were to see the Father or the Son, it is evidence that you are saved. We see here that

Joseph Smith does not yet have his calling and election made sure. In other words, he does not yet have his exaltation in celestial glory assured, even though he has seen both the Father and the Son, as well as Moroni, and several other angels. At this point in the Prophet's life, there is still an "if." By the way, in D&C 132:49, Joseph Smith will be told that his exaltation is assured.

Another thing we see here, in verse 22 (in the last phrase), is a strong hint that the Prophet will eventually give his life for the gospel.

Next, the instruction turns again from Joseph to Martin Harris. In His mercy, the Savior specifically gives Martin another chance, spelling out in considerable detail what he must do in order to qualify for the witness he desires.

23 **And now**, again, **I speak** unto you, my servant Joseph, **concerning the man** [*Martin Harris*] **that desires the witness**—

24 Behold, I say unto him, **he exalts himself** [*he is still afflicted with pride and arrogance*] and **does not humble himself sufficiently** before me; **but if he will bow down before me, and humble himself in mighty prayer and faith, in the sincerity of his heart, then will I grant unto him a view of the things which he desires to see.**

Having given Martin such tremendous and merciful encouragement, the Lord next gives strict instructions as to what he is to say by way of bearing witness to the Book of Mormon. He is to "say no more" (verse 26) than what he is told to say. Perhaps this is another chance for him to show strict obedience to the Lord's instruction, rather than giving in to his tendency to make his own rules.

25 And **then he shall** say unto the people of this generation: Behold, **I have seen the things which the Lord hath shown unto Joseph Smith, Jun.**, and **I know of a surety that they are true**, for **I have seen them**, for **they have been shown unto me by the power of God and not of man.**

26 And **I the Lord command him**, my servant Martin Harris, **that he shall say no more** unto them concerning these things, except he shall say: I have seen them, and they have been shown unto me by the power of God; and **these are the words which he shall say.**

We will pause here for a moment and turn to the Testimony of the Three Witnesses in the introductory pages of the Book of Mormon. Note how strictly Martin Harris and the other two witnesses (Oliver Cowdery and David Whitmer) held to this instruction from the Lord. We will use **bold** to point things out.

THE TESTIMONY OF THREE WITNESSES

BE IT KNOWN unto all nations, kindreds, tongues, and people, unto whom this work shall come: That **we**, through the grace of God the Father, and our Lord Jesus Christ, **have seen the plates** which contain this record, which is a record of the people of Nephi, and also of the Lamanites, their brethren, and also of the people of Jared, who came from the tower of which hath been spoken. And we also know that they have been translated by the gift and power of God, for his voice hath declared it unto us; wherefore **we know of a surety that the work is true**. And **we also testify that we have seen** the engravings which are upon the plates; and **they have been shown unto us by the power of God, and not of man**. And we declare with words of soberness, that an angel of God came down from heaven, and he brought and laid before our eyes, that we beheld and saw the plates, and the engravings thereon; and we know that it is by the grace of God the Father, and our Lord Jesus Christ, that **we beheld and bear record that these things are true**. And it is marvelous in our eyes. Nevertheless, the voice of the Lord commanded us that we should bear record of it; wherefore, to be obedient unto the commandments of God, **we bear testimony of these things**. And we know that if we are faithful in Christ, we shall rid our garments of the blood of all men, and be found spotless before the judgment-seat of Christ, and shall dwell with him eternally in the heavens. And the honor be to the Father, and to the Son, and to the Holy Ghost, which is one God. Amen.

OLIVER COWDERY
DAVID WHITMER
MARTIN HARRIS

We will now return to section 5. In verses 27–29, Joseph is told what to do and say if Martin Harris fails to comply with the strict instructions just given by the Lord.

27 But **if he deny this he will break the covenant** which he has before covenanted with me, **and** behold, **he is condemned** [*stopped in progress toward returning to live with God forever*].

In the instructions given for Martin Harris in verse 28, next, we find a concise summary of how to obtain forgiveness. Sometimes people seem to think that all that is required to obtain forgiveness is to stop committing the sin. There is more, including humbling oneself, confessing, making covenants, keeping other commandments of God, and fostering attitudes and taking actions that show faith in Christ as explained next.

28 And now, except he **humble himself** and **acknowledge unto me the things that he has done which are wrong**, and **covenant with me that he will keep my commandments**, and **exercise faith in me**, behold, I say unto him, he shall have no such views, for I will grant unto him no views of the things of which I have spoken.

In conclusion, Joseph is told to tell Martin that if he refuses to be obedient to these strict instructions, he is to have nothing more to do with the coming forth of the Book of Mormon and is to stop troubling the Lord about it.

29 And **if this be the case** [*if he declines to follow the instructions in verse 28, above*] I command you, my servant Joseph, that **you shall say unto him, that he shall do no more, nor trouble me any more concerning this matter**.

Next, the Lord tells Joseph what to do if Martin disregards this merciful offer. As you will see, in verse 31, Joseph is also warned what will happen if he himself fails to obey. As mentioned previously, this is, in effect, a "parenting scene."

30 And **if this be the case**, behold, I say unto thee Joseph, **when thou hast translated a few more pages thou shalt stop for a season, even until I command thee again; then thou mayest translate again**.

The following quote from the *Doctrine and Covenants Student Manual*, 2017 Edition, used in the Institutes of religion of the Church, gives possible Insights for verse 30, above:

"The Prophet Joseph Smith had made very little progress on the work of the translation since the Book of Mormon plates had been returned to him following the loss of the 116 manuscript pages. It is possible that during this time, both Emma Smith and her brother Reuben Hale assisted Joseph as scribes (see *The Joseph Smith Papers, Documents, Volume 1: July 1828–June 1831*, 4). When the revelation recorded in Doctrine and Covenants 5 was given in March 1829, the Lord indicated that Joseph should 'stop for a season' (D&C 5:30) and wait until He would 'provide means' to complete the translation of the Book of Mormon (D&C 5:34). This seems to have been fulfilled when Oliver Cowdery arrived in Harmony, Pennsylvania, a few weeks after Joseph received this revelation (see commentary in this manual for Doctrine and Covenants 6)."

31 And **except thou do this**, behold, **thou shalt have no more gift**, and **I will take away the things which I have entrusted with thee**.

Next, we see the Savior's kindness as He explains why He is being so strict with both Joseph and Martin. This, again, is a part of good "parenting" by explaining the reasons for the instructions given. We will see more of this when we study section 95, where the Lord disciplines His children for not having proceeded with the building of the Kirtland Temple.

32 And now, because **I foresee the lying in wait to destroy thee**, yea, **I foresee that if my servant Martin Harris humbleth not himself and receive a witness from my hand, that he will fall into transgression**;

33 And **there are many that lie in wait to destroy thee** from off the face of the earth [*many are even now plotting to kill you*]; and **for this cause, that thy days may be prolonged, I have given unto**

thee these commandments [*in other words, I have given you these commandments in order to save your life*].

34 Yea, **for this cause** [*for this reason*] **I have said: Stop, and stand still until I command thee** [*as stated in verse 30*], and I will provide means whereby thou mayest accomplish the thing which I have commanded thee.

35 And **if thou art faithful in keeping my commandments, thou shalt be lifted up** [*exalted in celestial glory*] **at the last day** [*on Judgment Day*]. Amen.

SECTION 6

Background

This revelation was given to Joseph Smith and Oliver Cowdery at Harmony, Pennsylvania, in April 1829. The 5-foot, 5-inch, small-boned Oliver (see *History of Seneca County, Ohio*, by W. Lang, 365) was 22 years old at the time and had been teaching school in Manchester, New York (next to Palmyra), where Joseph's parents lived.

We can see the hand of the Lord in bringing Oliver Cowdery to teach in the school that served some of the Smith children. Joseph's mother, Lucy Mack Smith, recorded that Joseph's older brother,

Hyrum, was a trustee for the local school district and that a man by the name of Lyman Cowdery applied to him to teach in the area. He was hired, but ended up not able to come, and asked if his brother, Oliver, could teach in his stead. The trustees held a meeting and agreed to the proposal. Oliver began boarding at the Smith residence at this time. (See *History of Joseph Smith by His Mother, Lucy Mack Smith*, 138.)

For their labors, such school teachers typically received a small salary plus room and board in the homes of students' parents. Oliver received 50 cents a day, plus room and board in various homes. As mentioned above, the Smiths were the first to have him board in their home.

It was during this time that Oliver heard of the gold plates from people in the community. He consequently asked the Smiths about them. They were reluctant at first to say anything due to the difficulties they had already endured. Eventually they told him about the Book of Mormon plates and the work of translating that Joseph was doing in Harmony, Pennsylvania. After asking many questions and being told some details by Joseph Smith Sr., Oliver became desirous to meet the Prophet. Joseph's mother, Lucy Mack Smith, wrote about what happened as follows:

"Shortly after receiving this information, he [Oliver] told Mr. Smith that he was highly delighted with what he had heard, that he had been in a deep study upon the subject all day, and that it was impressed upon his mind, that he should yet have the privilege of writing for Joseph. Furthermore, that he had determined to pay him a visit at the close of the school. . . .

"On coming in on the following day, he said, 'The subject upon which we were yesterday conversing seems working in my very bones, and I cannot, for a moment, get it out of my mind; finally, I have resolved on what I will do. Samuel [Smith], I understand, is going down to Pennsylvania to spend the spring with Joseph; I shall make my arrangements to be ready to accompany him thither, . . . for I have made it a subject of prayer, and I firmly believe that it is the will of the Lord that I should go. If there is a work for me to do in this thing, I am determined to attend to it.'"

It was in April 1829 that Samuel and Oliver traveled to Harmony, Pennsylvania, to visit Joseph and Emma. The Prophet's mother wrote the following:

"Joseph had been so hurried with his secular affairs that he could not proceed with his spiritual concerns so fast as was necessary for the speedy completion of the work; there was also another disadvantage under which he labored, his wife had so much of her time taken up with the care of her house, that she could write for him but a small portion of the time. On account of these embarrassments, Joseph called upon the Lord, three days prior to the arrival of Samuel and Oliver, to send him a scribe, according to the promise of the angel; and he was informed that the same should be forthcoming in a few days. Accordingly, when Mr. Cowdery told him the business that he had come upon, Joseph was not at all surprised." (*History of Joseph Smith by His Mother, Lucy Mack Smith*, 141.)

Of special note in the above record by Joseph's mother is the information that Oliver had already received a witness of the work that Joseph was doing. Joseph Smith later recorded that the "Lord appeared unto a young man by the name of Oliver Cowd[e]ry and showed unto him the plates in a vision. . . . Therefore he was desirous to come and write for me" (in *The Joseph Smith Papers, Histories, Volume 1: Joseph Smith Histories, 1832–1844*, ed. Karen Lynn Davidson and others [2012], 16; spelling, punctuation, and capitalization standardized). This witness will be referred to in this section, especially in verses 14, 15, 22, and 23.

We will now proceed to study section 6. Verses 1–5 are nearly identical to verses 1–5 in sections 11, 12, and 14 and are similar to verses 1–4 in section 4. The message is clear. The true Church of Jesus Christ is about to be restored to the earth.

1 **A GREAT and marvelous work is about to come forth unto the children of men.**

Next, in verse 2, the word of God will be compared to a living, powerful sword, symbolic of truth from God, which cuts quickly though false doctrine and misunderstanding so that people who are honest in heart can know the truth.

2 Behold, I am God; **give heed unto my word, which is quick** [*alive*] and **powerful**, sharper than a two-edged sword, to the dividing asunder [*cutting apart*] of both joints and marrow; therefore give heed unto my words.

Doctrine
Verse 3. A very important benefit of missionary work is that it can save the soul of the missionary.

3 Behold, the field [*symbolic of the inhabitants of the world*] is white [*ripe, as in a field of grain*] already to harvest; therefore, whoso desireth to reap, let him thrust in his sickle [*join in the work of harvesting; missionary work, etc.*] with his might, and reap [*harvest*] while the day lasts, **that he may treasure up for his soul**

everlasting salvation in the kingdom of God.

4 Yea, whosoever will thrust in his sickle and reap, the same is called of God.

5 Therefore, **if you will ask of me you shall receive; if you will knock it shall be opened unto you.**

The endorsement and instruction from the Lord personally to Oliver, in verse 5, above, must have been gratifying to Oliver who had acted in great faith to come visit Joseph.

As the Lord specifically addresses Oliver's desires in the next verses, we will be taught much too. Verse 7, for instance, is rather well-known and is often quoted in talks and gospel lessons. You may wish to mark it by putting a box around it or underlining it in your own scriptures or marking it in your electronic scriptures.

6 Now, as you [*Oliver Cowdery*] have asked, behold, I say unto you, **keep my commandments, and seek to bring forth and establish the cause of Zion** [*seek to help in the restoration of the gospel*];

7 **Seek not for riches but for wisdom, and behold, the mysteries** [*the plain and simple truths, doctrines, ordinances, etc. of the gospel of Christ; compare with the information given in the Bible*

Dictionary, at the back of your Latter-day Saint Bible, under "Mystery"] **of God shall be unfolded unto you, and then shall you be made rich. Behold, he that hath eternal life** [*exaltation in the highest degree of glory in the celestial kingdom*] **is rich.**

Joseph Fielding Smith said the following about the word "mysteries" as used in verse 7, above (**bold** added for emphasis):

"The Lord has promised to reveal his mysteries to those who serve him in faithfulness. . . . **There are no mysteries pertaining to the Gospel, only as we, in our weakness, fail to comprehend Gospel truth. . . . The 'simple' principles of the Gospel, such as baptism, the atonement, are mysteries to those who do not have the guidance of the Spirit of the Lord**" (*Church History and Modern Revelation*, 1:43).

8 Verily, verily, **I say unto you** [*Oliver*], even as you desire of me so it shall be unto you [*your desires will be granted*]; and **if you desire, you shall be the means of doing much good in this generation.**

Some people get a bit confused as they read verse 9, next, because of the phrase, "say nothing but repentance." They wonder if maybe they should only say "repent" in one form or another as they share the gospel or preach it formally. The solution to this momentary dilemma is simple: follow the Savior, follow the Brethren. Do they literally say more than "repent" as they teach and explain the gospel? Answer—yes, of course! Therefore, we come to understand that "say nothing but repentance" means to teach the gospel simply and directly, such that people have a chance to understand it and accept it. If they do, it will lead them to repentance and progress in coming unto Christ.

Joseph Fielding Smith explained this as follows:

"In the revelation to Oliver Cowdery, and to several others who came to ask what the Lord would have them do, the Lord said: 'Say nothing but repentance unto this generation; keep my commandments, and assist to bring forth my work.' We must not infer from this expression that those who went forth to preach were limited in their teachings so that all they could say was 'repent from your sins,' but in teaching the principles of the Gospel they should do so with the desire to teach repentance to the people and bring them in humility to a realization of the need for remission of sins. Even today in all of our preaching it should be with the desire to bring people to repentance and faith in God. That was the burden of John's message as he went forth to prepare the way for the Lord: 'Repent ye; for the kingdom of heaven is at hand,' he declared to the people, but he also taught them the necessity of baptism and officiated in that ordinance for all who repented of their sins. [Matt. 3:11.] (*CHMR*, 1947, 1:39–40.)" (Roy W. Doxey, *Latter-day Prophets and the Doctrine and Covenants*, 1:64–65).

9 **Say nothing but repentance** unto this generation; keep my commandments, and assist to bring forth my work, according to my commandments, and you shall be blessed.

In verse 10, next, Oliver is told by the Lord that he has a gift. There are various possibilities as to what this gift was. One possibility is that it was the "spirit of revelation," as explained in D&C 8:2–3. In D&C 8:4, Oliver is told that this is his "gift."

Another possibility is the ability and privilege of assisting in the translating of the Book of Mormon plates (see verse 25). Oliver attempted to translate but did not succeed, as explained in D&C 9.

Yet another possibility is that the gift referred to here, in D&C 6:10, is the "gift of Aaron," which is referred to in D&C 8:6–8. The *Doctrine and Covenants Student Manual*, used in the institutes of religion of the Church, 1981, page 19, contains the following quotes explaining this gift:

"There was another gift bestowed upon Oliver Cowdery, and that was the gift of Aaron. Like Aaron with his rod in his hand going before Moses as a spokesman, so Oliver Cowdery was to go before Joseph Smith. Whatever he should ask the Lord by power of this gift should be granted if asked in faith and in wisdom. Oliver was blessed with the great honor of holding the keys of this dispensation with Joseph Smith, and, like Aaron, did become a spokesman on numerous occasions. It was Oliver who delivered the first public discourse in this dispensation. (Smith, *Church History and Modern Revelation*, 1:52.)"

"Oliver Cowdery also had the 'gift of Aaron.' Aaron was the elder brother of Moses. Being prompted by the Spirit of the Lord, he met his younger brother in the wilderness and accompanied him to Egypt. He introduced him to the children of Israel in the land of Goshen. He was his spokesman before Pharaoh, and he assisted him in opening up the dispensation which Moses was commissioned to proclaim (Exodus 4:27–31). This was the gift of Aaron. In some respects, Oliver Cowdery was the Aaron of the new and last dispensation." (Smith and Sjodahl, Commentary, 44)

10 Behold **thou hast a gift**, and blessed art thou because of thy gift. Remember it is sacred and cometh from above—

11 And **if thou wilt inquire, thou shalt know mysteries** which are great and marvelous; therefore thou shalt **exercise thy gift**, that thou mayest find out mysteries [*the basics of the gospel of Christ; see note in verse 7, above*], that thou mayest bring many to the knowledge of the truth, yea, convince them of the error of their ways.

12 Make not **thy gift** known unto any save it be those who are of thy faith. Trifle not with sacred things.

Next, in verse 13, we are all reminded that there is more to being righteous and qualifying for exaltation than avoiding sins of commission. We must also do much good. In addition, in verse 13, we note that in this context, "saved" and "salvation" mean exaltation. This is often the doctrinal definition of these two words. However, one must always look carefully at the context in which these terms are used. For instance, the people spoken of in D&C 132:17 are "saved" but not "exalted."

Doctrine

Verse 13. Exaltation is the greatest gift to us from God. It means living with Heavenly Father forever, in the highest degree of glory within the celestial kingdom, in our own family units, and becoming gods ourselves, like our Heavenly Parents.

13 If thou wilt do good, yea, **and hold out faithful to the end,** thou shalt be **saved in the kingdom of God** [*In this context, "saved" means "exaltation"*], **which is the greatest of all the gifts of God**; for **there is no gift greater than the gift of salvation.**

In verses 14–15, next, we are reminded that we don't always realize it when we are being inspired, and it seems to take later events and experiences to confirm that we were indeed being prompted by the Spirit. Once we are aware of the fact that the Spirit spoke to us, we can think back and analyze how we felt or how we were inspired, and then learn from it to be better at recognizing how God speaks to us personally.

14 Verily, verily, I say unto thee, blessed art thou for what thou hast done; for thou hast inquired of me, and behold, **as often as thou hast inquired thou hast received instruction of my Spirit**. If it had not been so, thou wouldst not have come to the place where thou art at this time [*Harmony, Pennsylvania, to see Joseph Smith*].

15 Behold, thou knowest that thou hast inquired of me and **I did enlighten thy mind**; and now **I tell thee these things that thou mayest know that thou hast been enlightened by the Spirit of truth**;

You may have heard that Satan can't read our minds and may have wondered if this is indeed the case. Verse 16, next, gives the answer.

Doctrine
Verse 16. Satan cannot read our minds.

16 Yea, I tell thee, that thou mayest know that there is none else save God that knowest thy thoughts and the intents of thy heart.

In the context of the scriptures, we come to understand that the word "God," in verse 16, above, obviously means "members of the Godhead." Also, people may wonder how servants of the Lord can "read" peoples' minds when appropriate, as in the case of Alma and Amulek (Alma 12:3), in doing His work. The answer is simple. The Spirit can read the "thoughts and intents" of the heart and can put them in the minds of the servants of the Lord, including missionaries, teachers, parents, and others as needed when appropriate according to God's laws.

Next, the Lord confirms to Oliver that he has indeed been inspired to know that Joseph Smith has been called of God as a prophet. Oliver has obviously already begun serving as the scribe for the translation by the time this revelation is given.

17 **I tell thee these things as a witness unto thee—that the words or the work which thou hast been writing** [*as Joseph's scribe during the translating of the plates*] **are true**.

Verses 18–19 contain tender counsel to Oliver to be faithful and loyal to the Prophet, who is not perfect. This counsel applies to all of us as we, too, stand by and support our bishops and Church leaders, as well as family members and friends.

18 Therefore be diligent; **stand by my servant Joseph, faithfully**, in whatsoever difficult circumstances he may be for the word's sake.

19 **Admonish** [*counsel and advise*] **him in his faults**, and **also receive admonition of him** [*take counsel from him also*]. **Be patient**; be **sober** [*be serious about serious things*]; be **temperate**; **have patience, faith, hope** and **charity** [*all denote qualities needed in order to do the work of the Lord, as stated in D&C 4:5*].

20 Behold, thou art Oliver [*in other words, I know you personally*], and I have spoken unto thee because of thy desires; therefore treasure up these words [*the words of counsel I am now giving you*] in thy heart. **Be faithful and diligent in keeping the commandments** of God, **and I will encircle thee in the arms of my love.**

Next, the Savior personally introduces Himself to Oliver Cowdery.

21 **Behold, I am Jesus Christ, the Son of God**. I am the same that came unto mine own, and mine own received me not [*I am He whom the Jews rejected*]. **I am the light which shineth in darkness** [*spiritual darkness*], and the darkness comprehendeth it not.

Perhaps you have had the experience of being given a blessing by a faithful priesthood holder, during which blessing things were mentioned which you alone knew. Such occurrences are sweet reminders of the truthfulness of the work. In verses 22–24, next, Oliver is given such a testimony-strengthening experience.

At one point, while he was staying with the Smith family in the Manchester and Palmyra area, Oliver had prayed to the Lord concerning what he had heard about Joseph Smith and the gold plates. He had received a witness from the Lord, but had told absolutely no one about the experience. Now, through the Prophet Joseph Smith, the Savior reminds him of this witness.

22 Verily, verily, I say unto you, if you desire a further witness,

cast your mind [*look back*] **upon the night that you cried unto me in your heart, that you might know concerning the truth of these things.**

Doctrine

Verse 23. Peace is one of the greatest forms of testimony and communication that comes from God.

23 **Did I not speak peace to your mind concerning the matter? What greater witness can you have than from God**?

Joseph Smith said the following about verses 22–24 in this section:

"After we had received this revelation [D&C 6], Oliver Cowdery stated to me that after he had gone to my father's to board, and after the family had communicated to him concerning my having obtained the plates, that one night after he had retired to bed he called upon the Lord to know if these things were so, and the Lord manifested to him that they were true, but he had kept the circumstance entirely secret, and had mentioned it to no one; so that after this revelation was given, he knew that the work was true, because no being living knew of the thing alluded to in the revelation, but God and himself" (*History of the Church*, 1:35).

Also, from verse 23, above, we learn that peace is one of the greatest testimonies we can be given from God. Unfortunately, it is sometimes overlooked because of the expectation of more spectacular forms of communication from heaven.

24 And **now, behold, you have received a witness; for if I have told you things which no man knoweth have you not received a witness?**

As mentioned previously, one of the gifts given to Oliver Cowdery was the gift of translating. We see this in verses 25–28, next, and find in verse 26 that there are yet other ancient records containing the gospel that we have not yet received (compare with 2 Nephi 29:7–11).

25 And, behold, **I grant unto you a gift**, if you desire of me, **to translate, even as my servant Joseph.**

26 Verily, verily, I say unto you, that **there are records which contain much of my gospel, which have been kept back** because of the wickedness of the people;

27 And now I command you, that if you have good desires— a desire to lay up treasures for yourself in heaven—**then shall you assist in bringing to light,**

with your gift, those parts of my scriptures which have been hidden because of iniquity.

In verse 28, next, we are reminded of the law of witnesses, which is an important part of the gospel. One of the common uses of this law of witnesses is for baptism—two witnesses are required to view each baptism to assure that the person is baptized properly.

28 And now, behold, I give unto you, and also unto my servant Joseph, the keys of this gift, which shall bring to light this ministry; and **in the mouth of two or three witnesses shall every word be established**.

Next, the Savior addresses both Joseph and Oliver, giving them true perspective as to what matters most. Although what He says to them, namely that "they can do no more unto you than unto me," may at first be a bit of a shock, it is a strong reminder that whatever happens to us in mortality is but a small thing compared with eternity and will "soon" be over.

29 Verily, verily, I say unto you, if they reject my words, and this part of my gospel and ministry, blessed are ye [*in other words, you will be okay, no matter what, because you have done your part*], for **they can do no more unto you than unto me**.

30 **And even if they do** unto you even as they have done unto me, blessed are ye, for **you shall dwell with me in glory**.

31 But **if they reject not my words**, which shall be established by the testimony which shall be given, **blessed are they**, and then shall ye have joy in the fruit of your labors [*in other words, you will be all right, no matter what, but if they do heed My words, brought forth by you, it will be an extra blessing and additional joy for you*].

Next, we see that the Savior is very much involved in the day-to-day work of the kingdom here on earth.

32 Verily, verily, I say unto you, as I said unto my disciples, where two or three are gathered together in my name, as touching one thing, behold, **there will I be in the midst of them—even so am I in the midst of you**.

Next, the Lord states twice what we know as "the law of the harvest."

33 **Fear not to do good**, my sons [*a particularly tender form of addressing these men*], for **whatsoever ye sow** [*plant; in other words, the work that you do for Me*]**, that shall ye also reap** [*harvest; in other words, what you do for Me will*

come back to bless you]; therefore, **if ye sow good ye shall also reap good for your reward**.

Doctrine

Verse 34. If we build our lives upon Christ, nothing can stop us from obtaining exaltation.

34 Therefore, **fear not**, little flock; **do good; let earth and hell combine against you**, for **if ye are built upon my rock, they cannot prevail** [*ultimately win over us*].

We all have imperfections, sins, and shortcomings that can make us feel inadequate to accept callings and to do the work of the Lord. Christ's tender counsel to Joseph and Oliver, next, can give comfort to all of us. It is both reassuring and insightful as to the intended effect and power of the Atonement in our daily lives.

35 Behold, **I do not condemn you; go your ways and sin no more; perform with soberness** [*seriousness*] **the work** which I have commanded you.

36 **Look unto me in every thought; doubt not, fear not.**

We understand verse 37, next, to not be an actual appearance of the Savior to Joseph and Oliver, rather, an invitation to better understand the power of the Atonement to cleanse and heal. Thus,

along with them, all of us are given power and encouragement to continue striving to keep the commandments, with optimism and confidence in the final outcome.

Doctrine

Verse 37. The Savior's suffering paid the price for us to become free from sin. Those who are faithful will receive exaltation.

37 **Behold the wounds which pierced my side, and also the prints of the nails in my hands and feet** [*reflect on My Atonement*]; **be faithful, keep my commandments, and ye shall inherit the kingdom of heaven**. Amen.

SECTION 7

Background

We know from this section in the Doctrine and Covenants that the Apostle John, often referred to as "John the Beloved," was given the privilege of remaining alive and continuing to minister and teach the gospel until the time of the Second Coming of the Savior. Thus, he is what we refer to as a "translated being." However, without the revelation here in section seven, we would be like others who only have the Bible on this subject. The problem is that the wording in the Bible, John

21:22–23, is not entirely clear and leaves readers wondering as to whether or not John would remain on earth and continue to live until the Second Coming. Those verses in John follow Peter's question to the resurrected Christ as to what John would do after the Savior's departure. We will include these verses from the New Testament here so that you can see how the question remains unanswered by them as to whether or not John was allowed to stay on earth. As you can see, in John 21:22, next, there is a big **"if."**

John 21:22–23

22 Jesus saith unto him, If I will that he tarry [*remain on earth*] till I come, what *is that* to thee? follow thou me.

23 Then went this saying [*a tradition, a rumor*] abroad among the brethren, that that disciple [*John*] should not die: **yet Jesus said not unto him** [*Peter*]**, He** [*John*] **shall not die; but, If I will** that he tarry till I come, what *is that* to thee?

Joseph Smith tells us that he and Oliver Cowdery found themselves with differing opinions about whether or not John died, or is still alive on earth. Consequently, they asked the Lord through the Urim and Thummim. The Prophet said:

"During the month of April [*1829, at Harmony, Pennsylvania*] I continued to translate, and he [*Oliver Cowdery*] to write, with little cessation, during which time we received several revelations. **A difference of opinion arising between us about the account of John the Apostle, mentioned in the New Testament, as to whether he died or continued to live**, we mutually agreed to settle it by the Urim and Thummim" (*History of the Church*, 1:35–36).

Section 7 was given in response to their question. As you will see, in the heading to section 7 in your Doctrine and Covenants, this section "is a translated version of the record made on parchment by John." We don't know whether Joseph Smith had the actual parchment in his possession and translated it, was shown it in vision, or was given its contents by revelation. Whatever the case, the answer was given in section 7, and thus we know that John the Beloved Apostle is still alive and on earth, and he will be until the Savior comes. See also *Doctrine and Covenants Student Manual*, 2018, used by the institutes of religion of the Church, under "Doctrine and Covenants 7."

As mentioned above, we understand that John is a translated being (see Bruce R. McConkie, *Mormon Doctrine*, 806). For more information about translated beings, you may wish to read 3 Nephi 28, which gives some details about the Three Nephites, who will continue to live on earth as translated beings and will die and be resurrected instantly at the time of the Savior's Second Coming.

In 1831, Joseph Smith said that at that time, John was working with the Lost Ten Tribes, preparing them for their return. See *History of the Church*, 1:176.

We will now proceed with our study of the text of section 7. Remember, as stated above, that this is taken from the writings of John, on parchment, and thus Joseph Smith is giving us John's own words here. Again, the question leading up to this revelation was whether or not John the Apostle is still alive on earth.

1 AND **the Lord said unto me: John**, my beloved, **what desirest thou?** For if you shall ask what you will [*whatever you want*], it shall be granted unto you.

2 And **I said unto him: Lord, give unto me power over death, that I may live and bring souls unto thee**.

3 And the Lord said unto me: Verily, verily, I say unto thee, because thou desirest this **thou shalt tarry** [*remain alive on earth*] **until I come in my glory** [*until the Second Coming*], and shalt prophesy before nations, kindreds, tongues and people.

4 And **for this cause** [*this is why*] **the Lord said unto Peter: If I will that he** [*John*] **tarry till I come, what is that to thee?** For **he desired of me that he might bring souls unto me**, but **thou** [*Peter*] **desiredst that thou mightest speedily come unto me in my kingdom**.

As you have just read, both Peter and John made special requests to the resurrected Savior, as He appeared and taught them on the shores of the Sea of Galilee (see John 21). As you will see, in verse 8, both of these requests were granted.

Verses 5 and 6, next, use the word "greater." Because of this, some people may tend to think that the Lord is telling Peter that John's wish was more important than his. This is not the case, according to verses 5, 6, and 8. "Greater," in this context, simply means "more" or "additional." In other words, John wants to do more work, or a "greater" work here on earth, in bringing souls unto Christ, than he has done up to now. Whereas, Peter wants to return quickly to heaven to be with the Savior, when he has finished his mission on earth.

5 I say unto thee, Peter, **this was a good desire** [*Peter's desire, as expressed at the end of verse 4, above*]; but my beloved [*John*] has desired that he might do **more**, or

a **greater work yet among men** than what he has before done.

6 Yea, he has undertaken a greater work [*additional work*]; therefore I will make him as flaming fire and a ministering angel [*he will be a translated being*]; he shall minister for those who shall be heirs of salvation who dwell on the earth.

Next, the writings of John, on this parchment, inform us that the Savior told Peter that he would be privileged to help John, from the other side of the veil, and that he, along with James and John, would continue to work as a team, holding the keys of presidency. One manifestation of this fact is their appearing to Joseph Smith and Oliver Cowdery in 1829 and restoring the keys of the Melchizedek Priesthood to them. (See *History of the Church*, 3:387. See also D&C 81:1–2.)

7 And I will make thee [*Peter*] to minister for him and for thy brother James; and **unto you three I will give this power and the keys of this ministry until I come**.

Did you notice, in verse 7, above, that Peter is told, in effect, that he would preside in this "presidency" and as such, he would "minister" to his counselors, James and John? We see this pattern today in our first presidencies.

Finally, we are taught that the

Savior told both Peter and John that what they asked for was good, and that they would both be rewarded for their righteous desires.

8 Verily I say unto you, **ye shall both have according to your desires**, for ye both joy in that which ye have desired.

SECTION 8

Background

Both sections 8 and 9 deal with Oliver Cowdery's desire to assist with the actual translating of the gold plates. Oliver had been told that he had the gift to translate ancient records (see D&C 6:25–28). The Prophet Joseph Smith recorded the following with respect to Oliver's desire to do so: "Whilst continuing the work of translation, during the month of April, Oliver Cowdery became exceedingly anxious to have the power to translate bestowed upon him, and in relation to this desire the following revelations were obtained: [D&C 8–9]" (*History of the Church*, 1:36).

Section 8 was given to Oliver Cowdery in April 1829, at Harmony, Pennsylvania, where he was serving as scribe to Joseph Smith as he translated the gold plates. From it we gain valuable instruction concerning how to recognize and receive revelation.

In verse 1, next, we are taught some of the basic requirements for receiving knowledge and revelation from God.

1 OLIVER Cowdery, verily, verily, I say unto you, that assuredly as the Lord liveth, who is your God and your Redeemer, even so surely shall you receive a knowledge of whatsoever things you shall **ask in faith**, with an **honest heart** [*having pure motives*], **believing that you shall receive** a knowledge concerning the engravings of old records, which are ancient, which contain those parts of my scripture of which has been spoken by the manifestation of my Spirit.

Next, we are taught of two major ways, among others, in which the Holy Ghost communicates with us, namely, in our mind and in our heart. There is a difference between the two. In a stake presidents' training meeting, which I was privileged to attend in the fall of 2000, Elder Richard G. Scott of the Quorum of the Twelve explained that "heart" deals with general feelings and impressions, whereas "mind" refers to specific thoughts and instruction. In other words, "heart" is general and "mind" is very specific. He went on to teach us that an impression to the heart, when followed, will lead to more specific instruction to the mind.

Elder Scott used Enos, in the Book of Mormon, as an example. He pointed out that in Enos 1:3, tender feelings about the words and instructions from his father over the years sunk deep into Enos's heart. Then in Enos 1:4, Enos acted upon those feelings and left his hunting and turned to God in humble prayer. As a result, very specific teachings and instructions came into his mind. (See Enos 1:5–10, especially verse 10.)

We will now continue with section 8.

Doctrine

Verse 2. Two of the most common ways the Lord speaks to us are in our minds and in our hearts through the Holy Ghost.

2 Yea, behold, **I will tell you in your mind and in your heart, by the Holy Ghost**, which shall come upon you and which shall dwell in your heart.

Next, in verse 3, Oliver is instructed as to the "spirit of revelation" and is reminded that it is a powerful means of communication that is also used by prophets. This is a gift that all of us can enjoy. It is part of having the gift of the Holy Ghost. In verse 4, Oliver will be told that he has this gift of recognizing and understanding the voice of the Spirit, and if he carefully follows what it says, he will be spared much misery.

3 Now, behold, **this** [*being taught in your mind and heart by the Holy Ghost*] **is the spirit of revelation**; behold, this is **the spirit by which Moses brought the children of Israel through the Red Sea on dry ground.**

4 Therefore **this is thy gift; apply unto it, and** blessed art thou, for **it shall deliver you out of the hands of your enemies**, when, if it were not so, they would slay you and bring your soul to destruction.

> President M. Russell Ballard, then of the Quorum of the Twelve Apostles, gave powerful counsel regarding the sources we use in seeking knowledge and understanding about the Church and the gospel:
>
> "Today we live in a world in which people don't ask of God—they seem to want to ask of Google. Even when it comes to questions of faith, there are many who trust the Internet to provide accurate, fair, and balanced answers to their questions more than they trust the ultimate source of truth, our Heavenly Father. . . .
>
> ". . . Today the Internet is full of those lying in wait to deceive the uninformed and inexperienced.
>
> "In our search for gospel truth, we not only need to find reliable sources but we also need to give the Lord equal time in our daily pursuits. We need to study the scriptures and the words of the Lord's servants. We need to be living right before God—we need to be doing His will [see John 7:16–17]. And we can never overstate the importance of taking our spiritual concerns directly to God and trusting His inspiration and guidance" ("Women of Dedication, Faith, Determination, and Action" [address given at Brigham Young University Women's Conference, May 1, 2015], 5–6; see womensconference.ce.byu.edu/transcripts).
>
> Next, we are reminded that in order to recognize when the Holy Ghost speaks to our minds and hearts, we must be in tune by keeping the commandments of God.

5 Oh, **remember these words, and keep my commandments**. Remember, this is your gift.

> Next, Oliver Cowdery is told that he has another gift, namely, the "gift of Aaron."

6 Now this is not all thy gift; for **you have another gift, which is the gift of Aaron**; behold, it has told you many things;

7 Behold, there is no other power, save the power of God, that can cause this **gift of Aaron** to be with you.

Joseph Fielding Smith explained the "gift of Aaron" as follows:

"There was another gift bestowed upon Oliver Cowdery, and that was the gift of Aaron. Like Aaron with his rod in his hand going before Moses as a spokesman, so Oliver Cowdery was to go before Joseph Smith. Whatever he should ask the Lord by power of this gift should be granted if asked in faith and in wisdom. Oliver was blessed with the great honor of holding the keys of this dispensation with Joseph Smith, and, like Aaron [Ex. 4:10–17], did become a spokesman on numerous occasions. It was Oliver who delivered the first public discourse in this dispensation." (*Church History and Modern Revelation*, 1:48. See also Doxey, *Latter-day Prophets and the Doctrine and Covenants*, 1:82.)

8 Therefore, **doubt not** [*an important ingredient of powerful faith*], for it is the gift of God; and you shall hold it in your hands [*perhaps this is symbolic, in the sense that his gift to be a spokesman for Joseph Smith would be like Aaron's rod (Exodus 7:10–12, etc.), which symbolized his authority and calling to be a spokesman for Moses*], **and do marvelous works**; and no power shall be able to take it away out of your hands, for it is the work of God.

9 And, therefore, whatsoever you shall ask me to tell you by that means, that will I grant unto you, and you shall have knowledge concerning it.

Doctrine

Verse 10. Faith in Christ is the foundation principle upon which all successful religious behavior is based.

10 Remember that **without faith you can do nothing**; therefore **ask in faith**. Trifle not with these things; do not ask for that which you ought not.

We do not know what specific ancient records are being referred to in verse 11, next. But we do know that there are many ancient records yet to be brought forth. See 2 Nephi 27:7–8; 29:11–13; 3 Nephi 26:6–11; Ether 3:22–28; 4:5–7.

11 Ask that you may know the mysteries of God, and that you may translate and receive knowledge from **all those ancient records** which have been hid up, that are sacred; and according to your faith shall it be done unto you.

From verse 12, next, we get a hint that the Savior is much involved in our lives, even though we often don't realize the extent of his involvement.

12 Behold, it is I [*Jesus Christ*] that have spoken it; and **I am the same that spake unto you from the beginning** [*see D&C 6:14–15, 22–23*]. Amen.

SECTION 9

Background

Section 9 was given to Oliver Cowdery in Harmony, Pennsylvania, in April 1829, and goes together with section 8. You may wish to review the background notes for section 8 in this study guide.

It would appear from the context of verses 1 and 2 that Oliver, who had been serving as Joseph Smith's scribe during the translating of the gold plates, had attempted to do some translating himself with the Lord's permission. In fact, in D&C 6:25, he was told, "I grant unto you a gift, if you desire of me, to translate, even as my servant Joseph."

He apparently did not understand, among other things, that translating required work (see verses 7–8), and thus failed in his effort. While it was obviously a disappointment to both Oliver and Joseph (see end of verse 12), it served as an important lesson and provides an opportunity for all of us to learn more about the process of receiving revelation.

Pay special attention to the tender words used by the Savior in addressing Oliver and encouraging him in verses 1–6, next. We feel His compassion and kindness for this powerful young man who was in rather intense training for the role he was to play in the restoration of the gospel. We will **bold** some of these terms of tenderness.

1 BEHOLD, I say unto you, **my son** [*Oliver Cowdery*], that because you did not translate according to that which you desired of me, and did commence again to write [*to serve as a scribe*] for my servant, Joseph Smith, Jun., even so I would that ye should continue until you have finished this record [*finished writing down the translation of the gold plates, which was to become the Book of Mormon*], which I have entrusted unto him.

2 And then, behold, **other records have I, that I will give unto you power that you may assist to translate**.

While we don't know what "other records" are referred to here by the Lord, we do know from the Book of Mormon that there are many such records. For instance, additional records are mentioned in 2 Nephi 27:7–8; 29:11–13; 3 Nephi 26:6–11; Ether 3:22–28 and 4:5–7.

We also have a fascinating account given by President Brigham

Young of other records, as follows:

"When Joseph got the plates, the angel instructed him to carry them back to the hill Cumorah, which he did. Oliver says that when Joseph and Oliver went there, the hill opened, and they walked into a cave, in which there was a large and spacious room. He says he did not think, at the time, whether they had the light of the sun or artificial light; but that it was just as light as day. They laid the plates on a table; it was a large table that stood in the room. Under this table there was a pile of plates as much as two feet high, and there were altogether in this room more plates than probably many wagon loads; they were piled up in the corners and along the walls. The first time they went there the sword of Laban hung upon the wall; but when they went again it had been taken down and laid upon the table across the gold plates; it was unsheathed, and on it was written these words: 'This sword will never be sheathed again until the kingdoms of the world become the kingdom of our God and his Christ.' I tell you this as coming not only from Oliver Cowdery, but others who were familiar with it, and who understood it just as well as we understand coming to this meeting, enjoying the day, and by and by we separate and go away, forgetting most of what is said, but remembering some things." (*Journal of Discourses*, 19:38. See also Doxey, *Latter-day Prophets and*

the Doctrine and Covenants, 1:87.)

3 **Be patient, my son**, for it is wisdom in me, and it is not expedient that you should translate at this present time.

> Next, Oliver is told to continue serving as scribe for Joseph Smith. We will have to wait for further information as to what "continue as you commenced" refers to in verse 5.

4 Behold, the work which you are called to do is to write for my servant Joseph.

5 And, behold, it is because that you did not continue as you commenced, when you began to translate, that I have taken away this privilege from you.

6 **Do not murmur** [*complain*]**, my son**, for it is wisdom in me [*I know what I am doing*] that I have dealt with you after this manner.

> While verses 7–12 are very specific to Oliver's attempt to translate, we can nevertheless learn some principles regarding how to prepare for and qualify for receiving revelation by studying them.
>
> First of all, in verse 7, combined with the beginning of verse 8, we learn that effort is required on our part. We will use **bold** to point this out.

Doctrine

Verses 7 and 8. Receiving revelation often requires work and preparation on our part.

7 Behold, you have not understood; **you have supposed that I would give it unto you, when you took no thought save it was** [*other than*] **to ask me.**

8 But, behold, I say unto you, that **you must study it out in your mind; then you must ask me if it be right,** and if it is right I will cause that your bosom shall burn within you; therefore, you shall feel that it is right.

We must be a bit careful with the word "burn" in verse 8, above. The use of this word seems to be very specific to this context with Oliver Cowdery. Perhaps we need to wait until we have an opportunity to ask him about it in the next life to find out exactly what is meant.

In general applications, the word "peace" seems to apply to all of us as far as recognizing the Lord's approval of a course of action we have determined to take. See, for instance, D&C 6:23, where the Lord asks Oliver Cowdery, "Did I not speak peace to your mind concerning the matter?"

President Dallin H. Oaks, when he was a member of the Quorum of the Twelve Apostles, spoke about this burning in the bosom mentioned in verse 8. He taught:

"What does a 'burning in the bosom' mean? Does it need to be a feeling of caloric heat, like the burning produced by combustion? If that is the meaning, I have never had a burning in the bosom. Surely, the word 'burning' in this scripture signifies a feeling of comfort and serenity. That is the witness many receive. That is the way revelation works" ("Teaching and Learning by the Spirit," *Ensign*, Mar. 1997, 13).

Again, verse 9, next, is very specific to Oliver Cowdery and his attempts to translate.

9 But **if it be not right you shall have no such feelings, but you shall have a stupor of thought that shall cause you to forget the thing which is wrong**; therefore, you cannot write that which is sacred save it be given you from me.

In the April 1931 general conference of the Church, Elder Melvin J. Ballard showed how principles learned from the specific lessons given to Oliver Cowdery in these verses could apply to members of the Church in general. He taught:

"There is a key given in the ninth section of the book of Doctrine and Covenants, which would be very profitable for the Latter-day Saints to follow even now. You remember the circumstance of

Oliver Cowdery translating portions of the Book of Mormon, and then all became darkness to him and he could not proceed. He inquired of the Lord to know why it was, and the answer came that he had taken no thought save it was to ask the Lord, and left the burden of responsibility there. [Sec. 9:8–9, quoted.]

"You do not know what to do today to solve your financial problems, what to plant, whether to buy or sell cattle, sheep or other things. It is your privilege to study it out; counsel together with the best wisdom and judgment the Lord shall give you, reach your conclusions, and then go to the Lord with it, tell him what you have planned to do. If the thing you have planned to do is for your good and your blessing, and you are determined to serve the Lord, pay your tithes and your offerings and keep his commandments, I promise that he will fulfil that promise upon your head, and your bosom shall burn within by the whisperings of the Spirit that it is right. But if it is not right, you shall have no such feelings, but you shall have a stupor of thought, and your heart will be turned away from that thing.

"I know of nothing today that the Latter-day Saints need more than the guidance of the Holy Spirit in the solution of the problems of life" (In Conference Report, April 1931, 37–38).

Next, the Savior continues to instruct Oliver as to why he did not succeed in translating and explains that the opportunity is now past.

10 Now, **if you had known this you could have translated**; nevertheless, it is not expedient [*necessary*] that you should translate now.

11 Behold, it was expedient [*important*] when you commenced; but **you feared, and the time is past**, and it is not expedient [*necessary*] now;

12 For, do you not behold [*can't you see*] that I have given unto my servant Joseph sufficient strength, whereby it is made up? **And neither of you have I condemned**.

We understand from the last sentence in verse 12, above, that Joseph Smith must have been somewhat concerned and disappointed too when Oliver failed to translate. Perhaps he felt some responsibility himself for the failure. Whatever the case, we see the kindness of the Lord in assuring both of them that "neither of you have I condemned." The word "condemned," in this context, can mean "put a stop to your eternal progression."

In other words, all is not lost, and it is important to move ahead according to the Lord's instructions. If they do, they will "prosper," as they are told in verse 13, next. In fact, according to verses 13 and 14, if they move past this failure and follow God's counsel in the future, nothing will be lost as far as their eternal exaltation is concerned. This is perhaps one of the most important lessons for all of us in this section.

13 Do this thing which I have commanded you, and you shall prosper. Be faithful, and yield to no temptation.

14 Stand fast in the work wherewith I have called you, and a hair of your head shall not be lost [*a symbolic phrase, meaning that the Lord will take good care of you completely and lead you to exaltation*], and **you shall be lifted up** [*be exalted; receive the highest degree of glory in the celestial kingdom*] at the last day [*on the day of final judgment*]. Amen.

SECTION 10

Background

Sections 3 and 10 go together. They both deal with the loss of the 116 manuscript pages of the Book of Mormon translation by Martin Harris. For more background information, you may wish to read the notes given in this study guide at the beginning of section 3.

By way of brief review, Martin Harris came to Harmony, Pennsylvania, in February 1828, and served as scribe for Joseph Smith as he translated from the gold plates. By June 14, 1828, they had 116 handwritten pages (called "manuscript pages") containing the translation of the Book of Mormon plates up to that point. After repeated requests by Martin, and contrary to the Lord's initial instruction, Joseph finally let him take the manuscript back to Palmyra, New York. Martin's hope, among other things, was to convince his wife and others that he was not wasting his time with a false prophet.

Martin broke serious promises made with respect to safeguarding the precious manuscript pages, and they were lost. After about three weeks, when Martin had not returned to Joseph and Emma's home in Harmony with the 116 pages, Joseph went to Palmyra to check concerning the manuscript. Upon finding that the pages had been lost, he returned to Harmony, dejected and very discouraged.

After returning home, the Urim and Thummim was taken from the Prophet by Moroni, referred to as "an angel" by his mother in her account (see *History of Joseph Smith by His Mother*, pages 133–36). Shortly thereafter, it was returned to Joseph, at which point he received the revelation we now have as section 3 of the Doctrine and Covenants. Afterward, the Urim and Thummim, as well as the gold plates, were taken from him.

After a time, both the plates and the Urim and Thummim were returned to him. Of this, the Prophet's mother wrote the following, quoting her son, Joseph Smith Jr.:

"After the angel left me," said he, "I continued my supplications to God, without cessation, and on the twenty-second of September, I had the joy and satisfaction of again receiving the Urim and Thummim, with which I have again commenced translating, and Emma writes for me, but the angel said that the Lord would send me a scribe [*Oliver Cowdery*], and I trust his promise will be verified. The angel seemed pleased with me when he gave me back the Urim and Thummim, and he told me that the Lord loved me, for my faithfulness and humility" (Lucy Mack Smith, *History of Joseph Smith by His Mother*, 135).

We will now study the revelation recorded as section 10 that Joseph received after the gold plates and the Urim and Thummim were returned to him. We will learn much about what happened to the 116 lost pages and see what the Lord told Joseph Smith to do about it.

We can learn many lessons from these verses, several of which we will point out as we go. First, we will consider verses 1–9 as a unit and simply **bold** five phrases that remind us of the reality of our accountability when we intentionally go against the counsels of God. Pay special attention to the word,

"***you***," which we will **bold**, *italicize,* and <u>underline</u> for extra emphasis. When we finish with this, we will repeat this block of verses and do more with several of the verses.

1 NOW, behold, I say unto you, that because <u>***you***</u> **delivered up those writings which** you had power given unto you to translate by the means of the Urim and Thummim, into the hands of a wicked man, <u>***you***</u> **have lost them**.

2 And <u>***you***</u> **also lost your gift** at the same time, and your mind became darkened.

3 Nevertheless, it is now restored unto you again; therefore see that you are faithful and continue on unto the finishing of the remainder of the work of translation as you have begun.

4 Do not run faster or labor more than you have strength and means provided to enable you to translate; but be diligent unto the end.

5 Pray always, that you may come off conqueror; yea, that you may conquer Satan, and that you may escape the hands of the servants of Satan that do uphold his work.

6 Behold, they have sought to destroy you; yea, even the man in whom you have trusted has sought to destroy you.

7 And for this cause I said that he is a wicked man, for he has sought to take away the things wherewith you have been entrusted; and he has also sought to destroy your gift.

8 And because _you_ have **delivered the writings into his hands,** behold, wicked men have taken them from you.

9 Therefore, _you_ **have delivered them up, yea, that which was sacred, unto wickedness.**

As mentioned above, we will now start over with the first nine verses, and do many more things with them. We can see the Savior teaching His young prophet (Joseph Smith was 22 years old at this time) by giving him understanding and leading him on the path to wisdom and increased ability to do the work that has been entrusted to him. We will continue to **bold** the actual scriptural text for teaching purposes. First, in verses 1–2, the Master Teacher gives a lesson on "cause and effect."

1 NOW, behold, I say unto you, that **because you delivered up those writings** [_the 116 manuscript pages_] which you had power given unto you to translate by the means of the Urim and Thummim, **into the hands of a wicked man** [_Martin Harris_], **you have lost them.**

2 And **you also lost your gift** at the same time, **and your mind became darkened** [_an immediate result of intentional disobedience_].

Next, Christ teaches a lesson on mercy and hope, explaining how Joseph can successfully complete the work of translating. In other words, His Atonement allows and enables us to move ahead after having been stopped by our own poor choices.

Doctrine
Verse 3. Through our repentance, the Atonement of Christ allows and enables us to resume progress on the covenant path toward exaltation after having been stopped by our own wrong choices.

3 **Nevertheless, it** [_the gift of translating_] **is now restored unto you again**; therefore **see that you are faithful** and **continue on unto the finishing of the remainder of the work of translation** as you have begun.

Verse 4, next, is a rather well-known verse in the Doctrine and Covenants, and is often quoted in lessons, conversations and sermons. In context, it contains a number of insights and vital lessons for each of us.

First of all, having been given another chance, after having "feared man [*Martin Harris*] more than God" (D&C 3:7), it would be highly likely that Joseph would have worn himself out and ruined his health and ability to serve by spending all his time and energy in resuming the work. He could easily have been too anxious and thus neglected his family, his health, and other responsibilities.

In addition, being too anxious can give Satan power over us because we become too hard on ourselves. It is possible that Joseph may indeed have been too hard on himself or this verse and its message would not have been included here by the Lord.

Being unreasonably hard on ourselves can become a serious deterrent to personal progress and can lead to discouragement and maybe even giving up as far as hopes of exaltation are concerned. Elder Marvin J. Ashton of the Quorum of the Twelve Apostles gave counsel regarding this as follows: " . . . the speed with which we head along the straight and narrow path isn't as important as the direction in which we are traveling" (April 1989 general conference). You may wish to read his entire talk. It is full of wisdom and encouragement on this issue.

For those who wish to be faithful in all things, the phrase "means provided," in verse 4, could even include things such as health,

finances, time, family situation, and more. Having said this, we will now proceed to verse 4.

4 Do not run faster or labor more than you have strength and means provided to enable you to translate; but be diligent unto the end.

Mosiah 4:27 is an especially significant cross-reference for verse 4, above. We will include this counsel from King Benjamin here.

Mosiah 4:27

27 And see that all these things are done in wisdom and order; for it is not requisite [*required by the Lord*] **that a man should run faster than he has strength.** And again, it is expedient [*necessary*] that he should **be diligent**, that thereby he might win the prize [*exaltation in celestial glory*]; therefore, **all things must be done in order.**

Next, verse 5 teaches us the importance of prayer in gaining personal victory over Satan and his evil followers.

5 **Pray always**, that you may come off conqueror; yea, that you may conquer Satan, and that you may escape the hands of the servants of Satan that do uphold his work.

There are many ways we can apply the counsel to "pray always" as given in verse 5, above. We will list a few here.

1. Constantly remember God and your covenants with Him, no matter what you are doing.

2. Maintain a constant feeling of gratitude and reverence for God and His creations.

3. Have a constant prayer in your heart that you will be guided and directed to do right, no matter what others do.

4. Always be ready to ask, "What would Jesus do?" as you face temptations in daily living.

5. Say many little prayers throughout the day, including expressions of gratitude for kindnesses as well as pleas for help.

6. Have a constant awareness of who you are and your covenant to "stand as [a witness] of God at all times and in all things, and in all places" (Mosiah 18:9).

President Henry B. Eyring gave counsel regarding "pray always." "The Lord hears the prayers of your heart. The feelings in your heart of love for our Heavenly Father and for His Beloved Son can be so constant that your prayers will ascend always" ("Always," Ensign, Oct. 1999, 12).

President Marion G. Romney of the First Presidency taught the importance of taking time to ponder. He said, "Pondering is, in my feeling, a form of prayer" (April 1973 general conference). Therefore, "praying always" could include taking time to ponder the things of God, thus giving the Holy Ghost a chance to teach, inspire, and direct you more effectively.

Next, beginning with verse 6, the Lord explains to Joseph Smith why he called Martin Harris a "wicked" man and tells him what has happened to the lost 116 pages of the Book of Mormon translation.

6 Behold, **they** [*the wicked people who now have the 116 pages*] **have sought to destroy you**; yea, even **the man** [*Martin Harris*] in whom **you have trusted has sought to destroy you**.

7 And for this cause [*this is why*] I said that he is a wicked man, for **he has sought to take away the things wherewith you have been entrusted**; and he has also sought to destroy your gift [*of translating the gold plates—see D&C 10:2–3*].

8 And because you have delivered the writings [*the 116 manuscript pages*] into his hands, behold, **wicked men have taken them** from you.

9 Therefore, **you** have delivered

them up, yea, that which was sacred, unto wickedness.

> Next, Joseph is told of the plot which has been hatched in the minds of the evil men who now have the 116 pages. He learns that they have changed the wording on the manuscript pages with the intent to get him to retranslate from the gold plates. If they can get him to do so, they will then produce the stolen pages and compare them with the retranslation. They will make sure that the stolen pages do not agree with the retranslation, thus attempting to discredit the Prophet and make themselves popular with local people who oppose Joseph Smith and his work. We will use **bold** to summarize what Joseph is told by the Lord.

10 And, behold, **Satan hath put it into their hearts to alter the words** which you have caused to be written, or which you have translated, which have gone out of your hands [*which you have lost*].

11 And behold, I say unto you, that **because they have altered the words, they read contrary from that which you translated** and caused to be written;

12 And, on this wise [*this is how*], **the devil has sought to lay a cunning plan, that he may destroy this work**;

13 For he hath put into their hearts to do this, that **by lying they may say they have caught you in the words which you have pretended to translate**.

14 Verily, I say unto you, that **I will not suffer [*allow*] that Satan shall accomplish his evil design** in this thing.

> Next, we get a specific insight as to one way in which Satan works with people to accomplish his evil goals with them.

15 For behold, **he has put it into their hearts** to get thee to tempt the Lord thy God, in asking to translate it over again.

16 **And then**, behold, **they say and think in their hearts—We will see if God has given him power to translate; if so, he will also give him power again**;

> Did you notice in verse 16, above, how cunning Satan is? He is not telling these wicked men that there is no God. In fact, he has them so deceived and dulled spiritually and intellectually as to be thinking up a plan to destroy Joseph and work against God, even if God helps him translate again!

17 And **if God giveth him power again,** or if he translates again, or, in other words, **if he bringeth forth the same words**, behold, we have the same [*the original*

translation on the 116 pages] with us, and we have altered them;

18 Therefore they will not agree [*the two translations will not agree, because of what we do with the original*], and **we will say that he has lied in his words, and that he has no gift, and that he has no power** [*in other words, we will say that he is not a prophet*];

19 **Therefore we will destroy him, and also the work**; and we will do this **that we may not be ashamed** [*embarrassed*] in the end, and **that we may get glory of the world** [*so that we will be praised by wicked and foolish people*].

20 Verily, verily, I say unto you, that **Satan has great hold upon their hearts**; he **stirreth them up to iniquity** [*wickedness*] **against that which is good**;

Satan is a master of deception. One of his strongest "tools" is that of stirring up feelings and emotions that go against and defy rational thought. For instance, as the Lord points out to Joseph in verse 21, next, these men did not even ask God in prayer if Joseph Smith has indeed been called as a prophet and is in fact translating ancient scripture. Because the devil has stirred up their hearts (feelings) so effectively, they haven't even taken time to "ask of me" (verse 21). Thus, we are

taught that wickedness does not promote rational thought.

If Satan can get people to act according to feelings of hatred, jealousy, prejudice, and so forth as he has these men; or, in other words, if he can stir up wicked feelings within their hearts, he can usually ruin their ability to think clearly and thus successfully trap them.

21 And **their hearts** [*center of feelings*] **are corrupt**, and **full of wickedness and abominations** [*extreme wickedness*]; and **they love darkness rather than light**, because **their deeds are evil**; therefore **they will not ask of** me [*they won't approach Me in prayer about this*].

Next, we are clearly shown a major goal and tactic used by the devil. He loves to destroy destroyers.

22 Satan stirreth them up, **that he may lead their souls to destruction.**

23 And thus **he has laid a cunning plan**, thinking to destroy the work of God; but **I will require this at their hands** [*these men will be held accountable for what they are attempting to do*], and **it shall turn to their shame** [*what they were trying to avoid in verse 19, above*] **and condemnation** [*being stopped in progress toward exaltation*] in the day of judgment.

Next, we are given another lesson and review how Satan works against people.

24 Yea, **he stirreth up their hearts to anger** against this work.

25 Yea, **he saith unto them: Deceive** and **lie in wait to catch, that ye may destroy**; behold, **this is no harm.** And **thus he flattereth them, and telleth them that it is no sin to lie that they may catch a man in a lie, that they may destroy him**.

26 And thus **he flattereth them,** and **leadeth them along** until he **draggeth their souls down to hell**; and thus **he causeth them to catch themselves in their own snare** [they get caught in their own trap].

27 And **thus he** [Satan] **goeth up and down, to and fro in the earth, seeking to destroy the souls of men**.

28 Verily, verily, I say unto you, **wo be unto him that lieth to deceive because he supposeth that another lieth to deceive**, for such are not exempt from the justice of God.

Next, the Savior reminds Joseph Smith again (see verse 11, above) that these men have altered the 116 pages. He instructs him not to retranslate the portion of the gold plates from which the lost manuscript pages came.

29 Now, behold, **they have altered these words, because Satan saith unto them** [the men who have the 116 pages]: **He** [Joseph Smith] **hath deceived you**—and thus he flattereth them away to do iniquity, to get thee to tempt the Lord thy God.

30 Behold, I say unto you, that **you shall not translate again those words** [the lost 116 pages] which have gone forth out of your hands;

31 For, behold, **they shall not accomplish their evil designs in lying against those words.** For, behold, **if you should bring forth the same words** [if you were to retranslate them] **they will say that you have lied** and that you have pretended to translate, but that you have contradicted yourself.

32 And, behold, **they will publish this** [their lies about you and the translation], and **Satan will harden the hearts of the people** to stir them up to anger against you, that they will not believe my words.

33 Thus **Satan thinketh to overpower your testimony in this generation**, that the work may not come forth in this generation.

Next, Jesus tells Joseph what to do instead of retranslating. He also tells him not to make this plan public knowledge until the Book of Mormon is completed.

34 But behold, **here is wisdom** [*here is wise counsel regarding the plan for replacing the lost 116 pages*], and because I show unto you wisdom, and give you commandments concerning these things, what you shall do, **show it not unto the world until you have accomplished the work of translation**.

35 **Marvel not** [*don't be surprised and don't question it*] that I said unto you: Here is wisdom, show it not unto the world—[*here is why I said it*] **for I said, show it not unto the world, that you may be preserved** [*to save your life*].

36 Behold, I do not say that you shall not show it unto the righteous;

Remember that in verse 34, above, the Lord told Joseph that He would teach him wisdom. There is very wise counsel in verse 37, next. It will help the Prophet avoid being deceived by people who appear to be righteous but are not. It is a reminder that Joseph Smith, as a prophet, is still learning. Such is the case, of course, with all of us.

37 But as you cannot always judge [*discern*] the righteous, or **as** [*since*] **you cannot always tell the wicked from the righteous**, therefore I say unto you, **hold your peace** [*keep this plan to yourself*] until I shall see fit to make all things known unto the world concerning the matter.

Next, the Lord tells Joseph exactly what to do to replace the lost 116 pages. You may recall from your study of the Book of Mormon that Nephi was instructed to make an additional set of plates (known as the small plates of Nephi—see 1 Nephi 9:2–3). Nephi did not know why he was so instructed (1 Nephi 9:5) but was obedient, pointing out to us that the Lord "knoweth all things from the beginning; wherefore, he prepareth a way to accomplish all his works among the children of men" (1 Nephi 9:6).

Now we know why. In the set of gold plates delivered to Joseph Smith by Moroni, there was a small set—the small plates of Nephi. Joseph will now be instructed to translate them to address the same period of time covered by the lost 116 pages. These small plates are what we have today as the books of 1 Nephi, 2 Nephi, Jacob, Enos, Jarom, and Omni in the Book of Mormon.

Thus, knowing what would happen, the Lord had prepared for the loss of the 116 pages by having Nephi make another set of plates, which He explains to the Prophet Joseph in the following verses.

38 And now, verily I say unto you, that **an account of those things that you have written** [*translated; the lost 116 pages*], **which have gone out of your hands** [*which have been lost*]**, is engraven upon the plates of Nephi** [*the large plates of Nephi—see Words of Mormon 1:3–7*];

39 Yea, and you remember it was said in those writings [*1 Nephi 9:1–4; 2 Nephi 5:28–33*] that a more particular account was given of these things upon the plates of Nephi [*the small plates of Nephi*].

40 And now, **because the account which is engraven upon the plates of Nephi** [*the small plates*] **is more particular** [*has more detail about spiritual things— see, for instance, Words of Mormon 1:4*] concerning the things which, in my wisdom, I would bring to the knowledge of the people in this account—

41 Therefore, **you shall translate the engravings which are on the plates of Nephi** [*the small plates of Nephi*]**, down even till you come to the reign of king Benjamin** [*which starts in Words of Mormon and continues in Mosiah, chapters 1–6*], or until you come to that which you have translated, which you have retained;

42 And behold, **you shall publish it as the record of Nephi** [*coming from the small plates of Nephi*]; and **thus I will confound** [*stop; thwart*] **those who have altered my words.**

43 I will not suffer [*permit*] that they shall destroy my work; yea, **I will show unto them that my wisdom is greater than the cunning of the devil.**

44 Behold, **they have only got a part**, or an abridgment [*a condensed version*] **of the account of Nephi.**

With respect to the "abridgment" spoken of in verse 44, above, Words of Mormon 1:3 contains Mormon's explanation that he had "made an abridgment from the plates of Nephi [*the large plates of Nephi*] down to the reign of this King Benjamin." Thus, what the men who stole the 116 pages actually had was limited in what it covered.

Verse 45, next, explains that what Joseph Smith was to translate now to replace the lost 116 pages had a much richer and fuller account of that period of time among the Nephites.

45 Behold, **there are many things engraven upon the plates of Nephi** [*the small plates of Nephi*] **which do throw greater views**

upon my gospel; therefore, it is wisdom in me that you should translate this first part of the engravings of Nephi [*consisting of 1 Nephi, 2 Nephi, Jacob, Enos, Jarom, and Omni*], and send forth in this work.

From what the Savior explained to His young Prophet, Joseph, in the foregoing verses, it is interesting to note that we, as students of the Book of Mormon, actually came out ahead as far as the loss of the 116 manuscript pages are concerned. Elder Jeffrey R. Holland explains:

"At least six times in the Book of Mormon, the phrase 'for a wise purpose' is used in reference to the making, writing, and preserving of the small plates of Nephi (see 1 Ne. 9:5; [Words of Mormon] 1:7; Alma 37:2, 12, 14, 18). We know one such wise purpose—the most obvious one—was to compensate for the future loss of 116 pages of manuscript translated by the Prophet Joseph Smith from the first part of the Book of Mormon (see D&C 3; 10).

"But it strikes me that there is a 'wiser purpose' than that, or perhaps more accurately, a 'wiser purpose' *in* that. The key to such a suggestion is in D&C 10:45. As the Lord instructs Joseph Smith on the procedure for translating and inserting the material from the small plates into what had been begun as the translation of the abridged large plates, he says, 'Behold, there are many things engraven upon the [small] plates of Nephi which do throw greater views upon my gospel' (emphasis added).

"So clearly this was not a *quid pro quo* in the development of the final Book of Mormon product. It was not tit for tat, this for that—116 pages of manuscript for 142 pages of printed text. Not so. We got back more than we lost. And it was known from the beginning that it would be so. We do not know exactly what we have missed in the 116 pages, but we do know that what we received on the small plates was the personal declarations of the three great witnesses [Nephi, Jacob, and Isaiah], three of the great doctrinal voices of the Book of Mormon, testifying that Jesus is the Christ" ("For a Wise Purpose," *Ensign*, Jan. 1996, 13–14).

Next, the Savior points out that many Book of Mormon prophets prayed that these records might come forth in the last days.

46 And, behold, all the remainder of this work [*the Book of Mormon*] does contain all those parts of my gospel which **my holy prophets, yea, and also my disciples, desired in their prayers** [*for example, Enos in Enos 1:13*] **should come forth unto this people.**

47 And **I said unto them, that**

it should be granted unto them according to their faith in their prayers;

48 Yea, and **this was their faith— that my gospel**, which I gave unto them that they might preach in their days, **might come unto their brethren the Lamanites, and also all that had become Lamanites because of their dissensions.**

49 Now, **this is not all**—their faith in their prayers was that this gospel should be made known also, if it were possible that other nations should possess this land;

50 And thus **they did leave a blessing upon this land in their prayers, that whosoever should believe in this gospel in this land might have eternal life** [*exaltation*];

51 Yea, **that it might be free unto all** of whatsoever nation, kindred, tongue, or people they may be.

> Some members of the Church have a tendency to want to belittle or tear down the teachings and convictions of other religions. According to verse 52, next, this should not be. The proper approach to bringing the gospel to others is given by the Lord at the end of the verse.

52 And now, behold, according to their faith in their prayers [*the prayers of ancient Book of Mormon prophets*] will I bring this part of my gospel [*the Book of Mormon*] to the knowledge of my people. Behold, **I do not bring it to destroy that which they have received, but to build it up.**

> As you no doubt noticed in verse 52, above, the proper approach to teaching the gospel is to compliment people on what they do have and believe, and to offer the full and true gospel of Jesus Christ to fill in the gaps and complete the picture for them.

53 And for this cause have I said: If this generation harden not their hearts, I will establish my church among them.

54 Now I do not say this to destroy my church [*as defined in verses 67 and 69*], but I say this to build up my church;

> Next, the Lord teaches the contrast between those who join His Church and keep His commandments, and the wicked, including those who pretend to set up churches of God but have selfish and wicked motives in so doing. As you will see, fear and lack of fear is a major part of this contrast.

55 Therefore, whosoever belongeth to my church **need not fear**, for such shall inherit the kingdom of heaven.

56 But it is **they who do not fear me** [*who do not respect and obey God and his commandments*], neither keep my commandments **but build up churches unto themselves to get gain**, yea, **and all those that do wickedly and build up the kingdom of the devil**— yea, verily, verily, I say unto you, that **it is they that I will disturb, and cause to tremble and shake to the center.**

Next, the Master emphasizes who He is, using many descriptive phrases from the Bible, and explaining that the Book of Mormon peoples were the "other sheep" of which he spoke in John 10:16.

Doctrine

Verse 57. Jesus is the Christ, the Son of God.

57 **Behold, I am Jesus Christ, the Son of God. I came unto mine own, and mine own received me not** [*John 1:11*].

Doctrine

Verse 58. Jesus is the light of the world (see also verse 70). People who are caught up in spiritual darkness do not comprehend spiritual things.

58 **I am the light which shineth in darkness, and the darkness comprehendeth it not** [*John 1:5*].

59 **I am he who said—Other sheep have I which are not of this fold** [*John 10:16*]—unto my disciples, and many there were that understood me not.

Next, the Savior describes some of the purposes of the Book of Mormon as He briefly reviews what he did for these "other sheep."

60 And **I will show unto this people** [*in our day, via the Restoration through Joseph Smith*] **that I had other sheep** [*the people of the Book of Mormon*], and that they were a branch of the house of Jacob [*they were a part of the house of Israel, the covenant people*];

61 And **I will bring to light their marvelous works** [*the works of these "other sheep" as recorded in the Book of Mormon*], which they did in my name;

62 Yea, and **I will also bring to light my gospel which was ministered unto them**, and, behold, they shall not deny that which you have received [*the words and teachings of the Book of Mormon will not contradict what I have given you, Joseph*], but they shall build it up, and shall bring to light the true **points of my doctrine**, yea, and the only doctrine which is in me.

The phrase, "points of my doctrine," as found in both verse 62, above, and verse 63, below, are of particular significance. The word "points" denotes clear, well-defined, and specific as opposed to "foggy," "blurry," "poorly defined," and "vague." Perhaps you've noticed that Satan has scored major victories among most people in the world today in terms of destroying clear doctrines. It is indeed a fact, as stated in 1 Nephi 13:26, that "they have taken away from the gospel of the Lamb many parts which are plain and most precious; and also many covenants of the Lord."

As we continue our study of the Doctrine and Covenants, we will see example after example of the restoration of clear, beautiful doctrines of the plan of salvation, along with the restoration of priesthood covenants.

63 And this I do that I may establish my gospel, that there may not be so much contention [*doing away with contention is one of the sweet results of understanding pure doctrine*]; yea, Satan doth stir up the hearts of the people to contention concerning the **points of my doctrine**; and in these things they do err, for they do wrest [*twist, misinterpret*] the scriptures and do not understand them.

64 Therefore, I will unfold unto them this great mystery [*perhaps including that the Lord will restore the gospel with its "points of doctrine," thus reducing contention and confusion among the honest in heart*];

65 For, behold, **I will gather them** [*the latter-day gathering of Israel*] **as a hen gathereth her chickens under her wings**, if they will not harden their hearts;

66 Yea, **if they will come, they may, and partake of the waters of life** [*the gospel of Jesus Christ as explained by the Savior to the woman at the well; John 4:7–14*] **freely**.

Next, in verses 67–69, Jesus explains how one can "partake of the waters of life freely" as invited in verse 66, above.

Doctrine

Verse 67. Repentance is essential in coming unto Christ, as well as remaining a strong member of His Church.

67 Behold, this is my doctrine—whosoever repenteth and cometh unto me, the same is my church.

Doctrine

Verse 68. It is dangerous to subject the gospel to personal interpretations that divert away from the Savior's intent in giving it.

68 **Whosoever declareth more or less than this** [*a warning not to dilute, add to, or take away from the pure gospel*], the same is not of me, but is against me; therefore he is not of my church.

69 And now, behold, **whosoever is of my church, and endureth** of my church **to the end**, him will I establish upon my rock [*the absolutely safe and secure gospel of Jesus Christ*], and the gates of hell shall not prevail [*win*] against them.

> The Savior's closing words to Joseph Smith can easily apply to all of us.

70 And now, **remember the words of him who is the life and light of the world, your Redeemer, your Lord and your God**. Amen.

> Just a quick review of how the translation of the gold plates progressed after the Urim and Thummim and the gold plates were returned to Joseph Smith prior to his receiving the revelation that we have just studied, section 10.
>
> As mentioned in the notes at the beginning of section 10, Joseph Smith's wife, Emma, served as a scribe during part of the translation after the plates and Urim and Thummim were returned to her husband. Martin Harris, who had served as a scribe from February

1828 to June 14, 1828 (at which time they had 116 manuscript pages of the translation) was out of the picture, although he came back to visit the Prophet in February 1829 (see notes in this study guide at the beginning of section 5).

The translation proceeded very slowly until the arrival of Oliver Cowdery, who began serving as scribe on April 7, 1829. After Oliver was sent by the Lord to assist the work, things moved quickly such that the translation was completed near the end of June 1829.

SECTION 11

Background

This revelation, received through the Urim and Thummim, was given through the Prophet Joseph Smith at Harmony, Pennsylvania, to his older brother Hyrum in the latter part of May 1829. Hyrum (born February 9, 1800) was almost 6 years older than Joseph (born December 23, 1805) and was about 4 inches taller at 6 feet, 4 inches in height. The tender relationship between these two great men of God is exemplary. They supported each other throughout their lives and died together in Carthage Jail on June 27, 1844.

To me, this sweet relationship is like that between Nephi and his older brother Sam in the Book of Mormon. Sam was generally in the background, never seeking center stage and always faithful and supportive of his younger brother, the Prophet Nephi. So it was with Hyrum, never seeking to draw attention away from Joseph and faithfully supporting his younger brother, the Prophet of the Restoration.

One of the reasons we know that Hyrum Smith was about 6 feet, 4 inches tall is that the suit he was wearing when he was martyred in Carthage jail is still in existence (in the possession of Hyrum's descendants), and it would take a man of that height to wear it properly according to the fashions of that day. I have seen this suit and felt the great spirit and goodness of this humble man.

Hyrum will be baptized by his brother Joseph in Seneca Lake sometime in June 1829. He will become one of the Eight Witnesses and will bring the first installment of the Book of Mormon manuscript (24 pages) to the typesetter, John H. Gilbert, who will set the type for the printing of the Book of Mormon at Grandin Press in Palmyra, New York.

At the time this revelation was given, the Aaronic Priesthood had already been conferred upon Joseph Smith and Oliver Cowdery by John the Baptist. That took place on May 15, 1829 (see heading to D&C 13). At the time of the restoration of the Aaronic Priesthood, Joseph and Oliver had also been baptized, with John the Baptist as their instructor (see Joseph Smith—History 1:68–74).

Sometime after the coming of John the Baptist, Hyrum had journeyed to Harmony to visit Joseph and Emma. The Prophet recorded the background to section 11, noting that being baptized had had a significant effect upon their ability to understand the scriptures. Joseph gave the following (**bold** added for emphasis):

"Our minds being now enlightened, we began to have the Scriptures laid open to our understandings, and the true meaning and intention of their more mysterious passages revealed unto us in a manner which we never could attain to previously, nor ever before had thought of. In the meantime we were forced to keep secret the circumstances of having received the Priesthood and our having been baptized, owing to a spirit of persecution which had already manifested itself in the neighborhood. . . .

"After a few days, however, feeling it to be our duty, we commenced to reason out of the Scriptures with our acquaintances and friends, as we happened to meet with them. About this time my brother Samuel H. Smith came to visit us. . . .

"**Not many days afterwards, my brother Hyrum Smith came to us** to inquire concerning these things, when at his earnest request, I inquired of the Lord through the Urim and Thummim, and received for him the following: [D&C 11]" (*History of the Church*, 1:43–45).

We will now proceed to study section 11. First of all, you will perhaps notice that it seems like you have read verses 1–9 before. You have. With the exception of two words, two punctuations, and one capitalization, these verses are the same as verses 1–9 of section 6, given to Oliver Cowdery, who was also anxious to assist with the work. We will point out these differences with **bold**.

1 A GREAT and marvelous work is about to come forth **among** the children of men.

2 Behold, I am God; give heed to my word, which is quick and powerful, sharper than a two-edged sword, to the dividing asunder of both joints and marrow; therefore give heed unto my **word**.

3 Behold, the field is white already to harvest; therefore, whoso desireth to reap [*section 6 has a comma here*] let him thrust in his sickle with his might, and reap while the day lasts, that he may treasure up for his soul everlasting salvation in the kingdom of God.

4 Yea, whosoever will thrust in his sickle and reap, the same is called of God.

5 Therefore, if you will ask of me you shall receive; if you will knock it shall be opened unto you.

6 Now, as you have asked, behold, I say unto you, keep my commandments, and seek to bring forth and establish the cause of Zion.

7 Seek not for riches but for wisdom; and, behold, the mysteries of God shall be unfolded unto you, and then shall you be made rich. Behold, he that hath eternal life is rich.

8 Verily, verily, I say unto you, even as you desire of me so it shall be done unto you; and, if you desire, you shall be the means of doing much good in this generation.

9 Say nothing but repentance unto this generation. Keep [*section 6 has a semicolon here and "keep" is not capitalized*] my commandments, and assist to bring forth my work, according to my commandments, and you shall be blessed.

You may wish to review the notes for the above verses as given in section 6 in this study guide. They are a reminder that the same basic message from the Lord applied to many who were to assist as the restoration of the gospel got underway. A similar message is given in the initial verses of sections 4, 12, and 14.

Also, you may wish to review the note preceding verse 9 in section 6 of this study guide, which explains the instruction to preach "nothing but repentance unto this generation" in verse 9 of this section (section 11).

We will now proceed with the rest of section 11. First, we will note that the first five words in verse 10, next, are identical to the words the Lord spoke to Oliver Cowdery in D&C 6:10. This is perhaps a reminder that each member is given one or more spiritual gifts by the Lord (see D&C 46:11). Verse 10 also reminds us that these gifts of the Spirit require personal righteousness and faith.

10 **Behold, thou hast a gift**, or thou shalt have a gift if thou wilt desire of me in **faith**, with an **honest heart**, believing in the power of Jesus Christ, or in my power which speaketh unto thee;

Joseph Fielding Smith sheds additional light upon Hyrum's "gift" as follows:

"The Lord declared that Hyrum Smith had a gift. The great gift which he possessed was that of a tender, sympathetic heart; a merciful spirit. The Lord on a later occasion said: 'Blessed is my servant Hyrum Smith; for I, the Lord, love him because of the integrity of his heart, and because he loveth that which is right before me, saith the Lord.' (D&C 124:15.) This great gift was manifest in his jealous watch care over the Prophet lest some harm come to him" *(Church History and Modern Revelation, 1:57).*

Next, the Savior assures Hyrum that He is the one giving this revelation.

11 For, behold, **it is I that speak**; behold, I am the light which shineth in darkness, and by my power **I give these words unto thee**.

Verses 12–13, next, teach us some of the ways we can tell when we are feeling the Spirit.

Doctrine

Verses 12–13. You can tell when the Spirit is with you by paying attention to what the Spirit does to you and for you.

12 **And now, verily, verily, I say unto thee, put your trust in that Spirit** which **leadeth to do good**—yea, to **do justly**, to **walk humbly**, to **judge righteously**; and **this is my Spirit.**

13 Verily, verily, I say unto you, I will impart unto you of **my Spirit**, which **shall enlighten your mind**, which **shall fill your soul with joy**;

Some people still have difficulty recognizing when they are feeling the Spirit. Did you notice the two specific ways mentioned in verse 13, above, as to how you can recognize that the Spirit is with you and inspiring you? Your mind works better and you are filled with joy.

Next, in verse 14, we are taught how significant and meaningful these simple instructions can be when followed.

14 And then shall ye know, or **by this shall you know, all things whatsoever you desire of me**, which are pertaining unto things of righteousness, **in faith believing in me that you shall receive**.

From the context of verses 15–26, especially verse 26, we understand that Hyrum Smith was anxious to begin preaching the gospel, which was being restored by his brother Joseph. As we watch what the Lord told him at this time, among other things, we are taught an important lesson, namely, that we need to be prepared before we go out to preach. This certainly can apply to missionaries and members today in teaching and preaching the gospel. In these verses, Hyrum was told to wait to preach until he was better prepared in several ways. We will use **bold** to point them out and then repeat these verses for additional teachings. By the way, Hyrum will finally get the go ahead to preach

in D&C 23:3, about 11 months later in April 1830.

15 Behold, I command you that **you need not suppose that you are called to preach until you are called**.

16 **Wait a little longer**, until you shall have my word, my rock, my church, and my gospel, that you may know of a surety my doctrine.

17 And then, behold, according to your desires, yea, even according to your faith shall it be done unto you.

18 Keep my commandments; **hold your peace**; appeal unto my Spirit;

19 Yea, cleave unto me with all your heart, that you may assist in bringing to light those things of which has been spoken—yea, the translation of my work; be patient until you shall accomplish it.

20 Behold, this is your work, to keep my commandments, yea, with all your might, mind and strength.

21 **Seek not to declare my word, but first seek to obtain my word**, and then shall your tongue be loosed; then, if you desire, you shall have my Spirit and my word,

yea, the power of God unto the convincing of men.

22 **But now hold your peace; study my word** which hath gone forth among the children of men, and also study my word which shall come forth among the children of men, or that which is now translating, yea, until you have obtained all which I shall grant unto the children of men in this generation, and then shall all things be added thereto.

23 Behold thou art Hyrum, my son; seek the kingdom of God, and all things shall be added according to that which is just.

24 Build upon my rock, which is my gospel;

25 Deny not the spirit of revelation, nor the spirit of prophecy, for wo unto him that denieth these things;

26 Therefore, **treasure up in your heart until the time** which is in my wisdom **that you shall go forth**.

As mentioned previously, we will now repeat verses 15–26, gleaning many additional insights from them, and then we will continue to the end of the section.

First of all, in verse 15, next, we are reminded that God's kingdom is a kingdom of order, which makes it a kingdom we can trust and understand. Hyrum is taught here that we do not take positions and callings in the Lord's Church until we are properly called by those in authority.

15 Behold, I command you that **you need not suppose that you are called to preach until you are called**.

In verses 16–19, next, Hyrum is again taught the lesson of "first things first." In other words, as stated above, there is order in the way the Lord runs things, and we, as workers in the kingdom, must abide by this order. In this case, we must prepare properly before we undertake to do His work.

16 **Wait** a little longer, **until you shall have my word, my rock, my church, and my gospel, that you may know of a surety my doctrine** [*you must understand the doctrine before you can preach it*].

17 **And then**, behold, **according to your desires**, yea, even **according to your faith shall** it **be done unto you**.

18 **Keep my commandments**; hold your peace [*don't start yet*]; **appeal unto my Spirit** [*first, learn more from the Spirit*];

19 Yea, **cleave unto** [*hold on to*] **me with all your heart**, that you

may assist in bringing to light those things of which has been spoken—yea, the translation of my work [*the Book of Mormon*]; **be patient** until you shall accomplish it.

In verse 20, next, Hyrum is taught the importance of keeping the commandments as a means of personal preparation to serve the Lord.

20 Behold, **this is your work, to keep my commandments**, yea, with all your might, mind and strength.

Verse 21, next, is quite often quoted in lessons and sermons. You may wish to mark it in your own scriptures. It applies wonderfully to missionaries as well as teachers and speakers in church. It again reminds us all that we must study and do our part to qualify for the help of the Spirit in teaching and explaining the gospel. When we do, the Spirit then carries our words into the hearts and souls of others who are ready to hear them.

21 Seek not to declare my word, but first seek to obtain my word, and then shall your tongue be loosed [*then you will be given the ability to teach*]; **then, if you desire, you shall have my Spirit and my word** [*a powerful combination!*]**, yea, the power of God unto the convincing of men.**

22 **But now hold your peace** [*don't start preaching, yet*]; **study my word** which hath gone forth among the children of men [*the Bible plus what Joseph Smith has taught so far*], and also study my word which shall come forth among the children of men, or that which is now translating [*the Book of Mormon; see footnote 22d, for this section*], yea, until you have obtained all which I shall grant unto the children of men in this generation, and **then shall all things be added thereto.**

23 Behold **thou art Hyrum, my son** [*these are terms of tenderness and endearment used by the Lord*]; **seek the kingdom of God, and all things shall be added according to that which is just.**

According to verse 24, next, a vital part of Hyrum's preparation is to build his life upon the gospel of Jesus Christ. This applies, of course, to all of us. The symbolism of "rock" is that of a completely firm, immovable foundation, one that you can completely trust.

24 **Build upon my rock, which is my gospel;**

As you are no doubt aware, a basic doctrine or teaching of some religions is that revelation has ceased. As we see in verse 25, next, that is a very serious false doctrine.

25 Deny not the spirit of revelation, nor the spirit of prophecy, for wo [*trouble, sadness, misery will come*] unto him that denieth these things;

Yet again, in verse 26, next, Hyrum is told to keep studying and learning until the time is right for him to start preaching the restored gospel. As stated previously, he will be called to go forth and preach in D&C 23:3, which is about 11 months from the time this revelation was received.

26 Therefore, **treasure up in your heart until the time which is in my wisdom that you shall go forth.**

In verse 27, next, we are reminded that what the Lord says to specific individuals can often apply to all of us.

27 Behold, **I speak unto all** who have good desires, and have thrust in their sickle to reap.

28 Behold, **I am Jesus Christ, the Son of God. I am the life and the light of the world.**

You may wish to read D&C 88:41 to catch a glimpse of the extent to which Jesus Christ is "the life and the light of the world" in terms of the physical universe. Not only is He our life and light (verse 28, above), but His power and influence are also the means by which

the physical universe is held in place.

29 **I am the same who came unto mine own and mine own received me not** [*I am the one who was rejected by the people in the Holy Land*];

As the Savior closes this revelation to Hyrum Smith, we are reminded that through Christ, we can receive exaltation in the highest degree of glory within the celestial kingdom. The phrase "become the sons of God," in verse 30, means full heirs of all God has, or, in other words, exaltation. Thus, the phrase "become his sons and his daughters" (Mosiah 5:7) is another way of saying the same thing. One more example is from D&C 76:24 where it explains to us that people on Heavenly Father's other worlds are also given the opportunity for exaltation through the Atonement of our Savior. It uses the phrase "begotten sons and daughters unto God" to denote exaltation, which means to obtain the highest degree of glory in the celestial kingdom. We will quote that verse of section 76 here, using **bold** for emphasis.

D&C 76:24

24 That by him [*Jesus Christ*], and through him, and of him, the worlds are and were created, and the inhabitants thereof are begotten sons and daughters unto God.

We will now conclude our study of section 11 as we read verse 30.

30 But verily, verily, I say unto you, that **as many as receive me**, to them will I give power to **become the sons of God**, even to them that believe on my name. Amen.

One last comment about the term "sons of God" in verse 30, above. It is an important phrase in gospel doctrinal vocabulary. Once in awhile, a student of the scriptures will become a bit confused on this point, thinking, "Wait a minute—we are all sons and daughters of God. We were all born to our Heavenly Parents as spirit children. It says so right in the proclamation on the family, second paragraph (given September 23, 1995). So, what does it mean to *become* a son or daughter of God?"

Well, the fact is that we are indeed all spirit sons and daughters of God. But the term "become sons of God" or "become daughters of God," as used in the scriptures in the context of final judgment and the eternity which lies ahead of us, means to be "born again" through Christ and to ultimately receive exaltation.

SECTION 12

Background

This revelation was given in Harmony, Pennsylvania, in May 1829.

It was given through Joseph Smith to Joseph Knight Sr.

Joseph Knight was born on November 3, 1772, making him almost 33 years older than the Prophet Joseph Smith. At this point in history, Joseph Smith was 23 years old and Joseph Knight was 56.

Father Knight, as he was sometimes called, had first met Joseph Smith in 1826 when he hired him to do some work at his farm and grist mill in Colesville, New York, about 130 miles southeast of Palmyra. By this time, the 20-year-old prophet had already seen the Father and Son during the First Vision and had also seen Moroni and had learned of the gold plates. In fact, he had already returned to the Hill Cumorah twice, as instructed by Moroni, on September 22 each year since 1823.

Joseph Smith boarded with the Knight family while working for them, and he eventually told them of his visions and spiritual experiences. Joseph Knight Sr. believed, along with other members of his family, including his wife, Polly, and sons, Joseph Knight Jr. and Newel Knight.

Father Knight assisted Joseph Smith on numerous occasions, supplying provisions and money, which enabled the Prophet and his scribe to continue the work of translating. Among other things, Brother Knight gave Joseph money to buy paper for his scribe to write on during the translating of the gold plates. Father Knight was baptized on June 28, 1830.

The Prophet Joseph Smith gave us the background to the receiving of this section as follows:

"About the same time an old gentleman came to visit us of whose name I wish to make honorable mention—Mr. Joseph Knight, Sen., of Colesville, Broome county, New York, who, having heard of the manner in which we were occupying our time, very kindly and considerately brought us a quantity of provisions, in order that we might not be interrupted in the work of translation by the want of such necessaries of life; and I would just mention here, as in duty bound, that he several times brought us supplies, a distance of at least thirty miles, which enabled us to continue the work when otherwise we must have relinquished it for a season.

"Being very anxious to know his duty as to this work, I inquired of the Lord for him, and obtained the following: [D&C 12]" *(History of the Church*, 1:47–48).

As we study this section, you will probably notice that the first 6 verses sound familiar. You have already seen almost identical counsel from God in the first six verses of sections 6 and 11, and you will see it again in the first six verses of section 14. This counsel,

given to Joseph Knight and others, is obviously very important counsel to all of us who seek to help build up the kingdom of God in these last days.

You may wish to review the notes given for verses 1–6 in section 6 in this book.

1 **A GREAT and marvelous work** [*the restoration of the gospel in the last days, before the Second Coming of Christ*] **is about to come forth among the children of men** [*the people of the world*].

2 **Behold** [*see, pay attention*], **I am God; give heed to my word**, which is quick [*living, alive*] and powerful, sharper than a two-edged sword [*which is effective in all directions*], to the dividing asunder [*separating*] of both joints and marrow [*symbolic of cutting through false doctrines and philosophies, exposing them to the light of truth*]; therefore, **give heed unto my word**.

3 Behold, **the field** [*the world*] **is white already to harvest** [*ready for the final preaching of the gospel before the Second Coming of Christ*]; **therefore, whoso desireth to reap** [*to help with the harvesting*] **let him thrust in his sickle with his might**, and reap while the day lasts, **that he may treasure up for his soul everlasting salvation**

in the kingdom of God [*that he may save his own soul*].

4 Yea, **whosoever will** [*has the desire and will take action to do so*] thrust in his sickle and reap, the same **is called of God**.

5 Therefore, **if you will ask of me you shall receive; if you will knock it shall be opened unto you** [*constant revelation is available to those who help with this work*].

Next, the Lord will respond directly to Joseph Knight's request for counsel as to what the Lord would have him do in helping with the work of restoring the gospel. It is interesting to note that, just as was the case with Hyrum Smith (section 11), the Lord emphasizes personal preparation first as a top priority. We will use **bold** to point this out. The Lord will give Brother Knight additional instruction in section 23.

6 Now, as you [*Joseph Knight Sr.*] have asked, behold, I say unto you, **keep my commandments**, and **seek to bring forth and establish the cause of Zion**.

7 Behold, **I speak** unto you, and also **to all** those who have desires to bring forth and establish this work;

8 And no one can assist in this work except he shall **be humble** and **full of love, having faith, hope, and charity, being temperate** in all things, whatsoever shall be entrusted to his care.

The Savior concludes by personally introducing Himself to Joseph Knight.

9 Behold, **I am the light and the life of the world, that speak these words**, therefore give heed with your might, and then you are called. Amen.

SECTION 13

Background

This is a very short section, consisting of just one verse, but it has tremendous significance. It deals with the coming of John the Baptist as a resurrected being on May 15, 1829, to confer the Aaronic Priesthood upon Joseph Smith and Oliver Cowdery. John the Baptist told Joseph and Oliver that he was working under the direction of Peter, James, and John, and that the time would soon come that they would receive the Melchizedek Priesthood (see heading to section 13 in your Doctrine and Covenants).

We will study more about the Aaronic Priesthood in sections 20 and 107. Those who hold this priesthood are authorized to administer in the outward ordinances of the gospel. For instance, deacons can pass the sacrament. Teachers can do the above, plus prepare and pass the sacrament. Priests can do the above, plus bless the sacrament and perform baptisms. The Aaronic Priesthood and its associated ordinances prepare us to enjoy the blessings and benefits of the Melchizedek Priesthood ordinances.

At the time of this great event in the Restoration, Joseph and Oliver had been working on the translation of the Book of Mormon in Harmony, Pennsylvania. The Book of Mormon teaches that one must be baptized in order to be saved (see, for example, 3 Nephi 11:33–34). As Joseph and Oliver got to this point in the translating, they became concerned that they, themselves, had not been baptized. We will quote from the Institute of Religion Church history student manual, *Church History in the Fullness of Times*, 2003, page 55, chapter 5, for more about this (**bold** added for emphasis):

"Joseph and Oliver were thrilled as such doctrines as the resurrected Savior's visit to the inhabitants of the Western Hemisphere and his teachings about baptism were unfolded during the translation (see 3 Nephi 11:18–38). **At this point their souls were driven to mighty prayer to learn how they could obtain the blessing of baptism**. On 15 May 1829, Joseph and Oliver went into the nearby woods along the Susquehanna River to pray."

Imagine for a moment what a special occasion this would have been for John the Baptist, who ministered during his mortal mission by virtue of the Aaronic Priesthood and was beheaded by Herod after almost a year in prison (see Mark 6:17–29). We know that John was resurrected with the Savior (see D&C 133:55). Imagine how he must have felt as Joseph and Oliver walked to the banks of the Susquehanna River near Joseph's home to pray about baptism, knowing that the time had finally arrived when he could restore the Aaronic Priesthood to the earth. And imagine what feelings must have swelled up in his heart as he actually laid his hands upon their heads and conferred upon Joseph and Oliver this sacred Aaronic Priesthood and instructed them in the mode of proper baptism so that they could baptize each other (see Joseph Smith—History 1:68–72).

The words used by John are full of meaning and doctrine. We will study them now, making several notes as we go along, and repeating the verse several times. You will see that there are many powerful principles and much authority associated with this priesthood.

First of all, we note that the "Priesthood of Aaron," referred to in this section, is what we normally refer to as the "Aaronic Priesthood." It was named after Aaron, who was Moses's brother. He and his sons were called upon to officiate as priests in the rites and sacrifices that belonged to the Aaronic Priesthood among the Children of Israel as Moses led them in the wilderness (see Exodus 28).

1 UPON you my fellow servants, in the name of Messiah I confer **the Priesthood of Aaron**, which holds the keys of the ministering of angels, and of the gospel of repentance, and of baptism by immersion for the remission of sins; and this shall never be taken again from the earth, until the sons of Levi do offer again an offering unto the Lord in righteousness.

Next, we see that this priesthood holds "keys." Three specific keys are mentioned:

1. The ministering of angels.

2. The gospel of repentance.

3. Baptism by immersion for the remission of sins.

Doctrine

Verse 1. The blessings that come to us through the Aaronic Priesthood include repentance, baptism, and the ministering of angels, whether behind the scenes or by direct appearance.

Doctrine

Verse 1. Baptism is an Aaronic Priesthood ordinance.

1 UPON you my fellow servants, in the name of Messiah I confer the Priesthood of Aaron [*the Aaronic Priesthood*]**, which holds the keys of the ministering of angels**, and of **the gospel of repentance**, and **of baptism by immersion for the remission of sins**; and this shall never be taken again from the earth, until the sons of Levi do offer again an offering unto the Lord in righteousness.

In the wording used by John the Baptist in verse 1, above, you can see that repentance and baptism are closely associated with the ministering of angels. We will first consider the keys of the ministering of angels and of repentance, with Moroni as our instructor, and then turn to President Dallin H. Oaks, then a member of the Quorum of the Twelve Apostles, for more on how these three keys work together for our good. Concerning the ministering of angels, Moroni taught:

Moroni 7:29–31

29 And because he hath done this, my beloved brethren, have miracles ceased? Behold I say unto you, Nay; neither have angels ceased to minister

unto the children of men.

30 For behold, they are subject unto him [*Christ*], to minister according to the word of his command, **showing themselves unto them of strong faith** and a firm mind in every form of godliness.

31 And **the office of their ministry is to call men unto repentance**, and to fulfil and **to do the work of the covenants of the Father** [*example: Peter, James, and John restoring the Melchizedek Priesthood*], which he hath made unto the children of men, **to prepare the way** among the children of men, by **declaring the word of Christ unto the chosen vessels of the Lord**, that they may bear testimony of him.

As mentioned above, Elder Dallin H. Oaks spoke on the subject of the Aaronic Priesthood and the ministering of angels in the priesthood session of the October 1998 general conference as follows (**bold** added for emphasis):

"The scriptures recite numerous instances where an angel appeared personally. Angelic appearances to Zacharias and Mary (see Luke 1) and to King Benjamin and Nephi, the grandson of Helaman (see Mosiah 3:2; 3 Ne. 7:17–18) are only a few examples.

When I was young, I thought such personal appearances were the only meaning of the ministering of angels. As a young holder of the Aaronic Priesthood, I did not think I would see an angel, and **I wondered what such appearances had to do with the Aaronic Priesthood**.

"But **the ministering of angels can also be unseen**. Angelic messages can be **delivered by a voice** or merely by **thoughts** or **feelings communicated to the mind**. President John Taylor described 'the action of the angels, or messengers of God, upon our minds, so that the heart can conceive . . . revelations from the eternal world' (*Gospel Kingdom*, sel. G. Homer Durham [1987], 31).

"Nephi described three manifestations of the ministering of angels when he reminded his rebellious brothers that (1) they had '**seen an angel**,' (2) they had '**heard his voice from time to time**,' and (3) also that an angel had '**spoken** unto [them] **in a still small voice**' though they were 'past feeling' and 'could not feel his words' (1 Ne. 17:45). The scriptures contain many other statements that angels are sent to teach the gospel and bring men to Christ (see Heb. 1:14; Alma 39:19; Moro. 7:25, 29, 31–32; D&C 20:35). **Most angelic communications are felt or heard rather than seen**.

"**How does the Aaronic Priesthood hold the key to the**

ministering of angels? The answer is the same as for the Spirit of the Lord.

"**In general, the blessings of spiritual companionship and communication are only available to those who are clean**. As explained earlier, through the Aaronic Priesthood ordinances of **baptism** and the **sacrament**, we are cleansed of our sins and promised that if we keep our covenants we will always have His Spirit to be with us. **I believe that promise not only refers to the Holy Ghost but also to the ministering of angels**, for 'angels speak by the power of the Holy Ghost; wherefore, they speak the words of Christ' (2 Ne. 32:3). So it is that **those who hold the Aaronic Priesthood open the door for all Church members who worthily partake of the sacrament to enjoy the companionship of the Spirit of the Lord and the ministering of angels**" (Dallin H. Oaks, "The Aaronic Priesthood and the Sacrament," *Ensign*, Nov. 1998, 39).

Before we move on to section 14, we will take a closer look at the phrase, "until the sons of Levi do offer again an offering unto the Lord in righteousness."

1 UPON you my fellow servants, in the name of Messiah I confer the Priesthood of Aaron, which holds the keys of the ministering of angels, and of the gospel of repentance, and of baptism by immersion for the remission of sins; and this shall never be taken again from the earth, **until the sons of Levi do offer again an offering unto the Lord in righteousness**.

There seem to be many possibilities as to what this phrase means, and we will not venture to give a final answer. Rather, we will give some possibilities by way of quotes from the scriptures and Church leaders.

Joseph Fielding Smith addresses the question as to whether or not the Aaronic Priesthood will remain on earth now as follows:

"We may be sure that the Aaronic Priesthood will never be taken from the earth while mortality endures, for there will always be need for temporal direction and the performance of ordinances pertaining to 'the preparatory Gospel'" (*Church History and Modern Revelation*, 1:62).

Oliver Cowdery's account uses the word "that" instead of "until." Thus, in Oliver's rendition, it reads "that the Sons of Levi may yet offer an offering unto the Lord in righteousness!" (See Pearl of Great Price, 1989 edition, page 59, last phrase of the second to last paragraph.) With this in mind, it could be that the phrase means, in effect, that the Aaronic Priesthood is being restored and "shall never be taken again from the earth" in order that authorized Aaronic Priesthood ordinances such as the sacrament and baptism can once again be offered to the Lord by sincere Saints.

Third Nephi 24:3 also uses the word "that" in the context of the sons of Levi offering an offering. We will quote it here, using **bold** for emphasis:

3 Nephi 24:3

And he shall sit as a refiner and purifier of silver; and he shall purify the sons of Levi, and purge them as gold and silver, **that they may offer unto the Lord an offering in righteousness.**

D&C 128:24 also uses the word "that" and seems to indicate that the faithful members of the Church are, in a sense, the "sons of Levi." We will quote this verse here, again using **bold** for emphasis.

D&C 128:24

24 Behold, the great day of the Lord is at hand; and who can abide the day of his coming, and who can stand when he appeareth? For he is like a refiner's fire, and like fuller's soap; and he shall sit as a refiner and purifier of silver, and he shall purify the sons of Levi, and purge them as gold

and silver, **that they may offer unto the Lord an offering in righteousness.** Let **us**, therefore, **as a church** and **a people**, and **as Latter-day Saints**, offer unto the Lord an offering in righteousness; and let us present in his holy temple, when it is finished, a book containing the records of our dead, which shall be worthy of all acceptation.

Having noted above that the faithful members of the Church could be one definition of "sons of Levi" in a broad sense, we will continue, suggesting that modern priesthood holders could also be considered to be the "sons of Levi." In the days of Moses, the sons of Levi were the ones who officiated in the Aaronic Priesthood ordinances among the Children of Israel. Thus, symbolically, "sons of Levi" could mean those who hold the priesthood today and officiate in priesthood ordinances. This seems to be the meaning of "sons of Moses and Aaron," who were of the tribe of Levi, in D&C 84:31–32. In this revelation, the Lord is addressing a number of elders who had gathered in Kirtland, Ohio, after returning from their missions in the eastern states. In these verses, He uses the phrase "sons of Moses and also the sons of Aaron." These would be the same as "sons of Levi." In verse 32, He tells these priesthood holders that they are the sons of Moses and Aaron. We will quote these two verses here and use **bold** to point things out.

D&C 84:31–32

31 Therefore, as I said concerning the sons of Moses— for the sons of Moses and also the sons of Aaron [*sons of Levi*] **shall offer an acceptable offering** and sacrifice in the house of the Lord, which house [*the Kirtland Temple*] shall be built unto the Lord in this generation, upon the consecrated spot as I have appointed—

32 And **the sons of Moses and of Aaron** shall be filled with the glory of the Lord, upon Mount Zion in the Lord's house, **whose sons are ye** [*you are the "sons of Moses and of Aaron"*]; and also many whom I have called and sent forth to build up my church.

And finally, In the 2018 *Doctrine and Covenants Student Manual*, used by the institutes of religion of the Church, in chapter 6 we read (**bold** added for emphasis): "In ancient times, God commanded His people to offer up animal sacrifices as part of their worship. The purpose of shedding the blood of an animal was to help people look forward in faith to the time when the blood of Jesus Christ would be shed to atone for their sins. From Moses's time to the death of Je-

sus Christ, the law of Moses dictated that animal sacrifices and burnt offerings be performed by priests officiating at the tabernacle or temple. These priests were descendants of Levi who were designated by the Lord to serve in the sanctuary (see Numbers 18:20–21). Thus **the term 'sons of Levi' refers to holders of the priesthood.**"

The question is often asked as to whether or not sacrifice will be offered again as a part of the restoration of all things in the last days. We will conclude our study of section 13 by quoting the Prophet Joseph Smith on this subject and then quoting Joseph Fielding Smith (**bold** added for emphasis):

"It is generally supposed that sacrifice was entirely done away when the Great Sacrifice [i.e.,] the sacrifice of the Lord Jesus was offered up, and that there will be no necessity for the ordinance of sacrifice in the future; but those who assert this are certainly not acquainted with the duties, privileges and authority of the Priesthood, or with the Prophets.

"The offering of sacrifice has ever been connected and forms a part of the duties of the Priesthood. It began with the Priesthood, and will be continued until after the coming of Christ, from generation to generation. . . .

"These sacrifices, as well as every ordinance belonging to

the Priesthood, will, when the Temple of the Lord shall be built, and the sons of Levi be purified, be fully restored and attended to in all their powers, ramifications, and blessings. This ever did and ever will exist when the powers of the Melchizedek Priesthood are sufficiently manifest; else how can **the restitution of all things** spoken of by the Holy Prophets be brought to pass. **It is not to be understood that the law of Moses will be established again with all its rites and variety of ceremonies**; this has never been spoken of by the prophets; **but those things which existed prior to Moses' day, namely, sacrifice, will be continued**" (*Teachings of the Prophet Joseph Smith*, 172–73).

Joseph Fielding Smith explained that "we are living **in the dispensation of the fulness of times** into which all things are to be gathered, and **all things are to be restored since the beginning**. Even this earth is to be restored to the condition which prevailed before Adam's transgression. Now in the nature of things, **the law of sacrifice will have to be restored, or all things which were decreed by the Lord would not be restored**. It will be necessary, therefore, for the sons of Levi, who offered the blood sacrifices anciently in Israel, to offer such a sacrifice again to round out and complete this ordinance in this dispensation. Sacrifice by the

shedding of blood was instituted in the days of Adam and of necessity will have to be restored.

"The sacrifice of animals will be done to complete the restoration when the temple spoken of is built; **at the beginning of the millennium, or in the restoration, blood sacrifices will be performed long enough to complete the fulness of the restoration in this dispensation. Afterwards sacrifice will be of some other character**" (*Doctrines of Salvation*, 3:94).

SECTION 14

Background

Sections 14–16 go together in the sense that they are given to three brothers, David Whitmer, John Whitmer, and Peter Whitmer Jr., all of whom desired to know what the Lord wanted them to do at this point in the restoration of the gospel. These three brothers were sons of Peter Whitmer Sr. and Mary Whitmer of Fayette, New York, who would play a prominent role in enabling the Prophet to complete the translation of the Book of Mormon.

It is interesting to see how the Lord prepares things in advance in order for His work to proceed. Joseph Smith had previously become acquainted with the Whitmer family. Oliver Cowdery had become especially good friends with David Whitmer after having met him in Palmyra. He had developed a special interest in David's sister, Elizabeth, whom he will later marry. As Joseph and Oliver continued the work of translating the Book of Mormon in Harmony, Pennsylvania, persecution began to increase. As a result, Oliver wrote to David Whitmer, requesting that he come and take him and Joseph to the home of David's father, Peter Whitmer Sr., in Fayette where they could continue the translation in peace. Peter Whitmer Sr. invited them to stay as long as was needed to complete the work. David came and picked up Joseph, Emma, and Oliver and transported them back to Fayette in his two-horse wagon. The translation was thus completed rapidly, under peaceful circumstances, at the home of Peter Whitmer Sr. in Fayette, New York.

One more interesting note reminds us of the miracles that accompanied this part of the work of the Restoration. As soon as David Whitmer received the letter from Oliver Cowdery asking him to come get Joseph, Emma, and Oliver, he wanted to leave right away with a wagon and go to Harmony and get them. But it was springtime, and preparation of the soil for spring planting could not be delayed. Consequently, he hurriedly set out to plow the soil on the farm. "At the end of a day of plowing he found he had accomplished in one day what normally would have taken

two days to do. David's father was likewise impressed with this apparent miracle. Peter Whitmer Sr. said, 'There must be an overruling hand in this, and I think you would better go down to Pennsylvania as soon as your plaster of paris is sown.' (Plaster of paris was used to reduce the acidity of the soil.) The next day David went to the fields to sow the plaster, but to his surprise he found the work had been done. His sister, who lived near the field, said that her children had called her to watch three strangers the day before spread the plaster with remarkable skill. She assumed they were men David had hired.

"Grateful for this divine intervention, David Whitmer hurried off on the three-day journey to Harmony. Joseph Smith and Oliver Cowdery met him as he approached the town. Although David had not told them exactly when he was coming, Joseph had seen in vision the details of David's trip to Harmony" (*Church History in the Fulness of Times*, 2003, 56–57).

We will now study section 14, which was given through Joseph Smith to David Whitmer in Fayette, New York, in June 1829. By the way, David was born on January 7, 1805, and thus was a little over 11 months older than Joseph Smith. He will become one of the Three Witnesses to the Book of Mormon. The Prophet gave the background to this section as follows:

". . . in the beginning of the month of June, his [Peter Whitmer, Sr.,] son, David Whitmer, came to the place where we were residing, and brought with him a two-horse wagon, for the purpose of having us accompany him to his father's place, and there remain until we should finish the work. It was arranged that we should have our board free of charge, and the assistance of one of his brothers to write for me, and also his own assistance when convenient. Having much need of such timely aid in an undertaking so arduous, and being informed that the people in the neighborhood of the Whitmers were anxiously awaiting the opportunity to inquire into these things, we accepted the invitation, and accompanied Mr. Whitmer to his father's house, and there resided until the translation was finished and the copyright secured. Upon our arrival, we found Mr. Whitmer's family very anxious concerning the work, and very friendly toward ourselves. They continued so, boarded and lodged us according to arrangements; and John Whitmer, in particular, assisted us very much in writing during the remainder of the work.

"In the meantime, David, John and Peter Whitmer, Jun., became our zealous friends and assistants in the work; and being anxious to know their respective duties, and having desired with much earnestness that I should inquire of the Lord concerning them, I did so, through the means of the Urim and Thummim, and obtained for them in succession the following revelations: [D&C 14–16]" (*History of the Church*, 1:48–49).

Again, verses 1–6 may seem quite familiar to you, because very similar wording was used by the Lord at the beginning of sections 4, 6, 11, and 12.

1 **A GREAT and marvelous work** [*the restoration of the gospel*] **is about to come forth unto the children of men.**

2 Behold, **I am God; give heed to my word,** which is **quick** [*alive; living; continuing revelation*] and **powerful, sharper than a two-edged sword,** to the dividing asunder [*separating; symbolic of cutting through false philosophies and doctrines, separating truth from error*] of both joints and marrow; therefore **give heed unto my word.**

3 Behold, **the field** [*the world*] **is white already to harvest** [*the time for the final gathering of Israel has arrived*]; therefore, **whoso desireth to reap** [*to join in the harvest*] **let him thrust in his sickle with his might, and reap while the day lasts** [*while the opportunity is still available*], **that he may treasure up for his soul everlasting salvation in the kingdom of God**

[*that he may save his own soul in exaltation in celestial glory*].

4 Yea, **whosoever will thrust in his sickle and reap, the same is called of God**.

5 Therefore, if you will **ask** of me you shall **receive**; if you will **knock** it shall be **opened** unto you.

6 Seek to bring forth and establish my Zion. **Keep my commandments in all things**.

Doctrine

Verse 7. Exaltation, obtained through keeping the commandments, is the greatest of all God's gifts to us.

7 And, **if you keep my commandments** and **endure to the end you shall have eternal life** [*exaltation*], which gift is **the greatest of all the gifts of God**.

Next, David Whitmer is told that if he is faithful, he can have the privilege of teaching by the power of the Holy Ghost, as well as hearing and seeing marvelous things.

Doctrine

Verse 8. The Holy Ghost enables us to bear witness effectively.

8 And it shall come to pass, that if you shall ask the Father in my name, in faith believing, you shall receive the Holy Ghost, which giveth utterance, that you may stand as a witness of the things of which you shall both hear and see, and also that you may declare repentance [*preach the gospel of Jesus Christ, which leads to repentance and cleansing through the Atonement*] unto this generation.

9 Behold, **I am Jesus Christ**, the Son of the living God, who created the heavens and the earth, a light which cannot be hid in darkness;

10 Wherefore, **I must bring forth the fulness of my gospel from the Gentiles unto the house of Israel**.

The question comes up as to who the "Gentiles" are in verse 10, above. Perhaps you have already noticed that the term "Gentile" is very context sensitive. According to the Bible Dictionary, page 679, the word has various meanings, depending on context. For instance, it can mean non-Jews, non-Israelites, nonmembers of the Church, Israelites who don't have the gospel, and so forth.

As used in verse 10, above, "Gentiles" refers to Joseph Smith and the early members of the Church, as well as faithful members now, who are taking the gospel to all the world in the final gathering of Israel. They are considered to be Gentiles because they are not inhabitants of the Holy Land now. President Wilford Woodruff explained this as follows (**bold** added for emphasis):

"Sometimes our neighbors and friends think hard of us because we call them Gentiles; but, bless your souls, **we are all Gentiles. The Latter-day Saints are all Gentiles in a national capacity**. The Gospel came to us among the Gentiles. **We are not Jews, and the Gentile nations have got to hear the Gospel first**. The whole Christian world have got to hear the Gospel, and when they reject it, the law will be bound and the testimony sealed, and it will turn to the house of Israel. Up to the present day we have been called to preach the Gospel to the Gentiles, and we have had to do it. For the last time we have been warning the world, and we have been engaged in that work for forty-five years" (*Journal of Discourses*, 18:112).

As the Lord closes this revelation to David Whitmer, he is counseled to "assist." This is especially significant in view of the fact that later in life he rejected Joseph Smith's authority, claiming to be president of the Church in Missouri (see *Joseph Smith and the Restoration*, 371), which led, among other

things, to his excommunication in April 1838.

11 And behold, thou art **David, and thou art called to assist**; which thing **if ye do, and are faithful, ye shall be blessed both spiritually and temporally**, and great shall be your reward. Amen.

SECTION 15

Background

As mentioned in the background to section 14, John Whitmer, brother of David Whitmer, wanted to know what the Lord desired him to do at this point of his life. In June 1829, the Lord gave him this revelation through the Prophet Joseph Smith in Fayette, New York.

1 HEARKEN, my servant John, and **listen to the words of Jesus Christ**, your Lord and your Redeemer.

2 For behold, **I speak unto you with sharpness and with power**, for mine arm is over all the earth.

3 And I will tell you that which no man knoweth save me and thee alone—

Sometimes we worry that it is too selfish to ask what will be of most benefit to us personally in doing the work of the Lord. While it is true that we must avoid becoming self-centered, verses 4–6, next, suggest that within proper limits, it is appropriate to consider the benefits to ourselves that come from participating in the work of the Lord.

4 For **many times you have desired of me to know that which would be of the most worth unto you**.

5 Behold, **blessed are you for this thing** [*it was appropriate for you to ask about this*], and for speaking my words which I have given you according to my commandments.

Doctrine

Verse 6. Serving missions and teaching the gospel to others is one of the most beneficial things we can do for ourselves.

6 And now, behold, I say unto you, that **the thing which will be of the most worth unto you will be to declare repentance unto this people**, that you may bring souls unto me, that you may rest with them in the kingdom of my Father. Amen.

SECTION 16

Background

This section was given to Peter Whitmer Jr. under the same circumstances as those for his brothers, David and John, as explained in the background for sections 14 and 15.

Since this section is exactly the same as section 15 except for the name "Peter," the question comes up as to why the Lord would use the same wording for two different people. While we don't know the answer for sure, there are many possibilities. One likely answer is simply that they were both wondering the same thing and that the answer was exactly the same for both; namely, that the preaching of the gospel in missionary efforts would be of most worth to them personally at this point in their lives. This same answer could be given to thousands of potential young missionaries today, as well as to many thousands of potential senior missionaries.

Since sections 15 and 16 are identical except for the names John and Peter, we will review a few scriptural terms as we study section 16.

1 **HEARKEN** [*listen carefully with the intent to obey*], my servant Peter, and listen to the words of Jesus Christ, your Lord and your Redeemer.

2 For behold, I speak unto you with **sharpness** [*pointedly, with a specific answer to your question*] and with power, for mine **arm** [*in scriptural symbolism, "arm" means power and authority*] is over all the earth.

Doctrine

Verses 3–5. Only members of the Godhead can know the deepest thoughts of your heart. See also D&C 6:16.

3 And I will tell you that which **no man knoweth save me and thee alone**—

4 For **many times you have desired of me to know that which would be of the most worth unto you**.

5 Behold, **blessed are you for this thing**, and for speaking my words which I have given unto you according to my commandments.

We will define three more scriptural vocabulary words and phrases in verse 6, next.

6 And now, behold, I say unto you, that the thing which will be of the most worth unto you will be to **declare repentance** [*preach the gospel in its simplicity, which leads to repentance*] unto this people, that you may bring souls unto me, that you may **rest** [*the word "rest" is defined in D&C 84:24 as the "fulness" of God's glory, or, in other words, exaltation*] with them in the **kingdom of my Father** [*the celestial kingdom*]. Amen.

SECTION 17

Background

During the translation of the gold plates, it became apparent that they would be shown by the power of God to three special witnesses, who would then bear witness to the world that the Book of Mormon is the work of God. We see this in the Book of Ether as follows (**bold** used for emphasis):

Ether 5:2–4

2 And behold, ye [*Joseph Smith*] **may be privileged that ye may show the plates unto those** [*the Eight Witnesses*] **who shall assist to bring forth this work**;

3 And **unto three shall they be shown by the power of God**; wherefore they shall know of a surety that these things are true.

4 And **in the mouth of three witnesses shall these things be established**; and the testimony of three, and this work, in the which shall be shown forth the power of God and also his word, of which the Father, and the Son, and the Holy Ghost bear record—and all this shall stand as a testimony against the world at the last day.

Another place in the Book of Mormon where the Three Witnesses are mentioned is 2 Nephi 27:12. We will quote that verse here and again use **bold** to point things out.

2 Nephi 27:12

12 Wherefore, at that day when the book [*the gold plates*] shall be delivered unto the man [*Joseph Smith*] of whom I have spoken, the book shall be hid from the eyes of the world, that the eyes of none shall behold it save it be that **three witnesses shall behold it, by the power of God**, besides him to whom the book shall be delivered; and they shall testify to the truth of the book and the things therein.

Furthermore, Joseph Smith and Martin Harris had been told, as recorded in section 5, that there would be three special witnesses who would be shown these things by the power of God, and who would literally hear the voice of the Lord declaring the truthfulness thereof. We will quote those verses here and use **bold**, as usual, for emphasis:

D&C 5:11–13

11 And in addition to your testimony, the testimony of three of my servants, whom I shall call and ordain, **unto whom I will show these things**, and they shall go forth with my words that are given through you.

12 Yea, **they shall know of a surety that these things are true, for from heaven will I declare it unto them**.

13 I will give them power that **they may behold and view these things as they are;**

As the translation of the Book of Mormon continued, in June 1829, Oliver Cowdery, David Whitmer, and Martin Harris, who had come to Fayette to visit the Prophet, expressed a deep desire to be the three witnesses spoken of. At their continued urging, Joseph finally agreed to inquire of the Lord through the Urim and Thummim and received section 17 as a result. Imagine the feelings in their hearts as they heard the following from the Savior, including the specific things they would be privileged to see as witnesses:

1 BEHOLD, I say unto you, that **you must rely upon my word**, which **if you do** with full purpose of heart, **you shall have a view of the plates**, and also of **the breastplate**, the **sword of Laban**, the **Urim and Thummim**, which were given to the brother of Jared upon the mount, when he talked with the Lord face to face, and **the miraculous directors** [*the*

Liahona] which were given to Lehi while in the wilderness, on the borders of the Red Sea.

The Joseph Smith Papers publications give additional insights as to what these three witnesses saw. Later in his life, David Whitmer testified "We not only saw the plates of the B[ook] of M[ormon] but also the Brass plates, the Plates of the Book of ether [sic], the Plates containing the Record of the wickedness of the people of the world, and many other plates" (in *The Joseph Smith Papers, Documents, Volume 1: July 1828– June 1831*, 380).

2 And **it is by your faith that you shall obtain a view of them**, even by that faith which was had by the prophets of old.

3 And **after that you have obtained faith, and have seen them** with your eyes, **you shall testify of them**, by the power of God;

4 And **this you shall do that my servant Joseph Smith, Jun., may not be destroyed**, that I may bring about my righteous purposes unto the children of men in this work.

Next, the Lord gives them very specific commandments as to what they are to testify of as the Three Witnesses.

5 And **ye shall testify that you have seen them**, even as my servant Joseph Smith, Jun., has seen them; for it is by my power that he has seen them, and it is because he had faith.

6 **And he has translated the book,** even that part which I have commanded him, **and** as your Lord and your God liveth **it is true**.

7 Wherefore, **you have received the same power**, and **the same faith**, and **the same gift like unto him;**

We will include the Testimony of the Three Witnesses here so that you can see that they held very tightly to these instructions of the Lord given in verses 5–7, above. As usual, we will use **bold** for emphasis.

THE TESTIMONY OF THREE WITNESSES

BE IT KNOWN unto all nations, kindreds, tongues, and people, unto whom this work shall come: That **we**, through the grace of God the Father, and our Lord Jesus Christ, **have seen the plates** which contain this record, which is a record of the people of Nephi, and also of the Lamanites, their brethren, and also of the people of Jared, who came from the tower of which hath been spoken. And **we also know that they have been translated by the gift and power of God,** for **his voice hath declared it unto us;** wherefore **we know of a surety that the work is true.** And **we also testify that we have seen the engravings which are upon the plates;** and **they have been shown unto us by the power of God, and not of man.** And we declare with words of soberness, that **an angel of God came down from heaven, and he brought and laid before our eyes, that we beheld and saw the plates, and the engravings** thereon; and **we know** that it is by the grace of God the Father, and our Lord Jesus Christ, that **we beheld and bear record that these things are true.** And it is marvelous in our eyes. Nevertheless, the voice of the Lord commanded us that we should bear record of it; wherefore, to be obedient unto the commandments of God, **we bear testimony of these things.** And we know that if we are faithful in Christ, we shall rid our garments of the blood of all men, and be found spotless before the judgment-seat of Christ, and shall

dwell with him eternally in the heavens. And the honor be to the Father, and to the Son, and to the Holy Ghost, which is one God. Amen.

OLIVER COWDERY
DAVID WHITMER
MARTIN HARRIS

As this revelation comes to a close, we see an "if, then" clause, meaning that "if" they do their part, "then" the Lord will be enabled to do His part. Furthermore, as we apply this to ourselves, we see that "if" we do our best, the "grace" or help of the Lord will be sufficient for us to attain exaltation at the final judgment. This is a very encouraging and comforting fact.

8 And **if you do these last commandments** of mine, which I have given you, **the gates of hell shall not prevail against you;** for **my grace is sufficient for you,** and **you shall be lifted up** [*exalted*] **at the last day** [*at the final judgment*].

9 And **I, Jesus Christ, your Lord and your God, have spoken it** unto you, that I might bring about my righteous purposes unto the children of men. Amen.

Since the Three Witnesses are such an important part of Church history and the coming forth of the Book of Mormon, we will take extra time here to give some follow-up history to this revelation that informed Oliver Cowdery, David Whitmer, and Martin Harris that they could serve as the Three Witnesses. We have fascinating and wonderful accounts of how and what the Three Witnesses saw and heard. The Prophet Joseph Smith wrote the following:

"Not many days after the above commandment [*section 17*] was given, we four, viz., Martin Harris, David Whitmer, Oliver Cowdery and myself, agreed to retire into the woods, and try to obtain, by fervent and humble prayer, the fulfilment of the promises given in the above revelation—that they should have a view of the plates. We accordingly made choice of a piece of woods convenient to Mr. Whitmer's house, to which we retired, and having knelt down, we began to pray in much faith to Almighty God to bestow upon us a realization of these promises.

"According to previous arrangement, I commenced by vocal prayer to our Heavenly Father, and was followed by each of the others in succession. We did not at the first trial, however, obtain any answer or manifestation of divine favor in our behalf. We again observed the same order of prayer, each calling on and praying fervently to God in rotation, but with the same result as before.

"Upon this, our second failure, Martin Harris proposed that he should withdraw himself from us, believing, as he expressed himself, that his presence was the cause of our not obtaining what we wished for. He accordingly withdrew from us, and we knelt down again, and had not been many minutes engaged in prayer, when presently we beheld a light above us in the air, of exceeding brightness; and behold, an angel stood before us. In his hands he held the plates which we had been praying for these to have a view of. He turned over the leaves one by one, so that we could see them, and discern the engravings thereon distinctly. He then addressed himself to David Whitmer, and said, 'David, blessed is the Lord, and he that keeps His commandments;' when, immediately afterwards, we heard a voice from out of the bright light above us, saying, 'These plates have been revealed by the power of God, and they have been translated by the power of God. The translation of them which you have seen is correct, and I command you to bear record of what you now see and hear.'

"I now left David and Oliver, and went in pursuit of Martin Harris, whom I found at a considerable distance, fervently engaged in prayer. He soon told me, however, that he had not yet prevailed with the Lord, and earnestly requested me to join him in prayer, that he also might realize the same blessings which we had just received. We accordingly joined in prayer, and ultimately obtained our desires, for before we had yet finished, the same vision was opened to our view, at least it was again opened to me, and I once more beheld and heard the same things; whilst at the same moment, Martin Harris cried out, apparently in an ecstasy of joy, 'Tis enough; tis enough; mine eyes have beheld; mine eyes have beheld;' and jumping up, he shouted, 'Hosanna,' blessing God, and otherwise rejoiced exceedingly" (*History of the Church*, 1:54–55).

Elders Orson Pratt and Joseph F. Smith (who later became the President of the Church) interviewed David Whitmer on September 7, 1878, and asked him questions about his experience as one of the Three Witnesses. Their account of this interview is as follows:

"On Saturday morning, Sept. 7 [1878], we met Mr. David Whitmer (at Richmond, Ray Co., Mo.), the last remaining one of the Three Witnesses of the Book of Mormon.

"Elder O. Pratt to David Whitmer: 'Do you remember what time you saw the plates?'

"D. Whitmer: It was in June, 1829, the latter part of the month, and the eight witnesses saw them, I think, the next day or the day after (i.e., one or two days after). Joseph showed them the plates himself, but the angel showed us (the Three Witnesses) the plates, as I suppose to fulfill the words of the book itself. Martin Harris was not with us at this time; he obtained a view of them afterwards (the same day). Joseph, Oliver, and myself were together when I saw them. We not only saw the plates of the Book of Mormon, but also the brass plates, the plates of the Book of Ether, the plates containing the records of the wickedness and secret combinations of the people of the world down to the time of their being engraved, and many other plates. The fact is, it was just as though Joseph, Oliver and I were sitting just here on a log, when we were overshadowed by a light. It was not the light of the sun, nor like that of a fire, but more glorious and beautiful. It extended away round us, I cannot tell how far, but in the midst of this light about as far off as he sits (pointing to John C. Whitmer, sitting a few feet from him), there appeared as it were a table with many records or plates upon it, besides the plates of the Book of Mormon, also the sword of Laban, the directors (i.e., the ball which Lehi had) and the interpreters. I saw them just as plain as I see this bed (striking the bed beside him with his hand), and I heard the voice of the Lord, as distinctly as I ever heard anything in my life, declaring that the records of the plates of the Book of Mormon were translated by the gift and power of God" (*Historical Record, Church Encyclopedia*, Book I, May 1887, 207–208; see also Doxey, *Latter-day Prophets*

and the Doctrine and Covenants,
1:153).

Joseph Smith's mother, Lucy Mack Smith, writes of the relief felt by her son now that three others had a sure witness that the work he was doing was of God. She wrote (**bold** added for emphasis):

"AS SOON as the Book of Mormon was translated, Joseph despatched a messenger to Mr. Smith, bearing intelligence of the completion of the work, and a request that Mr. Smith and myself should come immediately to Waterloo [*near Fayette and the Peter Whitmer Sr. farm*].

"The same evening, we conveyed this intelligence to Martin Harris, for we loved the man, although his weakness had cost us much trouble. Hearing this, he greatly rejoiced, and determined to go straightway to Waterloo to congratulate Joseph upon his success. Accordingly, the next morning, we all set off together, and before sunset met Joseph and Oliver at Mr. Whitmer's.

"The evening was spent in reading the manuscript, and it would be superfluous for me to say, to one who has read the foregoing pages, that we rejoiced exceedingly. It then appeared to those of us who did not realize the magnitude of the work, as if the greatest difficulty was then surmounted; but Joseph better understood the nature of the dispensation of the Gospel which was committed unto him.

"The next morning, after attending to the usual services, namely, reading, singing and praying, Joseph arose from his knees, and approaching Martin Harris with a solemnity that thrills through my veins to this day, when it occurs to my recollection, said, 'Martin Harris, you have got to humble yourself before God this day, that you may obtain a forgiveness of your sins. If you do, it is the will of God that you should look upon the plates, in company with Oliver Cowdery and David Whitmer.'

"In a few minutes after this, Joseph, Martin, Oliver and David, repaired to a grove, a short distance from the house, where they commenced calling upon the Lord, and continued in earnest supplication, until he permitted an angel to come down from his presence, and declare to them, that all which Joseph had testified of concerning the plates was true.

"When they returned to the house it was between three and four o'clock p.m. (David Whitmer indicated that they left the house about 11 a.m. Therefore, it appears that they were gone from the house between four and five hours.) Mrs. Whitmer, Mr. Smith and myself, were sitting in a bedroom at the time. **On coming in, Joseph threw himself down beside me, and exclaimed, 'Father, mother, you do not know how** happy I am: the Lord has now caused the plates to be shown to three more besides myself. They have seen an angel, who has testified to them, and they will have to bear witness to the truth of what I have said, for now they know for themselves, that I do not go about to deceive the people, and I feel as if I was relieved of a burden which was almost too heavy for me to bear, and it rejoices my soul, that I am not any longer to be entirely alone in the world.' Upon this, Martin Harris came in: he seemed almost overcome with joy, and testified boldly to what he had both seen and heard. And so did David and Oliver, adding that no tongue could express the joy of their hearts, and the greatness of the things which they had both seen and heard" (*History of Joseph Smith by His Mother*, 151).

In conclusion, we will include one more quote, this time from Richard Lloyd Anderson's fascinating research, combining several documented interviews with David Whitmer into one "composite" interview, providing a number of additional details about the heavenly manifestation given the Three Witnesses. Brother Anderson put this composite of several interviews with David Whitmer into a question and answer format as follows:

Q: Is your published testimony accurate?

A: "As you read my testimony given many years ago, so it stands as my own existence, the same as when I gave it, and so shall stand throughout the cycles of eternity."

Q: When did this event take place?

A: "It was in June, 1829, the very last part of the month."

Q: What was the approximate time of day?

A: "It was about 11 a.m."

Q: What were the circumstances of the vision?

A: "[We] went out into the woods nearby, and sat down on a log and talked awhile. We then kneeled down and prayed. Joseph prayed. We then got up and sat on the log and were talking, when all at once a light came down from above us and encircled us for quite a little distance around, and the angel stood before us."

Q: Describe the angel.

A: "He was dressed in white, and spoke and called me by name and said, 'Blessed is he that keepeth His commandments.' This is all that I heard the angel say."

Q: Did the angel have the Book of Mormon plates?

A: "[He] showed to us the plates, the sword of Laban, the Directors, the Urim and Thummim, and other records. Human language could not describe heavenly things and that which we saw."

Q: Did the vision take place under natural circumstances?

A: "The fact is, it was just as though Joseph, Oliver and I were sitting right here on a log, when we were overshadowed by a light. It was not like the light of the sun, nor like that of a fire, but more glorious and beautiful. It extended away round us, I cannot tell how far, but in the midst of this light, immediately before us, about as far off as he sits (pointing to John C. Whitmer, who was sitting 2 or 3 feet from him) there appeared, as it were, a table, with many records on it—besides the plates of the Book of Mormon, also the sword of Laban, the Directors, and the Interpreters. I saw them as plain as I see this bed (striking his hand upon the bed beside him), and I heard the voice of the Lord as distinctly as I ever heard anything in my life declaring that they were translated by the gift and power of God."

Q: Can you explain the supernatural power that surrounded you?

A: "All of a sudden I beheld a dazzlingly brilliant light that surpassed in brightness even the sun at noonday, and which seemed to envelop the woods for a considerable distance around. Simultaneous with the light came a strange entrancing influence which permeated me so powerfully that I felt chained to the spot, while I also experienced a sensation of joy absolutely indescribable."

Q: "Did you see the Urim and Thummim?"

A: "I saw the Interpreters in the holy vision; they looked like whitish stones put in the rim of a bow—looked like spectacles, only much larger."

Q: Did you see an actual table?

A: "You see that small table by the wall? . . . Well, there was a table about that size, and the heavenly messenger brought the several plates and laid them on the table before our eyes, and we saw them."

Q: Did you handle the plates?

A: "I did not handle the plates—only saw them. Joseph, and I think Oliver and Emma told me about the plates, and described them to me, and I believed them, but did not see except at the time testified of."

Q: How clearly could you see the plates?

A: "[T]he angel stood before us, and he turned the leaves one by one." "[H]e held the plates and turned them over with his hands, so that they could be plainly visible."

Q: "Did the angel turn all the leaves before you as you looked on it?"

A: "No, not all, only that part of the book which was not sealed, and what there was sealed appeared as solid to my view as wood."

Q: "Can you describe the plates?"

A: "They appeared to be of gold, about six by nine inches in size, about as thick as parchment, a great many in number and bound together like the leaves of a book by massive rings passing through the back edges. The engraving upon them was very plain and of very curious appearance."

Q: Is it possible that you imagined this experience?

A: "[O]ur testimony is true. And if these things are not true, then there is no truth; and if there is no truth, there is no God; and if there is no God, there is no existence. But I know there is a God, for I have heard His voice and witnessed the manifestation of his power."

Q: "Do you remember the peculiar sensation experienced upon that occasion?"

A: "Yes, I remember it very distinctly. And I never think of it, from that day to this, but what that spirit is present with me" (*Investigating the Book of Mormon Witnesses*, 80).

SECTION 18

Background

This section is perhaps most well known and oft-quoted for its teaching about the worth of souls (verses 10–16). It has this and much more to teach us. It was given to Joseph Smith, Oliver Cowdery, and David Whitmer in June 1829 at the Peter Whitmer Sr. residence in Fayette, New York.

When John the Baptist restored the Aaronic Priesthood to Joseph Smith and Oliver Cowdery on May 15, 1829 (see D&C 13), he told them that he was acting under the direction of Peter, James, and John, and that, in due time, they would receive the Melchizedek Priesthood (see heading to D&C 13). Peter, James, and John did indeed come and confer the Melchizedek Priesthood as promised by John the Baptist, but the date was not recorded. It does appear, though, that by the time section 18 was given, the Melchizedek Priesthood had been restored. Research from the Joseph Smith Papers given in the *Doctrine and Covenants Student Manual*, 2018, chapter 6, confirms this thinking (**bold** added for emphasis).

"In June 1829, Joseph Smith and Oliver Cowdery continued the translation of the Book of Mormon in the home of Peter Whitmer Sr. in Fayette, New York. During this time, Joseph and Oliver also sought to know how to exercise **the keys of the Melchizedek Priesthood that had been recently conferred upon them by heavenly messengers**. While praying in a room of the Whitmer home, the word of the Lord came to them and directed them to exercise the priesthood to ordain elders, administer the sacrament, and bestow the gift of the Holy Ghost by the laying on of hands. However, the Lord instructed them to wait to perform these ordinances until a group of believers could be assembled. (See *The Joseph Smith Papers, Histories, Volume 1: Joseph Smith Histories, 1832–1844*, ed. Karen Lynn Davidson and others [2012], 326, 328.)

Joseph Smith gives us a bit more background to section 18. From his writings, we learn that sometime in June 1829, Oliver Cowdery and David Whitmer had joined with him in desiring additional instruction with regard to the Melchizedek Priesthood. Joseph tells what occurred as they sought the Lord in prayer in the chamber of Peter Whitmer's house. Note how the Lord is patiently teaching them about proper order and procedure in His true Church, including the principle of having members sustain their leaders as well as sustaining priesthood ordinations:

"We had for some time made this matter a subject of humble prayer, and at length we got together in the chamber of Mr. Whitmer's house, in order more particularly to seek of the Lord what we now so earnestly desired; and here, to our unspeakable satisfaction, did we realize the truth of the Savior's promise—'Ask, and it

shall be given you; seek, and ye shall find; knock, and it shall be opened unto you'—for we had not long been engaged in solemn and fervent prayer, when the word of the Lord came unto us in the chamber, commanding us that I should ordain Oliver Cowdery to be an Elder in the Church of Jesus Christ; and that he also should ordain me to the same office; and then to ordain others, as it should be made known unto us from time to time. We were, however, commanded to defer this our ordination until such times as it should be practicable to have our brethren, who had been and who should be baptized, assembled together, when we must have their sanction to our thus proceeding to ordain each other, and have them decide by vote whether they were willing to accept us as spiritual teachers or not; when also we were commanded to bless bread and break it with them, and to take wine, bless it, and drink it with them; afterward proceed to ordain each other according to commandment; then call out such men as the Spirit should dictate, and ordain them; and then attend to the laying on of hands for the gift of the Holy Ghost, upon all those whom we had previously baptized, doing all things in the name of the Lord. The following commandment will further illustrate the nature of our calling to this Priesthood, as well as that of others who were yet to be sought after: [D&C 18]" (*History of the Church*, 1:60–62).

First, in section 18, the Lord specifically addresses Oliver Cowdery, acknowledging that He is aware of a matter Oliver has had on his mind, and assuring him that he does have a testimony, especially of the Book of Mormon manuscript. This may sound a bit strange because of the great spiritual experiences Oliver has already had. But perhaps you know from personal experience or from the experiences of others that a testimony needs constant nourishment. Thus, we see the Lord's kindness here in strengthening Oliver's testimony. We will use **bold** to point this out.

1 NOW, behold, **because of the thing which you, my servant Oliver Cowdery, have desired to know of me, I give unto you these words:**

2 Behold, **I have manifested unto you, by my Spirit in many instances, that the things which you have written** [*as a scribe during the translation of the gold plates*] **are true**; wherefore **you know that they are true** [*you do have a testimony of the Book of Mormon*].

Doctrine

Verses 3–4. Studying the scriptures and strictly living by the things contained in them is vital for our salvation.

3 **And if you know that they are true,** behold, I give unto you a commandment, that you **rely upon the things which are written;**

Specifically, Oliver is being reminded of the benefits which will come to him personally through studying the scriptures and sticking strictly to the teachings contained in them.

4 For **in them are all things written concerning the foundation of my church, my gospel, and my rock.**

The word "rock," used in verse 4, above, can have various meanings depending on context. Obviously, it symbolizes something that is solid and safe to build our lives upon. Three of many scriptural definitions are as follows:

1. "Build upon my rock, which is my gospel" (D&C 11:24).

2. "Jesus in His teachings says, 'Upon this rock I will build my Church, and the gates of hell shall not prevail against it [Matt. 16:18].' What rock? Revelation" (*History of the Church*, 5:258).

3. Jesus Himself is "the Rock" upon which we are invited to build. For example, "I am the good shepherd, and the stone of Israel. He that buildeth upon this rock shall never fall" (D&C 50:44).

Some members of the Church hesitate or decline to accept callings. What the Savior tells Oliver Cowdery next in verse 5 applies to all of us and reminds us that if we accept and fulfill callings, thus helping to "build up" the Church, the "gates of hell" will not ultimately win against us. This is a great benefit of being faithfully engaged in our church responsibilities.

5 Wherefore, **if you shall build up my church**, upon the foundation of my gospel and my rock, **the gates of hell shall not prevail** [*win*] **against you**.

Next, the Lord tells Oliver that the world is getting more and more wicked. The phrase "ripening in iniquity" involves the imagery of fruit ripening toward the point that it becomes completely rotten and falls off the tree.

6 Behold, **the world is ripening in iniquity** [*moving toward complete wickedness*]; **and it must needs be** [*it is necessary*] **that the children of men** [*the inhabitants of the earth*] **are stirred up unto repentance**, both the Gentiles [*non-Israelites*] and also the house of Israel [*descendants of Abraham, Isaac, and Jacob (Israel, who was the father of the Twelve Tribes of Israel)*].

From the context of verses 7 and 8, next, it appears that Oliver may

have had a tendency to be critical of the Prophet Joseph because of his imperfections. The counsel given to Oliver in verse 8 applies to all of us as we sustain our church leaders.

Doctrine

Verses 7–8. The Lord knows what He is doing when He calls certain individuals to be leaders in His church. (So, don't be critical of them.)

7 **Wherefore, as thou hast been baptized by the hands of my servant Joseph Smith, Jun.**, according to that which I have commanded him, he **hath fulfilled the thing which I commanded him**.

8 And now, **marvel not** [*don't wonder or be surprised*] **that I have called him** unto mine own purpose, which purpose is known in me; wherefore, **if he shall be diligent in keeping my commandments he shall be blessed unto eternal life**; and his name is Joseph [*I know him perfectly well. (By the way, in Hebrew, "Joseph" means "he who gathers for God")*].

There can be much additional significance to the Lord's saying "and his name is Joseph" in verse 8, above. For instance, Oliver would likely be familiar with the prophecy of Joseph, who was sold into Egypt, about a great latter-day prophet named Joseph, through whom the Lord would restore the gospel. (See 2 Nephi 3:13–15.) Thus, we can easily see the Savior saying to Oliver, in effect, that Joseph Smith is *the* Joseph spoken of in prophecy.

Next, as mentioned in the introductory notes to this section, the Lord refers to these men's callings as that of Apostles. Quoting from the *Doctrine and Covenants Student Manual* used in the Institutes of Religion of the Church, 1981 edition, page 35, we read the following:

"Brigham Young taught that Joseph Smith, Oliver Cowdery, and David Whitmer were the first Apostles of this dispensation (see *Journal of Discourses*, 6:320). To these, according to Heber C. Kimball, Martin Harris was later added (see *Journal of Discourses*, 6:29). These men were instructed to find and ordain twelve others who would form the Quorum of the Twelve."

The Lord is telling these men that they have the same calling as Paul the Apostle. Included in this holy calling is the responsibility of preaching the gospel and crying "repentance unto this people" (see verse 14 of this section). And in order to fulfill this calling, they must understand the true worth of each soul.

9 And now, Oliver Cowdery, I speak unto you, and also unto David Whitmer, by the way of commandment; for, behold, I command all men everywhere to repent, and I speak unto you, even as unto Paul mine apostle, for you are called even with that same calling with which he was called.

As mentioned previously, verses 10–16, next, are oft-quoted in the Church. The message is vital and sweet, for it deals with the foundational doctrine and truth that each soul, each individual person, is of incalculable worth. Tyrants and despots, whether widely known or appearing as bullies in small settings, are inspired by Satan to violate this eternal principle.

Doctrine

Verse 10. The worth of each individual soul is great in the sight of God.

10 Remember the worth of souls is great in the sight of God;

Next, we are taught that the Savior's Atonement itself is a supreme measure of the worth of souls.

Doctrine

Verse 11. The Savior suffered for all of the sins of all people. (Then, if they repent, they accept His gift. If they don't repent, they, in effect, reject His payment, and thus suffer

for their own sins—see D&C 19:17.)

11 For, behold, the Lord your Redeemer suffered death in the flesh; wherefore [*for this reason*] he suffered the pain of all men, that all men might repent and come unto him.

12 And he hath risen again from the dead, that he might bring all men unto him, on conditions of repentance.

Doctrine

Verse 13. When we repent, it brings the Savior great personal joy.

13 And how great is his joy in the soul that repenteth!

14 Wherefore [*this is why*], you [*Oliver Cowdery and David Whitmer*] are called to cry repentance unto this people.

Did you notice the exclamation point at the end of verse 13, above? Also take note of them at the end of verses 15 and 16, next. They are reminders of the pure joy felt by the Savior, as well as by us when we help bring souls to Him.

15 And if it so be that you should labor all your days in crying repentance unto this people, and bring, save it be one soul unto me, how great shall be your joy with him in the kingdom of my Father!

16 And now, if your joy will be great with one soul that you have brought unto me into the kingdom of my Father, how great will be your joy if you should bring many souls unto me!

We often think of missionaries when we read these two verses, and rightly so. But we must not limit the application to full-time missionary service. For instance, what about the parents who teach their children the gospel such that their souls are saved? And what about the individual member who brings a spouse back into activity or is the motivation for a friend to return to the Church?

Or what about the kind act or the show of respect that plants a "seed" that takes years to begin to grow, eventually does grow, and ultimately leads to conversion and coming unto Christ? In other words, there are virtually infinite applications for these verses in our lives.

Next, we see the Master Teacher providing training to these men as to how best to go about preaching the gospel. First, He assures them that they have His true gospel with its stability and power to save souls. Then He gives them additional instructions and cautions.

17 Behold, **you have my gospel** before you, and **my rock**, and **my salvation.**

18 **Ask the Father in my name, in faith believing** that you shall receive, **and you shall have the Holy Ghost**, which manifesteth [*shows and teaches*] all things which are expedient [*necessary*] unto the children of men. [*In other words, obtain the help of the Holy Ghost and you will be given all the assistance you need to be effective in saving souls.*]

19 And **if you have not faith, hope, and charity, you can do nothing**.

20 **Contend against no church, save** [*except*] **it be the church of the devil.**

The advice in verse 20, above, is critical for missionary success. The word "church" can mean any organization, group or individual. The "church of the devil" refers to anything that would tend to lead someone away from God. In 1 Nephi 14:10, Nephi was taught, "Behold there are save **two churches only**; the one is **the church of the Lamb of God**, and the other is **the church of the devil**; wherefore, whoso belongeth not to the church of the Lamb of God belongeth to that great church, which is the mother of abominations; and she is the whore of all the earth."

For successful missionary work, we must show respect and courtesy toward others and that which is sacred to them. Yet, when the Holy Ghost inspires and prompts, we must help people understand things that lead away from God.

Thus, the instruction to "contend against no church, save it be the church of the devil" can include not getting caught up in endless and worthless debates with other religions or philosophies, nor debating and quarreling with others over matters of personal preference and opinion.

Next, the "missionary training" of these early brethren continues with the caution to be serious about sacred things.

21 **Take upon you the name of Christ** [*keep your covenants and represent Christ properly*], **and speak the truth in soberness** [*be serious about serious and sacred things*].

Doctrine

Verse 22. Being saved is a very simple process. Baptism is essential for salvation (except, of course, in the case of children under age eight—see D&C 29:46–47; 68:25—and the handicapped who are not able to understand the gospel

sufficiently—see D&C 29:50).

22 And as many as **repent** and are **baptized** in my name, which is Jesus Christ, and **endure to the end**, the same shall **be saved**.

Doctrine

Verses 23–25. There is absolutely no other way to be saved other than through the gospel of Jesus Christ.

23 Behold, **Jesus Christ is the name** which is given of the Father, and **there is none other name given whereby man can be saved**;

24 Wherefore, **all men must take upon them the name which is given of the Father**, for in that name shall they [*those who are to be saved in celestial glory*] be called at the last day [*on the day of final judgment*];

25 Wherefore [*therefore*], **if they know not the name by which they are called, they cannot have place in the kingdom of my Father** [*the celestial kingdom*].

The imagery of the **bolded** part of verse 25, above, is that of a common scene in the Holy Land at the time of Christ's earthly ministry. Shepherds gave their sheep individual names and the sheep recognized their own name and

the voice of their shepherd. In the evening, several shepherds would bring their sheep to a common enclosure for safe-keeping during the night. Thus, the sheep of many shepherds mingled together throughout the night, kept safe by one or two guards.

In the morning, each shepherd would come to the gate of the enclosure and call out the names of his sheep to come to him and follow him out to pasture. His sheep recognized their master and "the name by which they were called." They came out of the crowd unto the shepherd and followed him to their reward of nourishment and protection during the day.

The "name by which we are called" is the name of Christ, which we have taken upon ourselves by covenant. If we are faithful to the gospel, we keep that name and recognize the voice of our "Good Shepherd" when He calls us to come out from the ways of the world. We thus follow Him to the safety and joy of righteousness on earth, and eventually, of celestial glory.

Beginning with verse 26 and continuing to the end of section 18, the topic switches to the calling of twelve men who will serve as the first Quorum of the Twelve Apostles in this dispensation. The Lord instructs Oliver Cowdery and David Whitmer to find twelve men who will qualify for this holy calling. Later, Martin Harris will also be called to assist them in this responsibility. By way of additional background, we will quote from the Church History student manual used by our institutes of religion entitled *Church History in the Fulness of Times*. We will use **bold** for teaching purposes.

"One of the most important events in the restoration of the Savior's church was the formation of the Quorum of the Twelve Apostles. Even before the Church was organized, the members had anticipated this significant step. Joseph Smith and Oliver Cowdery had received the authority of the apostleship (see D&C 20:2–3) probably as early as **1829. During that same year, a revelation [D&C 18] directed Oliver Cowdery and David Whitmer to search out the twelve** who would be 'called to go into all the world to preach my gospel unto every creature' (D&C 18:28). **Later Martin Harris was also called to assist in this selection**. This meant that the Three Witnesses to the Book of Mormon, under the direction and consent of the First Presidency, would choose the Twelve Apostles who were to serve as special witnesses of the Savior in this dispensation" (*Church History in the Fulness of Times*, 2003, 153–54).

It will be almost six years before these twelve special witnesses will be selected. It will be done at a meeting held in Kirtland, Ohio, on Saturday, February 14, 1835, to which those men who participated in the march of Zion's Camp were invited. From these faithful men, who had been tried and proven, came the majority of the members of the leading quorums of the Church.

We will list the original members of the Quorum of Twelve Apostles in order of seniority and age (which determined their order of seniority since they were all called at the same time): Thomas B. Marsh (35), David W. Patten (35), Brigham Young (33), Heber C. Kimball (33), Orson Hyde (30), William E. McLellin (29), Parley P. Pratt (27), Luke S. Johnson (27), William B. Smith (23), Orson Pratt (23), John F. Boynton (23), Lyman E. Johnson (23).

With the above as background, we will now study the rest of the section.

Next, Oliver and David are given some of the criteria that will apply when it comes time to select the Twelve. They are also instructed as to the duties of these twelve Apostles.

26 And now, behold, **there are others who are called** [*perhaps meaning "foreordained," since these twelve won't be officially called here on earth for almost six years*] **to declare my gospel, both unto Gentile and unto Jew;**

27 Yea, even twelve; and **the Twelve shall be my disciples,** and **they shall take upon them my name**; and the Twelve are they who **shall desire to take upon them my name with full purpose of heart.**

28 And if they desire to take upon them my name with full purpose of heart, **they are called to go into all the world to preach my gospel unto every creature.**

29 And **they are they who are ordained of me to baptize in my name,** according to that which is written;

30 And **you have that which is written before you**; wherefore, **you must perform it according to the words which are written.**

Next, the Savior speaks in advance to the twelve men who will be chosen, and who will understandably be quite intimidated and humbled by such a calling from God.

31 And now I speak unto you, the Twelve—Behold, **my grace is sufficient for you** [*I will help you carry out your sacred duties*]; **you must walk uprightly before me and sin not.**

32 And, behold, **you are they who are ordained of me to ordain priests and teachers; to declare my gospel, according to the power of the Holy Ghost which is in you, and according to the callings and gifts of God unto men;**

33 And **I, Jesus Christ, your Lord and your God, have spoken it.**

34 **These words are not of men nor of man, but of me**; wherefore, **you shall testify they are of me and not of man;**

Next, in verses 35–36, as the Savior continues to instruct the Twelve, we, ourselves, are taught a beautiful and simple principle, namely that we can hear the voice of the Lord by reading the scriptures. S. Dilworth Young spoke of this fact in the April 1963 general conference as follows:

"The thing that impresses me about this is, and I have never thought of it before, when I read a verse in the Doctrine and Covenants, I am hearing the voice of the Lord as well as reading his words, if I hear by the Spirit.

"Now I have heard it said many times by men that they have often asked the Lord for a special testimony and oftentimes haven't had it. They seem to want to hear the voice of the Lord. I confess I have often wanted to hear the voice of the Lord, without knowing that all these years I have been hearing it with deaf ears. This woke me up" (In Conference Report, April 1963, 74).

35 For **it is my voice which speaketh them** [*the scriptures*] unto you; for **they are given by my Spirit** unto you, and **by my power you can read them one to another;** and save it were by my power you could not have them;

36 **Wherefore, you can testify that you have heard my voice**, and know my words.

Next comes the specific instruction to Oliver Cowdery and David Whitmer (who, as noted previously, will also be joined by Martin Harris in this assignment) to search out the twelve men who will become the first Quorum of Twelve in this dispensation.

37 And now, behold, **I give unto you, Oliver Cowdery, and also unto David Whitmer, that you shall search out the Twelve, who shall have the desires of which I have spoken**;

38 And **by their desires and their works you shall know them**.

39 **And when you have found them** you shall **show these things** [*this revelation, including what I say next*] **unto them.**

The remainder of the verses in this section are to the Twelve, who will be called in just under six years in February 1835. They are to hear these verses especially at this time. According to the following quote from S. Dilworth Young, Oliver Cowdery read section 18 to them at the time of their calling.

"In 1835 the Twelve were chosen, as you know, and on one occasion they were called together and given their instructions. Oliver Cowdery was the spokesman; and after having given them some very powerful and heartwarming instruction, so moved was he, himself, that he had to stop two or three times to weep. He finally read the revelation [now designated as section 18]" (*Doctrine and Covenants Student Manual*, 1981, 36).

40 And **you** [*the Twelve*] **shall fall down** [*humble yourselves*] **and worship the Father in my name.**

41 And **you must preach unto the world,** saying: You must repent and be baptized, in the name of Jesus Christ;

42 For all men must repent and be baptized, and not only men, but women, and children who have arrived at the years of accountability [*this is in preparation for D&C 68:25, in which the age of eight will be given as the age for baptizing children*].

43 And now, after that you have

received this, **you must keep my commandments in all things;**

44 And **by your hands I will work a marvelous work among the children of men,** unto the convincing of many of their sins, that they may come unto repentance, and that they may come unto the kingdom of my Father.

45 Wherefore, **the blessings which I give unto you are above all things.**

46 And **after that you have received this, if you keep not my commandments you cannot be saved in the kingdom of my Father.**

47 Behold, **I, Jesus Christ, your Lord and your God, and your Redeemer, by the power of my Spirit have spoken it.** Amen.

SECTION 19

Background

Research for *The Joseph Smith Papers* publications has resulted in a change for the date given in the heading for this revelation. If you have a Doctrine and Covenants printed before the most recent edition (2013), the date given in the heading to section 19 is "March 1830." However, the date given in the 2013 edition of the scriptures is "likely in the summer of 1829." We will Include a quote from the *Doctrine and Covenants Student Manual*, 2018, chapter 8, which explains this change:

"Note: Earlier editions of the Doctrine and Covenants give the date of the revelation recorded in Doctrine and Covenants 19 as March 1830. Recent research suggests that the revelation was likely received during the summer of 1829. This date is reflected in the 2013 edition of the scriptures and in this chapter.) On August 25, 1829, Martin Harris mortgaged his property to Grandin as payment for the publication (see *The Joseph Smith Papers, Documents, Volume 1: July 1828–June 1831,* ed. Michael Hubbard MacKay and others [2013], 86–89)."

Section 19 is one of the great revelations on the Atonement of Christ. In it, He teaches us about the extreme difficulty of His suffering for us and urgently invites us to repent so that we can be forgiven through His atoning gift and will not have to suffer the penalties for our own sins, which suffering will be far beyond our ability now to comprehend.

This revelation was given in the form of a commandment through Joseph Smith to Martin Harris at Manchester, New York. You may remember that Martin Harris lived in Palmyra, which was next to Manchester where Joseph Smith's parents lived.

Martin Harris had signed a contract that mortgaged his farm to guarantee payment for the printing of the Book of Mormon. The printer, 23-year-old Egbert B. Grandin, was manager and principal owner of the *Wayne Sentinel*, which was a newspaper printed in Palmyra. There was much local opposition to the printing of the Book of Mormon, and the only way Grandin would agree to proceed with the printing was if the printing costs were secured in this way. The plan had been to sell copies of the Book of Mormon and pay for the printing in that manner. But with opposition building, the only way Grandin would continue printing was through Martin's legal guarantee to pay the costs within eighteen months of the time printing began if sales failed to cover the amount owed. The agreement called for the printing of 5,000 copies for $3,000.

As the printing proceeded, opposition increased. In fact, a mass meeting was held by the people of Palmyra and the surrounding area in which it was agreed to boycott the purchase of Books of Mormon and to use their influence to prevent others likewise from buying it. The first completed copies of the Book of Mormon were ready for sale on March 26, 1830, according to an ad in the *Wayne Sentinel*. (See *Joseph Smith and the Restoration*, 114–17.)

With this as background, it doesn't take much imagination to suggest that Martin Harris was getting worried that he might actually end up losing some of his prime farm acreage to pay the debt and perhaps was beginning to hesitate to keep his part of the agreement. It is indeed a credit to him that he obeyed the word of the Lord in verses 26, 34, and 35, wherein he was told "Impart of thy property . . . Pay the debt." He did so, selling 151 acres of the approximately 240 to 300 acres that he owned to pay the $3,000 printing debt.

Martin Harris had seen the angel who brought the gold plates to the Three Witnesses, by permission of the angel had handled each of the plates that had been translated, had seen the Urim and Thummim, the breastplate, the sword of Laban, the Liahona (see D&C 17:1), and also the brass plates, the plates of Ether, and several other plates (see note after section 17, verse 1, in this study guide). He had also heard the voice of the Lord. Even with witnessing all of this, at the time of this revelation, he was still having difficulties keeping the commandments as you will sense from the context of the verses in this section. Still, one of the encouraging and endearing things about Martin Harris is that despite troubles along the way, including leaving the Church for several years, he came back and was faithful to the end of his life. This is a sweet reminder to each of us that the Lord keeps helping us in spite of our weaknesses and failures. This can give us great hope and encouragement along the way.

As indicated previously, this revelation is unusual in the sense that it is given as a commandment (see heading to section 19 in your Doctrine and Covenants). As you will see, the Savior is direct and to the point with Martin Harris, commanding him frequently on several different matters. As we study it, we will be taught many doctrines and principles that can bless our lives also.

The first thing we will do by way of studying section 19 is to go through the entire section **bolding** several of the gospel vocabulary words and phrases, doctrines, commandments, principles, gospel concepts, and counsel in order to get a better idea and feeling for how much is packed into these forty-one verses. Then we will repeat the verses, taking time to study several of them.

Doctrine

Verses 1–2. Under the Father's direction, Jesus is in charge of all things on earth.

1 **I AM Alpha and Omega** [*the beginning letter and the ending letter in the Greek alphabet*], Christ the Lord; yea, even I am he, **the beginning and the end**, the

Redeemer of the world.

2 **I**, having accomplished and **finished the will of** him whose I am, even **the Father**, concerning me—having done this **that I might subdue all things unto myself**—

Doctrine

Verse 3. Jesus will overcome Satan completely and will be our final judge—see also John 5:22.

3 **Retaining all power**, even to the **destroying of Satan and his works at the end of the world**, and the **last great day of judgment, which I shall pass upon the inhabitants** thereof, **judging every man according to his works and** the **deeds** which he hath done.

Doctrine

Verses 4–5. All of us must repent of our sins or suffer for them.

4 And surely **every man must repent or suffer**, for **I, God, am endless**.

5 Wherefore, I revoke not the judgments which I shall pass, but **woes shall go forth, weeping, wailing and gnashing of teeth,**

yea, to those who are found on my left hand. [*In scriptural symbolism, "left hand" is often symbolic of the wicked, whereas, "right hand" or "covenant hand," is symbolic of the righteous, those who make and keep covenants with God.*]

Doctrine

Verses 6–12. "Endless torment" does not last forever.

6 Nevertheless, it is not written that there shall be no end to this torment, but it is written *endless torment*.

7 Again, it is written *eternal damnation*; wherefore it is more express than other scriptures, that it might work upon the hearts of the children of men, altogether for my name's glory.

8 Wherefore, **I will explain unto you this mystery**, for it is meet unto you to know even as mine apostles.

9 I speak unto you that are chosen in this thing, even as one, that you may enter into **my rest** [*celestial glory*].

10 For, behold, the mystery of godliness, how great is it! For, behold, **I am endless**, and **the punishment which is given from my hand is endless punishment,**

for **Endless is my name**. Wherefore—

11 **Eternal punishment is God's punishment.**

12 **Endless punishment is God's punishment.**

13 Wherefore, **I command you to repent**, and keep the commandments which you have received by the hand of my servant Joseph Smith, Jun., in my name;

14 And it is by my almighty power that you have received them;

Doctrine

Verses 15–18. We cannot begin to imagine or comprehend the suffering endured by the Savior as He paid for our sins.

15 Therefore **I command you to repent**—repent, **lest** I smite you by **the rod of my mouth**, and by my wrath, and by my anger, and **your sufferings be sore**—how sore you know not, **how exquisite** you know not, yea, **how hard to bear** you know not.

16 For behold, **I, God, have suffered these things for all, that they might not suffer if they would repent;**

Doctrine

If we do not repent, we will have to suffer for our own sins.

17 But **if they would not repent they must suffer even as I**;

18 **Which suffering caused myself, even God, the greatest of all, to tremble because of pain, and to bleed at every pore, and to suffer both body and spirit— and would that I might not drink the bitter cup, and shrink—**

19 Nevertheless, glory be to the Father, and **I partook and finished my preparations unto the children of men.**

Doctrine

Verse 20. Confession is a necessary part of qualifying for forgiveness of sins.

Doctrine

Verse 20. Part of the suffering endured by the Savior for our sins was the withdrawal of the Spirit from Him so that He was alone without that help and support.

20 Wherefore, **I command you again to repent**, lest I humble you with my almighty power; and that you **confess your sins, lest you suffer these punishments** of

which I have spoken, of which in the smallest, yea, even in the least degree **you have tasted at the time I withdrew my Spirit**.

21 And **I command you** that you preach naught but repentance, and show not these things unto the world until it is wisdom in me.

22 For **they cannot bear meat now, but milk** they must receive; wherefore, they must not know these things, lest they perish.

23 **Learn of me, and listen to my words; walk in the meekness of my Spirit, and you shall have peace in me.**

Doctrine

Verse 24. Christ works under the direction of the Father and carried out His will in every detail.

24 **I am Jesus Christ; I came by the will of the Father, and I do his will.**

25 And again, **I command thee** that thou shalt not covet thy neighbor's wife; nor seek thy neighbor's life.

Doctrine

Verse 26. The Book of Mormon contains the word of God.

26 And again, **I command thee** that **thou shalt not covet thine own property, but impart it freely to the printing of the Book of Mormon**, which **contains the truth and the word of God**—

27 Which is my word to the **Gentile**, that soon it may go to the **Jew**, of whom the **Lamanites are a remnant**, that they may believe the gospel, and look not for a Messiah to come who has already come.

Doctrine

Verse 28. Public prayer as well as private prayer are part of proper worship.

28 And again, **I command thee** that thou shalt **pray vocally as well as in thy heart**; yea, before the world as well as in secret, in public as well as in private.

29 And thou shalt declare glad tidings, yea, **publish it upon the mountains**, and upon every high place, and among every people that thou shalt be permitted to see.

30 And thou shalt do it with all humility, trusting in me, **reviling not against revilers**.

31 And of **tenets** thou shalt not talk, but thou shalt declare **repentance** and **faith** on the Savior, and remission of sins by **baptism**, and by fire, yea, even the **Holy Ghost**.

32 Behold, this is a great and the last commandment which I shall give unto you concerning this matter; for this shall suffice for thy daily walk, even unto the end of thy life.

33 And **misery** thou shalt receive **if** thou wilt **slight these counsels, yea,** even the **destruction** of thyself and property.

34 Impart a portion of thy property, yea, even part of thy lands, and all save the support of thy family.

35 **Pay the debt** thou hast contracted with the printer. **Release thyself from bondage**.

36 Leave thy house and home, except when thou shalt desire to see thy family;

37 And **speak freely to all**; yea, **preach, exhort, declare the truth**, even with a loud voice, with a sound of rejoicing, crying— **Hosanna**, hosanna, blessed be the name of the Lord God!

38 **Pray always**, and I will pour out my Spirit upon you, and great shall be your blessing—yea, even more than if you should obtain treasures of earth and **corruptibleness** to the extent thereof.

39 Behold, canst thou read this without rejoicing and lifting up thy heart for gladness?

40 Or **canst thou run about longer as a blind guide?**

41 Or canst thou be humble and meek, and conduct thyself wisely before me? Yea, **come unto me thy Savior.** Amen.

Having looked at many of the gospel concept words and phrases contained in these 41 verses as stated previously, we will now go through and add notes and do a detailed study of many of the teachings contained in this section. First of all, in verses 1–3, next, the Savior introduces Himself. The names and titles He uses are often used elsewhere in the scriptures. Through them, we learn more about Him in His various stewardships and powers as our Savior and Redeemer. For instance, in verse 1, we see five titles by which He is identified in the scriptures and through which He teaches us much about Himself. We will **bold** them and add explanatory notes.

1 I AM **Alpha and Omega** [*the first and last letters of the Greek Alphabet; in other words, "I am the first and the last, the beginning and the end"; for instance, He created the earth in the beginning, under the Father's direction, and will be there at the end, as our final judge*], **Christ** [*the "Anointed One," the "Messiah" whom the prophets promised would come*] **the Lord** [*the God of this world, under the Father's direction*]; yea, even I am he, **the beginning and the end** [*same as Alpha and Omega*], the **Redeemer of the world** [*the Savior of all*].

As Jesus Christ continues introducing Himself in verses 2 and 3, next, we are taught much more about Him.

2 I, **having accomplished and finished the will of him whose I am, even the Father, concerning me** [*He carried out the Atonement and all aspects of His mortal mission perfectly, as assigned by the Father; see also verse 19*]—having done this **that I might subdue all things unto myself** [*having carried out the Atonement perfectly gave Christ personal power over all things (see verse 3) such that he could save all who are willing to come unto Him for salvation*]—

3 **Retaining all power, even to the destroying of Satan and his works at the end of the world** [*the "end of the world" is defined as "the destruction of the wicked" in Joseph Smith—Matthew 1:4*], and **the last great day of judgment** [*the final judgment*], **which I shall pass upon the inhabitants thereof** [*Christ is our final judge. John 5:22 tells us that "the Father*

judgeth no man, but hath committed all judgment unto the Son."], **judging every man according to his works and the deeds which he hath done.** [*Christ will judge us according to our works. In D&C 137:9, Jesus informs us that He will also judge us according to the desires of our hearts.*]

Some people wonder at times if there is any chance that Satan might win out in the end. The answer, at the beginning of verse 3, above, is clear. There is absolutely no chance at all of this happening. The devil and his evil hosts will ultimately be "cast away into their own place, that they shall not have power over the saints any more at all." See D&C 88:114. This absolute truth is most comforting.

Next, the Savior teaches Martin Harris (and us) about the suffering of those who choose not to repent. He will use the terms, "endless," and "eternal." Pay close attention to them and how He defines them. You will see that they are not the same in this context.

First of all, He will make two simple statements in verse 4, next.

4 And surely **every man must repent or suffer**, for **I, God, am endless.**

The first **bolded** statement in verse 4, above, needs no clarification, because it is an established and obvious fact.

For the last statement, we will quickly convene an English grammar class and review the use of adjectives. Adjectives describe a noun. For instance, in the sentence, "Go get the blue ball," the word "blue" is an adjective describing the noun "ball."

If we had a sentence describing God, we might have several adjectives. Example: "We worship a kind, loving, endless God." "Kind," "loving," and "endless" are all adjectives describing God. Let's take it one step farther. Supposing we were describing God's punishment of Laman and Lemuel and the others who had rebelled on the ship and tied Nephi up (1 Nephi 18:8–11), we could say it was "God's" punishment. We could say the same thing in our context here by saying it was "kind" punishment (because it was designed by God to help save their souls), or "loving" punishment, or "endless" punishment (meaning coming from God). In this case, "endless" would have nothing to do with how long it lasts (because the punishment was a raging storm which lasted four days [1 Nephi 18:15]); rather, it would be simply stating that the punishment came from God. "Endless" describes Him. Therefore, **"endless" can be used as an adjective to describe blessings or punishments that come from Him**. Just tuck this thinking into your mind for a moment and you will soon see where we are going with this.

Continuing, the Savior says that nothing will stop the punishments which will come upon the unrepentant.

5 Wherefore, **I revoke** [*cancel*] **not the judgments** [*punishments*] **which I shall pass,** but woes shall go forth, **weeping, wailing and gnashing of teeth** [*extreme misery*], yea, to those who are found on **my left hand.** [*"Left hand" is a scriptural term which refers to those who will have to suffer for their own sins. "Right hand" refers to those who have made and kept covenants ("right hand" is symbolic of covenant making), and are thus forgiven through the Savior's Atonement.*]

In verse 6, next, we come back to the idea that "endless" can sometimes be used simply as an adjective describing God, and thus describing punishments or blessings which come from Him. In this type of context, it is not describing the duration of things.

6 Nevertheless, **it is not written that there shall be no end to this torment, but it is written** *endless torment.*

Before we move on, let's do a bit more with "suffer," verse 4, "weeping, wailing and gnashing of teeth," verse 5, and "endless torment," verse 6. We have just been told

in verse 6 that this suffering and punishment doesn't last forever. So, when does it take place?

For the most part, the answer is that this punishment and suffering will take place when people who refuse to repent are turned over to Satan to suffer for their own sins. Generally speaking, this takes place while the Millennium is going on upon the earth. We don't know where Satan is at that time (he is not on earth tempting people, see D&C 101:28), but the wicked will be turned over to him, "thrust down to hell! These are they who shall not be redeemed from the devil until the last resurrection, until the Lord, even Christ the Lamb, shall have finished his work [the end of the Millennium—see D&C 76:84–85; compare with 88:100–101]."

Concerning being turned over to Satan to be punished, Apostle Bruce R. McConkie taught that it means to be turned over to Satan "with all the protective power of the priesthood, of righteousness, and of godliness removed so that Lucifer is free to torment, persecute and afflict such a person without let or hindrance" (*Mormon Doctrine*, 108).

Continuing, we know from the scriptures that the only ones who will spend eternity with Satan are sons of perdition. Thus, we know that the rest of the wicked who do not qualify for outer darkness will be among those spoken of in D&C

76:84–85 (quoted above) who will eventually be "redeemed from the devil" and will be completely free from his influence as they go to the telestial kingdom, which is so nice that it "surpasses all understanding." See D&C 76:89.

So, by way of summarizing all of the above concerning "endless" punishment, we see that it is the punishment, among other things, of being turned over to the buffetings of Satan to suffer for one's own sins, having refused to repent, and that it does not last forever. So, Martin Harris is being told, in very strong and serious terms, that unless he repents, he will suffer "endless" punishment, or God's punishments, and that he would do very well to reconsider some of the things he is doing, along with some of his attitudes and the commitments he ought to keep.

In fact, as you will see as we move on to verse 7, next, the Lord specifically tells Martin that He is using terminology designed to get Martin's full attention.

7 Again, **it is written** *eternal damnation;* wherefore **it is more express than other scriptures, that it might work upon the hearts of the children of men**, altogether for my name's glory.

As you noticed, the term "eternal damnation" is used in verse 7, above. The term "eternal punishment" will be used in verse 11. There is a difference between "damnation" and "punishment." We will quote from the *Doctrine and Covenants Student Manual*, 1981, page 37. Elder James E. Talmage is quoted there, explaining what "eternal punishment" means (**bold** added for emphasis):

"That is a direful expression; but in his mercy the Lord has made plain what those words mean. 'Eternal punishment,' he says, is God's punishment, for he is eternal; and that condition or state or possibility will ever exist for the sinner who deserves and really needs such condemnation; but **this does not mean that the individual sufferer or sinner is to be eternally and everlastingly made to endure and suffer. No man will be kept in hell** (turned over to the buffetings of Satan; see D&C 76:84–85) **longer than is necessary to bring him to a fitness for something better**. When he reaches that stage the prison doors will open and there will be rejoicing among the hosts who welcome him into a better state. The Lord has not abated in the least what he has said in earlier dispensations concerning the operation of his law and his gospel, but he has made clear unto us his goodness and mercy through it all, for it is his glory and his work to bring about the immortality and eternal life of man" (In Conference Report, April 1930, 97).

Again, quoting from the student manual mentioned above, page 37, we will see what "eternal damnation" means. Elder Bruce R. McConkie is quoted as follows (**bold** added for emphasis):

"**Eternal damnation is the opposite of eternal life**, and all those who do not gain eternal life, or exaltation in the highest heaven within the celestial kingdom, are partakers of **eternal damnation**. **Their eternal condemnation is to have limitations imposed upon them so that they cannot progress to the state of godhood and gain a fulness of all things**.

"They 'remain separately and singly, without exaltation, . . . to all eternity; and from henceforth are not gods, but are angels of God forever and ever.' (D&C 132:17.) **Their** kingdom or **progress has an 'end,'** and **they 'cannot have an increase**.' (D&C 131:4.) **Spirit children are denied to them to all eternity**, and they inherit 'the deaths,' meaning an absence of posterity in the resurrection. (D&C 132:16–25.)

"**They are never** redeemed from their spiritual fall and **taken back into the full presence and glory of God**. Only the obedient are 'raised in immortality unto eternal life.' The disobedient, 'they that believe not,' are raised in immortality 'unto eternal damnation; for they cannot be redeemed from their spiritual fall, because they repent not.' (D&C 29:42–44.)" (*Mormon Doctrine*, 234).

With the above as background, we will listen as the Lord explains these important concepts to Martin Harris.

8 Wherefore, **I will explain unto you this mystery**, for it is meet [*necessary*] unto you to know even as mine apostles.

9 I speak unto you that are chosen in this thing, even as one, **that you may enter into my rest** [*exaltation in celestial glory, the "fulness of his glory"; see D&C 84:24*].

10 For, behold, the mystery of godliness, how great is it! For, **behold, I am endless, and the punishment which is given from my hand is endless punishment, for Endless is my name**. Wherefore—

11 **Eternal punishment is God's punishment**.

12 **Endless punishment is God's punishment**.

13 Wherefore [*this is why*], **I command you to repent**, and keep the commandments which you have received by the hand of my servant Joseph Smith, Jun., in my name;

14 And it is by my almighty power that you have received them;

Verses 15–19, next, are quite well-known and often-quoted in sermons and lessons. You may wish to mark them in your own scriptures. In them, the Savior explains how difficult His suffering was, and pleads with all of us to accept His gift so that we don't have to "suffer even as I" (verse 17).

15 Therefore **I command you to repent**—repent, **lest I smite** [*punish*] **you by the rod** [*power and authority*] **of my mouth**, and **by my wrath**, and **by my anger, and your sufferings be sore** [*extremely severe*]—how sore you know not, how **exquisite** [*extremely difficult*] you know not, yea, how **hard to bear** you know not.

16 For behold, **I, God, have suffered these things for all, that they might not suffer if they would repent**;

17 **But if they would not repent they must suffer even as I;**

As you are perhaps aware, because of the wording in Luke 22:44, many Bible scholars and students have doubts as to whether or not Jesus actually bled from every pore. It reads as follows:

Luke 22:44

44 And being in an agony he prayed more earnestly: and his sweat was as it were [*as if it*

were] great drops of blood falling down to the ground.

In verse 18, next, in which the Savior describes the suffering required by His Atonement, He, Himself, tells us that He did, indeed, bleed from every pore because of the suffering He took upon Himself for the sins of all mankind.

18 **Which suffering caused myself, even God**, the greatest of all [*who have lived as mortals on this earth*], **to tremble because of pain**, and to **bleed at every pore**, and to **suffer both body and spirit**—and **would** [*desire*] **that I might not drink the bitter cup** [*follow through with the Atonement*], and **shrink** [*hesitate*]—

From the above description by the Savior Himself, it would appear that when it finally came right down to it, He was somewhat taken back by how difficult it really was. All the more reason for us to be eternally grateful to Him for His following through. He did, as stated by Him in the next verse.

19 **Nevertheless**, glory be to the Father, and **I partook and finished my preparations unto the children of men** [*the Savior's work to prepare the way for us to have forgiveness available*].

The rest of the verses in this section are very specific to Martin Harris. But, as usual, we can learn much which applies to ourselves from what the Lord says here.

20 Wherefore, **I command you** [*Martin Harris*] again to **repent, lest I humble you** with my almighty power; and that you **confess your sins, lest you suffer these punishments of which I have spoken**, of which in the smallest, yea, even in the least degree you have tasted at the time I withdrew my Spirit [*referring to some past experience in Martin's life*].

21 And I command you that you **preach naught but** [*nothing but*] **repentance**, and show not these things [*possibly referring to the teachings about eternal punishment, endless punishment, and so on*] unto the world until it is wisdom in me.

22 For **they cannot bear meat now, but milk they must receive**; wherefore, they must not know these things, lest they perish [*for fear that they would be overwhelmed, and thus would lose their interest in the gospel*].

23 **Learn of me**, and **listen to my words; walk in** the **meekness** [*part of the definition of meekness is the attribute of not being easily irritated*] of my Spirit, and **you shall have peace in me.**

24 **I am Jesus Christ; I came by the will of the Father, and I do his will.**

From verse 25, we are given to understand that Martin was struggling with some major temptations at this point in his life.

25 And again, **I command thee that thou shalt not covet thy neighbor's wife; nor seek thy neighbor's life.**

Next, Martin is commanded (for his own good) to keep his word, and sell some of his property to pay for the printing of the Book of Mormon, as he had formerly agreed to do.

26 And again, **I command thee** that **thou shalt not covet thine own property, but impart it freely to the printing of the Book of Mormon**, which contains the truth and the word of God—

27 Which is my word to the **Gentile** [*meaning, in this context, all who are not Jews*], that soon it may go to the **Jew**, of **whom the Lamanites are a remnant** [*meaning that the Lamanites are descendants of Lehi, who came from Jerusalem; all citizens of Jerusalem, regardless of which tribe of Israel they came from, were considered to be Jews*], that they may believe the gospel, and look not for a Messiah to come

who has already come [*meaning that the Jews will someday know, through the true gospel, that Christ has already come*].

Perhaps you've heard someone criticize the practice of public prayer on the basis that Jesus taught people to avoid praying in public like the hypocrites and taught instead to "enter into thy closet" and thus pray in secret (Matthew 6:5–6). We don't know whether or not Martin felt this way, but we do see the Savior's instruction, next, that both sincere public prayer as well as private prayer are part of His gospel. This is one of the reasons this book of scripture is called the "Doctrine and Covenants," because it gives us correct doctrine on such matters.

28 And again, I command thee that thou shalt **pray vocally as well as in thy heart**; yea, **before the world as well as in secret, in public as well as in private**.

29 And thou shalt **declare glad tidings** [*preach the gospel*], yea, publish it upon the mountains [*make it available to many people*], and upon every high place [*symbolic of making it easy for people to hear you and know what you stand for*], and among every people that thou shalt be permitted to see.

30 And thou shalt **do it with all**

humility, trusting in me, **reviling not against revilers** [*don't say mean things back to people who say mean things to you or about you*].

31 And of tenets thou shalt not talk [*don't get caught up in "bashing" other people's doctrines and beliefs*], but **thou shalt declare repentance** and **faith on the Savior**, and remission of sins by **baptism**, and by fire [*symbolic of how the Holy Ghost "burns" imperfections out of us, as in the refining of gold*], yea, even the **Holy Ghost.** [*In other words, don't waste time arguing and debating different ideologies, dogmas, and beliefs. Rather, teach the simple basics of the gospel*].

In verses 32–33, next, Martin is told, in effect, that this is a very important opportunity being given him by the Lord, and how he responds to it will affect him the rest of his life.

32 Behold, **this is a great and the last commandment which I shall give unto you concerning this matter**; for **this shall suffice for thy daily walk, even unto the end of thy life**.

33 And **misery thou shalt receive if thou wilt slight** [*ignore or underestimate the importance of*] **these counsels**, yea, even the **destruction of thyself and property**.

Next, the Savior once again instructs Martin to sell part of his land and pay the printing bill for the Book of Mormon. He does it, selling 151 acres to raise the $3,000 needed to pay for the printing of 5,000 Books of Mormon.

34 Impart a portion of thy property, yea, even part of thy lands, and all save the support of thy family.

35 Pay the debt thou hast contracted with the printer. Release thyself from bondage [*a simple reminder that debt is a form of bondage*].

According to the 2018 edition of the *Doctrine and Covenants Student Manual*, chapter 8, "Later in life, Martin testified that from the proceeds of the sale of the book, he recouped all of the money that he had advanced for the printing of the book. (See 'Additional Testimony of Martin Harris [One of the Three Witnesses] to the Coming forth of the Book of Mormon,' *The Latter-day Saints' Millennial Star*, vol. 21 [August 20, 1859], 545.)"

In the context of section 19, verses 36–37, next, seem to refer to missionary travel in order to preach the gospel rather than instructing Martin to leave home and never come back except on occasion to see his family.

36 Leave thy house and home [*to preach*], except when thou shalt desire to see thy family;

37 And **speak freely to all**; yea, **preach, exhort** [*urge people to obey the gospel*], **declare** the truth, even with a loud voice, **with a sound of rejoicing** [*be happy as you preach*], crying—Hosanna, hosanna, blessed be the name of the Lord God!

The word, "hosanna," as used in verse 37, above, means "Lord, please save now," or words to that effect. (See Bible Dictionary, under "Hosanna.") It is used in conjunction with praising the Lord and asking for his help and support, acknowledging our dependency on Him.

38 **Pray always** [*remember God constantly in your daily life, and your responsibility and opportunity to represent Him properly, and to get help from Him*], **and I will pour out my Spirit upon you**, and **great shall be your blessing**—yea, even more than if you should obtain treasures of earth and corruptibleness to the extent thereof.

39 Behold, **canst thou read this without rejoicing and lifting up thy heart for gladness?**

40 **Or canst thou run about longer as a blind guide?**

41 **Or canst thou be humble and meek, and conduct thyself wisely before me?** Yea, **come unto me thy Savior.** Amen.

The last phrase of verse 41, above, is especially tender, indicating that despite the severe reprimands Martin Harris received throughout section 19, our loving Savior wants to be his Redeemer too.

SECTION 20

Background

The heading to this section in the latest edition of the scriptures (2013) reads quite differently than in the previous editions of the Doctrine and Covenants. It is a direct result of the research for the Joseph Smith Papers Project. First, we will give the heading to recent editions prior to 2013, and then the heading for the 2013 edition.

Recent editions prior to 2013

"Revelation on Church Organization and Government, given through Joseph Smith the Prophet, April 1830. HC 1:64–70. Preceding his record of this revelation the Prophet wrote: We obtained of him [Jesus Christ] the following, by the spirit of prophecy and revelation; which not only gave us much information, but also pointed out to us the precise day upon which, according to his will and commandment, we should proceed to organize his Church once more here upon the earth."

The 2013 edition

"Revelation on Church organization and government, given through Joseph Smith the Prophet, at or near Fayette, New York. Portions of this revelation may have been given as early as summer 1829. The complete revelation, known at the time as the Articles and Covenants, was likely recorded soon after April 6, 1830 (the day the Church was organized). The Prophet wrote, 'We obtained of Him [Jesus Christ] the following, by the spirit of prophecy and revelation; which not only gave us much information, but also pointed out to us the precise day upon which, according to His will and commandment, we should proceed to organize His Church once more here upon the earth.'"

Section 20 could easily be called the first "Handbook of Instructions" for the Church. In it, the Lord tells the exact day upon which He wants His Church organized (verse 1). Among other things, He gives instructions on how people can qualify for baptism (verse 37), explains specific duties of elders, priests, teachers, deacons, and members (verses 38–69), gives instructions for people called to positions in the Church to be sustained by the members before they are ordained or set apart (verse 65), and gives instruction for blessing babies (verse 70).

Continuing, the Lord gives specific instructions on how to baptize and the exact words of the baptismal prayer (verses 73 and 74). Next, He gives instructions regarding the sacrament and the exact words of the prayers to be used by the priesthood holders in blessing the bread and wine (verses 75–79). We will discuss the use of water in the place of wine when we get to these verses in our detailed study of section 20.

The Savior goes on to give instructions on dealing with members who are involved in transgression (verse 80), instructs that membership records should be kept (verse 82), deals with excommunication (verse 83), and instructs that members moving into another area of the Church may take a signed certificate with them indicating that they are in good standing. This is somewhat similar to temple recommends today.

As you can see, this section is indeed a handbook of instructions for the early leaders of the Church in this dispensation.

Section 20 is also sometimes referred to as the "Articles and Covenants of the Church," as well as the "Constitution of the Church." It was a most important foundational revelation in the establishment of the Church through Joseph Smith and is a vital document for Church government and doctrine in our day.

Before we begin our detailed, verse-by-verse study, we will quote Joseph Smith and then Elder George Q. Cannon for a brief summary of the organization of the Church on April 6, 1830 (**bold** added for emphasis). First, Joseph Smith:

"In this manner did the Lord continue to give us instructions from time to time, concerning the duties which now devolved upon us; and among many other things of the kind, we obtained of him the following [section 20], by the spirit of prophecy and revelation; which not only gave us much information, but also **pointed out to us the precise day upon which, according to his will and commandment, we should proceed to organize his Church once more here upon the earth**" (*History of the Church*, 1:64, April 1830).

Next, George Q. Cannon:

"The Church of Jesus Christ of Latter-day Saints was organized on the 6th day of April, in the year of our Lord one thousand eight hundred and thirty, in Fayette, Seneca County, in the State of New York. Six persons were the original members: Joseph Smith the Prophet, Oliver Cowdery, Hyrum Smith, Peter Whitmer, Jun., Samuel H. Smith, and

David Whitmer. Each of the men had already been baptized by direct authority from heaven. The organization was made on the day and after the pattern dictated by God in a revelation given to Joseph Smith. The Church was called after the name of Jesus Christ; because he so ordered. Jesus accepted the Church, declared it to be his own and empowered it to minister on earth in his name.

"The sacrament, under inspiration from Jesus Christ, was administered to all who had thus taken upon them his name . . .

". . . It was necessary that God should define the mode and the principle of organization and should direct each step to be taken in this establishment of his kingdom . . .

"Joseph proceeded carefully, and exactly according to the instruction of the Almighty, and he laid the foundation of a work which will endure as long as earth shall last" (George Q. Cannon, *Life of Joseph Smith*, 1907, 52–54).

There were six original members of the Church, as stated in the George Q. Cannon quote above, which met the requirements of the state of New York for the organizing of a church. While there were several others present at the organization meeting who had likewise been baptized previously, only six were on the organization documentation, the minimum number required by state law. We will quote the Institute of Religion student manual for Church History, *Church History in the Fulness of Times*, for a brief summary of the actual organizing of the Church (**bold** added for teaching purposes):

"The meeting was simple. Joseph Smith, then twenty-four years old, called the group to order and designated five associates—Oliver Cowdery, Hyrum Smith, Peter Whitmer, Jr., Samuel H. Smith, and David Whitmer—to join him to meet New York's legal requirements for incorporating a religious society. After kneeling in solemn prayer, Joseph asked those present if they were willing to accept him and Oliver as their teachers and spiritual advisers. Everyone raised their hands in the affirmative. Although they had previously received the Melchizedek Priesthood, Joseph Smith and Oliver Cowdery then ordained each other to the office of elder. They did this to signify that they were elders **in the newly organized church**. The sacrament of the Lord's supper was administered next. The prayers used had been received through revelation (see D&C 20:75–79). **Joseph and Oliver then confirmed those who had previously been baptized as members of the Church of Jesus Christ** and bestowed upon them the gift of the Holy Ghost" (*Church History in the Fulness of Times*, 2003, 67–68).

We will now proceed with our verse-by-verse study.

1 THE rise of the Church of Christ in these last days, **being one thousand eight hundred and thirty years since the coming of our Lord and Savior Jesus Christ in the flesh** [*in other words, since the birth of Christ*], it being regularly organized and established agreeable to the laws of our country [*specifically, the laws of the state of New York*], by the will and commandments of God, in the fourth month, and on **the sixth day of the month which is called April—**

Both President Harold B. Lee and President Spencer W. Kimball explained the significance of this specific date as follows (**bold** added for emphasis):

President Lee: "**April 6**, 1973, is a particularly significant date because it commemorates not only the anniversary of the organization of The Church of Jesus Christ of Latter-day Saints in this dispensation, but also **the anniversary of the birth of the Savior**, our Lord and Master, Jesus Christ" (In Conference Report, April 1973, 4; or *Ensign*, April 1973, 2).

President Kimball: ". . . The name Jesus Christ and what it represents has been plowed deep into the history of the world, never to be uprooted. **Christ was born on the sixth of April**. Being one of the sons of God and His Only Begotten, his birth is of supreme importance" (In Conference Report, Apr. 1975, 3–4; or *Ensign*, May 1975, 4).

One more comment about April. The month of April appears to be very significant to the Savior. Not only was He born in April (in our calendar system), but He was also crucified and resurrected near this time of year.

2 Which commandments [*referred to near the end of verse 1*] were given to **Joseph Smith, Jun.**, who **was called of God**, and **ordained an apostle** of Jesus Christ, to be **the first elder of this church**;

3 And to **Oliver Cowdery**, who was also called of God, **an apostle** of Jesus Christ, to be **the second elder** of this church, and ordained under his [*Joseph Smith's*] hand;

4 And this according to the grace of our Lord and Savior Jesus Christ, to whom be all glory, both now and forever. Amen.

While the proper order of having one in charge (Joseph Smith as the "first elder" in verses 2–3, above) may seem standard procedure for us because we are used to it, this was somewhat unusual in many New England churches and congregations of Joseph Smith's day. For instance, in many religious organizations of the day, any one was considered authorized to have revelations for the entire congregation or for any individuals or groups.

God's kingdom is a "house of order" (D&C 132:8), with a living prophet at the head. And as you can see, the Lord established this principle among His Saints right at the beginning in our dispensation at the organization of His true Church.

From this point, with Joseph Smith as the first elder or presiding elder and Oliver Cowdery as the second elder, the Lord will continue to organize the leadership of the Church as the membership increases in numbers. Anthon H. Lund explained this process as follows:

"Now the Church was organized [April 1830], but not all the officers of the Church as we have them today, for the simple reason they did not have enough members in the Church to make a complete organization. Ten months after the Church was organized, Edward Partridge was ordained a Bishop to the Church, and in June following the first High Priests were ordained. In December, 1833, Joseph Smith, Senior, was ordained a Patriarch, and two months later the first High Council was organized. The Quorum of Twelve Apostles was organized [February 1835]. All the offices in the Priesthood were now established and men were ordained to fill them.

"In regard to Church government I will state that during the first thirteen months all Church business was done by conferences of Elders presided over by Joseph Smith and Oliver Cowdery. Several of the leading brethren were now ordained High Priests who afterwards formed the presiding quorum of the Church. In March, 1832, Joseph was called by revelation to be President of the Church, and a month later he was sustained as President of the High Priests' quorum. Next spring, March 18, 1833, the First Presidency was organized and sustained, consisting of three High Priests; Joseph Smith, President; Sidney Rigdon, First Counselor, and Frederick G. Williams, Second Counselor" (In Conference Report, April 1917, 14–15).

Continuing now with section 20, we will first read verse 5, next, and then read the Prophet Joseph Smith's explanation of what is meant by "entangled again in the vanities of the world."

5 After it was truly manifested unto this first elder [*Joseph Smith*] that he had received a remission of his sins [*which was one of his main concerns as he went into the grove to pray, which led to the First Vision in spring 1820*], he was entangled again in the vanities of the world;

As mentioned above, we will now turn to Joseph's account for help in understanding verse 5 (**bold** added for emphasis):

Pearl of Great Price, JS—History 1:28

"During the space of time which intervened between the time I had the vision and the year eighteen hundred and twenty-three—having been forbidden to join any of the religious sects of the day, and being of very tender years, and persecuted by those who ought to have been my friends and to have treated me kindly, and if they supposed me to be deluded to have endeavored in a proper and affectionate manner to have reclaimed me—I was left to all kinds of temptations; and, mingling with all kinds of society, I frequently fell into many foolish errors, and displayed the weakness of youth, and the foibles of human nature; which, I am sorry to say, led me into divers temptations, offensive in the sight of God. In making this confession, **no one need suppose me guilty of any great or malignant sins**. A disposition to commit such was never in my nature. But **I was guilty of levity, and sometimes associated with jovial company, etc., not consistent with that character which ought to be maintained by one who was called of God as I had been**. But this will not seem very strange to any one who recollects my youth, and is acquainted with my native cheery temperament."

Continuing with section 20, verses 6–12 refer to the appearance of Moroni to Joseph Smith and to the coming forth of the Book of Mormon.

6 But **after repenting, and humbling himself sincerely**, through faith, **God ministered unto him by an holy ange**l [*Moroni*], whose countenance [*face*] was as lightning, and whose garments [*robes; clothes*] were pure and white above all other whiteness;

7 **And gave unto him** [*Joseph Smith*] **commandments which inspired him**;

Too many people look upon commandments as restrictions which they must obey or they will be in trouble. This is sad. Verse 7, above, shows us the true role of commandments from God in our lives. They are to inspire us and bless us, to provide safety, security, and happiness for us. In fact, in D&C 59:4, the Savior tells us that if we are faithful, we will be blessed "with commandments not a few."

8 And **gave him power from on high, by the means** [*including the Urim and Thummim*] **which were before prepared** [*which were prepared in advance*], **to translate the Book of Mormon;**

9 **Which contains** a record of a fallen people [*the Nephites*], and **the fulness of the gospel** of Jesus Christ **to the Gentiles and to the Jews** also;

Verse 9, above, contains three words or phrases (**bolded**) which we will pause to examine.

Fullness of the gospel

Some people wonder how the Book of Mormon can have the "fulness" of the gospel when, for instance, nothing is specifically mentioned within its pages about temple marriage, the three degrees of glory, or work for the dead. No details are given about a number of doctrines contained in the Doctrine and Covenants. Since we know that the Book of Mormon is true, whenever we see something that appears on the surface to be a contradiction, we know that it is our understanding that is flawed rather than the word of God. Therefore, whenever we come to a word or phrase we may not understand, there is wisdom in looking at other possible meanings for it, especially paying attention to the context in which it is set.

When we do this, we find a number of possibilities. For instance, "fulness," in this context, could easily mean the gospel of faith, repentance, baptism, and gift of the Holy Ghost followed by the lifestyle of Christlike charity and humility which will lead to exaltation. An example of this would be the Nephites in the land of Zarahemla, who welcomed their former enemies, the Lamanites who had been converted, gave them land on which to live, and defended them with their lives. (See Alma 27:22–23.)

Charles W. Penrose, who served as a counselor in the First Presidency, explained "fulness of the gospel" as follows:

"We are told that the Book of Mormon contains the fulness of the gospel, that those who like to get up a dispute, say that the Book of Mormon does not contain any reference to the work of salvation for the dead, and there are many other things pertaining to the gospel that are not developed in that book, and yet we are told that book contains 'the fulness of the everlasting gospel.' Well, what is the fulness of the gospel? You read carefully the revelation in regard to the three glories, section 76, in the Doctrine and Covenants, and you find there defined what the gospel is [76:40–43]. There God, the Eternal Father, and Jesus Christ, his Son, and the Holy Ghost, are held up as the three persons in the

Trinity—the one God, the Father, the Word and the Holy Ghost, all three being united and being one God. When people believe in that doctrine and obey the ordinances which are spoken of in the same list of principles [20:17–28], you get the fulness of the gospel for this reason: If you really believe so as to have faith in our Eternal Father and in his Son, Jesus Christ, the Redeemer, and will hear him, you will learn all about what is needed to be done for the salvation of the living and the redemption of the dead.

"When people believe and repent and are baptized by Divine authority and the Holy Ghost is conferred upon them as a gift, they receive the everlasting gospel . . . and when the Holy Ghost as a gift is conferred upon people, young or old, as an 'abiding witness,' as a continuous gift, as a revelating spirit, they have the beginning, and I would not say the end, but they have the substance of the gospel of Jesus Christ. They have that which will bring salvation, for the gift of the Holy Ghost is such that it will highly enliven everyone who receives it" (In Conference Report, April 1922, 27–28).

Gentiles

As you no doubt have already noticed, the word, "Gentiles," has many different meanings and must be understood in context. According to the Bible Dictionary under "Gentiles," it can mean people who are not of the house of Israel or people who are of Israel but who do not have the gospel. In addition, "Gentile" can also mean someone who is not a Jew, either by blood line or by nationality. In this sense, Joseph Smith and most members of the Church are Gentiles. In the context of verse 9, above, "Gentiles" can easily refer to everyone other than the Jews.

Jews

"Jews," as used in the scriptures, usually refers to people who are blood line descendants of Judah, or to people who are residents of the Jerusalem area. Since Lehi and his family, including Laman and Lemuel, came from the Jerusalem area, they would be considered Jews, even though Lehi was from the tribe of Manasseh (Alma 10:3). Therefore, in the context of verse 9, above, "Jews" can be referring to the Lamanites, or descendants of Lehi, through Laman and Lemuel, and so on. This is clearly stated in D&C 19:27. Of course, the Jews, as we know them, will also be blessed by the teachings and testimony of Christ as contained in the Book of Mormon. This is also confirmed in D&C 19:27.

We will now continue with section 20, verses 10–16, in which the Savior tells us that angels are much involved in spreading the Book of Mormon throughout the world. He also teaches us more about the purposes of the Book of Mormon.

10 Which [*the Book of Mormon*] was given by inspiration, and is **confirmed to others by the ministering of angels**, and is declared unto the world by them—

In verse 11, next, we are taught that one of the important functions of the Book of Mormon is to bear witness of and support the Bible. Perhaps you've noticed that fewer and fewer "Christians" today seem to believe the Bible. In fact, it may well be said that members of the Church believe the Bible and the standards and principles taught in it much more than most Christians.

This is not bragging. It is a simple fact, especially when you look at the involvement of many Christians in premarital sex, homosexuality, lesbianism, and the like. The Bible preaches strongly against such behaviors, and the teachings of our Church substantiate and support the Bible.

Just one more comment regarding verse 11. The Prophet Ezekiel prophesied of the day when the Bible and the Book of Mormon would go hand-in-hand. We are living in the time of the fulfillment of that great prophecy. In fact, do you realize that the Topical Guide and Bible Dictionary, as well as the footnotes in the Book of Mormon, are a prominent part of the fulfillment of Ezekiel's prophecy? They are uniting the Bible and Book of Mormon as never before. We will

quote Ezekiel here, using **bold** for emphasis:

Ezekiel 37:15–19

15 The word of the LORD came again unto me, saying,

16 Moreover, thou son of man, **take** thee **one stick** [*the Bible*], and write upon it, **For Judah, and for the children of Israel his companions**: then take **another stick** [*the Book of Mormon*], and write upon it, **For Joseph, the stick of Ephraim, and** *for* **all the house of Israel his companions**:

17 And **join them one to another** into one stick; and **they shall become one in thine hand**.

18 ¶ And when the children of thy people shall speak unto thee, saying, Wilt thou not **shew us what thou** *meanest* by these?

19 Say unto them, **Thus saith the Lord GOD; Behold, I will take the stick of Joseph, which** *is* **in the hand of Ephraim, and the tribes of Israel his fellows, and will put them with him,** *even* **with the stick of Judah, and make them one stick, and they shall be one in mine hand.**

As you can well see, the 1982 addition of the words "Another Testament of Jesus Christ" to the title of the Book of Mormon is very significant in light of Ezekiel's prophecy.

Again, as taught in verse 11, next, one of the significant functions of the Book of Mormon is to prove that the Bible is true. It also shows that revelation has not ceased.

11 Proving to the world that the holy scriptures are true, and **that God does inspire men and call them to his holy work in this age and generation, as well as in generations of old**;

12 Thereby **showing that he is the same God yesterday, today, and forever**. Amen.

Be careful not to confuse policies with doctrines as you consider verse 12, above. Some members wonder how God can be the same "yesterday, today, and forever" when He changes the age for missionaries to go on missions; changes from separate meetings for priesthood and Relief Society, Sunday School, and sacrament meetings to a meeting block for all; eliminates seventies on a stake basis and only has general authority seventies, and so on.

While policies change as needed to meet the needs of an expanding and growing church, doctrines such as faith, repentance, baptism by immersion, the gift of the Holy Ghost, celestial marriage, and all things needed for exaltation and living in the family unit forever do not change. In this sense, God is the same "yesterday, today, and forever." He is completely fair to all people through work for the living and work for the dead. The requirements for exaltation are the same and must be met, whether in this life or in the next (through the preaching of the gospel in the spirit world and work for the dead).

Among other things, verses 13–16, next, bear witness that the Book of Mormon and those who bear witness of it and the restoration of the gospel will prepare the world for the final judgment.

13 Therefore, having so great witnesses [*among other things, the Book of Mormon and those called to the work of spreading the gospel—see verse 11, above*], **by them shall the world be judged**, even as many as shall hereafter come to a knowledge of this work [*the Book of Mormon and the ensuing restoration of the true Church*].

14 And **those who receive it in faith, and work righteousness**, shall **receive** a crown [*"crown" is symbolic of becoming gods*] of **eternal life** [*"eternal life" always means exaltation in the highest degree of glory in the celestial kingdom*];

15 But **those who harden their**

hearts in unbelief, and **reject it**, it shall turn to their own **condemnation**—

"Condemnation," as used in verse 15, above, simply defined, means "stopped."

16 For **the Lord God has spoken it**; and **we, the elders of the church**, have heard and **bear witness** to the words of the glorious Majesty on high, to whom be glory forever and ever. Amen.

In verses 17–36, we will be taught about the creation, the fall, the Atonement, and several accompanying doctrines. By way of reminder, one of the obvious reasons this book of scripture is called "The Doctrine and Covenants" is that it contains many "doctrines" that can be loosely defined as true facts about God and the gospel and includes teachings and requirements for exaltation, the proper procedures for use of the priesthood, the priesthood ordinances, and so on.

We will continue to point out many "doctrines" along the way by using "**Doctrine**" to emphasize them. Some may seem almost too obvious to even mention, but remember that they are not obvious to the majority of the residents of the earth in our day.

Doctrine

Verse 17. There is a God. This earth and its inhabitants are not a biological accident careening through interstellar space.

17 By these things we know that there is a God in heaven, who is **infinite and eternal**, from everlasting to **everlasting** the same **unchangeable** [*therefore, completely reliable*] God, the framer [*the Creator*] of heaven and earth, and all things which are in them;

Doctrine

Verse 18. We are created in the image of God.

18 And that he created man, male and female, after his own image and in his own likeness, created he them;

There is an important "order" or "sequence" pointed out in verses 19 through 31, next. It is a sequence that, in a significant way, is repeated over and over in our lives (although we use the sacrament rather than being rebaptized) as we grow and progress toward returning to our Father in Heaven. We will use **bold** to highlight key words in this sequence.

As you know, we were given **agency** clear back in premortality—see D&C 29:35–36. In order to have agency mean anything at all, we must have **knowledge**. Knowledge and agency bring the possibility of both **progression** on the covenant path and **transgression** with its accompanying **accountability**. Transgression leads to the need for the **Atonement**, which is accessed through **faith**, **repentance**, **baptism**, and the **gift of the Holy Ghost**. These, in turn, all combine together to bring **justification** and **sanctification**.

We will likewise **bold** most of the doctrines in verses 19–31 so that you can quickly see them in their context. Then we will repeat these verses and do more with them.

19 And gave unto them **commandments** that they should love and serve him, the only living and true God, and that he should be the only being whom they should worship.

20 But by the **transgression** of these holy laws man became sensual and devilish, and became **fallen** man.

21 Wherefore, the Almighty **God gave his Only Begotten Son**, as it is written in those scriptures which have been given of him.

22 He suffered temptations but gave no heed unto them.

23 **He was crucified, died, and rose again the third day**;

24 And **ascended into heaven**, to sit down on the right hand of the Father, to reign with almighty power according to the will of the Father;

25 **That as many as would believe and be baptized in his holy name, and endure in faith to the end, should be saved—**

26 Not only those who believed after he came in the meridian of time, in the flesh, but all those from the beginning, even as many as were before he came, who believed in the words of the holy prophets, who spake as they were inspired by **the gift of the Holy Ghost**, who truly testified of him in all things, should have eternal life,

27 As well as those who should come after, **who should believe in the gifts and callings of God by the Holy Ghost**, which beareth record of the Father and of the Son;

28 Which **Father, Son,** and **Holy Ghost** are one God, infinite and eternal, without end. Amen.

29 And we know that all men must **repent** and **believe on the name of Jesus Christ**, and **worship the Father in his name**, and endure in **faith** on his name to the

end, or they cannot be saved in the kingdom of God.

30 And we know that **justification** through the grace of our Lord and Savior Jesus Christ is just and true;

31 And we know also, that **sanctification** through the grace of our Lord and Savior Jesus Christ is just and true, to all those who love and serve God with all their mights, minds, and strength.

> As indicated above, we will now repeat verses 19 through 31 and do more with them. In these verses, the Lord gives us knowledge of many basics of the plan of salvation. Before we can exercise faith, be obedient, or even have effective agency, we must have knowledge, including knowledge of God and His commandments.

Doctrine

Verse 19. There is only one living and true God. (This is God the Father, as spoken of in Ephesians 4:6. Christ and the Holy Ghost are members of the Godhead but serve under the Father.)

19 And gave unto them com-mandments that they should **love and serve him, the only living and true God**, and that **he should be the only being whom they should worship.**

Doctrine

Verse 19, above. Heavenly Father is the only being we should worship. (Christ always directs us to worship the Father. We pray to the Father in the name of Jesus Christ. We reverence, love and respect the Savior, but in the strict sense of verse 19, we do not worship Him.)

Doctrine

Verse 20. The fall of Adam came through transgression. Also, we did not start out "carnal, sensual, and devilish" at birth. Rather, clean and pure at birth, all of us can "become carnal, sensual and devilish" through personal transgression.

20 But **by** the **transgression** of these holy laws **man became sensual and devilish**, and **became fallen man**.

> There is a commonly taught false doctrine that we are all, by nature, evil and unclean. In fact, this is the thinking behind the false doctrine of "original sin," which, in some belief systems, states that babies are unclean at birth and must be baptized as infants. In other words, such people believe that we are "fallen" at birth, inherently unclean

and evil by nature because we are human beings. Verse 20, above, contains the key word "became," showing that such thinking is not true. It says, in effect, that we can become evil through our choices. See also Alma 42:10.

Doctrine

Verse 21. Heavenly Father did give His Only Begotten Son to atone for our sins.

21 Wherefore, the Almighty God gave his Only Begotten Son, as it is written in those scriptures which have been given of him.

Some people get confused with the phrase "Only Begotten Son" because they realize that all of us are spirit sons and daughters of Heavenly Parents (see proclamation on the family, paragraph 2). They wonder how Jesus can be the "Only Begotten" when it is clear that we are all begotten spirit children of God. In other words, we are His literal spirit offspring. The answer is simple. The complete phrase is "the Only Begotten of the Father, in the flesh." Jesus is the only one born into a mortal body, begotten of the Father, in the flesh. In other words, the Father is the literal father of Christ's mortal body. President Heber J. Grant explained this as follows (**bold** added for emphasis):

"We believe absolutely that Jesus

Christ is the Son of God, begotten of God, the first-born in the spirit and **the only begotten in the flesh**; that He is the Son of God just as much as you and I are the sons of our fathers" (Heber J. Grant, "Analysis of the Articles of Faith," *Millennial Star*, Jan. 5, 1922, 2).

Doctrine

Verse 22. Christ was actually tempted but did not give in to it at all.

22 He suffered temptations but gave no heed unto them.

Doctrine

Verse 23. Christ was literally resurrected.

23 He was crucified, died, and rose again the third day;

24 And ascended into heaven, to sit down on the right hand of the Father, to reign with almighty power according to the will of the Father;

The title "Doctrine and Covenants" implies that there are "covenants" as well as "doctrines" included within the pages of this sacred volume of scripture we are studying. Verse 25, next, is an example of this.

Covenant

Verse 25. Baptism is a "covenant."

25 That as many as would be-lieve and **be baptized in his holy name**, and **endure in faith** [*live righteously*] to the end, should be saved—

Doctrine

Verse 26. The Atonement worked before it was actually performed by the Savior. (In other words, it is truly an "infinite" Atonement, covering present, past, and future.)

26 Not only those who believed after he came in the merid-ian of time, **in the flesh, but all those from the beginning**, even as many as were before he came, **who believed** in the words of the holy prophets, who spake as they were inspired by the gift of the Holy Ghost, who truly testified of him in all things, should have eternal life,

Doctrine

Verse 27. One of the major functions of the Holy Ghost is to bear witness to us of the Father and the Son.

27 As well as those who should **come after** [*all who have lived since Christ, or will live*], who should be-lieve in the gifts and callings of God by **the Holy Ghost**, which **beareth record of the Father and of the Son**;

Doctrine

Verse 28. The Godhead consists of the Father, the Son, and the Holy Ghost. They work in complete unity and harmony with each other as "one."

28 Which Father, Son, and Holy Ghost are one God, infinite and eternal, without end. Amen.

Joseph Fielding Smith gave ad-ditional instruction on what "one God" means (verse 28, above) in reference to the Godhead:

"It is perfectly true, as recorded in the Pearl of Great Price and in the Bible, that to us there is but one God [see Moses 1:6; Mark 12:32]. Correctly interpreted God in this sense means Godhead, for **it is composed of Father, Son, and Holy Spirit**. This Godhead pre-sides over us, and to us, the inhab-itants of this world, **they consti-tute the only God, or Godhead**. There is none other besides them [See 1 Corinthians 8:5–6]. To them we are amenable, and subject to their authority, and there is no other Godhead unto whom we are subject. However, as the Prophet has shown, there can be, and are, other Gods" (*Answers to Gospel Questions*, 2:142).

Doctrine

Verse 29. No one can be saved except through Jesus Christ.

29 And we know that all men **must repent** and **believe on the name of Jesus Christ**, and **worship the Father in his name**, and **endure in faith on his name to the end, or they cannot be saved** in the kingdom of God.

Verses 30 and 31, next, deal with the doctrines of justification and sanctification. There are many ways to approach and define both of these words. We will intentionally keep it simple for our purposes here. We will use Moses 6:60 from the Pearl of Great Price as the basis for our discussion:

Moses 6:60

For **by the water** [*in other words, through baptism*] ye keep the commandment [*to be baptized*]; **by the Spirit** [*the Holy Ghost*] **ye are justified**, and **by the blood** [*Christ's Atonement*] **ye are sanctified**;

From Moses 6:60, quoted above, we see that the Holy Ghost "justifies" us. Perhaps one of the simplest ways to envision being "justified" is to think in terms of computers and word processing. When we are typing a document and want to "justify" the left margin, we use the proper key strokes or the correct mouse click and the left margin lines up perfectly. If we choose to "justify" both margins and give the computer the proper commands, both left and right margins line up perfectly.

Applying this analogy to ourselves as members of the Church, we are given the gift of the Holy Ghost. If we follow His promptings faithfully throughout our lives, we will gradually be "justified" or lined up in harmony with the requirements for exaltation. This will allow us to fully qualify for the cleansing and purifying "blood" [*Atonement of Christ*] by which we are "sanctified." "Sanctified" can be defined as being cleansed from sin and made pure and holy, fit to be in the presence of God in celestial glory.

Thus, "justification" comes by following the promptings of the Holy Ghost and being lined up in harmony with God through the grace of [*help of*] the Savior. Additionally, one of the functions of the Holy Ghost, who is also known as the "Holy Spirit of promise" (D&C 132:7), is to ratify and approve all covenants, etc., that we enter into with God. When we qualify for our covenants to be "sealed by the Holy Spirit of promise" (132:7), it is another way of saying that we are "justified."

"Sanctification," as mentioned above, means to be made worthy to be in the presence of God. It is to have our sins remitted through the atoning blood of the Savior; or, in other words, to have our "garments [*symbolic of our lives*] . . . made white through the blood of the Lamb" (Alma 34:36).

In summary, the Holy Ghost prompts us and guides us as we strive to follow the teachings of Christ. As we follow His promptings, we are "justified," lined up in harmony with Christ, which allows us to be "sanctified" or cleansed from sin through His Atonement. Ultimately, our lives, covenants, promises, etc., can thus be ratified, approved, and sealed by the Holy Ghost, who is also known as the Holy Spirit of promise (or the Holy Spirit who was promised by the Savior to His disciples and who came to them on the day of Pentecost—see Acts 2). Through being justified and sanctified, we will be allowed entrance into exaltation in the celestial kingdom.

Doctrine

Verses 30 and 31. In order to be saved in celestial exaltation, we must be "justified" and "sanctified."

30 And we know that justification through the grace of our Lord and Savior Jesus Christ is just and true;

31 And we know also, that **sanctification through the grace of our Lord and Savior Jesus Christ is just and true**, to all those who

love and serve God with all their mights, minds, and strength.

Verses 32–34, next, are a reminder that we must be careful not to let our guard down because of past good deeds and success in being in harmony with God.

32 But **there is a possibility that man may fall from grace** and depart from the living God;

33 Therefore **let the church take heed** and pray always, **lest they fall into temptation**;

34 Yea, and even **let those who are sanctified take heed also**.

Verse 35, next, is a reference to Revelation 22:18–19, in which the Apostle John warns against adding unauthorized teachings or doctrines to or taking away from the pure gospel of Jesus Christ.

35 And we know that **these things are true and according to the revelations of John, neither adding to, nor diminishing from the prophecy of his book, the holy scriptures, or the revelations of God** which shall come hereafter by the gift and power of the Holy Ghost, the voice of God, or the ministering of angels.

36 And **the Lord God has spoken it**; and honor, power and glory be rendered to his holy

name, both now and ever. Amen.

From here to the end of the section, we see what we referred to at the beginning of this section as the first "Handbook of Instructions" of the Church. As you will see, it gives instructions on many matters concerning how to conduct and run the newly restored Church. First of all, verse 37, next, gives instructions as to how people are to qualify for baptism into the Church.

Doctrine

Verse 37. Baptism is the "gate" or entrance into the Lord's Church and onto the covenant path.

37 *And again, by way of commandment to the church concerning the manner of baptism*—All those who **humble themselves** before God, and **desire to be baptized**, and **come forth with broken hearts** and **contrite spirits** [*"contrite" means humbly desiring correction as needed*], and **witness before the church** that they have **truly repented of all their sins**, and are **willing to take upon them the name of Jesus Christ**, having a **determination to serve him to the end**, and truly **manifest by their works** that they **have received of the Spirit of Christ unto the remission of their sins**,

shall be received by baptism into his church.

Verses 38 through 60 explain various duties, responsibilities, and limitations of the different priesthood offices. Perhaps you've wondered why we refer to Apostles as "elders." The answer is found in verse 38, next. In fact, "elder" is a title that can appropriately refer to any Melchizedek Priesthood holder, including general authorities. Joseph Fielding Smith explained this as follows (**bold** added for emphasis):

"We learn at this time the Lord revealed that the designation of **'Elder' is one applicable to the apostles and likewise to all others who hold the Melchizedek Priesthood**. The use of this designation makes it needless to use unnecessarily sacred terms as 'Apostle,' 'Patriarch,' 'High Priest,' etc. It is proper in general usage to speak of the apostles, the seventies and all others holding the Melchizedek Priesthood as 'elders.' Of course, the term President, in speaking of the First Presidency, is the proper designation" (*Church History and Modern Revelation*, 1:95).

38 *The duty of the elders, priests, teachers, deacons, and members of the church of Christ*—An **apostle is an elder**, and it is his calling [*the calling of an elder*] to baptize;

In the next several verses, this "handbook of instructions" will explain the various duties of certain priesthood offices.

Duties of Elders—vv. 39–45

39 And **to ordain other elders, priests, teachers, and deacons**;

40 And to **administer bread and wine—the emblems of the flesh and blood of Christ—**

41 And to **confirm those who are baptized into the church, by the laying on of hands** [*confirmation must be done by holders of the Melchizedek Priesthood and cannot be done by holders of the Aaronic Priesthood*] for the baptism of fire and the Holy Ghost [*the gift of the Holy Ghost*], according to the scriptures;

The use of the word "fire" in conjunction with the Holy Ghost (see verse 41, above) is common in the scriptures and in sermons and lessons in the Church. The imagery is that of a refiner's fire. The refiner heats the gold ore to the point of melting it, at which point the pure gold remains and the slag containing imperfections and impurities floats to the top of the crucible and is discarded. The Holy Ghost can do the same for us. He "burns" the impurities out of our minds and hearts as we listen to His promptings. Thus, we ultimately become "pure gold," worthy to live in celestial glory.

42 And **to teach, expound** [*explain*], **exhort** [*urge and warn as needed*], **baptize**, and **watch over the church**;

43 And **to confirm the church** [*since confirming new members is already mentioned in verse 41, above, perhaps this means to set members apart to various callings, which is a Melchizedek Priesthood function*] by the laying on of the hands, and the giving of the Holy Ghost;

44 And to **take the lead of all meetings** [*when no one with higher authority is present*].

45 The elders are to **conduct the meetings as they are led by the Holy Ghost**, according to the commandments and revelations of God.

Duties of Priests—vv. 46–52

46 The priest's duty is **to preach, teach, expound, exhort, and baptize, and administer the sacrament,**

Neither teachers nor deacons can baptize, bless the sacrament, or lay on hands (see verse 58).

47 And **visit** the house of **each member** [*as in ministering to assigned members and families*], and **exhort** them to pray vocally and in secret and attend to all family duties.

48 And he may also **ordain other priests, teachers, and deacons**.

49 And he is to **take the lead of meetings when there is no elder present**;

50 But when there is an elder present, he is only to preach, teach, expound, exhort, and baptize,

51 And visit the house of each member, exhorting them to pray vocally and in secret and attend to all family duties.

52 **In all these duties the priest is to assist the elder if occasion requires.**

Duties of Teachers—vv. 53–57

53 The teacher's duty is to **watch over the church always, and be with and strengthen them**;

54 And **see that there is no iniquity in the church, neither hardness with each other, neither lying, backbiting, nor evil speaking**;

55 And **see that the church meet together often**, and also **see that all the members do their duty**.

56 And he is to **take the lead of meetings in the absence of the elder or priest—**

57 And is **to be assisted** always, in all his duties in the church, **by the deacons, if occasion requires**.

Duties of Deacons—vv. 57–59

58 But **neither teachers nor deacons have authority to baptize, administer the sacrament, or lay on hands**;

59 They are, however, to **warn, expound, exhort, and teach, and invite all to come unto Christ**.

Verse 60, next, among other things, reminds us that the one ordaining another to an office in the priesthood should seek the guidance of the Holy Ghost as he does so in order that the ordination and accompanying blessing might be specific to that person.

60 Every elder, priest, teacher, or deacon **is to be ordained according to the gifts and callings of God unto him**; and **he is to be ordained by the power of the Holy Ghost, which is in the one who ordains him**.

Next, this "handbook of instructions" deals with the topic of what we now refer to as "stake conferences." For many years, these stake conferences were held on a quarterly basis. Now, they are held every six months. A reminder that this is a "policy," not a "doctrine," and that we are led by living prophets.

Stake Conferences—vv. 61–62

61 The several elders compos-ing this church of Christ are to **meet in conference once in three months, or from time to time as said conferences shall direct or appoint**;

62 And said conferences are to do whatever church business is nec-essary to be done at the time.

Sustainings—vv. 63, 65–67

63 The elders are to receive their licenses [*recommends to perform ordinances or function in their priest-hood callings*] from other elders, **by vote of the church** [*the church unit, such as branches, wards, dis-tricts, stakes*] **to which they be-long, or from the conferences**.

Recommends to Perform Priesthood Ordinances and Duties—vv. 64

64 Each priest, teacher, or deacon, who is ordained by a priest, may **take a certificate** [*recommend to perform ordinances and so on*] from him at the time, **which certificate**, when presented to an elder, shall entitle him to a license, which **shall authorize him to perform the duties of his calling**, or he may receive it from a conference.

No Secret Ordinations—v. 65

65 **No person is to be ordained to any office** in this church, where there is a regularly organized branch of the same, **without the vote of that church**;

The instruction in verse 65, above, that no one is to be ordained with-out being sustained by the mem-bers of his appropriate church unit, is far more important that many members realize. It is a vital safe-guard against apostasy. Perhaps you are aware that many so-called break-offs from the Church claim that their leaders were secretly ordained and thus have authority to carry on the work of God. Such claims are in direct violation of the above instructions from the Savior Himself.

66 But the **presiding elders, trav-eling bishops, high councilors, high priests, and elders, may have the privilege of ordain-ing, where there is no branch of the church that a vote may be called.**

67 Every president of the high priesthood (or presiding elder), bishop, high councilor, and high priest, **is to be ordained by the direction of a high council or general conference**.

Verse 37 listed requirements for people to qualify for baptism. Once a person has been baptized, there is to be a waiting period before he or she is confirmed and begins partaking of the sacrament.

Waiting Period Between Baptism and Confirmation—vv. 68–69

68 *The duty of the members after they are received by baptism—* The **elders or priests are to have a sufficient time to expound all things concerning the church of Christ to their understanding, previous to their partaking of the sacrament and being confirmed** by the laying on of the hands of the elders, **so that all things may be done in order.**

69 And **the members shall manifest** before the church, and also before the elders, **by a godly walk and conversation, that they are worthy of it**, that there may be works and faith agreeable to the holy scriptures—walking in holiness before the Lord.

Blessing Babies—v. 70

70 Every member of the church of Christ having children is to bring them unto the elders before the church, who are to lay their hands upon them in the name of Jesus Christ, and **bless them in his name.**

No Infant Baptisms—v. 71

71 **No one** can be received [*baptized*] into the church of Christ **unless he has arrived unto the years of accountability** before God [*which is age eight; see D&C 68:25*], **and is capable of repentance.**

Baptismal Prayer and How to Baptize—vv. 72–74

72 Baptism is to be administered in the following manner unto all those who repent—

Doctrine

Baptism is to be performed by immersion—vv. 73–74.

73 The **person who** is called of God and **has authority** from Jesus Christ to baptize, **shall go down into the water with the person** who has presented himself or herself for baptism, and **shall say, calling him or her by name: Having been commissioned of Jesus Christ, I baptize you in the name of the Father, and of the Son, and of the Holy Ghost. Amen.**

74 Then shall he **immerse him or her in the water**, and come forth again out of the water.

The baptismal prayer, given in verse 73, above, is the one that is used today. Perhaps you are aware that a baptismal prayer is given in 3 Nephi 11:25, which was used by the Nephites. Its wording is just a bit different than the prayer given here.

In preparation for my first baptism as a young missionary in Austria, I memorized the baptismal prayer in German as given in 3 Nephi 11:25 rather than the one in D&C 20:73. I didn't know any better, and I never thought to ask my senior companion. I'm sure that he assumed that since I was from Utah, I would know to use the prayer given in the Doctrine and Covenants.

When the time of the actual baptism arrived, I nervously went down into the water with the man I was to baptize, got situated, and began saying the prayer from Third Nephi. The witnesses quickly corrected me, which did away with any composure I had left, and so they had to say almost each word or phrase of the prayer, which I repeated in halting German, in order to complete the ordinance. As you can imagine, I have always used the correct prayer since then.

If a person were to ask why we can't use the baptismal prayer given in Third Nephi, the answer is simple. The Lord gave us the prayer He wants us to use in our day, which is recorded in D&C 20:73, and we don't seek to counsel the Lord.

Also, some members wonder why we can't baptize someone in a bathtub or other container which is just large enough for the candidate for baptism to fit in and be successfully immersed. Again, we find the answer in verse 73, above. Both the priesthood holder and the candidate for baptism must go down into the water. In fact, I had an acquaintance who had to be rebaptized at age twelve when it was brought up that he was baptized at age eight in a watering trough at the farm, with the man performing the baptism standing on the ground outside the trough.

Sacrament Prayers and How to Conduct the Sacrament— vv. 75–79

75 It is expedient [*necessary, vital*] **that the church meet together often to partake of bread and wine in the remembrance of the Lord Jesus**;

As you know, we use water in place of wine in our sacrament services today. We will discuss this when we study section 27, verses 1–4. As we come to the sacrament prayers themselves, verses 77 and 79, we will use **bold** to point out the covenants we make and the promises the Lord gives us in return.

76 And **the elder** [*a Melchizedek Priesthood holder*] **or priest shall administer it**; and after this

manner shall he administer it—he shall kneel with the church and call upon the Father in solemn prayer, saying:

77 O God, the Eternal Father, we ask thee in the name of thy Son, Jesus Christ, to bless and sanctify this bread to the souls of all those who partake of it, that they may **eat in remembrance of the body of thy Son**, and **witness** unto thee, O God, the Eternal Father, **that they are willing to take upon them the name of thy Son**, and **always remember him** and **keep his commandments** which he has given them; **that they may always have his Spirit to be with them**. Amen.

78 The manner of administering the wine—he shall take the cup also, and say:

79 O God, the Eternal Father, we ask thee in the name of thy Son, Jesus Christ, to bless and sanctify this wine to the souls of all those who drink of it, that they may **do it in remembrance of the blood of thy Son, which was shed for them**; that they may **witness** unto thee, O God, the Eternal Father, **that they do always remember him**, that they may **have his Spirit to be with them**. Amen.

Thus, from verses 77 and 79, above, we see that when partaking of the sacrament, we do it in remembrance of His body and blood that were given for us, and make covenants to (1) take upon us the name of Jesus Christ, (2) to constantly remember Him and our commitments to Him, and (3) we promise to keep His commandments. In return, He promises that we will "always have his Spirit to be with" us, which is a most powerful promise. When we strive to keep our covenants, and thus have the strong influence of the Spirit with us, we will consistently be guided and directed toward exaltation!

Perhaps you've heard someone ask if we are renewing covenants or making covenants when we partake of the sacrament. The answer is that we do both. We make the same covenants again and again each time we partake of the sacrament. We also, in effect, renew these covenants as well as our covenants of baptism and other covenants we have made. This includes temple covenants, as explained by President Dallin H. Oaks in a talk about the sacrament. (**Bold** added for emphasis.)

"Our witness that we are willing to take upon us the name of Jesus Christ has several different meanings. . . .

". . . We take upon us the name of Christ when we are baptized in his name, when we belong to his Church and profess our belief in him, and when we do the work of his kingdom. . . .

"It is significant that when we partake of the sacrament we do not witness that we *take upon* us the name of Jesus Christ. We witness that we are *willing* to do so. (See D&C 20:77.) The fact that we only witness to our willingness suggests that something else must happen before we actually take that sacred name upon us in the most important sense. . . .

"Willingness to take upon us the name of Jesus Christ can . . . be understood as willingness to take upon us the authority of Jesus Christ. According to this meaning, **by partaking of the sacrament we witness our willingness to participate in the sacred ordinances of the temple** and to receive the highest blessings available through the name and by the authority of the Savior when he chooses to confer them upon us. . . .

". . . **When we witness our willingness to take upon us the name of Jesus Christ, we are signifying our commitment to do all that we can to achieve eternal life in the kingdom of our Father**. We are expressing our candidacy—our determination to strive for—exaltation in the celestial kingdom" ("Taking upon Us the Name of Jesus Christ," *Ensign*, May 1985, 80–82).

President Spencer W. Kimball explained that the covenants we renew in partaking of the sacrament include all of our covenants to live righteously:

"The Savior emphasized that the tangible bread and water of the Sacrament were to remind us continually of the sacrifice he made for us and **for renewal of our covenants of righteousness**" (*Teachings of Spencer W. Kimball*, 220).

Church Discipline, Including Excommunication—vv. 80 and 83

80 **Any member** of the church of Christ **transgressing**, or being overtaken in a fault, **shall be dealt with as the scriptures direct**.

Membership Records—vv. 81, 82, and 84

81 It shall be the duty of the several churches, composing the church of Christ, to send one or more of their teachers to attend the several conferences held by the elders of the church,

82 With a list of the names of the several members uniting themselves with the church since the last conference; or send by the hand of some priest; so that **a regular list of all the names of the whole church** may be **kept in a book by one of the elders**, whomsoever the other elders shall appoint from time to time;

83 And also, **if any have been expelled from the church** [*excommunication*], so that their **names** may be **blotted out** of the general church record of names.

84 All members removing from the church where they reside, if going to a church where they are not known, may take **a letter certifying that they are regular members and in good standing**, which certificate may be signed by any elder or priest if the member receiving the letter is personally acquainted with the elder or priest, or it may be signed by the teachers or deacons of the church.

SECTION 21

Background

This revelation was received by Joseph Smith on Tuesday, April 6, 1830, at the home of Peter Whitmer Sr. in Fayette, New York, during the actual meeting in which the Church was officially organized.

There were about sixty people present in Father Whitmer's home to witness this marvelous event. As the meeting began, the twenty-four-year-old Prophet Joseph designated five others to join him in order to meet the requirements of the state of New York for the organization of a church. The five were Oliver Cowdery, Hyrum Smith, Peter Whitmer Jr., Samuel H. Smith, and David Whitmer.

The meeting was opened with prayer, after which Joseph Smith asked those present to sustain him and Oliver Cowdery as their leaders in the kingdom of God. Everyone present raised their hands in support of this action. Unanimous approval was also given to organize the Church of Jesus Christ. Joseph recorded what followed these actions:

"I then laid my hands upon Oliver Cowdery, and ordained him an Elder of the 'Church of Jesus Christ of Latter-day Saints;' after which, he ordained me also to the office of an Elder of said Church. [*They had previously received the Melchizedek Priesthood but were told to wait to ordain each other to the office of elder until the Church was organized. See* History of the Church, *1:61).*] We then took bread, blessed it, and brake it with them; also wine, blessed it, and drank it with them. We then laid our hands on each individual member of the Church present, that they might receive the gift of the Holy Ghost, and be confirmed members of the Church of Christ. The Holy Ghost was poured out upon us to a very great degree—some prophesied, whilst we all praised the Lord, and rejoiced exceedingly. Whilst yet together, I received the following commandment: [D&C 21]" (*History of the Church*, 1:77–78).

After the meeting concluded, a number of people were baptized, including Orrin Porter Rockwell and Martin Harris, as well as Joseph Smith Sr. and Lucy Mack Smith, the parents of the Prophet.

As we begin our study of the verses in this section, which was given during the meeting in which the Church was officially organized, we will see that the Lord gave several instructions to the new members of the Restored Church. The very first phrase, in verse 1, emphasizes the importance of keeping records, which will include a history of the Church and a record of the revelations received.

1 BEHOLD, **there shall be a record kept among you**; and in it thou [*Joseph Smith*] shalt be called a seer, a translator, a prophet, an apostle of Jesus Christ, an elder of the church through the will of God the Father, and the grace of your Lord Jesus Christ,

We will repeat verse 1, this time emphasizing what the Lord teaches us about the role of the living prophet.

1 BEHOLD, there shall be a record kept among you; and in it **thou shalt be** called a **seer**, a **translator**, a **prophet**, an **apostle** of Jesus Christ, an **elder** of the church through the will of God the Father, and the grace [*help,*

mercy] of your Lord Jesus Christ,

The Institute of Religion *Doctrine and Covenants Student Manual, 1981,* defines the above terms as follows (**bold** added for emphasis and text rearranged slightly for use here):

Seer

Elder John A. Widtsoe defined a seer as "one who **sees with spiritual eyes. He perceives the meaning of that which seems obscure to others**; therefore he is an interpreter and clarifier of eternal truth. He **foresees the future** from the past and the present. This he does by the power of the Lord operating through him directly, or indirectly with the aid of divine instruments such as the Urim and Thummim. In short, he is one who sees, who walks in the Lord's light with open eyes" (Mosiah 8:15–17) (*Evidences and Reconciliations,* 1:205–6; see also Moses 6:36).

Translator

The title "translator" may refer to one who has received two blessings given a prophet by the spirit of God: (1) The power to convert the written or spoken word into another language (see D&C 20:8). (2) The power to give a clearer meaning to a given language.

Through the gift of translation, a prophet does not merely convey in the language of the reader the words that were recorded by the writer, but by revelation, he also **preserves for the reader the thoughts or intent of the original writer**.

Prophet

According to Elder Widtsoe, "**A prophet is a teacher. That is the essential meaning of the word**. He teaches the body of truth, the gospel, revealed by the Lord to man; and under inspiration explains it to the understanding of the people. He is an expounder of truth. Moreover, he shows that the way to human happiness is through obedience to God's law. He calls to repentance those who wander away from the truth. He becomes a warrior for the consummation of the Lord's purposes with respect to the human family. The purpose of his life is to uphold the Lord's plan of salvation. All this he does by close communion with the Lord, until he is 'full of power by the spirit of the Lord' (Micah 3:8; see also D&C 20:26; 34:10; 43:16).

"In the course of time the word 'prophet' has come to mean, perhaps chiefly, a man who receives revelations and directions from the Lord. **The principal business of a prophet has mistakenly been thought to foretell coming events, to utter prophecies, which is only one of the several prophetic functions**.

"In the sense that a prophet is a man who receives revelations from the Lord, the titles 'seer and revelator' merely amplify the larger and inclusive meaning of the title 'prophet'" (*Evidences and Reconciliations*, 1:204–5).

Scriptural insights into the role of a prophet are found in Exodus 4:15–16; 7:1–2.

Apostle

An Apostle is a special witness of Jesus Christ to all the world (see D&C 107:23). The Prophet Joseph Smith explained the important calling of an Apostle by asking a question and then giving the answer:

"What importance is there attached to the calling of these Twelve Apostles, different from the other callings or officers of the Church? . . .

"They are the Twelve Apostles, who are called to the office of the Traveling High Council, who are to preside over the churches of the Saints, among the Gentiles, where there is a presidency established; and they are to travel and preach among the Gentiles, until the Lord shall command them to go to the Jews. They are to hold the keys of this ministry, to unlock the door of the Kingdom of heaven unto all nations, and to preach the Gospel to every creature. This is the power, authority, and virtue of their apostleship" (*History of the Church*, 2:200).

Elder

The name of an office in the Melchizedek Priesthood, elder is also the general title used to address one who bears this priesthood. Elder Bruce R. McConkie added that an elder is a representative of the Lord:

"What is an elder? An elder is a minister of the Lord Jesus Christ. He holds the holy Melchizedek Priesthood. He is commissioned to stand in the place and stead of his Master—who is the Chief Elder—in ministering to his fellowmen. He is the Lord's agent. His appointment is to preach the gospel and perfect the Saints" ("Only an Elder," *Ensign*, June 1975, 66). (End of quote from the *Doctrine and Covenants Student Manual*, 1981 edition, 44.)

Before we move on, we will give one more quote, this time from the Prophet Joseph Smith, concerning the role of a "seer." As usual, we will use **bold** for emphasis.

"Wherefore, we again say, search the revelations of God; study the prophecies, and rejoice that God grants unto the world **Seers and Prophets**. They are **they who saw** the mysteries of godliness; **they saw** the flood before it came; **they saw** angels ascending and descending upon a ladder that reached from earth to heaven; **they saw** the stone cut out of the mountain, which filled the whole earth; **they saw** the Son of God come from the regions of bliss and dwell with men on earth; **they saw** the deliverer come out of Zion, and turn away ungodliness from Jacob; **they saw** the glory of the Lord when he showed the transfiguration of the earth on the mount; **they saw** every mountain laid low and every valley exalted when the Lord was taking vengeance upon the wicked; **they saw** truth spring out of the earth, and righteousness look down from heaven in the last days, before the Lord came the second time to gather his elect; **they saw** the end of wickedness on earth, and the Sabbath of creation crowned with peace; **they saw** the end of the glorious thousand years, when Satan was loosed for a little season; **they saw** the day of judgment when all men received according to their works, and **they saw** the heaven and the earth flee away to make room for the city of God, when the righteous receive an inheritance in eternity" (*Teachings of the Prophet Joseph Smith*, 12–13).

In this quote from Joseph Smith, we are taught that seers "see" the future. They "see" by the power of God and then tell us what they see. They are "watchmen on the tower," which is a scriptural phrase referring to guards who stand high upon towers where they can "see" a long way off and warn the citizens of the city when danger is coming. Thus, our modern "prophets, seers, and revelators" have been, in effect, called of God to stand upon high "towers" and are given spiritual sight to "see" when danger is coming and to warn us of it. For instance, in "The Family: A Proclamation to the World," our "prophets, seers, and revelators" have strengthened us and warned us of coming dangers and of dangers that have already come among us in our day.

Continuing with section 21, we hear the Lord bearing witness of Joseph Smith and his role in restoring the Church in the last days (verses 2 and 3).

2 **Being inspired of the Holy Ghost to lay the foundation thereof** [*the Church*], and to build it up unto the most holy faith.

3 Which church was organized and **established in** the year of your Lord **eighteen hundred and thirty**, in the **fourth month**, and on the **sixth day** of the month which is called **April.**

Next, in verses 4–6, we are clearly taught the importance of following the living prophet. In fact, we are specifically taught that if we do, there is not a chance that Satan's forces can succeed in ultimately taking us from God. Apostates and detractors do not seem to be able to comprehend this simple doctrine.

Doctrine

Verses 4–6. If we faithfully follow the living prophet, we are assured of exaltation.

4 Wherefore, meaning the church [*in other words, the members of the Church*], **thou shalt give heed unto all his words and commandments** which he shall give unto you as he receiveth them, walking in all holiness before me;

5 For **his word ye shall receive, as if from mine own mouth**, in all patience and faith.

6 For **by doing these things the gates of hell shall not prevail** [*win*] **against you**; yea, and the Lord God will disperse the powers of darkness from before you, and cause the heavens to shake for your good, and his name's glory.

Elder Harold B. Lee reminded us that the Lord will never allow our living Prophet to lead us astray. He taught (**bold** added for emphasis):

"We are not dependent only upon the revelations given in the past as contained in our standard works— as wonderful as they are . . . We have a mouthpiece to whom God does and is revealing his mind and will. **God will never permit him to lead us astray**. As has been said [D&C 43:3–4], God would remove us out of our place if we should attempt to do it. You have no concern. Let the management and government of God, then, be with the Lord. Do not try to find fault with the management and affairs that pertain to him alone and by revelation through his prophet—his living prophet, his seer, and his revelator. (*The Place of the Living Prophet* [address delivered to seminary and institute of religion personnel], 8 July 1964, 16.)" (*Doctrine and Covenants Student Manual*, 1981, 45).

In the remaining verses of this section, the Savior continues to instruct and bear witness to the members of the Church as to the importance and validity of the calling of Joseph Smith.

7 For thus saith the Lord God: **Him have I inspired to move the cause of Zion in mighty power for good**, and his diligence I know, and his prayers I have heard.

8 Yea, **his weeping for Zion I have seen**, and I will cause that he shall mourn for her no longer; for **his days of rejoicing are come unto the remission of his sins**, and the manifestations of my blessings upon his works.

9 For, behold, I will bless **all those who labor in my vineyard** with a mighty blessing, and they **shall believe on his words**, which

are given him through me by the Comforter [*the Holy Ghost*], which manifesteth that Jesus was crucified by sinful men for the sins of the world, yea, for the remission of sins unto the contrite [*humble and willing to be corrected as needed*] heart.

As previously mentioned, during the organization of the Church in the Peter Whitmer Sr. home, Oliver Cowdery ordained Joseph Smith an elder, and then Joseph ordained Oliver an elder, as instructed by the Lord. Next, we see these instructions.

10 Wherefore it behooveth me [*it is My desire*] that **he** [*Joseph Smith*] **should be ordained by you, Oliver Cowdery** mine apostle;

11 This being an ordinance unto you, that you are an elder under his hand, **he being the first** unto you [*Joseph Smith presides, is the highest officer in the Church, and is over you*], that you might be an elder unto this church of Christ, bearing my name—

12 And **the first preacher of this church** unto the church, and before the world, yea, before the Gentiles; yea, and thus saith the Lord God, lo, lo! to the Jews also. Amen.

SECTION 22

Background

Given through the Prophet Joseph Smith at Manchester, New York, in April 1830, this revelation addresses the issue of whether or not converts need to be baptized if they were previously baptized in their old church.

The Lord speaks clearly and to the point, as you can see in verses 2 and 4. It almost sounds like a parent speaking to children who keep bringing up the same question, even though they have already been told the answer.

First, in verses 1 and 2, next, the Lord explains the reason for requiring that all who desire to enter His true Church do so through proper, authorized baptism. Among other things, He explains that this is a new covenant, not an existing one contained in other religious organizations that is just being revised or updated. In other words, this is a "restoration" of the true Church, not a revitalization of an existing sect or church.

1 BEHOLD, I say unto you that **all old covenants** [*such as in the Law of Moses*] **have I caused to be done away in this thing** [*in the restoration of the Church of Jesus Christ through Joseph Smith*]; and **this is a new and an everlasting covenant** [*"new" for this dispensation (the last days), because all other*

churches have gone into apostasy and have no priesthood authority*], **even that which was from the beginning** [*this is a restoration of the true Church, with the power and authority that Adam had at the beginning of things on this earth; see Moses 6:64–68*].

The phrase "the new and everlasting covenant," seen in verse 1, above, is an important point of doctrine for anyone who understands the gospel. President Joseph Fielding Smith explained it as follows:

"The new and everlasting covenant is the fulness of the gospel. It is composed of 'All covenants, contracts, bonds, obligations, oaths, vows, performances, connections, associations, or expectations' that are sealed upon members of the Church by the Holy Spirit of promise, or the Holy Ghost, by the authority of the President of the Church who holds the keys. . . .

"Marriage for eternity is **a** new and everlasting covenant. Baptism is also **a** new and everlasting covenant, and likewise ordination to the priesthood, and every other covenant is everlasting and **a part** of **the new and everlasting covenant** which **embraces all things**" (*Answers to Gospel Questions*, 1:65).

2 Wherefore [*this is why*], **although a man should be baptized an**

hundred times it availeth him nothing [*it does him no good*], for you cannot enter in at the strait [*narrow*] gate by the law of Moses [*in other words, even the Law of Moses can't get you into the celestial kingdom*], neither by your dead works [*other religions and churches of the day don't have the necessary power and authority either*].

Next, in verse 3, the Lord explains that none of the existing churches of the day have the power and authority to save souls. In other words, the apostasy was universal.

3 For it is because of your dead works [*baptisms and other ordinances in existing churches that have no power or authority to perform them*] that I have caused this last covenant and this church to be built up unto me, even as in days of old [*just like I did in previous dispensations and restorations of the gospel*].

4 Wherefore, enter ye in at the gate [*be baptized by immersion by proper authority; it is the gate to the covenant path*], as I have commanded, and seek not to counsel your God. Amen.

SECTION 23

Background

This revelation (which is a series of five brief revelations) was given through Joseph Smith at Manchester, New York (which was located next to Palmyra), in April 1830. These revelations were given to five men, Oliver Cowdery, Hyrum Smith (Joseph's older brother), Samuel H. Smith (Joseph's younger brother), Joseph Smith Sr. (Joseph's father), and Joseph Knight Sr. Shortly after the official organization of the Church, on Tuesday, April 6, 1830, all five men had come to the Prophet to have him inquire of the Lord for them as to their duties. These 5 individual revelations were later combined to become section 23.

Joseph Smith recorded the following that led up to these revelations:

"The following persons being anxious to know of the Lord what might be their respective duties in relation to this word, I enquired of the Lord, and received for them the following:" (*History of the Church,* 1:80).

As you read this section, you may wish to pay attention to which of the five men listed above that is not told that he is under no condemnation.

The first message is to Oliver Cowdery, consisting of verses 1 and 2. At this point, he was the "second elder" of the Church and was a prominent and important player in the Restoration. However, he is warned about pride, which will ultimately lead to his excommunication in 1838. (He will return to the Church ten years later.)

1 BEHOLD, **I speak unto you, Oliver**, a few words. Behold, **thou art blessed, and art under no condemnation** [*Oliver is doing well at this point*]. **But beware of pride**, lest thou shouldst enter into temptation.

2 Make known thy calling unto the church, and also before the world, and **thy heart shall be opened to preach the truth** from henceforth and forever. Amen.

We will include just a bit here about the charges that led to Oliver Cowdery's excommunication in 1838 in Missouri. We will quote from the *Church History in the Fulness of Times* student manual, 2003, used by our institutes of religion:

"A much more serious matter was the case of Oliver Cowdery. He was charged by the high council for persecuting Church leaders with vexatious lawsuits, seeking to destroy the character of Joseph Smith, not abiding ecclesiastical authority in temporal affairs, selling lands in Jackson County, and leaving his calling as Assistant Presi-

dent of the Church and turning to the practice of law. Oliver refused to appear before the council, but he answered by letter. He denied the Church's right to dictate how he should conduct his life and asked that his fellowship with the Church be ended. The high council excommunicated him 12 April 1838. He spent a decade outside the Church, but later humbly submitted himself for rebaptism in October 1848 in Kanesville, Iowa" (*Church History in the Fulness of Times*, 2003, 186).

Next, the Lord speaks to Hyrum, who is five years older than his brother, Joseph. Perhaps you will remember, from section 11, that Hyrum Smith was anxious to go forth and preach the gospel. At that time, he was told to wait. Now, in this brief message, he is told that the time has come for his tongue to be "loosed" and that he can now "exhort" and "strengthen the church." Imagine his gratitude and feelings as he realizes that his obedience to the Lord's instructions in section 11 have paid off and he can now begin preaching.

Something in verse 3 appears to be prophetic, namely, "thy duty is unto the church." This would seem to be a reference to Hyrum's later being called to serve as patriarch to the Church. (See D&C 124:124.)

3 Behold, **I speak unto you, Hyrum**, a few words; for **thou also art under no condemnation**

[*the same as Oliver Cowdery in verse 1*], and **thy heart is opened, and thy tongue loosed** [*you can go forth and preach now; see section 11*]; **and thy calling is to exhortation, and to strengthen the church continually.** Wherefore **thy duty is unto the church forever,** and this because of thy family. Amen.

The next message is to Joseph's younger brother by about three years, Samuel, who is considered to be one of the first missionaries of the Church. He traveled to Lima, New York, in April 1830, where he preached the gospel. He was ordained an elder at the first conference of the Church held June 9, 1830.

His missionary efforts included selling a copy of the Book of Mormon in April 1830 to Phineas Young, a brother of Brigham Young. Brigham gave the book to his sister, Fanny Young Murray, who was the mother-in-law of Heber C. Kimball. All of these people were eventually baptized. (See *Church History in the Fullness of Times*, 1989 edition, 75.)

Samuel also left a copy of the Book of Mormon with a minister named John P. Greene, whose wife, Rhoda, was Brigham Young's sister. They, too, joined the Church.

4 Behold, **I speak a few words unto you, Samuel;** for **thou also art under no condemnation,** and **thy calling is to exhortation** [*teaching and explaining the gospel*], **and to strengthen the church;** and thou art **not as yet called to preach before the world.** Amen.

Next, the Lord speaks to Joseph Smith's father. He was born on July 12, 1771, and was 59 years old at the time of this revelation.

5 Behold, **I speak a few words unto you, Joseph;** for **thou also art under no condemnation,** and **thy calling also is to exhortation, and to strengthen the church;** and this is thy duty from henceforth and forever. Amen.

In the introduction to this section, we invited you to note which of the five men addressed by the Lord in these brief revelations was not told that he was under no condemnation. It is Joseph Knight Sr. The reason is that the other four have already been baptized, but Father Knight has not yet agreed to be baptized. Thus, he is under "condemnation," which is a word that basically means "stopped from progressing farther." Also, he apparently has not brought himself to pray yet.

You may wish to review the background notes for section 12 in this study guide for more information about Joseph Knight.

6 Behold, I manifest unto you [a

bit stronger wording than used with the other four men], Joseph Knight, by these words, that **you must take up your cross,** in the which **you must pray** vocally before the world as well as in secret, and in your family, and among your friends, and in all places.

7 And, behold, **it is your duty to unite with the true church** *[you must be baptized]*, and give your language to exhortation continually, that you may receive the reward of the laborer. Amen.

Joseph Knight Sr. was baptized on June 28, 1830, by Oliver Cowdery. It was the same day that Emma Smith, the Prophet's wife, was baptized. For a bit more background on this, we quote the following:

"In the latter part of June 1830, the Prophet, accompanied by his wife, Oliver Cowdery, and John and David Whitmer, visited the Knight family in Colesville, New York. Joseph Knight, Sr., who had read the Book of Mormon and was satisfied it was true, and a number of others in the area desired baptism. On Saturday, 26 June, the brethren dammed a stream to make a pond suitable for baptisms. That night a mob, incited by leaders of some area churches who feared losing members, demolished the dam. On Sunday the brethren proceeded with the meeting. The Prophet related,

'Oliver Cowdery preached, and others of us bore testimony to the truth of the Book of Mormon, the doctrine of repentance, baptism for the remission of sins, and laying on of hands for the gift of the Holy Ghost.' Some members of the mob attended the meeting and afterward harassed those in attendance.

"Early the next day, 28 June, the brethren repaired the dam and held the baptismal service. Thirteen people were baptized, including Emma Smith. Many neighbors mocked them, asking if they 'had been washing sheep'" *(Church History in the Fulness of Times,* 2003, 71).

SECTION 24

Background

Section 24 was given to Joseph Smith and Oliver Cowdery in July 1830 in Harmony, Pennsylvania, where Joseph and Emma were living on a small farm. In the approximately four months since the organization of the Church on April 6, 1830, persecution had increased significantly.

We know that during these months since the organization of the Church, there had been much harassment of the Saints and a number of lawsuits against Joseph based on trumped-up charges. He had been arrested more than once and hauled off to court. Although he was acquitted each time, it still was terribly time consuming and disruptive and had to be discouraging to him and his wife and the members of the Church.

George Q. Cannon, who served as a counselor in the First Presidency under Presidents John Taylor, Wilford Woodruff, and Lorenzo Snow, gave the following, which helps us understand the setting and background for sections 24–26:

"Accompanied by his wife and three of the Elders, he [Joseph Smith] went again to Colesville [New York, in late June 1830]. Here they found many people awaiting baptism. Joseph prepared to accede to their demand. A suitable portion of a little stream in that locality was prepared for the purpose of the administration of the ordinance; but in the night sectarian priests, fearful of losing their congregations and their hire, instigated evil men to desecrate the spot and to destroy all the preparations of the Elders. . . . A few days later the ordinance was administered by Oliver Cowdery to thirteen persons at Colesville. . . .

"While the baptisms were in progress an angry mob collected, and threatened destruction to the Elders and believers. The mob surrounded the house of Joseph Knight and his son Newel and railed with devilish hatred at the inmates. The Prophet spoke to them and made an effort to calm their passions, but without avail. Wearied with their own impotent wrath, the mobs departed; but only to concoct new plots.

"That night a meeting was to be held, and when the believers and sympathizers had assembled, and Joseph was about to offer them instruction and consolation, a constable approached and arrested him on a warrant charging him with being a disorderly person, for setting the country in an uproar by circulating the Book of Mormon and by preaching a gospel of revelation.

"A court was convened to consider the strange charges brought against the young man, Joseph Smith; and hateful lies, of every form which the father of falsehood could devise, were circulated to create popular dislike. . . . The bitter feeling of endangered priestcraft was visible throughout the trial; but all the accusations which were made were but lies, and none were sustained. The court declared an acquittal. The evidence in the trial was a high tribute to the character of Joseph Smith. . . .

"This paper [a warrant] was secured on the oath of a sectarian bigot; and no sooner was Joseph acquitted by the court in Chenango County than he was seized under the new warrant and dragged back to Colesville.

"When the morning came, Joseph was arraigned before the magistrate's court of Colesville. Arrayed against him were some of the people who had been discomfited at the trial in Chenango County. This time they were determined to secure a conviction. By the side of the Prophet were his friends and advocates who had aided him in the former trial. Despite the vindictive effort of the mob, the court discharged the Prophet, declaring that nothing was shown to his dishonor" (*Life of Joseph Smith the Prophet*, 64–67).

The Prophet, himself, does not give any specific reason for this revelation, but does write the following by way of general background to sections 24, 25, and 26:

"After our departure from Colesville [*in April 1830*], after the trial [*based on false charges and held in South Bainbridge, New York; see* Church History in the Fulness of Times, *2003, 71–73*], the Church there were very anxious, as might be expected, concerning our again visiting them, during which time Sister Knight, wife of Newel Knight, had a dream, which enabled her to say that we would visit them that day, which really came to pass, for a few hours afterwards we arrived; and thus was our faith much strengthened concerning dreams and visions in the last days, foretold by the ancient Prophet Joel; and although we this time were forced to seek safety from our enemies by flight, yet did we feel confident that eventually we should come off victorious, if we only continued faithful to Him who had called us forth from darkness into the marvelous light of the everlasting Gospel of our Lord Jesus Christ.

"Shortly after our return home, we received the following commandments [sections 24, 25, and 26]:" (*History of the Church*, 1:101).

With this background in mind, we will now watch as the Lord comforts the Prophet and counsels him in verses 1–9.

1 BEHOLD, **thou wast called and chosen to write** [*translate*] **the Book of Mormon**, and to my ministry; and **I have lifted thee up out of thine afflictions**, and have counseled thee, that **thou hast been delivered from all thine enemies**, and **thou hast been delivered from the powers of Satan and from darkness!**

The last phrase of verse 1, above, can refer to Satan's attempts to disrupt the work of restoration referred to in the background notes above, and could well also include the powers of darkness that overtook Joseph in the Sacred Grove preceding the First Vision.

Joseph is still not perfect, as the Lord reminds him in verse 2, next, but the encouragement, kindness, and power of the Atonement are made clear in the second half of the verse.

2 Nevertheless, **thou art not excusable in thy transgressions; nevertheless, go thy way and sin no more**.

Verse 3, next, reminds us that Joseph had the normal responsibilities of a husband and father to provide for his family.

3 Magnify thine office [*serve well in the calling you have*]; and **after thou hast sowed** [*planted*] **thy fields** and secured them, go speedily unto the church [*members of the Church*] which is in Colesville, Fayette, and Manchester, and they shall support thee; and I will bless them both spiritually and temporally;

As is the case with full-time general authorities and missionaries in our day, Joseph Smith was also to receive some support for him and his family from the members of the Church as explained in verse 3, above. Just as some members today decline to pay tithes and offerings, so also did some members in the early Church fail to give of their means to the Church, and thus came under condemnation as explained in verse 4, next.

4 But **if they receive thee not, I will send upon them a cursing instead of a blessing**.

In section 21, verses 1, 4, and 5, Joseph's role as the Prophet was briefly described by the Lord. In verse 5, next, he is told to continue in this role as Prophet and teacher to the Church. By the way, you can tell from the wording in verse 5 that the Savior is speaking.

5 And thou shalt continue in calling upon God [*the Father*] **in my name** [*Jesus Christ*], and writing the things [*the revelations and instructions*] which shall be given thee by the Comforter [*the Holy Ghost*], and expounding [*teaching and explaining*] all scriptures unto the church.

Verse 6, next, reminds us that the companionship of the Holy Ghost is a powerful help from God, and we can receive inspiration at the very moment we need it.

Also, in the last half of verse 6, we are reminded of the consequences to us as members if we ignore the words of our living Prophet.

6 And **it shall be given thee in the very moment what thou shalt speak and write**, and **they** [*the members of the Church*] **shall hear it** [*be obedient to it*]**, or I will send unto them a cursing instead of a blessing**.

In verses 7 and 9, next, Joseph Smith is told that he will have the help of the Lord in serving well as the Prophet, but that he will not become wealthy financially.

7 For thou shalt devote all thy service in Zion; and **in this thou shalt have strength**.

8 **Be patient in afflictions**, for thou shalt have many; but endure them, for, lo, **I am with thee**, even unto the end of thy days.

9 And **in temporal labors** [*pursuing wealth and worldly status*] **thou shalt not have strength, for this is not thy calling**. Attend to thy calling [*as the Prophet*] and thou shalt have wherewith [*the means necessary*] to magnify thine office, and to expound all scriptures, and continue in laying on of the hands and confirming the churches [*strengthening the branches of the Church; see Acts 15:41*].

Regarding the first sentence in verse 9, above, President Dallin H. Oaks, of the Quorum of the Twelve Apostles at the time, explained that: "[Joseph Smith] was almost continually on the edge of financial distress. In the midst of trying to fulfill the staggering responsibilities of his sacred calling, he had to labor as a farmer or merchant to provide a living for his family. He did this without the remarkable spiritual gifts that sustained him in his prophetic calling. The Lord had advised him that 'in temporal labors thou shalt not have strength, for this is not thy calling' (D&C

24:9)" ("Joseph, the Man and the Prophet," *Ensign*, May 1996, 71).

Next, the Savior gives Joseph counsel for Oliver Cowdery. He is to continue in preaching the gospel and is warned against slacking off in the work to which he has been called. He is also warned again against pride (see D&C 23:1) and seeking glory for himself rather than for the Lord. Great promises are given to him if he will follow this counsel.

10 And thy brother [*in the gospel*] **Oliver shall continue in bearing my name before the world, and also to the church**. And **he shall not suppose that he can say enough in my cause**; and lo, I am with him to the end.

11 **In me he shall have glory, and not of himself**, whether in weakness or in strength, whether in bonds or free;

12 And at all times, and in all places, **he shall open his mouth and declare my gospel** as with the voice of a trump, both day and night. **And I will give unto him strength such as is not known among men.**

Perhaps you have noticed that "the voice of a trump," verse 12, above, is a phrase used frequently in the scriptures. It carries with it the imagery of a message that is clear and simple, easy to pick out from other sounds. Thus, Oliver is to teach the gospel simply and clearly and is to make his voice reach far and wide to be heard by many.

Next, counsel is given regarding expecting and requesting miracles, except for those that naturally go along with the work of serving in the Church as a priesthood holder and as a missionary. People who demand miracles are, in effect, tempting the Lord to prove His power, and thus place themselves in a dangerous position. See Matthew 4:7, where the devil is told by the Savior, "Thou shalt not tempt the Lord thy God."

13 **Require not miracles, except** [*unless*] **I shall command you**, **except** casting out devils, healing the sick, and against poisonous serpents, and against deadly poisons;

The miracles listed in verse 13, above, are listed in Mark 16:17–18 and are associated with missionary work (see Mark 16:15) and faithful membership in the Church. We will quote Mark here (**bold** added for emphasis):

Mark 16:15–18

15 And he said unto them, **Go ye into all the world, and preach the gospel to every creature**.

16 He that believeth and is baptized shall be saved; but he that believeth not shall be damned.

17 And **these signs shall follow them that believe**; In my name shall they **cast out devils**; they shall speak with new tongues;

18 They shall **take up serpents**; and **if they drink any deadly thing, it shall not hurt them**: they shall **lay hands on the sick, and they shall recover**.

One example of "casting out devils," in verse 13 of section 24, above, occurred in behalf of Newel Knight, a son of Joseph Knight Sr. as follows:

"Newel, a son of Joseph Knight, became much interested in the Prophet's words. Many serious conversations ensued, and Newel became so far convinced of the divinity of the work that he gave a partial promise that he would arise in meeting and offer supplication to God before his friends and neighbors. But at the appointed moment he failed to respond to Joseph's invitation. Later he told the Prophet that he would pray in secret, and thus seek to resolve his doubts and gain strength. On the day following, Newel went into the woods to offer his devotions to heaven; but was unable to give utterance to his feelings, being held in bondage by some power which he could not define. He returned to his home ill in body, and depressed in mind. His appearance alarmed his wife, and in a broken voice he requested her to quickly find the Prophet and bring him to his bedside. When Joseph arrived at the house, Newel was suffering most frightful distortions of his visage and limbs, as if he were in convulsions. Even as the Prophet gazed at him, Newel was seized upon by some mysterious influence and tossed helpless about the room. Through the gift of discernment, Joseph saw his friend was in the grasp of the evil one, and that only the power of God could save him from the tortures under which he was suffering. He took Newel's hand and gently addressed him. Newel replied, 'I am possessed of a devil. Exert your authority, I beseech you, to cast him out.' Joseph replied, 'If you know that I have power to drive him from your soul, it shall be done.' And when these words were uttered, Joseph rebuked the destroyer and commanded him in the name of Jesus Christ to depart. The Lord condescended to honor his servant, in thus exercising the power which belonged to his Priesthood and calling, for instantly Newel cried out with joy that he felt the accursed influence leave him and saw the evil spirit passing from the room.

"Thus was performed the first miracle of the Church. . . . Since that hour thousands of miracles have been performed by the Elders of the Church, through the power of the Priesthood restored from heaven and in fulfillment of the promises made by the Lord Jesus" (*Life of Joseph Smith*, 61–63).

As we continue with verse 14, next, we see an important matter in conjunction with administering to the sick that is sometimes misunderstood by members of the Church. It is that Melchizedek Priesthood holders are not to solicit opportunities to give blessings and administer to the sick. Such blessings are to be requested by those who desire them, which is clearly stated in this verse.

14 And **these things ye shall not do, except it be required of you by them who desire it**, that the scriptures might be fulfilled; for ye shall do according to that which is written [*in the scriptures*].

One example of "do according to that which is written," at the end of verse 14, above, is found in James 5:14. We will quote James here, using **bold** to emphasize the principle that the one needing the blessing should be the one asking for it:

James 5:14

Is any sick among you? **let him call for the elders of the church**; and let them pray over him, anointing him with oil in the name of the Lord:

A serious difficulty that can arise when the proper order given in verse 14, above, is not followed, is that a blessing or administration could be imposed upon a member who does not feel comfortable having one. In such cases, damage can be done and embarrassment and alienation from the Church could occur. Obviously, in the case of a faithful member who is unconscious or a child who does not know enough to ask for a blessing, family or friends could properly ask that he or she be administered to. It is also appropriate, when the Spirit so prompts, for family or friends to ask an ill individual if he or she would like to be administered to. This still leaves it up to the sick person to "call for the elders."

We will continue now with section 24, verse 15. Many people have heard, in one form or another, the term, "casting off the dust of your feet against them." Such terminology is used many places in the scriptures. (See Topical Guide under "Dust.") We will first read verse 15, using **bold** for emphasis, and then include a quote from Joseph Fielding Smith about this matter.

15 And in whatsoever place ye shall enter, and they receive you not in my name, ye shall leave a cursing instead of a blessing, by **casting off the dust of your feet against them as a testimony**, and cleansing your feet by the wayside.

As you can see, in verse 15, above, "casting off the dust of your feet"

is basically a witness or testimony that the missionary has tried to teach them the gospel but was rejected by them. The *Doctrine and Covenants Student Manual*, 1981, 130–31, explains this and quotes Joseph Fielding Smith as follows (**bold** added for emphasis):

"The ordinance of washing the dust from one's feet was practiced in New Testament times and was reinstituted in this dispensation. (See D&C 88:139–40; John 11:2; 12:3; 13:5–14.) **The action of shaking or cleansing the dust from one's feet is a testimony against those who refuse to accept the gospel.** (See D&C 24:15; 84:92; 99:4.) Because of the serious nature of this act, Church leaders have directed that it be done only at the command of the Spirit. President Joseph Fielding Smith explained the significance of the action as follows: 'The cleansing of their feet, either by washing or wiping off the dust, would be recorded in heaven as a testimony against the wicked. This act, however, was not to be performed in the presence of the offenders, "lest thou provoke them, but in secret, and wash thy feet, as a testimony against them in the day of judgment." The missionaries of the Church who faithfully perform their duty are under the obligation of leaving their testimony with all with whom they come in contact in their work. This testimony will stand as a witness against those who reject the message, at the judgment.' (*Church History and Modern Revelation*, 1:223.)"

Perhaps you have found yourself wondering why it seems that the wicked get away with their evil deeds and don't seem to get punished by the Lord, while their victims suffer. The scriptures are clear that they will be punished, but there is a key phrase in verse 16, next, which explains the delay.

16 And it shall come to pass that whosoever shall lay their hands upon you by violence, ye shall command to be smitten in my name; and, behold, I will smite them according to your words, **in mine own due time**.

No doubt one of the key reasons for the Lord's waiting to "smite" the wicked is that there is still a chance that they might repent and come unto Christ. Think of how many times you, yourself, may have deserved "smiting" but it didn't happen to you, and then it becomes easier to let the Lord smite others in His "own due time."

17 And **whosoever shall go to law with thee** [*takes you to court*] shall be cursed by the law [*perhaps meaning that they will eventually be caught up with, either by the laws of the land or the laws of God*].

The Joseph Smith Papers publications shed additional light on the severe persecutions faced by

the early Church at this point, including vexatious law suits ("whosoever shall go to law with thee" in verse 17, above) as shown by a quote from the 2019 *Doctrine and Covenants Student Manual*, chapter 10, as follows:

"In late June 1830, Joseph Smith, Emma Smith, Oliver Cowdery, David Whitmer, and John Whitmer traveled from Harmony, Pennsylvania, to visit Church members and other believers in Colesville, New York. On Saturday, June 26, a stream was dammed to prepare for baptisms the next day (Sunday), but a hostile mob destroyed the dam during the night. Early Monday morning, the dam was rebuilt and 13 people were baptized, including Emma Smith. By the time the baptisms were completed, however, a mob of nearly 50 men gathered, insulting and threatening to harm the Saints. That evening, the Saints met to confirm those who had been baptized earlier that day, but before the confirmations could be performed, Joseph was arrested on charges of "being a disorderly person, of setting the country in an uproar by preaching the Book of Mormon" (in *The Joseph Smith Papers, Histories, Volume 1: Joseph Smith Histories, 1832–1844*, ed. Karen Lynn Davidson and others [2012], 396).

The terms "purse" and "scrip," in verse 18, next, are important for understanding this verse as well as other passages of scripture where they are used. Some people tend to think that "scrip" is a short form of "scriptures." It is not. We will read the verse and then turn to the Bible Dictionary for help.

18 And thou shalt **take no purse nor scrip**, neither staves, neither two coats, **for the church shall give unto thee in the very hour what thou needest** for food and for raiment [*clothing*], and for shoes and for money, and for scrip.

The Bible Dictionary, under "Scrip," defines both "scrip" and "purse" as follows (**bold** added for emphasis):

Bible Dictionary, under "Scrip"

"**Scrip.** A bag used by shepherds or by travelers (1 Sam. 17:40; Matt. 10:10; Mark 6:8; Luke 9:3; 10:4; 22:35–36). The **bag** was usually made of leather and was **used for carrying bread and other food**. It should not be confused with a **money bag**, which **was called a purse**."

As you can see from the above definitions, Joseph and Oliver were instructed to rely completely on the Lord for their upkeep while going out among the members and preaching to the world.

Finally, in verse 19, next, we

see that this is indeed the last dispensation (the last time the gospel is to be restored before the Second Coming of Christ). We see the imagery of pruning or cutting out false philosophies and false doctrines from people's lives so that they can enjoy the true gospel of Christ. We also see, at the end of the verse, that many of the counsels and instructions given in this section provide a pattern for others who have joined the Church and are assisting Joseph and Oliver in the work of the Restoration.

19 For **thou art called to prune my vineyard** [*the world*] with a mighty pruning, yea, even **for the last time** [*compare with Jacob 5:69 and 71*]; yea, and **also all those whom thou hast ordained**, and they **shall do even according to this pattern**. Amen.

SECTION 25

Background

Section 25 is perhaps best-known, because in it, Emma Smith is requested by the Lord to make a collection of sacred hymns, which became the first hymn book for the Church. See verse 11.

As noted in the background to section 24 in this book, this revelation was given through the Prophet Joseph Smith while at Harmony, Pennsylvania, in July 1830. It is directed to the Prophet's wife, Emma.

At this time, Joseph was 25 years old and Emma was 26. She was born on July 10, 1804, in Harmony, the seventh of nine children born to Isaac and Elizabeth Hale. Joseph was born on December 23, 1805.

Joseph and Emma had met in late 1825. He and some other men worked for about a month not far from the Hale residence in Harmony, Pennsylvania, as employees of Mr. Josiah Stowell. During this time, Joseph boarded at the Hale residence and was attracted to their daughter. She was also attracted to him.

Emma is described on page 50 of the *Doctrine and Covenants Student Manual, 1981,* as follows:

"Emma was a beautiful woman with an attractive personality, and she had the reputation of being a refined and dignified woman who was an excellent housekeeper and cook. Her Methodist upbringing had helped her develop a great love of music."

She was about five feet, nine inches tall, used excellent English grammar, had dark hair and brown eyes and was a schoolteacher in the area. Joseph continued to court her over time and eventually asked her father for permission to marry her. He refused, expressing concerns about Joseph's lack of education and involvement with "gold digging." As a result, Joseph and Emma eloped and were married in South Bainbridge, New York, on January 18, 1827, after which they lived for a time with Joseph's parents in Manchester, New York. They stayed in Manchester until after Moroni delivered the gold plates to Joseph, on September 22, 1827. In fact, Emma accompanied her husband to the Hill Cumorah on that occasion and waited at the bottom of the hill while Joseph climbed up the hill to his meeting place with Moroni.

As soon as Joseph brought the gold plates home to his parent's house in Manchester, persecutions raged. Finally, with Emma's father's permission, Joseph and Emma moved back to Harmony, Pennsylvania, to her parent's home. A short time later, they moved to a small home on 13 acres near Emma's parents in Harmony.

When time permitted, Joseph worked on translating the gold plates and Emma served as his scribe. Susan Easton Black writes of the time after Joseph brought the plates to his parent's home and later of Emma's serving as a scribe during the translation, as follows:

"On 22 September 1827 Emma was privileged to be the first to know that Joseph had acquired the plates from the angel Moroni. The plates 'lay in a box under our bed for months,' she said, 'but I never felt at liberty to look at them.' Emma was a scribe for the Book of Mormon translation, and said of her experience, 'It is marvelous to me . . . when acting as his scribe, [he] would dictate to me hour after hour; and when returning after meals, or after interruptions, he could at once begin where he had left off, without either seeing the manuscript or having any portion of it read to him.' She bore a continuing testimony, even in her seventy-fourth year, of her husband's prophetic calling: 'I believe he was everything he professed to be'" (*Who's Who in the Doctrine and Covenants*, 273–74).

Once, while Emma was serving as Joseph's scribe as he was translating the gold plates, she said that he dictated something about the walls of Jerusalem, upon which he stopped and asked, "Emma, did Jerusalem have walls around it?" (Taken from a letter from Emma to her children, published in the *Saint's Herald*, 1884, Number 2, 31.) Thus, she bore record that her husband did indeed translate the Book of Mormon plates.

You may remember that the Book of Mormon translation was completed, with Oliver Cowdery serving as scribe, and the book was printed and available for sale on March 26, 1830. Afterward, Emma did considerable traveling with her husband during the months of April to July 1830 and felt the

joy of the restored gospel as well as the wrath of persecutors who were constantly trying to thwart the Restoration.

At the time section 25 was given in July 1830, persecution was beginning to mount in Harmony, and the time was approaching when it would be necessary for Joseph and Emma to move to Fayette, New York, to escape it. Emma's Uncle Nathaniel (a minister) and others had tried to poison her mind regarding her "prophet" husband. Attempts were being made to persuade her to leave Joseph and stay in Harmony when he was forced to leave, where she would be well taken care of by family and friends. It is in this setting that she was given this revelation.

1 HEARKEN unto the voice of the Lord your God, while I speak unto you, Emma Smith, my daughter [*a term of tenderness and endearment*]; **for** verily I say unto you, **all those who receive my gospel are sons and daughters in my kingdom.**

The phrase "sons and daughters in my kingdom," in verse 1, above, is doctrinally significant vocabulary. It is one way of saying "are saved in the kingdom of heaven." In Mosiah 5:7, we see the same doctrine in slightly different wording as follows (**bold** added for emphasis):

Mosiah 5:7

And now, **because of the covenant which ye have made ye shall be called the children of Christ, his sons, and his daughters**; for behold, this day he hath spiritually begotten you; for ye say that **your hearts are changed through faith on his name**; therefore, ye are born of him and **have become his sons and his daughters**.

In summary, by way of doctrinal vocabulary, we find the following three classes of people referred to in the scriptures:

1. **Sons and daughters of God**—meaning those who have been baptized, are keeping covenants, and are heading for celestial glory. See D&C 76:24 and Moses 6:64–68.

2. **Sons and daughters of men**—meaning those who refuse to be baptized, and thus continue living according to the ways of the world. See Moses 8:14–15, and Genesis 6:2.

3. **Sons of perdition**—meaning those who sin to the extent that Cain did. See Moses 6:16–32 and D&C 76:30–38.

Continuing, in verse 2, next, the Lord gives Emma counsel to be faithful and He will preserve her life. This is no doubt especially meaningful in view of the threats and mobs that will confront her during her life. By the way, she died of natural causes, surrounded by family and friends, at the age of 74 on April 30, 1879, in Nauvoo, Illinois. Her last words, as recalled by her son Alexander, were "Joseph, Joseph, Joseph." Her son Joseph Smith III reported her last words as "Joseph! Yes, yes, I'm coming." (See *Zion's Ensign*, December 31, 1903.)

2 A revelation I give unto you concerning my will; and **if thou art faithful and walk in the paths of virtue before me**, I will preserve thy life, and **thou shalt receive an inheritance in Zion**.

3 Behold, **thy sins are forgiven thee**, and **thou art an elect lady**, whom I have called.

Joseph Smith explained the term "elect lady" in verse 3, above, as follows:

"I assisted in commencing the organization of 'The Female Relief Society of Nauvoo' in the Lodge Room. Sister Emma Smith, President, and Sister Elizabeth Ann Whitney and Sarah M. Cleveland, Counselors. I gave much instruction, read in the New Testament, and Book of Doctrine and Covenants, concerning the Elect Lady, and showed that the elect meant to be elected to a certain work . . . and that the revelation was then fulfilled by Sister Emma's election to the Presidency of the Society, she having previously been ordained to expound the Scriptures." (See *History of the Church*, 4:552–53.)

Verse 4, next, appears to be a reference to the gold plates and other things that Joseph saw but Emma didn't. The Lord assures her that He knows what He is doing by keeping these things from her.

4 **Murmur not because of the things which thou hast not seen**, for **they are withheld from thee** and from the world, **which is wisdom in me** in a time to come [*perhaps meaning that if Emma were to see these things, it would cause her extra trouble in the future*].

Next, we see some excellent marriage counsel. We need to include verse 9 in which Emma is told that "thy husband shall support thee."

5 And the office of thy calling shall **be** for **a comfort unto** my servant, Joseph Smith, Jun., **thy husband**, in his afflictions, **with consoling words, in the spirit of meekness.**

Only strong-willed, secure people are able to be meek, which, by definition, is strong but humble and not easily irritated.

Next, Emma is counseled to go with Joseph when he moves to Fayette. As mentioned in the background notes, above, she was being strongly pressured to use his leaving as a chance to leave him and live a peaceful, quiet life in the security and care of family and friends in Harmony.

She followed the counsel of the Lord given in verse 6, went with her husband, Joseph, and never saw her family again except for one brother in Nauvoo much later in life. The situation that was developing in Harmony at this time is described as follows:

"About this time a Methodist minister convinced Isaac Hale of many falsehoods about his son-in-law. As a result, life became unbearable for Joseph and his family in Harmony. Therefore, Joseph began to make preparations to permanently move to Fayette where he had been invited to live with Peter Whitmer Sr. again. In late August, Newel Knight took his team and wagon to Harmony to move Joseph and his family to Fayette" (*Church History in the Fulness of Times*, 1989, 77).

6 And **thou shalt go with him at the time of his going**, and be unto him for a scribe, while there is no one to be a scribe for him, that I may send my servant, Oliver Cowdery, whithersoever I will.

As mentioned previously, Emma was a school teacher. In verse 7, next, the Savior teaches her that she will be able to use her teaching talents, enhanced by the Holy Ghost, to strengthen members of the Church.

7 And **thou shalt be ordained** under his hand **to expound** [*explain and teach*] **scriptures**, and to **exhort** [*urge to be obedient*] the church, according **as it shall be given thee by my Spirit**.

Did you notice the word "ordain" in verse 7, above? Perhaps you've noticed that the doctrinal vocabulary of the Church has gradually developed over the years, and now, in many cases, we have more specifically defined words for specific practices and doctrines in the Church. In place of the word "ordained," as used in verse 7, we now use the phrase "set apart." Joseph Fielding Smith explained this as follows:

"The term 'ordain' was used generally in the early days of the Church in reference to both ordination and setting apart. . . . Men holding the Priesthood were said to have been 'ordained' to preside over branches and to perform special work. Sisters also were said to have been 'ordained' when they were called to some special duty or responsibility. In later years we developed a distinction between ordain and setting apart. Men are ordained to offices in the Priesthood and set apart to preside over stakes, wards, branches, missions, and auxiliary organizations. The sisters are set apart—not

ordained—as presidents of auxiliary organizations, to missions, etc. This saying that Emma Smith was 'ordained' to expound scripture, does not mean that she had conferred upon her the Priesthood, but that she was set apart to this calling, which found its fulfillment in the Relief Society of the Church" (*Church History and Modern Revelation*, 1:126).

As we move on to verse 8, next, we note that Emma was baptized on June 28, 1830, but had not yet been confirmed. It may sound strange that they would wait so long for confirmation, but Emma, along with 12 others, had been baptized in Colesville, New York, on June 28, 1830, despite the attempts of a mob to prevent it. The mobs did succeed in preventing their confirmation that evening as summarized in research from the Joseph Smith Papers Project summarized in the *Doctrine and Covenants Student Manual,* 2018, as follows:

"In late June 1830, Joseph Smith, Emma Smith, Oliver Cowdery, David Whitmer, and John Whitmer traveled from Harmony, Pennsylvania, to visit Church members and other believers in Colesville, New York. On Saturday, June 26, a stream was dammed to prepare for baptisms the next day (Sunday), but a hostile mob destroyed the dam during the night. Early Monday morning, the dam was rebuilt and 13 people were baptized, including Emma

Smith. By the time the baptisms were completed, however, a mob of nearly 50 men gathered, insulting and threatening to harm the Saints. That evening, the Saints met to confirm those who had been baptized earlier that day, but before the confirmations could be performed, Joseph was arrested on charges of "being a disorderly person, of setting the country in an uproar by preaching the Book of Mormon" (in *The Joseph Smith Papers, Histories, Volume 1: Joseph Smith Histories, 1832–1844,* ed. Karen Lynn Davidson and others [2012], 396).

Thus, in verse 8, the Lord instructs Emma to be confirmed and receive the gift of the Holy Ghost. She will be confirmed in August 1830 after section 27 is given.

8 For **he shall lay his hands upon thee, and thou shalt receive the Holy Ghost**, and thy time shall be given to writing, and to learning much.

9 And **thou needest not fear, for thy husband shall support thee in the church** [*in your work in the Church*]; for unto them is his calling [*perhaps a reminder to Emma that Joseph will not become wealthy— see D&C 24:9—because his calling is to excel in spiritual things*], that all things might be revealed unto them [*he is to be the Prophet*], whatsoever I will, according to their faith.

10 And verily I say unto thee that **thou shalt lay aside the things of this world, and seek for the things of a better.**

At the end of verse 10, above, Emma is told basically the same thing her husband was told in D&C 24:9, namely that her priorities were to be spiritual rather than on the pursuit of worldly wealth.

Next, in verse 11, Emma is told that she will be given the ability and the assignment to make a selection of sacred hymns for the Church. This was in harmony with her talent in music and singing in her local choir as she grew up in Harmony.

11 And **it shall be given thee, also, to make a selection of sacred hymns**, as it shall be given thee, which is pleasing unto me, to be had in my church.

She accepted this calling, and in 1835, her hymnbook was published. This collection of sacred hymns was printed in a book that was four inches by three inches and a third-inch thick. It contained ninety hymns, thirty-four of which were written by Church members. No music was printed with the hymns, therefore, they were sung to popular melodies of the day, and in many cases, a given hymn could be sung to several different melodies.

Several of the hymns selected by Emma, with the help of W. W. Phelps, are still included in our present hymnbook, including the following:

1. "Gently Raise the Sacred Strain"
2. "Guide Us, O Thou Great Jehovah"
3. "He Died! The Great Redeemer Died!"
4. "How Firm a Foundation"
5. "I Know That My Redeemer Lives"
6. "Joy to the World"
7. "Know Then That Every Soul Is Free"
8. "Now Let Us Rejoice"
9. "O God, the Eternal Father"
10. "Redeemer of Israel"
11. "The Spirit of God Like a Fire Is Burning"

The title page to her hymnal was roughly as follows:

A COLLECTION
OF
SACRED HYMNS,
FOR THE
CHURCH
OF THE
LATTER DAY SAINTS.
SELECTED BY
EMMA SMITH.
Kirtland, Ohio:
Printed by
F. G. Williams & co.
1835

The Preface to her book of sacred hymns was as follows:

PREFACE

In order to sing by the Spirit, and with the understanding, it is necessary that the church of the Latter Day Saints should have a collection of "Sacred Hymns," adapted to their faith and belief in the gospel, and, as far as can be, holding forth the promises made to the fathers who died in the precious faith of a glorious resurrection, and a thousand years' reign on earth with the Son of Man in his glory. Notwithstanding the church, as it were, is still in its infancy, yet, as the song of the righteous is a prayer unto god, it is sincerely hoped that the following collection, selected with an eye single to his glory, may answer every purpose till more are composed, or till we are blessed with a copious variety of the songs of Zion.

Next, the Savior expresses His feelings about these hymns He has asked Emma to collect and publish. From His words, we learn that participating in singing the hymns of Zion is a form of prayer, and that we will be blessed for so doing.

Doctrine

Verse 12. When the righteous sing hymns, the Lord considers them to be prayers.

12 For **my soul delighteth in the song of the heart**; yea, **the song of the righteous is a prayer unto me**, and **it shall be answered with a blessing upon their heads.**

In the final verses of this section, Emma is invited to be happy and to stick with the covenants she has made, which would include her marriage vows to Joseph as well as her baptismal covenants. She is also counseled to beware of pride.

13 Wherefore, **lift up thy heart and rejoice**, and **cleave unto the covenants which thou hast made.**

14 **Continue in the spirit of meekness**, and **beware of pride**. Let thy soul delight in thy husband, and the glory which shall come upon him.

We will repeat verse 14, here, and **bold** some valuable marriage counsel given by the Lord to Emma, which can easily apply to many of us. It is that rather than being jealous of our spouse when he or she accomplishes things and receives praise for them, we should rejoice and be happy for them. This can certainly apply to parents also when their children succeed and garner praise, as well as to children when their parents succeed.

14 Continue in the spirit of meekness, and beware of pride. **Let thy soul delight in thy husband, and the glory which shall come upon him.**

Finally, Emma is counseled to keep the commandments. In terms of gospel vocabulary, the word "crown," in verse 15, next, refers to exaltation. We understand this from D&C 20:14 in which we read, "crown of eternal life." In the scriptures, the phrase "eternal life" always means exaltation, becoming gods. See also Revelation 2:10 and 3:11, as well as numerous other references in the Topical Guide under "Crown."

15 **Keep my commandments continually, and a crown of righteousness thou shalt receive**. And except thou do this, where I am you cannot come.

In verse 16, next, we are reminded that, in most cases, the counsel given by the Lord to one person in the scriptures can apply to all of us. Hence, the great value in our studying them.

16 And verily, verily, I say unto you, that **this is my voice unto all**. Amen.

SECTION 26

Background

This revelation was given to Joseph Smith, Oliver Cowdery, and John Whitmer, a son of

Peter Whitmer Sr., at Harmony, Pennsylvania, in July 1830. It is the last of the three revelations for which the basic background given for section 24 in this study guide applies.

This section is most commonly referred to as the basis for our sustaining of officers and teachers in our church meetings. It is known as the principle of "common consent" as given in verse 2. This principle of common consent is also used in sustaining actions of the Church, such as dividing wards and stakes, etc.

First, we will be reminded in verse 1 of the importance of all of us studying the scriptures throughout our lives as a basic foundation for our performing our duties in the Church.

1 BEHOLD, I say unto you that you shall **let your time be devoted to the studying of the scriptures**, and to **preaching**, and to **confirming the church** [*strengthening the Church; see context of Acts 15:41*] at Colesville, and to performing your labors on the land [*probably meaning to take care of their farms and crops*], such as is required, until after you shall go to the west [*to Fayette, New York*] to hold the next conference [*which was held in Fayette on September 26–27, 1830*]; and then it shall be made known what you shall do.

With respect to the phrase "studying of the scriptures," in verse 1, above, it could also be a reference to the Joseph Smith Translation of the Bible. It appears that the Prophet's study and translation of the Bible got under way about this time in the history of the Church. The earliest manuscripts of the JST (Joseph Smith Translation of the Bible) were written in the summer and fall of 1830 and are in the handwriting of John Whitmer and Oliver Cowdery. (See Robert J. Mathew's *Joseph Smith's Translation of the Bible*, page 27.)

Next, in verse 2, the Lord teaches the principle of common consent.

Doctrine

Verse 2. No one can hold a calling in the Church without being sustained by the people he or she will serve.

2 And **all things shall be done by common consent in the church**, by much prayer and faith, for all things you shall receive by faith. Amen.

The question sometimes comes up as to what would happen if you voted against an action being proposed by the person conducting a meeting of the Church.

The answer is that the presiding authority would acknowledge your negative vote and invite you to visit with him, your bishop, or your stake president after the meeting to discuss your concerns. If, for instance, the business at hand were the sustaining of a person to a calling in the Church, and you questioned their worthiness. The presiding officer might then hold up the ordination or setting apart until the matter was resolved.

On the other hand, if you just didn't like the person, you would be out of order in letting your personal feelings get in the way. Joseph Fielding Smith explained this as follows:

"I have no right to raise my hand in opposition to a man who is appointed to any position in this Church, simply because I may not like him, or because of some personal disagreement or feeling I may have, but only on the grounds that he is guilty of wrong doing, of transgression of the laws of the Church which would disqualify him for the position which he is called to hold" (*Doctrines of Salvation*, 3:124).

It is important for you to know that the use of the principle of common consent in the Church is a powerful safeguard against apostasy. In effect, it means that there are no secret ordinations, which often form the basis of apostate groups that have broken away from the Church. In fact, a person cannot hold an office in this church without the knowledge of the people. We will again use a quote from Joseph Fielding Smith from the *Doctrine and Covenants Student Manual* for institutes of religion, 1981, page 54:

"No man can preside in this Church in any capacity without the consent of the people. The Lord has placed upon us the responsibility of sustaining by vote those who are called to various positions of responsibility. No man, should the people decide to the contrary, could preside over any body of Latter-day Saints in this Church, and yet it is not the right of the people to nominate, to choose, for that is the right of the priesthood" (*Doctrines of Salvation*, 3:123; see also D&C 20:65).

Finally, once we have sustained a person in a calling, it is our responsibility to do our part to cooperate and help that person's responsibility move forward successfully.

SECTION 27

Background

This revelation was received by Joseph Smith near Harmony, Pennsylvania, in August 1830. The Prophet had set out to obtain wine for the sacrament when he was met by an angel and instructed not to secure wine from enemies of the Church (see heading to section 27 in your Doctrine and Covenants and also verse 3 of this section).

This section contains the revelation and instruction that provides the basis for our using water for the sacrament rather than wine.

The Prophet Joseph Smith provides background information for section 27 as follows:

"Early in the month of August Newel Knight and his wife paid us a visit at my place in Harmony, Pennsylvania; and as neither his wife nor mine had been as yet confirmed, it was proposed that we should confirm them, and partake together of the Sacrament, before he and his wife should leave us. In order to prepare for this I set out to procure some wine for the occasion, but had gone only a short distance when I was met by a heavenly messenger, and received the following revelation, the first four paragraphs of which were written at this time, and the remainder in the September following: [D&C 27]" (*History of the Church*, 1:106).

As you will see, this section consists of three distinct portions. Verses 1–4 deal with the matter of what to eat and drink when preparing and partaking of the sacrament. Verses 5–14 deal with a great sacrament meeting which will be held in conjunction with the meeting with Adam and the Savior at Adam-ondi-Ahman in Missouri prior to the Second Coming. Verses 15–18 counsel us to put on the "whole armor" of God.

In verse 1, Joseph is told that the heavenly messenger is representing the Savior on this occasion.

1 **LISTEN to the voice of Jesus Christ**, your Lord, your God, and your Redeemer, whose word is quick [*alive, living; symbolic of continuous revelation*] and powerful.

Next, in verse 2, Joseph is instructed that it does not matter what is used in partaking of the sacrament as long as it is done "with an eye single to my glory." In other words, with pure intent.

This is the basis for our using water rather than wine in our sacrament. It is also the reason that an isolated group of Latter-day Saints under unusual circumstances, such as a group of LDS servicemen and women, could use crackers and juice for the sacrament under the direction of their authorized group leader.

Obviously, such circumstances are unusual, and "variety" in the emblems of the sacrament is to be avoided. Otherwise, the focus of many members would be on what was being used for the sacrament that day rather than on the ordinance itself. As a matter of standard practice, we simply use bread and water.

Perhaps you've wondered if it is proper to use wheat bread rather than white bread. Good question. Answer: it is proper. There are many places on earth where white bread is not available. Also, what about those members who are allergic to wheat flour and thus must use bread or wafers made from rice?

In summary, it is the ordinance itself which is sacred, and components and settings should not detract from that.

Doctrine

Verse 2. It does not matter what is used for the sacrament as long as it is done with proper intent.

2 For, behold, I say unto you, that it mattereth not what ye shall eat or what ye shall drink when ye partake of the sacrament, **if it so be that ye do it with an eye single to my glory—remembering unto the Father my body which was laid down for you, and my blood which was shed for the remission of your sins.**

Ezra Taft Benson, who later became the President of the Church, gave an example of the meaning of verse 2, above, in a conference talk, when he explained basically that when bread is not available, a substitute may be used, such as potatoes or potato peelings, which were used by members of the Church in Europe during World War II (in Conference Report, Oct. 1952, 120).

3 Wherefore, a commandment I give unto you, that **you shall not purchase wine neither strong drink of your enemies;**

4 Wherefore, **you shall partake of none except it is made new** [*fresh*] **among you**; yea, in this my Father's kingdom which shall be built up on the earth.

Joseph Smith recorded the following, which serves as follow-up to verses 1–4, above:

"In obedience to the above commandment, we prepared some wine of our own making, and held our meeting, consisting only of five: Newel Knight and his wife, myself and my wife, and John Whitmer. We partook together of the Sacrament, after which we confirmed these two sisters [*Newel Knight's wife, Sally, and Emma Smith*] into the Church, and spent the evening in a glorious manner. The Spirit of the Lord was poured out upon us, [and] we praised the Lord God, and rejoiced exceedingly" (*History of the Church*, 1:108).

According to the Prophet, as quoted earlier, the remainder of this section was written down in September 1830. See also the heading to section 27 in your Doctrine and Covenants.

What follows in verses 5–14, next, is a most wonderful and marvelous revelation. It keys off of the statement of the Savior to His Apostles on the night of the Last Supper. He said, in reference to the sacrament which He had just introduced to them, "But I say unto you, I will not drink henceforth of this fruit of the vine, until that day when I drink it new with you in my Father's kingdom" (Matthew 26:29). Now, in section 27, we are given much more detail about the meeting at which this prophecy will be fulfilled. For instance, we are told the names of some prominent past prophets who will be in attendance. In addition, we are told that all those who are worthy of living with Christ forever will be in attendance. This is exciting! In order to point these people out, we will go through verses 5–14 and **bold** them. Then we will repeat these verses and do much more with them.

5 Behold, this is wisdom in me; wherefore, marvel not, for **the hour cometh that I will drink of the fruit of the vine with you** on the earth, **and with Moroni**, whom I have sent unto you to reveal the Book of Mormon, containing the fulness of my everlasting gospel, to whom I have committed the keys of the record of the stick of Ephraim;

6 And **also with Elias**, to whom I have committed the keys of bringing to pass the restoration of all things spoken by the mouth of all the holy prophets since the world began, concerning the last days;

7 And **also John** the son of Zacharias, which Zacharias he (Elias) visited and gave promise that he should have a son, and his name should be John, and he should be filled with the spirit of Elias;

8 Which John I have sent unto you, my servants, Joseph Smith, Jun., and Oliver Cowdery, to ordain you unto the first priesthood which you have received, that you might be called and ordained even as Aaron;

9 And **also Elijah**, unto whom I have committed the keys of the power of turning the hearts of the fathers to the children, and the hearts of the children to the fathers, that the whole earth may not be smitten with a curse;

10 And **also with Joseph** and **Jacob**, and **Isaac**, and **Abraham**, your fathers, by whom the promises remain;

11 And **also with** Michael, or **Adam**, the father of all, the prince of all, the ancient of days;

12 And **also with Peter**, and **James**, and **John**, whom I have sent unto you, by whom I have ordained you and confirmed you to be apostles, and especial witnesses of my name, and bear the keys of your ministry and of the same things which I revealed unto them;

13 Unto whom I have committed

the keys of my kingdom, and a dispensation of the gospel for the last times; and for the fulness of times, in the which I will gather together in one all things, both which are in heaven, and which are on earth;

14 And also **with all those whom my Father hath given me out of the world.**

As stated previously, we will now go through verses 5–14 again and do much more with them by way of study. First of all, by way of additional background, we will quote from *Millennial Messiah*, by Bruce R. McConkie (**bold** added for emphasis):

"With reference to the use of sacramental wine in our day, the Lord said to Joseph Smith: 'You shall partake of none except it is made new among you; yea, in this my Father's kingdom which shall be built up on the earth.' In so stating, he is picking up the language he used in the upper room [at the Last Supper in Jerusalem, before His crucifixion]. Then he says: 'The hour cometh that I will drink of the fruit of the vine with you on the earth.' **Jesus is going to partake of the sacrament again with his mortal disciples on earth. But it will not be with mortals only.** He names **others who will be present** and who will participate in the sacred ordinance. These include **Moroni, Elias, John the Baptist, Elijah,** **Abraham, Isaac, Jacob, Joseph** (who was sold into Egypt), **Peter, James, and John,** 'and also with **Michael, or Adam,** the father of all, the prince of all, the ancient of days.' Each of these is named simply by way of illustration. **The grand summation of the whole matter comes in these words: 'And also with all those whom my Father hath given me out of the world.'** (D&C 27:4–14.) **The sacrament is to be administered** in a future day, on this earth, when the Lord Jesus is present, and when all the righteous of all ages are present. **This, of course, will be a part of the grand council at Adam-ondi-Ahman**" (*The Millennial Messiah*, 587).

Elder McConkie summarized this great sacrament meeting as follows: **"Every faithful person in the whole history of the world, every person who has so lived as to merit eternal life in the kingdom of the Father will be in attendance and will partake, with the Lord, of the sacrament"** (*The Promised Messiah*, 595).

This certainly answers the question you hear asked as to who is going to attend the meeting held at Adam-ondi-Ahman before the Second Coming (see section 116).

With this as background, we will now continue verse by verse repeating verses 5–14 and adding more commentary. In verse 5, next, we learn that Jesus gave Moroni the "keys" of bringing the

Book of Mormon to earth in the last days.

5 Behold, this is wisdom in me; wherefore, marvel not, for the hour cometh that I will drink of the fruit of the vine with you on the earth, and with **Moroni, whom I have sent unto you to reveal the Book of Mormon, containing the fulness of my everlasting gospel, to whom I have committed the keys of the record of the stick of Ephraim** [*the Book of Mormon; see Ezekiel 37:15–17*];

Next, we must define the term "Elias" or verse 6 will leave us confused. We will use a quote from the *Doctrine and Covenants Student Manual*, 1981 edition, pages 55–56, as used in institute of religion classes of the Church. In it, we will be told that "Elias," as often used in the scriptures, is a term meaning "messenger from God." The quote is as follows (**bold** added for emphasis):

"Since Elias refers to more than one person, it is sometimes confusing. Elder Bruce R. McConkie explained: 'Correcting the Bible by the spirit of revelation, the Prophet restored a statement of John the Baptist which says that **Christ is the Elias** who was to restore all things. (Inspired Version [JST], John 1:21–28.) By revelation we are also informed that the **Elias** who was to restore all

things **is the angel Gabriel** who was known in mortality as Noah. (D&C 27:6–7; Luke 1:5–25; *Teachings*, 157.) From the same authentic source we also learn that the promised **Elias is John the Revelator**. (D&C 77:9, 14.) Thus there are **three different revelations** which **name Elias as being three different persons**. What are we to conclude?

"'By finding answer to the question, by whom has the restoration been effected, we shall find who Elias is and find there is no problem in harmonizing these apparently contradictory revelations. Who has restored all things? **Was it one man? Certainly not**. Many angelic ministrants have been sent from the courts of glory to confer keys and powers, to commit their dispensations and glories again to men on earth. At least the following have come: Moroni, John the Baptist, Peter, James, and John, Moses, Elijah, Elias, Gabriel, Raphael, and Michael. (D&C 13; 110; 128:19–21.) Since it is apparent that no one messenger has carried the whole burden of the restoration, but rather that each has come with a specific endowment from on high, **it becomes clear that Elias is a composite personage. The expression must be understood to be a name and a title for those whose mission it was to commit keys and powers to men in this final dispensation'"

(*Mormon Doctrine*, 221; see also D&C 110:12–16).

With the above quote as background, we will now proceed with verse 6.

6 And also with **Elias** [*a composite of many heavenly beings sent by God to earth*], **to whom I have committed the keys of bringing to pass the restoration of all things** spoken by the mouth of all the holy prophets since the world began, concerning the last days;

7 And also **John the son of Zacharias** [*John the Baptist*], which Zacharias he (Elias) [*Gabriel; in other words, Noah; see Bible Dictionary under "Gabriel"*] visited and gave promise that he should have a son, and his name should be John, and he should be filled with the spirit of Elias;

8 **Which John** [*the Baptist*] **I have sent unto you** [*on May 15, 1829; see D&C 13*], my servants, **Joseph Smith, Jun., and Oliver Cowdery, to ordain you** unto the first priesthood [*the Aaronic Priesthood; see D&C 13*] which you have received, that you might be called and ordained even as Aaron;

9 And also **Elijah** [*the prophet who was translated and taken up into heaven—see 2 Kings 2:11; he was resurrected with Christ—see D&C 133:55*], unto whom I have committed the keys of the power of turning the hearts of the fathers to the children, and the hearts of the children to the fathers [*the keys of sealing families together*], that the whole earth may not be smitten with a curse [*these keys will be restored to Joseph Smith and Oliver Cowdery in the Kirtland Temple on April 3, 1836—see D&C 110:13–15*];

10 And also with **Joseph** [*who was sold into Egypt*] and **Jacob**, and **Isaac**, and **Abraham**, your fathers [*ancestors*], by whom the promises remain [*in other words, through whom the blessings of Abraham are to be carried to the whole earth—see Abraham 2:9–11*];

11 And also with **Michael, or Adam**, the father of all [*the ancestor of all; the first man—see D&C 84:16*], the prince of all, **the ancient of days** [*the first mortal on earth*];

The phrase, "the prince of all," in verse 11, above, implies authority and power to rule. Joseph Fielding Smith taught that Adam has authority over all people on earth, directly under Christ, as follows (**bold** added for emphasis):

"Michael, who is **Adam, holds the keys of salvation for the human family, under the direction and counsel of Jesus Christ**, who is the Holy One of Zion [see D&C 78:15–16]. **Adam will**, when the earth is cleansed and purified and becomes a celestial globe, **preside over the children of men, who are of his posterity**. He is Adam, 'the prince, the arch-angel.' In the eternities before this earth was formed he was the archangel. He became Adam when he came to this earth to be the father of the human family. (D&C 107:54–57.)

"The Prophet Joseph Smith said of Adam: 'Commencing with Adam, who was the first man, who is spoken of in Daniel as the "Ancient of Days," or in other words, the first and oldest of all, the great progenitor of whom it is said in another place is Michael. . . . **Adam holds the keys of all the dispensations** of the fulness of times, i.e. the dispensations of all times have been and will be revealed through him from the beginning'" (*Teachings of the Prophet Joseph Smith*, 167–68; *Church History and Modern Revelation*, 1:309).

Next, as the Savior continues to list names of those from the past who will attend this meeting with Him, He verifies that Peter, James, and John have already restored the Melchizedek Priesthood to the earth in this dispensation.

Perhaps you will recall that Joseph Smith did not record the exact date of this great event, which appears to have taken place between the restoration of the Aaronic Priesthood on May 15, 1829 (see D&C 13), and the end of June 1829 (see D&C 18:9; see also background notes to section 18 in this study guide). The Lord apparently did not choose to bring the exact date back to his mind, and thus, the fact that we do not have the date is a reminder to us of Joseph's honesty.

12 And also with **Peter**, and **James**, and **John**, **whom I have sent unto you, by whom I have ordained you and confirmed you to be apostles, and especial witnesses of my name, and bear the keys of your ministry and of the same things which I revealed unto them**;

There is another precious truth that we can glean from verse 12, above. Did you notice that the Savior said, in effect, that He ordained them to the Melchizedek Priesthood? In other words, when an authorized servant of the Lord places his hands upon our heads, it is the same as if the Savior, Himself, were doing it!

Next, Jesus reiterates that He personally gave Peter, James, and John their priesthood keys and authority.

13 **Unto whom I have committed the keys of my kingdom**, and a dispensation of the gospel for the last times [*this is the last time the gospel will be restored, before the*

Second Coming]; and for the fulness of times [*the "dispensation of the fulness of times"*], in the which I will gather together in one all things, both which are in heaven, and which are on earth [*in other words, all things have been restored in our last days*];

As we finish the topic dealt with in verses 5–14, verse 14, next, tells us, in effect, that all the righteous who qualify for celestial glory will attend this "sacrament meeting" with the Savior.

14 And also with all those whom my Father hath given me out of the world.

Verse 14, above, obviously includes all the righteous, living and dead. In other words, this will be a rather large meeting. Daniel saw this in vision and speaks of it and the numbers attending it. We will quote him and use **bold** to point things out:

Daniel 7:9–13

9 I [*Daniel*] beheld till the thrones were cast down, and **the Ancient of days** [*Adam*] **did sit**, whose garment *was* white as snow, and the hair of his head like the pure wool: **his throne** *was like* **the fiery flame**, *and* his wheels *as* burning fire.

10 A fiery stream issued and came forth from before him:

thousand thousands [*millions*] ministered unto him, and **ten thousand times ten thousand** [*a hundred million*] stood before him: the judgment was set, and the books were opened.

11 I beheld then because of the voice of the great words which the horn [*the power of heaven; "horn" symbolizes power, in Biblical symbolism*] spake: I beheld *even* till the beast [*symbolic of the devil*] was slain, and his body destroyed [*symbolic of Satan's kingdom*], and given to the burning flame [*destroyed by the power of Christ's glory*].

12 As concerning the rest of the beasts [*Satan's evil hosts, both mortal and evil spirits*], they had their dominion taken away: yet their lives were prolonged for a season and time [*they had their "glory days" of evil and wickedness in the last days before the coming of Christ*].

13 I [*Daniel*] saw in the night visions, and, behold, *one* like **the Son of man came** [*Christ came*] with the clouds of heaven, and came **to the Ancient of days**, and they brought him [*Adam*] near before him [*Christ*].

In concluding our consideration of verses 5–14, we will add one more quote as follows (**bold** added for emphasis):

"Before the Lord Jesus descends openly and publicly in the clouds of glory, attended by all the hosts of heaven; before the great and dreadful day of the Lord sends terror and destruction from one end of the earth to the other; before he stands on Mount Zion, or sets his feet on Olivet, or utters his voice from an American Zion or a Jewish Jerusalem; before all flesh shall see him together; before any of his appearances, which taken together comprise the second coming of the Son of God—before all these, there is to be a secret appearance to selected members of his Church. He will come in private to his prophet and to the apostles then living. Those who have held keys and powers and authorities in all ages from Adam to the present will also be present. And further, **all the faithful members of the Church then living and all the faithful saints of all the ages past will be present. It will be the greatest congregation of faithful saints ever assembled on planet earth. It will be a sacrament meeting**. It will be a day of judgment for the faithful of all the ages. And it will take place in Daviess County, Missouri, at a place called Adam-ondi-Ahman" (*The Millennial Messiah*, 578).

In verses 15–18, next, the Lord tells us how we can prepare to attend the great meeting spoken of in verses 5–14.

15 Wherefore, **lift up your hearts and rejoice** [*be happy; let the joy the gospel brings show on your faces and in your lives*], and **gird up your loins** [*prepare for action; dress your lives in the gospel of Jesus Christ*], and **take upon you my whole armor,** that ye may be able to withstand the evil day, having done all, that ye may be able to stand.

16 **Stand, therefore, having your loins girt about with** [*being dressed in*] **truth,** having on the breastplate of **righteousness,** and your feet shod with the preparation of **the gospel of peace,** which I have sent mine angels to commit unto you;

17 **Taking the shield of** [*protect yourselves with*] **faith** wherewith ye shall be able to quench all the fiery darts of the wicked;

18 And take **the helmet of salvation,** and the **sword of my Spirit** [*the Holy Ghost can cut through falsehood and deception*], which I will pour out upon you, and **my word** which I reveal unto you, and **be agreed as touching all things whatsoever ye ask of me** [*work together in harmony*],

and **be faithful** until I come, and ye shall be caught up [*you will be caught up to meet Christ, whether alive or dead—see D&C 88:96–98*], that where I am ye shall be also. Amen.

SECTION 28

Background

This section is a revelation given through Joseph Smith at Fayette, New York, in September 1830. Among other things, it deals with two important principles for Latter-day Saints that can protect them against deception. First, the Lord will not let His prophet lead the people astray. Second, the prophet is the only one who can receive revelation for the whole Church. Those who follow the living Prophet faithfully are fully assured of entrance into the celestial kingdom.

By way of background, Hiram Page, who was born in 1800, who studied medicine and traveled widely practicing it, and who was baptized into the Church on April 11, 1830 (five days after its organization), had found a stone that he considered to give him powers to receive revelations. He began using it and convinced others, including some members of the Whitmer family and Oliver Cowdery, that he was receiving revelations for the Church. These revelations included the supposed location of Zion and the proper order of the Church.

It is also helpful to know a bit about Hiram and Oliver and the Whitmer family. Hiram had married Catherine Whitmer, the oldest daughter of Peter Whitmer Sr., and Oliver had married her sister, Elizabeth Ann. So, they were all part of the same family.

Most of the people in that area of the country at the time were Congregationalists and believed that any person could receive revelation and pronounce doctrine for a whole congregation or any groups or individuals. Section 28 will preach correct doctrine with respect to the true Church of Jesus Christ; namely, that only one man is authorized to receive revelation and commandments for the whole church. That man is the living Prophet.

This "seer stone," or "peep stone" as it has variously been called, was handed down from generation to generation in the Whitmer family. It is now in the possession of what was known as the Reorganized Church of Jesus Christ of Latter Day Saints, which is now known as the Community of Christ Church. Cecil E. McGavin was permitted to examine it and described it as follows:

"The Page 'peep stone,' however, was preserved as a souvenir. It is now in the possession of the Reorganized Church. The writer was permitted to examine it. It is a flat stone about seven inches long, four wide, and one-quarter inch in thickness. It is dark gray in color with waves of brown and purple gracefully interwoven across the surface. A small hole has been drilled through one end of it as if a string had been threaded through it. It is simply impressive enough to make a good paper weight, yet it became a tool through which the adversary attempted to stir up strife and create a schism in the Church" (McGavin, *Historical Background of the Doctrine and Covenants* and Otten, *Historical Background and Setting for each section of the Doctrine and Covenants*).

Newel Knight, son of Joseph Knight Sr., recorded some valuable background to section 28 in his diary, as follows:

"After arranging my affairs at home, I again set out for Fayette, to attend our second conference, which had been appointed to be held at Father Whitmer's where Joseph then resided. On my arrival I found Brother Joseph in great distress of mind on account of Hyrum [Hiram] Page, who had managed to get up some dissension of feeling among the brethren by giving revelations concerning the government of the Church and other matters, which he claimed to have received through the medium of a stone he possessed. He had quite a roll of papers full of these revelations, and many in the Church were led astray by them. Even Oliver Cowdery and the Whitmer family had given heed to them, although

they were in contradiction to the New Testament and the revelations of these last days. Here was a chance for Satan to work among the little flock, and he sought by this means to accomplish what persecution failed to do. Joseph was perplexed and scarcely knew how to meet this new exigency. That night I occupied the same room that he did and the greater part of the night was spent in prayer and supplication. After much labor with these brethren they were convinced of their error, and confessed the same, renouncing the revelations as not being of God, but acknowledged that Satan had conspired to overthrow their belief in the true plan of salvation. In consequence of these things Joseph enquired of the Lord before conference commenced and received the revelation published on page 140 of the Doctrine and Covenants [section 28], wherein God explicitly states His mind and will concerning the receiving of revelations.

"Conference having assembled, the first thing done was to consider the subject of the stone in connection with Hyrum Page, and after considerable investigation and discussion, Brother Page and all the members of the Church present renounced the stone, and the revelations connected with it, much to our joy and satisfaction." (Journal History, 26 Sept. 1830. See also *Doctrine and Covenants Student Manual*, 1981, 57.)

Sometime during this same summer, prior to the conference mentioned above by Newel Knight, Oliver Cowdery had written a letter to Joseph Smith in which he commanded him to change the wording of verse 37 of section 20 of the Doctrine and Covenants. Joseph, who was working at the time on arranging the revelations received so far for eventual publication, wrote of this as follows (**bold** added for emphasis):

"I began to arrange and copy the revelations, which we had received from time to time; in which I was assisted by John Whitmer, who now resided with me.

"Whilst thus employed in the work appointed me by my Heavenly Father, **I received a letter from Oliver Cowdery**, the contents of which gave me both sorrow and uneasiness. Not having that letter now in my possession, I cannot of course give it here in full, but merely an extract of the most prominent parts, which I can yet, and expect long to, remember.

"**He wrote to inform me that he had discovered an error in one of the commandments**—Book of Doctrine and Covenants [20:37]: **'And truly manifest by their works that they have received of the Spirit of Christ unto a remission of their sins.'**

"The above quotation, he said, was erroneous, and added: **'I command you in the name of God to erase those words, that no priestcraft be amongst us!'**

"I immediately wrote to him in reply, in which I asked him by what authority he took upon him to command me to alter or erase, to add to or diminish from, a revelation or commandment from Almighty God.

"A few days afterwards I visited him and Mr. Whitmer's family, when I found the family in general of his opinion concerning the words above quoted, and it was not without both labor and perseverance that I could prevail with any of them to reason calmly on the subject. However, Christian Whitmer at length became convinced that the sentence was reasonable, and according to Scripture; and finally, with his assistance, I succeeded in bringing, not only the Whitmer family, but also Oliver Cowdery to acknowledge that they had been in error, and that the sentence in dispute was in accordance with the rest of the commandment. And thus was this error rooted out, which having its rise in presumption and rash judgment, was the more particularly calculated (when once fairly understood) to teach each and all of us the necessity of humility and meekness before the Lord, that He might teach us of His ways, that we might walk in His paths, and live by every word that proceedeth forth from His mouth" (*History of the Church*, 1:104–5).

One of the things we see in all of

this is that the Lord waited until the need arose in the minds and hearts of the members and then taught principles of Church government that are vital to all of us today. We will now study this section. Notice how gentle the Lord is with Oliver, even though he has caused much anguish and concern for Joseph as well as others. In verse 1, next, He assures this "second elder" (D&C 20:3) of the Church that he is still important.

1 BEHOLD, I say unto thee, Oliver, that it shall be given unto thee that **thou shalt be heard by the church in all things whatsoever thou shalt teach them by the Comforter, concerning the revelations and commandments which I have given**.

Next, the Savior teaches the principle of having one man, the living Prophet, at the head of the Church, and the principle that no one is authorized to receive revelation for the whole Church except him.

2 But, behold, verily, verily, I say unto thee, **no one shall be appointed to receive commandments and revelations in this church excepting my servant Joseph Smith, Jun.**, for he receiveth them even as Moses [*he is the living Prophet now, just like Moses was then*].

3 And **thou** [*Oliver Cowdery*] **shalt be obedient unto the things which I shall give unto him**, even as Aaron, to **declare** [*explain and teach*] **faithfully** [*don't change them one bit, because of your own personal opinions*] **the commandments and the revelations, with power and authority unto the church**.

An important cross-reference for verse 2, above, is found in D&C 43:3–4, where the Lord teaches clearly that He will never allow the living Prophet to lead us astray. He thus bears testimony to us that there is complete safety and reliability in following the living Prophet.

Next, in verses 4 and 5, Oliver is told that he may speak and teach and even command under the direct supervision of the Holy Ghost, but he is not to write commandments to the Church. That is the Prophet's job. The Prophet is the only one who should give commandments and have them written down so that members can refer to them and abide by them.

This is an important distinction. Even elders can command the water to be calmed or an evil spirit to leave when clearly and definitely inspired to do so by the Holy Ghost. But written commandments and new doctrines are the specific jurisdiction of the living Prophet.

4 And **if thou art led at any time by the Comforter** [*the Holy Ghost*] **to speak or teach, or** at all times **by** the **way of commandment unto the church,** thou mayest do it.

5 But **thou shalt not write by way of commandment,** but by wisdom;

> Verse 6, next, appears to be a direct reference to the incident, quoted in the background notes above, in which Oliver Cowdery had written to the Prophet, commanding him to delete the words "and truly manifest by their works that they have received of the Spirit of Christ unto a remission of their sins" from D&C 20:37.

6 And **thou shalt not command him who is at thy head, and at the head of the church;**

> In verse 7, we are taught that the living Prophet is the only one on earth who has all the priesthood keys and is authorized to use them. (The counselors in the First Presidency and the members of the Quorum of the Twelve Apostles all have the keys—given to each one upon being ordained an Apostle—but they must use them under the direction of the President of the Church.)

Doctrine

Verse 7. The living Prophet is the only one on earth authorized to exercise all the priesthood keys available to man on earth today.

7 For **I have given him the keys** of the mysteries, and the revelations which are sealed, **until I shall appoint unto them another in his stead** [*in other words, the next Prophet*].

> Next, Oliver Cowdery is called to go on a mission to the Lamanites. He will be joined by Peter Whitmer Jr. (D&C 30:5), Parley P. Pratt, and Ziba Peterson (D&C 32:2–3). This will be a dangerous and difficult journey of about 1,500 miles into the western frontier (just west of Missouri at that time). We will talk more about it when we get to section 32. Once again, Oliver is counseled not to take over as Prophet by writing commandments.

8 And now, behold, I say unto **you that you shall go unto the Lamanites and preach my gospel unto them**; and inasmuch as they receive thy teachings thou shalt cause my church to be established among them; and **thou shalt have revelations, but write them not by way of commandment.**

In the background notes to this revelation, we mentioned that one of the purported revelations claimed by Hiram Page apparently was that of giving the location of the city of Zion. We now know that it is to be located in Independence, Missouri, because the Lord revealed it to Joseph Smith on July 20, 1831, as recorded in D&C 57:2–3. But verse 9, next, informs Oliver that there has been no revelation from God yet on that matter. Thus, the source of Hiram Page's "revelations" becomes obvious.

9 And now, behold, I say unto you that **it is not revealed, and no man knoweth where the city Zion shall be built**, but it shall be given hereafter [*D&C 57:2–3*]. Behold, I say unto you that it shall be on the borders by the Lamanites.

10 Thou shalt not leave this place [*Fayette, New York*] until after the conference [*the second conference of the Church, scheduled to be held at the Peter Whitmer Sr. home in Fayette on September 26, 1830*]; and **my servant Joseph shall be appointed to preside over the conference** by the voice of it [*and will be sustained again by the members at the conference; similar to what we do in general, stake, and ward conferences*], **and what he saith to thee thou shalt tell** [*yet another reminder to Oliver to follow*

the Prophet and not go off on his own on doctrine and commandments].

Next, we are taught a kind principle, namely, keep it as private as possible when it becomes our responsibility to correct another person. It is gratifying to know that Hiram Page accepted counsel, renounced the stone he was using to receive false revelations, and supported the Prophet at the conference.

11 And again, **thou shalt take thy brother, Hiram Page, between him and thee alone,** and tell him that **those things which he hath written from that stone are not of me and that Satan deceiveth him;**

Just a bit more information derived from the Joseph Smith Papers research that shows how Satan deceived Hiram Page with his stone. We will use a quote from the *Doctrine and Covenants Student Manual*, 2018, chapter 11.

"In northwestern New York during the early 1800s, many people believed individuals could receive knowledge supernaturally through an instrument such as a stone or a divining rod. Hiram Page claimed that words would appear on the stone he possessed. He said that after he dictated the words and had them copied to paper, the words would disappear from the stone and others would appear (see *The Joseph Smith Papers,*

Documents: Volume 1: July 1828–June 1831, ed. Michael Hubbard MacKay and others [2013], 184). The Lord denounced Hiram Page's false revelations."

Next, the Lord continues advising Oliver as to what to say to Hiram.

12 For, **behold, these things have not been appointed unto him** [*it is not his stewardship to receive revelation for the Church*], **neither shall anything be appointed unto any of this church contrary to the church covenants** [*no member of the Church will ever be given power and authority that goes contrary to the order established by God*].

13 For **all things must be done in order, and by common consent in the church**, by the prayer of faith.

14 And **thou** [*Oliver*] **shalt assist to settle all these things, according to the covenants of the church** [*according to the proper order of the true Church*], before thou shalt take thy journey among the Lamanites.

15 And it shall be given thee from the time thou shalt go, until the time thou shalt return, what thou shalt do [*you will be inspired to know what to do as you go on your missionary journey to the Lamanites—verse 8*].

Last of all, the Lord gives Oliver counsel about being willing to preach wherever he goes, having a good attitude about it, and making sure that his preaching reflects the positive nature of the gospel to those who heed it.

16 And thou must **open thy mouth at all times**, declaring my gospel **with the sound of rejoicing**. Amen.

SECTION 29

Background

This revelation was given through the Prophet Joseph Smith at Fayette, New York, in September 1830, some days before the conference mentioned in section 28, verse 10. This next conference would be the second conference of the Church since its organization on April 6, 1830, and was to be held in the Whitmer home. It would last for three days.

As already mentioned, this revelation, known now as section 29, was given some days prior to the conference. It was given through the Prophet in the presence of six elders, Oliver Cowdery, David Whitmer, John Whitmer, Peter Whitmer, Samuel H. Smith, and Thomas B. Marsh, along with three other members of the Church (see *The Joseph Smith Papers, Documents, Volume 1: July 1828–June 1831*, ed. Michael Hubbard MacKay and others [2013], 177–78).

It is filled with specific doctrines of the gospel. Perhaps you remember that the Lord showed Nephi in vision that he was going to restore many "plain and precious things" (1 Nephi 13:40) through "other books" (1 Nephi 13:39). One of these "other books" is the Doctrine and Covenants, in which the Lord said that He would "bring to light the true points of my doctrine" (D&C 10:62). Section 29 brings together many of these "points of doctrine."

We will first go through the entire section with no notes added, using **bold** to highlight many of these teachings and doctrines, so that you can see at a glance how powerful section 29 is. You may want to just read the **bolded** words and phrases this time through. Then we will repeat the section, adding several notes as we go.

1 LISTEN to the voice of **Jesus Christ**, **your Redeemer**, the **Great I AM**, whose **arm of mercy hath atoned for your sins**;

2 Who **will gather** his people even as a hen gathereth her chickens under her wings, even **as many as will hearken to my voice** and **humble themselves** before me, and **call upon me in mighty prayer**.

3 Behold, verily, verily, I say unto you, that **at this time your sins are forgiven you, therefore ye receive these things**; but remember to **sin no more, lest perils shall come upon you**.

4 Verily, I say unto you that **ye are chosen out of the world to declare my gospel** with the sound of rejoicing, as with the voice of a trump.

5 Lift up your hearts and be glad, for **I am in your midst**, and am **your advocate with the Father**; and it is his good will to give you the kingdom.

6 And, as it is written—**What-so-ever ye shall ask in faith, being united in prayer according to my command, ye shall receive**.

7 And **ye are called to bring to pass the gathering of mine elect**; for **mine elect hear my voice and harden not their hearts**;

8 Wherefore the decree hath gone forth from the Father that **they shall be gathered** in unto one place upon the face of this land, **to prepare** their hearts and be prepared **in all things against the day when tribulation and desolation are sent forth upon the wicked**.

9 For **the hour is nigh** and the day soon at hand when the earth

is ripe; and **all the proud and they that do wickedly shall be as stubble**; and **I will burn them up**, saith the Lord of Hosts, that wickedness shall not be upon the earth;

10 For **the hour is nigh**, and that which was spoken by mine apostles must be fulfilled; for as they spoke so shall it come to pass;

11 For **I will reveal myself from heaven with power and great glory**, with all the hosts thereof, and **dwell in righteousness with men on earth a thousand years**, and the wicked shall not stand.

12 And again, verily, verily, I say unto you, and it hath gone forth in a firm decree, by the will of the Father, that mine apostles, **the Twelve** which were with me in my ministry at Jerusalem, **shall stand at my right hand at the day of my coming** in a pillar of fire, being **clothed with robes of righteousness**, with **crowns upon their heads**, in glory even as I am, **to judge the whole house of Israel**, even **as many as have loved me and kept my commandments, and none else.**

13 For **a trump shall sound both long and loud**, even as upon Mount Sinai, and **all the earth shall quake**, and **they shall come forth**—yea, even **the dead which died in me**, to **receive a crown of righteousness**, and to be **clothed upon, even as I am**, to **be with me**, that we may be one.

14 But, behold, I say unto you that **before this great day** shall come the **sun shall be darkened**, and the **moon shall be turned into blood**, and the **stars shall fall** from heaven, and **there shall be greater signs** in heaven above and in the earth beneath;

15 And **there shall be weeping and wailing** among the hosts of men;

16 And there shall be **a great hailstorm** sent forth to destroy the crops of the earth.

17 And it shall come to pass, **because of the wickedness of the world**, that **I will take vengeance upon the wicked**, for they will not repent; for **the cup of mine indignation is full**; for behold, **my blood shall not cleanse them if they hear me not**.

18 Wherefore, I the Lord God will send forth **flies** upon the face of the earth, which shall take hold of the inhabitants thereof, and shall eat their flesh, and shall cause **maggots** to come in upon them;

19 And their **tongues shall be**

stayed that they shall not utter against me; and **their flesh shall fall from off their bones**, and their **eyes from their sockets**;

20 And it shall come to pass that **the beasts of the forest and the fowls of the air shall devour them up.**

21 And **the great and abominable church**, which is **the whore of all the earth**, shall be **cast down** by devouring fire, according as it is spoken by the mouth of Ezekiel the prophet, who spoke of these things, which have not come to pass but surely must, as I live, for abominations shall not reign.

22 And again, verily, verily, I say unto you that **when the thousand years are ended**, and **men again** begin to **deny their God**, then will I spare the earth but for **a little season**;

23 And **the end shall come**, and the heaven and the earth shall be consumed and pass away, and there shall be a **new heaven** and a **new earth**.

24 For **all old things shall pass away**, and **all things shall become new**, even the **heaven** and the **earth**, and all the fulness thereof, both **men** and **beasts**, the **fowls** of the air, and the **fishes** of the sea;

25 And **not one hair**, neither mote, **shall be lost**, for it is the workmanship of mine hand.

26 But, behold, verily I say unto you, **before the earth shall pass away, Michael, mine archangel, shall sound his trump**, and then shall **all the dead awake**, for their graves shall be opened, and they shall come forth—yea, **even all**.

27 And **the righteous shall be gathered on my right hand unto eternal life**; and **the wicked on my left hand will I be ashamed to own before the Father**;

28 **Wherefore I will say unto them—Depart from me, ye cursed, into everlasting fire, prepared for the devil and his angels**.

29 And now, behold, I say unto you, never at any time have I declared from mine own mouth that they should return, for **where I am they cannot come**, for they have no power.

30 But remember that **all my judgments are not given unto men**; and as the words have gone forth out of my mouth even so shall they be fulfilled, that **the first shall be last, and that the last shall be first** in all things whatsoever I have created by the

word of my power, which is the power of my Spirit.

31 For **by the power of my Spirit created I** them; yea, **all things both spiritual and temporal**—

32 **First spiritual, secondly temporal**, which is the beginning of my work; and again, **first temporal, and secondly spiritual**, which is the last of my work—

33 Speaking unto you that you may naturally understand; but unto myself **my works have no end, neither beginning**; but it is given unto you that ye may understand, because ye have asked it of me and are agreed.

34 Wherefore, verily I say unto you that **all things unto me are spiritual**, and not at any time have I given unto you a law which was temporal; neither any man, nor the children of men; neither **Adam, your father**, whom I created.

35 Behold, **I gave unto him that he should be an agent unto himself**; and I gave unto him commandment, but no temporal commandment gave I unto him, for **my commandments are spiritual**; they are **not natural nor temporal, neither carnal nor sensual**.

36 And it came to pass that **Adam**, being **tempted of the devil**—for, behold, **the devil** was before Adam, for he **rebelled against me**, saying, Give me thine **honor**, which **is my power**; and also a **third part** of the hosts of heaven **turned he away from me because of their agency**;

37 And they were thrust down, and **thus came the devil and his angels**;

38 And, behold, **there is a place prepared for them** from the beginning, which place is **hell**.

39 And **it must needs be that the devil should tempt the children of men, or they could not be agents unto themselves**; for **if they never should have bitter they could not know the sweet**—

40 Wherefore, it came to pass that **the devil tempted Adam**, and **he partook of the forbidden fruit** and transgressed the commandment, wherein **he became subject to the will of the devil**, because he yielded unto temptation.

41 Wherefore, I, the Lord God, caused that he should be **cast out from the Garden of Eden**, from my presence, because of his transgression, wherein he became **spiritually dead**, which is **the**

first death, even that same death which is **the last death**, which is spiritual, which **shall be pronounced upon the wicked** when I shall say: Depart, ye cursed.

42 But, behold, I say unto you that **I, the Lord God, gave unto Adam and unto his seed, that they should not die as to the temporal death, until I**, the Lord God, should send forth angels to **declare unto them repentance and redemption, through faith on the name of mine Only Begotten Son**.

43 And **thus did I, the Lord God, appoint unto man the days of his probation**—that **by his natural death he might be raised in immortality unto eternal life**, even as many as would believe;

44 And **they that believe not unto eternal damnation**; for they cannot be redeemed from their spiritual fall, because they repent not;

45 For **they love darkness rather than light**, and their deeds are evil, and **they receive their wages** of whom they list to obey.

46 But behold, I say unto you, that **little children are redeemed** from the foundation of the world through mine Only Begotten;

47 Wherefore, **they cannot sin**, for **power is not given unto Satan to tempt little children, until they begin to become accountable before me;**

48 For it is given unto them even as I will, according to mine own pleasure, that great things may be required at the hand of their fathers.

49 And, again, I say unto you, that **whoso having knowledge, have I not commanded to repent?**

50 And **he that hath no understanding, it remaineth in me to do according as it is written**. And now I declare no more unto you at this time. Amen.

As stated previously, we will now repeat all fifty verses of section 29 and take a closer look at the doctrines and teachings of the gospel and the plan of salvation that are given in them by the Lord. Basically, you could preach the entire gospel using this section as a springboard.

We will begin by pointing out what is known as "divine investiture." We will use verse 1 in combination with verses 42 and 46 to define this term. "Divine investiture" is probably not a term that you will have to recall and explain in order to make it through the final judgment successfully, but as you will see, it can be helpful to know what it means.

Perhaps you've been confused occasionally as to who is speaking in scripture—the Father or the Son. Some of this confusion comes from the fact that Jesus often quotes His Father without first telling us that He is going to do so. This is called "divine investiture." In other words, Christ is authorized or "invested" with the right to speak for the "Divine" Father, and when He does so, it is binding on us, just as if the Father had spoken it. There is nothing strange about His doing this, because He and His Father are "one." It just sometimes throws us off a bit.

"Divine investiture" can also refer to when the Holy Ghost is speaking for Christ, as in Moses 5:9, or when an angel is speaking for Christ, as if He were speaking, as is the case in Judges 2:1–3. Let's look now at our example of Christ speaking as if the Father were speaking. We will put the three verses together here, which we need in order to demonstrate this. We will **bold** words and phrases that point out the transition from when Christ is speaking for Himself and when He begins to speak directly for the Father.

D&C 29:1, 42 and 46

1 **LISTEN** to the voice of Jesus Christ, your Redeemer, the Great I AM, whose arm of mercy hath atoned for your sins;

42 But, behold, I say unto you

that I, the Lord God, gave unto Adam and unto his seed, that they should not die as to the temporal death, until I, the Lord God, should send forth angels to declare unto them repentance and redemption, **through faith on the name of mine Only Begotten Son.**

46 But behold, I say unto you, that little children are redeemed from the foundation of the world **through mine Only Begotten;**

We see this same thing in Moses 1:6, where the Savior addresses Moses and speaks for the Father. By way of summary for the topic of "divine investiture," Joseph Fielding Smith explains:

"CHRIST MAY SPEAK AS THE FATHER. In giving revelations our Savior speaks at times for himself; at other times for the Father, and in the Father's name, as though he were the Father, and yet it is Jesus Christ, our Redeemer who gives the message. So, we see, in Doctrine and Covenants 29:1, that he introduces himself as 'Jesus Christ, your Redeemer,' but in the closing part of the revelation he speaks for the Father, and in the Father's name as though he were the Father, and yet it is still Jesus who is speaking, for the Father has put his name on him for that purpose" (*Doctrines of Salvation,* 1:27).

Next, we will point out more doctrine contained in verse 1.

Doctrine

Verse 1. Jesus Christ is the God (Jehovah) of the Old Testament, the God who gave commandments to Abraham, Moses, and others.

1 LISTEN to the voice of Jesus Christ, your Redeemer, the Great I AM, whose arm [*symbolic of power in scriptural symbolism*] of mercy hath atoned for your sins;

> "I AM" is an Old Testament name for Jehovah, which is another name for the premortal Jesus Christ. During Jehovah's appearance at the burning bush, when Moses asked Him who he should tell the people gave him authority to be their prophet, Jesus told him to tell them that it was "I AM" who sent him. (See Exodus 3:14.)

Doctrine

Verse 2. It is time for the final gathering of Israel before the Second Coming.

2 Who will gather his people [*it is time for the last days' gathering of Israel*] even as a hen gathereth her chickens under her wings [*symbolic of the warmth, comfort, and security of the gospel*], even as many as will hearken to my voice

and humble themselves before me, and call upon me in mighty prayer.

> One of the great blessings of the Atonement is that we don't have to wait until Judgment Day to find out if our sins are forgiven. As illustrated in verse 3, next, as well as elsewhere in the scriptures, through proper repentance, we can receive forgiveness enroute. This means that we are clean, but we are obviously not yet perfect.

Doctrine

Verse 3. Sins can be and are forgiven as we strive to go through life on the covenant path. It is a merciful way of giving us encouragement enroute to exaltation.

3 Behold, verily, verily, I say unto you, that at this time your sins are forgiven you, therefore [*this is why*] ye receive these things; but remember to sin no more, lest perils shall come upon you.

> In verses 4 and 5, next, we are reminded to be upbeat and pleasant as we take the gospel to others.

Doctrine

Verses 4 and 5. We are to be primarily upbeat and pleasant about preaching the gospel.

4 Verily, I say unto you that ye are chosen out of the world to declare my gospel with the sound of rejoicing, as with the voice of a trump [*symbolizing that the gospel is a clear, easy to recognize, pure message*].

5 **Lift up your hearts and be glad**, for **I am in your midst**, and am your advocate with the Father; and it is his good will to give you the kingdom.

Did you notice in verse 5, above, that the Savior is in our midst and that the Father loves to give His children His kingdom?

Doctrine

Verse 5, above. The Savior is not an "absentee" God. Rather, He spends much time in our midst.

Next, we are taught the importance of unity and harmony as we pray together for desired blessings.

Doctrine

Verse 6. There is much power in working together in harmony, as far as influencing the powers of heaven for desired blessings is concerned.

6 And, as it is written—Whatsoever ye shall ask in faith, **being united in prayer** according to my command, ye shall receive.

Doctrine

Verse 7. The "elect," those whose hearts are pure, recognize the gospel message when they hear it.

7 And ye are called to bring to pass the gathering of mine elect; for mine elect hear my voice and harden not their hearts;

Verse 8, next, tells us that there is one gathering place for the early Saints (when the Church was just starting out), but there are many "gathering places" now; namely, the stakes of Zion. (See D&C 115:6.)

8 Wherefore the decree hath gone forth from the Father that **they shall be gathered in unto one place upon the face of this land, to prepare their hearts** and be prepared in all things against the day when tribulation and desolation are sent forth upon the wicked.

There is an important message to us in verse 8, above, as to how best to prepare for the trouble and devastations of the last days. Did you notice the key word in verse 8? It is "hearts." Symbolically, our hearts are the center of our feelings and emotions. The Spirit often speaks to our heart, giving us feelings and testimony concerning the gospel. We tend to act according to our feelings, even more so than according to our minds. Thus, a major preparation for remaining strong and loyal to God during times of trial and trouble comes in the form of having the word of God and the testimony of the Spirit written in our hearts. This type of spiritual nourishment comes in large measure from scripture study, listening to the words of the living prophets, meeting with other Saints whose values and standards reflect the Lord, sincere prayer, serving others, and so on.

Doctrine

Verse 9. The wicked will be burned at the time of the Second Coming.

9 For **the hour is nigh** [*getting close*] and the day soon at hand **when the earth is ripe** [*when the majority of people on earth are fully wicked*]; and all **the proud** and **they that do wickedly shall be as stubble** [*very flammable stalks of dry straw*] ; and **I will burn them up**, saith the Lord of Hosts, that **wickedness shall not be upon the earth** [*for the beginning of the Millennium*];

A quote from the 2018 *Doctrine and Covenants Student Manual* for institutes of religion in the Church informs us that the wicked will not be able to survive the intensity of the Savior's glory when He comes. Therefore, they will be consumed by it. (**Bold** added for emphases.)

"The Lord warned that those who are 'proud and they that do wickedly shall be as stubble' and burn at His coming (D&C 29:9). While pride is a common sin that affects everyone to some degree, in this case 'the proud' refers to **those who cannot abide the Lord's glory because of wickedness**. In a later revelation, the Lord clarified that this group includes 'they who are liars, and sorcerers, and adulterers, and whoremongers, and whosoever loves and makes a lie. These are they who suffer the wrath of God on earth' (D&C 76:103–4)."

That the glory of the Savior at His coming will be the cause of the burning of the wicked is confirmed by D&C 5:19, as well as 2 Nephi 12:10, 19, and 21.

10 For **the hour is nigh, and that which was spoken by mine apostles** [*the "signs of the times," especially the prophecies about the Second Coming and the destruction of the wicked*] **must be fulfilled;** for **as they spoke so shall it come to pass** [*their prophecies will be fulfilled*];

Doctrine

Verse 11. The Savior's Coming ushers in the beginning of the Millennium, which will last for 1000 years. Also, there will be no wicked people at the beginning of the Millennium.

11 For I will reveal myself from heaven with power and great glory, with all the hosts thereof, **and dwell in righteousness with men on earth a thousand years**, and **the wicked shall not stand.**

Doctrine

The Twelve Apostles, who ministered with the Savior at Jerusalem, will assist the Savior in judging the righteous people of the House of Israel.

12 And again, verily, verily, I say unto you, and it hath gone forth in a firm decree, by the will of the Father [*this is all done under the direction of the Father*], that mine apostles, **the Twelve which were with me in my ministry at Jerusalem**, shall stand at my right hand [*symbolic of covenants; symbolic of personal righteousness and qualifying to enter celestial glory*] at the day of my coming in a pillar of fire [*with glory*], being clothed with robes of righteousness [*symbolic, among other things, of having kept temple covenants*], with crowns [*symbolic of the power and authority of gods, in exaltation*] upon their heads, **in glory even as I am** [*with the same glory that Christ has*], **to judge the whole house of Israel**, even **as many as have loved me and kept my commandments** [*the*

Twelve will judge the righteous of the House of Israel], and **none else.**

As you can see, verse 12, above, is set in the context of the time of the Second Coming. This will usher in the Millennium. The Savior explains that the Twelve will only be involved with judging the righteous (see end of verse 12). This makes sense, since only the righteous dead will be resurrected at that time. Bruce R. McConkie gives added explanation as follows (**bold** added for emphasis):

"Be it remembered that the Twelve Apostles of the Lamb, who were with the Lord in his ministry in Jerusalem, shall judge the whole house of Israel, **meaning that portion of Israel who have kept the commandments**, 'and none else.' (D&C 29:12.) There will be a great hierarchy of judges in that great day, of whom Adam, under Christ, will be the chief of all. **Those judges will judge the righteous ones** under their jurisdiction, **but Christ himself, he alone, will judge the wicked** (*The Millennial Messiah*, 584).

Doctrine

Verse 13. The righteous who have died since the resurrection of Christ will be resurrected at the time of the Savior's Second Coming (except for Peter, James, and Moroni, who have already

been resurrected). They will be "clothed upon" (verse 13) with power and authority to rule and reign with Christ during the Millennium (see also Revelation 20:4).

13 For **a trump shall sound** both long and loud, even as upon Mount Sinai [*announcing the presence of the Lord—see Exodus 19:16–20*], and **all the earth shall quake**, and **they shall come forth**—yea, even **the dead which died in me** [*those who died faithful to Christ*], **to receive a crown of righteousness** [*these righteous people will have power and authority to rule and reign with the Savior during the Millennium; they will also know that they are heading toward celestial glory because they are included in this resurrection*], and **to be clothed upon, even as I am** [*perhaps also including the imagery of being clothed in personal righteousness—see Revelation 19:8*], **to be with me, that we may be one.**

Doctrine

Verses 14–21. Many signs of the times (prophecies that will be fulfilled as the Second Coming gets closer and finally arrives) will take place, alerting the righteous who study the scriptures and listen to the living prophets that the Second Coming is getting close.

14 But, behold, I say unto you that before this great day shall come [*before the Second Coming and the destruction of the wicked*] **the sun shall be darkened**, and the **moon shall be turned into blood**, and the **stars shall fall from heaven**, and there shall be **greater signs in heaven above and in the earth beneath**;

15 And **there shall be weeping and wailing** [*there will be much of agony and distress, gloom and doom*] **among the hosts of men**;

16 And there shall be **a great hailstorm** sent forth to destroy the crops of the earth.

17 And it shall come to pass, **because of the wickedness of the world**, that **I will take vengeance upon the wicked, for they will not repent**; for the cup of mine indignation [*righteous anger*] is full [*mercy cannot hold justice back any longer*]; for behold, **my blood shall not cleanse them if they hear me not** [*if they do not listen to and obey the gospel*].

18 Wherefore, **I the Lord God will send forth flies** upon the face of the earth, which shall take

hold of the inhabitants thereof, and shall eat their flesh, and shall cause **maggots** to come in upon them;

19 And **their tongues shall be stayed** [*perhaps they will be speechless because of horror; can also mean that the destruction of the wicked will stop their blasphemy against God*] that they shall not utter against me; and **their flesh shall fall from off their bones,** and **their eyes from their sockets** [*indicating horrible conditions on earth prior to the Second Coming*];

20 And it shall come to pass that **the beasts of the forest and the fowls of the air shall devour them up.**

21 And **the great and abominable church** [*the "church of the devil" (1 Nephi 14:10), "kingdom of the devil" (1 Nephi 22:22–23)*], which is **the whore** [*a highly symbolic word, meaning one who perverts that which is right and holy and good for evil purposes; thus symbolic of Satan and his evil hosts*] **of all the earth,** shall be **cast down by devouring fire,** according as it is spoken by the mouth of Ezekiel the prophet [*see Ezekiel 38:22 and 39:6; see also heading for Ezekiel 38 as background*], who spoke of these things, **which have not**

come to pass [*yet in 1830, at the time of this revelation*] **but surely must,** as I live, for abominations shall not reign [*wickedness will not ultimately rule the earth*].

Doctrine

Verse 22. After the end of the Millennium, there will be a "little season," during which many will again turn wicked and deny God.

22 And again, verily, verily, I say unto you that when the thousand years are ended, and **men again begin to deny their God,** then will I spare the earth but for **a little season;**

Joseph Fielding Smith wrote of this "little season" as follows, telling us that there would be many sons of perdition during that time (**bold** added for emphasis):

"After the thousand years Satan will be loosed again and will go forth again to deceive the nations. Because men are still mortal, Satan will go out to deceive them. Men will again deny the Lord, but in doing **so they will act with their eyes open and because they love darkness rather than light, and so they become sons of perdition.** Satan will gather his hosts, both those on the earth and the wicked dead who will eventually also be brought forth in the resurrection. Michael, the prince,

[Adam] will gather his forces and the last great battle will be fought. Satan will be defeated with his hosts. Then will come the end. Satan and those who follow him will be banished into outer darkness" (*Doctrines of Salvation*, 1:87).

Doctrine

Verses 23–25. The heaven and the earth and everything on it will die and be resurrected. This includes pets.

23 And **the end** [*of the 7,000 years of this earth's temporal existence— see D&C 77:6*] **shall come**, and the **heaven and the earth shall be consumed and pass away** [*die—see D&C 88:26*], and **there shall be a new heaven and a new earth** [*not new in the sense of being replaced; rather, new in the sense of being renewed, or celestialized— see D&C 130:9*].

24 For **all old things shall pass away**, and **all things shall become new**, even the **heaven** and the **earth**, and **all the fulness thereof** [*everything on the earth*], both **men** and **beasts**, the **fowls of the air**, and the **fishes of the sea**;

25 And **not one hair, neither mote, shall be lost, for it is the workmanship of mine hand**.

We will give a quote from the *Doctrine and Covenants Student*

Manual, 1981, used previously by our institutes of religion, by way of follow-up on verses 23–25, above (**bold** added for emphasis):

"President Joseph Fielding Smith explained that this passage '**does not mean that this earth shall pass away and another take its place**, and the heaven thereof shall pass away, and another heaven take its place, but that the earth and its heaven shall, after passing away through death, be renewed again in immortality. **This earth is living and must die**, but since it keeps the law it shall be restored through the resurrection by which **it shall become celestialized** and the abode of celestial beings. The next verse of this revelation explains this as follows: [D&C 29:24–25]

'So we see that the Lord intends to save, not only the earth and the heavens, not only man who dwells upon the earth, but all things which he has created. The animals, the fishes of the sea, the fowls of the air, as well as man, are to be re-created, or renewed, through the resurrection, for they too are living souls.' (In Conference Report, Oct. 1928, 99–100; see also D&C 88:17–19, 25–26.)" [As quoted in *Doctrine and Covenants Student Manual*, 1981, 62.]

Doctrine

Verse 26. There will be a final resurrection after the end of

the Millennium that will be the resurrection of the wicked (see also D&C 88:100–102).

26 But, behold, verily I say unto you, **before the earth shall pass away**, Michael [*Adam*], mine archangel, shall sound his trump, and **then shall all the dead awake**, for their graves shall be opened, and **they shall come forth** [*will be resurrected*]—**yea, even all**.

Although the Lord will reveal more details, especially in section 76 about the three degrees of glory and perdition, and in section 88, concerning the various resurrections, at this point in time (verses 27–29, next), He uses the Biblical imagery of being on God's "right hand" or "left hand" to emphasize that the righteous will gain eternal life and the wicked will not be privileged to live with God.

"Right hand," in this context, means that you are righteous, having made and kept covenants with God. "Right hand" symbolizes making covenants with God. "Left hand" means that a person is wicked, having refused to repent, and having either made and then violated covenants with God or refused to make such covenants.

27 And **the righteous shall be gathered on my right hand unto eternal life**; and **the wicked on my left hand** will I be ashamed to own before the Father;

28 Wherefore [*this is why*] I will say unto them—**Depart from me, ye cursed, into everlasting fire** [*hell*], **prepared for the devil and his angels**.

29 And now, behold, I say unto you, **never at any time have I declared from mine own mouth that they should return**, for **where I am they cannot come**, for **they have no power**.

30 But **remember that all my judgments are not given unto men** [*perhaps meaning that the Lord has not explained everything to us yet and does not give all His reasons to us for what He does; He doesn't have to explain to us in order to proceed with His work*]; and as the words have gone forth out of my mouth even so shall they be fulfilled, that **the first shall be last, and that the last shall be first** in all things whatsoever I have created by the word of my power, which is the power of my Spirit.

The Joseph Smith Translation of the Bible rendition of Mark 10:31 (which is Mark 10:30 in the JST) helps us understand the phrase "the first shall be last, and . . . the last shall be first" in verse 30, above. We will quote it here, with **bold** added for emphasis:

JST Mark 10:30

But **there are many who make themselves first, that shall be last**, and the last first. [*In other words, those who are prideful and make themselves priority, even above God's commandments, will find themselves in "last place" on Judgment Day.*]

Verses 31 and 32, next, sometimes confuse members of the Church a bit. While there are many things that could be done with these verses, we will take a simple approach. In effect, what the Lord is saying first is that He initially created all things in spirit form and then in physical form in conjunction with the Fall of Adam and Eve. This was the creation or "beginning" of the earth. Then, He speaks of the "last of my work" (verse 32), which could be understood to mean the final stage of our progression before Judgment Day, beginning with our mortal life and continuing to resurrection and final judgment.

Doctrine

Verses 31 and the first part of verse 32. God created all things in spirit form before they were created physically. (See also Moses 3:5.)

31 For by the power of my Spirit **created** I them; yea, **all things both spiritual and temporal**

[*having to do with mortality, earthly time, earthly things*]—

32 **First spiritual, secondly temporal** [*all things were first created in spirit form in premortality and then created in physical form on earth in conjunction with the Fall of Adam and Eve*], which is the beginning of my work [*"to bring to pass the immortality and eternal life of man" (See Moses 1:39)*]; and **again, first temporal, and secondly spiritual** [*meaning, perhaps, among other things that the final phase of our progression toward Judgment Day and exaltation begins with mortality and then proceeds to the spirit world, the Second Coming, our work and progress during the Millennium, and on to final judgment, which are all designed to help us become more spiritual*], **which is the last of my work** [*which is the final part of the Savior's work before He turns all things back over to the Father—see D&C 76:107–8*]—

As the Lord continues, He explains that He is speaking in terms that we can understand as mortals, because, in fact, His works do not have a beginning, neither do they have an end. Also, since all that He does is designed to promote our spirituality and eternal well-being, everything is "spiritual" to Him, whereas we tend to make a distinction between physical things and spiritual things.

33 **Speaking unto you that you may naturally** [as mortals] **understand**; but unto myself my works have no end, neither beginning; but it is given unto you [I'm speaking to you in this simpler way] that ye may understand, because ye have asked it of me and are agreed [are united together in asking Me].

34 Wherefore, verily I say unto you that **all things unto me are spiritual** [are designed to promote your spirituality], and **not at any time have I given unto you a law which was temporal**; neither any man, nor the children of men; **neither Adam**, your father [first ancestor], whom I created.

35 Behold, **I gave unto him that he should be an agent unto himself** [Adam was given agency]; and I gave unto him commandment [so that he had an environment of knowledge in which to exercise his agency], but no temporal commandment gave I unto him, for **my commandments are spiritual; they are not natural nor temporal, neither carnal nor sensual.**

We will add one quote here from the *Doctrine and Covenants Student Manual*, 1981, in conjunction with verses 31–35:

"When the Lord created the earth, he first created all things spiritually (Moses 3:5–9). After the Fall all things became temporal (D&C 77:6). At the end of the earth, the temporal will again become spiritual (Articles of Faith 1:10). Thus, in the beginning things were spiritual first and temporal second. In the end things will be temporal first and spiritual second (McConkie, *Doctrinal New Testament Commentary*, 1:669). These expressions are given by the Lord only for the sake of man's understanding in mortality, however. From God's point of view there is neither beginning nor end, and all things are spiritual.

"Man makes a distinction between temporal and spiritual laws, and some are very much concerned about keeping the two separate. To the Lord everything is both spiritual and temporal, and the laws He gives are consequently spiritual because they concern spiritual beings. When He commanded Adam to eat bread in the sweat of his brow, or Moses to strike the rock that the people might drink, or the Prophet Joseph to erect the Nauvoo House, or the Saints in Utah to build fences and roads, such laws were for their spiritual welfare as well as physical. To obey such laws, when given, is a spiritual duty. One who performs his daily labor 'as to the Lord, and not to men' (Eph. 6:7) derives spiritual benefit from whatever his duties are (Smith and

Sjodahl, *Commentary*, 156)."

Doctrine

Verse 36. The ultimate source of God's power is His honor and integrity.

36 And it came to pass that Adam, being tempted of the devil—for, behold, **the devil was before Adam** [*Lucifer became the devil before Adam was placed on earth*], for he **rebelled against me, saying, Give me thine honor, which is my power**; and also a third part of the hosts of heaven turned he away from me **because of their agency;**

Doctrine

Verse 36, above. We had agency in premortality.

Some people wonder to what extent we had agency in our premortal life as spirit children of our Heavenly Parents (see *The Family: A Proclamation to the World*, September 23, 1995, second paragraph). The answer is obviously "yes," since Lucifer and the spirits who followed him exercised their agency to rebel against God. Thus, it is clear that we were given knowledge and agency there such that we could make choices, make mistakes, repent, be forgiven, and thus make progress there. In other words, our situation there was very similar to our situation here in mortality. It had to be in order for us to progress. A summary of this is given in the New Testament student manual, used in our institutes of religion, as follows (**bold** added for emphasis):

"**We were given laws** and **agency**, and **commandments to have faith** and **repent** from the wrongs that we could do there." "**Man could and did in many instances, sin before he was born** . . ." (*Life and Teachings of Jesus and His Apostles*, New Testament student manual, used by the institutes of religion, 336).

In conjunction with the above quote, it is important to note that the Atonement of Christ is infinite. It works in the present, past, and future and thus operated for us there in premortality also. A quote from Elder Jeffrey R. Holland, in which he speaks of things we might think about during the sacrament, verifies this as follows (**bold** added for emphasis):

"We could remember that even in the Grand Council of Heaven [*held in premortality*] He loved us and was wonderfully strong, that **we triumphed even there by the power of Christ and our faith in the blood of the Lamb**" ("This Do in Remembrance of Me," *Ensign*, Nov. 1995).

As the Lord continues the instructions given in section 29, we are taught that Lucifer and the rebellious spirits from our premortal life became the devil and his evil spirits.

Doctrine

Verse 37. Lucifer and the spirits who rebelled with him in premortality were thrust down to earth. Thus, Lucifer became the devil and they became his evil spirit followers.

37 And **they were thrust down** [*to earth—see Revelation 12:4*]**, and thus came the devil and his angels**;

Doctrine

Verse 38. The plan of salvation, which was taught us in premortality, included a final place for the devil and those who follow him completely.

38 And, behold, **there is a place prepared for them from the beginning** [*in other words, as explained to us in the council in heaven in our premortality*], which place is **hell** [*perdition, outer darkness*].

Doctrine

Verse 39. Temptation is necessary in order for us to exercise our agency and progress.

39 And it must needs be [*it is necessary*] **that the devil should tempt the children of men** [*people*]**, or they could not be agents unto themselves**; for if they never should have bitter they could not know the sweet—

In our battle against Satan and the evil spirits who follow him, it is important to know that people with physical bodies have power over those who do not. We will quote from the 2018 *Doctrine and Covenants Student Manual*, chapter 12, to show this.

"President James E. Faust (1920–2007) of the First Presidency explained: We need not become paralyzed with fear of Satan's power. He can have no power over us unless we permit it. He is really a coward, and if we stand firm, he will retreat. The Apostle James counseled: 'Submit yourselves therefore to God. Resist the devil, and he will flee from you' [James 4:7]. And Nephi states that 'he hath no power over the hearts' of people who are righteous [1 Nephi 22:26].

"We have heard comedians and others justify or explain their misdeeds by saying, 'The devil made me do it.' I do not really think the devil can make us do anything; certainly he can tempt and he can deceive, but he has no authority over us which we do not give him.

"The power to resist Satan may

be stronger than we realize. The Prophet Joseph Smith taught: 'All beings who have bodies have power over those who have not. The devil has no power over us only as we permit him. The moment we revolt at anything which comes from God, the devil takes power' [*Teachings of the Prophet Joseph Smith*, sel. Joseph Fielding Smith (1976), 181]. He also stated, 'Wicked spirits have their bounds, limits, and laws by which they are governed' [in *History of the Church*, 4:576]. So Satan and his angels are not all-powerful. . . ."

Doctrine

Verses 40–41. The Fall of Adam was a necessary part of the plan of salvation.

40 Wherefore [*this is why*], it came to pass that **the devil tempted Adam, and he partook of the forbidden fruit** and **transgressed the commandment, wherein he became subject to the will of** [*temptations of*] **the devil**, because he yielded unto temptation. [*In other words, by partaking of the forbidden fruit, Adam and Eve got things going for us on earth, including the necessary element of being subject to the temptations of the devil.*]

Because of our agency, we "own" the consequences of our own actions. So it was with Adam and

Eve, because they were taught sufficiently to be accountable for their choices. Elder John A. Widtsoe, of the Quorum of the Twelve, explained this as follows (**bold** added for emphasis):

"Such was the problem before our first parents: to remain forever at selfish ease in the Garden of Eden, or to face unselfishly tribulation and death, in bringing to pass the purposes of the Lord for a host of waiting spirit children. They chose the latter . . . This they did with open eyes and minds as to consequences. The memory of their former estates may have been dimmed, but **the gospel had been taught them during their sojourn in the Garden of Eden** . . . the choice that they made raises Adam and Eve to preeminence among all who have come on earth" (*Evidences and Reconciliations*, 193–94).

Also, from the *Encyclopedia of Mormonism* we read (**bold** added for emphasis):

"Satan was present to tempt Adam and Eve, much as he would try to thwart others in their divine missions: 'and he sought also to beguile Eve, for he knew not the mind of God, wherefore he sought to destroy the world' (Moses 4:6). **Eve faced the choice between selfish ease and unselfishly facing tribulation and death** (Widtsoe, 193). As befit her calling, **she** realized that there was no other way and **deliberately**

chose mortal life so as to further the purpose of God and bring children into the world" (*Encyclopedia of Mormonism*; see "Eve").

One more note here. Elder Joseph Fielding Smith, of the Quorum of the Twelve, discussed the topic as to whether or not Adam's transgression was a sin and whether or not Adam and Eve got cursed as follows:

Was Adam and Eve's partaking of the fruit a sin? (Genesis 3:6, Moses 4:12)

Answer

"What did Adam do? The very thing the Lord wanted him to do; and I hate to hear anybody call it a sin, for it wasn't a sin . . . I see a great difference between transgressing the law and committing a sin." (Joseph Fielding Smith, "Fall, Atonement, Resurrection, Sacrament," in *Charge to Religious Educators*, 124, quoted in *Doctrines of the Gospel Student Manual*, 20).

If it wasn't a sin, then why did the Lord "curse" them for doing it? (Gen. 3:13–19.)

Answer

He didn't curse Adam and Eve. Read Genesis 3:13–19 more carefully. He cursed the serpent (verse 14) and the ground (verse 17). In fact, the ground was cursed "for thy sake"; i.e., it was a blessing for them. Joseph

Fielding Smith explained this as follows:

"When Adam was driven out of the Garden of Eden, the Lord passed a sentence upon him. Some people have looked upon that sentence as being a dreadful thing. It was not; it was a blessing. In order for mankind to obtain salvation and exaltation it is necessary for them to obtain bodies in this world, and pass through the experiences and schooling that are found only in mortality . . . The fall of man came as a blessing in disguise, and was the means of furthering the purposes of the Lord in the progress of man, rather than a means of hindering them" (*Doctrines of the Gospel Student Manual*, 1981, 21).

41 **Wherefore** [*this is why*], **I, the Lord God, caused that he should be cast out from the Garden of Eden**, from my presence, **because of his transgression, wherein he became spiritually dead** [*cut off from the direct presence of God*], which is **the first death**, even **that same death which is the last death** [*which those who refuse to repent will suffer, meaning that they will be cut off from the presence of God forever*], which is spiritual, [*the "death" of their spirituality*] **which shall be pronounced upon the wicked when I shall say: Depart, ye cursed** [*at the final judgment—see verse 28, above*].

Next, in verse 42, the Savior quotes His Father, explaining our "probationary period" or "testing period" here on earth. First, He emphasizes the necessity of our having knowledge of the plan of salvation.

42 But, behold, I say unto you that **I, the Lord God, gave unto Adam and unto his seed** [*posterity*], **that they should not die as to the temporal death** [*physical death*], **until I**, the Lord God, **should send forth angels to declare** [*teach and explain*] **unto them repentance and redemption, through faith on the name of mine Only Begotten Son**.

Doctrine

Verse 43. Physical death is a necessary part of the plan of salvation. Without it, we could not gain resurrected bodies, nor would we have the opportunity to attain eternal life, which is exaltation, which is having our own family unit forever, becoming gods, having spirit children, and creating worlds to send them to.

43 And thus did I, the Lord God, appoint unto man the days of his probation—that by his natural death [*physical death*] he

might be raised in immortality [*living forever as resurrected beings*] unto **eternal life**, even as many as would believe;

Doctrine

Verse 44. Those who refuse to come unto Christ will still be resurrected but will be damned, which means "stopped in their progression."

44 And they that believe not unto [*will be resurrected unto*] **eternal damnation** [*those who refuse to believe in Christ will still be resurrected but will be damned*]; for **they cannot be redeemed from their spiritual fall, because they repent not**;

Next, we are taught why some people refuse to be saved.

45 For **they love darkness rather than light**, and **their deeds are evil**, and they receive their wages [*rewards*] of whom they list [*desire*] to obey. [*In other words, they choose to be rewarded by the devil.*]

Next, in verses 46 and 47, we are given powerful doctrine regarding the salvation of little children. Among other things that come from these two verses, we understand that parents have the first eight years of their children's lives to teach them without Satan's direct temptations entering into their minds. Obviously, children can be tempted and influenced by others and conditions in their environment, so parents and others need to do their best to minimize such bad influences and teach their children to walk uprightly before the Lord.

Doctrine

Verses 46–47. Little children are saved. Little children cannot commit sin. Satan is not allowed to tempt little children.

46 But behold, I say unto you, that little children are redeemed from the foundation of the world [*according to the plan that was presented in the premortal council*] **through mine Only Begotten;**

47 Wherefore, **they cannot sin,** for **power is not given unto Satan to tempt little children, until they begin to become accountable** before me;

Perhaps you have wondered if the above means that little children will be saved in the celestial kingdom's lowest degree or if they will gain exaltation. The answer is that they will receive exaltation, which is the highest degree of glory in the celestial kingdom. President Joseph F. Smith taught that they "will inherit their exaltation." (See *Gospel Doctrine*, 453.) Thus, we

understand that they will have the opportunity to choose a spouse (perhaps in the spirit world or during the Millennium), will be sealed together by proxies in temples during the Millennium, will enter celestial exaltation as husbands and wives in their own family units, and live forever as gods, having their own spirit offspring and creating worlds for them.

Next, the Lord emphasizes that because of being given this period of time during which Satan cannot directly put temptation into their children's minds (until the age of accountability, which is eight; see D&C 68:25), He expects great things of their parents!

48 For it is given unto them even as I will, according to mine own pleasure, **that great things may be required at the hand of their fathers.**

Next, we are reminded that those who are accountable and have knowledge are under obligation to repent.

49 And, again, I say unto you, that **whoso having knowledge, have I not commanded to repent?**

Finally, in this doctrinally packed section, we have a beautiful and merciful doctrine that applies, among other things, to the intellectually handicapped and others whose minds are not capable of full accountability.

Doctrine

Verse 50. The intellectually handicapped and others whose minds are not capable of full accountability are treated by the same rules and blessings as little children who are not accountable. Thus, their exaltation is assured.

50 And **he that hath no understanding, it remaineth in me to do according as it is written** [*for instance, in the Book of Mormon, Moroni, chapter 8, concerning the redemption of little children*]. And now I declare no more unto you at this time. Amen.

SECTION 30

Background

This revelation was given through Joseph Smith to David Whitmer (who was one of the Three Witnesses to the Book of Mormon), Peter Whitmer Jr. (who was one of the Eight Witnesses), and John Whitmer (who was also one of the Eight Witnesses). It was given at Fayette, New York, in September 1830, following the three-day conference of the Church that began on September 26, 1830.

As you can see in the heading to section 30 in your Doctrine and Covenants, this material was originally published as three revelations for the Book of Commandments but was later combined by the Prophet Joseph into one section for the 1835 edition of the Doctrine and Covenants. He gave some background to these revelations as follows:

"At length our conference assembled [September 26–28, 1830]. The subject of the stone previously mentioned [see Historical Background for D&C 28] was discussed, and after considerable investigation, Brother Page, as well as the whole Church who were present, renounced the said stone, and all things connected therewith, much to our mutual satisfaction and happiness. We now partook of the Sacrament, confirmed and ordained many, and attended to a great variety of Church business on the first and the two following days of the conference, during which time we had much of the power of God manifested amongst us; the Holy Ghost came upon us, and filled us with joy unspeakable; and peace, and faith, and hope, and charity abounded in our midst" (in *The Joseph Smith Papers, Histories, Volume 1: Joseph Smith Histories, 1832–1844,* ed. Karen Lynn Davidson and others [2012], 452).

As you will see in verses 1–4, David Whitmer is chastised by the Lord. From the context and historical background, we have reason to believe that he was thus scolded on account of his siding with his brother-in-law, Hiram Page, who was receiving false revelations by means of his seer stone (see notes for section 28).

As you have no doubt sensed, in the New England environment in which the Church was restored, it was quite a struggle to establish the principle of having only one person at the head of the Church; namely, the Prophet. In that same environment, it was a common belief that anyone could receive revelation for any group or individual. As the Lord instructs David Whitmer, we see firm instruction on these matters.

1 BEHOLD, I say unto you, **David**, that **you have feared man and have not relied on me** for strength as you ought.

2 But **your mind has been on the things of the earth more than on the things of me**, your Maker, and the ministry whereunto you have been called; and **you have not given heed unto my Spirit, and to those who were set over you** [*such as Joseph Smith*], **but have been persuaded by those whom I have not commanded** [*such as peer pressure from Hiram Page with his "peep stone" and family members who went along with him and opposed Joseph Smith as a result*].

Next, in verses 3 and 4, the Lord gives David some time to sort things out and ponder. Such time is often needed in order for real change to take place, especially change in one's heart and feelings about matters that have been a source of frustration and misunderstanding.

3 Wherefore [*for this reason*], **you are left to inquire for yourself at my hand** [*you need to do some praying about these matters and let Me help you understand*], and **ponder upon the things which you have received**.

4 And **your home shall be at your father's house, until I give unto you further commandments**. And you shall attend to the ministry in the church, and before the world, and in the regions round about. Amen.

Next, Peter Whitmer Jr. (David Whitmer's younger brother, born September 27, 1809, who never left the Church but remained faithful the rest of his life) is told to go on the mission to the Lamanites with Oliver Cowdery, who was called to this mission as recorded in D&C 28:8. Two others will be instructed by the Lord to join them (Parley P. Pratt and Ziba Peterson—see D&C 32). This will be a 1,500-mile journey that will start on October 18, 1830. We will do more with this mission when we study section 32.

5 Behold, I say unto you, **Peter,** that **you shall take your journey with your brother Oliver** [*on the mission to the Lamanites*]; for the time has come that it is expedient in me that you shall open your mouth to declare my gospel [*your preparation time is over and it is time for you to preach the gospel to the world*]; therefore, fear not, but give heed unto the words and advice of your brother [*Oliver Cowdery*], which he shall give you.

Next, we see some rather tender advice for missionary companions.

6 And **be you afflicted in all his afflictions, ever lifting up your heart unto me in prayer and faith, for his and your deliverance**; for I have given unto him [*Oliver Cowdery*] power to build up my church among the Lamanites;

Next, the Lord teaches another brief lesson about order and leadership in the Church. In this case, Oliver Cowdery is serving as "second elder" in the Church, next in authority to Joseph Smith, who is the "first elder" (see D&C 20:2–3).

7 And **none have I appointed to be his counselor over him in the church, concerning church matters, except it is his brother, Joseph Smith, Jun.**

8 Wherefore, give heed unto these things and be diligent in keeping my commandments, and you shall be blessed unto eternal life [*exaltation*]. Amen.

In the final revelation within this section, the Lord addresses John Whitmer, David Whitmer's older brother, born August 27, 1802. By the way, John will be called by the Lord to be the historian of the Church (D&C 47:1). He wrote 96 pages of history while actively serving in this position but refused to give them to the Church. This was one of the causes for his excommunication on March 10, 1838, in Missouri.

At the time of this revelation, John is given specific instructions to spend his time among the members of the Church in the area around Fayette, including in the home of Philip Burroughs, who was a neighbor of the Whitmers. There is no record indicating that Philip Burroughs was baptized, but his wife was (see *Doctrine and Covenants Student Manual*, 2018, chapter 13).

9 Behold, I say unto you, my servant **John,** that **thou shalt commence from this time forth to proclaim my gospel,** as with the voice of a trump.

10 And **your labor shall be at your brother Philip Burroughs', and in that region round about,**

yea, wherever you can be heard, **until I command you to go from hence** [*from here*].

11 And your whole labor shall be in Zion [*among the members of the Church*], **with all your soul**, from henceforth [*from this time forward*]; yea, you shall ever **open your mouth** in my cause, **not fearing what man can do**, for I am with you. Amen.

SECTION 31

Background

This revelation is given to Thomas B. Marsh through the Prophet Joseph Smith in September 1830 in Fayette, New York. Brother Marsh had been baptized on September 3, 1830, by David Whitmer in Seneca Lake, and had already been ordained an elder by Oliver Cowdery by the time of this revelation. He would become the first president of the Quorum of the Twelve Apostles.

Born on November 1, 1799, Thomas left his parents' home when he was 14 and wandered for many years from city to city. He finally tried to find success in the grocery business but failed. During this time, he joined the Methodist Church, but it never did seem to "take" in his soul. In the course of events, he ended up in western New York, where he heard of Joseph Smith. He

pursued his interest in Joseph Smith and his "golden book" and finally ended up at E. B. Grandin's printing shop in Palmyra, New York, where the Book of Mormon was in the process of being printed. He met Martin Harris there, who gave him proof sheets of the first sixteen printed pages of the Book of Mormon.

Martin took Thomas to the Smith home in Manchester, next to Palmyra, where Oliver Cowdery spent the better part of two days telling Thomas about Joseph Smith and the restoration of the gospel. After this, Thomas returned to Boston, Massachusetts, where he taught his family what he had learned. Soon, the family moved with him to Palmyra, where he was baptized. In section 31, verse 3, he is called on a mission.

It will be helpful, by way of perspective and hindsight as we study section 31, to know that Brother Marsh was warned in advance by the Lord in this revelation, especially in verse 9, about keeping his own household in proper order and to "revile not against those that revile." If followed, this advice may well have kept him from leaving the Church and being excommunicated on March 17, 1839. He returned to the Church, although it was much later in his life, on July 16, 1857, in Florence, Nebraska. He came to the Salt Lake Valley and later settled in Ogden, about 35 miles north of Salt Lake City, where he died in poverty and broken health in January 1866.

A rather well-known incident in the life of Thomas Marsh that reflects the need for the counsel given in verse 9, was an argument that developed between His wife, Elizabeth, and Lucinda Harris, wife of George W. Harris, over milk strippings. Sister Marsh and Sister Harris made an agreement with each other in August 1838 to exchange milk, including the last of the milk, or "strippings" from their cows (which contains more cream than the first of the milking) so that each would have the cream needed for making cheese. Apostle George A. Smith, speaking of the importance of not letting little irritations in life develop into prideful battles, used this situation of milk strippings to illustrate his point as follows:

"You may think that these small matters amount to but little, but sometimes it happens that out of a small matter grows something exceedingly great. For instance, while the Saints were living in Far West, there were two sisters wishing to make cheese, and, neither of them possessing the requisite number of cows, they agreed to exchange milk.

"The wife of Thomas B. Marsh, who was then President of the Twelve Apostles, and sister Harris concluded they would exchange milk, in order to make a little larger cheese than they otherwise could.

To be sure to have justice done, it was agreed that they should not save the strippings, but that the milk and strippings should all go together. Small matters to talk about here, to be sure, two women's exchanging milk to make cheese.

"Mrs. Harris, it appeared, was faithful to the agreement and carried to Mrs. Marsh the milk and strippings, but Mrs. Marsh, wishing to make some extra good cheese, saved a pint of strippings from each cow and sent Mrs. Harris the milk without the strippings.

"Finally it leaked out that Mrs. Marsh had saved strippings, and it became a matter to be settled by the Teachers. They began to examine the matter, and it was proved that Mrs. Marsh had saved the strippings, and consequently had wronged Mrs. Harris out of that amount.

"An appeal was taken from the Teacher to the Bishop, and a regular Church trial was had. President Marsh did not consider that the Bishop had done him and his lady justice, for they decided that the strippings were wrongfully saved, and that the woman had violated her covenant.

"Marsh immediately took an appeal to the High Council, who investigated the question with much patience, and I assure you they were a grave body. Marsh being extremely anxious to maintain the character of his wife, as he was the President of the Twelve Apostles, and a great man in Israel, made a desperate defense, but the High Council finally confirmed the Bishop's decision.

"Marsh, not being satisfied, took an appeal to the First Presidency of the Church, and Joseph and his Counsellors had to sit upon the case, and they approved the decision of the High Council.

"This little affair, you will observe, kicked up a considerable breeze, and Thomas B. Marsh then declared that he would sustain the character of his wife, even if he had to go to hell for it.

"The then President of the Twelve Apostles, the man who should have been the first to do justice and cause reparation to be made for wrong, committed by any member of his family, took that position, and what next? He went before a magistrate and swore that the 'Mormons' were hostile towards the State of Missouri.

"That affidavit brought from the government of Missouri an exterminating order, which drove some 15,000 Saints from their homes and habitations, and some thousands perished through suffering the exposure consequent on this state of affairs.

"Do you understand what trouble was consequent to the dispute about a pint of strippings?" (Talk by George A. Smith, *Journal of Discourses*, 3:283).

Remember, Brother Marsh did return to the Church, a reminder that the mercy of the Lord is constantly extended to us, but he paid a bitter price for pride and for not following the Lord's counsel regarding his family in this revelation. We are reminded that although we obtain promises from the Lord by way of blessings, including patriarchal blessings, there is still an obligation for us to do our part in order for the blessings to be fulfilled.

We will now proceed to study section 31.

1 **THOMAS**, my son [*a term of tenderness and endearment*], blessed are you because of your faith in my work.

2 Behold, **you have had many afflictions because of your family**; nevertheless, **I will bless you and your family**, yea, your little ones; and the day cometh that they will believe and know the truth and be one with you in my church.

3 Lift up your heart and rejoice, for **the hour of your mission is come**; and your tongue shall be loosed [*you will be given power and skill in teaching and preaching*], and **you shall declare glad tidings of great joy unto this generation.**

4 You shall declare the things

which have been revealed to my servant, **Joseph Smith**, Jun. You shall begin to preach from this time forth, yea, to reap in the field which is white already to be burned.

5 Therefore, thrust in your sickle with all your soul, and **your sins are forgiven you** [*you are given a fresh start*], and **you shall be laden with sheaves upon your back** [*you will have a good harvest of souls brought into the Church*], for the laborer is worthy of his hire [*the laborers in the Church must earn their keep*]. Wherefore, your family shall live.

"Sheaves," in verse 5, above, are grain stalks at harvest time, which have been bundled in order to make it easier to carry them to the threshing floor for harvest. They are symbolic of the "harvest" of souls being brought into the Lord's Church, as well as souls in the Church being brought to Christ.

6 Behold, verily I say unto you, go from them [*your family*] only for a little time, and declare my word [*preach the gospel*], and I will prepare a place for them.

7 Yea, **I will open the hearts of the people, and they will receive you**. And I will establish a church [*branches of the Church*] by your hand;

8 And **you shall strengthen them and prepare them** against the time [*for the time*] when they shall be gathered.

As mentioned previously, following the counsel of the Lord, given in verse 9, next, would have spared Thomas B. Marsh much agony.

9 **Be patient in afflictions, revile not against those that revile. Govern your house in meekness, and be steadfast.**

10 Behold, I say unto you that you shall be a physician unto the church, but not unto the world [*the worldly*], for they will not receive you.

11 Go your way whithersoever I will, and **it shall be given you by the Comforter** [*the Holy Ghost*] **what you shall do and whither you shall go.**

12 **Pray always, lest you enter into temptation and lose your reward**.

13 **Be faithful unto the end**, and lo, I am with you. **These words are not of man nor of men, but of me, even Jesus Christ**, your Redeemer, by the will of the Father [*Jesus always gives credit to the Father*]. Amen.

SECTION 32

Background

Section 32 is a revelation given through the Prophet Joseph Smith in October 1830 to Parley P. Pratt and Ziba Peterson. In verses 2 and 3, these two men will be called to join with Oliver Cowdery and Peter Whitmer Jr., who have already been called to prepare to go on a mission to the Lamanites (see D&C 28:8 and 30:5). These faithful brethren will depart on their mission from Fayette, New York, on October 18, 1830, for what will be about a 1,500-mile journey to Independence, Missouri, and a little beyond to the Indian lands. Among many others, Sidney Rigdon will be brought into the Church as a result of this mission.

Parley Parker Pratt was born April 12, 1807, and was baptized by Oliver Cowdery early in September 1830 after having read the Book of Mormon straight through. He was ordained an elder shortly after his baptism.

Some years prior to this, while still in his teens, Parley had become disgusted with society, purchased a Bible and an axe, and had moved west to the frontier, where he spent the winter alone, eating venison, studying his Bible, and reading about the Lewis and Clark expedition.

The Lord managed to get Parley back into society by having him think of a girl he liked back home in New York. He went to see her, and they married and moved back to his cabin. The frontier continued moving west, and so society caught up with him and his wife. They turned the cabin into a pleasant home and met others as they came west and settled in the area.

Among others, Parley met a Campbellite preacher and minister named Sidney Rigdon, whose views about religion matched his very nicely. Sidney felt strongly that there needed to be a return to the New Testament Church established by Christ. He also had a concern as to whether or not the proper authority to perform ordinances was even upon the earth any more. They became good friends and often studied and preached together. On this mission to the Lamanites, Parley would meet his old friend Sidney, who, by this time, was minister to a large congregation in Mentor, Ohio, not far from Kirtland. Sidney Rigdon and a large number of his congregation would be converted to the gospel, and in fact, as a result, the center of population for the Church would soon end up being in the Kirtland area. (For more information and fascinating reading, see *Autobiography of Parley P. Pratt*, edited by Parley P. Pratt Jr., Deseret Book, 1985.)

Ziba Peterson was baptized on April 18, 1830, and was probably in his late teens or early twenties at the time. He was ordained an elder not long thereafter, at least by June 1830.

As mentioned above, Parley Pratt and Ziba Peterson would be called by the Lord to join with Oliver Cowdery and Peter Whitmer Jr. in preaching to the Indians in western lands.

1 AND **now concerning my servant Parley P. Pratt**, behold, I say unto him that as I live **I will that he shall declare my gospel and learn of me, and be meek and lowly of heart**.

2 And that which I have appointed unto him is that **he shall go with my servants, Oliver Cowdery and Peter Whitmer, Jun., into the wilderness among the Lamanites**.

3 And **Ziba Peterson also shall go with them**; and **I myself will go with them and be in their midst**; and I am their advocate with the Father, and nothing shall prevail against them.

It is most comforting and encouraging, in verse 3, above, to learn that the Savior spends time with His missionaries.

Next, in verses 4 and 5, the Savior gives counsel that applies to all missionaries today; namely, to stick with the scriptures in their teaching.

4 And they shall **give heed to that which is written**, and **pretend to no other revelation**; and they shall pray always that I may unfold the same to their understanding.

5 And they shall **give heed unto these words** and **trifle not**, and I will bless them. Amen.

Here we will include a summary of this missionary journey to the Lamanites, taken from the Sunday School Gospel Doctrine teacher's supplement for 1978:

"The Lamanite missionaries commenced their work with the Cattaraugus tribe near Buffalo, New York. Here they were fairly well received, and after leaving copies of the Book of Mormon they continued their journey west. They took a slight detour to teach the gospel to a minister friend of Parley P. Pratt and his congregation near Kirtland, Ohio . . . What must have been thought to be a diversion from their mission turned out to be a major accomplishment. Here lived Sidney Rigdon, a Reformed Baptist preacher. Parley P. Pratt was apparently convinced that with the feelings and beliefs that Sidney Rigdon held he would respond to the gospel message. He was not disappointed.

"Not only Sidney Rigdon but many of his congregation joined the Church. In a short period of time, 130 people were baptized into the

Church in that area, making it the largest single group of Latter-day Saints on the earth at the time. After introducing Sidney Rigdon and the others to the gospel, the missionaries pursued their journey west toward more populous Lamanite tribes. The missionaries now numbered five, with the addition of a convert from Kirtland, Frederick G. Williams. Their missionary labors were temporarily delayed with the arrest of Parley P. Pratt [*as part of the attempt to prevent the missionaries from further successes*] . . .

"The missionaries visited the Wyandot tribe at Sandusky, Ohio. From here they commenced the most difficult part of their journey through the wilderness, to the frontier village of Independence, Missouri . . .

"Upon arriving at Independence, two of the missionaries took work to help finance their mission while the other three continued a short distance to the Indian lands. Here it appeared they would have their greatest success among the Delaware Indians. Although the Indians were at first suspicious of the missionaries because they had been exploited by some previous Christian missionaries, this suspicion was soon alleviated by the moving address delivered by Oliver Cowdery . . .

"Chief Anderson of the Delaware Tribe was very impressed and asked the missionaries to remain during the winter and teach them the Book of Mormon. Success appeared imminent, but it was shattered when other Christian missionaries influenced the Indian agent to evict the Mormon elders from Indian lands. Asked to leave, the disappointed missionaries made their way back to Independence. Here they stayed, with the exception of Parley P. Pratt, who was chosen to report their labors to Joseph Smith and to visit the Saints they had left behind in Kirtland" (Doctrine and Covenants, section 1 through 102 [Sunday School Gospel Doctrine teacher's supplement, 1978], 69–70).

SECTION 33

Background

This section is a revelation given through Joseph Smith to Ezra Thayre and Northrop Sweet in October 1830 at Fayette, New York.

As you can see, at this point in the Restoration, the Lord is gathering individuals and giving them specific instructions as they embark to spread the gospel, establish the Church, and gather Israel for the last time in preparation for the Second Coming.

Ezra Thayre was born October 14, 1791, and was 14 years older than Joseph Smith. He was converted by the preaching of Hyrum Smith and was baptized by Parley P. Pratt in October 1830. After much faithful service in building the kingdom, accompanied by periods when he was out of harmony with the leaders of the Church, Ezra Thayre refused to follow the Twelve after the martyrdom of the Prophet Joseph Smith and ultimately ended up a high priest in the Reorganized Church of Jesus Christ of Latter Day Saints. (See Susan Easton Black's *Who's Who in the Doctrine and Covenants*, pages 318–21.)

We know very little about Northrop Sweet, other than that he was born in 1802 and was baptized in October 1830. He apostatized in 1831 and formed his own church, which had six members including himself, and which never grew beyond that number.

In this revelation, we will see a number of things that apply to us. We will bold them now and then come back to do a bit more.

1 BEHOLD, I say unto you, my servants Ezra and Northrop, **open ye your ears** and **hearken to the voice of the Lord your God**, whose word is quick and powerful, sharper than a two-edged sword, to the dividing asunder of the joints and marrow, soul and spirit; and is a discerner of the thoughts and intents of the heart.

2 For verily, verily, I say unto you that ye are called to **lift up your voices** as with the sound of a trump, to declare my gospel unto a crooked and perverse generation.

3 For behold, the field is white already to harvest; and **it is the eleventh hour, and the last time that I shall call laborers into my vineyard**.

4 And **my vineyard has become corrupted every whit**; and **there is none which doeth good save it be a few**; and **they err in many instances because of priestcrafts**, all having corrupt minds.

5 And verily, verily, I say unto you, that **this church have I established** and called forth out of the wilderness.

6 And **even so will I gather mine elect** from the four quarters of the earth, even as many as will believe in me, and hearken unto my voice.

7 Yea, verily, verily, I say unto you, that **the field is white already to harvest**; wherefore, thrust in your sickles, and reap with all your might, mind, and strength.

8 **Open your mouths** and they shall be filled, and you shall become even as Nephi of old, who journeyed from Jerusalem in the wilderness.

9 **Yea, open your mouths** and

spare not, and you shall be laden with sheaves upon your backs, for lo, I am with you.

10 Yea, **open your mouths** and they shall be filled, saying: Repent, repent, and prepare ye the way of the Lord, and make his paths straight; for the kingdom of heaven is at hand;

11 Yea, repent and be baptized, every one of you, for a remission of your sins; yea, be baptized even by water, and then cometh the baptism of fire and of the Holy Ghost.

12 Behold, verily, verily, I say unto you, this is my gospel; and remember that they shall have faith in me or they can in nowise be saved;

13 And upon this rock I will build my church; yea, upon this rock ye are built, and if ye continue, the gates of hell shall not prevail against you.

14 And **ye shall remember the church articles and covenants to keep them**.

15 And **whoso having faith you shall confirm** in my church, by the laying on of the hands, **and I will bestow the gift of the Holy Ghost upon them**.

16 And **the Book of Mormon and the holy scriptures are given of me for your instruction**; and the power of my Spirit quickeneth all things.

17 Wherefore, **be faithful, praying always, having your lamps trimmed and burning, and oil with you**, that you may be ready at the coming of the Bridegroom—

18 For behold, verily, verily, I say unto you, that **I come quickly**. Even so. Amen.

We will now repeat the above verses and add some notes and commentary. As you perhaps noticed, there are a number of words and phrases that require a person to be familiar with the scriptures already in order to best understand them. We will add notes in brackets for a number of these.

1 BEHOLD, I say unto you, my servants Ezra and Northrop, **open ye your ears** [*listen carefully; pay attention*] and **hearken to the voice of the Lord your God**, whose word is quick [*living; consists of on-going revelation*] and powerful, sharper than a two-edged sword [*symbolic of being effective in all directions*], to the dividing asunder [*cutting apart*] of the joints and marrow [*literally, butchering an animal; symbolically, getting to the very essence of life*], soul and spirit;

and is a discerner [*one who knows*] of the thoughts and intents of the heart.

2 For verily, verily, I say unto you that ye are called to **lift up your voices** [*preach the gospel; let others hear your testimony*] as with the sound of a trump [*symbolic of pure, easy to understand, easy to pick out from the "noise" of the world*], **to declare my gospel unto a crooked and perverse generation** [*wicked people who pervert truth and do not walk the "strait and narrow" path*].

3 For behold, the field is white already to harvest; and **it is the eleventh hour** [*the Second Coming is getting close*], and **the last time that I shall call laborers into my vineyard** [*this is the last Restoration before the Second Coming*].

4 And **my vineyard** [*the world*] **has become corrupted every whit** [*every bit*]; and **there is none which doeth good save it be a few**; and **they err in many instances because of priestcrafts** [*in other words, they don't have the truth available to them*], all having corrupt minds.

5 And verily, verily, I say unto you, that **this church have I established** and called forth out of the wilderness [*out of apostasy*].

6 And **even so will I gather mine elect** [*among other things, those who are the noble and great from the premortal life who have been "planted" throughout the earth and will respond to the gospel message and gather with the Saints*] from the four quarters of the earth [*from all over the world*], **even as many as will believe in me, and hearken** [*listen and obey*] **unto my voice**.

7 Yea, verily, verily, I say unto you, that **the field is white already to harvest**; wherefore, thrust in your sickles [*go to work harvesting*], and reap with all your might, mind, and strength.

Next, in verses 8–10, the Lord reminds all of us of the importance of our being willing to "open our mouths" and teach the gospel. Many baptisms have been delayed because an acquaintance was afraid to "open his or her mouth." Notice that in the next three verses, the Savior says "Open your mouths" three times. In Biblical symbolism, saying something three times means that it is most important!

8 **Open your mouths** and they shall be filled [*with what you should say, by the Holy Ghost*], and you shall become even as Nephi of old [*a most powerful promise!*], who journeyed from Jerusalem in the wilderness.

9 **Yea, open your mouths** and spare not [*don't hold back*], and you shall be laden with sheaves upon your backs [*you will have much success, a bounteous "harvest" of souls; see Alma 26:5*], for lo, I am with you.

Since the phrase "laden with sheaves" is often used in scripture, we will take a moment and quote from Alma (as Ammon rejoices in the missionary work accomplished during their missions to the Lamanites) in order to explain this imagery. It deals with harvesting.

Alma 26:5

Behold, the field was ripe [*the missionary opportunities were abundant*], and blessed are ye, for ye did thrust in the sickle [*you went on missions*], and did reap [*harvest*] with your might, yea, all the day long did ye labor; and **behold the number of your sheaves** [*look at your bounteous harvest*]! And they [*the converts*] shall be gathered into the garners [*the storage bins, the Lord's barns; in other words, the celestial kingdom, to be with God forever*], that they are not wasted.

10 Yea, **open your mouths** and they shall be filled, saying: Repent, repent, and prepare ye the way of the Lord, and make his paths straight [*apply the ways of God in your lives; walk the "strait and narrow"*]; for the kingdom of heaven is at hand [*the gospel is here now and available to you*];

11 Yea, **repent and be baptized**, every one of you, **for a remission of your sins**; yea, be baptized even by water, and **then cometh the baptism of fire** [*symbolic of the Holy Ghost's burning the sin and impurities out of you*] **and of the Holy Ghost**.

12 Behold, verily, verily, I say unto you, **this is my gospel** [*repentance, baptism, gift of the Holy Ghost, faith (mentioned next, in this verse)*]; and remember that they shall have **faith in me** or they can in nowise be saved;

13 And upon this rock [*the gospel of Jesus Christ; Christ Himself*] I will build my church; yea, upon this rock ye are built [*you are building your lives upon the true Church*], and if ye continue, the gates of hell shall not prevail against you [*Satan and his evil hosts will not ultimately take you away from God*].

14 And **ye shall remember the church articles and covenants** [*the things given in section 20*] **to keep them**.

Next, these missionaries are reminded that they have the authority to confirm baptized converts as members of the Church, by the laying on of hands, and to bestow the gift of the Holy Ghost.

15 And whoso having faith **you shall confirm** in my church, **by the laying on of the hands** [*a specific, tangible ordinance, rather than just a "feeling"*], **and I will bestow the gift of the Holy Ghost upon them**.

We need to be aware that when we are confirmed and given the gift of the Holy Ghost, it still doesn't necessarily come upon us until we "receive" it and the Lord gives it to us. In other words, the gift of the Holy Ghost is not necessarily "automatic" after hands have been laid upon our heads. The Bible Dictionary, at the back of your LDS Bible, addresses this issue as follows:

Bible Dictionary under "Holy Ghost"

"The gift of the Holy Ghost is the right to have, whenever one is worthy, the companionship of the Holy Ghost."

16 And the Book of Mormon and the holy scriptures are given of me for your instruction; and the power of my Spirit quickeneth all things [*makes all things come alive in our understanding*].

17 Wherefore, **be faithful, praying always, having your lamps** [*symbolic of our lives*] **trimmed** [*a reference to the Parable of the Ten Virgins in Matthew 25:1–13*] **and burning, and oil with you, that you may be ready at the coming of the Bridegroom** [*the coming of Christ*]—

Perhaps you've noticed when you've read the Parable of the Ten Virgins, that all ten of the virgins had oil in their lamps. The problem came when five of them did not have a reserve supply of oil. These "reserves" come from faithfully living and keeping covenants. Those who do so have the "reserve" strength and spiritual stamina to remain faithful when it takes longer than they thought for the Savior to come into their lives and rescue them from difficulties.

18 For behold, verily, verily, I say unto you, that **I come quickly** [*not "I come soon"; rather, "when I come, it will be quickly, and there will be no time left for you to prepare to meet Me"*]. Even so. Amen.

SECTION 34

Background

This revelation was given through Joseph Smith to Orson Pratt, younger brother of Parley P. Pratt, in the Peter Whitmer Sr. home on November 4, 1830, at Fayette,

New York. Orson was born September 19, 1811, was baptized on his 19th birthday, September 19, 1830, and had been a member of the Church just six weeks when this revelation was given.

The Prophet recorded the following as background to this section:

"In the fore part of November, Orson Pratt, a young man nineteen years of age, who had been baptized at the first preaching of his brother, Parley P. Pratt, September 19th (his birthday), about six weeks previous, in Canaan, New York, came to inquire of the Lord what his duty was, and received the following answer [section 34]:" (*History of the Church*, 1:127–28).

Orson Pratt wrote in his journal about receiving this revelation as follows:

"In October, 1830, I traveled westward over two hundred miles to see Joseph Smith the Prophet. I found him in Fayette, Seneca County, New York, residing at the home of Mr. Whitmer. I soon became intimately acquainted with this good man, and also with the witnesses of the Book of Mormon. By my request, on the 4th of November, the Prophet Joseph inquired of the Lord for me and received the revelation published in the Doctrine and Covenants, Section 34" (Journal History, Nov. 1830, 1).

In verses 1–3, the Savior personally introduces Himself to Orson Pratt.

1 **MY son Orson, hearken and hear and behold what I, the Lord God, shall say unto you, even Jesus Christ your Redeemer;**

2 **The light and the life of the world, a light which shineth in darkness and the darkness comprehendeth it not;**

3 **Who so loved the world that he gave his own life, that as many as would believe might become the sons of God** [*"sons of God" is a scriptural term that means "exalted"; see Mosiah 5:7, D&C 76:24, D&C 25:1, Moses 6:64–68*]. **Wherefore you are my son;**

Next, in verses 4–6, the Lord issues the call for Orson Pratt to serve as a missionary.

4 And **blessed are you because you have believed;**

5 And more blessed are you [*you are going to receive additional blessings*] because **you are called of me to preach my gospel—**

6 To lift up your voice as with the sound of a trump, both long and loud, **and cry repentance unto a crooked and perverse generation, preparing the way**

of the Lord for his second coming.

Next, in verse 7, we are taught that the Second Coming of Christ is getting close.

7 For behold, verily, verily, I say unto you, **the time is soon at hand that I shall come in a cloud with power and great glory.**

Perhaps you've wondered why the scriptures say that Christ will come in a "cloud." In scriptural symbolism, "cloud" represents the presence and glory of the Lord, as in Exodus 13:21, where the Children of Israel were led by a cloud during the day, and as in Exodus 16:10, where the glory of the Lord appeared in the cloud. Also, when the Savior ascended into heaven, He was taken up into a cloud, and His Apostles were told that He would "so come in like manner as ye have seen him go into heaven." (See Acts 1:9–11. In D&C 84:5, the "cloud" is the "glory of the Lord.")

Thus, when we read that the Savior will come in clouds of glory, the clouds symbolize His presence and His glory.

Next, in verse 8, we see that, in context, the "great day" spoken of at the time of the Lord's coming will be, in effect, a "great day" of trouble for the wicked; or, in other words, a "day of great fear and trembling."

8 And it shall be **a great day** at the time of my coming, **for all nations shall tremble.**

Next, the Savior reminds Orson Pratt that many signs of the times will be fulfilled before His coming. Remember, "signs of the times" are prophecies that will be fulfilled in the last days, alerting the faithful that the Second Coming is indeed getting close.

9 But **before that great day** shall come, the **sun shall be darkened**, and the **moon** be **turned into blood**; and the **stars shall refuse their shining,** and **some shall fall,** and **great destructions await the wicked.**

Having shown Orson why the world needs the gospel so badly, the Savior now calls him on a mission.

10 Wherefore [*for this reason*], **lift up your voice and spare not** [*don't hold back*], for the Lord God hath spoken; therefore **prophesy,** and it shall be given **by the power of the Holy Ghost.**

As you are aware, the blessings promised us by the Lord have an "if," reminding us that we, too, have things to do in order for them to be fulfilled. We see this in the Lord's instruction to Orson Pratt in verse 11, next.

11 And **if** you are faithful, behold, **I am with you** until I come—

12 And verily, verily, I say unto you, I come quickly. I am your Lord and your Redeemer. Even so. Amen.

SECTION 35

Background

This revelation was given to Joseph Smith and Sidney Rigdon in the Fayette, New York, area in December 1830.

Sidney Rigdon was born on February 19, 1793, and was about 12 years older than the Prophet. Thus, at the time of this revelation, Joseph was about 25 years old and Sidney was 37. Brother Rigdon was described as being about five feet, nine and one-half inches tall, and at one time weighed about 215 pounds.

In the background to section 32, we mentioned that a highly successful and popular minister by the name of Sidney Rigdon, in Mentor, Ohio (near Kirtland), had been converted to the gospel, along with around 120–130 of his congregation. When approached by his old friend, Parley P. Pratt, and Parley's three missionary companions, who were enroute on their mission to the Lamanites, Sidney had accepted a copy of the Book of Mormon. In so doing, he told Parley not to push him, rather, that he would read the book and determine whether or not it was of God. He read it and

was converted. He was baptized on November 14, 1830.

Once converted, Sidney realized that he would lose his lucrative job as a preacher in the Kirtland area. He asked his wife, Phoebe, if she was willing to follow him in this new religion, saying, "My Dear you have followed me once into poverty, are you again willing to do the same[?]" She responded, "I have weighed the matter, I have contemplated on the circumstances in which we may be placed, I have counted the cost, and I am perfectly satisfied to follow you. [Y]ea, it is my desire to do the will of God, come life or come death" (in *The Joseph Smith Papers, Documents, Volume 1: July 1828–June 1831*, 213, note 91).

Soon after his baptism, he traveled to Fayette, New York, along with another convert from his congregation, Edward Partridge, to see the Prophet Joseph Smith. At this time, the Prophet was working on the translation of the Bible (which we know today as the Joseph Smith Translation of the Bible or the "JST"). Oliver Cowdery and John Whitmer had been serving as scribes for Joseph during this work of translation but had both been called on missions (Oliver Cowdery in D&C 28:8, John Whitmer in D&C 30:9–11), which left the Prophet without a scribe. In verse 20 of this section, Sidney Rigdon is called to fill this vacancy and serve as scribe.

As has been previously stated, Sidney was a very effective preacher and a successful minister, having attracted large numbers of people to his congregation, many of whom joined the Church when he did. Thus, in verse 4 of this section, Brother Rigdon is compared to John the Baptist, having prepared the way for Joseph Smith in the same sense that John the Baptist prepared the way for the Savior.

In verses 1 and 2, the Savior introduces Himself to Sidney Rigdon.

1 **LISTEN to the voice of the Lord your God**, even Alpha and Omega [*the "A" and "Z" of the Greek alphabet*], the beginning and the end, whose course is one eternal round [*He always uses the same gospel to bring salvation to people; the same principles of faith, repentance, baptism, gift of the Holy Ghost, ordinances, and so on*], the same today as yesterday, and forever.

2 **I am Jesus Christ**, the Son of God, who was crucified for the sins of the world, even as many as will **believe on my name** [*part of the "one eternal round" spoken of in verse 1, above*], **that they may become the sons of God** [*a scriptural term meaning attaining exaltation*], even one in me [*united in complete harmony with Christ*]

as I am one in the Father [*united, working in complete harmony with the Father*], as the Father is one in me, that we may be one.

Next, the Savior reminds Sidney that He has been watching over him and knows of his past accomplishments. He has heard his prayers (no doubt including his prayers as to whether or not the Book of Mormon is true). He informs him that He has been preparing him for the work that now lies before him.

3 Behold, verily, verily, I say unto my servant Sidney, **I have looked upon thee and thy works. I have heard thy prayers, and prepared thee for a greater work**.

Imagine how Sidney Rigdon must have felt as he heard the next words addressed to him by the Savior! The Lord tells him, in verses 4–5, next, that he has been preparing the way, just like John the Baptist did for Jesus, but Sidney wasn't aware of it. This is a reminder to all of us that we are often prompted and led by the Lord to do something without even being aware that we are being inspired.

4 Thou art blessed, for thou shalt do great things. Behold **thou wast sent forth, even as John** [*John the Baptist*], **to prepare the way before me, and before Elijah** which should come, **and thou knewest it not**.

Did you notice in verse 4, above, that the Savior also mentioned that Sidney was sent to prepare the way for Elijah to come? He appeared in the Kirtland Temple on April 3, 1836, and restored the keys of sealing (D&C 110:13–15).

Next, the Lord addresses the issue of proper priesthood authority to perform saving ordinances of the gospel.

5 Thou didst baptize by water unto repentance, **but they received not the Holy Ghost;**

6 But **now** [*as a member of the Church, with proper priesthood authority*] I give unto thee a commandment, that **thou shalt baptize by water, and they shall receive the Holy Ghost** by the laying on of the hands, even as the apostles of old.

Joseph Fielding Smith wrote about verses 5 and 6 as follows:

"The Lord told Sidney that he had looked upon him and his works, having reference to his ministry as a Baptist and later as one of the founders of the 'Disciples' with Alexander Campbell and Walter Scott. During those years the hand of the Lord was over him and directing him in the gathering of many earnest souls who could not accept the teachings of the sects of the day. His prayers in which he sought further light than the world was able to give, were now to be answered. The Lord informed him that he had been sent to prepare the way, and in the gathering of his colony and the building up of his congregation in and around Kirtland, the hand of the Lord was directing him, and the way for the reception of the fulness of truth was being prepared. It should be carefully noted that a great number of forceful, intelligent men who became leaders in the Church had been gathered by Sidney Rigdon, with the help of the Lord, in this part of the land. Without any question, the Spirit of the Lord had rested upon these men, as it did on Sidney Rigdon and Parley P. Pratt, to direct them to gather in Kirtland at that early day. When, therefore, Parley P. Pratt, Ziba Peterson and their companions came to Kirtland they found the way prepared for them through the preaching, very largely, of Sidney Rigdon, so that it was not a difficult matter for these missionaries to convince this group of the truth. While Sidney was preaching and baptizing by immersion without authority, which the Lord informed him in this revelation, yet it all resulted in good when the Gospel message reached them. These men were not only convinced and ready for baptism, but were in a condition by which the Priesthood could be given them, and this was done" (*Church History and Modern Revelation*, 1:160).

Next, the Lord gives Sidney a perspective of the magnitude and importance of the Restoration, in which Sidney would now be a significant participant.

7 And it shall come to pass that **there shall be a great work in the land,** even **among the Gentiles,** for their folly and their abominations shall be made manifest in the eyes of all people.

The word "Gentile," as used in verse 7, above, generally refers to anyone who does not have the true gospel of Jesus Christ. Let's look at the Bible Dictionary in the back of our Latter-day Saint scriptures for the definition of Gentile.

Bible Dictionary, under "Gentile"

"As used throughout the scriptures it has a dual meaning, sometimes to designate peoples of non-Israelite lineage and **other times to designate nations that are without the gospel, even though there may be some Israelite blood therein.** This latter usage is especially characteristic of the word as used in the Book of Mormon."

You may wish to read more definitions of "Gentile" in your Bible Dictionary.

8 For I am God, and mine arm is not shortened [*I haven't lost My*

power]; and **I will show miracles, signs, and wonders, unto all those who believe on my name.**

Elder Dallin H. Oaks taught about two types of miracles as follows: "First, miracles worked by the power of the priesthood are always present in the true Church of Jesus Christ. The Book of Mormon teaches that 'God has provided a means that man, through faith, might work mighty miracles' (Mosiah 8:18). The 'means' provided is priesthood power (see James 5:14–15; D&C 42:43–48), and that power works miracles through faith (see Ether 12:12; Moro. 7:37). . . .

"A second type of genuine miracle is the miracle worked through the power of faith, without specifically invoking the power of the priesthood. Many of these miracles occur in our Church, such as by the prayers of faithful women, and many occur outside it. As Nephi taught, God 'manifesteth himself unto all those who believe in him, by the power of the Holy Ghost; yea, unto every nation, kindred, tongue, and people, working mighty miracles, signs, and wonders, among the children of men according to their faith' (2 Ne. 26:13; see also 1 Ne. 7:12; James 5:15)" ("Miracles," *Ensign*, June 2001, 8–9).

Elder Oaks further explained why some miracles may not happen even when our faith is sufficient:

"I have been speaking of miracles that happen. What about miracles that don't happen? Most of us have offered prayers that were not answered with the miracle we requested at the time we desired. Miracles are not available for the asking. . . . The will of the Lord is always paramount. The priesthood of the Lord cannot be used to work a miracle contrary to the will of the Lord. We must also remember that even when a miracle is to occur, it will not occur on our desired schedule. The revelations teach that miraculous experiences occur 'in his own time, and in his own way' (D&C 88:68)" ("Miracles," 9).

As the Savior continues to give Brother Rigdon this perspective of the latter-day work that is about to come forth, He reminds him that the same miracles that followed the true Church in past dispensations will be present in this last dispensation.

9 And whoso shall ask it in my name in faith, **they shall cast out devils**; they shall **heal the sick**; they shall **cause the blind to receive their sight**, and **the deaf to hear**, and **the dumb** [*a person who is unable to talk*] **to speak**, and **the lame to walk.**

10 And the time speedily cometh that **great things are to be shown forth** unto the children of men [*in other words, there will be plenty of*

evidence for the honest in heart that the gospel is true];

The word, "faith," in verse 11, next, must be looked upon as "faith in the Lord Jesus Christ" in order to make sense in this context. The basic message is that without faith in Christ, which involves following Him and keeping His commandments, nothing is ultimately left for society except wickedness and disaster.

11 But **without faith shall not anything be shown forth except desolations upon Babylon** [*symbolic of Satan's kingdom and the intense wickedness that goes with it*], the same **which has made all nations drink of the wine of the wrath of her fornication.**

We will take a moment to analyze the phrase "drink of the wine of the wrath of her fornication," in verse 11, above. "Fornication," in this context, means perverting the ways of God and being thus involved in deep and gross wickedness. Its definition comes from "fornication," as in sexual transgression, in which the powers of procreation (which are holy, good, and proper within the protective bonds of marriage) are perverted, misused, and put to evil designs and purposes, leading to destruction of spirituality.

The word "adultery" is also often used the same way in the scriptures; that is, meaning wickedness and breaking God's commandments. We will quote from the Bible Dictionary in the back of your LDS Bible (**bold** added for emphasis):

Bible Dictionary under "Adultery"

"**Adultery.** The unlawful association of men and women. Although generally having reference to illicit activity of married persons, the scripture often does not distinguish between the married and the unmarried. While adultery is usually spoken of in the individual sense, **it is sometimes used to illustrate the apostasy of a nation or a whole people from the ways of the Lord**, such as Israel forsaking her God and going after strange gods and strange practices (Ex. 20:14; Jer. 3:7–10; Matt. 5:27–32; Luke 18:11; D&C 43:24–25). Severe penalties were given in the O.T. for adultery (Lev. 20:10); and unrepentant adulterers will suffer the judgments of God in the world to come (Heb. 13:4; Rev. 18:3–18; D&C 76:103)."

Now, with the above definitions in place, we will repeat the last half of verse 11, adding notes.

Verse 11, last half

. . . **the same** [*Satan's kingdom, Babylon*] **which has made all nations** [*the wicked throughout the world, throughout history*] **drink** [*participate in*] **of the wine** [*the temptations*] **of the wrath** [*the destructive power*] **of her** [*Satan's kingdom, the "whore of all the earth" (1 Nephi 14:10)*] **fornication** [*sin, wickedness, rebellion, etc.; Satan's intentional perversion of righteousness*].

Finally, we will just mention that Babylon was a huge, wicked city in ancient times, and thus came to be symbolic of Satan's kingdom. The city of Babylon was surrounded by 56 miles of walls that were 335 feet high and 85 feet wide. See Bible Dictionary under "Babylon or Babel."

Continuing, in verses 12 through 15, next, the Lord explains that He will use "the weak things of the world" to spread His gospel, and that they will be successful. This is a comforting reminder that all of us, regardless of intellect and educational background, can be effective instruments in the hands of the Lord.

12 And there are none that doeth good except those who are ready to receive the fulness of my gospel, which I have sent forth unto this generation [*the Restoration through the Prophet Joseph Smith*].

13 Wherefore, **I call upon the weak things of the world**, those who are unlearned and despised, to thrash the nations by the power of my Spirit;

14 And **their arm shall be my arm**, and **I will be their shield and their buckler; and I will gird up their loins** [*I will prepare them for battle*], and they shall fight manfully for me; and **their enemies shall be under their feet** [*they will succeed; the gospel will go forth*]; and **I will let fall the sword in their behalf** [*I will defend them*], and **by the fire of mine indignation** [*the Lord's righteous anger*] **will I preserve them.**

15 And **the poor and the meek shall have the gospel preached unto them**, and they shall be looking forth for the time of **my coming**, for it **is nigh at hand**—

Next, the Lord uses a parable that Sidney Rigdon no doubt knows well. Perhaps he has used it in his preaching over many years. It deals with how people can know that the Second Coming of Christ is getting close. Sidney would know what it means when the Lord says, "summer is nigh."

16 And they shall learn **the parable of the fig-tree**, for even now already **summer is nigh.**

We will take a moment and quote the parable of the fig-tree. It is a reference to the signs of the times, which will alert the faithful that the Second Coming is getting close. There are several places in scripture where this parable is given. We will use Matthew (**bold** added for emphasis):

Matthew 24:32–33

32 Now learn a parable of **the fig tree; When** his branch is yet tender, and **putteth forth leaves, ye know that summer** *is* **nigh**:

33 So likewise ye, **when ye shall see all these things, know that it** [*the Second Coming of Christ*] **is near,** *even* **at the doors.**

With this in mind, Sidney Rigdon can sense the urgency of the work to which he is now being called by the Savior; namely, to assist Joseph Smith in the spreading forth of the restored gospel of Jesus Christ. Sidney will be reminded, in verses 17–19, next, that Joseph has weaknesses too.

As you can imagine, it might be difficult for an accomplished gospel scholar and minister like Sidney Rigdon, who is 37 years old, to work under the direction of a 25-year-old Prophet whose weaknesses and inexperience he may well notice. This is certainly a reminder for all of us that our leaders are not perfect, yet we are commanded to sustain them and support them in the work to which they have been called. It is perhaps one of the greatest miracles of all that in the work of saving souls, the Lord does a perfect work with imperfect people.

17 And **I have sent forth the fulness of my gospel by the hand of my servant Joseph**; and **in weakness have I blessed him**;

18 And **I have given unto him the keys** [*he is the Prophet*] of the mystery of those things which have been sealed [*such as the Book of Mormon*], even things which were from the foundation of the world, and the things which shall come from this time until the time of my coming [*I will continue to reveal things to My Prophet*], **if he abide in me** [*if he remains faithful*], and **if not, another will I plant in his stead**.

Did you notice that we have a guarantee from the Lord, Himself, in verse 18, above, that He will not let the Prophet lead us astray? In effect, at the last of verse 18, we are taught that if the Prophet were ever to depart from the Lord, He would remove him and replace him. Thus, we are always completely safe in following our living Prophet.

Next, we feel the tenderness of the Lord as He instructs the much

older and much more experienced Sidney Rigdon to "watch over" His young Prophet.

19 Wherefore, **watch over him** that his faith fail not, and it shall be given by the Comforter, the Holy Ghost [*you will be helped in "watching over him" by the Holy Ghost*], that knoweth all things [*including Joseph's needs*].

Next, Sidney Rigdon will be called by the Lord to serve as a scribe for the Prophet as he continues to work on the Joseph Smith Translation of the Bible. Can you imagine how fascinating it would be for Sidney, who no doubt had come upon many questions about the Bible during his own studies of it, to sit in the presence of the Prophet of God and hear corrections to the Bible? Just think how many of his questions would be answered during this process!

20 And a commandment I give unto thee—that **thou shalt write** [*serve as a scribe*] **for him**; and the scriptures [*the inspired translation of the Bible*] shall be given, even as they are in mine own bosom [*the way that I gave them originally*], **to the salvation of mine own elect** [*the honest in heart, who recognize and respond to the gospel when they hear it; this also includes members of the Church as they continue to study the gospel*];

21 For **they will hear my voice,** and **shall see me,** and **shall not be asleep** [*as was the case in the parable of the 10 virgins (see Matthew 25:1–13), in other words, will not be caught unprepared*], and **shall abide the day of my coming** [*they will not be burned at the Second Coming*]; **for they shall be purified** [*by the gospel and the Atonement, such that they can be in His presence when He comes in full glory*], **even as I am pure** [*through the Atonement of Christ, we can become as pure and clean as the Savior Himself*].

Next, Sidney is instructed to remain for a time in Fayette with the Prophet and to accompany him in his travels.

22 And now I say unto you, **tarry with him,** and he shall journey with you; **forsake him not,** and surely these things [*the things spoken of in this revelation*] shall be fulfilled.

Next, Sidney is given a brief but concise lesson in what the Prophet's role is and what his own role is. Joseph can "prophesy," but Sidney is limited to "preaching" and explaining what the living Prophet has revealed.

Perhaps you've noticed that it is the same today. The role of our living Prophet includes that of revealing new doctrine, whereas, all others are limited to explaining and clarifying existing revealed doctrine. This is one of the very significant safeguards for us to prevent deception. It is often the case that apostates claim new doctrines and revelations that change existing doctrines and the current order of the Church.

23 And inasmuch as ye do not write [*when you are not involved in being a scribe for the Prophet*], behold, **it shall be given unto him** [*Joseph Smith*] **to prophesy;** and **thou shalt preach** my gospel and call on the holy prophets [*use your knowledge of the teachings of ancient prophets in the Bible and the Book of Mormon*] **to prove his words,** as they shall be given him.

Next, the Lord gives Sidney an inkling of his potential for good if he follows this counsel.

24 **Keep all the commandments and covenants** [*including baptism*] **by which ye are bound;** and **I will cause the heavens to shake for your good,** and **Satan shall tremble** and **Zion shall rejoice upon the hills** [*symbolic of getting closer to heaven and God*] **and flourish;**

"Israel," as used in verse 25, next, refers to the "house of Israel," which means "descendants of Jacob (Israel)," which means "descendants of Abraham, Isaac, and Jacob," who are the Lord's covenant people (see Abraham 2:9–11). All who come into the Church by baptism, whether direct descendants of Israel or not, become covenant Israel and are on the covenant path that leads to exaltation.

25 And **Israel shall be saved** in mine own due time [*when the time is right*]; and **by the keys** [*the keys of the priesthood*] **which I have given shall they be led**, and **no more be confounded** [*confused or stopped in their progression toward exaltation*] **at all**.

26 **Lift up your hearts and be glad**, your redemption draweth nigh.

Have you noticed how many times the Lord tells these early Saints to be happy? This is counter to a commonly held notion, especially in the New England environment of Joseph Smith's day, that truly religious people were unsmiling and sour of disposition.

27 **Fear not, little flock**, the kingdom is yours until I come [*you will run the Church until I come to rule on earth for a thousand years*]. Behold, I come quickly. Even so. Amen.

SECTION 36

Background

This revelation was given to Edward Partridge through the Prophet Joseph Smith, near Fayette, New York, in December 1830. In the background notes given in this study guide for section 35, we mentioned that Sidney Rigdon was accompanied by Edward Partridge in coming to Fayette to meet the Prophet Joseph Smith personally.

Edward Partridge was born August 27, 1793, and thus was 37 years old when he met the 25-year-old Prophet in Fayette. By profession, he was a hatter (a maker of hats), having served a four-year apprenticeship and having become a journeyman hatter in Clinton, New York, by age twenty. He eventually moved to Painesville, Ohio, where he married his wife, Lydia, and owned his own hat shop, plus other property. He was a respected family man and business owner in 1830 when Oliver Cowdery, Parley P. Pratt, Peter Whitmer Jr., and Ziba Peterson came through on their 1,500-mile mission to the Lamanites, preaching the gospel as they went along.

Lydia was baptized, but Edward was not favorably impressed at first by the message of these missionaries. However, he did send an employee to get a copy of the Book of Mormon for him to read. As he read, he was converted, but did not agree to be baptized at this point.

After traveling with Sidney Rigdon to Fayette and meeting Joseph

Smith there, he listened to a talk by the Prophet and then agreed to be baptized if Joseph would baptize him. The Prophet agreed. Edward Partridge was thus baptized on December 11, 1830, and ordained an elder four days later on December 15. Within three days of his return to his home in Ohio, near the first of February 1831, he would be called to be the first Bishop of the Church (see D&C 41:9).

The Prophet gave a brief description of Edward Partridge as follows (**bold** added for emphasis):

"In December Sidney Rigdon came to inquire of the Lord, and with him came **Edward Partridge**, the latter was **a pattern of piety**, and **one of the Lord's great men.** Shortly after the arrival of these two brethren, thus spake the Lord [*sections 35 and 36 follow*]:" (*History of the Church,* 1:128).

We will now proceed with section 36. Verse 1, next, contains two major messages for Edward Partridge. First, he is forgiven of sins, which will give him confidence to do the work of the Lord. Second, he is called to preach the gospel.

1 **THUS saith the Lord God, the Mighty One of Israel** [*another "name-title" for Christ*]: Behold, I say unto you, **my servant Edward**, that **you are blessed**, and **your sins are forgiven you**, and **you are called to preach my gospel** as with the voice of a trump;

Another part of the symbolism, which is a part of the word "trump," in verse 1, above (in addition to its being a clear, simple message, easy to pick out from the noise of the world), is that the sounding of a horn is a clear signal to gather, to rally together for a common cause. In this case, it symbolizes, among other things, the gathering of Israel in the last days.

Next, as the Lord instructs Edward to be confirmed a member of the Church, we are taught that when a worthy priesthood holder places his hands upon our head, it is the same as if the Lord were placing His hands upon our heads and blessing us. We are also taught about the benefit of receiving the gift of the Holy Ghost.

2 And **I will lay my hand upon you by the hand of my servant Sidney Rigdon**, and **you shall receive** my Spirit, **the Holy Ghost**, even **the Comforter** [*another "name-title" for the Holy Ghost, which reminds us of His role in bringing peace and comfort to us*], **which shall teach you the peaceable things of the kingdom;**

As you can see from the last part of verse 2, above, one of the major roles of the Holy Ghost is to teach us the gospel. This role of the Holy Ghost as our teacher was also emphasized in John, as follows:

John 14:26

But the Comforter, which is the Holy Ghost, whom the Father will send in my name, he shall teach you all things, and bring all things to your remembrance, whatsoever I have said unto you.

Moving forward with section 36, the Savior continues to instruct Edward Partridge about his missionary service.

3 And you shall **declare it** [*the gospel message*] **with a loud voice**, saying: **Hosanna**, blessed be the name of the most high God.

The word "Hosanna," as used in verse 3, above, is a special word for the followers of God. It is used in many settings, including in our dedication services for new temples. And President Russell M. Nelson led members of the Church worldwide in the Hosanna Shout during the April 2020 general conference. Basically, it means "Lord, save us now, please" or "Lord, grant us salvation." See Bible Dictionary, under "Hosanna." Yet another way of defining it would be "Come now, O thou great Jehovah, deliver us, O we plead!"

The waving of palm leaves (which symbolized triumph and victory in Biblical cultures) often accompanied the shouting of Hosanna. In *Mormon Doctrine*,

under "Hosanna Shout," Bruce R. McConkie mentions the waving of white handkerchiefs in conjunction with the Hosanna Shout during our temple dedications. Our waving of white handkerchiefs is symbolic of the waving of palm branches. We invite the Savior to come into our lives and save us, thus giving us triumph and victory over all things that could prevent us from returning to the presence of God forever.

Next, the Lord tells Edward Partridge that what He is saying applies to all who go forth in missionary service. As you know, this period in the restoration of the gospel was a time when the Lord inspired many of the great and noble, who had been sent to earth at that time, to join the Church and go forth in missionary service. We have been watching them "gather" for the last several sections of the Doctrine and Covenants. As they gather to the Prophet, they are then sent forth to gather others.

4 And now **this calling and commandment** give I unto you **concerning all men**—

5 That **as many as shall come before my servants Sidney Rigdon and Joseph Smith, Jun.**, embracing this calling and commandment, shall be ordained [*"ordained" can mean to be ordained to an office in the priesthood, or, it can mean "set apart" to serve*] and **sent forth**

to preach the everlasting gospel among the nations—

6 **Crying repentance**, saying: Save yourselves from this untoward [*rebellious, wicked, unruly*] generation, and come forth out of the fire [*come away from the fires of hell*], hating even the garments [*clothing*] spotted with the flesh [*symbolic of lives dirtied by the wickedness of the world*].

7 And this commandment shall be given unto the elders of my church, that **every man which will embrace it with singleness of heart may be ordained and sent forth** [*sent on missions*], even as I have spoken.

8 **I am Jesus Christ, the Son of God**; wherefore, gird up your loins [*prepare for action*] and I will suddenly come to my temple. Even so. Amen.

SECTION 37

Background

As previously mentioned, the population center of the Church began switching from New York to the Kirtland, Ohio, area with the conversion of Sidney Rigdon and over 100 members of his congregation in Mentor, Ohio, and the Kirtland, Ohio, area. In this revelation, given to Joseph Smith and Sidney Rigdon near Fayette, New York, in December 1830, the Lord instructs the Church to gather in Ohio (see especially verse 3). At this time, there were about 200 members of the Church in New York.

First, though, in verse 1, the Lord instructs Joseph and Sidney to stop work on the Joseph Smith Translation of the Bible (the JST) for now. After they relocate to Ohio, they will resume the work of translating the Bible. You may wish to look at the map of the Ohio area in the back of your Doctrine and Covenants to get oriented as to where "the Ohio" (verses 1 and 3) is. If you look at your map, "the Ohio" is basically the area in and around Kirtland.

1 BEHOLD, I say unto you that **it is not expedient** [*necessary*] in me **that ye should translate** [*translate the Bible, which will become the JST*] **any more until ye shall go to the Ohio** [*the Ohio River Valley area in northeastern Ohio*], and this because of the enemy [*including the enemies of the Church in New York*] and for your sakes [*it will be to your advantage*].

Next, though, in verse 2, the Lord instructs them not to rush off to Ohio before they have completed their current callings to preach the gospel in New York, etc.

2 And again, I say unto you **that ye shall not go until ye have preached my gospel in those parts**, and have **strengthened up the church** whithersoever it is found, and more **especially in Colesville**; for, behold, they pray unto me in much faith.

> Next, in verse 3, the Savior tells them that He wants them in Ohio by the time that Oliver Cowdery and his companions get back from their mission to the Lamanites (see D&C 28:8, 30:5, 32:1–3). These missionaries left on October 18, 1830, for their 1,500-mile missionary journey to the western frontier and points in between. (See notes for section 32 in this study guide.)

3 And again, a commandment I give unto the church, that it is expedient in me [*necessary according to My knowledge*] that they should **assemble together at the Ohio, against the time that my servant Oliver Cowdery shall return unto them**.

4 Behold, here is wisdom [*there is wisdom in following My counsel*], and let every man choose for himself [*you now have knowledge and are invited to use your agency*] until I come. Even so. Amen

SECTION 38

Background

This revelation was given through Joseph Smith at the third conference of the Church, held in Fayette, New York, on January 2, 1831. Members from the branches of the Church in various locations in New York gathered for this conference in the home of Peter Whitmer Sr. During the conference, several members asked about the commandment to move to Ohio.

As you saw in section 37, the Lord had commanded the members of the Church in the New York area to move some 300 miles west to Ohio in the dead of winter. In fact, it seems that every time they have to relocate, it is in the cold and misery of winter—New York to Kirtland, Kirtland to Missouri, Missouri to Nauvoo, Nauvoo to the Salt Lake Valley. Perhaps it was a kindness to them since it was less convenient for their enemies and persecutors to follow them under such miserable conditions.

During the conference, Joseph Smith prayed to the Lord in the presence of those in attendance and received this revelation. Here, in section 38, among other things, they will be told why they have been commanded to move to Ohio, especially in verse 32, where they are informed that they will be given the "law" in Ohio (section 42) and be "endowed with power from on high" (in the Kirtland Temple, which they will yet build).

This section is filled with powerful teachings and gospel doctrine, including much of doctrinal vocabulary. At this point in time, the Church has only been organized for about 9 months. It is a credit to the new converts to the restored gospel that the Lord is able to give them so much at this time. It would take humble and grateful people to change their ways and accept so much that was new to them.

There are many approaches that can be taken to study this section. First, we will simply go through it, using **bold** to point out several of the teachings, doctrines, and important gospel vocabulary words and phrases contained in it. This way, you can see "at-a-glance" what a precious and power-packed revelation this is for these early Saints, as well as for us. Then, we will repeat the section again, demonstrating just one approach to gospel study, and yet again, adding a number of notes.

As a suggestion, you may wish to read only the **bolded** segments this time through and see how many of them you understand.

1 THUS saith **the Lord your God**, even **Jesus Christ**, the **Great I AM, Alpha and Omega**, the **beginning and the end, the same which looked upon the wide expanse of eternity, and all** the seraphic hosts of heaven, before the world was made;

2 The same **which knoweth all things**, for **all things are present before mine eyes**;

3 **I** am the same which **spake, and the world was made**, and **all things came by me.**

4 **I am the same which have taken the Zion of Enoch into mine own bosom; and** verily, I say, **even as many as have believed in my name, for I am Christ, and in mine own name, by the virtue of the blood which I have spilt, have I pleaded before the Father for them.**

5 But behold, **the residue of the wicked have I kept in chains of darkness** until the **judgment** of the great day, which **shall come at the end of the earth**;

6 And even so will I cause the wicked to be kept, that will not hear my voice but harden their hearts, and **wo, wo, wo**, is their doom.

7 But behold, verily, verily, I say unto you that **mine eyes are upon you. I am in your midst** and ye cannot see me;

8 But the day soon cometh that ye shall see me, and know that I

am; for **the veil of darkness shall soon be rent**, and **he that is not purified shall not abide the day**.

9 Wherefore, **gird up your loins** and be prepared. Behold, **the kingdom is yours**, and the enemy shall not overcome.

10 Verily I say unto you, **ye are clean, but not all**; and there is none else with whom I am well pleased;

11 For **all flesh is corrupted before me**; and **the powers of darkness prevail upon the earth**, among the children of men, in the presence of all the hosts of heaven—

12 **Which causeth silence to reign**, and all **eternity is pained**, and the **angels are waiting** the great command **to reap down the earth**, to **gather the tares** that they may be burned; and, behold, **the enemy is combined**.

13 And now **I show unto you a mystery, a thing which is had in secret chambers, to bring to pass even your destruction** in process of time, and ye knew it not;

14 But now I tell it unto you, and ye are blessed, not because of your iniquity, neither your hearts of unbelief; for verily some of you are guilty before me, but **I will be merciful unto your weakness**.

15 Therefore, **be ye strong** from henceforth; **fear not, for the kingdom is yours**.

16 And for your salvation I give unto you a commandment, for I have heard your prayers, and the poor have complained before me, and the rich have I made, and all flesh is mine, and **I am no respecter of persons**.

17 And **I have made the earth rich**, and behold **it is my footstool**, wherefore, **again I will stand upon it.**

18 And **I hold forth and deign to give unto you greater riches**, even a land of promise, **a land flowing with milk and honey**, upon which there shall be no curse when the Lord cometh;

19 And I will give it unto you for **the land of your inheritance**, if you seek it with all your hearts.

20 And this shall be **my covenant** with you, **ye shall have it for the land of your inheritance**, and for the inheritance of your children forever, **while the earth shall stand**, and **ye shall possess it again in eternity**, no more to pass away.

21 But, verily I say unto you that

in time ye shall have no king nor ruler, for **I will be your king and watch over you**.

22 Wherefore, **hear my voice and follow me**, and you shall be a free people, and **ye shall have no laws but my laws when I come**, for **I am your lawgiver**, and **what can stay my hand?**

23 But, verily I say unto you, **teach one another** according to the office wherewith I have appointed you;

24 And **let every man esteem his brother as himself**, and **practice virtue** and **holiness** before me.

25 And again I say unto you, **let every man esteem his brother as himself**.

26 For what man among you having twelve sons, and is no respecter of them, and they serve him obediently, and he saith unto the one: Be thou clothed in robes and sit thou here; and to the other: Be thou clothed in rags and sit thou there—and looketh upon his sons and saith **I am just**?

27 Behold, this I have given unto you as a parable, and it is even as I am. I say unto you, be one; and **if ye are not one ye are not mine**.

28 And again, I say unto you that the enemy in the secret chambers seeketh your lives.

29 **Ye hear of wars in far countries**, and you say that there will soon be great wars in far countries, but **ye know not the hearts of men in your own land**.

30 I tell you these things because of your prayers; wherefore, **treasure up wisdom in your bosoms**, lest the wickedness of men reveal these things unto you by their wickedness, in a manner which shall speak in your ears with a voice louder than that which shall shake the earth; but **if ye are prepared ye shall not fear**.

31 And that ye might escape the power of the enemy, and be gathered unto me a righteous people, **without spot and blameless—**

32 Wherefore, for this cause I gave unto you the commandment that ye should go to the Ohio; and there I will give unto you **my law** [*section 42*]; and there you shall be **endowed with power from on high**;

33 And from thence, whosoever I will shall go forth among all nations, and it shall be told them what they shall do; for I have a great work laid up in store, for **Israel shall be saved**, and I will lead

them whithersoever I will, and **no power shall stay my hand**.

34 And now, I give unto the church in these parts a commandment, that certain men among them shall be appointed, and they shall be **appointed by the voice of the church**;

35 And **they shall look to the poor and the needy, and administer to their relief** that they shall not suffer; and send them forth to the place which I have commanded them;

36 And this shall be their work, to govern the affairs of the property of this church.

37 And they that have farms that cannot be sold, let them be left or rented as seemeth them good.

38 See that all things are preserved; and when men are endowed with power from on high and sent forth, all these things shall be **gathered unto the bosom of the church**.

39 And **if ye seek the riches which it is the will of the Father to give unto you**, ye shall be the richest of all people, for ye shall have **the riches of eternity**; and **it must needs be** that the riches of the earth are mine to give; but **beware of pride**,

lest ye become as the Nephites of old.

40 And again, I say unto you, I give unto you a commandment, that every man, both elder, priest, teacher, and also member, go to with his might, with the labor of his hands, to prepare and accomplish the things which I have commanded.

41 And **let your preaching be** the warning voice, every man to his neighbor, **in mildness and in meekness**.

42 And **go ye out from among the wicked**. Save yourselves. **Be ye clean that bear the vessels of the Lord**. Even so. Amen.

As mentioned above, there are many important messages and teachings contained in this section. For instance, one of the principles in section 38 that is taught often in talks and lessons in the Church by using the last phrase of verse 30 is the value of preparation. It says, "If ye are prepared ye shall not fear." This section also often serves as a springboard for a talk or sermon based on the last part of verse 42 in which the Lord says, "Be ye clean that bear the vessels of the Lord."

Yet another vital message is that of avoiding being abrasive and harsh in our gospel teaching and preaching. This counsel is given in verse 41, wherein the Lord counsels to "let your preaching be the warning voice . . . in mildness and in meekness."

There are also many approaches to studying the scriptures. We will take time to demonstrate one here. It is to select a theme or topic and then go through a section or block of scripture picking out only those verses, words, and phrases that tie in with that theme. For instance, section 38 lends itself well to picking out what we might call "the ten commandments of good teaching." We will take the time and space here to repeat verses 22 to 42 again, but this time we will only **bold** those passages associated with effective and inspired teaching. You will no doubt be able to pick out other words and phrases that could be added to these rules of good teaching. We will place numbers from one to ten by each of these "commandments" and list ten of them, starting with verse 22. You will see that many of these suggestions for effective teaching have to do with the preparation of the teacher himself or herself.

Just one more bit of explanation. You will no doubt observe that some of the **bolded** items are not really well connected with the verses or context in which they lie. One of the points we are making is that under the direction of the Holy Ghost, you may find much inspiration and help as you read the scriptures, which does not really relate to the context of the passage of scripture at hand. Rather, words and concepts "jump out at you" in answer to your own specific needs. Such is the case demonstrated by these "ten commandments" of effective teaching.

So, suppose you are a newly called teacher in one of the church classes and are searching in the scriptures for help in fulfilling your new calling. By the help of the Spirit, these ten items "jump out at you." Remember, our first item is found in verse 22.

22 Wherefore, **hear my voice and follow me [*1. You must be following Christ yourself.*]**, and you shall be a free people, and ye shall have no laws but my laws when I come, for I am your lawgiver, and what can stay my hand?

23 But, verily I say unto you, **teach one another [*2. Some of the most important teaching in the Church is done when we teach and strengthen each other in gospel knowledge and principles and living.*]** according to the office wherewith I have appointed you;

24 And **let every man esteem his brother as himself [*3. We must respect those we teach.*]**, and **practice virtue and holiness before me [*4. You must have a deep, inner commitment to live the gospel.*]**.

25 And again I say unto you, let every man esteem his brother as himself.

26 For what man among you having twelve sons, and is no respecter of them, and they serve him obediently, and he saith unto the one: Be thou clothed in robes and sit thou here; and to the other: Be thou clothed in rags and sit thou there—and looketh upon his sons and saith I am just?

27 Behold, this I have given unto you as a parable, and it is even as I am. I say unto you, **be one [5.** *You must try to avoid contention in order to have the Spirit.*]; and if ye are not one ye are not mine.

28 And again, I say unto you that the enemy in the secret chambers seeketh your lives.

29 Ye hear of wars in far countries, and you say that there will soon be great wars in far countries, but ye know not the hearts of men in your own land.

30 I tell you these things because of your prayers; wherefore, **treasure up wisdom in your bosoms [6.** *Study the scriptures; learn wisdom and use wisdom in your teaching.*]**, lest the wickedness of men reveal these things unto you by their wickedness, in a manner which shall speak in your ears with a voice louder than that which shall shake the earth; but if ye are prepared ye shall not fear.

31 And that ye might escape the power of the enemy, and be gathered unto me a righteous people, without spot and blameless—

32 Wherefore, for this cause I gave unto you the commandment that ye should go to the Ohio; and there I will give unto you my law; and there you shall be endowed with power from on high;

33 And from thence, whosoever I will shall go forth among all nations, and it shall be told them what they shall do; for I have a great work laid up in store, for Israel shall be saved, and I will lead them whithersoever I will, and no power shall stay my hand.

34 And now, I give unto the church in these parts a commandment, that certain men among them shall be appointed, and they shall be appointed by the voice of the church;

35 And they shall look to the poor and the needy, and administer to their relief that they shall not suffer; and send them forth to the place which I have commanded them;

36 And this shall be their work, to govern the affairs of the property of this church.

37 And they that have farms that cannot be sold, let them be left or rented as seemeth them good.

38 See that all things are preserved; and when men are endowed with power from on high and sent forth, all these things shall be gathered unto the bosom of the church.

39 And if ye seek the riches which it is the will of the Father to give unto you, ye shall be the richest of all people, for ye shall have the riches of eternity; and it must needs be that the riches of the earth are mine to give; but **beware of pride [7. *Pride alienates others, including students, in a hurry.*]**, lest ye become as the Nephites of old.

40 And again, I say unto you, I give unto you a commandment, that every man, both elder, priest, teacher, and also member, go to with his might, with the labor of his hands, to **prepare [8. *Good teaching requires much preparation and study on your part.*]** and accomplish the things which I have commanded.

41 And **let your preaching be** the warning voice, every man to his neighbor, **in mildness and in meekness [9. *Be pleasant with your students and try not to alienate them.*]**.

42 And go ye out from among the wicked. Save yourselves. **Be ye clean that bear the vessels of the Lord [10. *strive to be clean in mind and body in order to teach effectively.*]**. Even so. Amen.

Having done the above, we will now go through the entire section again, adding several notes and teaching comments. Beginning with verse 1, next, we find three of the many "name-titles" for Jesus Christ. We will list them here:

1. **The Lord God**—the God of this world, under the direction of the Father.

2. **The Great I AM**—"I AM" means "the Living God" (as opposed to idols, etc., that are, of course, inanimate objects). "I AM" is another name for Jehovah, the name by which Christ is often known, as the God of the Old Testament. (See Exodus 3:14.)

3. **Alpha and Omega**—the first and last letters of the Greek alphabet, symbolizing that Jesus is in charge of all things under the direction of the Father. It also means that He was there in premortality, "in the beginning" helping us, and that He

will be there for us at the end on Judgment Day as our Advocate (see D&C 45:3–5), making those who are worthy completely free from sin and worthy to enter celestial glory.

In verses 1–6, after giving three of His names by which He is known in scripture, the Savior describes a number of His powers and functions.

1 THUS saith **the Lord your God,** even **Jesus Christ, the Great I AM, Alpha and Omega**, the beginning and the end [*in charge of all things under the direction of the Father*], the same [*the Creator*] which looked upon the wide expanse of eternity, and all the seraphic hosts of heaven [*including all the premortal spirit children of the Father*], before the world was made;

We will include a quote from the *Doctrine and Covenants Student Manual*, 1981, page 75, which gives added insight for the phrase "seraphic hosts of heaven" in verse 1, above:

"Seraphs are angels who reside in the presence of God. . . . it is clear that seraphs include the unembodied spirits of pre-existence, for our Lord 'looked upon the wide expanse of eternity, and all the seraphic hosts of heaven, before the world was made' (D&C 38:1). Whether the name seraphs also applies

to perfected and resurrected angels is not clear."

"In Hebrew the plural of seraph is seraphim" (*Mormon Doctrine*, 702–3).

2 The same which **knoweth all things**, for **all things are present before mine eyes**;

3 I am **the same which spake** [*I am the Creator*], **and the world was made**, and **all things came by me.**

Next, Jesus informs these early Saints that He is the God who caused the City of Enoch to be taken up to heaven.

4 **I am the same which have taken the Zion of Enoch into mine own bosom**; and verily, I say, even as many as have believed in my name, for I am Christ, and in mine own name, by the virtue of the blood which I have spilt, have I pleaded before the Father for them.

Verse 4, above, regarding the City of Enoch, is particularly significant in this context, because in December 1830, shortly before this conference of the Church (January 2, 1831), the Savior had revealed the seventh chapter of the Book of Moses (which is in the Pearl of Great Price). In Moses 7:69, the City of Enoch (Zion) is taken up. Can you imagine the excitement of these new members as they received the Book of Moses, which restores so much that had been left out of the Bible? And then to hear the Lord refer specifically to this as He introduced Himself to them during this conference, in this revelation!

By the way, the Lord began revealing the chapters of Moses to the Prophet Joseph Smith, which we have in the Pearl of Great Price, in June 1830 (as you can see if you look at the headings for each chapter of Moses) and finished by revealing Moses, chapter 8, in February 1831.

Next, the Lord continues telling these Saints about Himself and what He does. He refers to the captivity of wickedness, in which the rebellious find themselves, and to the final judgment. In a very real sense, the Savior is bearing witness here also that He respects agency so completely that He allows people to get themselves into real trouble.

5 But behold, the residue of the wicked have I kept in **chains of darkness** until the judgment of the great day, which shall come at the end of the earth [*after the Millennium is over, and after the "little season" (see D&C 88:111–14) that comes after the Millennium*];

Behaviors that lead up to being held captive in the "chains of darkness" are described in Alma as follows (**bold** added for emphasis):

Alma 12:11

And they that will harden their hearts [*reject the gospel*], to them is given the lesser portion of the word **until they know nothing concerning his mysteries** [*the basics of the gospel, which are "mysteries" to those who know nothing about Christ*]; and then they are taken captive by the devil, and led by his will down to destruction. Now **this is what is meant by the chains of hell**.

6 And even so will I cause the wicked to be kept, that will not hear my voice [*who refuse to pay attention to the gospel when it is brought to them*] but harden their hearts, and wo, wo, wo [*"wo" means, basically, "deep trouble"*], is their doom.

Next, the Savior assures these Saints that He knows their needs and is among them.

7 But behold, verily, verily, I say unto you that **mine eyes are upon you. I am in your midst** and ye cannot see me;

Perhaps you've seen or heard of the "all seeing eye" carved on the east center tower of the Salt Lake Temple. The symbolism of that, according to the architect, Truman O. Angell, is that of verse 7, above; namely, that the Lord can see us and knows how best to help and support us.

Also, concerning the statement, "I am in your midst and ye cannot see me," in verse 7, above: I recall, as a young missionary, attending the mission home in Salt Lake City where the Church Office Building now stands. Part of our training consisted of a meeting in an upper room of the Salt Lake Temple with Elder Harold B. Lee. He invited us to ask any questions we wanted to ask. A meeting similar to this is described by Elder Lee in the following quote (**bold** added for emphasis):

"I have a session with the missionary groups as they go out, in the temple, where they are permitted to ask intimate questions that wouldn't be proper to be discussed elsewhere. They sometimes ask, 'Could you tell us a certain place in the temple where the Savior has been seen?' My answer is, 'Keep in mind that this is the house of the Lord; this is the place that we try to keep as pure and holy and sacred as any building we have. This is the most likely place He would come when He comes on earth. Don't ask for a certain place because He has walked these halls. How do you know but what He is here in your midst?'" (In Conference Report, British Area Conference 1971, 135–36; or *Ensign*, Nov. 1971, 12–13).

8 But **the day soon cometh** [*the*

Second Coming] **that ye shall see me**, and know that I am; for the veil of darkness shall soon be rent [*torn aside*], and **he that is not purified shall not abide the day** [*will not survive the Second Coming*].

In reference to the phrase "shall not abide the day," in verse 8, above, we will quote four verses contained in the scriptures that teach that the wicked will be burned by the glory of the coming Christ. We will add **bold** for emphasis.

D&C 5:19

For a desolating scourge shall go forth among the inhabitants of the earth, and shall continue to be poured out from time to time, if they repent not, until the earth is empty, and the inhabitants thereof are **consumed away and utterly destroyed by the brightness of my coming**.

2 Nephi 12:10, 19, 21

10 O ye wicked ones, enter into the rock, and hide thee in the dust, for the fear of the Lord and **the glory of his majesty shall smite thee.**

19 And they shall go into the holes of the rocks, and into the caves of the earth, for the fear of the Lord shall come upon them and **the glory of his majesty**

shall smite them, when he ariseth to shake terribly the earth.

21 To go into the clefts of the rocks, and into the tops of the ragged rocks, for the fear of the Lord shall come upon them and the majesty of **his glory shall smite them**, when he ariseth to shake terribly the earth.

Next, the Savior counsels to be prepared and explains that nothing can prevent faithful Saints from attaining celestial glory.

9 Wherefore, **gird up your loins** [*prepare for action*] and **be prepared.** Behold, **the kingdom is yours,** and **the enemy shall not overcome.**

In verse 10, next, the Lord encourages these humble members by telling them, in effect, that He is pleased with them even though they still have a distance to go in terms of gospel progress.

10 Verily I say unto you, **ye are clean, but not all**; and **there is none else with whom I am well pleased;**

Next, in verses 11 to 12, we are given a brief lesson on "cause and effect," in this case being why communication from heaven to the inhabitants of the earth has been curtailed so severely.

11 For **all flesh is corrupted before me**; and **the powers of darkness prevail upon the earth,** among the children of men, in the presence of all the hosts of heaven [*perhaps meaning "as witnessed by all the hosts of heaven"*]—

12 **Which causeth silence to reign** [*which cuts off communication from heaven to the inhabitants of the earth*], and **all eternity is pained** [*all the beings in heaven are very concerned about this*], and **the angels** [*the destroying angels*] **are waiting the great command to reap down the earth** [*to harvest the wicked on earth*], **to gather the tares** [*the wicked*] that they may be burned; and, behold, **the enemy is combined** [*all the forces of evil are combining together to destroy the spirituality of the inhabitants of the earth*].

Verse 12, above, is a reference to the parable of the Wheat and the Tares, given in Matthew 13:24–30, 36–43, and explained in D&C 86:1–7. Since an understanding of this parable is a must for understanding verse 12, above, we will take time to review the parable here. We will use a quote from *New Testament Made Easier*, part 1, 28–29.

The Parable of the Wheat and the Tares (Matthew 13:24–30, 36–43)

24 Another parable put he forth unto them, saying, The kingdom of heaven is likened unto a man [*Christ, see verse 37*] which sowed [*planted*] good seed [*faithful followers of Christ, verse 38*] in his field [*the world, verse 38*]:

25 But while men slept, his enemy [*the devil, verse 39*] came and sowed tares [*wicked people, verse 38*] among the wheat [*faithful members of the Church*], and went his way.

A tare is a weed that looks very much like wheat while it is growing. Often, the roots of tares intertwine with the roots of the wheat while both are growing.

26 But when the blade was sprung up, and brought forth fruit, then appeared the tares also.

27 So the servants of the householder [*Christ*] came and said unto him, Sir, didst not thou sow [*plant*] good seed [*wheat*] in thy field? from whence then hath it tares [*where did the tares come from*]?

28 He said unto them, An enemy hath done this. The servants said unto him, Wilt thou then that we go and gather them up [*would you like us to weed out the tares now*]?

29 But he said, Nay [*No*]; lest [*for fear that*] while ye gather up the tares, ye root up also the wheat with them.

There are several messages here in verse 29. One message might be that there are usually insincere and unrighteous members living among the righteous members of wards and branches of the Church. Another message could be that each of us has some "tares" in our own lives and personalities, and we would be wise to weed them out as our righteous attributes mature. Jacob 5:65–66 in the Book of Mormon reminds us that as the good in people grows, the bad can gradually be cleared away. See also D&C 86:6.

30 Let both grow together until the harvest: and in the time of harvest I will say to the reapers [*harvesters, angels in verse 39*], Gather ye together first the tares [*the wicked*], and bind them in bundles to burn them: but gather the wheat [*the righteous*] into my barn [*my kingdom*].

D&C 86:7 changes the order of the harvesting, as does JST Matt. 13:29. The correct order is that the wheat is gathered first, then the tares are gathered, bundled (bound), and burned. This is significant doctrinally, because it indicates that, at the Second Coming, the righteous will be taken up first (D&C 88:96), and then the wicked will be burned.

36 Then Jesus sent the multitude away, and went into the house: and his disciples came unto him, saying, Declare [*explain*] unto us the parable of the tares of the field [*verses 24–30*].

37 He answered and said unto them, He that soweth [*plants*] the good seed [*wheat; righteousness*] is the Son of man [*Christ; Son of Man of Holiness—see Moses 6:57*];

38 The field is the world; the good seed are the children of the kingdom [*faithful members of the Church; the righteous*]; but the tares are the children of the wicked *one* [*followers of Satan; the wicked*];

39 The enemy that sowed them is the devil; the harvest is the end of the world; and the reapers [*harvesters*] are the angels.

40 As therefore the tares [*the wicked*] are gathered and burned in the fire; so shall it be in the end of this world [*the wicked will be burned at the Second Coming*].

41 The Son of man [*Christ*] shall send forth his angels, and they shall gather out of his kingdom all things that offend, and them which do iniquity [*the wicked*];

42 And shall cast them into a furnace of fire [*the burning at the Second Coming—see note above*]: there shall be wailing [*bitter crying*] and gnashing [*grinding*] of teeth.

43 Then shall the righteous shine forth as the sun [*symbolic of celestial glory for the righteous Saints*] in the kingdom of their Father. Who hath ears to hear, let him hear [*those who are spiritually in tune will understand what I am saying*].

We will now continue with section 38. In verse 13, next, the Savior alerts these New York Saints that their enemies are in the process of hatching some plots and conspiracies to bring about their destruction.

13 And **now I show unto you** a mystery, **a thing which is had in secret chambers, to bring to pass even your destruction in process of time,** and ye knew it not;

There is a rather encouraging message for all of us in verse 14, next. It is that even though we have our weaknesses and faults, the Lord still extends mercy to us and blesses us, which fosters growth and progress in people whose hearts are honest.

14 But now I tell it unto you, and **ye are blessed**, not because of your iniquity, neither your hearts of unbelief; for verily **some of you are guilty before me, but I will be merciful unto your weakness**.

15 Therefore, **be ye strong from henceforth** [*use this as an opportunity to improve from now on*]; **fear not** [*fear is the opposite of faith and is an enemy to personal progress*], **for the kingdom is yours** [*if we allow God to keep working with us, we will ultimately "make it"*].

Next, at the end of verse 16, we are reminded that the Lord loves all people, and everyone, regardless of their status or financial state, will be given a completely fair chance to understand and accept or reject the gospel by using their individual agency (whether on earth or in the postmortal spirit world).

Doctrine

Verse 16. God is completely fair to all people.

16 **And for your salvation I give unto you a commandment** [*through which you can obtain all the blessings I have in store for you—*]

see verses 23–27, below], for I have heard your prayers, and the poor have complained before me, and the rich have I made, and all flesh is mine, and **I am no respecter of persons** [*the Lord treats all people fairly, and we must also if we expect to become like Him; this is part of the "setting" for the commandments given in verses 23–27*].

As we study verses 17–20, next, we will use a quote from the *Doctrine and Covenants Student Manual*, 1981, page 77, as background to what we will be taught.

"To better understand the Lord's promise in these verses, one needs to understand that the earth was designed by the Lord as a place of habitation for his children. The earth itself reflects the level of life that is lived on it. Elder Bruce R. McConkie described four of the stages the earth has gone through and will yet go through:

"Edenic earth. Following its physical creation, the earth was pronounced good. It was a terrestrial or paradisiacal state. There was no death either for man or for any form of life, and 'all the vast creation of animated beings breathed naught but health, and peace, and joy.' (2 Ne. 2:22; *Voice of Warning*, 89–91.)

"Telestial earth. When Adam fell, the earth fell also and became a mortal sphere, one upon which worldly and carnal people can live. This condition was destined to continue for a period of 6,000 years, and it was while in this state that the earth was baptized in water. (D&C 77:6–7, 12; *Man: His Origin and Destiny*, 415–36, 460–66.)

"Terrestrial earth. 'We believe . . . that the earth will be renewed and receive its paradisiacal glory.' (Tenth Article of Faith.) Thus, the earth is to go back to the primeval, paradisiacal, or terrestrial state that prevailed in the days of the Garden of Eden. Accompanying this transition to its millennial status the earth is to be burned, that is, receive its baptism of fire. It will then be a new heaven and a new earth, and again health, peace, and joy will prevail upon its face. (D&C 101:23–32; Isa. 65:17–25; Mal. 3:1–6; 4:1–6; *Man: His Origin and Destiny*, 380–97.)

"Celestial earth. Following the millennium plus 'a little season' (D&C 29:22–25), the earth will die, be resurrected, and becoming like a 'sea of glass' (D&C 130:7), attain unto 'its sanctified, immortal, and eternal state.' (D&C 77:1–2.) Then the poor and the meek—that is, the godfearing and the righteous—shall inherit the earth; it will become an abiding place for the Father and the Son, and celestial beings will possess it forever and ever. (D&C 88:14–26, 111.) (*Mormon Doctrine*, 211.)

"The statement that there will be no curse on the land when the Lord comes (see D&C 38:18) refers to the terrestrial earth during the Millennium, whereas the promise that the Saints will possess it during eternity (see D&C 38:18) reflects the earth's eventual celestial state."

With the above quote from the *Doctrine and Covenants Student Manual* as background, we will proceed with verses 17–20.

17 And **I have made the earth rich** [*there is plenty for all; it is man's mismanagement that causes problems; compare with D&C 104:17*], and behold it is my footstool [*this earth is Christ's; see D&C 130:9, end of verse*], wherefore, **again I will stand upon it** [*during the Millennium, and then on through eternity, after it is celestialized; see D&C 130:9–11*].

18 And **I hold forth** [*have in mind*] **and deign** [*plan*] **to give unto you greater riches, even a land of promise, a land flowing with milk and honey** [*the very best; the celestial earth*], **upon which there shall be no curse** [*during the Millennium, when the earth is once again a paradise, like it was before the Lord cursed it at the time of the Fall of Adam*] **when the Lord cometh** [*for the Millennium*];

19 And **I will give it unto you for the land of your inheritance,**

if you seek it with all your hearts [*you will obtain celestial glory and live on this earth forever, as it becomes your celestial planet; see D&C 130:9*].

Doctrine

Verse 20. The righteous will live on this earth forever.

20 And this shall be my covenant with you, ye shall have it for the land of your inheritance, and **for the inheritance of your children forever,** while the earth shall stand, and **ye shall possess it again in eternity** [*when the earth is celestialized*], no more to pass away.

21 But, verily I say unto you that in time [*during the Millennium*] ye shall have no king nor ruler, for **I will be your king and watch over you.**

22 Wherefore, **hear my voice and follow me** [*listen carefully to what the Savior says as He describes the commandment mentioned in verse 16, above, which, if followed, will gain you all the millennial and celestial blessings described above*], and **you shall be a free people,** and **ye shall have no laws but my laws when I come** [*during the Millennium*], **for I am your lawgiver,** and what can stay my hand [*what can stop the hand of the Lord*]?

Next, the Savior describes some of the components of the "commandment" that He said He would give these Saints in verse 16, above.

23 But, verily I say unto you, **teach one another** according to the office wherewith I have appointed you;

24 And **let every man esteem his brother as himself, and practice virtue and holiness before me.**

25 And again I say unto you, **let every man esteem his brother as himself.** [*This is basically the "golden rule."*]

Next, using a parable, Jesus reasons with all of us, the point being that He is completely fair with all people. Thus, all who earn exaltation will be given it.

26 For **what man among you having twelve sons,** and is no respecter of them [*is not prejudiced for or against any of them*], **and they serve him obediently,** and he saith unto the one: Be thou clothed in robes [*symbolic of royalty; in other words, exaltation*] and sit thou here; and to the other: Be thou clothed in rags [*received much less than he earned*] and sit thou there—and looketh upon his sons and saith I am just [*completely fair*]?

27 Behold, **this I have given unto you as a parable**, and it is even as I am [*the parable represents the Savior and that He would never deprive any people of what they have earned*]. I say unto you, **be one** [*live in harmony; be united in righteousness; avoid contention*]; and **if ye are not one ye are not mine**.

Now, the Lord returns to the topic of dangers that are developing against the Saints at this time in New York.

28 And again, I say unto you that **the enemy in the secret chambers** [*secret plots against you are developing*] **seeketh your lives**.

29 **Ye hear of wars in far countries**, and you say that there will soon be great wars in far countries, **but ye know not the hearts of men in your own land** [*there are dangers you are unaware of in your home areas*].

Next, we are reminded that our prayers can be effective in helping save us from dangers.

30 **I tell you these things because of your prayers**; wherefore, treasure up wisdom in your bosoms [*take what the Lord says to heart*], lest the wickedness of men reveal these things unto you by their wickedness [*otherwise, you will find out the hard way*], in a manner which shall speak in your ears with a voice louder than that which shall shake the earth; **but if ye are prepared ye shall not fear**.

Among the many lessons that could be taught from the last phrase of verse 30, above, is the fact that if we are prepared to meet the Savior, we need not fear anything else, even death at the hand of enemies. The righteous have a type of peace about them that the wicked can't have or understand.

As the Lord continues, and with the above background in place, He answers the question on the minds of many members who are attending this conference of the Church. The question? Why were they commanded to move to Ohio (see D&C 37:3). The answer? Verses 31–33. In fact, the Lord gives five specific reasons for having the Saints move to Ohio.

31 And **(1) that ye might escape the power of the enemy**, and **(2) be gathered unto me a righteous people, without spot and blameless—**

32 Wherefore, **for this cause** [*for this reason*] **I gave unto you the commandment that ye should go to the Ohio**; and **(3) there I will give unto you my law** [*section 42*]; and **(4) there you shall be endowed with power from on**

high [*in the Kirtland Temple, after it is built; see especially D&C 110, which records the visits of Christ, Moses, Elias, and Elijah in the Kirtland Temple*];

33 And **(5) from thence, whosoever I will shall go forth among all nations** [*from Kirtland, Ohio, missionaries will go out to all the world*], and it shall be told them what they shall do; for I have a great work laid up in store, for **Israel shall be saved**, and I will lead them whithersoever I will, and **no power shall stay my hand**.

Next, instructions are given concerning the immediate problems faced by the members as they deal with leaving homes and property, or, in some cases, by those who do not have the means to move to Ohio.

34 And now, I give unto the church in these parts [*New York*] a commandment, that **certain men among them shall be appointed**, and they shall be appointed by the voice of the church [*they are to be sustained by the members of the Church*];

35 And **they shall look to the poor and the needy, and administer to their relief that they shall not suffer**; and send them forth to the place which I have commanded them;

36 And this shall be their work, **to govern the affairs of the property of this church**.

Next, the Savior teaches a lesson in priorities. If material things are standing in the way of following the commandments of God, leave material concerns and possessions behind.

37 And **they that have farms that cannot be sold, let them be left or rented** as seemeth them good.

38 See that all things are preserved; and **when men are endowed with power from on high and sent forth, all these things shall be gathered unto the bosom of the church** [*perhaps meaning that the time will come that the Church will prosper and much more than what is being left behind by members in New York will be owned by the Church and its members*].

In verse 39, we are reminded that true riches are the things of eternal value. These include the gospel, exaltation, and eternal families. However, in the last half of verse 39, it is noted that the wealth of the world is also available to members, but if they gain it, they must beware of pride.

39 And if ye seek **the riches which it is the will of the Father to give unto you**, ye shall be the richest of all people, for ye shall

have **the riches of eternity**; and it must needs be that **the riches of the earth are mine to give; but beware of pride**, lest ye become as the Nephites of old [*who were destroyed by the "prosperity, pride, wickedness, destruction" cycle of apostasy*].

In Jacob 2:18–19, we are taught the proper order of priorities regarding financial success and being loyal to God as follows (**bold** added for emphasis):

Jacob 2:18–19

18 But **before ye seek for riches, seek ye for the kingdom of God.**

19 And **after ye have obtained a hope in Christ** [*after you have proven that you can live the gospel no matter what*] **ye shall obtain riches, if ye seek them**; and **ye will seek them for the intent to do good**—to clothe the naked, and to feed the hungry, and to liberate the captive, and administer relief to the sick and the afflicted.

Before we leave verse 39, above, we will do just a bit more with the last warning, "beware of pride, lest ye become as the Nephites of old." Throughout the Book of Mormon, we see what is commonly known as the "cycle of apostasy." It is basically that when people prosper, they become prideful. Then they forget God and turn wicked. Then He has to humble them. After they get humbled by pestilence and destruction, they repent and start being righteous. As they become more righteous, they prosper. As they prosper, they become prideful and forget God. And the whole cycle starts over.

Of course, there is an easy way to avoid going round and round through this cycle. It is to remain humble and faithful to God when prosperity comes your way, and follow the pattern in Jacob 2:18–19, above. By doing this, you can avoid the "cycle of apostasy" and continue to enjoy the blessings of the gospel *and* prosperity.

As we return to section 38, we see in verse 40, next, that the Lord commands the priesthood holders as well as all members to do everything they can to fulfill the commandments He has given them in this section.

40 And again, I say unto you, **I give unto you a commandment**, that **every** man, both **elder, priest, teacher,** and also **member,** go to with his might, with the labor of his hands, to **prepare and accomplish the things which I have commanded.**

As all of us fulfill the commandment to share and spread the gospel, we are reminded that it is to be done in kindness and wisdom.

The Lord also reminds us in verse 41, next, that often the most likely candidates for joining the Church are our neighbors (those around us, whether in our neighborhoods, at work, school, etc.). Often, the best and most effective "preaching" is a good example.

41 And let your preaching be the warning voice, every man to his neighbor, in mildness and in meekness.

Perhaps you've noticed the symbolism in verse 42, next, in the actual moving of these Saints from New York to Ohio. They must physically flee the wicked in New York who are plotting to destroy them, just as all of us must "go out from among the wicked" in terms of avoiding the filth and spiritual corruption of our day in order to "save ourselves."

42 And go ye out from among the wicked. Save yourselves. Be ye clean that bear the vessels of the Lord. Even so. Amen.

The final phrase of verse 42, above, is a reference to the priesthood holders of ancient Israel whose responsibilities included handling the bowls, containers, instruments, and such that were used in the sacrifices and rituals of the Law of Moses. They were expected to keep themselves clean and worthy to officiate in these rites.

So also today are those who officiate in the ordinances of salvation expected to keep themselves clean and worthy of doing the work of the Lord. In a broader sense, this applies to all members, who are expected to be worthy examples to all as they "bear" the gospel of Jesus Christ to all the world.

SECTION 39

Background

Sections 39 and 40 go together. They both deal with an elderly Methodist minister named James Covel. Section 39 was given to him in Fayette, New York, through the Prophet Joseph Smith, on January 5, 1831. Section 40 was given to Joseph Smith and Sidney Rigdon on the following day, January 6, 1831, regarding him.

Up until the 2013 edition of the Doctrine and Covenants, his name was given as "James Covill," but recent research, including that for *The Joseph Smith Papers* publications, shows that his name was "James Covel." You can see this by comparing the headings to section 39 in earlier editions and the 2013 edition. Also, recent research tells us that he was a Methodist minister rather than a Baptist minister as indicated in the heading of section 39 in previous editions of the Doctrine and Covenants

James had been a Methodist minister for about forty years at the time of his becoming interested in the Church. There is disagreement among historians as to when he was born, so we will simply note that he was probably somewhere near seventy years old when he received the revelation given him by the Lord as recorded in section 39. John Whitmer, one of the Eight Witnesses to the Book of Mormon, said that James Covel "covenanted with the Lord that he would obey any commandment that the Lord would give through his servant Joseph" (in *The Joseph Smith Papers, Documents, Volume 1: July 1828–June 1831*, 233–34).

In section 39, James Covel is told that if he listens to the Lord and gets baptized, he will receive blessings beyond his fondest dreams (see verse 10). He is called to do a great work, even at his age, and is told that he has tremendous potential for good. The sad thing about him is that he accepted the Church with great enthusiasm, and then, within a short time, rejected it and the marvelous promises of the Lord to him. We don't even know for sure if he was baptized.

There is much for us to learn from this revelation, including some significant comparisons to our patriarchal blessings, which we will point out along the way. As is the case with several previous revelations in the Doctrine and Covenants that were given to individuals or groups,

the Lord will first introduce Himself to James Covel, particularly in verses 1–5. The Savior will use several Biblical words and phrases with which this Methodist minister is no doubt familiar.

1 HEARKEN and **listen to the voice of him who is** from all eternity to all eternity, **the Great I AM** [*Exodus 3:14; one of the many names for Jehovah, the God of the Old Testament, the premortal Jesus Christ*], even **Jesus Christ—**

2 **The light and the life of the world** [*compare with John 8:12, etc.*]; **a light which shineth in darkness and the darkness comprehendeth it not** [*John 1:5*];

3 **The same which came in the meridian of time** unto mine own, **and mine own received me not** [*compare with Isaiah 53:3*];

4 But **to as many as received me, gave I power to become my sons** [*John 1:12*]; and even so will I give unto as many as will receive me, power to become my sons [*a scriptural phrase meaning exaltation; see Mosiah 5:7, D&C 76:24, etc.*].

5 And verily, verily [*listen very carefully*], I say unto you, **he that receiveth my gospel receiveth me** [*compare with John 13:20*]; **and he that receiveth not my gospel receiveth not me.**

Next, the Savior teaches James Covel and all of us a brief course in some gospel basics, emphasizing the role of the gift of the Holy Ghost in teaching us throughout our lives after baptism and confirmation.

6 And **this is my gospel—repentance** and **baptism** by water, and **then cometh** the baptism of fire and **the Holy Ghost**, even the Comforter, **which showeth all things, and teacheth the peaceable things of the kingdom**.

Next, in verses 7–9, the Savior gets very personal with James Covel, encouraging him and telling him of concerns He has had about him in the past.

7 And now, behold, I say unto you, my servant James, I have looked upon thy works and **I know thee**.

8 And verily I say unto thee, **thine heart is now right before me at this time**; and, behold, **I have bestowed great blessings upon thy head** [*a reminder that God likes to bless all His children, whether members of the Church or not; perhaps referring also to the blessing of hearing the true gospel just recently*];

9 Nevertheless, thou hast seen great sorrow, for **thou hast rejected me many times because of pride and the cares of the world** [*a clear warning about weaknesses that have caused problems*

for him in the past. Unfortunately, they will yet lead him away from the great blessings that are now ready for him, as explained in verses 10–23].

You will see the word "if" in both verses 10 and 11. Patriarchal blessings often have "ifs" in them, meaning that the promised blessings are conditional upon the person's faithfulness and obedience to the Lord. President Harold B. Lee spoke of "iffy" blessings as follows:

"I sat in a class in Sunday School in my own ward one day, and the teacher was the son of a patriarch. He said he used to take down the blessings of his father, and he noticed that his father gave what he called 'iffy' blessings. He would give a blessing, but it was predicated on . . . 'if you will cease doing that.' And he said, 'I watched these men to whom my father gave the "iffy" blessings, and I saw that many of them did not heed the warning that my father as a patriarch had given, and the blessings were never received because they did not comply.'

"You know, this started me thinking. I went back into the Doctrine and Covenants and began to read the 'iffy' revelations that have been given to the various brethren in the Church. If you want to have an exercise in something that will startle you, read some of the warnings that were given through the Prophet Joseph Smith to Thomas B. Marsh, Martin Harris, some of the Whitmer brothers, William E. McLellin—warnings which, had they heeded, some would not have fallen by the wayside. But because they did not heed, and they didn't clear up their lives, they fell by the wayside, and some had to be dropped from membership in the Church" (In Conference Report, Oct. 1972, 130; or *Ensign,* Jan. 1973, 107–8).

We will look at these "ifs" and at the great blessings promised to James Covel if he would follow the counsel of the Lord. But first, as mentioned previously in this study guide, the Doctrine and Covenants contains many "doctrines," but there are just a few "covenants." The covenants we make with God pertain to obtaining celestial glory and exaltation in the highest degree of glory thereof. These covenants include baptism and confirmation, sacrament, ordination to Melchizedek Priesthood for men, endowments, and celestial marriage. They also include covenants we make with the Lord through our priesthood leaders during temple recommend interviews, including payment of tithing, sabbath observance, and keeping the Word of Wisdom.

Two of these "covenants" mentioned now by the Savior to James Covel are those of baptism and

confirmation, in verse 10. They are given in conjunction with the "ifs" in this revelation.

Covenants

Verse 10. Baptism and Confirmation

10 But, behold, the days of thy deliverance are come [*you can be delivered from this pride, etc., now*], **if thou wilt hearken to my voice**, which saith unto thee: Arise and **be baptized**, and **wash away your sins**, calling on my name, and you shall **receive my Spirit** [*receive the gift of the Holy Ghost*], **and a blessing so great as you never have known.**

11 And **if thou do** this, **I have prepared thee for a greater work** [*you will be able to do even greater things than you have in the past*]. **Thou shalt preach the fulness of my gospel** [*rather than the incomplete gospel you have been preaching in the past*], which I have sent forth in these last days, **the covenant** [*that the Lord made that He would gather Israel in the last days*] which I have sent forth **to recover** [*gather*] **my people**, which are of **the house of Israel** [*the twelve tribes of Israel*].

12 And it shall come to pass that **power shall rest upon thee; thou shalt have great faith**, and **I will**

be with thee and go before thy face [*among other things, the Lord will prepare people to hear Brother Covel's preaching*].

13 **Thou art called to labor in my vineyard** [*the earth*], **and to build up my church**, and to **bring forth Zion** [*help establish the restored Church*], that it may rejoice upon the hills and flourish.

Next, the Lord specifically tells James Covel that He does not want him to do missionary work in the eastern United States. While we do not know, we have to wonder if that is where James Covel wanted to go, perhaps because he would be among former members of his congregations and other friends. Whatever the case, he is told to gather with the Saints in Ohio, which means that he would be leaving basically everything and starting over new. This was a real test of faith and of the depth of his commitment to the covenant (see background notes above) he had made with the Lord before this revelation, to follow whatever instructions were given him through Joseph Smith.

14 Behold, verily, verily, I say unto thee, **thou art not called to go into the eastern countries** [*eastern United States and perhaps Canada*], **but thou art called to go to the Ohio.**

Next, the Savior gives James

Covel an idea of the great blessings that await him if he will gather with the Saints to Ohio.

15 And **inasmuch as** [*if*] **my people shall assemble themselves at the Ohio**, I have kept in store **a blessing such as is not known among the children of men**, and **it shall be poured forth upon their heads** [*among other things, they will build the Kirtland Temple and receive the tremendous blessings of the visits of the Savior, Moses, Elias, and Elijah; see D&C 110*]. And **from thence men shall go forth into all nations.**

Next, we are given an insight into the fact that people have agency, and if they use it to be disobedient, the Lord is obligated by eternal laws to punish them if they continue to refuse to repent, even though kind and merciful Saints continue to pray that He will hold back the punishments.

16 Behold, verily, verily, I say unto you, that **the people in Ohio call upon me in much faith, thinking I will stay my hand in judgment** [*thinking that I will hold back the punishments*] upon the nations, **but I cannot deny my word.**

Nephi was taught this same lesson (verse 16, above) early on in his life, at a time when he prayed fervently for Laman and Lemuel.

We will quote this short scripture block from First Nephi and use **bold** to point out this lesson:

<u>1 Nephi 2:17–21</u>

17 And **I spake unto Sam, making known unto him the things which the Lord had manifested unto me by his Holy Spirit**. And it came to pass that **he believed in my words**.

18 But, behold, **Laman and Lemuel would not hearken unto my words; and being grieved** because of the hardness of their hearts **I cried unto the Lord for them**.

19 And it came to pass that **the Lord spake unto me**, saying: **Blessed art thou, Nephi, because of thy faith**, for thou hast sought me diligently, with lowliness of heart.

20 And **inasmuch as ye shall keep my commandments, ye shall prosper**, and shall be led to a land of promise; yea, even a land which I have prepared for you; yea, a land which is choice above all other lands.

21 And **inasmuch as thy brethren shall rebel against thee, they shall be cut off from the presence of the Lord**.

As we continue with section 39, the Savior informs James Covel that there is one way in which the judgments (punishments) of God can be held back. If people like him accept the gospel and spread it successfully to others (verse 17), then the punishments will not come (verse 18).

17 Wherefore **lay to** [*go to work*] **with your might** and call faithful laborers into my vineyard [*bring others into the Church to join you*], that it [*the "vineyard," the inhabitants of the world*] may be pruned [*have false doctrines, false philosophies, pride, wickedness, etc. cut out of their thinking and their lives*] for the last time [*before the Second Coming of Christ*].

18 And **inasmuch as** [*if*] **they do repent and receive the fulness of my gospel, and become sanctified** [*made clean, pure, and fit to be in the presence of God*], **I will stay mine hand in judgment**.

Yet again, in verse 19, next, James Covel is instructed to go forward in missionary work. Imagine how the skills and knowledge he gained as a Methodist minister for over forty years would bless him and those he would teach in this effort!

19 Wherefore, **go forth** [*in this missionary work*], **crying with a loud voice, saying: The kingdom of heaven is at hand** [*the true gospel*

is now available to you]; crying: Hosanna! [*see notes about "Hosanna" after D&C 36:3 in this study guide*] blessed [*praised*] be the name of the Most High God.

If James Covel will obey the Lord's counsel to him in this revelation, he will be baptized and ordained to the Melchizedek Priesthood such that as he goes forth preaching, he can baptize converts and confirm them, giving them the gift of the Holy Ghost. He will then have proper priesthood authority to do this (which he did not have formerly, as a minister). In other words, the Lord is clearly telling him what his potential is, much the same as He tells us our potential in our patriarchal blessings.

20 Go forth baptizing with water [*by immersion*], preparing the way before my face for the time of my coming [*the Second Coming*];

In verse 21, next, we are reminded that no one knows the "day or the hour" when Christ will come in power and glory to start His millennial reign on earth, which will last for a thousand years.

Doctrine

Verse 21. No man knows the day or hour of the Second Coming.

21 For the time is at hand [*the Second Coming is getting close*];

the day or the hour no man knoweth; but it surely shall come.

It is interesting that some people can't seem to accept what the Lord said in verse 21, above, at face value. For instance, some teach that our living prophets, the First Presidency, and the Quorum of the Twelve Apostles will know the day and hour but will just not be allowed to tell us. Elder M. Russell Ballard of the Twelve addressed this issue in a BYU devotional on March 12, 1996, as follows (**bold** added for emphasis):

"Now with the Lord's help I would like to speak to you about a subject that is on a lot of people's minds. My intention is not to alarm or to frighten, but to discuss the significant and interesting times in which we are now living, to consider some of the events and circumstances we can anticipate in the future and to suggest a few things we can all do to fortify ourselves and our families for the challenges and trials that will surely come into all of our lives at one time or another."

Elder Ballard continued, reading from Matthew 24:3–7, reading and commenting, and then paused, saying, "I want to pause here for a moment and suggest to you, if you haven't been aware, that some of these things seem to be occurring with ever-increasing regularity. If you measured the natural disasters that have occurred in the world during the last 10 years and plotted that year-by-year, you would see an acceleration. The earth is rumbling, and earthquakes are occurring in 'divers places.' Human nature being what it is, we don't normally pay much attention to these natural phenomena until they happen close to where we are living. But when we contemplate what has happened during the past decade, not only with earthquakes but also with regards to hurricanes, floods, tornadoes, volcanic eruptions, and the like, you would see an accelerating pattern.

"So, can we use this scientific data to extrapolate that the Second Coming is likely to occur during the next few years, or the next decade, or the next century? Not really. I am called as one of the apostles to be a special witness of Christ in these exciting, trying times, and **I do not know when He is going to come again**. As far as I know, none of my brethren in the Council of the Twelve or even in the First Presidency knows. And I would humbly suggest to you, my young brothers and sisters, that **if we do not know, then nobody knows**, no matter how compelling their arguments or how reasonable their calculations."

We will now finish our study of section 39. In verse 22, next, we see, among other things, the commonly used phrase in the Church "in time and eternity," which means on this earth as well as throughout eternity.

22 And he that receiveth these things [*the blessings and message of the restored gospel*] receiveth me [*receives Christ*]; and they shall be gathered unto me **in time and in eternity**.

23 And again, it shall come to pass that on as many as ye shall baptize with water, **ye shall lay your hands, and they shall receive the gift of the Holy Ghost**, and shall be looking forth for the signs of my coming [*the signs of the times*], and shall know me.

24 Behold, **I come quickly** [*can mean that when the Savior comes, it will be quickly, worldwide, rather than meaning He is coming right away*]. Even so. Amen.

SECTION 40

Background

Section 40 goes together with section 39. Please refer to the background notes for section 39 in this study guide. By way of summary, James Covel, who had been a Methodist minister (see *Doctrine and Covenants Student Manual*, 2018 edition, chapter 14) for about forty years, had approached joining the Church with great enthusiasm, covenanting with the Lord that he would do whatever he was told to do by way of revelation through the Prophet

Joseph Smith. As a result, he was given the revelation contained in section 39 at Fayette, New York, on January 5, 1831, three days after the third general conference of the Church was held there.

But on the next day, James Covel abruptly left Fayette. This was no doubt a big disappointment to Joseph Smith and Sidney Rigdon. On this day, January 6, 1831, the Lord gave the revelation recorded in section 40 to Joseph and Sidney, explaining why James went back on his word and that He, the Lord, would handle the matter from that point on. The Prophet recorded the following regarding James Covel at this point:

"As James Covill [*Covel*] rejected the word of the Lord, and returned to his former principles and people, the Lord gave unto me and Sidney Rigdon the following revelation, explaining why he obeyed not the word: [D&C 40]" (*History of the Church,* 1:145).

Among the lessons we might learn from this very brief revelation is that agency plays a pivotal role in our lives. The Lord teaches us what our potential is, and then we use our agency to accept or reject it. This is the case with many patriarchal blessings. We are shown our potential and given great blessings and promises. But we are free to reject those blessings, and some do, as did James Covel.

Some people might be inclined to ask why the Lord would pronounce such a marvelous revelation upon this man, James Covel, when He knew that he would reject the gospel. The answer comes in the form of an important principle; namely that **the Lord does not withhold present blessings from us because of our future misbehavior** (see *Doctrine and Covenants Student Manual*, 1981, page 306).

Yet another lesson for us here might be that we should not try to second guess such people to any great degree; rather, we should hope and pray for the best for them and turn the matter over to the Lord (verse 3).

One more observation. As you know, it is possible for a person's heart to be right before the Lord, which opens the door to view available blessings. The door can be closed again through a change of heart. This principle is taught clearly in the parable of the sower (Matthew 13:3–9, 18–23).

1 BEHOLD, verily I say unto you, that **the heart of my servant James Covill was right before me**, for he covenanted with me [*before the revelation was given; see notes for section 39 in this study guide*] that he would obey my word.

2 And **he received the word with gladness**, but straightway [*right away*] Satan tempted him;

and the **fear of persecution** and the **cares of the world caused him to reject the word.**

3 Wherefore he broke my covenant, and **it remaineth with me to do with him as seemeth me good** [*in other words, the Lord will handle it from here*]. Amen.

SECTION 41

Background

This revelation was given to the members of the Church on February 4, 1831, at Kirtland, Ohio. It is the first of many revelations in the Doctrine and Covenants given in Ohio. By now a large number of members had gathered in Ohio according to the commandment of the Lord (D&C 37:1, 3; 38:32) with the central location for gathering being in Kirtland.

The Prophet Joseph Smith and his wife, Emma, along with Sidney Rigdon and Edward Partridge, arrived in Kirtland from New York in early February, a few days before this revelation was given. This 300-mile trip in winter cold was difficult for Emma, who had already moved seven times since their marriage four years before. To make things more trying, she was just recovering from a month of being sick and was six months pregnant with twins. Joseph Knight provided a good sleigh to make the trip a bit more bearable for her.

Upon their arrival, the sleigh stopped in front of a store owned by Newel K. Whitney. What followed is another testimony of the prophetic calling of Joseph Smith:

"About the first of February the sleigh pulled up in front of Newel K. Whitney's store in Kirtland. Joseph sprang from the sleigh and entered the store. 'Newel K. Whitney! Thou art the man,' he exclaimed, extending his hand cordially, as if to an old and familiar acquaintance. 'You have the advantage of me,' replied the merchant, . . . I could not call you by name as you have me.' 'I am Joseph the Prophet,' said the stranger smiling. 'You've prayed me here, now what do you want of me?' Joseph explained to the amazed merchant that back in New York he had seen Newel in a vision praying for him to come to Kirtland. The Whitney's received Joseph and Emma Smith with kindness and invited them to live temporarily with them. During the next several weeks the Smiths 'received every kindness and attention which could be expected, and especially from Sister Whitney'" (*Church History in the Fulness of Times*, 2003, 90–91).

The Prophet Joseph Smith gave background to this section as follows:

"The branch of the Church in this part of the Lord's vineyard, which had increased to nearly one hundred members, were striving to do the will of God, so far as they knew it, though some strange notions and false spirits had crept in among them. With a little caution and some wisdom, I soon assisted the brethren and sisters to overcome them. The plan of 'common stock,' which had existed in what was called 'the family,' whose members generally had embraced the everlasting Gospel, was readily abandoned for the more perfect law of the Lord; and the false spirits were easily discerned and rejected by the light of revelation.

"The Lord gave unto the Church the following: [D&C 41]" (*History of the Church*, 1:146–47).

One other bit of background for understanding this section, as well as section 42, is that many of the members in the Kirtland area had been living a type of "united order" prior to joining the Church. In other words, they had all things in common. Joseph Smith had succeeded in persuading these new converts to leave this order and told them that the Lord would reveal to them the proper form of the law of consecration. A first step toward the proper order of the Lord with respect to this matter was the appointing of the first bishop of the Church (Edward Partridge in verse 9).

As we begin our study of the verses in this section, we find some strong wording against hypocrites in verse 1. It is a strong contrast between faithful Saints, who do their best to obey the Lord, and others, who claim membership in the Church, but who do not really want to live the gospel.

Doctrine

Verse 1. The Lord loves to bless us.

1 HEARKEN and hear, O ye my people, saith the Lord and your God, ye whom I delight to bless with the greatest of all blessings, ye that hear me [*listen and obey*]; and **ye that hear me not** [*disregard the Lord's commandments*] **will I curse, that have professed my name** [*who claim to be members but don't follow the Lord's commandments; in other words, you who are hypocrites*], with the heaviest of all cursings.

You may recall that in the New Testament, the Savior was patient toward all kinds of sinners, with the exception of those who were deeply hypocritical, whom He called "whited sepulchres." We will quote this verse from Matthew:

Matthew 23:27

Woe unto you, scribes and Pharisees, **hypocrites!** for ye are like unto **whited sepulchres** [*whitewashed graves*], which indeed **appear beautiful outward, but are within** [*inside*] **full of dead** *men's* **bones, and of all uncleanness.**

Next, in verses 2–3, the Lord teaches these members the importance of unity and harmony as preparation to receive revelation from God.

2 Hearken, O ye elders of my church whom I have called, behold **I give unto you a commandment**, that ye shall **assemble yourselves together to agree upon my word;**

3 And **by the prayer of your faith ye shall receive my law** [*which will be given in section 42*], **that ye may know how to govern my church and have all things right before me.**

It is hoped that from this section you will sense the importance of what the Lord reveals in section 42. The main purpose of section 41 is to prepare the Lord's people for what He gives them in section 42, which is often referred to as "The Law."

Next, especially in verse 5, you can sense that with the added knowledge that is coming to these early members of the Church, comes a considerable increase in accountability.

4 And I will be your ruler when I come [*for the Millennium*]; and behold, I come quickly, and **ye**

shall see that my law is kept.

5 **He that receiveth my law and doeth it, the same is my disciple** [*a true follower of Christ*]; and **he that saith he receiveth it and doeth it not, the same is not my disciple, and shall be cast out from among you** [*otherwise, they will ruin the harmony and unity that are required in order to become a "Zion" people*];

6 **For it is not meet** [*good, proper, appropriate*] **that the things which belong to the children of the kingdom** [*faithful members of the Church*] **should be given to them that are not worthy** [*in other words, who are hypocritical and don't desire to live the gospel*], or to dogs [*a reference to Matthew 7:6*], or the pearls [*precious gospel truths, experiences, testimonies, etc.*] to be cast before swine [*see Matthew 7:6*].

In verses 7–8, the members are instructed to provide a house for Joseph and Emma. They will build a small frame house for them on the Isaac Morley farm. The instruction for Sidney Rigdon's accommodations is a bit different, perhaps because he is from this area and has many friends and acquaintances. In fact, Leman Copley, who has a large farm about 20 miles east of Kirtland, will offer to provide a house and supplies for Sidney and his wife, Phoebe.

7 And again, it is meet [*needed*] that my servant **Joseph Smith, Jun., should have a house built, in which to live and translate** [*resume work on translating the Bible, which will become the Joseph Smith Translation of the Bible or JST*].

8 And again, it is meet that my servant **Sidney Rigdon should live as seemeth him good**, inasmuch as he keepeth my commandments.

Next, Edward Partridge is called to be the first Bishop of the Church. Among other things, this is an important step in setting things in place for the Saints to live the law of consecration. Notice that the law of "common consent," established in section 26, is now firmly in place in the Church.

9 And again, I have called my servant **Edward Partridge**; and I give a commandment, that he should be appointed [*sustained*] **by the voice of the church** [*by the members of the Church, according to the law of common consent*], and ordained a **bishop unto the church**, to leave his merchandise [*his hat shop (he was a journeyman hatter) and other property*] and to **spend all his time in the labors of the church**;

10 **To see to all things** as it shall be appointed unto him **in my laws** in the day that I shall give them.

As you can see, based on the end of verse 10, above, the Lord is telling these members that He is going to reveal much more concerning the law of consecration and other laws and principles soon.

As this revelation draws to a close, the Lord pays Edward Partridge a high complement.

11 And this because **his heart is pure before me**, for **he is like unto Nathanael of old** [*see John 1:47*]**, in whom there is no guile** [*deceit; selfish motives; fraud*].

Finally, the Lord warns them not to change or alter the words of this revelation. We are also reminded that accountability increases with additional knowledge of the gospel. Of course, it is worth it, but it is good to be reminded of the consequences of sinning against knowledge. See D&C 82:3.

12 **These words are given unto you, and they are pure before me**; wherefore, **beware how you hold them**, for they are to be answered upon your souls [*you are accountable to live by them*] in the day of judgment. Even so. Amen.

SECTION 42

Background

This revelation is often referred to as "The Law" or "The Law of the Lord." If you truly want to be a disciple of Christ and return to the Father in celestial exaltation, you will follow the principles and commandments taught in this section.

The Lord promised the Saints that He would give them this "law" in Ohio (D&C 38:32).

Given through the Prophet Joseph Smith, section 42 was actually revealed in two parts. Verses 1 through 72 were given February 9, 1831, in the presence of twelve elders (see heading to section 42 in your Doctrine and Covenants), and verses 74–93 were given two weeks later on February 23, 1831. Verse 73 was added by Joseph Smith at the time the Doctrine and Covenants was published. (See institutes of religion, *Doctrine and Covenants Student Manual*, 2018, chapter 16.)

An additional quote from the 2018 *Doctrine and Covenants Student Manual*, chapter 16, is also helpful in setting the stage for our study of section 42:

"In obedience to the Lord's direction recorded in Doctrine and Covenants 41:2–3, the Prophet Joseph Smith and 12 elders met on February 9, 1831, and prayed together, supplicating the Lord to manifest

His law. These brethren asked the Lord about five matters in particular: (1) whether the various communities of Saints should gather in one place or remain separate for the time being, (2) what the Lord's law was for governing and regulating the Church, (3) how they should care for the families of those called to serve as missionaries, (4) how the Saints living under the principles of consecration should deal with nonmembers, and (5) what preparations should be made in order to care for the Saints arriving from the East (see *The Joseph Smith Papers, Documents, Volume 1: July 1828– June 1831,* ed. Michael Hubbard MacKay and others [2013], 246–47, note 42). In response, the Prophet received the revelation recorded in Doctrine and Covenants 42:1–72, which is a composite of revelatory answers that the Lord gave these brethren in answer to the first three questions. The revealed answers to the remaining questions were not published as part of the Doctrine and Covenants.

"Two weeks later, on February 23, 1831, Joseph Smith and seven elders approached the Lord with further questions regarding implementing the law of the Church. The Lord gave these men additional direction. This direction was added to the February 9 revelation and is now recorded in Doctrine and Covenants 42:74–93. The additional details recorded in Doctrine and Covenants 42:73 were added later by the Prophet at the time the

Doctrine and Covenants was prepared for publication. It is important to note that the Prophet Joseph Smith occasionally made changes or additions to previously recorded revelations to clarify or reflect additional understanding that the Lord had revealed. These inspired revisions illustrate the ongoing nature of revelation and are an example of the right and authority of the Lord and His prophet to amend or clarify previous revelation."

This section is one of the great doctrinal revelations from the Lord, as explained by Apostle George Q. Cannon as follows:

"Altogether this was a most important revelation. It threw a flood of light upon a great variety of subjects and settled many important questions. Faithful men and women were greatly delighted at being members of a Church which the Lord acknowledged as His own, and to which He communicated His word through his inspired Prophet as he did at this time" (*Life of Joseph Smith*, Good Press, 109).

We will first go through this section, using **bold** to point out several of the many "laws" contained in this revelation. Then we will repeat the verses, doing yet more as we go through again.

The Law of Listening and Obeying

1 **HEARKEN**, O ye elders of my church, who have assembled yourselves together in my name, even Jesus Christ the Son of the living God, the Savior of the world; inasmuch as ye believe on my name and **keep my commandments**.

2 Again I say unto you, **hearken** and **hear** and **obey** the law which I shall give unto you.

The Law of Unity

3 **For verily I say, as ye have assembled yourselves together according to the commandment wherewith I commanded you, and are agreed** as touching this one thing, and have asked the Father in my name, even so ye shall receive.

The Law of Missionary Work

4 Behold, verily I say unto you, I give unto you this first commandment, that **ye shall go forth in my name**, every one of you, excepting my servants Joseph Smith, Jun., and Sidney Rigdon.

5 And I give unto them a commandment that they shall go forth for a little season, and it shall be given by the power of the Spirit when they shall return.

6 And ye shall **go forth in the power of my Spirit**, preaching my gospel, **two by two**, in my

name, lifting up your voices as with the sound of a trump, declaring my word like unto angels of God.

7 And ye shall go forth **baptizing with water, saying: Repent ye, repent ye, for the kingdom of heaven is at hand**.

8 And from this place ye shall go forth into the regions westward; and inasmuch as ye shall find them that will receive you ye shall **build up my church in every region—**

9 **Until the time shall come when it shall be revealed unto you from on high, when the city of the New Jerusalem shall be prepared**, that ye may be gathered in one, that ye may be my people and I will be your God.

The Law of Replacing Church Leaders Who Transgress

10 And again, I say unto you, that my servant Edward Partridge shall stand in the office whereunto I have appointed him. And it shall come to pass, that **if he transgress another shall be appointed in his stead**. Even so. Amen.

The Law of No Secret Ordinations

11 Again I say unto you, that **it shall not be given to any one to go forth to preach my gospel, or to build up my church, except he be ordained by some one who has authority, and it is known to the church that he has authority and has been regularly ordained by the heads of the church**.

The Law of Teaching

12 And again, the elders, priests and teachers of this church shall **teach the principles of my gospel, which are in the Bible and the Book of Mormon**, in the which is the fulness of the gospel.

13 And they shall **observe the covenants and church articles** [*Doctrine and Covenants, section 20*] **to do them**, and **these shall be their teachings, as they shall be directed by the Spirit**.

The Law of Obtaining the Spirit in Order to Teach

14 And **the Spirit shall be given unto you by the prayer of faith**; and **if ye receive not the Spirit ye shall not teach**.

The Law of Continuing Revelation and Additional Scripture

15 And **all this ye shall observe to do as I have commanded concerning your teaching, until the fulness of my scriptures is given**.

16 And as **ye shall lift up your voices by the Comforter, ye shall speak and prophesy as seemeth me good**;

17 For, behold, **the Comforter knoweth all things, and beareth record of the Father and of the Son**.

The Law of Avoiding Going to Telestial Glory

18 And now, behold, I speak unto the church. **Thou shalt not kill** [*intentional murder*]; and he that kills shall not have forgiveness in this world, nor in the world to come.

19 And again, I say, thou shalt not kill; but he that killeth shall die.

20 **Thou shalt not steal**; and he that **stealeth and will not repent** shall be cast out.

21 Thou shalt **not lie**; he that lieth and will **not repent** shall be cast out.

22 Thou shalt **love thy wife with all thy heart, and shalt cleave unto her and none else**.

23 And **he that looketh upon a woman to lust after her shall deny the faith, and shall not have the Spirit**; and **if he repents not he shall be cast out**.

24 **Thou shalt not commit adultery**; and he that **committeth adultery, and repenteth not, shall be cast out**.

25 **But he that has committed adultery and repents with all his heart, and forsaketh it, and doeth it no more, thou shalt forgive**;

26 But if he doeth it again, he shall not be forgiven, but shall be cast out.

27 **Thou shalt not speak evil of thy neighbor**, nor **do him** any **harm**.

28 Thou knowest my laws concerning these things are given in my scriptures; he that sinneth and **repent**eth **not** shall be cast out.

The Law of Obtaining Celestial Glory

29 If thou **love**st **me** thou shalt **serve me** and **keep all my commandments**.

30 And behold, thou wilt **remember the poor**, and **consecrate of thy properties for their support** that which thou hast to impart unto them, with a covenant and a deed which cannot be broken.

31 And inasmuch as ye **impart of your substance unto the poor**, ye will do it unto me; and they shall be laid before the bishop of my church and his counselors, two of the elders, or high priests, such as he shall appoint or has appointed and set apart for that purpose.

32 And it shall come to pass, that after they are laid before the bishop of my church, and after that he has received these testimonies concerning the consecration of the properties of my church, that they cannot be taken from the church, agreeable to my commandments, every man shall be made accountable unto me, a steward over his own property, or that which he has received by consecration, as much as is sufficient for himself and family.

33 And again, if there shall be properties in the hands of the church, or any individuals of it, more than is necessary for their support after this first consecration, which is a residue to be consecrated unto the bishop, it shall

be kept to administer to those who have not, from time to time, that every man who has need may be amply supplied and receive according to his wants.

34 Therefore, the residue shall be kept in my storehouse, to administer to the poor and the needy, as shall be appointed by the high council of the church, and the bishop and his council;

35 And for the purpose of purchasing lands for the public benefit of the church, and building houses of worship, and building up of the New Jerusalem which is hereafter to be revealed—

36 That my covenant people may be gathered in one in that day when I shall come to my temple. And this I do for the salvation of my people.

37 And it shall come to pass, that he that sinneth and repenteth not shall be cast out of the church, and shall not receive again that which he has consecrated unto the poor and the needy of my church, or in other words, unto me—

38 For **inasmuch as ye do it unto the least of these, ye do it unto me**.

39 For it shall come to pass, that which I spake by the mouths of

my prophets shall be fulfilled; for I will consecrate of the riches of those who embrace my gospel among the Gentiles unto the poor of my people who are of the house of Israel.

40 And again, **thou shalt not be proud in thy heart**; let all thy garments be plain, and their beauty the beauty of the work of thine own hands;

41 And **let all things be done in cleanliness before me**.

The Law of Work

42 **Thou shalt not be idle**; for he that is idle shall not eat the bread nor wear the garments of the laborer.

The Law of Healing

43 And **whosoever among you are sick**, and **have not faith to be healed, but believe**, shall be **nourished with** all **tenderness**, with **herbs** and **mild food,** and that not by the hand of an enemy.

44 And the **elders of the church, two or more**, shall be called, and shall pray for and **lay their hands upon them in my name**; and **if they die they shall die unto me, and if they live they shall live unto me.**

45 **Thou shalt live together in love**, insomuch that thou shalt **weep for the loss of them that die**, and **more especially for those that have not hope of a glorious resurrection**.

46 And it shall come to pass that **those that die in me shall not taste of death, for it shall be sweet unto them**;

47 And **they that die not in me**, wo unto them, for **their death is bitter**.

The Law of Faith

48 And again, it shall come to pass that he that hath **faith in me to be healed**, and is **not appointed unto death, shall be healed**.

49 He who hath **faith** to see shall see.

50 He who hath **faith** to hear shall hear.

51 The lame who hath **faith** to leap shall leap.

52 And **they who have not faith to do these things, but believe in me, have power to become my sons** [*can be saved in celestial glory also*]; and inasmuch as they break not my laws thou shalt bear their infirmities.

The Law of Consecration

53 **Thou shalt stand in the place of thy stewardship**.

54 **Thou shalt not take thy brother's garment**; thou shalt **pay for that which thou shalt receive of thy brother**.

55 And **if thou obtainest more than that which would be for thy support, thou shalt give it into my storehouse**, that all things may be done according to that which I have said.

The Law of Continuing with the Work of Translating the Bible (the JST)

56 Thou shalt **ask, and my scriptures shall be given** as I have appointed, and they shall be preserved in safety;

57 And it is expedient that thou shouldst hold thy peace concerning them, and **not teach them until ye have received them in full**.

58 And I give unto you a commandment that **then ye shall teach them unto all men**; for they shall be taught unto **all nations, kindreds, tongues and people**.

59 Thou shalt take the things which thou hast received, which have been given unto thee in my

scriptures for a law, to be my law to govern my church;

The Law of Being Saved

60 And **he that doeth according to these things shall be saved**, and **he that doeth them not shall be damned if he so continue**.

The Law of Gaining Additional Knowledge

61 **If thou shalt ask, thou shalt receive** revelation upon revelation, knowledge upon knowledge, that thou mayest know the mysteries and peaceable things—that which bringeth joy, that which bringeth life eternal.

62 **Thou shalt ask**, and it shall be revealed unto you in mine own due time where the New Jerusalem shall be built.

The Law of Missionary Work (continued)

63 And behold, it shall come to pass that **my servants shall be sent forth to the east** and to the **west**, to the **north** and to the **south**.

64 And even now, let him that goeth to the east teach them that shall be converted to flee to the west, and this in consequence of that which is coming on the earth, and of secret combinations.

The Law of Knowing the Mysteries (details of the gospel, which are a mystery to those caught up in the ways of the world)

65 Behold, thou shalt **observe all these things**, and **great shall be thy reward; for unto you it is given to know the mysteries of the kingdom**, but unto the world it is not given to know them.

66 Ye shall **observe the laws which ye have received and be faithful**.

67 And **ye shall hereafter receive** church **covenants, such as shall be sufficient to establish you**, both here and in the New Jerusalem.

68 Therefore, **he that lacketh wisdom, let him ask of me, and I will give him liberally and upbraid him not**.

69 Lift up your hearts and rejoice, for unto you the kingdom, or in other words, the keys of the church have been given. Even so. Amen.

The Law of Using Consecrated Property to Support Church Officers

70 **The priests and teachers shall have their stewardships**, even as the members.

71 And **the elders or high priests who are appointed to assist the bishop** as counselors in all things, **are to have their families supported out of the property which is consecrated to the bishop**, for the good of the poor, and for other purposes, as before mentioned;

72 **Or they are to receive a just remuneration for all their services**, either a stewardship or otherwise, as may be thought best or decided by the counselors and bishop.

73 **And the bishop, also, shall receive his support, or a just remuneration for all his services in the church**.

The Law for Dealing with Divorce Because of Fornication

74 Behold, verily I say unto you, that **whatever persons among you, having put away their companions for the cause of fornication**, or in other words, **if they shall testify before you in all lowliness of heart that this is the case, ye shall not cast them out from among you**;

The Law for Dealing with Divorce Because of Adultery

75 **But if ye shall find that any persons have left their**

companions for the sake of adultery, and **they themselves are the offenders**, and their companions are living, they **shall be cast out from among you**.

76 And again, I say unto you, that ye shall be watchful and careful, with all inquiry, that ye **receive none such among you if they are married**;

The Law of Allowing Persons Guilty of Sexual Sin into Membership in the Church

77 And **if they are not married, they shall repent of all their sins or ye shall not receive them.**

The Law of Maintaining Good Standing in the Church

78 **And again, every person who belongeth to this church of Christ, shall observe to keep all the commandments and covenants of the church.**

The Law for Dealing with Murderers

79 And it shall come to pass, that **if any persons among you shall kill they shall be delivered up and dealt with according to the laws of the land**; for remember that he hath **no forgiveness**; and it shall be proved according to the laws of the land.

The Law for Dealing with Members Who Commit Adultery

80 And **if any man or woman shall commit adultery, he or she shall be tried before two elders of the church, or more**, and **every word shall be established** against him or her **by two witnesses of the church**, and not of the enemy; but **if there are more than two witnesses it is better**.

81 But **he or she shall be condemned by the mouth of two witnesses**; and **the elders shall lay the case before the church, and the church shall lift up their hands against him or her**, that they may be dealt with according to the law of God.

82 And **if it can be, it is necessary that the bishop be present also**.

83 And thus ye shall do in all cases which shall come before you.

The Laws of Dealing with Members Who Steal, Rob, Lie.

84 And if a man or woman shall **rob**, he or she shall be **delivered up unto the law of the land.**

85 And if he or she shall **steal**, he or she shall be **delivered up unto the law of the land.**

86 And if he or she shall **lie**, he or she shall be **delivered up unto the law of the land**.

The Law of Final Judgment by God

87 And **if he or she do any manner of iniquity, he or she shall be delivered up unto the law, even that of God**.

The Law Governing How Members Are to Deal with Those Who Have Offended Them

88 And if thy brother or sister offend thee, thou shalt **take him or her between him or her and thee alone**; and **if he or she confess thou shalt be reconciled**.

89 And **if he or she confess not** thou shalt **deliver him or her up unto the church**, not to the members, but **to the elders** [*turn the matter over to the leaders of the branch or ward, etc.*]. And it shall be done **in a meeting**, and that **not before the world** [*keep it as private as possible*].

90 And **if** thy brother or sister **offend many**, he or she shall be **chastened before many**.

91 And **if** any one **offend openly**, he or she shall be **rebuked openly**, that he or she may be ashamed.

And **if** he or she **confess not**, he or she shall be **delivered up unto the law of God**.

92 **If** any shall **offend in secret, he or she shall be rebuked in secret, that he or she may have opportunity to confess in secret to him or her whom he or she has offended, and to God**, that the church may not speak reproachfully of him or her [*so that there is not a lot of gossip about him or her*].

93 And **thus shall ye conduct in all things**.

> We will now repeat section 42, adding additional notes and commentary. As is the case in previous revelations, the Savior identifies Himself as the one giving this revelation.

1 **HEARKEN**, O ye elders of my church, who have assembled yourselves together in my name, even **Jesus Christ the Son of the living God** [*as opposed to "dead" or inanimate gods, idols, etc.*]**, the Savior of the world**; inasmuch as ye believe on my name and keep my commandments.

2 Again I say unto you, **hearken** and **hear** and **obey the law** which I shall give unto you.

3 For verily I say, **as ye have assembled yourselves together**

according to the commandment wherewith I commanded you [*in D&C 41:2–3*], **and are agreed** as touching this one thing [*are unified and in harmony on this matter of seeking the "Law of the Lord"*], and have asked the Father in my name, even so **ye shall receive**.

It is crucial that the membership of the Church increase rapidly at this point in the beginnings of the Restored Church. Perhaps you have noticed that the Lord had a great many people in place to accept the gospel. The first commandment the Savior gives here has to do with this need for rapid membership growth.

4 Behold, verily I say unto you, I give unto you **this first commandment**, that **ye shall go forth in my name, every one of you, excepting** my servants **Joseph Smith, Jun.,** and **Sidney Rigdon**.

Perhaps one of the reasons Joseph Smith and Sidney Rigdon were told not to spend much time in missionary efforts in verse 4, above, and in verse 5, next, was that they were to continue with the translation of the Bible (corrections, revisions, etc.), as commanded in verse 56. Joseph was the translator and Sidney was the scribe in this important work that will become The Joseph Smith Translation of the Bible, commonly referred to as the JST.

5 And I give unto them a commandment that **they shall go forth for a little season**, and it shall be **given by the power of the Spirit when they shall return**.

The Savior continues explaining and instructing regarding His commandment to go forth on missions in verses 6–9, next.

6 And ye shall **go forth in the power of my Spirit, preaching** my gospel, **two by two**, in my name, lifting up your voices as **with the sound of a trump** [*a clear, easy-to-pick-out sound as compared to all the confusion about religion in the world*], **declaring my word like unto angels of God**.

In the New England of the day, as is the case in our day, there was much controversy among various religions as to whether or not literal baptism was even necessary, let alone whether or not it could properly be done by sprinkling or should be done by immersion.

7 And ye shall go forth **baptizing with water** [*by immersion*], **saying: Repent ye**, repent ye, for **the kingdom of heaven is at hand** [*meaning, among other things, that the gospel is now being made available to you*].

8 And from this place [*Kirtland*] ye shall **go forth into the regions westward**; and inasmuch as ye

shall find them that will receive you ye shall **build up my church in every region—**

Next, in verse 9, it is made clear that Kirtland, Ohio, is a temporary gathering place. It will be a headquarters and gathering place for about five years (see D&C 64:21), and then the Saints will gather to Missouri, including Independence, Missouri, the location where the New Jerusalem will be built (see D&C 57:1–3).

Doctrine

Verse 9. A city called "New Jerusalem" will be built.

9 **Until the time shall come** when it shall be revealed unto you from on high, **when the city of the New Jerusalem shall be prepared, that ye may be gathered** in one, **that ye may be my people and I will be your God.**

Next, the Lord explains that Church leaders are not above the laws of the Lord, and if they transgress seriously, they must be replaced.

10 And again, I say unto you, that my servant Edward Partridge shall stand in the office whereunto I have appointed him [as the first Bishop of the Church. See section 41, verse 9]. And it shall come to pass, that **if he transgress**

another shall be appointed in his stead [in his place]. Even so. Amen.

It may be that relatively few members realize how important the law of common consent (raising our hands to sustain those called to positions, etc.; see D&C 26:2) is to the stability and security of the Church. Among other things, it protects against apostasy by assuring that there are no secret ordinations in the Church.

For instance, anyone who presides over a group in the Church must have been sustained by that group and ordained or set apart by one who has the proper authority and who has likewise been sustained by members. A number of break-off groups from the Church claim secret ordinations as the source of their authorization to create a new church. Verse 11, next, teaches this principle of having no secret ordinations in the Lord's true Church.

11 Again I say unto you, that **it shall not be given to any one** to go forth to preach my gospel, or **to build up my church, except** [unless] **he be ordained by some one who has authority, and it is known to the church that he has authority** and has been **regularly ordained** by the heads of the church.

Next, in verse 12, those who teach the gospel are instructed to stick with the scriptures in their teaching.

12 And again, the elders, priests and teachers of this church shall **teach the principles of my gospel, which are in the Bible and the Book of Mormon**, in the which is the fulness of the gospel.

Next, those who teach the gospel are counseled to live the gospel themselves and to follow the Spirit as to what to teach.

13 And **they shall observe the covenants and church articles** [another name for section 20; see background notes to section 20 in this study guide] to **do them**, and **these shall be their teachings, as they shall be directed by the Spirit**.

14 And **the Spirit shall be given unto you by the prayer of faith; and if ye receive not the Spirit ye shall not teach**.

There are at least two ways to look at verse 14, above. One is to understand that it is saying that if you do not have the Spirit with you, don't try to teach. The other way is to consider it to be saying that if you try to teach without the Spirit, your efforts will be unsuccessful. Either way, without the Spirit, your teaching will be ineffective.

15 And **all this ye shall observe to do as I have commanded**

concerning your teaching, until the fulness of my scriptures is given.

16 And as ye shall **lift up your voices by the Comforter** [as directed by the Holy Ghost], ye shall speak and prophesy as seemeth me good;

Doctrine

Verse 17. The Holy Ghost knows all things.

17 For, behold, the Comforter [the Holy Ghost] **knoweth all things, and beareth record of the Father and of the Son.**

Next, in verses 18–28, the Lord reinforces the fact that the Ten Commandments are still in force today. This message is badly needed in our world.

The word "kill," as used in the context of verse 18, next, means the intentional murdering of another human being by one who has sufficient knowledge of the gospel to be accountable for the deed. The Prophet Joseph Smith taught about murderers as follows:

"A murderer, for instance, one that sheds innocent blood, cannot have forgiveness" (Teachings of the Prophet Joseph Smith, 339).

The Doctrine and Covenants Student Manual, used by our institutes of religion, 1981 edition, page 83, teaches the following about murder:

"There is no forgiveness in this world or in the world to come, because the Atonement of Christ does not cover murder committed by one who has joined the Church—a murderer must suffer for the sin himself (see Smith, *Teachings of the Prophet Joseph Smith*, 339)."

We will now read verses 18 and 19.

Doctrine

Verses 18–28. The Ten Commandments are still in force today.

18 And now, behold, I speak unto the church. Thou shalt not kill; and **he that kills shall not have forgiveness in this world, nor in the world to come.**

19 And again, I say, thou shalt not kill; but he that killeth shall die [*according to D&C 42, footnote 19b, this is a reference to capital punishment; verse 79 instructs that murderers are to be dealt with by the laws of the land*].

20 Thou shalt not steal; and he that stealeth and will not repent shall be cast out.

21 Thou shalt not lie; he that lieth and will not repent shall be cast out.

Verse 22, next, gives counsel for successful marriage. It is interesting to note that there is only one other person, in addition to our spouse, whom we are commanded to love "with all our heart"; namely, the Lord (Matthew 22:37). That puts spouses in a high and exclusive category as well as priority.

22 **Thou shalt love thy wife with all thy heart**, and shalt cleave unto her and none else.

Did you notice also, in verse 22, above, that the Lord leaves absolutely no room for flirting on the part of married people? Spencer W. Kimball taught this subject as follows:

"There are those married people who permit their eyes to wander and their hearts to become vagrant, who think it is not improper to flirt a little, to share their hearts, and have desire for someone other than the wife or the husband, the Lord says in no uncertain terms: [D&C 42:22 quoted]

"And, when the Lord says *all* thy heart, it allows for no sharing nor dividing nor depriving. And, to the woman it is paraphrased: 'Thou shalt love thy husband with *all* thy heart and shalt cleave unto him and none else.' The words *none else* eliminate everyone and everything. The spouse then becomes pre-eminent in the life of the husband or wife, and neither social life nor occupational life nor political life nor any other interest nor person nor thing shall ever take precedence over the companion spouse. We sometimes find women who absorb and hover over the children at the expense of the husband, sometimes even estranging them from him. The Lord says to them: '. . . Thou shalt cleave unto *him* and none else.'" (*Improvement Era*, December 1962, 65:928).

"Marriage presupposes total allegiance and total fidelity. Each spouse takes the partner with the understanding that he or she gives totally to the spouse all the heart, strength, loyalty, honor, and affection, with all dignity. Any divergence is sin; any sharing of the heart is transgression. As we should have 'an eye single to the glory of God,' so should we have an eye, an ear, a heart single to the marriage and the spouse and family" (*Faith Precedes the Miracle*, 142–43).

Next, in verse 23, we learn the dangers and penalties of entertaining lustful thoughts. "Entertaining" means to intentionally continue in engaging in lustful thinking rather than getting such thoughts out of your mind.

A student once asked me why it was such a "big deal" to abstain from sex outside of marriage since the medical technology is readily available to prevent conception. The class, as you can imagine, was at full attention.

I complemented her for asking the question and then invited the class to turn to D&C 42:23 to find the answer. (Obviously, if one is involved in sex outside of marriage, that person's mind is entertaining lustful thoughts.) Verse 23 points out two major dangers.

Doctrine

Verse 23. Sexual immorality drives the Spirit away.

23 And he that looketh upon a woman to lust after her shall deny the faith, and **shall not have the Spirit**; and if he repents not he shall be cast out.

Referring back to verse 23, above, denying the faith or rejecting your loyalty to God is a most serious consequence of lustful thinking. In addition, driving the Spirit away through intentionally continuing in lustful thinking leaves you wide open to Satan's temptations and input into your mind. Thus, it leaves you vulnerable to much damage from the devil.

Next, in verses 24–26, the issue of adultery and Church disciplinary action (probation, disfellowship, or excommunication) are addressed.

24 Thou shalt not commit adultery; and **he that committeth adultery, and repenteth not, shall be cast out** [*subject to Church discipline*].

25 But he that has committed adultery and repents with all his heart, and **forsaketh it** [*stops doing it*], and **doeth it no more**, thou shalt **forgive**;

26 But if he doeth it again, he shall not be forgiven, but shall be **cast out**.

Sometimes a misunderstanding results from misreading verse 26, above. It is that if a person has committed adultery more than once, he or she must be excommunicated. This is not necessarily the case. That decision is left up to what the Spirit tells the presiding authority (for example, the bishop or stake president) who is conducting the disciplinary council.

The following First Presidency statement from Heber J. Grant, J. Reuben Clark, and David O. McKay is instructional concerning the Church and sexual transgression of members (**bold** added for emphasis):

"To us in this Church the Lord has declared that adulterers should not be admitted to membership (D&C 42:76); that adulterers in the Church, if unrepentant should be cast out (D&C 42:75) but if repentant should be permitted to remain (D&C 42:74, 42:25) and, He said, 'By this ye may know if a man repenteth of his sins—behold, he will confess them and forsake them' (D&C 58:43).

"In the great revelation on the three heavenly glories, the Lord said, speaking of those who will inherit the lowest of these, or the telestial glory: 'These are they who are liars, and sorcerers, and adulterers, and whoremongers, and whosoever loves and makes a lie' (D&C 76:103).

"The doctrine of this Church is that sexual sin—the illicit sexual relations of men and women—stands, in its enormity, next to murder. (Alma 39:3–5)

"The Lord has drawn no essential distinctions between fornication and adultery and harlotry or prostitution. Each has fallen under His solemn and awful condemnation.

"You youths of Zion, you cannot associate in nonmarital, illicit sex relationships, which is fornication, and escape the punishments and the judgments which the Lord has declared against this sin. The day of reckoning will come just as certainly as night follows day. They who would palliate this crime and say that such indulgence is but a sinless gratification of a normal desire, like appeasing hunger and thirst, speak filthiness with their lips. Their counsel leads to destruction; their wisdom comes from the Father of Lies.

"You husbands and wives who have taken on solemn obligations of chastity in the Holy Temples of the Lord and who violate those sacred vows by illicit sexual relations with others, you not only commit the vile and loathsome sin of adultery, but you break the oath you yourselves made with the Lord himself before you went to the altar for your sealing. You become subject to the penalties which the Lord has prescribed for those who breach their covenants with Him. . . .

"But they who sin may repent and they repenting, God will forgive them, for the Lord has said, "Behold, he who has repented of his sins, the same is forgiven and I, the Lord, remember them no more" (D&C 58:42).

"By virtue of the authority in us vested as the First Presidency of the Church, we warn our people who are offending of the degradation, the wickedness, the punishment that attend upon unchastity; we urge you to **remember the blessings which flow from the living of the clean life**; we call upon you to keep, day in and day out, the way of strictest chastity, through which only can God's choice gifts come to you and His Spirit abide with you.

"How glorious is he who lives the chaste life. He walks unfearful in the full glare of the noon-day sun, for he is without moral infirmity. He can be reached by no shafts of base calumny, for his armor is without flaw. His virtue cannot be challenged by any just accuser, for he lives above reproach.

His cheek is never blotched with shame for he is without hidden sin. He is honored and respected by all mankind, for he is beyond their censure. He is loved by the Lord, for he stands without blemish. The exaltations of eternities await his coming" (In Conference Report, October 1942, 10–12).

Next, the Lord reminds us that if we want to be true disciples, we will treat others with kindness.

27 Thou shalt not speak evil of thy neighbor, nor do him any harm.

Finally, as far as the above scripture block is concerned, the Savior bears witness that the Bible and Book of Mormon contain His commandments concerning the above sins.

28 Thou knowest my laws concerning these things are given in my scriptures; he that sinneth and repenteth not shall be cast out.

As we move on to the next several verses, we are taking a large step from the avoiding of telestial behaviors to the living of celestial law, including the law of consecration in a "Zion" society, which involves treating others the way the Savior would treat them.

Perhaps you have wondered whether or not you could live successfully and comfortably in the celestial kingdom in the presence of God. The personal qualities needed for living the law of consecration are evident, and the "ground rules" for living in a Zion environment are given in the next several verses. You may be interested in evaluating your own preparation for celestial glory against these criteria.

Before we continue, we will quote just one verse from the Doctrine and Covenants that deals with the above:

D&C 105:5

And **Zion** cannot be **built up** unless it **is by the principles of the law of the celestial kingdom**; otherwise I cannot receive her unto myself.

Verses 30–42, next, give some details of how to administer and live the law of consecration. Remember that many more details will be added in later revelations. We will use **bold** to point out celestial traits and law of consecration details.

29 If thou lovest me thou shalt serve me and **keep all my commandments** [*since none of us are perfect, we understand this to mean to earnestly strive to keep all of God's commandments*].

30 And behold, thou wilt **remember the poor**, and **consecrate of thy properties for their support** [*be generous*] **that which thou**

hast [*your surplus, after your own needs and wants—see D&C 51:3—are taken care of*] to impart unto them, with a covenant and a deed [*willing to deed your properties to the Church*] which cannot be broken.

31 And **inasmuch as ye impart of your substance unto the poor, ye will do it unto me** [*when you are generous with the poor, it is the same as being generous with God*]; and **they shall be laid before the bishop** of my church and his counselors [*the bishop is the main administrator of the law of consecration*], two of the elders, or high priests, such as he shall appoint or has appointed and set apart for that purpose.

32 And it shall come to pass, that **after they** [*the properties that have been deeded to the Church by members willing to live the law of consecration*] **are laid before the bishop of my church**, and after that he has received these testimonies [*written deeds*] concerning the consecration of the properties of my church, that **they cannot be taken from the church** [*if a person "quits" this "united order," he or she does not get the property back that was originally deeded to the Church*], agreeable to my commandments, **every man shall be made accountable unto me, a**

steward over his own property [*everyone will be deeded—see D&C 51:4—some property back*], or that which he has received by consecration [*deeded to him by the bishop*], as much as is sufficient for himself and family [*according to his family's needs*].

As you no doubt noticed, in verse 32, above, **private ownership of property is a major part of living the true law of consecration**. Most people do not understand this. Private ownership of property was one of the major differences between the "united order" that some of Sidney Rigdon's congregation had been living on Isaac Morley's farm in the Kirtland area, and the proper "united order" set up according to the Lord's rules.

By now you can see that unselfishness and generosity would be major personality traits needed by participants in living the law of consecration. These are celestial qualities.

Next, in verses 33–35, the Lord instructs further that if, after all participating members have deeded their property to the Church (the initial step in living the law of consecration), and after the bishop has deeded back to each family according to their needs, there is still some left over, it is to be kept by the bishop for assisting the poor, helping members now and then when their needs exceed their resources, for purchasing public lands for the Church, building churches, and so on.

33 And again, **if there shall be properties in the hands of the church**, or any individuals of it, **more than is necessary** for their support **after this first consecration**, which is a residue to be consecrated unto the bishop, **it shall be kept to administer to those who have not, from time to time**, that **every man who has need may be amply supplied and receive according to his wants**.

34 Therefore, **the residue shall be kept in my storehouse, to administer to the poor and the needy**, as shall be appointed by the high council of the church, and the bishop and his council;

35 And **for the purpose of purchasing lands for the public benefit of the church**, and **building houses of worship**, and **building up of the New Jerusalem** which is hereafter to be revealed [*the location will be revealed as being in Independence, Jackson County, Missouri; see D&C 57:2–3*]—

36 That my covenant people may be gathered in one in that day when I shall come to my temple. And **this I do for the salvation of my people**.

Next, the Lord instructs concerning what to do about members who join in with the law of consecration but later drop out and leave the Church. They do not receive back the properties they originally deeded to the Church.

37 And it shall come to pass, that he that sinneth and repenteth not shall be cast out of the church, and **shall not receive again that which he has consecrated unto the poor and the needy of my church, or in other words, unto me**—

38 For **inasmuch as ye do it unto the least of these, ye do it unto me** [*another principle of living the law of consecration*].

39 For it shall come to pass, that which I spake by the mouths of my prophets shall be fulfilled; for **I will consecrate of the riches of those who embrace my gospel among the Gentiles unto the poor of my people who are of the house of Israel.**

Have you noticed how much the Church is doing today to fulfill the Savior's prophecy, **bolded** in verse 39, especially through tithing, fast offerings, missionary donations, the Humanitarian Fund, and the Perpetual Education Fund? In some very real ways, we are living the law of consecration today with very gratifying results!

In verses 40–42, next, the Lord gives added instructions for living the law of consecration, including that those who are lazy cannot be a part of such groups.

40 And again, **thou shalt not be proud in thy heart**; **let all thy garments be plain** [*this can be carried to extremes; it was designed to avoid the fashion "caste system" which often exists in society*], and their beauty the beauty of **the work of thine own hands** [*in other words, the clothes they made were to have individual beauty and reflect the individuality of the owner; this point was missed by some in early "united orders"*];

41 And **let all things be done in cleanliness** before me.

42 **Thou shalt not be idle**; for he that is idle shall not eat the bread nor wear the garments [*clothing*] of the laborer.

In verses 43–52, next, the Lord gives much counsel and direction concerning the healing of the sick. First, he counsels those who do not have faith to be healed but who still believe in God. You will see that He treats them with kindness rather than criticism for their lack of faith.

43 And whosoever among you are **sick, and have not faith to be healed, but believe, shall be**

nourished with all tenderness, with herbs and mild food, and that not by the hand of an enemy [*in other words, members should take care of their own*].

Next, instructions are given for administering to the sick.

44 And **the elders of the church, two or more, shall be called,** and shall pray for **and lay their hands upon them in my name; and if they die they shall die unto me, and if they live they shall live unto me** [*in other words, they will be fine either way; the Lord has a different perspective on death than most people*].

45 **Thou shalt live together in love,** insomuch that thou shalt **weep for the loss of them that die,** and **more especially for those** [*the wicked*] **that have not hope of a glorious resurrection.**

The counsel given in the last half of verse 45, above, is somewhat difficult to follow for those who tend to "rejoice" when a wicked leader or cruel terrorist is killed or dies. This would seem to be an additional lesson for us from the Lord on developing Christlike love for all people, regardless of how offensive they might be, if we desire someday to enter celestial glory.

Next, we are taught that dying holds no fear for the righteous.

46 And it shall come to pass **that those that die in me** [*who have been faithful to the Lord*] **shall not taste of death, for it shall be sweet unto them;**

Brigham Young gives a perspective on dying that is truly enlightening:

"We shall turn round and look upon it [the valley of death] and think, when we have crossed it, why this is the greatest advantage of my whole existence, for I have passed from a state of sorrow, grief, mourning, woe, misery, pain, anguish and disappointment into a state of existence, where I can enjoy life to the fullest extent as far as that can be done without a body. My spirit is set free, I thirst no more, I want to sleep no more, I hunger no more, I tire no more, I run, I walk, I labor, I go, I come, I do this, I do that, whatever is required of me, nothing like pain or weariness, I am full of life, full of vigor, and I enjoy the presence of my heavenly Father" (*Journal of Discourses*, 17:142).

President Joseph F. Smith taught the following:

"All fear of this death has been removed from the Latter-day Saints. They have no dread of the temporal death, because they know that as death came upon them by the transgression of Adam, so by the righteousness of

Jesus Christ shall life come unto them, and though they die, they shall live again. Possessing this knowledge, they have joy even in death, for they know that they shall rise again and shall meet again beyond the grave. They know that the spirit dies not at all; that it passes through no change, except the change from imprisonment in this mortal clay to freedom and to the sphere in which it acted before it came to this earth" (*Gospel Doctrine*, 428).

And finally, Spencer W. Kimball gave the following concerning death:

"If we say that early death is a calamity, disaster or a tragedy, would it not be saying that mortality is preferable to earlier entrance into the spirit world and to eventual salvation and exaltation? If mortality be the perfect state, then death would be a frustration but the Gospel teaches us there is no tragedy in death, but only in sin" ("Tragedy or Destiny," Brigham Young University Speeches of the Year [Dec. 6, 1955], 3).

As we continue, the Lord teaches, in effect, that death is not sweet for the wicked.

47 And they **that die not in me, wo unto them, for their death is bitter.**

Next, we are taught the importance of faith in the healing of the sick.

48 And again, it shall come to pass that **he that hath faith in me to be healed, and is not appointed unto death, shall be healed.**

Spencer W. Kimball taught the following regarding the phrase "appointed unto death" in verse 48, above:

"If not 'appointed unto death' and sufficient faith is developed, life can be spared. But if there is not enough faith, many die before their time. It is evident that even the righteous will not always be healed and even those of great faith will die when it is according to the purpose of God. Joseph Smith died in his thirties as did the Savior. Solemn prayers were answered negatively.

"If he is not 'appointed unto death!' That is a challenging statement. I am confident that there is a time to die. I am not a fatalist. I believe that many people die before 'their time' because they are careless, abuse their bodies, take unnecessary chances, or expose themselves to hazards, accidents, and sickness. . . .

"God can control our lives. He guides and blesses us, but gives us our agency. We may live our lives in accordance with His plan for us or we may foolishly shorten or terminate them.

"I am positive in my mind that the Lord has planned our destiny. We can shorten our lives but I think we cannot lengthen them very much. Sometime we'll understand fully, and when we see back from the vantage point of the future we shall be satisfied with many of the happenings of this life which seemed too difficult for us to comprehend" ("Tragedy or Destiny," 6, 9, 11–12).

Wilford Woodruff gave a rather fascinating discourse on the phrase, "appointed unto death," as follows:

"The Prophet Joseph Smith held the keys of this dispensation on this side of the veil, and he will hold them throughout the countless ages of eternity. He went into the spirit world to unlock the prison doors and to preach the Gospel to the millions of spirits who are in darkness, and every Apostle, every Seventy, every Elder, etc., who has died in the faith, as soon as he passes to the other side of the veil, enters into the work of the ministry, and there is a thousand times more to preach there than there is here. I have felt of late as if our brethren on the other side of the veil had held a council, and that they had said to this one, and that one, 'Cease thy work on the earth, come hence, we need help,' and they have called this man and that man. It has appeared so to me in seeing the many men who have been called from our midst lately. Perhaps I may be permitted to relate a circumstance with which I am acquainted in relation to Bishop Roskelley, of Smithfield, Cache Valley. On one occasion he was suddenly taken very sick— near to death's door. While he lay in this condition, President Peter Maughan, who was dead, came to him and said: 'Brother Roskelley, we held a council on the other side of the veil. I have had a great deal to do, and I have the privilege of coming here to appoint one man to come and help. I have had three names given to me in council, and you are one of them. I want to inquire of your circumstances.' The Bishop told him what he had to do, and they conversed together as one man would converse with another. President Maughan then said to him: 'I think I will not call you. I think you are wanted here more than perhaps one of the others.' Bishop Roskelley got well from that hour. Very soon after, the second man was taken sick, but not being able to exercise sufficient faith, Brother Roskelley did not go to him. By and by this man recovered, and on meeting Brother Roskelley he said: 'Brother Maughan came to me the other night and told me he was sent to call one man from the ward,' and he named two men as had been done to Brother Roskelley. A few days afterwards the third man was taken sick and died. Now, I name this to show a principle. They have work on the other side of the veil; and they want men, and they call them. And that was my view in regard to Brother George A. Smith. When he was almost at death's door, Brother Cannon administered to him, and in thirty minutes he was up and ate breakfast with his family. We labored with him in this way, but ultimately, as you know, he died. But it taught me a lesson. I felt that man was wanted behind the veil. We labored also with Brother Pratt; he, too, was wanted behind the veil.

"Now . . . those of us who are left here have a great work to do. We have been raised up of the Lord to take this kingdom and bear it off. This is our duty; but if we neglect our duty and set our hearts upon the things of this world, we will be sorry for it (*Journal of Discourses*, 22:333–34).

Next, more examples of the principle of faith are given.

49 He who hath faith to see shall see.

50 He who hath faith to hear shall hear.

51 The lame who hath faith to leap shall leap.

In verse 52, next, the Savior comforts those who do not have sufficient faith to be healed by telling them that they can still attain exaltation. This puts "faith to be healed" into a proper perspective as compared to being true to covenants and living the gospel.

52 And they who have not faith to do these things, but believe in me, have power to become my

sons [*"power to become my sons (and daughters)" means power to attain exaltation; see Mosiah 5:7, D&C 76:24, etc.*]; and inasmuch as they break not my laws thou shalt bear their infirmities.

53 Thou shalt stand in the place of thy stewardship [*take care of your stewardship (properties, callings, etc.) with diligence, honor, and integrity*].

Before you read the next verse, it will be helpful to have a bit more background. Before the conversion of Sidney Rigdon and many of his rather large congregation (he was a successful minister and preacher on the western frontier in Ohio), several former members of his congregation were living in a type of "united order" in which all things were owned in common. They had set it up according to their understanding of Acts 2:44–45 and 4:32. There was no private ownership of property, and some problems developed. We will quote some commentary on this from the institute of religion student manual, *Church History in the Fullness of Times*, 1989, page 95 (**bold** added for teaching purposes):

"Now settled in Kirtland, the Prophet was eager to know the Lord's will concerning the economic salvation of the Saints, many of whom were impoverished, particularly those who had left their homes in New York. His interest in the Lord's economic program was aroused when he arrived in Ohio and discovered a group of about fifty people who had established a cooperative venture based on their interpretation of statements in the book of Acts, describing the early Saints as having all things in common (see Acts 2:44–45; 4:32). This group, known as 'the family,' formerly followers of Sidney Rigdon, were members of the Church living on Isaac Morley's farm near the village of Kirtland. When John Whitmer arrived in mid-January, he noted that what they were doing created many problems. For example, **Heman Bassett took a pocket watch belonging to Levi Hancock and sold it. When asked why, Heman replied, 'Oh, I thought it was all in the family.' Levi responded that he did not like such 'family doing'** and would not endure it any longer."

With the above as specific context, verse 54, next, is even more meaningful as a principle of the law of consecration.

54 **Thou shalt not take thy brother's garment**; thou shalt pay for that which thou shalt receive of thy brother.

Perhaps you've noticed that nowhere in the specific instructions given so far by the Lord regarding the law of consecration does He define for these Saints what "surplus" is. In other words, it is up to

them to determine what it is. This would definitely require "celestial" type generosity and integrity on the part of the people involved. But just in case you are thinking that it would be extremely difficult to be "that good," have you noticed that the leaders of our Church today apply the same principle to our tithes and offerings? In fact, they even apply it to our temple attendance. They don't tell us how often to go to the temple, they don't tell us how much fast offering to pay, and they don't tell us how to calculate our tithing, other than to quote D&C 119:3, which says tithing is to be paid on "one tenth of all their interest annually." They have defined "interest" as being "income."

In summary, all of these things involve the consecration of our time and money, and it is up to the individuals to determine how much fast offering they pay, how they calculate their tithing, and how much of their time they dedicate to temple attendance. So, being a faithful Saint in our day requires celestial qualities also. This principle is given again in verse 55, next.

55 And **if thou obtainest more than that which would be for thy support, thou shalt give it into my storehouse**, that all things may be done according to that which I have said.

Next, in verses 56–58, the topic

is the translation of the Bible. See D&C 42, footnote 56a, as well as 45:60–61. This translation is now referred to as the Joseph Smith Translation of the Bible, or the JST.

56 Thou shalt **ask, and my scriptures** [*the inspired translation of the Bible*] **shall be given as I have appointed** [*according to the instructions of the Lord, for instance in D&C 35:20*], and **they shall be preserved in safety** [*possibly a reference to the lost 116 manuscript pages of the translation from the gold plates that were lost by Martin Harris; in other words, be very careful not to lose the translation notes from your work on the Bible*];

57 And it is expedient [*necessary*] that thou shouldst **hold thy peace concerning them** [*don't start preaching about them yet*], and not teach them until ye have received them in full.

One significant way in which the JST is being taken to all the world as instructed in verse 58, next, is in our Latter-day Saint edition of the Bible, which contains numerous footnotes using the JST, as well as a section in the back for longer excerpts from the JST.

58 And I give unto you a commandment that then ye shall teach them unto all men; for **they shall be taught unto all nations,**

kindreds, tongues and people.

Verses 59–60, next, are a "straight to the point" summary of the importance of taking these laws seriously. Such things raise our accountability level as well as our opportunities for growth.

59 **Thou shalt take the things which thou hast received**, which have been given unto thee **in my scriptures for a law**, to be my law **to govern my church**;

60 And **he that doeth according to these things shall be saved**, and **he that doeth them not shall be damned** if he so continue [*unless he repents*].

Next, these Saints are encouraged to keep asking questions and learning. The benefits far outweigh the risks of additional accountability.

61 **If thou shalt ask, thou shalt receive revelation upon revelation, knowledge upon knowledge, that thou mayest know the mysteries** [*spiritual truths; see Bible Dictionary under "Mystery"*] **and peaceable things—that which bringeth joy, that which bringeth life eternal** [*exaltation in the highest degree of glory in the celestial kingdom*].

Next, the topic turns briefly to the future New Jerusalem.

62 Thou shalt **ask, and it shall be revealed** unto you **in mine own due time where the New Jerusalem shall be built**.

New Jerusalem is often referred to as the City of Zion and will be built in Independence, Jackson County, Missouri (see D&C 57:2–3). The following quote from the Bible Dictionary points this out (**bold** added for emphasis):

Zion

"The word *Zion* is used repeatedly in all the standard works of the Church, and is defined in latter-day revelation as 'the pure in heart' (D&C 97:21). Other usages of Zion have to do with a geographical location. For example, Enoch built a city that was called Zion (Moses 7:18–19); Solomon built his temple on Mount Zion (1 Kgs. 8:1; cf. 2 Sam. 5:6–7); and Jackson County, Missouri, is called Zion in many of the revelations in the D&C, such as 58:49–50; 62:4; 63:48; 72:13; 84:76; 104:47. **The city of New Jerusalem, to be built in Jackson County, Missouri, is to be called Zion** (D&C 45:66–67). The revelations also speak of 'the cause of Zion' (D&C 6:6; 11:6). In a wider sense all of North and South America are Zion (HC 6:318–19). For further

references see 1 Chr. 11:5; Ps. 2:6; 99:2; 102:16; Isa. 1:27; 2:3; 4:3–5; 33:20; 52:1–8; 59:20; Jer. 3:14; 31:6; Joel 2:1–32; Amos 6:1; Obad. 1:17, 21; Heb. 12:22–24; Rev. 14:1–5; and many others. (In the N.T., *Zion* is spelled *Sion*.)"

The Book of Mormon has a number of references to the New Jerusalem, including in Third Nephi as follows:

3 Nephi 20:22

22 And behold, this people will I establish in this land, unto the fulfilling of the covenant which I made with your father Jacob; and it shall be a **New Jerusalem**. And the powers of heaven shall be in the midst of this people; yea, even I will be in the midst of you.

Apostle Bruce R. McConkie explains more about "New Jerusalem":

"'We believe . . . that Zion (the New Jerusalem) will be built upon the American continent.' So specified the seer of latter days in our Tenth Article of Faith. Zion, the New Jerusalem, on American soil! And we hasten to add, so also shall there be Zions in all lands and New Jerusalems in the mountains of the Lord in all the earth. But the American Zion shall be the capital city, the source whence the law shall go forth to govern all the earth [*during the Millennium*]. It shall be the city of the Great King. His throne shall be there, and from there he shall reign gloriously over all the earth" (*The Millennial Messiah*, 301).

In 1879, Apostle Orson Pratt gave a brief description of the temple that will be built in conjunction with the New Jerusalem:

"There [*New Jerusalem*] . . . we expect to build a temple different from all other temples in some respects. It will be built much larger, cover a larger area of ground, far larger than this Tabernacle covers and this Tabernacle will accommodate from 12,000 to 15,000 people. We expect to build a temple much larger, very much larger, according to the revelation God gave to us forty years ago in regard to that temple. But you may ask in what form will it be built? Will it be built in one large room, like this Tabernacle? No; there will be 24 different compartments in the temple that will be built in Jackson County. The names of these compartments were given to us some 45 or 46 years ago; the names we still have, and when we build these 24 rooms, in a circular form and arched over the centre, we shall give the names to all these different compartments just as the Lord specified through Joseph Smith. . . . Perhaps you may ask for what purpose these 24 compartments are built. I answer not to assemble the outside world in, nor to assemble the Saints all in

one place, but these buildings will be built with a special view to the different orders, or in other words the different quorums or councils of the two Priesthoods that God has ordained on the earth. That is the object of having 24 rooms so that each of these different quorums, whether they be High Priests or Seventies, or Elders, or Bishops, or lesser Priesthood, or Teachers, or Deacons, or Patriarchs, or Apostles, or High Councils, or whatever may be the duties that are assigned to them, they will have rooms in the temple of the Most High God, adapted, set apart, constructed, and dedicated for this special purpose. . . . But will there be any other buildings excepting those 24 rooms that are all joined together in a circular form and arched over the center—are there any other rooms that will be built—detached from the temple? Yes. There will be tabernacles, there will be meeting houses for the assembling of the people on the Sabbath day. There will be various places of meeting so that the people may gather together; but the temple will be dedicated to the Priesthood of the Most High God, and for the most sacred and holy purposes" (*Journal of Discourses*, 25:24–25).

The Tenth Article of Faith refers to the yet-to-be-built New Jerusalem as follows:

10 We believe in the literal gathering of Israel and in the restoration of the Ten Tribes; that **Zion (the**

New Jerusalem) **will be built upon the American continent**; that Christ will reign personally upon the earth; and, that the earth will be renewed and receive its paradisiacal glory.

We will learn more about the coming New Jerusalem when we study section 45. The instruction in verses 63–64, next, seems to apply especially to these early Saints. They are to go on missions in all directions, but those who go east to New York and the surrounding area are to counsel their converts to go west and gather with the Saints in Ohio.

63 And behold, it shall come to pass that my servants shall be sent forth to the east and to the west, to the north and to the south.

64 And even now, **let him that goeth to the east teach them** that shall be converted to flee to the west, and this in consequence of that which is coming on the earth, and of secret combinations [*see D&C 38:13 and 28–29*].

In verses 65–66, next, we all learn, again, the lesson that obedience brings great blessings. Perhaps this is the reason that obedience is sometimes referred to as "the first law of heaven."

65 Behold, **thou shalt observe** [*obey*] **all these things, and great shall be thy reward**; for unto you

it is given to know the mysteries [*spiritual truths, simple basics of the gospel—see verse 61, above*] of the kingdom, but unto the world [*those who reject the gospel and thus remain "worldly"*] it is not given to know them.

66 **Ye shall observe the laws which ye have received and be faithful.**

Can you see the "progression" in these verses? First, the Lord has reminded the Saints of the value of obedience (verses 65 and 66, above). Then, in verse 67, next, He tells them that if they are obedient to what they have been given, they will receive more! This process of going from one level up to the next, and then to the next and so on, will continue for the faithful until they qualify for exaltation.

67 And **ye shall hereafter receive church covenants, such as shall be sufficient to establish you, both here and in the New Jerusalem.** [*Those in the New Jerusalem will be "Zion" people; in other words, worthy of celestial glory and living in the presence of the Savior; see 3 Nephi 20:22.*]

Next, the Savior encourages all of us to continue seeking wisdom, which, among other things, can be defined as planning wisely for a pleasant future.

68 Therefore, **he that lacketh wisdom, let him ask of me**, and I will give him liberally and upbraid him not.

The word "upbraid," in verse 68, above, is familiar to Latter-day Saints since it is also used in James 1:5, which led Joseph Smith to go into the grove to pray, which led to the First Vision. It means "to scold" and is derived from the practice in ancient times of disciplining disobedient children by taking hold of their braids and jerking upward.

In verse 69, next, the Savior invites the Saints to cheer up and be happy. Remember, they are facing many hardships and sacrifices. Many of them have recently relocated from New York to Kirtland in wintertime, and many more hardships are yet to come, especially as the Saints make their way west.

69 **Lift up your hearts and rejoice**, for unto you the kingdom, or in other words, the keys of the church have been given. Even so. Amen.

Verses 70–73, next, are additional instructions as to the use of consecrated properties to support those who are called to serve full time in the Church.

70 The priests and teachers shall have their stewardships, even as the members.

71 And **the elders or high priests who are appointed to assist the bishop** as counselors in all things, **are to have their families supported out of the property which is consecrated to the bishop**, for the good of the poor, and for other purposes, as before mentioned;

72 **Or they are to receive a just remuneration** [*payment*] **for all their services**, either a stewardship or otherwise, as may be thought best or decided by the counselors and bishop.

73 And **the bishop, also, shall receive his support**, or a just remuneration for all his services in the church.

As mentioned at the beginning of the background notes for section 42 in this study guide, verses 74–93 were given two weeks later than verses 1–72. (Verse 73 was added later by Joseph Smith at the time the Doctrine and Covenants was published.) Verses 74–93 are instructions about dealing with transgressors in the Church. We will study about disciplinary councils when we get to section 102.

In the meantime, keep in mind that in these next verses, the Lord is setting up the proper order for helping members guilty of serious sin get their lives back in order with the help of the Atonement of Jesus Christ. It is a kindness and a show of love to help people straighten out their lives before Judgment Day.

President N. Eldon Tanner, of the First Presidency, spoke on this subject as follows:

"Every mission president, stake president, and bishop is directed and instructed how to investigate and handle all cases of transgression. A person who is guilty of a serious transgression cannot progress, and he is not happy while the guilt is upon him. Until he has confessed and repented he is in bondage. The transgressor who is dealt with as he should be, with love and with proper discipline, will later express his appreciation for your concern, your interest, and your leadership. As he is properly dealt with, he is in a position to repent and come back to full activity. But he must be dealt with.

"It has been reported to me that some bishops and even stake presidents have said that they never have excommunicated or disciplined anyone and that they do not intend to. This attitude is entirely wrong. Judges in Israel have the responsibility to sit in righteous judgment where it becomes necessary. Let me read from the twentieth section of the Doctrine and Covenants an important reminder to those who have the responsibility of judging: 'Any member of the Church of Christ transgressing, or being overtaken

in a fault, shall be dealt with as the scriptures direct.' (D&C 20:80.)

"Brethren, study the scriptures and the handbook and do as they direct and discipline the members of the Church when necessary. Remember that it is no kindness to a transgressor for his local authority to ignore or overlook or try to cover up his iniquity" (In Conference Report, Oct. 1974, 110; or *Ensign*, Nov. 1974, 78).

In verses 74–75, next, instructions are given for dealing with divorces caused by sexual transgression.

74 Behold, verily I say unto you, that whatever persons among you, **having put away** [*divorced*] **their companions for the cause of fornication,** or in other words, **if they shall testify before you in all lowliness of heart that this is the case** [*if they repent humbly*], **ye shall not cast them out** from among you [*don't excommunicate them*];

75 But if ye shall find that any persons have **left their companions for the sake of** [*divorced because of*] **adultery,** and **they themselves are the offenders,** and their companions are living, **they shall be cast out** [*excommunicated*] from among you.

Next, instructions are given with

respect to letting such transgressors join the Church.

76 And again, I say unto you, that ye shall **be watchful and careful,** with all inquiry, **that ye receive none such among you if they are married;**

Keep in mind that these instructions, above, were given at the beginnings of the Church. Be aware that an overriding principle in disciplinary action is that the Holy Ghost reveals to the presiding priesthood authority what type of disciplinary action is best suited to help the transgressor return to good standing with the Lord.

Verse 77, next, reminds us that it is possible to repent completely of sexual sin.

77 And if they are not married, **they shall repent of all their sins or ye shall not receive them.**

78 And again, **every person who belongeth to this church of Christ, shall observe to keep all the commandments and covenants of the church.**

In verses 79–87, we are reminded that there are limits to the jurisdiction of Church discipline, and that some situations must be dealt with by civil courts according to the laws of the land. This is a strong example of the

principle of separation of church and state.

79 And it shall come to pass, that **if any persons among you** [*members of the Church*] shall **kill** [*murder*] **they shall be delivered up and dealt with according to the laws of the land**; for remember that he hath no forgiveness [*D&C 42:18*]; and it shall be proved according to the laws of the land.

Next, in verses 80–83, the Lord instructs that being disciplined properly for sexual immorality comes under the jurisdiction of the Church.

80 And **if any man or woman shall commit adultery, he or she shall be tried before two elders of the church, or more**, and every word shall be established against him or her by two witnesses of the church, and not of the enemy; but if there are more than two witnesses it is better.

81 But he or she shall be condemned by the mouth of two witnesses; and the elders shall lay the case before the church, and the church shall lift up their hands against him or her, that they may be **dealt with according to the law of God.**

82 And **if it can be, it is necessary that the bishop be present also.**

83 And thus ye shall do in all cases which shall come before you.

Verses 84–86 specify more situations which must be dealt with by the laws of the land. In other words, the Church can't put people in jail or fine them.

84 **And if a man or woman shall rob**, he or she shall be **delivered up unto the law of the land.**

85 And **if he or she shall steal**, he or she shall be **delivered up unto the law of the land.**

86 And **if he or she shall lie**, he or she shall be **delivered up unto the law of the land.**

We must not miss the point made by the Lord in verse 87, next, that all of the above, including sins that are to be handled by the laws of the land, are also sins against God and against the covenants of baptism and so forth. Therefore, as you have no doubt seen, members of the Church who commit serious crimes against society also must face Church disciplinary action as part of their repentance process.

87 And **if he or she do any manner of iniquity, he or she shall be delivered up unto the law, even that of God.**

Finally, as this tremendous revelation on the "Law" comes to a close, the Lord gives instructions regarding the handling of both personal offenses and offenses against large numbers of people. First of all, the Lord is concerned about protecting the privacy of the offender wherever possible. This obviously helps avoid gossip and unnecessary additional pain.

88 And **if thy brother or sister offend thee**, thou shalt **take him or her between him or her and thee alone** [*handle it in private*]; and **if he or she confess thou shalt be reconciled** [*if they confess and apologize, forgive them and let it go*].

Obviously, some refuse to confess and ask forgiveness when invited to do so, thus continuing their abusive behavior. Next, the Savior gives instructions for dealing with this situation among members.

89 And **if he or she confess not thou shalt deliver him or her up unto the church** [*turn him or her over to the Church, usually the bishop or branch president*], not to the members, but to the elders [*the presiding priesthood authority*]. And it shall be done in a meeting, and that not before the world [*still keep it as private as possible*].

If the transgression of a member has hurt the feelings and testimonies of many members, the above-given "privacy rules" do not apply, as explained next in verses 90–91.

90 And if thy brother or sister offend many, he or she shall be chastened [*disciplined*] **before many** [*as many as need to be informed about the disciplinary action*].

91 And if any one offend openly, he or she shall be rebuked openly, that he or she may be ashamed. And **if he or she confess not** [*if he or she does not acknowledge being in the wrong*]**, he or she shall be delivered up unto the law of God** [*this can mean at least two things; namely, be subject to disciplinary action of the Church, or be dealt with by the Lord on or before Judgment Day; see D&C 40:3 and 64:11*].

It is significant that the Lord, as He brings this instructional session to a close, chooses to emphasize that whenever possible, the privacy of persons who have sinned should be maintained. It is a strong reminder to us of the "worth of souls" (D&C 18:10) and strong counsel to each of us in our personal relationships with others.

92 If any shall offend in secret, he or she shall be rebuked in secret, that he or she may have opportunity to confess in secret to him or her whom he or she has offended, and to God, that the church [*members of the Church*] may not speak reproachfully of [*gossip about*] him or her.

93 And thus shall ye conduct in all things.

BONUS SECTION

A

BRIEF CHRONOLOGY

OF

MAJOR CHARACTERS

IN

EARLY CHURCH HISTORY

BY DAVID J. RIDGES

INTRODUCTION

Who was Where, When, in Early Church History?

Years ago, I got to wondering where other significant players in the Restoration were and what they were doing about the time Joseph Smith had the First Vision in the spring of 1820. I wondered how the Lord got them prepared and in the right place at the right time to do their part in the marvelous work that was coming forth. With some research, I found, for instance, that:

John Taylor, who would become the third president of the Church, was twelve years old, in England, working on his father's farm. Four years later, he would join the Methodist Church in England. During this period of his life, he would see a vision of an angel in heaven with a trumpet and a message to all nations. In five years, he would have strong thoughts come into his mind of preaching the gospel in the Americas.

Wilford Woodruff, who would become the fourth president of the Church, was thirteen years old and had already suffered through eleven serious accidents (that obviously didn't kill him). They, among other things, seemed to toughen him up to issue the Manifesto stopping the practice of plural marriage.

Sidney Rigdon was twenty-seven years old, already on the western frontier in Ohio, and would marry Phebe Brooks in June 1820.

Lorenzo Snow, who would become the fifth president of the Church, was six years old and wanted to be a soldier. His older sister was Eliza R. Snow.

The Peter Whitmer Sr. Family by 1820 had already lived in Fayette, New York, for eleven years. They were Pennsylvania Germans and attended German church services (Anderson, *Investigating the Book of Mormon Witnesses*, 67). In ten years, on April 6, 1030, the true Church would be organized in their home.

Martin Harris was thirty-seven years old and an established farmer, textile manufacturer, and civic leader in Palmyra, New York. He was respected and meticulous, known for his integrity, and thus would make a reliable witness to the Book of Mormon.

Parley P. Pratt was thirteen years old and had already read much of the Bible. The previous year he had read Revelation chapter 20 in the Bible, which concerns the First Resurrection (the resurrection of those who will attain celestial glory), and had a fervent desire to be a part of that resurrection. In a few years, he would become disgusted with all white men and their corrupt society, would move a bit beyond the western frontier of civilization, and would meet a frontier preacher named Sidney Rigdon.

Now, let's go chronologically, starting with Martin Harris, and watch the Lord prepare and move these people around geographically to be where they were needed, when they were needed for the work of the Restoration.

1783—Martin Harris is born in New York (thirty-seven years before the First Vision and twenty-two years before Joseph Smith is born). Martin will be highly respected and prominent in the community affairs of Palmyra, New York. He will also be known as one who constantly reads the scriptures and can quote the Bible at surprising length (Anderson, *Investigating the Book of Mormon Witnesses*, chapter 7). He will come to Utah at age eighty-seven and die at age ninety-two.

1793—Sidney Rigdon is born in Pennsylvania on February 19. He will love books, the Bible, and history. His father, a strict Baptist, will strongly oppose young Sidney's constant reading but will not be able to stop him. He will be five feet, nine and one-half inches tall, and later in life will weigh 215 pounds. He will be twelve years older than Joseph Smith and will be instructed to watch over him in D&C 35:19. Joseph Smith will be twenty-five and Sidney Rigdon thirty-seven when they meet. Sidney will be told that his role is similar to that of John the Baptist (D&C 35:4).

1800—A respected friend of Wilford Woodruff's parents, "Father" Robert Mason, receives a vision concerning the Restoration. In thirty years, he will tell his young friend, twenty-three-year-old Wilford Woodruff, about it (*Teachings of Presidents of the Church*, 1–3). Mason taught Wilford Woodruff much during his youth, including that true authority did not exist on earth and that the day was near when God would again restore His Church.

1801—Brigham Young is born in Vermont, the ninth child in the family. He will be four years older than Joseph Smith. He will be five feet, ten inches tall, with red hair and freckles (Susan Easton Black lecture, summer 1985).

1802—Joseph Smith's mother-to-be, Lucy Mack Smith, comes down with "a heavy cold, which caused a severe cough. A hectic fever set in which threatened to prove fatal" (Proctor, *Revised and Enhanced History of Joseph Smith*, 47). The doctors gave up on saving her. One night, as her husband sat by her side, expecting her to die, she begged and pled with the Lord to spare her life so she could bring up her children and so that her husband would be comforted. She "covenanted with God that if he would let me live, I would endeavor to get that religion that would enable me to serve him right, whether it was in the Bible or wherever it might be found, even if it was to be obtained from heaven by prayer and faith. At last a voice spoke to me and said, 'Seek, and ye shall find; knock, and it shall be opened unto you. Let your heart be comforted. Ye believe in God, believe also in me'" (ibid., 48). From that time forward, she gained strength, and when her health had returned sufficiently, she began to diligently search for "some pious person who knew the ways of God to instruct me in the things of heaven" (ibid.). In this search, she was repeatedly disappointed, which finally led her to say in her heart, "There is not on earth the religion which I seek. I must again turn to my Bible, take Jesus and his disciples for an example. I will try to obtain from God that which man cannot give nor take away" (ibid., 50). Surely these feelings and conclusions in Mother Smith's heart and mind prepared her to support her son when he was called to restore the gospel.

1803—Lucy Mack Smith has a dream in which she is told that the "pure and undefiled gospel of the Son of God . . . will be made available when her husband . . . was more advanced . . . in life" (Proctor, *Revised and Enhanced History*, 58–60). This great lady was well prepared to be the mother of the prophet of the Restoration.

1804—Emma Hale is born in Harmony, Pennsylvania, on July 10 (one and one-half years before Joseph Smith is born), the seventh child in the family. She will grow to be a beautiful young woman, five feet, nine inches tall, with dark hair and brown eyes (Black, *Who's Who in the Doctrine and Covenants*, 273). She will have a good singing voice and will be intelligent, capable, and particular with grammar and her choice of words, never using slang expressions. She will be a meticulous housekeeper and an excellent cook. She will also be a "rural schoolteacher" (Anderson, *Investigating the Book of Mormon Witnesses*, 5).

Brigham Young's parents move to eastern New York. In those days, a man could be fined five schillings for kissing his wife on Sunday (Rebecca Cornwall and Richard F. Palmer, "The Religious and Family Background of Brigham Young," *BYU Studies*, vol. 18:3, spring 1978, 288). Sometime in Brigham's young life he will be taught that dancing and violin music are evil. Later, as a prophet, he will be given D&C 136:28, in which the members of the Church are told to "praise the Lord with singing, with music, with dancing, and with a prayer of praise and thanksgiving."

Joseph Smith Sr. moves his family to eastern New York, not far from where Brigham Young is living.

1805—Joseph Smith Sr. moves back to Vermont.

Joseph Smith is born on December 23 in Vermont (the fourth of ten children in the Smith Family—Alvin, Hyrum, Sophronia, Joseph Smith Jr., Samuel, Ephraim (died in infancy), William, Catherine, Don Carlos, and Lucy, who was born in 1821, after the First Vision).

1806—Oliver Cowdery is born on October 3 in Vermont, the youngest of eight children. His mother will die when he is about three years old. He has brown eyes and will be five feet, five inches tall (Lang, *History of Seneca County (Ohio)*, 365). His oldest brother, Warren, will join the Church late in 1831, will hold responsible positions, but will leave the Church in 1838 (the same year Oliver is excommunicated) and never return (Black, *Who's Who in the Doctrine and Covenants*, 77). Oliver's father, William Cowdery, will join the Church in February 1836.

1807—Wilford Woodruff is born on March 1 in Connecticut. His mother will die when he is not quite one year old. He will be toughened up by life, having had numerous life-threatening accidents, and will be well prepared to handle the tough task of issuing the Manifesto stopping polygamy. He will write a journal of nine volumes with more than seven thousand pages, including a "Chapter on Accidents." He will live ninety-one years.

Parley P. Pratt is born April 12. In twenty-three years, he will be ready for baptism (1830). He will be murdered while on a mission in Arkansas on May 13, 1857, at age fifty.

1808—Joseph Smith will turn three on December 23.

Martin Harris will marry his first cousin Lucy Harris in March. They will have three children.

John Taylor is born November 1 in England. He will grow to more than six feet tall. Parley P. Pratt will preach to him in Canada, and he will be baptized in 1836. He will carry a bullet from Carthage to the time of his death. He will be a double martyr. He will nearly die in Carthage Jail, when the Prophet Joseph is martyred. He will die at age 78, on July 25, 1887, of congestive heart failure while in hiding in Davis County, Utah, unable to get proper medical help because of persecutors.

Wilford Woodruff's mother dies of spotted fever on January 11 when she is twenty-eight years old. Wilford is not quite one year old.

1809—Oliver Cowdery's mother dies. He is three years old.

The Whitmers move from Pennsylvania to Fayette, New York. They will be well established in twenty-one years, when the Lord will use their home for the organization of the Church on April 6, 1830.

1810—Wilford Woodruff falls into a cauldron of scalding water. He is three years old, and it will be nine months before he will be out of danger of dying from this accident (*Teachings of Presidents of the Church—Woodruff*, 6).

Sidney Rigdon's father dies. Sidney is seventeen years old and must support his mother on the farm. He doesn't like farming.

1811—Joseph Smith Sr. has a vision closely paralleling Lehi's dream (Smith, *History of Joseph Smith*, 48–50). This is one of at least seven visions this great father had. No wonder he supported his son! Joseph's parents were well prepared to be the parents of a prophet, just as others like Elizabeth and Zacharias (John the Baptist), Abraham and Sarah (Isaac), and Joseph and Mary (Jesus). Joseph, of course, was not the Savior's father, but was well prepared through dreams and visions to help raise Him.

1812—Twenty-nine-year-old Martin Harris serves in the War of 1812 against Britain. He is wealthy enough to hire a substitute but doesn't (Anderson, *Investigating the Book of Mormon Witnesses*, 99). He is a man of high principles.

1812–1813—When he is five and six, Wilford Woodruff has many accidents.

He will fall from the top of a barn flat on his face on the bare floor. Later, he will fall from the top to the bottom of the stairs but will only break one arm in one place.

Wilford is feeding a pumpkin to his favorite cow when a bull leaves his own pumpkin, pushes away the cow that young Wilford likes, and starts eating her pumpkin. Wilford is furious, picks up the pumpkin and marches toward his cow to give it to her. The bull sees him carrying the pumpkin and lunges toward him. Wilford starts running but does not drop the pumpkin despite his father's frantic shouts to do so. The enraged bull is upon him—he trips and falls, the pumpkin rolls away, and the bull jumps over little Wilford, gores the pumpkin, and tears it to shreds. Wilford escapes.

Wilford falls from his uncle's porch and breaks his other arm. Wilford hasn't yet broken a leg, so he does that. He lies in pain in the house for nine hours before help arrives. Wilford gets kicked in the abdomen by an ox. (If he hadn't been standing so close, he probably would have been killed. As it was, he was thrown more than kicked, probably saving his life.) Later, a wagon load of hay tips on top of him, but he suffers no harm (Cowley, *Wilford Woodruff*, 6–8).

1813—Joseph Smith Jr., going on eight, has bone surgery on his left leg. Fourteen pieces of bone will work their way to the surface before the wound heals. He will use crutches for three years and walk with a slight limp in later life (LeRoy S. Wirthlin, "Joseph Smith's Boyhood Operation: An 1813 Surgical Success," *BYU Studies,* vol. 21, no. 2, 153). By the time he has the First Vision, he will already be familiar with overcoming obstacles.

1814—Lorenzo Snow is born in Mantua, Ohio. As he grows up, he will want to pursue a military career. His sister Eliza R. Snow and the Lord have other plans for him.

Parley P. Pratt, seven years old, reads selections from the Old Testament under the direction of his mother.

1815—Brigham Young's mother dies. He is fourteen. Wilford Woodruff's mother, Oliver Cowdery's mother, and Sidney Rigdon's Father have all died by now.

Wilford Woodruff is about eight years old and still alive, but his horse has bolted, tipping the wagon over on top of him and his father. Later this year, Wilford climbs an elm tree and steps on a dry limb when he is fifteen feet up. It breaks and he falls, landing flat on his back on the ground. The fall knocks the wind out of him. A cousin runs and tells Wilford's folks that Wilford is dead. He isn't. A Baptist revival this year in Farmington, Connecticut, gets his hopes up with respect to religion, but he is disappointed. It seems to him that preachers don't preach a living gospel (Cowley, *Wilford Woodruff*, 21).

1816—Brigham Young's father moves farther west, settling in Genoa, New York, which is about sixty miles southeast of Palmyra.

1817—Sidney Rigdon, about twenty-four years of age, joins with the United Baptists in Pennsylvania.

1818—Joseph Smith starts earnestly seeking the truth concerning God and which church to join. He is twelve years old and will search diligently for two years, encountering much frustration.

Sidney Rigdon becomes a licensed Baptist preacher. He is five feet, nine inches tall, will weight up to 215 pounds, and is an excellent preacher and speaker. Later, on the western frontier, he will bring many to him who will eventually join the true Church. He will be a type of John the Baptist for the Prophet Joseph Smith (see D&C 35:4).

1819—Twelve-year-old Parley P. Pratt reads Revelation 20 in the Bible, which concerns the First Resurrection. He has an urgent desire to secure for himself a place in the resurrection of the just.

Sidney Rigdon moves to Warren, Ohio, to preach as an apprentice to Adamson Bentley. This gets Sidney closer to the western frontier, where he will need to be in eleven years when Elder Parley P. Pratt and his three missionary companions come through Kirtland, Ohio. Sidney and many of his congregation at that time will be converted.

Twelve-year-old Wilford Woodruff is drowning in thirty feet of water. A man saves him. He suffers much as he is revived (Cowley, *Wilford Woodruff*, 7).

1820—Joseph Smith is visited by the Father and the Son in the First Vision.

John Taylor, age twelve, is working on his father's farm in England.

Sidney Rigdon marries Phebe Brooks in Ohio on June 12. They are on the western frontier.

Thirteen-year-old Wilford Woodruff is freezing to death. Hypothermia has set in. He is asleep in the hollow of a large apple tree. A man in the distance, who sees him crawl into the hollow, comes to his aid. He has much difficulty waking him but saves his life.

1821—Sidney Rigdon becomes an ordained Baptist minister, attracting large crowds wherever he preaches. During the summer of this year, he will visit Alexander Campbell and be converted to Campbell's ways of thinking, which include faith, repentance, baptism by immersion, and the gift of the Holy Ghost. Later this year, Sidney will move back to Pittsburgh, Pennsylvania, to accept a position as pastor for a Campbellite congregation.

Wilford Woodruff has accidently sunk an ax into his left instep, passing nearly through his foot. It will be nine months before it is healed. He is fourteen years old (Cowley, *Wilford Woodruff*, 8).

1822—Parley Pratt is working on a farm. He is fifteen years old and away from home.

Wilford Woodruff is fifteen years old and has just been bitten on the hand by a dog with rabies. The dog did not draw blood, and Wilford is spared again.

1823—Moroni visits Joseph Smith the first time.

Brigham Young joins the Methodist Reform Church (some think it was in 1824), but it will not satisfy his desire for truth.

Sixteen-year-old Parley P. Pratt is living with his Aunt VanCott and is able to attend a few months of school. He does well, and his teacher holds him up as an exemplary student, a fact he mentions in his autobiography: "I made such extraordinary progress that the teacher often spoke of me to the whole school, and exhorted them to learn as Parley Pratt did" (Pratt, *Autobiography*, 1938, 21).

John Taylor, 15, has decided to be a cooper (barrel maker) in England. Little does he know what God has in mind!

Martin Harris will win eight prizes this year at the fair for cloth manufacturing. He produces linen, cotton, wool ticking, blankets, and worsted and flannel fabrics (Anderson, *Investigating the Book of Mormon Witnesses*, 99).

1824—Sixteen-year-old John Taylor joins the Methodist Church in England. This year he will see a vision of an angel in the heavens with a trumpet and a message to all nations. He wonders what the dream means. (See Revelation 14:6–7.)

Parley P. Pratt is working with his father to clear seventy acres in New York, above Palmyra, as a homesite for his father's family. While working with his father, he asks why there are so many discrepancies between the biblical church and churches now. Where are the simple doctrines of repentance, baptism, and the gift of the Holy Ghost? He is much perplexed over these matters. Furthermore, he wonders if the authority of God is even on earth. His father can't give satisfactory answers.

Joseph Smith visits Moroni as scheduled. He is being taught by other Book of Mormon prophets as well.

Sidney Rigdon has been fired as a pastor for teaching too many of his own doctrines. He is working as a tanner in Pittsburgh and will continue to do so through 1826.

Wilford Woodruff has just been dislodged from the saddle on a runaway horse careening wildly down a hillside. He has slid up the horse's neck and is on its head, hanging onto its ears for dear life as it continues to plummet down a steep, rocky hillside. The horse slams into a breast-high boulder, stopping it dead in its tracks, and Wilford flies through the air, landing on his feet almost one rod (sixteen feet) in front of the horse (otherwise he would have been killed instantly). He breaks one leg in two places and displaces both ankles. The dazed horse almost rolls over him as it attempts to get up. In eight weeks, he will be able to walk with the aid of crutches.

1825—John Taylor, in England, is strongly impressed that he will someday preach the gospel in America. He is seventeen years of age and will preach his first sermon this year for the Methodists.

Parley P. Pratt, eighteen, is baptized into the Baptist Church.

Joseph Smith continues to be taught by Moroni and others.

1826—Parley Pratt has become disgusted with corrupt white-man society. He buys a Bible and leaves the civilized world. He later buys a gun, earns an ax, and moves a bit past the western frontier, where he builds a shack in the forest about thirty-two miles west of Cleveland, Ohio (Sidney Rigdon territory). Parley is nineteen. He is now in a position to meet Sidney Rigdon, who teaches faith, repentance, baptism, and the gift of the Holy Ghost.

Sidney Rigdon moves to Mentor, Ohio, near Cleveland, to become pastor of a congregation there.

Joseph Smith continues his visits and discussions with Moroni. He is getting so familiar with Book of Mormon places, architecture, dress styles, and so forth that his parents and brothers and sisters often gather around him in the evening and listen to him tell stories of ancient American history.

Joseph and Emma wish they could get her parents' permission to marry.

Parley P. Pratt is sitting in a shack in the forest, eating venison, reading the Bible, and reading about the Lewis and Clark expedition. Once in a while he will have a refreshing conversation with a red man, whom he still respects, but he wants nothing to do with white men because of their generally corrupt ways.

1827—Joseph Smith elopes with Emma Hale on January 18. They are married in South Bainbridge, New York, by a justice of the peace. Nine children will come (see information sheet at the end of this section), and four will live to maturity. Three will live a few hours, one fourteen months, and one will be stillborn. In addition, they will adopt twins.

Parley P. Pratt, still living on the western frontier, clears an area for a farm and replaces his shack with a house, which triggers thoughts about the girl he left behind in New York. He is now twenty, tanned by the sun and weather, and has a heavy growth of whiskers. On July 4, he finds himself in Canaan, Columbia, New York, near the house where the girl of his dreams, Thankful Halsey, lived the last time he saw her three years before. She is home! Later that evening he proposes to her with the following words: "If you still love me and desire to share my fortune you are worthy to be my wife." She accepts. They will marry on September 9 (Pratt, *Autobiography,* 29).

Joseph Smith brings the gold plates home to his parent's place in Palmyra from the Hill Cumorah.

Martin Harris sends his wife, Lucy, and his daughter, Lucy, to the Smiths to investigate whether Joseph really has obtained the gold plates. He is a careful man and wants to be sure before he gets involved. Lucy and Lucy are allowed to heft the box the plates are in. It convinces them, and they report as much to Martin. They say that the plates must weigh close to sixty pounds.

In December, Joseph and Emma move to Harmony, Pennsylvania, to live with her parents.

Wilford Woodruff is twenty years old and still alive, but he is standing on a water wheel, clearing away ice. Another worker, unaware that Wilford is there, opens the water head gate, which starts the wheel in motion. Wilford falls off and narrowly escapes being crushed in the machinery.

1828—Oliver Cowdery, who will become one of the Three Witnesses to the Book of Mormon, comes to Manchester, near Palmyra, where Joseph Smith's parents live, to teach school (his brother, Lyman, got the job in the first place but wasn't able to keep his commitment, so Oliver was cleared by Hyrum Smith and others on the board of education to take his place). Thus, Oliver meets the Smith family. Also, he finds himself quite impressed by one of his students in the school. She is Elizabeth Ann Whitmer, the sister of David Whitmer. Oliver will marry her in 1832. They will have six children: five girls and one boy. Only one will live to maturity, a girl. She will marry but will have no children.

David Whitmer, who will also become one of the Three Witnesses, comes to Palmyra on business and becomes fast friends with Oliver Cowdery. They discuss various rumors they've heard about the gold plates. They are both curious about the matter.

Martin Harris, who likewise will become one of the Three Witnesses, visits Joseph Smith in Harmony, Pennsylvania, where Joseph and Emma are living. He obtains a copy of some of the characters from the plates and takes them to a professor of ancient languages, Dr. Charles Anthon, in New York City, who will initially confirm their authenticity. In April, Martin begins serving as scribe for Joseph, and by June 14, 116 pages of the translation will be completed. Martin will plead with Joseph to let him take the 116 pages of translation home to Palmyra to show them to his wife, Lucy, in order to counter her caustic criticism of his spending time and wasting money on foolish pursuits with Joseph Smith, and also in order to stop the waging tongues about him among the citizens in Palmyra. The 116 manuscript pages will soon be lost.

Because of the loss of 116 pages, Joseph loses the gift of translation for a season. Moroni takes the Urim and Thummin and the plates. He will return them to Joseph on September 22.

1829—Parley P. Pratt meets Sidney Rigdon near the western frontier and is excited about Sidney's preaching of faith, repentance, baptism, and the gift of the Holy Ghost. Parley joins with Sidney but is still uncomfortable about the matter of authority to perform ordinances.

Oliver Cowdery decides he must visit Joseph Smith in Harmony, Pennsylvania, to investigate the gold plates. He stops along the way and talks to his friend, David Whitmer, in Fayette, New York, and agrees to write and tell David what he finds out. He arrives in Harmony and within two days (April 7) he begins as scribe in the work of translation.

Brigham Young and his wife move to Mendon, New York, fifteen miles from Palmyra. At Palmyra, he hears rumors regarding a man named Joe Smith and a gold Bible he dug out of a mountain.

In early spring of this year, Oliver writes to the Whitmers, informing them that Joseph is indeed involved in the work of the Lord. Moved by Oliver's statements, Peter Whitmer Sr. and some members of his family journey to Harmony and meet Joseph personally. David Whitmer is apparently not with them on this visit.

Later, David Whitmer brings a wagon to Harmony and transports Joseph and Oliver to Fayette to complete the work of translation. Emma will follow shortly. In fact, Emma's Uncle Nathaniel has tried to talk her into not going with Joseph. Instead, she will follow the Lord's counsel given later (in D&C 25:6) and join Joseph in Fayette. She never saw her family again except for one brother in Nauvoo. Moroni transports the plates to Fayette, meets Joseph in the garden there, and returns the plates to him.

John the Baptist restores the Aaronic Priesthood by conferring it upon Joseph Smith and Oliver Cowdery.

Peter, James, and John restore the Melchizedek Priesthood.

The Book of Mormon is completed, and a printer is hired.

1830—Robert Mason tells young Wilford Woodruff of the coming Restoration of the true Church, and that Wilford will play a major role in it. It will be two years before Wilford hears about the Latter-day Saints and three years before he is baptized. Wilford will be baptized for Robert Mason in the Nauvoo Temple. Much later in his life, he will have the signers of the Declaration of Independence and others appear to him in the St. George Temple and will supervise work for the dead for them.

By March 26, the first copies of the Book of Mormon are printed.

The Church is organized at the Whitmer home in Fayette, New York, on April 6.

Parley P. Pratt is impressed to search the scriptures and pray for understanding. He is impressed to sell the farm and return with his wife to New York. He does. When they arrive at Rochester, he is impressed to change plans and head south from there. He bids his wife "goodbye," says he will catch up to her later, and heads south. He obtains a copy of the Book of Mormon from a Baptist Deacon named Hamlin, who happens to have one. He then reads it through, hardly stopping for food or sleep. He then hurries to the Palmyra area, finds Hyrum Smith, and keeps him up all night asking about the gospel. Shortly thereafter, on September 1, he is baptized by Oliver Cowdery.

Sidney Rigdon is baptized after being visited by the newly baptized Parley P. Pratt, who, with his missionary companions, is on his way to the western frontier to fulfill his mission to the Lamanites (D&C 32).

Wilford Woodruff concludes that the only real peace of mind or true happiness comes through righteousness and service to God (Cowley, *Wilford Woodruff*, 26).

Samuel Smith gives a copy of the Book of Mormon to John P. Greene, who gives it to his wife, who gives it to her brother, Brigham Young, who is one of Heber C. Kimball's best friends. Brigham will not be an instant baptism. He will study and compare the Book of Mormon and the Bible for almost two years before baptism. Brigham's father reads and believes it too.

1831—Lorenzo Snow hears Joseph Smith preach at Hiram, Ohio. Lorenzo is seventeen years old.

Brigham Young and Heber C. Kimball listen to LDS missionaries in Phineas Young's home.

Wilford Woodruff has another bout with a water wheel. He survives again. He wonders why no apostles are on earth. He has desired baptism but doubts the authority of Christian ministers. He is twenty-four years old. He finally talks a Baptist minister into baptizing him on condition that he does not have to join the minister's church.

1832—John Taylor moves to Canada with his parents. He is twenty-four years old, is a skilled wood turner, and serves as a Methodist Sunday school teacher. He meets Leonora Cannon, George Q. Cannon's sister. (George Q. Cannon will become a counselor to John Taylor, Wilford Woodruff, and Lorenzo Snow in the First Presidency.) John Taylor proposes to Leonora, but she says, "No." That night she has a dream in which she sees herself married to John Taylor. Consequently, she accepts his proposal. John will get into trouble with his church by comparing it with the Bible and sticking to Bible teachings.

Brigham Young is baptized on April 14. He is instrumental in converting all of his brothers and sisters, his father, and his dying wife (Barrett, *Joseph Smith and the Restoration*, 210). Heber C. Kimball takes care of his children. Heber Kimball is baptized June 15. He is over six feet tall with a barrel chest that measures the same from front to back as from side to side (ibid., 210–11).

Wilford Woodruff, age twenty-five, reads about Joseph Smith and the new church in a slanderous newspaper article. He is deeply impressed and has a strong desire to meet some Latter-day Saints, who claim to possess gifts of the Spirit as in Bible times (Cowley, *Wilford Woodruff*, 30).

Oliver Cowdery and Elizabeth Ann Whitmer are married in Jackson County, Missouri, where the Whitmer family has immigrated. He is twenty-six, she is almost eighteen. Of their children, three will live less than a month, one will live five months, and the remaining child will live six and one-half years.

Brigham Young meets Joseph Smith in September in Kirtland, Ohio.

1833—Brigham Young marries Mary Ann Angell. (She is buried with him in Salt Lake City.) She will move alone from Far West. Her child will be run over in a wagon accident and will be miraculously healed.

Wilford Woodruff, age twenty-six, is baptized on December 31, two days after first hearing missionaries preach. "The snow was about three feet deep, the day was cold, and that water was mixed with ice and snow, yet I did not feel the cold," he wrote (Cowley, *Wilford Woodruff*, 35). That same day, his horse with newly caulked shoes kicks Wilford's hat off his head, missing his head by just two inches. Ten minutes later, Wilford has hitched the horse with another to a sled and is driving away. Some loose boards on the sled slide forward, slip end first to the ground, and fly up endwise, picking Brother Woodruff up and pitching him forward between the horses. The frightened animals run down the hill, dragging him under the sled behind them. He escapes without injury.

1834—Wilford Woodruff and Brigham Young are marching with Zion's Camp. Wilford is nearly shot by a rifle ball that is accidently discharged by a camp member. The ball passes through three tents with a dozen men in each without hurting anyone and passes within inches of Wilford's chest (Cowley, *Wilford Woodruff*, 9).

A musket, heavily loaded with buckshot and pointing directly at Wilford Woodruff's chest, is accidently snapped but misfires.

1835—Lorenzo Snow enters Oberlin College. He is disenchanted with organized religion. He is twenty-one. His sister, Eliza R. Snow, invites him to Kirtland to study Hebrew. He will rub shoulders with many of the Church leaders and become especially fond of Joseph Smith Sr.

1836—John Taylor has been converted in Canada by Parley P. Pratt and is baptized.

1837—Wilford Woodruff marries Phoebe Carter.

1838—Wilford Woodruff baptizes his father, Aphek Woodruff, on July 1.

1839—In April, Wilford Woodruff is pinned in a wagon accident and dragged by the frightened team for about half a mile with his head and shoulders dragging on the ground. Despite his awkward position, he manages somehow to steer the frightened horses into the corner of a high fence, where he and the team land in a pile together. Of this incident he said, "I was considerably bruised, but escaped without any broken bones, and after one day's rest was able to attend to my labors again" (Cowley, *Wilford Woodruff*, 10).

1846—On October 15, while cutting down a tree a couple of miles outside of Winter Quarters, Nebraska (just across the western border of Iowa), Wilford Woodruff is struck by the tree, knocked into the air, and thrown against an oak tree. His left thigh, hip, and left arm are badly bruised, and his breastbone and three left ribs are broken. His lungs, internal organs, and left side are badly bruised. He must ride his horse two and one-half miles over rough road to get back to the settlement. Pain forces him off the horse twice. Upon arriving back at Winter Quarters, men carry him in a chair to his wagon. Before putting him in bed, Brigham Young, Heber C. Kimball, Willard Richards, and others bless him. He lays upon his bed, unable to move until his breastbone begins to knit together. In about twenty days he begins to walk, and in thirty days, he returns to his normal duties.

Of his accidents, Wilford said, "I have broken both legs, one of them in two places; both arms, both ankles, my breastbone, and three ribs. I have been scalded, frozen and drowned. I have been in two water wheels while turning under a full head. I have passed through a score of other hairbreadth escapes" (Cowley, *Wilford Woodruff*, 11).

Taught By Whom?

(Heavenly Messengers Who Taught Joseph Smith)

The Prophet Joseph Smith was taught by many from beyond the veil. President John Taylor, in various talks, mentioned many of these "teachers" of the Prophet. The following combined quotes from some of his talks help us realize how many heavenly personages were involved:

"When God selected Joseph Smith to open up the last dispensation . . . the **Father** and the **Son** appeared to him . . . **Moroni** came to Joseph. . . . Then comes another personage, whose name is **John the Baptist**. . . . Afterwards came **Peter, James** and **John**. . . . Then we read again of **Elias** or **Elijah**, . . . who committed to him the powers and authority associated with his position. Then **Abraham**, who had the Gospel, the Priesthood and Patriarchal powers in his day; and **Moses** who stood at the head of the gathering dispensation in his day. . . . We are informed that **Noah**, who was a Patriarch, **and all in the line of the Priesthood, in every generation back to Adam**, who was the first man, possessed the same. Why was it that all these people . . . could communicate with Joseph Smith? Because he stood at the head of the dispensation of the fullness of times. . . . If you were to ask Joseph what sort of a looking man **Adam** was, he would tell you at once; he would tell you his size and appearance and all about him. You might have asked him what sort of men **Peter**, **James** and **John** were, and he could have told you. Why? Because he had seen them." (*Journal of Discourses*, 18:325–26).

"And when Joseph Smith was raised up as a Prophet of God, **Mormon**, **Moroni**, **Nephi** and others of the ancient Prophets who formerly lived on this Continent, and **Peter** and **John** and others who lived on the Asiatic Continent, came to him and communicated to him certain principles pertaining to the gospel of the son of God" (*Journal of Discourses*, 17:374).

"I know of what I speak for I was very well acquainted with him (Joseph Smith) and was with him a great deal during his life, and was with him when he died. The principles which he had, placed him in communication with the Lord, and not only with the Lord, but with the ancient apostles and prophets; such men, for instance, as **Abraham**, **Isaac**, **Jacob**, **Noah**, **Adam**, **Seth**, **Enoch**, and **Jesus** and the **Father**, and the **apostles that lived on this continent** as well as **those who lived on the Asiatic Continent**. He seemed to be as familiar with these people as we are with one another" (*Journal of Discourses*, 21:94).

APPENDIX

CHILDREN OF JOSEPH SMITH SR AND LUCY MACK SMITH

Name	Birth Date	Place of Birth	Death Date
1. Child	about 1797	Tunbridge, VT	about 1797
2. Alvin	11 Feb. 1798	Tunbridge, VT	19 Nov. 1823
3. Hyrum	9 Feb. 1800	Tunbridge, VT	27 June 1844
4. Sophronia	16 May 1803	Tunbridge, VT	about 1876
5. Joseph Jr.	23 Dec. 1805	Sharon, VT	27 June 1844
6. Samuel Harrison	13 March 1808	Tunbridge, VT	30 July 1844
7. Ephraim	13 March 1810	Royalton, VT	24 March 1810
8. William	13 March 1811	Royalton, VT	13 Nov. 1893
9. Catherine	28 July 1812	Lebanon, NH	1 Feb. 1900
10. Don Carlos	25 March 1816	Norwich, VT	7 Aug. 1841
11. Lucy	18 July 1821	Palmyra, NY	9 Dec. 1882

(See *Church History in the Fulness of Times*, 21.)

CHILDREN OF JOSEPH SMITH AND EMMA HALE SMITH

1. Alvin—Born and died on June 15, 1828, at Harmony, Pennsylvania. Some historians say his name was Alva.

2. Louisa—Born April 30, 1831, at Kirtland, Ohio. A girl, one of the twins, lived about three hours.

3. Thaddeus—Born April 30, 1831, at Kirtland, Ohio. A boy, one of the twins, lived about three hours.

4. Joseph Smith III—Born November 6, 1832, at Kirtland, Ohio. Died December 10, 1914, at Independence, Missouri.

5. Frederick G. Williams—Born June 20, 1836, at Kirtland, Ohio. Died April 13, 1862, at Nauvoo.

6. Alexander Hale—Born June 2, 1838, at Far West, Missouri. Died August 12, 1909, at Nauvoo.

7. Don Carlos—Born June 13, 1840, at Nauvoo. Died August 15, 1841, at 14 months at Nauvoo, Illinois.

8. A boy—Born December 26, 1842, at Nauvoo. He did not survive his birth.

9. David Hyrum—Born November 17, 1844, at Nauvoo. Died August 29, 1904, in Elgin, Illinois.

ADOPTED CHILDREN

10. Joseph Smith Murdock—A twin, born April 30, 1831, at Kirtland, Ohio. Died one year later on March 29, 1832.

11. Julia Murdock—A twin, born April 30, 1831, at Kirtland, Ohio. Died in 1880 near Nauvoo.

FINAL SITUATION OF THE FIVE SURVIVING CHILDREN OF JOSEPH AND EMMA

1. **Julia Murdock**. Twins were born to John Murdock's wife the same day that Emma Hale Smith gave birth to twins, a boy and a girl. Emma's infants did not survive their birth. Sister Murdock passed away, leaving her twins motherless. John Murdock asked that Joseph and Emma raise his infants in place of their lost twins. The boy died after a year. The girl survived.

Julia grew up in the Smith household and at about age eighteen married Elisha Dixon. They resided in Nauvoo for some years. The couple later moved to Texas, where Elisha was killed in a boiler explosion on a steamship trafficking the Red River. Still in her early twenties, Julia returned to Nauvoo. She subsequently married John J. Middleton and moved with him to St. Louis. John was a Catholic, and she joined his faith. He became a chronic alcoholic. Julia left him and returned to Nauvoo, where she lived in the Mansion House until the death of Emma in 1879. Sick, penniless, and suffering from breast cancer, Julia passed away in 1880 at the home of Mr. and Mrs. James Moffatt, near Nauvoo.

2. **Joseph Smith III**. The eldest son was not yet twelve years old when his father, the Prophet Joseph Smith, was martyred, on June 27, 1844. His mother, Emma Smith, elected not to move the family to the west with the body of Saints, and so Joseph grew up in Nauvoo. As a young man he studied law and held various offices of public trust. At twenty-four, Joseph married Emmeline Griswold and subsequently two other wives, Ada Rachel Clark and Bertha Madison. Seventeen children were born to Joseph and his three wives.

He was contacted in 1856 by a church body calling itself the "New Organization." Its members requested that he assume the presidency of their church, but he declined. However, in his twenty-eighth year, he wrote to William Marks, former Nauvoo stake president and a leader in the "New Organization," stating that he was now ready to take his father's place as the head of the Reorganized Church. William Marks, W. W. Blair, and Israel Rogers visited Joseph in Nauvoo and discussed the proposed reorganization. Consequently, Joseph and his Mother, Emma Smith, attended a special conference at Amboy, Illinois, April 6, 1860, where, under the hands of Zenos H. Gurley, William Marks, Samuel Powers, and W. W. Blair, he was ordained prophet, seer, and revelator and successor to his father.

Joseph Smith III retained his office as president of the Reorganized Church of Jesus Christ of Latter Day Saints until his death on December 10, 1914. Frederick G. Smith, third child of Joseph and Bertha Madison, succeeded his father.

3. **Frederick G. Williams Smith**. The Prophet's second living son married Annie Marie Jones when he was twenty-one years old. They lived in Nauvoo for many years, where he was a farmer and merchant. Only one daughter was born to them, Alice Fredericka. Alice was contacted in Chicago by missionaries from the Church in Utah and was baptized into the faith of the "Utah Mormons" on January 6, 1915. However, her family prevailed upon her to give up this affiliation, and she returned to the Reorganized Church. Frederick Granger Williams Smith passed away in Nauvoo at the age of twenty-six on April 13, 1863.

4. **Alexander Hale Smith**. The prophet's third living son married Elizabeth Kendall and became the father of four sons and five daughters. He farmed near Nauvoo for many years and was recognized as a skilled wrestler, hunter, and marksman. Alexander gave his full support to his elder brother in the work of the Reorganized Church. He became one of the most popular ministers of the organization, traveling extensively in America and in many foreign lands. Alexander served as an apostle and as a counselor to the president. His last years were spent as the presiding patriarch. While visiting

Nauvoo, he passed away in the old Mansion House at age seventy-one on August 12, 1909.

5. **David Hyrum Smith**. The prophet's last son was born five months after the Martyrdom, receiving the name his father had suggested at the time of his leaving for Carthage. David and his brother, Alexander, were sent as missionaries to Utah in 1869. At the age of twenty-six, he married Clara Hartshorn, and they had one son named Elbert. Elbert served as a counselor to his Uncle Joseph and later to President Frederick M. Smith. Subsequently he was called as presiding patriarch of the Reorganized Church. David Hyrum was a popular missionary, preacher, hymn writer, and poet for the Reorganized Church. Early in his mature life, his activity was curtailed by illness. He died at age sixty in the State Mental Hospital at Elgin, Illinois.

Sources

Anderson, Richard Lloyd. *Investigating the Book of Mormon Witnesses.* Salt Lake City: Deseret Book, 1981.

Barrett, Ivan J. *Joseph Smith and the Restoration.* Provo, UT: Brigham Young University, 1982.

Black, Susan Easton. *Who's Who in the Doctrine and Covenants.* Salt Lake City: Bookcraft, 1997.

Cannon, George Q. *Life of Joseph Smith the Prophet.* Good Press, 1888.

————. *Life of Joseph Smith the Prophet.* Salt Lake City: Deseret News Press, 1907.

Church History in the Fulness of Times. Salt Lake City: The Church of Jesus Christ of Latter-day Saints (Institutes of Religion), 1989, 2003.

Clark, James R. (Compiler.) *Messages of the First Presidency of The Church of Jesus Christ of Latter-day Saints.* 6 vols. Salt Lake City: Bookcraft, 1965–75.

Conference Reports of The Church of Jesus Christ of Latter-day Saints. Salt Lake City: The Church of Jesus Christ of Latter-day Saints, 1898 to the present.

Cowley, Matthias F. *Wilford Woodruff: History of His Life and Labors.* 2d ed. Salt Lake City: Bookcraft, 1964.

Doctrine and Covenants Student Manual. Salt Lake City: The Church of Jesus Christ of Latter-day Saints (Institutes of Religion), 1981, 2018.

Doctrines of the Gospel Student Manual. Salt Lake City: The Church of Jesus Christ of Latter-day Saints (Institutes of Religion), 1981.

Doxey, Roy W. (Compiler.) *Latter-day Prophets and the Doctrine and Covenants.* Salt Lake City: Deseret Book, 1978.

"The Family: A Proclamation to the World." *Ensign or Liahona,* Nov. 2010, 129.

Hancock, Levi Ward. Autobiography. Typescript. L. Tom Perry Special Collections, Harold B. Lee Library, Brigham Young University, Provo, Utah.

Joseph Smith Papers, The. Salt Lake City: Church Historian's Press. (These books consist of several volumes now [2020] and will consist of more than 30 volumes when they are complete.)

Journal of Discourses. 26 vols. London: Latter-day Saints' Book Depot, 1854–86.

Kimball, Spencer W. *The Teachings of Spencer W. Kimball.* Edited by Edward L. Kimball. Salt Lake City: Bookcraft, 1982.

Lang, W. *History of Seneca County [Ohio], from the Close of the Revolutionary War to July, 1880.* Woburn, MA: Unigraphic, 1973.

Latter-day Saints' Millennial Star, The. Manchester, Liverpool, and London, England: The Church of Jesus Christ of Latter-day Saints, 1840–1970.

Life and Teachings of Jesus and His Apostles: New Testament Student Manual, The. Salt Lake City: The Church of Jesus Christ of Latter-day Saints, 1979.

Ludlow, Daniel H. *Encyclopedia of Mormonism.* Edited by Daniel H. Ludlow. 5 vols. New York: Macmillan, 1992.

Lundwall, N. B. *Temples of the Most High.* Salt Lake City: Bookcraft, 1971.

Matthews, Robert J. *A Plainer Translation: Joseph Smith's Translation of the Bible—A History and Commentary.* Provo, Utah: Brigham Young University Press, 1975.

McConkie, Bruce R. *Doctrinal New Testament Commentary.* 3 vols. Salt Lake City: Bookcraft, 1965–73.

———. *The Millennial Messiah: The Second Coming of the Son of Man.* Salt Lake City: Deseret Book, 1982.

———. *Mormon Doctrine.* 2d ed. Salt Lake City: Bookcraft, 1966.

———. *The Mortal Messiah: From Bethlehem to Calgary.* 4 vols. Salt Lake City: Deseret Book, 1979–81.

———. *The Promised Messiah: The First Coming of Christ.* Salt Lake City: Deseret Book, 1978.

McGavin, Cecil E. *Historical Background of the Doctrine and Covenants.* Salt Lake City: Literary Licensing, 2011.

Otten, L. G. *Historical Background and Setting for each section of the Doctrine and Covenants.* Privately published, 1970.

Pratt, Parley P. *Autobiography of Parley P. Pratt.* Salt Lake City: Deseret Book, 1938–1985.

Proctor, Scott and Maurine. *The Revised and Enhanced History of Joseph Smith by His Mother.* Salt Lake City: Bookcraft, 1996.

Roberts, B. H. *A Comprehensive History of The Church of Jesus Christ of Latter-day Saints, Century One.* 6 vols. Salt Lake City: Deseret Press, 1930.

Smith, Hyrum M. and Janne M. Sjodahl. *Doctrine and Covenants Commentary.* Salt Lake City: Deseret Book, 1951.

Smith, Joseph. *History of The Church of Jesus Christ of Latter-day Saints.* Edited by B. H. Roberts. 2d ed. rev., 7 vols. Salt Lake City: The Church of Jesus Christ of Latter-day Saints, 1932–51.

————. *Teachings of the Prophet Joseph Smith.* Selected by Joseph Fielding Smith. Salt Lake City: Deseret Book, 1976.

Smith, Joseph F. *Gospel Doctrine.* Salt Lake City: Deseret Book, 1939.

Smith, Joseph Fielding. *Answers to Gospel Questions.* Compiled by Joseph Fielding Smith Jr. 5 vols. Salt Lake City: Deseret Book, 1957–66.

————. *Church History and Modern Revelation—A Course Study for Melchizedek Priesthood Quorums.* Salt Lake City: The Council of the Twelve Apostles of The Church of Jesus Christ of Latter-day Saints, 1946.

————. *Doctrines of Salvation.* Compiled by Bruce R. McConkie. 3 vols. Salt Lake City: Bookcraft, 1954–56.

————. *Way to Perfection.* Salt Lake City: Deseret Book, 1975.

Smith, Lucy Mack. *History of Joseph Smith by His Mother, Lucy Mack Smith.* Salt Lake City: Bookcraft, 1958.

Talmage, James E. *The Articles of Faith.* Salt Lake City: Deseret Book, 1984.

Teachings of Presidents of the Church—Wilford Woodruff. Salt Lake City: The Church of Jesus Christ of Latter-day Saints, 2004.

————. *Jesus the Christ.* Salt Lake City: Deseret Book, 1977.

Times and Seasons. Commerce (later Nauvoo), Illinois, 1839–46.

Widtsoe, John A. *Evidences and Reconciliations.* Salt Lake City: Bookcraft, 1943.

————. *The Message of the Doctrine and Covenants.* Salt Lake City: Bookcraft, 1978.

————. *The Word of Wisdom: A Modern Interpretation.* Salt Lake City: Deseret Book, 1938.

Young, Brigham. *Discourses of Brigham Young.* Selected by John A. Widtsoe. Salt Lake City: Deseret Book, 1954.

Additional sources for the notes given in this work are as follows:

- The Standard Works of The Church of Jesus Christ of Latter-day Saints.
- Footnotes in the Latter-day Saint version of the King James Bible.
- The Joseph Smith Translation of the Bible.
- The Bible Dictionary in the back of the Latter-day Saint version of the King James Bible.

- Various dictionaries.
- Various student manuals provided for our institutes of religion.
- Other sources as noted in the text.

ABOUT THE AUTHOR

David J. Ridges was raised in southeastern Nevada until his family moved to North Salt Lake City, Utah, when he was in fifth grade. He is the second of eight children.

Brother Ridges graduated from Bountiful High, served a two-and-a-half-year German-speaking mission to Austria, attended the University of Utah and BYU, and then graduated from BYU with a major in German and a physics minor. He later received a master's degree in educational psychology with a Church History minor from BYU.

He taught seminary and institute of religion as his chosen career for thirty-five years. He taught BYU Campus Education Week, Especially for Youth, Adult Religion, and Know Your Religion classes for over twenty-five years.

Brother Ridges has served as a Sunday School and seminary curriculum writer. He has had many callings, including Gospel Doctrine teacher, bishop, stake president, and patriarch. He and Sister Ridges have served two full-time, eighteen-month CES missions. He has written over forty books, which include several study guides for the standard works, Isaiah, Revelation, and many doctrinal publications on gospel topics such as the signs of the times, plan of salvation, and temples.

Brother and Sister Ridges met at the University of Utah. They were married in the Salt Lake Temple, are the parents of six children, and have sixteen grandchildren and one great-granddaughter so far. They make their home in Springville, Utah.

Scan to visit

www.davidjridges.com

NOTES

NOTES

NOTES

NOTES

YOUR STUDY OF

THE

DOCTRINE AND COVENANTS MADE EASIER

PART 3

SECTION 94 THROUGH SECTION 138

OFFICIAL DECLARATION—1

OFFICIAL DECLARATION—2

SECOND EDITION

DAVID J. RIDGES

YOUR STUDY OF

THE

DOCTRINE AND COVENANTS MADE EASIER

PART 3

SECTION 94 THROUGH SECTION 138

OFFICIAL DECLARATION—1

OFFICIAL DECLARATION—2

SECOND EDITION

DAVID J. RIDGES

CFI, AN IMPRINT OF

CEDAR FORT
Publishing & Media

SPRINGVILLE, UTAH

This book is not an official publication of The Church of Jesus Christ of Latter-day Saints. The opinions and views expressed herein belong solely to the author and do not necessarily represent the opinions or views of Cedar Fort, Inc. Permission for the use of sources, graphics, and photos is also solely the responsibility of the author.

ISBN 13: 978-1-4621-3897-5

Published by CFI, an imprint of Cedar Fort, Inc.
2373 W. 700 S., Springville, UT, 84663
Distributed by Cedar Fort, Inc., www.cedarfort.com

Library of Congress Control Number: 2020945612

Cover design by Shawnda T. Craig
Cover design © 2020 Cedar Fort, Inc.

Printed in the United States of America

10 9 8 7 6 5 4 3 2 1

Printed on acid-free paper

DEDICATION

To my wife, Janette, who
is my greatest blessing.

CONTENTS

SECTIONS

PREFACE

The Doctrine and Covenants is the Savior's book to us in our day. It teaches the "doctrines" and "covenants" necessary to live a righteous, rewarding life, which can bring joy and satisfaction during mortality, as well as exaltation in the eternities. In the October 1986 general conference of the Church, in reference to the importance of understanding the doctrines of the gospel, Elder Boyd K. Packer said:

> True doctrine, understood, changes attitudes and behavior. The study of the doctrines of the gospel will improve behavior quicker than a study of behavior will improve behavior. ("Little Children," *Ensign*, Nov. 1986)

Briefly put, "doctrines" are the teachings of the plan of salvation, the answers to questions about the meaning and purpose of life, instructions, rules, and commandments that, if followed, will lead to salvation. In D&C 10:62, the Lord tells His people that He is going to "bring to light the true points" of His doctrine. The Doctrine and Covenants does this.

This book is a brief, to-the-point guide to a better understanding of the doctrines of the gospel. The style is somewhat conversational to help you feel as if you were being guided through the Doctrine and Covenants by a teacher. It is designed to give you instant understanding of basic doctrines and principles, as well as to provide you with a background for deeper understanding and testimony.

INTRODUCTION

I have had a number of friends who have told me that they "don't get much out of reading the Doctrine and Covenants." This study guide is intended to remedy that. Through background and setting notes for each section, plus brief in-the-verse notes, along with the help of the Holy Ghost, I hope you will be enabled to feel and relive the excitement and effects of these revelations on the Prophet Joseph Smith and the early participants in the Restoration and see how they apply to you. Indeed, a key to understanding and enjoying studying the Doctrine and Covenants is seeing the application of its doctrines and teachings in your own life and in the lives of your family and friends. There are boundless applications and blessings available to us directly from the Savior through the study of this book of scripture. This study guide points them out.

As was the case with the first edition, this second edition comes in three volumes. This is part three. This new three-volume set contains many updates and much additional historical information based on research made available through the Joseph Smith Papers Project. I have used the 2013 edition of the Doctrine and Covenants, as published by The Church of Jesus Christ of Latter-day Saints, as the basic text. References to the Bible come from the King James Version, also as published by The Church of Jesus Christ of Latter-day Saints. JST references refer to the Joseph Smith Translation of the Bible.

Every verse of the Doctrine and Covenants from section 94 through section 138 and Official Declarations 1 and 2 are included in this volume. All the remaining verses of the Doctrine and Covenants are contained in parts one and two of this three-volume study guide set. All three volumes have background and setting notes for each section, as well as brief notes of explanation between and within the verses to clarify and help you learn and grow in your appreciation and understanding of this sacred volume of scripture. The notes within the verses are printed in italics and enclosed in brackets in order to make it easy for you to distinguish between the actual scripture text and my teaching comments.

Notes between the verses are indented and printed in a different font than the scripture text. **Bold** is often used to highlight things for teaching purposes.

You may be aware, as mentioned above, that, as a result of recent research for the Joseph Smith Papers Project, there are a number of changes to the section headings in the 2013 printing of the Doctrine and Covenants compared to previous editions. Such adjustments, most of them minor, have been made to 78 sections. One example of this is found in sections 39 and 40, where the name "James Covel" is now used rather than "James Covill." Another example of these Joseph Smith Papers Project research-based changes is this: If you are using an edition of the Doctrine and Covenants prior to the 2013 edition, you will see a number of corrected or added dates for the sections in this study guide. For example, prior to the 2013 edition of the Doctrine and Covenants, the date given for section 80 is March 1832. Based on recent research, the date is now given as March 7, 1832. Furthermore, at the time I wrote the first edition of this study guide, the then-current research for when living the Word of Wisdom became a temple recommend requirement was documented as being in the 1930s under President Heber J. Grant. However, current research has established it as being in 1919, shortly after President Grant became the Prophet. The Second Edition of *Doctrine and Covenants Made Easier* incorporates these changes as well as adding hundreds of additional helps and clarifications to assist you in your study.

This study guide is designed to be a user-friendly, "teacher in your hand" introductory study of this portion of the Doctrine and Covenants, as well as a refresher course for more advanced students of the scriptures. It is also designed to be a quick-reference resource that will enable readers to look up a particular passage or block of scripture for use in lessons, talks, or personal study as desired. It is my hope that you will incorporate some of the notes given in this study guide into your own scriptures, whether paper copy or on digital devices, to assist you in reading and studying this portion of the Doctrine and Covenants in the future. Thus, your own scriptures will become one of your best tools in your continued study of the gospel.

—David J. Ridges

SECTION 94

Background

This revelation was given through the Prophet Joseph Smith on August 2, 1833, at Kirtland, Ohio. Prior to the publication of the 2013 edition of the Doctrine and Covenants, the date for this revelation was given as May 6, 1833. However, recent research has proved this to be Incorrect. You can see, though, that the order in which the revelations appear in the Doctrine and Covenants has not been changed.

Perhaps you've noticed that many of the revelations contained in the Doctrine and Covenants were given in Kirtland, Ohio, or the surrounding communities. In fact, sixty-three of them were, which constitutes over 40 percent of the Doctrine and Covenants. You can verify this by going to the front of your Doctrine and Covenants and browsing through the "Chronological Order of Contents," looking to the far right of the page to see how many revelations were given during a specific month for that location.

There is a lesson to be learned from this. On occasion, you may hear someone wonder why the Lord required the Saints to put so much work and effort into building up the Kirtland area when they were only going to be there for about five years (see D&C 64:21). But when you see what happened in this area—the receiving of these revelations, the building of the Kirtland Temple, the appearance of the Savior in it, the appearance of Moses, Elias, and Elijah restoring priesthood keys (see D&C 110), and the gathering and strengthening of valiant converts to provide a firm foundation (see D&C 58:7) for the spreading of the gospel into all the world—you understand the wisdom of the Lord in having Kirtland as "a strong hold . . . for the space of five years" (D&C 64:21). It temporarily became a vital hub for missionary work and for the education of a strong core of faithful members in the ways of the Lord.

You may know of several strong and faithful members who have been guided by the Lord to locate in a particular area for a season, and then, after renovating their homes and yards just the way they wanted them, they were transferred by an employer to another location or were compelled to relocate for other reasons. Years later, they look back and see that they were strengthened by each move and are now in a position to do more good than would otherwise have been possible.

At this point in Church history, the Saints have a little over three years left in Kirtland before they will be driven out, especially by apostates.

As you can see from the heading

to this section in your Doctrine and Covenants, as well as in verses 13 and 14, Hyrum Smith, Reynolds Cahoon, and Jared Carter are appointed to be the building committee that supervises the construction work required by the Lord for this area now.

Instructions for the layout of a "Zion" city and the eventual formation of the first stake of the Church in Kirtland will be given in verse 1, next.

1 AND again, verily I say unto you, my friends, a commandment I give unto you, that **ye shall commence a work of laying out and preparing a beginning and foundation of the city of the stake of Zion, here in the land of Kirtland**, beginning at my house [*beginning at the site for the building of the Kirtland Temple*].

The first stake of the Church, the Kirtland Stake, was officially organized on February 17, 1834.

2 And behold, **it must be done according to the pattern which I have given unto you**.

The Prophet Joseph Smith received the layout for a typical "city of Zion" by revelation. It was a plan for a city, one mile square, which would accommodate from fifteen to twenty thousand residents. It was the basic plan for the layout of Kirtland, and the Prophet sent it

to the brethren in Missouri in late June 1833. It is described in the 1989 Institute of Religion's Church history manual as follows:

"Late in June 1833 the Prophet sent a plan for the building up of the city of Zion and its accompanying temple to the Saints in Missouri. The city was designed for fifteen to twenty thousand people and 'was to be one mile square, with ten-acre blocks, divided into one-half-acre lots, one house to the lot.' A complex of twenty-four 'temples' was to be built and used as houses of worship. The schools were to be located on two central city blocks. Lands on the north and south of the city were to be used for barns, stables, and farms. The farmer, as well as the merchant and mechanic, was to live in the city to enjoy all the social, cultural, and educational advantages. Unfortunately, mob interference prevented the implementation of this plan, although many of its basic ideas were later used by the Latter-day Saints in northern Missouri, Nauvoo, Illinois, and in hundreds of other settlements in the West" (*Church History in the Fulness of Times*, 1989, 130).

You can read more about this in *The Joseph Smith Papers, Documents, Volume 3: February 1833– March 1834*, 208–11.

Next, beginning in verse 3, the Lord specifies that a building is to be built next to the site of the

Kirtland Temple for the use of the First Presidency in receiving revelations and conducting the business of the Church.

3 And **let the first lot on the south** [*of the temple site*] **be consecrated** [*set aside*] unto me **for the building of a house for the presidency** [*the First Presidency*], for the work of the presidency, in obtaining revelations; and for the work of the ministry of the presidency, in all things pertaining to the church and kingdom.

In verses 4–9, the Savior gives specific instructions for constructing this headquarters building for the First Presidency and outlines worthiness guidelines for entering it. You will notice that these are similar to the requirements for entering holy, dedicated Church buildings today.

4 Verily I say unto you, that **it shall be built fifty-five by sixty-five feet in the width thereof and in the length thereof**, in the inner court.

5 And there shall be a lower court and a higher court, according to the pattern which shall be given unto you hereafter.

6 And **it shall be dedicated unto the Lord** from the foundation thereof, according to the order of the priesthood, according to the pattern which shall be given unto you hereafter.

7 And **it shall be wholly dedicated unto the Lord for the work of the presidency.**

8 And **ye shall not suffer** [*permit*] **any unclean thing to come in unto it**; and **my glory shall be there, and my presence shall be there.**

9 **But if there shall come into it any unclean thing, my glory shall not be there; and my presence shall not come into it.**

The second lot to the south of the temple site is to be set aside for a building in which Church publications could be printed and in which Joseph Smith and his scribes could continue work on the translation of the Bible (the Joseph Smith Translation of the Bible, or JST).

10 And again, verily I say unto you, **the second lot on the south shall be dedicated unto me for the building of a house unto me, for the work of the printing of the translation of my scriptures** [*the Joseph Smith Translation of the Bible (JST)*], **and all things whatsoever I shall command you.**

11 **And it shall be fifty-five by sixty-five feet** in the width thereof and the length thereof, in the

inner court; and there shall be a lower and a higher court.

12 And **this house shall be wholly dedicated unto the Lord** from the foundation thereof, for the work of the printing, in all things whatsoever I shall command you, **to be holy, undefiled**, according to the pattern in all things as it shall be given unto you.

> Verses 13–15 instruct that the three men of the Church building committee are to have their homes near the printing office.

13 And **on the third lot** [*south of the temple site*] **shall my servant Hyrum Smith receive his inheritance**.

14 And **on the first and second lots on the north** [*north of the temple site*] **shall my servants Reynolds Cahoon and Jared Carter receive their inheritances**—

15 **That they may do the work** which I have appointed unto them, **to be a committee to build mine houses**, according to the commandment, which I, the Lord God, have given unto you.

> Having given the above instructions for a building for the First Presidency and a printing office, the Lord instructs the Saints to delay actually beginning construction until He tells them to move ahead.

16 **These two houses are not to be built until I give unto you a commandment concerning them**.

> Although neither of these two buildings was actually built since constructing the temple took all the members' time and resources and then the Saints were driven out, this revelation did lay the foundation for building church office buildings in Salt Lake City, Utah, as well as establishing facilities for Church publications.
>
> Thus, we see the Lord preparing the faithful Saints in the present for the future. He does much of the same thing with us.

17 And now **I give unto you no more at this time.** Amen.

SECTION 95

Background

> This revelation was given through the Prophet Joseph Smith on June 1, 1833, in Kirtland, Ohio.
>
> Applying the teachings, doctrines, and principles found in the Doctrine and Covenants in our own lives gives life and deep meaning to our study of this sacred volume of scripture. This section provides an excellent example of such application.
>
> In December 1832, the Lord commanded the Saints to build

a temple in Kirtland (see D&C 88:119). It was not to be the same kind of temple as those we build now, where sacred ordinances are performed for the living and the dead, and where a temple recommend is required for entering. Rather, it was to be a building where the Saints could meet, where revelations could be given, where the School of the Prophets could meet, and so forth.

As you can see, section 95 was given on June 1, 1833, five months after the commandment to build the Kirtland Temple. Because of poverty and perhaps a lack of understanding of the importance of this temple, nothing had yet been done as far as actually beginning construction was concerned.

As you study this revelation, you will see that the Saints are severely chastised by the Lord for this lack of action on their part (verses 2–3). This gives us an opportunity to observe how the Lord disciplines His children. We will thus be taught a lesson in parenting skills or skills for effectively supervising others.

Among the steps used by the Lord in disciplining, we see Him:

1. Reassuring them that He loves them (verse 1).

2. Informing them that they are in trouble (verse 2).

3. Not leaving them guessing as to what they have done wrong.

Rather, He tells them exactly what the problem is (verse 3).

4. Explaining why it is a problem (verses 4–8).

5. Giving them a way to get out of the trouble they're in (verse 13).

We will note these steps as we proceed. No doubt, you will be able to see others also. As usual, we will use **bold** type to point things out.

Step 1

1 VERILY, thus saith the Lord unto you whom I love, and **whom I love I also chasten** [*scold, reprove; the fact that the Lord scolds us as needed is proof that He loves us; so also with parents*] **that their sins may be forgiven**, for with the chastisement I prepare a way for their deliverance in all things out of temptation, and **I have loved you** [*I have always loved you*]—

Step 2

2 Wherefore, **ye must needs be chastened and stand rebuked** before my face;

Step 3

3 For **ye have sinned against me a very grievous** [*serious*] **sin, in that ye have not considered the great commandment** in all things, that **I have given unto you concerning the building of mine house** [*the Kirtland Temple—see D&C 88:119*];

Step 4

4 **For the preparation wherewith** [*the temple is to be built in preparation for the following:*] I design [*plan*] **to prepare mine apostles** [*a broad reference; those who have been called to preach the gospel—the Quorum of the Twelve Apostles will not be organized until February 1835*] **to prune my vineyard** [*to cut out false doctrines and philosophies, to shape and form people's lives with the gospel throughout the world*] **for the last time** [*before the Second Coming; see Jacob 5:71*], **that I may bring to pass my strange act** [*as prophesied by Isaiah—see Isaiah 28:21; the Restoration, the "marvelous work and a wonder"—2 Nephi 27:26*], **that I may pour out my Spirit upon all flesh—**

5 **But behold, verily I say unto you, that there are many who have been ordained among you,** whom I have called **but few of them are chosen** [*to have true power in doing the work of the Lord*].

6 **They who are not chosen** [*to be effective tools in the hand of the Lord*] **have sinned** a very grievous sin, **in that they are walking in darkness at noon-day** [*they are not living the gospel when it is "shining" all around them*].

7 And **for this cause** [*this reason*] **I gave unto you a commandment that you should call your solemn assembly** [*including building a temple in which to hold solemn assemblies—D&C 88:70–119*], **that your fastings and your mourning might come up into the ears of the Lord of Sabaoth** [*the Savior—see notes for D&C 87:7 in part 2 of this series*], **which, by interpretation, is the creator of the first day, the beginning and the end.**

President Spencer W. Kimball gave a few details about "solemn assemblies" and some of the reasons for holding them. He said that they "have been known among the Saints since the days of Israel. They have been of various kinds but generally have been associated with the dedication of a temple or a special meeting appointed for the sustaining of a new First Presidency or a meeting for the priesthood to sustain a revelation, such as the tithing revelation to President Lorenzo Snow. . . .

"Each of the presidents of the Church has been sustained by the priesthood of the Church in solemn assembly down to and including President Harold B. Lee, who was sustained October

6, 1972" (in Conference Report, April 1974, 64–65; or "What Do We Hear?" *Ensign,* May 1974, 45).

8 Yea, verily I say unto you, **I gave unto you a commandment that you should build a house** [*the Kirtland Temple*], **in the which house I design** [*plan*] **to endow** [*bless*] **those whom I have chosen with power from on high** [*which will include the appearance of the Savior, Moses, Elias, and Elijah— see D&C 110*];

Next, in verse 9, the Master explains that these are some of the reasons why He wants these Saints to remain in the Kirtland area for a period of time, even though He has already told them that it will only be for about five years (see D&C 64:21).

9 For **this is the promise of the Father unto you; therefore** [*for this reason*] **I command you to tarry** [*to remain in the Kirtland area for a time*], even as mine apostles at Jerusalem [*see Acts 1:4*].

10 Nevertheless [*in spite of these wonderful promises*], **my servants sinned** a very grievous sin; and **contentions arose in the school of the prophets** [*in spite of the commandment given in D&C 88:123–24 to "love one another" and to "cease to find fault one with another"*]; **which was very grievous unto**

me, saith your Lord; therefore I sent them forth to be chastened.

11 Verily I say unto you, **it is my will that you should build a house** [*the temple*]. **If you keep my commandments you shall have power to build it.**

12 **If you keep not my commandments, the love of** [*the blessings of*] **the Father shall not continue with you, therefore you shall walk in darkness**.

In the context of verse 12, above, "the love of the Father" means "the blessings of the Father," which are earned by obedience to His commandments. You may wish to read "Divine Love," an article by then Elder Russell M. Nelson in the February 2003 *Ensign*, in which he teaches this concept of the Father's love.

Step 5

13 **Now here is wisdom** [*this is how you can get out of the trouble you are in*], and the mind of the Lord—**let the house be built**, not after the manner of the world, for I give not unto you that ye shall live after the manner of the world;

The Saints responded quickly to this revelation, and the day after they received it, they began digging trenches for the foundation of the temple.

14 Therefore, **let it be built after the manner which I shall show unto three of you**, whom ye shall appoint and ordain unto this power.

The promise of the Lord, given to Joseph Smith, Frederick G. Williams, and Sidney Rigdon in verse 14, above, was marvelously fulfilled according President Williams. He said:

"Joseph [Smith] received the word of the Lord for him to take his two counselors, [Frederick G.] Williams and [Sidney] Rigdon, and come before the Lord, and He would show them the plan or model of the house to be built. We went upon our knees, called on the Lord, and the building appeared within viewing distance, I being the first to discover it. Then all of us viewed it together. After we had taken a good look at the exterior, the building seemed to come right over us" (in *Teachings of Presidents of the Church: Joseph Smith* [2007], 271). When the temple was nearing completion, President Williams said it looked like the building he had seen in vision to the smallest detail, and he could not tell the difference between the temple he saw in vision and the temple as built (Tait and Rogers, "A House for Our God," *Revelations in Context*, 167).

Next, in verses 15–17, the Savior gives the dimensions for the building of the Kirtland Temple as well

as the uses for various parts of the building.

15 And the size thereof shall be **fifty and five feet in width**, and let it be **sixty-five feet in length**, in the inner court thereof.

16 And **let the lower part of the inner court be dedicated unto me for your sacrament offering**, and for your **preaching**, and your **fasting**, and your **praying**, **and the offering up of your most holy desires unto me**, saith your Lord.

17 And **let the higher part of the inner court be dedicated unto me for the school of mine apostles** [*the School of the Prophets*], **saith Son Ahman** [*the Son of God*]; or, in other words, Alphus; or, in other words, Omegus [*another form of "Alpha and Omega," the first and last letters of the Greek alphabet, meaning Christ*]; even Jesus Christ your Lord. Amen.

"Ahman," used in verse 17, above, is the name of God in the pure language. This is explained by Elder Orson Pratt as follows (**bold** added for emphasis):

"There is one revelation that this people are not generally acquainted with. I think it has never been published, but probably it will be in the Church History. It is given in questions and answers. The first question is, **'What is the name of God in the pure language?'** The answer says, **'Ahman.'** 'What is the name of the Son of God?' Answer, 'Son Ahman—the greatest of all the parts of God excepting Ahman'" (*Journal of Discourses*, 2:342).

SECTION 96

Background

This revelation was given to the Prophet Joseph Smith on June 4, 1833, in Kirtland, Ohio.

In the heading to this section in your Doctrine and Covenants, the "French farm" (103 acres) is mentioned. Some months prior to this revelation, the Church had purchased some farms for the purpose of settling the members and establishing the Kirtland Stake. The Prophet Joseph Smith spoke of this in his history. He said (**bold** added for emphasis):

"*March 23* [1833].—A council was called for the purpose of appointing a committee to purchase land in Kirtland, upon which the Saints might build a Stake of Zion. Brother Joseph Coe and Moses Dailey were appointed to ascertain the terms of sale of certain farms; and Brother Ezra Thayre to ascertain the price of **Peter French's farm**. The brethren agreed to continue in prayer and fasting for the ultimate success of their mission. After an absence of about three

hours Brothers Coe and Dailey returned and reported that Elijah Smith's farm could be obtained for four thousand dollars; and Mr. Morley's for twenty-one hundred; and **Brother Thayre reported that Peter French would sell his farm for five thousand dollars**. The council decided to purchase the farms, and appointed Ezra Thayre and Joseph Coe to superintend the purchase; and they were ordained under the hands of Sidney Rigdon, and set apart as general agents of the Church for that purpose" (*History of the* Church, 1:335).

The Peter French farm had a good stone quarry and the facilities needed for making brick. Thus, it was an ideal tract of land on which to build the temple and other buildings and homes associated with the establishing of Kirtland as a temporary gathering place for the Saints. About fifteen hundred members had gathered to Kirtland by this time.

At the time of this revelation, a committee of high priests had met to consider a number of issues associated with the dividing up of the French farm for a temple site and for lots upon which members could settle and build homes. One issue was who should be in charge. Since these men could not agree on the matter, they agreed to ask the Lord through the Prophet.

You will see answers to this and other matters as we study this section.

1 BEHOLD, I say unto you, **here is wisdom, whereby ye may know how to act concerning this matter,** for **it is expedient** [*urgent, necessary*] in me **that this stake** [*the Kirtland Stake*] that I have set for the strength of Zion **should be made strong.**

2 Therefore, **let my servant Newel K. Whitney** [*the bishop in Kirtland*] **take charge** of the place which is named among you, upon which I design to build mine holy house.

3 And again, **let it be divided into lots, according to wisdom** [*you decide and use wisdom and common sense*], for the benefit of those who seek inheritances, **as** it shall be **determined in council** among you.

> Verse 3, above, is a good example of the use of councils in the Church for making decisions and taking action to move the work of the Lord ahead. The council process can lead to revelation. As you know, councils, such as ward councils, are still a vital part of the Church today.

4 Therefore, take heed that ye **see to this matter** [*move ahead on this*], and that portion that is necessary to benefit mine order [*the United Order or United Firm in Kirtland—see D&C 92:1*], **for the purpose of bringing forth my word to the children of men** [*the ultimate purpose of the Church*].

> A quote from the 2018 *Doctrine and Covenants Student Manual*, chapter 37, helps us understand verse 4, above.
>
> "A portion of the property was to be used to benefit the Lord's 'order, for the purpose of bringing forth [His] word to the children of men' (D&C 96:4). This had reference to the United Order, or United Firm. 'A subset of the United Firm, the Literary Firm, was responsible for publishing the revelations' [see D&C 70]. 'That portion' [D&C 96:4] to be devoted to bringing forth God's word may refer either to acreage allotted for building a print shop or to land-sale proceeds that could be used to support such a printing operation" (in *The Joseph Smith Papers, Documents, Volume 3: February 1833– March 1834*, 111, note 277).

5 For behold, verily I say unto you, **this** [*referring to the last phrase in verse 4, above*] **is the most expedient in me** [*the most important thing of all*], **that my word should go forth unto the children of men** [*people*], for the purpose of subduing the hearts of the children of men for your good. Even so. Amen.

> Next, in verses 6–9, the Lord instructs that John Johnson should

be invited to join the United Firm in the Kirtland area. Brother and Sister Johnson joined the Church in the spring of 1831, after Sister Johnson's arm was miraculously healed in Kirtland when Joseph Smith commanded in the name of Jesus Christ that she be made whole.

Joseph and Emma accepted the Johnson's invitation to live with them in their spacious farm home in Hiram, Ohio, about thirty miles southeast of Kirtland. They moved in on September 12, 1831. They lived there until September 1832, and the Johnson home became the headquarters of the Church during that time. The Prophet received many revelations while there, including section 76, which deals with the three degrees of glory and perdition. It was also while living at the Johnson home that Joseph was tarred and feathered by a mob (on the night of March 24, 1832). John Johnson heard the noise of the mob and went outside to help the Prophet but was knocked down and suffered a broken collarbone. He was later administered to by David Whitmer and was immediately healed.

The above brief background about John Johnson gives added meaning to the phrase "whose offering I have accepted" in verse 6, next.

6 And again, verily I say unto you, it is wisdom and expedient in me,

that my servant **John Johnson whose offering I have accepted**, and whose prayers I have heard, unto whom I give a promise of eternal life [*exaltation*] inasmuch as [*if*] he keepeth my commandments from henceforth—

7 For **he is a descendant of Joseph and a partaker of the blessings of the promise made unto his fathers** [*in other words, he is an heir to the blessings of Abraham, Isaac, and Jacob (see Abraham 2:9–11) if he lives worthy of them (verse 6, above)*]—

8 Verily I say unto you, it is expedient in me that he **should become a member of the order** [*the United Firm, operating under the law of consecration*], that he may assist in bringing forth my word unto the children of men.

9 Therefore **ye shall ordain him unto** [*set him apart for*] **this blessing**, and he shall seek diligently to take away incumbrances [*the financial obligations*] that are upon the house named among you, that he may dwell therein. Even so. Amen.

Just a quick note about the term *ordain* as used in verse 9, above. Perhaps you've noticed that the vocabulary of the Church gradually developed over many years. For example, the words *intelligence*, spirits, and souls were used interchangeably early on (see Abraham 3:18–23). Whereas now we use intelligence to mean what we were before spirit birth, spirit means that which leaves the body at death, and soul means the "spirit and the body" (see D&C 88:15).

The term ordain was used interchangeably in the early days of the restored Church to mean ordained to the priesthood as well as being set apart to a calling or assignment in the Church. For example, Emma Smith was "ordained" to be an instructor in the Church (D&C 25:7). Whereas, now, the term ordained is used in reference to priesthood offices, and set apart is used for all other callings that are accompanied by the laying on of hands. This includes serving in a stake presidency, in a Relief Society presidency, as a missionary, and many other such callings.

SECTION 97

Background

This revelation dealing with the situation of the members in Missouri was given through the Prophet Joseph Smith on August 2, 1833, in Kirtland, Ohio. As requested by the Lord (D&C 88:77–80, 117–41), the members in Missouri had started a School of the Elders with Parley P. Pratt as the teacher. Of this he wrote:

"A school of Elders was . . .

organized, over which I was called to preside. This class, to the number of about sixty, met for instruction once a week. The place of meeting was in the open air, under some tall trees, in a retired place in the wilderness, where we prayed, preached and prophesied, and exercised ourselves in the gifts of the Holy Spirit. Here great blessings were poured out, and many great and marvelous things were manifested and taught. The Lord gave me great wisdom, and enabled me to teach and edify the Elders, and comfort and encourage them in their preparations for the great work which lay before us. I was also much edified and strengthened" (Autobiography of Parley P. Pratt, 93–94).

Mob violence broke out against the members in Independence, Missouri, on July 20, 1833. The home of W. W. Phelps (who would later write "Praise to the Man" and other Church hymns) was destroyed along with the Church's printing press (underway with the printing of the Book of Commandments). Bishop Edward Partridge was taken to the town square of Independence and tarred and feathered, as was Brother Charles Allen. A brief account of these events is given in History of the Church as follows:

"On the 20th of July, the mob collected, and demanded the discontinuance of the Church printing establishment in Jackson county, the closing of the store, and the cessation of all mechanical labors. The brethren refused compliance, and the consequence was that the house of W. W. Phelps, which contained the printing establishment, was thrown down, the materials taken possession of by the mob, many papers destroyed, and the family and furniture thrown out of doors.

"The mob then proceeded to violence towards Edward Partridge, the Bishop of the Church, as he relates in his autobiography:

"'I was taken from my house by the mob, George Simpson being their leader, who escorted me about half a mile, to the court house, on the public square in Independence [Missouri]; and then and there, a few rods from said court house, surrounded by hundreds of the mob, I was stripped of my hat, coat and vest and daubed with tar from head to foot, and then had a quantity of feathers put upon me; and all this because I would not agree to leave the county, and my home where I had lived two years.

"'Before tarring and feathering me I was permitted to speak. I told them that the Saints had suffered persecution in all ages of the world; that I had done nothing which ought to offend anyone; that if they abused me, they would abuse an innocent person; that I was willing to suffer for the sake of Christ; but, to leave the country, I

was not then willing to consent to it. By this time the multitude made so much noise that I could not be heard: some were cursing and swearing, saying, 'call upon your Jesus,' etc.; others were equally noisy in trying to still the rest, that they might be enabled to hear what I was saying.

"'Until after I had spoken, I knew not what they intended to do with me, whether to kill me, to whip me, or what else I knew not. I bore my abuse with so much resignation and meekness, that it appeared to astound the multitude, who permitted me to retire in silence, many looking very solemn, their sympathies having been touched as I thought; and as to myself, I was so filled with the Spirit and love of God, that I had no hatred towards my persecutors or anyone else.'

"Charles Allen was next stripped and tarred and feathered, because he would not agree to leave the county, or deny the Book of Mormon. Others were brought up to be served likewise or whipped" (*History of the Church,* 1:390–91).

The Prophet Joseph Smith later reflected on the tarring and feathering of Edward Partridge and Charles Allen as follows:

"When Bishop Partridge, who was without guile, and Elder Charles Allen, walked off, coated like some unnamed, unknown bipeds, one of the sisters cried aloud: '*While you, who have done this wicked deed, must suffer the vengeance of God, they, having endured persecution, can rejoice, for henceforth for them, is laid up a crown eternal in the heavens.'*

"Surely this was a time for awful reflection; man, unrestrained, like the brute beast, may torment the body; but God will punish the soul!" (*History of the Church*, 1:390–93).

Some of the local leaders of the Church in Missouri even offered themselves to the mob if they would leave the other members in peace. We read:

"It was at this point, too, that several of the brethren stepped forward and offered themselves as a ransom for the Church, expressing themselves as being willing to be scourged or to die if that would appease the anger of the mob against the Saints. The mob would not accept the sacrifice of the brethren, however, but renewed their threats of violence against the whole Church. The brethren who offered themselves as a ransom for the Saints were John Corrill, John Whitmer, William W. Phelps, Algernon S. Gilbert, Edward Partridge, and Isaac Morley" (*History of the Church,* footnote 5, 1:394–95).

On July 23, 1833, local leaders of the Church were forced to sign an agreement stating that the Saints would leave Jackson County. The Prophet recorded: "On the same day (July 23rd), while the brethren in Missouri were preparing to leave the county, through the violence of the mob, the corner stones of the Lord's House were laid in Kirtland, after the order of the Holy Priesthood" (*History of the* Church, 1:400).

It is significant that, with the slow communication methods of the day, the Prophet Joseph Smith had no way of knowing what had so recently transpired among the members in Missouri. This revelation is another witness that he was truly a prophet of God, as it addresses the causes of these troubles, of which he had not yet heard by communication from Missouri.

First, in this section, the Savior addresses the members in Kirtland and assures them that the faithful among the membership of the Church in Missouri will not lose their eternal reward, regardless of what happens to the Church in general in Zion. Notice as He begins this revelation that we are taught that "hearing" the voice of the Spirit is essentially the same as hearing the literal voice of the Lord.

1 VERILY **I say unto you my friends** [*the faithful in Kirtland*], **I speak unto you with my voice, even the voice of my Spirit,** that I may show unto you my will **concerning your brethren in the land of Zion** [*Jackson County,*

Missouri], **many of whom are truly humble and are seeking diligently to learn wisdom and to find truth.**

2 Verily, verily I say unto you, **blessed are such, for they shall obtain** [among other things, they will obtain exaltation]; **for I, the Lord, show mercy unto all the meek**, and upon all whomsoever I will, that I may be justified when I shall bring them unto judgment. [In other words, all will receive the opportunity to know of the mercy and kindness of God. And because the Lord is completely fair, all who are faithful will ultimately receive their reward of exaltation in celestial glory regardless of the seemingly unfair things that happen to them on earth.]

Next, in verses 3–5, the Master expresses His pleasure with the work of Parley P. Pratt as the director of the "school in Zion."

3 Behold, I say unto you, **concerning the school in Zion** [School of the Elders], **I, the Lord, am well pleased** that there should be a school in Zion, and **also with my servant Parley P. Pratt, for he abideth in me** [he carefully stays true to the teachings and commandments of God as he teaches this School of the Elders].

4 **And inasmuch as** [if] **he continueth to abide in me** [continues to remain faithful] **he shall continue to preside over the school** in the land of Zion until I shall give unto him other commandments.

5 And **I will bless him with a multiplicity of blessings, in expounding** [explaining and teaching] **all scriptures and mysteries** [basics of the gospel, which are a "mystery" to most inhabitants of the world—see Bible Dictionary under "Mystery"] **to the edification** [building up and enlightenment] **of the school, and of the church in Zion.**

Next, in verses 6–7, the Savior tells those in the School of the Elders that He will give them another chance to repent, but if they don't, the "ax" is about to fall.

6 And **to the residue of the school** [the others who are attending this school], **I, the Lord, am willing to show mercy; nevertheless, there are those that must needs be chastened** [punished if they don't repent], **and their works shall be made known.**

7 **The ax is laid at the root of the trees; and every tree** [trees are often symbolic of people in the scriptures] **that bringeth not forth good fruit** [that does not repent and live righteously] **shall be hewn down and cast into the fire** [will

be destroyed; can also mean that they will be turned over to Satan to suffer for their sins]. I, the Lord, have spoken it.

Next, the Savior again assures those who are doing their best to live the gospel that they are not included in the chastisement He has just given.

8 Verily I say unto you, **all among them who know their hearts are honest, and are broken, and their spirits contrite, and are willing to observe their covenants by sacrifice—yea, every sacrifice which I, the Lord, shall command—they are accepted of me.**

Did you notice the answer in verse 8, above, to a question that often comes up in gospel discussions; namely, whether we can know if we are doing alright in the eyes of God? The answer is yes.

The Lord goes on to use beautiful imagery to describe the growth and productivity of faithful members of the Church who are willing to grow under the direction of God.

9 For **I, the Lord, will cause them to bring forth** [*produce*] **as a very fruitful tree which is planted in a goodly land, by a pure stream, that yieldeth much precious fruit.**

Next, the topic turns to the building

of a temple in Zion. Verses 10–17 provide a short course in financing temple construction and in the value and blessings of temple attendance.

10 Verily I say unto you, that **it is my will that a house** [*a temple*] **should be built unto me in the land of Zion,** like unto the pattern which I have given you.

11 Yea, **let it be built speedily, by the tithing of my people.**

12 Behold, **this is the tithing and the sacrifice which I, the Lord, require at their hands,** that there may be **a house** [*temple*] **built unto me for the salvation of Zion—**

13 **For a place of thanksgiving** for all saints, and for a place **of instruction** for all those who are called to the work of the ministry in all their several callings and offices;

14 **That they may be perfected in the understanding of their ministry, in theory,** in **principle,** and in **doctrine,** in **all things pertaining to the kingdom of God on the earth,** the keys of which kingdom have been conferred upon you.

Next, in verses 15–17, we see the reason for requiring temple recommends for entrance into our holy temples.

15 And **inasmuch as** [*if*] **my people build a house unto me** in the name of the Lord, **and do not suffer any unclean thing to come into it**, that it be not defiled, **my glory shall rest upon it**;

16 Yea, and **my presence shall be there**, for **I will come into it**, and **all the pure in heart that shall come into it shall see God**.

There are many ways to interpret the phrase "shall see God" in verse 16, above. First, when the conditions are right and it is in harmony with His will, people can literally see God. Another way of "seeing" the Lord is through studying the scriptures. Example: "The scriptures shall be given . . . they will hear my voice, and shall see me" (D&C 35:20–21). Yet another meaning of "seeing" God is to have a firm testimony of His existence, through the power of the Holy Ghost.

In D&C 88:68, we learn that "the days will come that you shall see him; for he will unveil his face unto you, and it shall be **in his own time**, and **in his own way**, and **according to his own will**."

17 **But if it be defiled I will not come into it**, and my glory shall not be there; for I will not come into unholy temples.

In verses 18–19, next, the promise is given that if the members of the Church in Zion repent and live according to the laws and commandments given above, Zion will be established. This will require truly living in accordance with celestial law, including the law of consecration, which is the law upon which Zion will be built. See D&C 105:5.

18 And, now, behold, **if Zion do these things she shall prosper, and spread herself and become very glorious, very great, and very terrible** [*frightening to enemies who would like to destroy the Church*].

19 And **the nations of the earth shall honor her**, and shall say: Surely Zion is the city of our God, and surely Zion cannot fall, neither be moved out of her place, for God is there, and the hand of the Lord is there;

20 **And he hath sworn by the power of his might to be her salvation and her high tower** [*symbolic of protection*].

The "high tower" spoken of in verse 20, above, calls to mind the imagery of a watch tower, built onto the city wall in ancient times, from which danger could be seen while yet far off. Thus, "high tower" symbolizes safety and protection from God, who sees danger coming and warns and protects against it. Another way to say it is that those who exercise their agency so that they live within the safe haven of the gospel walls and protection will come under the safety and protection of God.

Next, the Savior gives us His definition of *Zion*. You will see that it is primarily a condition of the heart. Thus, in effect, Zion can be wherever we are, if we are pure in heart. Zion is wherever the Saints are gathered, if they are pure in heart.

21 Therefore, verily, thus saith the Lord, let Zion rejoice, for **this is Zion—THE PURE IN HEART**; therefore, let Zion rejoice, while all the wicked shall mourn.

Sometimes confusion arises with respect to the word *Zion*. This is because there are so many different meanings to it in addition to the basic definition given in verse 21, above. The Bible Dictionary gives a number of definitions as follows:

Zion

"The word *Zion* is used repeatedly in all the standard works of the Church, and is defined in latter-day revelation as 'the pure in heart' (D&C 97:21). Other usages of Zion have to do with a geographical location. For example, Enoch built a city that was called Zion (Moses 7:18–19); Solomon built his temple on Mount Zion (1 Kgs. 8:1; cf. 2 Sam. 5:6–7); and Jackson County, Missouri, is called Zion in many of the revelations in the D&C, such as 58:49–50; 62:4;

63:48; 72:13; 84:76; 104:47. The city of New Jerusalem, to be built in Jackson County, Missouri, is to be called Zion (D&C 45:66–67). The revelations also speak of 'the cause of Zion' (D&C 6:6; 11:6). In a wider sense all of North and South America are Zion (HC 6:318–19). For further references see 1 Chr. 11:5; Ps. 2:6; 99:2; 102:16; Isa. 1:27; 2:3; 4:3–5; 33:20; 52:1–8; 59:20; Jer. 3:14; 31:6; Joel 2:1–32; Amos 6:1; Obad. 1:17, 21; Heb. 12:22–24; Rev. 14:1–5; and many others. (In the N.T., *Zion* is spelled *Sion*.)"

Next, in verses 22–24, the Savior foretells the destructions that will go forth upon the earth because of wickedness. He informs us that people will become tired of the constant barrage of negative news (verse 23) and that things will not get better until the Second Coming and Millennium (end of verse 23).

22 For behold, and lo, **vengeance cometh speedily upon the ungodly as the whirlwind**; and who shall escape it?

23 **The Lord's scourge shall pass over by night and by day,** and **the report thereof** [*the news*] **shall vex all people**; yea, **it shall not be stayed** [*it won't be stopped*] **until the Lord come**;

24 **For the indignation of the Lord is kindled against their**

abominations [*gross wickedness*] and all their wicked works.

In verses 25–26, next, the members in Jackson County are, in effect, told that if they repent, Zion can still be established at this time. But if they fail to repent, they will be subject to "sore affliction."

25 Nevertheless, **Zion shall escape if she observe to do all things whatsoever I have commanded her.**

26 **But if she observe not to do whatsoever I have commanded her, I will visit** [*punish*] **her according to all her works, with sore affliction, with pestilence, with plague, with sword, with vengeance, with devouring fire.**

Yet again, in verses 27–28, the Savior invites these Saints to repent and do much better at living according to the laws and commandments upon which Zion can be successfully built. If they do, they will be spared further serious affliction and can remain in Missouri. He is giving them one more chance. Otherwise, it will be far in the future when Zion will be established in Missouri.

27 **Nevertheless, let it be read this once** to her ears, that I, the Lord, have accepted of her offering; and **if she sin no more none of these things shall come upon her;**

28 **And I will bless her with blessings, and multiply a multiplicity of blessings upon her, and upon her generations forever and ever, saith the Lord your God.** Amen.

Unfortunately, too many of the members in Missouri failed to repent sufficiently for the above blessings to be provided in 1833. Parley P. Pratt wrote the following:

"This revelation [section 97] was not complied with by the leaders and Church in Missouri as a whole (notwithstanding many were humble and faithful); therefore, the threatened judgment was poured out to the uttermost, as the history of the five following years will show" (*Autobiography of Parley P. Pratt*, 96).

SECTION 98

Background

This revelation was given through the Prophet Joseph Smith on August 6, 1833, at Kirtland, Ohio, and primarily concerned the difficulties between the old settlers in Missouri and the newly arrived members of the Church there.

In 1833, the original settlers of Missouri had become greatly concerned about the large influx of Latter-day Saints coming into their state. Shortly after the Lord revealed in July 1831 (section 57) that the city of Zion as well as a temple were to be built in Independence, Missouri, hundreds of members began gathering to Jackson county. By summer of 1833, it appears that more than 1,200 Saints had settled there. (For more information, see *The Joseph Smith Papers, Documents, Volume 3: February 1833–March 1834, ed. Gerrit J. Dirkmaat and others* [2014], 121.)

There were obviously significant lifestyle differences and differences in religious beliefs between the two groups, which led the old settlers to form mobs and persecute the members of the Church, often with the encouragement of local ministers of other churches.

Sections 97 and 98 go together and were sent from Kirtland at the same time—August 6, 1833—in a letter from the Prophet to the Saints in Missouri. The members in Missouri had already suffered mob violence, beginning on July 20, 1833 (see background information for section 97 in this study guide). There was much sentiment on the part of many members in Jackson County to retaliate and get revenge for the atrocities already committed against them (see heading to section 98 in your Doctrine and Covenants).

While section 98 is often referred to as a revelation giving the laws and principles of self-defense, which it definitely is, it can also be considered a revelation on character development and self-control.

If we hope to someday become like our Father in Heaven, we must develop self-control. Otherwise, we would never succeed in being sufficiently patient with our own spirit children whom we send to worlds to undergo the training and lessons that we are now undergoing. Without self-control and the other character traits that go along with it, including love, patience, and the ability to forgive, we would quite likely prematurely destroy the worlds we create for our spirit children. In other words, we would never qualify to become gods.

We will first go through the entire section, **bolding** some of the words and phrases that exemplify the Christlike character traits we need to develop if we are to become gods. We will also bold things that show how this mortal life is a test or proving ground. Then we will repeat the section and add notes and commentary.

1 VERILY I say unto you my friends, fear not, let your hearts be comforted; yea, rejoice evermore, and in everything give thanks;

2 **Waiting patiently** on the Lord, for your prayers have entered into the ears of the Lord of Sabaoth, and are recorded with this seal and testament—the Lord hath sworn and decreed that they shall be granted.

3 Therefore, he giveth this promise unto you, with an immutable covenant that they shall be fulfilled; and all things wherewith you have been afflicted shall work together for your good, and to my name's glory, saith the Lord.

4 And now, verily I say unto you **concerning the laws of the land, it is my will that my people should observe to do all things whatsoever I command them**.

5 **And that law of the land which is constitutional**, supporting that principle of freedom in maintaining rights and privileges, **belongs to all mankind, and is justifiable before me**.

6 **Therefore, I, the Lord, justify you**, and your brethren of my church, **in befriending that law which is the constitutional law of the land**;

7 And as pertaining to law of man, whatsoever is more or less than this, cometh of evil.

8 I, the Lord God, make you free, therefore ye are free indeed; and the law also maketh you free.

9 Nevertheless, when the wicked rule the people mourn.

10 **Wherefore, honest men and wise men should be sought for diligently, and good men and wise men ye should observe to uphold**; otherwise whatsoever is less than these cometh of evil.

11 And I give unto you a commandment, that ye shall **forsake all evil and cleave unto all good**, that ye shall **live by every word which proceedeth forth out of the mouth of God**.

12 For he will give unto the faithful line upon line, precept upon precept; and **I will try you and prove you herewith**.

13 And whoso layeth down his life in my cause, for my name's sake, shall find it again, even life eternal.

14 Therefore, be not afraid of your enemies, for I have decreed in my heart, saith the Lord, that **I will prove you in all things**, whether you will abide in my covenant, even unto death, that you may be found worthy.

15 For **if ye will not abide in my covenant ye are not worthy of me**.

16 Therefore, **renounce war and proclaim peace**, and seek diligently to turn the hearts of the children to their fathers, and the hearts of the fathers to the children;

17 And again, the hearts of the Jews unto the prophets, and the prophets unto the Jews; lest I come and smite the whole earth with a curse, and all flesh be consumed before me.

18 Let not your hearts be troubled; for in my Father's house are many mansions, and I have prepared a place for you; and where my Father and I am, there ye shall be also.

19 Behold, I, the Lord, am not well pleased with many who are in the church at Kirtland;

20 For they do not forsake their sins, and their wicked ways, the pride of their hearts, and their covetousness, and all their detestable things, and observe the words of wisdom and eternal life which I have given unto them.

21 Verily I say unto you, that I, the Lord, will chasten them and will do whatsoever I list, if they do not repent and observe all things whatsoever I have said unto them.

22 And again I say unto you, if ye observe to do whatsoever I command you, I, the Lord, will turn away all wrath and indignation from you, and the gates of hell shall not prevail against you.

23 Now, I speak unto you concerning your families—**if men will smite you, or your families, once, and ye bear it patiently and revile not against them, neither seek revenge, ye shall be rewarded**;

24 **But if ye bear it not patiently, it shall be accounted unto you as being meted out as a just measure unto you**.

25 And again, **if your enemy shall smite you the second time**, and you revile not against your enemy, and **bear it patiently**, your reward shall be an hundred fold.

26 And again, **if he shall smite you the third time**, and ye **bear it patiently**, your reward shall be doubled unto you four-fold;

27 And these three testimonies shall stand against your enemy if he repent not, and shall not be blotted out.

28 And now, verily I say unto you, if that enemy shall escape my vengeance, that he be not brought into judgment before me, then ye shall see to it that ye warn him in my name, that he come no more upon you, neither upon your family, even your children's children unto the third and fourth generation.

29 And then, if he shall come upon you or your children, or your children's children unto the

third and fourth generation, I have delivered thine enemy into thine hands;

30 And then **if thou wilt spare him**, thou shalt be rewarded for thy righteousness; and also thy children and thy children's children unto the third and fourth generation.

31 Nevertheless, thine enemy is in thine hands; and if thou rewardest him according to his works thou art justified; if he has sought thy life, and thy life is endangered by him, thine enemy is in thine hands and thou art justified.

32 Behold, this is the law I gave unto my servant Nephi, and thy fathers, Joseph, and Jacob, and Isaac, and Abraham, and all mine ancient prophets and apostles.

33 And again, this is the law that I gave unto mine ancients, that they should not go out unto battle against any nation, kindred, tongue, or people, save I, the Lord, commanded them.

34 And if any nation, tongue, or people should proclaim war against them, they should first lift a standard of peace unto that people, nation, or tongue;

35 And if that people did not accept the offering of peace, neither the second nor the third time, they should bring these testimonies before the Lord;

36 Then I, the Lord, would give unto them a commandment, and justify them in going out to battle against that nation, tongue, or people.

37 And I, the Lord, would fight their battles, and their children's battles, and their children's children's, until they had avenged themselves on all their enemies, to the third and fourth generation.

38 Behold, this is an ensample unto all people, saith the Lord your God, for justification before me.

39 And again, verily I say unto you, if after thine enemy has come upon thee the first time, he repent and come unto thee praying thy forgiveness, **thou shalt forgive him**, and shalt hold it no more as a testimony against thine enemy—

40 And so on unto the second and third time; and **as oft as thine enemy repenteth** of the trespass wherewith he has trespassed against thee, thou shalt **forgive him**, until seventy times seven.

41 And if he trespass against thee and repent not the first time, nevertheless thou shalt **forgive him**.

42 And if he trespass against thee the second time, and repent not, nevertheless thou shalt **forgive him**.

43 And if he trespass against thee the third time, and repent not, thou shalt also **forgive him**.

44 But if he trespass against thee the fourth time thou shalt not forgive him, but shalt bring these testimonies before the Lord; and they shall not be blotted out until he repent and reward thee fourfold in all things wherewith he has trespassed against thee.

45 And if he do this, thou shalt **forgive him with all thine heart**; and if he do not this, I, the Lord, will avenge thee of thine enemy an hundred-fold;

46 And upon his children, and upon his children's children of all them that hate me, unto the third and fourth generation.

47 But if the children shall repent, or the children's children, and turn to the Lord their God, with all their hearts and with all their might, mind, and strength, and restore four-fold for all their trespasses wherewith they have trespassed, or wherewith their fathers have trespassed, or their fathers' fathers, then **thine indignation shall be turned away**;

48 And vengeance shall no more come upon them, saith the Lord thy God, and their trespasses shall never be brought any more as a testimony before the Lord against them. Amen.

Having gone through section 98 pointing out the instructions that when followed lead to character development (including self-control), we will now repeat section 98 adding notes and commentary.

To begin with, the Savior calls these early members His "friends," which is a term of closeness and endearment. And, at the end of verse 1, He counsels them to develop the character trait of gratitude. As you have perhaps noticed, those who have gratitude live a much more pleasant and peaceful life, regardless of their circumstances and what is going on around them. In fact, all commandments are given for our good and to promote inner peace, happiness, and joy, here as well as hereafter. And the Lord specifically commanded us to show gratitude (see D&C 59:21).

Section 98 repeated, with notes and commentary added

1 **VERILY I say unto you my friends**, fear not, let your hearts be comforted; yea, rejoice evermore, and **in everything give thanks**;

As we watch the Master school and help His "children" (Mosiah 5:7) move toward exaltation, we see Him next counsel them to have patience and reassure them that their prayers are heard. Those who do not have patience often develop bitterness toward God. Perhaps you've noticed that things usually happen according to the timetable of the Lord rather than according to the demands of people.

2 **Waiting patiently on the Lord,** for **your prayers have entered into the ears of the Lord of Sabaoth** [*the Savior, "the creator of the first day, the beginning and the end"—see D&C 95:7*], and are recorded with this seal and testament—[*covenant—see Bible Dictionary under "Covenant"*]—**the Lord hath sworn** [*promised*] **and decreed that they shall be granted.**

If you were to stop at the end of verse 2, above, and fail to read verse 3, next, you would miss the connection between what we ask for in prayer and what we get from the Lord. A major lesson here is that we get what is best for us rather than simply what we ask for.

3 **Therefore, he giveth this promise unto you**, with an immutable [*unchangeable*] covenant that they shall be fulfilled; and **all things wherewith you have been afflicted shall work together for your good,** and to my name's glory [*His work and "glory" is "to bring to pass the immortality and eternal life of man"—see Moses 1:39*], saith the Lord.

As we approach verses 4–6, next, wherein the Saints are counseled to support the laws of the land and the Constitution of the United States, it is helpful to remember that the members of the Church in Missouri had not been protected by the laws of the land thus far. In fact, the Prophet Joseph Smith recorded his thoughts on how the Missouri Saints had been treated by civil authorities and others who should have sustained and invoked the laws of the land in behalf of all citizens, including members of the Church. He recorded:

"In the course of this day's wicked, outrageous, and unlawful proceedings, many solemn realities of human degradation, as well as thrilling incidents were presented to the Saints [in Missouri]. An armed and well organized mob, in a government professing to be governed by law, with the Lieutenant Governor (Lilburn W. Boggs), the second officer in the state [of Missouri], calmly looking on, and secretly aiding every movement, saying to the Saints, 'You now know what our Jackson boys can do, and you must leave the county;' and all the justices, judges, constables, sheriffs, and military officers, headed by such western missionaries and clergymen as the Reverends McCoy, Kavanaugh, Hunter, Fitzhugh, Pixley, Likens, and Lovelady, consisting of Methodists, Baptists, Presbyterians, and all the different sects of religionists that inhabited that country, with that great moral reformer, and register of the land office at Lexington, forty miles east, known as the head and father of the Cumberland Presbyterians, even the Reverend Finis Ewing, publicly publishing that 'Mormons were the common enemies of mankind, and ought to be destroyed'—all these solemn realities were enough to melt the heart of a savage; while there was not a *solitary offense* on record, or proof, that a Saint had broken the law of the land" (*History of the Church*, 1:391–92).

As you will see, in verses 4–6, despite all of these violations and the lack of help from the government and laws of the land, the Lord still counsels the Saints to support the constitutional laws of the land.

4 And now, verily I say unto you **concerning the laws of the land**, it is my will that my people should observe to do all things whatsoever I command them.

5 And **that law of the land which is constitutional, supporting that principle of freedom in maintaining rights and privileges, belongs to all**

mankind, and is justifiable before me.

6 Therefore, **I, the Lord, justify you, and your brethren of my church, in befriending that law which is the constitutional law of the land**;

> You may wish to read D&C 101:77–80, in which the Lord gives His reasons for inspiring the writers of the Constitution of the United States. In verse 7, next, it implies that the Missouri mobbers were not abiding by the constitutional laws established by God, therefore, their behaviors were evil.

7 And **as pertaining to law of man, whatsoever is more or less than this** [*the Constitution*], **cometh of evil**.

> In verses 8–10, next, we are all given counsel about exercising our right to vote and about supporting good and wise political leaders.

8 **I, the Lord God, make you free** [*we were all given the freedom by the Lord to exercise moral agency— see D&C 29:35*], **therefore ye are free indeed** [*we truly are free to make choices*]; **and the law also maketh you free** [*good laws that adhere to the principles found in the Constitution allow people freedom and accountability—see D&C 101:77–78*].

9 Nevertheless, when the wicked rule the people mourn.

10 Wherefore [*for this reason*], honest men and wise men should be sought for diligently [*for public office*], and good men and wise men ye should observe to uphold; otherwise whatsoever is less than these cometh of evil.

Next, the topic turns to what God expects and requires of those who desire to be His true followers, regardless of circumstances. In other words, the distressed Saints in Missouri cannot use the wicked behavior of others to justify evil behavior on their part.

11 And I give unto you a commandment, that ye shall forsake all evil and cleave unto all good, that ye shall live by every word which proceedeth forth out of the mouth of God.

Verses 12–15, next, teach about the support of the Lord and the personal growth that will come to all who apply verse 11 in their lives, regardless of what those around them do. They will continue to grow and make progress toward eternal exaltation in celestial glory.

12 For he will give unto the faithful line upon line, precept upon precept [*principle upon principle*]; and I will try you and prove [*test*] you herewith.

13 And whoso layeth down his life in my cause, for my name's sake, shall find it again, even life eternal [*a scriptural term meaning exaltation*].

In verses 14–15, we are given to understand that the real enemy is not those who might even go so far as to kill us. Rather, it is the breaking of our covenants that we have made with God to live the gospel.

14 Therefore, be not afraid of your enemies, for I have decreed in my heart, saith the Lord, that I will prove you in all things, whether you will abide in my covenant, even unto death, that you may be found worthy.

15 For if ye will not abide in my covenant ye are not worthy of me [*in other words, if we do not do our best to keep our covenants, regardless of pressures to break them, we will not be found worthy of exaltation*].

Next, in verses 16–18, among other things, we are taught that true Saints strive to be peacemakers. However, sometimes our efforts to make peace and "renounce war" are not successful because of the behavior of others. Under those circumstances, there are rules and principles concerning self-defense, which the Lord will give us in verses 23–48.

16 Therefore, **renounce war** and **proclaim peace**, and **seek diligently to turn the hearts of the children to their fathers** [*among other things, perhaps including teaching the gospel so that people's hearts turn toward the ancient "fathers" or prophets*], and the hearts of the fathers to the children [*implying, among other things, the tying or binding of generations together; the sealing power will be restored by Elijah in section 110, as he restores the keys of sealing families together to Joseph Smith and Oliver Cowdery*];

> Continuing the message given in verse 16, above, the Savior informs us that the day will come when our brothers and sisters of the tribe of Judah (the Jews) will have their hearts softened. Large numbers of them will accept the gospel of Jesus Christ as their hearts are also turned "unto the prophets."

17 And again, **the hearts of the Jews unto the prophets, and the prophets unto the Jews**; lest I come and smite the whole earth with a curse, and all flesh be consumed before me.

> President Ezra Taft Benson spoke of the Jews and verse 17, above, as follows:
>
> "In Jacob's blessing to Judah, he declared: 'Judah is . . . as an old lion: who shall *rouse* him up?' (Gen. 49:9; italics added.) We come as messengers bearing the legitimate authority to arouse Judah to her promises. We do not ask Judah to forsake her heritage. We are not asking her to leave father, mother, or family. We bring a message that Judah does not possess. That message constitutes 'living water' from the fountain of living water.
>
> "Our prophet, Joseph Smith, was given a commandment by the Lord to turn 'the hearts of the Jews unto the prophets, and the prophets unto the Jews.' (D&C 98:17.) We are presently sending our messengers to every land and people whose ideology permits us entrance. We have been gathering Joseph's descendants for 146 years. We hope you, who are of Judah, will not think it an intrusion for us to present our message to you. You are welcome to come to our meetings. We display no crosses. We collect no offerings. We honor your commitment to your unique heritage and your individuality. We approach you in a different way than any other Christian church because we represent the restored covenant to the entire house of Israel.
>
> "Yes, we understand the Jews, as David Ben-Gurion said. We understand them because we belong to the same house of Israel. We are your brothers—Joseph. We look forward to the day of fulfillment of

God's promise when 'the house of Judah shall walk with the house of Israel' (Jer. 3:18.)" ("A Message to Judah from Joseph," *Ensign,* December 1976, 72).

Before we leave verse 17, above, take another look at the last half of the verse. A major doctrine we gain from it is that the primary purpose of the creation of this earth is to provide the opportunity for exaltation for Father's spirit children. If the "hearts of the children" were not turned to their "fathers," and the "hearts of the fathers to the children" (verse 16, above), this purpose would not be fulfilled. Temple work for the dead would not take place. The gospel of Christ would not be here; thus, all would turn to wickedness, and all would be "consumed" (verse 17) at the Second Coming, leaving none on earth during the Millennium to do temple work for the dead.

In verse 18, next, the Savior comforts the faithful, assuring them that there is plenty of room in celestial glory for all who qualify to come there.

18 **Let not your hearts be troubled**; for **in my Father's house are many mansions**, and **I have prepared a place for you; and where my Father and I am, there ye shall be also**.

The phrase "many mansions," found in verse 18, above, is often used to teach the doctrine that there are different degrees of glory. But in the context of verse 18, it seems to be saying that there are "many mansions" within the Father's "house," or, in other words, there is room for the "innumerable" (D&C 76:67) righteous people who will return to His presence to live forever.

Although this section deals primarily with the plight of the members in Missouri, the Lord sees similar lack of faithfulness, pride, and so forth among the members in Kirtland. We would do well to check our own lives against the concerns of the Lord spoken of in verses 19–22. The promise given at the end of verse 22 can also apply to us.

19 Behold, **I, the Lord, am not well pleased with many who are in the church at Kirtland**;

20 For **they do not forsake their sins, and their wicked ways**, the **pride** of their hearts, and their **covetousness**, and **all their detestable things**, and **observe the words of wisdom and eternal life** [*the knowledge and counsel already given them by the Lord*] **which I have given unto them.**

21 **Verily** [*listen up—what comes next is important*] I say unto you, that **I, the Lord, will chasten them and will do whatsoever I**

list [*whatever is necessary to purify them*], **if they do not repent and observe all things whatsoever I have said unto them**.

22 And again I say unto you, **if ye observe to do whatsoever I command you, I, the Lord, will turn away all wrath and indignation** [*punishments*] from you, **and the gates of hell shall not prevail against you** [*will not ultimately win against you*].

It is important to understand that there is a difference between being punished by the "indignation" (verse 22, above) of God, because of sin and wickedness on our part, and being tried and proven "in the furnace of affliction," which can come upon the righteous even though they are living the gospel. The punishments of God are designed to stop the downward spiral in the lives of people who have turned to sin. Trials and tribulations that come upon the righteous are designed to solidify progress already made and to provide more growth toward godhood.

Next, in verses 23–48, the Savior will give these beleaguered Saints the laws of self-defense that He gave to the ancient prophets, including Nephi, Abraham, Isaac, Jacob, and Joseph (see verse 32). As mentioned in the background notes to this section in this study guide, section 98 is well-known for this counsel regarding self-de-

fense. As you read, pay close attention to how much self-control is required in order to obey this law. Also, be aware that the first, second, and third offense scenarios given in verses 23–26 are not life-and-death situations when someone is threatening to kill you or your family and is raising a gun to shoot you. Such cases are dealt with in the last half of verse 31.

The Lord's Law of Self-Defense

The First Offense

23 Now, I speak unto you concerning your families—if men will **smite you, or your families, once,** and ye **bear it patiently and revile not against them, neither seek revenge, ye shall be rewarded** [*by the Lord*];

The reward spoken of at the end of verse 23, above, could include the peace and satisfaction of having exercised self-control, freedom from personal hatred, the developing of additional Christlike virtues, the peace and calm that are given to the obedient by the Holy Ghost, and so forth.

Verse 24, next, may sound somewhat harsh, but remember that we are dealing with the high laws and expectations that pertain to those who wish to become "Zion" people. Behaviors expected of "Zion" people are the same behaviors required of gods, or, in other words, "celestial" (D&C 105:5). Gods must be patient with their children and exercise much self-control.

24 But if ye bear it not patiently, it shall be accounted unto you as being meted out as a just measure unto you [*in other words, you deserve what you get*].

The Second Offense

25 And again, **if your enemy shall smite you the second time**, and you **revile not** against your enemy, and **bear it patiently**, your **reward shall be an hundred fold**.

The Third Offense

26 And again, if he shall smite you **the third time**, and ye **bear it patiently**, your **reward** shall be doubled unto you four-fold;

27 **And these three testimonies shall stand against your enemy if he repent not**, and shall not be blotted out.

As indicated in verse 28, next, the Lord does not always "smite" the enemies of the righteous upon the first offense, nor the second, nor the third. Sometimes He never does during their mortal lives. This can be hard at times for the righteous to understand and difficult for them to bear. The Savior

reminds us in D&C 64:21 that the reason He often holds back is that He may yet save more of the wicked if He gives them more chances to repent.

Also, in verses 28–31, next, we are told that there are circumstances under which we are justified in fighting against our enemies. Captain Moroni used these principles in defending his people against their enemies (see Alma 46:12–13, 18; see also Alma 43–63).

28 And now, verily I say unto you, **if that enemy shall escape my vengeance**, that he be not brought into judgment before me, **then ye shall see to it that ye warn him in my name**, that he come no more upon you, neither upon your family, even your children's children unto the third and fourth generation.

29 And **then, if he shall come upon you** or your children, or your children's children unto the third and fourth generation, **I have delivered thine enemy into thine hands** [*you may go ahead and defend yourselves*];

Did you see what happened between verse 29, above, and verse 30, next? Even though we are justified in defending ourselves, as stated in verse 29, there is a great reward for us and our posterity if we still forgive as indicated in verse 30. The good examples given by patient and forgiving parents or grandparents continue to live on and influence their children and grandchildren down through the ages.

30 And **then if thou wilt spare him, thou shalt be rewarded** for thy righteousness; and **also thy children** and **thy children's children** unto the third and fourth generation.

As previously mentioned, immediate danger to life and limb are covered by a different law. It is given in the last half of verse 31, next.

In Case of Immediate Danger to Life and Limb

31 **Nevertheless, thine enemy is in thine hands; and if thou rewardest him according to his works thou art justified** [*in other words, if you chose to extract justice from your enemy, at this point, you are not being wicked*]; **if he has sought thy life, and thy life is endangered by him, thine enemy is in thine hands and thou art justified** [*you may take immediate action; in other words, you do not give him the first three shots at point blank range*].

In verses 32–38, the Master informs us that the laws of self-defense given in this revelation are those that He gave the righteous in ancient times, and they apply to nations as well as individuals.

32 Behold, **this is the law I gave unto my servant Nephi, and thy fathers** [*ancestors*], **Joseph**, and **Jacob**, and **Isaac**, and **Abraham**, and **all mine ancient prophets and apostles**.

33 And again, **this is the law that I gave unto mine ancients**, that **they should not go out unto battle against any nation, kindred, tongue, or people, save** [*unless*] **I, the Lord, commanded them**.

34 And **if any nation, tongue, or people should proclaim war against them**, they should **first lift a standard of peace** unto that people, nation, or tongue;

35 And **if that people did not accept** the offering of peace, **neither the second nor the third time**, they should **bring these testimonies before the Lord**;

36 **Then I, the Lord, would** give unto them a commandment, and **justify them in going out to battle** against that nation, tongue, or people.

Those individuals and nations who adhere to these laws are entitled to special help from the Lord in battle.

37 And **I, the Lord, would fight**

their battles, and their children's battles, and their children's children's, until they had avenged themselves on all their enemies, to the third and fourth generation.

38 Behold, **this is an ensample** [*example; a precedent that may be safely followed*] **unto all people**, saith the Lord your God, **for justification before me** [*if you want to be justified in self-defense*].

President David O. McKay summarized the doctrine of self-defense as follows:

"There are, however, two conditions which may justify a truly Christian man to enter—mind you, I say enter, not begin—a war: (1) An attempt to dominate and to deprive another of his free agency, and (2) Loyalty to his country. Possibly there is a third, viz., Defense of a weak nation that is being unjustly crushed by a strong, ruthless one.

"Paramount among these reasons, of course, is the defense of man's freedom. An attempt to rob man of his free agency caused dissension even in heaven. . . .

"To deprive an intelligent human being of his free agency is to commit the crime of the ages. . . .

"So fundamental in man's eternal progress is his inherent right to choose, that the Lord would defend it even at the price of war. Without freedom of thought, freedom of choice, freedom of action within lawful bounds, man cannot progress. . . .

"The greatest responsibility of the state is to guard the lives, and to protect the property and rights of its citizens; and if the state is obligated to protect its citizens from lawlessness within its boundaries, it is equally obligated to protect them from lawless encroachments from without—whether the attacking criminals be individuals or nations" (in Conference Report, April 1942, 72–73).

In verses 39–48, next, the Savior provides a summary of His laws of self-defense, emphasizing the importance of forgiving our enemies.

39 And again, verily I say unto you, **if** after thine enemy has come upon thee **the first time, he repent and come unto thee praying thy forgiveness, thou shalt forgive him**, and **shalt hold it no more as a testimony against thine enemy** [*this is, among other things, strong counsel not to hold grudges*]—

40 And so on unto the second and third time; and **as oft as thine enemy repenteth of the trespass wherewith he has trespassed against thee, thou shalt forgive**

him, until seventy times seven [*in effect, with no limits*].

Remember we said earlier that these laws are those that gods follow. Verse 40, above, is similar to Mosiah 26:30, which says:

"Yea, and as often as my people repent will I forgive them their trespasses against me."

The extreme importance of our developing the ability to forgive others is obvious in light of the fact that Jesus repeats these laws yet again as this revelation draws to a close.

41 And **if he trespass against thee and repent not the first time, nevertheless thou shalt forgive him**.

42 And if he trespass against thee **the second time, and repent not, nevertheless thou shalt forgive him**.

43 And if he trespass against thee **the third time, and repent not, thou shalt also forgive him**.

After so many offenses without repentance on the part of the offender, the matter is to be turned over to the Lord (compare with D&C 64:9–11).

44 But **if he trespass against thee the fourth time thou shalt not forgive him**, but shalt **bring these testimonies before the**

Lord; and **they shall not be blotted out until he repent and reward thee** [*make restitution*] **four**fold in all things wherewith he has trespassed against thee.

Paying back "four fold" (verse 44, above) is most likely a reference to the laws of restitution given by Moses to the children of Israel. For example, if a man robbed a sheep from another, he was to restore four sheep as part of his repentance (see Exodus 22:1).

Yet again, the importance of our forgiving others with all our heart is emphasized in verse 45, next.

45 And if he do this, **thou shalt forgive him with all thine heart**; and if he do not this, I, the Lord, will avenge thee of thine enemy an hundred-fold [*in other words, if he or she does not repent and make restitution, he or she will answer to the Lord in His own due time*];

Verse 46 shows the natural consequence of bad example on the part of parents. It is natural that the pattern set by the parents influences their children down through the generations. But verses 47–48 teach that this chain can be broken at any time by righteous offspring (compare with Ezekiel 18).

46 And **upon his children, and upon his children's children of all them that hate me, unto the third and fourth generation**.

47 **But if the children shall repent**, or the children's children, and turn to the Lord their God, **with all their hearts** and with all their might, mind, and strength, **and restore four-fold for all their trespasses wherewith they have trespassed**, or wherewith their fathers have trespassed, or their fathers' fathers, then **thine indignation** [*your justifiable anger*] **shall be turned away**;

48 And vengeance shall no more come upon them, saith the Lord thy God, and **their trespasses shall never be brought any more as a testimony before the Lord against them**. Amen.

The wording in the last half of verse 48, above, pertaining to the fact that we should forgive and forget when people ask us for forgiveness is similar to the rules that the Lord follows, as given in D&C 58:42–43 (**bold** added for emphasis).

D&C 58:42–43

42 **Behold, he who has repented of his sins, the same is forgiven, and I, the Lord, remember them no more.**

43 By this ye may know if a man repenteth of his sins—behold, he will confess them and forsake them.

SECTION 99

Background

This revelation was given through the Prophet Joseph Smith to John Murdock on August 29, 1832, at Hiram, Ohio. At the time of this revelation, Brother Murdock had been a widower with four living children for about fifteen months. His three oldest children were still under his care, and the fourth, a one-year-old daughter, had been adopted by Joseph and Emma Smith.

John Murdock was born on July 15, 1792. Thus, he was about thirteen and a half years older than Joseph Smith. Early in life, John had a vision in which he was asked if he were participating in the ordinances of the gospel. He was not. This led him to earnestly search for a religion that made gospel ordinances an important part of worship.

As he pursued his search for such a church, he joined several different religions, being ultimately disappointed with each. First, he joined a Lutheran sect but eventually decided that they did not follow the Bible. Next, he affiliated with the Presbyterians, then the Baptists, and after that, the Methodists. By 1827, he and his wife of just over three years, Julia, were residing in the Kirtland, Ohio, area where he had joined the Cambellite faith started by Alexander Campbell. However, he gradually became disappointed with them, too, because many Cambellites did not believe in the gift of the Holy Ghost as spoken of in the scriptures.

By the time Parley P. Pratt, Oliver Cowdery, Ziba Peterson, and Peter Whitmer Jr. came through the Kirtland, Ohio, area in the winter of 1830, preaching the restored gospel as they traveled to teach the Lamanites on the western frontier (D&C 32), John had decided that all religions were wrong because they had departed from the teachings of the Bible.

As a result, when he heard of the four missionaries and that they taught the restoration of the ancient church, he traveled twenty miles to hear them for himself. He read the Book of Mormon and knew it was true. Parley P. Pratt baptized him on November 5, 1830. He had already been baptized by immersion twice in other churches, but this time he felt the power and authority of the true priesthood and forgiveness of sins.

At the time of their baptism, John and his wife, Julia, had three children, and she was expecting twins. On April 30, 1831, she gave birth to a girl and a boy. Julia died six hours afterward. John named the girl Julia Murdock and the boy Joseph Smith Murdock. Emma Smith also gave birth the same day, but her twins, a girl, Louisa, and a boy, Thaddeus, lived only

about three hours and died. In deep sorrow, John gave his twins to Joseph and Emma to raise.

On June 7, 1831, John Murdock was called to serve a mission to Missouri with Hyrum Smith (see D&C 52:8). Upon returning home, he found that his little son, Joseph, had died as a result of exposure after a mob broke into the home (March 24, 1832) where Joseph and Emma Smith were staying. The Prophet had stayed up late caring for little Joseph Smith Murdock, who was sick with the measles. The mob broke in and dragged the Prophet out over the frozen ground to tar and feather him. The door was left open, and the resulting cold air led to the baby's death.

Sometime during the winter of 1832–1833, John Murdock received a vision of the Savior. He said, "I saw the form of a man, most lovely, the visage of his face was sound and fair as the sun. His hair a bright silver grey, curled in most majestic form, His eyes a keen penetrating blue, and the skin of his neck a most beautiful white and he was covered from the neck to the feet with a loose garment, pure white, whiter than any garment I have ever before seen. His countenance was most penetrating, and yet most lovely" (Typescript of the journal of John Murdock, 18).

In section 99, Brother Murdock is called on another mission, this time to the "eastern countries" (verse 1). He will preach in the Kirtland area from September 1832 to April 1833, at which time he will depart on a mission to New York. He will serve for a year with his companion Zebedee Coltrin.

John will participate in Zion's Camp, serve a mission to New York beginning on March 5, 1835, and will marry Amoranda Turner on February 4, 1836, in New York. They will have no children. He will help settle Far West, Missouri, in 1836 and will serve on the high council there. His wife will die on August 16, 1837. He will marry Electa Allen on May 3, 1838, and they will have three children.

He will be ordained bishop of the Nauvoo Twentieth Ward on August 20, 1842, and will be called to serve a mission to the East in November 1844. His wife will die on October 16, 1845. He will marry Sarah Zuflet on March 13, 1846. They will have two children. In May 1846, he will go west with the Saints and serve as a high councilor, a bishop in Salt Lake City, and a delegate to the House of Representatives in 1849. John will be called to serve a mission to Australia and will serve for about two years, after which he will be released by President Brigham Young, who will gently tell him his missionary days are over and to come home permanently and be at peace. He will be called as a patriarch, serving many Saints in

Utah County for thirteen years. He will reside in Lehi, Utah, from 1854 to 1867 and will die faithful to the Church on the Prophet Joseph Smith's birthday, December 23, 1871, at the age of seventy-nine in Beaver County, Utah.

We will now proceed with this revelation to John Murdock, given August 29, 1832.

1 BEHOLD, thus saith the Lord unto my servant John Murdock— **thou art called to go into the eastern countries** from house to house, from village to village, and from city to city, **to proclaim mine everlasting gospel** unto the inhabitants thereof, in the midst of persecution and wickedness.

In verses 2–3, next, we are taught a simple truth, along with John Murdock, that when people receive the missionaries, they receive the Lord.

2 And **who receiveth you receiveth me**; and you shall have power to declare my word in the demonstration of my Holy Spirit [*you will have the help of the Holy Ghost in your teaching*].

3 And **who receiveth you as a little child** [*with pure, simple faith*], **receiveth my kingdom**; and blessed are they, for they shall obtain mercy.

4 And **whoso rejecteth you shall be rejected of my Father** and his house; and you shall **cleanse your feet** in the secret places [*not in public, which would stir people up against you unnecessarily*] by the way **for a testimony against them**.

When we see the phrase "I come quickly," as in verse 5, next, we probably should not think of it as meaning "soon." Rather, we should know that when the Second Coming begins, there will be no more time for repenting, since He will come "quickly" or "suddenly" (D&C 133:2) when He comes.

5 And behold, and lo, **I come quickly** to judgment, to convince all of their ungodly deeds which they have committed against me, as it is written of me in the volume of the book [*perhaps meaning "in the scriptures," as in 2 Nephi 26:18, 1 Thessalonians 5:3, Mark 13:36, and so forth, but we don't know for sure*].

As we approach verse 6, next, it is helpful to remember that although Brother Murdock had given the twins to Joseph and Emma to raise after Julia's death, he still had three older children whose ages would range from about seven down.

6 And now, verily I say unto you, that **it is not expedient** [*necessary*] **that you should go** [*on your mission to the East—verse 1*] **until your** [*three older*] **children are**

provided for, and sent up kindly [*suitably, appropriately*] unto the bishop of Zion [*to Bishop Edward Partridge in Missouri who arranged for the children to be cared for by Latter-day Saint families there*].

Next, in verses 7–8, we are reminded of another gospel principle—the Lord leaves many things up to our own choosing. There are many situations in which either choice would be righteous, and the Lord will support us in whichever we choose. You may wish to cross-reference these verses with D&C 58:26–28. In this case, the Savior is telling Brother Murdock, who loves missionary work, that after a few years he may settle down and stay home, or he may continue going on missions throughout his life.

7 And **after a few years, if thou desirest of me, thou mayest go up also unto the goodly land**, to possess thine inheritance;

8 **Otherwise thou shalt continue proclaiming my gospel until thou be taken** [*until the end of your life*]. Amen.

SECTION 100

Background

This revelation was given to the Prophet Joseph Smith and Sidney Rigdon on October 12, 1833, at Perrysburg in southwestern New

York, which was located about one hundred and forty miles northeast of Kirtland.

Having left Kirtland on October 5, 1833, they were going on a mission to Canada, preaching along the way. They returned home to Kirtland and their families on November 4, 1833. The Prophet recorded:

"*October 5.*—I started on a journey to the east, and to Canada, in company with Elders Rigdon and Freeman Nickerson, and arrived the same day at Lamb's tavern, in Ashtabula; and the day following, the Sabbath, we arrived in Springfield, whilst the brethren were in meeting, and Elder Rigdon spoke to the congregation. A large and attentive congregation assembled at Brother Rudd's in the evening, to whom we bore our testimony. We continued at Springfield until the 8th of October, when we removed to Brother Roundy's at Elk Creek; and continuing our journey on the evening of the 9th, we arrived at a tavern, and on the 10th, at Brother Job Lewis' in Westfield where we met the brethren according to previous appointment, and spoke to them as the Spirit gave utterance, greatly to their gratification.

"On the 11th of October, we left Westfield, and continuing our journey, staid that night with a man named Nash . . . with whom we reasoned, but to no purpose. On the 12th, arrived at Father Nickerson's, at Perrysburg, New York, where I received the following revelation [section 100]" (*History of the Church*, 1:416–17, 419–20).

In footnote 6, for *History of the Church*, 1:419, we are informed of an entry made by the Prophet in his private journal, in his own handwriting, on October 11, 1833. He said, "I feel very well in my mind. The Lord is with us, but have much anxiety about my family" (Joseph's journal, 7. See also *The Joseph Smith Papers, Documents, Volume 3: February 1833–March 1833*, 321–23).

Having received this revelation in section 100, Joseph and Sidney then continued to Canada where they preached for over a week, baptizing fourteen people.

Knowing that Joseph was worried about being away from his family, we hear the Lord's answer to his concern, next, in verse 1.

1 VERILY, thus saith the Lord unto you, **my friends** Sidney and Joseph, **your families are well; they are in mine hands**, and I will do with them as seemeth me good; for in me there is all power.

We will pause for just a moment to consider the significance of the Lord's calling these brethren His "friends" in verse 1 and elsewhere in the Doctrine and Covenants. While many religions teach that God is unapproachable and that it is blasphemous and demeaning to God to even think that one could have a tender relationship with Him, others believe that it is proper and appropriate for one to think of God as being approachable and near. The debate continues among other groups, but the answer is given here by pure revelation. "Friends" is a term of closeness, approachability, and endearment.

2 Therefore, follow me, and **listen to the counsel which I shall give unto you**.

3 Behold, and lo, **I have much people in this place, in the regions round about**; and **an effectual door shall be opened** [*Joseph and Sidney are opening an effective door for future missionary work in Canada as well as in New York*] **in the regions round about in this eastern land**.

> Verse 3 is prophetic. Many converts will come from Canada through this "door," including John Taylor, who will eventually serve as the third president of the Church.

4 **Therefore** [*for this reason*], **I, the Lord, have suffered you to come unto this place** [*have permitted and requested you to come here, even though you are needed at home*]; **for thus it was expedient in me** [*it was necessary*] **for the salvation of souls**.

5 Therefore, verily I say unto you, **lift up your voices unto this people; speak the thoughts that I shall put into your hearts, and you shall not be confounded** [*confused and stopped*] before men;

> Verse 6, next, contains a promise that can apply to all of us as we serve in our callings to teach and preach. It happens often to missionaries, to teachers in the classroom, to speakers in sacrament meetings and so forth.

6 For **it shall be given you in the very hour, yea, in the very moment, what ye shall say**.

> When the Spirit of the Lord helps us, as stated in verse 6, above, things often go very well, and it could be tempting to take glory to ourselves and become prideful. In verses 7–8, next, we are reminded that we must remain humble and speak with reverence about the blessings we receive.

7 But a commandment I give unto you, that **ye shall declare whatsoever thing ye declare** in my name, **in solemnity of heart, in the spirit of meekness** [*in humility*], in all things.

8 And I give unto you this promise, that **inasmuch as ye do this the Holy Ghost shall be shed**

forth in bearing record unto all things whatsoever ye shall say.

Next, in verses 9–11, Sidney Rigdon is given specific instructions by the Savior regarding his role compared to the role of the Prophet. He is to represent the Prophet to the people, whereas, Joseph is to represent the Lord to him. It is vital for Sidney not to begin thinking that he is the prophet.

9 And it is expedient in me that you, my servant **Sidney, should be a spokesman unto this people**; yea, verily, I will ordain you unto this calling, even to be **a spokesman unto my servant Joseph.**

10 And **I will give unto him** [*Joseph Smith*] **power to be mighty in testimony.**

11 And **I will give unto thee** [*Sidney Rigdon*] **power to be mighty in expounding** [*teaching and explaining*] **all scriptures,** that **thou** [*Sidney*] **mayest be a spokesman unto him,** and **he** [*Joseph*] **shall be a revelator unto thee**, that thou mayest know the certainty of all things pertaining to the things of my kingdom on the earth.

12 Therefore, **continue your journey and let your hearts rejoice**; for behold, and lo, I am with you even unto the end.

As this revelation concludes, the Savior gives counsel regarding the status of Zion in Jackson County, Missouri. At this time in 1833, acts of mob violence are commonly occurring there, and the members of the Church will soon be driven from Jackson County.

In late August 1833, Orson Hyde and John Gould (verse 14) had been sent from Kirtland on the dangerous journey to Jackson County with instructions to the Missouri Saints.

First, in verse 13, next, we learn that Zion will someday be redeemed. However, she will be "chastened for a little season." From our vantage point in time, we see that this "little season" was to last many years. The day will yet come when the prophecies about building Zion and the New Jerusalem in Missouri will be fulfilled (see 3 Nephi 20:22; 21:23–25; Ether 13:2–6; D&C 45:65–69; 84:2–4).

13 And now I give unto you a word concerning Zion. **Zion shall be redeemed, although she is chastened for a little season.**

14 Thy brethren, my servants **Orson Hyde and John Gould, are in my hands**; and inasmuch as they keep my commandments they shall be saved.

A quote from the 2018 *Doctrine and Covenants Student Manual* helps us understand verse 14, above.

"In late August 1833 the Prophet Joseph Smith sent Orson Hyde and John Gould to Jackson County, Missouri, with letters and other documents to comfort the suffering Church members there. These two men returned to Kirtland, Ohio, on November 25, 1833, with the unfortunate news that attacks on the Saints in Jackson County had resumed. (See *The Joseph Smith Papers, Documents, Volume 3: February 1833–March, 1834*, 325, note 39.)"

There is an important message for all of us in verse 15, next. This message is particularly helpful at times when things are not going as we expected and prayed for.

15 Therefore, **let your hearts be comforted**; for **all things shall work together for good to them that walk uprightly**, and to the sanctification of the church.

16 **For I will raise up unto myself a pure people, that will serve me in righteousness** [*the reason for the delay in building up Zion at this time in Jackson County*];

17 And **all that call upon the name of the Lord, and keep his commandments, shall be saved** [*in celestial glory*]. Even so. Amen.

SECTION 101

Background

This revelation was given to the Prophet Joseph Smith on December 16 and 17, 1833, at Kirtland, Ohio. It explains why the members of the Church in Missouri had been driven from their homes in Zion.

Beginning in July 1833, mobs began attacking the Saints in Zion (Jackson County, Missouri), destroying their homes and driving them from the county. During the night of Thursday, October 31, 1833, "a mob of about fifty horsemen attacked the Whitmer Settlement on the Big Blue River west of Independence. They unroofed thirteen houses and nearly whipped to death several men, including Hiram Page, one of the eight witnesses of the Book of Mormon" (*Church History in the Fulness of Times*, 135–36).

On November 25, 1833, Joseph Smith learned that mobs had driven the Saints from Jackson County. This news caused him great sorrow. On December 10, 1833, he wrote a letter to the Church leaders in Missouri in which he said:

"I have always expected that Zion would suffer some affliction, from what I could learn from the commandments which have been given. . . . I know that Zion, in the own due time of the Lord will be redeemed; but how many will be the days of her purification, tribulation and affliction, the Lord has kept hid from my eyes; and when I enquire concerning this subject, the voice of the Lord is, Be still, and know that I am God! All those who suffer for my name shall reign with me, and he that layeth down his life for my sake, shall find it again. Now, there are two things of which I am ignorant, and the Lord will not shew them [unto] me; . . . why God hath suffered so great calamity to come upon Zion; and what the great moving cause of this great affliction is: And again, by what means he will return her back to her inheritance" (in *Manuscript History of the Church*, vol. A-1, page 393, josephsmithpapers.org). Joseph continued praying for answers, and finally, on December 16 and 17, he received this revelation now known as section 101.

By the time of this revelation, most Church members in Jackson County had fled across the Missouri River into Clay County, Missouri, where local citizens helped them by offering shelter, food, clothing, and work as much as their own circumstances permitted. The Saints lived in abandoned slave cabins, built crude shacks, and lived in tents throughout the rest of the winter. Members of the mobs in Jackson County called the citizens of Clay County "Jack-Mormons" because they were friendly toward the Mormons.

Needless to say, this was a great disappointment to the members of the Church. They had anticipated that Zion would be built up at this time in Missouri and looked forward to being a part of it. As we look back, we see that many were doing well at living the gospel as required to establish a Zion society. But many were not (see verse 41). They had been warned many times by the Lord that they must do better at being true followers of Christ if they were to establish Zion. They were warned in D&C 97:26 that if they did not repent and do better at being true Saints, they would be subject to "sore affliction, with pestilence, with plague, with sword, with vengeance, with devouring fire."

This should be somewhat sobering and thought-provoking to us since we are constantly being counseled by the Lord to do better at keeping the Sabbath Day holy, avoiding the evils that surround us, studying the scriptures, carrying out our ministering sisters and ministering brothers service, and so forth.

Because section 101 is such a major revelation in the Doctrine and Covenants and contains such significant doctrine, counsel, and perspective, we will take extra time here to give a somewhat detailed overview. If you "stand back" and look at it as a whole, you will see that the Lord begins by explaining why these Saints have been driven from their lands and homes (verses 1–8). He then holds out hope to them (verse 9) and gives them perspective, telling them that the day is coming when troubles and punishments will be poured out upon the whole earth because of wickedness, which will ultimately open the doors for His people to build up the Church (verses 10–11).

Perspective of future blessings can provide strength and encouragement to endure present troubles. The Savior next takes the minds and hearts of these battered Saints into the future, showing them the gathering of Israel (verses 12–13), the comforting of the faithful who have been persecuted (verses 14–16), giving assurance that Zion will yet be established (verses 17–21), and promising that the faithful among them will participate in the glory that will accompany His Second Coming (verses 22–35). This blessing will come upon the faithful Saints, whether living or dead (see D&C 88:96–98). In addition, the faithful will have all their questions answered at the beginning of the Millennium (verse 32).

Continuing to give perspective, the Savior reminds the members in Missouri, as well as those in the Kirtland area, that the highest joys and blessings come to the faithful in the next life, and that one should work even more diligently to care for the soul than for physical life (verses 36–38). A major role and

obligation of true Saints is to be the "salt of the earth," which includes being a good example to others regardless of circumstances (verses 39–40).

Next, in verses 41–62, the Master Teacher sets the stage and then gives a parable, which once again explains why the Saints in Missouri were driven out, thus failing to establish Zion at this time. The Savior continues by emphasizing the work of gathering that must continue and by reviewing the parable of the wheat and the tares, implying that the "tares" among the Missouri Saints were the cause of the members being driven out of Jackson County (verses 63–66). Tares will be found among the Church membership until the Second Coming, but it's comforting to know that the "tares" in the Church often convert to "wheat."

Even though the members of the Church have been driven out of Jackson County, all members are given another opportunity to demonstrate their faith in the Lord by continuing to purchase land in Jackson County (verses 67–75). This may be one of the most difficult tests of all for the members at this time in history (see verse 75).

Another very difficult issue was the fact that the Saints were not protected by the Constitution, because local and state officials in Missouri refused to enforce the constitutional rights of the Latter-day Saints.

Thus, the value and importance of the Constitution of the United States was in doubt in the minds of many. In verses 76–80, the Savior leaves no doubt as to the validity and importance of this inspired document.

In verses 81–95, Jesus gives instructions that the Saints themselves are to adhere to the constitutional laws of the land and are to follow those laws in attempting to get redress and justice.

Finally, in verses 96–101, the Church is given specific instructions regarding land and property in Missouri owned by members.

With this overview as background, we will now begin our verse-by-verse study of this section. As stated previously, in verses 1–8 the Lord gives the reasons for the Saints not being allowed to establish Zion at this time. Remember that this revelation was given to Joseph Smith in Kirtland, Ohio, informing him and others about the situation in Jackson County.

1 VERILY I say unto you, **concerning your brethren** [*the members of the Church in Jackson County, Missouri*] **who have been** afflicted, and persecuted, and **cast out from the land of their inheritance—**

2 **I, the Lord, have suffered** [*permitted*] **the affliction** to come upon them, wherewith they have been afflicted, **in consequence of their transgressions;**

Note the encouragement given in verse 3, next. This can apply to all of us who diligently and humbly repent as needed.

3 **Yet I will own them,** and **they shall be mine** in that day when I shall come to make up my jewels [*when He assigns people to celestial glory*].

4 Therefore, **they must needs be chastened** [*scolded and punished for wrongdoing*] **and tried** [*tested*], even as Abraham, who was commanded to offer up his only son [*see Genesis 22:1–14; Hebrews 11:17–19*].

5 For **all those who will not endure chastening** [*those who will not accept correction from God*]**, but deny me, cannot be sanctified.**

Remember that the laws upon which Zion is to be established are the same laws that apply to the celestial kingdom (see D&C 105:5). Harmony, purity, and pleasantness are among these laws. We would all do well to seek to avoid succumbing to the sins and tendencies listed in verses 6–8, next.

6 Behold, I say unto you, there were **jarrings,** and **contentions,** and **envyings,** and **strifes,** and **lustful and covetous desires**

among them; therefore **by these things they polluted their inheritances** [*in other words, they ruined their opportunity to build a Zion society*].

7 They were slow to hearken unto the voice of the Lord their God; therefore, the Lord their God is slow to hearken unto their prayers, to answer them in the day of their trouble.

8 In the day of their peace they esteemed lightly my counsel; but, in the day of their trouble, of necessity they feel after me.

> Verse 9, next, assures that the law of mercy can still be made active in behalf of those who have fallen short through the sins mentioned in verses 6–8, above.

9 Verily I say unto you, **notwithstanding** [*in spite of*] **their sins, my bowels** [*a scriptural term meaning the deepest center of feeling and tenderness*] **are filled with compassion towards them**. I will not utterly cast them off; and in the day of wrath I will remember mercy.

> Next, in verses 10–11, we are taught that the days will come when the wicked who persecute the righteous will feel the wrath of God. This is one of the "signs of the times" (prophecies that will be fulfilled in the last days before the

Second Coming). One of many references to this is found in D&C 88:89–91.

10 **I have sworn** [*promised*], and the decree hath gone forth by a former commandment which I have given unto you [*see D&C 1:13–14*], **that I would let fall the sword of mine indignation** [*righteous anger*] **in behalf of my people**; and even as I have said, it shall come to pass.

11 **Mine indignation is soon to be poured out without measure** [*without limits*] **upon all nations**; and this will I do when the cup of their iniquity [*their wickedness*] is full.

> Some people get impatient, hoping that the Lord will smite the wicked now. They have apparently missed the last of verse 11, above, where it says, in effect, that the wicked will feel the anger of God when "the cup of their iniquity is full," meaning when they have become extremely wicked.

> Next, the Savior gives counsel as to how we can be saved, and foretells the gathering of Israel and the rewarding of the righteous.

12 And in that day [*when pestilence, plagues, natural disasters, and so forth are poured out upon the earth because of wickedness*] **all who are found upon the**

watch-tower [*who have gathered to the gospel and joined with the prophets who watch for and defend against evil*], **or in other words, all mine Israel** [*all of Israel who have come to Christ*], **shall be saved.**

13 And **they that have been scattered shall be gathered** [*this would be especially comforting to the Saints in Jackson County who have been "scattered" from their homes and lands in Zion*].

14 And **all they who have mourned shall be comforted.**

15 And **all they who have given their lives for my name shall be crowned.**

16 **Therefore, let your hearts be comforted concerning Zion; for all flesh is in mine hands; be still and know that I am God.**

Next, we are taught that the location for the city of Zion, the New Jerusalem, has not been changed. It will yet be built in Independence, Jackson County, Missouri.

Doctrine

Zion, New Jerusalem will yet be built in Jackson County, Missouri.

17 **Zion shall not be moved out of her place,** notwithstanding [*even though*] her children [*the members*

of the Church in Jackson County in 1833*] are scattered.

By the way, did you know that the Garden of Eden was located where the city of Zion will be built? Joseph Fielding Smith taught this as follows:

"In accord with the revelations given to the Prophet Joseph Smith, we teach that the Garden of Eden was on the American continent located where the City Zion, or the New Jerusalem, will be built. When Adam and Eve were driven out of the Garden, they eventually dwelt at a place called Adam-ondi-Ahman, situated in what is now Daviess County, Missouri" (*Doctrines of Salvation,* 3:74).

18 **They that remain** [*likely meaning the righteous remnant of Israel in the last days who are gathered to the gospel*], **and are pure in heart, shall return, and come to their inheritances** [*will help build the city of Zion*], **they and their children, with songs of everlasting joy, to build up the waste places of Zion—**

19 And **all these things** [*will take place in order*] **that the prophets might be fulfilled** [*in order that the prophecies about Zion given by the Lord's prophets might be fulfilled*].

In verses 20–21, next, the Savior tells these early Saints that as the latter-day gathering of Israel goes forth, the day will come when stakes of Zion will be added as gathering places for the Lord's people throughout the world. We are witnessing the fulfillment of this prophecy on a grand scale in our day!

20 And, behold, **there is none other place appointed** than that which I have appointed; neither shall there be any other place appointed than that which I have appointed, **for the work of the gathering of my saints—**

21 **Until the day cometh when there is found no more room for them**; and then **I have other places which I will appoint unto them, and they shall be called stakes**, for the curtains or the strength of Zion.

The counsel given at the end of verse 22, next, applies to all of us as we prepare to meet the Savior (verse 23), whether it is at His Coming or when we die, if we pass away before He comes.

22 Behold, it is my will, that **all they who call on my name, and worship me according to mine everlasting gospel, should gather together, and stand in holy places** [*such as temples, righteous homes, church, seminaries and institutes of religion, associating with righteous friends, and so forth*];

Doctrine

Everyone will see the Savior when He comes again. This includes those who have already died and are in the spirit world.

23 And **prepare for the revelation which is to come** [*the Second Coming*], **when the veil** [*which keeps us from seeing heaven and the spirits around us, etc.*] of the covering of my temple, in my tabernacle, **which hideth the earth, shall be taken off**, and **all flesh shall see me together** [*at the same time*].

Orson Pratt taught that it will not only be those living at the time of the Second Coming who will see the coming Lord. The dead will also see Him. Elder Pratt said (**bold** added for emphasis):

"The second advent of the Son of God is to be something . . . accompanied with great power and glory, something that will not be done in a small portion of the earth like Palestine, and seen only by a few; but it will be an event that will be seen by all—all flesh shall see the glory of the Lord; when he reveals himself the second time, every eye, **not only those living at that time in the flesh, in mortality on the earth, but also the very dead themselves**" (*Journal of Discourses*, 18:170; also quoted in the 1981

Doctrine and Covenants Student Manual, 241).

Revelation 1:7 teaches that "every eye shall see him" and that even those who crucified Him will see His coming. We will quote the verse here:

Revelation 1:7

7 Behold, he cometh with clouds [*from heaven in glory*]; and every eye shall see him, and they *also* which pierced him [*those who crucified Him*]: and all [*the wicked*] kindreds of the earth shall wail because of him. Even so, Amen.

Watch now as the Savior takes the minds of these Saints into a "high mountain," high above their present troubles and concerns, and gives them perspective and details about His Second Coming (verses 23, 25, 32–34), the destruction of all "corruptible" things (verse 24), and the Millennium (verses 25–31, 35).

Since we understand that animals, birds, fish, and so forth, are not capable of sin, we interpret "every corruptible thing" in verse 24, next, as being a symbolic statement that anything that would disturb the peace and righteousness on earth as the thousand years of peace begins will be destroyed at the time of the Second Coming.

Doctrine

All things that do not belong on earth during the Millennium (including wicked people, pornographic materials, the occult, things that promote evil, destroy peace, and so forth) will be burned by the glory of the coming Christ. See D&C 5:19.

24 And every corruptible thing, both of man, or of the beasts of the field, or of the fowls of the heavens, or of the fish of the sea, that dwells upon all the face of the earth, **shall be consumed**;

25 And also that of **element shall melt with fervent heat**; and **all things shall become new** [*"the earth will be renewed and receive its paradisiacal glory"—tenth article of faith*], **that my knowledge and glory may dwell upon all the earth.**

Doctrine

There will be peace on earth during the Millennium.

26 And **in that day** [*during the Millennium*] the enmity [*animosity*] of man, and the enmity of beasts, yea, **the enmity of all flesh, shall cease** from before my face [*in other words, the Millennium will truly be a time of peace*].

It appears from verse 27, next, that among other things, because of personal righteousness during the Millennium, people will be close enough to the Spirit to know what they may ask for and thus will have their requests granted (compare with D&C 46:30; 50:30).

27 And in that day whatsoever any man shall ask, it shall be given unto him.

People sometimes wonder whether Satan will literally be bound by God's power during the Millennium so he can't even try to tempt, or if he will go about tempting but no one will listen. The answer is given in verse 28, next.

Doctrine

Satan will not be allowed to tempt mortals on earth during the Millennium.

28 And in that day [*during the Millennium*] **Satan shall not have power to tempt any man.**

Occasionally someone refers to 1 Nephi 22:26 and asserts that it will be "because of the righteousness of his people" that "Satan has no power" during the Millennium. In other words, Satan will still be here, tempting and attempting to lead people astray, but no one will follow him. Joseph Fielding Smith addressed this issue as follows:

"There are many among us who teach that the binding of Satan will

be merely the binding which those dwelling on the earth will place upon him by their refusal to hear his enticings. This is not so. He will not have the privilege during that period of time to tempt any man. (D. & C. 101:28)" (*Church History and Modern Revelation*, 1:192).

Next, in verses 29–31, the Savior teaches these Saints who are refugees from mob violence and have lost loved ones that there will be no death as we know it (in the sense of mourning, having funerals, burying loved ones, and so forth) during the Millennium. During the thousand years of peace, people will die but will be resurrected in the "twinkling of an eye" (verse 31).

29 And there shall be no sorrow because there is no death [*as we have come to know it, burying loved ones in graves until we meet again*].

30 In that day [*during the Millennium*] **an infant shall not die until he is old; and his life shall be as the age of a tree;**

The "age of a tree," as given at the end of verse 29, above, means one hundred years old (see Isaiah 65:20). Elder Joseph Fielding Smith taught (**bold** added for emphasis):

"When Christ comes the saints who are on the earth will be quickened and caught up to meet him. This does not mean that those who are living in mortality at that time will be changed and pass through the resurrection, for mortals must remain on the earth until after the thousand years are ended. A change, nevertheless, will come over all who remain on the earth; they will be quickened so that they will not be subject unto death until they are old. **Men shall die when they are one hundred years of age**, and the change shall be made suddenly to the immortal state. Graves will not be made during this thousand years. . . . death shall come as a peaceful transition from the mortal to the immortal state" (*Way to Perfection*, 298–99, 311).

31 And **when he dies he shall not sleep**, that is to say **in the earth** [*he will not be buried in a grave*], **but shall be changed in the twinkling of an eye**, and shall be caught up, and his rest shall be glorious.

Doctrine

All of our questions will be answered at the beginning of the Millennium, including how the earth was created, how long it took, the role of dinosaurs, and so forth (see verses 32–34).

32 Yea, verily I say unto you, **in that day when the Lord shall come, he shall reveal all things**—

33 Things which have passed, and hidden things which no man knew, **things of the earth, by which it was made**, and the purpose and the end thereof—

34 **Things most precious**, things that are above, and things that are beneath, things that are in the earth, and upon the earth, and in heaven.

Apostle Bruce R. McConkie taught us what "reveal all things" (verse 32) includes:

"All things are to be revealed in the millennial day. The sealed part of the Book of Mormon will come forth; the brass plates will be translated; the writings of Adam and Enoch and Noah and Abraham and prophets without number will be revealed. We shall learn a thousand times more about the earthly ministry of the Lord Jesus than we now know. We shall learn great mysteries of the kingdom that were not even known to those of old who walked and talked with the Eternal One. We shall learn the details of the creation and the origin of man."

Elder McConkie concluded that in the millennial day, "Nothing in or on or over the earth will be withheld" (*The Millennial Messiah: The Second Coming of the Son of Man*, 676.

Next, in verses 35–38, the Savior gives us a brief lesson in eternal perspective.

35 And **all they who suffer persecution for my name, and endure in faith**, though they are called to lay down their lives for my sake **yet shall they partake of all this glory** [*spoken of in verses 23–34, above*].

36 Wherefore, **fear not even unto death**; for **in this world your joy is not full, but in me your joy is full**.

In verse 37, next, we are counseled not to make physical well-being a priority over spiritual well-being.

37 Therefore, **care not for the body, neither the life of the body; but care for the soul, and for the life of the soul**.

38 And **seek the face of the Lord always, that in patience ye may possess your souls, and ye shall have eternal life** [*"eternal life," as used in the scriptures, always means "exaltation" in the highest degree of glory in the celestial kingdom, or, in other words, becoming gods and living in our own family units forever*].

One of the things we are taught in verses 39–40, next, is that when we make covenants with God, we are covenanting to be the "salt of the earth." In other words, we commit to be an influence for good and to spread the gospel by word and deed throughout our lives.

39 **When men** are called unto mine everlasting gospel, and **covenant with an everlasting covenant, they are accounted as the salt of the earth** and the savor of men [*they add pleasantness and goodness to people's lives*];

40 **They are called to be the savor of men**; therefore, **if that salt of the earth lose its savor** [*if they do not keep these covenants to live the gospel and be an influence for good, etc.*], behold, **it is thenceforth good for nothing** only to be cast out and trodden under the feet of men.

Next, in verses 41–42, the Lord specifically addresses the issue of the Saints' having been driven out of Jackson County.

41 Behold, **here is wisdom** [*counsel*] **concerning the children of Zion** [*the members who were driven out of Zion in Jackson County, Missouri*], even **many, but not all**; they **were found transgressors, therefore they must needs be chastened** [*corrected and disciplined*]—

42 **He that exalteth himself** [*is prideful*] **shall be abased** [*humbled*], and **he that abaseth** [*humbles*] **himself shall be exalted** [*strengthened and supported by the Lord*].

Next, the Savior gives a parable explaining why the Saints were driven from Jackson County. This parable is a strong witness of the fact that Joseph Smith was a prophet of God. It consists of verses 44–62.

As with all parables, there can be different levels of meaning and interpretation. As we go through it, we will provide one possible interpretation. You will likely see additional possibilities.

Parable

43 And now, I will show unto you a parable, that you may know my will **concerning the redemption of Zion**.

44 A certain **nobleman** [*Christ— see verse 52*] had a **spot of land** [*Zion, in Jackson County, Missouri*], **very choice; and he said unto his servants** [*members of the Church who were called to go to Zion*]: **Go ye unto my vineyard** [*Jackson County*], even upon **this very choice piece of land** [*Zion*], and **plant twelve olive-trees** [*establish Latter-day Saint settlements*];

Twelve, in scriptural symbolism, means "God's divine organization and work." Thus, twelve in verse 44, above, would not literally mean twelve settlements but rather communities that represent God and His work.

45 And set **watchmen** [*prophets; Church leaders*] round about them, and build a **tower** [*temple*], that **one** [*the local leaders of the Church*] **may overlook the land round about** [*may see and spot approaching danger, especially spiritual dangers*], **to be a watchman upon the tower** [*to guard against the evils and dangers of the world*], **that mine olive-trees** [*covenant Israel; the members and their new settlements*] **may not be broken down when the enemy shall** [*not if but when dangers come*] **come to spoil** and take upon themselves the fruit of my vineyard.

46 Now, **the servants of the nobleman** [*the Saints who went to Missouri*] went and did as their lord commanded them [*moved to the land of Zion*], and planted the olive-trees [*established Latter-day Saint settlements*], and **built a hedge round about** [*established their territory*], and **set watchmen** [*local leaders of the Church*], and **began to build a tower** [*began to build a temple*].

Remember that the Lord had already designated the site for this temple (see D&C 57:3), and the Prophet Joseph Smith had already dedicated it (see D&C 84:3).

Watch now, as the parable continues, how the members

in Zion rationalized away the importance of the temple and began making their own rules and priorities rather than obeying the Lord's commandments.

47 And **while they were yet laying the foundation thereof** [*of the temple; they did lay the cornerstones of the temple*], **they began to say among themselves:** And **what need hath my lord of this tower?**

48 **And consulted for a long time** [*began procrastinating*], saying among themselves: **What need hath my lord of this tower, seeing this is a time of peace?** [*See verse 8.*]

49 **Might not this money be given to the exchangers?** [*Couldn't we make better use of this money?*] For **there is no need of these things**.

Remember, the Lord said in verse 41 that some were faithful but others were not. This obviously led to disharmony, "jarrings and contentions" (verse 6), which are not compatible with the celestial laws and principles upon which Zion was to be established (D&C 105:5).

As we see, beginning with verse 50, next, because of such lack of harmony and unity with respect to commitments and covenants each of them had already made with the Lord, they lost His help, which

opened the door to mob violence against them and the failure to establish Zion at that time.

50 And **while they were at variance one with another they became very slothful, and they hearkened not unto the commandments of their lord**.

51 **And the enemy came by night** [*symbolizing that they did not expect trouble*], **and broke down the hedge** [*broke through the inadequate defenses of the Saints, spiritually as well as physically*]; **and the servants of the nobleman** [*the members of the Church in Zion*] **arose and were affrighted, and fled; and the enemy** [*the mobs, symbolic of Satan*] **destroyed their works**, and **broke down the olive-trees** [*destroyed the Saints' settlements in Zion*].

Next, the Lord chastens these members for failing to obey His commandments and establish Zion.

52 Now, **behold, the nobleman, the lord of the vineyard, called upon his servants, and said** unto them, **Why! what is the cause of this great evil?**

53 **Ought ye not to have done even as I commanded you, and**—after ye had planted the vineyard, and built the hedge

round about, and set watchmen upon the walls thereof—**built the tower also, and set a watchman upon the tower, and watched for my vineyard, and not have fallen asleep, lest the enemy should come upon you?**

Verse 54, next, gives us strong reason to carefully study and heed the words of our living prophets!

54 And behold, **the watchman upon the tower would have seen the enemy while he was yet afar off**; and **then ye could have made ready** and kept the enemy from breaking down the hedge thereof, **and saved my vineyard from the hands of the destroyer.**

Next, beginning with verse 55, Joseph Smith is instructed to gather a small army from the members in the Kirtland area and elsewhere, which will become known as Zion's Camp. They are to march to Missouri to help the Saints there.

55 And **the lord of the vineyard** [*Christ*] **said unto one of his servants** [*Joseph Smith—see D&C 103:21*]: **Go and gather together the residue of my servants** [*in the Kirtland area*], **and take** all the strength of mine house, which are **my warriors**, my young men, and they that are of middle age also among all my servants, who are

the strength of mine house, save [*except*] those only whom I have appointed to tarry [*those who are to remain behind to lead the Church while Joseph and the others march the nine hundred miles to Missouri*];

56 **And go ye** straightway [*right away*] **unto the land of my vineyard** [*Jackson County, Missouri*], and **redeem my vineyard**; for it is mine; **I have bought it with money** [*the Saints in Zion had paid for their properties and had legal title to the lands from which they were driven*].

As you can see, verse 57, next, contains terms and symbolism of warfare in ancient times.

57 **Therefore, get ye straightway** [*right away*] **unto my land; break down the walls of mine enemies; throw down their tower, and scatter their watchmen.**

Have you noticed that there is a significant lesson in the timing of the Lord in these verses? We see the phrase "by and by" in verse 58, next. And in verses 59–60, we see the servant asking, in effect, when will Zion be redeemed? And the Lord answers, "When I will." One of the lessons we must learn is that when the Lord commands, we must obey—now. In some cases, people basically say that they will obey after they see the blessings and make sure that they make the effort to obey worthwhile. That is not how it works.

In this case, the Saints are told what to do "straightway" (verses 56–57, 60, 62), but the desired results will take place "when I will" (verse 60)—in other words, in the Lord's due time.

58 And inasmuch as they gather together against you, avenge me of mine enemies, **that by and by** [*eventually, in the Lord's due time*] **I may come with the residue** [*perhaps meaning the righteous remnant of Israel—compare with 3 Nephi 5:24; Ether 13:10*] **of mine house and possess the land.**

59 **And the servant said unto his lord: When shall these things be?**

60 And he said unto his servant: **When I will**; go ye straightway, and **do all things whatsoever I have commanded you;**

In verse 61, next, the Savior compliments and gives approval to His prophet, Joseph Smith. At the end of verse 62, we see that it will be a long time before Zion will be established in Missouri.

61 And **this shall be my seal** [*the Lord's approval and covenant*] **and blessing upon you** [*Joseph Smith—see verse 55*]—**a faithful and wise steward in the midst of**

mine house, a ruler in my kingdom.

62 And **his servant went straightway, and did all things whatsoever his lord commanded him**; and **after many days all things were fulfilled.**

In the *Doctrine and Covenants Student Manual*, 1981 edition, page 243, which is used by the institutes of religion of the Church, a quote by Sidney B. Sperry is given in which he explains the above parable as follows:

"It would seem that the parable is to be interpreted in this way: the nobleman is the Lord, whose choice land in His vineyard is Zion in Missouri. The places where the Saints live in Zion are the olive trees. The servants are the Latter-day Saint settlers, and the watchmen are their officers in the Church. While yet building in Zion, they become at variance with each other and do not build the tower or Temple whose site had been dedicated as early as August 3, 1831. Had they built it as directed, it would have been a spiritual refuge for them, for from it the Lord's watchmen could have seen by revelation the movements of the enemy from afar. This foreknowledge would have saved them and their hard work when the enemy made his assault.

"But the Saints in Missouri were slothful, lax, and asleep. The enemy came, and the Missouri persecutions were the result. The Lord's people were scattered and much of their labors wasted. The Almighty rebuked His people, as we have already seen, but He commanded one of His servants (v. 55), Joseph Smith (103:21), to gather the 'strength of Mine house' and rescue His lands and possessions gathered against them.

"Subsequently, the Prophet and his brethren in the famous Zion's Camp did go to Missouri in 1834 in an attempt to carry out the terms of the parable. Before they went, additional revelation was received (see 103:21–28) concerning the redemption of Zion. The brethren were instructed to try to buy land in Missouri, not to use force; and if the enemy came against them, they were to bring a curse upon them. Zion was not redeemed at that time but we may look for it in the not-too-distant future. Verily, it will be redeemed when the Lord wills it (*Compendium*, 521–22)."

That same manual goes on to say:

"Though Joseph Smith followed the Lord's instructions to gather together the 'strength of my house' (D&C 103:22) by organizing Zion's Camp to go forth to redeem Zion, the Lord's purpose in sending them and his will concerning the redemption of Zion were not fully understood by his people. The redemption of Zion did not take place at that time.

When the servant in the parable asked when the land would be possessed, the Lord responded, 'When I will' (D&C 101:60).

"The parable further states that all things will be fulfilled 'after many days' (v. 62), which passage indicates that a long period of time will pass before Zion will be redeemed. The redemption of Zion still had not taken place even after the Saints had been expelled from Missouri and from Nauvoo. The Lord then told Brigham Young that 'Zion shall be redeemed in mine own due time' (D&C 136:18). The redemption of Zion (meaning, the city of New Jerusalem in Missouri) is still future, although of course it is much closer now than it was when the Saints first sought to regain their inheritance in the land of Zion.

"The time of Zion's redemption is referred to in Doctrine and Covenants 58:44; 105:15, 37. Compare the parable in Doctrine and Covenants 101 with those given in Isaiah 5:1–7 and Matthew 21:33–46."

The Savior now changes the subject to the importance of continuing the work of gathering the Saints in many different locations. In verse 63, next, He implies that all the Saints can learn wisdom if they are willing to listen more effectively than they have in the past.

63 Again, verily I say unto you,

I will show unto you wisdom in me concerning all the churches [*groups, branches, wards, stakes, and the like*], **inasmuch as [***if***] they are willing to be guided in a right and proper way for their salvation**—

64 **That the work of the gathering** together of my saints **may continue**, that I may build them up unto my name upon holy places [*note that this is plural; in other words, there are now many gathering places for the Saints*]; **for the time of harvest is come** [*it is time for the prophesied last days gathering of Israel*], and my word must needs [*must*] be fulfilled.

Next, the Lord refers to the parable of the wheat and the tares (Matthew 13:24–30, 36–43). Tares are undesirable weeds that are hard to distinguish from wheat when both are young and growing together. But, when they both mature, it is easy to tell the wheat from the tares. The wheat symbolizes the righteous members of the Church and the tares represent the wicked among them.

65 Therefore, **I must gather together my people, according to the parable of the wheat and the tares, that the wheat may be secured** [*through righteous living and keeping covenants*] **in the garners** [*anciently, barns; symbolically to be gathered to celestial exaltation*] **to possess eternal life** [*exaltation*], and be crowned with celestial glory, **when I shall come** in the kingdom of my Father **to reward every man according as his work shall be** [*this is often referred to as the "law of the harvest"; in other words, what you plant is what you will harvest*];

66 While **the tares shall be bound** in bundles, and **their bands made strong** [*the time will come for the unrepentant in which the law of justice cannot be satisfied by the law of mercy; in other words, the wicked will be "bound" by their sins*], **that they may be burned with unquenchable fire**.

You may wish to reread the parable of the wheat and the tares in Matthew 13:24–30, 36–43. Additional helps for understanding it are given in D&C 86.

The commandment for these early Saints to continue to gather in various places is given in verse 67, next, but in verse 68, they are cautioned not to hurry so much that they are poorly prepared.

67 Therefore, **a commandment I give unto all the churches, that they shall continue to gather together** unto the places which I have appointed.

68 **Nevertheless**, as I have said

unto you in a former commandment [D&C 58:56; 63:24], **let not your gathering be in haste, nor by flight; but let all things be prepared before you.**

It may be a bit of a surprise at this point that the Lord is going to ask the members of the Church to continue donating money to purchase land in Missouri, including in Jackson County (verses 70–71). However, when we realize that faith and obedience are some of the most important lessons we can learn in this life, we soon see that humble obedience is the key issue here, not whether or not these early members of the Church will be permitted to build Zion in Missouri during their lifetime.

69 And **in order that all things be prepared before you, observe [keep] the commandment which I have given concerning these things**—

70 **Which saith**, or teacheth, to **purchase all the lands with money, which can be purchased** for money [which are for sale], **in the region round about the land** which I have appointed to be the land **of Zion**, for the beginning of the gathering of my saints;

71 **All the land which can be purchased in Jackson county, and the counties round about, and leave the residue** [the rest

of what needs to be done] **in mine hand.** [In other words, do what you've been commanded to do and leave the rest to the Lord.]

In verses 72–73, next, the Lord gives more specific detail about what the members of the Church should do in order to qualify for Him to take it from there. You will see that these things are to be done with wisdom and order, not helter-skelter—a most important principle that must be followed in building up the Lord's Church on earth.

With hindsight made possible by histories kept by early members, we note that many of those who originally moved to Missouri to establish Zion came poorly prepared, apparently thinking that if they came, God would provide. This was counter to the instructions given them in D&C 58:56 and 63:24, and, if repeated, would go against the instructions given in verse 72, here.

72 Now, verily I say unto you, **let all the churches** [the wards and branches throughout the Church] **gather together all their moneys** [their donations]; **let these things be done in their time** [in a timely manner]**, but not in haste**; and observe to have all things prepared before you.

73 And **let honorable men be appointed, even wise men, and**

send them to purchase these lands.

Verse 74, next, may mean that the Lord is inviting the wards and branches already established in the eastern United States and Canada to likewise buy lands upon which they can settle, thus establishing Zion communities in various locations. This seems to be a part of the fulfillment of verse 21, which indicates that stakes will become gathering places for Zion people. Perhaps you have noticed that we often refer to stakes as "stakes of Zion," in our gospel vocabulary today.

However, verse 74 could also mean that members of the Church in "eastern countries" should pool their resources and buy land in and around Jackson County and then settle there, thus building Zion.

74 And **the churches in the eastern countries** [*generally meaning areas in the United States and Canada, which are north and east of Ohio*], when they are built up, if they will hearken unto this counsel they **may buy lands and gather together upon them; and in this way they may establish Zion**.

The Lord gives an interesting perspective in verse 75, next. We generally see the poverty of these early members and feel sorry for them as they scrape together donations from their meager means in order to obey God's commandments on financial matters. Yet, in verse 75, the Savior informs us that these Saints had more than enough money among them to purchase the needed land in Missouri at this time!

No doubt, there is an important lesson for us here. It is that with our means, no matter how small or large, plus the help of the Lord (see verse 71), we can accomplish what He asks the Church to do financially.

75 **There is even now already in store sufficient, yea, even an abundance** [*there is more than enough*], **to redeem Zion**, and establish her waste places, **no more to be thrown down, were the churches, who call themselves after my name, willing to hearken to my voice** [*if the members of the Church who claim to be the Lord's people were willing to be obedient on this matter*].

Perhaps you have occasionally wondered (as many of us have) whether you would have been a faithful member of the Church had you lived in the days of these Saints. It may be that one way to tell is whether we are generous with our donations to the Church today.

Next, the topic switches to the Constitution of the United States of America. These Saints have not been protected from mobs and atrocities committed against them. Thus, the importance and validity of the Constitution has come into serious question in the hearts and minds of many of them. We will now be taught important doctrine by the Savior regarding the inspiration that went into the framing of the Constitution.

First, in verse 76, He counsels adherence to constitutional law as the Saints seek redress and compensation for their losses in Missouri.

Doctrine

The Constitution of the United States is an inspired document.

76 And again I say unto you, those who have been scattered by their enemies [*the members of the Church who lived in Jackson County, Missouri*]**, it is my will that** they **should continue to importune for redress** [*compensation; amends, satisfaction*]**, and redemption, by the hands of those who are placed as rulers and are in authority over you—**

77 According to the laws and constitution of the people, **which I have suffered** [*caused*] **to be established** [*the Savior inspired the writing of the Constitution*]**, and** should be maintained for the

rights and protection of all flesh, **according to just and holy principles;**

We are taught about the basic purposes and goals of the Constitution as an inspired document, in verses 78–79, next. As you will see, the preservation of individual moral agency and accountability are key principles. These are principles over which the War in Heaven was fought (see Moses 4:3).

78 **That every man may act** in doctrine and principle pertaining to futurity, **according to the moral agency which I have given unto him** [*we were given agency way back in our premortal existence—see D&C 29:35*]**, that every man may be accountable for his own sins in the day of judgment.**

79 Therefore, **it is not right that any man should be in bondage one to another.**

80 And **for this purpose have I established the Constitution of this land, by the hands of wise men whom I raised up unto this very purpose, and redeemed the land by the shedding of blood.**

Did you notice what kind of men the Lord used to frame the Constitution (in verse 80, above)? They were great men whom the Lord sent to earth at that time for that exact purpose! Undoubtedly, they were among the "noble and great ones" seen by Abraham as recorded in Abraham 3:22.

Perhaps you have noticed that some current historians seem to delight in "dethroning" our founding fathers as heroes. They take pleasure in pointing out their faults and shortcomings, as if to say, "They weren't that great." Verse 80, above, quickly puts things back into proper perspective, and shows that these commentators and historians are wrong.

By the way, did you know that most of these great men are now members of the Church? The signers of the Declaration of Independence, many of whom helped write the Constitution, appeared to Wilford Woodruff in the St. George Utah Temple and requested that their temple work be done. Their baptisms were performed on August 21, 1877. We will get some details about this from Wilford Woodruff, who was serving at the time as the president of the St. George Temple. He said:

"I will here say, before closing, that two weeks before I left St. George, the spirits of the dead gathered around me, wanting to know why we did not redeem them. Said they, 'You have had the use of the Endowment House [in Salt Lake City] for a number of years, and yet nothing has ever been done for us. We laid the foundation of the government you now enjoy, and we never apostatized from it, but we remained true to it and were faithful to God.' These were the signers of the Declaration of Independence, and they waited on me for two days and two nights. I thought it very singular, that notwithstanding so much work had been done, and yet nothing had been done for them. The thought never entered my heart, from the fact, I suppose, that heretofore our minds were reaching after our more immediate friends and relatives. I straightway went into the baptismal font and called upon brother McCallister to baptize me for the signers of the Declaration of Independence, and fifty other eminent men, making one hundred in all, including John Wesley, Columbus, and others; I then baptized him for every President of the United States, except three [Buchanan, Van Buren, and Grant]; and when their cause is just, somebody will do the work for them (*Journal of Discourses*, 19:229–30).

It is interesting to note that the "fifty other eminent men" included Benjamin Franklin, Daniel Webster, Henry Clay, John Wesley, and Benito Juarez. Also, after the work was done for these men, Sister Luc Bigelow Young was baptized for seventy prominent women, including Martha Washington and Elizabeth Barrett Browning (see Richard Cowan, *Temples to Dot the Earth*, 79–80).

Next, in verses 81–84, Jesus compares the situation of the Missouri Saints and their unsuccessful attempts to get help and protection from civil authorities to the parable of the woman and the unjust judge, which was given by Him and recorded in Luke 18:1–8. The main point of this parable is given in Luke 18:1 as follows:

Luke 18:1

1 AND he spake a parable unto them to this end [*in other words, the main point is*], **that men ought always to pray, and not to faint** [*not give up; not give up on the Lord*];

Notice that the Savior repeats the main point of this parable in the last part of verse 81, next.

81 Now, unto what shall I liken the children of Zion [*the members of the Church who were driven out of Jackson County*]**? I will liken** [*compare*] **them unto the parable of the woman and the unjust judge, for men ought always to pray and not to faint, which saith—**

82 There was in a city a judge which feared not God, neither regarded man.

83 And there was a widow in that city, and she came unto him, saying: Avenge me of mine adversary.

84 And he would not for a while [*implying that it will be a considerable time before the Saints return to build up Zion*], but afterward he said within himself: Though I fear not God, nor regard man, yet **because this widow troubleth me I will avenge her, lest by her continual coming she weary me**.

In verses 85–92, next, the Master teaches how this parable applies to these discouraged Saints.

85 **Thus** [*to this parable*] **will I liken the children of Zion** [*the Saints driven from Zion*]**.**

86 **Let them importune at the feet of the judge** [*let them formally request of the local civil authorities in Jackson County to insure them their rights as citizens*]**;**

87 And **if he heed them not** [*if they do not receive justice, protection and their civil rights from local government officials*]**, let them importune at the feet of the governor** [*let them go to the governor of the state*]**;**

88 And **if the governor heed them not, let them importune at the feet of the president** [*of the United States*]**;**

The Saints did ask for redress and help from both Presidents Andrew Jackson (in 1834) and Martin Van

Buren (on November 29, 1839—see *Church History in the Fulness of Times*, 220) but to no avail. Late in 1839, the Prophet and Elias Higbee traveled to Washington D.C. and met with President Van Buren. Joseph recorded this interview with the President of the United States as follows:

"During my stay I had an interview with Martin Van Buren, the President, who treated me very insolently, and it was with great reluctance he listened to our message, which, when he had heard, he said: *"Gentlemen, your cause is just, but I can do nothing for you;"* and *"If I take up for you I shall lose the vote of Missouri."* His whole course went to show that he was an office-seeker, that self-aggrandizement was his ruling passion, and that justice and righteousness were no part of his composition. I found him such a man as I could not conscientiously support at the head of our noble Republic. I also had an interview with Mr. John C. Calhoun, whose conduct towards me very ill became his station. I became satisfied there was little use for me to tarry, to press the just claims of the Saints on the consideration of the President or Congress, and stayed but a few days, taking passage in company with Porter Rockwell and Dr. Foster on the railroad and stages back to Dayton, Ohio" (*History of the Church*, 4:80).

After the Saints have done all in their power through legal means to right the wrongs against them, the Lord will take over (verses 89–91). Remember, though, that He will intervene when the timing is right (verse 90).

89 And **if the president heed them not, then will the Lord arise and come forth out of his hiding place, and in his fury vex the nation;**

90 **And in his hot displeasure,** and **in his fierce anger, in his time** [*when the time is right, according to the will and wisdom of the Lord*], **will cut off those wicked, unfaithful, and unjust stewards, and appoint them their portion among hypocrites, and unbelievers;**

91 Even **in outer darkness**, where there is weeping, and wailing, and gnashing of teeth [*symbolic of the extreme misery of those who reject the Savior's Atonement and thus are punished for their own sins*].

The "outer darkness" spoken of in verse 91, above, is not the outer darkness we often associate with the final fate of the sons of perdition. Rather, it refers more to the wicked who will end up in the telestial kingdom and who will first be turned over to Satan to be punished for their own sins (thus, the "weeping, and wailing, and gnashing of teeth") because they rejected the pleas of the Saints for redress and justice and, ultimately, the Savior's Atonement for their sins (see Alma 40:13; D&C 19:15–17).

Many people tend to look forward to the punishment of the wicked and gain considerable satisfaction in realizing that they will someday get what they deserve. However, as we draw closer and closer to the Lord, we will have more of a tendency to follow the counsel given in verse 92, next.

92 Pray ye, therefore, that their ears may be opened unto your cries, **that I may be merciful unto them, that these things may not come upon them**.

Next, the Savior gives us a general lesson in the principle of accountability and explains that the civil authorities mentioned in verses 86–88 must be given a chance to respond positively to the requests for redress from the Saints in order for them to be held accountable for their responses to fair claims from citizens.

93 What I have said unto you must needs be [*the members must take their complaints to the government authorities as instructed; this is a basic principle that goes with agency, knowledge and accountability*], **that all men may be left without excuse** [*in order for all to be held accountable*];

94 That wise men and rulers may hear and know that which they have never considered [*in other words, they will be surprised when they see the hand of the Lord in behalf of the righteous—compare with Isaiah 52:10*];

As the Savior continues to tell why the Saints must follow His instructions, He explains that the world will look upon the restoration of the gospel and the faithful members of the Church as "strange" or unusual.

95 That I may proceed to bring to pass my act, my strange act [*the restoration of the gospel—see D&C 95:4*], and perform my work, **my strange work** [*Isaiah 28:21*], **that men may discern between the righteous and the wicked** [*the Restoration will provide the people of the world with a choice between good examples and bad examples*], saith your God.

In verses 96–99, the displaced members who had lived in Jackson County are instructed not to sell their lands and properties in Zion, even though they have been driven out and prospects for returning look doubtful. This was a difficult test for them.

Oliver Cowdery failed this test. On April 12, 1838, he was excommunicated from the Church. One of the charges brought against him was selling land in Jackson County, Missouri, in direct opposition to the counsel of the Lord on this matter (*Church History in the Fulness of Times*, 186–87).

96 And again, I say unto you, **it is contrary to my commandment and my will that my servant Sidney Gilbert should sell my storehouse** [*the store (D&C 58:37) that he established in Independence, Jackson County, Missouri*], which I have appointed unto my people, into the hands of mine enemies.

97 **Let not that which I have appointed be polluted by mine enemies, by the consent of those who call themselves after my name** [*by those who claim to be faithful members of the Church*];

98 For **this is a very sore and grievous sin against me, and against my people** [*against the faithful members of the Church*], **in consequence of those things which I have decreed and which are soon to befall the nations.**

99 Therefore, **it is my will that my people should claim, and hold claim upon that which I have appointed unto them** [*do not sell their properties in Jackson County, which they own by legal deed, according to the laws of the land*], **though they should not be permitted to dwell thereon** [*even if they do not get to return and live there again*].

Finally, in verses 100–101, the Savior tells the members who were driven from their land and homes in Jackson County that there is still a chance for them to return if they will repent sufficiently and live the higher laws required of a Zion people.

100 Nevertheless, **I do not say they shall not dwell thereon; for inasmuch as** [*if*] **they bring forth fruit and works meet for my kingdom** [*if they demonstrate that they are willing to live the celestial laws upon which Zion is to be built (D&C 105:5)*] **they shall dwell thereon.**

101 **They shall build, and another shall not inherit it; they shall plant vineyards, and they shall eat the fruit thereof** [*compare with Isaiah 65:21*]. Even so. Amen.

It appears that the opportunity to return to their lands in Jackson County was dependent not only on the faithfulness of the Saints who had been displaced, but also upon the faithfulness of the general membership of the Church at that time, particularly in Ohio and the eastern United States and Canada.

Members throughout the Church had been instructed (D&C 101:69–

73) to donate money for additional purchase of land in Jackson County. Many were slow to do so or did not contribute at all.

When it came to gathering men, as instructed in D&C 101:55–57, to march to Jackson County and help the members return to their lands there, many would not go. We will study more about this when we get to section 103. Suffice it to say, at this point, that the Lord initially requested an "army" of five hundred (D&C 103:30). Recruiting efforts, which lasted a month, yielded an army of 207.

SECTION 102

Background

Perhaps you've noticed that most sections in the Doctrine and Covenants are revelations to Joseph Smith, or are, through him, given to others. Section 102 is a record of the minutes taken by Elders Oliver Cowdery and Orson Hyde of the organization of the first high council of the Church on February 17, 1834, at Kirtland, Ohio. These minutes were revised by Joseph Smith the next day and presented the following day to the high council. They unanimously accepted them. Verses 30–32 were added to the minutes later in preparation for this section to be included in the 1835 publication of the Doctrine and Covenants. They explain the difference between local high councils and the Council of the Twelve Apostles.

In this section, many of the principles and procedures followed in modern-day membership councils are given by the Lord. You can read details about membership councils (formerly referred to as "disciplinary councils") in the General Handbook, Section 32, which has been revised and was made available to all members on the Church's website in 2020.

Before we study section 102 verse by verse, we will give a bit more background.

It is important to distinguish between this first "high council" for which the First Presidency of the Church served as the presidency and stake high councils as they are organized today. In our day, a stake presidency serves as the presidency of the high council in their stake.

It is interesting to watch the gradual development of various levels of organization within the Church from the time of the Restoration to the present day. It is wonderful evidence of ongoing revelation.

The first stake in the Church was organized in Kirtland, Ohio, on February 17, 1834. The First Presidency of the Church, with Joseph Smith as the president, served as the stake presidency. In conjunction with the organizing of this first stake of Zion, a high council was called. Some of section 102 applies only to this first high council (verses 9–10), but much of it applies to stake high councils today.

The Prophet Joseph Smith taught that the high council is organized according to the pattern used by the Saints in ancient times. He said:

"I then declared the council organized according to the ancient order, and also according to the mind of the Lord" (*History of the Church,* 2:32–33).

One of the primary functions of the first high council of the Church was to serve as a second level of judiciary; in other words, to handle difficult issues that could not be settled satisfactorily by local leaders such as bishoprics and branch presidencies (see verse 2). Decisions of the bishopric could be appealed to the high council, and decisions of the high council could be appealed to the first presidency (verse 27).

As we proceed to study this section, we will emphasize, among other things, procedures that apply to high councils as well as to membership councils today. Remember, this section is the minutes kept by Oliver Cowdery and Orson Hyde for the meeting during which this high council was organized and was later revised by Joseph Smith.

1 THIS day [*February 17, 1834*] a general council of twenty-four high priests assembled at the house of Joseph Smith, Jun., by revelation, and **proceeded to organize the high council of the church of Christ, which was to consist of twelve high priests, and one or three presidents as the case might require**.

Next, the purpose of this high council is given.

2 **The high council was appointed** by revelation **for the purpose of settling important difficulties** [*including serious transgressions on the part of individual members*] **which might arise in the church, which could not be settled by the church or the bishop's council** [*conducted by a bishop and his counselors*] **to the satisfaction of the parties**.

We see in verse 3, next, that this high council consisted of a presiding presidency and twelve high priests to serve as high councilors.

3 **Joseph Smith, Jun.** [*president of the Church*]**, Sidney Rigdon** [*first counselor in the First Presidency*] **and Frederick G. Williams** [*second counselor in the First Presidency*] **were acknowledged presidents** [*sustained, as required by D&C 26:2*] **by the voice of the council**; and **Joseph Smith, Sen.** [*the Prophet's father*]**, John Smith, Joseph Coe,**

John Johnson, Martin Harris, John S. Carter, Jared Carter, Oliver Cowdery, Samuel H. Smith, Orson Hyde, Sylvester Smith, and Luke Johnson, high priests, **were chosen to be a standing council** [*one that continues to function on an on-going basis*] **for the church**, by the unanimous voice of the council.

> Proper procedure in the Church is to allow the person who has been called the opportunity to accept or turn down the position. This is demonstrated next in verse 4.

4 **The above-named councilors were then asked whether they accepted their appointments, and whether they would act in that office according to the law of heaven**, to which they all answered that they accepted their appointments, and would fill their offices according to the grace of God bestowed upon them.

5 **The number composing the council** [*the group attending this meeting where this high council was selected*], **who voted in the name and for the church in appointing the above-named councilors were forty-three**, as follows: nine high priests, seventeen elders, four priests, and thirteen members.

> According to verse 6, next, in order to conduct and conclude any

official business, a minimum of seven high councilors must be in attendance at a high council meeting.

6 Voted: that **the high council cannot have power to act without seven of the above-named councilors**, or their regularly appointed successors are present.

> Verse 6, above, does not apply in the case of a stake disciplinary council. Twelve high priests must be present, in addition to the stake president and two other high priests (usually his counselors). If any of the high councilors cannot be in attendance, other high priests may be asked to fill in (see verse 7, next). If the stake president cannot attend, the disciplinary council cannot be held unless a General Authority gives permission for one of the stake president's counselors to take his place.

7 **These seven shall have power to appoint other high priests**, whom they may consider worthy and capable **to act in the place of absent councilors**.

> Next, instructions are given for replacing high councilors. As you will see, the stake president and his counselors nominate the replacements.

8 Voted: that **whenever any vacancy shall occur** by the

death, removal from office for transgression, or removal from the bounds of this church government [*if a high councilor moves to a location outside the jurisdiction of this high council*], of any one of the above-named councilors, **it shall be filled by the nomination of the president or presidents**, and sanctioned [*sustained*] by the voice of a general council of high priests, convened for that purpose, to act in the name of the church.

Next, in verses 9–10, instructions are given that apply only to the president of the Church and his counselors. Remember that at this early stage in the growth of the Church, the First Presidency was also the stake presidency for the Kirtland Stake, the first stake in the Church.

9 **The president of the church**, who is also the president of the council [*the Kirtland Stake high council*], **is appointed by revelation, and acknowledged** [*sustained—see D&C 26:2*] **in his administration by the voice of the church** [*by the general membership of the Church*].

Next, in verse 10, these early Saints are reminded that the president presides over the entire Church. This is nothing unusual to us because we are used to it. However, we must realize that it

was not the normal thing among various religious groups and sects in Joseph Smith's day. Many Christian churches of his day had their own local leaders and did not have a strong central organization. Thus, many of the converts to the Church were not accustomed to having one central leader with strong authority over all local units of the Church.

10 And **it is according to the dignity of his** [*the president of the Church*] **office that he should preside over the council of the church** [*the whole Church*]; and **it is his privilege to be assisted by two other presidents** [*the counselors in the First Presidency*], appointed after the same manner that he himself was appointed.

Verse 11, next, applies both to the First Presidency of the Church as well as to stake presidencies. Again, in order to understand how important these specific organizational instructions are, we must be aware that such strong organizational rules were not common among religions in the Prophet's day, nor are they generally common among many religious organizations in our day.

11 And **in case of the absence of one or both of those** [*counselors*] who are appointed to assist him, **he has power** [*authority*] **to preside over the council without an**

assistant; and **in case he himself is absent, the other presidents** [*his counselors*] **have power to preside in his stead, both or either of them**.

Verse 12, next, foreshadows the establishment of many stakes as the Church grows.

Beginning with verse 12 and continuing through verse 33, procedures and instructions are given that apply directly to stake membership councils (formerly called disciplinary councils). You will see the reason for drawing numbers (verse 12, next) when you read verse 17. As you will see in verse 34, the members of this first high council did draw numbers that arranged them in order from one to twelve for purposes of disciplinary councils.

12 **Whenever a high council of the church of Christ is regularly organized**, according to the foregoing pattern, it shall be the duty of the twelve councilors to **cast lots by numbers**, and thereby ascertain who of the twelve shall speak first, commencing with number one and so in succession to number twelve.

13 **Whenever this council convenes to act upon any case** [*in other words, whenever a stake membership council is convened*], the twelve councilors shall consider whether it is a difficult one or not; if it is not [*if it is not a difficult or complex case*], **two only** of the councilors **shall speak upon it** [*make a recommendation as to what the decision of the council should be*], according to the form above written.

14 But **if** it is thought to be **difficult, four** shall be appointed; and **if more difficult, six**; but in no case shall more than six be appointed to speak [*make recommendations as to what the outcome of the council should be*].

The importance of preserving the worth of the individual (D&C 18:10) is a basic principle of the gospel of Jesus Christ. Verse 15, next, shows this principle in action. Half of the high councilors are assigned to make sure that the individual is treated with respect during the proceedings.

15 **The accused, in all cases, has a right to half of the council, to prevent insult or injustice**.

16 And **the councilors appointed to speak** [*the two, four, or six— verses 13–14, above*] before the council **are to present the case, after the evidence is examined** [*make their recommendation as to what disciplinary action should be applied to the person appearing before the council, after the whole council has examined and discussed*

the case together], **in its true light before the council**; and every man is to speak according to equity and justice [*personal biases and prejudices are to be set aside*].

17 **Those councilors who draw even numbers**, that is, 2, 4, 6, 8, 10, and 12, are the individuals who **are to stand up in behalf of the accused, and prevent insult and injustice.**

The high councilors mentioned in verse 17, above, are not "defense attorneys." Membership councils in the Church are not like courts of civil law in which there are prosecuting attorneys and defense attorneys. Rather, the six high councilors who are to "stand up in behalf of the accused" are responsible to stand up for him or her in the sense of insuring respect, courtesy, and fairness.

In most disciplinary councils held today, there are not "accusers" and "accused" (verse 18, next). Rather, a member has already confessed serious transgression and desires help in repenting and doing whatever is necessary to put things back in order with God. However, in cases where a member is accused of serious sin and does not confess (if guilty), both the person or persons who claim to know of the transgression and the accused are to be heard by the council.

18 In all cases **the accuser and the accused shall have a privilege of speaking for themselves before the council, after the evidences are heard and the councilors who are appointed to speak on the case have finished their remarks.**

Verse 19, next, instructs that the stake president is to make the final decision as to what disciplinary action is to be taken by the council and that his decision is to be presented to the other members of the membership council for their sustaining vote.

In the case of a bishop's membership council, the bishop makes the final decision and presents it to his counselors for sustaining.

19 After the evidences are heard, the councilors, accuser and accused have spoken, **the president shall give a decision** according to the understanding which he shall have of the case, and call upon **the twelve councilors** to **sanction the same by their vote.**

20 **But should the remaining councilors, who have not spoken** [*who were not part of the two, four, or six (verses 13–14) who were chosen to make recommendations as to the outcome of the council*], **or any one of them** [*any council member*], after hearing the evidences and

pleadings impartially, **discover an error in the decision of the president**, they can manifest it, and **the case shall have a re-hearing** [*in other words, unless the decision of the stake president is sustained unanimously at this point by the other council members, the council must be continued*].

21 And **if, after a careful rehearing, any additional light is shown upon the case, the decision shall be altered accordingly**.

If, after rehearing, which would include the discussion of any new evidence or points of view, nothing basically has changed, then the decision can be given based on the majority (verse 22) of council members sustaining it. In practice, few stake presidents go ahead with a decision unless it is sustained unanimously by the council members.

22 **But in case no additional light is given, the first decision shall stand, the majority of the council having power to determine the same.**

Verse 23, next, applies directly to the prophet in this context, but obviously can apply within their stewardships to stake presidents and bishops.

23 **In case of difficulty respecting doctrine or principle**, if there

is not a sufficiency written to make the case clear to the minds of the council, **the president may inquire and obtain the mind of the Lord by revelation**.

Verses 24–25 apply primarily to the early days of the Church, before there were stakes in other locations.

24 **The high priests, when abroad, have power to call and organize a council** [*a membership council*] after the manner of the foregoing, to settle difficulties, **when the parties or either of them shall request it**.

25 And **the said council** of high priests **shall have power to appoint one of their own number to preside** over such council for the time being.

Membership councils today follow the same practice, given in verse 26, next, of reporting the results of disciplinary action to the First Presidency.

26 **It shall be the duty of said council to transmit, immediately, a copy of their proceedings**, with a full statement of the testimony accompanying their decision, **to the** high council of the seat of the **First Presidency of the Church**.

If a member is dissatisfied with

the result of a bishop's council, it can be referred to the stake president with a request that a stake membership council be convened. Likewise, if a member is not satisfied with the outcome of a stake membership council, he or she may appeal it to the First Presidency as indicated in verse 27, next.

27 Should the parties or either of them be dissatisfied with the decision of said council, **they may appeal to** the high council of the seat of **the First Presidency of the Church**, and have a rehearing, which case shall there be conducted, according to the former pattern written, as though no such decision had been made.

In order to prevent the time and energies of the high council from being consumed by frivolous arguments and disagreements among members, the Lord gives the instruction in verses 28–29, next.

28 This council of high priests abroad is only to be called on the most difficult cases of church matters; and no common or ordinary case is to be sufficient to call such council.

29 The traveling or located high priests abroad have power to say whether it is necessary to call such a council or not.

Verses 30–33, next, distinguish between the authority of the Twelve Apostles, which will be organized as a quorum in 1835, and the authority of the high council or high councils referred to in this section.

30 There is a distinction between the high council or traveling high priests abroad, and the traveling high council composed of the twelve apostles, in their decisions.

31 From the decision of the former [*the local high council*] **there can be an appeal; but from the decision of the latter** [*the Apostles*] **there cannot.**

32 The latter can only be called in question by the general authorities of the church **in case of transgression.**

33 Resolved: that the president or presidents of the seat of **the First Presidency of the Church shall have power to determine whether any such case, as may be appealed, is justly entitled to a re-hearing,** after examining the appeal and the evidences and statements accompanying it.

Among the many things we learn from this section is that the Lord's kingdom is indeed a "house of order" (D&C 132:8).

Verse 34, next, is a record of the outcome of drawing lots on the part of the first high council. The purpose for this was mentioned previously in verses 15 and 17.

34 The twelve councilors then proceeded to cast lots or ballot, to ascertain who should speak first, and the following was the result, namely: 1, Oliver Cowdery; 2, Joseph Coe; 3, Samuel H. Smith; 4, Luke Johnson; 5, John S. Carter; 6, Sylvester Smith; 7, John Johnson; 8, Orson Hyde; 9, Jared Carter; 10, Joseph Smith, Sen.; 11, John Smith; 12, Martin Harris. After prayer the conference adjourned.

OLIVER COWDERY,
ORSON HYDE, Clerks.

By the way, the first case heard by the Kirtland Stake high council was the case of Brother Curtis Hodges. Ezra Thayer, who later left the Church, brought charges against Brother Hodges. The minutes of this disciplinary council, held on February 19, 1834 (two days after the date of section 102) are available in *History of the Church*, kept by Joseph Smith, as follows:

"To the President of the High Council of the Church of Christ.

"The following charges I prefer against Elder Curtis Hodges, Sen., of this Church: First, for an error in spirit; second, for an error in the manner of his address, which consisted in loud speaking, and a want of clearness in articulation, which was calculated to do injury to the cause of God; and also, for contending that that was a good and proper spirit that actuated him thus to speak—all of which I consider unbecoming in an Elder in this Church, and request a hearing before the High Council.

(Signed) Ezra Thayer.

"Elder Hodges pleaded 'not guilty' of the above charges.

"Father Lions was called on to substantiate the above charges, and his testimony was pointed against Brother Hodges. Brother Story testified that Elder Hodges talked so loud at a prayer meeting that the neighbors came out to see if some one was hurt. At another meeting, he said that Elder Thayer rebuked him for his error, but he did not receive the rebuke; that he raised his voice so high, that he could not articulate so as to be understood; and that his teaching brought a damper upon the meeting, and was not edifying. Brother Erastus Babbitt was then called upon, who testified that Elder Hodges was guilty of hollowing [making noise without value] so loud that in a measure he lost his voice, and uttered but little else distinctly than 'Glory to heaven's King.' His testimony against Brother Hodges was pointed. Brother Truman Wait testified much to the same effect.

"Councilor Oliver Cowdery stood up on the part of the accuser, and opened the case clearly.

"Councilor Joseph Coe stood up on the part of the accused, but could say but a few words.

"The accuser and the accused then spoke for themselves, after which the President arose and laid open the case still more plainly, and gave his decision, which was, that the charges in the declaration had been sustained by good witnesses; also, that Elder Hodges ought to have confessed when rebuked by Elder Thayer; also, if he had the Spirit of the Lord at the meetings, where he hollowed [made so much noise], he must have abused it, and grieved it away. All the Council agreed with the decision.

"Elder Hodges then rose and said he now saw his error, but never saw it before; and appeared to feel thankful that he saw it. He said he had learned more during this trial than he had since he came into the Church; confessed freely his error, and said he would attend to the overcoming of that evil, the Lord being his helper.

"The Council forgave him, and adjourned to the evening of the 20th" (*History of the Church*, 2:34).

SECTION 103

Background

This revelation was given through the Prophet Joseph Smith on February 24, 1834, at Kirtland, Ohio. We will give somewhat more background for this section than usual, in order to help you gain a more detailed understanding and a better feel for what the Saints were going through at this time. It is hoped also that it will better enable you to see how the Lord works with people who have not yet quite caught the vision of what it means to be totally committed to the Church and the covenants they have made to God.

Mob action and violence against the Saints in Jackson County, Missouri, had begun in July 1833. By early November 1833, the members of the Church who had settled in Zion, Jackson County, Missouri, had been driven by mobs from their homes and across the Missouri River to Clay County, Missouri. Though they were kindly received by the citizens of Clay County and were able to subsist there for a brief season, they desired to know what their longer-term future was. As mentioned in the background notes for section 101 in this study guide, being driven out of Zion was a severe blow to these Saints. In section 101, the Lord gave them the reasons they had been driven out, as well as some instructions for the future.

By the winter of 1834, the Saints determined to send two men to Kirtland to counsel with the Prophet Joseph Smith and the members there about their situation in Missouri. Elder Parley P. Pratt wrote about this as follows:

"After making our escape into the county of Clay—being reduced to the lowest poverty—I made a living by day labor, jobbing, building, or wood cutting, till some time in the winter of 1834, when a general Conference was held at my house, in which it was decided that two of the Elders should be sent to Ohio, in order to counsel with President Smith and the Church at Kirtland, and take some measures for the relief or restoration of the people thus plundered and driven from their homes. The question was put to the Conference: 'Who would volunteer to perform so great a journey?'

"The poverty of all, and the inclement season of the year made all hesitate. At length Lyman Wight and myself offered our services, which were readily accepted. I was at this time entirely destitute of proper clothing for the journey; and I had neither horse, saddle, bridle, money nor provisions to take with me; or to leave with my wife, who lay sick and helpless most of the time.

"Under these circumstances I knew not what to do. Nearly all had been robbed and plundered, and all were poor. As we had to start without delay, I almost trembled at the undertaking; it seemed to be all but an impossibility; but 'to him that believeth all things are possible.' [Mark 9:23.] I started out of my house to do something towards making preparation; I hardly knew which way to go, but I found myself in the house of brother John Lowry, and was intending to ask him for money; but as I entered his miserable cottage in the swamp, amid the low, timbered bottoms of the Missouri river, I found him sick in bed with a heavy fever, and two or three others of his family down with the same complaint, on different beds in the same room. He was vomiting severely, and was hardly sensible of my presence. I thought to myself, 'well, this is a poor place to come for money, and yet I must have it; I know of no one else that has got it; what shall I do?' I sat a little while confounded and amazed. At length another Elder happened in; at that instant faith sprung up in my heart; the Spirit whispered to me, 'is there anything too hard for the Lord?' I said to the Elder that came in: 'Brother, I am glad you have come; these people must be healed, for I want some money of them, and must have it.'

"We laid hands on them and rebuked the disease; brother Lowry rose up well; I did my errand, and readily obtained all I asked. This provided in part for my family's sustenance while I should leave them. I went a little further into the woods of the Missouri bottoms, and came to a camp of some brethren, by the name of Higbee, who owned some horses; they saw me coming, and, moved by the Spirit, one of them said to the other, 'there comes brother Parley; he's in want of a horse for his journey—I must let him have old Dick;' this being the name of the best horse he had. 'Yes,' said I, 'brother, you have guessed right; but what will I do for a saddle?' 'Well,' says the other, 'I believe I'll have to let you have mine.' I blessed them and went on my way rejoicing.

"I next called on Sidney A. Gilbert [actually, A. Sidney Gilbert—see D&C 53, heading], a merchant, then sojourning in the village of Liberty—his store in Jackson County having been broken up, and his goods plundered and destroyed by the mob. 'Well,' says he, 'brother Parley, you certainly look too shabby to start a journey; you must have a new suit; I have got some remnants left that will make you a coat,' etc. A neighboring tailoress and two or three other sisters happened to be present on a visit, and hearing the conversation, exclaimed, 'Yes, brother Gilbert, you find the stuff and we'll make it up for him.' This arranged, I now lacked only a cloak; this was also furnished by brother Gilbert.

"Brother Wight was also prospered in a similar manner in his preparations. Thus faith and the blessings of God had cleared up our way to accomplish what seemed impossible. We were soon ready, and on the first of February we mounted our horses, and started in good cheer to ride one thousand or fifteen hundred miles through a wilderness country. We had not one cent of money in our pockets on starting.

"We travelled every day, whether through storm or sunshine, mud, rain or snow; except when our public duties called us to tarry. We arrived in Kirtland early in the spring, all safe and sound; we had lacked for nothing on the road, and now had plenty of funds in hand. President Joseph Smith and the Church in Kirtland received us with a hospitality and joy unknown except among the Saints; and much interest was felt there, as well as elsewhere, on the subject of our persecution (*Autobiography of Parley P. Pratt,* 107–9).

Elders Pratt and Wight arrived in Kirtland on February 22, 1834. Two days later, the Kirtland Stake high council, which had been organized for less than a week—see D&C 102, met in the home of the Prophet Joseph Smith and heard the report of these two brethren concerning the plight of the Saints in Missouri. That same day, section 103 was received.

As you will see, this revelation reviews two major reasons that the Saints were driven out of Jackson County (verses 1–4), encourages these members of the Church to do better at keeping all the commandments the Lord has given about being a Zion people, and warns of the consequences if they do not (verses 5–10). It also teaches a lesson about the blessings that will come after faithfully enduring tribulation (verses 11–14), explains part of the parable given in D&C 101:43–62 in which Joseph Smith is told to lead men to Missouri (verses 15–21), instructs Joseph Smith to begin gathering this army of men (verse 22), and instructs all members of the Church to continue contributing money and purchasing land in Zion (verse 23). In addition, it explains that some will lose their lives in the cause of redeeming Zion (verses 24–28), sends eight men (four companionships) on brief missions to gather funds and recruit men to serve in what will become known as Zion's Camp—the name of the small army that is to march to Zion (verses 29–40)—and gives specific instructions as to how many men are needed and what to do if that number cannot be obtained (verses 30–34).

Near the end of February, the eight men listed, including the Prophet (verses 37–40), left on recruiting missions to gather funds and men for Zion's Camp. They traveled throughout the eastern United States, visiting the various branches of the Church there, but had little success. The Prophet expressed his concern about the lack of support for Zion's Camp in a letter written by the First Presidency to Orson Pratt (verse 40), who was still in the East recruiting. The Prophet wrote:

"Kirtland, April 7, 1834.

"Dear Brother Orson:—We received yours of the 31st ultimo in due course of mail, and were much grieved on learning that you were not likely to succeed according to our expectations. Myself, Brothers Newel, Frederick and Oliver, retired to the translating room, where prayer was wont to be made, and unbosomed our feelings before God; and cannot but exercise faith yet that you, in the miraculous providences of God, will succeed in obtaining help. The fact is, unless we can obtain help, I myself cannot go to Zion, and if I do not go, it will be impossible to get my brethren in Kirtland, any of them, to go; and if we do not go, it is in vain for our eastern brethren to think of going up to better themselves by obtaining so goodly a land, (which now can be obtained for one dollar and one quarter per acre,) and stand against that wicked mob; for unless they do the will of God, God will not help them; and if God does not help them, all is vain.

"Now the fact is, this is the head of the Church and the life of the body; and those able men, as members of the body, God has appointed to be hands to administer to the necessities of the body. Now if a man's hand refuses to administer to the necessities of his body, it must perish of hunger; and if the body perish, all the members perish with it; and if the head fail, the whole body is sickened, the heart faints, and the body dies, the spirit takes its exit, and the carcase remains to be devoured by worms.

"Now, Brother Orson, if this Church, which is essaying to be [claiming to be] the Church of Christ will not help us, when they can do it without sacrifice, with those blessings which God has bestowed upon them, I prophesy—I speak the truth, I lie not— God shall take away their talent, and give it to those who have no talent, and shall prevent them from ever obtaining a place of refuge, or an inheritance upon the land of Zion; therefore they may tarry, for they might as well be overtaken where they are, as to incur the displeasure of God, and fall under His wrath by the way side, as to fall into the hands of a merciless mob, where there is no God to deliver, as salt that has lost its savor, and is thenceforth good for nothing, but to be trodden under foot of men" (*History of the Church*, 2:48).

The Camp of Israel (later known as Zion's Camp) left for the thousand-mile journey to Missouri on May 1, 1834, from Kirtland. Many groups of recruits joined along the way, coming from the surrounding country, including Indiana and Illinois. Even though the total number of recruits for Zion's Camp was below the initial five hundred requested in this revelation (verse 30), a number of strong and valiant Saints were among its numbers. Many future leaders of the Church would come from this group. The average age of the recruits was 29, the age of the Prophet Joseph Smith at the time. The youngest member was 16, and the oldest, 79. Ultimately, there were 207 men, 11 women, 11 children, and 25 baggage wagons in Zion's Camp.

We will now proceed to study section 103 verse by verse. First, the Lord refers to the Prophet and others in Kirtland as His "friends," a term of closeness and endearment. He informs them that He will now tell them what to do regarding the plight of the Saints in Missouri, about which they have just heard from Parley Pratt and Lyman Wight.

1 VERILY I say unto you, **my friends,** behold, **I will give unto you a revelation and commandment, that you may know how to act** in the discharge of your duties **concerning the salvation and redemption of your brethren, who have been scattered on the land of Zion;**

Next, in verse 2, we are reminded again that the Lord does things according to His own timetable and wisdom. Although this is sometimes a difficult lesson to accept, especially when we have a need or want that we would like fulfilled now, it is a vital concept to accept. Otherwise, we are likely to become bitter toward the Lord and lose our faith and testimony.

2 Being driven and smitten by the hands of mine enemies, on whom I will pour out my wrath without measure **in mine own time.**

Next, even though it is a difficult lesson, especially if you are the victim, we are reminded that the wicked are sometimes allowed to persecute the righteous in order that there be sufficient evidence against them to convict them on Judgment Day. If the Lord were to intervene every time a person chooses to be wicked, the whole system of moral agency would be defeated, and there would be no real agency. This is the first reason the Lord gives in this revelation as to why the wicked were allowed to drive the Saints from Jackson County.

3 For **I have suffered them thus far** [allowed the mobbers to do what they have done so far], **that they might fill up the measure of their iniquities** [in order that their agency choices might convict them on Judgment Day—compare with Alma 14:11], **that their cup might be full** [in order that their punishments might be fair];

The second reason for the Lord's allowing the persecution of the Saints in Missouri is given next in verse 4.

4 And **that those who call themselves after my name** [who claim to be the people of the Lord] **might be chastened** [disciplined because of their sins] for a little season **with a sore** [severe] **and grievous chastisement, because they did not hearken altogether unto the precepts** [specific rules and instructions about living in Zion] **and commandments which I gave unto them.**

In verses 5–10, next, the Savior explains what can happen if the members of the Church do much better from now on and also what will happen if they don't.

5 But verily I say unto you, that **I have decreed a decree which my people shall realize** [which will be fulfilled in behalf of the persecuted Saints], **inasmuch as** [if] **they hearken from this very hour unto the counsel which I,** the Lord their God, **shall give unto them.**

6 Behold **they shall,** for I have decreed it, **begin to prevail** [win] **against mine enemies from this very hour.**

Did you notice the important statement by the Savior, in verse 6, above, as to whose enemies the enemies of the Lord's people are?

Next, in verse 7, the Master again emphasizes the importance of adhering to all His words, not just picking and choosing from among His teachings. This lesson applies to all of us.

7 And **by hearkening to observe** [*obey*] **all the words which I, the Lord their God, shall speak unto them, they shall never cease to prevail** until the kingdoms of the world are subdued under my feet, and the earth is given unto the saints, to possess it forever and ever [*in other words, such Saints will "inherit the earth" (Matthew 5:5) and will live on the earth forever as their celestial kingdom—D&C 130:9–11*].

8 **But inasmuch as they keep not my commandments, and hearken not to observe all my words,** the kingdoms of **the world shall prevail against them.**

9 For **they were set to be a light unto the world, and to be the saviors of men;**

10 And **inasmuch as they are not the saviors of men, they are as salt that has lost its savor, and is thenceforth good for nothing but to be cast out and trodden under foot of men.**

Next, in verses 11–14, the Savior specifically says that the Saints who have been driven off their land will return. But it will be after much tribulation. Also, note how the Lord includes the rest of the members of the Church (verse 13). In other words, they too must live the gospel according to the laws of Zion (the laws of the celestial kingdom—see D&C 105:5). Without verse 14, we would not have the complete context of the Savior's promise that they "shall return" (verse 11), and thus might be inclined to claim that the Lord did not fulfill His promise to these Saints (see verse 31 and compare with D&C 58:31–33).

11 But verily I say unto you, **I have decreed that your** [*referring to the members in the Kirtland area*] **brethren** [*in Missouri*] **which have been scattered shall return** to the lands of their inheritances, and shall build up the waste places of Zion.

12 For **after much tribulation**, as I have said unto you in a former commandment [*D&C 58:2–4*], **cometh the blessing**.

13 Behold, **this is the blessing which I have promised after your tribulations** [*the members in Kirtland and other locations besides Missouri*], **and the tribulations of your brethren** [*the Saints in Missouri*]—your redemption, and the redemption of your brethren, **even their restoration to the land of**

Zion, to be established, no more to be thrown down.

14 **Nevertheless, if they pollute** [*through personal sin and unworthiness*] **their inheritances they shall be thrown down**; for I will not spare them if they pollute their inheritances.

15 Behold, I say unto you, **the redemption of Zion must needs come by power** [*the power of God, which will come only if they fulfill the requirements given in verse 7, above*];

16 **Therefore** [*because Zion can only be redeemed by the power of God*], **I will raise up unto my people a man** [*Joseph Smith*], **who shall lead them like as Moses led the children of Israel** [*compare to D&C 107:91*].

17 For **ye are the children of Israel**, and of **the seed** [*descendants*] **of Abraham, and ye must needs be led out of bondage by power**, and with a stretched-out arm [*scriptural symbolism for the power of God*].

18 And **as your fathers** [*ancestors*] **were led at the first, even so shall the redemption of Zion be.**

19 **Therefore, let not your hearts faint** [*don't get discouraged*], for I say not unto you as I said unto your fathers: Mine angel shall go up before you, **but not my presence**.

Note, in comparison to the last phrase in verse 19, above, that the Savior promises that His presence will accompany the Saints who eventually go to redeem Zion (verse 20).

Also, don't miss the phrase "in time" in verse 20, next. As you have no doubt already noticed, there are many hints in these verses that the redemption of Zion will take longer than most Saints perhaps anticipated.

20 But I say unto you: **Mine angels shall go up before you, and also my presence**, and **in time ye shall possess the goodly land**.

Next, the Savior provides the interpretation as to who the "servant" is in verse 55 of section 101.

21 Verily, verily I say unto you, that **my servant Joseph Smith, Jun. is the man to whom I likened the servant** to whom the Lord of the vineyard spake **in the parable** [*D&C 101:43–62*] which I have given unto you.

In verse 22, next, the Prophet Joseph Smith is instructed to proceed to gather the men for the march of Zion's Camp. It has been over two months since the revelation was given (section 101) in which he was alerted that this time would come.

22 Therefore let my servant Joseph Smith, Jun. say unto the strength of my house, my young men and the middle aged—**Gather yourselves together unto the land of Zion**, upon the land **which I have bought with money that has been consecrated unto me** [*in other words, the Saints, with money they had consecrated to the Lord under the law of consecration, had legally purchased the lands from which they had been driven, and they had legal deeds to that property*].

Next, the members of the Church in all locations are counseled to continue contributing money for the purpose of purchasing land in Jackson County, Missouri, in spite of the fact that the Missouri Saints had been driven off their land. This is a real test of faith and obedience!

23 And **let all the churches** [*the branches of the Church*] **send up wise men with their moneys, and purchase lands even as I have commanded them**.

One possible interpretation of "curse" as used in verses 24–26 is to be cursed in the sense that the righteous obedience of the Saints will bring down condemnation from God against their enemies until

their enemies or their children, grandchildren, or later posterity stop fighting against truth and righteousness.

Another possible meaning of the word is that the Lord will "hide [his] face from them" (Deuteronomy 32:20) such that they will not receive His blessings and protections (see Deuteronomy 32:20–25).

Yet another possible meaning of curse is that the Saints and their leaders would actively pray that the Lord would stop their enemies and that He would curse their enemies by smiting them in various ways.

24 And **inasmuch as** [*if*] **mine enemies come against you to drive you from my goodly land**, which I have consecrated to be **the land of Zion, even from your own lands after these testimonies** [*after you have fulfilled these commandments*], **which ye have brought before me against them, ye shall curse them**;

25 **And whomsoever ye curse, I will curse**, and ye shall avenge me of mine enemies.

26 And **my presence shall be with you** even in avenging me of mine enemies, unto the third and fourth generation of them that hate me.

The phrase "unto the third and fourth generation of them that hate me," in verse 26, above, shows that hatred and wickedness on the part of the parents normally spreads to their children, grandchildren, and so forth. However, any of them or their posterity can "break the chain" by turning to God (see Ezekiel 18, especially verses 14–17).

Verses 27–28, next, emphasize the necessity of total dedication to the Lord at all costs if one desires exaltation.

27 Let no man be afraid to lay down his life for my sake; for whoso layeth down his life for my sake shall find it again [*will find eternal life, exaltation*].

28 And whoso is not willing to lay down his life for my sake is not my disciple [*true follower*].

In verse 29, next, Sidney Rigdon is instructed to go on a brief recruiting mission to the eastern United States, explaining to the members of the Church there what the Lord has said concerning that which must be done to redeem Zion. He is to urge them to keep the commandments and instructions of the Lord given in the above verses respecting the redemption of Zion. Lyman Wight will be assigned to go with him (verse 38).

29 It is my will that my servant Sidney Rigdon shall lift up his voice in the congregations in the eastern countries, in preparing the churches to keep the commandments which I have given unto them **concerning the restoration and redemption of Zion.**

In verse 30, Parley P. Pratt and Lyman Wight are instructed not to go back to the Saints in Clay County until recruits have been gathered to join the cause of Zion's Camp. Parley will go on a brief recruiting mission with Joseph Smith (verse 37) and, as mentioned above, Lyman will go with Sidney Rigdon (verse 38). Five hundred men are to be sought for to join Zion's Camp, as the small army of Saints will be called.

30 It is my will that my servant Parley P. Pratt and my servant **Lyman Wight should not return to the land of their brethren** [*the Saints temporarily staying in Clay County, Missouri—across the Missouri River from Jackson County*], **until they have obtained companies** [*of "soldiers" for Zion's Camp*] **to go up unto the land of Zion,** by tens, or by twenties, or by fifties, or by an hundred, **until they have obtained** to the number of **five hundred** of the strength of my house [*of the able-bodied men who are members of the Church*].

Next, in verse 31, the Lord makes

an understatement. It is some-what similar to the understatement made by Abraham, when his life was in imminent danger. Abraham said, "I, Abraham, saw that it was needful for me to obtain another place of residence" (Abraham 1:1).

31 Behold this is my will; ask and ye shall receive; but **men do not always do my will.**

In verses 32–34, the Lord tells them what to do if they cannot get five hundred men to join Zion's Camp.

32 Therefore, **if you cannot obtain five hundred**, seek diligently that peradventure [*perhaps*] you may obtain **three hundred.**

33 And **if ye cannot obtain three hundred**, seek diligently that peradventure ye may obtain **one hundred.**

34 **But** verily I say unto you, a commandment I give unto you, that **ye shall not go up unto the land of Zion until you have obtained a hundred** of the strength of my house, to go up with you unto the land of Zion.

Do you realize that, as members of the Church, we have both the privilege and the obligation to pray for our living prophet? We see this principle in verses 35–36, next.

35 Therefore, as I said unto you [*in*

Matthew 7:7, D&C 4:7, and so forth], ask and ye shall receive; **pray earnestly that peradventure my servant Joseph Smith, Jun., may go with you**, and preside in the midst of my people, and organize my kingdom upon the consecrated land, and establish the children of Zion upon the laws and commandments which have been and which shall be given unto you.

36 **All victory and glory is brought to pass unto you through your diligence, faithfulness, and prayers of faith.**

In verses 37–40, the Savior organizes companionships for brief recruiting missions for Zion's Camp.

37 Let my servant **Parley P. Pratt** journey with my servant **Joseph Smith, Jun.**

38 Let my servant **Lyman Wight** journey with my servant **Sidney Rigdon.**

39 Let my servant **Hyrum Smith** journey with my servant **Frederick G. Williams.**

40 Let my servant **Orson Hyde** journey with my servant **Orson Pratt**, whithersoever my servant Joseph Smith, Jun., shall counsel them, in obtaining the fulfilment of these commandments which

I have given unto you, and leave the residue in my hands. Even so. Amen.

By the way, Oliver Cowdery and Sidney Rigdon did not march with Zion's Camp to Missouri. Rather, they were left behind in Kirtland to lead the Church there in the absence of the Prophet and other brethren. Among their responsibilities was supervising the ongoing construction on the Kirtland Temple.

SECTION 104

Background

This revelation concerning the United Firm (see headings to sections 78 and 82 in the 2013 edition of the Doctrine and Covenants) was given to the Prophet Joseph Smith on April 23, 1834. The exact location is not recorded, although the Prophet had just returned to Kirtland the day before, on April 22, 1834 (see *History of the Church*, 2:54). The setting was likely that of a council meeting of members belonging to the United Firm, which was in financial difficulties.

By way of background, we will quote from the 2018 Doctrine and Covenants Student Manual, chapter 40:

"In March and April of 1832, the Lord commanded the Prophet Joseph Smith and a small group

of priesthood leaders in Ohio and Missouri to organize the United Firm (also referred to as the United Order). They covenanted to consecrate property to the Church and to work together to manage the Church's storehouses and printing business (see D&C 78:1–3; 82:11–12). In addition, United Firm members 'supervised farms and residential real estate, an ashery, a tannery, a stone quarry, a sawmill, and a brick kiln' (in *The Joseph Smith Papers, Documents, Volume 2: July 1831– January 1833*, ed. Matthew C. Godfrey and others [2013], 498). The profits made from these businesses were to be used to finance the work of building Zion as well as to provide income to United Firm members (see D&C 82:17–19).

"By April 1834 the United Firm was experiencing serious financial problems. Because of mob violence in Missouri in 1833, William W. Phelps's printing office in Jackson County had been destroyed and Sidney Gilbert was forced to close his storehouse. Consequently, neither the printing office nor the store could produce income for the firm, but the firm still had to repay the debts it had acquired to establish and supply these businesses. In Ohio, United Firm members increasingly became indebted to New York companies as they borrowed money to supply the Kirtland storehouse and to purchase land and a new printing press in Kirtland. In addition, some of the firm's members 'manifest[ed] a covetous spirit toward the firm's property for which they were responsible' (in *The Joseph Smith Papers, Documents, Volume 4: April 1834–September 1835*, 20). Because of these difficulties, 'members of the Kirtland branch of the United Firm met on 10 April 1834 and decided "that the firm should be [dissolved] and each one" receive a stewardship, or property, to oversee and manage' (in *The Joseph Smith Papers, Documents, Volume 4: April 1834–September 1835*, 21; see also *The Joseph Smith Papers, Journals, Volume 1: 1832–1839*, ed. Dean C. Jessee and others [2008], 38). About two weeks later the Prophet Joseph Smith received the revelation recorded in Doctrine and Covenants 104, which contained further instructions from the Lord regarding the United Firm and its properties."

The United Firm was originally set up based upon the laws and principles of the law of consecration.

1 VERILY I say unto you, my friends, **I give unto you counsel, and a commandment, concerning all the properties which belong to the order** [*the United Firm, headquartered in Kirtland*] **which I commanded to be organized and established, to be a united order**, and an everlasting order for the benefit of my church, and

for the salvation of men until I come—

Beginning with verse 2, next, the Lord explains that those called to belong to the United Firm must be faithful and keep their covenants. If so, they would receive the high blessings that attend living according to the law of consecration. But those who were not faithful and violated the covenants made when joining the United Firm were subject to the "buffetings of Satan" (verse 9).

2 **With promise immutable** [*not subject to being revoked*] **and unchangeable, that inasmuch as those whom I commanded were faithful they should be blessed with a multiplicity of blessings;**

3 **But inasmuch as** [*if*] **they were not faithful they were nigh unto cursing.**

In verse 4, next, we are shown two major stumbling blocks to living the law of consecration.

4 **Therefore, inasmuch as some of my servants have not kept the commandment, but have broken the covenant through covetousness**, and **with feigned words** [*pretended sincerity*], **I have cursed them with a very sore and grievous curse.**

The seriousness of breaking the covenant made (as in D&C 78:11;

82:15) in order to participate in the United Firm is pointed out in verses 5–9, next.

5 For I, the Lord, have decreed in my heart, that **inasmuch as any man belonging to the order shall be found a transgressor**, or, in other words, **shall break the covenant with which ye are bound** [compare with D&C 78:11–12; 82:15], **he shall be cursed in his life, and shall be trodden down by whom I will** [in other words, will not receive the protection from enemies which would otherwise be available from the Lord];

6 For **I, the Lord, am not to be mocked in these things**—

As you will see in verse 7, next, even if the United Firm is dissolved because of the transgressions and selfishness of some participants, those who did strive to keep their covenants and live the law of consecration would ultimately receive their reward in heaven.

7 **And all this that the innocent among you** [those who did their best to live according to the law of consecration] **may not be condemned with the unjust; and that the guilty among you may not escape;** because **I, the Lord, have promised unto you a crown of glory** [a scriptural term symbolizing exaltation] **at my right hand**

[the covenant hand, symbolizing those who made and kept covenants with God].

8 Therefore, **inasmuch as** [if] **you are found transgressors, you cannot escape my wrath in your lives**.

9 Inasmuch as ye are cut off for transgression, **ye cannot escape the buffetings of Satan** until the day of redemption.

The "buffetings of Satan" are described by Bruce R. McConkie as follows:

"To be turned over to the buffetings of Satan is to be given into his hands; it is to be turned over to him with all the protective power of the priesthood, of righteousness and of godliness removed, so that Lucifer is free to torment, persecute, and afflict such a person without let [interference] or hindrance" (*Mormon Doctrine*, 108).

Verse 10, next, points out that repentance and forgiveness are still available to transgressors who have not kept their covenants in the United Order. However, if they refuse to repent, the leaders of the Church are authorized to subject them to Church discipline, including excommunication if needed, which will turn them over to the buffetings of Satan.

10 And **I now give unto you power** from this very hour, that

if any man among you, of the order [*who belongs to the United Firm*], **is found a transgressor and repenteth not** of the evil, that **ye shall deliver him over unto the buffetings of Satan**; and he shall not have power to bring evil upon you.

Next, in verses 11–18, the Savior gives a brief review of the principles of "stewardship" and accountability as they relate to the United Firm and the law of consecration. These principles also apply to our lives and what we do with the blessings (stewardships) we are given by the Lord.

11 It is wisdom in me; therefore, a commandment I give unto you, that **ye shall organize yourselves and appoint every man his stewardship**;

12 **That every man may give an account unto me of the stewardship which is appointed unto him.**

13 For **it is expedient** [*necessary*] **that I, the Lord, should make every man accountable, as a steward over earthly blessings**, which I have made and prepared for my creatures.

Next, in verses 14–16, the Savior explains that He is the Creator and that all things belong to Him. In other words, we are stewards over

things that belong to God and are thus obligated to use them as He would.

14 **I, the Lord, stretched out the heavens, and built the earth** [*created the heaven and the earth—Genesis 1:1*], my very handiwork; and **all things therein are mine**.

15 And **it is my purpose to provide for my saints, for all things are mine**.

16 **But it** [*providing for the Saints—verse 15, above*] **must needs be done in mine own way**; and behold **this is the way** [*the laws, rules, and attitudes inherent in the law of consecration*] **that I, the Lord, have decreed to provide for my saints, that the poor shall be exalted** [*strengthened and nourished spiritually and physically*], **in that the rich are made low** [*kept humble and generous*].

Perhaps you have heard some people claim that the earth is not capable of supporting the large populations that are upon it and that are yet coming. Verse 17, next, answers that concern.

17 For **the earth is full, and there is enough and to spare**; yea, I prepared all things, and have given unto the children of men to be agents unto themselves.

As you can see, referring back to

verse 17, above, the real problem when it comes to poverty and starvation is man's mismanagement of the natural resources that God has placed upon the earth. It is the selfishness, greed, malicious destruction of resources, and oppression that cause the problems we see in the world around us, not the lack of preparation on the part of God to provide for all His children whom He will send to this earth.

Verse 18, next, explains the importance of generosity and sharing with others, as a major component of the law of consecration.

18 Therefore, **if any man shall take of the abundance which I have made, and impart not his portion** [*refuse to use his means for the benefit of others*], **according to the law of my gospel** [*including the law of consecration; see D&C 42:30*], **unto the poor and the needy, he shall, with the wicked, lift up his eyes in hell, being in torment** [*as was the case with the selfish rich man in the parable given by the Savior—see Luke 16:22–23*].

Remember, as explained in the background notes at the beginning of this section, that the United Firm in Kirtland was to be dissolved and reorganized at this time as instructed by the Lord. One of the lessons we learn from this is that the Lord gives us opportunities to

live higher laws, but when we fail, He patiently has us live according to other laws that, if obeyed, will lead eventually to our being able to live higher celestial laws.

Beginning with verse 19, next, the Savior gives instructions for the dividing up of the properties of the Kirtland United Firm among the members of that order.

19 And now, verily I say unto you, **concerning the properties of the order—**

20 **Let** my servant **Sidney Rigdon have** appointed unto him **the place where he now resides, and the lot of the tannery** [*Sidney Rigdon's father was a tanner, therefore, Sidney had some training in tanning leather for leather goods*] **for his stewardship, for his support while he is laboring in my vineyard,** even as I will, when I shall command him.

According to verse 21, next, the principle of common consent (sustaining—see D&C 26:2) is to be applied to this distribution of property among the members of the Kirtland United Firm.

21 And **let all things be done according to** the counsel of the order, and **united consent or voice of the order,** which dwell in the land of Kirtland.

22 And this stewardship and

blessing, I, the Lord, confer upon my servant Sidney Rigdon for a blessing upon him, and his seed [*posterity*] after him;

23 And I will multiply blessings upon him, inasmuch as he will be humble before me.

24 And again, **let** my servant **Martin Harris have** appointed unto him, for his stewardship, **the lot of land which my servant John Johnson obtained in exchange for his former inheritance**, for him and his seed after him;

25 And inasmuch as he is faithful, I will multiply blessings upon him and his seed after him.

26 And **let** my servant **Martin Harris devote his moneys for the proclaiming of my words**, according as my servant Joseph Smith, Jun., shall direct.

27 And again, **let** my servant **Frederick G. Williams have the place upon which he now dwells.**

28 And **let** my servant **Oliver Cowdery have the lot which is set off joining the house, which is to be for the printing office**, which is lot number one, and **also the lot upon which his father resides**.

29 And **let** my servants **Frederick G. Williams and Oliver Cowdery have the printing office** and all things that pertain unto it.

30 And this shall be their stewardship which shall be appointed unto them.

31 And inasmuch as they are faithful, behold I will bless, and multiply blessings upon them.

32 And this is the beginning of the stewardship which I have appointed them, for them and their seed after them.

33 And, inasmuch as they are faithful, I will multiply blessings upon them and their seed after them, even a multiplicity of blessings.

34 And again, **let** my servant **John Johnson have the house in which he lives, and the inheritance, all save** [*except*] **the ground which has been reserved for the building of my houses** [*see D&C 94:3, 10, 16*], which pertains to that inheritance, and those lots which have been named for my servant Oliver Cowdery.

35 And inasmuch as he is faithful, I will multiply blessings upon him.

36 And **it is my will that he should sell the lots that are laid off** [*designated*] **for the building up of the city of my saints**, inasmuch as it shall be made known to him by the voice of the Spirit, and according to the counsel of the order, and by the voice of the order.

37 And this is the beginning of the stewardship which I have appointed unto him, for a blessing unto him and his seed after him.

38 And inasmuch as he is faithful, I will multiply a multiplicity of blessings upon him.

39 And again, **let** my servant **Newel K. Whitney** [*the bishop in the Kirtland area*] **have** appointed unto him **the houses and lot where he now resides, and the lot and building on which the mercantile establishment stands** [*the Newel K. Whitney Store*]**, and also the lot which is on the corner south of the mercantile establishment, and also the lot on which the ashery is situated**.

40 And all this I have appointed unto my servant Newel K. Whitney for his stewardship, for a blessing upon him and his seed after him, for the benefit of the mercantile establishment of my order which I have established for my stake in the land of Kirtland.

41 Yea, verily, this is the stewardship which I have appointed unto my servant N. K. Whitney, even this whole mercantile establishment, him and his agent, and his seed after him.

42 And inasmuch as he is faithful in keeping my commandments, which I have given unto him, I will multiply blessings upon him and his seed after him, even a multiplicity of blessings.

43 And again, **let** my servant **Joseph Smith, Jun., have** appointed unto him **the lot which is laid off for the building of my house** [*the Kirtland Temple—see D&C 95:8*]**, which is forty rods long** [*a rod is 16.5 feet long*] **and twelve wide, and also the inheritance upon which his father now resides**;

44 And this is the beginning of the stewardship which I have appointed unto him, for a blessing upon him, and upon his father.

45 For behold, **I have reserved an inheritance for his father, for his support**; therefore he shall be reckoned in the house of my servant Joseph Smith, Jun.

46 And I will multiply blessings upon the house of my servant Joseph Smith, Jun., inasmuch as he

is faithful, even a multiplicity of blessings.

When the United Firm was first organized, there was one group, and the Saints in Kirtland, as well as the Saints in Missouri, belonged to it. In verses 47–51, next, the Savior instructs that the members in Kirtland and those in Missouri were to become separate, independent organizations at this time.

47 And now, a commandment I give unto you concerning Zion [*in Missouri*], that **you shall no longer be bound as a united order to your brethren of Zion**, only on this wise [*except as follows*]—

48 After you are organized, **you shall be called the United Order of the Stake of Zion, the City of Kirtland**. And **your brethren** [*in Missouri*], after they are organized, **shall be called the United Order of the City of Zion**.

49 And **they shall be organized in their own names**, and in their own name; and they **shall do their business in their own name**, and in their own names;

50 And **you shall do your business in your own name**, and in your own names.

In verses 51–53, next, the Lord explains why they are to divide

these two groups into two separate organizations.

51 And **this I have commanded to be done for your salvation, and also for their salvation, in consequence of their being driven out and that which is to come.**

52 **The covenants being broken through transgression**, by **covetousness** and **feigned words** [*see verse 4, above*]—

53 **Therefore, you are dissolved as a united order with your brethren**, that you are not bound only up to this hour unto them, only on this wise, as I said, by loan as shall be agreed by this order in council, as your circumstances will admit and the voice of the council direct.

Beginning with verse 54, next, the Lord gives instructions to those in Kirtland as to what is to be done with the stewardships He distributed, starting with verse 19 of this section. First, He reminds them that all things belong to Him and that they are to be faithful stewards over them.

54 And again, **a commandment I give unto you concerning your stewardship which I have appointed unto you.**

55 Behold, **all these properties are mine**, or else your faith is vain

[*otherwise, your faith in God would be of no value*], and ye are found hypocrites, and the covenants which ye have made unto me are broken;

56 And **if the properties are mine, then ye are stewards**; otherwise ye are no stewards.

57 But, verily I say unto you, **I have appointed unto you to be stewards** over mine house, even stewards indeed.

One of the things the Savior requires these Saints to do with the proceeds from their stewardships is to print the "fulness of my scriptures" and the revelations that He had given and would yet give (verse 58, next). This would no doubt include the Doctrine and Covenants (published in Kirtland in 1835), as well as the Joseph Smith Translation of the Bible (see D&C 104, footnote 58a). It could also include the book of Moses and the book of Abraham, which were first published in Church periodicals and later became part of the Pearl of Great Price.

The Savior explains the importance of making the fullness of the scriptures and the revelations available to all to read and study. One of the purposes is to prepare us to live with Him someday.

58 And **for this purpose I have commanded you to organize yourselves, even to print my words, the fulness of my scriptures**, the **revelations which I have given unto you, and which I shall, hereafter, from time to time give unto you—**

59 **For the purpose of building up my church and kingdom on the earth**, and **to prepare my people for the time when I shall dwell with them**, which is nigh at hand.

Another instruction from the Savior is that the Saints in the Kirtland area are to organize two separate funds, a "treasury" (verses 60–66) that is to be called the "sacred treasury" (verse 66) and "another treasury" (verse 67), into which surplus money from individual stewardships is to be placed.

60 And ye shall **prepare** for yourselves **a place for a treasury,** and consecrate it unto my name.

61 And ye shall **appoint one among you to keep the treasury**, and he shall be ordained unto this blessing.

Verse 62, next, explains that the funds given to the treasury in Kirtland are to be kept separate from other funds.

62 And **there shall be a seal upon the treasury,** and **all the sacred things shall be delivered into the treasury; and no man**

among you shall call it his own, or any part of it, for **it shall belong to you all** with one accord.

63 And I give it unto you from this very hour; and now see to it, that ye go to and **make use of the stewardship** which I have appointed unto you, **exclusive of the sacred things** [*verse 62, above*], **for the purpose of printing these sacred things** as I have said.

64 And **the avails** [*profits, proceeds—see D&C 104, footnote 64a*] **of the sacred things shall be had in the treasury**, and a seal shall be upon it; and **it shall not be used or taken out of the treasury by any one**, neither shall the seal be loosed which shall be placed upon it, **only** [*except*] **by the voice of the order, or by commandment**.

65 And thus shall ye preserve the avails of the sacred things in the treasury, for sacred and holy purposes.

66 And **this shall be called the sacred treasury of the Lord**; and a seal shall be kept upon it that it may be holy and consecrated unto the Lord.

67 And again, **there shall be another treasury prepared**, and a treasurer appointed to keep the treasury, and a seal shall be placed upon it;

J. Reuben Clark Jr., of the First Presidency, gave a general conference talk in which he spoke of these funds. He said:

"The Lord created two other institutions besides the [bishop's] storehouse: one was known as the Sacred Treasury, into which was put 'the avails of the sacred things in the treasury, for sacred and holy purposes.' While it is not clear, it would seem that into this treasury were to be put the surpluses which were derived from the publication of the revelations, the Book of Mormon, the Pearl of Great Price, and other similar things, the stewardship of which had been given to Joseph and others. (D. & C. 104:60–66)

"The Lord also provided for the creation of 'Another Treasury,' and into that other treasury went the general revenues which came to the Church, such as gifts of money and those revenues derived from the improvement of stewardships as distinguished from the residues of the original consecrations and the surpluses which came from the operation of their stewardships. (D. & C. 72:11)

"We have in place of the two treasuries, the 'Sacred Treasury' and 'Another Treasury,' the general funds of the Church.

"Thus you will see, brethren, that in many of its great essentials, we have, as the Welfare Plan has now developed, the broad essentials of the United Order" (in Conference Report, October 1942, 56–58).

As you will see in the next verses, the amount of money we donate to the Church for the work of the Lord is not the important thing. The key issue is that we donate according to our ability.

68 And **all moneys that you receive in your stewardships, by improving upon the properties which I have appointed unto you**, in houses, or in lands, or in cattle, or in all things save it be the holy and sacred writings, which I have reserved unto myself for holy and sacred purposes, **shall be cast into the treasury** as fast as you receive moneys, **by hundreds**, or by **fifties**, or by **twenties**, or by **tens**, or by **fives**.

69 Or in other words, if any man among you obtain five dollars let him cast them into the treasury; or if he obtain ten, or twenty, or fifty, or an hundred, let him do likewise;

Since donating to this general fund of the Church is a rather new concept for these Saints, the Lord emphasizes that this is a general fund of the Church and is to be used by the Church only by the sustaining vote of the pertinent members.

70 And **let not any among you say that it is his own; for it shall not be called his, nor any part of it.**

71 And **there shall not any part of it be used, or taken out of the treasury, only by the voice and common consent of the order.**

72 And **this shall be the voice and common consent** [*see D&C 26:2*] of the order—**that any man among you say to the treasurer: I have need of this** [*money from the "other" treasury—verse 67*] **to help me in my stewardship**—

73 If it be five dollars, or if it be ten dollars, or twenty, or fifty, or a hundred, **the treasurer shall give unto him the sum which he requires to help him in his stewardship**—

Next, in verses 74–77, warning and instruction are given with respect to how to handle transgressors who are participating in the use of the funds.

74 **Until he be found a transgressor**, and it is manifest before the council of the order plainly [*it is clear that he has transgressed*] that he is an unfaithful and an unwise steward.

75 **But so long as he is in full fellowship, and is faithful and wise in his stewardship, this shall be his token unto the treasurer that the treasurer shall not withhold** [*the faithful and worthy Saints are to be helped as needed from this fund*].

76 **But in case of transgression, the treasurer shall be subject unto the council and voice of the order** [*the vote of the order as to what to do regarding a transgressor*].

77 And **in case the treasurer is found** an **unfaithful** and an **unwise** steward, he shall be subject to the council and voice of the order, and **shall be removed out of his place, and another shall be appointed in his stead** [*in his place*].

At this point, the Church in Kirtland was heavily in debt. The burden of providing for the steady flow of new converts was exhausting to the financial resources of the Church. In verses 78–86, the Lord gives instructions about dealing with this heavy burden. Note how He stresses that this should be a one-time dilemma for them (verses 83 and 86).

78 And again, verily I say unto you, **concerning your debts**— behold it is my will that **you shall pay all your debts**.

79 And it is my will that you shall humble yourselves before me, and obtain this blessing by your diligence and humility and the prayer of faith.

80 And **inasmuch as you are diligent and humble, and exercise the prayer of faith**, behold, **I will soften the hearts of those to whom you are in debt, until I shall send means unto you for your deliverance** [*until the Lord provides the means to pay them*].

81 Therefore **write speedily to New York** and write **according to that which shall be dictated by my Spirit; and I will soften the hearts of those to whom you are in debt,** that it shall be taken away out of their minds to bring affliction upon you.

82 And **inasmuch as** [*if*] **ye are humble and faithful and call upon my name**, behold, **I will give you the victory**.

83 **I give unto you a promise, that you shall be delivered this once** out of your bondage [*the bondage of debt*].

In verses 84–85, next, the Prophet and the Church leaders in Kirtland are given permission to use the property they were given (beginning with verse 19) as collateral for loans that could help pay off the debts of the Church at this time.

84 **Inasmuch as you obtain a chance to loan money** by hundreds, or thousands, even **until you shall loan enough to deliver yourself from bondage** [*from debt*], **it is your privilege**.

85 And **pledge** [*use for collateral to secure the loans*] **the properties** which I have put into your hands, **this once**, by giving your names by common consent or otherwise, as it shall seem good unto you.

86 **I give unto you this privilege, this once**; and behold, **if you proceed to do the things which I have laid before you**, according to my commandments, all these things are mine, and ye are my stewards, and **the master** [*Christ*] **will not suffer his house to be broken up** [*if these Saints faithfully follow the Lord's instructions given here, the Church will not be broken up*]. Even so. Amen.

SECTION 105

Background

This revelation was given through the Prophet Joseph Smith on June 22, 1834, on the Fishing River in Missouri.

In obedience to the instructions given by the Lord (D&C 103), the Camp of Israel, a small "army" of about 100 men from northeastern Ohio, led by the Prophet Joseph Smith (later referred to as Zion's Camp) had departed from Kirtland in early May 1834 for the purpose of marching to Missouri and, with the promised assistance of Missouri Governor Daniel Dunklin's militia, restoring the displaced Latter-day Saints to their lands in Jackson County. Others, including men from Michigan Territory recruited by Hyrum Smith and Lyman Wight, joined as they marched along and ultimately, 207 men, 11 women, and 11 children had joined the 900-mile march of Zion's Camp. They brought 25 baggage wagons with them, containing clothing and provisions for the journey, as well as for the Saints in Missouri.

Upon arriving near Jackson County, the leaders of Zion's Camp negotiated with Governor Dunklin to have him keep his word. However, he backed out of his agreement, stating as his reason the threat of civil war in his state if he assisted the Latter-day Saints.

Mobbers had gathered together in wild bands, and, on June 19, five leaders of the Missouri mobs had ridden into the camp on Fishing River, bragging that they had four hundred men who would destroy the members of Zion's Camp before morning. What happened next is recorded as follows:

"A few minutes after the Missourians left, a small black cloud appeared in the clear western sky. It moved eastward, unrolling like a scroll, filling the heavens with darkness. As the first ferry load of mobbers crossed the Missouri River to the south, a sudden squall made it nearly impossible for the boat to return to pick up another load. The storm was so intense that Zion's Camp abandoned their tents and found shelter in an old Baptist meetinghouse nearby. When Joseph Smith came in, he exclaimed, 'Boys, there is some meaning to this. God is in this storm.' It was impossible for anyone to sleep, so the group sang hymns and rested on the rough benches. One camp member recorded that during this time the whole canopy of the wide horizon was in one complete blaze with terrifying claps of thunder.

"Elsewhere the beleaguered mobbers sought any refuge they could. The furious storm broke branches from trees and destroyed crops. It soaked and made the mobbers' ammunition useless, frightened and scattered their horses, and raised the level of the Fishing River, preventing them from attacking Zion's Camp. The Prophet recalled, 'It seemed as if the mandate of vengeance had gone forth from the God of battles, to protect His servants from the destruction of their enemies.'

"Two days later, on 21 June, Colonel John Sconce and two associates of the Ray County militia rode into Zion's Camp to learn of the Mormons' intentions. 'I see that there is an Almighty power that protects this people,' Sconce admitted. The Prophet explained that the only purpose of Zion's Camp was to help their brethren be reinstated on their lands and that their intent was not to injure anyone. He said, 'The evil reports circulated about us were false, and got up by our enemies to procure our destruction.' Sconce and his companions were so affected by the stories of the unjust trials and suffering of the Saints that they promised to use their influence to offset feelings against the Mormons (*Church History in the Fulness of Times*, 2003, 148).

From *The Joseph Smith Papers, Documents, Volume 4: April 1834–September 1835*, 71–72, we learn that, in order to calm the minds of Missouri citizens, Joseph Smith along with some other members of Zion's Camp, on June 21, 1834, signed a statement stating that they did not plan "to commence hostilities against any man or body of men," rather were seeking a peaceful way to help the displaced Latter-day Saints to return to their homes and lands in Jackson County.

The next day, on June 22, 1834, the Prophet Joseph Smith held a council with camp members to determine how to proceed from there. During the council, he received the revelation now known as section 105, disbanding Zion's Camp. It was officially disbanded in Clay County, Missouri, across the River north of Jackson County, on June 24, 1834.

On the same day as the camp was disbanded, an earlier prophecy given by the Prophet Joseph Smith before Zion's Camp entered Missouri began to be fulfilled. Heber C. Kimball, a member of the Camp and later a member of the First Presidency of the Church, wrote:

"Brother Joseph got up in a wagon and said he would deliver a prophecy. After giving the brethren much good advice, he exhorted them to faithfulness and humility, and said the Lord had told him that there would be scourge come upon the camp in consequence of the fractious and unruly spirits that appeared among them, and they would die like sheep with the rot; still if they would repent and humble themselves before the Lord, the scourge in great measure might be turned away; 'but, as the Lord lives, this camp will suffer for giving way to their unruly temper'; which afterwards actually did take place to the sorrow of the brethren" (Whitney, *The Life of Heber C. Kimball*, 47–48).

As stated above, this prophecy began to be fulfilled at the time the Camp was disbanded on June 24, 1834. According to the 2018 *Doctrine and Covenants Student Manual*, chapter 41, "The camp experienced the beginnings of an outbreak of cholera, causing vomiting and severe diarrhea. As a result, 68 people, including the Prophet Joseph Smith, suffered from the sickness, and 13 members of the camp and 2 other Latter-day Saints who were living in Clay County died (see *The Joseph Smith Papers, Documents, Volume 4: April 1834–September 1835*, 72, note 334)."

As we study the Lord's word here, we will see that His purposes often reach beyond our current circumstances and expectations. This can sometimes cause disappointment and frustration on our part, but if we steadfastly remain true to God and continue in faith, the day will come that we will see as He sees and rejoice that He answered our prayers the way He did.

In verses 1–6, the Savior explains to the members of Zion's Camp (and to the entire Church) why the Missouri Saints cannot be put back on the land of Zion at this time.

1 VERILY I say unto you who have assembled yourselves together **that you may learn my will concerning the redemption of mine afflicted people** [*the members who were driven out of Zion, Jackson County*]—

2 Behold, I say unto you, **were it not for the transgressions of my people,** speaking concerning

the church and not individuals [*in other words, many were living in harmony with the laws required of a Zion people, but too many were not*], **they might have been redeemed even now.**

3 But behold, **they have not learned to be obedient** to the things which I required at their hands**, but are full of all manner of evil, and do not impart of their substance, as becometh saints, to the poor and afflicted among them;**

4 **And are not united according to the union required by the law of the celestial kingdom;**

5 And **Zion cannot be built up unless it is by the principles of the law of the celestial kingdom;** otherwise I cannot receive her unto myself.

6 And **my people must needs be chastened until they learn obedience,** if it must needs be [*if necessary*], by the things which they suffer.

Next, in verse 7, the Lord explains that He is not referring to all of the leaders of the Church in what He said in verses 1–6, above.

7 **I speak not concerning those who are appointed to lead my people,** who are **the first elders**

[*the leaders*] **of my church,** for they are not all under this condemnation;

Next, in addition to the members in Missouri, the Savior includes the members of the Church in other areas who are failing to live the gospel as they should. As we see, from verse 8, next, some of them, especially those in the eastern United States, have been saying, in effect, that if God does not protect the Saints in Missouri, then they will not plan on moving to Missouri, nor will they waste their money by contributing to the cause of building up Zion in Missouri, even though the Lord commanded it (see D&C 101:69–75; 103:23).

8 But **I speak concerning my churches** [*branches of the Church*] **abroad** [*in other locations*]—**there are many who will say: Where is their God** [*why doesn't God protect them*]? **Behold, he will deliver them in time of trouble, otherwise we will not go up unto Zion, and will keep our moneys.**

In verses 9–12, next, the Lord gives several reasons for not redeeming Zion by putting the Saints back on their land now.

9 Therefore, **in consequence of the transgressions of my people** [*in all locations of the Church*], **it is expedient in me** [*it is according to the Lord's wisdom*]

that mine elders [*Zion's Camp*] should wait for a little season for the redemption of Zion—

10 That they themselves may be prepared, and that my people may be taught more perfectly, and have experience, and know more perfectly concerning their duty, and the things which I require at their hands.

According to verses 11–12, next, in addition to the strengthening and preparation mentioned in verses 9 and 10, above, the members of the Church, in order to establish Zion, need the endowment of power that will not be available to them until they finish building the temple in Kirtland, Ohio. This power will come, especially when the Savior, Moses, Elias, and Elijah appear in the Kirtland Temple on April 3, 1836, and priesthood keys are restored (see D&C 110). The "endowment" of "power from on high" spoken of in verses 11–12 should not be confused with the "endowment" that we receive in temples today.

11 And this [*the redemption of Zion—verse 9*] cannot be brought to pass until mine elders are endowed with power from on high.

12 For behold, I have prepared a great endowment and blessing to be poured out upon them, inasmuch [*if*] as they are faithful

and continue [*endure tribulation*] in humility before me.

13 Therefore it is expedient in me [*this is the reason it is wise in the Lord's sight*] that mine elders should wait for a little season, for the redemption of Zion [*for Zion to be built up*].

Next, the Lord says, in effect, that if the Saints will fight and win their personal battles against selfishness and sin (with the help of the Atonement), He will fight the battles necessary to reclaim the land of Zion.

14 For behold, I do not require at their hands to fight the battles of Zion; for, as I said in a former commandment [*see D&C 98:37*], even so will I fulfil—I will fight your battles.

15 Behold, the destroyer [*perhaps meaning destroying angels, such as mentioned in Revelation 7:1–3, the destruction of the wicked by the wicked (Mormon 4:5) or by plagues, pestilences, and so on (D&C 88:87–90)*] I have sent forth to destroy and lay waste mine enemies; and not many years hence [*in the future*] they shall not be left to pollute mine heritage, and to blaspheme [*speak disrespectfully of*] my name upon the lands which I have consecrated for the gathering together of my saints.

Did you notice the word "lands" (plural) in verse 15, above? This implies that the scope of this prophecy extends beyond Jackson County to various gathering places of the Saints throughout the whole earth.

Next, in verses 16–19, the Lord gives comforting and encouraging words to those who were faithful in Zion's Camp.

16 Behold, **I have commanded my servant Joseph Smith, Jun., to say unto the strength of my house** [*the members of the Church in the Kirtland area and in the eastern United States*], **even my warriors, my young men, and middle-aged,** to **gather together** [*Zion's Camp*] **for the redemption of my people**, and throw down the towers of mine enemies, and scatter their watchmen;

17 But **the strength of mine house have not hearkened unto my words** [*including the members of the Church in the eastern United States at the time did not respond with sufficient money or men to provide the five hundred recruits for Zion's Camp as initially requested by the Lord—see D&C 103:30–34*].

18 But **inasmuch as there are those who have hearkened unto my words** [*since there were many who did obey and march with Zion's*

Camp], I have prepared **a blessing and an endowment for them, if they continue faithful**.

19 **I have heard their prayers, and will accept their offering** [*they will receive the blessings despite the failure of the Church as a whole to carry out the commandments of the Lord*]; **and it is expedient in me** [*it is according to the Lord's wisdom*] **that they** [*the faithful members of Zion's Camp*] **should be brought thus far for a trial of their faith**.

Although it might appear to some that Zion's Camp was a failure, it was not. Many great blessings came to faithful individuals and to the Church as a result of the march of Zion's Camp. For example, nine of the original twelve Apostles of the restored Church were selected from the members of Zion's Camp. All seven presidents of the Seventy's quorum came from this faithful group, and all sixty-three members of that original quorum of the Seventy also came from among those who had marched to Missouri.

Additionally, the members of the "army of Israel," as it was sometimes called, had the privilege of associating closely with and being taught by the Prophet Joseph Smith during the nearly one-thousand-mile journey. Another blessing that came from it was that the members of the Church in Missouri, some of whom had felt neglected by the Prophet and other Church leaders who stayed in the Kirtland area, now felt supported and sustained by the Church at large.

Next, the Lord gives instructions regarding what the members of Zion's Camp should do now they are being disbanded.

20 And now, verily I say unto you, a commandment I give unto you, that as many as have come up hither [*to Missouri*]**, that can stay in the region round about, let them stay;**

21 And those that cannot stay, who have families in the east [*in the Kirtland area and elsewhere in the eastern United States*]**, let them tarry** [*remain in Missouri*] **for a little season, inasmuch as my servant Joseph shall appoint unto them** [*according to instructions given them by the Prophet*]**;**

22 For I will counsel him concerning this matter, and all things whatsoever he shall appoint unto them shall be fulfilled.

Did you notice what is happening in verses 21–22, above? As you can no doubt understand, a few members of the Church, including some members of Zion's Camp, became disgruntled with the Prophet and apostatized from the Church when the "army" was

disbanded rather than fighting and restoring the Saints to their lands. In these two verses, the Lord is obviously sustaining and supporting His Prophet in the eyes of the people.

Another issue is addressed in verses 23–24, next. The Saints themselves could do much damage to the prospects of peace in Missouri by boasting and bragging to the local citizens that this land was eventually going to be their land. In these verses, the Lord counsels them to avoid such behavior.

23 And let all my people who dwell in the regions round about be very faithful, and prayerful, and humble before me, and reveal not the things which I have revealed unto them [*about the future destiny of Zion in Missouri*]**, until it is wisdom in me that they should be revealed** [*in other words, until the timing is right*]**.**

24 Talk not of judgments, neither boast of faith nor of mighty works, but carefully gather together, as much in one region as can be, consistently with the feelings of the people [*in other words, don't stir up feelings of the old settlers unnecessarily*]**;**

If the members of the Church in Missouri at this time will be obedient to this counsel, and keep the commandments and instructions the Lord gives next, then they will receive the blessings promised in verses 25–40.

25 And behold, **I will give unto you favor and grace in their eyes, that you may rest in peace and safety**, while you are saying unto the people: Execute judgment and justice for us according to law, and redress us of our wrongs [*while petitioning the government for redress, as instructed in D&C 101:85–89*].

26 Now, behold, I say unto you, my friends, **in this way you may find favor in the eyes of the people, until the army of Israel becomes very great**.

27 And **I will soften the hearts of the people, as I did the heart of Pharaoh, from time to time, until my servant Joseph Smith, Jun., and mine elders**, whom I have appointed, **shall have time to gather up the strength of my house**,

28 **And to have sent wise men, to fulfil that which I have commanded concerning the purchasing of all the lands in Jackson county that can be purchased, and in the adjoining counties** round about [*as instructed in D&C 101:72–74*].

29 For **it is my will that these lands should be purchased**; and after they are purchased **that my saints should possess them according to the laws of consecration** which I have given.

30 And **after these lands are purchased, I will hold the armies of Israel guiltless in taking possession of their own lands**, which they have previously purchased with their moneys [*in other words, this is how the Saints who have been driven from Jackson County can return to their lands*], and of throwing down the towers of mine enemies that may be upon them, and scattering their watchmen, and avenging me of mine enemies unto the third and fourth generation of them that hate me.

31 **But first let my army become very great, and let it be sanctified** [*become pure and holy*] before me, that it may become fair as the sun, and clear as the moon, and that her banners may be terrible unto all nations [*may command respect from all nations*];

32 **That the kingdoms of this world may be constrained** [*forced*] **to acknowledge that the kingdom of Zion is in very deed the kingdom of our God and his**

Christ; therefore, **let us become subject unto her laws** [*in other words, by setting a good example, the members of the Church will see people throughout the world desire to join the Church and enjoy the blessings of being subject to the kind and merciful laws of God*].

Before this can happen, the Kirtland Temple must be completed, as stated in verse 33, next.

33 Verily I say unto you, **it is expedient in me that the first elders** [*the leaders*] **of my church should receive their endowment** [*not endowments, as we know them, rather, the endowment spoken of in verses 11–12, above*] **from on high in my house** [*the Kirtland Temple*], which I have commanded to be built unto my name in the land of Kirtland.

34 And **let those commandments which I have given concerning Zion and her law be executed and fulfilled, after her redemption**.

You have probably heard the phrase "many are called but few are chosen" (D&C 121:34) several times. In verses 35–37, next, we get some help in understanding what this means.

35 **There has been a day of calling, but the time has come for**

a **day of choosing** [*choosing those who are to receive the promised blessings from the Lord*]; **and let those be chosen that are worthy**.

36 And **it shall be manifest unto my servant, by the voice of the Spirit, those that are chosen**; and **they shall be sanctified** [*made pure and holy, fit to participate in the building up of Zion; the same as being made worthy to dwell in the celestial kingdom*];

37 And **inasmuch as** [*if*] **they follow the counsel which they receive, they shall have power after many days** [*another reminder that it will be some time before Zion is redeemed from her enemies in Missouri*] **to accomplish all things pertaining to Zion** [*symbolic of accomplishing all that is necessary to enter into celestial glory*].

In summary, from verses 35–37, above, we learn that "many are called but few are chosen" means, in effect, that all are called to receive the highest blessings from God, but relatively few are chosen at this time in the history of the earth to be so blessed because they do not follow the counsels of the Lord.

Finally, as the Lord brings this revelation to a close, He counsels the Saints to be peacemakers.

38 And again I say unto you, **sue**

[*petition the government and the mobbers*] **for peace**, not only to the people that have smitten you, but also to all people;

39 And **lift up an ensign of peace**, and **make a proclamation of peace** unto the ends of the earth;

40 And **make proposals for peace unto those who have smitten you, according to the voice of the Spirit which is in you**, and all things shall work together for your good.

41 Therefore, **be faithful**; and behold, and lo, I am with you even unto the end. Even so. Amen.

SECTION 106

Background

This revelation was given through the Prophet Joseph Smith on November 25, 1834, at Kirtland, Ohio, regarding Warren Cowdery, the oldest brother of Oliver Cowdery (Oliver was the youngest of eight children—see Church History Topics under Oliver Cowdery).

Warren Cowdery had joined the Church through the efforts of his brother, Oliver, and also the influence of Joseph Smith. He was living in Freedom, New York, at the time of this revelation calling him to preside over the small branch of the Church there. About forty converts had been baptized in that area over the past several months.

One of the significant doctrinal contributions of this revelation is the fact that the righteous will not be caught off guard by the Second Coming, whereas, the wicked will (verses 4–5).

1 IT is my will that my servant **Warren A. Cowdery should be appointed and ordained a presiding high priest over my church** [*the branch of the Church*], **in the land of Freedom** [*in Freedom, New York*] **and the regions round about;**

In addition to his duties as presiding high priest over the Freedom Branch of the Church, Brother Cowdery is to serve as a missionary in the area also.

2 **And should preach my everlasting gospel**, and lift up his voice and warn the people, **not only in his own place, but in the adjoining counties;**

3 And devote his whole time to this high and holy calling, which I now give unto him, **seeking diligently the kingdom of heaven and its righteousness, and all things necessary shall be added thereunto**; for the laborer is worthy of his hire [*those who earn the needed blessings are given them*].

Next, in verses 4–5, we are taught that the Second Coming is getting close, that the worldly and the wicked will be caught off guard by it, but the righteous who are acquainted with the word of God will not be.

4 And again, verily I say unto you, **the coming of the Lord draweth nigh**, and **it overtaketh the world** [*the wicked as well as those who do not study the word of God*] **as a thief in the night** [*it will catch them by surprise*]—

Doctrine

The righteous, those who study and live the gospel, will not be caught off guard by the Second Coming of Christ.

5 Therefore, **gird up your loins** [*get prepared*], **that you may be the children of light** [*those who know and live the gospel*], **and that day** [*the Second Coming*] **shall not overtake you as a thief.**

In verses 6–8, next, Warren Cowdery is cautioned about pride and arrogance and counseled to be humble and faithful in his leadership and missionary responsibilities.

6 And again, verily I say unto you, **there was joy in heaven when my servant Warren bowed to my scepter** [*when he accepted the gospel*], **and separated himself from the crafts of men** [*from the ways of the world*];

7 Therefore, blessed is my servant Warren, for **I will have mercy on him**; and, **notwithstanding the vanity of his heart** [*even though he now has a tendency to be prideful*]**, I will lift him up inasmuch as** [*if*] **he will humble himself before me.**

8 And **I will give him grace** [*the help which the Savior gives us*] **and assurance wherewith he may stand** [*which will give him the strength and ability to live the gospel and carry out his callings*]; and **if he continue to be a faithful witness and a light unto the church I have prepared a crown** [*symbolic of exaltation*] **for him in the mansions of my Father.** Even so. Amen.

Unfortunately, Warren Cowdery did not heed the counsel to avoid vanity and eventually left the Church, having become critical of its leaders. He left at about the same time his brother, Oliver Cowdery, was excommunicated in 1838. He had moved to Kirtland and continued to live there until his death in 1851 at age sixty-two.

SECTION 107

Background

We will quote the heading to this section as given in the 2013 edition of the Doctrine and Covenants.

Revelation on the priesthood, given through Joseph Smith the Prophet, at Kirtland, Ohio, about April 1835. Although this section was recorded in 1835, the historical records affirm that most of verses 60 through 100 incorporate a revelation given through Joseph Smith on November 11, 1831. This section was associated with the organization of the Quorum of the Twelve in February and March 1835. The Prophet likely delivered it in the presence of those who were preparing to depart May 3, 1835, on their first quorum mission.

As you can see, this revelation is a composite of several revelations given at various times up to and including April 1835. Parts of this section were given as early as November 11, 1831.

This is one of the great revelations on priesthood. In it we are taught about the Aaronic and Melchizedek Priesthoods, the quorums of the First Presidency, the Twelve, and the Seventy, the organization of elders, priests, teachers, and deacons into quorums, and the responsibility of individual priesthood holders to actively learn their duties and responsibilities and carry them out.

Among other things in this section, we are taught the priesthood line of authority from Adam to Noah, and of the meeting held in the valley of Adam-ondi-Ahman three years prior to Adam's death when he was 927 years old.

It is rather exciting to see verse 98, which authorizes Area Seventies. This verse was little noticed until President Gordon B. Hinckley pointed it out several years ago when Area Seventies were first called to serve. It had always been there, placed in this section by the Lord for future use when the time came.

And we live in the marvelous day when additional Quorums of the Seventy are being added as authorized in verses 93–98, to keep up with the leadership needs of the rapidly growing Church.

Before we begin our verse-by-verse study, we will add a bit more background.

The information and instruction in this section paved the way for the restoration and organization of the Quorum of the Twelve Apostles again in our day. During a special conference held on Saturday, February 14, 1835, the

Three Witnesses to the Book of Mormon (Oliver Cowdery, David Whitmer, and Martin Harris), under the direction of the Prophet Joseph Smith, selected the twelve men who were to become the first Quorum of Twelve Apostles in this dispensation. Earlier, in June 1829, the Book of Mormon witnesses Oliver Cowdery and David Whitmer had been told that they would someday do this (see D&C 18:37). Martin Harris was later called to assist them. Now that day had come. The twelve men they chose, listed according to age at the time they were called, were:

Thomas B. Marsh (35)

David W. Patten (35)

Brigham Young (33)

Heber C. Kimball (33)

Orson Hyde (30)

William E. McLellin (29)

Parley P. Pratt (27)

Luke S. Johnson (27)

William B. Smith (23)

Orson Pratt (23)

John F. Boynton (23)

Lyman E. Johnson (23)

Almost a month later, on March 12, 1835, the newly called Twelve met with the Prophet Joseph Smith. During that meeting, he proposed that they prepare to leave on their first missions through the eastern United States, traveling as far as the Atlantic Ocean. They determined that their departure date should be May 4, 1835.

The *History of the Church* records the feelings and anxieties of these brethren as the weight of their calling as Apostles of Christ began to settle on them. In the minutes of a meeting held by the Twelve, kept by Orson Hyde and William E. McLellin acting as clerks, we read:

"This afternoon [28 March 1835] the Twelve met in council, and had a time of general confession. On reviewing our past course [*spelling in context*] we are satisfied, and feel to confess also, that we have not realized the importance of our calling to that degree that we ought; we have been light-minded and vain, and in many things have done wrong. For all these things we have asked the forgiveness of our heavenly Father; and wherein we have grieved or wounded the feelings of the Presidency, we ask their forgiveness. The time when we are about to separate is near; and when we shall meet again, God only knows; we therefore feel to ask of him whom we have acknowledged to be our Prophet and Seer, that he inquire of God for us, and obtain a revelation, (if consistent) [if appropriate] that we may look upon it when we are separated, that our hearts may be comforted. Our worthiness has not inspired us to make this request, but our unworthiness. We have unitedly asked God our heavenly Father to grant unto us through His Seer, a revelation of His mind and will concerning our duty [during] the coming season, even a great revelation, that will enlarge our hearts, comfort us in adversity, and brighten our hopes amidst the powers of darkness" (*History of the Church,* 2:209–10).

The beginning portion of section 107 was dictated by the Prophet Joseph Smith sometime between March and early May 1835 as the newly called Twelve were preparing to serve their first missions as apostles. This instruction and clarification regarding the priesthood blessed the lives of these early brethren and are invaluable also to us.

We will now proceed with our verse-by-verse study of this section.

In verses 1–6, we are taught that there are two major categories of priesthood in the Church—Aaronic and Melchizedek. In verse 5, further clarification is given, stating that the Aaronic Priesthood is an "appendage" to the Melchizedek Priesthood.

1 **THERE are, in the church, two priesthoods**, namely, the **Melchizedek** and **Aaronic**, including the Levitical Priesthood.

Referring back to verse 1, above, sometimes in gospel conversations, "Aaronic Priesthood" means priests, teachers, and deacons, and "Levitical Priesthood" means teachers and deacons. The terms *Aaronic* and *Levitical* are explained in the Bible Dictionary as follows (**bold** added for teaching emphasis. Note that the quote below picks up about half way through the first paragraph given under "Aaronic Priesthood"):

Aaronic Priesthood

Bible Dictionary under "Aaronic Priesthood"

"**The terms *Aaronic* and *Levitical* are sometimes used synonymously** [*in other words, to mean the same thing*] (D&C 107:1, 6, 10), although there are some specific differences in the offices existing within the Levitical Priesthood. For example, the lesser [*Aaronic*] priesthood was conferred only upon men of the tribe of Levi. However, **within the tribe, only Aaron and his sons could hold the office of priest**. And, still further, from the firstborn of Aaron's sons (after Aaron) was selected the high priest (or president of the priests). Thus Aaron and his sons after him had greater offices in the Levitical Priesthood than did the other Levites.

"**The privileges of the priests were greater than those who functioned in the other Levitical offices**, and a distinction between the two is evident when the scripture speaks of them as 'the priests and the Levites' (1 Kgs. 8:4; Ezra 2:70; John 1:19). **The priests could offer sacrifices for the people, burn incense on the altar, and teach the law, whereas the other Levites were employed in more menial tasks**, such as the housekeeping of the tabernacle, keeping oil in the lamps, transporting the Ark of the Covenant, taking down and setting up the tabernacle when moving, and related tasks in assisting the priests (Num. 3:5–10; 18:1–7; 1 Chr. 23:27–32)."

Next, the Savior teaches us why the higher priesthood is called Melchizedek Priesthood.

Melchizedek Priesthood

2 Why the first [*Melchizedek, the first to be mentioned in verse 1, above*] **is called the Melchizedek Priesthood is because Melchizedek was such a great high priest**. [*He was the high priest and king of Salem or Jerusalem. To learn more about him, see JST Genesis 14:25–40 in the Joseph Smith Translation section at the back of your Latter-day Saint edition of the Bible; Alma 13:14–19; D&C 84:14.*]

3 Before his day [*about 2000 B.C.*] **it was called** *the Holy Priesthood, after the Order of the Son of God*.

4 But out of respect or reverence to the name of the Supreme Being, to avoid the too frequent repetition of his name, they, the church, in ancient days, **called that priesthood after Melchizedek,** or the Melchizedek Priesthood.

5 All other authorities or offices in the church are appendages to this priesthood [*to the Melchizedek Priesthood*].

6 But there are two divisions or grand heads—one is the **Melchizedek Priesthood,** and the other is the **Aaronic** or Levitical **Priesthood**.

Next, in verses 7–12, the Master Teacher trains us with more specifics about the Melchizedek Priesthood and the offices within it.

7 The office of an elder comes under the priesthood of Melchizedek.

8 The Melchizedek Priesthood holds the right of presidency, and has power and authority over all the offices in the church in all ages of the world, **to administer in spiritual things.**

The First Presidency

9 The Presidency of the High Priesthood [*the First Presidency— see D&C 81:2; 107:22, 65–66*], after the order of Melchizedek, **have a right to officiate in all the offices in the church.**

Next, in verse 10, we are taught that high priests can officiate in the callings and duties normally filled by elders, priests, teachers, and deacons at the local level. An example of this is when a high priest blesses or passes the sacrament.

Melchizedek Priesthood

10 High priests after the order of the Melchizedek Priesthood have a right to officiate in their own standing [in their own offices and callings], **under the direction of the presidency** [the First Presidency], in administering spiritual things, **and also in the office of an elder, priest** (of the Levitical order), **teacher, deacon, and member.**

Next, in verse 12, we see that in the absence of a high priest, an elder may conduct.

11 An elder has a right to officiate in his stead [in the place of a high priest] when the high priest is not present.

In verse 8, above, we were taught that the primary stewardship of the Melchizedek Priesthood is to "administer in spiritual things." Verse 12, next, emphasizes this again and also explains that high priests and elders may preside and function at the local level when no General Authorities are present.

Perhaps you've noticed that when a General Authority is present, he is designated as the "presiding authority" by the one conducting the meeting. This is often seen at stake conferences.

12 **The high priest and elder are to administer in spiritual things,** agreeable to the covenants and commandments of the church; and **they have a right to officiate in all these offices of the church when there are no higher authorities present.**

Next, in verses 13–17, we are given more details about the Aaronic Priesthood.

Aaronic Priesthood

13 **The second priesthood** [as mentioned in verse 1, above] **is called the Priesthood of Aaron, because it was conferred upon Aaron** [the brother of Moses—see Exodus 7:7] **and his seed** [posterity], throughout all their generations.

14 Why it is called the lesser priesthood is because **it is an appendage to** [attached to or a lesser part of] **the greater, or the Melchizedek Priesthood, and has power in administering outward ordinances** [such as passing the sacrament, collecting fast offerings, preparing the sacrament,

blessing the sacrament, and baptizing—compare with D&C 20:46–60].

Next, as the Savior continues giving this great revelation on priesthood, He explains that the bishop is the president of the Aaronic Priesthood. The concept and principle of priesthood keys is also tied in with the bishop.

15 The bishopric is the presidency of this priesthood [*Aaronic*], **and holds the keys or authority of the same.**

Verses 16–17, next, must be kept in the context of the presiding bishop of the Church (Bishop Edward Partridge at this time in Church history). It deals only with that office, not with the office of local bishops in the various wards of the Church.

The Presiding Bishop of the Church

16 No man has a legal right to this office [*Presiding Bishop of the Church*]**, to hold the keys of this priesthood, except he be a literal descendant of Aaron** [*compare with D&C 68:15–21*]**.**

17 But as a high priest of the Melchizedek Priesthood has authority to officiate in all the lesser offices, **he may officiate in the office of bishop** [*Presiding Bishop*] **when no literal descendant of Aaron can be found, provided**

he is called and set apart and ordained unto this power by the hands of the Presidency of the Melchizedek Priesthood [*the First Presidency*]**.**

We will quote from the teachings of Joseph Fielding Smith for additional explanation of verses 16–17, above.

"It has no reference whatever to bishops of wards. Further, such a one must be designated by the First Presidency of the Church and receive his anointing and ordination under their hands. The revelation comes from the Presidency, not from the patriarch, to establish a claim to the right to preside in this office. In the absence of knowledge concerning such a descendant, any high priest, chosen by the Presidency, may hold the office of Presiding Bishop and serve with counselors" (*Doctrines of Salvation,* 3:92–93).

"The office of Presiding Bishop of the Church is the same as the office which was held by Aaron. . . . It was this office which came to John the Baptist, and it was by virtue of the fact that he held the keys of this power and ministry that he was sent to Joseph Smith and Oliver Cowdery to restore that Priesthood, May 15, 1829. The person who has the legal right to this presiding office has not been discovered; perhaps is not in the Church, but should it be shown by revelation that there is one who is the 'firstborn among the sons of Aaron,' and thus entitled by birthright to this presidency, he could 'claim' his 'anointing' and the right to that office in the Church" (*Church History and Modern Revelation*, 1:259).

Next, in verses 18–19, we are taught more about the role and authority of Melchizedek Priesthood. Yet again, we are reminded that it deals with the spiritual blessings and ordinances that attend the faithful in the true Church of Jesus Christ. Without it, we would not have the gift of the Holy Ghost, administering to the sick, patriarchal blessings, temple ordinances, the privilege of being set apart, fathers' blessings, ongoing revelation, and so forth.

Melchizedek Priesthood

18 The power and authority of the higher, or **Melchizedek Priesthood, is to hold the keys of all the spiritual blessings of the church—**

19 To have the privilege of receiving the mysteries of the kingdom of heaven, [*"spiritual truths known only through revelation"—see Guide to the Scriptures; the basic teachings and truths of the gospel of Jesus Christ—see Bible Dictionary under "Mystery"*] **to have the heavens opened unto them,** to **commune with the general assembly and church**

of the Firstborn [*to be taught the doctrines that pertain to exaltation; "church of the Firstborn" refers to those who obtain exaltation in the celestial kingdom—see D&C 76:94–95; 93:21–22*], and to **enjoy the communion and presence of God the Father, and Jesus the mediator of the new covenant.**

Verses 20–21 provide more detail about Aaronic Priesthood.

Aaronic Priesthood

20 The power and authority of the lesser, or Aaronic Priesthood, is to hold the keys of the ministering of angels [*see D&C 13; Moroni 7:29–31*], and **to administer in outward ordinances**, the letter of the gospel, the **baptism** of repentance for the remission of sins, agreeable to the covenants and commandments.

Beginning with verse 21, next, the Savior gives details about the structure and role of General Authority quorums in the Church.

General Authority Quorums

21 Of necessity there are presidents, or presiding officers growing out of, or appointed of or from among those who are ordained to the several offices in these two priesthoods.

The First Presidency

22 Of the Melchizedek Priesthood, three Presiding High Priests, chosen by the body, appointed and ordained to that office, and upheld by the confidence, faith, and prayer of the church, **form a quorum of the Presidency of the Church**.

The Quorum of the Twelve Apostles

23 The twelve traveling councilors are called to be **the Twelve Apostles**, or **special witnesses of the name of Christ in all the world**—thus differing from other officers in the church in the duties of their calling.

24 And they **form a quorum, equal in authority and power to the three presidents** [*the First Presidency*] previously mentioned.

We must not stop reading at the end of verse 24, above. To do so would leave us with a false concept about the authority of the Quorum of the Twelve with respect to the First Presidency. We might think that the two quorums are absolute equals. This is not the case. To complete this doctrine, we must read verse 33, which states that the Twelve "officiate . . . under the direction of the Presidency of the Church."

What we do learn from verse 24 is that when the President of the Church dies and the Quorum of the First Presidency is thus dissolved, the Quorum of the Twelve Apostles temporarily has full authority to lead the Church until the next president is ordained and set apart to serve as president of the Church.

For example, after the martyrdom of the Prophet Joseph Smith, Brigham Young led the Church for three and a half years as president of the Twelve. The First Presidency was again organized in December 1847 and sustained by the members of the Church on December 27, 1847, during a conference held in Kanesville, Iowa, near Council Bluffs.

The Quorum of the Seventy

25 The Seventy are also called to preach the gospel, and **to be especial witnesses unto the Gentiles and in all the world**—thus differing from other officers in the church in the duties of their calling.

26 And **they form a quorum, equal in authority to that of the Twelve** special witnesses or Apostles just named.

As was the case with the Twelve (verse 24), we must not stop here with verse 26; rather we must read verse 34, which states that the Seventy "act in the name of the

Lord, under the direction of the Twelve."

President Gordon B. Hinckley explained the "equality" of these quorums as follows: "The question arises, How can they [the three quorums] be equal in authority? Speaking to this question, President Joseph F. Smith (1838–1918) taught: 'I want here to correct an impression that has grown up to some extent among the people, and that is, that the Twelve Apostles possess equal authority with the First Presidency in the Church. This is correct when there is no other Presidency but the Twelve Apostles; but so long as there are three presiding Elders who possess the presiding authority in the Church, the authority of the Twelve Apostles is not equal to theirs. If it were so, there would be two equal authorities and two equal quorums in the Priesthood, running parallel, and that could not be, because there must be a head' (Elders' Journal, Nov. 1, 1906, 43).

"Likewise, the Seventy, who serve under the direction of the Twelve, would become equal in authority only in the event that the First Presidency and the Quorum of the Twelve were somehow destroyed" ("The Quorum of the First Presidency," *Ensign*, Dec. 2005, 47).

Next, the Lord explains that decisions made by these General Authority quorums as they lead and guide the Church should be made unanimously. An exception to this is found in verse 28, below.

27 And **every decision** made by either [*any*] of these quorums **must be by the unanimous voice** of the same; that is, every member in each quorum must be agreed to its decisions, in order to make their decisions of the same power or validity one with the other—

28 **A majority may form a quorum when circumstances render it impossible to be otherwise** [*such as when some are traveling and cannot attend a quorum meeting*]—

In verse 29, we are taught that this structure of a presiding presidency of three high priests was used anciently also.

29 Unless this is the case, their decisions are not entitled to the same blessings which the decisions of **a quorum of three presidents** were **anciently**, who were ordained after the order of Melchizedek, and were righteous and holy men.

The personal qualities of character and integrity listed in verse 30, next, can also apply to any of us as we function in presidencies of priesthood quorums or auxiliaries of the Church on the local and stake level.

30 **The decisions of these quo-rums**, or either [*any*] of them, **are to be made in all righteous-ness, in holiness, and lowliness of heart** [*humility*], **meekness and long suffering, and in faith, and virtue, and knowledge, temper-ance, patience, godliness, broth-erly kindness and charity**;

31 **Because the promise is, if these things abound in them they shall not be unfruitful** in the knowledge of the Lord.

If it were ever necessary, verse 32, next, gives the structure for appealing a decision of any of the General Authority quorums.

32 And **in case that any decision of these quorums is made in un-righteousness, it may be brought before a general assembly of the several quorums** [*the First Presi-dency, the Quorum of the Twelve Apostles, and the First Quorum of the Seventy—see* Doctrine and Cov-enants Student Manual, *1981, 264*], **which constitute the spiritual authorities of the church**; other-wise there can be no appeal from their decision.

Next, in verses 33–35, additional duties of the Twelve and the Sev-enty are given.

The Quorum of the Twelve Apostles

33 **The Twelve are a Traveling Presiding High Council**, to of-ficiate in the name of the Lord, **under the direction of the Pres-idency of the Church**, agreeable to the institution of heaven; **to build up the church, and regu-late all the affairs of the same in all nations,** first unto the Gentiles and secondly unto the Jews [*in the last days, the "Gentiles" (in this con-text, meaning all who are not Jews) will get the first chance to accept the gospel, and then the Jews will get another opportunity to accept it—see 1 Nephi 13:42*].

Elder David A. Bednar of the Quo-rum of the Twelve Apostles taught about the role of the Quorum of the Twelve. He said "Our com-mission is to go into all the world and proclaim 'Jesus Christ, and him crucified' (see Mark 16:15; 1 Corinthians 2:2). An Apostle is a missionary and a special witness of the name of Christ. The 'name of Christ' refers to the totality of the Savior's mission, death, and resurrection—His authority, His doctrine, and His unique qualifi-cations as the Son of God to be our Redeemer and our Savior. As special witnesses of the name of Christ, we bear testimony of the reality, divinity, and resurrection of Jesus Christ, His infinite and eter-nal Atonement, and His gospel"

("Special Witnesses of the Name of Christ," *The Religious Educator: Perspectives on the Restored Gospel*, vol. 12, no. 2 [2011], 1; quoted in the 2018 *Doctrine and Covenants Student Manual*, chapter 42).

The Quorum of the Seventy

34 The Seventy are to act in the name of the Lord, **under the direction of the Twelve** or the traveling high council, in building up the church and regulating all the affairs of the same **in all nations**, first unto the Gentiles and then to the Jews;

35 The Twelve being sent out, **holding the keys**, to open the door by the proclamation of the gospel of Jesus Christ, and first unto the Gentiles and then unto the Jews.

Verses 36–37, next, provide a pattern for local stake presidencies and high councils in the stakes of the Church.

Local Stake Presidencies and High Councils

36 The standing high councils, at the stakes of Zion, form a quorum equal in authority in the affairs of the church, in all their decisions, to the quorum of the presidency [*stake presidencies today*], or to the traveling high council.

37 The high council in Zion form a quorum equal in authority in the affairs of the church, in all their decisions, to the councils of the Twelve at the stakes of Zion.

We will again quote from the *Doctrine and Covenants Student Manual*, 1981, this time for clarification of verses 36–37, above:

"'At the time this Revelation was given, there were two standing High Councils in the Church: One in Kirtland, organized February 17th, 1834, and one in Clay County, Mo., organized July 3rd, the same year.' (Smith and Sjodahl, *Commentary*, p. 702.)

"'This indicates the importance attached to the organization of the High Council in Zion,' wrote Smith and Sjodahl, since the government of the Church would not be in danger of being centralized, but the model of a high council in each stake of Zion had been set. 'The standing High Councils in the various Stakes are presided over by the Stake presidency, and their jurisdiction is confined to the Stakes in which they are located.' (*Commentary*, p. 703.)

"Sperry said: 'The Lord indicates that the High Council in Zion (Missouri) was to form a quorum equal in authority, in the affairs of the Church, to the councils of Twelve (High Councils) at the Stakes of Zion (vs 37). And so today a High Council in any Stake of Zion is as important as that in any other Stake. The authority and power of any Stake High Council is local and confined to the boundaries of the Stake concerned'" (*Compendium*, 565; quoted in *Doctrine and Covenants Student Manual*, 1981, 265).

Additional instructions for the Quorum of the Twelve and the Seventy are given in verses 38–39, next.

The Twelve and the Seventy

38 It is the duty of the traveling high council [*the Twelve*] **to call upon the Seventy, when they need assistance**, to fill the several calls for preaching and administering the gospel, instead of any others.

Stake Patriarchs

39 It is the duty of the Twelve, in all large branches of the church, **to ordain evangelical ministers** [*patriarchs*], as they shall be designated unto them by revelation—

As you are probably aware, many of the duties originally assigned to the Twelve have now been delegated to stake presidents. This is one of the blessings of ongoing revelation, one of the basic factors that distinguishes our Church from all others. Among these duties is the ordaining of patriarchs. If you will excuse me for being a bit personal, I had the privilege

of ordaining a new patriarch for our stake when I was serving as a stake president. I was acting under the direction of the President of the Quorum of the Twelve. Years later, as I was released, our patriarch was called to be the new stake president. Subsequently, he ordained me as the new stake patriarch. Because we are close personal friends, these were extra sweet experiences for both of us.

Next, in verses 40–52, the Savior gives the patriarchal line of priesthood authority from Adam to Noah. This "patriarchal priesthood" will be the order of priesthood in the celestial kingdom, highest degree, where the family unit is preserved. These verses serve to illustrate that the priesthood must be passed from one worthy man to another, by proper authority and by the process of ordination by the laying on of hands.

40 The order of this priesthood was confirmed to be handed down from father to son, and rightly belongs to the literal descendants of the chosen seed [*Israel*], to whom the promises were made.

All who join the Church in these last days are considered to be "Israel" and are a part of the much-prophesied last days gathering of Israel. Priesthood holders today are encouraged to keep a record of their priesthood line of authority and to pass a copy of it on to others they ordain.

41 This order was instituted in the days of Adam, and came down by lineage in the following manner:

42 From Adam to **Seth**, who **was ordained by Adam** at the age of sixty-nine years, and was blessed by him three years previous to his (Adam's) death, and received the promise of God by his father, that his posterity should be the chosen of the Lord, and that they should be preserved unto the end of the earth;

43 Because he (**Seth**) was a perfect man, and his likeness **was the express likeness of his father**, insomuch that **he seemed to be like unto his father in all things**, and could be **distinguished** from him **only by his age**.

44 **Enos was ordained** at the age of one hundred and thirty-four years and four months, **by** the hand of **Adam**.

45 God called upon **Cainan** in the wilderness in the fortieth year of his age; and he **met Adam** in journeying to the place Shedolamak. He was eighty-seven years old when he **received his ordination**.

46 **Mahalaleel** was four hundred and ninety-six years and seven days old when he **was ordained by** the hand of **Adam**, who also blessed him.

47 **Jared** was two hundred years old when he **was ordained under the hand of Adam**, who also blessed him.

48 **Enoch** was twenty-five years old when he **was ordained under the hand of Adam**; and he was sixty-five and Adam blessed him.

49 And **he saw the Lord, and he walked with him, and was before his face continually; and he walked with God three hundred and sixty-five years, making him four hundred and thirty years old when he was translated** [*with the whole City of Enoch— see Moses 7:69*].

It is interesting to note that President Brigham Young taught that the City of Enoch was taken up with houses, lands, gardens, cattle, and all their possessions. (See *Discourses of Brigham Young*, 105.)

50 **Methuselah** was one hundred years old when he **was ordained under the hand of Adam**.

Did you notice that all of these men so far were ordained by Adam? This is one of the interesting evidences that Adam and the inhabitants of the earth before the flood did indeed live hundreds of years. Methuselah (verse 50, above), was Adam's great-great-great-great-great-grandson, and Adam still had fifty-six years to live after ordaining him! Counting Adam and going to Methuselah, we have eight generations.

51 Lamech was thirty-two years old when he **was ordained under the hand of Seth.**

52 Noah was ten years old when he **was ordained under the hand of Methuselah.**

Adam lived to be 930 years old (see Genesis 5:5). Three years prior to his death, a great council was held in the Valley of Adam-ondi-Ahman (about seventy miles north, northeast of Independence, Missouri), to which the righteous posterity of Adam and Eve were invited. We learn about this in verses 53–57.

53 Three years previous to the death of Adam, he called Seth, Enos, Cainan, Mahalaleel, Jared, Enoch, and Methuselah [all of whom Adam had ordained to the Melchizedek Priesthood—see verses 42–50], who were all high priests, **with the residue** [remainder] **of his posterity who were righteous, into the valley of Adam-ondi-**

Ahman, and there bestowed upon them his last blessing.

54 And **the Lord appeared unto them,** and **they rose up and blessed** [blessed often means praised in this type of context] **Adam,** and called him Michael, the prince, the archangel.

Adam Presides over This Earth under the Direction of Christ

55 And **the Lord administered comfort unto Adam, and said** unto him: **I have set thee to be at the head;** a multitude of nations shall come of thee, and **thou art a prince over them forever.**

In verse 55, above, we are taught that Adam stands next to Christ as far as authority over this earth is concerned.

56 And **Adam stood up in the midst of the congregation;** and, notwithstanding [even though] he was bowed down with age, **being full of the Holy Ghost, predicted whatsoever should befall his posterity unto the latest generation.**

57 **These things were all written in the book of Enoch,** and are to be testified of in due time [in other words, we will get the Book of Enoch someday in the future].

Sometime before the Savior's Second Coming, a similar meeting will be held at Adam-ondi-Ahman. It is spoken of in D&C 116 and is described in Daniel 7:9–14, D&C 27:5–14, and *The Millennial Messiah*, by Bruce R. McConkie, pages 578–87, which confirms, along with D&C 27:14, that all of the righteous, living and dead, will attend that glorious meeting.

In verses 58–63, next, additional duties of the Twelve are given. Among other things, we learn that priesthood quorums are to be organized on the local level, with presiding officers over each.

58 It is the duty of the Twelve, also, to ordain and set in order all the other officers of the church, agreeable to the revelation [*apparently one of the revelations referred to in the heading of this section, which were "received at sundry (various) times"*] **that says:**

59 To the church of Christ in the land of Zion, **in addition to the church laws respecting church business—**

Presiding Officers for Local Priesthood Quorums

60 Verily, I say unto you, saith the Lord of Hosts, there must needs be presiding elders to preside over those who are of the office of an elder;

61 And also priests to preside over those who are of the office of a priest;

62 And also teachers to preside over those who are of the office of a teacher, in like manner, and also the deacons—

63 Wherefore, **from deacon to teacher,** and from **teacher to priest,** and from **priest to elder,** [*in other words, each quorum is to have local presiding priesthood officers*] severally as they are appointed, according to the covenants and commandments of the church.

The Living Prophet Is the President of the High Priesthood and, as Such, Presides Over All Other Officers in the Church

64 Then comes the High Priesthood, which is the greatest of all.

65 Wherefore, **it must needs be that one be appointed of the High Priesthood to preside over the priesthood, and he shall be called President of the High Priesthood of the Church;**

66 Or, in other words, **the Presiding High Priest** over the High Priesthood of the Church.

The Living Prophet Holds All the Priesthood Keys and Thus Directs All Priesthood Functioning in the Church.

67 **From the same** [*from the President of the Church*] **comes the administering of ordinances and blessings upon the church, by the laying on of the hands**.

Duties of Bishops

68 Wherefore, **the office of a bishop is not equal unto it** [*not equal to the president of the Church*]; for the office of a bishop is in administering all temporal things;

> While we are familiar with the fact that a bishop is not equal in authority to the living prophet (verse 68, above), we do well to keep in mind that to many of the early members of the Church in this last dispensation, it was not obvious. Most of them had come as converts from religious groups in which the local minister or pastor had all the authority. And if there were any central organization and leadership at all associated with that particular religion, it was at best a relatively weak advisory body that could be hearkened to or ignored, depending on the desires of the local minister. Thus, verse 68 required a rather dramatic change in thinking and understanding for many early Saints.
>
> Next, we are taught that a bishop of a ward must be a high priest.

A Local Bishop Must Be a High Priest

69 **Nevertheless a bishop must be chosen from the High Priesthood**, unless he is a literal descendant of Aaron [*see notes associated with verses 16–17 in this section*];

70 For unless he is a literal descendant of Aaron he cannot hold the keys of that priesthood.

71 Nevertheless, **a high priest**, that is, after the order of Melchizedek, **may be set apart unto the ministering of temporal things** [*may be ordained a bishop*], having a knowledge of them by the Spirit of truth;

> In verses 72–74, next, special emphasis is given to the role and responsibility of bishops to serve as judges among the members within their stewardship. This is a great blessing for members, because it allows them to go to someone close by who is authorized by God to assist them in overcoming sin and other difficulties that may arise in their lives. Bishops are often referred to as "common judges in Israel."

72 And also **to be a judge in Israel**, to do the business of the church, **to sit in judgment upon transgressors** upon testimony as it shall be laid before him according to

the laws, **by the assistance of his counselors**, whom he has chosen or will choose among the elders of the church.

73 **This is the duty of a bishop who** is not a literal descendant of Aaron, but **has been ordained to the High Priesthood after the order of Melchizedek.**

74 **Thus shall he be a judge**, even **a common judge** among the inhabitants of Zion, or in a stake of Zion, or in any branch of the church where he shall be set apart unto this ministry, until the borders of Zion are enlarged and it becomes necessary to have other bishops or judges in Zion or elsewhere.

Verse 75, next, alerts these members in 1835 that the Church will continue to grow and that as it does so, additional bishops will be needed, and they will have the same responsibilities and duties as listed above.

75 And **inasmuch as there are other bishops appointed they shall act in the same office.**

You have seen the term "literal descendant of Aaron" (as in verse 76, next) a number of times now. This may be one of those things that will be put to use someday in the future, at which time we will be delighted to finally understand what it

means and how it is implemented. We will have to wait and see.

Looking ahead to verses 81 and 84, we see that no one is exempt from accountability in this Church, including members of the First Presidency. The last part of verse 76, next, explains that if a member of the First Presidency were to exercise his agency to commit serious transgression, the Presiding Bishop, with two counselors, would preside at the disciplinary council for him.

76 But **a literal descendant of Aaron has a legal right to the presidency of this priesthood** [*the office of Presiding Bishop—see notes and commentary for verses 16–17*], **to the keys of this ministry, to act** in the office of bishop independently, **without counselors, except in a case where a President of the High Priesthood** [*a member of the First Presidency*], after the order of Melchizedek, **is tried, to sit as a judge in Israel** [*in other words, to preside at that membership council, formerly called "disciplinary council"*].

We will include two quotes here that give additional clarification for verse 76, above. The first is by Joseph Fielding Smith; the second is by John A. Widtsoe (**bold** added for emphasis):

"The bishop is a common judge in Israel, and members are amenable to his jurisdiction. **In case of** an accusation made against one of the First Presidency, the case would be tried before the presiding bishop and a council of high priests" (*Church History and Modern Revelation*, 2:21).

"The Presiding Bishop's Court [*membership council*] consists of the Presiding Bishop with his two counselors, and twelve High Priests especially chosen for the purpose. It is a tribunal extraordinary, from which there is no appeal, to be convened if it should be necessary to try a member of the First Presidency for crime or neglect of duty" (*Priesthood and Church Government*, 212).

Next, beginning with verse 77, the Lord explains that extra difficult local issues, including the results of local membership councils, may be appealed to the First Presidency (compare with D&C 102:27).

The Decisions of Local "Judges," Including Those in Wards and Stakes, Regarding Extra Difficult Matters May Be Appealed to the First Presidency

77 And **the decision of either of these councils** [*any of these local councils*], agreeable to the commandment which says:

78 Again, verily, I say unto you, the most important business of the church, and **the most difficult cases** of the church [*at the local level*], **inasmuch as there is not satisfaction upon the decision of the bishop or judges, it shall be handed over and carried up** [*appealed*] unto the council of the church, **before the Presidency of the High Priesthood** [*the First Presidency*].

79 And **the Presidency of the council of the High Priesthood shall have power to call other high priests, even twelve, to assist as counselors**; and thus the **Presidency of the High Priesthood and its counselors shall have power to decide** upon testimony according to the laws of the church.

80 And after this decision it shall be had in remembrance no more before the Lord; for **this is the highest council of the church of God, and a final decision** upon controversies in spiritual matters.

81 **There is not any person belonging to the church who is exempt from this council of the church** [*see also verse 84*].

82 And **inasmuch as** [*if*] **a President of the High Priesthood** [*a member of the First Presidency*] **shall transgress**, he shall be had in remembrance before [*he shall*

be brought before] the common council of the church [*a membership council presided over by the Presiding Bishop of the Church—see verse 76*], who shall be assisted by twelve counselors of the High Priesthood [*by twelve high priests especially assembled for this membership council*];

83 And **their decision upon his head shall be an end of controversy concerning him**.

84 Thus, **none shall be exempted from the justice and the laws of God**, that all things may be done in order and in solemnity before him, according to truth and righteousness.

Next, in verses 85–89, the numbers of priesthood holders making up full quorums at the local level are given.

Deacons Quorum

85 And again, verily I say unto you, the duty of a president over the office of a deacon is to preside over twelve deacons, to sit in council with them, and to teach them their duty, edifying one another, as it is given according to the covenants.

Teachers Quorum

86 And also the duty of **the president over the office of the** teachers is to preside over twen-ty-four of the teachers, and to sit in council with them, teaching them the duties of their office, as given in the covenants.

Priests Quorum

87 Also the duty of **the president** over the Priesthood of Aaron **is to preside over forty-eight priests**, and sit in council with them, to teach them the duties of their office, as is given in the covenants—

The Bishop Is the President of the Priests Quorum in His Ward

88 This president is to be a bishop; for this is one of the duties of this priesthood.

Elders Quorum

89 Again, **the duty of the president** over the office of elders **is to preside over ninety-six** elders, and to sit in council with them, and to teach them according to the covenants.

By the way, it is significant that a deacons quorum is the smallest in terms of members. In this way, in a general sense, those who are newest in the priesthood can be given the most individual attention by quorum leaders.

In our day, we have witnessed a significant revelation regarding the membership of elders quorums.

As you may recall, as of the April 2018 general conference (the Saturday evening priesthood session on March 31), all high priests and elders in a given ward are now members of the elders quorum of their ward. President Russell M. Nelson announced the following in that priesthood session: "Tonight we announce a significant restructuring of our Melchizedek Priesthood quorums to accomplish the work of the Lord more effectively. In each ward, the high priests and the elders will now be combined into one elders quorum."

This is a marvelous example of continuing revelation. It is a very real example of the fact that the words of the living Prophet take precedence over the words in the scriptures.

Next, in verse 90, emphasis is given to the fact that elders quorums serve locally in their wards and are not expected to travel as is the case with General Authority Seventies.

90 **This presidency** [*the elders quorum presidency—verse 89*] **is a distinct one from that of the seventy,** and **is designed for those who do not travel into all the world.**

The President of the Church Presides over the Whole Church and Possesses All the Gifts of God

91 **And again, the duty of the President of the office of the**

High Priesthood is to preside over the whole church, and to be like unto Moses—

92 Behold, here is wisdom; yea, **to be a seer, a revelator, a translator, and a prophet, having all the gifts of God** which he bestows upon the head of the church.

As you know, we live in an exciting time in the growth of the Church. In verses 93–98, next, we see the organization of the Seventy, put in place by the Savior in the early 1830s and being used to handle the expanding General Authority leadership needs of the Church in our day.

The General Authority Seventy Quorums Have Seven Presidents

93 **And it is according to the vision showing the order of the Seventy,** that **they should have seven presidents to preside over them, chosen out of the number of the seventy;**

94 And **the seventh president of these presidents is to preside over the six;**

Verses 95–97, next, point out that General Authority Seventies and Quorums of Seventy can be added as needed to keep up with the growth of the Church.

95 And **these seven presidents**

are to choose other seventy be-sides the first seventy to whom they belong, **and are to preside over them**;

96 **And also other seventy**, until seven times seventy, **if the labor in the vineyard of necessity requires it**.

97 And **these seventy are to be traveling ministers**, unto the Gentiles first and also unto the Jews.

> President Gordon B. Hinckley pointed out verse 98, next, at the time area authority Seventies were called. They are now referred to as "Area Seventies." This verse allows for these brethren to continue working in their occupations and live in their own homes while holding "as high and responsible offices in the church" (end of verse 98) as the Seventy who are called upon to travel constantly throughout the world.

98 Whereas **other officers** [*Area Seventies*] of the church, who belong not unto the Twelve, neither to the Seventy, **are not under the responsibility to travel among all nations, but are to travel as their circumstances shall allow**, notwithstanding [*even though*] they may hold as high and responsible offices in the church.

You may recall from the background notes given at the beginning of this section in this study guide that the twelve men who were called to serve in the first Quorum of the Twelve Apostles in this dispensation felt the heavy weight of responsibility settling in upon them. As a result, they asked the Prophet Joseph Smith to seek a revelation from the Lord for them "that we may look upon it when we are separated [*serving missions throughout the Church*], that our hearts may be comforted."

The Savior has granted their request and taught them much about priesthood and the offices within it in this section. Now, in conclusion, He invites them to "learn [their] duty, and to act in the office in which [they] are appointed, in all diligence" (verse 99, next). This council applies to all of us who accept callings in the Church. We have the revelations of the Lord to study, through which we too can learn our duty.

99 Wherefore, now **let every man learn his duty, and to act in the office in which he is appointed, in all diligence**.

100 **He that is slothful shall not be counted worthy to stand, and he that learns not his duty and shows himself not approved shall not be counted worthy to stand**. Even so. Amen.

SECTION 108

Background

This revelation was given through the Prophet Joseph Smith to Lyman Sherman, a personal friend of the Prophet, on December 26, 1835, in Kirtland, Ohio. Brother Sherman and his wife, Delcena, had joined the Church in January 1832 in New York and subsequently moved to Kirtland.

Brother Sherman had been a faithful member of Zion's Camp and was called to serve as one of the Seven Presidents of the First Quorum of the Seventy (see D&C 107:93). He'd had concerns about his worthiness for some time and came to the Prophet on the day after Christmas, seeking the word of the Lord in his behalf. Joseph Smith gave some background to this revelation. He said:

"Brother Lyman Sherman came in, and requested to have the word of the Lord through me; 'for,' said he, 'I have been wrought upon to make known to you my feelings and desires, and was promised that I should have a revelation which should make known my duty'" (*History of the Church*, 2:345).

Having been concerned about his worthiness before the Lord, the first three verses of this revelation were no doubt sweet indeed to him. The Savior told him that his sins were forgiven and confirmed the fact that he had been prompted by the Spirit to come to the Prophet. Furthermore, he was given a gentle warning to avoid resisting the promptings of the Lord in the future and to be more strict in keeping his covenants with the Lord.

1 VERILY thus saith the Lord unto you, my servant Lyman: **Your sins are forgiven you, because you have obeyed my voice in coming up hither this morning to receive counsel of him whom I have appointed** [*Joseph Smith*].

2 Therefore, **let your soul be at rest concerning your spiritual standing,** and **resist no more my voice.**

3 And arise up and **be more careful henceforth in observing your vows, which you have made and do make, and you shall be blessed with exceeding great blessings.**

The "solemn assembly" spoken of in verse 4, next, could well be the upcoming dedication of the Kirtland Temple, or one of the meetings associated with it. Also, the Saints held additional solemn assemblies after the Kirtland Temple dedication. A quote from the 2018 *Doctrine and Covenants Student Manual* is helpful here:

"A solemn assembly was held three days after the dedication of the

Kirtland Temple on March 27, 1836, and may have been a fulfillment of the command to 'call a solemn assembly . . . of those who are the first laborers in this last kingdom' (D&C 88:70; see also D&C 88:117; 95:7; 108:4; 109:6, 10). The Prophet Joseph Smith recorded that on March 30, 1836, a congregation of about three hundred Church leaders and members met in the Kirtland Temple and participated in the ordinances of the washing of feet and the sacrament. The Prophet gave instruction, and Church leaders pronounced blessings and prophesied. Joseph Smith recorded that he left the meeting 'at about 9 o'clock in the evening,' and the members of the Quorum of the Twelve Apostles continued the meeting, during which there was 'exhorting, prophesying and speaking in tongues until 5 o'clock in the morning—the Savior made His appearance to some, while angels ministered unto others, and it was a Pentecost and [an] endowment indeed, long to be remembered' (in *The Joseph Smith Papers, Journals, Volume 1: 1832–1839*, 215–16; spelling, punctuation, and capitalization standardized)."

"Solemn assemblies continue to be held in modern times, as explained by Elder David B. Haight (1906–2004) of the Quorum of the Twelve Apostles: 'A solemn assembly, as the name implies, denotes a sacred, sober, and reverent occasion when the Saints assemble under the direction of the First Presidency. Solemn assemblies are used for three purposes: the dedication of temples, special instruction to priesthood leaders, and sustaining a new President of the Church' ("Solemn Assemblies," *Ensign*, Nov. 1994, 14)."

4 **Wait patiently until the solemn assembly shall be called** of my servants [*by the leaders of the Church*], then you shall be remembered with the first of mine elders [*apparently a reference to the leaders of the Church, including the Seventies—compare D&C 88:85, 105:7*], and receive right by ordination with the rest of mine elders whom I have chosen.

President Spencer W. Kimball taught the following about solemn assemblies:

Solemn assemblies "have been known among the Saints since the days of Israel. They have been of various kinds but generally have been associated with the dedication of a temple or a special meeting appointed for the sustaining of a new First Presidency or a meeting for the priesthood to sustain a revelation, such as the tithing revelation to President Lorenzo Snow. . . .

"Joseph Smith and Brigham Young were first sustained by a congregation, including a fully organized priesthood. Brigham Young was sustained on March 27, 1846, and was 'unanimously elected president over the whole Camp of Israel' by the council. (B. H. Roberts, *A Comprehensive History of the Church,* vol. 3, p. 52.) Later he was sustained, and the Hosanna Shout was given.

"Each of the presidents of the Church has been sustained by the priesthood of the Church in solemn assembly down to and including President Harold B. Lee, who was sustained October 6, 1972" (in Conference Report, April 1974, 64–65; or "What Do We Hear?" *Ensign,* May 1974, 45).

In verse 5, next, Brother Sherman is promised that the blessings mentioned in verse 4, above, will come to him if he remains faithful.

5 Behold, this is the promise of the Father unto you **if you continue faithful**.

6 And it shall be fulfilled upon you in that day that **you shall have right to preach my gospel wheresoever I shall send you**, from henceforth from that time.

Using hindsight, the "wheresoever" in verse 6, above, may have been a foreshadowing of a mission in the spirit world (D&C 138:57) for Brother Lyman since he died faithful to the Church on January 27, 1839, in Far West, Missouri, at the age of thirty-four.

The counsel given by the Savior in verse 7, next, certainly applies to all of us.

7 Therefore, **strengthen your brethren in all your conversation, in all your prayers, in all your exhortations, and in all your doings**.

8 And behold, and lo, **I am with you to bless you and deliver you forever**. Amen.

SECTION 109

Background

This section consists of the dedicatory prayer given by the Prophet Joseph Smith at the dedication of the Kirtland Temple on March 27, 1836. As you can see in the heading to section 109 in your Doctrine and Covenants, the Prophet confirmed that this prayer was given to him by revelation.

At the end of December 1832 and on January 3, 1833, the Saints were given what is now known as section 88 (see heading to section 88 in your Doctrine and Covenants) in which they were commanded by the Lord to build a temple in Kirtland (D&C 88:119). By June 1833, they had still not begun. Consequently, the Savior chastised them rather severely (D&C 95:2–3) and said, "Let the house [*the Kirtland Temple*] be built" (D&C 95:13). Four days later, they began digging foundation trenches and hauling stones for the temple construction (see the gospel doctrine teacher's manual, *Doctrine and Covenants and Church History,* 100).

The temple was constructed at a cost estimated to be between $40,000 and $60,000 during a time of extreme poverty and hardship for the members of the Church. Nevertheless, after almost three years, it was completed and ready for this dedicatory prayer on Sunday, March 27, 1836.

Some people have wondered why the Lord would have the members go through such extreme hardship and sacrifice to build a temple that would soon be abandoned. In D&C 64:21, the Saints were clearly told that Kirtland would be a stronghold of the Church for only five years, and at the time of the dedication of the temple, about four and a half of the five years was up. Perhaps there is some important symbolism in this. A chart has been included (at right) to illustrate some possible symbolism.

When we stop to think about it, as illustrated in the chart, the temporary nature of the Kirtland Temple was not a problem at all in the eternal nature of things, just as the temporary nature of mortality is not a problem when viewed from the perspective of eternity. We come to mortality, accomplish its purposes by keeping the commandments if we so choose, and then leave, having been better prepared for the highest blessings of eternity. The Saints built the Kirtland Temple, benefited beyond words from its eternal purposes, and then left it having been better prepared for the future.

Mortality	Kirtland Temple	Mortality	Kirtland Temple
Is temporary	Was for temporary use.	Designed to bring us back into God's presence through our obedience to God's commandments.	Designed to bring God's presence to the Saints (D&C 110:1–8) upon their obedience to the commandment to build a temple.
Requires sacrifice and prioritizing in order to keep God's commandments.	Required sacrifice and prioritizing in order to keep God's commandment to build a temple.		
Requires that we put our best into serving God and keeping His commandments in order to progress toward our exaltation.	Required that the Saints put their best into building the temple in order to qualify for the promised blessings that would enable them to progress toward exaltation. These blessings included the appearance of the Savior and the coming of Moses, Elias, and Elijah who restored priesthood keys necessary for sealing families together forever (D&C 110).	Designed to develop in us the power to become like God (in other words, to attain exaltation), through gaining physical bodies and learning obedience to God's commandments, during our temporary mortal state.	Built for the purpose (during its temporary service as a holy temple) of giving revelation, instruction (D&C 95:4, 8; 109:14–15, etc.), and restoring priesthood keys (D&C 110) which empower the righteous to become like God (in other words, to attain exaltation).

It is interesting to note that the day of the dedication of the Kirtland Temple was Palm Sunday, the Sunday before Easter, on which day many celebrate the Savior's triumphal entry into Jerusalem. The Master's entry into Jerusalem was accompanied by the spreading of palm branches along His path (John 12:13; Matthew 21:1–9), thus the name Palm Sunday. In biblical culture, palm branches symbolize triumph and victory.

In *History of the Church,* volume 2, beginning on page 416, we find an account of the dedication of the Kirtland Temple. We will include a brief summary of the day and the dedicatory services:

- Hundreds of people gathered early in the morning, hoping to get a seat in the temple for the services.

- The doors of the Kirtland Temple were opened at 8:00 A.M.

- About a thousand members were seated inside, but hundreds remained who could not get in. They were eventually seated in the schoolhouse, and the services were repeated for them the following Thursday.

- At 9:00 A.M., President Sidney Rigdon began the seven-hour-long services by reading Psalms 24 and 96.

- The choir sang.

- Sidney Rigdon offered an opening prayer.

- A hymn was sung.

- Sidney Rigdon spoke for two and a half hours.

- Joseph Smith was sustained as the Prophet and Seer of the Church.

- The hymn "Now Let Us Rejoice" was sung.

- A twenty-minute intermission followed.

- Services were resumed by singing "Adam-ondi-Ahman."

- Joseph Smith spoke briefly.

- The First Presidency and Twelve were then sustained as prophets, seers, and revelators, followed by the sustaining of other officers and leaders.

- The Prophet then "prophesied to all, that inasmuch as they would uphold these men in their several stations, (alluding to the different quorums in the Church), the Lord would bless them; yea, in the name of Christ, the blessings of heaven should be theirs; and when the Lord's anointed go forth to proclaim the word, bearing testimony to this generation, if they receive it they shall be blessed; but if not, the judgments of God will follow close upon them, until that city or that house which rejects them, shall be left desolate" (*History of the Church*, 2:418–19).

- A hymn was sung.

- The dedicatory prayer was offered by the Prophet Joseph Smith (as recorded in section 109).

- Following the dedicatory prayer, the choir sang "The Spirit of God," composed especially for the occasion by W. W. Phelps.

- The Prophet "then asked the several quorums separately, and then the congregation, if they accepted the dedication prayer, and acknowledged the house dedicated. The vote was unanimous in the affirmative, in every instance" (*History of the Church*, 2:427).

- The sacrament was then administered and passed to the congregation.

- Various testimonies were given, including the witness that several angels had been seen during the services thus far.

- Sidney Rigdon gave some closing remarks.

- Sidney Rigdon gave a closing prayer.

- The congregation stood and participated in the Hosanna Shout.

Thus, the first temple in this dispensation was dedicated. Of the final portion of the dedicatory service, beginning with the administration of the sacrament, the Prophet recorded:

"The Lord's Supper was then administered; President Don Carlos Smith blessed the bread and the wine, which was distributed by several Elders to the Church; after which I bore record of my mission, and of the ministration of angels.

"President Don Carlos Smith also bore testimony of the truth of the work of the Lord in which we were engaged.

"President Oliver Cowdery testified of the truth of the Book of Mormon, and of the work of the Lord in these last days.

"President Frederick G. Williams arose and testified that while President Rigdon was making his first prayer, an angel entered the window and took his seat between Father Smith and himself, and remained there during the prayer.

"President David Whitmer also saw angels in the house.

"President Hyrum Smith made some appropriate remarks congratulating those who had endured so many toils and privations to build the house" (*History of the Church,* 2:427).

The Prophet continued by describing the Hosanna Shout (**bold** added for emphasis):

Hosanna Shout

"President Rigdon then made a few appropriate closing remarks, and a short prayer, at the close of which we sealed the proceedings of the day by shouting **hosanna, hosanna, hosanna to God and the Lamb**, three times, sealing it each time with **amen, amen, and amen**.

"President Brigham Young gave a short address in tongues, and David W. Patten interpreted, and gave a short exhortation in tongues himself, after which I blessed the congregation in the name of the Lord, and the assembly dispersed a little past four o'clock, having manifested the most quiet demeanor during the whole exercise" (*History of the Church,* 2:428).

That evening, a special priesthood meeting was held in the temple. Joseph Smith recorded special manifestations during that meeting. He said:

"Brother George A. Smith arose and began to prophesy, when a noise was heard like the sound of a rushing mighty wind, which filled the Temple, and all the congregation simultaneously arose, being moved upon by an invisible power; many began to speak in tongues and prophesy; others saw glorious visions; and I beheld the Temple was filled with angels, which fact I declared to the congregation. The people of the neighborhood came

running together (hearing an unusual sound within, and seeing a bright light like a pillar of fire resting upon the Temple), and were astonished at what was taking place. This continued until the meeting closed at eleven p. m." (*History of the Church,* 2:428).

Before we study the dedicatory prayer for the Kirtland Temple as given in this section, we will pause to say a bit more about the Hosanna Shout.

The basic meaning of the word *Hosanna* is "save now" (see Bible Dictionary under "Hosanna"). You may wish to turn to Psalm 118:25, where you will see a beautiful context demonstrating its meaning. It is essentially a plea to the Lord to "save us now, please."

In biblical times, the waving of palm branches (palm fronds) was symbolic of triumph and victory. The hoped-for victory over enemies was demonstrated with palm fronds during the triumphal entry of the Savior into Jerusalem (Matthew 21:9). Spiritually, palm branches are used to symbolize triumph and victory over sin and imperfection because of the Savior's Atonement. An example of this is seen in Revelation 7:9.

White handkerchiefs used in the Hosanna Shout at temple dedications today are symbolic of the waving of palm fronds and represent our humble and enthusiastic plea that the Savior and His

Atonement give us victory over sin and save us in His Father's kingdom forever.

Keep in mind that in just seven days following this dedicatory prayer, in a series of glorious manifestations, Christ, Moses, Elias, and Elijah will appear to the Prophet and Oliver Cowdery in the Kirtland Temple (D&C 110).

As we proceed with our study of this section, our primary focus will be the blessings of the temple, along with our responsibilities to prepare for temple worship. We will use **bold** exclusively in this section to point these things out and make less than usual use of notes and commentary, thus letting the scripture speak for itself. We will use *Our Responsibilities* to point out some things we should do in order to gain the blessings of the temple, and *Blessings of Temple Attendance* to indicate what some of the precious benefits of temple attendance are. In cases where both responsibilities and blessings occur in the same verse, we will repeat the verse. You will no doubt find additional blessings and responsibilities beyond what we have listed.

1 THANKS be to thy name, O Lord God of Israel, who keepest covenant and showest mercy unto thy servants who walk uprightly before thee, with all their hearts—

2 Thou who hast commanded thy servants to build a house to thy name in this place [*Kirtland*].

Our Responsibilities

3 And now thou beholdest, O Lord, that **thy servants have done according to thy commandment**.

4 And now we ask thee, Holy Father, in the name of Jesus Christ, the Son of thy bosom, in whose name alone salvation can be administered to the children of men, we ask thee, O Lord, to accept of this house, the workmanship of the hands of us, thy servants, which thou didst command us to build [*the Savior will accept it in one week, as recorded in D&C 110:7*].

Blessings of Temple Attendance

5 For thou knowest that we have done this work through great tribulation; and out of our poverty we have given of our substance to build a house to thy name, that **the Son of Man** might have a place to **manifest** himself **to his people**.

6 And as thou hast said in a revelation, given to us, calling us thy friends, saying—Call your solemn assembly, as I have commanded you;

Our Responsibilities

7 And as all have not faith, **seek ye diligently** and **teach**

one another words of wisdom; yea, **seek ye out of the best books words of wisdom**, seek learning even by study and also by faith;

Our Responsibilities

8 **Organize** yourselves; **prepare** every needful thing, and **establish** a house, even **a house of prayer**, a house of **fasting**, a house of **faith**, a house of **learning**, a house of **glory**, a house of **order, a house of God**;

Our Responsibilities

One of the things we learn from verse 9, next, is that we need to have a constant awareness of who we are and of the covenants we make in the name of Jesus Christ. Also, while in the temple, everything we do is in the name of the Lord. We are in a celestial environment and gain firsthand knowledge and feelings of what heaven is like.

9 **That your incomings** may be **in the name of the Lord**, that your **outgoings** may be **in the name of the Lord, that all your salutations may be in the name of the Lord**, with uplifted hands unto the Most High—

Blessings of Temple Attendance

10 And now, Holy Father, we ask thee to **assist us**, thy people, **with thy grace**, in calling our solemn assembly, that it may be done to thine honor and to thy divine acceptance;

Blessings of Temple Attendance

11 And in a manner that we may be found worthy, in thy sight, to **secure a fulfilment of the promises** which thou hast made unto us, thy people, **in the revelations given unto us**;

Blessings of Temple Attendance

12 **That thy glory may rest down upon thy people**, and upon this thy house, which we now dedicate to thee, that it may be sanctified and consecrated to be holy, and **that thy holy presence may be continually in this house**;

Blessings of Temple Attendance

13 And **that all people who shall enter** upon the threshold of the Lord's house **may feel thy power**, and feel constrained to acknowledge that thou hast sanctified it, and that it is thy house, a place of thy holiness.

Blessings of Temple Attendance

14 And do thou grant, Holy Father, **that all those who shall**

worship in this house may be taught words of wisdom out of the best books, and that they may seek learning even by study, and also by faith, as thou hast said [*in D&C 88:118*];

Blessings of Temple Attendance

15 And **that they may grow up in thee**, and **receive a fulness of the Holy Ghost**, and **be organized according to thy laws, and be prepared to obtain every needful thing**;

16 And **that this house may be a house of prayer, a house of fasting, a house of faith, a house of glory and of God**, even thy house;

17 **That all** the incomings of thy people, into this house, **may be in the name of the Lord**;

18 **That all** their outgoings from this house **may be in the name of the Lord**;

19 And **that all** their salutations **may be in the name of the Lord**, with holy hands, uplifted to the Most High;

Our Responsibilities

20 And **that no unclean thing shall be permitted to come into thy house to pollute it**;

Blessings of Temple Attendance

21 And **when thy people transgress**, any of them, **they may speedily repent and return unto thee, and find favor in thy sight, and be restored to the blessings which thou hast ordained to be poured out upon those who shall reverence thee in thy house.**

Our Responsibilities

(Verse 21, repeated)

21 And **when thy people transgress**, any of them, they may **speedily repent and return unto thee**, and find favor in thy sight, and be restored to the blessings which thou hast ordained to be poured out upon those who shall **reverence thee in thy house.**

Blessings of Temple Attendance

22 And we ask thee, Holy Father, **that thy servants may go forth from this house armed with thy power**, and **that thy name may be upon them**, and **thy glory be round about them**, and **thine angels have charge over them**;

Blessings of Temple Attendance

23 And from this place they may bear exceedingly great and glorious tidings, in truth, unto the ends of the earth, that **they may know that this is thy work**, and that thou hast put forth thy hand, to fulfil that which thou hast spoken by the mouths of the prophets, concerning the last days.

Blessings of Temple Attendance

24 We ask thee, Holy Father, to **establish the people that shall worship**, and honorably hold a name and standing in this thy house, **to all generations and for eternity**;

Our Responsibilities

(Verse 24, repeated)

24 We ask thee, Holy Father, to establish the people that shall worship, and **honorably hold a name and standing in this thy house**, to all generations and for eternity;

Blessings of Temple Attendance

25 That **no weapon formed against them shall prosper**; that he who diggeth a pit for them shall fall into the same himself [*the*

wicked who attempt to snare and destroy the righteous will ultimately fall into their own trap, meaning the buffetings of Satan and answering to God for their wickedness];

The fulfilling of verses 25–26 is best seen in an eternal, spiritual context since many righteous throughout history have gone through misery and even death because of their faithfulness to God. But in the eternal scheme of things, no wicked ever triumph over the righteous who endure to the end.

Blessings of Temple Attendance

26 That no combination of wickedness shall have power to rise up and prevail [*ultimately win*] **over thy people upon whom thy name shall be put in this house**;

27 And **if any people shall rise against this people**, that **thine anger be kindled against them**;

Blessings of Temple Attendance

28 And **if they shall smite this people thou wilt smite them; thou wilt fight for thy people** as thou didst in the day of battle, **that they may be delivered from the hands of all their enemies** [*especially the enemies of their spirituality*].

29 We ask thee, Holy Father, to **confound, and astonish, and to bring to shame and confusion, all those who have spread lying reports abroad, over the world, against thy servant or servants, if they will not repent**, when the everlasting gospel shall be proclaimed in their ears;

30 And **that all their works may be brought to naught**, and be swept away by the hail, and by the judgments which thou wilt send upon them in thine anger, that there may be an end to lyings and slanders against thy people.

31 For thou knowest, O Lord, that thy servants have been innocent before thee in bearing record of thy name, for which they have suffered these things.

32 Therefore we plead before thee for **a full and complete deliverance** from under this yoke;

Blessings of Temple Attendance

33 Break it off, O Lord; break it off from the necks of thy servants, by thy power, **that we may rise up in the midst of this generation and do thy work**.

Blessings of Temple Attendance

34 O Jehovah, have **mercy** upon this people, and as all men sin **forgive the transgressions of thy people, and let them be blotted out forever.**

Blessings of Temple Attendance

35 **Let the anointing** of thy ministers **be sealed upon them** with power from on high.

36 Let it be fulfilled upon them, as upon those on the day of Pentecost; let the gift of tongues be poured out upon thy people, even cloven tongues as of fire, and the interpretation thereof.

37 And let thy house be filled, as with a rushing mighty wind, with thy glory.

Blessings of Temple Attendance

38 Put upon thy servants the testimony of the covenant, that when they go out and proclaim thy word they may seal up the law, and **prepare the hearts of thy saints for all those judgments thou art about to send**, in thy wrath, **upon the inhabitants of the earth**, because of their transgressions, **that thy people may not faint** [give up;

lose hope; get caught up in despair, gloom and doom] **in the day of trouble.**

Blessings of Temple Attendance

39 And whatsoever city thy servants shall enter, and the people of that city receive their testimony, let thy peace and thy salvation be upon that city; that they may gather out of that city **the righteous, that they may come forth to Zion, or to her stakes,** the places of thine appointment, with songs of everlasting joy;

> Verse 40, next, is an inspired plea for mercy upon the wicked, requesting that they be given a chance to repent (verse 39, above). This is a major insight into how God works with all of us and a doctrinal reminder that everyone must have a perfect opportunity to hear and understand the gospel before the final judgment. Verse 43 reminds us that all souls are precious.

40 And **until this be accomplished, let not thy judgments fall upon that city.**

41 And whatsoever city thy servants shall enter, and the people of that city receive not the testimony of thy servants, and thy servants warn them to save themselves from this untoward [*wicked*] generation, let it be upon that city according to that which thou hast spoken by the mouths of thy prophets.

42 But **deliver thou**, O Jehovah, we beseech thee, **thy servants from their hands**, and cleanse them from their blood [*the sins and abominations of the wicked*].

43 O Lord, we delight not in the destruction of our fellow men; their souls are precious before thee;

44 But thy word must be fulfilled. Help thy servants to say, with thy grace assisting them: Thy will be done, O Lord, and not ours.

45 We know that thou hast spoken by the mouth of thy prophets terrible things concerning the wicked, in the last days—that thou wilt pour out thy judgments, without measure;

Blessings of Temple Attendance

46 Therefore, O Lord, **deliver thy people from the calamity of the wicked**; enable thy servants to seal up the law, and bind up the testimony, **that they may be prepared against the day of burning.**

47 We ask thee, Holy Father, to remember those who have been driven by the inhabitants of Jackson county, Missouri, from the lands of their inheritance, and break off, O Lord, this yoke of affliction that has been put upon them.

48 Thou knowest, O Lord, that they have been greatly oppressed and afflicted by wicked men; and our hearts flow out with sorrow because of their grievous burdens.

49 O Lord, how long wilt thou suffer this people to bear this affliction, and the cries of their innocent ones to ascend up in thine ears, and their blood come up in testimony before thee, and not make a display of thy testimony in their behalf?

Verses 50 and 53–55 contain yet another inspired reminder of the Christlike mercy that must be developed in the hearts of those who strive to become gods.

50 Have mercy, O Lord, upon the wicked mob, who have driven thy people, that they may cease to spoil, that they may repent of their sins if repentance is to be found;

51 But if they will not, make bare thine arm, O Lord, and redeem that which thou didst appoint a Zion unto thy people.

52 And if it cannot be otherwise, that the cause of thy people may not fail before thee may thine anger be kindled, and thine indignation fall upon them, that they may be wasted away, both root and branch, from under heaven;

53 But inasmuch as they will repent, thou art gracious and merciful, and wilt turn away thy wrath when thou lookest upon the face of thine Anointed.

54 Have mercy, O Lord, upon all the nations of the earth; have mercy upon the rulers of our land; may those principles, which were so honorably and nobly defended, namely, the Constitution of our land, by our fathers, be established forever.

55 **Remember the kings, the princes, the nobles, and the great ones of the earth, and all people**, and the churches, all the poor, the needy, and afflicted ones of the earth;

56 **That their hearts may be softened** when thy servants shall go out from thy house, O Jehovah, to bear testimony of thy name; **that their prejudices may give way before the truth, and thy people may obtain favor in the sight of all**;

On occasion, a student will ask why Joseph Smith addresses Jehovah (as in verse 56, above), since we know that we are to pray only to the Father (as in verse 47, above). One possible answer appears to be rather simple and straightforward. The Prophet is praying to the Father, as evidenced in the prayer, but occasionally speaks directly to the Savior who is present at the dedicatory services.

Blessings of Temple Attendance

57 That all the ends of the earth may know that we, thy servants, have heard thy voice, and that thou hast sent us;

58 That from among all these, thy servants, the sons of Jacob [*the literal and spiritual descendants of Abraham, Isaac, and Jacob*], may gather out the righteous to build a holy city to thy name, as thou hast commanded them.

Blessings of Temple Attendance

59 We ask thee to appoint unto Zion other stakes besides this one which thou hast appointed, **that the gathering of thy people may roll on in great power and majesty**, that thy work may be cut short in righteousness.

60 Now these words, O Lord, we

have spoken before thee, concerning the revelations and commandments which thou hast given unto us, who are identified with the Gentiles.

61 But thou knowest that thou hast a great love for the children of Jacob, who have been scattered upon the mountains for a long time, in a cloudy and dark day.

Beginning with verse 62, we see that the collective righteousness of the Saints, endowed with power from on high in temples (see D&C 95:8), can have a beneficial effect on the rest of the world.

The Potential Effects of Our Temple Attendance Upon Others

62 We therefore ask thee to have mercy upon the children of Jacob [*the house of Israel*], **that Jerusalem, from this hour, may begin to be redeemed;**

63 **And the yoke of bondage may begin to be broken off from the house of David** [*the Jews*];

64 **And the children of Judah may begin to return to the lands which thou didst give to Abraham**, their father [*their ancestor*].

65 And cause that **the remnants of Jacob** [*Israel*], who have been cursed and smitten because of their transgression, be **converted**

from their wild and savage condition to the fulness of the everlasting gospel;

66 **That they may lay down
their weapons of bloodshed, and
cease their rebellions**.

67 And may all the scattered remnants of Israel, who have been
driven to the ends of the earth,
come to a knowledge of the truth,
believe in the Messiah, and be redeemed from oppression, and rejoice before thee.

68 O Lord, remember thy servant,
Joseph Smith, Jun., and all his afflictions and persecutions—how
he has covenanted with Jehovah,
and vowed to thee, O Mighty God
of Jacob—and the command-
ments which thou hast given unto
him, and that he hath sincerely
striven to do thy will.

69 **Have mercy, O Lord, upon
his wife and children**, that they
may be exalted in thy presence,
and preserved by thy fostering
hand.

70 **Have mercy upon all their immediate connections, that their
prejudices may be broken up
and swept away as with a flood**;
that they may be converted and
redeemed with Israel, and know
that thou art God.

71 Remember, O Lord, the presidents, even all the presidents of
thy church, that thy right hand
may exalt them, with all their
families, and their immediate
connections, that their names may
be perpetuated and had in everlasting remembrance from generation to generation.

72 Remember all thy church, O
Lord, with all their families, and all
their immediate connections, with
all their sick and afflicted ones,
with all the poor and meek of the
earth; **that the kingdom, which
thou hast set up without hands,
may become a great mountain
and fill the whole earth**;

73 **That thy church may come
forth out of the wilderness** of
darkness [*of apostasy and spiritual
darkness*], **and shine forth fair as
the moon, clear as the sun, and
terrible as an army with banners**;

74 **And be adorned as a bride for
that day** [*be prepared for the Second
Coming*] when thou shalt unveil the
heavens, and cause the mountains
to flow down at thy presence, and
the valleys to be exalted, the rough
places made smooth; that thy glory
may fill the earth;

Blessings of Temple Attendance

75 That when the trump shall sound for the dead, we shall be caught up in the cloud to meet thee, that we may ever be with the Lord;

Blessings of Temple Attendance

76 That our garments [*symbolic of our lives*] may be pure, that we may be clothed upon with robes of righteousness, with palms in our hands [*symbolic of triumph and victory over all things that could keep us from celestial glory*], and crowns of glory upon our heads [*crowns symbolize being kings and queens (see* Mormon Doctrine*, pages 173 and 613) and ruling as gods (see D&C 132:20) in exaltation*], and reap eternal joy for all our sufferings.

77 O Lord God Almighty, hear us in these our petitions, and answer us from heaven, thy holy habitation, where thou sittest enthroned, with glory, honor, power, majesty, might, dominion, truth, justice, judgment, mercy, and an infinity of fulness, from everlasting to everlasting.

78 O hear, O hear, O hear us, O Lord! And answer these petitions, and accept the dedication of this house unto thee, the work of our hands, which we have built unto thy name;

Blessings of Temple Attendance

79 And also this church, to put upon it thy name. And help us by the power of thy Spirit, **that we may mingle our voices with those bright, shining seraphs around thy throne, with acclamations of praise, singing Hosanna to God and the Lamb!**

Blessings of Temple Attendance

80 And let these, thine anointed ones, be clothed with salvation, and thy saints shout aloud for joy. Amen, and Amen.

SECTION 110

Background

This section records four visions in which the Savior, Moses, Elias, and Elijah appeared to the Prophet Joseph Smith and Oliver Cowdery in the Kirtland Temple on Easter Sunday, April 3, 1836, just one week after the temple dedication. The Prophet recorded these visions in his Journal and it was later published as section 110.

On that very special Sunday morning, about 1,000 Saints had gathered in the temple to worship.

Remember that the Kirtland Temple was not like the temples we attend to perform ordinance work for the living and the dead. Rather, it was more like a tabernacle or large meeting house where meetings and conferences were held. However, it served its function as a temple magnificently as these four visions took place in it.

The Prophet Joseph Smith gave the following background to the events of that day:

"*Sunday, 3 [April 3, 1836].—At*tended meeting in the Lord's House, and assisted the other Presidents of the Church in seating the congregation, and then became an attentive listener to the preaching from the stand. Thomas B. Marsh and David W. Patten [*the senior members of the Quorum of the Twelve* Apostles] spoke in the forenoon to an attentive audience of about one thousand persons. In the afternoon, I assisted the other Presidents in distributing the Lord's Supper [*the sacrament*] to the Church, receiving it from the Twelve, whose privilege it was to officiate at the sacred desk this day. After having performed this service to my brethren, I retired to the pulpit, the veils [*the canvas curtains that were used to divide the large meeting room into classrooms*] being dropped, and bowed myself, with Oliver Cowdery, in solemn and silent prayer. After rising from prayer, the following vision was opened to both of us

[section 110]—" (*History of the Church*, 2:434–35).

It is interesting to note, based on D&C 67:11 and Moses 1:11, that in order to see the Savior while in a mortal body, a person would have to be "transfigured," or, in other words, "quickened," changed temporarily by the Spirit of God to a higher spiritual state in order to not be destroyed in the flesh by the intense glory of God. Thus, we understand that Joseph and Oliver were quickened during this vision of the Savior.

The appearance of Christ on Easter Sunday, the yearly anniversary and celebration of His coming forth from the tomb, was certainly a special reconfirmation of His literal resurrection.

It is also of special significance that Elijah came on April 3, 1836, which was Easter Sunday that year. As you may recall, the Jews celebrate Passover at the time of year during which we celebrate Easter. They faithfully believe that Elijah will come as promised in Malachi 4:5–6 and that he will come during Passover. Furthermore, as part of their Passover observance, a vacant seat is reserved for Elijah and the door is opened to invite him in, in the hope that this may be the year of his coming (see Bible Dictionary under "Elijah").

Elijah did indeed come on Easter Sunday during the time that faithful

Jews around the world were celebrating Passover! He came to the Kirtland Temple where he restored the keys of work for the dead, including sealing families together. Our belief in the coming of Elijah can be a strong bond between us and our Jewish friends.

This series of glorious visions certainly made all the sacrifice and trials of the Saints in building the temple worthwhile.

We will now proceed with our verse-by-verse study. As mentioned above, there were four marvelous visions.

Vision #1
The Savior

1 THE veil was taken from our [*Joseph Smith and Oliver Cowdery*] minds, and the eyes of our understanding were opened [*by the power of the Holy Ghost*].

Next, in verses 2–3, we are given a description of the Savior, which includes much biblical symbolism.

2 We saw the Lord [*Jesus Christ*] standing upon the breastwork of the pulpit [*the small wall that extends out from both sides of the pulpit*], before us; and under his feet was a paved work of pure gold [*in biblical symbolism, gold represents the very best, celestial glory, God*], in color like amber [*symbolic of divine glory—compare with Ezekiel 1:3–4*].

3 His eyes were as a flame of fire [*symbolic of celestial glory*]; the hair of his head was white [*symbolic of purity; celestial glory*] like the pure snow [*symbolic of the Savior's ability to cleanse—compare with Isaiah 1:18*]; his countenance shone above the brightness of the sun; and his voice was as the sound of the rushing of great waters, even the voice of Jehovah, saying:

Next, in verse 4, the Savior specifically identifies Himself and personally introduces Himself to the Prophet and Oliver Cowdery.

4 I am the first and the last [*Jesus Christ is involved in all things for our potential exaltation under the direction of the Father*]; I am he who liveth [*He is resurrected*], I am he who was slain [*crucified*]; I am your advocate with the Father. [*He is constantly working with us to save us.*]

All of us worry somewhat about whether we will be found worthy to meet the Savior. Next, we see the Lord's kindness and mercy as He quickly puts Joseph and Oliver at ease on this matter.

5 Behold, your sins are forgiven you; you are clean before me;

therefore, **lift up your heads and rejoice** [*compare with Mosiah 3:3–9, where King Benjamin is told that he may rejoice and that he can tell his people that they, too, may have joy because of the Atonement and their efforts to live worthy of it*].

6 **Let the hearts of your brethren rejoice, and let the hearts of all my people rejoice, who have,** with their might, **built this house to my name**.

In verse 7, next, the Savior answers the Prophet's plea, given one week previously in the dedicatory prayer of the Kirtland Temple, wherein he said, "We ask thee, O Lord, to accept of this house, the workmanship of the hands of us, thy servants, which thou didst command us to build" (D&C 109:4).

7 For behold, **I have accepted this house,** and my name shall be here; and **I will manifest myself to my people in mercy in this house**.

As you probably know, the Savior can be represented by the Holy Ghost, as well as by angels as if it were the Savior Himself speaking (as was the case with the angel in Revelation 1:1; 19:9–10). This is sometimes referred to as "divine investiture." In verse 8, next, however, the Savior says that He, personally, will appear and speak to them with His own voice if they will remain worthy.

8 Yea, **I will appear unto my servants, and speak unto them with mine own voice,** if my people will keep my commandments, and do not pollute this holy house [*by unworthiness*].

Next, in verses 9–10, the Savior prophesies concerning the Kirtland Temple. The "endowment" spoken of in verse 9 is not what we do in temples today when we "receive our endowment." Rather, it involves the endowment (gift) of power and priesthood keys that will be bestowed upon Joseph Smith and Oliver Cowdery by Moses, Elias, and Elijah on this day, as well as revelations, inspiration, and instruction that will be given during the remaining time of the Kirtland Temple's authorized use.

Next, the Savior prophesies about the Kirtland Temple:

9 Yea **the hearts of thousands and tens of thousands shall greatly rejoice in consequence of the blessings which shall be poured out, and the endowment with which my servants have been endowed in this house.**

10 And **the fame of this house shall spread to foreign lands;** and **this is the beginning of the blessing which shall be poured out upon the heads of my people.** Even so. Amen.

Next, in verse 11, the appearance of Moses is recorded. He will restore the keys of the gathering of Israel throughout the earth and the leading of the ten tribes from the north.

Vision #2
Moses

11 After this vision closed, the heavens were again opened unto us; and Moses appeared before us, **and committed unto us the keys of the gathering of Israel** from the four parts of the earth, **and the leading of the ten tribes from the land of the north**.

The work of gathering Israel in the last days is one of the most often-prophesied events in the scriptures and is a prominent sign of the times being fulfilled in our day. Our modern prophets speak of it very often and of gathering Israel on both sides of the veil. Also, you can read more about the "leading of the ten tribes from the land of the north" in D&C 133:26–33.

Regarding the gathering of Israel, President Russell M. Nelson, then an Apostle, taught: "The choice to come unto Christ is not a matter of physical location; it is a matter of individual commitment. People can be "brought to the knowledge of the Lord" without leaving their homelands. True, in the early days of the Church, conversion often meant emigration as well.

But now the gathering takes place in each nation. The Lord has decreed the establishment of Zion in each realm where He has given His Saints their birth and nationality. Scripture foretells that the people "shall be gathered home to the lands of their inheritance, and shall be established in all their lands of promise." "Every nation is the gathering place for its own people." The place of gathering for Brazilian Saints is in Brazil; the place of gathering for Nigerian Saints is in Nigeria; the place of gathering for Korean Saints is in Korea; and so forth. Zion is "the pure in heart." Zion is wherever righteous Saints are. Publications, communications, and congregations are now such that nearly all members have access to the doctrines, keys, ordinances, and blessings of the gospel, regardless of their location" (October 2006 general conference, Sunday morning session).

Elder Bruce R. McConkie spoke of the keys restored by Moses. He said (**bold** added for emphasis):

"Israel's great lawgiver, the prophet whose life was in similitude of the Messiah himself, the one who delivered Israel from Egyptian bondage and led them to their land of promise, came to Joseph Smith and Oliver Cowdery on 3 April 1836, in the Kirtland Temple. **He gave them: (1) 'the keys of the gathering of Israel from the four parts of the earth,' and (2)** the keys of 'the leading of the ten tribes from the land of the north' (D&C 110:11).

"Since then, with increasing power and in great glory, **we have gathered**, from their Egyptian bondage as it were, the dispersed of Ephraim and few others, initially to the mountains of America, but now **into the stakes of Zion in the various nations** of the earth. The gathering of Israel is a reality. **When the ten tribes return they will come at the direction of the President of The Church of Jesus Christ of Latter-day Saints**, for he now holds and will then hold the keys of presidency and direction for this mighty work" ("This Final Glorious Gospel Dispensation," *Ensign,* April 1980, 22; quoted in *Doctrine and Covenants Student Manual,* 1981, 275).

Many people wonder and speculate as to where the lost ten tribes are. Joseph Fielding Smith gave the following advice on this matter:

"Whether these tribes are in the north or not, I am not prepared to say. As I said before, they are 'lost' and until the Lord wishes it, they will not be found. All that I know about it is what the Lord has revealed, and He declares that they will come from the North. He has also made it very clear and definite that these lost people are separate and apart from the scattered Israelites now being gathered out" (*Signs of the Times,* 186; quoted

in *Doctrine and Covenants Student Manual,* 1981, 275).

Next, in verse 12, Elias appears and restores the keys and blessings related to the Abrahamic Covenant (see Genesis 12:1–3, 17:1–8, 22:17–18, Abraham 2:9–11). These blessings relate to attaining exaltation ourselves and taking the gospel to all people so they likewise have the opportunity to do so.

According to the Bible Dictionary, we do not know who this Elias was, other than that he lived during the days of Abraham (see Bible Dictionary under "Elias," definition number 4). It will be interesting someday to meet him and find out more about his life and mission.

Vision #3
Elias

12 After this, Elias appeared, and committed the dispensation of the gospel of Abraham, saying that **in us and our seed all generations after us should be blessed.**

We will say just a bit more about the "dispensation of the gospel of Abraham," spoken of in verse 12, above. The covenants that the Lord made with Abraham figure prominently in our lives, too, if we seek them and live worthy of them. The last phrase of verse 12 reminds us of Abraham 2:9–11, which is a summary of the blessings and responsibilities of the descendants of Abraham, Isaac, and Jacob if they desire to receive exaltation. The "blessings of Abraham, Isaac, and Jacob" (as often mentioned in patriarchal blessings) definitely have reference to exaltation, since all three of these ancient prophets have already become gods (see D&C 132:37).

We will quote Abraham 2:9–11 and add notes and commentary in order to gain additional insights as to the keys restored by Elias in this appearance in the Kirtland Temple. As you read through these three verses, which provide a summary of the Abrahamic Covenant, keep in mind that we are seeking instruction as to what the "dispensation of the gospel of Abraham" is. You will find that it involves promises and covenants of exaltation as well as responsibilities of those who desire to attain it. It also deals with blessings needed along the way. We will use **bold** for emphasis.

The Abrahamic Covenant

Abraham 2:9–11

9 And I will make of thee a great nation [*symbolically, a reference to having innumerable spirit children of our own as gods (compare with "a continuation of the seeds forever and ever"— D&C 132:19*], and I will bless thee above measure [*exaltation*], and make thy name great among all nations [*symbolic of exaltation, becoming gods*], and thou shalt be a blessing unto thy seed [*posterity*] after thee, that in their hands they shall bear this ministry and Priesthood unto all nations [*missionary work; part of our responsibility as members of the Church*];

10 And I will bless them through thy name; for as many as receive this Gospel shall be called after thy name [*will be called the descendants of Abraham*], and **shall be accounted thy seed** [*will be given the same blessings and promises of exaltation that Abraham was given; they will be considered to be of Abraham, Isaac, and Jacob (Israel), or, in other words, will be called Israel and will be gathered home to God*], and shall rise up and bless thee, as their father [*ancestor*];

11 And I will bless them that bless thee, and curse them that curse thee [*the Lord's blessings and spiritual protection will be poured out upon righteous Israel*]; **and in thee** [*that is, in thy priesthood*] **and in thy seed** [*that is, thy Priesthood*], for I give unto thee a promise that this right shall continue in thee, and in thy seed after thee [*that is to say, the literal seed, or the seed of the body*] **shall all the families of the earth be blessed, even with the blessings of the Gospel, which are the blessings of salvation, even of life eternal** [*exaltation; life eternal is another scriptural term for exaltation*].

Next, in verses 13–15, Elijah appears. You may wish to read a summary of his life and mission in the Bible Dictionary under "Elijah." Imagine how humbled and pleased he must have been to be the one chosen to restore these priesthood keys as prophesied in Malachi 4:5–6.

Vision #4
Elijah

13 After this vision had closed, another great and glorious vision burst upon us; for **Elijah** the prophet, who was taken to heaven without tasting death [*2 Kings 2:11*], **stood before us, and said**:

14 Behold, **the time has fully come, which was spoken of by the mouth of Malachi** [*Malachi 4:5–6*]—**testifying that he** [*Elijah*] **should be sent, before the great and dreadful day of the Lord come** [*the Second Coming*]—

Next, in verse 15, we learn that a

major function of the priesthood keys restored by Elijah was to get the work of family history and work for the dead going upon the earth before the Second Coming of Christ.

15 **To turn the hearts of the fathers to the children, and the children to the fathers**, lest the whole earth be smitten with a curse [*in other words, if families are not sealed together in exaltation by the power of the priesthood for time and all eternity, then a major purpose of the earth and its creation would not have been fulfilled*]—

Joseph Fielding Smith explained the importance of family history work and the keys restored by Elijah as follows:

"What was the nature of this restoration? It was the conferring upon men in this dispensation of the sealing power of the priesthood, by which all things are bound in heaven as well as on earth. It gave the authority to Joseph Smith to perform in the temple of God all the ordinances essential to salvation for both the living and the dead.

"Through the power of this priesthood which Elijah bestowed, husband and wife may be sealed, or married for eternity; children may be sealed to their parents for eternity; thus the family is made eternal, and death does not separate the members. This is the great principle that will save the world from utter destruction.

"Vicariously the dead may obtain the blessings of the gospel—baptism, confirmation, ordination, and the higher blessings, which are sealed upon them in the temples of the Lord, by virtue of the authority restored by Elijah. Through the restoration of these keys, the work of the Lord is fully inaugurated before the coming of Jesus Christ in glory.

"These keys of the binding, or sealing power, which were given to Peter, James, and John in their dispensation, are keys which make valid all the ordinances of the gospel. They pertain more especially to the work in the temples, both for the living and for the dead. They are the authorities which prepare men to enter the celestial kingdom and to be crowned as sons and heirs of God.

"These keys hold the power to seal husbands and wives for eternity as well as for time. They hold the power to seal children to parents, the key of adoption, by which the family organization is made intact forever. This is the power that will save the obedient from the curse in the coming of the great and dreadful day of the Lord. Through these keys the hearts of the children have turned to their fathers" (*Doctrines of Salvation,* 2:118–19; quoted in *Doctrine and Covenants Student Manual,* 277).

It could be that in verse 16, next, Elijah is referring to the keys that he restored to Joseph Smith and Oliver Cowdery. However, it may also be that he is summarizing the restoration of priesthood keys in the Kirtland Temple on that day by Moses, Elias, and himself. This restitution of keys is a sign of the times (one of many prophecies that will be fulfilled in the last days prior to the Savior's coming), indicating that the Second Coming of the Lord is getting relatively close.

16 Therefore, **the keys of this dispensation are committed into your hands**; and **by this ye may know that the great and dreadful day of the Lord** [*the Second Coming of Christ*] **is near, even at the doors**.

In conclusion, the marvelous manifestations and revelations, including the restoration of vital priesthood keys, which took place on Easter Sunday, April 3, 1836, in the Kirtland Temple, continue to bless the lives of faithful Saints throughout the world, as well as millions who have passed beyond the veil. The work of sealing families, living and dead, accelerates, accompanied by the blessings of heaven and advances in technology.

These blessings alone, which came on this special Easter Sunday, more than justify every effort to build the Kirtland Temple in spite of being forced to abandon it relatively soon thereafter such as these early Saints were compelled to do. The blessings of eternity, conferred by those having these restored priesthood keys and accepted by individuals through the gift of moral agency under temporary mortal conditions, are part of the perspective and schooling designed by a loving Father for His children as they follow the Savior back home.

SECTION 111

Background

This revelation was given through the Prophet Joseph Smith on August 6, 1836, at Salem, Massachusetts.

The Church was still deeply in debt at this time due to the building of the Kirtland Temple as well as expenses incurred in funding Zion's Camp and providing for the Saints who had been driven from their homes in Missouri. Many of them had been left destitute and relied on the generosity of impoverished members in Kirtland and elsewhere.

In the midst of this financial difficulty came news from Brother William Burgess that he knew of a large amount of money hidden in the basement of a deceased widow's house in Salem, Massachusetts, which was available for the taking. Upon hearing of this, Joseph Smith, Sidney Rigdon,

Hyrum Smith, and Oliver Cowdery departed for Salem. B. H. Roberts, a prominent early historian of the Church, explained what happened.

"Ebenezer Robinson, for many years a faithful and prominent elder in the church, and at Nauvoo associated with Don Carlos Smith—brother of the Prophet—in editing and publishing the *Times and Seasons,* states that the journey to Salem arose from these circumstances. There came to Kirtland a brother by the name of Burgess who stated that he had knowledge of a large amount of money secreted in the cellar of a certain house in Salem, Massachusetts, which had belonged to a widow (then deceased), and thought he was the only person who had knowledge of it, or of the location of the house. The brethren accepting the representations of Burgess as true made the journey to Salem to secure, if possible, the treasure. Burgess, according to Robinson, met the brethren in Salem, but claimed that time had wrought such changes in the town that he could not for a certainty point out the house 'and soon left'" (*Comprehensive History of the Church,* 1:411).

Imagine the feelings in the minds and hearts of these brethren after Burgess acknowledged that he could not remember which house it was and left them. The Lord's kindness and mercy, in response to this venture, is encouraging to all of us who have likewise been involved in "follies" (verse 1).

In fact, when we understand the background, this section becomes one of the great sections in the Doctrine and Covenants because it reveals so clearly the tenderness of the Master as He continues to patiently school His little flock. Watch as He picks them up and looks at the bright side of things in verses 1–4 while acknowledging to them that their main motivation for coming here was folly.

1 **I, THE Lord your God, am not displeased** with your coming this journey, **notwithstanding your follies** [*likely referring to their coming here to find treasure*].

2 **I have much treasure** [*souls*] **in this city** for you, for the benefit of Zion, **and many people in this city, whom I will gather out in due time** for the benefit of Zion, through your instrumentality.

3 Therefore, it is expedient that you should **form acquaintance with men in this city, as you shall be led, and as it shall be given you**.

4 And it shall come to pass **in due time** [*according to the Lord's schedule*] that **I will give this city into your hands**, that you shall have power over it, insomuch that

they shall not discover your secret parts [*embarrass you or put you to shame—compare with Isaiah 3:17*]; and its wealth pertaining to gold and silver shall be yours [*obviously a prophecy of the future; possibly referring to the many converts in the Salem area who joined the Church within the next few years, many of whom moved to Nauvoo and then on west. Their financial resources would be a "treasure" indeed to the Church's financial needs*].

By 1842, there were ninety members in the Salem Branch of the Church, and on April 11, 1843, Elder Erastus Snow recorded in his journal that he had baptized more than one hundred converts from Salem (quoted in *Doctrine and Covenants Student Manual,* 1981, 278).

As you no doubt know, the Lord could easily point out to our Church leaders today the location of oil, gold, precious minerals, and so forth, which could free the members of the Church from the necessity of sacrificing and making financial contributions. But this would not bless us. Rather, it would curse us, because we would be denied the blessings of personal, voluntary sacrifice, which leads us to focus on eternal priorities.

As this section continues, the Savior counsels these brethren concerning the debts of the Church.

5 **Concern not yourselves about your debts, for I will give you power to pay them.**

6 **Concern not yourselves about Zion** [*the Church and its members in Missouri*]**, for I will deal mercifully with her.**

Next, in verses 7–9, the Savior instructs them to stay for a while in the Salem area and tells them that the Spirit will point out a place that they can rent. One of the lessons we learn here is that the Holy Ghost communicates with us and approves our decisions by giving us peace.

7 **Tarry in this place, and in the regions round about;**

8 And **the place** [*housing accommodations*] where it is my will that you should tarry, for the main, **shall be signalized unto you by the peace and power of my Spirit, that shall flow unto you.**

9 This place you may obtain by hire [*rent*]. And **inquire diligently concerning the more ancient inhabitants and founders of this city** [*learn what you can about the original inhabitants of Salem*]**;**

10 For **there are more treasures than one for you in this city.**

A quote from the 2018 *Doctrine and Covenants Student Manual,*

chapter 44, sheds additional light on verses 9 and 10, above.

"In obedience to the Lord's command to 'inquire diligently concerning the more ancient inhabitants and founders of this city' (D&C 111:9), during their stay in Salem, Massachusetts, the Prophet Joseph Smith and his companions traveled throughout Salem and its surrounding areas visiting museums, historical sites, and libraries (see *The Joseph Smith Papers, Documents, Volume 5: October 1835–January 1838*, 278, note 248). They learned more about the city's founding by the Puritan pilgrims in the early 1600s and about the American Revolutionary War and the establishment of the United States (see *Manuscript History of the Church*, vol. B-1, page 749, josephsmithpapers.org).

"Some of the brethren spent time learning about the Salem witch trials (see Oliver Cowdery, 'Prospectus,' *Latter Day Saints' Messenger and Advocate*, Oct. 1836, 388–91). In addition, the Prophet Joseph Smith and his companions visited the remains of the Charlestown Ursuline Convent, which had been destroyed by an anti-Catholic mob motivated by religious intolerance. Referring to this experience, the Prophet wrote: 'When will man cease to war with man, and wrest from him his sacred right, of worshiping his God according as his conscience dictates? Holy Father, hasten the day' (in *Manuscript History of the Church*, vol. B-1, page 749, josephsmithpapers.org)."

Finally, from verse 1, above, we get the impression that the initial motivation for the trip to Salem was not thought through very well. As the Savior concludes this merciful and encouraging revelation, He appears to be gently counseling these leaders to be wiser in the future and assures them that He will continue helping and guiding them as they grow.

11 Therefore, **be ye as wise** as serpents and yet without sin; **and I will order all things for your good, as fast as ye are able to receive them**. Amen.

SECTION 112

Background

This revelation was given through the Prophet Joseph Smith to Thomas B. Marsh, one of the original Twelve Apostles in this dispensation, on July 23, 1837, at Kirtland, Ohio.

At this time, Brother Marsh was the president of the Quorum of the Twelve. Verses 1–12 are mainly to him personally. Verses 13–34 are primarily instructions for him to give to the Twelve.

Thomas Baldwin Marsh was six years older than Joseph Smith,

having been born on November 1, 1799, in Massachusetts. He was baptized on September 3, 1830, by David Whitmer and became a member of the Quorum of the Twelve Apostles when it was organized in 1835.

As mentioned above, verses 1–12 were given as personal counsel and instruction to Thomas Marsh. When we study these verses, we will see advice to control the feelings of the heart (verse 2) and warnings to avoid pride and be humble (verses 3 and 10). Sadly, Brother Marsh failed to heed these specific words of the Lord to him. His life provides a disappointing lesson about the results of failure to follow the Lord's counsel.

Perhaps you have heard of the case involving milk strippings, which led to his apostasy and excommunication from the Church. Briefly put, Brother Marsh's wife, Elizabeth, and Lucinda Harris, wife of George Harris, wanted to make cheese, but neither had enough cows to do it alone. Therefore, they agreed to exchange milk, including the strippings (the last of the milking, which is extra rich with cream). Sister Harris kept her part of the bargain, but when it was Sister Marsh's turn to provide milk, she cheated, keeping back a pint of strippings from each cow. George A. Smith spoke of this in a talk delivered some years later in Salt Lake City. He was warning about how small matters can lead to big troubles if not quickly resolved. He said:

"For instance, while the Saints were living in Far West, there were two sisters wishing to make cheese, and, neither of them possessing the requisite number of cows, they agreed to exchange milk.

"The wife of Thomas B. Marsh, who was then President of the Twelve Apostles, and sister Harris concluded they would exchange milk, in order to make a little larger cheese than they otherwise could. To be sure to have justice done, it was agreed that they should not save the strippings, but that the milk and strippings should all go together. Small matters to talk about here, to be sure, two women's exchanging milk to make cheese.

"Mrs. Harris, it appeared, was faithful to the agreement and carried to Mrs. Marsh the milk and strippings, but Mrs. Marsh, wishing to make some extra good cheese, saved a pint of strippings from each cow and sent Mrs. Harris the milk without the strippings.

"Finally it leaked out that Mrs. Marsh had saved strippings, and it became a matter to be settled by the Teachers. They began to examine the matter, and it was proved that Mrs. Marsh had saved the strippings, and consequently had wronged Mrs. Harris out of that amount.

"An appeal was taken from the Teacher to the Bishop, and a regular Church trial was had. President Marsh did not consider that the Bishop had done him and his lady justice, for they decided that the strippings were wrongfully saved, and that the woman had violated her covenant.

"Marsh immediately took an appeal to the High Council, who investigated the question with much patience, and I assure you they were a grave body. Marsh being extremely anxious to maintain the character of his wife, as he was the President of the Twelve Apostles, and a great man in Israel, made a desperate defence, but the High Council finally confirmed the Bishop's decision.

"Marsh, not being satisfied, took an appeal to the First Presidency of the Church, and Joseph and his Counsellors had to sit upon the case, and they approved the decision of the High Council.

"This little affair, you will observe, kicked up a considerable breeze, and Thomas B. Marsh then declared that he would sustain the character of his wife, even if he had to go to hell for it.

"The then President of the Twelve Apostles, the man who should have been the first to do justice and cause reparation to be made for wrong, committed by any member of his family, took that position, and what next? He went before a magistrate and swore that the 'Mormons' were hostile towards the State of Missouri.

"That affidavit brought from the government of Missouri an exterminating order, which drove some fifteen thousand Saints from their homes and habitations, and some thousands perished through suffering the exposure consequent on this state of affairs" (George A. Smith, in *Journal of Discourses*, 3:284).

Thomas B. Marsh was excommunicated on March 17, 1839, and was out of the Church for eighteen years. He was rebaptized on July 16, 1857, in Florence, Nebraska, a weak and emaciated shadow of what he once was. He came to Salt Lake City and then moved to Ogden, Utah, where he died penniless and in poor health in January 1866.

We will now proceed with our study of section 112. Remember, as stated above, that verses 1–12 are personal counsel to Thomas B. Marsh.

1 VERILY thus saith the Lord unto you my servant Thomas: I have heard thy prayers; and thine alms [*offerings and personal sacrifices*] have come up as a memorial before me, in behalf of those, thy brethren [*the other members of the Twelve*], who were chosen to bear testimony of my name and to send it abroad among all nations, kindreds, tongues, and people, and ordained through the instrumentality of my servants,

Next, in verses 2–12, Thomas is given direct, gentle counsel, which, if followed, could have saved him much anguish. He is also given the encouragement of having his sins forgiven (verse 3), which gives him a whole new start.

2 Verily I say unto you, **there have been some few things in thine heart and with thee with which I, the Lord, was not well pleased.**

3 **Nevertheless,** inasmuch as thou hast abased [*humbled*] thyself thou shalt be exalted; therefore, **all thy sins are forgiven thee.**

4 **Let thy heart be of good cheer** [*be positive and upbeat*] before my face; and **thou shalt bear record of my name, not only unto the Gentiles, but also unto the Jews; and thou shalt send forth my word unto the ends of the earth.**

In the next verses, Brother Marsh is told of the good he can do in spreading the gospel, locally and among the nations of the earth.

5 Contend thou, therefore, morning by morning; and day after day **let thy warning voice go forth;** and when the night cometh let not

the inhabitants of the earth slumber, because of thy speech.

6 Let thy habitation be known in Zion, and **remove not thy house** [*don't leave the Church*]; for I, the Lord, have a great work for thee to do, in publishing my name among the children of men [*people*].

7 Therefore, **gird up thy loins** [*prepare*] **for the work**. Let thy feet be shod also, for thou art chosen, and thy path lieth **among the mountains, and among many nations**.

8 And by thy word many high ones shall be brought low [*humbled*], and by thy word many low ones [*humble people*] shall be exalted.

9 Thy voice shall be a rebuke unto the transgressor; and at thy rebuke let the tongue of the slanderer cease its perverseness.

Verse 10, next, is one of the often-quoted verses in the Doctrine and Covenants. You may wish to mark it in your own Doctrine and Covenants.

10 **Be thou humble; and the Lord thy God shall lead thee by the hand, and give thee answer to thy prayers**.

11 **I know thy heart, and have heard thy prayers** concerning

thy brethren. **Be not partial towards them in love above many others** [*don't show more love toward your colleagues in the Quorum of the Twelve and other Church leaders than to others*], but **let thy love be for them as for thyself**; and **let thy love abound unto all men, and unto all who love my name**.

As we read verse 12, next, it is helpful to remember that all members, including the leaders, are basically new in the Church at this time in the Restoration. None of them are seasoned veterans, because the Church has been organized for only a little more than seven years. Many are still working on making the transitions from other belief systems and lifestyles to those of the true gospel. In order to help the Twelve continue to change into the understanding and worthiness needed to serve as Apostles, and to accelerate these changes, Brother Marsh is counseled by the Lord to be very direct in teaching and correcting these brethren as needed.

Also, be aware that in many settings, it is common for men and women of position and power to believe that they can do no wrong and are not subject to the same rules that apply to those over whom they preside. The Lord makes it clear that such is not the case in the true Church.

12 And **pray for thy brethren**

of the Twelve. **Admonish them sharply** [*be very direct with them as you warn them about unworthiness*] for my name's sake, and **let them be admonished for all their sins** [*the Twelve must repent if they sin; there is no privileged class in the Church, who are exempt from the penalties of sin*], and **be ye faithful before me unto my name** [*can include being faithful to covenants made in the name of Jesus Christ*].

As mentioned above, in serving as the President of the Quorum of the Twelve Apostles, Thomas B. Marsh had the responsibility of instructing and teaching the other members of the Twelve. Verses 13–34 instruct him as to his duties as president and teach him things he is to pass on to the other members of the Quorum.

First, in verse 13, next, we see that some of these quorum members are still in the process of being thoroughly converted to the restored gospel of Jesus Christ. This should not surprise us, since we, ourselves, are still going through the conversion process when it comes to living some aspects of the gospel. A beautiful message is given to these men and to all of us. It is that as we go through trials and tribulations, if we will humble ourselves and remain teachable instead of getting angry at the Lord because of hardships, we will be converted more deeply, and He will heal us.

13 And **after their temptations,** and **much tribulation,** behold, **I, the Lord, will feel after them** [*the Lord's tender heart will reach out to them*], and **if they harden not their hearts, and stiffen not their necks** [*if they do not become prideful*] **against me, they shall be converted, and I will heal them.**

Much sacrifice is required on the part of the Twelve Apostles and their families in our day. These Brethren travel throughout the world to preach the gospel and to keep the Church in order (see D&C 107:33). In verse 14, next, the Lord tells Thomas and the rest of the Twelve at the time of this revelation to "take up your cross." This is biblical terminology meaning to sacrifice whatever is necessary in order to fulfill their callings. The taking up of one's cross implies that there will be very difficult times. As you know, crucifixion was common in the days of the Bible. Thus, cross implies severe trial and tribulation.

14 Now, I say unto you, and what I say unto you, I say unto all the Twelve: Arise and **gird up your loins** [*prepare for action*], **take up your cross** [*give whatever is required in order to fulfill your calling*], **follow me, and feed my sheep.**

In verse 15, next, the Savior gives a special warning not to rebel against the Prophet Joseph

Smith. At this time, there was much of dissension and rebellion in Kirtland and elsewhere against the Prophet. One of the big factors was the failing Kirtland Safety Society (a banking system owned by the Prophet and others) that, along with hundreds of other banks throughout the nation, was failing during what was called "the Panic of 1837." Even some members of the Quorum of the Twelve Apostles were rebelling against Joseph Smith and calling him a fallen prophet.

In fact, back in February 1837, several who considered Joseph to be a fallen Prophet had called a meeting in the temple for the purpose of installing David Whitmer as the leader of the Church (see *Church History in the Fulness of Times,* 2003, 173–74). Their attempt met with failure but serves as a reminder of the spirit of apostasy that was prominent at the time section 112 was given. And in August 1837, while Joseph Smith and most of the Apostles were away on missions, John F. Boynton (one of the Apostles) joined other apostates in attempting to take over the Kirtland Temple by storming it, armed with pistols and bowie knives. They, too, failed (see *Church History in the Fulness of Times,* 2003, 176–77).

This next verse serves as a strong warning to all of us to avoid rebelling against the Prophet Joseph Smith and also against our living prophet.

15 **Exalt not yourselves** [*don't get caught up in pride and thinking you should lead the Church*]; **rebel not against my servant Joseph; for verily I say unto you, I am with him**, and my hand shall be over him; and **the keys which I have given unto him**, and also to you-ward [*to the Twelve*], **shall not be taken from him till I come.** [*We understand that all the prophets, living and dead, will turn their priesthood keys back over to the Savior prior to the Second Coming. This is to be done at the council in Adam-ondi-Ahman. We will say more about this when we get to section 116.*]

There is perhaps another message we should get by implication from verse 15, above. It is that the Lord will not let the living prophet lead us astray. This is found also in D&C 28:2 and 43:3–5.

Next, in verse 16, Brother Marsh is taught that he holds the keys of directing the Twelve in their ministry to all the world. And, in verse 17, he is taught his role in using his "keys" to "unlock doors" in places where the First Presidency does not have the time to travel and serve directly.

16 Verily I say unto you, **my servant Thomas, thou art the man whom I have chosen to hold the keys of my kingdom, as**

pertaining to the Twelve [*just as the President of the Quorum of the Twelve does today*], abroad among all nations—

17 **That thou mayest be my servant to unlock the door of the kingdom in all places where my servant Joseph, and my servant Sidney, and my servant Hyrum** [*the First Presidency at this time*], **cannot come;**

We will quote from the 1981 Institute of Religion *Doctrine and Covenants Student Manual* in order to get a brief background as to why Hyrum Smith is serving in the First Presidency at the time of this revelation.

"The passage in verse 17 about Joseph, Hyrum, and Sidney refers to the First Presidency as it was constituted when the revelation was given. When the First Presidency of the Church was originally organized, Jesse Gause and Sidney Rigdon were called to be counselors to the Prophet. After Jesse Gause's apostasy (see Historical Background for D&C 81 [*in the 1981* Doctrine and Covenants Student Manual]), the Presidency was reorganized in 1833 with Frederick G. Williams as Second Counselor. At a conference held at Far West, Missouri, on 7 November 1837, Frederick G. Williams was replaced by Hyrum Smith (see *History of the Church,* 2:522–23)" (*Doctrine and*

Covenants Student Manual, 1981, 282).

Next, in verses 18–22, we see a short course on authority and delegation as it pertains to the leading quorums of the Church. It is a reminder that the Twelve function under the direction of the First Presidency (as stated in D&C 107:33) and that many others function under the authority and direction of the Twelve.

18 For **on them** [*the First Presidency*] **have I laid the burden of all the churches** [*the branches, wards, and stakes*] for a little season.

19   Wherefore, **whithersoever they** [*the First Presidency*] **shall send you, go ye,** and **I will be with you**; and in whatsoever place ye shall proclaim my name an effectual door shall be opened unto you, that they may receive my word.

Verse 20, next, is a simple, straightforward reminder that you cannot be a member of this Church in good standing with the Lord unless you support and sustain the First Presidency in your words and actions.

20 **Whosoever receiveth my word receiveth me,** and **whosoever receiveth me, receiveth** those, **the First Presidency**, whom I have sent, whom I have made counselors [*advisors and*

supervisors] for my name's sake unto you [*the Twelve*].

21 And again, I say unto you, that **whosoever ye shall send** in my name, **by the voice of your brethren, the Twelve**, duly recommended and authorized by you, **shall have power to open the door of my kingdom unto any nation whithersoever ye shall send them—**

22 **Inasmuch as they shall humble themselves** before me, and **abide in my word** [*stick with the scriptures and the words of the living prophets*], and **hearken to the voice of my Spirit**.

Next, beginning with verse 23, Brother Marsh is told that spiritual darkness is covering the earth, that wickedness is taking over, and that the need for repentance will be preached by calamities and troubles upon the earth.

23 Verily, verily, I say unto you, **darkness covereth the earth**, and **gross darkness the minds of the people**, and **all flesh** [*everyone*] **has become corrupt** before my face.

24 Behold, **vengeance cometh speedily upon the inhabitants of the earth, a day of wrath**, a day of **burning**, a day of **desolation**, of **weeping**, of **mourning**, and of **lamentation**; and **as a whirlwind** [*which spares none in its path*] **it shall come upon all the face of the earth, saith the Lord**.

As mentioned in previous notes, there was already much of apostasy in Kirtland at the time of this revelation. Verses 25–28 point this out. First, the Lord points out that the Church must be cleansed (a major purpose of trials and tribulation of the Saints) before it can fulfill its role in taking the gospel to others.

25 And **upon my house** [*the Church*] **shall it** [*the troubles spoken of in verses 23–24*] **begin**, and **from my house shall it go forth**, saith the Lord;

26 **First among those among you**, saith the Lord, **who have professed to know my name** [*who have claimed to be faithful members of the Church*] **and have not known me** [*but are not*], **and have blasphemed against me in the midst of my house** [*likely meaning the Kirtland Temple; see notes following verse 14, above*], saith the Lord.

In verses 27–29, next, the Twelve, including Thomas B. Marsh, are told to get their own lives in order before they try to direct and teach others in living the gospel. In verse 27, they are told not to worry about the apostasy taking place at that time in Kirtland.

27 Therefore, see to it that ye trouble not yourselves concerning the affairs of my church in this place [*Kirtland*], saith the Lord.

28 **But purify your hearts before me; and then go ye into all the world**, and preach my gospel unto every creature who has not received it;

29 And **he that believeth and is baptized shall be saved, and he that believeth not, and is not baptized, shall be damned** [*stopped in their progression*].

Next, the Savior gives a brief review concerning the priesthood keys that have been given to the Twelve and the First Presidency in this last dispensation, which is known as "the dispensation of the fullness of times" (the last time the gospel will be restored before the Second Coming and the dispensation in which all the priesthood keys and authority from previous dispensations have been restored).

30 For **unto you, the Twelve, and** those, **the First Presidency**, who are appointed with you to be your counselors [*advisors*] and your leaders, **is the power of this priesthood given**, for the last days and **for the last time**, in the which is the dispensation of the fulness of times.

31 **Which power you hold, in connection with all those who have received a dispensation at any time from the beginning of the creation**;

32 For verily I say unto you, **the keys of the dispensation, which ye have received, have come down from the fathers** [*ancient prophets*], **and last of all, being sent down from heaven unto you**.

33 Verily I say unto you, behold **how great is your calling. Cleanse your hearts and your garments** [*garments in this context symbolize our lives*], **lest the blood of this generation be required at your hands** [*in other words, if you don't get your lives in order so you can teach the gospel to the world, you will bear a responsibility for their sins*].

34 **Be faithful until I come**, for I come quickly; and **my reward is with me to recompense** [*reward*] **every man according as his work shall be**. I am Alpha and Omega [*"the beginning and the end," Jesus Christ*]. Amen.

SECTION 113

Background

This section consists of questions and answers about Isaiah, chapters 11 and 52, given by the Prophet Joseph Smith in March 1838. From the context of *History of the Church,* volume 3, pages 9–10, in which this section is recorded, it appears likely that these questions and answers were given in the last half of March in Far West, Missouri.

Isaiah uses much symbolism, and, as a result, his writings and imagery can be difficult to understand without help. The inspired teachings of the Prophet Joseph Smith, here and elsewhere, provide us with significant help in understanding Isaiah.

We will first go through section 113, using **bold** to point out the questions and answers. Then we will quote the referenced Isaiah verses, adding Joseph Smith's helps by way of notes.

Question

1 WHO is the Stem of Jesse [*Jesse was King David's father—see 1 Samuel 16:19, and thus, an ancestor of Christ—see Matthew 1:5–6, 16–17*] spoken of in the 1st, 2d, 3d, 4th, and 5th verses of the Isaiah?

Answer

2 Verily thus saith the Lord: **It is Christ**.

Question

3 What is the rod spoken of in the first verse of the 11th chapter of Isaiah, that should come of the Stem of Jesse?

Answer

4 Behold, thus saith the Lord: **It is a servant in the hands of Christ, who is partly a descendant of Jesse as well as of Ephraim, or of the house of Joseph, on whom there is laid much power.**

Question

5 **What is the root of Jesse** spoken of in the 10th verse of the 11th chapter?

Answer

6 Behold, thus saith the Lord, **it is a descendant of Jesse, as well as of Joseph, unto whom rightly belongs the priesthood, and the keys of the kingdom, for an ensign, and for the gathering of my people in the last days.**

Question

7 Questions by Elias Higbee: **What is meant by** the command in Isaiah, 52d chapter, 1st verse,

which saith: **Put on thy strength, O Zion—and what people had Isaiah reference to?**

Answer

8 He had reference to those whom God should call in the last days, who should hold the power of priesthood to bring again Zion, and the redemption of Israel; and **to put on her strength is to put on the authority of the priesthood**, which she, Zion, has a right to by lineage; **also to return to that power which she had lost**.

Question

9 **What are we to understand by Zion loosing herself from the bands of her neck**; 2d verse?

Answer

10 **We are to understand that the scattered remnants** [*of Israel*] **are exhorted to return to the Lord** from whence they have fallen; which **if they do, the promise of the Lord is that he will speak to them**, or **give them revelation**. See the 6th, 7th, and 8th verses. **The bands of her neck are the curses of God upon her, or the remnants of Israel in their scattered condition among the Gentiles**.

As you can see, verses 1–5 in this section deal with Isaiah 11:1–5, 10. When Moroni appeared to Joseph Smith on September 21, 1823, he quoted Isaiah, chapter 11, "saying that it was about to be fulfilled" (Joseph Smith–History 1:40). Thus, we understand that Isaiah 11 has directly to do with Joseph Smith and the restoration of the gospel in the last days. We will now quote these Isaiah verses, adding the helps from Joseph Smith as we go.

Isaiah 11:1–5

1 **AND there shall come forth a rod** [*a servant of Christ (see D&C 113:3–4) who will serve in the last days (according to Moroni—Joseph History 1:40)*] **out of the stem of Jesse** [*Christ—see D&C 113:1–2*], and a Branch shall grow out of his roots:

Verses 2–3 appear to list a number of leadership qualities, which apply to the Savior and could also apply to faithful leaders, including Joseph Smith.

2 And **the spirit of the LORD shall rest upon him, the spirit of wisdom** and **understanding**, the spirit of **counsel** and **might**, the spirit of **knowledge** and of the **fear of the LORD** [*respect for God*];

3 And shall make him **of quick understanding** in the fear of

the LORD: and **he shall not judge after the sight of his eyes, neither reprove after the hearing of his ears**:

Verse 4, next, appears to apply to Christ (the "stem of Jesse," verse 1).

4 But **with righteousness shall he judge** the poor, **and reprove with equity** [*fairness*] for the meek of the earth: and **he shall smite the earth with the rod of his mouth, and with the breath of his lips shall he slay the wicked.**

Verse 5, next, certainly applies to Christ and could also apply to any great leader who is humble and has respect for God. In effect, it says that such leaders would be clothed with personal righteousness and would be deeply faithful to God.

5 And **righteousness shall be the girdle of his loins** [*clothed with righteousness*], and **faithfulness the girdle of his reins** [*deepest thoughts and desires*].

Isaiah 11:10

10 And in that day there shall be **a root of Jesse** [*a mighty leader in the kingdom of God in the last days (see D&C 113:5–6); this could easily be Joseph Smith*], which shall stand for an ensign of the people; to it shall the

Gentiles seek: and **his rest** [*exaltation—see D&C 84:24*] **shall be glorious**.

Verses 7–10 of section 113 refer to Isaiah 52:1–2, 6–8. We will quote them here and then add Joseph Smith's explanations as notes.

Isaiah 52:1–2, 6–8

1 **AWAKE, awake; put on thy strength** [*From D&C 113:8 "put on the authority of the priesthood*], **O Zion** [*"those whom God should call in the last days, who should hold the power of priesthood to bring again Zion, and the redemption of Israel"—see D&C 113:8*]; **put on thy beautiful garments, O Jerusalem**, the holy city: for henceforth there shall no more come into thee the uncircumcised and the unclean.

2 Shake thyself from the dust; arise, *and* sit down, O Jerusalem: **loose thyself from the bands of thy neck** [*from D&C 113:10; "the curses of God upon her, or the remnants of Israel in their scattered condition among the Gentiles"—see D&C 113:10*], O captive daughter of Zion.

6 [*From D&C 113:10; "The scattered remnants are exhorted to return to the Lord from whence they have fallen; which if they do,*

the promise of the Lord is that he will speak to them, or give them revelation. See the 6th, 7th, and 8th verses"—see D&C 113:10] **Therefore my people shall know my name: therefore *they shall know* in that day that I *am* he that doth speak: behold, *it is* I.**

7 How beautiful upon the mountains are the feet of him that bringeth good tidings, that publisheth peace; that bringeth good tidings of good, that publisheth salvation; that saith unto Zion, Thy God reigneth!

8 Thy watchmen shall lift up the voice; with the voice together shall they sing: for they shall see eye to eye, when the LORD shall bring again Zion.

SECTION 114

Background

This revelation was given through the Prophet Joseph Smith on April 11, 1838, in Far West, Missouri.

In verse 1, David W. Patten is addressed. Brother Patten was a faithful member of the original Quorum of the Twelve Apostles called in this last dispensation. At the time of this revelation, he had been living with the Saints in

Missouri for some time, and was a stabilizing influence there. It was a difficult time in Missouri, with much dissension and apostasy among the members, including some of the leaders of the Church there. In fact, the members of the stake presidency in Missouri, David Whitmer, William W. Phelps, and John Whitmer, were themselves in a state of apostasy at this time. This is helpful background for verse 2.

We will provide a bit more background on David Patten. He was born on November 14, 1799, in New York and was thus a little over six years older than Joseph Smith. He was a bit over six feet, one inch tall and weighed over two hundred pounds when he was baptized in the early 1830s. He was ordained an Apostle and member of the Twelve on February 15, 1835.

As we look back through the eyes of history, the mission call given to him in verse 1, next, may well have foreshadowed his martyrdom, and the mission was to the spirit world mission field.

He was fatally shot in Missouri in the abdomen by a member of a Missouri mob during the Battle of Crooked River on October 25, 1838. He was thirty-eight years of age.

We know through revelation that he returned to the presence of God, as stated by the Savior as follows:

D&C 124:130

130 David Patten I have taken unto myself; behold, his priesthood no man taketh from him; but, verily I say unto you, another may be appointed unto the same calling.

We will now read the two verses of section 114.

1 VERILY thus saith the Lord: It is wisdom in my servant David W. Patten, that he **settle up all his business as soon as he possibly can,** and make a disposition of his merchandise, **that he may perform a mission unto me** next spring, in company with others, even twelve including himself, to testify of my name and bear glad tidings unto all the world.

In verse 2, next, the Savior gives instruction regarding replacing those leaders who have gone into apostasy.

2 For verily thus saith the Lord, that **inasmuch as there are those among you who deny my name** [*who have apostatized and left the Church*], **others shall be planted in their stead and receive their bishopric** [*their leadership positions*]. Amen.

As implied in verse 2, above, this was indeed a difficult time in Missouri and an especially trying time as far as apostasy was concerned. Among the prominent members of the Church who left during this period were the following:

The Stake Presidency in Missouri

• David Whitmer—excommunicated on April 13, 1838.

• John Whitmer (also one of the Eight Witnesses of the Book of Mormon)—excommunicated on March 10, 1838.

• William W. Phelps—excommunicated on February 10, 1838.

Apostles

• Luke S. Johnson—excommunicated spring 1837.

• Lyman E. Johnson—excommunicated on April 13, 1838.

• John F. Boynton—excommunicated on April 12, 1838.

• William E. McLellin—excommunicated spring 1837.

Other

• Oliver Cowdery (one of the Three Witness)—excommunicated on April 12, 1838.

• Hiram Page (one of the Eight Witnesses)—excommunicated during this period in Far West, Missouri.

• Martin Harris (one of the Three Witnesses)—left the Church near the end of 1837.

SECTION 115

Background

This revelation was given through the Prophet Joseph Smith on April 26, 1838, at Far West, Missouri.

By the time of this revelation, Far West, Missouri, had become the main gathering place for members of the Church. It is located in Caldwell County, some fifty miles northeast of Independence.

In January 1838, the Prophet and other leaders of the Church left Kirtland, Ohio, forced to leave because of the apostasy there. The exodus continued, with most other faithful members following.

By this time, the citizens of Clay County, Missouri (to which the majority of the Missouri Saints had fled upon their expulsion from Jackson County), had requested that the Mormons move on. These citizens had been kind and generous to the impoverished Saints in the meantime, but the time had come when it was becoming a serious difficulty for Clay County to have the Latter-day Saints continue in their communities.

As a result, the state legislature of Missouri had exclusively established Caldwell County as a gathering place for the Saints. Far West, in Caldwell County, became the central gathering place. The Prophet and others joined the members of the Church there.

This revelation is addressed to the officers and members of the Church, and particularly to the First Presidency and the Presiding Bishopric.

1 VERILY **thus saith the Lord unto you,** my servant **Joseph Smith, Jun.,** and also my servant **Sidney Rigdon,** and also my servant **Hyrum Smith** [*the First Presidency*], **and your counselors who are and shall be appointed hereafter;**

It appears from the wording in verse 1, above, that President Joseph Smith had more than two counselors at this time. Indeed, this was the case. We will quote from the 1981 *Doctrine and Covenants Student Manual* in order to explain this (**bold** added for emphasis):

"At a conference held at Kirtland, Ohio, on 3 September 1837, Oliver Cowdery, Joseph Smith, Sr., Hyrum Smith, and John Smith were sustained as **assistant counselors**.

"At the time the revelation in Doctrine and Covenants 115 was given, however, only Joseph Smith, Sr., and John Smith were serving as assistant counselors (26 April 1838). Hyrum Smith had taken the place of Frederick G. Williams in the First Presidency, and Oliver Cowdery had lost his membership in the Church (see *History of the*

Church, 2:509; Smith, *Essentials in Church History,* 569).

"Later, in Nauvoo, others served as counselors to the Prophet: John C. Bennett (who served a short time because Sidney Rigdon was ill), William Law, and Amasa Lyman (see *History of the Church,* 4:255, 264, 282–86, 341)" (*Doctrine and Covenants Student Manual,* 1981, 286).

2 And also unto you, my servant Edward Partridge, and his counselors [*the Presiding Bishopric*];

Perhaps you have noticed in your reading of Church history that it was not until this time that the name of the Church was firmly established. Until this revelation was given, it was referred to by various names, including The Church of Christ, The Church of Jesus Christ, The Church of the Latter Day Saints, The Church of Christ of Latter Day Saints, and the Church of God. In verses 3 and 4, the Lord instructs as to the exact name of His Church in the last days.

The Official Name
of the Church

3 And also unto my faithful servants who are of the high council of my church in Zion, for thus it shall be called, and unto all the elders and people of my Church of Jesus Christ of Latter-day Saints, scattered abroad **in all the world;**

4 For **thus shall my church be called in the last days, even The Church of Jesus Christ of Latter-day Saints.**

In summing up a landmark address regarding our using the correct, revealed name of the Church (verse 4, above), the Prophet, President Russell M. Nelson, taught the following in the Sunday morning session of the October 2018 session of general conference:

"My dear brothers and sisters, I promise you that if we will do our best to restore the correct name of the Lord's Church, He whose Church this is will pour down His power and blessings upon the heads of the Latter-day Saints, the likes of which we have never seen. We will have the knowledge and power of God to help us take the blessings of the restored gospel of Jesus Christ to every nation, kindred, tongue, and people and to prepare the world for the Second Coming of the Lord.

"So, what's in a name? When it comes to the name of the Lord's Church, the answer is 'Everything!' Jesus Christ directed us to call the Church by His name because it is His Church, filled with His power."

Verse 5, next, is given to all members (see verse 3, above).

5 Verily I say unto you all: **Arise and shine forth, that thy light may be a standard for the nations;**

Verse 6, next, is quite often quoted in sermons and classes in the Church. It clearly states that a major purpose of stakes throughout the world is to serve as a "defense, and for a refuge" for the Saints. Wherever stakes exist, members have the full program of the Church available to them, including patriarchs who can give them their patriarchal blessings. They can associate with others who have similar beliefs and commitments to God. In our day, we are watching the continuing organization of stakes throughout the world.

6 And **that the gathering together upon the land of Zion, and upon her stakes, may be for a defense, and for a refuge from the storm**, and from wrath when it shall be poured out without mixture [*without being diluted*] upon the whole earth.

One other note about stakes, as mentioned in verse 6, above. In scriptural imagery and symbolism, stakes hold up the Church, just as stakes are used to hold up a tent. Isaiah uses this imagery to prophesy the last days' growth of the Church:

Isaiah 54:2

2 **Enlarge the place of thy tent** [*keep building new chapels, temples, and so forth to accommodate the growth of the Church*], and let them stretch forth the curtains of thine habitations: spare not, **lengthen thy cords,** and **strengthen thy stakes**;

Next, beginning with verse 7, the Lord teaches these members that they are on holy ground and that a temple is to be built in Far West. If you have ever been to Far West, you can testify that it is indeed holy ground because of the Spirit that abides there. The Lord commands them to begin laying the foundation on July 4, 1838.

7 **Let the city, Far West, be a holy and consecrated land unto me**; and it shall be called most holy, for **the ground upon which thou standest is holy**.

8 Therefore, **I command you to build a house** [*a temple*] **unto me**, for the gathering together of my saints, that they may worship me.

9 And **let there be a beginning of this work, and a foundation, and a preparatory work**, this following summer;

10 And **let the beginning be made on the fourth day of July next**; and from that time forth let

my people labor diligently to build a house unto my name;

In obedience to this commandment, more than five hundred men gathered on July 4, 1838, and dug a five-foot-deep foundation, 120 feet by 80 feet, in less than half a day. They also laid the four corner stones of the Far West Temple that day.

Beginning with verse 11, additional instructions are given regarding the building of the Far West Temple, including that this time the brethren are not to go into debt to build the temple, as was the case with the Kirtland Temple.

Looking at the difference in instructions for the Kirtland Temple and the Far West Temple, we are reminded that the leaders of the Church are guided by the Lord through ongoing revelation. And, when things are changed in the Church, we should rejoice in continuous revelation to the brethren, rather than wonder why they don't do things the same as in times past.

11 And **in one year from this day let them re-commence laying the foundation of my house.**

12 Thus **let them from that time forth labor diligently until it shall be finished,** from the corner stone thereof unto the top thereof, until there shall not anything remain that is not finished.

13 Verily I say unto you, **let not my servant Joseph, neither my servant Sidney, neither my servant Hyrum, get in debt any more for the building of a house unto my name;**

14 But **let a house be built unto my name according to the pattern which I will show unto them.**

15 And **if my people build it not according to the pattern which I shall show unto their presidency, I will not accept it** at their hands.

16 But **if my people do build it according to the pattern which I shall show unto their presidency,** even my servant Joseph and his counselors, **then I will accept it** at the hands of my people.

Beginning with verse 17, next, we see another example of a change in how things are to be done (in other words, an example of ongoing revelation). In D&C 58:56, the Saints were instructed not to gather "in haste, nor by flight." Again, in D&C 63:24, they were told to gather to Zion, in Missouri, "not in haste." Yet, here, they are told to gather "speedily" to Far West.

17 And again, verily I say unto you, it is my will that the city of **Far West should be built up speedily by the gathering of my saints;**

Have you noticed that the Lord specifically shows support for His prophet in the eyes of the people? He has done this a number of times already (see D&C 28:2; 43:3–5; 112:15) and does it again in verses 18–19, next. This is yet another reminder to us that the Lord sustains His living prophet and that we are completely safe following him.

It is also particularly significant considering the apostasy taking place in Ohio and Missouri at the time of this revelation, as pointed out in the notes accompanying section 114 in this study guide.

18 And **also that other places should be appointed for stakes in the regions round about, as they shall be manifested unto my servant Joseph**, from time to time.

19 For behold, **I will be with him, and I will sanctify him before the people; for unto him have I given the keys of this kingdom and ministry**. Even so. Amen.

SECTION 116

Background

This revelation was given to the Prophet Joseph Smith on May 19, 1838, at a place called Spring Hill in the area the Lord refers to as Adam-ondi-Ahman in Missouri.

The Prophet recorded the following (**bold** added for emphasis):

"In the afternoon I went up the river [*the Grand River*] about half a mile to Wight's Ferry, accompanied by President Rigdon, and my clerk, George W. Robinson, for the purpose of selecting and laying claim to a city plat near said ferry in Daviess County, township 60, ranges 27 and 28, and sections 25, 36, 31, and 30, **which the brethren called 'Spring Hill,' but by the mouth of the Lord it was named Adam-ondi-Ahman**" (*History of the Church,* 3:35).

Adam-ondi-Ahman is located in Missouri roughly seventy miles north, northeast of Independence. While we do not know the exact meaning of the name Adam-ondi-Ahman, Bruce R. McConkie explains that we do have some clues. He said:

"Adam was the first man of all men; Ahman is one of the names by which God was known to Adam [D&C 78:20, 95:17]. Adam-ondi-Ahman, a name carried over from the pure Adamic language into English, is one for which we have not been given a revealed, literal translation. As near as we can judge—and this view comes down from the early brethren who associated with the Prophet Joseph Smith, who was the first one to use the name in this dispensation—Adam-ondi-Ahman means the place or land of God where Adam dwelt" (*Mormon Doctrine,* 19).

We will first go through the verse and then add additional commentary.

1 Spring Hill is named by the Lord **Adam-ondi-Ahman**, because, said he, it **is the place where Adam shall come to visit his people**, or the Ancient of Days [*Adam*] shall sit, as spoken of by Daniel the prophet [*in Daniel 7:9–14*].

In the Doctrine and Covenants we are taught that a great conference of Adam and Eve's righteous posterity was held in Adam-ondi-Ahman, three years prior to Adam's death. We read:

D&C 107:53–56

53 **Three years previous to the death of Adam, he called Seth, Enos, Cainan, Mahalaleel, Jared, Enoch, and Methuselah**, who were all high priests, **with the residue of his posterity who were righteous, into the valley of Adam-ondi-Ahman**, and there bestowed upon them his last blessing.

54 And **the Lord appeared unto them**, and **they rose up and blessed Adam**, and called him Michael, the prince, the archangel.

55 And **the Lord administered comfort unto Adam**, and said

unto him: I have set thee to be at the head; a multitude of nations shall come of thee, and thou art a prince over them forever.

56 **And Adam stood up** in the midst of the congregation; **and, notwithstanding he was bowed down with age, being full of the Holy Ghost, predicted whatsoever should befall his posterity unto the latest generation**.

Shortly before the Second Coming of Christ, another great council will be held at Adam-ondi-Ahman. We read of this in the book of Daniel in the Old Testament. He had a vision in which he saw that millions of righteous people will attend this great meeting.

Daniel 7:9–10, 13–14

9 **I beheld till the thrones were cast down** [*Daniel saw the future, including the downfall of governments in the last days, as spoken of in D&C 87:6*], and **the Ancient of days** [*Adam*] **did sit** [*compare with the last part of this section*], whose garment *was* white as snow, and the hair of his head like the pure wool: his throne [*Adam is in a position of great power and authority*] *was like* the fiery flame, *and* his wheels *as* burning fire.

10 A fiery stream issued and came forth from before him: **thousand thousands** [*millions*] **ministered unto him, and ten thousand times ten thousand** [*a hundred million*] **stood before him**: the judgment was set, and the books were opened.

13 **I** [*Daniel*] **saw in the night visions,** and, behold, *one* **like the Son of man** [*a biblically respectful way of saying Jehovah, or in other words, Christ*] came with the clouds of heaven, and **came to the Ancient of days**, and they brought him near before him.

Next, we see, in Daniel's vision that the keys of leadership are given back to Christ during this grand council in preparation for His ruling and reigning as "Lord of lords, and King of kings" (Revelation 17:14) during the Millennium.

14 And **there was given him** [*Christ*] **dominion,** and **glory,** and **a kingdom, that all people, nations, and languages, should serve him** [*during the Millennium*]: his dominion *is* an everlasting dominion, which shall not pass away, and his kingdom *that* which shall not be destroyed.

Joseph Fielding Smith taught about this meeting at Adam-ondi-Ahman before the Second

Coming. He said that "all who have held keys will make their reports and deliver their stewardships, as they shall be required. Adam will . . . then . . . make his report, as the one holding the keys for this earth, to his Superior Officer, Jesus Christ. Our Lord will then assume the reins of government; directions will be given to the Priesthood; and He, whose right it is to rule, will be installed officially by the voice of the Priesthood there assembled. This grand council of Priesthood will be composed, not only of those who are faithful who now dwell on this earth, but also of the prophets and apostles of old, who have had directing authority. Others may also be there, but if so they will be there by appointment, for this is to be an official council called to attend to the most momentous matters concerning the destiny of this earth" (*Way to Perfection,* 1984 hardcover edition, 290–91).

Among other things, Bruce R. McConkie taught the following about this council at Adam-ondi-Ahman (**bold** added for emphasis):

"But Daniel has yet more to say about the great events soon to transpire at Adam-ondi-Ahman. And we need not suppose that all these things shall happen in one single meeting or at one single hour in time. It is proper to hold numerous meetings at a general conference, some for the instruction of leaders, others for edification of all the saints. In some, business is transacted; others are for worship and spiritual refreshment. And so Daniel says: 'I saw in the night visions, and, behold, one like the Son of man came with the clouds of heaven, and came to the Ancient of days, and they brought him near before him.' **Christ comes to Adam**, who is sitting in glory. He comes to conform to his own priestal order. He comes to hear the report of Adam for his stewardship. **He comes to take back the keys of the earthly kingdom**. He comes to be invested with glory and dominion so that he can reign personally upon the earth" (*Millennial Messiah,* 585).

You may wish to read more about this meeting at Adam-ondi-Ahman in *The Millennial Messiah* (quoted above), 578–88.

Brother McConkie also taught:

"At this council, all who have held keys of authority will give an accounting of their stewardship to Adam. Christ will then come, receive back the keys, and thus take one of the final steps preparatory to reigning personally upon the earth. (Dan. 7:9–14; *Teachings*, p. 157.)" (*Mormon Doctrine,* 21).

Before we leave section 116, we will consider one other insight. It is interesting to note that the Garden of Eden was located in what is now Jackson County, Missouri.

Joseph Fielding Smith taught this as follows:

"In accord with the revelations given to the Prophet Joseph Smith, we teach that the Garden of Eden was on the American continent located where the City Zion [in Jackson County, Missouri], or the New Jerusalem, will be built. . . . When Adam and Eve were driven out of the Garden, they eventually dwelt at a place called Adam-ondi-Ahman, situated in what is now Daviess County, Missouri" (*Doctrines of Salvation,* 3:74).

Thus, when Adam and Eve were cast out from the Garden of Eden, they went to the area of Adam-ondi-Ahman to dwell. In other words, things got started in Missouri in the Garden of Eden as far as mortal life on this earth is concerned. It will have gone full-circle back to Missouri with the council at Adam-ondi-Ahman as the time for the Millennium approaches.

SECTION 117

Background

This revelation was given through the Prophet Joseph Smith to William Marks, Newel K. Whitney, and Oliver Granger on July 8, 1838, at Far West, Missouri. It is the first of five given on this date and recorded in the Prophet's journal. Sections 118, 119, 120, and an unpublished one to

Frederick G. Williams and William W. Phelps are the other four.

Because of the apostasy and dangerous conditions that had developed in Kirtland, Joseph Smith and Sidney Rigdon had fled to Far West in January 1838. William Marks had been assigned to remain in Kirtland and take care of the Church's temporal concerns there. Newell Whitney was the bishop in Kirtland. Oliver Granger was a member of the Kirtland high council as well as a financial agent for the Church there. He traveled to Far West, arriving by July 8, 1838.

In section 115, verse 17, the Lord commanded the Saints in Kirtland to come "speedily" to Far West. That commandment was given April 26, 1838. On July 6, 1838, a company of 515, known as the "Kirtland Camp," left Kirtland for Far West. However, some of the members of the Church in Kirtland who owned property had a hard time parting with it. Among these were William Marks and Bishop Newel K. Whitney. They were not with this company.

Two days later, in this revelation, the Lord revealed to the Prophet that Brother Marks and Bishop Whitney were not coming with the company from Kirtland. Their hearts were set on their temporal properties and concerns to the point that they would not comply with the command to come quickly to Far West. The fact that the

Prophet Joseph Smith knew their situation just two days after the Kirtland Camp left is a testimony of his calling as the Prophet.

In verses 1–9, the Savior teaches a short course in perspective to William Marks (*a member of the Kirtland high council and an "agent" called to assist Bishop Whitney*) and Newel K. Whitney (*the Bishop in Kirtland*) regarding the relative worth of "property" (verse 4) compared to eternal blessings and the worth of the "drop" compared to "the more weighty matters" (verse 8). This is an important course for all of us.

1 VERILY **thus saith the Lord unto** my servant **William Marks, and also** unto my servant **Newel K. Whitney,** let them **settle up their business speedily and journey from the land of Kirtland,** before I, the Lord, send again the snows upon the earth.

2 **Let them awake, and arise, and come forth, and not tarry, for I, the Lord, command it.**

3 Therefore, **if they tarry it shall not be well with them.**

4 **Let them repent of all their sins, and of all their covetous desires** [*including coveting their own property and finances over and above the value of obedience to the Lord's commands to quickly relocate*

to *Far West*], before me, saith the Lord; **for what is property unto me? saith the Lord.**

Next, in verse 5, the Lord instructs these men to sell their property and Church property to pay the debts of the Church, and if any is left over after that, they may keep it.

5 Let the properties of Kirtland be turned out for debts, saith the Lord. **Let them go** [*let go of your holdings*], saith the Lord, and **whatsoever remaineth, let it remain in your hands**, saith the Lord.

Next, in verses 6–7, the Savior reminds them who it is who is giving them this command, with special emphasis on the fact that He has the power to keep His promises to them if they obey Him and come quickly to Far West.

6 For have I not the fowls of heaven, and also the fish of the sea, and the beasts of the mountains? Have I not made the earth? Do I not hold the destinies of all the armies of the nations of the earth?

7 Therefore, will I not make solitary places to bud and to blossom, and to bring forth in abundance? saith the Lord.

8 Is there not room enough on the mountains of Adam-ondi-Ahman,

and on the plains of Olaha Shinehah [*perhaps a part of Adam-ondi-Ahman; Shinehah means "sun" according to Abraham 3:13*], or the land where Adam dwelt, **that you should covet that which is but the drop, and neglect the more weighty matters?**

9 Therefore, come up hither unto the land of my people, even Zion.

Verse 10, next, is given to Brother Marks. He will accept the counsel and will come to Far West. But he will not be completely successful in overcoming the tendencies that caused him to hesitate in the first place. Eventually, he will apostatize, join the conspirators against Joseph Smith, and after the Martyrdom, he will join one break-off group from the Church after another, finally settling in the Reorganized Church of Jesus Christ of Latter-Day Saints where he stayed until his death at age seventy-nine on May 22, 1872.

10 Let my servant William Marks be faithful over a few things, and he shall be a ruler over many [*a formula for obtaining exaltation*]. **Let him preside in the midst of my people in the city of Far West, and let him be blessed with the blessings of my people.**

As you can see, verse 11, next, is a rather stinging rebuke to Bishop

Whitney. The "Nicolaitane band" is a reference to Revelation 2:6 and refers to people who want to be in the world and in the Church at the same time. In other words, they want to be loyal to the Church, but they also want to be loyal to their worldly pursuits and selfish interests. It can't be done.

11 **Let my servant Newel K. Whitney be ashamed of the Nicolaitane band** and of all their secret abominations, **and of all his littleness of soul** before me, saith the Lord, **and come up to the land of Adam-ondi-Ahman, and be a bishop** unto my people, saith the Lord, **not in name but in deed** [*you must carry out your duties as bishop, not just have the title*], saith the Lord.

Bishop Whitney accepted this counsel and rebuke and came to Far West. He humbly worked on overcoming the weaknesses spoken of by the Lord in verse 11, above, and grew in wisdom and ability to serve faithfully. He remained a dear friend of the Prophet, and after the Martyrdom, he was called as the Presiding Bishop of the Church.

He and his family came west with the Saints, arriving in the Salt Lake Valley in 1848. He passed away, faithful to the end, on Monday, September 23, 1850.

Next, the Lord compliments Oliver Granger, who had already come to Far West from Kirtland. He was a humble man of faith who had great business skills. He personally carried a copy of this revelation to his associates William Marks and Newel K. Whitney in Kirtland after the Prophet received it.

12 And again, I say unto you, **I remember my servant Oliver Granger**; behold, verily I say unto him that **his name shall be had in sacred remembrance from generation to generation**, forever and ever, saith the Lord.

Next, in verse 13, Brother Granger is appointed to help settle the debts of the Church in Kirtland. He was so successful and demonstrated such high integrity in accomplishing this that he became highly respected in the Kirtland area.

13 Therefore, **let him contend earnestly for the redemption of the First Presidency** of my Church [*among other things, help them pay off their debts and the debts of the Church incurred at Kirtland*], saith the Lord; and when he falls he shall rise again, for **his sacrifice shall be more sacred unto me than his increase** [*his personal profits from business ventures*], saith the Lord.

14 Therefore, **let him come up hither speedily** [*return quickly from*

Kirtland back to Far West], **unto the land of Zion**; and in the due time he shall be made a merchant unto my name, saith the Lord, for the benefit of my people.

15 Therefore **let no man despise my servant Oliver Granger, but let the blessings of my people be on him forever and ever.**

Oliver Granger moved with the Saints to Commerce (Nauvoo), Illinois, and became a land agent for the First Presidency. He was again sent to Kirtland in 1840, representing the Prophet to settle remaining financial matters of the Church. He died faithful in Kirtland in 1841 at age forty-seven.

Verse 16, next, is addressed to all members of the Church in the Kirtland area. The phrase "in mine own due time" is a reminder that the Lord's timetable is often different than ours.

16 And again, verily I say unto you, **let all my servants in the land of Kirtland remember the Lord their God, and mine house** [*the Kirtland Temple*] **also, to keep and preserve it holy,** and to overthrow the moneychangers [*probably a reference to those who are taking dishonest advantage of the Saints as they move out to go to Far West*] **in mine own due time**, saith the Lord. Even so. Amen.

SECTION 118

Background

This revelation was given through the Prophet Joseph Smith on July 8, 1838, at Far West, Missouri. It is one of five given on the same day (as explained in the background notes to section 117 in this study guide).

As you can see in the heading to section 118 in your Doctrine and Covenants, this revelation came in response to the request, "Show us thy will, O Lord, concerning the Twelve."

By way of background, by now Apostles John F. Boynton, Luke Johnson, Lyman Johnson, and William E. McLellin had apostatized and been excommunicated.

In verse 1, the Savior instructs that the Quorum of the Twelve should be reorganized with new Apostles called to replace those who apostatized. In verse 6, He will give the names of those who are to be called as Apostles in order for this reorganization to take place.

1 VERILY, thus saith the Lord: **Let a conference be held immediately; let the Twelve be organized; and let men be appointed to supply the place of those who are fallen.**

Next, in verse 2, Thomas B. Marsh is told to stay in Missouri and preach the gospel there for the time being.

2 Let my servant Thomas remain for a season in the land of Zion, to publish my word.

Brother Marsh was publishing the *Elders' Journal* in Far West at this time, which he had already been publishing in Kirtland. It ran from October 1837 to August 1838.

Next, the remaining faithful Apostles are given a conditional promise regarding their families.

3 Let the residue [*the rest of the Twelve*] **continue to preach** from that hour, **and if they will do this in all lowliness of heart, in meekness and humility, and long-suffering, I, the Lord, give unto them a promise that I will provide for their families;** **and an effectual door shall be opened for them, from henceforth** [*from now on*]**.**

Perhaps you've noticed that temporal blessings are conditional upon our faithfulness and sometimes upon the faithfulness of others.

Ultimately, however, our exaltation is based upon our own use of moral agency, coupled with the Savior's Atonement. We cannot blame anyone else if we fail. In other words, each person is ultimately responsible for whether he or she is saved. Brigham Young

taught this. He said (**bold** added for emphasis):

"Who has influence over any one of you, to cause you to miss salvation in the celestial kingdom of God? I will answer these questions for myself. If brother Brigham and I shall take a wrong track, and be shut out of the kingdom of heaven, no person will be to blame but brother Brigham and I. **I am the only being in heaven, earth, or hell, that can be blamed**.

"This will equally apply to every Latter-day Saint. **Salvation is an individual operation. I am the only person that can possibly save myself**. When salvation is sent to me, I can reject or receive it" (*Journal of Discourses*, 1:312).

Next, in verses 4–5, the members of the Twelve, including the new ones to be called, are commanded to go on an overseas mission, leaving from Far West on April 26, 1839. The specifying of such an exact date by the Lord sets the groundwork for a marvelous miracle.

4 And next spring let them depart to go over the great waters, and there promulgate [*spread, preach*] **my gospel,** the fulness thereof, **and bear record of my name.**

5 Let them take **leave** of my saints **in the city of Far West, on the twenty-sixth day of April**

next, on the building-spot of my house [*from the Far West Temple site*], saith the Lord.

We will explain the "marvelous miracle" mentioned above. By the time April 26, 1839, arrived, the Saints had been completely driven from Missouri and into Illinois. Not only that, but also some of the Missourians knew of the plan of the Twelve to leave from Far West on that date. They were determined to prevent it so that Joseph Smith would become a false prophet, at least as far as this prophecy was concerned. Any members of the Church who entered Missouri were "fair game."

Nevertheless, the prophecy was fulfilled. Just after midnight on April 26, 1839, Apostles Brigham Young, Heber C. Kimball, Orson Pratt, John E. Page, John Taylor, Wilford Woodruff, and George A. Smith, along with about twenty other members of the Church, gathered at the Far West Temple site as a preliminary to the mission of several of the Twelve to England. They sang part of a hymn, and Elder Alpheus Cutler, the master workman of the house, then recommenced laying the foundation of the Lord's House by rolling a large stone near the southeast corner. All seven of the Apostles present offered prayers, and the group sang the hymn "Adam-ondi-Ahman." We will quote from *History of the Church* for what happened after this:

"Thus was fulfilled a revelation of July 8, 1838, which our enemies had said could not be fulfilled, as no 'Mormon' would be permitted to be in the state.

"As the Saints were passing away from the meeting, Brother Turley said to Elders Page and Woodruff, 'Stop a bit, while I bid Isaac Russell [*an apostate and enemy to the Church*] good bye;' and knocking at the door, called Brother Russell. His wife answered, 'Come in, it is Brother Turley.' Russell replied, 'It is not; he left here two weeks ago;' and appeared quite alarmed; but on finding it was Brother Turley, asked him to sit down; but the latter replied, 'I cannot, I shall lose my company.' 'Who is your company?' enquired Russell. 'The Twelve.' '*The Twelve!*' 'Yes, don't you know that this is the twenty-sixth, and the day the Twelve were to take leave of their friends on the foundation of the Lord's House, to go to the islands of the sea? The revelation is now fulfilled, and I am going with them.' Russell was speechless, and Turley bid him farewell.

"The brethren immediately returned to Quincy, taking with them the families from Tenney's Grove" (*History of the Church,* 3:340).

Wilford Woodruff recorded what happened:

"When the revelation was given [in 1838], all was peace and quietude in Far West, Missouri, the city where most of the Latter-day Saints dwelt; but before the time came for its fulfillment, the Saints of God had been driven out of the State of Missouri into the State of Illinois, under the edict of Governor Boggs; and the Missourians had sworn that if all the other revelations of Joseph Smith were fulfilled, that [one] should not be. It stated the day and the place where the Twelve Apostles should take leave of the Saints, to go on their mission across the great waters, and the mobocrats of Missouri had declared that they would see that it should not be fulfilled. . . .

"Having determined to carry out the requirement of the revelation, . . . we started for Far West. . . .

"On the morning of the 26th of April, 1839, notwithstanding the threats of our enemies that the revelation which was to be fulfilled this day should not be, and notwithstanding that ten thousand of the Saints had been driven out of the State by the edict of the governor, . . . we moved on to the temple ground in the city of Far West, and held a council, and fulfilled the revelation and commandment given unto us, and we performed many other things at this council. . . .

"Bidding good-by to the small remnant of Saints who remained on the temple ground to see us fulfill the revelation and commandments of God, we turned our back on Far West and Missouri, and returned to Illinois. We had accomplished the mission without a dog moving his tongue at us [see Exodus 11:7], or any man saying, 'Why do you so?'" (*Teachings: Wilford Woodruff*, 139–41).

As mentioned previously, verse 6, next, names four men to replace the four Apostles who had apostatized.

6 Let my servant **John Taylor,** and also my servant **John E. Page,** and also my servant **Wilford Woodruff,** and also my servant **Willard Richards,** be appointed to fill the places of those who have fallen, and be officially notified of their appointment.

Of the four men called to be Apostles in verse 6, above, all but John E. Page will remain faithful, and as you can see, two of them, John Taylor and Wilford Woodruff, will eventually serve as presidents of the Church.

Elder Page was called in April 1840 to accompany Orson Hyde to dedicate Palestine for the return of the Jews. He started out on the journey but would not leave the United States, thus forcing Elder Hyde to go alone. After the martyrdom of Joseph Smith, Page affiliated with apostate James Strang and was excommunicated on June 26, 1846. He left the Strangites in 1849 and joined the Brewsterites (another break-off from the Church). He left them in 1850 and joined another faction.

Finally, he joined the Hedrikites and became an apostle in that break-off organization. He helped them secure ownership of the temple site in Independence, Missouri, which they still own today. He died on October 14, 1867, at age sixty-eight.

SECTION 119

Background

This revelation was one of five given through the Prophet Joseph Smith on the same day—July 8, 1838—in Far West, Missouri. See the background for section 117 in this study guide for more information.

This section and section 120 go together since they both involve the law of tithing. This is the section in which we are instructed that tithing is ten percent of our income annually. For additional background, we will quote the heading to section 119 as given in your Doctrine and Covenants.

"*Revelation given through Joseph Smith the Prophet, at Far West, Missouri, July 8, 1838, in answer to his supplication: 'O Lord, show unto thy servants how much thou requirest of the properties of thy people for a tithing.' HC 3:44. The law of tithing, as understood today, had not been given to the Church previous to this revelation.*

The term 'tithing' in the prayer just quoted and in previous revelations (64:23; 85:3; 97:11) had meant not just one-tenth, but all free-will offerings, or contributions, to the Church funds. The Lord had previously given to the Church the law of consecration and stewardship of property, which members (chiefly the leading elders) entered into by a covenant that was to be everlasting. Because of failure on the part of many to abide by this covenant, the Lord withdrew it for a time, and gave instead the law of tithing to the whole Church. The Prophet asked the Lord how much of their property he required for sacred purposes. The answer was this revelation."

Joseph Fielding Smith also explained the background to this section. He said:

"The Lord had given to the Church the law of consecration and had called upon the members, principally the official members, to enter into a covenant that could not be broken and to be everlasting in which they were to consecrate their properties and receive stewardships, for this is the law of the celestial kingdom. Many of those who entered into this solemn covenant broke it and by so doing brought upon their heads, and the heads of their brethren and sisters, dire punishment and persecution. This celestial law of necessity was thereupon withdrawn for the time, or until the time of the redemption of Zion. While suffering intensely because of their debts and lack of means to meet their obligations Joseph Smith and Oliver Cowdery, November 29, 1834, in solemn prayer promised the Lord that they would give one tenth of all that the Lord should give unto them, as an offering to be bestowed upon the poor; they also prayed that their children, and the children's children after them should obey this law. (*History of the Church,* 2:174–75.) Now, however, it became necessary for the law to be given to the whole Church so the Prophet prayed for instruction. The answer they received [came] in the revelation [D&C 119]" (*Church History and Modern Revelation,* 2:90–91).

The "covenant" made by Joseph Smith and Oliver Cowdery in 1834, referenced by Joseph Fielding Smith in the above quote, was recorded by the Prophet as follows:

"On the evening of the 29th of November, I united in prayer with Brother Oliver for the continuance of blessings. After giving thanks for the relief which the Lord had lately sent us by opening the hearts of the brethren from the east, to loan us $430; after commencing and rejoicing before the Lord on this occasion, we agreed to enter into the following covenant with the Lord, viz.:

"That if the Lord will prosper us in our business and open the way before us that we may obtain means to pay our debts; that we be not troubled nor brought into disrepute before the world, nor His people; after that, of all that He shall give unto us, we will give a tenth to be bestowed upon the poor in His Church, or as He shall command; and that we will be faithful over that which He has entrusted to our care, that we may obtain much; and that our children after us shall remember to observe this sacred and holy covenant; and that our children, and our children's children, may know of the same, we have subscribed our names with our own hands.

"(Signed)

Joseph Smith, Jun.

Oliver Cowdery"

(*History of the Church,* 2:174–75).

Tithing is an established principle in the Bible and is required of worthy temple recommend holders today. It was paid by Abraham to Melchizedek (see Genesis 14:20), is taught strongly in Malachi 3:8–12, and was commonly paid in New Testament times (see Matthew 23:23, Luke 18:12).

As noted in the background given above, at the time of this revelation the Church and its leaders were deeply in debt. In answer to the Prophet's question that led up to this revelation, the Lord spelled out what was to be done. First, as stated in verses 1–3, all members of the Church were to donate their "surplus property" (verse 1) to the

Church, for several purposes as given in verse 2. In this context, surplus meant all that they could spare, above and beyond their basic needs.

1 VERILY, thus saith the Lord, **I require all their surplus property to be put into the hands of the bishop** of my church in Zion,

2 **For the building of mine house** [*the temple in Far West*], and **for the laying of the foundation of Zion** [*establishing the Church in Missouri*] and **for the priesthood, and for the debts of the Presidency of my Church**.

3 And **this shall be the beginning of the tithing of my people**.

In other words, this will set the stage for beginning to practice the law of tithing, meaning that, from this time on, members will pay ten percent of their annual income as tithing to the Church, through the bishop, as stated in verse 4, next.

4 And **after that**, those who have thus been tithed [*who have given all their surplus, as commanded in verses 1–3, above*] shall **pay one-tenth of all their interest annually**; and this shall be a standing law unto them forever, for my holy priesthood, saith the Lord.

The word "interest," in verse 4, above, needs to be defined as commonly used at the time of this revelation. Otherwise, there could be many different definitions, which would affect how much tithing we pay. The word "interest" means income as used in D&C 124:89.

Also, an entry in John Taylor's *Nauvoo Journal,* dated Saturday, January 11, 1845, defines the term. Regarding the payment of tithing, he wrote (**bold** added for emphasis):

"One tenth of their interest, or **income** yearly afterward" (*BYU Studies,* Vol. 23 [Summer 1983]: 20).

Even if we didn't have Elder Taylor's definition of "interest" as being "income," we have the words of our modern prophets and Apostles instructing us on this matter. For example, Apostle John A. Widtsoe taught (**bold** added for emphasis):

"Tithing means one-tenth. Those who give less do not really pay tithing; they are lesser contributors to the Latter-day cause of the Lord. **Tithing means one-tenth of a person's income**, interest, or increase. The merchant should pay tithing upon the net income of his business, the farmer upon the net income of his farming operations; the wage earner or salaried man upon the wage or salary earned by him. Out of the remaining nine-tenths he pays his current expenses, taxes, savings, etc. To deduct living costs, taxes, and similar expenses from the income and pay tithing upon the remainder does not conform to the Lord's commandment. Under such a system most people would show nothing on which to pay tithing. There is really no place for quibbling on this point. **Tithing should be given upon the basis of our full earned income**. If the nature of a business requires special interpretation, the tithepayer should consult the father of his ward, the bishop" (*Evidences and Reconciliations,* 86).

In general conference, President Spencer W. Kimball taught (**bold** used for emphasis):

"Inquiries are received at the office of the First Presidency from time to time from officers and members of the Church asking for information as to what is considered a proper tithe.

"We have uniformly replied that the simplest statement we know of is the statement of the Lord himself, namely, that the members of the Church should pay '**one-tenth of all their interest annually**' which **is understood to mean income** (see D&C 119:4)" ("The Law of Tithing," *Ensign,* November 1980, 77).

Verse 5, next, summarizes verses 1–4, above, stating that all members at the time who are gathering to Missouri are to donate all their surplus to the Church and then pay tithing (as defined in verse 4) thereafter.

5 Verily I say unto you, it shall come to pass that **all those who gather unto the land of Zion shall be tithed of their surplus properties, and shall observe this law** [*pay ten percent of their income annually*], or they shall not be found worthy to abide among you.

Verse 6, next, contains a warning about what will happen if the Saints do not keep these commandments.

6 And I say unto you, **if my people observe not this law**, to keep it holy, and by this law sanctify the land of Zion unto me, that my statutes and my judgments may be kept thereon, that it may be most holy, behold, verily I say unto you, **it shall not be a land of Zion unto you**.

The same lesson (end of verse 6, above) could be applied to members of the Church today who have tithing to pay but don't. In effect, the Church will not be Zion to them because they are not qualifying for the blessings of faithful membership.

Next, in verse 7, the Savior applies the law of tithing to all members of the Church, not just those emigrating to Missouri at the time of this revelation. Thus, worthy members pay an honest tithe today.

7 And **this shall be an ensample** [*example*] **unto all the stakes of Zion**. Even so. Amen.

Elder David A. Bednar taught what the payment of tithing does for each of us:

"The honest payment of tithing is much more than a duty; it is an important step in the process of personal sanctification" ("The Windows of Heaven," *Ensign*, Nov. 2013, 20).

By the way, "sanctification" means made pure and holy and fit to be in the presence of God.

SECTION 120

Background

This revelation was given through the Prophet Joseph Smith on July 8, 1838, at Far West, Missouri.

According to *The Joseph Smith Papers,* from the time of the organization of the Church on April 6, 1830, the funds of the Church were managed and distributed by various leaders, including bishops and members of the United Firm, the First Presidency, stake presidencies, and the high council (see *The Joseph Smith Papers, Documents, Volume 6: February 1838–August 1839*, 189).

This revelation specifically specifies and defines the committee that oversees the use and spending of the tithing funds of the

Church. As you will see, the Savior is a member of this committee. There are nineteen members who serve on this council. We will use **bold** to point them out.

1 VERILY, thus saith the Lord, the time is now come, that **it** [*tithing—see section 119*] **shall be disposed of** [*spent*] **by a council**, composed of **the First Presidency** [*who are three members serving on this Council on the Disposition of the Tithes*] of my Church, and of **the bishop and his council** [*the Presiding Bishopric—three more members*], and by **my high council** [*the Quorum of the Twelve Apostles—twelve more members*]; and by **mine own voice** [*the Savior, making 19 members in all who serve on this council that oversees the spending of the tithing funds of the Church*] **unto them**, saith the Lord. Even so. Amen.

As you can see from the above revelation, we have absolutely no concerns or worries about the use and spending of the tithing we pay.

SECTION 121

Background

This section, as well as sections 122 and 123, are taken from two letters written between March 20–25, 1839 (see footnote in *History of the* Church, 3:289), by the

Prophet Joseph Smith from Liberty Jail in Liberty, Missouri. They were addressed to Bishop Edward Partridge and the Saints who had now taken refuge in Quincy, Illinois, and surrounding locations. We will include the complete text of these letters at the end of section 123 in this study guide, with sections 121, 122, and 123 in **bold.**

As the Saints continued to gather to Missouri, tensions continued to rise. Even though the Missouri state legislature had established two new counties, Caldwell and Daviess in northwestern Missouri, with the express purpose of providing a place for members to gather, many old settlers opposed this gathering. They formed mobs and began persecuting the Saints anew in the summer of 1838. Parley P. Pratt described the situation as follows:

"Soon after these things the war clouds began again to lower with dark and threatening aspect. Those who had combined against the laws in the adjoining counties [especially Jackson County], had long watched our increasing power and prosperity with jealousy, and with greedy and avaricious eyes. It was a common boast that, as soon as we had completed our extensive improvements, and made a plentiful crop, they would drive us from the State, and once more enrich themselves with the spoils" (*Autobiography of Parley P. Pratt,* 150).

Persecution of the Saints continued through the rest of the summer and into the fall. Mobs burned houses and crops, stole domestic animals, took prisoners, beat men, and ravished Mormon women.

On October 27, 1838, Gov. Lilburn W. Boggs of Missouri, believing false reports about the Saints and refusing to investigate the reports himself, issued the infamous "extermination order" that stated: "The Mormons must be treated as enemies and must be exterminated or driven from the state, if necessary for the public good. Their outrages are beyond all description" (*History of the Church,* 3:175).

Among the atrocities committed against the Saints was the Haun's Mill Massacre. On Tuesday afternoon, October 30, 1838, about 240 mobbers approached the small LDS settlement of Haun's Mill (sometimes spelled "Hawn's Mill") about twelve miles east of Far West. As the women and children fled into the surrounding woods, most of the men ran into the blacksmith shop. The mob shot without mercy at women and children, as well as men, and with devilish glee, hacked one of the men to death with a corn knife. In all, at least seventeen settlers of Haun's Mill were killed and about thirteen were wounded. It is sad to note that Jacob Haun, the leader of this settlement, had disregarded the counsel of the

Prophet in which he counseled all of the Saints in nearby settlements to gather immediately to Far West where they could take a stand together against the mobs.

By October 31, 1838, more than two thousand Missourians surrounded Far West, threatening to carry out the governor's orders to drive the Mormons from the state or exterminate them. On the same day, Joseph Smith and other Church leaders were betrayed into the hands of General Samuel D. Lucas, leader of the Missouri state militia. They were mistreated, imprisoned, and tried. By the end of November, the Prophet and five others, including his brother Hyrum and Sidney Rigdon, were placed in Liberty Jail, where they languished in the most miserable winter conditions from November 30, 1838, to the first part of April 1839.

Liberty Jail was a cold, poorly ventilated stone dungeon, with four-foot-thick walls and two small barred windows. The outside measured twenty-two and a half feet long, twenty-two feet wide, with twelve-foot-high walls, making the interior measurements about fourteen by fourteen by twelve feet. It had an upper level and a lower level, with access to the lower level through a hole in the upper floor. Joseph Smith was six feet tall and could not stand up straight in the lower level. They were forced to sleep on filthy straw on the hard floor or on split logs. They were served filthy food and suffered terribly from the winter cold.

And perhaps worst of all, they were helpless to assist their families and the rest of the Saints who were at the same time being driven completely from the state. Imagine the feelings of the Prophet Joseph Smith, who had seen the Father and the Son, Moroni, John the Baptist, Peter, James, and John, Moses, Elias, Elijah, and many others, and whose prayers had been answered countless times, who had been saved and protected on so many occasions. He now found himself in such a miserable prison, with the days turning to weeks and then to months. Imagine the anguish in his heart that caused him, after almost four months in this vile prison, to cry out:

1 **O GOD, where art thou?** And where is the pavilion [*in biblical imagery, the place where Jehovah dwells in His majesty—compare with Psalm 27:4–5*] that covereth thy hiding place?

2 **How long shall thy hand be stayed**, and thine eye, yea thy pure eye, behold from the eternal heavens the wrongs of thy people and of thy servants, and thine ear be penetrated with their cries?

3 Yea, O Lord, **how long shall they suffer these wrongs and**

unlawful oppressions, before thine heart shall be softened toward them, and thy bowels be moved with compassion toward them?

4 O Lord God Almighty, maker of heaven, earth, and seas, and of all things that in them are, and who controllest and subjectest the devil, and the dark and benighted dominion of Sheol—stretch forth thy hand [*exercise Thy power*]; let thine eye pierce; let thy pavilion be taken up; let thy hiding place no longer be covered; let thine ear be inclined; let thine heart be softened, and thy bowels [*a biblical term for deepest feelings and emotions*] moved with compassion toward us.

5 Let thine anger be kindled against our enemies; and, in the fury of thine heart, with thy sword avenge us of our wrongs.

6 Remember thy suffering saints, O our God; and thy servants will rejoice in thy name forever.

We will pause here to point out one of the many great lessons to be learned from sections 121, 122, and 123. As mentioned in the background notes to this section, all three sections are taken from the same two letters written by the Prophet from Liberty Jail.

Now that you have felt the pain and anguish of the Prophet's heart and his desperate plea for God's intervention in verses 1–6, above, please go to the last verse of section 123, and read it (verse 17).

Did you notice the difference in the Prophet's feelings and emotions? He is still in the same prison, under the same circumstances. The Lord has not said anything about getting him and the others out of prison. Yet the words cheerfully describe his feelings and accurately represent the tone at the end of section 123. What has happened in such a short time, from the first of section 121 to the end of section 123? Watch carefully for the answer as we continue with the Lord's response to the Prophet's humble and desperate plea in the first six verses of section 121. You will see that it has to do with perspective, confidence in your standing with the Lord, and seeing things the way the Lord sees them.

We will continue using **bold** to emphasize things, letting these precious words of the Savior speak mainly for themselves.

Perspective

7 My son, peace be unto thy soul; thine adversity and thine afflictions shall be but a small moment;

Perspective

8 And then, **if thou endure it well, God shall exalt thee on high; thou shalt triumph over all thy foes.**

Perspective

9 **Thy friends do stand by thee, and they shall hail thee again with warm hearts and friendly hands** [*a very comforting prophecy for Joseph at this moment*].

Perspective

10 **Thou art not yet as Job**; thy friends do not contend against thee, neither charge thee with transgression, as they did Job.

Perspective

11 And **they who do charge thee with transgression, their hope shall be blasted, and their prospects shall melt away as the hoar frost** [*the frost on things just before the sun comes up and melts it*] **melteth before the burning rays of the rising sun;**

12 And also that **God hath set his hand** and seal **to change the times and seasons** [*to disrupt their plans*], and to blind their minds, that they may not understand his marvelous workings; **that he may prove them also and take them in their own craftiness;**

13 Also **because their hearts are corrupted, and the things which they are willing to bring upon others, and love to have others suffer, may come upon themselves to the very uttermost;**

14 **That they may be disappointed** [*among other things, in the fact that they will not stop the work of the Lord and the growth and spread of the Church*] **also, and their hopes may be cut off;**

As you read verse 15 about the fate of these persecutors of the Saints and their posterity, you would do well to read Ezekiel 18, which explains that if the children of wicked people choose not to follow in the footsteps of their wayward parents but rather turn to God, the chain of wickedness will not continue with them. Among other things, verse 15 could be a reference to the destruction of the wicked at the Second Coming.

15 And **not many years hence**, that **they and their posterity shall be swept from under heaven**, saith God, that not one of them is left to stand by the wall.

Perspective

16 **Cursed are all those that shall lift up the heel against mine anointed** [*a term that usually means the leaders of the Church*], saith the Lord, **and cry they**

have sinned when they have not sinned before me, saith the Lord, but have done that which was meet [*required*] in mine eyes, and which I commanded them.

17 But those who cry transgression do it because they are the servants of sin [*they are the ones who are caught up in sin*], and are the children of disobedience themselves.

18 And those who swear falsely against my servants, that they might bring them into bondage and death—

19 Wo unto them; because they have offended my little ones they shall be severed from the ordinances of mine house [*they will be cut off from the Church and from the temple blessings of exaltation*].

20 Their basket shall not be full, their houses and their barns shall perish, and they themselves shall be despised by those that flattered them [*those who encouraged them to betray and mob the Saints and their leaders*].

21 They shall not have right to the priesthood, nor their posterity after them from generation to generation.

22 It had been better for them that a millstone had been hanged about their necks, and they drowned in the depth of the sea.

23 Wo unto all those that discomfort my people, and drive, and murder, and testify against them, saith the Lord of Hosts; a generation of vipers shall not escape the damnation of hell [*there is no ultimate escape for the wicked except repentance*].

Verse 24, next, appears to be a direct response to Joseph's plea in verse 2, above.

24 Behold, mine eyes see and know all their works, and I have in reserve a swift judgment in the season thereof [*when the time is right, after they have had a fair opportunity to repent*], for them all;

Sometimes it is difficult for the righteous to be patient with the Lord while He gives the wicked more time to repent. Verse 25, next, is a reminder that everyone's time to face the consequences of their evil will come if they do not repent.

25 For there is a time appointed for every man, according as his works shall be [*everyone gets a completely fair opportunity and then will ultimately be judged according to agency choices*].

In verses 26–32, the Lord takes

the Prophet's mind far away from Liberty Jail and gives him a perspective of great knowledge and blessings that await him, including the fact that through his faithfulness, he will eventually understand the universe, the gods, the orbits and revolutions of the stars and planets, and so forth. Abraham, who was also persecuted (see Abraham 1), was given similar perspective (see Abraham 3) as preparation for him to continue his great mission as a prophet.

Perspective

26 God shall give unto you knowledge by his Holy Spirit, yea, by the unspeakable gift of the Holy Ghost, that has not been revealed since the world was until now [*Joseph will be given knowledge that has not been revealed on earth before—for example, details of the resurrection found in D&C 88, compared with Alma 40:19–21; details about the three degrees of glory, D&C 76, compared with 1 Corinthians 15:39–42*];

27 **Which our forefathers have awaited with anxious expectation to be revealed in the last times** [*the last days*], which their minds were pointed to by the angels, as held in reserve **for the fulness of their glory** [*for their exaltation*];

28 **A time to come in the which nothing shall be withheld,** **whether there be one God or many gods** [*Joseph Smith was later privileged to reveal to us that there are many gods—see, for example, D&C 132:20, which tells that righteous, temple-married husbands and wives will become gods; see also the Prophet's explanation of 1 Corinthians 8:5 in* Teachings of the Prophet Joseph Smith, *370–71*], **they shall be manifest.**

29 **All thrones and dominions, principalities and powers, shall be revealed** and set forth upon [*given to*] all who have endured valiantly for the gospel of Jesus Christ [*in other words, all those who are worthy of exaltation*].

30 **And also, if there be bounds set to the heavens** or to the **seas,** or to the dry **land,** or to the **sun, moon,** or **stars**—

31 **All the times of their revolutions,** all the appointed days, months, and years, and all the days of their days, months, and years, and **all their glories, laws,** and **set times,** shall be revealed in the days of the dispensation of the fulness of times [*chiefly through the Prophet Joseph Smith; compare with D&C 35:17*]—

32 **According to that which was ordained in the midst of the Council of the Eternal God of**

all other gods before this world was, that should be reserved unto the finishing and the end thereof, when every man [*every worthy person*] shall enter into his eternal presence and into his immortal rest.

Perspective

33 **How long can rolling waters remain impure? What power shall stay the heavens** [*what can stop the power of heaven? Nothing!*] **As well might man stretch forth his puny arm to stop the Missouri river in its decreed course, or to turn it up stream, as to hinder the Almighty from pouring down knowledge from heaven upon the heads of the Latter-day Saints.**

Next, in verses 34–44, all of us are given a brief lesson in the prerequisites for using the priesthood effectively and how to use it properly. It is also a warning about the effects of uncontrolled negative personality traits upon our relationships with others.

This is one of the greatest sermons ever given on proper use of the priesthood.

Perspective

34 **Behold, there are many called** [*to serve God and keep His commandments*] **but few are chosen** [*to use the priesthood effectively and, ultimately, receive all the blessings of the gospel, including exaltation*]. **And why are they not chosen?**

35 **Because their hearts are set so much upon the things of this world**, and **aspire to the honors of men** [*they desire praise of man more than approval from God*], that **they do not learn this one lesson—**

Perspective

36 That **the rights of the priesthood are inseparably connected with the powers of heaven, and that the powers of heaven cannot be controlled nor handled only** [*except*] **upon the principles of righteousness.**

37 **That they may be conferred upon us**, it **is true; but when we undertake to cover our sins, or to gratify our pride**, our **vain ambition**, or to **exercise control** or **dominion** or **compulsion** upon the souls of the children of men, **in any degree of unrighteousness**, behold, **the heavens withdraw** themselves; **the Spirit of the Lord is grieved; and when it is withdrawn, Amen to the priesthood or the authority of that man.**

38 Behold, **ere he is aware, he is left unto himself, to kick against the pricks** [*sharp, pointed sticks used in olden times to drive cattle; symbolic of conscience; the promptings of the Spirit*], **to persecute the saints, and to fight against God.**

Verse 39, next, is a short course in human nature, a word to the wise to those who will humbly listen.

39 **We have learned by sad experience that it is the nature and disposition of almost all men, as soon as they get a little authority, as they suppose, they will immediately begin to exercise unrighteous dominion.**

40 **Hence** [*this is why*] **many are called, but few are chosen** [*as stated in verse 34, above*].

Next, in verses 41–45, the Savior explains how priesthood holders should use the priesthood as they lead others. The principles taught apply to anyone in leadership positions, man or woman.

41 **No power or influence can or ought to be maintained by virtue of the priesthood** [*because one holds the priesthood*], **only** [*except*] **by persuasion, by long-suffering** [*patience, pure love*], **by gentleness** and **meekness, and by love unfeigned** [*genuine love*];

42 **By kindness,** and **pure knowledge** [*including knowledge of gospel doctrines and principles, knowledge of the people's needs and backgrounds within one's stewardship, and so forth*], **which shall greatly enlarge the soul** [*including the ability to be compassionate*] **without hypocrisy, and without guile** [*without ulterior motives*]—

Many people misunderstand the word "betimes" in verse 43, next, and think it means "occasionally." Instead, it means "soon, right away, early on in the situation" (see any good dictionary of the English language).

43 **Reproving** [*offering correction; scolding*] **betimes** [*right away, immediately, while the situation is still in focus*] **with sharpness** [*with directness; can also mean with clarity, explaining what the problem or concern is*], **when moved upon by the Holy Ghost; and then showing forth afterwards an increase of love toward him whom thou hast reproved, lest he esteem thee to be his enemy;**

44 **That he may know that thy faithfulness is stronger than the cords of death.**

The last part of verse 43, above, beginning with "showing forth afterwards an increase of love," is a vital part of leading others in righteousness. There is a tendency on the part of many leaders who exercise "unrighteous dominion" (verse 39, above) to ostracize, cut off, ignore, or avoid those whom they have reproved. The Savior "stretches forth his hands unto them all the day long" (Jacob 6:4), inviting them to repent and return to the fold.

So it is that parents, teachers, priesthood and auxiliary leaders, and all who have influence on others should show "forth afterwards an increase of love," helping those who have been scolded or disciplined to return to confident fellowship in the fold, knowing that your correcting him or her was done out of love as explained in verse 43–44.

As we move on to verse 45, next, don't forget the "classroom" (the dungeon) that Joseph finds himself in as he is being taught these lessons in Christlike leadership and care for others. It is a setting in which it would be most difficult to have "charity towards all men" as instructed in verse 45. It is a great credit to the Prophet and an insight into his great strength of character that he becomes genuinely cheerful at the end of section 123 (see 123:17). Of course, these lessons apply to us also.

45 **Let thy bowels** [*your whole being*] **also be full of charity towards all men** [*including those*] *who influenced your being placed in Liberty Jail*], **and to the household of faith** [*to the faithful members of the Church*], and **let virtue garnish** [*adorn, decorate, give beauty to*] **thy thoughts unceasingly; then shall thy confidence wax** [*grow*] **strong in the presence of God** [*then you will feel more and more comfortable with God, including praying for help from Him*]; **and the doctrine of the priesthood** [*proper understanding and use of the priesthood*] **shall distil upon** [*gently come upon*] **thy soul as the dews from heaven** [*symbolic of pure truth coming down from above*].

46 **The Holy Ghost shall be thy constant companion,** and **thy scepter** [*symbolic of power and priesthood authority; exaltation; becoming gods*] **an unchanging scepter of righteousness and truth** [*just as is the case with God*]; and **thy dominion shall be an everlasting dominion** [*as a god*], **and without compulsory means it** [*perhaps referring back to dominion; it could also refer back to "righteousness and truth"*] **shall flow unto thee forever and ever.**

One possible meaning of the phrase "without compulsory means," in verse 46, above, is that all things in the universe voluntarily honor and obey God because of the righteousness and truth that is in Him (compare with D&C 29:36, where we see that God's honor is the source of His power). This principle would naturally apply to any who become gods.

SECTION 122

Background

As stated in the background notes for section 121 in this study guide, sections 121 through 123 go together, being excerpts from two letters written by the Prophet Joseph Smith from the jail in Liberty, Missouri. One is dated March 20, 1839, and the other about two days later. The full text of these letters is included at the end of section 123 in this study guide.

Section 122 is much quoted. It contains poignant feelings and a sweet reminder that the Savior is acquainted with any and all of our griefs and sorrows, because He suffered far beyond what any of us can. He understands our troubles and suffering better than we possibly can. Thus, He is in a position to strengthen and bless us according to our real needs and what is best for us, no matter what our condition or grief.

An amazing prophecy is given in this section, which echoes what Moroni told young Joseph in 1823 when he said that Joseph's "name should be had for good and evil among all nations" (Joseph Smith—

History 1:33). It is verses 1–2 in which the Lord prophecies that all the world will know of Joseph Smith. Some will seek after his work and teachings as a prophet of God and come to salvation. Others will mock and ridicule.

Any time you see or hear anti-Latter-day Saint rhetoric belittling Joseph Smith, you can, in a significant way, say in your heart, "There is another proof that Joseph Smith was indeed a true prophet! They know about him! This is prophecy being fulfilled! The Church is true!"

Likewise, whenever you hear a conversion story or read about the Prophet Joseph Smith being honored in faraway places as well as close by, you can rejoice, knowing that this prophecy, given when he was but an obscure farm boy in upstate New York (when Moroni told him he would be known throughout the earth) and repeated here in section 122 when he was still relatively unknown, is being fulfilled.

We will now proceed with our study of section 122. Among other things, we will continue to point out perspectives given the Prophet by the Lord that enable him to understand and become cheerful by the end of the letters from Liberty Jail (see D&C 123:17) in spite of the oppressive and terribly difficult conditions and suffering he has been forced to endure over the past almost four months.

Perspective

1 THE ends of the earth shall inquire after thy name [*will want to know more about you*], and **fools shall have thee in derision, and hell shall rage against thee;**

2 **While the pure in heart**, and **the wise**, and the **noble**, and the **virtuous, shall seek counsel, and authority, and blessings constantly from under thy hand** [*those things restored by the Lord through the Prophet Joseph will constantly bless countless lives*].

Perspective

3 **And thy people shall never be turned against thee by the testimony of traitors.**

Perspective

4 And **although their** [*traitors and enemies*] **influence shall cast thee into trouble**, and into bars and walls [*jails and prisons*], **thou shalt be had in honor; and but for a small moment** [*just a little while longer*] and **thy voice shall be** more **terrible in the midst of thine enemies** than the fierce lion, **because of thy righteousness** [*an affirmation of his good standing with the Lord, no doubt a great comfort to Joseph*]; and **thy God shall stand by thee forever and ever.**

Did you notice an important lesson for all of us at the end of verse 4, above? It has to do with the Lord's statement "thy God shall stand by thee forever and ever." Sometimes we may tend to believe that "stand by" means "not allow anything bad to happen to us." Such is obviously not the case. In fact, that would not be good for us eternally. Rather, it means that He will support us and help us "in every time of trouble" (see D&C 3:8).

Virtually every trial and tribulation mentioned in verses 5–7 happened to the Prophet Joseph Smith. Feel the power of these lines as they lead up to two of the most powerful quotes in all of the scriptures. We will **bold** these well-known lines at the end of verse 7 and in verse 8.

5 If thou art called to pass through tribulation; if thou art in perils among false brethren [*traitors, betrayers*]; if thou art in perils among robbers; if thou art in perils by land or by sea;

6 If thou art accused with all manner of false accusations; if thine enemies fall upon thee; if they tear thee from the society of thy father and mother and brethren and sisters; and if with a drawn sword thine enemies tear thee from the bosom of thy wife, and of thine offspring, and thine elder

son, although but six years of age, shall cling to thy garments, and shall say, My father, my father, why can't you stay with us? O, my father, what are the men going to do with you? and if then he shall be thrust from thee by the sword, and thou be dragged to prison, and thine enemies prowl around thee like wolves for the blood of the lamb [*no doubt symbolic of the evil people who persecuted the Savior*];

7 And if thou shouldst be cast into the pit, or into the hands of murderers, and the sentence of death passed upon thee; if thou be cast into the deep; if the billowing surge conspire against thee; if fierce winds become thine enemy; if the heavens gather blackness, and all the elements combine to hedge up the way; and above all, if the very jaws of hell shall gape open the mouth wide after thee, **know thou, my son, that all these things shall give thee experience, and shall be for thy good.**

8 **The Son of Man** [*the Savior; the Son of Man of Holiness; in other words, the Son of Heavenly Father— see Moses 6:57*] **hath descended below them all. Art thou greater than he?**

One of the important lessons we learn from verse 9, next, is that Satan and his evil followers have limits set by God.

Perspective

9 Therefore, hold on thy way, and **the priesthood shall remain with thee**; for **their bounds are set, they cannot pass**. Thy days are known, and thy years shall not be numbered less; therefore, **fear not what man can do, for God shall be with you forever and ever.**

A question that sometimes comes up regarding verse 9, above, is whether there was a set time for Joseph Smith to die. From what we know about agency and that predestination is a false doctrine, we may probably conclude that there was not a set time for the Prophet to die. Rather, the Lord may have been telling him that, in spite of his enemies, he would accomplish his mission successfully.

During the last seven months of his life, Joseph seemed to feel that his life was drawing to a close. Consequently, he met with the Quorum of the Twelve almost every day, preparing them for his departure. "In an extraordinary council meeting in late March 1844, he solemnly told the Twelve that he could now leave them, because his work was done and the foundation was laid so the kingdom of God could be reared" (*Church History in the Fulness of Times,* 2003, 293–94).

SECTION 123

Background

This section goes together with sections 121 and 122. All three are excerpts from two letters written by Joseph Smith to Bishop Edward Partridge and members of the Church who had taken refuge in Quincy, Illinois. Joseph wrote the letters while in Liberty Jail, just a few days apart, starting on March 20, 1839. The complete text of the two letters is included at the end of this section.

You may wish to read the background notes for section 121 in this study guide if you haven't already done so. In them, the question is asked as to what happened to the Prophet between the first six verses of section 121 and the last verse of section 123? What was it that led to such an upbeat approach to things at the end of the second letter as opposed to the desperate cry for help at the first of section 121?

The answer, in part, is that the Lord gave the Prophet perspective. He allowed Joseph to see things as He sees them in the perspective of eternity. He assured him that he was in good standing with God and that his work was acceptable and would eternally benefit countless souls.

This perspective and assurance, coupled no doubt with blessings and strengthening from the Lord, led to a tremendous change in the thirty-three-year-old Prophet's feelings and outlook. The Lord spoke to him in sections 121 and 122, and Joseph speaks to the Saints and teaches them as their prophet in this section.

The first topic addressed here by Joseph Smith and his fellow prisoners is that the members of the Church should keep records and gather evidence of the persecutions and illegal acts against them to be presented to government officials (verse 6). This is in harmony with the Lord's counsel in D&C 101:86–89.

1 AND again, **we** [*the Prophet and the others in Liberty Jail*] **would suggest for your consideration the propriety of** [*the importance of*] **all the saints gathering up a knowledge of all the facts, and sufferings and abuses put upon them by the people of this State;**

2 **And also of all the property and amount of damages which they have sustained, both of character and personal injuries, as well as real property** [*homes, farms, livestock, and so forth*];

3 And **also the names of all persons that have had a hand in their oppressions,** as far as they

can get hold of them and find them out.

4 And perhaps a committee can be appointed to find out these things, and to **take statements and affidavits; and also to gather up the libelous** [*lies and slander that break the law*] **publications that are afloat**;

As you perhaps are aware, many of the Prophet Joseph Smith's enemies have characterized him as an unlearned and illiterate farm boy. They forget that he was tutored by the Lord and His angels, as well as constantly being taught by the Holy Ghost. In light of the thinking and attitude of his critics, it is almost humorous to see the vocabulary words he used in verse 5, next. We will **bold** them to point them out. In fact, you may want to see how many of them you can define yourself.

5 And all that are in the magazines, and in the encyclopedias, and all the **libelous** histories that are published, and are writing, and by whom, and present the whole **concatenation** of **diabolical rascality** and **nefarious** and murderous **impositions** that have been practised upon this people—

As you can see, the Prophet was indeed highly educated. We will repeat verse 5 and provide definitions for the words in **bold**.

Verse 5 repeated

5 And all that are in the magazines, and in the encyclopedias, and all the **libelous** [*slanderous*] histories that are published, and are writing, and by whom, and present the whole **concatenation** [*series of related items*] of **diabolical** [*devilish*] **rascality** [*trouble causing*] and **nefarious** [*wicked, evil*] and murderous **impositions** [*trouble; persecutions; disruptions of normal life and liberty*] that have been practised upon this people—

We will now continue, moving ahead to verse 6, where the Prophet explains why he is asking the Saints to gather evidence against their persecutors.

6 **That we may not only publish to all the world, but present them to the heads of government in all their dark and hellish hue**, as the last effort which is enjoined on [*required from*] us by our Heavenly Father, **before we can fully and completely claim that promise which shall call him forth from his hiding place** [*as explained in D&C 101:86–90*]; and **also that the whole nation may be left without excuse before he can send forth the power of his mighty arm**.

Many students of the Doctrine and Covenants miss one of the major messages contained in verses 7–10, next. **It is that false creeds and beliefs hold an iron grip on the hearts and behaviors of most of mankind. Satan has been highly successful in accomplishing this.** Note the power words such as *riveted, iron yoke, strong band, handcuffs, chains, shackles,* and *fetters* used by the Prophet to describe the "inherited lies" (verse 7) that bind people to false doctrine, unrighteous behaviors, and bitter prejudice against the Lord's true Church and its members.

We will **bold** a number of these power words and phrases that describe the terrible damage caused by false creeds passed down from generation to generation.

7 It is an imperative duty that we owe to God, to angels, with whom we shall be brought to stand, and also to ourselves, to our wives and children, who have been made to bow down with grief, sorrow, and care, under the most damning hand of **murder, tyranny, and oppression**, supported and urged on and upheld by the influence of that spirit which hath so **strongly riveted** the **creeds of the fathers**, who have inherited lies, **upon the hearts of the children**, and **filled the world with confusion**, and has been growing stronger and stronger, and is now **the very mainspring of all corruption**, and the whole earth groans under the weight of its iniquity.

8 **It is an iron yoke**, it is **a strong band**; they are the very **handcuffs**, and **chains**, and **shackles**, and **fetters of hell** [*the chains and shackles of hell*].

9 Therefore it is an imperative duty that we owe, not only to our own wives and children, but to the widows and fatherless, whose husbands and fathers have been murdered under **its iron hand**;

10 **Which dark and blackening deeds are enough to make hell itself shudder**, and to stand aghast and pale, **and the hands of the very devil to tremble and palsy**.

11 And **also it** [*the work of recording and exposing the atrocities against the Saints*] **is an imperative duty that we owe to all the rising generation, and to all the pure in heart**—

Note the merciful teaching that many "are only kept from the truth because they know not where to find it" in verse 12, next.

Perspective

12 **For there are many yet on the earth** among all sects, parties, and denominations, who are blinded by the subtle craftiness of

men, whereby they lie in wait to deceive, and **who are only kept from the truth because they know not where to find it—**

13 **Therefore,** that **we should waste** [*use up our energies*] **and wear out our lives in bringing to light all the hidden things of darkness, wherein we know them**; and they are truly manifest from heaven—

14 **These** [*the instructions to collect evidence of persecution*] **should then be attended to with great earnestness.**

Verse 15, next, is prophetic, and we are seeing some of its fulfillment today as government entities and public figures apologize to the Church and its people for persecutions of the past.

15 Let no man count them [*the evidences of persecution*] as small things; for **there is much which lieth in futurity** [*there is much in the future*], pertaining to the saints, **which depends upon these things.**

Next, the Prophet emphasizes how seemingly small things can profoundly influence much larger matters.

16 You know, brethren, that **a very large ship is benefited very much by a very small helm** [*tiller; steering wheel of a ship*] **in the time of a storm**, by being kept workways [*at the proper angle*] with the wind and the waves.

Finally, in verse 17, next, we see and feel the effects of the blessings and counsels of the Lord upon the Prophet Joseph Smith since the opening six verses of section 121. He has been given perspective, knowledge, and understanding that have strengthened and cheered him, even though his physical circumstances have not been altered. He is still in Liberty Jail and at the mercy of bigotry and hatred. This verse holds a powerful lesson for all of us.

17 Therefore, dearly beloved brethren, **let us cheerfully do all things that lie in our power;** and **then may we stand still, with the utmost assurance, to see the salvation of God, and for his arm to be revealed** [*as taught by the Lord in D&C 101:85–93*].

The Prophet and his fellow inmates were kept in Liberty Jail until early April 1839. In the meantime, public opinion in Missouri had turned against Governor Boggs, the mobs, and the corrupt legal system because of their treatment of the Latter-day Saints. Some government officials and people in law enforcement quietly began trying to figure a way to let the prisoners "escape." Finally, they were granted a change of venue and transferred to Gallatin, Missouri, for trial where a drunken jury made a mockery of the judicial system.

Joseph and his brethren were then given a change of venue to Boone County. About mid-April, the company, consisting of the prisoners, a sheriff, and four guards, left Gallatin for the new court venue. The sheriff had been privately instructed to let the prisoners escape. Hyrum Smith relates what happened next (**bold** added for emphasis):

"We went down that day as far as Judge Morin's—a distance of some four or five miles. There we stayed until the next morning, when we started on our journey to Boone county, and traveled on the road about twenty miles distance. There we bought a jug of whisky, with which we treated the company; and while there the sheriff showed us the mittimus before referred to, without date or signature, and said that Judge Birch told him never to carry us to Boone county, and never to show the mittimus; and, said he, **I shall take a good drink of grog and go to bed, and you may do as you have a mind to**.

"Three others of the guard drank pretty freely of whisky, sweetened with honey. They also went to bed, and were soon asleep, and **the other guard went along with us, and helped to saddle the horses**.

"Two of us mounted the horses, and the other three started on foot, and we took our change of venue for the state of Illinois, and in the course of nine or ten days arrived safe at Quincy, Adams county [*April 22, 1839*], where we found our families in a state of poverty, although in good health, they having been driven out of the state previously by the murderous militia, under the exterminating order of the executive of Missouri" (*History of the Church*, 3:423).

As mentioned in the background notes for section 121, we will here include the complete text of the letters written from Liberty Jail by the Prophet Joseph Smith, which contain sections 121, 122, and 123. We will **bold** the verses of the three sections as they appear in the text of the letters. We are quoting from *History of the Church*, 3:289–303.

"Liberty Jail, Clay County, Missouri,

"March 25, 1839.

(Note that more recent research dates these letters as starting on March 20, 1839. Quoting from the 2018 *Doctrine and Covenants Student Manual*, we read: "On March 20, 1839, the Prophet dictated a letter to Bishop Edward Partridge and Church members in Quincy, Illinois, and in other locations. It was followed approximately two days later by another letter to Bishop Partridge and the Saints, in which the Prophet offered comfort and provided counsel. (See *The Joseph Smith Papers, Documents, Volume 6: February 1838–August 1839*, 357, 389.) Portions of these letters are recorded in Doctrine and Covenants 121–23.")

"To the Church of Latter-day Saints at Quincy, Illinois, and Scattered Abroad, and to Bishop Partridge in Particular:

"Your humble servant, Joseph Smith, Jun., prisoner for the Lord Jesus Christ's sake, and for the Saints, taken and held by the power of mobocracy, under the exterminating reign of his excellency, the governor, Lilburn W. Boggs, in company with his fellow prisoners and beloved brethren, Caleb Baldwin, Lyman Wight, Hyrum Smith, and Alexander McRae, send unto you all greeting. May the grace of God the Father, and of our Lord and Savior Jesus Christ, rest upon you all, and abide with you forever. May knowledge be multiplied unto you by the mercy of God. And may faith and virtue, and knowledge and temperance, and patience and godliness, and brotherly kindness and charity be in you and abound, that you may not be barren in anything, nor unfruitful.

"For inasmuch as we know that the most of you are well acquainted with the wrongs and the high-handed injustice and cruelty that are practiced upon us; whereas we have been taken prisoners charged falsely with every kind of evil, and thrown into prison, enclosed with strong walls, surrounded with a strong guard, who continually watch day and night as indefatigable as the devil does in tempting and laying snares for the people of God:

"Therefore, dearly beloved brethren, we are the more ready and willing to lay claim to your fellowship and love. For our circumstances are calculated to awaken our spirits to a sacred remembrance of everything, and we think that yours are also, and that nothing therefore can separate us from the love of God and fellowship one with another; and that every species of wickedness and cruelty practiced upon us will only tend to bind our hearts together and seal them together in love. We have no need to say to you that we are held in bonds without cause, neither is it needful that you say unto us, We are driven from our homes and smitten without cause. We mutually understand that if the inhabitants of the state of Missouri had let the Saints alone, and had been as desirable of peace as they were, there would have been nothing but peace and quietude in the state unto this day; we should not have been in this hell, surrounded with demons (if not those who are damned, they are those who shall be damned) and where we are compelled to hear nothing but blasphemous oaths, and witness a scene of blasphemy, and drunkenness and hypocrisy, and debaucheries of every description.

"And again, the cries of orphans and widows would not have ascended up to God against them. Nor would innocent blood have stained the soil of Missouri. But oh! the unrelenting hand! The inhumanity and murderous disposition of this people! It shocks all nature; it beggars and defies all description; it is a tale of woe; a lamentable tale; yea a sorrowful tale; too much to tell; too much for contemplation; too much for human beings; it cannot be found among the heathens; it cannot be found among the nations where kings and tyrants are enthroned; it cannot be found among the savages of the wilderness; yea, and I think it cannot be found among the wild and ferocious beasts of the forest—that a man should be mangled for sport! women be robbed of all that they have—their last morsel for subsistence, and then be violated to gratify the hellish desires of the mob, and finally left to perish with their helpless offspring clinging around their necks.

"But this is not all. After a man is dead, he must be dug up from his grave and mangled to pieces, for no other purpose than to gratify their spleen against the religion of God.

"They practice these things upon the Saints, who have done them no wrong, who are innocent and virtuous; who loved the Lord their God, and were willing to forsake all things for Christ's sake. These things are awful to relate, but they are verily true. It must needs be that offenses come, but woe unto them by whom they come.

"[*Section 121:1–6*] **Oh God! where art Thou? And where is the pavilion that covereth Thy hiding place? How long shall Thy hand be stayed, and Thine eye, yea Thy pure eye, behold from the eternal heavens, the wrongs of Thy people, and of Thy servants, and Thy ear be penetrated with their cries? Yea, O Lord, how long shall they suffer these wrongs and unlawful oppressions, before Thine heart shall be softened towards them, and Thy bowels be moved with compassion towards them?**

"O Lord God Almighty, Maker of Heaven, Earth and Seas, and of all things that in them are, and who controllest and subjectest the devil, and the dark and benighted dominion of Sheol! Stretch forth Thy hand, let Thine eye pierce; let Thy pavilion be taken up; let Thy hiding place no longer be covered; let Thine ear be inclined; let Thine heart be softened, and Thy bowels moved with compassion towards us, Let Thine anger be kindled against our enemies; and in the fury of Thine heart, with Thy sword avenge us of

our wrongs; remember Thy suffering Saints, O our God! and Thy servants will rejoice in Thy name forever.

"Dearly and beloved brethren, we see that perilous times have come, as was testified of. We may look, then, with most perfect assurance, for the fulfillment of all those things that have been written, and with more confidence than ever before, lift up our eyes to the luminary of day, and say in our hearts, Soon thou wilt veil thy blushing face. He that said "Let there be light," and there was light, hath spoken this word. And again, Thou moon, thou dimmer light, thou luminary of night, shalt turn to blood.

"We see that everything is being fulfilled; and that the time shall soon come when the Son of Man shall descend in the clouds of heaven. Our hearts do not shrink, neither are our spirits altogether broken by the grievous yoke which is put upon us. We know that God will have our oppressors in derision; that He will laugh at their calamity, and mock when their fear cometh.

"O that we could be with you, brethren, and unbosom our feelings to you! We would tell, that we should have been liberated at the time Elder Rigdon was, on the writ of habeas corpus, had not our own lawyers interpreted the law, contrary to what it reads, against us; which prevented us from introducing our evidence before the mock court.

"They have done us much harm from the beginning. They have of late acknowledged that the law was misconstrued, and tantalized our feelings with it, and have entirely forsaken us, and have forfeited their oaths and their bonds; and we have a come-back on them, for they are co-workers with the mob.

"As nigh as we can learn, the public mind has been for a long time turning in our favor, and the majority is now friendly; and the lawyers can no longer browbeat us by saying that this or that is a matter of public opinion, for public opinion is not willing to brook it; for it is beginning to look with feelings of indignation against our oppressors, and to say that the "Mormons" were not in the fault in the least. We think that truth, honor, virtue and innocence will eventually come out triumphant. We should have taken a habeas corpus before the high judge and escaped the mob in a summary way; but unfortunately for us, the timber of the wall being very hard, our auger handles gave out, and hindered us longer than we expected; we applied to a friend, and a very slight incautious act gave rise to some suspicions, and before we could fully succeed, our plan was discovered; we had everything in readiness, but the last stone, and we could have made our escape in one minute, and should have succeeded admirably, had it not been for a little imprudence or over-anxiety on the part of our friend.

"The sheriff and jailer did not blame us for our attempt; it was a fine breach, and cost the county a round sum; but public opinion says that we ought to have been permitted to have made our escape; that then the disgrace would have been on us, but now it must come on the state; that there cannot be any charge sustained against us; and that the conduct of the mob, the murders committed at Haun's Mills, and the exterminating order of the governor, and the one-sided, rascally proceedings of the legislature, have damned the state of Missouri to all eternity. I would just name also that General Atchison has proved himself as contemptible as any of them.

"We have tried for a long time to get our lawyers to draw us some petitions to the supreme judges of this state, but they utterly refused. We have examined the law, and drawn the petitions ourselves, and have obtained abundance of proof to counteract all the testimony that was against us, so that if the supreme judge does not grant us our liberty, he has to act without cause, contrary to honor, evidence, law or justice, sheerly to please the devil, but we hope better things and trust before many days God will so order our case, that we shall be set at liberty and take up our habitation with the Saints.

"We received some letters last evening—one from Emma, one from Don C. Smith, and one from Bishop Partridge—all breathing a kind and consoling spirit. We were much gratified with their contents. We had been a long time without information; and when we read those letters they were to our souls as the gentle air is refreshing, but our joy was mingled with grief, because of the sufferings of the poor and much injured Saints. And we need not say to you that the floodgates of our hearts were lifted and our eyes were a fountain of tears, but those who have not been enclosed in the walls of prison without cause or provocation, can have but little idea how sweet the voice of a friend is; one token of friendship from any source whatever awakens and calls into action every sympathetic feeling; it brings up in an instant everything that is passed; it seizes the present with the avidity of lightning; it grasps after the future with the fierceness of a tiger; it moves the mind backward and forward, from one thing to another, until finally all enmity, malice and hatred, and past differences, misunderstandings and mismanagements are slain victorious at the feet of hope; and when the heart is sufficiently contrite, then the voice of inspiration steals along and whispers, [*section 121:7–25*] **My son, peace be unto** thy soul; thine adversity and thine afflictions shall be but a small moment; and then if thou endure it well, God shall exalt thee on high; thou shalt triumph over all thy foes; thy friends do stand by thee, and they shall hail thee again, with warm hearts and friendly hands; thou art not yet as Job; thy friends do not contend against thee, neither charge thee with transgression, as they did Job; and they who do charge thee with transgression, their hope shall be blasted and their prospects shall melt away as the hoar frost melteth before the burning rays of the rising sun; and also that God hath set His hand and seal to change the times and seasons, and to blind their minds, that they may not understand His marvelous workings, that He may prove them also and take them in their own craftiness; also because their hearts are corrupted, and the things which they are willing to bring upon others, and love to have others suffer, may come upon themselves to the very uttermost; that they may be disappointed also, and their hopes may be cut off; and not many years hence, that they and their posterity shall be swept from under heaven, saith God, that not one of them is left to stand by the wall. Cursed are all those that shall lift up the heel against mine anointed, saith the Lord, and cry they have sinned when they have not sinned before me, saith the Lord, but have done that which was meet in mine eyes, and which I commanded them; but those who cry transgression do it because they are the servants of sin and are the children of disobedience themselves; and those who swear falsely against my servants, that they might bring them into bondage and death; wo unto them; because they have offended my little ones; they shall be severed from the ordinances of mine house; their basket shall not be full, and their houses and their barns shall perish, and they themselves shall be despised by those that flattered them; they shall not have right to the Priesthood, nor their posterity after them, from generation to generation; it had been better for them that a millstone had been hanged about their necks, and they drowned in the depth of the sea.

"Wo unto all those that discomfort my people, and drive and murder, and testify against them, saith the Lord of Hosts; a generation of vipers shall not escape the damnation of hell. Behold mine eyes see and know all their works, and I have in reserve a swift judgment in the season thereof, for them all; for there is a time appointed for every man according as his work shall be.

"And now, beloved brethren, we say unto you, that inasmuch as God hath said that He would have a tried people, that He would purge them as gold, now we think that this time He has chosen His own crucible, wherein we have been tried; and we think if we get through with any degree of safety, and shall have kept the faith, that it will be a sign to this generation, altogether sufficient to leave them without excuse; and we think also, it will be a trial of our faith equal to that of Abraham, and that the ancients will not have whereof to boast over us in the day of judgment, as being called to pass through heavier afflictions; that we may hold an even weight in the balance with them; but now, after having suffered so great sacrifice and having passed through so great a season of sorrow, we trust that a ram may be caught in the thicket speedily, to relieve the sons and daughters of Abraham from their great anxiety, and to light up the lamp of salvation upon their countenances, that they may hold on now, after having gone so far unto everlasting life.

"Now, brethren, concerning the places for the location of the Saints, we cannot counsel you as we could if we were present with you; and as to the things that were written heretofore, we did not consider them anything very binding, therefore we now say once for all, that we think it most proper that the general affairs of the Church, which are necessary to be considered, while your humble servant remains in bondage, should be transacted by a general conference of the most faithful and the most respectable of the authorities of the Church, and a minute of those transactions may be kept, and forwarded from time to time, to your humble servant; and if there should be any corrections by the word of the Lord, they shall be freely transmitted, and your humble servant will approve all things whatsoever is acceptable unto God. If anything should have been suggested by us, or any names mentioned, except by commandment, or thus saith the Lord, we do not consider it binding; therefore our hearts shall not be grieved if different arrangements should be entered into. Nevertheless we would suggest the propriety of being aware of an aspiring spirit, which spirit has often times urged men forward to make foul speeches, and influence the Church to reject milder counsels, and has eventually been the means of bringing much death and sorrow upon the Church.

"We would say, beware of pride also; for well and truly hath the wise man said, that pride goeth before destruction, and a haughty spirit before a fall. And again, outward appearance is not always a criterion by which to judge our fellow man; but the lips betray the haughty and overbearing imaginations of the heart; by his words and his deeds let him be judged. Flattery also is a deadly poison. A frank and open rebuke provoketh a good man to emulation; and in the hour of trouble he will be your best friend; but on the other hand, it will draw out all the corruptions of corrupt hearts, and lying and the poison of asps is under their tongues; and they do cause the pure in heart to be cast into prison, because they want them out of their way.

"A fanciful and flowery and heated imagination beware of; because the things of God are of deep import; and time, and experience, and careful and ponderous and solemn thoughts can only find them out. Thy mind, O man! if thou wilt lead a soul unto salvation, must stretch as high as the utmost heavens, and search into and contemplate the darkest abyss, and the broad expanse of eternity—thou must commune with God. How much more dignified and noble are the thoughts of God, than the vain imaginations of the human heart! None but fools will trifle with the souls of men.

"How vain and trifling have been our spirits, our conferences, our councils, our meetings, our private as well as public conversations—too low, too mean, too vulgar, too condescending for the dignified characters of the called and chosen of God, according to the purposes of His will, from before the foundation of the world!

We are called to hold the keys of the mysteries of those things that have been kept hid from the foundation of the world until now. Some have tasted a little of these things, many of which are to be poured down from heaven upon the heads of babes; yea, upon the weak, obscure and despised ones of the earth. Therefore we beseech of you, brethren, that you bear with those who do not feel themselves more worthy than yourselves, while we exhort one another to a reformation with one and all, both old and young, teachers and taught, both high and low, rich and poor, bond and free, male and female; let honesty, and sobriety, and candor, and solemnity, and virtue, and pureness, and meekness, and simplicity crown our heads in every place; and in fine, become as little children, without malice, guile or hypocrisy.

"And now, brethren, after your tribulations, if you do these things, and exercise fervent prayer and faith in the sight of God always, [section 121:26–32] **He shall give unto you knowledge by His Holy Spirit, yea by the unspeakable gift of the Holy Ghost, that has not been revealed since the world was until now; which our forefathers have waited with anxious expectation to be revealed in the last times, which their minds were pointed to by the angels, as held in reserve for the fullness of their glory; a time to come in the which** nothing shall be withheld, whether there be one God or many Gods, they shall be manifest; all thrones and dominions, principalities and powers, shall be revealed and set forth upon all who have endured valiantly for the Gospel of Jesus Christ; and also if there be bounds set to the heavens, or to the seas; or to the dry land, or to the sun, moon or stars; all the times of their revolutions; all the appointed days, months and years, and all the days of their days, months and years, and all their glories, laws, and set times, shall be revealed, in the days of the dispensation of the fullness of times, according to that which was ordained in the midst of the Council of the Eternal God of all other Gods, before this world was, that should be reserved unto the finishing and the end thereof, when every man shall enter into His eternal presence, and into His immortal rest.

"But I beg leave to say unto you, brethren, that ignorance, superstition and bigotry placing itself where it ought not, is oftentimes in the way of the prosperity of this Church; like the torrent of rain from the mountains, that floods the most pure and crystal stream with mire, and dirt, and filthiness, and obscures everything that was clear before, and all rushes along in one general deluge; but time weathers tide; and notwithstanding we are rolled in the mire of the flood for the time being, the next surge peradventure, as time rolls on, may bring to us the fountain as clear as crystal, and as pure as snow; while the filthiness, floodwood and rubbish is left and purged out by the way.

"[Section 121:33] **How long can rolling water remain impure? What power shall stay the heavens? As well might man stretch forth his puny arm to stop the Missouri river in its decreed course, or to turn it up stream, as to hinder the Almighty from pouring down knowledge from heaven, upon the heads of the Latter-day Saints**.

"What is Boggs or his murderous party, but wimbling willows upon the shore to catch the flood-wood? As well might we argue that water is not water, because the mountain torrents send down mire and roil the crystal stream, although afterwards render it more pure than before; or that fire is not fire, because it is of a quenchable nature, by pouring on the flood; as to say that our cause is down because renegades, liars, priests, thieves and murderers, who are all alike tenacious of their crafts and creeds, have poured down, from their spiritual wickedness in high places, and from their strongholds of the devil, a flood of dirt and mire and filthiness and vomit upon our heads.

"No! God forbid. Hell may pour forth its rage like the burning lava of mount Vesuvius, or of Etna, or of the most terrible of the burning mountains; and yet shall "Mormonism" stand. Water, fire, truth and God are all realities. Truth is "Mormonism." God is the author of it. He is our shield. It is by Him we received our birth. It was by His voice that we were called to a dispensation of His Gospel in the beginning of the fullness of times. It was by Him we received the Book of Mormon; and it is by Him that we remain unto this day; and by Him we shall remain, if it shall be for our glory; and in His Almighty name we are determined to endure tribulation as good soldiers unto the end.

"But, brethren, we shall continue to offer further reflections in our next epistle. You will learn by the time you have read this, and if you do not learn it, you may learn it, that walls and irons, doors and creaking hinges, and half-scared-to-death guards and jailers, grinning like some damned spirits, lest an innocent man should make his escape to bring to light the damnable deeds of a murderous mob, are calculated in their very nature to make the soul of an honest man feel stronger than the powers of hell.

"But we must bring our epistle to a close. We send our respects to fathers, mothers, wives and children, brothers and sisters; we hold them in the most sacred remembrance.

"We feel to inquire after Elder Rigdon; if he has not forgotten us, it has not been signified to us by his writing. Brother George W. Robinson also; and Elder Cahoon, we remember him, but would like to jog his memory a little on the fable of the bear and the two friends who mutually agreed to stand by each other. And perhaps it would not be amiss to mention uncle John [Smith], and various others. A word of consolation and a blessing would not come amiss from anybody, while we are being so closely whispered by the bear. But we feel to excuse everybody and everything, yea the more readily when we contemplate that we are in the hands of persons worse that a bear, for the bear would not prey upon a dead carcass.

"Our respects and love and fellowship to all the virtuous Saints. We are your brethren and fellow-sufferers, and prisoners of Jesus Christ for the Gospel's sake, and for the hope of glory which is in us. Amen.

"We continue to offer further reflections to Bishop Partridge, and to the Church of Jesus Christ of Latter-day Saints, whom we love with a fervent love, and do always bear them in mind in all our prayers to the throne of God.

"It still seems to bear heavily on our minds that the Church would do well to secure to themselves the contract of the land which is proposed to them by Mr. Isaac

Galland, and to cultivate the friendly feelings of that gentleman, inasmuch as he shall prove himself to be a man of honor and a friend to humanity; also Isaac Van Allen, Esq., the attorney-general of Iowa Territory, and Governor Lucas, that peradventure such men may be wrought upon by the providence of God, to do good unto His people. We really think that Mr. Galland's letter breathes that kind of a spirit, if we may judge correctly. Governor Lucas also. We suggest the idea of praying fervently for all men who manifest any degree of sympathy for the suffering children of God.

"We think that the United States Surveyor of the Iowa Territory may be of great benefit to the Church, if it be the will of God to this end; and righteousness should be manifested as the girdle of our loins.

"It seems to be deeply impressed upon our minds that the Saints ought to lay hold of every door that shall seem to be opened unto them, to obtain foothold on the earth, and be making all the preparation that is within their power for the terrible storms that are now gathering in the heavens, "a day of clouds, with darkness and gloominess, and of thick darkness," as spoken of by the Prophets, which cannot be now of a long time lingering, for there seems to be a whispering that the angels of heaven who have been entrusted with the counsel of these matters

for the last days, have taken counsel together; and among the rest of the general affairs that have to be transacted in their honorable council, they have taken cognizance of the testimony of those who were murdered at Haun's Mills, and also those who were martyred with David W. Patten, and elsewhere, and have passed some decisions peradventure in favor of the Saints, and those who were called to suffer without cause.

"These decisions will be made known in their time; and the council will take into consideration all those things that offend.

"We have a fervent desire that in your general conferences everything should be discussed with a great deal of care and propriety, lest you grieve the Holy Spirit, which shall be poured out at all times upon your heads, when you are exercised with those principles of righteousness that are agreeable to the mind of God, and are properly affected one toward another, and are careful by all means to remember, those who are in bondage, and in heaviness, and in deep affliction far your sakes. And if there are any among you who aspire after their own aggrandizement, and seek their own opulence, while their brethren are groaning in poverty, and are under sore trials and temptations, they cannot be benefited by the intercession of the Holy Spirit, which maketh intercession for us day and night with groanings that cannot be uttered.

"We ought at all times to be very careful that such high-mindedness shall never have place in our hearts; but condescend to men of low estate, and with all long-suffering bear the infirmities of the weak.

"[*Section 121:34–46*] **Behold, there are many called, but few are chosen. And why are they not chosen? Because their hearts are set so much upon the things of this world, and aspire to the honors of men, that they do not learn this one lesson—that the rights of the Priesthood are inseparably connected with the powers of heaven, and that the powers of heaven cannot be controlled nor handed only upon the principles of righteousness. That they may be conferred upon us, it is true; but when we undertake to cover our sins, or to gratify our pride, our vain ambition, or to exercise control, or dominion, or compulsion, upon the souls of the children of men, in any degree of unrighteousness, behold, the heavens withdraw themselves; the Spirit of the Lord is grieved; and when it is withdrawn, *Amen to the Priesthood,* or the authority of that man. Behold! ere he is aware, he is left unto himself, to kick against the pricks; to**

persecute the Saints, and to fight against God.

"We have learned by sad experience that it is the nature and disposition of almost all men, as soon as they get a little authority, as they suppose, they will immediately begin to exercise unrighteous dominion. Hence many are called, but few are chosen.

"No power or influence can or ought to be maintained by virtue of the Priesthood, only by persuasion, by long-suffering, by gentleness, and meekness, and by love unfeigned; by kindness, and pure knowledge, which shall greatly enlarge the soul without hypocrisy, and without guile, reproving betimes with sharpness, when moved upon by the Holy Ghost, and then showing forth afterwards an increase of love toward him whom thou hast reproved, lest he esteem thee to be his enemy; that he may know that thy faithfulness is stronger than the cords of death; let thy bowels also be full of charity towards all men, and to the household of faith, and virtue garnish thy thoughts unceasingly, then shall thy confidence wax strong in the presence of God, and the doctrine of the Priesthood shall distill upon thy soul as the dews from heaven. The Holy Ghost shall be thy constant companion, and thy

sceptre an unchanging sceptre of righteousness and truth, and thy dominion shall be an everlasting dominion, and without compulsory means it shall flow unto thee forever and ever.

"[Section 122:1–9] The ends of the earth shall inquire after thy name, and fools shall have thee in derision, and hell shall rage against thee, while the pure in heart, and the wise, and the noble, and the virtuous, shall seek counsel, and authority and blessings constantly from under thy hand, and thy people shall never be turned against thee by the testimony of traitors; and although their influence shall cast thee into trouble, and into bars and walls, thou shalt be had in honor, and but for a small moment and thy voice shall be more terrible in the midst of thine enemies, than the fierce lion, because of thy righteousness; and thy God shall stand by thee forever and ever.

"If thou art called to pass through tribulations; if thou art in perils among false brethren; if thou art in perils among robbers; if thou art in perils by land or by sea; if thou art accused with all manner of false accusations; if thine enemies fall upon thee; if they tear thee from the society of thy father and mother and brethren and sisters, and if with a drawn sword thine enemies tear thee from the bosom of thy wife, and of thine offspring, and thine elder son, although but six years of age, shall cling to thy garment, and shall say, My father, my father, why can't you stay with us? O, my father, what are the men going to do with you? and if then he shall be thrust from thee by the sword, and thou be dragged to prison, and thine enemies prowl around thee like wolves for the blood of the lamb; and if thou shouldst be cast into the pit, or into the hands of murderers, and the sentence of death passed upon thee; if thou be cast into the deep; if the billowing surge conspire against thee; if fierce winds become thine enemy; if the heavens gather blackness, and all the elements combine to hedge up the way; and above all, if the very jaws of hell shall gape open the mouth wide after thee, know thou, my son, that all these things shall give thee experience, and shall be for thy good. The Son of Man hath descended below them all; art thou greater than he?

"Therefore, hold on thy way, and the Priesthood shall remain with thee, for their bounds are set, they cannot pass. Thy days are known, and thy years shall not be numbered less; therefore, fear not what man can do, for God shall be with you forever and ever.

"Now, brethren, I would suggest for the consideration of the conference, its being carefully and wisely understood by the council or conferences that our brethren scattered abroad, who understand the spirit of the gathering, that they fall into the places and refuge of safety that God shall open unto them, between Kirtland and Far West. Those from the east and from the west, and from far countries, let them fall in somewhere between those two boundaries, in the most safe and quiet places they can find; and let this be the present understanding, until God shall open a more effectual door for us for further considerations.

"And again, we further suggest for the considerations of the Council, that there be no organization of large bodies upon common stock principles, in property, or of large companies of firms, until the Lord shall signify it in a proper manner, as it opens such a dreadful field for the avaricious, the indolent, and the corrupt hearted to prey upon the innocent and virtuous, and honest.

"We have reason to believe that many things were introduced among the Saints before God had signified the times; and notwithstanding the principles and plans may have been good, yet aspiring men, or in other words, men who had not the substance of godliness about them, perhaps undertook to handle edged tools. Children, you know, are fond of tools, while they are not yet able to use them.

"Time and experience, however, are the only safe remedies against such evils. There are many teachers, but, perhaps, not many fathers. There are times coming when God will signify many things which are expedient for the well-being of the Saints; but the times have not yet come, but will come, as fast as there can be found place and reception for them.

"[*Section 123:1–17*] **And again, we would suggest for your consideration the propriety of all the Saints gathering up a knowledge of all the facts and sufferings and abuses put upon them by the people of this state; and also of all the property and amount of damages which they have sustained, both of character and personal injuries, as well as real property; and also the names of all persons that have had a hand in their oppressions, as far as they can get hold of them and find them out; and perhaps a committee can be appointed to find out these things, and to take statements, and affidavits, and also to gather up the libelous publications that are afloat, and all that are in the magazines, and in the encyclopaedias, and all the libelous histories that are published, and are writing, and by whom, and present** the whole concatenation of diabolical rascality, and nefarious and murderous impositions that have been practiced upon this people, that we may not only publish to all the world, but present them to the heads of government in all their dark and hellish hue, as the last effort which is enjoined on us by our Heavenly Father, before we can fully and completely claim that promise which shall call Him forth from His hiding place, and also that the whole nation may be left without excuse before He can send forth the power of His mighty arm.

"It is an imperative duty that we owe to God, to angels, with whom we shall be brought to stand, and also to ourselves, to our wives and children, who have been made to bow down with grief, sorrow, and care, under the most damning hand of murder, tyranny, and oppression, supported and urged on and upheld by the influence of that spirit which hath so strongly riveted the creeds of the fathers, who have inherited lies, upon the hearts of the children, and filled the world with confusion, and has been growing stronger and stronger, and is now the very mainspring of all corruption, and the whole earth groans under the weight of its iniquity.

"It is an iron yoke, it is a strong band; they are the very handcuffs, and chains, and shackles, and fetters of hell.

"Therefore it is an imperative duty that we owe, not only to our own wives and children, but to the widows and fatherless, whose husbands and fathers have been murdered under its iron hand; which dark and blackening deeds are enough to make hell itself shudder, and to stand aghast and pale, and the hands of the very devil to tremble and palsy. And also it is an imperative duty that we owe to all the rising generation, and to all the pure in heart, (for there are many yet on the earth among all sects, parties, denominations, who are blinded by the subtle craftiness of men, whereby they lie in wait to deceive, and who are only kept from the truth because they know not where to find it); therefore, that we should waste and wear out our lives in bringing to light all the hidden things of darkness, wherein we know them; and they are truly manifest from heaven.

"These should then be attended to with great earnestness. Let no man count them as small things; for there is much which lieth in futurity, pertaining to the Saints, which depends upon these things. You know, brethren, that a very large ship is benefited very much by a very small helm in the time of a storm, by being kept workways with the wind and the waves.

"Therefore, dearly beloved brethren, let us cheerfully do all things that lie in our power, and then may we stand still with the utmost assurance, to see the salvation of God, and for His arm to be revealed.

"And again, I would further suggest the impropriety of the organization of bands or companies, by covenant or oaths, by penalties or secrecies; but let the time past of our experience and sufferings by the wickedness of Doctor Avard suffice and let our covenant be that of the Everlasting Covenant, as is contained in the Holy Writ and the things that God hath revealed unto us. Pure friendship always becomes weakened the very moment you undertake to make it stronger by penal oaths and secrecy.

"Your humble servant or servants, intend from henceforth to disapprobate everything that is not in accordance with the fullness of the Gospel of Jesus Christ, and is not of a bold, and frank, and upright nature. They will not hold their peace—as in times past when they see iniquity beginning to rear its head—for fear of traitors, or the consequences that shall follow by reproving those who creep in unawares, that they may get something with which to destroy the flock. We believe that the experience of the Saints in times past has been sufficient, that they will from henceforth be always ready to obey the truth without having men's persons in admiration because of advantage. It is expedient that we should be aware of such things; and we ought always to be aware of those prejudices which sometimes so strangely present themselves, and are so congenial to human nature, against our friends, neighbors, and brethren of the world, who choose to differ from us in opinion and in matters of faith. Our religion is between us and our God. Their religion is between them and their God.

"There is a love from God that should be exercised toward those of our faith, who walk uprightly, which is peculiar to itself, but it is without prejudice; it also gives scope to the mind, which enables us to conduct ourselves with greater liberality towards all that are not of our faith, than what they exercise towards one another. These principles approximate nearer to the mind of God, because it is like God, or Godlike.

"Here is a principle also, which we are bound to be exercised with, that is, in common with all men, such as governments, and laws, and regulations in the civil concerns of life. This principle guarantees to all parties, sects, and denominations, and classes of religion, equal, coherent, and indefeasible rights; they are things that pertain to this life; therefore all are alike interested; they make our responsibilities one towards another in matters of corruptible things, while the former principles do not destroy the latter, but bind us stronger, and make our responsibilities not only one to another, but unto God also. Hence we say, that the Constitution of the United States is a glorious standard; it is founded in the wisdom of God. It is a heavenly banner; it is to all those who are privileged with the sweets of its liberty, like the cooling shades and refreshing waters of a great rock in a thirsty and weary land. It is like a great tree under whose branches men from every clime can be shielded from the burning rays of the sun.

"We, brethren, are deprived of the protection of its glorious principles, by the cruelty of the cruel, by those who only look for the time being, for pasturage like the beasts of the field, only to fill themselves; and forget that the "Mormons," as well as the Presbyterians, and those of every other class and description, have equal rights to partake of the fruits of the great tree of our national liberty. But notwithstanding we see what we see, and feel what we feel, and know what we know, yet that fruit is no less precious and delicious to our taste; we cannot be weaned from the milk, neither can we be driven from the breast; neither will we deny our religion because of the hand of oppression; but we will hold on until death.

"We say that God is true; that the Constitution of the United States is true; that the Bible is true; that the Book of Mormon is true; that the Book of Covenants is true; that Christ is true; that the ministering angels sent forth from God are true, and that we know that we have an house not made with hands eternal in the heavens, whose builder and maker is God; a consolation which our oppressors cannot feel, when fortune, or fate, shall lay its iron hand on them as it has on us. Now, we ask, what is man? Remember, brethren, that time and chance happen to all men.

"We shall continue our reflections in our next.

"We subscribe ourselves, your sincere friends and brethren in the bonds of the everlasting Gospel, prisoners of Jesus Christ, for the sake of the Gospel and the Saints.

"We pronounce the blessings of heaven upon the heads of the Saints who seek to serve God with undivided hearts, in the name of Jesus Christ. Amen.

"Joseph Smith, Jun.,
Hyrum Smith,
Lyman Wight,
Caleb Baldwin,
Alexander McRae."

SECTION 124

Background

This revelation was given to the Prophet Joseph Smith on January 19, 1841, in Nauvoo, Illinois. It is the longest section in the Doctrine and Covenants and deals with several topics, including the following:

- Reassurance to the Prophet Joseph Smith that his work is acceptable to the Lord (verse 1)

- A command to make a proclamation to all the world (verses 2–14)

- Specific instructions and assignments to several brethren (verses 15–21)

- An assignment to build a hotel for guests and visitors in Nauvoo, to be called the "Nauvoo House" (verses 22–24, 56–83, 119–22)

- A commandment to build the Nauvoo Temple (verses 25–28, 40–48, 55)

- Instructions that baptisms for the dead are normally to be performed in temples and that permission to perform them temporarily in the Mississippi River will soon be withdrawn (verses 29–36)

- Additional instructions on the purposes of temples throughout the ages (verses 37–39)

- Doctrine concerning faithful members who try with all their hearts to keep God's commandments but are prevented by circumstances beyond their control (verses 49–54)

- Instructions to individuals to settle in Nauvoo and remain there (verses 84–86)

- Instructions for William Law to serve as a counselor to Joseph Smith (verses 87–91)

- Hyrum Smith is called to be patriarch to the Church and replace Oliver Cowdery in several functions in the Church (verses 91–96)

- Instructions to several individuals, including warnings to some (verses 97–118)

- Additional instructions regarding Hyrum Smith's call to serve as patriarch and a review of priesthood keys, quorums, and presidencies, including several callings of brethren to serve in quorum presidencies (verses 123–45)

As we proceed, we will make considerable use of **bold**, letting the scriptures speak for themselves, and point out some important lessons along the way with notes and commentary.

Reassurance to the Prophet Joseph Smith that his work is acceptable to the Lord (verse 1)

1 VERILY, thus saith the Lord unto you, my servant Joseph Smith, **I am well pleased with your offering** and acknowledgments, which you have made; for unto this end have I raised you up, that I might show forth my wisdom through the weak things of the earth.

A command to make a proclamation to all the world (verses 2–14)

The Proclamation to All the World, spoken of here, was completed in 1845 by the Quorum of the Twelve after the martyrdom of the Prophet Joseph Smith and his brother, Hyrum. You can read a summary of the main content of this proclamation in an article by President Ezra Taft Benson ("A Message to the World," *Ensign,* November 1975, 32–34).

2 Your prayers are acceptable before me; and in answer to them I say unto you, that **you are now called immediately to make a solemn proclamation** of my gospel, and of this stake which I have planted to be a cornerstone of Zion, which shall be polished with the refinement which is after the similitude of a palace.

3 **This proclamation shall be made to all the kings of the world, to the four corners thereof,** to the honorable president-elect, and the high-minded governors of the nation in which you live, and **to all the nations of the earth** scattered abroad.

4 Let it be **written in the spirit of meekness and by the power of the Holy Ghost, which shall be in you at the time of the writing** of the same;

5 For **it shall be given you by the Holy Ghost** to know my will concerning those kings and authorities, even what shall befall them in a time to come.

6 For, behold, I am about **to call upon them to give heed to the light and glory of Zion**, for the set time has come to favor her.

7 **Call ye, therefore, upon them** with loud proclamation, and **with your testimony**, fearing them not, for they are as grass [*they are only temporarily in power*], and all their glory as the flower thereof which soon falleth, **that they may be left also without excuse—**

8 And **that I may visit them** in the day of visitation [*the day of punishment—see Isaiah 10, footnote 3a*], **when I shall unveil the face**

of my covering, to appoint the portion [*the just reward*] of the oppressor among hypocrites, where there is gnashing of teeth, **if they reject my servants and my testimony** which I have revealed unto them.

> The "if" in the last part of verse 8, above, is an important reminder that they will have a fair chance to understand and accept the gospel before the day of final judgment. And verse 9, next, reminds us that the Lord will continue to work with them.

9 And again, **I will visit and soften their hearts**, many of them for your good, that ye may find grace in their eyes, **that they may come to the light of truth,** and the Gentiles to the exaltation or lifting up of Zion.

10 For **the day of my visitation cometh speedily, in an hour when ye think not** of; and where shall be the safety of my people, and refuge for those who shall be left of them?

11 **Awake, O kings of the earth! Come ye, O, come ye, with your gold and your silver, to the help of my people**, to the house of the daughters of Zion.

12 And again, verily I say unto you, **let my servant Robert B. Thompson help you to write this proclamation**, for I am well pleased with him, and that he should be with you;

13 **Let him, therefore, hearken to your counsel**, and I will bless him with a multiplicity of blessings; let him be faithful and true in all things from henceforth, and he shall be great in mine eyes;

> Verse 14, next, is a quick reminder that accountability goes along with responsibility.

14 But **let him remember that his stewardship will I require at his hands**.

Specific instructions and assignments to several brethren (verses 15–21)

> Verse 15, next, is quite often quoted in church classes and discussions. You may wish to mark it in your scriptures.

15 And again, verily I say unto you**, blessed is my servant Hyrum Smith; for I, the Lord, love him because of the integrity of his heart, and because he loveth that which is right before me**, saith the Lord.

> Next, in verses 16–17, John C. Bennett, who will eventually have his membership withdrawn (the terminology now requested by the leaders of the Church in place of

"excommunication"), is instructed to help write the proclamation and to stand by the Prophet in times of trouble. Notice the "ifs" in these verses, which I have pointed out.

16 Again, **let my servant John C. Bennett help you in your labor in sending my word to the kings and people of the earth, and stand by you**, even you my servant Joseph Smith, **in the hour of affliction**; and his reward shall not fail *if* he receive counsel.

17 And for his love he shall be great, for he shall be mine *if* he do this, saith the Lord. I have seen the work which he hath done, which I accept *if* he continue, and will crown him with blessings and great glory.

Unfortunately, Bennett apostatized from the Church and became one of Joseph's most bitter and destructive enemies.

Over my years of teaching, students occasionally asked why the Lord would call such people as John C. Bennett to high and trusted positions in the Church when he would apostatize later and cause much trouble. The 1981 *Doctrine and Covenants Student Manual* has an excellent answer (**bold** added for emphasis):

"Smith and Sjodahl summarized John C. Bennett's introduction to the Church and his eventual apostasy to explain why the Lord commended him:

"'[John C. Bennett] was well educated and possessed many gifts and accomplishments. He was a physician, a university professor, and a brigadier-general. On the 27th of July, 1840, he offered his services to the Church. The Prophet Joseph replied, inviting him to come to Commerce [*Nauvoo*], if he felt so disposed, but warned him at the same time not to expect exaltation "in this generation," from devotion to the cause of truth and a suffering people; nor worldly riches; only the approval of God. The outcome of the correspondence was that he joined the Church and rose to prominent positions among the Saints. His fellowship with the people of God did not last long, however. On the 25th of May, 1842, he was notified that the leaders of the Church did no longer recognize him as a member, because of his impure life, and shortly afterwards the Church took action against him. Then he became one of the most bitter enemies of the Church. His slanders, his falsehoods and unscrupulous attacks, which included perjury and attempted assassination were the means of inflaming public opinion to such an extent that the tragedy at Carthage became possible.

"'Why, then, did his name appear, in this Revelation, as that of a trusted assistant of Joseph?

John Taylor furnishes the answer to that question. He says, "Respecting John C. Bennett: I was well acquainted with him. At one time he was a good man, but fell into adultery, and was cut off from the Church for his iniquity" (*History of the Church,* Vol. V, p. 81). **At the time of the revelation he was a good man.** But he was overcome by the adversary and made the slave of his carnal desires. The Lord knew him and warned him. "His reward shall not fail if he receive counsel." "He shall be great . . . if he do this," etc. **Bennett did not heed these warning "ifs"** from Him who knew what was in his heart.' (Commentary, pp. 770–71.)

"**The Lord does not withhold present blessings because of future sinful behavior.** He blessed King David as long as he was faithful and did not withhold opportunity, although he had foreknowledge of David's future transgressions with Bathsheba. As long as one obeys, the blessings come. With the perspective of history one may be tempted to ask why the Lord chose men who would eventually falter to be leaders in the Church, but one should remember that at the time of their calling they were faithful and true" (*Doctrine and Covenants Student Manual,* 1981, 306).

18 And again, I say unto you that it is my will that my servant **Lyman Wight should continue**

in preaching for Zion, in the spirit of meekness, confessing me before the world; and I will bear him up as on eagles' wings; and he shall beget glory and honor to himself and unto my name.

Next, in verse 19, we are told that three faithful men, including the Prophet's father, who have died by the date of this revelation, are with the Lord in heaven.

19 That when he shall finish his work I may receive him unto myself, even as I did my servant **David Patten,** who **is with me at this time, and also my servant Edward Partridge, and also my aged servant Joseph Smith, Sen., who sitteth with Abraham** [*symbolic of exaltation*] at his right hand, and blessed and holy is he, for he is mine.

You may wish to make a cross-reference in your scriptures from Abraham, in verse 19, above, to D&C 132:29 and 37, wherein we are informed that Abraham has now become a god.

20 And again, verily I say unto you, my servant **George Miller** is without guile [*without ulterior motives; has a pure heart*]; he **may be trusted** because of the integrity of his heart; and for the love which he has to my testimony I, the Lord, love him.

21 I therefore say unto you, **I seal upon his head the office of a bishopric** [*Brother Miller is to be called and ordained a bishop*], like unto my servant Edward Partridge, that he may receive the consecrations [*donations to the Church*] of mine house, that he may administer blessings upon the heads of the poor of my people, saith the Lord. Let no man despise my servant George, for he shall honor me.

An assignment to build a hotel for guests and visitors in Nauvoo, to be called the "Nauvoo House" (verses 22–24, 56–83, 119–22)

22 **Let** my servant **George** [*Miller*], and my servant **Lyman** [*Wight*], **and** my servant **John Snider, and others, build a house** [*a hotel, the Nauvoo House—see verse 60—which still exists today on the banks of the Mississippi River*] unto my name, such a one as my servant Joseph shall show unto them, upon the place which he shall show unto them also.

23 And it shall be for **a house for boarding**, a house **that strangers may come from afar to lodge therein**; therefore let it be a good house, worthy of all acceptation, **that the weary traveler may find health and safety while he shall contemplate the word of the**

Lord; and the corner-stone I have appointed for Zion.

24 **This house shall be a healthful habitation** if it be built unto my name, and if the governor which shall be appointed unto it shall not suffer any pollution [*crude or evil activities*] to come upon it. It shall be holy, or the Lord your God will not dwell therein.

A commandment to build the Nauvoo Temple (verses 25–28, 40–48, 55)

25 And again, verily I say unto you, **let all my saints come from afar**.

26 And send ye swift messengers, yea, chosen messengers, and say unto them: **Come ye, with all your gold, and your silver, and your precious stones**, and with all your antiquities [*perhaps including knowledge of ancient temples and construction materials, as described in the Bible for the Tabernacle, Solomon's Temple, and so forth*]; **and with all who have knowledge of antiquities** [*possibly meaning building skills for constructing such things*], that will come, may come, and bring the box-tree [*used in building the Tabernacle used by the Children of Israel— see Exodus 26:15*], and the fir-tree, and the pine-tree, together with all the precious trees of the earth;

27 And **with iron**, with **copper,** and with **brass**, and with **zinc,** and with **all your precious things** of the earth; **and build a house to my name,** for the Most High to dwell therein.

28 For **there is not a place** [*temple*] found on earth **that he may come to and restore again that which was lost unto you, or which he hath taken away, even the fulness of the priesthood.**

Instructions that baptisms for the dead are normally to be performed in temples and that permission to perform them temporarily in the Mississippi River will soon be withdrawn (verses 29–36)

29 For **a baptismal font there is not upon the earth, that they, my saints, may be baptized for those who are dead**—

At this time, the Saints were performing baptisms for the dead in the Mississippi River near Nauvoo.

30 For **this ordinance belongeth to my house** [*should be done in a temple*], and cannot be acceptable to me, only [*except*] in the days of your poverty, wherein ye are not able to build a house unto me.

31 **But I command you**, all ye my saints, **to build a house unto**

me [*the Nauvoo Temple*]; and **I grant unto you a sufficient time to build a house** unto me; and **during this time your baptisms** [*for the dead in the Mississippi River*] **shall be acceptable unto me.**

32 **But** behold, **at the end of this appointment** [*the time granted by the Lord for the building of the Nauvoo Temple*] **your baptisms for your dead shall not be acceptable unto me**; and if you do not these things at the end of the appointment ye shall be rejected as a church, with your dead, saith the Lord your God.

In verse 33, next, we are told, in effect, that we were taught about the purpose of temples in the premortal councils. Thus, we understood that if we were sent to earth during a time when the gospel was not available to us, our work would be done by proxies in temples and we would have a completely fair opportunity to attain exaltation also.

33 For verily I say unto you, that **after you have had sufficient time to build a house to me, wherein the ordinance of baptizing for the dead belongeth,** and for which **the same** [*the plan to have temples on earth*] **was instituted from before the foundation of the world** [*was a part of the plan of salvation, instituted and taught by the Father in premortality*], **your**

baptisms for your dead cannot be acceptable unto me;

34 For **therein** [*in temples*] **are the keys of the holy priesthood ordained**, that you may receive honor and glory.

35 And **after this time** [*after the time allotted by the Lord for the building of the Nauvoo Temple*], **your baptisms for the dead**, by those who are scattered abroad, **are not acceptable** unto me, saith the Lord.

Next, in verse 36, these Saints are told that there are to be many temples built, including one in Jerusalem in the last days.

36 For **it is ordained** [*it is part of the Father's plan*] **that in Zion**, and **in her stakes**, and **in Jerusalem**, those places which I have appointed for refuge [*a major purpose of stakes—see D&C 115:6*], **shall be the places** [*the temples—compare with the first phrase of verse 30, above*] **for your baptisms for your dead.**

Additional instructions on the purposes of temples throughout the ages (verses 37–39)

37 And again, verily I say unto you, how shall your washings be acceptable unto me, except ye perform them in a house [*temple*] which you have built to my name?

38 For, for this cause I commanded Moses that he should build a tabernacle, that they should bear it with them in the wilderness, and to build a house [*temple*] in the land of promise, that those ordinances might be revealed which had been hid from before the world was.

39 Therefore, verily I say unto you, that your **anointings**, and your **washings**, and your **baptisms for the dead**, and your **solemn assemblies,** and your memorials for your **sacrifices by the sons of Levi**, and for **your oracles** [*revelations from God—see D&C 90, footnote 4a*] in your most holy places wherein you receive **conversations**, and your **statutes and judgments**, for the beginning of the revelations and foundation of Zion, and for the glory, honor, and endowment of all her municipals [*citizens*], are ordained [*authorized*] by the ordinance of **my holy house, which my people are always commanded to build unto my holy name**.

More instructions regarding the building of the Nauvoo Temple (verses 40–48)

40 And verily I say unto you, **let this house be built** unto my

name, **that I may reveal mine ordinances therein unto my people**;

Remember, although Moses, Elias, and Elijah came to the Kirtland Temple and restored priesthood keys, the endowment as we know it, as well as celestial marriage, had not been available to the Saints yet. Therefore, "mine ordinances" (verse 40, above) would not be made available until the construction of the Nauvoo Temple.

41 For **I deign** [*plan*] **to reveal unto my church things which have been kept hid from before the foundation of the world**, things **that pertain to the dispensation of the fulness of times** [*our dispensation, meaning the time from the Restoration of the gospel to the earth through the Prophet Joseph Smith to the time of the Savior's Second Coming*].

42 And **I will show unto my servant Joseph all things pertaining to this house, and the priesthood thereof, and the place whereon it shall be built.**

43 And **ye shall build it on the place where you have contemplated building it**, for that is the spot which I have chosen for you to build it.

44 **If ye labor with all your**

might, I will consecrate that spot that it shall be made holy.

45 And **if my people will hearken unto my voice, and unto the voice of my servants whom I have appointed to lead my people, behold, verily I say unto you, they shall not be moved out of their place.**

46 **But** *if* **they will not hearken to my voice, nor unto the voice of these men whom I have appointed, they shall not be blest,** because they pollute mine holy grounds, and mine holy ordinances, and charters, and my holy words which I give unto them.

Verses 47–48, next, contain a clear explanation of the principle found in D&C 82:10, which declares, "I, the Lord, am bound when ye do what I say; but when ye do not what I say, ye have no promise."

47 And it shall come to pass **that if you build a house unto my name, and do not do the things that I say, I will not perform the oath which I make unto you, neither fulfil the promises which ye expect at my hands**, saith the Lord.

48 **For instead of blessings, ye, by your own works, bring cursings** [*troubles*]**, wrath, indignation,**

and judgments upon your own heads, by your follies, and by all your abominations, which you practise before me, saith the Lord.

Doctrine concerning faithful members who try with all their hearts to keep God's commandments but are prevented by circumstances beyond their control (verses 49–54)

49 Verily, verily, I say unto you, that when I give a commandment to any of the sons of men to do a work unto my name, and those sons of men go with all their might and with all they have to perform that work, and cease not their diligence, and their enemies come upon them and hinder them from performing that work, behold, it behooveth me [*I am obligated*] to require that work no more at the hands of those sons of men, but to accept of their offerings [*their efforts to perform the work required by the Lord*].

Next, in verse 50, the Savior explains that the responsibility for the required work not being done will be transferred from the person who tried to do it, to those who prevented it from being done.

50 And the iniquity and transgression of my holy laws and commandments I will visit upon the heads of those who hindered my work, unto the third and fourth generation, so long as they repent not, and hate me, saith the Lord God.

The principle explained in verses 49–50, above, applies to the faithful Saints who tried to build Zion, including the temple, in Jackson County, Missouri.

51 Therefore, for this cause [*because of this principle*] have I accepted the offerings of those whom I commanded to build up a city and a house unto my name, in Jackson county, Missouri, and were hindered by their enemies, saith the Lord your God.

52 And I will answer judgment, wrath, and indignation, wailing, and anguish, and gnashing of teeth upon their heads [*they will be held accountable*], unto the third and fourth generation, so long as they repent not, and hate me, saith the Lord your God.

People are sometimes bothered by the scriptural phrase "unto the third and fourth generation" (verse 52, above) when it comes to the sins of the parents being passed to their children, grandchildren, and so forth. It seems unfair that children get punished for the sins of their parents.

This can easily be misunderstood as an unfair "curse." But did you notice the answer to this concern at the end of verse 52, above? It is quite natural in most cases for children to learn from their parents, including from their sins and wickedness. However, if people repent, no matter how they became acquainted with sin, the wickedness is gone and the chain is broken. Read Ezekiel 18 for a more thorough explanation of this principle.

53 And **this** [*the principles taught in verses 49–52, above*] **I make an example unto you, for your consolation** [*comfort; relief*] **concerning all those who have been commanded to do a work and have been hindered by the hands of their enemies, and by oppression**, saith the Lord your God.

As summarized in verse 54, next, being pure in heart is the important factor in eventually receiving exaltation.

54 For **I am the Lord your God, and will save all those of your brethren who have been pure in heart, and have been slain in the land of Missouri**, saith the Lord.

More instruction regarding the building of the Nauvoo Temple (verse 55)

55 And again, verily I say unto

you, **I command you again to build a house to my name, even in this place** [*Nauvoo*]**, that you may prove yourselves unto me that ye are faithful in all things** whatsoever I command you, **that I may bless you, and crown you with honor, immortality, and eternal life** [*exaltation*]**.

More about building the Nauvoo House (verses 56–83)

56 And now I say unto you, **as pertaining to my boarding house** [*the Nauvoo House*] which I have commanded you to build [*see verses 22–24*] **for the boarding of strangers, let it be built** unto my name, and **let my name be named upon it** [*let it be a pleasant, righteous environment—see verse 60*]**, and **let my servant Joseph and his house have place therein**, from generation to generation.

57 **For this anointing** [*blessing*] **have I put upon his head, that his blessing shall also be put upon the head of his posterity** after him.

58 And **as I said unto Abraham** concerning the kindreds of the earth, **even so I say unto my servant Joseph: In thee and in thy seed shall the kindred of the earth be blessed**.

59 Therefore, **let my servant Joseph and his seed** [*posterity*] **after him have place in that house, from generation to generation,** forever and ever, saith the Lord.

60 And **let the name of that house be called Nauvoo House**; and **let it be a delightful habitation for man, and a resting-place for the weary traveler, that he may contemplate the glory of Zion** [*the beauties of the gospel*], and the glory of this, the corner-stone thereof;

61 **That he may receive also the counsel from those whom I have set to be** as plants of renown, and as **watchmen** upon her walls [*in other words, from the leaders of the Church*].

Next, in verse 62, the Lord organizes a building committee for the purpose of building the Nauvoo House.

62 Behold, verily I say unto you, **let** my servant **George Miller,** and my servant **Lyman Wight,** and my servant **John Snider,** and my servant **Peter Haws, organize themselves, and appoint one of them to be a** president over their quorum [*their committee*] **for the purpose of building that house.**

Beginning with verse 63, next, and coming into play in many more verses, we see that these brethren were authorized to sell stock to finance the construction of the Nauvoo House. Rules and regulations concerning the selling of this stock are spelled out. Stock is to be issued in minimum amounts of fifty dollars and maximum amounts of fifteen thousand dollars for one individual stockholder.

63 And **they shall form a constitution** [*draw up an agreement*], **whereby they may receive stock for the building of that house.**

64 And **they shall not receive less than fifty dollars for a share of stock** in that house, and they shall be permitted to receive **fifteen thousand** dollars from any one man for stock in that house.

65 But **they shall not be permitted to receive over fifteen thousand dollars stock from any one man.**

66 And **they shall not be permitted to receive under fifty dollars for a share of stock** from any one man in that house.

67 And **they shall not be permitted to receive any man, as a stockholder** in this house, **except the same shall pay** his stock into their hands **at the time he receives stock;**

68 And **in proportion to the amount of stock he pays into their hands he shall receive stock** in that house; but **if he pays nothing into their hands he shall not receive any stock** in that house.

This stock is to be transferable to descendants of the stockholders.

69 And if any pay stock into their hands **it shall be for stock in that house, for himself, and for his generation after him, from generation to generation**, so long as he and his heirs shall hold that stock, and do not sell or convey the stock away out of their hands by their own free will and act, if you will do my will, saith the Lord your God.

No monies received for stock in the Nauvoo House are to be used for any other purposes.

70 And again, verily I say unto you, if my servant George Miller, and my servant Lyman Wight, and my servant John Snider, and my servant Peter Haws, receive any stock into their hands, in moneys, or in properties wherein they receive the real value of moneys, **they shall not appropriate any portion of that stock to any other purpose**, only in that house.

The penalty for violating the rule given in verse 70, above, is severe.

71 And **if they do appropriate any portion of that stock anywhere else**, only in that house, **without the consent of the stockholder, and do not repay fourfold** for the stock which they appropriate anywhere else, only in that house, **they shall be accursed, and shall be moved out of their place**, saith the Lord God; for I, the Lord, am God, and cannot be mocked in any of these things.

One of the major messages from the Lord that we are seeing as we go along here is that it is a sacred trust and responsibility to handle the funds of the Church. Anyone who mishandles or misappropriates them is in serious trouble with Him.

Next, in verse 72, we are reminded that the prophet of the Church is subject to the same rules and commandments to which the members are held.

72 Verily I say unto you, let my servant Joseph pay stock into their hands for the building of that house, as seemeth him good; but **my servant Joseph cannot pay over fifteen thousand dollars stock in that house, nor under fifty dollars; neither can any other man, saith the Lord.**

73 And there are **others also** who **wish to know my will concerning them**, for they have asked it at my hands.

74 Therefore, I say unto you concerning my servant **Vinson Knight**, if he will do my will **let him put stock into that house** for himself, and for his generation after him, from generation to generation.

75 And **let him lift up his voice long and loud, in the midst of the people, to plead the cause of the poor and the needy**; and let him not fail, neither let his heart faint [*give up*]; **and I will accept of his offerings**, for they shall not be unto me as the offerings of Cain [*which were rejected by the Lord—see Moses 5:19–21*], for he shall be mine, saith the Lord.

76 Let his family rejoice and turn away their hearts from affliction; for I have chosen him and anointed him, and he shall be honored in the midst of his house, for **I will forgive all his sins**, saith the Lord. Amen.

77 Verily I say unto you, **let** my servant **Hyrum** [*Smith*] **put stock into that house** [*buy stock in the Nauvoo House*] as seemeth him good, for himself and his generation after him, from generation to generation.

78 **Let** my servant **Isaac Galland put stock into that house**; for **I, the Lord, love him for the work he hath done, and will forgive all his sins**; therefore, let him be remembered for an interest in that house from generation to generation.

Have you noticed how often the Savior tells people in this section that He forgives them of their sins? They get a new start! This applies to us too as we honestly strive to live the gospel and improve. In fact, each time we honestly and sincerely partake of the sacrament, thus renewing our covenants, it is as if we had been rebaptized!

Perhaps you've noticed that on many occasions the Lord has told members to follow the instructions given them by His Prophet. We see this next in verse 79. This carries the strong message that the Lord supports His Prophet, and we would be very wise to follow his counsel.

79 Let my servant Isaac Galland be appointed among you, and be ordained by my servant William Marks, and be blessed of him, to go with my servant Hyrum [*Smith*] **to accomplish the work that my servant Joseph shall point out to them, and they shall be greatly blessed**.

80 **Let** my servant **William Marks pay stock into that house**, as seemeth him good, for himself and his generation, from generation to generation.

81 **Let** my servant **Henry G. Sherwood pay stock into that house**, as seemeth him good, for himself and his seed after him, from generation to generation.

82 **Let** my servant **William Law pay stock into that house**, for himself and his seed after him, from generation to generation.

William Law had planned to take his family back to Kirtland but is counseled by the Lord to remain in Nauvoo. He is told here that hard times are coming to residents of Kirtland. He stayed and became second counselor to Joseph in the First Presidency.

83 **If he will do my will let him not take his family unto the eastern lands, even unto Kirtland**; nevertheless, I, the Lord, will build up Kirtland, but I, the Lord, have a scourge prepared for the inhabitants thereof.

Instructions to individuals to settle in Nauvoo and remain there (verses 84–86)

The counsel of the Prophet and the First Presidency at this time was for the Saints to gather in the Nauvoo area and build it up. Apparently, Almon W. Babbitt was counseling members to leave Nauvoo to settle elsewhere, including Kirtland. The imagery of the golden calf in verse 84, next, is symbolic of someone who attempts to lead the people away from the Prophet's counsel, as was the case with Moses's brother, Aaron, when he set up the golden calf for the Children of Israel to worship while Moses was on the mountain communing with the Lord (see Exodus 32:1–4).

84 And **with** my servant **Almon Babbitt, there are many things with which I am not pleased**; behold, **he aspireth to establish his counsel instead of the counsel which I have ordained** [*authorized, approved*], **even that of the Presidency of my Church**; and **he setteth up a golden calf** for the worship of my people [*he is attempting to lead the Saints astray*].

85 **Let no man go from this place** [*Nauvoo*] **who has come here essaying** [*attempting; planning*] **to keep my commandments**.

We learn an important and comforting doctrine in verse 86, next. It is that if we die faithful to God, we are allowed to continue working toward our exaltation in the next life.

86 If they live here let them live

unto me [*be faithful and loyal to God*]; and **if they die let them die unto me; for they shall rest from all their labors here, and shall continue their works** [*in the next life*].

Instructions for William Law to serve as a counselor to Joseph Smith (verses 87–91)

87 Therefore, **let my servant William** [*Law*] **put his trust in me,** and cease to fear concerning his family, because of the sickness of the land [*perhaps a reference to the malaria and sickness suffered initially by the Saints before they successfully drained the swampy lands of Nauvoo*]. **If ye love me, keep my commandments; and the sickness of the land shall redound to your glory** [*will end up being a blessing to you*].

88 **Let my servant William** go and **proclaim my everlasting gospel** with a loud voice, and with great joy, as he shall be moved upon by my Spirit, **unto the inhabitants of Warsaw** [*Illinois, a few miles south of Nauvoo*], and also unto the inhabitants of **Carthage**, and also unto the inhabitants of **Burlington**, and also unto the inhabitants of **Madison**, and await patiently and diligently for further instructions at my general conference, saith the Lord.

89 **If he will do my will** [*if he really wants to do the will of the Lord*] **let him from henceforth** [*from now on*] **hearken to the counsel of my servant Joseph, and with his interest** [*financial means; income—see D&C 119:4*] **support the cause of the poor, and publish the new translation of my holy word** [*the Joseph Smith Translation of the Bible*] **unto the inhabitants of the earth.**

90 And **if he will do this I will bless him with a multiplicity of blessings, that he shall not be forsaken, nor his seed be found begging bread.**

91 And again, verily I say unto you, **let** my servant **William** [*Law*] **be appointed, ordained, and anointed, as counselor unto my servant Joseph** [*as second counselor in the First Presidency*], **in the room of** [*in place of*] **my servant Hyrum** [*Smith*], **that my servant Hyrum may take the office of** Priesthood and **Patriarch**, which was appointed unto him by his father, by blessing and also by right;

Hyrum Smith is called to be patriarch to the Church and replace Oliver Cowdery in several functions in the Church (verse 91, above, and verses 92–96)

The Prophet's father, Joseph Smith Sr., had been serving as the patriarch to the Church prior to his death on September 14, 1840, in Nauvoo. Now Hyrum was called to fill that position, serving the general population of the Church as needed.

92 That **from henceforth he shall hold the keys of the patriarchal blessings upon the heads of all my people,**

93 That **whoever he blesses shall be blessed,** and **whoever he curses shall be cursed;** that **whatsoever he shall bind on earth shall be bound in heaven;** and **whatsoever he shall loose on earth shall be loosed in heaven.**

94 And from this time forth I appoint unto him **that he may be a prophet, and a seer, and a revelator unto my church, as well as my servant Joseph;**

95 **That he may act in concert also with my servant Joseph;** and **that he shall receive counsel from my servant Joseph** [*in other words, he is to work under the direction of Joseph, the Prophet*], who shall show unto him the keys whereby he may ask and receive, **and be crowned with the same blessing, and glory, and honor, and priesthood, and gifts of the priesthood, that once were put**

upon him that was my servant Oliver Cowdery;

Remember that Oliver Cowdery had apostatized and had been excommunicated in April 1838. At this time, he is still out of the Church but will return and request rebaptism during a conference of the Church held at Kanesville, Iowa, in October 1848. His request will be approved, and he will be rebaptized in November 1848.

96 That my servant Hyrum may bear record of the things which I shall show unto him, **that his name may be had in honorable remembrance from generation to generation, forever and ever** [*as you know, this prophecy has been thoroughly and marvelously fulfilled*].

Instructions to several individuals, including warnings to some (verses 97–118)

97 **Let my servant William Law** also receive the keys by which he may ask and receive blessings; let him **be humble before me, and be without guile, and he shall receive of my Spirit, even the Comforter** [*the Holy Ghost*], **which shall manifest unto him the truth of all things, and shall give him, in the very hour, what he shall say.**

As you can see, William Law is

given marvelous promises if he will "be humble before me" (verse 97, above). Unfortunately, he will not follow this counsel, and will apostatize, becoming one of the Prophet's most bitter enemies.

One of the lessons we can learn from this is that blessings, including patriarchal blessings, can point out to us what our potential is. But we still have agency and can lose the blessings by poor agency choices.

98 And **these signs shall follow him—he shall heal the sick**, he shall **cast out devils**, and shall **be delivered** from those who would administer unto him deadly poison;

99 And **he shall be led in paths where the poisonous serpent** [*can be symbolic of Satan and his temptations and poisonous false doctrines and philosophies*] **cannot lay hold upon his heel, and he shall mount up in the imagination of his thoughts as upon eagles' wings.**

100 And **what if I will that he should raise the dead, let him not withhold his voice.**

101 Therefore, **let my servant William cry aloud and spare not, with joy and rejoicing, and** with hosannas to him [*God*] that sitteth upon the throne forever

and ever, saith the Lord your God.

Next, in verse 102, we see that both William Law and Hyrum Smith are to take pressure off the Prophet Joseph.

102 Behold, I say unto you, **I have a mission in store for my servant William, and my servant Hyrum, and for them alone; and let my servant Joseph tarry at home, for he is needed.** The remainder I will show unto you hereafter. Even so. Amen.

103 And again, verily I say unto you, **if** my **servant Sidney** [*Rigdon*] **will serve me and be counselor unto my servant Joseph, let him arise and come up and stand in the office of his calling, and humble himself before me.**

104 And **if he will offer unto me an acceptable offering, and acknowledgments** [*perhaps meaning that Sidney must confess his tendencies toward apostasy that were in his heart at this time*], **and remain with my people** [*in Nauvoo*], behold, **I, the Lord your God, will heal him** [*he was suffering from poor health at this time*] that he shall be healed; **and he shall lift up his voice again** on the mountains, **and be a spokesman** before my face.

105 **Let him come and locate**

his family in the neighborhood in which my servant Joseph resides.

106 And in all his journeyings **let him lift up his voice** [*preach the gospel*] as with the sound of a trump, and warn the inhabitants of the earth to flee the wrath to come.

Next, both Sidney Rigdon and William Law, counselors in the First Presidency, are instructed to help the Prophet write the proclamation spoken of in verses 2–3, at the beginning of this section.

107 **Let him assist my servant Joseph, and also let my servant William Law assist my servant Joseph, in making a solemn proclamation** unto the kings of the earth, even as I have before said unto you.

108 **If my servant Sidney will do my will** [*if Sidney Rigdon truly desires to be obedient*], **let him not remove his family unto the eastern lands** [*probably meaning Kirtland—see verse 83*], but let him change their habitation, even as I have said [*in other words, they need to relocate to live near the Prophet as stated in verse 105*] .

109 Behold, **it is not my will that he shall seek to find safety and refuge out of** the city which I

have appointed unto you, even the city of **Nauvoo.**

110 Verily I say unto you, even now, **if he will hearken unto my voice, it shall be well with him.** Even so. Amen.

Have you noticed that there are a lot of "ifs" to many of these individuals? It is certainly a reminder that we do indeed have agency.

111 And again, verily I say unto you, **let** my servant **Amos Davies pay stock** into the hands of those whom I have appointed **to build** a house for boarding, even **the Nauvoo House.**

112 This let him do if he will have an interest [*if he wants to be a stockholder*]; and **let him hearken unto the counsel of my servant Joseph**, and labor with his own hands that he may obtain the confidence of men.

A principle that applies to all of us is taught to Brother Amos Davies in verse 112, next.

113 And **when he shall prove himself faithful in** all things that shall be entrusted unto his care, yea, even **a few things, he shall be made ruler over many** [*this usually refers to exaltation—see verse 114—when we become gods*];

114 **Let him therefore abase**

[*humble*] **himself that he may be exalted**. Even so. Amen.

Robert Foster, spoken of in verse 115, next, became one of the most bitter and dangerous apostates, bringing false charges against the Prophet and conspiring with others to bring about his death.

115 And again, verily I say unto you, **if** my servant **Robert D. Foster will** [*truly desires to*] **obey my voice**, let him build a house for my servant Joseph, according to the contract which he has made with him, as the door shall be open to him from time to time.

116 And **let him repent of all his folly, and clothe himself with charity; and cease to do evil, and lay aside all his hard** [*mean, bitter*] **speeches**;

117 And pay stock also into the hands of the quorum [*building committee*] of the Nauvoo House, for himself and for his generation after him, from generation to generation;

There is much more to the picture here than merely donating money for the building of the Nauvoo House by buying stock in it (verse 117, above). It is the principle of joining with others in supporting and sustaining the work of the Lord and unselfishly doing whatever it takes to be obedient and follow the Prophet.

118 **And hearken unto the counsel of my servants Joseph, and Hyrum, and William Law, and unto the authorities** which I have called to lay the foundation of Zion; and **it shall be well with him forever and ever**. Even so. Amen.

More instructions regarding the Nauvoo House (verses 119–22)

119 **And again, verily I say unto you, let no man pay stock to the quorum** [*the building committee—see verse 62*] **of the Nauvoo House unless he shall be a believer in the Book of Mormon, and the revelations I have given unto you**, saith the Lord your God;

The policy that no one could buy stock in the Nauvoo House unless they believed in the scriptures (verse 119, above) is similar to the policy today, that no one may pay tithing unless he or she is a member of the Church. Verse 120 is a stern warning not to change that rule.

120 For **that which is more or less than this cometh of evil, and shall be attended with cursings** [*trouble*] **and not blessings**, saith the Lord your God. Even so. Amen.

Next, in verse 121, the Lord shows a high degree of trust in the honesty and integrity of those serving on the Nauvoo House building committee by allowing them to set their own wages.

121 And again, verily I say unto you, **let the quorum of the Nauvoo House** [*the building committee*] **have** a **just** recompense of **wages** [*be paid a fair salary*] **for all their labors** which they do in building the Nauvoo House; and let their wages be **as shall be agreed among themselves,** as pertaining to the price thereof.

122 **And let every man who pays stock bear his proportion of their wages,** if it must needs be, for their support, saith the Lord; otherwise, their labors shall be accounted [*credited*] unto them for stock in that house [*otherwise, they can be credited with stock in the Nauvoo House as wages*]. Even so. Amen.

Additional instructions regarding Hyrum Smith's call to serve as patriarch and a review of priesthood keys, quorums, and presidencies, including several callings of brethren to serve in quorum presidencies (verses 123–45)

In these next verses, the Savior gives a brief review and overview of the priesthood organization of the Church. The Nauvoo Stake will be organized with a presidency and a high council, and several priesthood quorums will be organized.

In verse 123, next, we are reminded that the Savior, Himself, holds the Melchizedek Priesthood and is a high priest, as was Melchizedek.

123 Verily I say unto you, **I now give unto you the officers belonging to my Priesthood,** that ye may hold the keys thereof, even **the Priesthood** which is **after the order of Melchizedek** [*the priesthood that Melchizedek held*], **which is after the order of** [*which is the same as that held by*] **mine Only Begotten Son.**

Did you notice what just happened at the end of verse 123, above? The Savior spoke for the Father without alerting us first that He was going to do so. This is often referred to as "Divine Investiture" and means that the Savior speaks directly for the Father, as if the Father were doing the talking. You can see other examples of this in D&C 29:1, 42, and 46, as well as in Moses 1:6 as explained in *Doctrines of Salvation,* 1:27.

124 First, **I give unto you Hyrum Smith to be a patriarch unto you, to hold the sealing blessings of my church,** even the Holy Spirit of promise [*the sealing power exercised by the Holy Ghost—see*

D&C 132:7, 19], whereby ye are sealed up unto the day of redemption, that ye may not fall notwithstanding the hour of temptation that may come upon you.

125 I give unto you my servant **Joseph** [*the Prophet*] to be a **presiding elder over all my church**, to be **a translator, a revelator, a seer, and prophet**.

126 I give unto him for **counselors** my servant **Sidney Rigdon** and my servant **William Law**, that these may **constitute a quorum and First Presidency**, to receive the oracles [*revelations*] for the whole church.

127 I give unto you my servant **Brigham Young** to be a **president over the Twelve** traveling council [*the Twelve Apostles*];

128 **Which Twelve hold the keys to open up the authority of my kingdom upon the four corners of the earth** [*the whole world*]**, and after that to send my word to every creature**.

129 They are **Heber C. Kimball, Parley P. Pratt, Orson Pratt, Orson Hyde, William Smith, John Taylor, John E. Page, Wilford Woodruff, Willard Richards, George A. Smith**;

130 David Patten [*who was killed in the Battle of the Big Blue during mob violence in Missouri*] I have taken unto myself; behold, **his priesthood no man taketh from him**; but, verily I say unto you, **another may be appointed unto the same calling** [*to replace him as an Apostle in the Quorum of the Twelve Apostles*].

131 And again, I say unto you, **I give unto you a high council, for the corner-stone of Zion** [*for the Nauvoo Stake*]—

132 Namely, **Samuel Bent, Henry G. Sherwood, George W. Harris, Charles C. Rich, Thomas Grover, Newel Knight, David Dort, Dunbar Wilson**—Seymour Brunson I have taken unto myself; no man taketh his priesthood, but another may be appointed unto the same priesthood in his stead; and verily I say unto you, let my servant **Aaron Johnson** be ordained unto this calling in his stead—**David Fullmer, Alpheus Cutler, William Huntington**.

133 And again, **I give unto you Don C. Smith** [*Joseph Smith's younger brother*] **to be a president over a quorum of high priests**;

134 Which ordinance [*procedure*] is instituted for the purpose of qualifying those who shall be appointed **standing presidents**

[*presidents of local quorums as opposed to General Authorities*] or servants **over different stakes scattered abroad**;

Can you see that this is a sweeping panorama of how the priesthood is organized to handle the expansion of the Church? While it is quite familiar to us in our day, it was new and vital instruction for these early Saints.

135 And they may travel also if they choose, but rather be **ordained for standing presidents** [*to serve as local quorum presidencies*]; this is the office of their calling, saith the Lord your God.

136 **I give unto him** [*Don Carlos Smith*] **Amasa Lyman and Noah Packard for counselors**, that they may **preside over the quorum of high priests** of my church, saith the Lord.

137 And again, I say unto you, **I give unto you John A. Hicks, Samuel Williams, and Jesse Baker, which priesthood is to preside over the quorum of elders**, which quorum is instituted for **standing ministers** [*priesthood leaders who preside over local quorums and are not required to travel throughout the world as is the case with General Authorities*]; nevertheless **they may travel, yet they are ordained to be standing**

ministers to my church, saith the Lord.

138 And again, **I give unto you Joseph Young, Josiah Butterfield, Daniel Miles, Henry Herriman, Zera Pulsipher, Levi Hancock, James Foster, to preside over the quorum of seventies** [*to serve as the seven presidents of the General Authority Seventies*];

Verse 139, next, instructs that the General Authority Seventies are presided over by the Quorum of the Twelve Apostles (see D&C 107:34).

139 Which quorum is instituted for **traveling elders to bear record of my name in all the world, wherever the traveling high council, mine apostles, shall send them** to prepare a way before my face.

140 The difference between this quorum and the quorum of elders is that one is to travel continually [*the Apostles*], and the other [*the Seventies*] is to preside over the churches from time to time; the one has the responsibility of presiding from time to time, and the other has no responsibility of presiding [*at this time in the development of the Church*], saith the Lord your God.

141 And again, I say unto you, **I**

give unto you Vinson Knight, Samuel H. Smith, and Shadrach Roundy, if he will receive it, to preside over the bishopric; a knowledge of said bishopric is given unto you in the book of Doctrine and Covenants.

142 And again, I say unto you, Samuel Rolfe and his counselors for priests [a priests quorum presidency], and the president of the teachers and his counselors [a teachers quorum presidency], and also the president of the deacons and his counselors [a deacons quorum presidency], and also the president of the stake and his counselors [the stake presidency for the Nauvoo Stake].

Next, the Savior summarizes the above instructions for expanding the priesthood organization of the Church. It will be essential for the continued growth of the Church to have these quorum presidencies function properly in the new stakes and wards as they are formed.

143 The above offices I have given unto you, and the keys thereof, for helps and for governments, for the work of the ministry and the perfecting of my saints.

The sustaining of officers in conference is addressed in verse 144, next, and is based on the law of common consent as given in D&C 26:2.

144 And a commandment I give unto you, that you should fill all these offices and approve of those names which I have mentioned, or else disapprove of them at my general conference;

145 And that ye should prepare rooms [offices] for all these offices [priesthood leaders] in my house [the Nauvoo Temple—see footnote 145a] when you build it unto my name, saith the Lord your God. Even so. Amen.

SECTION 125

Background

This revelation was given through the Prophet Joseph Smith in March 1841 at Nauvoo, Illinois.

When the Saints were driven from Missouri and began settling in what became Nauvoo, Illinois, some of them settled across the Mississippi River in the territory of Iowa to the west of Nauvoo and began establishing settlements there. Church leaders had arranged to buy 700 acres in Illinois in what became Nauvoo, and around 18,000 acres of land in Lee County, Iowa Territory.

With the large numbers of Saints fleeing persecution elsewhere, having these large tracts of land available for settlement was most helpful. It obviously allowed the members to find homesites and begin building without overcrowding certain locations. Branches of the Church were established in Iowa Territory in Zarahemla (see verse 3) and Nashville (near Montrose), as well as in small settlements near the existing settlement of Montrose.

By October 5, 1839, the Iowa Stake was created. About a year and a half later, as mentioned above, in March 1841, the Prophet Joseph Smith received this revelation after asking the Lord about the settlements across the Mississippi River in Iowa Territory.

Question

1 WHAT is the will of the Lord concerning the saints in the Territory of Iowa?

Answer

2 Verily, thus saith the Lord, I say unto you, **if those who call themselves by my name** [*members of the Church who have taken upon themselves the name of Jesus Christ through baptism*] **and are essaying** [*attempting, endeavoring, striving*] **to be my saints**, if they **will do my will and keep my commandments** concerning them [*in other words, if they truly want to be obedient*], **let them gather** themselves together **unto the places which I**

shall appoint unto them by my servant Joseph, and build up cities unto my name, that they may be prepared for that which is in store for a time to come.

One of the important messages in the scriptures is that the Lord supports His prophets. In verse 2, above, we see yet another example of this in which the Lord points the people to the Prophet Joseph for inspired instructions concerning the settlements in the Territory of Iowa.

3 **Let them build** up a city unto my name upon the land **opposite the city of Nauvoo**, and let the name of **Zarahemla** be named upon it.

Zarahemla was near Montrose, Iowa, and at one time had over three hundred members living in it.

Next, in verse 4, the Lord tells the Saints that they are free to choose any of the named locations or to live in any stakes that were established.

4 And **let all those** who come from the east, and the west, and the north, and the south, **that have desires to dwell therein, take up their inheritance in the same** [*in other words, those who desire to live in Zarahemla are welcome to do so*], **as well as in** the city of **Nashville** [*in Lee County, Iowa*], **or in the city**

of Nauvoo, and in all the stakes which I have appointed, saith the Lord.

In August 1841, the Iowa Stake name was changed to the Zarahemla Stake. Some months later, in January 1842, the Iowa Territory settlements had served their temporary purpose and the Zarahemla Stake was dissolved because so many members had moved to Nauvoo to help build the temple and assist in other construction projects.

SECTION 126

Background

This revelation was given through the Prophet Joseph Smith to Brigham Young (the president of the Quorum of the Twelve Apostles at the time—see D&C 124:127) on July 9, 1841, in Nauvoo, Illinois.

Brigham Young had studied the Book of Mormon extensively for two years before being baptized in his own millpond by Eleazar Miller on April 15, 1832. After his baptism, he traveled extensively on missions in Upper Canada and several eastern states, including New York. He faithfully participated in the march of Zion's Camp from Ohio to Missouri in 1834. He became a member of the Quorum of the Twelve Apostles on February 14, 1835. He left Montrose, Iowa, on September 14, 1839, to serve a mission in England. On July 1, 1841, having completed his mission to England, he rejoined his wife Mary Ann and his children who were living in Nauvoo. Now, in this revelation, the Lord tells him to send other missionaries abroad (verse 3) and to stay home with his family from now on.

One of the things we see here is the fact that the Lord is keeping Brigham closer to the Prophet, no doubt, to train him to become the next prophet. He spent twenty-eight of the last thirty-six months of the Prophet's life in close contact with him. On July 9, 1841, Joseph visited Brigham in his home and dictated this revelation to him.

Brigham Young gave his all in whatever he was called to do by the Lord, and in verse 1, we hear the Lord compliment him and accept his work.

1 **DEAR and well-beloved brother, Brigham Young,** verily thus saith the Lord unto you: My servant Brigham, **it is no more required at your hand to leave your family as in times past, for your offering is acceptable to me.**

2 **I have seen your labor and toil in journeyings for my name.**

3 I therefore command you to **send my word abroad** [*as President of the Twelve, direct others in*

missionary work], and **take espe-cial care of your family from this time, henceforth** and forever. Amen.

SECTION 127

Background

This is a letter written by the Prophet Joseph Smith to the Saints in Nauvoo, Illinois, dated September 1, 1842.

At the time Joseph Smith wrote this letter, he was in hiding in the home of John Taylor's father in Nauvoo (see *Doctrine and Covenants Student Manual,* 1981, 314). Persecution against him had increased in Illinois, and repeated attempts by Missourians to trap him and take him to Missouri had forced him into hiding.

In the first two verses of this letter, we get insights into the indomitable and cheerful personality of the Prophet of the Restoration.

1 **FORASMUCH as** the Lord has revealed unto me **that my enemies, both in Missouri and this State, were again in the pursuit of me**; and inasmuch as **they pursue me without a cause, and have not the least shadow or coloring of justice or right on their side** in the getting up of their prosecutions against me; and inasmuch as their pretensions are all founded in falsehood of the blackest dye, **I have thought it expedient** [*necessary*] and wisdom in me **to leave the place for a short season, for my own safety and the safety of this people.** I would say to all those with whom I have business, that I have left my affairs with agents and clerks who will transact all business in a prompt and proper manner, and will see that all my debts are canceled [*paid off*] in due time, by turning out property, or otherwise, as the case may require, or as the circumstances may admit of. **When I learn that the storm is fully blown over, then I will return to you again.**

2 And **as for the perils which I am called to pass through, they seem but a small thing to me**, as the envy and wrath of man have been my common lot all the days of my life; and for what cause it seems mysterious, unless I was ordained from before the foundation of the world for some good end, or bad, as you may choose to call it. Judge ye for yourselves. God knoweth all these things, whether it be good or bad. But nevertheless, **deep water is what I am wont** [*accustomed*] **to swim in. It all has become a second nature to me**; and I feel, like Paul, to glory in tribulation; for to this day has the God of my fathers

delivered me out of them all, and will deliver me from henceforth; for behold, and lo, **I shall triumph over all my enemies, for the Lord God hath spoken it.**

3 **Let all the saints rejoice, therefore, and be exceedingly glad**; for Israel's God is their God, and he will mete out a just recompense of reward upon the heads of all their oppressors.

Next, in verse 4, the Prophet urges the Saints to continue work on building the Nauvoo Temple, as well as other projects.

4 And again, verily thus saith the Lord: **Let the work of my temple, and all the works which I have appointed unto you, be continued on and not cease**; and let your diligence, and your perseverance, and patience, and your works be redoubled [*increased*], and you shall in nowise lose your reward, saith the Lord of Hosts. And **if they persecute you, so persecuted they the prophets and righteous men that were before you**. For all this there is a reward in heaven.

Perhaps one of the important messages we gain from the last part of verse 4, above, is that the righteous are always persecuted by the wicked. And if the Church is not being persecuted on occasion,

it may be that we are not living our religion as we should.

Next, the Prophet writes and instructs about baptism for the dead. He had introduced the topic as early as August 15, 1840, in a funeral sermon for Brother Seymore Brunson, after which baptisms for the dead were conducted in the Mississippi River. In section 124, verses 29–33, given January 19, 1841, the Saints were warned that the time would soon come in which their baptisms for the dead would no longer be valid unless they built the Nauvoo Temple and performed them in it.

The first baptisms for the dead in the Nauvoo Temple baptismal font (the rest of the building was not yet completed) were performed on Sunday, November 21, 1841 (see *Doctrine and Covenants Student Manual,* 1981, 314).

5 And again, **I give unto you a word in relation to the baptism for your dead**.

Any of you who have had the privilege of being baptized for the dead know that there is a recorder present who makes sure that the baptisms are officially and accurately recorded in the records of the temple. The instruction for this is seen in verse 6, next. The reasons for it are given in verses 7 and 9.

6 Verily, thus saith the Lord unto you concerning your dead: When

any of you are baptized for your dead, **let there be a recorder**, and let him be eye-witness of your baptisms; let him hear with his ears, that he may testify of a truth, saith the Lord;

7 **That in all your recordings it may be recorded in heaven; whatsoever you bind on earth, may be bound in heaven; whatsoever you loose on earth, may be loosed in heaven**;

8 For I am about to restore many things to the earth, pertaining to the priesthood, saith the Lord of Hosts.

9 And again, **let all the records be had in order, that they may be put in the archives of my holy temple**, to be held in remembrance from generation to generation, saith the Lord of Hosts.

In verses 10–12, next, we feel the loneliness and yearning of the Prophet to again be able to openly associate with the Saints.

10 I will say to all the saints, that **I desired, with exceedingly great desire, to have addressed them from the stand** [*the pulpit; in other words, in public meetings of the Church*] on the subject of baptism for the dead, on the following Sabbath. **But inasmuch as it is out of my power to do so, I will**

write the word of the Lord from time to time, on that subject, and send it to you by mail, as well as many other things.

11 **I now close my letter for the present, for the want of more time; for the enemy is on the alert**, and as the Savior said, **the prince of this world cometh** [*a quote from John 14:30, meaning the devil is much involved in the persecutions*], **but he hath nothing in me** [*he will not take me*].

12 Behold, **my prayer to God is that you all may be saved**. And **I subscribe myself** [*I present myself to you as*] **your servant in the Lord** [*in the work of the Lord*], **prophet and seer of the Church of Jesus Christ of Latter-day Saints**.

JOSEPH SMITH.

SECTION 128

Background

As was the case with section 127, this letter from the Prophet was also written while he was in hiding. This time he was hiding in the attic of Edward Hunter's home, which was accessed by a trap door. There was not enough room for Joseph to stand up. We read (**bold** added for emphasis), "President Smith, accompanied by

Brother Erastus Derby, left Brother Whitney's about nine o'clock, and went to Brother Edward Hunter's, where he was welcomed, and made comfortable by the family, and **where he can be kept safe from the hands of his enemies**" (*History of the Church,* 5:146).

The letter was dated September 6, 1842, in Nauvoo, Illinois. In it the Prophet gives additional instruction on work for the dead.

1 AS I stated to you in my letter [*section 127*] before I left my place, that I would write to you from time to time and give you information in relation to many subjects, **I now resume the subject of the baptism for the dead,** as that subject seems to occupy my mind, and **press itself upon my feelings** the strongest, since I have been pursued by my enemies.

In verse 1, above, we gain an important insight as to one of the ways the Spirit of the Lord communicates with us. The Holy Ghost "presses" things upon our minds and feelings.

Next, in verses 2–5, Joseph Smith gives instruction regarding the role of temple recorders. The importance of record-keeping is strongly emphasized.

2 I wrote a few words of revelation to you **concerning a recorder** [*a*

person who witnesses and officially records baptisms for the dead—see D&C 127:6]. **I have had a few additional views in relation to this matter, which I now certify**. That is, it was declared in my former letter that **there should be a recorder, who should be eye-witness, and also to hear with his ears, that he might make a record of a truth before the Lord**.

3 Now, in relation to this matter, **it would be very difficult for one recorder to be present at all times, and to do all the business**. To obviate [*eliminate*] this difficulty, **there can be a recorder appointed in each ward of the city, who is well qualified for taking accurate minutes**; and **let him be very particular and precise** in taking the whole proceedings, certifying in his record that he saw with his eyes, and heard with his ears, giving the date, and names, and so forth, and the history of the whole transaction; **naming also some three individuals that are present**, if there be any present, who can at any time when called upon certify to the same, **that in the mouth of two or three witnesses every word may be established**.

4 Then, **let there be a general recorder,** to whom these other

records can be handed, being attended with certificates over their own signatures, certifying that the record they have made is true. **Then the general church recorder can enter the record on the general church book**, with the certificates and all the attending witnesses, with his own statement that he verily believes the above statement and records to be true, from his knowledge of the general character and appointment of those men by the church. And when this is done on the general church book, the record shall be just as holy, and shall answer the ordinance just the same as if he had seen with his eyes and heard with his ears, and made a record of the same on the general church book.

5 **You may think this order of things to be very particular; but let me tell you that it is only to answer the will of God**, by conforming to the ordinance and preparation that the Lord ordained and prepared before the foundation of the world, **for the salvation of the dead who should die without a knowledge of the gospel**.

Next, the Prophet emphasizes the importance of keeping accurate records by quoting the Apostle John, who recorded his vision in the Book of Revelation.

6 And further, I want you to remember that **John the Revelator** was contemplating this very subject in relation to the dead, when he declared, as you will find recorded in **Revelation 20:12**—*And I saw the dead, small and great* [relatively unknown as well as famous], *stand before God; and the books were opened; and another book was opened, which is the book of life* [the record of our lives, which is kept in heaven—see verse 7, next]; *and the dead were judged out of those things which were written in the books, according to their works.*

7 **You will discover in this quotation that the books were opened; and another book was opened, which was the book of life; but the dead were judged out of those things which were written in the books,** according to their works; consequently, **the books spoken of must be the books which contained the record of their works, and refer to the records which are kept on the earth.** And the book which was **the book of life is the record which is kept in heaven;** the principle agreeing precisely with the doctrine which is commanded

you in the revelation contained in the letter which I wrote to you previous to my leaving my place—that in all your recordings it may be recorded in heaven.

Next, in verse 8, the Prophet teaches of the power of the priesthood to bind and loose in heaven and earth and continues to emphasize the importance of records. Perhaps you know of someone whose records were lost or whose ordinance, such as baptism or a priesthood ordination, was not recorded. In such cases, the ordinance must be performed again, and a proper record kept and submitted to the Church.

Also, the Prophet Joseph Smith explains that the work done for the dead by proxy counts just the same as if the dead had received the ordinances themselves.

8 Now, the nature of this ordinance consists in the power of the priesthood, by the revelation of Jesus Christ, wherein it is granted that **whatsoever you bind on earth shall be bound in heaven, and whatsoever you loose on earth shall be loosed in heaven.** Or, in other words, taking a different view of the translation, **whatsoever you record on earth shall be recorded in heaven, and whatsoever you do not record on earth shall not be recorded in heaven; for out of the books**

shall your dead be judged, according to their own works, whether they themselves have attended to the ordinances in their own *propria persona* [*in person*], **or by the means of their own agents** [*proxies*], according to the ordinance which God has prepared for their salvation from before the foundation of the world, according to the records which they have kept concerning their dead.

9 **It may seem to some to be a very bold doctrine that we talk of—a power which records or binds on earth and binds in heaven. Nevertheless, in all ages of the world, whenever the Lord has given a dispensation of the priesthood to any man by actual revelation, or any set of men, this power has always been given.** Hence, whatsoever those men did in authority, in the name of the Lord, and did it truly and faithfully, **and kept a proper and faithful record of the same, it became a law on earth and in heaven,** and could not be annulled, according to the decrees of the great Jehovah. This is a faithful saying. Who can hear it?

Beginning with verse 10, next, the Prophet explains to the Saints that the doctrine of sealing and loosing on earth and heaven through the power of the priesthood delegated to man is not a new doctrine. Rather, it is clearly taught in the Bible.

10 **And again, for the precedent, Matthew 16:18, 19**: *And I say also unto thee, That thou art Peter, and upon this rock I will build my church; and the gates of hell shall not prevail against it. And I will give unto thee the keys of the kingdom of heaven: and* **whatsoever thou shalt bind on earth shall be bound in heaven; and whatsoever thou shalt loose on earth shall be loosed in heaven**.

11 Now the great and grand secret of the whole matter, and **the *summum bonum*** [*the main point*] **of the whole subject** that is lying before us, **consists in obtaining the powers of the Holy Priesthood. For him to whom these keys are given there is no difficulty in obtaining a knowledge of facts in relation to the salvation of the children of men, both as well for the dead as for the living.**

Next, we are instructed about the necessity for baptism and the symbolism of baptism.

12 **Herein is** glory and honor, and immortality and **eternal life** [*exaltation*]—The ordinance of **baptism by water** [*in other words,*

baptism is required for exaltation unless an individual dies before age eight—see D&C 137:10)], **to be immersed therein in order to answer to the likeness of** [*symbolic of*] **the dead** [*in being baptized, our old self is buried, like the dead—compare with Romans 6:4–6*], that one principle might accord with [*work in harmony with*] the other; **to be immersed in the water and come forth out of the water is in the likeness of the resurrection of the dead in coming forth out of their graves**; hence, this ordinance [*baptism by immersion—see first of this verse*] **was instituted to form a relationship with the ordinance of baptism for the dead**, being in likeness of the dead.

Perhaps you have noticed that, wherever possible, our baptismal fonts are constructed so that they are below ground level. The symbolism behind this is explained in verse 13, next.

13 Consequently, **the baptismal font was instituted as a similitude of** [*to symbolize*] **the grave, and was commanded to be in a place underneath** [*below ground level*] where the living are wont to assemble, **to show forth the living and the dead, and that all things may have their likeness,** and that they may accord [*agree;*

harmonize] one with another—**that which is earthly conforming to that which is heavenly, as Paul hath declared**, 1 Corinthians 15:46, 47, and 48:

14 Howbeit [*however*] **that was not first which is spiritual, but that which is natural; and afterward that which is spiritual** [*in other words, first we get our mortal bodies; next, we get our immortal, resurrected bodies*]. The first man [*Adam*] is of the earth, earthy [*Adam received a mortal body first, made of earthly elements*]; the second man [*Christ*] is the Lord from heaven. As is the earthy [*just like Adam*], such are they also that are earthy [*all of us get a mortal body subject to death*]; and as is the heavenly [*just as Christ received a resurrected celestial body*], such are they also that are heavenly [*so also will all the righteous get a celestial, resurrected body*]. **And as are the records on the earth in relation to your dead, which are truly** [*accurately*] **made out, so also are the records in heaven. This, therefore, is the sealing and binding power**, and, in one sense of the word, the keys of the kingdom, which consist in the key of knowledge.

Joseph Fielding Smith explained the reason for having baptismal fonts in our temples below ground level, as follows:

"The Lord has placed the baptismal font in our temples below the foundation, or the surface of the earth. This is symbolical, since the dead are in their graves, and we are working for the dead when we are baptized for them. Moreover, baptism is also symbolical of death and the resurrection, in fact, is virtually a resurrection from the life of sin, or from spiritual death, to the life of spiritual life. (See D. & C. 29:41–45.) Therefore when the dead have had this ordinance performed in their behalf they are considered to have been brought back into the presence of God, just as this doctrine is applied to the living" (*Church History and Modern Revelation,* 2:332).

Verse 15, next, teaches vital doctrine about our own salvation and doing the work for our dead.

Doctrine

When we can do the work for our dead, doing it is essential for our own salvation.

15 **And now, my dearly beloved brethren and sisters, let me assure you that these are principles in relation to the dead and the living that cannot be lightly passed over, as pertaining to our salvation. For their salvation is necessary and essential to our salvation,** as Paul

says concerning the fathers—that **they without us cannot be made perfect—neither can we without our dead be made perfect** [*you may wish to cross-reference this phrase with the similar phrase in verse 18*].

Remember that this concept of doing work for the dead is a new, even startling doctrine for these early Saints. Next, the Prophet helps them understand that it is not new; rather, it was taught by the Apostle Paul in the Bible, as well as being a part of Elijah's mission as prophesied in Malachi.

16 And now, **in relation to the baptism for the dead, I will give you another quotation of Paul**, 1 Corinthians 15:29: *Else what shall they do which are baptized for the dead, if the dead rise not at all? Why are they then baptized for the dead?*

17 And again, in connection with this quotation I will give you a quotation from one of the prophets, who had his eye fixed on the restoration of the priesthood, the glories to be revealed in the last days, and in an especial manner this most glorious of all subjects belonging to the everlasting gospel, namely, the **baptism for the dead**; for **Malachi says**, last chapter, verses 5th and 6th: *Behold, I will send you Elijah the prophet*

*before the coming of the great and dreadful day of the Lord: And **he shall turn the heart of the fathers to the children, and the heart of the children to their fathers**, lest I come and smite the earth with a curse.*

Sometimes we find ourselves wishing that the Prophet Joseph Smith had clarified and rewritten almost every verse in the Bible. In verse 18, next, we see that he could have done much in that regard, but it was not necessary in many cases.

18 **I might have rendered a plainer translation to this, but it is sufficiently plain to suit my purpose as it stands.** It is sufficient to know, in this case, that **the earth will be smitten with a curse** [*won't fulfill its ultimate purpose of providing the opportunity for exaltation in family units for all who qualify*] **unless there is a welding link of some kind or other between the fathers and the children**, upon some subject or other—and **behold what is that subject? It is the baptism for the dead.** For **we without them cannot be made perfect; neither can they without us be made perfect.** Neither can they nor we be made perfect without those who have died in the gospel also; **for it is necessary** in the ushering in of the dispensation

of the fulness of times, which dispensation is now beginning to usher in, **that a whole and complete and perfect union, and welding together of dispensations, and keys, and powers, and glories should take place, and be revealed from the days of Adam even to the present time**. And not only this, but those things which never have been revealed from the foundation of the world, but have been kept hid from the wise and prudent, shall be revealed unto babes and sucklings in this, the dispensation of the fulness of times.

Having mentioned how important and special the dispensation of the fullness of times is (verse 18, above), the Prophet will now summarize several aspects of the restoration, including appearances of past prophets who have come to restore things pertaining to their dispensations to our dispensation, which is the last dispensation before the Second Coming. As you can see, we do indeed have the restored gospel, restored from the past.

19 Now, **what do we hear** in the gospel which we have received? **A voice of gladness! A voice of mercy from heaven;** and **a voice of truth out of the earth** [*the Book of Mormon*]; **glad tidings for the dead; a voice of gladness for the living and the dead** [*because*

work for the dead has been restored]; glad tidings of great joy. How beautiful upon the mountains are the feet of those that bring glad tidings of good things, and that say unto Zion: Behold, thy God reigneth! As the dews of Carmel, so shall the knowledge of God descend upon them!

20 And again, what do we hear? Glad tidings from Cumorah! **Moroni**, an angel from heaven, declaring the fulfilment of the prophets—the book to be revealed. **A voice of the Lord** in the wilderness of Fayette, Seneca county, declaring the three witnesses to bear record of the book! The voice of **Michael** [*Adam*] on the banks of the Susquehanna, detecting the devil when he appeared as an angel of light [*this is all we know about this appearance*]! The voice of **Peter, James, and John** in the wilderness between Harmony, Susquehanna county, and Colesville, Broome county, on the Susquehanna river, declaring themselves as possessing the keys of the kingdom, and of the dispensation of the fulness of times!

21 And again, **the voice of God** in the chamber of old Father Whitmer, in Fayette, Seneca county, and at sundry times, and

in divers [*various*] places through all the travels and tribulations of this Church of Jesus Christ of Latter-day Saints! And the voice of **Michael, the archangel** [*Adam*]; the voice of Gabriel, and of **Raphael** [*we don't know who this is*], and of **divers** [*various*] **angels**, from Michael or Adam down to the present time, **all declaring their dispensation, their rights, their keys, their honors, their majesty and glory, and the power of their priesthood; giving line upon line, precept upon precept**; here a little, and there a little; giving us consolation by holding forth that which is to come, confirming our hope!

As indicated in the above verses, the Prophet Joseph Smith was taught by many who came from beyond the veil. We will include a partial list here, quoting from President John Taylor:

"When God selected Joseph Smith to open up the last dispensation . . . the **Father** and the **Son** appeared to him . . . **Moroni** came to Joseph . . . Then comes another personage, whose name is **John the Baptist** . . . Afterwards came **Peter, James and John** . . . Then we read again of **Elias or Elijah**, . . . who committed to him the powers and authority associated with his position. Then **Abraham**, who had the Gospel, the Priesthood

and Patriarchal powers in his day; and **Moses** who stood at the head of the gathering dispensation in his day. . . . We are informed that **Noah**, who was a Patriarch, and all in the line of the Priesthood, in every generation back to **Adam**, who was the first man, possessed the same. Why was it that all these people could communicate with Joseph Smith? Because he stood at the head of the dispensation of the fullness of times. . . . If you were to ask Joseph what sort of a looking man **Adam** was, he would tell you at once; he would tell you his size and appearance and all about him. You might have asked him what sort of men **Peter, James, and John** were, and he could have told you. Why? Because he had seen them" (in *Journal of Discourses*, 18:325–26).

"And when Joseph Smith was raised up as a Prophet of God, **Mormon, Moroni, Nephi and others of the ancient Prophets who formerly lived on this Continent, and Peter and John and others who lived on the Asiatic Continent**, came to him and communicated to him certain principles pertaining to the gospel of the Son of God" (in *Journal of Discourses*, 17:374).

"I know of what I speak for I was very well acquainted with him (Joseph Smith) and was with him a great deal during his life, and was with him when he died. The principles which he had, placed him in communication with the Lord, and not only with the Lord, but with the ancient apostles and prophets, such men, for instance, as **Abraham, Isaac, Jacob, Noah, Adam, Seth, Enoch, and Jesus and the Father, and the apostles that lived on this continent as well as those who lived on the Asiatic Continent.** He seemed to be as familiar with these people as we are with one another" (in *Journal of Discourses*, 21:94).

Also, the Prophet Joseph Smith gave the following description of the **Apostle Paul**: "He is about five feet high; very dark hair; dark complexion; dark skin; large Roman nose; sharp face; small black eyes, penetrating as eternity; round shoulders; a whining voice, except when elevated, and then it almost resembled the roaring of a lion. He was a good orator, active and diligent, always employing himself in doing good to his fellow man" (*Teachings of the Prophet Joseph Smith,* 180).

We feel the enthusiasm and great spirit of the Prophet Joseph Smith as he brings this letter to a close. Remember, he himself is in relatively miserable circumstances again at the time he wrote this epistle to the Saints.

22 **Brethren, shall we not go on in so great a cause? Go forward and not backward. Courage,** **brethren; and on, on to the victory!** Let your hearts rejoice, and be exceedingly glad. Let the earth break forth into singing. **Let the dead speak forth anthems of eternal praise to the King Immanuel, who hath ordained, before the world was, that which would enable us to redeem them out of their prison; for the prisoners shall go free**.

23 Let the mountains shout for joy, and all ye valleys cry aloud; and all ye seas and dry lands tell the wonders of your Eternal King! And ye rivers, and brooks, and rills, flow down with gladness. Let the woods and all the trees of the field praise the Lord; and ye solid rocks weep for joy! And let the sun, moon, and the morning stars sing together, and let all the sons of God shout for joy! And let the eternal creations declare his name forever and ever! **And again I say, how glorious is the voice we hear from heaven, proclaiming in our ears, glory, and salvation, and honor, and immortality, and eternal life; kingdoms, principalities, and powers!**

Verse 24, next, is a cross-reference for the phrase "until the sons of Levi do offer again an offering unto the Lord in righteousness," as found in section

13. Upon close examination, we see that one possible interpretation of this phrase is that we are, in effect, the sons of Levi.

They held the priesthood and performed ordinances among the children of Israel. In our day, we hold the priesthood and perform ordinances, including saving ordinances for the dead. Therefore, symbolically, we can be considered to be the "sons of Levi." And, because of the restoration of the priesthood, including the keys of sealing by Elijah (D&C 110:13–16), we can "offer again an offering unto the Lord in righteousness." In other words, we can once again perform valid saving priesthood ordinances upon the earth.

24 Behold, **the great day of the Lord is at hand** [*the Second Coming of Christ is getting close*]; and who can abide [*survive*] the day of his coming, and who can stand when he appeareth? For he is like a refiner's fire, and like fuller's soap; and he shall sit as a refiner and purifier of silver, and **he shall purify the sons of Levi**, and purge them as gold and silver, **that they may offer unto the Lord an offering in righteousness. Let us, therefore**, as a church and a people, and as Latter-day Saints, **offer unto the Lord an offering in righteousness**; and let us present in his holy temple, when it is finished, a book containing the records of our dead, which shall be worthy of all acceptation.

25 Brethren, **I have many things to say to you on the subject; but shall now close for the present**, and continue the subject another time. I am, as ever, your humble servant and never deviating friend,

JOSEPH SMITH.

SECTION 129

Background

This section consists of instructions by the Prophet Joseph Smith given on February 9, 1843, in Nauvoo, Illinois, regarding how to tell the difference between angels with resurrected bodies, righteous spirits, and evil spirits attempting to make people believe they are from God.

Most members of the Church have probably heard about "offering to shake hands" (verse 4) with messengers from the other side as a means of detecting impostors. This was an important issue in the early days of the Church, because Satan and his evil spirits were using every possible ploy to deceive the Saints with false revelations.

As you will see, three kinds of beings beyond the veil are mentioned by the Prophet in this instruction:

1. Resurrected beings with bodies of flesh and bone.

2. Righteous spirits who have only a spirit body and either have been to earth already but are not yet resurrected, or who have not yet been born on earth.

3. Evil spirits who have only their spirit bodies, which they obtained in premortality.

Before we study this section verse by verse, there is an additional major message implied here that we will just mention. It is the wonderful assurance that Satan and his evil hosts are bound by God and His laws. They are limited by Him. He has power to command, and they must obey!

Otherwise, any of Satan and his evil spirits could simply read section 129 of the Doctrine and Covenants and fool us by refusing to shake hands (verses 6–7). Thus, we would think him to be from God and would listen to his message with obedience in mind. As it is, however, Satan, or any other evil spirit, must offer his hand (because God requires it of them) when requested to do so (verse 8), and thus can be detected as evil by the righteous and informed.

Parley P. Pratt and others were present on February 9, 1843,

when the Prophet gave this instruction. We will use **bold**, as usual, for teaching purposes.

1 **THERE are two kinds of beings in heaven**, namely: **Angels**, who are **resurrected personages, having bodies of flesh and bones**—

2 For instance, Jesus said: *Handle me and see, for a spirit hath not flesh and bones, as ye see me have.*

3 **Secondly**: the **spirits of just** [*righteous men who faithfully obey the laws and ordinances of the gospel*] **made perfect**, they **who are not resurrected**, but inherit the same glory [*meaning righteous "spirits who have once had a mortal body and are awaiting resurrection"—see Guide to the Scriptures under "Angels," churchofjesuschrist. org*].

4 **When a messenger comes saying he has a message from God, offer him your hand** and request him to shake hands with you.

5 **If he be an angel** [*a resurrected being—see verse 1*] **he will do so, and you will feel his hand**.

6 **If he be the spirit of a just man made perfect** he will come in his glory; for that is the only way he can appear—

7 **Ask him to shake hands with you, but he will not move**, because it is contrary to the order of heaven for a just man to deceive; but he will still deliver his message.

8 **If it be the devil** as an angel of light [*trying to masquerade as a messenger from God*], **when you ask him to shake hands he will offer you his hand, and you will not feel anything**; you may therefore detect him.

9 **These are three grand keys whereby you may know whether any administration is from God.**

We receive further clarification on this topic from the 2018 *Doctrine and Covenants Student Manual* as follows:

"While the Prophet Joseph Smith referred only to resurrected beings as angels, President George Q. Cannon (1827–1901) of the First Presidency explained, 'In the broadest sense, any being who acts as a messenger for our Heavenly Father is an angel, be he a God, a resurrected man, or the spirit of a just man' ("Editorial Thoughts," *The Juvenile Instructor*, Jan. 15, 1891, 53). Thus, in addition to the heavenly messengers described in Doctrine and Covenants 129, God's angels also include spirits who 'have not yet obtained a body of flesh and bone' (*Guide to*

the Scriptures, "Angels," scriptures .lds.org; see also Ether 3:6–16; Moses 5:6) as well as translated beings—individuals whose mortal bodies are changed so that they do not experience pain or death (see 3 Nephi 28:6–9; Mormon 8:10–11; D&C 7:1–3)."

Over the years, some of my students have asked why we don't hear more of this now. One possible reason is that we have the gift of the Holy Ghost and thus can be warned by Him when evil approaches. Also, the Church is well-established now and the leadership is solidly in place as opposed to the frequent apostasy of Church leaders in the early days of the Restoration.

Whatever the case, the counsel and guidance in this section is still in force should it be needed by the righteous.

SECTION 130

Background

This section consists of items of instruction given by the Prophet Joseph Smith on Sunday, April 2, 1843, while accompanied by some of the brethren for dinner and visiting at his sister's home (Sophronia; see Joseph Smith–History 1:4 for a listing of his siblings) in Ramus, Illinois, about twenty miles southeast of Nauvoo.

The Prophet gave a little background for this Sunday as follows:

"*Sunday, 2.*—Wind N.E. Snow fell several inches, but melted more or less.

"At ten a.m. went to meeting. Heard Elder Orson Hyde preach. . . . Alluding to the coming of the Savior, he said, 'When He shall appear, we shall be like Him, &c. He will appear on a white horse as a warrior, and maybe we shall have some of the same spirit. Our God is a warrior (John 14:23). It is our privilege to have the Father and Son dwelling in our hearts, &c.'

"We dined with my sister Sophronia McCleary, when I told Elder Hyde that I was going to offer some corrections to his sermon this morning. He replied, 'They shall be thankfully received'" (*History of the Church*, 5:323).

The Prophet recorded these teachings in his journal and they became the instruction on a variety of topics given here in section 130.

Doctrine

The Savior is a glorified man, with a glorified resurrected body of flesh and bones—see also verse 22)

1 WHEN the Savior shall appear we shall see him as he is. We shall see that he is a man like ourselves.

Doctrine

We will enjoy socializing in the next life but will have the capacity to enjoy it even more.

2 And **that same sociality which exists among us here will exist among us there**, only it will be coupled with eternal glory, which glory we do not now enjoy.

Doctrine

The Father and the Son do not dwell in our heart.

3 John 14:23—The appearing of the Father and the Son in that verse is a personal appearance; and **the idea that the Father and the Son dwell in a man's heart is an old sectarian** [*coming from other religions*] **notion, and is false**.

Doctrine

Time systems are controlled by the planets upon which beings live. No angels minister to us other than those who belong to this earth.

4 In answer to the question—**Is not the reckoning of God's time, angel's time, prophet's time, and man's time, according to the planet on which they reside?**

5 I answer, **Yes**. But there are **no angels** who **minister to this**

earth but those who do belong or have belonged to it.

Doctrine

The planet upon which the Father resides serves as a Urim and Thummim.

6 **The angels do not reside on a planet like this earth;**

7 **But they reside in the presence of God, on a globe like a sea of glass and fire, where all things for their glory are manifest, past, present, and future,** and are continually before the Lord.

8 **The place where God resides is a great** [*huge*] **Urim and Thummim**.

Doctrine

This earth will become a Urim and Thummim for those who belong to it and attain celestial glory.

Christ will live on this earth when it is celestialized.

9 **This earth**, in its sanctified and immortal state [*in its glorified, celestial state*], will be made like unto crystal and **will be a Urim and Thummim to the inhabitants who dwell thereon,** whereby all things pertaining to an inferior kingdom, or **all kingdoms of a lower order, will be manifest to those who dwell on it**; and **this earth will be Christ's.**

Joseph Smith taught that this earth will be moved back into the presence of God when it finishes up. He said:

"This earth will be rolled back into the presence of God, and crowned with celestial glory" (*Teachings of the Prophet Joseph Smith,* 181).

Brigham Young taught about the earth when it is celestialized. He said:

"When it [the earth] becomes celestialized, it will be like the sun, and be prepared for the habitation of the saints, and be brought back into the presence of the Father and the Son [near Kolob], it will not then be an opaque body as it now is, but it will be like the stars of the firmament, full of light and glory; it will be a body of light. John compared it, in its celestial state, to a sea of glass" (in *Journal of Discourses,* 7:163).

He also taught: "This earth, when it becomes purified and sanctified, or celestialized, will become like a sea of glass; and a person, by looking into it, can know things past, present, and to come; though none but celestialized beings can enjoy this privilege. They will look into the earth, and the things they desire to know will be exhibited to them, the same as the face is seen by looking into a mirror" (in *Journal of Discourses*, 9:87).

Orson Pratt taught that other worlds will also become celestial kingdoms for their worthy inhabitants. Speaking of the celestialization of other worlds and their inhabitants, he said (**bold** added for emphasis):

"By and by, when each of these creations has fulfilled the measure and bounds set and the times given for this continuance in a temporal state [*their mortal time period*], **it and its inhabitants who are worthy will be made celestial and glorified together**. Then, from that time henceforth and for ever, there will be no intervening veil between God and his people who are sanctified and glorified, and he will not be under the necessity of withdrawing from one to go and visit another, because **they will all be in his presence**" (in *Journal of Discourses*, 17:332–33; quoted also in *Doctrine and Covenants Student Manual*, 1981, 201).

Doctrine

Everyone who attains the celestial kingdom will be given a white stone that will serve as a Urim and Thummim for them.

10 Then the **white stone** mentioned in Revelation 2:17, **will become a Urim and Thummim** to each individual who receives one, **whereby things pertaining to a higher order of kingdoms will be made known**;

11 And **a white stone is given to each of those who come into the celestial kingdom,** whereon is a new name written, which no man knoweth save he that receiveth it. The new name is the key word [*those who have received their endowments know about the "new name"*].

Doctrine

The Civil War would start in South Carolina (of course, this prophecy has already been fulfilled).

This prophecy, given 18 years before the beginning of the Civil War, in verses 12–13, next, is a strong reminder that Joseph Smith was indeed a prophet of God. Shortly before the Civil War began, popular opinion was that the Northern States, with their superior power and financial capability, would start the war. It appeared unlikely that South Carolina would start it.

However, on April 12, 1861, South Carolina fired on Union Troops at Fort Sumter, and thus the Civil War was underway. This exacting prophecy was given eighteen years before its precise fulfillment.

12 I prophesy, in the name of the

Lord God, that **the commencement of the difficulties** which will cause much bloodshed previous to the coming of the Son of Man **will be in South Carolina**.

13 It may probably arise through the slave question. This a voice declared to me, while I was praying earnestly on the subject, December 25th, 1832.

Doctrine

No one knows the exact timing of the Second Coming.

14 **I was once praying very earnestly to know the time of the coming of the Son of Man**, when I heard a voice repeat the following:

15 Joseph, my son, if thou livest until thou art eighty-five years old, thou shalt see the face of the Son of Man; therefore let this suffice, and **trouble me no more on this matter.**

16 **I was left thus, without being able to decide whether this coming referred to the beginning of the millennium or to some previous appearing, or whether I should die and thus see his face.**

17 I believe the coming of the Son of Man will not be any sooner than that time.

Doctrine

The knowledge and intelligence we gain in this life will continue with us in the resurrection and be advantageous for us.

18 **Whatever principle of intelligence we attain unto in this life, it will rise with us in the resurrection**.

19 And **if a person gains more knowledge and intelligence in this life** through his diligence and obedience than another, **he will have so much the advantage in the world to come**.

I was once chatting with an elderly sister in her early eighties when she expressed her concern about continuing to study the scriptures. Her problem was that the next day, she couldn't even remember what she had been reading the day before. She was somewhat comforted when I reminded her that verses 18–19 say nothing about when we rise in the "morning," rather, in the "resurrection."

Thus, we understand it to be worthwhile to continue studying and learning, because we are filing it away now to come forth with us in the resurrection, whether or not we can retrieve it from our memories now. There, it will become an advantage to us.

Doctrine

All blessings received
are based on laws.

20 There is a law, irrevocably
decreed   [cannot be revoked] in
heaven before the foundations of
this world [in premortality], **upon
which all blessings are predicated** [based]—

21 And **when we obtain any
blessing from God, it is by obedience to that law upon which it
is predicated.**

Doctrine

**The Father and Son have
glorified, resurrected bodies
of flesh and bones. The Holy
Ghost is a spirit and must be
a spirit in order to fulfill His
calling.**

22 **The Father has a body of flesh
and bones** as tangible [as touch-
able] as man's; **the Son also**; but
the Holy Ghost has not a body of
flesh and bones, but **is a personage of Spirit. Were it not so, the
Holy Ghost could not dwell in
us.**

Doctrine

**A person can receive
temporary help from the
Holy Ghost but must join the
Church in order to have the**
constant companionship of the
Holy Ghost.

23 **A man may receive the Holy
Ghost, and it may descend upon
him and not tarry** [remain] **with
him.**

One of the common applications
of verse 23, above, is when a prospective convert is being taught
the gospel. The Holy Ghost can
bear strong witness that what he
or she is hearing is the truth. However, unless the person acts upon
that witness and joins the Church,
the Holy Ghost withdraws and the
testimony often fades.

A common question asked by my
students over the years has been
whether the Holy Ghost will ever
get a body. While there are many
things we do not know about Him,
we can read a quote from the Ensign which informs us that Joseph
Smith taught that He will someday
get a body (**bold** added for emphasis):

"**The Holy Ghost**. The Bible gives
little detail about the personage
of the Holy Ghost. The Prophet,
however, gave us a number of insights about that spirit being and
his office. On several occasions,
especially in Nauvoo in 1842–43,
the Prophet spoke of the Holy
Ghost as a being 'in the form of
a personage,' as a 'spirit without
tabernacle,' separate and distinct
from the personages of the Father and the Son. According to

the George Laub journal, on another occasion Joseph taught that "**the Holy Ghost is yet a spiritual body and waiting to take to himself a body**" (Donald Q. Cannon, Larry E. Dahl, and John W. Welch, "The Restoration of Major Doctrines through Joseph Smith: The Godhead, Mankind, and the Creation," *Ensign,* January 1989, 29).

SECTION 131

Background

This section consists of instructions given by the Prophet Joseph Smith on May 16–17, 1843, at Ramus, Illinois, a settlement about twenty miles southeast of Nauvoo.

Verses 1–4 were given to William Clayton that evening (May 16). Verses 5 and 6 were given the next morning (May 17) in a meeting, and verses 7–8 were given in the evening (May 17).

Four important doctrines are taught here.

Doctrine

The celestial kingdom has three degrees of glory in it. Celestial marriage is required for entrance into the highest. The family unit exists only in the highest of the three.

1 In the celestial glory there are three heavens or degrees;

2 And in order to obtain the highest, a man must enter into this order of the priesthood [*meaning the new and everlasting covenant of marriage*];

Apostle Parley P. Pratt described how wonderful the Prophet Joseph's teachings were to him regarding celestial marriage.

"It was from [Joseph Smith] that I learned that the wife of my bosom might be secured to me for time and all eternity. . . . It was from him that I learned that we might cultivate these affections, and grow and increase in the same to all eternity; while the result of our endless union would be an offspring as numerous as the stars of heaven, or the sands of the sea shore. . . .

"I had loved before, but I knew not why. But now I loved—with a pureness—an intensity of elevated, exalted feeling" (*The Autobiography of Parley Parker Pratt,* 297).

3 And if he does not, he cannot obtain it.

4 He may enter into the other, but that is the end of his kingdom; he cannot have an increase [*he cannot become a God and have children eternally—compare with what he and his wife can have as stated in D&C 132:19–20*].

The Prophet gave background for what is included as the next two verses of this section (**Bold** added for emphasis):

"*Wednesday, 17.*—Partook of breakfast at Brother Perkins'; after which we took a pleasure ride through Fountain Green.

"At ten A.M. **preached from 2nd Peter, 1st chapter** and showed that knowledge is power; and the man who has the most knowledge has the greatest power.

"Salvation means a man's being placed beyond the power of all his enemies.

"The more sure word of prophecy means a man's knowing that he is sealed up into eternal life by revelation and the spirit of prophecy, through the power of the holy priesthood. It is impossible for a man to be saved in ignorance.

"Paul saw the third heavens, **and I more**. Peter penned the most sublime language of any of the apostles" (*History of the Church*, 5:392).

As you can see, verses 5 and 6 were taken from the second to last paragraph of the quote, above.

You may wish to read all of 2 Peter 1 as a background for the Prophets statements in these verses.

Doctrine

It is possible to know that you have qualified for exaltation.

5 (May 17th, 1843.) The more sure word of prophecy [*2 Peter 1:19*] **means a man's knowing that he is sealed up unto eternal life** [*exaltation*], by revelation and the spirit of prophecy, through the power of the Holy Priesthood.

We understand from D&C 132:49 that the Prophet Joseph Smith was "sealed up unto eternal life"; in other words, his calling and election were made sure. We will quote it here and add **bold** for teaching purposes.

D&C 132:49

49 **For I am the Lord thy God, and will be with thee even unto the end of the world, and through all eternity**; for verily I seal upon you your exaltation, and prepare a throne for you in the kingdom of my Father, with Abraham your father.

Elder Bruce R. McConkie taught the following (**bold** added for emphasis):

"Those members of the Church who devote themselves wholly to righteousness, living by every word that proceedeth forth from the mouth of God, **make their calling and election sure**. That is, they **receive the more sure word of prophecy, which means that the Lord seals their exaltation upon them while they are yet in this life**. Peter summarized the course of righteousness which the saints must pursue to make their calling and election sure and then (referring to his experience on the Mount of Transfiguration with James and John) said that those three had received this more sure word of prophecy (2 Pet. 1.)" (*Mormon Doctrine*, 109).

Having one's "calling and election made sure" does not have to happen in mortality. No doubt, for most Saints, it will happen in the next life. This will be true of those who died after age eight without having had the opportunity to accept the gospel and who accept the gospel fully in the spirit world mission field.

Doctrine

It is impossible to be saved without knowing the gospel.

6 It is impossible for a man to be saved in ignorance [*of the gospel*].

President Marion G. Romney of the First Presidency years ago explained what type of knowledge is meant in verse 6, above. He taught:

"By receiving the Savior's message and accepting him for what he was and is, the Apostles obtained eternal life [see John 17:1–2, 6–8].

"This knowledge of 'the only true God, and Jesus Christ' (John 17:3)

is the most important knowledge in the universe; it is the knowledge without which the Prophet Joseph Smith said no man could be saved. The lack of it is the ignorance referred to in the revelation wherein it is written: 'It is impossible for a man to be saved in ignorance.' (D&C 131:6.)" ("Except a Man Be Born Again," *Ensign*, Nov. 1981, 14).

The Prophet recorded some background for verses 7–8, next, as follows:

"In the evening went to hear a Methodist preacher lecture. After he got through, offered some corrections as follows:

"The 7th verse of 2nd chapter of Genesis ought to read—God breathed into Adam his spirit [*i.e. Adam's spirit*] or breath of life; but when the word "rauch" applies to Eve, it should be translated lives.

"Speaking of eternal duration of matter, I said:

"There is no such thing as immaterial matter. All spirit is matter, but is more fine or pure, and can only be discerned by purer eyes. We cannot see it, but when our bodies are purified, we shall see that it is all matter.

"The priest seemed pleased with the correction, and stated his intention to visit Nauvoo" (*History of the Church*, 5:393).

Doctrine

Spirit is matter. Our spirit bodies are made out of actual matter.

7 There is no such thing as immaterial matter. All spirit is matter, but it is more fine or pure, and can only be discerned by purer eyes;

8 We cannot see it; but when our bodies are purified we shall see that it is all matter.

One of the things the beautiful and simple doctrine given by the Prophet in verses 7–8, above, helps us understand is that we were "real" people in our premortal existence as spirit children of our Heavenly Parents ("The Family—A Proclamation to the World," *Ensign,* November 1995, 102). "Spirit is matter," and thus, we were made out of actual matter, rather than being in some strange, wispy, indefinable state of existence.

Another lesson we learn here is that some things cannot be discovered by scientific methods; rather, it must be given to us through pure revelation from God.

SECTION 132

Background

This great revelation on eternal marriage was dictated by the Prophet Joseph Smith on July 12, 1843, in Nauvoo, Illinois. As you can see in the heading to section 132 in your Doctrine and Covenants, we understand that the doctrines and principles taught in this section were given to the Prophet as early as 1831.

Generally speaking, as indicated in the *Doctrine and Covenants Student Manual,* 2018, chapters 51–52, this revelation can be divided into two main sections:

1. Verses 3–33 deal mainly with the doctrine of celestial marriage, meaning eternal marriage, often referred to as the "new and everlasting covenant of marriage" (D&C 131:2). This is the beautiful, eternal marriage covenant that we enter into together as husband and wife when we are sealed in the temple.

2. Having explained the law of celestial marriage in verses 3–33, the Lord then returns to Joseph's original question about plural marriage (verse 1) and answers it in verses 34–66.

If we fail to note the above two general divisions within this revelation, we can get caught up in some false doctrines and serious misunderstandings, including believing that plural marriage should still be actively practiced among members of the Church today. In other words, if you interpret the phrase "this law," in verse 3, to mean plural marriage, you will be off track and could easily be led astray.

However, if you correctly interpret "this law" in verse 3 to mean the law of celestial marriage itself and how you can make yours last eternally, you will have a correct understanding of verses 3–33 specifically, and section 132 generally.

First, we see in verse one that Joseph Smith had asked the Lord why plural marriage was allowed in Old Testament times. This question may well have come into his mind while he was working on the Joseph Smith Translation of the Bible in 1831. He would have been working on the Old Testament at that time and would have encountered plural marriage practiced by Abraham, Isaac, Jacob, and others in ancient times.

As you can see, the Lord expresses His willingness to answer Joseph's question (verses 1 and 2) but first He will teach His Prophet about the foundational principle of eternal marriage before returning to the topic of plural marriage.

1 VERILY, thus saith the Lord unto you my servant Joseph, that **inasmuch as you have inquired** of my hand **to know and understand wherein I, the Lord, justified my servants Abraham, Isaac, and Jacob, as also Moses,**

David and Solomon, my servants, as touching the principle and doctrine of their having many wives and concubines [*legally married, second class wives, according to the social and cultural system of the day*]—

2 Behold, and lo, **I am the Lord thy God, and will answer thee** as touching this matter.

By the way, "polygamy" is often used to mean plural marriage in discussions about the subject, but if you want to be accurate, "polygamy" means having more than one wife or more than one husband, whereas "plural marriage" means having more than one wife.

As we continue, verses 3–33 will teach us the law of celestial marriage, not to be confused with the explanation of plural marriage in verses 34–66.

Verses 3–33

The Law of Celestial Marriage

As stated above, the law of celestial marriage is that law that must be complied with by a husband and wife who desire to be sealed for time and eternity, to live in the family unit forever. In order to emphasize that verses 3–33 are dealing with this law, we will first go through these verses without commentary, using **bold** to point out various forms of the phrase "**this law**." Our purpose is to further point out the fact that these verses are explaining the law of eternal, celestial marriage, not plural marriage. After we have done this, we will repeat the verses, adding notes and commentary.

You may wish to mark or highlight what we **bold** in these verses in your own Doctrine and Covenants as a simple way of pointing out in your own scriptures that verses 3–33 are given in reference to the law and principle of celestial marriage.

3 Therefore, prepare thy heart to receive and obey the instructions which I am about to give unto you; for all those who have **this law** revealed unto them must obey the same.

4 For behold, I reveal unto you a new and an everlasting covenant; and if ye abide not that covenant, then are ye damned; for no one can reject this covenant and be permitted to enter into my glory.

5 For all who will have a blessing at my hands shall abide **the law** which was appointed for that blessing, and the conditions thereof, as were instituted from before the foundation of the world.

6 And as pertaining to the new and everlasting covenant, it was instituted for the fulness of my glory; and he that receiveth a fulness thereof must and shall abide **the law**, or he shall be damned, saith the Lord God.

7 And verily I say unto you, that the conditions of **this law** are these: All covenants, contracts, bonds, obligations, oaths, vows, performances, connections, associations, or expectations, that are not made and entered into and sealed by the Holy Spirit of promise, of him who is anointed, both as well for time and for all eternity, and that too most holy, by revelation and commandment through the medium of mine anointed, whom I have appointed on the earth to hold this power (and I have appointed unto my servant Joseph to hold this power in the last days, and there is never but one on the earth at a time on whom this power and the keys of this priesthood are conferred), are of no efficacy, virtue, or force in and after the resurrection from the dead; for all contracts that are not made unto this end have an end when men are dead.

8 Behold, mine house is a house of order, saith the Lord God, and not a house of confusion.

9 Will I accept of an offering, saith the Lord, that is not made in my name?

10 Or will I receive at your hands that which I have not appointed?

11 And will I appoint unto you, saith the Lord, except it be by **law**, even as I and my Father ordained unto you, before the world was?

12 I am the Lord thy God; and I give unto you this commandment—that no man shall come unto the Father but by me or by my word, which is **my law**, saith the Lord.

13 And everything that is in the world, whether it be ordained of men, by thrones, or principalities, or powers, or things of name, whatsoever they may be, that are not by me or by my word, saith the Lord, shall be thrown down, and shall not remain after men are dead, neither in nor after the resurrection, saith the Lord your God.

14 For whatsoever things remain are by me; and whatsoever things are not by me shall be shaken and destroyed.

15 Therefore, if a man marry him a wife in the world, and he marry her not by me nor by my word, and he covenant with her so long as he is in the world and she with him, their covenant and marriage are not of force when they are dead, and when they are out of the world; therefore, they are not bound by any law when they are out of the world.

16 Therefore, when they are out of the world they neither marry nor are given in marriage; but are appointed angels in heaven, which angels are ministering servants, to minister for those who are worthy of a far more, and an exceeding, and an eternal weight of glory.

17 For these angels did not abide **my law**; therefore, they cannot be enlarged, but remain separately and singly, without exaltation, in their saved condition, to all eternity; and from henceforth are not gods, but are angels of God forever and ever.

18 And again, verily I say unto you, if a man marry a wife, and make a covenant with her for time and for all eternity, if that covenant is not by me or by my word, which is **my law**, and is not sealed by the Holy Spirit of promise, through him whom I have anointed and appointed unto this power, then it is not valid neither of force when they are out of the world, because they are not joined by me, saith the Lord, neither by my word; when they are out of the world it cannot be received there,

because the angels and the gods are appointed there, by whom they cannot pass; they cannot, therefore, inherit my glory; for my house is a house of order, saith the Lord God.

19 And again, verily I say unto you, if a man marry a wife by my word, which is **my law**, and by the new and everlasting covenant, and it is sealed unto them by the Holy Spirit of promise, by him who is anointed, unto whom I have appointed this power and the keys of this priesthood; and it shall be said unto them—Ye shall come forth in the first resurrection; and if it be after the first resurrection, in the next resurrection; and shall inherit thrones, kingdoms, principalities, and powers, dominions, all heights and depths—then shall it be written in the Lamb's Book of Life, that he shall commit no murder whereby to shed innocent blood, and if ye abide in **my covenant**, and commit no murder whereby to shed innocent blood, it shall be done unto them in all things whatsoever my servant hath put upon them, in time, and through all eternity; and shall be of full force when they are out of the world; and they shall pass by the angels, and the gods, which are set there, to their exaltation and glory in all things, as hath

been sealed upon their heads, which glory shall be a fulness and a continuation of the seeds forever and ever.

20 Then shall they be gods, because they have no end; therefore shall they be from everlasting to everlasting, because they continue; then shall they be above all, because all things are subject unto them. Then shall they be gods, because they have all power, and the angels are subject unto them.

21 Verily, verily, I say unto you, except ye abide **my law** ye cannot attain to this glory.

22 For strait is the gate, and narrow the way that leadeth unto the exaltation and continuation of the lives, and few there be that find it, because ye receive me not in the world neither do ye know me.

23 But if ye receive me in the world, then shall ye know me, and shall receive your exaltation; that where I am ye shall be also.

24 This is eternal lives—to know the only wise and true God, and Jesus Christ, whom he hath sent. I am he. Receive ye, therefore, **my law**.

25 Broad is the gate, and wide the way that leadeth to the deaths; and many there are that go in thereat,

because they receive me not, neither do they abide in **my law**.

26 Verily, verily, I say unto you, if a man marry a wife according to my word, and they are sealed by the Holy Spirit of promise, according to mine appointment, and he or she shall commit any sin or transgression of the new and everlasting covenant whatever, and all manner of blasphemies, and if they commit no murder wherein they shed innocent blood, yet they shall come forth in the first resurrection, and enter into their exaltation; but they shall be destroyed in the flesh, and shall be delivered unto the buffetings of Satan unto the day of redemption, saith the Lord God.

27 The blasphemy against the Holy Ghost, which shall not be forgiven in the world nor out of the world, is in that ye commit murder wherein ye shed innocent blood, and assent unto my death, after ye have received my new and everlasting covenant, saith the Lord God; and he that abideth not **this law** can in nowise enter into my glory, but shall be damned, saith the Lord.

28 I am the Lord thy God, and will give unto thee **the law of my Holy Priesthood**, as was ordained by me and my Father before the world was.

29 Abraham received all things, whatsoever he received, by revelation and commandment, by my word, saith the Lord, and hath entered into his exaltation and sitteth upon his throne.

30 Abraham received promises concerning his seed, and of the fruit of his loins—from whose loins ye are, namely, my servant Joseph—which were to continue so long as they were in the world; and as touching Abraham and his seed, out of the world they should continue; both in the world and out of the world should they continue as innumerable as the stars; or, if ye were to count the sand upon the seashore ye could not number them.

31 This promise is yours also, because ye are of Abraham, and the promise was made unto Abraham; and by **this law** is the continuation of the works of my Father, wherein he glorifieth himself.

32 Go ye, therefore, and do the works of Abraham; enter ye into **my law** and ye shall be saved.

33 But if ye enter not into **my law** ye cannot receive the promise of my Father, which he made unto Abraham.

As you can see from the above **bolding**, verses 3–33 clearly refer to the law of celestial marriage, which applies to all who wish to qualify for exaltation, meaning to have their own eternal family unit as gods. After we have repeated verses 3–33 in order to add commentary, we will then deal with the topic of plural marriage, as explained in verses 34–66.

Now, a repeat of verses 3–33.

In verse 3, Joseph is told that once he becomes aware of the law of celestial marriage, he will be held accountable to obey it.

3 Therefore, **prepare thy heart to receive and obey the instructions which I am about to give unto you**; for **all those who have this law** [*the law of celestial marriage*] **revealed unto them must obey the same**.

4 For behold, I reveal unto you **a new and an everlasting covenant**; and **if ye abide not** [*do not enter into and obey*] **that covenant, then are ye damned** [*stopped in progression as far as exaltation is concerned*]; for no one can reject this covenant and be permitted to enter into my glory.

President Spencer W. Kimball defined the phrase "new and everlasting covenant" **as used in verse 4**, above, **as celestial marriage**. He said (**bold** added for emphasis):

"Though relatively few people in this world understand it, **the new and everlasting covenant is the marriage ordinance in the holy temple** by the properly constituted leaders who hold the genuine, authoritative keys. This glorious blessing is available to men and women on this earth" ("Temples and Eternal Marriage," *Ensign*, August 1974, 5).

Elder Marcus B. Nash of the Seventy further expanded our knowledge of the meaning of "**the new and everlasting covenant**" to include marriage and all other ordinances of the restored gospel.

"The new and everlasting covenant 'is the sum total of all gospel covenants and obligations' [Joseph Fielding Smith, *Doctrines of Salvation*, comp. Bruce R. McConkie (1955), 1:156] given anciently [see Jeremiah 32:40; D&C 22:1] and again restored to the earth in these latter days. . . . Because the covenant has been restored in the last dispensation of time, it is 'new,' and because it spans all eternity [see D&C 132:7], it is 'everlasting.'

"In the scriptures the Lord speaks of both 'the' new and everlasting covenant and 'a' new and everlasting covenant. For example, in Doctrine and Covenants 22:1, He refers to baptism as 'a new and an everlasting covenant, even that which was from the beginning.' In Doctrine and Covenants 132:4, He likewise refers to eternal marriage as 'a new and an everlasting covenant.' When He speaks of 'a' new and everlasting covenant, He is speaking of one of the many covenants encompassed by His gospel.

"When the Lord speaks generally of 'the' new and everlasting covenant, He is speaking of the fulness of the gospel of Jesus Christ, which embraces all ordinances and covenants necessary for the salvation and exaltation of mankind. Neither baptism nor eternal marriage is 'the' new and everlasting covenant; rather, they are each parts of the whole" ("The New and Everlasting Covenant," *Ensign*, Dec. 2015, 42–43).

5 For **all who will have a blessing at my hands shall abide the law which was appointed** [*established*] **for that blessing** [*as stated in D&C 130:20–21*], **and the conditions thereof, as were instituted from before the foundation of the world** [*before the world was created; in other words, in premortality*].

Doctrine
Celestial marriage is required for exaltation.

6 And as pertaining to the new and everlasting covenant, it was instituted for the fulness of my glory [*in other words, for exaltation*]; and he that receiveth a fulness thereof must and shall abide the law [*of celestial marriage*], or he

shall be damned [*stopped, held back from the highest blessings*], saith the Lord God.

Doctrine
All ordinances must be ratified and sealed by the Holy Ghost (the Holy Spirit of promise) in order to be valid in the next life.

7 And verily I say unto you, that **the conditions of this law** [*the rules that apply to the law of celestial marriage*] **are these: All covenants, contracts, bonds, obligations, oaths, vows, performances, connections, associations, or expectations**, that are **not made and entered into and sealed by the Holy Spirit of promise** [*the Holy Ghost, who was promised by the Savior to come upon His Apostles*], **of him who is anointed** [*by authorized priesthood holders*], both as well for time and for all eternity, and that too most holy, by revelation and commandment **through the medium of mine anointed** [*under the direction of the living Prophet who holds and exercises all the priesthood keys*], whom I have appointed on the earth to hold this power (and I have appointed unto my servant Joseph to hold this power in the last days, and there is never but one on the earth at a time on whom this power and the keys of

this priesthood are conferred), **are of no efficacy, virtue, or force in and after the resurrection from the dead**; for **all contracts that are not made unto this end** [*not performed by proper authority and not sealed by the Holy Ghost*] **have an end when men are dead**.

The phrase "there is never but one on the earth at a time on whom this power and the keys of this priesthood are conferred," in verse 7, above, bears added explanation.

At the present time, we have fifteen Apostles. They are the three members of the First Presidency and the twelve members of the Quorum of the Twelve Apostles. Each of them was given all the priesthood keys at the time he was ordained an Apostle and set apart as a member of the Twelve.

However, only the prophet himself is authorized to exercise all of these priesthood keys (as stated in one of the temple recommend interview questions). The others hold them, but they are, in effect, latent, until if and when he becomes the Prophet, the President of the Church.

The Prophet, in his position of holding and exercising all the priesthood keys, may delegate to any other member of the First Presidency or the Twelve, as well as to any other man who holds the proper priesthood, the privilege and responsibility of performing specific priesthood ordinances. Thus, temple sealers are authorized to perform celestial marriages and sealings in holy temples.

In verses 8–14, the Savior explains that there is to be no confusion on this and other issues because His "house is a house of order." In other words, He operates according to laws and rules; therefore, we can trust Him completely and can rely on salvation if we follow the rules.

8 Behold, **mine house is a house of order**, saith the Lord God, and not a house of confusion.

9 Will I accept of an offering, saith the Lord, that is not made in my name?

10 Or will I receive at your hands that which I have not appointed?

11 And will I appoint unto you, saith the Lord, except it be by law, even as I and my Father ordained unto you, before the world was?

12 **I am the Lord thy God; and I give unto you this commandment—that no man shall come unto the Father but by me or by my word, which is my law, saith the Lord.**

Doctrine

All ordinances not authorized by God or His authorized

servants, regardless of who authorized or performed them, are not valid in the next life.

13 And **everything that is in the world**, whether it be ordained [*authorized*] of men, by thrones, or principalities, or powers, or things of name, whatsoever they may be, that are **not by me or by my word**, saith the Lord, shall be thrown down, and **shall not remain after men are dead**, neither in nor after the resurrection, saith the Lord your God.

14 For **whatsoever things remain** [*are valid in eternity*] **are by me** [*are those things done by proper priesthood authority*]; and whatsoever things are not by me shall be shaken and destroyed.

Doctrine

All marriages not performed by proper priesthood authority for time and all eternity are not valid in eternity.

15 Therefore, **if a man marry him a wife in the world** [*during this mortal life*], and he marry her **not by me nor by my word**, and he covenant with her so long as he is in the world and she with him, **their covenant and marriage are not of force when they are dead**, and when they are out of the world; therefore, **they are not bound** [*together as husband and wife*] **by any law when they are out of the world.**

16 **Therefore**, when they are out of the world **they** neither marry nor are given in marriage; but **are appointed angels in heaven** [*the celestial kingdom*], which angels are ministering servants, **to minister for those who are worthy of a far more, and an exceeding, and an eternal weight of glory** [*as gods in family units forever*].

Did you notice the great difference between exaltation and even the other two categories in the celestial kingdom, as pointed out in verse 16, above? This is certainly another reminder that it is more than worth every effort to attain celestial exaltation.

17 **For these angels did not abide my law** [*did not keep the law of celestial marriage*]; **therefore, they cannot be enlarged** [*procreate, have children; have the power and privilege of increasing power and dominion as gods eternally*], **but remain separately and singly, without exaltation**, in their saved condition, **to all eternity**; and from henceforth [*from then on*] **are not gods, but are angels of God forever and ever.**

Question

What if a faithful person wanted to marry in the temple but did not have a valid opportunity to do so during mortality?

Also, what if a faithful member did marry in the temple, but due to circumstances beyond the individual's control, the marriage did not work out?

Answer

In the postmortal spirit world, such individuals will be given a completely fair opportunity to meet and choose an eternal companion whom they can love and respect. Then, mortal proxies will perform the sealing for them in a temple during the Millennium. Thus, by the time of the final judgment, they will have kept the law of celestial marriage and can be judged worthy of exaltation.

President Spencer W. Kimball addressed this concern as follows:

"To you we say this: You are making a great contribution to the world as you serve your families and the Church and the world. You must remember that the Lord loves you and the Church loves you. To you women, we can only say we have no control over the heartbeats or the affections of men, but pray that you may find fulfillment. And in the meantime, we promise you that insofar as eternity is concerned, no soul will be deprived of rich and high and eternal blessings for anything which that person could not help, that the Lord never fails in his promises, and that every righteous person will receive eventually all to which the person is entitled and which he or she has not forfeited through any fault of his or her own. We encourage both men and women to keep themselves well-groomed, well-dressed, abreast of the times, attractive mentally, spiritually, physically, and especially morally, and then they can lean heavily upon the Lord's promises for these heavenly blessings" ("The Importance of Celestial Marriage," *Ensign*, October 1979, 5).

In verse 18, next, the Savior repeats what He has said above, emphasizing that even if the wording of a ceremony says "for time and for all eternity," it is still not valid unless performed by proper priesthood authority and then sealed by the Holy Ghost. He also explains that it cannot be received after the world is finished up, meaning after the earth has become a celestial planet (see D&C 130:9), and there are no more mortals upon it who can serve as proxies for work for the dead.

18 And **again**, verily I say unto you, **if a man marry a wife, and make a covenant with her for time and for all eternity**, if that covenant is **not by me or by my word** [*not according to the laws of*

the gospel], which is **my law, and is not sealed by the Holy Spirit of promise, through him whom I have anointed and appointed unto this power** [*under the direction of the keys held by the living Prophet*], **then it is not valid** neither of force **when they are out of the world**, because they are not joined by me, saith the Lord, neither by my word; **when they are out of the world** [*after the final Judgment Day; after this world has become a celestial planet*] **it cannot be received there**, because the angels and the gods are appointed there, by whom they cannot pass; **they cannot, therefore, inherit my glory** [*exaltation*]; for my house is a house of order, saith the Lord God.

After quoting D&C 132:13, President Spencer W. Kimball taught about the above verses as follows:

"How final! How frightening! Since we know well that mortal death does not terminate our existence, since we know that we live on and on, how devastating to realize that marriage and family life, so sweet and happy in so many homes, will end with death because we fail to follow God's instructions or because we reject his word when we understand it.

"It is clear in the Lord's announcement that righteous men and women will receive the due rewards of their deeds. They will not be damned in the commonly accepted terminology but will suffer many limitations and deprivations and fail to reach the highest kingdom, if they do not comply. They become ministering servants to those who complied with all laws and lived all commandments.

"[The Lord] then continues concerning these excellent people who lived worthily but failed to make their contracts binding:

"'For these angels did not abide my law; therefore, they cannot be enlarged, but remain separately and singly, without exaltation, in their saved condition, to all eternity; and from henceforth are not gods, but are angels of God forever and ever.' (D&C 132:17.)

"How conclusive! How bounded! How limiting! And we come to realize again as it bears heavily upon us that this time, this life, this mortality is the time to prepare to meet God. How lonely and barren will be the so-called single blessedness throughout eternity! How sad to be separate and single and apart through countless ages when one could, by meeting requirements, have happy marriage for eternity in the temple by proper authority and continue on in ever-increasing joy and happiness, growth and development toward godhood. . . .

"Are you willing to jeopardize your eternities, your great continuing happiness, your privilege to see God and dwell in his presence? For the want of investigation and study and contemplation; because of prejudice, misunderstanding, or lack of knowledge, are you willing to forego these great blessings and privileges? Are you willing to make yourself a widow for eternity or a widower for endless ages—a single, separate individual to live alone and serve others? Are you willing to give up your children when they die or when you expire, and make them orphans? Are you willing to go through eternity alone and solitary when all of the greatest joys you have ever experienced in life could be 'added upon' and accentuated, multiplied, and eternalized? Are you willing, with the Sadducees, to ignore and reject these great truths? I sincerely pray you stop today and weigh and measure and then prayerfully proceed to make your happy marriage an eternal one. Our friends, please do not ignore this call. I beg of you, open your eyes and see; unstop your ears and hear" ("Temples and Eternal Marriage," *Ensign*, August 1974, 6).

Verses 19–21, next, are one of the most powerful sets of verses in all the scriptures. In them, we are clearly taught the law of celestial marriage.

Doctrine

The law of celestial marriage.

19 And again, verily I say unto you, if a man **marry** a wife **by**
my word**, which is **my law**, and by the new and everlasting covenant** [*according to the law of celestial marriage*], **and it is sealed** unto them **by the Holy Spirit of promise,** [*and it is performed*] **by him who is anointed** [*authorized*], **unto whom I have appointed this power and the keys of this priesthood** [*in other words, who has the authority to seal on earth and in heaven*]; and it shall be said unto them—Ye shall come forth in the first resurrection [*by basic definition, first resurrection means those who enter celestial glory*]; and if it be after the first resurrection, in the next resurrection [*no matter when you are resurrected*]; and **shall inherit thrones, kingdoms, principalities,** and **powers, dominions, all heights and depths** [*these are all terms that refer to gods*]—**then shall it be written in the Lamb's Book of Life** [*the record in heaven in which the names of the exalted are written—compare with D&C 88:2, Revelation 3:5; see also Bible Dictionary under "Book of Life," as well as the notes for D&C 131:5 in this study guide*], **that he shall commit no murder whereby to shed innocent blood** [*the sin against the Holy Ghost—see verse 27; in other words, if he does not commit an unpardonable sin and deeply and sincerely repents of all*]

other sins he commits], and **if ye abide in my covenant** [*if you keep the law of celestial marriage, keep all of the commandments, and repent of your sins*], **and commit no murder whereby to shed innocent blood, it shall be done unto them in all things** [*all the promises of celestial marriage and exaltation will be given them*] **whatsoever my servant** [*authorized priesthood holder*] **hath put upon them** [*through authorized priesthood ordinances*]**, in time, and through all eternity; and shall be of full force when they are out of the world; and they shall pass by the angels, and the gods,** which are set there [*celestial glory is not intruded upon by unauthorized entry of evil or people who are not qualified to be there*], **to their exaltation and glory in all things,** as hath been sealed upon their heads, which glory shall be **a fulness** [*exaltation, the Father's lifestyle*] and **a continuation of the seeds** [*powers of procreation*] **forever and ever** [*having spirit children and living in the family unit forever*].

Next, in verse 20, we are clearly taught the equality of the husband and wife as they serve together as gods in their own eternal family unit.

20 **Then shall they** [*the husband and wife*] **be gods,** because they have no end [*among other things, no end of children*]; **therefore shall they be from everlasting to everlasting** [*will be doing the same thing the Father does*], because they continue; **then shall they** [*the husband and wife*] **be above all, because all things are subject unto them. Then shall they be gods, because they** [*the husband and wife*] **have all power, and the angels are subject unto them.**

Bruce R. McConkie explained verse 20, above, as follows (**bold** added for emphasis):

"If righteous men have power through the gospel and its crowning ordinance of celestial marriage to become kings and priests to rule in exaltation forever, it follows that the women by their side (without whom they cannot attain exaltation) will be queens and priestesses. (Rev. 1:6; 5:10.) Exaltation grows out of the eternal union of a man and his wife. Of those whose marriage endures in eternity, the Lord says, "Then shall they be gods" (D. & C. 132:20); that is, **each of them, the man and the woman, will be a god. As such they will rule over their dominions forever**" (*Mormon Doctrine*, 613).

21 Verily, verily, I say unto you, **except ye abide** [*keep, obey*] **my law** [*the law of celestial marriage*] **ye cannot attain to this glory** [*becoming gods, exaltation*].

22 For **strait is the gate, and narrow the way** [*the rules for exaltation are very strictly defined*] that leadeth unto the **exaltation and continuation of the lives** [*becoming gods and having children forever, in the eternal family unit, which is exaltation*], and few there be that find it, because ye receive me not in the world neither do ye know me.

23 But **if ye receive me in the world, then shall ye know me, and shall receive your exaltation**; that **where I am ye shall be also.**

Note the difference between verse 24, next, and John 17:3.

24 **This is eternal lives** [*this is the privilege of having children forever*]—to know the only wise and true God, and Jesus Christ, whom he hath sent. I am he. Receive ye, therefore, my law.

John 17:3

3 **And this is life eternal**, that they might know thee the only true God, and Jesus Christ, whom thou hast sent.

Question

What will we do with our spirit children if we become gods and have spirit offspring forever?

Answer

We will create worlds for them and send them to them, just as our Father in Heaven has done for us.

Question

Will we use the same plan of salvation for our spirit children as is used by the Father for us?

Answer

Yes. The First Presidency explained this as follows (bold added for emphasis):

"Only resurrected and glorified beings can become parents of spirit offspring. Only such exalted souls have reached maturity in the appointed course of eternal life; and **the spirits born to them in the eternal worlds will pass in due sequence through the several stages or estates by which the glorified parents have attained exaltation**" ("1916 First Presidency Statement," *Improvement Era*, August 1916, 942).

25 **Broad is the gate, and wide the way that leadeth to the deaths** [*the end of the privilege of having children; in other words, they will not become gods and, consequently, will not be privileged to have eternal increase*]; and many there are that go in thereat, **because they receive me not, neither do they abide in my law** [*of celestial marriage*].

Joseph Fielding Smith explained verse 25, above, as follows:

"The term 'deaths' mentioned here has reference to the cutting off of all those who reject this eternal covenant of marriage and therefore they are denied the power of exaltation and the continuation of posterity. To be denied posterity and the family organization, leads to the 'deaths,' or end of increase in the life to come" (*Church History and Modern Revelation*, 2:360).

Verse 26, next, is one of the most misquoted and misunderstood of all the scriptures. Some people take it to mean that as long as a couple can somehow manage to get married in the temple, they have no further worries as far as exaltation is concerned, as long as they don't commit an unpardonable sin. We will use **bold** to suggest how such individuals read this verse.

26 Verily, verily, I say unto you, **if a man marry a wife according to my word** [*in other words, in the temple*]**,** and they are sealed by the Holy Spirit of promise, according to mine appointment, **and he or she shall commit any sin or transgression** of the new and everlasting covenant **whatever,** and all manner of blasphemies, and **if they commit no murder wherein they shed innocent blood,** yet **they shall** come forth in the first resurrection, and **enter into their exaltation**; but they shall be

destroyed in the flesh, and shall be delivered unto the buffetings of Satan unto the day of redemption, saith the Lord God.

Obviously, there is something seriously wrong with the above approach leading up to verse 26! No doubt you can see that it is completely contrary to the overall context of the gospel and the scriptures. What this verse is saying is that, upon deep and thorough repentance, all but unforgivable sins can be forgiven. Therefore, if a person is guilty of extremely serious transgression, including adultery, he or she can still be forgiven, and exaltation is still available. The key issue is that deep and life-changing repentance must take place, so that the individual is a "new" person, "born again," with "a mighty change of heart."

Joseph Fielding Smith explained this aspect of verse 26 as follows:

"Verse 26, in Section 132, is the most abused passage in any scripture. The Lord has never promised any soul that he may be taken into exaltation without the spirit of repentance. While repentance is not stated in this passage, yet it is, and must be, implied. It is strange to me that everyone knows about verse 26, but it seems that they have never read or heard of Matthew 12:31–32, where the Lord tells us the same thing in substance as we find in verse 26, section 132. . . .

"So we must conclude that those spoken of in verse 26 are those who, having sinned, have fully repented and are willing to pay the price of their sinning, else the blessings of exaltation will not follow. Repentance is absolutely necessary for the forgiveness, and the person having sinned must be cleansed" (*Doctrines of Salvation*, 2:95–96).

One of the things that people sometimes forget, in verse 26, is that all celestial marriages must be "sealed by the Holy Spirit of promise," and the Holy Ghost would certainly not seal a marriage in which the spouses intentionally do not keep the other commandments of God.

Next, in verse 27, the Lord explains what the "sin against the Holy Ghost" consists of. It is unforgivable and leads to becoming a son of perdition.

27 **The blasphemy against the Holy Ghost, which shall not be forgiven** in the world nor out of the world, **is in that ye commit murder wherein ye shed innocent blood, and assent unto my death** [*would gladly crucify Christ if given the opportunity*], **after ye have received my new and everlasting covenant** [*including knowing full well that the gospel is true by the power of the Holy Ghost*], **saith the Lord God; and he that abideth not this law can in nowise**

enter into my glory, but shall be damned, saith the Lord.

Bruce R. McConkie taught more about "murder, wherein ye shed innocent blood"; in other words, the sin against the Holy Ghost, as spoken of in verse 27, above. He said:

"The innocent blood is that of Christ; and those who commit blasphemy against the Holy Ghost, which is the unpardonable sin (Matt. 12:31–32), thereby 'crucify to themselves the Son of God afresh, and put him to an open shame.' (Heb. 6:6.) They are, in other words, people who would have crucified Christ, having the while a perfect knowledge that he was the Son of God" (*Doctrinal New Testament Commentary*, 3:345).

You may wish to read the notes and commentary given in this series of study guides for D&C 76:30–35 for more information about what leads to becoming sons of perdition.

Verses 28–32, next, relate back to verses 1–2 in which the Lord told Joseph that He would answer his question about Abraham and other ancient prophets regarding plural marriage. Thus far, in verses 3–27, He has revealed the law of celestial marriage itself to Joseph. As previously noted, He will give instruction about plural marriage, beginning with verse 34. In the meantime, in verse 28, next, He teaches the Prophet that the law of celestial marriage was presented as part of the plan of salvation in the premortal councils.

28 I am the Lord thy God, and will give unto thee **the law of my Holy Priesthood** [*the law of celestial marriage*], as **was ordained** [*established*] **by me and my Father before the world was.**

Next, in verses 29–30, Joseph is reminded that Abraham accepted all of God's laws, including the law of celestial marriage, and that this obedience has already led Abraham to exaltation. In other words, Abraham is already a god. And the promises given to him that his posterity would be innumerable are already under way toward being fulfilled.

29 **Abraham received all things,** whatsoever he received, by revelation and commandment, by my word, saith the Lord, **and hath entered into his exaltation and sitteth upon his throne.**

30 **Abraham received promises concerning his seed** [*his posterity*], and of the fruit of his loins [*his descendants*]—from whose loins ye are, namely, my servant Joseph [*Joseph Smith is a descendant of Abraham*]—**which were to continue so long as they were in the world; and as touching Abraham and his seed, out of the world they**

should continue [*he would continue having children (spirit offspring—compare with Acts 17:28–29) in the next life*]; both in the world and out of the world should they continue **as innumerable as the stars; or, if ye were to count the sand upon the seashore ye could not number them.**

Next, in verses 31–33, Joseph Smith is told that he too can be exalted if he will obey the law of celestial marriage as did Abraham.

31 **This promise is yours also,** because ye are of Abraham, and the promise was made unto Abraham; and **by this law** [*through the law of celestial marriage, by which we can indeed become like God*] **is the continuation of the works of my Father, wherein he glorifieth himself** [*in other words, it is through bringing His spirit children to the point of becoming gods like He is and having worlds of their own that the Father increases in glory and dominion—compare to Moses 1:39*].

32 Go ye, therefore, and **do the works of Abraham** [*be obedient in all things like Abraham was*]; **enter ye into my law** [*enter into celestial marriage*] **and ye shall be saved** [*exalted, like Abraham is*].

The phrase "do the works of Abraham," in verse 32, above, is explained in the *Doctrine and*

Covenants Student Manual as follows:

"This is not a commandment to engage in plural marriage (that commandment is given [to Joseph Smith] in verses 34 through 37) but rather a commandment for the Saints to receive the covenants and commandments of God in the same faith and righteousness as Abraham did" (*Doctrine and Covenants Student Manual*, 1981, 332).

33 But if ye enter not into my law [*celestial marriage*] ye cannot receive the promise of my Father, which he made unto Abraham [*in other words, you cannot attain exaltation*].

Verses 34–66

Plural Marriage

As stated several times in the notes and commentary for verses 3–33, the explanation of plural marriage requested by Joseph Smith (according to verses 1–2) began with the Lord's teaching the Prophet the law of celestial marriage in verses 3–33.

Now, having done that, the Savior will answer the specific question regarding why it was approved by the Lord for Abraham and other ancient prophets to have more than one wife.

Before we go farther with this topic, we will quote Bruce R. McConkie, wherein he teaches that

plural marriage is not required for exaltation.

"Plural marriage is not essential to salvation or exaltation. Nephi and his people were denied the power to have more than one wife [*see Jacob 2:27*] and yet they could gain every blessing in eternity that the Lord ever offered to any people. In our day, the Lord summarized by revelation the whole doctrine of exaltation and predicated it upon the marriage of one man to one woman. (D. & C. 132:1–28.) Thereafter he added the principles relative to plurality of wives with the express stipulation that any such marriages would be valid only if authorized by the President of the Church (D. & C. 132:7, 29–66.)" (*Mormon Doctrine*, 578).

Now, to the Lord's answer to the Prophet's question about plural marriage.

By way of review, remember that Abraham and Sarah were not able to have children for many years (Isaac was finally born to them when Abraham was a hundred years old and Sarah was ninety—see Genesis 21:1–5). Abraham had been promised that his posterity would be great (see Genesis 12:2), but the years came and went with no child. Finally, when Abraham was eighty-five, Sarah requested that he marry her servant, Hagar, and have children for them. This was according to the custom of the day (Genesis 16:1–3).

Consequently, a son, Ishmael (see Genesis 16:11) was born to them.

This comes into play, now, as the Lord explains plural marriage to Joseph Smith.

34 God commanded Abraham, and Sarah gave Hagar to Abraham to wife. And why did she do it? Because this was the law; and from Hagar sprang many people. This, therefore, was fulfilling, among other things, the promises.

35 Was Abraham, therefore, under condemnation? Verily I say unto you, **Nay; for I, the Lord, commanded it.**

Next, the Lord teaches Joseph a principle; namely, that whatever He commands is right, regardless of any other issues involved.

36 Abraham was commanded to offer his son Isaac; nevertheless [even though], **it was written: Thou shalt not kill** [one of the Ten Commandments—see Exodus 20:13]. **Abraham,** however, **did not refuse,** and **it was accounted unto him for righteousness** [Abraham was given credit for being obedient].

Verse 37, next, informs us that Abraham, Isaac, and Jacob have already become gods. This, of course, means that their righteous

wives have likewise attained their exaltation (compare with verses 19–20).

The Lord is illustrating to Joseph Smith the principle that obedience to God's commands brings exaltation.

37 Abraham received concubines [legally married secondary wives according to the customs of the day], and **they bore him children; and it was accounted unto him for righteousness, because** they were given unto him, and **he abode in my law**; as **Isaac also and Jacob** did none other things than that which they were commanded; and **because they did none other things than that which they were commanded, they have entered into their exaltation,** according to the promises, and sit upon thrones, **and are not angels but are gods.**

Next, in verse 38, the Lord uses David and others as examples of those who were authorized to practice plural marriage, with the caution that it must be authorized by Him; otherwise, it is sin.

38 David also received many wives and concubines, and **also Solomon and Moses** my servants, as **also many others** of my servants, from the beginning of creation until this time; and

in nothing did they sin save in those things which they received not of me.

In verse 39, next, King David is used as an example of one who started out faithful but who lost his exaltation through disobedience.

By way of quick review before studying verse 39, it is helpful to recall that Uriah was Bathsheba's husband. While Uriah was away in the army serving the King faithfully, King David pursued an illicit relationship with Bathsheba, resulting in her being with child. In an attempt to cover up his adultery, David commanded Uriah to come home on leave from the army, obviously in the hopes that it would appear that Uriah was the father of Bathsheba's child.

David's plot did not work. Uriah would not go home while his men were giving their lives on the battlefield. Consequently, King David commanded that Uriah be placed in battle where he would be killed. He was (see 2 Samuel 11:2–17). Thus, David attempted to cover up a forgivable sin, adultery, with murder.

In verse 39, next, the Lord tells what happened to David as a result.

39 David's wives and concubines were given unto him of me [were authorized by the Lord],

by the hand of Nathan [an Old Testament prophet—see 2 Samuel 7:2], my servant, and others of the prophets who had the keys of this power; and in none of these things did he sin against me save [except] in the case of Uriah and his wife [Bathsheba]; and, therefore he hath fallen from his exaltation, and received his portion [punishment]; and he shall not inherit them [his wives] out of the world [in the next life], for I gave them unto another, saith the Lord.

As you can see from verse 39, above, David has tragically "fallen from his exaltation."

We must be extremely careful not to misinterpret the phrase "I gave them unto another," in verse 39, above, to mean that David's wives, who were worthy of exaltation, are treated as mere property without consideration of their feelings on the matter of being eternal mates.

This is one of those cases where we must look at the larger context of the scriptures and the words of the brethren for correct understanding. From them, we know that individual agency is always respected by God. Thus, we know that in exaltation, each spouse, whether husband or wife, will be in that eternal relationship by agency choice. And we can with full confidence apply this principle to David's worthy wives. It will be interesting someday to meet them and see whom they chose to marry for eternity.

In verse 40, next, the Savior encourages Joseph to keep asking questions.

40 I am the Lord thy God, and I gave unto thee, my servant Joseph, an appointment, and restore all things [*the Lord called Joseph Smith to be the Prophet of the Restoration*]. **Ask what ye will, and it shall be given unto you according to my word.**

As we read verses 41–45, next, it is apparent that the Prophet had asked whether people involved in plural marriage were committing adultery as far as the laws of God are concerned. The answer is clearly that plural marriage, when approved by God, is not adultery. But violating the marriage covenant through illicit sex does constitute adultery and brings spiritual destruction.

41 And as ye have asked concerning adultery, verily, verily, I say unto you, **if a man receiveth a wife in the new and everlasting covenant** [*if a man and his wife are married for time and eternity*], **and if she be with another man**, and I have not appointed unto her by the holy anointing, **she hath committed adultery and shall be destroyed** [*spiritually—compare with D&C 42:23 which tells us*

that lustful thinking drives the Spirit away].

Next, we are informed that anyone who is unfaithful to his or her spouse, whether married in the temple or having a civil marriage, is guilty of adultery.

42 If she be not in the new and everlasting covenant, and she be with another man, she has committed adultery.

43 And if her husband be with another woman, and he was under a vow, **he hath** broken his vow and hath **committed adultery.**

44 And if she [*referring to the man's wife in verse 43, above, whose husband has been unfaithful*] **hath not committed adultery**, but is innocent and hath not broken her vow, and she knoweth it, and I reveal it unto you, my servant Joseph, then shall you have power, by the power of my Holy Priesthood, to take her and give her unto him that hath not committed adultery but hath been faithful [*in other words, the doctrine here is that a man or a woman can be sealed to someone else in the temple if his or her marriage is broken up because of unfaithfulness on the part of the spouse*]; for he shall be made ruler over many.

The doctrine taught in verse 44, above, is an important insight into a correct understanding of Matthew 5:32, which, if misunderstood, could lead one to believe that to marry a divorced person is committing adultery. Obviously, worthy individuals whose marriage was broken up by adultery may marry worthily in the temple.

Next, Joseph is taught more about the sealing power.

45 For I have conferred upon you the keys and power of the priesthood, wherein I restore all things, and make known unto you all things in due time.

46 And verily, verily, I say unto you, that whatsoever you seal on earth shall be sealed in heaven; and whatsoever you bind on earth, in my name and by my word, saith the Lord, it shall be eternally bound in the heavens; and **whosoever sins you remit on earth shall be remitted eternally in the heavens; and whosoever sins you retain on earth shall be retained in heaven.**

We know that ultimately God is the only one who can forgive sins. Bruce R. McConkie explained verse 46, above, as follows:

"Revelation from the Lord is always required to retain or remit sins. Since God is the one who must cleanse and purify a human soul, the use of his priestly powers to do so must be authorized

and approved by him, and this approval comes by revelation from his Holy Spirit. In many cases in this dispensation the Lord by revelation announced that the sins of certain persons were forgiven. (D. & C. 60:7; 61:2; 62:3; 64:3.) Accordingly, if by revelation he should tell his apostles to act for him, using his power which is priesthood, and to thus retain or remit sins, they would do so, and their acts would in effect be his. See Matt. 16:13–20; 17:1–9; 18:18.

"This same apostolic power is always found in the true Church, and hence we find the Lord saying to Joseph Smith: 'I have conferred upon you the keys and power of the priesthood, . . . and whosoever sins you remit on earth shall be remitted eternally in the heavens; and whosoever sins you retain on earth shall be retained in heaven' (D. & C. 132:45–46.)" (*Doctrinal New Testament Commentary*, 1:857–58).

Continuing, the Master gives additional examples of the sealing power which He has restored through Joseph Smith.

47 And again, verily I say, whomsoever you bless I will bless, and whomsoever you curse I will curse, saith the Lord; for I, the Lord, am thy God.

48 And again, verily I say unto you, my servant Joseph, that

whatsoever you give on earth, and **to whomsoever you give** [*in marriage*] **any one on earth, by my word and according to my law** [*in compliance with the gospel and the sealing power of the priesthood*], **it shall be visited with blessings and not cursings** [*in other words, it is approved by God*], and with my power, saith the Lord, **and shall be without condemnation on earth and in heaven**.

Next, in verse 49, the Lord seals the Prophet Joseph Smith up to exaltation. In other words, his calling and election is made sure. And in verse 50, He gives the reasons that this blessing can come upon Joseph at this time.

49 For I am the Lord thy God, and will be with thee even unto the end of the world, and through all eternity; for verily **I seal upon you your exaltation**, and prepare a throne for you in the kingdom of my Father, with Abraham your father [*Joseph's ancestor, who has already received his exaltation— see verses 29 and 37*].

50 Behold, **I have seen your sacrifices**, and will forgive all your sins; **I have seen your sacrifices in obedience** to that which I have told you. Go, **therefore, and I make a way for your escape, as**

I accepted the offering of Abraham of his son Isaac.

As far as the next several verses are concerned, there is much more that we do not know than there is that we do know. We will have to wait for further clarification. When it comes to verse 51, for example, we do not know what the test was. All we know is that they passed the test.

51 Verily, I say unto you: **A commandment I give unto mine handmaid, Emma Smith**, your wife, whom I have given unto you, **that she stay herself and partake not of that which I commanded you to offer unto her** [*stop and do not go ahead with whatever it was that the Lord asked her to do*]; for **I did it, saith the Lord, to prove you all, as I did Abraham**, and that I might require an offering at your hand, by covenant and sacrifice.

Verses 52–54 briefly summarize the fact that Joseph Smith practiced plural marriage.

52 And **let mine handmaid, Emma Smith, receive all those** [*wives*] **that have been given unto my servant Joseph**, and who are virtuous and pure before me; and those who are not pure, and have said they were pure, shall be destroyed [*spiritually*], saith the Lord God.

53 For I am the Lord thy God, and ye shall obey my voice; and **I give unto my servant Joseph that he shall be made ruler over many things; for he hath been faithful over a few things, and from henceforth I will strengthen him**.

54 And **I command mine handmaid, Emma Smith, to abide and cleave unto my servant Joseph**, and to none else. But if she will not abide [*keep*] this commandment she shall be destroyed [*spiritually as far as exaltation is concerned*], saith the Lord; for I am the Lord thy God, and will destroy her if she abide not in my law.

Occasionally, you may run into claims that Joseph Smith did not participate in plural marriage and that Emma Smith made statements to that effect. President Wilford Woodruff discussed these claims. He said:

"Emma Smith, the widow of the Prophet, is said to have maintained to her dying moments that her husband had nothing to do with the patriarchal order of marriage, but that it was Brigham Young that got that up. I bear record before God, angels and men that Joseph Smith received that revelation, and I bear record that Emma Smith gave her husband in marriage to several women while he was living, some of whom are to-day living in this city, and some may be present in this congregation, and who, if called upon, would confirm my words. But lo and behold, we hear of publication after publication now-a-days, declaring that Joseph Smith had nothing to do with these things. Joseph Smith himself organized every endowment in our Church and revealed the same to the Church, and he lived to receive every key of the Aaronic and Melchizedek priesthoods from the hands of the men who held them while in the flesh, and who hold them in eternity" (in *Journal of Discourses*, 23:131).

55 But **if she will not abide this commandment, then shall my servant Joseph do all things for her** [*keep his commitments to her*], even as he hath said; **and I will bless him and multiply him and give unto him an hundredfold in this world** [*in other words, many blessings—compare with Mark 10:29–30*], of fathers and mothers, brothers and sisters, houses and lands, wives and children, and crowns of eternal lives [*exaltation*] in the eternal worlds.

Next, we see a gentle and tender lesson on what forgiving others can do for us personally, including receiving blessings that will enable us to overcome obstacles to our individual happiness.

56 And again, verily I say, **let mine handmaid** [*Emma Smith*] **forgive my servant Joseph his trespasses**; and **then shall she be forgiven her trespasses**, wherein she has trespassed against me; **and I, the Lord thy God, will bless her**, and **multiply her**, and make **her heart to rejoice**.

We do not know what "property" is being referred to in verse 57.

57 And again, I say, let not my servant Joseph put his property out of his hands, lest an enemy come and destroy him; for Satan seeketh to destroy; for I am the Lord thy God, and he is my servant; and behold, and lo, I am with him, as I was with Abraham, thy father, even unto his exaltation and glory.

Next, the Savior reminds the Prophet that there are yet many things for him to learn (verse 58). Among other things, the Master reviews again the fact that if the Lord gives a commandment, it becomes the right thing to do, no matter what is written elsewhere (verse 59). If we fail to understand this · principle, we could easily go into apostasy.

For example, there were many instances in the Book of Mormon where individuals and peoples were told by the Lord not to retaliate against their enemies, such

as when Alma told his people to surrender to Amulon and the Lamanites (Mosiah 23:29). However, Captain Moroni rallied the Nephites to fight against their enemies (Alma 46:12–21). It was not sin to surrender, and it was not sin to fight, because in both cases it was the commandment of the Lord through His authorized servant in that particular situation.

58 **Now, as touching the law of the priesthood, there are many things pertaining thereunto.**

59 Verily, **if a man be called of my Father,** as was Aaron [*in other words, by proper authority*], by mine own voice, and by the voice of him that sent me, and I have endowed him with the keys of the power of this priesthood, **if he do anything in my name, and according to my law and by my word, he will not commit sin,** and I will justify him.

60 **Let no one, therefore, set on my servant Joseph** [*accuse Joseph Smith of being a fallen prophet*]; **for I will justify** [*support and uphold*] **him**; for **he shall do the sacrifice which I require at his hands for his transgressions** [*Joseph had to repent as needed—for example, after the loss of the 116 manuscript pages (see D&C 3 and 10)—just like everyone else has to in order to be forgiven*], saith the Lord your God.

Perhaps you have heard that before a man could enter into a plural marriage authorized by the Lord through the Prophet, the consent of his first wife was required. This is found in verse 61, next.

61 And again, **as pertaining to the law of the priesthood** [*as it applies to the principle of plural marriage*]—if any man espouse [*marry*] a virgin, and desire to espouse another, and **the first give her consent**, and if he espouse the second, and they are virgins, and have vowed to no other man, then is he justified; he cannot commit adultery for they are given unto him; for he cannot commit adultery with that that belongeth unto him and to no one else.

62 And **if he have ten virgins given unto him by this law** [*the law of the priesthood—see verse 61*]**, he cannot commit adultery** [*the answer to the basic question asked by Joseph—see verses 1–2, 34–35*], for they belong to him, and they are given unto him; therefore is he justified [*he is not committing sin, adultery*].

63 But **if one or either** [*any*] **of the ten virgins, after she is espoused** [*married*]**, shall be with another man, she has committed adultery**, and shall be destroyed [*spiritually*]; for they are given unto

him to multiply and replenish the earth, according to my commandment, and to fulfil the promise which was given by my Father before the foundation of the world [*in premortality*], and for their exaltation in the eternal worlds, that they may bear the souls of men [*motherhood is an eternal privilege only for those who attain exaltation*]; for **herein** [*giving spirits the opportunity to attain immortality and eternal life—Moses 1:39*] **is the work of my Father continued**, that he may be glorified.

64 And again, verily, verily, I say unto you, **if any man** have a wife, **who holds the keys of this power**, and he **teaches unto her the law of my priesthood**, as pertaining to these things, then shall she believe and administer unto him, or she shall be destroyed [*spiritually*], saith the Lord your God; for I will destroy her [*probably by withdrawing His Spirit, as is the case anytime we break a commandment*]; for I will magnify my name upon all those who receive and abide in my law.

65 Therefore, it shall be lawful in me, **if she receive not this law**, for him to receive all things whatsoever I, the Lord his God, will give unto him, because she did not believe and administer

unto him according to my word; and **she then becomes the transgressor**; and **he is exempt from the law of Sarah** [*plural marriage*], who administered unto Abraham according to the law when I commanded Abraham to take Hagar to wife.

66 And now, **as pertaining to this law** [*concerning plural marriage*], verily, verily, I say unto you, **I will reveal more unto you, hereafter; therefore, let this suffice for the present**. Behold, I am Alpha and Omega [*Jesus Christ*]. Amen.

SECTION 133

Background

This revelation was given through the Prophet Joseph Smith on November 3, 1831, at Hiram, Ohio, about 15 miles southeast of Kirtland.

As you can see, this section is not placed in the Doctrine and Covenants in chronological order. In fact, it was given during the same conference of the Church at which section one was given. The conference was convened to consider details of publishing the Book of Commandments, which was a collection of several revelations received by the Prophet up to that time. The Book of Commandments was the predecessor to the Doctrine and Covenants.

Joseph Smith gave some background for this section. He recorded:

"It had been decided by the conference that Elder Oliver Cowdery should carry [*copies of*] the commandments and revelations to Independence, Missouri, for printing, and that I should arrange and get them in readiness by the time that he left, which was to be by—or, if possible, before—the 15th of the month [November]. At this time there were many things which the Elders desired to know relative to preaching the Gospel to the inhabitants of the earth, and concerning the gathering; and in order to walk by the true light, and be instructed from on high, on the 3rd of November, 1831, I inquired of the Lord and received the following important revelation [section 133], which has since been added to the book of Doctrine and Covenants, and called the Appendix" (*History of the Church*, 1:229).

Thus, section 1 is the Lord's preface, and section 133 is the Lord's appendix to the Doctrine and Covenants. In effect, these two sections are bookends to the sections between them.

Section 133 contains an unusually large number of major scriptural references and concepts that assume that the reader is already familiar with many scriptural terms and passages. For example, "Go ye out from Babylon" (verse 5) means to flee sin and evil. "Go forth to meet the Bridegroom" (verse 10) means to prepare to meet the Savior. "He that goeth, let him not look back" (verse 15), referring to Lot's wife and her turning into a pillar of salt, means that once you have made commitments to follow Christ, don't look wistfully back at your old worldly lifestyle. Thus, when a familiar scriptural word or phrase is mentioned in this revelation, it brings up a whole concept and message with just a few words.

In fact, if you become familiar with the words and phrases used by the Savior in this revelation, you will be better equipped to understand much more as you read and study the scriptures and the words of Church leaders throughout your life. We will list twenty of them here. You may wish to see how many of them you already understand before we define them in context as we proceed with this section.

1. "Shall suddenly come to his temple" (verse 2).

2. "He shall make bare his holy arm" (verse 3).

3. "Sanctify yourselves" (verse 4).

4. "Go ye out from Babylon" (verse 5).

5. "Be ye clean that bear the vessels of the Lord" (verse 5).

6. "Awake and arise and go forth to meet the Bridegroom" (verse 10).

7. "He that goeth, let him not look back" (verse 15).

8. "Prepare ye the way of the Lord, and make his paths straight" (verse 17).

9. "Having his Father's name written on their foreheads" (verse 18).

10. "And he shall utter his voice out of Zion, and he shall speak from Jerusalem" (verse 21).

11. "Their enemies shall become a prey unto them" (verse 28).

12. "Living water" (verse 29).

13. "Children of Ephraim" (verse 30).

14. "Crowned with glory" (verse 32).

15. "Who is this that cometh down from God in heaven with dyed garments?" (verse 46).

16. "Their blood have I sprinkled upon my garments, and stained all my raiment" (verse 51).

17. "This was the day of vengeance which was in my heart" (verse 51).

18. "Stand on the right hand of the Lamb" (verse 56).

19. "They shall sing the song of the Lamb, day and night forever and ever" (verse 56).

20. "It shall leave them neither root nor branch" (verse 64).

We will define these phrases in context as we study this section verse by verse.

This section is a call from the Savior to the Saints to come unto Him, to repent and separate themselves from the evil ways of the world, to spread the gospel, and to prepare to meet Him. Among other things, He teaches them about the lost ten tribes (verses 26–33), why He will wear red at His Coming (verses 46–51), the first resurrection at the time of His resurrection (verses 54–55), the resurrection of the righteous (verse 56), His purposes for restoring the gospel (verses 57–61), the destruction of the wicked at His coming (verse 64), and the destiny of those who continue to reject Him (verses 65–73).

The Savior begins by requesting the Saints' attention and introducing Himself.

1 HEARKEN, O ye people of my church, saith the Lord your God, and **hear the word of the Lord concerning you**—

2 The Lord **who shall suddenly come to his temple** [*can be a reference to the Second Coming—see heading to Malachi 3,* but can also be a reference to other appearances of the Savior prior to the Second Coming*]; the Lord **who shall come down upon the world with a curse** [*punishment*] **to judgment**; yea, **upon all the nations that forget God**, and **upon all the ungodly** [*the wicked*] **among you.**

3 For **he shall make bare his holy arm** [*will demonstrate His power; "arm" is symbolic of power in biblical symbolism*] **in the eyes of all the nations** [*it will be obvious that there is a God to those who are willing to see*], and **all the ends of the earth shall see the salvation of their God** [*salvation will be made available to all people on earth*].

4 Wherefore, **prepare ye, prepare ye**, O my people; **sanctify yourselves** [*come unto Christ and become pure, clean, fit to be in the presence of God*]; **gather ye together**, O ye people of my church, **upon the land of Zion** [*gather in Missouri*], **all you that have not been commanded to tarry** [*to stay in the Kirtland, Ohio, area*].

5 **Go ye out from Babylon** [*flee from evil and wickedness; do not join in the wickedness of the world*]. **Be ye clean that bear the vessels of the Lord** [*be clean and pure in heart as members of the Church and holders of the priesthood*].

6 Call your **solemn assemblies** [*sacred meetings attended by invitation by those who wish to keep God's commandments and separate themselves from the evil ways of the world; these include temple dedications and sustaining a new First Presidency of the Church*], and **speak often one to another.** And **let every man call upon the name of the Lord.**

7 Yea, verily I say unto you again, the time has come when the voice of the Lord is unto you: **Go ye out of Babylon** [*separate yourselves from the wickedness of the world*]; **gather ye out from among the nations,** from the four winds [*from every direction*], from one end of heaven to the other.

Next, the Savior instructs the Church to send missionaries to preach to all the world. He commands that the gospel is to be taken first to the Gentiles (in this context, it means everyone except the Jews), and then to the Jews.

Currently, we are in the stage of missionary work referred to as the "times of the Gentiles," meaning that the gospel is now to be taken to everyone except the Jews. We have not yet been allowed to make an all-out effort to take the gospel to the Jews. It is one of the "signs of the times" that is yet to be fulfilled.

8 **Send forth the elders of my church unto the nations** which are afar off; **unto the islands of the sea**; send forth **unto foreign lands**; call upon all nations, **first** upon **the Gentiles,** and **then** upon **the Jews.**

9 And behold, and lo, **this shall be their cry** [*the missionaries' message*], and **the voice of the Lord unto all people**: Go ye forth unto the land of Zion [*gather to Zion—literally to Missouri, at the time of this revelation; in our day, it means gathering to the stakes of Zion throughout the world*], that the borders of my people may be enlarged, and that her stakes may be strengthened, and **that Zion may go forth** unto the regions round about.

10 Yea, **let the cry** [*message*] **go forth among all people**: Awake **and arise and go forth to meet the Bridegroom** [*prepare to meet the Savior; a reference to the parable of the ten virgins in Matthew 25:1–13*]; behold and lo, **the Bridegroom cometh** [*the Second Coming is getting close*]; go ye out to meet him. **Prepare yourselves for the great day of the Lord.**

There are still people in and out of the Church who claim to be able to pinpoint the time of the Second Coming with considerable accuracy. Verse 11, next, is yet another reminder not to join with them in their false claims.

11 **Watch** [*be constantly prepared by living righteously*], therefore, **for ye know neither the day nor the hour.**

As mentioned earlier, there are two major gatherings in the last days prior to the Second Coming. We see these in verses 12 and 13, next. First, the Gentiles are to be gathered to the gospel. While this is happening, the Jews are to be gathered to the Holy Land. Then, when the time is right, they will be converted to the Savior in large numbers.

12 **Let them, therefore, who are among the Gentiles flee unto Zion** [*let the non-Jewish converts gather to Zion*].

13 And **let them who be of Judah** [*the Jews*] **flee unto Jerusalem** [*gather to Jerusalem, the Holy Land*], **unto the mountains of the Lord's house.**

Babylon is defined for us in verse 14, next.

14 Go ye out from among the nations, even from **Babylon**, from the midst of **wickedness**, which is **spiritual Babylon**.

By the way, the term "*Babylon*," as used here, comes from the ancient wicked city of Babylon located where modern-day Iraq now is. It was a stronghold of evil and unrighteousness. The city itself was surrounded by 56 miles of walls that were 335 feet high and 85 feet wide (see Bible Dictionary under "Babylon"). It looked to be completely invincible, much the same as Satan's kingdom does to some today. It fell completely. Such will also be the case with the devil's kingdom at the Second Coming.

Next, the Master reminds the Saints that their gathering is to be undertaken with wisdom and order.

15 But verily, thus saith the Lord, **let not your flight be in haste, but let all things be prepared before you**; and **he that goeth, let him not look back** lest sudden destruction shall come upon him.

The phrase "he that goeth, let him not look back" is a reference to Lot's wife in the Old Testament. As Lot and his family fled the evil city of Sodom, they were instructed by the Lord not to look back, but his wife did and became a pillar of salt (see Genesis 19:26). We may assume that she looked back longingly at the lifestyle they were abandoning. Thus, to "look back" after an individual has been baptized and become active in the Church, has been sealed in the temple and had children, etc. is symbolic of wishing to participate in some of the evils and temptations that must be left behind when covenants are made with God.

Next, the Lord emphasizes a major part of the missionary message to all the world.

16 Hearken and hear, O ye inhabitants of the earth. Listen, ye elders of my church together [*in harmony one with another*], and hear the voice of the Lord; for **he calleth upon all men**, and **he commandeth all men everywhere to repent**.

17 For behold, **the Lord God hath sent forth the angel crying through the midst of heaven** [*as prophesied in Revelation 14:6–7; in other words, we are in the last days*], saying: **Prepare ye the way of the Lord, and make his paths straight** [*repent and go straight forward in righteousness*], for the hour of his coming is nigh—

The 144,000 mentioned in verse 18, next, are high priests, 12,000 out of each tribe of Israel, who will "administer the everlasting gospel" and "bring as many as will come to the church of the Firstborn" (see D&C 77:11).

18 When the Lamb [*Christ*] shall stand upon Mount Zion (the City of New Jerusalem—see D&C 84:2), and with him **a hundred and forty-four thousand**, having his **Father's name written on their foreheads** [*in biblical symbolism, "forehead" means "loyalty"*].

As indicated in the note at the end of verse 18, above, "forehead" in biblical symbolism means "loyalty." Thus, symbolically speaking, if you were to have the Savior's name on your forehead, it would indicate to God and others your intent and determination to be loyal to Christ. On the other hand, if you were to have the devil's name or any of his front organizations, so-to-speak, on your forehead, you would be indicating that you are loyal to evil and wickedness.

19 Wherefore, **prepare ye for the coming of the Bridegroom** [*the Second Coming*]; go ye, **go ye out to meet him** [*in other words, come unto Christ; be constantly prepared to meet the Savior*].

Before the actual Second Coming to all the world, the Savior will make some other prophesied appearances, including those spoken of in verse 20, next.

20 For behold, **he shall stand upon the mount of Olivet** [*the Mount of Olives in the Holy Land east of Jerusalem*], and **upon the mighty ocean**, even the great deep, and **upon the islands of the sea**, and **upon the land of Zion** [*which can include appearances at both New Jerusalem and Adam-on-di-Ahman*].

Ezra Taft Benson spoke of two of these appearances as follows (**bold** added for emphasis):

"His first appearance will be to the righteous Saints who have gathered to the **New Jerusalem**. In this place of refuge they will be safe from the wrath of the Lord, which will be poured out without measure on all nations . . .

"The second appearance of the Lord will be **to the Jews**. To these beleaguered sons of Judah, surrounded by hostile Gentile armies, who again threaten to overrun Jerusalem, the Savior—their Messiah—will appear and set His feet on the Mount of Olives, 'and it shall cleave in twain, and the earth shall tremble, and reel to and fro, and the heavens also shall shake' (D&C 45:48).

"The Lord Himself will then rout the Gentile armies, decimating their forces (see Ezek. 38, 39). Judah will be spared, no longer to be persecuted and scattered" ("Five Marks of the Divinity of Jesus Christ," *New Era,* December 1980, 49–50).

Joseph Smith spoke of the appearance of the Savior at a meeting to be held at Adam-ondi-Ahman in Missouri, which is about seventy miles north northeast of Independence.

"Daniel in his seventh chapter speaks of the Ancient of Days; he means the oldest man, our Father Adam, Michael, he [who] will call his children together and hold a council with them to prepare them for the coming of the Son of Man. He (Adam) is the father of the human family, and presides over the spirits of all men, and all that have had the keys must stand before him in this grand council. . . The Son of Man stands before him, and there is given him glory and dominion. Adam delivers up his stewardship to Christ, that which was delivered to him as holding the keys of the universe, but retains his standing as head of the human family" (*Teachings of the Prophet Joseph Smith,* 157).

Bruce R. McConkie also taught about the Savior's appearance at Adam-ondi-Ahman. He said:

"Before the Lord Jesus descends openly and publicly in the clouds of glory, attended by all the hosts of heaven; before the great and dreadful day of the Lord sends terror and destruction from one end of the earth to the other; before he stands on Mount Zion, or sets his feet on Olivet, or utters his voice from an American Zion or a Jewish Jerusalem; before all flesh shall see him together; before any of his appearances, which taken together comprise the second coming of the Son of God—before all these, there is to be a secret appearance to selected members of his Church. He will come in private to his prophet and to the apostles then living. Those who have held keys and powers and authorities in all ages from Adam to the present will also be present [*at the meeting at Adam-ondi-Ahman*]" (*The Millennial Messiah,* 578–79).

21 And **he shall utter his voice out of Zion** [*New Jerusalem, in America*], **and he shall speak from Jerusalem** [*Old Jerusalem; both of these cities will serve as headquarters for the Savior during the Millennium*], and **his voice shall be heard among all people;**

Next, we are taught that there will be changes in the earth's surface in conjunction with the Second Coming and in preparation for the Millennium. It is interesting to note that changes in the earth's surface also accompanied the destruction of the wicked at the time of the resurrected Savior's coming to the Nephites. You may wish to read about these in 3 Nephi 8:17–18.

22 And it shall be a voice as the voice of many waters, and as the voice of a great thunder, which **shall break down the mountains, and the valleys shall not be found.**

23 **He shall command the great deep** [*the water, oceans*], **and it shall be driven back** into the north countries, and **the islands shall become one land;**

24 And **the land of Jerusalem and the land of Zion shall be turned back into their own place** [*returned to their original locations*], **and the earth shall be like as it was in the days before it was divided.**

Under the direction of the Prophet Joseph Smith, an article was published that helps us understand verses 23–24, above.

"The Eternal God hath declared that the great deep shall roll back into the north countries and that the land of Zion and the land of Jerusalem shall be joined together, as they were before they were divided in the days of Peleg [*Genesis 10:25*]. No wonder the mind starts at the sound of the last days!" ("The Last Days," *Evening and Morning Star,* February 1833, 1).

Joseph Fielding Smith taught:

"If, however, the earth is to be restored as it was in the beginning, then all the land surface will again be in one place as it was before the days of Peleg, when this great division was accomplished. Europe, Africa, and the islands of the sea including Australia, New Zealand, and other places in the Pacific must be brought back and joined together as they were in the beginning" (*Answers to Gospel Questions,* 5:74).

Next, in verse 25, the Savior speaks of His millennial reign.

25 And the Lord, even **the Savior, shall stand in the midst of his people, and shall reign over all flesh** [*during the Millennium, all people will be governed by the Savior; this form of government is called a "theocracy," meaning government by God*].

Verses 26–33, next, deal with the return of the Lost Ten Tribes.

As recorded in D&C 110:11, Moses restored the keys of "leading the ten tribes from the land of the north" to Joseph Smith and Oliver Cowdery. These keys have been transferred from prophet to prophet and reside with the President of the Church today.

Because of wickedness, the ten tribes of Israel were carried away captive by Shalmaneser about 721 B.C. and taken away into Assyria (2 Kings 17:6–7). Since then, they have been lost to us. They will return from the north (see Jeremiah 23:8). The resurrected Savior told the Nephites that He was to visit the Lost Ten Tribes at that time (3 Nephi 17:4).

In 1831, the Prophet Joseph Smith told some of the brethren that John, the Beloved Apostle, was at that time working with the Ten Tribes, preparing them for their return. The following quote comes from the history kept by John Whitmer:

"The Spirit of the Lord fell upon Joseph in an unusual manner, and he prophesied that John the Revelator was then among the Ten Tribes of Israel who had been led away by Shalmaneser, king of Assyria, to prepare them for their return from their long dispersion, to again possess the land of their fathers" (*History of the Church,* 1:176, footnote).

We do not know where the lost ten tribes are, so it is fruitless to speculate and draw definite conclusions from it.

26 And **they who are in the north countries** [*the Lost Ten Tribes of Israel*] **shall come in remembrance before the Lord** [*the Lord will fulfill His promises to bring them back*]; and **their prophets shall hear his voice,** and shall no longer stay themselves [*will no longer hold back*]; and they shall smite the rocks, and the ice shall flow down at their presence.

27 And **an highway** [*can be literal; "highway" can also mean the gospel*] **shall be cast up in the midst of the great deep.**

28 **Their enemies shall become a prey unto them** [*no one will stop them*],

From verse 29, next, it appears that geological changes will be made in order to accommodate the travel and arrival of the lost ten tribes.

In addition, there may be considerable symbolism in verse 29 in the sense that barren deserts can symbolize apostasy, and living water usually refers to the Savior and His gospel (see John 4:10). Thus, one possible interpretation of verse 29 may be that the ten tribes will return from the apostasy that led to their being lost spiritually and carried away into captivity. They will once again be nourished by the living water.

29 And **in the barren deserts there shall come forth pools of living water;** and **the parched ground shall no longer be a thirsty land.**

Verses 30–32 indicate that Ephraim will be gathered first. We see this in lineage declarations in many patriarchal blessings. Ephraim is to prepare the way for the return of the others.

30 **And they shall bring forth their rich treasures unto the children of Ephraim** [*descendants of Ephraim*], **my servants.**

The ten tribes will consist of large numbers of people when they arrive, as indicated in verse 31, next.

31 And **the boundaries of the everlasting hills** [*the Rocky Mountains*] **shall tremble at their presence.**

32 And **there shall they** fall down

and **be crowned with glory** [*receive their temple blessings*], even in Zion, **by the hands of the servants of the Lord, even the children of Ephraim.**

President Joseph Fielding Smith explained that the tribe of Ephraim will play a prominent role in the gathering of Israel in the last days. He said: "The Lord called upon the descendants of Ephraim to commence his work in the earth in these last days. . . . The keys are with Ephraim. It is Ephraim who is to be endowed with power to bless and give to the other tribes . . . their blessings" (*Doctrines of Salvation*, 2:250–51; see also D&C 113:5–6).

33 And **they shall be filled with songs of everlasting joy.**

34 Behold, **this** [*gathering them again, in the last days*] **is the blessing of the everlasting God upon the tribes of Israel**, and **the richer blessing** [*the birthright blessing—see Genesis 48:13–20*] **upon the head of Ephraim and his fellows.**

Referring back to verse 34, above, in Old Testament culture, the holder of the birthright blessing had the responsibility of taking care of the other family members. Thus, Ephraim has the responsibility of preparing the way for the other tribes of Israel to return to the Savior. Much is being done now by way of missionary work and temple building to prepare for the continued gathering of Israel, including the return of the ten tribes.

Next, the return of the Jews to Christ is prophesied. This will take place after much pain, as stated in verse 35. This can be referred to as the "spiritual gathering" of the Jews and appears to be yet future as far as large-scale conversions are concerned.

35 And they also of the tribe of Judah, after their pain, shall be sanctified [*cleansed by the Atonement of Christ*] **in holiness before the Lord** [*they will become righteous, faithful Saints*], to dwell in his presence day and night, forever and ever.

Next, the Master speaks of the Restoration. The angel spoken of in verse 36 appears to be representative of many angelic beings who participated in restoring the gospel to Joseph Smith, including Moroni, John the Baptist, Peter, James and John, Moses, Elias, and Elijah.

36 And now, verily saith the Lord, **that these things might be known among you**, O inhabitants of the earth, **I have sent forth mine angel flying through the midst of heaven** [*Revelation 14:6–7*], having the everlasting gospel, **who hath** appeared unto some and hath **committed it unto man**,

who shall appear unto many that dwell on the earth.

37 And **this gospel shall be preached unto every nation, and kindred, and tongue, and people**.

A brief missionary training course is given next, beginning with verse 38.

38 And **the servants of God shall go forth, saying with a loud voice**: Fear [*respect and honor*] God and give glory to him, for **the hour of his judgment is come** [*the much-prophesied last days' punishments and calamities are now coming*];

39 And **worship him that made heaven, and earth**, and the sea, and the fountains of waters—

Verses 40–44, next, summarize the prayers of the righteous in the last days as they plead for the coming of the Savior.

40 Calling upon the name of the Lord day and night, saying: O that thou wouldst rend the heavens [*perhaps meaning "tear the veil away" as will be the case at the time of the Second Coming—see D&C 88:95*], that thou wouldst come down, that the mountains might flow down at thy presence [*the Second Coming*].

The unrestrained glory of the Lord at His coming is described in verse 41, next. It is this glory that will destroy the wicked (see D&C 5:19, 2 Nephi 12:10, 19, 21).

41 And it shall be answered upon their heads [*their prayers will be answered*]; for **the presence of the Lord shall be as the melting fire that burneth, and as the fire which causeth the waters to boil.**

The plight of the wicked is briefly described in verses 42–43, next.

42 O Lord, thou shalt come down to make thy name known to thine adversaries, and all nations shall tremble at thy presence—

43 When thou doest terrible things, things they look not for [*the wicked do not expect to be destroyed; most of them do not believe in Christ or His Second Coming*];

The righteous will rejoice when Christ comes, as foretold in verse 44, next.

44 Yea, when thou comest down, and the mountains flow down at thy presence, **thou shalt meet him who rejoiceth and worketh righteousness, who remembereth thee in thy ways.**

In verse 45, next, we are informed

that we cannot even begin to imagine the wonderful blessings that lie in store for the righteous.

45 For since the beginning of the world have not men heard nor perceived by the ear, neither hath any eye seen, O God, besides thee, how great things thou hast prepared for him [*the faithful, righteous*] **that waiteth** [*trusts, relies; waits with faith for promised blessings*] **for thee.**

Next, in verses 46–51, we are taught more about the Second Coming. Among other things, the Savior will wear red at the time of His coming. Whether this color is literal or symbolic, the message is the same. It represents the blood of the wicked (see verse 51) as they are destroyed at the time of his Second Advent.

46 And it shall be said: Who is this that cometh down from God in heaven with dyed [*red*] **garments** [*clothing*]; yea, from the regions which are not known [*from heaven*], clothed in his glorious apparel [*in His full glory*], traveling in the greatness of his strength [*this time, He comes in power*]?

47 And he shall say: I am he who spake in righteousness, mighty to save [*in other words, "I am the Messiah"*].

48 And **the Lord shall be red in his apparel**, and his garments like him that treadeth in the wine-vat [*His clothing will be "stained" (like the clothing of a worker who tramples grapes to make wine) with the blood of the wicked, symbolic of their destruction*].

The Savior's glory will be far more intense than the light of the sun as explained in verse 49, next. Symbolically, the sun and the moon are embarrassed to compete with the Savior as far as glory is concerned.

49 **And so great shall be the glory of his presence that the sun shall hide his face in shame, and the moon shall withhold its light**, and the stars shall be hurled from their places.

Next, in verses 50–51, the Savior explains why His clothing will be red when He comes.

50 And his voice shall be heard: **I have trodden the wine-press alone** [*He performed the Atonement alone*], **and have brought judgment upon all people** [*through His atoning sacrifice, He qualified to have all people subject to Him, both to His mercy where possible and to His judgments and condemnations where required by the law of justice*]; and **none were with me** [*He had to do the Atonement alone—compare with Matthew 27:46*];

51 And **I have trampled them** [*the wicked*] **in my fury** [*symbolic of the demands of the law of justice*], and I did tread upon them in mine anger, and **their blood have I sprinkled upon my garments, and stained all my raiment** [*the wicked will have been destroyed at this point of His coming*]; for **this was the day of vengeance** [*justice; punishment of the wicked*] **which was in my heart** [*which is part of the plan of salvation*].

Next, more is said about the happy state of the righteous as the Savior comes on earth to reign for a thousand years. Note the contrast between the state of the wicked in the above verses and the feelings in the hearts of the faithful.

52 And **now** [*when the Savior comes*] **the year of my redeemed is come** [*finally, the righteous are set free from the oppressions they've endured*]; and **they shall mention the loving kindness of their Lord, and all that he has bestowed upon them according to his goodness, and according to his loving kindness**, forever and ever.

Verse 53, next, speaks of the Atonement.

53 In all their afflictions he was afflicted. And the angel of his presence saved them; and in his love, and in his pity, he redeemed them, and bore them, and carried them all the days of old;

One of the teachings of the gospel is that the faithful Saints from the time of Adam and Eve up to the time of the Savior's resurrection came forth with Christ at His resurrection. It is found in verses 54–55, next. All these Saints qualified for celestial glory. No terrestrials or telestials have been resurrected yet.

It is interesting to note that the inhabitants of the city of Enoch, who were translated, were resurrected with Christ.

54 Yea, and **Enoch** also, **and they who were with him**; the **prophets who were before him**; and **Noah** also, and they who were before him; and **Moses** also, and they who were before him;

55 And **from Moses to Elijah**, and from **Elijah to John**, who **were with Christ in his resurrection**, and the holy apostles, with Abraham, Isaac, and Jacob, shall be in the presence of the Lamb.

The resurrection spoken of in verses 54–55, above, is part of what is termed the "first resurrection." First resurrection is, in fact, often used as a general term

meaning celestial resurrection regardless of when a particular righteous person is resurrected.

Another major portion of the first resurrection will take place at the time of the Savior's coming, as discussed next in verse 56.

56 And **the graves of the saints shall be opened** [*the righteous who have died since the resurrection of Christ*]; and **they shall come forth** and stand **on the right hand of the Lamb** [*a phrase meaning those worthy of celestial glory; right hand symbolizes having made and kept covenants*], when he shall stand upon Mount Zion [*when He comes*], and upon the holy city, the New Jerusalem; and **they shall sing the song of the Lamb, day and night forever and ever** [*symbolism, in effect, meaning "We are saved, we are saved"*].

Verses 57–61 review again the purposes of the Restoration of the true gospel through the Prophet Joseph Smith.

57 And for this cause, **that men might be made partakers of the glories which were to be revealed,** the Lord sent forth [*restored*] the fulness of his gospel, his everlasting covenant, reasoning in plainness and simplicity—

58 **To prepare the weak** [*those who are looked down upon by*

skeptics and nonbelievers; also can mean that anyone can live the gospel] **for those things which are coming on the earth**, and **for the Lord's errand** [to do the work of the Lord] in the day when **the weak shall confound the wise**, and the little one become a strong nation [from very small beginnings, the Church will grow to very large numbers], and **two shall put their tens of thousands to flight** [symbolic of the fact that the small Church will become very influential].

59 And **by the weak things of the earth** [the humble, meek members of the Church] **the Lord shall thrash the nations by the power of his Spirit.**

60 And **for this cause these commandments were given;** they were commanded to be kept from the world in the day that they were given [see D&C 105:23–24], but now are to go forth unto all flesh—

61 And **this according to the mind and will of the Lord**, who ruleth over all flesh.

62 And **unto him that repenteth and sanctifieth himself** [keeps the commandments] **before the Lord shall be given eternal life** [exaltation].

63 And upon **them that hearken not to the voice of the Lord** shall be fulfilled that which was written by the prophet Moses, that **they should be cut off** from among the people [in other words, the wicked will be destroyed].

64 And also **that which was written by the prophet Malachi:** For, behold, **the day cometh** [the Second Coming] **that shall burn as an oven, and all the proud, yea, and all that do wickedly, shall be stubble** [dry grain stocks in a field]; and **the day that cometh shall burn them up**, saith the Lord of hosts, that it shall **leave them neither root nor branch** [they will have neither ancestors nor descendants in eternity; in other words, they will not be part of a family unit in eternity].

As the Master Teacher, the Savior sets the stage for the wicked to ask, "Why were we destroyed?" The answer is given in verses 65–67.

65 Wherefore, **this shall be the answer of the Lord unto them** [the wicked, when they ask why they were burned]:

66 In that day when I came unto mine own, **no man among you received me**, and you were driven out.

67 **When I called** [*when I invited you to come unto Me*] again **there was none of you to answer**; yet my arm was not shortened at all that I could not redeem, neither my power to deliver [*I still had power to redeem you; it still was not too late*].

In the last half of verse 67, above, and in verses 68–69, the Savior is quoting Isaiah 50:2–3.

In effect, He is asking why the wicked and foolish, referred to in verses 66–67, above, refused to listen to Him when He brought his gospel to them. He reminds them that He has not lost His power to redeem them, so it does not make sense for them to reject Him.

68 Behold, **at my rebuke** [*command*] **I dry up the sea** [*as in the Red Sea and the children of Israel*]. **I make the rivers a wilderness** [*the Lord has power over nature*]; their fish stink, and die for thirst.

69 **I clothe the heavens with blackness, and make sackcloth their covering** [*the Lord can cause the sky to be dark during the day; in other words, He has power over all things*].

Next, in verses 70–74, the Savior explains what will happen to the wicked because they reject Him and the saving principles of the gospel after they are given the opportunity to accept it.

70 And **this shall ye have of my hand—ye shall lie down in sorrow.**

71 **Behold, and lo, there are none to deliver you** [*no one other than the Savior can save us*]; for **ye obeyed not my voice when I called to you out of the heavens; ye believed not my servants** [*missionaries, prophets, teachers, parents, and so forth*]**, and when they were sent unto you ye received them not.**

72 **Wherefore** [*this is why*]**, they sealed up the testimony and bound up the law** [*their testimonies are recorded against you—compare with Isaiah 8:16*]**, and ye were delivered over unto darkness.**

73 **These** [*the wicked*] **shall go away into outer darkness, where there is weeping, and wailing, and gnashing of teeth.**

The "outer darkness" spoken of in verse 73, above, cannot mean "sons of perdition," because it is used with respect to the wicked in general. Rather, it denotes being turned over to Satan to be punished because they would not repent (see Alma 40:13). The qualifications for becoming sons of perdition are given in D&C 76:31–35.

74 Behold the Lord your God hath spoken it. Amen.

SECTION 134

Background

This section is not a revelation in the sense that most other sections in the Doctrine and Covenants are. Rather, it consists of a declaration of the Church's position regarding governments and laws in general, which was prepared for a general meeting of the Saints in Kirtland, Ohio, on August 17, 1835. During that meeting, this article entitled "Of Governments and Laws in General" was read by Oliver Cowdery and sustained by the Saints as a proper representation of the Church's position on the subject.

Be sure to read the heading to this section in your Doctrine and Covenants.

It is important to know that this statement of beliefs about governments was given as a direct response to accusations by bitter enemies of the Church that the Latter-day Saints were opposed to any government other than their own church and that they were opposed to law and order.

We will use **bold** to highlight the main points of this important document. First of all, we do believe in man-made governments and in law and order.

1 **WE believe that governments were instituted of God for the benefit of man**; and **that he holds** men accountable for their acts in relation to them, both in making laws and administering them, for the good and safety of society.

Next, this article on governments states that without appropriate laws and enforcement, God-given agency cannot function as it is intended to (compare with D&C 101:78).

2 We believe that **no government can exist in peace, except such laws are framed and held inviolate** [*enforced*] **as will secure to each individual the free exercise of conscience, the right and control of property, and the protection of life.**

3 **We believe that all governments necessarily require civil officers and magistrates to enforce the laws of the same**; and that such as will administer the law in equity and justice should be sought for and upheld by the voice of the people if a republic, or the will of the sovereign.

The issue of separation of church and state is addressed in verse 4, next.

4 We believe that religion is instituted of God; and that men are amenable [*accountable*] to him, and to him only, for the exercise

of it, unless their religious opinions prompt them to infringe upon the rights and liberties of others; but **we do not believe that human law has a right to interfere in prescribing rules of worship to bind the consciences of men, nor dictate forms for public or private devotion**; that the civil magistrate should restrain crime, but never control conscience; should punish guilt, but never suppress the freedom of the soul.

Members of the Church are expected to sustain and honor their government wherever they live, no matter what form their government takes, as long as their basic rights are protected.

5 We believe that **all men are bound to sustain and uphold the respective governments in which they reside, while protected in their inherent and inalienable rights** by the laws of such governments; and that **sedition and rebellion are unbecoming every citizen thus protected**, and should be punished accordingly; and that **all governments have a right to enact such laws as in their own judgments are best calculated to secure the public interest**; at the same time, however, **holding sacred the freedom of conscience**.

Looking back through history, it is clear that almost any government, no matter the form, is better than no government.

6 We believe that every man should be honored in his station, rulers and magistrates as such, being placed for the protection of the innocent and the punishment of the guilty; and that to the laws all men show respect and deference, as **without them peace and harmony would be supplanted by anarchy and terror**; human laws being instituted for the express purpose of regulating our interests as individuals and nations, between man and man; and divine laws given of heaven, prescribing rules on spiritual concerns, for faith and worship, both to be answered by man to his Maker.

Verse 7, next, is another statement relating to the separation of church and state.

7 We believe that **rulers, states, and governments have a right, and are bound to enact laws for the protection of all citizens in the free exercise of their religious belief**; but **we do not believe that they have a right in justice to deprive citizens of this privilege**, or proscribe [*attempt to control*] them in their opinions, **so long as a regard and reverence**

are shown to the laws and such religious opinions do not justify sedition nor conspiracy.

Verse 8, next, is a clear statement that the Church does believe in law and order.

8 **We believe that the commission of crime should be punished** according to the nature of the offense; that murder, treason, robbery, theft, and the breach of the general peace, in all respects, should be punished according to their criminality and their tendency to evil among men, **by the laws of that government** in which the offense is committed; and for the public peace and tranquility **all men should step forward and use their ability in bringing offenders against good laws to punishment.**

Verse 9, next, is a clear statement of our position on the separation of church and state as far as the state having a "state religion" is concerned. It is common in many nations of the world for the state to have an official religion, which then is given perks and privileges not available to other religious bodies.

9 **We do not believe it just to mingle religious influence with civil government, whereby one religious society is fostered and another proscribed** [*limited*] in its spiritual privileges, and the individual rights of its members, as citizens, denied.

The right of a church organization to discipline its members, including excommunication (holding a membership council, imposing membership restrictions, or membership withdrawal), is spoken of in verse 10, next. However, such religious organizations must not take it upon themselves to inflict any penalties upon their members other than restrictions in religious privileges. In other words, they must not overlap into the jurisdiction of civil law and punishment.

10 We believe that **all religious societies have a right to deal with their members for disorderly conduct**, according to the rules and regulations of such societies; provided that such dealings be for fellowship and good standing; but **we do not believe that any religious society has authority to try men on the right of property or life**, to take from them this world's goods, or to put them in jeopardy of either life or limb, **or to inflict any physical punishment upon them. They can only excommunicate them from their society, and withdraw from them their fellowship.**

Verse 11, next, deals with the issue of self-defense when the government cannot protect us or refuses to protect us according to our rights as citizens.

11 **We believe that men should appeal to the civil law** [*the laws of the land*] **for redress** [*correction and restitution*] **of all wrongs and grievances, where personal abuse is inflicted or the right of property or character infringed, where such laws exist as will protect the same; but we believe that all men are justified in defending themselves, their friends, and property, and the government, from the unlawful assaults and encroachments of all persons in times of exigency** [*emergency*], **where immediate appeal cannot be made to the laws, and relief afforded**.

Verse 12, next, should be understood in the context in which it was given; namely, 1835 pre-Civil War American society.

12 We believe it just to preach the gospel to the nations of the earth, and warn the righteous to save themselves from the corruption of the world; but **we do not believe it right to interfere with bond-servants, neither preach the gospel to, nor baptize them contrary to the will and wish of their masters, nor to meddle with or influence them in the least to cause them to be dis-** **satisfied with their situations in this life, thereby jeopardizing the lives of men**; such interference we believe to be unlawful and unjust, and dangerous to the peace of every government allowing human beings to be held in servitude [*slavery*].

Joseph Smith taught that it is not the role of the Church and its missionaries to overthrow the established laws of societies and governments:

"It should be the duty of an Elder, when he enters into a house, to salute the master of that house, and if he gain his consent, then he may preach to all that are in that house; but if he gain not his consent, let him not go unto his slaves, or servants, but let the responsibility be upon the head of the master of that house, and the consequences thereof, and the guilt of that house is no longer upon his skirts. . . . But if the master of that house give consent, the Elder may preach to his family, his wife, his children and his servants, his man-servants, or his maid-servants, or his slaves" (*History of the Church*, 2:263).

SECTION 135

Background

The tribute that appears here as section 135 was written based on the eyewitness accounts of John

Taylor and Willard Richards who were prisoners in the same room with Joseph and Hyrum Smith at the time of the Martyrdom at Carthage Jail, Carthage, Illinois, on June 27, 1844, at about 5:00 p.m.

We will include a copy of the heading to section 135 from the 2013 edition of the Doctrine and Covenants for your information:

Announcement of the martyrdom of Joseph Smith the Prophet and his brother, Hyrum Smith the Patriarch, at Carthage, Illinois, June 27, 1844. This document was included at the end of the 1844 edition of the Doctrine and Covenants, which was nearly ready for publication when Joseph and Hyrum Smith were murdered.

Elder Taylor was in the jail with them, along with Willard Richards at the time the mob entered the jail and carried out their cowardly deeds. Hyrum was shot first and fell dead on the floor. John Taylor was shot several times, including being hit by a lead ball that smashed the pocket watch in his left vest pocket. It no doubt saved his life. The watch was stopped at twenty-two minutes and twenty seconds after 5:00 P.M. The Prophet was shot and fell from the window onto the ground, dead. At about this time, someone shouted, "The Mormons are coming!" (which was not the case), and

the mob quickly dispersed. Elder Richards was not hit by any bullets except for a tiny nick on one ear. We read about this as follows:

"Dr. Richards' escape was miraculous; he being a very large man, and in the midst of a shower of balls, yet he stood unscathed, with the exception of a ball which grazed the tip end of the lower part of his left ear. His escape fulfilled literally a prophecy which Joseph made over a year previously, that the time would come that the balls would fly around him like hail, and he should see his friends fall on the right and on the left, but that there should not be a hole in his garment" (*History of the Church*, 6:619).

Thus, the Prophet of the Restoration and his beloved brother sealed their missions with their blood. We will add minimal notes and commentary to this section, letting the inspired words of John Taylor speak for themselves.

1 TO seal the testimony of this book and the Book of Mormon, **we announce the martyrdom** [*being killed because of a specific mission*] **of Joseph Smith the Prophet, and Hyrum Smith the Patriarch**. They were shot in Carthage jail, on the 27th of June, 1844, about five o'clock P.M., by an armed mob—painted black—of from 150 to 200 persons. Hyrum was shot first and fell calmly,

exclaiming: *I am a dead man!* Joseph leaped from the window, and was shot dead in the attempt, exclaiming: *O Lord my God!* They were both shot after they were dead, in a brutal manner, and both received four balls [*bullets*].

2 **John Taylor** and Willard Richards, two of the Twelve, were the only persons in the room at the time; the former **was wounded in a savage manner with four balls**, but has since recovered; the latter, through the providence of God, escaped, without even a hole in his robe.

Verse 3, next, tells us the relative position of the Prophet Joseph Smith among all the prophets who have ever lived.

3 **Joseph Smith, the Prophet and Seer of the Lord, has done more, save** [*except*] **Jesus only, for the salvation of men in this world, than any other man that ever lived in it**. In the short space of twenty years, he has brought forth the Book of Mormon, which he translated by the gift and power of God, and has been the means of publishing it on two continents; has sent the fulness of the everlasting gospel, which it contained, to the four quarters of the earth; has brought forth the revelations and commandments which compose this book of Doctrine and Covenants, and many other wise documents and instructions for the benefit of the children of men; gathered many thousands of the Latter-day Saints, founded a great city [*Nauvoo*], and left a fame and name that cannot be slain. He lived great, and he died great in the eyes of God and his people; and like most of the Lord's anointed in ancient times, has sealed his mission and his works with his own blood; and so has his brother Hyrum. In life they were not divided, and in death they were not separated!

4 When Joseph went to Carthage to deliver himself up to the pretended requirements of the law, two or three days previous to his assassination, he said: **"I am going like a lamb to the slaughter; but I am calm as a summer's morning; I have a conscience void of offense towards God, and towards all men. I SHALL DIE INNOCENT, AND IT SHALL YET BE SAID OF ME—HE WAS MURDERED IN COLD BLOOD."**—The same morning, after Hyrum had made ready to go—shall it be said to the slaughter? yes, for so it was—he read the following paragraph, near the close of the twelfth chapter of Ether, in the

Book of Mormon, and turned down the leaf upon it:

We understand from the last of verse 4, above, and the passage quoted in verse 5, next, that Hyrum also was informed by the Lord that he would die in Carthage Jail.

5 *And it came to pass that I prayed unto the Lord that he would give unto the Gentiles grace, that they might have charity. And it came to pass that the Lord said unto me: If they have not charity it mattereth not unto thee, thou hast been faithful; wherefore thy garments shall be made clean. And because thou hast seen thy weakness, thou shalt be made strong, even unto the sitting down in the place which I have prepared in the mansions of my Father. And now I . . . bid farewell unto the Gentiles; yea, and also unto my brethren whom I love, until we shall meet before the judgment-seat of Christ, where all men shall know that my garments are not spotted with your blood.* The testators are now dead, and their testament is in force.

The word *testator,* as used in verse 5, above, means "one who has made a legally valid will" (see any dictionary). The will becomes valid after the death of the testator. This word usage here denotes that Joseph and Hyrum have made

their testimonies binding and valid by giving their lives for the cause.

6 Hyrum Smith was forty-four years old in February, 1844, and Joseph Smith was thirty-eight in December, 1843; and henceforward **their names will be classed among the martyrs of religion; and the reader in every nation will be reminded that the Book of Mormon, and this book of Doctrine and Covenants of the church, cost the best blood of the nineteenth century to bring them forth** for the salvation of a ruined world; and that if the fire can scathe a green tree for the glory of God, how easy it will burn up the dry trees [*the wicked*] to purify the vineyard [*the earth*] of corruption. They lived for glory; they died for glory; and glory is their eternal reward. **From age to age shall their names go down to posterity as gems for the sanctified**.

7 They were innocent of any crime, as they had often been proved before, and were only confined in jail by the conspiracy of traitors and wicked men; and **their *innocent blood* on the floor of Carthage jail is a broad seal affixed to "Mormonism" that cannot be rejected by any court on earth**, and their *innocent blood* on the

escutcheon [*coat of arms; seal*] of the State of Illinois, with the broken faith of the State as pledged by the governor, is a witness to the truth of the everlasting gospel that all the world cannot impeach [*refute*]; and **their innocent blood** on the banner of liberty, and on the *magna charta* of the United States, is an ambassador for the religion of Jesus Christ, that **will touch the hearts of honest men among all nations**; and their *innocent blood,* with the innocent blood of all the martyrs under the altar that John saw [*which John the Revelator saw, recorded in Revelation 6:9*], will cry unto the Lord of Hosts till he avenges that blood on the earth. Amen.

SECTION 136

Background

This revelation was given through President Brigham Young on January 14, 1847, at Winter Quarters on the west bank of the Missouri River near Council Bluffs, Iowa.

At this point in time, the Saints were preparing to undertake the final stretch of the westward journey to the Salt Lake Valley.

After the death of the Prophet Joseph Smith, Brigham Young led the Church as the President of the Quorum of the Twelve Apostles. Because of continued threats from the enemies of the Church and mob violence, the Saints began leaving Nauvoo and the surrounding area in February 1846. The first group left on February 4, and others followed. The main body of Saints traveling west at this time was called the Camp of Israel. During February alone, over three thousand Saints crossed the Mississippi River and headed west.

With so many preparing now to journey on from Winter Quarters to the Salt Lake Valley, the need for careful and effective organization was met by the Lord through Brigham Young. In addition to the specific organization of these Saints into companies of hundreds, fifties, and tens, the most important consideration of all, as stated in verses 2 and 4, was that the members of the Church and others traveling with them maintain their personal righteousness. This same principle applies to us today, no matter how we are organized in stakes and wards, districts, and branches, and regardless of who is called to preside over us.

1 **THE Word and Will of the Lord concerning the Camp of Israel in their journeyings to the West**:

2 Let all the people of the Church of Jesus Christ of Latter-day Saints, and those who journey with them, be organized into

companies, **with a covenant and promise to keep all the commandments and statutes of the Lord our God.**

3 Let the companies be organized with captains of hundreds, captains of fifties, and captains of tens, with a president and his two counselors at their head, under the direction of the Twelve Apostles.

4 And **this shall be our covenant**—that **we will walk in all the ordinances of the Lord**.

5 Let each company provide themselves with all the teams, wagons, provisions, clothing, and other necessaries for the journey, that they can.

6 When the companies are organized let them go to with their might, to prepare for those who are to tarry.

7 Let each company, with their captains and presidents, decide how many can go next spring; then choose out a sufficient number of able-bodied and expert men, to take teams, seeds, and farming utensils, to go as pioneers to prepare for putting in spring crops.

Next, in verse 8, we see the principles of the law of consecration and our modern welfare system of the Church in action.

8 **Let each company bear an equal proportion**, according to the dividend of their property, **in taking the poor, the widows, the fatherless, and the families of those who have gone into the army** [*the Mormon Battalion*], that the cries of the widow and the fatherless come not up into the ears of the Lord against this people.

As indicated in verse 9, next, fields were planted by these advanced companies to provide for those who would come along later.

9 Let each company **prepare houses, and fields for raising grain**, for those who are to remain behind this season; and this is the will of the Lord concerning his people.

10 Let every man use all his influence and property to remove this people to the place where the Lord shall locate a stake of Zion.

11 And **if ye do this with a pure heart, in all faithfulness, ye shall be blessed**; you shall be blessed in your flocks, and in your herds, and in your fields, and in your houses, and in your families.

12 Let my servants Ezra T. Benson and Erastus Snow organize a company.

13 And let my servants Orson Pratt and Wilford Woodruff organize a company.

14 Also, let my servants Amasa Lyman and George A. Smith organize a company.

15 And appoint presidents, and captains of hundreds, and of fifties, and of tens.

16 And let my servants that have been appointed go and teach this, my will, to the saints, that they may be ready to go to a land of peace.

Next, in verses 17–18 we have yet another reminder that the enemies of the Saints will not stop the work of the Lord (compare with D&C 121:33 and Daniel 2:35, 44–45).

17 Go thy way and do as I have told you, and **fear not thine enemies; for they shall not have power to stop my work**.

18 **Zion shall be redeemed in mine own due time**.

Verse 19, next, cautions us that pure motives are essential in serving the Lord.

19 **And if any man shall seek to build up himself**, and seeketh not my counsel, **he shall have no power**, and his folly shall be made manifest.

In verses 20–30, next, some of the Ten Commandments are re-emphasized, and other commandments are given that will assist us in having a peaceful journey throughout life as well as lead us to salvation.

20 Seek ye; and keep all your pledges one with another; and **covet not that which is thy brother's**.

21 **Keep yourselves from evil to take the name of the Lord in vain**, for I am the Lord your God, even the God of your fathers, the God of Abraham and of Isaac and of Jacob.

22 **I am he who led the children of Israel out of the land of Egypt**; and my arm [*symbolic of the power of the Lord*] is stretched out in the last days, to save my people Israel.

23 **Cease to contend one with another; cease to speak evil one of another** [*this certainly includes gossip*].

24 **Cease drunkenness** [*the Word of Wisdom was not yet a commandment—see D&C 89:2*]; and **let your words tend to edifying one another**.

25 **If thou borrowest of thy neighbor, thou shalt restore that**

which thou hast borrowed; and if thou canst not repay then go straightway and tell thy neighbor, lest he condemn thee.

26 **If thou shalt find that which thy neighbor has lost, thou shalt make diligent search till thou shalt deliver it to him again.**

27 Thou shalt **be diligent in preserving what thou hast** [*don't be wasteful*], that thou mayest be a wise steward; for it is the free gift of the Lord thy God, and thou art his steward.

28 If thou art merry, **praise the Lord with singing, with music, with dancing, and with a prayer of praise and thanksgiving.**

29 If thou art sorrowful, **call on the Lord thy God with supplication, that your souls may be joyful.**

30 **Fear not thine enemies, for they are in mine hands** and I will do my pleasure with them.

Next, the Savior explains the role of trials and tribulations in the growth and development of the Saints (compare with D&C 58:2–4).

31 **My people must be tried in all things, that they may be prepared to receive the glory that I have for them**, even the glory of

Zion; and **he that will not bear chastisement is not worthy of my kingdom.**

32 **Let him that is ignorant learn wisdom by humbling himself and calling upon the Lord his God, that his eyes may be opened that he may see, and his ears opened that he may hear;**

33 For **my Spirit is sent forth into the world to enlighten the humble and contrite** [*those who desire correction from the Lord as needed*], and to the condemnation of the ungodly.

Next, in verses 34–36, we see that those who drove the Saints out of the United States, including apostates as well as government officials, may still repent if they so chose.

34 **Thy brethren** have rejected you and your testimony, even **the nation that has driven you out;**

35 And now cometh the day of their calamity, even the days of sorrow, like a woman that is taken in travail; and **their sorrow shall be great unless they speedily repent, yea, very speedily.**

36 For **they killed the prophets, and them that were sent unto**

them; and they have shed innocent blood, which crieth from the ground against them.

Next, in the first half of verse 37, the Savior gives us a formula, in effect, for gaining additional light and knowledge from Him.

37 Therefore, marvel not at [*don't doubt or question*] these things, for **ye are not yet pure; ye can not yet bear my glory**; but **ye shall behold it if ye are faithful in keeping all my words** that I have given you, from the days of Adam to Abraham, from Abraham to Moses, from Moses to Jesus and his apostles, and from Jesus and his apostles to **Joseph Smith, whom I did call upon by mine angels, my ministering servants, and by mine own voice out of the heavens, to bring forth my work**;

In verse 37, above, and verses 38–39, next, the Savior bears His personal testimony to us as to the calling of the Prophet Joseph Smith.

38 **Which foundation he did lay, and was faithful; and I took him to myself.**

39 Many have marveled because of his death; but **it was needful that he should seal his testimony with his blood**, that he might be honored and the wicked might be condemned.

40 Have I not delivered you from your enemies, only in that I have left a witness of my name?

41 Now, therefore, hearken, O ye people of my church; and ye elders listen together; you have received my kingdom [*the Church has been restored*].

This revelation started out with the importance and necessity of the Saints' keeping their personal righteousness at a high level (verse 2). It has come full circle now and closes with the same emphasis.

42 **Be diligent in keeping all my commandments**, lest judgments come upon you, and your faith fail you, and your enemies triumph over you. So no more at present. Amen and Amen.

SECTION 137

Background

This section is the record of a vision given to the Prophet Joseph Smith on January 21, 1836, in the Kirtland Temple. According to the heading for the 2013 edition, "the occasion was the administration of ordinances in preparation for the dedication of the temple."

This section and section 138 were unanimously accepted as scripture in the April 1976 general conference of the Church. They were originally provided as an addition to the Pearl of Great Price and were added as sections 137 and 138 of the Doctrine and Covenants when the next edition of the Latter-day Saint scriptures was printed.

This section contains pleasant insights and powerful doctrines. One of the best-known doctrines from this vision is found in verse ten in which the Prophet saw the salvation of little children.

Vision of the Celestial Kingdom

1 THE heavens were opened upon us, and I beheld the celestial kingdom of God, and the glory thereof, whether in the body or out I cannot tell.

It is interesting that the Prophet could not tell whether he was "in the body or out" (verse 1). One of the things we learn from this is that spiritual manifestations are given to us through our spirits. Joseph Smith explained this as follows:

"All things whatsoever God in his infinite wisdom has seen fit and proper to reveal to us, while we are dwelling in mortality, in regard to our mortal bodies, are revealed to us in the abstract, and independent of affinity of this mortal tabernacle, but are revealed to our spirits precisely as though we had no bodies at all; and those revelations which will save our spirits will save our bodies. God reveals them to us in view of no eternal dissolution of the body, or tabernacle" (*Teachings of the Prophet Joseph Smith*, 355).

Continuing his account of this vision, the Prophet describes the beauty and glory of the celestial kingdom.

2 I saw the transcendent beauty of the gate through which the heirs [*those who attain celestial glory*] **of that kingdom will enter**, which was **like unto circling flames of fire;**

3 Also the blazing throne of God, whereon was seated **the Father and the Son**.

4 I saw the beautiful streets of that kingdom, which had the appearance of being paved with gold.

In biblical color symbolism, gold represents the very best, the highest blessings from God (see, for example, Revelation 1:13 describing Christ, and Revelation 4:4 describing the reward of the righteous).

5 I saw Father Adam and Abraham; and **my father and my mother; my brother Alvin**, that has long since slept [*who had already died*];

336 DOCTRINE AND COVENANTS MADE EASIER, SECOND EDITION, PART 3

At the time of this vision, Joseph's father and mother were still alive. Thus, the vision was showing the Prophet the future status of his parents. However, his oldest brother, Alvin (seven years older than Joseph), had died on November 17, 1823. It had been a source of concern to the Prophet that his beloved brother, Alvin, had not been baptized, knowing that baptism was a requirement for entrance into celestial glory.

Thus, when he saw Alvin in the celestial kingdom in this vision, it caused him to wonder how this could be. The Master Teacher created a question in His young prophet's mind, as evidenced in verse 6, next, and then answered it in verses 7 and 8.

6 And marveled how it was that he had obtained an inheritance in that kingdom, seeing that he had departed this life before the Lord had set his hand to gather Israel the second time, and **had not been baptized for the remission of sins.**

Doctrine

All who would have accepted the gospel had they had a sufficient opportunity in this life will accept it in the next life (see section 138) and will attain celestial glory.

Doctrine

God is completely fair to all of His children.

7 Thus came the voice of the Lord unto me, saying: All who have died without a knowledge of this gospel, who would have received it if they had been permitted to tarry [*if they had not died when they did*]**, shall be heirs of the celestial kingdom of God;**

8 Also all that shall die henceforth without a knowledge of it, who would have received it with all their hearts, shall be heirs of that kingdom;

Verse 9, next, is an example of the importance of answering questions in the bigger, overall context of the scriptures. We read often that we will be judged by our works, by our deeds. But what about the faithful member who wants to keep all of God's commandments but is prevented from paying tithing, for example, by a cruel spouse or parent?

What about the spouse who wants to be sealed in the temple but is prevented because the husband or wife is not converted? And what about the faithful single member who is prevented from celestial marriage because of health conditions or lack of finding a mate?

The questions go on and on, but the answer is clearly and simply given in verse 9.

Doctrine

Because of the complete fairness of God, He will judge us by the desires of our hearts as well as our deeds.

9 For I, the Lord, will judge all men according to their works, according to the desire of their hearts.

Thus, the honest and faithful Saint who is prevented from keeping all of the commandments upon which exaltation is contingent during mortality will be given the opportunity to keep them in the next life because of the sincere desires of his or her heart in this life (compare with D&C 124:49).

Verse 10, next, abolishes a terrible false doctrine that is commonly found among the belief systems of some religions.

10 And I also beheld that all children who die before they arrive at the years of accountability are saved in the celestial kingdom of heaven.

Question

Does verse 10, above, mean that little children who die before age eight are saved, at least in the lowest degree within the celestial kingdom (see D&C 131:1–4), or does it mean that they will receive exaltation in the highest degree of that kingdom?

Answer

They will be exalted. President Joseph F. Smith taught this wonderful doctrine, speaking of little children who die. He said (**bold added for emphasis**):

"Under these circumstances, our beloved friends who are now deprived of their little one, have great cause for joy and rejoicing, even in the midst of the deep sorrow that they feel at the loss of their little one for a time. They know he is all right; they have the assurance that their little one has passed away without sin. Such children are in the bosom of the Father. **They will inherit their glory and their exaltation**, and they will not be deprived of the blessings that belong to them; for, in the economy of heaven, and in the wisdom of the Father, who doeth all things well, those who are cut down as little children are without any responsibility for their taking off, they, themselves, not having the intelligence and wisdom to take care of themselves and to understand the laws of life; and, in the wisdom and mercy and economy of God our Heavenly Father, all that could have been obtained and enjoyed by them if they had been permitted to live in the flesh will be provided for them hereafter. **They will lose nothing by being taken away from us in this way**" (*Gospel Doctrine,* 1977, 452–53).

Question

How can they be exalted since they are not married?

Answer

They will choose a mate in the spirit world or during the Millennium. Then they will introduce themselves and their fiancée to mortals during the Millennium who will be sealed for them by proxy in a temple. Joseph Fielding Smith taught this. He said:

"DECEASED CHILDREN
TO CHOOSE MATES
IN MILLENNIUM

"We have people coming to us all the time just as fearful as they can be that a child of theirs who has died will lose the blessings of the kingdom of God unless that child is sealed to someone who is dead. They do not know the wishes of their child who died too young to think of marriage, but they want to go straight to the temple and have a sealing performed. Such a thing as this is unnecessary and in my judgment wrong.

"The Lord has said through his servants that during the millennium those who have passed beyond and have attained the resurrection will reveal in person to those who

are still in mortality all the information which is required to complete the work of these who have passed from this life. Then the dead will have the privilege of making known the things they desire and are entitled to receive. In this way no soul will be neglected and the work of the Lord will be perfected" (*Doctrines of Salvation,* 3:65).

SECTION 138

Background

This section is the record of a vision given to President Joseph F. Smith, the sixth president of the Church in this dispensation, on October 3, 1918. It was given to him six weeks before he passed away. (See background notes for section 137 for additional background information.)

In 1979, the First Presidency and the Quorum of the Twelve Apostles announced that President Joseph F. Smith's vision would be added to the Doctrine and Covenants as section 138 in the 1981 edition of the scriptures.

This vision gives much detail about the postmortal spirit world and the work of preaching the gospel to the dead that is going on there. Thus, it is one of the major doctrinal sections of the Doctrine and Covenants.

In verses 1–11, we see the importance of pondering as a means of opening up the channels of communication with heaven, as President Smith provides us with information as to what led up to this vision.

1 ON the third of October, in the year nineteen hundred and eighteen, **I sat in my room pondering over the scriptures**;

2 **And reflecting** upon the great atoning sacrifice that was made by the Son of God, for the redemption of the world;

3 And the great and wonderful love made manifest by the Father and the Son in the coming of the Redeemer into the world;

4 That through his atonement, and by obedience to the principles of the gospel, mankind might be saved.

5 **While I was thus engaged, my mind reverted to the writings of the apostle Peter,** to the primitive saints [*the members of the Church in the New Testament*] scattered abroad throughout Pontus, Galatia, Cappadocia, and other parts of Asia, where the gospel had been preached after the crucifixion of the Lord.

6 **I opened the Bible and read the third and fourth chapters of the first epistle of Peter,** and as

I read I was greatly impressed, more than I had ever been before, with the following passages:

7 "For Christ also hath once suffered for sins, the just for the unjust, that he might bring us to God, being put to death in the flesh, but quickened by the Spirit:

8 "By which also **he went and preached unto the spirits in prison**;

9 "Which sometime were disobedient, when once the long-suffering of God waited in the days of Noah, while the ark was a preparing, wherein few, that is, eight souls were saved by water." (1 Peter 3:18–20.)

10 "**For for this cause was the gospel preached also to them that are dead, that they might be judged according to men in the flesh, but live according to God in the spirit.**" (1 Peter 4:6.)

11 **As I pondered** over these things which are written, **the eyes of my understanding were opened**, and **the Spirit of the Lord rested upon me, and I saw the hosts of the dead, both small** [*relatively unknown*] **and great** [*well-known, powerful, influential*].

The Vision of Paradise

12 And there were gathered together in one place [*paradise*] an innumerable company of **the spirits of the just** [*those who are worthy of celestial glory—see D&C 76:69–70*], **who had been faithful in the testimony of Jesus while they lived in mortality;**

13 And who had offered sacrifice in the similitude of the great sacrifice of the Son of God, and had suffered tribulation in their Redeemer's name.

Bruce R. McConkie described paradise as follows:

"Paradise—the abode of righteous spirits, as they await the day of their resurrection; paradise—a place of peace and rest where the sorrows and trials of his life have been shuffled off, and where the saints continue to prepare for a celestial heaven; paradise—not the Lord's eternal kingdom, but a way station along the course leading to eternal life, a place where the final preparation is made for that fulness of joy which comes only when body and spirit are inseparably connected in immortal glory!" (*The Mortal Messiah*, 4:222).

14 **All these had departed the mortal life, firm in the hope of a glorious resurrection** [*the* celestial resurrection—see D&C 88:28–29, 97–98*], **through the grace of God the Father and his Only Begotten Son, Jesus Christ** [*because of the Father's plan and the Atonement of Christ*].

Doctrine

The righteous spirits in paradise were anxiously awaiting their resurrection, knowing that Christ had been crucified and would soon be visiting them prior to their resurrection with Him.

15 I beheld that **they were filled with joy and gladness,** and were rejoicing together **because the day of their deliverance** [*resurrection—see verses 16 and 50*] **was at hand.**

16 **They were assembled awaiting the advent** [*coming*] **of the Son of God into the spirit world, to declare their redemption from the bands of death.**

17 Their sleeping dust [*their dead mortal body*] was to be restored unto its perfect frame [*compare with Alma 40:23*], bone to his bone, and the sinews and the flesh upon them, **the spirit and the body to be united never again to be divided,** that they might receive a fulness of joy.

Doctrine

When the Savior visited the postmortal spirit world after His crucifixion, He visited the righteous spirits in paradise.

18 While this vast multitude [*of righteous postmortal spirits*] waited and conversed, rejoicing in the hour of their deliverance from the chains of death, **the Son of God appeared**, declaring liberty to the captives who had been faithful;

> Imagine the tenderness and joy in the Savior's heart at this time! He had just left an environment of cruelty, deep evil, and vile hypocrisy in which He had been crucified. Now, he was among humble, righteous people who had already died and who welcomed Him with all their hearts and listened to His every word.

19 And **there he preached to them** the everlasting gospel, the doctrine of the resurrection and the redemption of mankind from the fall, and from individual sins on conditions of repentance.

> As you know, "We believe the Bible to be the word of God as far as it is translated correctly" (eighth article of faith). The version of Peter's teachings that we have in the Bible leaves us with the idea that Christ personally preached to the spirits in prison.

1 Peter 3:18–19

18 For Christ also hath once suffered for sins, the just for the unjust, that he might bring us to God, being put to death in the flesh, but quickened by the Spirit:

19 By which also he went and preached unto the spirits in prison;

Verses 20–22, next, show that this was not the case.

Doctrine

Christ did not preach personally to the wicked in spirit prison.

20 But unto the wicked he did not go, and among the ungodly and the unrepentant who had defiled themselves while in the flesh, his voice was not raised;

21 **Neither did the rebellious** who rejected the testimonies and the warnings of the ancient prophets **behold his presence** [*see Him*], **nor look upon his face**.

22 **Where these were, darkness reigned, but among the righteous there was peace;**

> On occasions, a student will ask why we refer to it as spirit prison. The answer is simple and important. Sin and ignorance of truth

place a person in "prison" in the sense that they cannot progress. For example, without knowledge of the gospel, we cannot live the gospel and pursue eternal joy and happiness in exaltation. If individuals get caught up in worldliness and evil, they are in bondage, because there are eternal limits placed upon them unless they repent. Thus, they are in "prison."

President Smith continues now with his description of the righteous spirits in paradise as he saw the Savior visit them and prepare them to be resurrected (verse 19).

23 And **the saints rejoiced in their redemption, and bowed the knee and acknowledged the Son of God** as their Redeemer and Deliverer from death and the chains of hell.

24 **Their countenances shone**, and the radiance from the presence of the Lord rested upon them, and **they sang praises unto his holy name**.

Next, in verses 25–28, a question comes up in President Smith's mind, which will lead to additional answers given in the vision.

25 I marveled [*became curious*], for **I understood that the Savior spent about three years in his ministry among the Jews and those of the house of Israel**, endeavoring to teach them the ever-

lasting gospel and call them unto repentance;

26 And yet, notwithstanding his mighty works, and miracles, and proclamation of the truth, in great power and authority, there were but few who hearkened to his voice, and rejoiced in his presence, and received salvation at his hands.

27 **But his ministry among those who were dead was limited to the brief time intervening between the crucifixion and his resurrection**;

28 **And I wondered at the words of Peter—wherein he said that the Son of God preached unto the spirits in prison**, who sometime were disobedient, when once the long-suffering of God waited in the days of Noah—and **how it was possible for him to preach to those spirits and perform the necessary labor among them in so short a time**.

Doctrine

The righteous spirits in paradise are sent on missions into the spirit prison (the spirit world mission field) to teach the gospel to them.

29 And **as I wondered, my eyes were opened**, and my

understanding quickened, **and I perceived that the Lord went not in person among the wicked** and the disobedient who had rejected the truth, to teach them;

30 **But** behold, **from among the righteous, he organized his forces** and appointed messengers, clothed with power and authority, **and commissioned them to go forth and carry the light of the gospel to them that were in darkness,** even **to all** the spirits of men [*everyone will ultimately be given a perfect opportunity to understand and then accept or reject the gospel, before final judgment*]; and **thus was the gospel preached to the dead**.

Doctrine

All will receive a perfect opportunity to understand and then accept or reject the gospel of Jesus Christ before they are brought before the judgment bar of God.

Of course, children who die before the "years of accountability" (D&C 137:10) will be saved in celestial glory; thus, they do not need the opportunity to receive the gospel spoken of above. They already have it. The intellectually handicapped are in the same category as children who die

before the age of accountability (see D&C 29:50 and 137:7).

31 And the chosen messengers went forth **to declare the acceptable day of the Lord** [*Isaiah 61:1–2, meaning that it was time to begin preaching the gospel to the dead according to the timetable predetermined in the plan of salvation*] and proclaim liberty to the captives who were bound, even unto all who would repent of their sins and receive the gospel.

According to verse 32, next, there are two major categories of people in the spirit world mission field (spirit prison).

32 Thus was the gospel preached to **(1) those who had died** in their sins, **without a knowledge of the truth, or (2) in transgression, having rejected the prophets.**

From verse 32, above, we understand that there are good and honorable people in the spirit world mission field who have not had the gospel adequately preached to them or have not heard it at all. Also, there are intentionally wicked individuals. Obviously, there are also many people who fit somewhere in between these two categories. It is much the same as here on earth as far as missionary work is concerned. They all need to have the gospel preached to them, and that takes place in the spirit prison. Joseph Fielding Smith addressed the topic of who goes to paradise and who goes to the spirit world mission field as follows:

"As I understand it, *the righteous—meaning* **those who have been baptized and who have been faithful**—are gathered **in one part [paradise] and all the others in another part of the spirit world**. This seems to be true from the vision given to President Joseph F. Smith [See D&C 138]" (*Doctrines of Salvation,* 2:230).

This whole doctrine should be very comforting to those who worry about good and honorable loved ones and friends who have died but are not yet in paradise. They realize that these loved ones are not being punished by being sent to the spirit prison or mission field; rather, they are being given an opportunity to hear, understand, and accept the gospel, just as is the case with people on the earth. Furthermore, they must accept it in an environment of opposition and diversity of thinking and belief systems, just as we here on earth must. If they accept it and are faithful there, they have every opportunity of obtaining the highest degree of glory in the celestial kingdom (exaltation) that we here on earth have once their temple work is done by mortals, either here or during the Millennium.

Next, in verses 33–34, we see that the very same gospel principles are taught in the spirit world mission field as are taught by missionaries here on earth.

33 These were taught **faith** in God, **repentance** from sin, vicarious **baptism** for the remission of sins, **the gift of the Holy Ghost** by the laying on of hands,

34 And **all other principles of the gospel** that were necessary for them to know in order to qualify themselves that they might be judged according to men in the flesh, but live according to God in the spirit [*in other words, they will be judged by the same standards as mortals who have the opportunity to live the gospel here*].

Verse 35, next, summarizes the fact that all the dead are given the opportunity to hear and understand the gospel of Jesus Christ.

35 **And so it was made known among the dead**, both small and great, the unrighteous as well as the faithful, **that redemption had been wrought through the sacrifice of the Son of God upon the cross.**

Verses 36–37, next, summarize the fact that the spirits of the righteous were organized into a mighty missionary force to preach the gospel to all the dead who had not yet qualified for the privilege of being in the presence of the Savior.

36 Thus was it made known that **our Redeemer spent his time during his sojourn in the world of spirits, instructing and preparing the faithful spirits** of the prophets who had testified of him in the flesh;

37 **That they might carry the message of redemption unto all the dead, unto whom he could not go personally, because of their rebellion and transgression,** that they through the ministration of his servants might also hear his words.

Next, in verses 38–49, President Smith points out a number of ancient prophets whose spirits he saw in the vision as they awaited the Savior's arrival to visit them in the spirit world paradise.

38 Among the great and mighty ones who were assembled in this vast congregation of the righteous were Father **Adam**, the Ancient of Days and father of all,

39 And our glorious **Mother Eve**, with **many of her faithful daughters** who had lived through the ages and worshiped the true and living God.

40 **Abel**, the first martyr, was there, and his brother **Seth**, one of the mighty ones, who was in the express image of his father, Adam.

41 **Noah**, who gave warning of the flood; **Shem**, the great high priest; **Abraham**, the father [*ancestor*] of the faithful; **Isaac, Jacob,** and **Moses**, the great law-giver of Israel;

42 And **Isaiah**, who declared by prophecy that the Redeemer was anointed to bind up the broken-hearted, to proclaim liberty to the captives, and the opening of the prison to them that were bound, were also there.

43 Moreover, **Ezekiel**, who was shown in vision the great valley of dry bones, which were to be clothed upon with flesh [*who were to be resurrected*], to come forth again in the resurrection of the dead, living souls;

44 **Daniel**, who foresaw and foretold the establishment of the kingdom of God in the latter days, never again to be destroyed nor given to other people;

45 **Elias** [*Elijah—see Bible Dictionary under "Elias"*], who was with Moses on the Mount of Transfiguration;

46 And **Malachi**, the prophet who testified of the coming of Elijah—of whom also Moroni spake to the Prophet Joseph Smith, declaring that he should come before the ushering in of the great and dreadful day of the Lord—were also there.

In verses 47–48, next, President Smith briefly explains the role and mission of Elijah in restoring the sealing power (see D&C 110:13–15) so that work for the dead can be performed in temples during our dispensation.

47 The Prophet Elijah was to plant in the hearts of the children the promises made to their fathers,

48 Foreshadowing the great work to be done in the temples of the Lord in the dispensation of the fulness of times [*our dispensation*], for the redemption of the dead, and the sealing of the children to their parents, lest the whole earth be smitten with a curse and utterly wasted at his coming.

49 **All these and many more, even the prophets who dwelt among the Nephites** and testified of the coming of the Son of God, **mingled in the vast assembly and waited for their deliverance,**

Doctrine

We will miss our mortal bodies after we die. We will consider the limitations of not having a physical body to be a type of bondage.

50 For **the dead had looked upon the long absence of their spirits from their bodies as a bondage**.

Next, in verse 51, President Smith teaches that the Savior gave these righteous spirits in paradise, to whom He appeared during the time His body lay in the tomb, the power to be resurrected with Him.

51 These [*the spirits in paradise*] the Lord taught, and **gave them power to come forth, after his resurrection from the dead**, to enter into his Father's kingdom, there to be crowned with immortality [*living forever with a resurrected body of flesh and bone*] and eternal life [*exaltation*],

Among other things, verse 52, next, teaches us that we can continue to progress in celestial glory.

52 **And continue thenceforth their labor** as had been promised by the Lord, and be partakers of all blessings which were held in reserve for them that love him.

The Prophet Joseph Smith also taught that the faithful can continue to progress after they have died. He said (**bold** added for emphasis):

"When you climb up a ladder, you must begin at the bottom, and ascend step by step, until you arrive at the top; and so it is with the principles of the Gospel—you must begin with the first, and go on until you learn all the principles of exaltation. But **it will be a great while after you have passed through the veil before you will have learned them. It is not all to be comprehended in this world; it will be a great work to learn our salvation and exaltation even beyond the grave**" (*Teachings of the Prophet Joseph Smith*, 348).

Next, in verses 53–56, President Joseph F. Smith sees many modern prophets, including his own father, and other righteous spirits in the spirit world. He explains that many righteous spirits were reserved to come forth in the dispensation of the fullness of times.

Doctrine

Many choice spirits were reserved to come to earth during the last days.

53 The Prophet Joseph Smith, and my father, **Hyrum Smith, Brigham Young, John Taylor, Wilford Woodruff,** and **other choice spirits** who were **reserved**

to come forth in the fulness of times to take part in laying the foundations of the great Latter-day work,

54 Including the building of the temples and the performance of ordinances therein for the redemption of the dead, **were also in the spirit world**.

55 I observed that they were also among the noble and great ones who were **chosen in the beginning to be rulers** [*leaders—see Abraham 3:25*] **in the Church of God**.

As you know, we were taught the gospel of Jesus Christ in premortality, given agency (see D&C 29:35–36), and allowed to make agency choices that led to growth and progress, or to rebellion (as was the case with the devil and his one third; see Revelation 12:4, 7–9). Verse 56, next, is one of the places in scripture in which we see the doctrine that we were taught the gospel in premortality.

Doctrine

We were taught the gospel of Jesus Christ during our premortal lives as spirit children of God.

56 Even before they were born, they, with many others, received their first lessons in the world of

spirits and were prepared to come forth in the due time of the Lord to labor in his vineyard for the salvation of the souls of men.

Next, in verse 57, we find the doctrine that after faithful men die, they serve as missionaries in the spirit world, preaching to the spirits in the spirit world mission field.

Doctrine

After faithful men die, they serve as missionaries in the spirit world.

57 I beheld that the faithful elders of this dispensation, when they depart from mortal life, continue their labors in the preaching of the gospel of repentance and redemption, through the sacrifice of the Only Begotten Son of God, **among those who are in darkness and under the bondage of sin in the great world of the spirits of the dead.**

Question

Do faithful sisters, after they die, also serve as missionaries in the spirit world?

Answer

Yes. President Joseph F. Smith taught (**bold** added for emphasis):

"Now, among all these millions of spirits that have lived on the earth and have passed away, from generation to generation, since the beginning of the world, without the knowledge of the gospel—among them you may count that at least one-half are women. Who is going to preach the gospel to the women? Who is going to carry the testimony of Jesus Christ to the hearts of the women who have passed away without a knowledge of the gospel? Well, to my mind, it is a simple thing. **These good sisters** who have been set apart, ordained to the work, called to it, authorized by the authority of the holy Priesthood to minister for their sex, in the House of God for the living and for the dead, **will be fully authorized and empowered to preach the gospel and minister to the women** while the elders and prophets are preaching it to the men. The things we experience here are typical of the things of God and the life beyond us. There is a great similarity between God's purposes as manifested here and his purposes as carried out in his presence and kingdom. **Those who are authorized to preach the gospel here and are appointed here to do that work will not be idle after they have passed away, but will continue to exercise the rights that they obtained here under the Priesthood of the Son of God to minister for the salvation of those who have died without a knowledge of the truth**" (*Gospel Doctrine*, 461).

Next, in verses 58–59, we see that the dead must repent of their sins and be cleansed by the Atonement of Christ in order to accept the ordinance work which is done for them by us in the temples.

58 The **dead who repent will be redeemed, through obedience to the ordinances of the house of God** [*temples*],

59 And **after they have paid the penalty of their transgressions, and are washed clean**, shall receive a reward according to their **works**, for they are heirs of salvation.

President Smith closes by bearing his testimony to us of the truthfulness of his marvelous vision of the redemption of the dead.

60 **Thus was the vision of the redemption of the dead revealed to me**, and **I bear record, and I know that this record is true**, through the blessing of our Lord and Savior, Jesus Christ, even so. Amen.

OFFICIAL DECLARATION—1

Background

The heading for Official Declaration—1, used in the 2013 edition of the Doctrine and Covenants, is as follows:

The Bible and the Book of Mormon teach that monogamy is God's standard for marriage unless He declares otherwise (see 2 Samuel 12:7–8 and Jacob 2:27, 30). Following a revelation to Joseph Smith, the practice of plural marriage was instituted among Church members in the early 1840s (see section 132). From the 1860s to the 1880s, the United States government passed laws to make this religious practice illegal. These laws were eventually upheld by the U.S. Supreme Court. After receiving revelation, President Wilford Woodruff issued the following Manifesto, which was accepted by the Church as authoritative and binding on October 6, 1890. This led to the end of the practice of plural marriage in the Church.

The Official Declaration—1 is sometimes referred to as the "Manifesto" and is the official document from the Church announcing the end of the practice of plural marriage.

The practice of plural marriage had been revealed to the Prophet Joseph Smith as early as 1831 (see heading to section 132) and had first been publicly preached in the Salt Lake Valley on August 29, 1852, by Elder Orson

Pratt under the direction of President Brigham Young (see *Doctrine and Covenants Student Manual,* 1981 edition, page 327).

Although the Saints and the Church had been severely persecuted because of this practice, President Wilford Woodruff, the president of the Church at the time plural marriage was discontinued, clearly stated that public pressure was not the reason for its discontinuance. Rather, it was commanded by the Lord that it be stopped. In a minute, we will use **bold** to point this out in the excerpts from addresses by President Woodruff, which follow Official Declaration—1 in the Doctrine and Covenants.

We will now read the Manifesto, using **bold** at times for emphasis.

To Whom It May Concern:

Press dispatches having been sent for political purposes, from Salt Lake City, which have been widely published, to the effect that the Utah Commission, in their recent report to the Secretary of the Interior, allege that plural marriages are still being solemnized and that forty or more such marriages have been contracted in Utah since last June or during the past year, also that in public discourses the leaders of the Church have taught, encouraged and urged the continuance of the practice of polygamy—

I, therefore, as President of the Church of Jesus Christ of Latter-day Saints, do hereby, in the most solemn manner, declare that these charges are false. **We are not teaching polygamy or plural marriage, nor permitting any person to enter into its practice**, and I deny that either forty or any other number of plural marriages have during that period been solemnized in our Temples or in any other place in the Territory.

One case has been reported, in which the parties allege that the marriage was performed in the Endowment House, in Salt Lake City, in the Spring of 1889, but I have not been able to learn who performed the ceremony; whatever was done in this matter was without my knowledge. In consequence of this alleged occurrence the Endowment House was, by my instructions, taken down without delay.

Inasmuch as laws have been enacted by Congress forbidding plural marriages, which laws have been pronounced constitutional by the

court of last resort, I hereby declare my intention to submit to those laws, and to use my influence with the members of the Church over which I preside to have them do likewise.

There is nothing in my teachings to the Church or in those of my associates, during the time specified, which can be reasonably construed to inculcate or encourage polygamy; and when any Elder of the Church has used language which appeared to convey any such teaching, he has been promptly reproved. And **I now publicly declare that my advice to the Latter-day Saints is to refrain from contracting any marriage forbidden by the law of the land.**

WILFORD WOODRUFF
President of the Church of Jesus Christ
of Latter-day Saints.

President Lorenzo Snow offered the following:

"I move that, recognizing Wilford Woodruff as the President of the Church of Jesus Christ of Latter-day Saints, and the only man on the earth at the present time who holds the keys of the sealing ordinances, we consider him fully authorized by virtue of his position to issue the Manifesto which has been read in our hearing, and which is dated **September 24th, 1890**, and that as a Church in General Conference assembled, we accept his declaration concerning plural marriages as authoritative and binding."

The vote to sustain the foregoing motion was unanimous.

Salt Lake City, Utah, October 6, 1890.

EXCERPTS FROM THREE ADDRESSES BY PRESIDENT
WILFORD WOODRUFF REGARDING THE MANIFESTO
[*Official Declaration—1*]

The Lord will never permit me or any other man who stands as President of this Church to lead you astray. It is not in the programme. It is not in the mind of God. If I were to attempt that, the Lord would remove me out of my place, and so He will any other man who attempts to lead the children of men astray from the oracles of God and from their duty. (Sixty-first Semiannual General Conference of the Church, Monday, October 6, 1890, Salt Lake City, Utah. Reported in *Deseret Evening News,* October 11, 1890, p. 2.)

It matters not who lives or who dies, or who is called to lead this Church, they have got to lead it by the inspiration of Almighty God. If they do not do it that way, they cannot do it at all. . . .

I have had some revelations of late, and very important ones to me, and I will tell you what the Lord has said to me. Let me bring your minds to what is termed the manifesto. . . .

The Lord has told me to ask the Latter-day Saints a question, and He also told me that if they would listen to what I said to them and answer the question put to them, by the Spirit and power of God, they would all answer alike, and they would all believe alike with regard to this matter.

The question is this: Which is the wisest course for the Latter-day Saints to pursue—to continue to attempt to practice plural marriage, with the laws of the nation against it and the opposition of sixty millions of people, and at the cost of the confiscation and loss of all the Temples, and the stopping of all the ordinances therein, both for the living and the dead, and the imprisonment of the First Presidency and Twelve and the heads of families in the Church, and the confiscation of personal property of the people (all of which of themselves would stop the practice); or, after doing and suffering what we have through our adherence to this principle to cease the practice and submit to the law, and through doing so leave the Prophets, Apostles and fathers at home, so that they can instruct the people and attend to the duties of the Church, and also leave the Temples in the hands of the Saints, so that they can attend to the ordinances of the Gospel, both for the living and the dead?

The Lord showed me by vision and revelation exactly what would take place if we did not stop this practice. If we had not stopped it, you would have had no use for . . . any of the men in this temple at Logan; for all ordinances would be stopped throughout the land of Zion. Confusion would reign throughout Israel, and many men would be made prisoners. This trouble would have come upon the whole Church, and we should have been compelled to stop the practice. Now, the question is, whether it should be stopped in this manner, or in the way the Lord has manifested to us, and leave our Prophets and Apostles and fathers free men, and the temples in the hands of the people, so that the dead may be redeemed. A large number has already been delivered from the prison house in the spirit world by this people, and shall the work go on or stop? This is the question I lay before the Latter-day Saints. You have to judge for yourselves. I want you to answer it for yourselves. I shall not answer it; but I say to you that that is exactly the condition we as a people would have been in had we not taken the course we have.

. . . I saw exactly what would come to pass if there was not something done. I have had this spirit upon me for a long time. But **I want to say this: I should have let all the temples go out of our hands; I should have gone to prison myself, and let every other man go there, had not the God of heaven commanded me to do what I did do**; and when the hour came that I was commanded to do that, it was all clear to me. **I went before the Lord, and I wrote what the Lord told me to write. . . .**

I leave this with you, for you to contemplate and consider. The Lord is at work with us. (Cache Stake Conference, Logan, Utah, Sunday, November 1, 1891. Reported in *Deseret Weekly,* November 14, 1891.)

Now I will tell you what was manifested to me and what the Son of God performed in this thing. . . . All these things would have come to pass, as God Almighty lives, had not that Manifesto been given. Therefore, **the Son of God felt disposed to have that thing presented to the Church and to the world for purposes in his own mind**. The Lord had decreed the establishment of Zion. He had decreed the finishing of this temple. He had decreed that the salvation of the living and the dead should be given in these valleys of the mountains. And Almighty God decreed that the Devil should not thwart it. If you can understand that, that is a key to it. (From a discourse at the sixth session of the dedication of the Salt Lake Temple, April 1893. Typescript of Dedicatory Services, Archives, Church Historical Department, Salt Lake City, Utah.)

OFFICIAL DECLARATION—2

Background

The heading for Official Declaration—2, used in the 2013 edition of the Doctrine and Covenants, is as follows:

The Book of Mormon teaches that "all are alike unto God," including "black and white, bond and free, male and female" (2 Nephi 26:33). Throughout the history of the Church, people of every race and ethnicity in many countries have been baptized and have lived as faithful members of the Church. During Joseph Smith's lifetime, a few black male members of the Church were ordained to the priesthood. Early in its history, Church leaders stopped conferring the priesthood on black males of African descent. Church records offer no clear insights into the origins of this practice. Church leaders believed that a revelation from God was needed to alter this practice and prayerfully sought guidance. The revelation came to Church President Spencer W. Kimball and was affirmed to other Church leaders in the Salt Lake Temple on June 1, 1978. The revelation removed all restrictions with regard to race that once applied to the priesthood.

Official Declaration—2 is the official statement of the Church that the priesthood can now be given to any worthy man. It is marvelous to live in the day and age when this blessing is given to all the world.

As we read this declaration, we will use **bold** for emphasis:

To Whom It May Concern:

On September 30, 1978, at the 148th Semiannual General Conference of The Church of Jesus Christ of Latter-day Saints, the following was presented by President N. Eldon Tanner, First Counselor in the First Presidency of the Church:

In early June of this year, the First Presidency announced that a revelation had been received by President Spencer W. Kimball extending priesthood and temple blessings to all worthy male members of the Church. President Kimball has asked that I advise the conference that after he had received this revelation, which came to him after extended meditation and prayer in the sacred rooms of the holy temple, he presented it to his counselors, who accepted it and approved it. It was then presented to the Quorum of the Twelve Apostles, who unanimously approved it, and was subsequently presented to all other General Authorities, who likewise approved it unanimously.

President Kimball has asked that I now read this letter:

June 8, 1978

To all general and local priesthood officers of The Church of Jesus Christ of Latter-day Saints throughout the world:

Dear Brethren:

As we have witnessed the expansion of the work of the Lord over the earth, we have been grateful that people of many nations have responded to the message of the restored gospel, and have joined the Church in ever-increasing numbers. This, in turn, has inspired us with a desire to extend to every worthy member of the Church all of the privileges and blessings which the gospel affords.

Aware of the promises made by the prophets and presidents of the Church who have preceded us that at some time, in God's eternal plan, all of our brethren who are worthy may receive the priesthood, and witnessing the faithfulness of those from whom the priesthood has been withheld, we have pleaded long and earnestly in behalf of these, our faithful brethren, spending many hours in the Upper Room of the Temple supplicating the Lord for divine guidance.

He has heard our prayers, and **by revelation** has confirmed that the long-promised day has come when **every faithful, worthy man in the Church may receive the holy priesthood**, with power to exercise its divine authority, and enjoy with his loved ones every blessing that flows therefrom, including the blessings of the temple. Accordingly, **all worthy male members of the Church may be ordained to the priesthood without regard for race or color.** Priesthood leaders are instructed to follow the policy of carefully interviewing all candidates for ordination to either the Aaronic or the Melchizedek Priesthood to insure that they meet the established standards for worthiness.

We declare with soberness that the Lord has now made known his will for the blessing of all his children throughout the earth who will hearken to the voice of his authorized servants, and prepare themselves to receive every blessing of the gospel.

Sincerely yours,

SPENCER W. KIMBALL
N. ELDON TANNER
MARION G. ROMNEY

The First Presidency

Recognizing Spencer W. Kimball as the prophet, seer, and revelator, and president of The Church of Jesus Christ of Latter-day Saints, it is proposed that we as a constituent assembly accept this revelation as the word and will of the Lord. All in favor please signify by raising your right hand. Any opposed by the same sign.

The vote to sustain the foregoing motion was unanimous in the affirmative.

Salt Lake City, Utah, September 30, 1978.

SOURCES

Anderson, Richard Lloyd. *Investigating the Book of Mormon Witnesses.* Salt Lake City: Deseret Book, 1981.

Barrett, Ivan J. *Joseph Smith and the Restoration.* Provo, UT: Brigham Young University, 1982.

Black, Susan Easton. *Who's Who in the Doctrine and Covenants.* Salt Lake City: Bookcraft, 1997.

Book of Mormon Student Manual. Salt Lake City: The Church of Jesus Christ of Latter-day Saints (Institutes of Religion), 1982.

Cannon, George Q. *Life of Joseph Smith the Prophet.* Salt Lake City: Deseret News Press, 1907.

Church History in the Fulness of Times. Salt Lake City: The Church of Jesus Christ of Latter-day Saints (Institutes of Religion), 1989, 2003.

Clark, James R. (Compiler.) *Messages of the First Presidency of The Church of Jesus Christ of Latter-day Saints.* 6 vols. Salt Lake City: Bookcraft, 1965–75.

Conference Reports of The Church of Jesus Christ of Latter-day Saints. Salt Lake City: The Church of Jesus Christ of Latter-day Saints, 1898 to the present.

Cowan, Richard. *Temples to Dot the Earth.* Salt Lake City: Deseret Book, 1989.

Cowley, Matthias F. *Wilford Woodruff: History of His Life and Labors.* 2d ed. Salt Lake City: Bookcraft, 1964.

Doctrine and Covenants and Church History: Gospel Doctrine Teacher's Manual. Salt Lake City: The Church of Jesus Christ of Latter-day Saints, 1999.

Doctrine and Covenants Student Manual. Salt Lake City: The Church of Jesus Christ of Latter-day Saints (Institutes of Religion), 1981, 2018.

Doctrines of the Gospel Student Manual. Salt Lake City: The Church of Jesus Christ of Latter-day Saints (Institutes of Religion), 1981.

Doxey, Roy W. (Compiler.) *Latter-day Prophets and the Doctrine and Covenants.* Salt Lake City: Deseret Book, 1978.

"The Family: A Proclamation to the World." *Ensign or Liahona,* Nov. 2010, 129.

Hancock, Levi Ward. Autobiography. Typescript. L. Tom Perry Special Collections, Harold B. Lee Library, Brigham Young University, Provo, Utah.

Hinckley, Bryant S. *Sermons and Missionary Services of Melvin J. Ballard.* Salt Lake City: Deseret Book, 1949.

Joseph Smith Papers, The. Salt Lake City: Church Historian's Press. See also josephsmithpapers.org. (These books consist of several volumes now [2020] and will consist of more than 30 volumes when they are complete.)

Journal of Discourses. 26 vols. London: Latter-day Saints' Book Depot, 1854–86.

Kimball, Spencer W. *The Teachings of Spencer W. Kimball.* Edited by Edward L. Kimball. Salt Lake City: Bookcraft, 1982.

Lang, W. *History of Seneca County [Ohio], from the Close of the Revolutionary War to July, 1880.* Woburn, MA: Unigraphic, 1973.

Latter-day Saints' Millennial Star, The. Manchester, Liverpool, and London, England: The Church of Jesus Christ of Latter-day Saints, 1840–1970.

Life and Teachings of Jesus and His Apostles: New Testament Student Manual, The. Salt Lake City: The Church of Jesus Christ of Latter-day Saints, 1979.

Ludlow, Daniel H. *Encyclopedia of Mormonism.* Edited by Daniel H. Ludlow. 5 vols. New York: Macmillan, 1992.

Lundwall, N. B. *Temples of the Most High.* Salt Lake City: Bookcraft, 1971.

Matthews, Robert J. *A Plainer Translation: Joseph Smith's Translation of the Bible—A History and Commentary.* Provo, Utah: Brigham Young University Press, 1975.

McConkie, Bruce R. *Doctrinal New Testament Commentary.* 3 vols. Salt Lake City: Bookcraft, 1965–73.

———. *The Millennial Messiah: The Second Coming of the Son of Man.* Salt Lake City: Deseret Book, 1982.

———. *Mormon Doctrine.* 2d ed. Salt Lake City: Bookcraft, 1966.

———. *The Mortal Messiah: From Bethlehem to Calgary.* 4 vols. Salt Lake City: Deseret Book, 1979–81.

———. *The Promised Messiah: The First Coming of Christ.* Salt Lake City: Deseret Book, 1978.

McGavin, Cecil E. *Historical Background of the Doctrine and Covenants.* Salt Lake City: Literary Licensing, 2011.

Murdock, John. Typescript of the Journal of John Murdock. Harold B Lee Library, Brigham Young University.

Otten, L. G. *Historical Background and Setting for each section of the Doctrine and Covenants.* Privately published, 1970.

Pratt, Parley P. *Autobiography of Parley P. Pratt.* Edited by Parley P. Pratt Jr. Salt Lake City: Deseret Book, 1938–1985.

Proctor, Scott and Maurine. *The Revised and Enhanced History of Joseph Smith by His Mother.* Salt Lake City: Bookcraft, 1996.

"Special Witnesses of the Name of Christ," *The Religious Educator: Perspectives on the Restored Gospel,* vol. 12, no. 2. BYU Religious Studies Center. Provo, UT: Brigham Young University, 2011.

Revelations in Context. Edited by Matthew McBride and James Goldberg (2016). See history.lds.org.

Roberts, B. H. *A Comprehensive History of The Church of Jesus Christ of Latter-day Saints, Century One.* 6 vols. Salt Lake City: Deseret Press, 1930.

Smith, Hyrum M. and Janne M. Sjodahl. *Doctrine and Covenants Commentary.* Salt Lake City: Deseret Book, 1951.

Smith, Joseph. *History of The Church of Jesus Christ of Latter-day Saints.* Edited by B. H. Roberts. 2d ed. rev., 7 vols. Salt Lake City: The Church of Jesus Christ of Latter-day Saints, 1932–51.

―――――. *Teachings of the Prophet Joseph Smith.* Selected by Joseph Fielding Smith. Salt Lake City: Deseret Book, 1976.

Smith, Joseph F. *Gospel Doctrine.* Salt Lake City: Deseret Book, 1939.

Smith, Joseph Fielding. *Answers to Gospel Questions.* Compiled by Joseph Fielding Smith Jr. 5 vols. Salt Lake City: Deseret Book, 1957–66.

―――――. *Church History and Modern Revelation—A Course Study for Melchizedek Priesthood Quorums.* Salt Lake City: The Council of the Twelve Apostles of The Church of Jesus Christ of Latter-day Saints, 1946.

―――――. *Doctrines of Salvation.* Compiled by Bruce R. McConkie. 3 vols. Salt Lake City: Bookcraft, 1954–56.

―――――. *Way to Perfection.* Salt Lake City: Deseret Book, 1975.

Smith, Hyrum M. and Janne M. Sjodahl. *Doctrine and Covenants Commentary.* Salt Lake City: Deseret Book, 1951.

Smith, Lucy Mack. *History of Joseph Smith by His Mother, Lucy Mack Smith.* Salt Lake City: Bookcraft, 1958.

Sperry, Sidney B. *Doctrine and Covenants Compendium.* Salt Lake City: Bookcraft, 1960.

Tait, Lisa Olsen and Brent Rogers. "A House for Our God." *Revelations in Context.* See churchofjesuschrist.org/study/manual/revelations-in-context/a-house-for-our-god?lang=eng.

Talmage, James E. *The Articles of Faith.* Salt Lake City: Deseret Book, 1984.

————. *Jesus the Christ.* Salt Lake City: Deseret Book, 1977.

Teachings of Presidents of the Church—Wilford Woodruff. Salt Lake City: The Church of Jesus Christ of Latter-day Saints, 2004.

Times and Seasons. Commerce (later Nauvoo), Illinois, 1839–46.

Widtsoe, John A. *Evidences and Reconciliations.* Salt Lake City: Bookcraft, 1943.

————. *Priesthood and Church Government.* Salt Lake City: Deseret Book, 1962.

————. *The Message of the Doctrine and Covenants.* Salt Lake City: Bookcraft, 1978.

————. *The Word of Wisdom: A Modern Interpretation.* Salt Lake City: Deseret Book, 1938.

Whitney, Orson F. *The Life of Heber C. Kimball.* Salt Lake City: Steven and Wallis, 1945.

Young, Brigham. *Discourses of Brigham Young.* Selected by John A. Widtsoe. Salt Lake City: Deseret Book, 1954.

Additional sources for the notes given in this work are as follows:

- The Standard Works of The Church of Jesus Christ of Latter-day Saints.
- Footnotes in the Latter-day Saint version of the King James Bible.
- The Joseph Smith Translation of the Bible.
- The Bible Dictionary in the back of the Latter-day Saint version of the King James Bible.
- Various dictionaries.
- Various student manuals provided for our institutes of religion.
- Other sources as noted in the text.

ABOUT THE AUTHOR

David J. Ridges was raised in southeastern Nevada until his family moved to North Salt Lake City, Utah, when he was in fifth grade. He is the second of eight children.

Brother Ridges graduated from Bountiful High, served a two-and-a-half-year German-speaking mission to Austria, attended the University of Utah and BYU, and then graduated from BYU with a major in German and a physics minor. He later received a master's degree in educational psychology with a Church History minor from BYU.

He taught seminary and institute of religion as his chosen career for thirty-five years. He taught BYU Campus Education Week, Especially for Youth, Adult Religion, and Know Your Religion classes for over twenty-five years.

Brother Ridges has served as a Sunday School and seminary curriculum writer. He has had many callings, including Gospel Doctrine teacher, bishop, stake president, and patriarch. He and Sister Ridges have served two full-time, eighteen-month CES missions. He has written over forty books, which include several study guides for the standard works, Isaiah, Revelation, and many doctrinal publications on gospel topics such as the signs of the times, plan of salvation, and temples.

Brother and Sister Ridges met at the University of Utah. They were married in the Salt Lake Temple, are the parents of six children, and have sixteen grandchildren and one great-grand-daughter so far. They make their home in Springville, Utah.

Scan to visit

www.davidjridges.com

NOTES

NOTES

NOTES

NOTES

NOTES

NOTES